SCOTS ADMINISTRATIVE LAW:
CASES AND MATERIALS

AUSTRALIA
LBC Information Services
Sydney

CANADA and USA
Carswell
Toronto

NEW ZEALAND
Brooker's
Auckland

SINGAPORE and MALAYSIA
Sweet & Maxwell Asia
Singapore and Kuala Lumpur

SCOTS ADMINISTRATIVE LAW:
CASES AND MATERIALS

Scott Blair, LL.B. (Hons), Dip.L.P.
Solicitor

W. GREEN/Sweet & Maxwell
EDINBURGH
1999

Published in 1999 by W. Green & Son Ltd
21 Alva Street
Edinburgh EH2 4PS

Typeset by Trinity Typesetting Services
East Linton, East Lothian

Printed and bound in Great Britain by Redwood Books
Kennet Way, Trowbridge, Wiltshire

No natural forests were destroyed to make this product;
only farmed timber was used and replanted

A CIP catalogue record for this book is available from the British Library

ISBN 0 414 01296 8

To the memory of my parents

Tom and Margaret

Foreword

My aim in writing this book had been to provide a set of materials covering as much of what is taught in administrative law courses in universities and colleges throughout Scotland. The book is essentially a basis for teaching and discussion by providing a readily accessible collection of case law, statute and other material. The emphasis throughout the book is on illustrating the general principles of administrative law and I hope that I have selected material which will allow evaluation of the doctrines used by the courts, for example in relation to abuse of discretion, as well as suggestions for reform and the relative strengths and weaknesses of methods of control of administrative action, such as between judicial and parliamentary control of delegated legislation.

When work on the book began there was no Scottish Parliament or Executive and these together with the incorporation of the European Convention on Human Rights were the election pledges of a party in opposition. They are now reality and the pace of rapid development over the past couple of months has meant that the book has had to undergo several substantial rewrites and these at a relatively late stage. Whilst I have endeavoured to give as full a commentary as I could on these aspects, inevitably practical considerations of available space and concern that speculation on my part is likely to be overtaken by events has meant that some areas have been given less full treatment than their significance might otherwise dictate. By way of example, shortly after the book was submitted for publication, a statutory instrument creating a Scottish Parliamentary Ombudsman was made. The discussion of the role of this new official, in Chapter 16, is therefore brief, although I hope that I have given the reader sufficient information so as to provide a basic understanding of the conditions under which this official will operate. It is intended that in any future edition of this book fuller treatment of those areas will be given when those developments are no longer innovations, but the practical reality of the Scottish legal system as it enters the twenty-first century. Similarly, I have not been able to take account of the proposals of the MacIntosh Commission on Local Government, whose proposals in relation to a number of areas, including the creation of a power of general competence could have wide reaching implications. The materials on *ultra vires* and the powers of local authorities, discussed in Chapter 3, will now require to be read alongside the proposals contained in the report of the Commission.

The reader will note that there is no separate chapter on the types of administrative authority or their functions or the nature of their administrative power. As originally conceived the book was to have such a chapter, but given the sheer scale of constitutional change it was thought that such a chapter would of necessity be superficial and likely to be overtaken by events very quickly. Instead it was decided to focus on the interplay of familiar doctrines and familiar concepts in administrative law and some of these new constitutional developments. Thus the legislative powers of the Scottish Parliament are examined primarily from the angle of the *ultra vires* doctrine. The procedures viable for judicial control of the Scottish Parliament and Scottish administration are examined as an aspect of the general procedures of judicial control in administrative law. Similarly the concept of the unity of the Crown is used as a way of examining the relationship between the Scottish and the United Kingdom Executives.

At a lower and more detailed level, where topics on administrative law are in a state of flux, the approach I have taken has been dependent on whether the area in question is likely to be the subject of immediate legislative reform. Thus in the area of freedom of information I have merely sought to draw the readers' attention to the existence of the Government's proposals in relation to reform in those areas not devolved to Holyrood and have noted the possibility of separate Scottish reform in devolved areas. As the United Kingdom Government's most recent proposals in the form of a draft Bill were only published towards the end of May and as there are currently no proposals before the Scottish Parliament to legislate on freedom of information, any comment thereon was thought likely to be rapidly overtaken by events. I have taken a similar approach in relation to my brief comments on 'Best Value'. Where however an area is likely to be subject to legislative change whether at Westminster or Holyrood, relatively soon, such as in the area of declaration of interests by local authority councillors, then I have sought to give a more detailed treatment and this is borne out by my discussion of the Nolan Report's proposals in this area, detailed in Chapter 9.

This book would not have been published but for the assistance of a great number of people. Especially I want to thank the staff of W. Green and Son Ltd, in particular Karen Taylor, Charlotte Pache and Noel Keenan for their help and encouragement and to Deirdre Lothian for working her way through the manuscript and the endless drafts, redrafts and amendments. Their patience I have tried a number of times. I also wish to record my thanks to the Clark Foundation for Legal Scholarship and for their generous support in providing financial assistance for the project. My colleague in the School of Law of Glasgow University, Professor Tony Prosser, was good enough to take time out of a busy schedule to comment on the text, and suggest areas for improvement, although I of course remain responsible for its final form. I also want to thank Mrs Edith McCrae and Mr Derek Flynn of the Scottish Committee of the Council on Tribunals, the Constitutional Unit of the Scottish Office and the staff of Glasgow University library. I also wish to record my thanks to my secretary, Mrs Jess Aikman who helped deal with a number of editorial queries. Finally I would like to record my thanks to Wendy Bruce who took the task of transforming the spoken word via the dictaphone to the written word through her excellent keyboard skills. This task she undertook without complaint even although I am sure that she could more usefully have used her time in more agreeable ways. My debt of gratitude is immeasurable.

One or two specific points in terms of updating should be borne in mind. I have relied on the third edition of Paul Craig's book, *Adminstrative Law*, as a source material. Shortly before submission that book went into it's fourth edition. Equally, the reader should be aware that the decision in *Stannifer Developments Ltd v. Glasgow Development Agency* discussed at para. 10–15, has now been heard by the Inner House: 1999 S.C. 156. Lord MacFadyen's decision was upheld. Similarly the Water Authority Bill referred to in Chapter 1 is now law. Apart from that I have sought to state the law as at June 20, 1999, although where possible I have incorporated some subsequent matters.

Scott Blair
Paisley
July 20, 1999

Contents

Table of Cases

Table of Statutes

Table of Statutory Instruments

Table of European Legislation

Table of Acknowledgments

We reproduce with kind permission by Butterworth & Co. Publishers Ltd extracts from:
R v. Sheer Metalcraft Ltd [1954] 1 All E.R. 542
D.P.P. v. Hutchinson [1990] 2 All E.R. 836
R. v. Secretary of State for the Home Department, ex parte Khan [1985] 1 All E.R. 40
Agricultural, Horticultural and Forestry Industry Training Board v. Aylesbury [1972] 1 All E.R. 280
R. v. Inner London Education Authority, ex parte Westminster City Council [1986] 1 All E.R. 19
Padfield v. Minister of Agriculture, Fisheries and Food [1968] 1 All E.R. 694
R. v. Ministry of Defence, ex parte Smith [1996] 1 All E.R. 257
Western Fish Products Ltd v. Penwith District Council [1981] 2 All E.R. 204
R. v. Inland Revenue Commissioners, ex parte MFK Underwriting Agents Ltd [1990] 1 All E.R. 91
Lavender (H.) and Son Ltd v. Minister of Housing and Local Government [1970] 3 All E.R. 871
McInnes v. Onslow Fane [1978] 3 All E.R. 211
R. v. Devon County Council, ex parte Baker [1995] 1 All E.R. 73
R. v. Higher Education Funding Council, ex parte Institute of Dental Surgery [1994] 1 All E.R. 651
R. v. Gaming Board for Great Britain, ex parte Benaim and Khaida [1970] 2 All E.R. 528
Ashbridge Investments Ltd v. Minister of Housing and Local Government [1965 3 All E.R. 371
Bendles Motors Ltd v. Bristol Corporation [1963] 1 All E.R. 578
Crake v. Supplementary Benefits Commission [1982] 1 All E.R. 498
X (Minors) v. Bedfordshire County Council [1995] 3 All E.R. 353
Bourgoin SA v. Ministry of Agriculture, Fisheries and Food [1985] 3 All E.R. 585
R. v. Parliamentary Commissioner for Administration, ex parte Dyer [1994] 1 All E.R. 375
R. v. Local Commissioner for Administration for the South, ex parte Eastleigh Borough Council [1988]
    3 All E.R. 151
National & Provincial Building Society v. United Kingdom [1997] S.T.C. 1466

We reproduce with kind permission by The Incorporated Council of Law Reporting for England and Wales extracts from:
Associated Provincial Picture Houses Ltd v. Wedensbury Corporation [1948] 1 K.B. 223
Laker Airways Ltd v. Department of Trade [1977] Q.B. 643
R. Port of London Authority, ex parte Kynoch Ltd [1919] 1 K.B. 176
Sagnata Investments Ltd v. Norwich Corporation [1971] 2 Q.B. 614
Re HK (An Infant) [1964] 2 Q.B. 617
R. v. Army Board of the Defence Council, ex parte Anderson [1992] 1 Q.B. 169
British Lauderers' Association v. Borough of Hendon Rating Authority [1949] 1 K.B. 462
Rederiaktiebolaget Amphitrite v. R. [1921] 3 K.B. 500
Commission for Crown Lands v. Page [1960] 2 Q.B. 274
McEldowney v. Forde [1971] A.C. 632
R. v. Secretary of State for the Home Department, ex parte Khawaja [1984] A.C. 74
Anisminic v. Foreign Compensation Commission [1969] 2 A.C. 147
Wheeler v. Leicester City Council [1985] A.C. 1054
Westminster Corporation v. London and Northe Western Ry [1905] A.C. 426
Nakkuda Ali v. M.F. de S. Jayaratne [1951] A.C. 66
Secretary of State for Education and Science v. Tameside Metropolitan Borough Council
    [1977] A.C. 1014
R. v. Secretary of State for the Home Department, ex parte Brind [1991] 1 A.C. 696
Re Preston [1985] A.C. 835
Re Findlay [1985] A.C. 318
British Oxygen Co. Ltd v. Minister of Technology [1971] A.C. 610
Ridge v. Baldwin [1964] A.C. 40
Bushell v. Secretary of State for the Environment [1981] A.C. 75
Calvin v. Carr [1980] A.C. 574
Lloyd v. McMahon [1987] A.C. 325
Durayappah v. Fernando [1967] 2 A.C. 337
Council of Civil Service Unions v. Minister for the Civil Service [1985] A.C. 374

R. v. Secretary of State for the Home Department, ex parte Doody [1994] 1 A.C. 531
Al-Mehdawi v. Secretary of State for the Home Department [1990] 1 A.C. 876
Franklin v. Minister of Town and Country Planning [1948] A.C. 87
R. v. Gough [1993] A.C. 646
Kingsway Investments Ltd v. Kent County Council [1971] A.C. 72
Wandsworth London Borough Council v. Winder [1985] A.C. 461
Edwards (Inspector of Taxes) v. Bairstow [1956] A.C. 14
Cozens v. Brutus [1973] A.C. 854
Birkdale District Electric Supply Co. Ltd v. Southport Corporation [1926 A.C. 355
British Transport Commission v. Westmorland County Council [1958] A.C. 126
Stovin v. Wise [1996] A.C. 923
Woolwich Equitable Building Society v. Inland Revenue Commissioners [1993] A.C. 70
Conway v. Rimmer [1968] A.C. 910
R. v. Chief Constable of the West Midlands Police, ex parte Wiley [1995] 1 A.C. 274
Stringer v. Minister of Housing and Local Government [1970] 1 W.L.R. 1281
Cinnamond v. British Airports Authority [1980] 1 W.L.R. 582
R. v. Secretary of State for Home Affairs, ex parte Hosenball [1977] 1 W.L.R. 766
R.v. Secretary of State for Transport, ex parte Pegasus Holdings (London) Ltd [1988] 1 W.L.R. 990
R. v. Amber Valley District Council, ex parte Jackson [1985] 1 W.L.R. 298
British Heritage v. Number 1 Poultry Ltd [1991] 1 W.L.R. 153

We reproduce with kind permission by The Law Society of Scotland extracts from:
Commission for Local Authority Accounts in Scotland v. City of Edinburgh District Council, 1988
    S.C.L.R. 352
Cinderella Rockafella's Ltd v. Glasgow District Licensing Board, 1994 S.C.L.R. 591
Aitken v. City of Glasgow District Council, 1988 S.C.L.R. 287
London and Clydeside Estates Ltd v. Secretary of State for Scotland, 1987 S.C.L.R. 195
Mahmood v. West Dunbartonshire Licensing Board, 1998 S.C.L.R. 843
WP v. Tayside Regional Council, 1989 S.C.L.R. 165
Hemming v. H.M. Advocate, 1997 S.C.C.R. 257

We reproduce with kind permission by The Scottish Council of Law Reporting extracts from:
Marshall v. Clark, 1957 J.C. 68
Robert Baird and Sons Ltd v. Glasgow Corporation, 1935 S.C. (H.L.) 21
County Council of the County of Banff v. Scottish Education Department, 1934 S.C. 353
Moss' Empires Ltd v. Assessor for Glasgow, 1917 S.C. (H.L.) 1
London and Clydeside Estates Ltd v. Aberdeen District Council, 1980 S.C. (H.L.) 1
School Board of the Parish of Dalziel v. Scottish Education Department, 1915 S.C. 234
Macbeth v. Ashley (1874) 1 R. (H.L.) 14
Donaldson's Hospital v. Educational Endowments Commissioners, 1932 S.C. 585
Kilmarnock Magistrates v. Secretary of state for Scotland, 1961 S.C. 350
McDonald v. Burns, 1940 S.C. 376
Malloch v. Aberdeen Corporation, 1971 S.C. (H.L.) 85
Wildridge v. Anderson (1897) 25 R. (J.) 27
Barrs v. British Wool Marketing Board, 1957 S.C. 72
Tehrani v. Argyll and Clyde Health Board (No. 2), 1989 S.C. 342
West v. Secretary of State for Scotland, 1992 S.C. 385
Pryde v. The Heritors and Kirk session of Ceres (1843) 5 D. 552
Nicol (D. & J.) v. Trustees of the Harbour of Dundee, 1915 S.C. (H.L.) 7
Portobello Magistrates v. Edinburgh Magistrates (1882) 10 R. 130
Rossi v. Magistrates of Edinburgh (1904) 7 F. (H.L.) 85
Forbes v. Underwood (1886) 13 R. 465
British Oxygen Co. Ltd v. South West Scotland Electricity Board, 1956 S.C. (H.L.) 112
Scottish Milk Marketing Board v. Paris, 1935 S.C. 287
Bell v. McGlennan, 1992 S.C. 41
Hallett v. Nicholson, 1979 S.C. 1
Glasgow Corporation v. Central Land Board, 1956 S.C. (H.L.) 1
Friel v. Chief Constable of Strathclyde, 1981 S.C. 1

Chapter 1

ADMINISTRATIVE TECHNIQUES 1: DECISION MAKING

Governmental decision making exists in many forms. The interplay of law and various forms **1–1**
of decision making can take a number of guises. Accordingly, the concept of *ultra vires*, both in
its simplest form discussed in Chapter 3 and in its more complex forms discussed in Chapters 6
and 7, its role in determining the nature and range of decisions a decision maker can lawfully
reach. The rules of natural justice discussed in Chapters 8 and 9 set minimum standards of
fairness for those affected by decisions. Judicial review and appeals discussed in Chapters 10
and 12 provide mechanisms for ensuring that grounds of legal control are made real and
jurisdictional control discussed in Chapter 4 ensures that whilst basic legality is maintained,
decision makers are not unduly inhibited by concern for judicial challenge.

A detailed study of decision making is beyond the scope of this work. Instead we focus on
four areas of particular importance to administrative lawyers: tribunals, inquiries, inspection and
regulation. For a more detailed account of the thinking behind these options of particular forms of
decision making see generally P. P. Craig, *Administrative Law* (3rd ed., 1994), pp. 445–456; V. Finch
and C. Ashton, *Administrative Law in Scotland* (1997), Chaps 4, 8; W. Wade and C. Forsyth
Administrative Law (7th ed., 1994), pp. 904–1003; and C. Harlow and R. Rawlings, *Law and
Administration* (2nd ed., 1997), Chaps 1, 3–5, 10, 11.

TRIBUNALS

Many disputes or conflicts in administrative law are resolved by the application of rules. The nature of **1–2**
these rules is varied: see Chapter 2). The ordinary courts of law are typically concerned with the
application rules of law in settling disputes but the settlement of disputes by the adjudicative process is
not confined to the courts. In the modern administrative state, tribunals have a very significant role to
play. They settle far more disputes each year than the courts do or could hope to do. As the next extract
shows, the use of tribunals for this purpose has a long history in Scots law but it was only around 40
years ago when the Committee on Administrative Tribunals and Inquiries (the Franks Committee) met
that any systematic attempt was made to assess what tribunals did and, in making suggestions for
reform, what they should do. Many, but not all of its recommendations, were accepted, the main ones
being included in the Tribunals and Inquiries Act 1958 (consolidated in the Act of 1992) and also by the
creation of the Council on Tribunals. For the role of the council see paras 1–41 to 1–50.

The literature on tribunals is large, but for a general survey see Craig, Chap. 4; J. Pey,
Tribunals on Trial (1989); P. Birkinshaw, *Grievances, Remedies in the State* (2nd ed., 1994);
Wade and Forsyth, Chap. 23; Finch and Ashton, Chap. 8; Harlow and Rawlings, Chap. 14; and
Laws of Scotland: Stair Encyclopaedia, Vol. 23, "Tribunals and Inquiries". For articles see
H. W. R. Wade, "Administrative Tribunals and Administrative Justice" (1981) 55 A. L.J. 374;
N. V. Lowe and H. F. Rawlings, "Tribunals and the Laws Protecting the Administration of
Justice" [1982] P.L. 418; R. Sainsbury, "Social Security Appeals: in Need of Review:" in
Edinburgh Essays in Public Law (W. Finnie *et al.* eds, 1991), p. 335; and N. Wikeley and
R. Young, "The Administration of Benefits in Britain: Adjudication Officers and the
Influence of Social Security Appeal Tribunals" [1992] P.L. 238.

R. E. Wraith and P. G. Hutchesson, *Administrative Tribunals*

(1973), pp. 29–33

1–3   "Scottish legal history points to a much closer relationship between the administration of justice and the conduct of government than a superficial understanding of the separation of powers doctrine would admit. As in England, there was a period before the modern differentiation of legislative, executive and judicial institutions and functions had developed. Distant judicial institutions appeared later still: indeed the differentiation of functions was probably never complete so long as Scotland was an independent kingdom. Three or four centuries ago, both at national and local levels, the same governmental organs exercised administrative, legislative and judicial functions. The growth of separate arrangements for judicial work during the sixteenth century was as much for reasons of practical convenience as for reasons of principle. The College of Justice was formally constituted in 1532 to give a firm and continuing basis to the Court of Session and the High Court of Justiciary with criminal jurisdiction was established in 1672. Yet the King's Council continued to exercise both civil and criminal jurisdiction and today it is difficult to see why certain cases came to the Council rather than to the Court of Session or the High Court of Justiciary.

          Since its inception, the Court of Session had been able to exercise some control over the jurisdiction of subordinate and inferior courts, a task which during the sixteenth and seventeenth centuries was itself subject to intervention from the Council. After the Union of 1707, the abolition of the separate Privy Council for Scotland had repercussions for the role of the central civil court similar to those arising from the disappearance of conciliar jurisdiction in England: it was thereafter the duty of the Court of Session to provide redress for citizens' grievances which formerly had gone properly to the Privy Council. By comparison with the common law courts in England, the supervisory control of the Court of Session was marked by a greater inflexibility that must in part have been due to the fact that no separate court of equity developed in Scotland. Through the exercise of the 'nobile officium', the Court of Session had an ultimate right to provide an extraordinary equitable remedy in a situation in which the strict law provided none. The eighteenth-century Scottish law reports provide numerous examples of an extensive supervisory jurisdiction being exercised by the Court of Session over inferior courts and tribunals, and this jurisdiction was not ignored in legal scholarship.

          For certain purposes, the Court of Session itself could take on a different form to exercise a specialised jurisdiction. By what the late Lord President Cooper called 'a remarkable anticipation of the modern *ad hoc* tribunal' the multifarious ecclesiastical business arising after the reformation and associated with parish churches, manses, stipends and teinds (or tithes) was vested first in statutory commissions and then transferred to the Court of Session itself, sitting as the "Commission for the Plantation of Kirks and the Valuation of Teinds". In this capacity between 1707 and 1725, the Court of Session performed a wide variety of administrative and judicial functions for the church, during a period when the church itself had major public responsibilities in the government of Scotland, for example in the poor law and in education. (Since 1925, what remains of this jurisdiction is undertaken by a judge sitting as Lord Ordinary on teinds.) In a similar way today, senators of the College of Justice may sit to exercise a specialised statutory jurisdiction as the Lands Valuation Appeal Court, hearing appeals against rating assessments made by local Valuation Appeal Committees, and, less frequently, as the Registration of Voters Appeal Court and the Election Petition Court. In 1708, a Court of Exchequer for Scotland was reconstituted and equipped with procedures similar to those in the English Court of Exchequer but in 1856 its jurisdiction was transferred to the Court of Session, which still deals with revenue cases by procedures derived from English revenue practice … many other inferior courts and tribunals, often exercising administrative functions, have existed in Scotland.… .

          During the nineteenth century many specialised organs of central and local government were established, often with power to settle disputes arising out of the exercise of their administrative functions. [They were] superseded by government departments and local authorities."

Notes

1–4   (1) It will be seen from the foregoing that even prior to the twentieth century there were a considerable number of what we would now regard as tribunals in operation dealing with an extremely varied range of issues. It was the field of social welfare that led to the creation of the tribunal system as we currently know it. This development was noted with some concern by Lord Hewart in *The New Despotism* (1929). His concerns about perceived partiality and lack of accountability were noted in 1932 by the Committee on Minsters' Powers (Cmd. 4060) (the Donoughmore Committee). However, by the time that the Franks Committee met in 1957 it was accepted that tribunals carried out a useful task and that the focus should be on lending coherence to a structure which was by then well established.

Report of the Committee on Administrative Tribunals and Inquiries

Cmnd. 218 (1957), paras 35–37

"The development of tribunals

35. At the time of the Donoughmore Committee (1929–32) there were few kinds of tribunal (although **1–5** some of them, for example the Courts of Referees under the Unemployment Insurance Acts, dealt with important issues affecting large numbers of the population), and the Committee was able to regard tribunals as somewhat exceptional, to be resorted to only in special circumstances and requiring strict safeguards. The position today is different. The continuing extension of governmental activity and responsibility for the general well-being of the community has greatly multiplied the occasions on which an individual may be at issue with the administration, or with another citizen or body, as to his rights, and the post-war years have seen a substantial growth in the importance and activities of tribunals. In some cases new policies or regulatory legislation have meant new tribunals, for example those established under the Agriculture Act, 1947, and under the Rent Acts. In other cases an earlier system has been adapted to wider purposes: for example, the local tribunals under the National Insurance Act, 1946, are the successors of the Courts of Referees. In other cases tribunals now perform functions previously carried out by the courts: for example, under the National Insurance (Industrial Injuries) Act, 1946, many of the issues previously tried in the courts under the Workmen's Compensation Acts are now determined by tribunals.

36. Tribunals today vary widely in constitution, function and procedure. Appointments of chairmen and members are usually made by the Minister responsible for the legislation under which they operate, but some are made by the Crown and some by the Lord Chancellor, even though he may have no direct responsibility for the subject-matter of their work. Most tribunals deal with cases in which an individual citizen is at issue with a Government Department or other public body concerning his rights or obligations under a statutory scheme. But a few (for example Rent Tribunals) are concerned with disputes between citizens. Still others (for example the Licensing Authorities for Public Service and Goods Vehicles) have regulatory functions and are therefore justa s much administrative bodies as they are adjudicating tribunals. Some tribunals, like the courts, have a detailed code of procedure, with testimony on oath and strict rules of evidence. Most have a simple procedure, usually without the oath and sometimes with a ban on legal representation. Finally, there are differences regarding appeals. Sometimes there is no appeal, and further redress can only be had by seeking a court order to set aside the decision. But in most cases there is an appeal — either to an appellate tribunal, a Minister or the courts.

37. Reflection on the general social and economic charges of recent decades convinces us that tribunals as a system for adjudication have come to stay. The tendency for issues arising from legislative schemes to be referred to special tribunals is likely to grow rather than to diminish. It is true that the Restrictive Trade Practices Act, 1956, provides for cases to be determined by a new branch of the High Court, the Restrictive Practices Court, and not by a tribunal, and that the Rent Act, 1957, has transferred part of the jurisdiction of Rent Tribunals to the courts. These recent preferences for determinations by courts of law do not, however, alter our general conviction."

Notes

One of the features that has remained consistent about the tribunal system from its modern **1–6** beginnings in the years before the turn of century to the system as we now know it post-Franks is that it is difficult to generalise about the nature and characteristics of tribunals. Tribunals cover too wide a spectrum of function. They range from employment tribunals to children's hearings, from lands valuation appeal committees to the Value Added Tax Tribunal for Scotland. Some have a UK-only jurisdiction such as the immigration appeal tribunal while others have an exclusively Scottish jurisdiction, such as the Crofters' Commission and children's hearings. Some tribunals are in daily session. Some such as the wireless telegraphy tribunal have never met. The employment appeal tribunal, despite its name, is a superior court of record, which normally sits with the judge of the Court of Session and two or four lay members. Tribunal procedure also varies. Some procedures are more formal than others: some, such as social security appeal tribunals, can be inquisitorial and others, such as employment tribunals or the immigration adjudicators, are adversarial in format. The basis for comparison of tribunals has been the traditional court model. That assumption was implicit in the criticisms made by Lord Hewart and the Donoughmore Commitee and remained so in the Franks Report.

Franks Report

paras 23–33, 38–42

"Openness, fairness and impartiality

1–7   23. When we regard our subject in this light, it is clear that there are certain general and closely linked characteristics which should mark these special procedures. We call these characteristics openness, fairness and impartiality.

24. Here we need only give brief examples of their application. Take openness. If these procedures were wholly secret, the basis of confidence and acceptability would be lacking. Next take fairness. If the objector were not allowed to state his case, there would be nothing to stop oppression. Thirdly, there is impartiality. How can the citizen be satisfied unless he feels that those who decide has case come to their decision with open minds?

25. To assert that openness, fairness and impartiality are essential characteristics of our subject-matter is not to say that they must be present in the same way and to the same extent in all its parts. Difference in the nature of the issue for adjudication may give good reason for difference in the degree to which the three general characteristics should be developed and applied. Again, the method by which a Minister arrives at a decision after a hearing or inquiry cannot be the same as that by which a tribunal arrives at a decision. This difference is brought out later in the Report. For the moment it is sufficient to point out that when Parliament sets up a tribunal to decide cases, the adjudication is placed outside the department concerned. The members of the tribunal are neutral and impartial in relation to the policy of the Minister, except in so far as that policy is contained in the rules which the tribunal has been set up to apply. But the Minister, deciding in the cases under the second part of our terms of reference, is committed to a policy which he has been charged by Parliament to carry out. In this sense he is not, and cannot be, impartial.

The allocation of decisions to tribunals and Ministers

26. At this stage another question naturally arises. On what principle has it been decided that some adjudications should be made by tribunals and some by Ministers? If from a study of the history of the subject we could discover such a principle, we should have a criterion which would be a guide for any future allocation of these decisions between tribunals and Ministers.

27. The search for this principle has usually involved the application of one or both of two notions, each with its antithesis. Both notions are famous and have long histories. They are the notion of what is judicial, its antithesis being what is administrative, and the notion of what is according to the rule of law, its antithesis being what is arbitrary.

28. What is judicial has been worked out and given expression by generations of judges. Its distinction from what is administrative recalls great constitutional victories and marks the essential difference in the nature of the decisions of the judiciary and of the executive.

29. The rule of law stands for the view that decisions should be made by the application of known principles or laws. In general such decisions will be predictable, and the citizen will know where he is. On the other hand there is what is arbitrary. A decision may be made without principle, without any rules. It is therefore unpredictable, the antithesis of a decision taken in accordance with the rule of law.

30. Nothing that we say diminishes the importance of these pairs of antitheses. But it must be confessed that neither pair yields a valid principle on which one can decide whether the duty of making a certain decision should be laid upon a tribunal or upon a Minister or whether the existing allocation of decisions between tribunals and Ministers is appropriate. But even if there is no such principle and we cannot explain the facts, we can at least start with them. An empirical approach may be the most useful.

31. Starting with the facts, we observe that the methods of adjudication by tribunals are in general not the same as those of adjudication by Ministers. All or nearly all tribunals apply rules. No ministerial

decisions of the kind denoted by the second part of our terms of reference is reached in this way. Many matters remitted to tribunals and Ministers appear to have, as it were, a natural affinity with one or other method of adjudication. Sometimes the policy of the legislation can be embodied in a system of detailed regulations. Particular decisions cannot, single case by single case, alter the Minster's policy. Where this is so, it is natural to entrust the decisions to a tribunal, if not to the courts. On the other hand it is sometimes desirable to preserve flexibility of decision in the pursuance of public policy. Then a wise expediency is the proper basis of right adjudication, and the decision must be left with a Minister.

32. But in other instances there seems to be no such natural affinity. For example, there seems to be no natural affinity which makes it clearly appropriate for appeals in good vehicle licence cases to be decided by the Transport Tribunal when appeals in a number of road passenger cases are decided by the Minister.

33. We shall therefore respect this factual difference between tribunals and Ministers and deal separately with the two parts of the subject. When considering tribunals we shall see how far the three characteristics of openness, fairness and impartiality can be developed and applied in general and how far their development and application must be adapted to the circumstances of particular tribunals. We shall then proceed to the decisions of Ministers after a hearing or inquiry and consider how far the difference in method of adjudication requires a different development and application of the three characteristics… .

The choice between tribunals and courts of law

38. We agree with the Donoughmore Committee that tribunals have certain characteristics which often give them advantages over the courts. These are cheapness, accessibility, freedom from technicality, expedition and expert knowledge of their particular subject. It is no doubt because of these advantages that Parliament, once it has decided that certain decisions ought not to be made by normal executive or departmental processes, often entrusts them to tribunals rather than to the ordinary courts. But as a matter of general principle we are firmly of the opinion that a decision should be entrusted to a court rather than to a tribunal in the absence of special considerations which make a tribunal more suitable.

39. Moreover, if all decisions arising from new legislation were automatically vested in the ordinary courts the judiciary would by now have been grossly overburdened. The Permanent Secretary to the Lord Chancellor said in his written evidence (Days 6–7, pp. 191–192): 'It is plain, I think, that if all the disputes now determined by administrative tribunals had to be transferred to the ordinary courts, such a transfer would necessarily involve the creation of a large number of additional judges, particularly in the county court … many of the disputes in question do not warrant, at least in my judgment, the services of a highly remunerated judge… . I believe that it is essential for the administration of justice as a whole that, because the Bench should be of the highest possible quality, any proposals for dilution should be jealously regarded… . These are some of the reasons why I believe, with others, that the system of administrative tribunals as it has grown up in this country has positively contributed to the preservation of our ordinary judicial system.' We agree with the Permanent Secretary to the Lord Chancellor that any wholesale transfer to the courts of the work of tribunals would be undesirable. We have not excluded from consideration whether the jurisdiction of any existing tribunal should be transferred to the ordinary courts, though we make no such recommendation. We therefore proceed to consider what improvements and safeguards, including appeals to the courts, should be introduced into the present structure.

Tribunals as machinery for adjudication

40. Tribunals are not ordinary courts, but neither are they appendages of government departments. Much of the official evidence, including that of the Joint Permanent Secretary to the Treasury, appeared to reflect the view that tribunals should properly be regarded as part of the machinery of administration, for which the Government must retain a close and continuing responsibility. Thus, for example, tribunals in the social service field would be regarded as adjuncts to the administration of the services themselves. We do not accept this view. We consider that tribunals should properly be regarded as machinery provided by Parliament for adjudication rather than as part of the machinery of administration. The essential point is that in all the cases Parliament has deliberately provided for a decision outside and independent of the department concerned, either at first instance (for example in the case of Rent Tribunals and the Licensing Authorities for Public Service and Goods Vehicles) or on appeal from a decision of a Minister or of an official in a special statutory position (for example a valuation officer or an insurance officer). Although the relevant statutes do not in all cases expressly enact that tribunals are to consist entirely of persons outside the government service, the use of the term 'tribunal' in legislation undoubtedly bears this connotation, and the intention of Parliament to provide for the independence of tribunals is clear and unmistakable.

The application of the principles of openness, fairness and impartiality

41. We have already expressed our belief, in Part I, that Parliament in deciding that certain decisions should be reached only after a special procedure must have intended that they should manifest three basic characteristics: openness, fairness and impartiality. The choice of a tribunal rather than a Minister as the deciding authority is itself a considerable step towards the realisation of these objectives, particularly the third. But in some cases the statutory provisions and the regulations thereunder fall short of what is required to secure these objectives. Our main task in this Part and in Part III will be to assess the extent to which the three objectives are capable of attainment in the field of tribunals and to suggest appropriate measures.

42. In the field of tribunals openness appears to us to require the publicity of proceedings and knowledge of the essential reasoning underlying the decisions; fairness to require the adoption of a clear procedure which enables parties to know their rights, to present their case fully and to know the case which they have to meet; and impartiality to require the freedom of tribunals from the influence, real or apparent, of departments concerned with the subject-matter of their decisions."

Notes

1–8   (1) The basis for comparison adopted by Franks has not, however, met with universal acceptance. J. A. Farmer, *Tribunals and Government* (1974), pp. 18–97 takes a different approach. He is sceptical of the criteria of openness, fairness, and impartiality. He sees these as being "unduly restrictive and serves to exclude certain tribunals which have an indistinguishable constitutional purpose from some of those which are included". He sees a distinction between "court substitute" and "policy oriented" tribunals. In the latter, but not the former, the Minister often retains a real degree of control and power to issue directions on procedure or even policy. Consider, for example, section 3(2) of the Civil Aviation Act 1971 considered in *Laker Airways v. Department of Trade* [1977] Q.B. 643, C.A. and noted at para. 7–21. Note too the comments of B. Abel-Smith and R. Stevens, *In Search of Justice* (1968), pp. 227–228:

> "Courts are said to be administering rules of law while tribunals are thought to be administering both law and policy. We would maintain that no such clear line can or should be drawn. Indeed it was the evolution of this myth which helped establish the tribunal system by convincing the judges of the ordinary courts that they were concerned with legal but not with policy questions. But continued insistence on this unsatisfactory distinction makes it increasingly difficult to entrust new matters to the courts or to merge courts and tribunals."

(2) Other important criticisms, noted by Farmer, include: "that the judicial system itself cannot necessarily be regarded as falling outside the business of the State" (p. 4), and that the allocation of a new jurisdiction to a court or tribunal has not always been done rationally (p. 4). Other criticisms are directed at the way in which tribunals perceive themselves, so he is critical of the argument that court-substitute tribunals do not have a system of precedent when in practice precedents are followed. On this see generally Chapter 7 of his book.

(3) Other writers question the traditional justification for rights of appeal to tribunals rather than courts, espoused by Franks, and suggest that the tribunals are based primarily on political and cost considerations, not that they will provide greater access to justice. T. Prosser, "Poverty, Ideology and Legality: Supplementary Benefit Appeal Tribunals and their Predecessors" [1977] Brit. J. Law & Soc. 44, stated:

> "The tribunals were not established to make up for defects in the judicial system. The choice was never between appeal to tribunals and appeal to the courts, but between appeal to tribunals and no appeal. Their introduction did not represent an incorporation of the idea of legality into new areas of society for its own sake. The provision of a formal right of appeal … was introduced as a counter-measure to political protest and as a means of making oppressive changes in the relief of poverty more palatable by giving it the symbolic appearance of legality whilst ensuring that this had no real effect."

(4) The quality of decision making espoused by Franks is not always reflected in practice. Professor Genn, "Tribunal Review of Administrative Decision-Making" in *Administrative Law and Government Action* (G. Richardson and H. Genn, eds., 1994), Chap. 11, p. 285, has written that:

"In practice, however, from the perspective of tribunal applicants, the conditions that operate in any tribunals are far from perfect. Despite their conventional characterisation as informal, accessible, and non-technical, frequently tribunals are not particularly quick, there is considerable variation in the degree of informality, and the issues dealt with are highly complex in terms of both the regulations to be applied and the factual situation of applicants. This study of processes and decision making has high-lighted the complexity of many areas of law with which tribunals must deal in the impact of this complexity on decision making. Although tribunal procedures are generally more flexible and straightforward in court hearings, the nature of tribunal adjudication means that those who appear before tribunals without representation are often at a disadvantage. The shortcomings of tribunals as effective checks on administrative decisions are the result of misdescription of procedures as informal and misconceptions about simple decision making in the scope for unrepresented applicants to prepare, present and advocate convincing cases."

For similar comments see Farmer, pp. 167–169 and N. Lewis, "Supplementary Benefits Appeal Tribunals" [1972] P.L. 257. Lewis, in particular, argues that the decision making of these tribunals did not fulfil the basic standards required by law, such as adherence to the rules against fettering or abuse of discretion.

(5) For discussion of the Franks Report generally see J. A. G. Griffith (1956) III J.S.P.T.L. (N.S.) 207–219; W. A. Robson, "Administrative Justice and Injustice: A Commentary on the Franks Report" [1958] P.L. 12; and E. S. Wade, "Administration Under the Law" (1957) 73 L.Q.R. 470.

(6) Do you consider that the Franks Committee's recommendations on the characteristics of tribunals is consistent with its statement of the reasons for adjudication by tribunals rather than by the courts? Consider some of the issues examined above in light of the next extract:

K. H. Hendry, "The Tasks of Tribunals: Some Thoughts"

1 C.J.Q. 253, 255–256, 259–266

"Tribunals are seen as providing a form of 'administrative justice' as opposed to 'judicial justice'. To   **1–9** the English administrative lawyer this simply asks the average tribunal to be simpler, quicker, cheaper, more accessible, more expert and more flexible than the ordinary courts. As important as these characteristics are I hope to suggest that a concept of 'administrative justice' ought to go further than this. Linked to all these qualities a tribunal should have, is the need contemporaneously to act 'justly'. The Franks Committee, and using the ensuing Report as their basis, the Council on Tribunals, equated the task to act justly with a task to act judicially. One is forced to ask whether acting administratively, justly and acting 'judicially' are in fact co-terminous?

Furthermore, since tribunals are meant to provide a system of administrative justice outside the normal courts we can infer that one of the tasks of tribunals is to lighten the regular courts' case-load, or to put it negatively, to avoid judicial justice in these matters. In keeping with classic constitutional principles, however, the ordinary courts were still to have powers of review and appeal; despite the fact that a rudimentary system of administrative justice was identifiable it was to go so far and no further — ultimately judicial justice would be paramount. This built-in paradox bears some examination, as does a further issue, namely the tension which must bear in on bodies that inhabit the twilight world of being theoretically divorced from the ordinary judicial hierarchy and at the same time independent of the administration.

It will have been gathered that tribunals could be classified as machinery for adjudication or for administration. The writer's view is that they are probably machinery for both — there seems to be no reason why the two functions cannot exist within one body. To fully understand this it is essential that a cogent concept of 'administrative justice' is developed and not to stop there: questions must be asked about the role and meaning of 'administrative law' and furthermore, about the nature of 'public law'. To some of these matters I now turn in greater detail.

The task of tribunals to provide 'administrative justice'

Writing in 1958 William A. Robson expressed the view that the Franks Report and, by implication, ensuing legislation have the effect of importing administrative justice into the general system of adjudication; in short there had been a reception of administrative justice.

There can be no doubt that an overriding purpose of the creation of specialised administrative tribunals was to institute a means of dealing with disputes outside the normal court hierarchies, but can this be described as 'administrative justice'? In England, the concept, if there is one, is rather woolly; it seems to mean no more and no less than those alternative means of dispute-settlement provided by statute under various administrative schemes. These alternative means, by and large, tribunals have certain advantages over the normal courts and they are preferable in certain circumstances; in essence, they do the same job (they resolve disputes) — thus the one is 'judicial justice,' if you like, and the other is 'administrative justice.'

The tendency is to leave it at that, to ask no more and to look no further. The Franks Committee was not asked to look at 'administrative justice' as a whole but only to consider and make recommendations in respect of the constitution and working of tribunals. The Committee could not, therefore, look at Departmental/Ministerial decisions in disputes between the citizen and public authorities. As Franks put it, in these circumstances the citizen was 'less protected against unfair or wrong decision.' The impact of Franks was to see tribunals as a rather specialised part of the machinery of justice. In consequence, and in accordance with traditional constitutional principle, tribunals were not to be severed from the regular courts who would, on the contrary, supervise their activities. Furthermore the Franks Committee favoured the view that all decisions of tribunals should be subject to review by the courts on points of law.

Classic systems of administrative justice provide a fully fledged hierarchy of administrative courts, equal in status to 'ordinary courts,' staffed by specialised judges, within a separate and self-contained structure. Common law 'ad-hocery' spawned tribunals devoid of any real concept of administrative justice, devoid also of the context of administrative justice, namely public law. Shocked eventually at the sight of 'tribunal proliferation,' reform did not attempt a uniform structure but concentrated rather on 'minimum standards' (fairness, openness, impartiality, etc.). The guardians of the system were, of course, to be the regular courts — any notion of the evolution of two distinct systems of law was deprecated, despite the fact that if one looked closely enough it was clear that two systems in fact existed. Would not tribunals have stood a better chance of fulfilling their essential tasks had the approach been different?

Despite the palpable lack of any principled, theoretical approach, it was felt by some that a form of 'administrative justice' existed in the system of tribunals. Tribunals, it was said, were possessed of certain characteristics, or at least, *should* be possessed of these characteristics, which when compared to 'judicial justice' made them, in certain circumstances, preferable. These characteristics are well known and self-explanatory, but a few words on each is not out of place for the simple reason that it is possible to argue that one of the major tasks of tribunals as a whole is to maintain these features which make them preferable to the ordinary courts.

(i) Simplicity and informality

It is argued that tribunals can adopt more informal methods, making it easier for the inexperienced to present their cases. Courts, on the other hand, adhere to the adversarial system (a judge sitting on high, observing the context, ensuring that the rules are obeyed, assessing the performance, and giving judgment according to the evidence before him). This is, apparently, true of some tribunals, notably if they have to deal with a *lis inter partes*, but very often the issues before tribunals are essentially non-combative, such as: is X entitled to supplementary benefit? or, is Y well enough to be released from a mental hospital? Wraith and Hutchesson found that this factor very often went hand in hand with an informal atmosphere in many tribunals; the appellant was greeted by name, invited to sit down, the procedures casually explained and the surroundings were conspicuously devoid of the grandeur of judicial proceedings. Through simplicity and informality it would seem that there has been a fairly large measure of success in making tribunals acceptable to the average man in the street. Indeed, there is a suggestion that the relatively more informal atmosphere of county court proceedings is in large measure due to the success it has had in tribunal operations.

On the other hand, there would appear to be a number of factors which, due to the view of tribunals in the United Kingdom, would detract from the simplicity and informality of tribunals; in particular the need and stress laid on the necessity for a legal chairman and quasi-legal procedures before, during and after hearings could well be counter-productive in this area. In this respect, the Tribunals and Inquiries Act requires consultation with the Council on Tribunals for the making, approving, confirming or concurring in Schedule 1, Tribunals' rules of procedure.

(ii) Speed

The delays occasioned by redress through the ordinary courts are notorious. Thus it has been stressed that an overriding advantage of specialised tribunals is their alacrity. It would be easy to take this for granted. The situation as a whole is undoubtedly better than in the courts, but the expedition of tribunals will vary from one to another. In 1973 it was found that Supplementary Benefit Appeal Tribunals matters were determined within two to four weeks, an appeal to a national insurance local tribunal took three to five weeks, and rent assessment committees dealt with their matters in two to three months. It can only be said that in this respect one cannot generalise; it is probably true that most tribunals are not immune from delay. In this respect the work of the Council of Tribunals has been valuable; they have highlighted delays and suggested improvements. Generally they have shown concern that tribunals should be able to cope effectively with the volume of business coming before them. More specifically, the Council has highlighted delays in Immigration Appeals and also for National Insurance Commissioners. Furthermore, it should be noted that the whole purpose of speedy administrative justice can be obliterated by appeal/review by the ordinary courts — a subject returned to below.

(iii) Cheapness

Use of the normal courts is often an expensive way of resolving a dispute. Tribunals, on the other hand, are meant to be cheaper. This is undoubtedly so: the cost of officials and building comes out of public funds and in neither case is as expensive or grandiose as the courts with their well-paid officials. Similarly, the proceedings being flexible and informal, will normally not require expensive involvement of lawyers and officials in gathering evidence, presenting cases, and so on. It is probably this characteristic which most sharply distinguishes tribunals from the ordinary courts of law. The Franks Committee recognised that if tribunals were to be made truly accessible 'the citizen must be able to have recourse to them without running the risk of being out of pocket' and thus proposed that as a general principle a successful applicant should be given a reasonable allowance in respect of expenses and that an unsuccessful applicant should not only never have to pay any costs but should be entitled to the same reasonable allowance as the successful applicant. The proposal was largely accepted by the Government of the day, but even today a fairly wide spectrum of practice with regard to costs still operates. The attitude of the Council of Tribunals is to deal with this problem in an ad hoc, tribunal by tribunal, way; in particular they have consistently advocated that legal aid should be available in all tribunals in which legal representation is permitted.

(iv) Accessibility

The whole system fails if recourse to a tribunal is in any way difficult. Wraith and Hutchesson noted tartly that with regard to publicity, this was not one of the most conspicuous features of tribunals except in so far as it was conspicuous by its absence; this relates to publicity to potential applicants and to the publicity of actual proceedings — the two go hand in hand. There is the added difficulty here of the extreme complexity of some of the statutory schemes involved, and the likely difficulty the layman will have firstly with dealing with what he considers to be faceless, uninterested bureaucracy in attempting to make a claim and generally the paperwork involved. In the latter respect the Council on Tribunals has stressed that the wording of official forms and leaflets should be as clear and simple as possible, but the problem still remains. The Franks Committee itself stressed that the citizen should be both aware and understand his right to apply to a tribunal.

There is a further danger of a larger kind here: the system of tribunals as is known resists uniformity and simplicity — under new social legislation the line of least resistance will be to create a new tribunal rather than to reorganise in a systematic way. The result is naturally a maze of different jurisdictions which, for the citizen, is not only inconvenient but also perplexing. At the time of the Franks Report there was, it was felt, little scope for fundamental reorganisation or amalgamation. Subsequently there has been piecemeal rationalisation but the attractiveness of a complete system of tribunals increases when one considers the in-built, day to day, difficulties of accessibility.

(v) Expertise

The courts are, in the main, fundamentally generalist. An advantage, characteristic and task of a specialised tribunal on the other hand is its expertness. This is achieved by ensuring that the composition of the body consisted of persons who have special skills, knowledge or expertise of the matter in hand. Ideally, therefore, tribunals are the embodiment of expert adjudication.

It should be noted that expertise is a somewhat elastic notion and will vary from tribunal to tribunal; further the Franks Committee clearly felt that the term should include legal expertise, generally in the chairman. This will to some extent guarantee the objectivity of proceedings and perhaps the proper sifting of facts, but as regards the expertness of non-legal members the range of skills and knowledge will vary from tribunal to tribunal. More will be said about the composition of tribunals later.

(vi) Flexibility

The avowed flexibility of tribunals exists not only in the informal procedures they adopt, their more or less ready accessibility and speed, but more importantly in that they to some extent avoid the rigidity of precedent to be found in the regular courts. Tribunals, more often than not have been created because the change required had to be rapid and effective; a tribunal was unlikely, as Jackson says, to 'achieve the futility of saying that a conclusion is ridiculous and yet necessary because of the system of precedent'.

Yet it must be borne in mind that because of the present supervision of tribunals by the ordinary courts, all tribunals are, in principle, bound to follow precedents set by decisions of the ordinary courts. Similarly where there is an appellate tribunal it binds lower tribunals in its system. But the more important element is the arbitrary intrusion of the regular courts' 'law' into the so-called flexibility of tribunal activities. Writers have noted that some tribunals pay great devotion to judicial precedent.

The question has to be asked whether allowing the generalist normal courts to, in effect, dictate to specialists on 'questions of law', which to a skilful lawyer could cover almost any aspect of an administrative scheme, ensures the flexible ascertainment of the objectives of an administrative scheme. Indeed, it has been strongly argued that the intrusion of the ordinary courts into what should be administrative adjudication is clearly harmful.

The characteristics of tribunals listed above are well known. It is recognised though that quick, simple, informal, cheap and flexible adjudication runs the risk of being arbitrary — the wise man under a palm tree could adjudicate in exactly this way. Thus an overriding task of tribunals was to be intrinsically *just* in their adjudications. As we have seen the Franks Report explicitly saw tribunals as 'machinery for adjudication' that is as essential components of the machinery of justice. Therefore (said Franks) the activities of tribunals had to be marked by 'openness, impartiality and fairness.' Recognising that secrecy would destroy confidence they stressed the publicity of proceedings and knowledge of the essential reasoning underlying decisions; similarly oppression could result from a party not being able to state his case, therefore they suggested procedures which would enable parties to know their rights, present their cases and know the case against them; finally, parties had to be satisfied that the body adjudicating had an open mind and in this respect the Report stressed especially the freedom of tribunals from Government Departments most concerned with the subject-matter.

In more detail, the Franks Report's recommendations suggest that a task to act 'justly' is not in essence different from a duty to act 'judicially'. One finds suggestions for public hearings, privilege for witnesses, legal representation, legal aid, the power to administer the oath, the power to subpoena witnesses and documents, the right to cross-examine directly, the publication of decisions and their circulation amongst tribunals and so on. Many of these separate ideas have been taken up and developed by the Council on Tribunals.

Now there are quite clearly safeguards of a fundamentally legal kind and their value is not in dispute. However, there would appear to be some tension between these clearly 'judicial' procedures and the essential worth of tribunals as cheap, flexible and fast dispensers of administrative justice. As stated, the Franks Committee was not concerned with a coherent concept of administrative justice, but it is suggested that a task to be 'just' is somewhat wider than the simple adoption of quasi-legal procedures. Franks expressly avoided any involvement in the policy behind particular administrative schemes — indeed many of the complaints the Council on Tribunals receive seem to relate to a rather wider concept of justice than simple 'judicialised procedures' — but their power to deal with general complaints are not very well defined. In the light of the terms of reference of the Franks Committee, namely to 'review the constitution and working of tribunals', it would have been difficult to review the multiplicity of policies involved, but it seems a pity not to have at least mentioned that the operation of tribunals ought, at the end of the day, to promote the objectives of the scheme for which they were constituted, and to perhaps suggest ways in which this could be achieved. Within this context it is of some worth to make the following ancillary comments.

(a) Tribunals' independence from Government Departments

It has been argued that Departments and Ministers, and not 'Parliament,' will have been largely responsible for the drafting of the rules relating to the constitution, functions and operation of tribunals. To some extent the statements of the Council on Tribunals and the Franks stress on independence from Departments, however, is impossible if taken literally. What is possible, and indeed desirable, is that a Department should not attempt to influence a decision: of this there is no evidence. What one cannot evade, it is suggested, is that tribunals are part of administrative schemes and to these schemes they have some responsibility. The Franks attempt at, and the Council of Tribunals stress on, the independence of tribunals, one cannot help but feel, is a rather charming attempt to approximate tribunals to ordinary courts of law.

(c) Procedure

Finally in this regard, a word about tribunal procedures: as stated the impact of Franks was to apply 'judicial' principles to them. On the other hand the Report rejected the idea of a single code of procedure since flexibility would be jeopardised if this took place. However, each statutory tribunal had to have a definite procedure specified by statute or statutory instrument. Informality was to be retained but within an orderly procedure. The Council on Tribunals has a consultative role with regard to the making of Schedule 1 tribunals' rules of procedure and as we have seen this is largely handled by their Legal Committee. We have already seen that the vast majority of procedural recommendations by Franks have been followed and persisted in by the Council on Tribunals; of these we will undoubtedly approve for they guarantee a very basic procedural justice. One is left wondering, however, whether the Franks Committee was 'asked to look at already open, fair and impartial administrative procedures and asked to see if they could be made more so?''

Notes

(1) To what extent do you consider that Hendry's views support, and in some respects   **1–10** undermine, the analysis adopted by the Franks Report? What aspects of the Tribunals and Inquiries Act 1992 does Hendry consider to be supportive in referring matters to tribunals rather than courts? A number of the sections of the Act are noted in the following pages. Is it possible to derive proposals for reform from the views expressed?

(2) One point not mentioned by Hendry is the structural method of ensuring that tribunals are regarded as part of the system of adjudication rather than the administrative structure in the development of "presidential systems". By this it is meant that a full-time national or regional officer — usually, but not always with legal qualifications — is to be responsible for co-ordinating the administration and practice of the tribunals in question. Examples of this include the Lands Tribunal for Scotland (president), the social security appeal tribunals (president) (see now the unified appeal tribunals under the Social Security Act 1998) and employment tribunals (president and regional chairmen).

Annual Report of the Council on Tribunals 1982–83

(1983–84) (H.C. 129), paras 2.15–2.16

"Tribunal constitution — presidential system

2.15   We have frequently recommended the presidential system of organisation under which a   **1–11** particular class of tribunal has a national president or chairman and, where the number of tribunals in that class justifies it, regional chairmen as well. We have made a further study of the presidential system this year. We see as its advantages:

(a) there is an obvious independence from the Government departments responsible either for decisions appealable to the tribunal or for its financing;

(b) a president can be responsible for the administrative arrangements, instead of a Government department having that role;

(c) he can appoint or advise on the appointment of tribunal chairmen, members, clerks and other staff;

(d) he can monitor the performance of tribunals, arrange for necessary training, and encourage consistency;

(e) co-ordination and communication between tribunals of the same type are facilitated and a sense of corporate identity and team spirit is fostered;

(f) the tribunal has a spokesman and a focal point for relationships and communication with other bodies; and

(g) a president may make interlocutory decisions and may give guidance about the allocation of cases and about other matters of practice and procedure.

In our view a presidential system ought to be established for a particular type of tribunal when a significant number of cases is dealt with every year and there is also an appreciable number of tribunals within the system, whether or not they sit in many locations or already have a regional organisation.

2.16 We favour the introduction of regional chairman for certain types of tribunals where both the appointment of a national president is justified and the number of tribunals would make administration easier through regional centres. The appointment of regional chairmen also helps to spread the workload and responsibility, while keeping a central focus. However, we accept that in those types of tribunal which handle a comparatively small number of cases a looser structure of quasi-autonomous regional chairmen without a national president would be acceptable. In such circumstances we would expect the regional chairmen to meet reasonably frequently to plan and co-ordinate their work in relation to administration, training and the other matters which would otherwise be the responsibility of a president. One of the senior regional chairmen could act as a focal point and take responsibility for organising the regional chairmen's activities."

Notes

1–12   (1) Does the presidential system help to resolve some of the difficulties in relation to policy-oriented tribunals? Does the presidential system contribute to the realisation of the aims of the Franks Committee? What are the possible disadvantages?

(2) There is some support for the view that the presidential system does improve standards. M. Partington, "The Restructuring of Social Security Appeal Tribunals: a Personal View" in *Public Law and Politics* (C. Harlow, ed., 1986), at p. 173, states that the presidential system in social security appeal tribunals created a focus for the whole system and moreover addressed both managerial and policy issues by implementation of training programmes and the monitoring of standards. He notes, however, that where the president has, to some extent, been required by statute to upgrade the system, the effect of this is more readily apparent than where the president is not subject to such an obligation (p. 178).

(3) The Council on Tribunals issued a special report in 1997, *Tribunals: Their Organisation and Independence*, Cmnd. 3744. Its support for presidential systems continued. The council had been concerned that matters of administration and funding, over which the government departments sponsoring the relevant tribunals had most control, were potentially threatening to the independence of many tribunals. It concluded that for a tribunal to be truly independent, it required, *inter alia*, high-quality appointments of chairmen and members, proper training for chairmen and members, appropriate standards of judicial performance with guidance and support for members, the freedom to take decisions uninfluenced by resources or other external considerations, proper administrative support such as support staff and text books, appropriate accommodation and proper rules and procedure: para. 2.3. It concluded that "the independence and integrity of the tribunal system is best served if someone from the judicial side of the tribunal is given a specific role in meeting some or all of these preconditions": para. 2.4. Specifically, while accepting that questions of finance and budgeting might more appropriately be handled by a senior tribunal administrator, the president should be given a central effective role in determining what resources were needed to ensure the efficient and effective working of the tribunal itself: paras 2.10–2.12. In addition, a president could monitor the performance of tribunal chairmen and members and ensure efficient use of judicial resources: para. 2.13; ensure the promotion of proper rules of procedure and consistency between individual tribunals in their decision making; have a central role in the appointment of tribunal chairmen and members; ensure that proper training and guidance is provided: para. 2.14; and liaise with Ministers on policy decisions which affect tribunals, such as changes to jurisdiction or procedure or the composition or make-up of a tribunal: para. 2.16. Apart from these specific goals, a president would provide a focus by giving central direction, particularly in dealing with a sponsoring department: paras 2.18–2.22. It concluded that in terms of appointment status, the judicial head need not necessarily be called "president", but he should stand apart from, if not above, his judicial colleagues and that his appointment should be made by the Lord Chancellor or Lord Advocate as appropriate, with his office and main functions provided for in statute: paras 2.23–2.24. These aspirations have, however, to be set against the reality of current government policy. In particular, note the provisions of the Social Security Act 1998, discussed at para. 1–17.

(4) One should be careful to exclude the easy assumption that the only model of administrative dispute resolution is adjudicative. Just as there has been a move towards a presidential system in relation to some important areas of decision making, so too has there been a move away from the use of the adjudicative model in other areas. One of the most controversial was that in relation to the social fund. The following extract explains the Government's reasoning.

The Reform of Social Security

Cmnd. 9518 (1985), paras 2.107–2.112

"How the social fund will be run

1–13   2.107 The fund will be run from DHSS local offices by a group of specialist officers. Special expertise will be needed, based on specific training in relevant skills, such as interviewing, counselling, and knowledge of help available from other sources. Decision-making will rest more on casework, liaison with other bodies and discussion with claimants. There will need to be clear links with the work of social service and health professionals who may also be involved in helping the same person. The views of outside professionals may have a part to play in helping officers reach judgments on individual cases.

2.108 Such expertise is to an extent already possessed by special case officers who since 1980 have had a remit to help claimants whose cases present special difficulty. Special case officers' concerns include: claimants with difficulties in adjusting to major changes in their circumstances (such as marital breakdown or discharge after a long stay in hospital); cases where there are doubts about claimants' ability to care for themselves or their children; those who have problems in managing essential living expenses; and others whose characteristics may create tension in dealing with staff. The Government believe it is right to develop existing good practice in this area and to expand the responsibilities of special case officers.

2.109 Specialist staff will exercise their judgment in reaching decisions on individual cases. The basis of deciding social fund payments is rather different from traditional benefit decision-making. There is widespread recognition that the present adjudication arrangements for handling special needs have not worked satisfactorily. There is also widespread agreement that, in handling the special difficulties of a minority of claimants, the scheme needs a degree of flexibility that is only possible with discretion.

2.110 The Government recognise that people who have asked for help with particular pressures should have an effective means of questioning the outcome. In all organisations, management has the first responsibility to see that services are well handled. This basic principle applies just as much to the administration of benefits as it does to other areas. It is however clear that the present appeal arrangements in special needs areas can have a sledgehammer effect. The full weight of legal consideration can be brought to bear on matters which may involve small sums of money for particular items with considerable delays between initial decision and formal review. We do not believe that the present system of appeals has best served the claimant's prime interest of a quick and effective reconsideration of decisions. The result is now too slow, too cumbersome, and too inflexible.

2.111 The first safeguard for claimants under the new arrangements will be a professional approach to the administration of the social fund. That is the reason for using specialist officers. Reviews which turn on judgment in difficult individual circumstances are best handled as near to the point of decision as possible. The further the review gets from the initial judgment both in terms of formality and time, the less equipped the reviewing authority is to judge whether the outcome is sensible. The Government therefore intend to provide for review by management as near as possible to where responsibility for the original decision rests. Just as social service and health care decisions are best taken locally by those directly responsible, so should the social fund be seen as an important responsibility of those administering it in local offices. The arrangements proposed by the Government involve judgment — local people are best placed to make that judgment.

2.112 The fund will work successfully only if there is a clear limit to its role; that is, if it concentrates on the special needs of a limited number of claimants. The fund will have a fixed annual budget. Some form of budgeting is the reality in most areas of social provision. The Government do not consider that this specialist part of the new arrangements should be any different."

Notes

(1) Until 1986 an appeal existed from all claims concerning supplementary benefit, which was the then available means test of benefit available to the unemployed or those on low incomes. These appeals were dealt with by the supplementary benefits appeal tribunal until 1984 and thereafter by social security appeal tribunals. Supplementary benefit was replaced by income support in 1986 and a social fund was established to consider claims for specific items, such as furniture and clothing. Until then claims such as this had been made under the single payments regulations and appeals concerning single payments were dealt with by SSAT. For a general account of the tribunal system prior to the introduction of the social fund see Sainsbury, below, especially pp. 336–338.

1–14

(2) The denial of right of appeal does not mean that judicial control is excluded. Judicial review exists: *Murray v. Social Fund Inspector*, 1996 S.L.T. 38 noted at para. 4–16. From the nature of the broad discretion conferred on the inspector making the decision in *Murray*, successful challenges are likely to be few and far between, although see *R. v. Secretary of State for Social Security, ex parte Stitt, The Times*, July 5, 1990.

(3) Does either the Franks Committee Report or Hendry's article provide an explanation for this development?

(4) The removal of the right of appeal was criticised by the Council on Tribunals: see Annual Reports for 1984–85, para. 2.34; 1985–86, para. 3.86.

(5) The social fund legislation is now contained in the Social Security Administration Act 1992, ss. 12, 64–66, 78, 167, 168. From a date to be appointed, however, the Social Security Act 1998 revokes sections 64–66 and replaces them with sections 36–38 of the 1998 Act. Under section 1 of the 1998 Act, from a date to be appointed, the function of the social fund officer is to be transferred to the Secretary of State. Section 36 provides for discretionary social fund decisions to be made by appropriate officers appointed by the Secretary of State and allows the Secretary of State to nominate officers who may issue guidance to other officers on his behalf. Section 37 confirms the continued existence of the social fund commissioner, whose duties include monitoring the quality of the decisions of appropriate officers and arranging for the training of such officers: s. 38(a), (b). Detailed provision for review of the determination of an appropriate officer is contained in section 38. In substance the provisions of section 38 on internal review mirror those contained in section 66 of the 1992 Act. Both independent and official reports suggest that the scheme in operation is in fact fast and generally perceived to be objective: see, for example, the Annual Report of the Social Fund Commissioner for 1987–88 and R. Drabble and T. Lynes, "The Social Fund — Discretion or Control?" [1989] P.L. 297. For a detailed account of the social fund see D. Feldman, "The Constitution and the Social Fund: A Novel Form of Legislation" (1991) 107 L.Q.R. 39; T. Buck, *The Social Fund: Law and Practice* (1969); and *Stair Memorial Encyclopaedia*, Vol. 21, "Social Security", paras 1123–1147.

(6) The social fund inspector system can be regarded as a system of internal administrative review. This phenomenon has been the subject of academic study (J. Mashaw, *Bureaucratic Justice* (Yale University Press, 1983) and has received the support of the Council on Tribunals, at least outwith the social fund system. In its 1985–86 Report at para. 3.92 the council accepted the value of such a procedure and expressed a view that all first-level adjudicative authorities should have power to review their decisions on the basis of ignorance, mistake of law or relevant change of circumstances. Prior to the creation of the social fund, there was some evidence to suggest that in appeals lodged with the then social security appeal tribunals, there existed a good proportion of appeals being withdrawn on the basis that internal review had satisfied the appellant. In 1985 195,902 appeals were lodged with the social security appeal tribunals throughout the United Kingdom. Most were withdrawn or not admitted as either being time-barred or not within the tribunals' jurisdiction. 77,734 appeals were heard of which 23 per cent were decided in the appellant's favour. However, a large number of withdrawn appeals followed administrative review of the appellant's case and in the chief adjudication officer's report for 1985–86 it was estimated that approximately 33 per cent of initial decisions on supplementary benefit were in fact inaccurate.

(7) The compromise between a tribunal-oriented system and one based on internal review is found in relation to review of housing benefit discussions. Decisions on housing benefit applications are made by a local authority inspector. A further hearing before an internal review board of local authority councillors exists: see generally the Social Security and Housing Benefit (General) Regulations 1987 (as amended); and M. Partington and H. Bolderson, *Housing Benefit Review Procedures: A Preliminary Analysis* (Brunel University, 1984). Such decisions are subject to judicial review: see *Malcolm v. Tweeddale District Housing Benefit Review Board*, 1994 S.L.T. 1212 and *Wilson v. Nithsdale District Council*, 1992 S.L.T. 1131 noted at para. 4–16.

THE PERSONNEL OF TRIBUNALS

Franks Commitee Report

paras 45–49, 55–58

"The appointment of chairmen and members

1–15   45. We have already said that it is important to secure the independence of the personnel of tribunals from the Departments concerned with the subject-matter of their decisions. This is particularly so when a Government Department is a frequent party to proceedings before a tribunal. We wish to make it clear that we have received no significant evidence that any influence is in fact exerted upon members of tribunals by Government Departments. But present practice can give no guarantee for the future. It appears to us undesirable in principle that the appointment of so many chairmen and members of tribunals should rest solely with the Ministers concerned, and we have received some evidence that this method of appointment can lead to misunderstanding.

46. A substantial volume of the evidence has advocated the appointment of all chairmen and members of tribunals by the Lord Chancellor. There is no doubt that such a change would serve to stress the independence of tribunals; it might also, by reason of the esteem in which the office of Lord Chancellor is held, enhance their status. The change would not involve any new principle, since the Lord Chancellor is already responsible for the appointment not only of a number of chairmen of tribunals but in some cases for the appointment of members also.

47. On the other hand some evidence placed before us, particularly by the Permanent Secretary to the Lord Chancellor, while accepting as reasonable that the Lord Chancellor should appoint all chairmen whether legally qualified or not, opposed the suggestion that the Lord Chancellor should appoint all members of tribunals.... [I]t was argued that responsibility for all appointments to tribunals would involve duplication of work with those Departments which already have, in their own regional or local organisations or in local advisory committees, adequate facilities for scrutinising nominations for such appointments. It was also urged upon us that to require the Lord Chancellor to exercise patronage in cases so numerous that it would be obvious that he could not give personal consideration to the choice of the candidates would be to weaken his authority as an instrument of judicial patronage.

48. We appreciate the force of the contention that all appointments to tribunals should be made by the Lord Chancellor so as to demonstrate clearly the intention that tribunals should be wholly independent of departmental influence. But we feel that the best practical course would be for the responsibility of the Lord Chancellor for such appointments not to be extended beyond the chairman, though we consider that he should retain his present responsibility for appointing members of certain tribunals and that there may be scope for extending this responsibility to a few other tribunals.

49. Although we are unable to recommend that all members of tribunals should be appointed by the Lord Chancellor we are satisfied that their appointment should not rest with the Ministers concerned with the subject-matter of the adjudications. In order to enhance the independence of tribunals, both in appearance and in fact, we consider that the Council on Tribunals should make these appointments. We see no need for the Council to review any existing appointments.

The qualifications of chairmen and members

55. There has been substantial agreement among witnesses that at any rate the majority of chairmen of tribunals should have legal qualifications. We attach great importance to the quality of chairmanship. Objectivity in the treatment of cases and the proper sifting of facts are most often best secured by having a legally qualified chairman, though we recognise that suitable chairmen can be drawn from fields other than the law. We therefore recommend that chairmen of tribunals should ordinarily have legal qualifications but that the appointment of persons without legal qualifications should not be ruled out when they are particularly suitable.

56. It is impossible, we think, to lay down any such general desideratum in the case of members because of the wide variety of experience which has to be drawn on for the different tribunals. Such evidence as we have received indicates that the quality of members is on the whole satisfactory, and we have ourselves no general proposals to make with regard to their qualifications. The new arrangements which we have recommended for the appointment of members will maintain and may well improve their quality.

The chairmen and members of appellate tribunals

58. Everything we have said so far in this Chapter applies also to tribunals which hear appeals from tribunals of first instance, except that all chairmen of appellate tribunals should have legal qualifications. Also the quality of membership should be higher than that in tribunals of first instance."

Tribunals and Inquiries Act 1992

s. 5

"Composition and procedure of tribunals and inquiries

Recommendations of Council as to appointment of members of tribunals

5.—(1) Subject to section 6 but without prejudice to the generality of section 1(1)(a), the Council may **1–16** make to the appropriate Minister general recommendations as to the making of appointments to membership of any tribunals mentioned in Schedule 1 or of panels constituted for the purposes of any such tribunals;

and (without prejudice to any statutory provisions having effect with respect to such appointments) the appropriate Minister shall have regard to recommendations under this section.

(2) In this section 'the appropriate Minister', in relation to appointments of any description, means the Minister making the appointments or, if they are not made by a Minister, the Minister in charge of the government department concerned with the tribunals in question.

(3) The following provisions shall have effect as respects any tribunal specified in Part II of Schedule 1—

    (a) the Council shall not make any recommendations under this section until—

        (i)   they have referred to the matter of the recommendations for consideration, and report to the Council, by the Scottish Committee, and

        (ii) they have considered the report of that Committee,

    (b) without prejudice to the generality of section 4(5), the Scottish Committee may of its own motion propose any such general recommendations as expedient to be made by the Council to the appropriate Minister, and

    (c) if the Council—

        (i)   in making recommendations under this section on any matter which they have referred to the Scottish Committee or on which that Committee has made proposals, do not adopt the report or proposals of that Committee without modification, or

        (ii) do not make recommendations on matters on which the Scottish Committee may submit its report or proposals to the Lord Advocate."

Notes

1–17   (1) The recommendation that the Council on Tribunals be responsible for membership of bodies under its remit has not been accepted. Section 5 contains the legislative response: section 6 is extracted at para. 1–20.

(2) Some of the most significant changes to the constitution of tribunals are contained in sections 5–6 of the Social Security Act 1998. The personnel of the new unified appeal tribunal established by the Act consists of a president appointed by the Lord Chancellor after consultation with the Lord Advocate who requires to be an advocate, barrister or solicitor of at least 10 years' standing: section 5(1), (3). The membership of the appeals tribunals will consist of persons appointed by the Lord Advocate after consultation, where appropriate, with the Lord President and the Chief Medical Officer for Scotland: section 6(1), (2). The qualifications of persons appointed to the panel of persons available to hear appeals as well as the number to be appointed and the terms and conditions of their appointment will be determined by the Lord Advocate with the consent of the Secretary of State: section 6 (3), (4). The person may be removed from the panel by the Lord Advocate on the grounds of incapacity or misbehaviour: section 6(5). The legislation governing appeals to the social security appeal tribunal, is the Social Security Administration Act 1992. Under it the president appointed persons to the panel from whom tribunal members would be drawn. He was further obliged to appoint persons having a knowledge or experience of the area from which appeals would come and would also be required to take into account any recommendations from organisations or persons considered appropriate. No such considerations apply to section 6. The tenure of panel members was also determined by the president. Partington, above, commenting on the relevant sections — sections 40 and 41 of the 1992 Act — felt that this form of selection "could lead to the establishment of a more active committed panel of members" (p. 176). The Council on Tribunals in its Annual Report 1996–97 (1996–97 H.C. 376) was concerned that there would be less scope for experienced lay membership under section 6. The Government countered by arguing that the new system would promote a body of professional people who would develop their own expertise. The council concluded that this was a "most significant and very unwelcome change": para. 1.21: see also para. 1.41 and Appendix A of the report for further comments and see too Report of the Scottish Committee, 1996–97, para. 1.39. How significant in your view is lay membership of a tribunal? Consider this in light of the article by Wikeley and Young above. Compare and contrast these provisions with the views expressed by the council in its 1997 Special Report, below, on the utility of the presidential approach. How far do these provisions weaken the role of the president? Is there a way in which the council's objectives could still be achieved within the new system? Arguably an even greater innovation than sections 5 and 6 is to be found in section 7 of the Act. Sections 5 to 7 are not yet in force.

Social Security Act 1998

s. 7

"Constitution of appeal tribunals

7.—(1) Subject to subsection (2) below, an appeal tribunal shall consist of one, two or three members **1–18** drawn by the President from the panel constituted under section 6 above.

(2) The member, or (as the case may be) at least one member, of an appeal tribunal must—

(a)   have a general qualification (construed in accordance with section 71 of the Courts and Legal Services Act 1990); or

(b)   be an advocate or solicitor in Scotland.

(3) Where an appeal tribunal has more than one member—

(a)   the President shall nominate one of the members as chairman;

(b)   decisions shall be taken by a majority of votes; and

(c)   unless regulations otherwise provide, the chairman shall have any casting vote.

(4) Where it appears to an appeal tribunal that a matter before it involves a question of fact of special difficulty, then, unless regulations otherwise provide, the tribunal may require one or more experts to provide assistance to it in dealing with the question.

(5) In subsection (4) above 'expert' means a member of the panel constituted under section 6 above who appears to the appeal tribunal concerned to have knowledge or experience which would be relevant in determining the question of fact of special difficulty.

(6) Regulations shall make provision with respect to—

(a)   the composition of appeal tribunals;

(b)   the procedure to be followed in allocating cases among differently constituted tribunals; and

(c)   the manner in which expert assistance is to be given under subsection (4) above… ."

Notes

(1) Under the Social Security Administration Act 1992, ss. 41 (1), 43 (1) the social security **1–19** appeal tribunal required to consist of a chairman and two other persons. There is no obligation for the new unified tribunal to consist of any more than one member. As originally drafted, there was no requirement that a chair, or any member, or indeed a single member, be legally qualified. This proposal proved extremely controversial, with lobbying groups pointing both to the difficulties encountered in the past with having non-legally qualified chairmen in the old supplementary benefit appeal tribunals, prior to the 1984 merger with national insurance local tribunals into SSATS, and to the increasing complexity of social security law. Subsection (2) now provides for the legal qualification of at least one member, but note that there is no specific requirement in the primary legislation that the lawyer member be the chairman. What are the advantages and disadvantages of the chairman being a lawyer? As a matter of practice, however, appeals relating to child support maintenance assessments will always go to a tribunal, with a legally qualified member who will be chairman if the tribunal consists of more than one member. The Government has given some indication as to which types of cases are likely to be heard by the one-, two- and three-person tribunals. About 75 per cent of appeal hearings will be heard by three-person tribunals, *per* Lord Hardie, the Lord Advocate: *Hansard*, H.L. Deb., Vol. 558, col. 135 (March 30, 1998). Cases relating to care or mobility component of disability living allowance will be heard by a three-person tribunal, comprising a legal and medical member, along with the person who has knowledge or experience of the needs of disabled persons. Two-person tribunals may be used where the appeal relates to labour market conditions for jobseekers' allowance, *per* Baroness Hollis of Higham: *Hansard*, H.L. Deb., Vol. 584, col. 144 (January 15, 1998). A legally qualified member sitting alone might hear an appeal which relates solely to whether a claimant satisfies the residence and present requirements for jobseekers' allowance, *per* Lord Hardie: *Hansard*, H.L. Deb., Vol. 588, col. 958 (April 20, 1998). Full details of the criteria for allocation will be contained in regulations to be issued under subsection (6)(*a*). Others suggest that such a structured or coherent approach to the constitution of tribunals may not be followed in practice — for example, M. Dailly, "Social Security Bill" (1997) 244 SCOLAG 127 suggests that in practice "simple" appeals

will always be sent to a one-member tribunal for a determination with a decision on what is a simple appeal being determined by DSS-appointed staff.

(2) Note the provisions in subsections (4)–(6) on the use of experts. However, the decision to use an expert rests with the tribunal and there is no obligation to obtain expert help. The Council on Tribunals certainly felt that the potential implication of this change was a "retrograde step", taking social security appeals back to where they were before the transfer of adjudication functions to adjudication officers and SSATs. In its view, the person hearing the appeal should be qualified and trained in the particular skills necessary to chair that tribunal: see paras 1.13 and 1.24 of the 1997 Report. Note also the comments of the council that there is no right of appeal if the appellant should not agree with the constitution of the tribunal: para. 1.22. The council also noted that one cause of frequent adjournment in the existing tribunal system was the apparent lack of expertise on the tribunal member hearing the appeal. Single-member tribunals are also competent in the field of employment rights disputes: see the Employment Rights (Dispute Resolution) Act 1998. In its 1996–97 Report the Scottish Committee of the Council on Tribunals, commenting on the Green Paper leading to that Act, had (at para. 1.42):

> "some misgivings that the proposals indicated an even closer move towards an industrial 'court'. We noted that the proposals allowed for a full time legal chairman to sit on his own, not only with power to determine the case but also initially to decide if the appeal should proceed in the first place. We firmly believe that there is a real need for lay input to be maintained."

(3) In its 1984–85 Report the Council on Tribunals noted that the transfer of responsibility for the special commissioners of income tax, value added tax tribunals, and social security commissioners to the Lord Chancellor's department strengthened independence and the perception of that independence and that generally, where important questions of public finance are involved or policies with a high degree of political content, then generally the oversight of such tribunals should be in the hands of a judicial department. Do you agree? What significance does the involvement of the Lord Chancellor and the Lord Advocate have in the appointment of presidents and panel members under sections 5 and 6 of the 1998 Act? is the suggestion of independence contained in such provisions undermined by the abolition of the independent tribunal service in the same Act? On this see para. 1–47.

(4) However, by far the most common pattern of appointment of chairmen is found in section 6 of the Tribunals and Inquiries Act 1992.

Tribunals and Inquires Act 1992

s. 6(1), (2), (5)–(8)

"Appointment of chairmen of certain tribunals

1–20   6.—(1) The chairman, or any person appointed to act as chairman, of any of the tribunals to which this subsection applies shall (without prejudice to any statutory provisions as to qualifications) be selected by the appropriate authority from a panel of persons appointed by the Lord Chancellor.

(2) Members of panels constituted under this section shall hold and vacate office under the terms of the instruments under which they are appointed, but may resign office by notice in writing to the Lord Chancellor; and any such member who ceases to hold office shall be eligible for re-appointment... .

(5) The person or persons constituting any tribunal specified in paragraph 31 of Schedule 1 shall be appointed by the Lord Chancellor, and where such a tribunal consists of more than one person the Lord Chancellor shall designate which of them is to be the chairman.

(6) In this section, 'the appropriate authority' means the Minister who apart from this Act would be empowered to appoint or select the chairman, person to act as chairman, members or member of the tribunal in question.

(7) A panel may be constituted under this section for the purposes either of a single tribunal or of two or more tribunals, whether or not of the same description.

(8) In relation to any of the tribunals referred to in this section which sits in Scotland, this section shall have effect with the substitution for any reference to the Lord Chancellor of a reference to the Lord President of the Court of Session."

Notes

(1) The Council on Tribunals recommended that chairmen of tribunals should normally be **1–21** legally qualified. In one of its earliest reports, that of 1959, it stated that experience showed that proceedings did not tend to become formal with a legally qualified chairman: para. 29. In 1982 only 36 per cent of supplementary benefit appeal tribunal chairmen were legally qualified, although most national insurance local tribunal chairmen were and the Council on Tribunals criticised the loss of good, experienced chairmen: see the Annual Report for 1982–3, para. 3.36. Compare with the provisions of section 6 of the 1998 Act at para. 1–17.

(2) There is also concern over the independence of clerks: see the Annual Report of the Council on Tribunals for 1973–4, paras 77–8 and see too the concerns of Dailly, above, in relation to the Social Security Act 1998. The officers and staff administering the new appeals agency which replaces the independent tribunal service, on which see para. 1–47, are to be appointed by the Secretary of State, see Sched. 1, para. 11, and have powers under para. 12 (other than determining appeals) delegated to them by the Secretary of State. These powers could conceivably include power to determine whether a case goes to a one-, two- or three-member tribunal. In Dailly's view, not only do such staff lack independence, there still remains the question of the scope for bias to enter the appeals process prior to a tribunal decision.

So far we have been concerned with formal requirements in connection with appointment to tribunals. However, these only tell half the story. Of equal importance is the way in which persons available for selection come to be in the pool and, once selected, how they carry out their functions. Consider the following excerpt in relation to the previous system of social security appeal tribunals.

N. Wikeley and R. Young, "The Marginalisation of Lay Members in Social Security Appeal Tribunals" in Judging Social Security (1992).

pp. 131–133

"Chairman were generally rather younger than lay members. Nearly half of the chairmen we interviewed **1–22** were in their fifties; a quarter were under 50 and a further quarter aged 60 or more. By contrast the great majority of members (63%) were over 60 years old. One quarter of the chairmen were female, indicating that there has been some success in appointing a larger number of women to such posts (in 1982 the proportion was only 17%: Harris, 1983).

Earlier studies were critical of the unrepresentative nature of those appointed to serve as lay members on tribunals (Lister, 1974, Fulbrook, 1978). The two lay members on each social security appeal tribunal, who receive expenses but no fee, are now drawn from a single list of people 'appearing to the President to have knowledge or experience of conditions in the area and to be representative of persons living or working in the area' (Social Security Act 1975, Sched. 10, para. 1(2)). Formerly both of the old tribunals had employed a two panel system. In national insurance local tribunals there were separate lists for employees and employers, with the members nominated by Trades Councils and business interests respectively to reflect the role of both sides of industry in contributing to the national insurance fund. Supplementary benefit appeal tribunals were constituted rather differently. One member, called the Secretary of State's member, was meant to have knowledge or experience of conditions in the area concerned and of the problems of the people living on low incomes. The other, the Trades Council member, was drawn from a panel representing work people.

The Government's plan to abolish the two panel system, and with it the automatic presence of at least one trade unionist on each tribunal, proved to be so politically controversial that it was dropped to ensure the passage of the HASSASSA Act 1983, before that year's General Election. The proposal was subsequently reintroduced and enacted in the Health and Social Security Act 1984. The rationale for the change, according to Government spokesmen, was the need to provide a more broadly representative base for tribunal membership. Critics feared that the middle class bias in the tribunals' composition would only become more pronounced (Wikeley, 1985).

In practice it seems that the creation of a single panel has made little difference as yet to the make-up of tribunals. In our sample by far the largest single group of members, some 37%, had been nominated by trade unions, almost twice as many as fell into the next largest category, those nominated by somebody within the tribunal system itself. These trade union nominees were also amongst the longest serving members of the tribunals, two thirds of them having been members for between five and 15 years. As indicated above, members were on average older than chairmen, although the proportion of women (38%) was higher than amongst chairmen. Notwithstanding the continuing role of trade union nominees, our findings suggest that the tribunal system has failed to build up a broader base of lay membership to reflect in some measure the range of people that appear as appellants. Only one of the 97 members we interviewed described himself as unemployed. It is still the case that most appellants find themselves facing a row of white, rather elderly faces across the tribunal table."

Notes

1–23   (1) For the full report see J. Baldwin, N. Wikeley and R. Young, *Judging Social Security* (1992). For a commentary on the previous system of SBATS see I. Flockhart, "Some Aspects of Tribunal Membership" in *"Justice, Discretion and Poverty"* (M. Adler and A. W. Bradley, eds., 1975).

(2) In some other situations the problem relates more to a lack of understanding of the role of the tribunal members. Where a legally qualified chairman sits, there is sometimes a tendency for the lay members to adopt a more passive role, particularly where issues may be legally complex, as in social security law, housing law or employment law. It is also sometimes assumed that where there is lay input into a tribunal there is also an assumption that where a lay member sits on the tribunal, they in some way represent a "side". That view does not appear to be borne out in practice: see, for example, the findings of K. Bell, "National Insurance Local Tribunals" (1974) 3 *Journal of Social Policy* 289 and (1975) 4 *Journal of Social Policy* 1. Often this arises because of a misunderstanding of the purpose of the legislation on which tribunal membership is based. For example, employment tribunals often consist of a chairman and two other members, one having experience of the employer's role, the other the employee's role. The difficulties of perception which this creates were noted by W. E. Cavenagh and D. Newton, "Administrative tribunals: How people become members" (1971) 49 *Public Administration* 197 at 210:

> "Ambiguity about what lay members are supposed to contribute seems to have been the cause of practical problems in the Industrial Tribunal, where some lay members, particularly on the workers' side, appear to come on with the idea that they are there to 'represent' their own 'side' of industry; yet this conflicts fundamentally with the view of the previous Lord Chancellor [Lord Gardiner] as expressed in 1968 in a speech circulated to all members:
>
> 'One sometimes hears the members erroneously referred to as "the employers' representative" or "the employees' representative". They are not. They represent no one, except the interests of justice. Each is an entirely independent judicial officer, who decides a case upon its merits, upon the evidence and law applicable'.
>
> But despite these words the problem persists and the misconception still seems quite widespread."

(3) Some attempt to address the question of passivity has been made. For example, in England, the Judicial Studies Board has become responsible for supervising the training of chairmen and members of many tribunals. There is a statutory obligation to arrange training for members of children's hearings: the Social Work (Scotland) Act 1968, Sched. 3, para. 7 and the Children (Scotland) Act 1995, s. 39(2), Sched. 1, paras 9, 10. Under the system of social security appeal tribunals, there is a statutory obligation to arrange training. Under the system of unified appeal tribunals created by section 1 of the Social Security Act 1998, this is no longer the case. Both Wikeley and Young, pp. 137–139, and Partington below, pp. 176–178, believed such training to be valuable. However, not everyone has been satisfied with training programmes: see, for example, C. Jones and M. Adler, "Can Anyone Get On These?" Scottish Consumer Council (1990). Similarly, the Scottish Committee of the Council on Tribunals has expressed concern about training in a number of its reports. Concern has, for example, been expressed about the training of those who take part in the decisions of education appeal committees, on which see the Annual Report 1996–97, paras 1.30–1.33, and in relation to local valuation appeal committees: see, for example, the Annual Report 1995–96, paras 1.32 and 2.7. Part of the difficulty appears to be that in the statute creating the tribunal there is, with a few exceptions, no obligation on the part of the constituting authority to train tribunal members. In its 1997–98 Report the committee reported with regret that (p. 18):

"Unfortunately we cannot report any progress towards recognising the need for tribunal training to be raised to the same level as that in other judicial processes. There will always be room for improvement in this vital area and when the opportunity arises the Committee will continue to press that a more professional attitude be adopted by tribunals and their funding Departments. We will encourage the implementation of training programmes for chairmen and members, but our efforts have not yet borne fruit."

It went on to observe that:

"The problem is the more pressing because of the impending introduction into U.K. law of the European Convention on Human Rights. Grappling with the complexities of this is going to be as much a difficulty for us as it will be for individual tribunals. We can see that even tribunals with good existing training programmes are going to have problems introducing the legislation to their procedures. How much more will that be the case when the programmes are less good? For all tribunals, this is a challenge."

LEGAL AID AND REPRESENTATION

Many of the issues which tribunals have to consider involve complex issues of law and the outcome of the tribunal's decision can be of great practical significance to the claimant or appellant. It is therefore unsurprising that many of those who become involved in the tribunal system wish to engage the services of an adviser, whether a lawyer or other expert. The most detailed study that exists took place in the context of the tribunal system in England and was carried out by Professor H. Genn. She considered the operation of SSAT's immigration adjudicators, industrial tribunals and mental health tribunals. There is, however, no reason to conclude that her findings would be markedly different in Scotland. **1–24**

H. Genn, "Tribunals and Informal Justice"

(1993) 56 M.L.R. 393 at 398 [Footnotes have been omitted.]

"A common characteristic of tribunals and informal courts is the relative infrequency with which one or both parties are represented. This absence of representation, especially for the weakest party, may be a deliberate design feature of the tribunal or informal court, and is generally justified on the grounds that the simplified procedures, absence of formality and, sometimes, interventionist role permitted to the judge or tribunal renders representation either unnecessary or inimical to the spirit of the hearings. All of these arguments can be found in literature concerning tribunals in England and Wales and in studies from abroad. For example: **1–25**

'Although the point has been cogently — many would say persuasively — disputed … informality is commonly thought to be not only a strength of, but also a reason for creating, tribunals that are not bound by the usual rules of legal procedure. One of the purported virtues of informal tribunals is that they are thought to allow litigants who cannot afford, or would be unwise to invest in, legal counsel to comprehend what is occurring and to present meaningful arguments to the decisionmaker.'

Arguments about the lack of necessity for representation in tribunals and small claims courts come in many different guises, but at bottom the rationale is simply one of resources. As Lempert and Monsma point out in a footnote: 'There is nothing natural about people lacking counsel when they cannot afford it or when the cost would be greater than the amount at stake. Society could, as it does for many misdemeanours, subsidise counsel for everyone facing informal hearings. Such a decision might soon transform the informal character of such tribunals while at the same time making informality less necessary.' Informality is therefore only *necessary* when a prior decision has been taken that representation will not be subsidised. The resources issue that often underpins decisions to opt for 'informal,' 'non-technical' proceedings should not, therefore, be obscured in debates about the drawbacks of conventional courts. The two issues are separate.

Despite the frequent absence of representatives from informal court and tribunal hearings, evidence from empirical research carried out in some tribunals and small claims courts consistently indicates that when present, representation can give an advantage to the represented party. Empirical studies in the UK on the contribution of representation to tribunals generally suggests that represented tribunal applicants are more likely to achieve a favourable outcome to their hearing than unrepresented applicants. However, some of the findings have been criticised for failing to take account of the possibility that representatives select the strongest cases.

The research by Lempert and Monsma on Housing Eviction Boards in Hawaii similarly concludes that legal representation makes a difference to the outcome before informal tribunals. In a study of alternatives in dispute processing procedures in the U.S. Sarat found that inequality in legal representation worked to the advantage of the party with legal counsel, enabling represented defendants to escape without suffering any loss. He concludes that: 'Of all the steps in the process by which disputes develop and settlement activity occurs, none is more significant than the decision to retain an attorney.' The reasons for the apparent advantage bestowed by representation have not received much close scrutiny by researchers. Indeed, policymakers and researchers have appeared reluctant to elaborate on such evidence, and the question of what it is that representatives *do* in hearings has received remarkably little attention in the literature on tribunals, informal justice, or on traditional court adjudication.

One of the chief results of the official view of tribunals in this country is their virtual exclusion from the Legal Aid scheme, although legal or lay representation is permitted in all tribunals. The absence of legal aid is generally explained or defended on the ground that tribunal procedures have been so designed that applicants should be able to bring their cases in person and without legal representation. Tribunal procedures are generally flexible; strict rules of evidence do not apply; applicants are permitted to tell their story in their own words; and tribunal chairs are free to take a more interventionist role than judges in court. Indeed, it is argued not only that legal representation is unnecessary in tribunals, but that the presence of lawyers might undermine the speed and informality that are the hallmarks of tribunal procedures. Despite the absence of legal aid for representation, however, some of those who bring their cases before tribunals pay for legal representation or obtain free representation from law centres, tribunal representation units, the Free Representation Unit and a host of specialist advice agencies across the country who provide a limited representation service. Repeated calls for the extension of legal aid to tribunals have fallen on deaf ears, although the research upon which this paper is based was commissioned specifically by the Lord Chancellor's Department to address some of the arguments made about the need for representation to be available to tribunal applicants.

The research looked at two broad questions: does representation increase the likelihood of winning at a tribunal hearing, holding other factors constant? If so, why? What is it about tribunal procedures, about the behaviour of tribunals, about the activities of representatives or the inadequacies of unrepresented appellants that gives represented applicants an advantage, and what, if anything, does this tell us about informal procedures generally?

The Effect of Representation on the Outcome of Tribunal Hearings

An analysis of the effect of representation on the outcome of hearings established that, in all four tribunals, the presence of a skilled representative significantly and independently increased the probability that a case would succeed. In social security appeals tribunals, the presence of a skilled representative increased the likelihood of success from 30 to 48 per cent. In hearings before immigration adjudicators, the overall likelihood of success was increased by the presence of a representative from 20 to 38 per cent. In mental health review tribunals, the likelihood of a favourable change in conditions rose from 20 to 35 per cent as a result of representation. The effect of representation on the outcome of industrial tribunal hearings is more complicated to state since both parties to hearings are able to appear with a representative. If the respondent was not represented and the applicant was represented by a lawyer, the applicant's success figure was increased from 30 to 48 per cent. Where the respondent was legally represented and the applicant was unrepresented, the applicant's probability of success fell to 10 per cent.

The research indicated clearly that the presence of a representative influences the *substantive* outcome of hearings, irrespective of the process value that representation may provide. It also showed that the type of representation used by appellants was very important, and that specialist representatives exerted the greatest influence on the outcome of hearings. In seeking to understand why representation appeared to have such a significant effect on the outcome of hearings that are intended to be 'informal,' the research raises questions about a number of assumptions and possible misconceptions concerning informal procedures in general. These can be summarised as:
   (a) the 'small equals simple" fallacy
   (b) the mismatch between informal procedure and decision-making in informal tribunals
   (c) the ability of appellants to prepare and advocate their own cases
   (d) the ability of tribunals to assist appellants in the absence of representation.

(a) The Problem of Complexity — 'Small' is not Necessarily 'Simple'
Much of the justification for establishing small claims courts or informal machinery for resolving low value claims rests on the reasonable assumption that such claims do not warrant a large investment by the claimant and, in any case, most claimants would not have the necessary resources to invest. It does not follow, however, that claims of small value are always, or ever, legally and factually simple, amenable to conveyor-belt resolution that would deliver substantively just outcomes. Indeed, it is generally accepted

that specialist tribunals are necessary because the regulations concerning, for example, social security benefits and immigration cases are so complex that generalist judges in the county court would be unlikely to be able to provide a high enough standard of decision-making.

Many of the views expressed by tribunal chairs and representatives during interviews were prefaced with complaints about the technicality and complexity of the legal framework within which the tribunals operated. Although most tribunal hearings are more informal and procedurally more flexible than courts, such informality has been wrongly assumed to extend to all aspects of tribunal processes. The fact that hearings are conducted across a table and that an appellant may choose whether he puts his case first are positive characteristics that should be protected and perhaps extended. However, none of the procedural informality of tribunals can overcome or alter the need for applicants to bring their cases within the regulations or statute, and prove their factual situation with evidence. Nor do informal procedures relieve tribunals from the obligation to make reasoned and consistent decisions.

Interviews with tribunal chairs and representatives revealed repeatedly a perception of, and concern about, the complexity of the law with which tribunals were required to deal:

> 'The process is very complex. I have problems understanding it all, so I don't know how the appellants manage — I am legally trained.' [SSAT Chair]
> 'Social security law is very underrated, but it is very finicky and these are people that need help more than any.' [SSAT Chair]
> 'There are so many precedents and anyone who didn't know the ins and outs of the law would think "Ah, I can go along to an adjudicator and I can put my case." But unless you know all the pitfalls you are liable to fall flat on your fact.' [Immigration Adjudicator]
> 'Industrial law is so complex now. Joe Bloggs is not going to distinguish between whether we think he nicked something or whether we are looking at the employer acting reasonably. People just don't appreciate these distinctions. The law has become silted up. We have unhappily got ourselves into a situation of high technicality.' [Industrial Tribunal Chair]

The 'small is simple' fallacy conveniently supports some of the justifications for establishing tribunals in which ordinary people might present their own cases, but the weakness in the argument was exposed in the statements of those whose job it is to decide such cases. It has also been challenged by other evaluations of procedures in small claims courts and tribunals... .

(c) Advocating the Case

Interviews with appellants carried out while they waited for their hearing to commence revealed that many were vague about what was likely to happen during the course of the hearing. This was especially so with appellants in SSATs who often had almost no idea about what 'appealing' actually meant. Many of those who bring their cases before tribunals have no accurate knowledge about the powers of tribunals or what the possible outcome of their hearing could be. Although tribunals issue information about appeals, this does little to explain what hearings will be like in practical terms. Most importantly, appellants are not informed in advance about their own role in the hearing and what they will have to do in order to persuade a tribunal to allow their case.

Tribunal information tends to stress the informality of proceedings. The danger of this is that, in the absence of direct experience, appellants develop misconceptions about the nature of the hearing and the way in which decisions are likely to be reached. Some may presume that informality is synonymous with a quiet chat or, at worst, an interview. They may also take the word 'independent' to mean 'on their side'. These problems were found to be particularly pronounced with appellants attending SSATs, which are the most informal of the tribunals studied. For example:

> 'I'm just going to tell them the truth.'
> 'You only need someone to speak for you if you are telling lies.'
> 'It's an open and shut case. It will only take me a few minutes.'
> 'It's the law that makes it difficult, and my case isn't in law.'

Most of those interviewed during the course of the research were experiencing their first tribunal hearing. Applicants therefore have no direct experience on which to base their expectations of the hearing. Although a substantial number of those interviewed felt confident whilst waiting for their hearing, many others expressed anxiety and concern about what they were going to face. In the event, some found the experience less difficult than they had expected, but many found the process traumatic. Apart from an inability to understand the law and the procedure, many unrepresented appellants said that they found difficulty in simply explaining the details of their case. This was confirmed in observation when applicants who had been reasonably confident and articulate in the waiting room became confused and hesitant once inside the hearing room.

Their conviction about the merit of their claim withered under close questioning which was often interpreted as hostile (even though in practice the purpose of the questioning was merely clarification). This was true of unrepresented appellants in SSATs, and even more so of unrepresented applicants in industrial tribunals who are cross-examined on their evidence and offered the opportunity to carry out cross-examination themselves.

A common complaint amongst those interviewed was that they had not known how they should have put their case and had not been prepared for what was required of them at the hearing. IN SSATs particularly, many appellants seemed unprepared for the importance of law.

> 'They said there was a clause for this and a clause for that, and that I didn't come into such and such clause. What are all these clauses anyway?'

Many were dismayed at the binding nature of regulations and did not understand why they had to be rigidly followed. Many appellants had believed that the tribunal were capable of looking at the case in a different manner from the DSS, at least with 'humanity and sympathy', and were frustrated that decisions were being made in accordance with regulations:

> 'They don't look at you as a person. They have got the rule book there and they have got to go by the book.'
> 'They should bring a bit of humanity or common sense into the thing. All I have heard up until now is section this and subsection that, which are very rigid.'
> 'I couldn't understand what they were talking about at all because everything was schedule such and such, you know, different numbers, but not saying to me why. It's hard, it's confusing. I'd sooner be told point blank. It's too complicated for me.'

Given that there is such a high level of confusion about the law and how it operates, it is not surprising that appellants do not comprehend the significance of case law and precedent:

> 'I just don't understand. That Chairman kept going on about this other bloke's case all those years back, and not looking at mine. I mean, I don't care what happened to a bloke down a quarry however many years ago it was.' [SSAT Appellant, confused by a leading case on industrial injuries introduced during his hearing.]

Even in SSATs, appellants found the language of the tribunal formal and difficult to follow, despite the efforts of tribunal chairman to 'enable' appellants to put their case. Appellants were often inarticulate, and some had literacy problems, which meant that they were easily intimidated by the fluency of the DSS Presenting Officer's submission and the jargon of the tribunal.

Unrepresented appellants were often successful but, in spite of winning appeals, there were still complaints about the difficulties of the hearing. Those who were successful were more likely than those who lost their case to say that they would go through the process again, but only if there was no alternative:

> 'If you are entitled, you should get it and shouldn't be put through a hearing.'
> 'Even though I won, I wouldn't like to do it again.'

Observation of hearings revealed that, despite the relative informality of surroundings and procedure, and despite the fact that many chairs are at some pains to put unrepresented appellants at ease, they are frequently at a disadvantage."

Notes

1–26   (1) The other factors noted by Genn, of the limits of informality and the ability of tribunals to assist an appellant (and their relationship to representation), are extracted and discussed at paras 1–33 and 1–37 respectively.

(2) Such Scottish research as exists indicates a fairly low level of representation. Adler and Bradley, pp. 109–127, established that in 1974 in Edinburgh and East Fife only 41 per cent of applicants were represented before NILTs and 30 per cent before SBATs. Similar findings are contained in the 1984 Report of the Scottish Consumer Council, "Tackling Tribunals".

(3) Undoubtedly one of the contributing factors to the relatively low level of representation is the difficulty in obtaining legal aid for tribunal representation. Some limited assistance is sometimes provided for legal advice leading up to the tribunal hearing, but not representation at the hearing. For example, at Housing Benefit Review Boards, the Scottish Legal Aid Board

will pay for a solicitor to give advice and assistance in preparing for a case before the board but will not pay for advocacy at the board. There is also limited provision for making assistance by way of representation at specific tribunals such as the mental health review tribunal. Legal aid is available in connection with a few tribunal proceedings such as the Lands Tribunal for Scotland and the employment appeal tribunal and for certain court proceedings relating to children's hearings. On legal aid generally see *Stair Memorial Encyclopaedia*, Vol. 13, "Legal Aid". What are the arguments for extending legal aid further?

Royal Commission on Legal Services in Scotland (Hughes Commission)

Cmnd. 7846 (1980), pp. 72–73, 91–93

"We recommend in Chapter 8 an extension of legal aid to enable claimants to be represented before tribunals by a solicitor — but only in limited circumstances. We believe that the best way to meet the needs of claimants before many tribunals is to encourage the development of lay representation at tribunals. Although a number of organisations such as Citizens Advice Bureaux, trade unions and claimants rights groups do excellent work in representing tribunal claimants, there is considerable variation in the help and advice available to claimants appearing before tribunals. The availability of representation also varies with the subject matter of the particular tribunal. Most claimants making an application to a tribunal both lodge the application and appear before the tribunal without the benefit of any informed and independent advice. This is unsatisfactory.   **1–27**

We know that a number of projects to try to build up lay representation before tribunals have been encouraged in England. From our observations such projects have helped both to extend the amount of representation and advice before tribunals, and also to improve the quality of such representation and advice. There have, however, only been a few projects of this nature. Some projects have concentrated on the training of lay representatives while others have built up teams who could provide representation before particular tribunals. Yet another scheme was aimed at providing a 'duty representative' at National Insurance Tribunals, who could advise all claimants and appear on their behalf if necessary. The source of funding of the different projects varies and is often only guaranteed for a short period. The future of the existing tribunal representation units, given the present funding basis, appears to be very insecure. While the inquisitorial approach of a tribunal may mean that the quality of presentation of a claimant's case is less critical to the outcome of his case, there is considerable scope for developing the system of lay representation before tribunals, and we are strongly of the opinion that finance should be made available for this purpose. While we recognise that there are a variety of kinds of tribunal, we recommend that encouragement should be given to developing the provision of lay advice and representation before those tribunals in which lay participation is appropriate, and that adequate training should be provided for lay representatives …"

Justice — All Souls Report 1988

paras 68–70

"The Lord Chancellor's Advisory Committee on Legal Aid considered the question of legal aid for tribunals in its Annual Report published in 1974 (HC20(1974–75)) and concluded that it was essential for applicants (a term it used to include appellants, claimants and, where appropriate, respondents) to have (i) access to competent advice as to their rights, the advisability of appealing and the consequences of doing so; (ii) frequently, assistance in gathering information and preparing the case; and (iii), in a limited number of cases, representation at the hearing (para. 31). 'There is a wide spectrum of need on the part of tribunal applicants, ranging from moral support and encouragement at one extreme to experienced legal advocacy on difficult issues of law at the other' (para. 33). The Committee found that there were many types of case that were too complex for the applicant to handle in which welfare organisations and trade unions had developed skills and expertise. It rejected the suggestion made to it that there should be a specialised body, decentralised in its administration throughout the country, for providing non-legal representation wherever that was needed, and preferred a system of financial support to those existing agencies that were providing non-legal help as part of their general service of advice and assistance (para. 34). The Committee did not consider that a tribunal could itself provide a satisfactory substitute for effective representation, especially where the other side was represented (para. 37)."   **1–28**

Notes

1–29   (1) The present Government is not likely to extend legal aid to tribunal representation notwithstanding the recommendation of the Hughes Commission and the Lord Chancellor's 1974 Report referred to in the JUSTICE-All Souls Report. The Council on Tribunals proposed in its evidence to the Royal Commission on Legal Services, Cmnd., 7648, para. 15–28, that if legal aid were made available, it should be limited to where a significant point of law arises or where the evidence is likely to be too complex for laymen to deal with or it is a test case where an issue of deprivation of liberty or an ability to earn is at stake.

(2) Under the Special Immigration Appeals Commission Act 1997 there is a right to legal representation before the Commission: section 5 (2). The lack of a right was one of the defects identified by the European Court of Human Rights in relation to the previous advisory panel procedures: see *Chahal v. United Kingdom* (1997) 23 E.H.R.R. 413, noted at para. 844, and see also the Immigration Appeals Committee Report for 1996–97, para. 1.52.

(3) Any development in representation is likely to come from organisations such as trade unions, the Citizens Advice Bureaux, welfare rights groups or the United Kingdom Immigration Advisory Service. There is arguably some merit in that Genn's findings suggest that it is not necessarily the case that lawyers are any more successful than lay advisers in securing positive results for clients. This has been noticed by the Council on Tribunals. For example, in its Annual Report for 1974–75, para. 85 it observed that:

> "In addition to applicants who would benefit from the provision of legal aid, there is a substantial number of applicants for whom non legal advice or representation is required and is indeed the more appropriate form of aid."

On the relative merits of lawyers as compared to lay advisers see generally R. Lawrence, "Solicitors and Tribunals" [1980] J.S.W.L. 13; A. Frost and C. Howard, *Representation and Administrative Tribunals* (1977): and the JUSTICE-All Souls Report, pp. 222–261. For a more recent discussion of the role and impact of CAB lay representatives see M. Dailly, "Lay representation in courts and tribunals — the evidence of CAB lay representatives in Scotland" (1998) 253 SCOLAG 110 and for reply see S. McPhee (1998) 254 SCOLAG 127.

TRIBUNAL PROCEDURE

Franks Report

paras 62–64

"Codes of procedure
1–30   62. Most of the evidence we have received concerning tribunals has placed great emphasis upon procedure, not only at the hearing itself but also before and after it. There has been general agreement on the broad essentials which the procedure, in this wider sense, should contain, for example provision for notice of the right to apply to a tribunal, notice of the case which the applicant has to meet, a reasoned decision by the tribunal and notice of any further right of appeal.

63. We agree that procedure is of the greatest importance and that it should be clearly laid down in a statute or statutory instrument. Because of the great variety of the purposes for which tribunals are established, however, we do not think it would be appropriate to rely upon either a single code or a small number of codes. We think that there is a case for greater procedural differentiation and prefer that the detailed procedure for each type of tribunal should be designed to meet the particular circumstances... .

Informality of atmosphere
64. There has been considerable emphasis, in much of the evidence we have received, upon the importance of preserving informality of atmosphere in hearings before tribunals, though it is generally conceded that in some

tribunals, for example the Lands Tribunal, informality is not an over-riding necessity. We endorse this view, but we are convinced that an attempt which has been made to secure informality in the general run of tribunals has in some instances been at the expense of an orderly procedure. Informality without rules of procedure may be positively inimical to right adjudication, since the proceedings may well assume an unordered character which makes it difficult, if not impossible, for the tribunal properly to sift the facts and weigh the evidence. It should be remembered that by their very nature tribunals may be less skilled in adjudication than courts of law. None of our witnesses would seek to make tribunals in all respects like courts of law, but there is a wide measure of agreement that in many instances their procedure could be made more orderly without impairing the desired informality of atmosphere. The object to be aimed at in most tribunals is the combination of a formal procedure with an informal atmosphere. We see no reason why this cannot be a formal procedure with an informal atmosphere. We see no reason why this cannot be achieved. On the one hand it means a manifestly sympathetic attitude on the part of the tribunal and the absence of the trappings of a court, but on the other hand such prescription of procedure as makes the proceedings clear and orderly."

Tribunals and Inquiries Act 1992

s. 8

"Procedural rules for tribunals

8.—(1) The power of a Minister, the Lord President of the Court of Session, the Commissioners of Inland Revenue or the Foreign Compensation Commission to make, approve, confirm or concur in procedural rules for any tribunal specified in Schedule 1 and shall be exercisable only after consultation with the Council.

(2) The power of the Treasury to make—

(a)   regulations under section 48(3) of the Building Societies Act 1986 (regulations with respect to appeals to the tribunal established under section 47 of that Act), or

(b)   regulations under section 30 of the Banking Act 1987 (regulations with respect to appeals under Part I of that Act),

shall be exercisable only after consultation with the Council.

(3) The Council shall consult the Scottish Committee in relation to the exercise of their functions under this section—

(a)   with respect to any tribunal specified in Part II of Schedule 1, or

(b)   with respect to any regulations under section 30 of the Banking Act 1987 which (by virtue of subsection (4) of that section) are made by the Lord Advocate.

(4) In this section 'procedural rules' includes any statutory provision relating to the procedure of the tribunal in question."

1–31

Notes

(1) Many of the tribunals subject to the supervision of the Council on Tribunals now have statutory rules and procedure. A range of procedural matters have been examined by the council, including the extent to which a hearing might be held in private, restriction on the right of representation by lawyers, see, for example, the Scottish Betting Levy Appeal Tribunal Rules, whether the formal rules of evidence should apply to tribunals, reasons for decisions, time-limits, procedure and general complexity. In its 1982–83 Report at para. 2.20 the council noted that it was generally not appropriate for tribunals to make their own rules because of a lack of expertise and, because unlike other rule makers, they are not accountable to Parliament. Is this realistic? In its most recent form, this concern has been expressed by the publication by the Council on Tribunals of a model code of procedure.

(2) The full text of the code can be found in Appendix C to the 1986–87 Annual Report (1987–88 H.C. 234). The code in turn is bolstered by a code for consultation with the council and the Scottish Committee which details the minimum requirements the council and the committee expect in relation to consultation on certain subordinate legislation affecting tribunals and the general desirability of being consulted on proposals for primary legislation. It also sets out the form in timing for such consultations. The current code is found in Appendix D of the Annual Report of the Scottish Committee for 1997–98.

1–32

(3) The extent to which departments will have regard to those codes is not clear. Compliance is purely voluntary and in the past the council has criticised departments which failed to consult it at an early stage when procedural rules were in fact subject to section 8 of the 1992 Act. Sometimes consultation has been 'farcical": see, for example, the DHSS (as it was then called) which sent draft regulations to the council on July 26 and then laid them before Parliament on August 2 — Annual Report 1984–85 (1985–86 H.C. 54). See also the 1995–96 Report of the Scottish Committee, where it regretted a 10-day time-limit being imposed by the Scottish Office Department of Health on draft regulations on the procedure of NHS committees. It described the time-limit as 'unsatisfactory and unrealistic' (para. 1.17).

The Scottish Committee of the council has been asked to comment on good practice guides for particular tribunals issued by the relevant government departments. Here, consultation has often been of real assistance: see, for example, in relation to the guide on valuation appeal committee, the Annual Report 1996–97, paras 1.86–1.71; in relation to the Code for Local Planning Inquiries, the 1995–96 Report, para. 1.44 and the 1996–97 Report, paras 1.5–1.6. While the Council on Tribunals has endeavoured to ensure that tribunal procedure is kept as close to the Franks' ideals of openness, fairness and impartiality, others question whether tribunal procedure meets those ideals.

H. Genn, "Tribunals and Informal Justice"

(1993) 56 M.L.R. 393 at 402 [Footnotes have been omitted.]

1–33   "Decision-making in tribunals is accomplished within the context of rules and case law which determine the existence of entitlements, or the limits of 'reasonableness.' The task of SSATs and immigration adjudicators is to scrutinise administrative decisions and to check that they have been made in accordance with regulations. Industrial tribunals are required to adjudicate between employers and employees on questions governed by statute and case law. MHRTs are intended to give effect to statutory provisions, although in practice they regard their role to be rather wider than this. SSATs, industrial tribunals and immigration hearings all have appellate tiers whose decisions affect future determinations, and the decisions of all tribunals are subject to judicial review. To succeed before such a tribunal an applicant must bring his case within the regulations or statute and prove his factual situation with evidence. Applicants do not succeed with cases for social security benefits because they cannot manage on their money; immigrants are not permitted to stay in the country because they want to; debtors are not permitted to avoid their debts in small claims courts because they cannot afford to pay. All must assert and establish a legal right, entitlement or defence: 'the assertion of a right is a form of moral criticism: besides the expression of a demand, it involves an appeal to the authority of principle in support of one's claims.' This represents the 'limit' of informality.

The decisions of judges and tribunals are taken on the basis of what has been heard of presented in relation to the relevant law. The crucial link between the process of receiving and evaluating information and reaching a decision ought not to be overlooked. It is via this linkage that procedure influences decision-making.

Lempert in his study of housing eviction tribunals in Hawaii clearly, and persuasively, identifies the limits of procedural informality and the way in which those appearing before tribunals can be deceived by the appearance of informality. He distinguishes between 'procedural' and 'substantive' informality and derives a set of principles that identify the circumstances which lead to the 'trap of hidden legalism':

> 'Whenever a party's participation is procedurally and substantively informal and the court's stance is procedurally informal and substantively legalistic, the party will believe her case is being heard in an informal tribunal, but we will in fact have a situation of hidden legalism. If one party and the judge are procedurally informal and substantively legalistic while the other party proceeds informally in both respects, the latter is seriously disadvantaged, for only her opponent is addressing the normative issues that concern the court. This is essentially the situation of non-payment tenants before the eviction board today. They may respond expansively when the board asks them why they could not pay their rent, but they soon learn their responses do not matter.'

A similar situation faces appellants in tribunals who have no representation or who come with an unskilled representative. The relative simplicity with which proceedings can be initiated, the literature from tribunals stressing their informality, the physical appearance of hearings and the approach of the tribunal to the conduct of hearings can convey the impression that decision-making processes are carried out in a rather relaxed and informal manner. This impression is misleading. In interviews with tribunals, chairs stressed the need for those appearing before them to 'make their case' by providing legally relevant factual information and evidence of those facts. The following statements provide typical examples of the way in which tribunal chairs perceive the difficulty in their own tribunals:

> 'People often have a generalised sense of injustice in the breakdown of relationships. They find it hard to appreciate that we are not concerned with a generalised sense of injustice. When applicants are unrepresented we get a lot of irrelevant information. It may be important to the applicant, but it is not important to us. We are in the business of applying the facts to the law.' [Industrial Tribunal Chair]
>
> 'Some people feel that this is just a matter of where they are going to tell their story and that's all that is necessary. They think that their story is good enough … but without expert knowledge of the law, it is unwise… . When they are not represented, either they give a lot of evidence which is quite irrelevant or they don't produce the most relevant evidence to us.' [Immigration Adjudicator]
>
> 'The importance of representation is to set the case within its legal context with a view to submissions on the law, and that is what patients and social workers don't always perceive.' [MHRT Judicial Member]
>
> 'You are dealing with rules and regulations and a person who is a lawyer or somebody who deals in that field will be able to know what is required; what evidence is required before the tribunal. It takes a long time for someone who isn't associated with the tribunals or who isn't a lawyer to understand what the regulations mean, what the words mean and what are the conditions under one regulation or another.' [SSAT Chair]

Thus, although unrepresented appellants are free to 'speak for themselves' before tribunals, and many value this freedom, it has hidden dangers. As the extracts from tribunal chairs suggest, decision-making processes in tribunals require legally relevant and sufficient accounts. Applicants tell stories which may or may not be relevant. The result is often that they may feel satisfied with the process but ultimately lose their case.

Interesting linguistic research carried out in the US describes in detail the difficulties facing parties to hearings in small claims courts. Although these informal courts allow the parties to give accounts of their case in a relatively unconstrained manner, problems arise when plaintiffs fail to give accounts that adequately deal with issues in the way that the court can test against evidence presented. O'Barr and Conley argue that although the freedom to speak without the assistance of representation and without being constrained by formal rules of evidence was welcomed by many litigants, 'this may be the mechanism by which informal procedures substitute expressive satisfaction for the enforcement of rights'.

Although appellants who come before tribunals may not appreciate the importance of sifting and selecting material relevant to the law, representatives do. Analysis of the activities of representatives before hearings as well as during hearings points to the importance of case preparation in the outcome of hearings. The most significant pre-hearing function is the construction of winnable cases. Unrepresented applicants have difficulty in identifying the facts which are relevant to their case and they therefore may fail to produce the evidence necessary to prove their case. In these situations, it becomes the responsibility of the tribunal to elicit relevant information from those who appear at tribunal hearings, and even when this can be accomplished to the satisfactory of the tribunal, the necessary evidence may not be immediately available.

Representatives, on the other hand, can conduct a careful examination of the facts of the appellant's situation, and then, within the context of the regulations or the statute, marshal such evidence as is necessary to convince a tribunal of the truth of those facts. In social security appeals this might involve provision of medical certificates, evidence of attempts to find work, or availability of work in the area, etc. In immigration cases, evidence may e required of resources or of family connections. In addition to documentary evidence, representatives can also arrange for witnesses to provide verbal evidence at an appeal hearing. Expert case construction requires a thorough knowledge of the law or regulations and the ability to sift the factual information given by the appellant in order to isolate those facts that will establish the appellants entitlement or case. This requires patience and sensitivity to the problems of anxious, inarticulate and occasionally illiterate applicants.

Unrepresented appellants are disadvantaged in this respect because they cannot, without advice, know what facts they must prove, nor what items of evidence might constitute sufficient proof to establish their case.

> 'Different cases demand different things. In this tribunal we are very much concerned with fact. Cases are won or lost on fact and so really a representative can help us most by marshalling the facts and seeing that we get proved the facts that we need.' [SSAT Chair]
>
> 'It's the preparation of the appeal which is the most important thing. The representative has the opportunity which no one else has to marshal the facts: to elicit from his client all the facts of the case. Then the representative has to decide for himself what is relevant to the issues and what is not, and the manner in which to present the case.' [Immigration Adjudicator]

Case preparation and the provision of evidence is fundamental to the outcome of tribunal hearings. Tribunals and representatives are well aware of this fact. Appellants, on the other hand, are not."

HEARINGS, EVIDENCE AND PRECEDENT

Franks Report

paras 71, 72, 76–77, 90

"Knowledge of the case to be met

1–34   71. The second most important requirement before the hearing is that citizens should know in good time the case which they will have to meet... .

72. We do not suggest that the procedure should be formalised to the extent of requiring documents in the nature of legal pleadings. What is needed is that the citizen should receive in good time beforehand a document setting out the main points of the opposing case. It should not be necessary and indeed in view of the type of person frequently appearing before tribunals it would in many cases be positively undesirable, to require the parties to adhere rigidly at the hearing to the case previously set out, provided always that the interests of another party are not prejudiced by such flexibility.

Public hearings

76. We have already said that we regard openness as one of the three essential features of the satisfactory working of tribunals. Openness includes the promulgation of reasoned decisions, but its most important constituent is that the proceedings should be in public. The consensus of opinion in the evidence received is that hearings before tribunals should take place in public except in special circumstances.

77. We are in no doubt that if adjudicating bodies, whether courts or tribunals, are to inspire that confidence in the administration of justice which is a condition of civil liberty they should, in general, sit in public. But just as on occasion the courts are prepared to try certain types of case wholly or partly *in camera* so, in the wide field covered by tribunals, there are occasions on which we think that justice may be better done, and the interests of the citizen better served, by privacy.

[The Committee went on to outline three types of case: where considerations of public security are involved, where intimate personal or financial circumstances have to be disclosed and where there are preliminary hearings involving professional capacity and reputation.]

Evidence

90. Tribunals are so varied that it is impossible to lay down any general guidance on the requirement of evidence at hearings. In the more formal tribunals, for example, the Lands Tribunal, there seems no good reason why some of the rules of evidence as in courts of law should not apply. In the majority of tribunals, however, we think it would be a mistake to introduce the strict rules of evidence of the courts. The presence of a legally qualified chairman should enable the tribunal to attach the proper weight to such matters as hearsay and written evidence."

JUSTICE-All Souls Report

paras 51–56

"(a) Openness

1–35   With few exceptions the courts perform in public. In the case of tribunals there is much variation but private sessions are common (though this is scarcely noticed as in practice very few tribunal hearings are attended by members of the public or the press). Likewise judges have all the papers read to them in open court. Tribunal members, in order to save time, prepare for the hearings by reading the entire dossier in private.

(b) Evidence

Tribunals may rely on evidence that would be inadmissible in a court of law. The extent to which they do so varies according to the nature of the tribunal, and the nature of the case. Evidence is admitted if logically probative. Thus, hearsay is admissible. 'No doubt in admitting it, the tribunal must observe the rules of natural justice, but this does not mean that it must be tested by cross-examination. It only means that the ... other side [must have] a fair opportunity of commenting on it and contradicting it', Lord Denning observed in *T. A. Miller Ltd v. Minister of Housing and LG* [1968] 1 W.L.R. 992. Naturally tribunal members make considerable use of their own expertise in the subject matter.

(c) Standard of proof

The usual standard of proof, as in the civil courts, is the balance of probabilities, but there are some instances where the criminal standard ('beyond reasonable doubt') is adopted. The burden of proof is, as in the courts, on he who asserts, but there are a number of presumptions prescribed by statute that favour applicants/appellants in some tribunals.

(d) Rules of procedure

Most tribunals have a general power to regulate their own proceedings, and they may adopt quite different rules. Franks found that there was 'general agreement on the broad essentials which the procedure (of tribunals) in this wider sense (of before and after as well as during the hearing) should contain'. They included the provision of notice of the right to apply to a tribunal, knowledge of the case to be met, a reasoned decision by the tribunal, and notice of any further right of appeal. Franks was not in favour either of a standard code of procedure or of a small number of codes (para. 63) but did envisage that the Council on Tribunals would have a statutory power to formulate rules of procedure. Neither this nor the ... proposal that [there] should [be] a central supervisory drafting department was adopted. Regulations containing rules of procedure are drafted in the legal sections of the various departments. This accounts for much of their variety. The Council on Tribunals try to achieve a unifying effect through the process of consultation. Sometimes their advice is ignored."

Notes

(1) For further general reading see Wraith and Hutchesson, pp. 140–148: national assistance **1–36** appeal tribunals later became social security appeal tribunals. For the new system of unified appeal tribunals see para. 1–47.

(2) The rules of natural justice provide a framework within which procedural fairness operates. On these see Chapters 8 and 9. Although the rules do not of themselves require a public hearing, many tribunals allow oral hearings. In some circumstances procedural rules prevent such a hearing and these have been held not to be in violation of natural justice: *Young v. Criminal Injuries Compensation Board*, 1997 S.L.T. 297, extracted at para. 8–24. The Council on Tribunals tries to ensure that rules of procedure provide for an oral hearing although sometimes all this means is that the chairman of the tribunal has a discretion to permit such a hearing: see the Annual Report 1971–72, paras 51–3, 65.

(3) Tribunals "are entitled to act on any material which is logically probative, even though it is not evidence in a court of law", Lord Denning M.R. in *T. A. Miller Ltd v. Minister of Housing and Local Government* [1968] 1 W.L.R. 992 at 995. Tribunals may therefore admit hearsay evidence: *R. v. Hull Prison Board of Visitors, ex parte St Germain (No. 2)* [1979] 1 W.L.R. 1401. For discussion of the relationship between matters of fact and evidence and the jurisdiction of tribunals, see Chapter 4.

(4) The Franks Committee (recommendation 18) recommended that tribunals should have power to order witnesses to give evidence or produce documents. This general recommendation has not been taken up although some tribunals have these powers, such as the Civil Aviation Authority, employment tribunals and the Lands Tribunal for Scotland. Such powers verge on the inquisitorial and do not sit readily with the adversarial context in which the courts who ultimately supervise the activities of tribunals operate. Even where such inquisitorial powers exist, they are often not utilised: see Wraith and Hutchesson, p. 147. Sometimes there is greater acceptance of an inquisitorial approach. For example, the guide to procedure in social security appeal tribunals made it clear that the proceedings are to be regarded as inquisitorial and that the tribunal is under a duty, when it identifies a point in favour of a claimant, to consider it and to reach its decision in light of it even if the point is not put forward by the claimant: para. 17. The utility of an inquisitorial approach is examined in the next extract. Again the question of representation appears to be a significant one.

H. Genn, "Tribunals and Informal Justice"

(1993) M.L.R. 393 at 406 [Footnotes have been omitted.]

"(d) The Role of Tribunals in Informal Proceedings

Most of the accounts of tribunals and informal courts make claims for the special role of judges and **1–37** tribunals in those forums. They are presumed to possess an awe-inspiring range of skills and qualities.

They have expert knowledge of their field and can unravel complicated regulations and case law without the assistance of representation; can hear and evaluate evidence that would be excluded in conventional courts as unreliable (e.g. hearsay) and be capable of giving it due weight; they can assess the credibility of witnesses and the value of written evidence; assist unrepresented parties and compensate for lack of representation by interventionist (inquisitorial) behaviour; and they are able to reach consistent, reasoned decisions in accordance with law without bias, without technicality, and with speed. The difficulty of carrying out all of the functions simultaneously has been authoritatively stated by Fuller:

> '[T]he integrity of the adjudicative process itself depends upon the participation of the advocate. This becomes apparent when we contemplate the nature of the task assumed by an arbiter who attempts to decide a dispute without the aid of partisan advocacy. Such an arbiter must undertake, not only the role of judge, but that of representative for both of the litigants. Each of these roles must be played to the full. When he resumes his neutral position, he must be able to view with distrust the fruits of this identification and be ready to reject the products of his own best mental efforts. The difficulties of this undertaking are obvious. If it is true that a man in his time must play many parts, it is scarcely given to him to play them all at once.'

Although Fuller's account is based on the role of the adjudicator in adversarial proceedings, it is nonetheless relevant for informal court and tribunal hearings. Despite relaxation of procedural rules and the greater freedom of intervention permitted to informal court judges and tribunals, it is clear that the majority of informal court and tribunal proceedings continue to follow an adversarial model. In SSATs which are described as being 'inquisitorial', proceedings continue to conform to a classically adversarial model: two parties, the Department and the applicant who tell their story; after which the tribunal delivers a simple binary decision on the basis of their preference for one or other account of the law or facts and their own understanding of the applicable law. Industrial tribunals and immigration hearings are explicitly adversarial and include cross-examination of witnesses. The same appears to be true for small claims procedures, as Yngvesson and Hennessey concluded in their survey of small claims literature:

> 'In spite of these assumptions the typical model for small claims procedure was, and is, basically adversary in its orientation, although greatly 'stripped down'. The judge is expected to adjudicate disputes, and many litigants behave as though they *are* engaged in a contest and bring to bear whatever skills they have to effect a judgment in their favour ... this puts some unrepresented litigants ... at a disadvantage, especially in cases which are factually or legally complex. In such cases, a fact-finder is required, yet the role of the fact-finder cannot adequately be filled by a judge who first hears of a case a few minutes before he is asked to bring judgment.'

Those who appear before tribunals without assistance may be disadvantaged because there is an imbalance of power between the parties, because they do not understand the law, are unable to present their cases coherently and are unaware of the need to furnish the tribunal with evidence of the facts they are asserting. Although it is the job of tribunals to 'compensate' for these disadvantages, representatives, and indeed many tribunals themselves, do not believe that this is possible. These beliefs were largely supported by observation and the results of analysis of tribunal outcome.

Observations of SSAT hearings (which are the most informal and the most 'inquisitorial' of all tribunal hearings) revealed great differences in the level of questioning and time spent on unrepresented appellants. In some hearings, tribunals would painstakingly go through the submissions, checking calculations and questioning applicants. At other hearings, the chair would simply ask the appellant what she would like to say, and then, without reference to any materials or delving for further information, would proceed to dismiss the case. This occurred in situations where there were clearly arguments that could have been made on the appellant's behalf. The tendency among appellants in SSATs is simply to respond to the questions put to them and rarely to offer additional information. The requirement that chairs be responsible for eliciting all of the necessary information from appellants, for correctly applying the law and adjudicating the case, involves the performance of several different roles. Even if chairs succeed in obtaining the information they think they require, there may still be scope for creative argument on the application of regulations which they are unlikely to undertake on behalf of an unrepresented appellant.

'It is not inherently impossible for claimants to come on their own, but to be honest the type of people coming here are among the most disadvantaged and they are inhibited by the whole process. Representation is important to be fair to the claimant, to hear everything they have got to say and a rep can do that. Of course it is different here to any other court of law, because it is not adversarial, it is inquisitorial. It's true that we can ask questions and get information out of appellants, but that is not going to be anything like what the representative could find out.' [SSAT Chair]

Even with the best intentions, tribunals are rarely able to spend the time necessary to elicit relevant information from the undifferentiated stream in which most appellants present their stories. Nor can they always know, in advance of hearing the evidence, what questions should be asked.

'The job of a representative is sifting out the grains from the chaff and then producing the evidence that can assist us.' [SSAT Chair]

The problems facing tribunals are compounded in more explicitly adversarial tribunal hearings. Chairs and members of industrial tribunals were well aware that hearings were a contest between two parties, and there were substantial differences in their opinion as to their proper role, especially when faced with a represented respondent and an unrepresented applicant. Some industrial tribunal chairs perceived no particular problem in adopting an active role, asking questions and intervening in hearings. For example:

'An applicant on his own has the advantage of being very carefully looked after by the Chairman. The only disadvantage is that the Chairman is only aware of the applicant's case in so far as it has been written down in the document, and if the documents are very meagre then his case comes out as he talks and you have to go along with him.' [IT Chair]
    'We have a very different approach to unrepresented parties. It is much more like conducting a seminar. Many Chairmen see unrepresented parties as a pain. I see them as a challenge. They have come for their day. You have got to explain everything in very careful detail.' [IT Chair]

Other chairs of industrial tribunals had more reservations about their ability to assist unrepresented parties and the propriety of so doing. For example:

'In industrial tribunals you've got to be a bit careful if you are a chairman. You have got to be strictly impartial because it is adversarial. If somebody doesn't put his case well, that's his hard luck. You can't put it for him or help him on his way because you have got to be absolutely down the centre. So you see in industrial tribunals a lot of cases get lost by default. You know, the applicant is shooting himself in the foot, but you mustn't help him. It would be absolutely wrong.' [Industrial Tribunal Chair]
    'When the tribunals were set up it was hoped that it would be on a not too formal basis, but over the years we have had legislation, precedent and that can put the applicant at a disadvantage without a representative. The chairman tries to be helpful, posing questions, getting the relevant evidence, but he must not descend into the arena. He must not become adversarial. It might be better if applicants were legally represented.' [IT Chair]

A substantial minority of industrial tribunal chairs had misgivings about assisting unrepresented parties on a number of counts. Some felt that it was difficult to perform the roles of adjudicator and representative at the same time. They also feared that where only one party was represented, giving assistance to the unrepresented party might be perceived as partiality.

'We'd like to say representation makes no difference because it is a confession of failure if it does. On difficult points of law you have to play so many different roles with unrepresented applicants.... It is dangerous to say that industrial tribunals are cosy and informal. In fact they are very demanding and complex.' [Industrial Tribunal Chair]

The contribution of representatives is to overcome these advantages. Representatives characterised their roles as those of advocates, enablers and translators.

'I think that they are legalistic hearings on the whole and the claimant, even if they were themselves an advice worker, would benefit from representation, because it is much easier to put somebody else's case than it is to put your own. It is often very difficult for unrepresented appellants to put their case clearly, objectively and straightforwardly to the tribunal.' [Lay Representative]

The influence of tribunal chairs or adjudicators in informal proceedings should not be underestimated. In the absence of representation, tribunal chairs bear responsibility for the fairness of the proceedings, although there are few immediate controls on their behaviour and there is no formal monitoring of their performance. The central importance of the tribunal chair not only to the conduct of the hearings but, more importantly, to the outcome of tribunal hearings was clearly illustrated by our research. In addition to estimating the effect of representation on outcome, we also estimated the effect of other circumstances of hearings on the likelihood of winning. In SSATs and immigration hearings, and to a lesser extent in industrial tribunals, the identity of the tribunal chair significantly and independently affected the chances of a successful outcome to a hearing. In SSATs it was found that the identity of a chair could cause a reduction in the chance of success for a case which might on average have a 30 per cent chance of winning, to around 5 per cent, after controlling for case type and other factors. Other results suggested that the identity of the chair could produce a higher chance of success, in one case increasing the chance of winning from 30 per cent to 50 per cent after controlling for other factors. Analysis of outcome in immigration hearings indicated that the effective chance of success for a typical appellant, depending solely on the choice of adjudicator, lay somewhere between 5 per cent and 50 per cent after controlling for other factors.

These figures are unlikely to surprise those who are in the habit of representing parties in courts or tribunals, although it is rare for the effects of differences between individual members of the judiciary to be quantified in this way. It is, however, possible that in informal proceedings, in the absence of strict procedural rules and in the absence of representatives, there are fewer constraints on the development of idiosyncratic judicial behaviour."

Notes

1–38   (1) For further reading on the inquisitorial method see A. Chayes, "The Role of the Judge in Public Law Litigation" [1976] 89 Harv.L.Rev. 1281 and L. Fuller, "The Forms and Limits of Adjudication" [1978] 92 Harv.L.Rev. 353 at 382.

(2) On the question of precedent J. D. B. Mitchell, *Constitutional Law* (1968) noted (p. 296) that:

> "the tribunal must have general principles, or else the random quality of its decisions provokes criticism; clearly, too, it must use expert knowledge. It was created for that purpose, but the borderline between correct and incorrect methods of decision may perhaps be easier sensed than described."

JUSTICE-All Souls Report

para. 60

1–39   "Tribunals follow the precedents of the superior courts and, where appropriate, their own appellate tribunals. But they are not obliged to follow their own precedents and, indeed, are sometimes discouraged from doing so (e.g. *Merchandise Transport Ltd v. British Transport Commission* [1962] 2 Q.B. 173). It is fundamental to any system of precedent that the existence of the precedents should be known, and the chairman and clerks of tribunals bear the chief responsibility for keeping abreast of them. The Franks Committee recommended that all final appellate tribunals should publish selected decisions and circulate them to any lower tribunals. It is plainly desirable that the precedents followed by tribunals should be made public but the extent to which they can be published is subject to limitations of cost."

Notes

1–40   (1) In *Chief Supplementary Benefit Officer v. Leary* [1985] 1 W.L.R. 84 at 89 it was held that a tribunal was bound by decisions of the English High Court, in exercising its supervisory jurisdiction, it was entitled to treat such decisions exercised by way of original jurisdiction, later transferred to the tribunal itself, as of persuasive force only. By implication this is the case with decisions of the tribunal itself. While consistency is desirable, rigid adherence to a tribunal's own precedents could be an unlawful fettering of discretion, on which see *Merchandise Transport Ltd v British Transport Commission* [1962] 2 Q.B. 173 at 193 *per* Devlin L.J., noted at para. 7–9.

(2) For discussion of another aspect of tribunal hearings, the duty to give reasons, see section 10 of the Tribunals and Inquiries Act 1992, extracted at para. 12–34.

THE COUNCIL ON TRIBUNALS

The Franks Committee recommended the creation of two standing councils, one for Scotland and one for England and Wales, to keep the working of tribunals under review. It saw the role of the councils as an advisory one although it also thought it would be appropriate to allocate some executive functions to them, such a the appointment of tribunal members. Parliament created one Council on Tribunals for the whole of the United Kingdom (but with a Scottish Committee) in the Tribunals and Inquiries Act 1958. The current legislation is contained in sections 1–4 of the Tribunals and Inquiries Act 1992.   **1–41**

For general reading on the council's role see H. W. R. Wade "Administrative Tribunals and Administrative Justice" (1981) 55 Aus. L.J. 374; Harlow and Rawlings, Chap. 14; Craig, Chap. 4; and Wade and Forsyth, Chap. 23.

The Constitution and the Functions of the Council and the Scottish Committee 1997–98

Appendix A

"1. The Council on Tribunals and its Scottish Committee are independent bodies first established in 1958 and now operating under the Tribunals and Inquiries Act 1992.   **1–42**

2. The principal functions of the Council, as laid down in the 1992 Act, are:

2.1 to keep under review the constitution and working of the tribunals specified in Schedule 1 to the Act, and, from time to time, to report on their constitution and working;

2.2 to consider and report on matters referred to the Council under the Act with respect to tribunals other than the ordinary courts of law, whether or not specified in Schedule 1 to the Act; and

2.3 to consider and report on these matters, or matters the Council may consider to be of special importance, with respect to administrative procedures which involve or may involve the holding of a statutory inquiry by or on behalf of a Minister.

3. The term 'statutory inquiry' means (i) an inquiry or hearing held in pursuance of a statutory duty, or (ii) a discretionary inquiry or hearing designated by an Order under section 16(2) of the Act. The relevant Order now in force is the Tribunals and Inquiries (Discretionary Inquiries) Order 1975 (SI 1975/1379) as amended (SI 1976/293, SI 1983/1287, SI 1990/526 and SI 1992/2171).

4. The 1992 Act stipulates that the Council must be consulted before procedural rules are made for any tribunal specified in Schedule 1 and on procedural rules made by the Lord Chancellor or Lord Advocate which relate to statutory inquiries. They must also be consulted before any exemption is granted from the requirement in section 10 of the Act to give reasons for decisions. In turn, the Council must consult the Scottish Committee on any rules relating to tribunals which come under its direct supervision or on any matter referred by the Lord Advocate prior to finalising any report. In addition, the Scottish Committee has the right in certain circumstances to report directly to the Lord Advocate.

5. In general terms the Scottish Committee supervises those tribunals and inquiries that are constituted under Scottish legislation and acts for the Council in overseeing tribunals held in Scotland that have a basis in 'United Kingdom' legislation. It has long been accepted practice for Departments to approach the Scottish Committee directly with proposals relating to tribunals and inquiries in Scotland.

6. The Council consists of 15 members appointed by the Lord Chancellor and the Lord Advocate, one of whom is appointed as Chairman. The Scottish Committee is made up of 3 members of the Council designated by the Lord Advocate plus a further 4 persons, not Council members, whom he also appoints. The Parliamentary Commissioner for Administration (Ombudsman) has a right to sit on both the Council and the Scottish Committee by virtue of his office. Appointees to the Scottish Committee normally hold office for a 3 year period which can, with the agreement of the Lord Advocate and member concerned, be extended by a further 3 year appointment. Salaries and expenses are paid to all members of the Council and Scottish Committee.

7. The Scottish Committee meets on a quarterly basis with those members who sit on the Council additionally attending a monthly meeting in London.

8. The Council is required to make an annual report which must be presented to Parliament and may, at any time, make a special report on its own initiative under paragraphs 2.1 or 2.3 above. Although not required

by statute, the Scottish Committee also produces an annual report which covers in more depth the Scottish issues included in the main report of the Council and details of other issues handled directly by the Scottish Committee. The report is given a very wide circulation to interested bodies throughout Scotland."

Notes

1–43   (1) The Scottish Committee has, of course, had to respond to the creation of the Scottish Parliament. In its response to the White Paper, *Scotland's Parliament*, Cm. 3658 (1997) the committee's "overriding recommendation, however, [was] that there will be a continuing need for an independent organisation responsible for overseeing tribunals in Scotland". The Scotland Act 1998 does not specifically mention the Council on Tribunals or the Scottish Committee. It is inevitable that in changes to tribunals subject to the devolved competence of the Parliament, the committee will have a role to play: see the 1996–97 Report, para. 1.3 and the 1997–98 Report, p. 7. To date, the committee has not been willing to suggest a wholly independent Scottish organisation. In its response to the White Paper, the committee noted that it "enjoyed extensive autonomous powers with regard to a supervision of the working of tribunals in Scotland" and that there was "an existing harmonious relationship between the Committee and the Council on Tribunals and a 'two way' interflow of ideas engendered by the present arrangement whereby our chairman and two other members are appointed to membership of the Council", 1996–97 Report, para. 1.4. The committee, however, went on to recommend that consideration be given to renaming the committee "the Scottish Council on Tribunals" which it felt would give the public a true perspective of its position and moreover that it should report to the Scottish Parliament and that Schedule 1 to the Tribunals and Inquiries Act 1992, which lists tribunals subject to the Scottish Committee, should be revised to take account of devolved legislative competence.

             (2) Among the tribunals subject to the Scottish Committee's supervision are the (exclusively Scottish) Crofters' Commission, the Lands Tribunal for Scotland, the Parole Board for Scotland, the Police Appeals Tribunal for Scotland, children's hearings and education appeal committees. Others, which were part of a U.K. legislative framework but which sit in Scotland subject to the committee's supervision, include the Criminal Injuries Compensation Authority, employment tribunals, the immigration appeal tribunal, social security appeal tribunals and the general and special commissioners of income tax. For discussion of it's role in relation to inquires see para. 1–54.

Special Report on the Functions of the Council on Tribunals

Cmnd. 7805 (1980)

1–44   "5.1 The Functions of the Council Committee examined a number of weaknesses in our statutory powers and material resources.
             5.2 These weaknesses are particularly striking when the scope of our statutory task is taken into account. The number of different types of tribunal within our jurisdiction has greatly increased since the Tribunals and Inquiries Act 1958 was passed, and now exceeds 50. Tribunals placed under our supervision since that time include the Local Valuation Courts, Immigration Adjudicators and the Immigration Appeal Tribunal, the Director General of Fair Trading (in respect of certain of his functions), Mental Health Review Tribunals, Rent Assessment Committees, Value Added Tax Tribunals, Children's Hearings (in Scotland) and Industrial Tribunals....
             5.4 Under the heading of matters requiring statutory attention, our committee considered the lack of clarity as to the extent of our general jurisdiction in relation to tribunals; our lack of a specific power to investigate complaints; and the absence of any requirement that we be consulted on proposed primary legislation affecting tribunals or inquiries, and of any power to require our views (expressed in response to statutory prescribed consultation) to be made public....
             5.6 Other matters governed by statute are the difference between the statutory expression of our powers in relation to inquiries and that in relation to tribunals; the absence of any obligation on the part of Ministers (other than the Lord Chancellor) to consult us on draft rules in connection with statutory inquiries; and the need to clarify the right of our members to attend private hearings and to remain at the deliberation stage of tribunals' proceedings ... we consider that all of them require suitable attention from Parliament, so that we can act with greater confidence and authority under a clear, logical and somewhat broadened remit.

5.7 Under the heading of resources, we refer to our constitution ... We believe that the Council should not be larger than now, and should continue to rely on the standing and the distinctive contribution of each member; but there is an obvious connection between our resources and the strength of our secretariat. A part-time body requires a great deal of professional and technical support if it is to do its job effectively. A staff as small as ours must be occupied almost exclusively by day-to-day business, and find hardly any opportunity for undertaking the wider studies and preparation of background material which are so important in our specialist field of work. We therefore recommend a modest increase in our staff....

8.6 Lord Franks made it clear, in discussion with our Functions of the Council Committee, that after a period of more than 20 years he still attached significance to the phrase 'supervision of tribunals' which appears in his report as the hearing to the chapter dealing with the creation of the Council of Tribunals. He felt that we should not lose sight of this rôle, because for him it still embodied the Council's essential function. Other witnesses, with practical experience as tribunal chairmen, voiced their concern about the lack of supervision of the kind envisaged by the Franks Committee — notably the absence of detailed knowledge about how tribunals are actually working, the appropriateness of their jurisdictions, the quality of decision-making in different classes of tribunals and, in general, what in fact happens at ground level. Sporadic visiting, although valuable in other respects, cannot provide this kind of systematic knowledge. It can come only from studies in depth....

8.10 We envisage that some of the research to which we have just referred would be carried out directly by our own staff. Particularly sensitive subjects would certainly have to be dealt with in this way. On other matters we would commission studies from outside researchers, or advise on research mounted on their own initiative by academic investigators. We see particular scope for directly commissioning research by academic consultants. The Administrative Conference of the United States succeeds in engaging consultants at a very modest cost to prepare reports on specific subjects on collaboration with committees of the Conference....

9.9 Looking ahead, therefore, we see an increasingly important constitutional role for the Council on Tribunals. In the changing constitutional climate our organisation has potentialities as yet unrealised — a point of view we share with all those with whom we had discussions. At present, movement generally is towards greater openness in public administration; there is growing demand for opening up procedures which have hitherto been closed, for explanations of how official decisions have been reached and for adjudication external to the agency in cases of unresolved disputes. Emphasis is on the legal aspects of citizens' rights and on effective procedures for their protection. In fact, the reconciliation of the requirements of efficient government with the rule of law has assumed greater significance within recent years. Indeed, some authorities are thinking in terms of a new constitutional settlement starting from a reaffirmation of the fundamental importance of the rule of law.

Specific Recommendations

10.1 We divide our proposals into those which would require legislation and those which could be given effect by administrative action, either with or without accompanying legislation.

Proposals requiring legislation

(i) The Council should be given a clear general power (in addition to the supervision of the tribunals named in Schedule 1 to the Act of 1971) to act as an advisory body over the whole area of administrative adjudication and the general pattern and organisation of tribunal structure.

(ii) The Council should be given a clear right to be consulted, and empowered to offer views, in relation to matters arising on draft primary legislation affecting our area of jurisdiction.

(iii) The entitlement of the Council to be consulted about procedural rules should be restated in clearer and more general terms.

(iv) When primary or secondary legislation on which the Council have been consulted is brought before Parliament, the Minister concerned should be obliged to disclose the substance of the Council's final advice.

(v) The differences between the wording of the Council's jurisdiction in connection with tribunals and that in connection with inquiries should be removed. In relation to both tribunals and inquiries, the Council should have a wide power to offer advice on general or particular matters, whether or not on request and without a matter having to be regarded as one of 'special importance'.

(vi) The Council should have a statutory power to investigate and issue findings upon certain complaints raising matters of principle in relation to the proceedings of tribunals and inquiries. In this connection the Council should be empowered to call for relevant papers from tribunals and government departments.

(vii) Members of the Council should be specifically empowered to visit private hearings of tribunals under the Council's supervision and to attend the deliberation stage of the proceedings of those tribunals.

(viii) At an appropriate time, further consideration should be given to the supervision of administrative tribunals and public inquiries in Northern Ireland.

Proposals not requiring legislation

(ix) A code for consultation with the Council should be agreed by the Lord Chancellor and government departments.

(x) The financial and staff resources of the Council should be strengthened.

10.2 We appreciate that the developments advocated in this report will need to be spread over a period of time. We are also mindful of economic restraints. The intention, therefore, is to indicate the way forward by setting out a programme which can be initiated in the near future and thereafter progressively implemented."

Notes

1–45   (1) In its response to the Special Report, the Government did not accept that the case for widening the council's powers had been made out. The cost of implementing the recommendations was of particular concern. It accepted that the council's right to be consulted about procedural rules should be restated in clearer terms and that from time to time it would be appropriate for departments to consult with the council about draft primary legislation on matters within the council's jurisdiction. For the terms of the Government's response and the council's reaction to it see its Annual Report 1980–81 (1981–82 H.C. 89).

(2) Notwithstanding the concerns of the council detailed in the 1980 Report, the council has no right to be consulted in relation to proposed primary legislation affecting its jurisdiction. Continuing with some of the concerns in the 1980 Report, the council has continued to insist on new legislation giving it power to advise on proposals to establish new tribunals, proposals affecting existing tribunals and changes to procedures of statutory inquiries. The council also wants removal of inconsistencies in its existing powers, such as its different powers of scrutiny over tribunals and inquiries. While the Government in general accepts that there is some merit to these proposals no legislative measures have yet been laid. For the council's most recent views on this see its 1993–94 Report (1994–95 H.C. 22), p. 9.

(3) The JUSTICE-All Souls Report, Chap. 9, suggested that the council should continue to exist with widened jurisdiction and with greater financial resources. All tribunals should be subject to jurisdiction of the council. An administrative review commission should also be created to work with the council and co-ordinate concerns arising from tribunal issues with the general trends in administrative law: (Chapter 4. Current thinking, however, is that such proposals are unlikely to find favour: see, for example, Professor Sir David Williams, "The Tribunal System — Its Future Control and Supervision" [1984] P.L. 87. Others take the view that reform is not necessary. D. M. Yardley, "The Functions of the Council on Tribunals" [1980] J.S.W.L. 265 at 271, commenting on the council's 1980 Report, wrote:

> "The main message coming from this report is nowhere directly expressed. But it is implicit from the comparatively minor nature of the recommendations that the Council is in fact working well, and that its achievement in the field of tribunals and inquiries have been substantial. It is a paradox that a body with a statutory constitution, but with no powers actually to achieve anything directly, should be so valuable. But it is submitted that this paradox is nonetheless true."

Do you agree? Consider the following.

WORK OF THE COUNCIL

Annual Report of the Council on Tribunals 1985–86

(1986–87 H.C. 42), paras 2.5–2.11

1–46   "2.5 In all our work we have been persistent in pursuing certain basic aims, as illustrated below. A good general guide to the Council's approach is embodied in the phrase 'openness, fairness and impartiality'. This was a constant theme of the Franks Report. However, over the years other standards have been significant. For example, efficiency, expedition and economy have also been prominent. Openness has to be expressed in practical steps to ensure accountability, so that it is clear where the responsibilities for different tribunals lie. The needs of users of the system have, rightly, received more emphasis.

2.6 We recommend that tribunals be clearly independent of the bodies over whose decisions they adjudicate: this has recently been implemented in connection with Social Security Appeal Tribunals: their members are no longer appointed by the Secretary of State in the department which was seen to be a party to appeals; they are now appointed and administered by the President of SSATs. It has been implemented in other ways in connection with Social Security Commissioners and specialist tax appeals (VAT Tribunals and Special Commissioners of Income Tax): the administrative responsibility for these tribunals has been transferred to the Lord Chancellor's Department....

2.8 We have been vigilant in seeking to ensure that people are granted a hearing in connection with proposals which affect their interests; that rights of appeal against administrative decisions are given wherever appropriate and are not eroded where they already exist, *e.g.* concerning the Social Fund, immigration appeals, expulsion and suspension from school, the Social Security Commissioners, the Transport Tribunal, and patents; that parties to tribunal proceedings are treated equitably and neither side is given an unfair advantage; that clerks to tribunals play a defined and appropriate part in the proceedings; that reasons are normally given in writing for all decisions and that they are adequate and comprehensible; that proceedings should be simple and clear, and should normally be in public: the proceedings must be 'not done in a corner'; and that resources should not be wasted — for example in Local Valuation Panels where many appeals are lodged but few are heard.

2.9 In short the procedure should make the tribunal easily accessible to the public; it should be cheap, swift and free from technicality. The whole proceedings should be, and be seen to be, independent and impartial, and fair to the powerful and the professional, but also to the vulnerable....

2.11 We have long stood out for the right of representation for parties before tribunals and inquiries. We believe that non-legal aid would sometimes be more suitable for parties before tribunals than professional assistance from a lawyer. We also believe that legal aid or assistance by way of representation should be extended to virtually all kinds of tribunal but subject to a 'sieve' to ensure that it would not be granted in cases which did not really merit it. At present legal aid is only available in the Lands Tribunals and the Commons Commissioners, and free legal representation before Mental Health Review Tribunals."

Notes

(1) Scrutiny of tribunal procedure is the most important function performed by the council. A **1–47** number of themes have been apparent in recent reports. In its Annual Report for 1989–90 (1990–91 H.C. 64) concern was expressed that financial factors were leading to a lowering of standards in tribunal procedure. That concern was apparent in relation to the creation of the one-person tribunals, such as the pension ombudsman under the Social Security Act 1990: see para. 1.11 of the report. More recently in its 1996–97 Report (1997–98 HC. 376) it expressed concern about the creation of one-person tribunals in relation to a wide range of social security appeals: see para. 1.15.

(2) As noted below, the council has produced a special report, *Tribunals: Their Organisation and Independence*, Cm. 3744 (1997). The report contained guidance examining the preconditions requiring for the establishment and maintenance of the independence and integrity of tribunals. It stressed the need to ensure that adequate resources and funds were secured by the department sponsoring the tribunal. We have already noted the importance of the president or judicial head in connection. The report expressed concern that some departments were of the view that budgetary matters were matters for the tribunal administrators in sponsoring department and not for the tribunals themselves. This was of concern to the council and, as we have noted at para. 1–12, it stressed the need to ensure that there was judicial input: see generally paras 2.5–2.13. In the Social Security Act 1998 the Independent Tribunal Service is, from a date to be appointed, to be abolished. Administration of appeals under that Act will become the responsibility of the Secretary of State: section 1. A new executive appeals agency is to be established. Although the role of the president is clearly a judicial one, with no responsibility for the agency, the council in its report for 1997–98 (1998–99 H.C. 45) expressed pleasure that "the Lord Advocate, in addressing issues of independence and accountability in the Parliamentary debate, made reference to our special report Tribunals: Their Organisation and Independence" (para. 1.10).

In its report for 1996–97 (1997–98 H.C. 376), it expressed reservations on the abolition of the ITS. It said it would be "wrong" to use the issue of financial accountability as a reason for destroying the existing appeal body — the ITS — and that one feature of a president-led system like the ITS was that the president ensured that there was sufficient manpower of sufficient ability to carry out the tasks required of the system. While its most recent report suggests that its initial concern over the abolition of the ITS may have been exaggerated, it remains to be seen whether in practice the philosophy of its special report will permeate the relationship of the president of the tribunals and the appeals agency.

(3) In its 1997–98 Report the council also flagged up the importance of the Human Rights Act 1998. It emphasised the role that tribunals will have to play as follows:

> "1.52 The incorporation of the Convention into domestic law will clearly have major implications for tribunals. Hitherto, the Convention has had only a limited impact on tribunals. Convention cases have sometimes resulted in changes to domestic law governing tribunals, but the tribunals themselves have not generally had to take account of the Convention. There are some exceptions to this. For example, it is Government policy that planning inspectors should take the Convention into account. Moreover, tribunals dealing with matters with an EU dimension, such as VAT and duties tribunals, have sometimes addressed Convention issues where these have fed in to the EU jurisprudence in particular areas of the law. But after incorporation, all tribunals will have to take account of relevant Convention jurisprudence and so far as possible to interpret legislation in a way compatible with Convention rights. It will be unlawful for tribunals, as public authorities, to act in a way incompatible with the Convention rights unless they are constrained to do so by domestic legislation."

The council also expressed concern in relation to the level of training that was taking place in the tribunal system in relation to the issues raised by the Act: see paras 1.53–1.55 and for the concerns of the Scottish Committee see para. 1–23.

(4) The removal of appeal rights from foreign visitors and a number of other categories, because of administrative pressures, was "deplored" by the council. See its comments on the Asylum and Immigration Appeals Act 1993: Annual Report 1992–93 (1993–94 H.C. 78), p. 2.

(5) The council has also criticised failings of bodies outside of its scope which led to knock-on problems from tribunals under its supervision. See, for example, its comments in relation to delays and decisions by child support appeal tribunals caused by delays in dealing with cases by Child Support Agency officers in its 1994–95 Report (1995–96 H.C. 64), p. 11.

(6) For the views of the Scottish Committee on the consultation paper, "A New Ethical Framework for Local Government in Scotland", see para. 9–18.

VISITS TO TRIBUNALS AND INQUIRIES

Annual Report of the Scottish Committee of the Council on Tribunals 1997–98

Appendix C

1–48   "Committee members made the following visits during the year:

Tribunals	No.	Locations Visited
Child Support Appeal Tribunal	3	Edinburgh, Glasgow, Inverness
Children's Hearings	4	Inverness, Lanarkshire, Perth, Stirling
Criminal Injuries Compensation Appeal Panel	1	Glasgow
Crofters Commission	1	Inverness
Crofters Commission — Plenary meeting	1	Inverness
Designated Lifer Tribunal	1	Greenock
Disability Appeal Tribunal	3	Dundee, Galashiels, Glasgow
Disability Appeal Tribunal — domiciliary	1	Greenock
Education Appeal Committee	4	Greenock, Glasgow, Inverness, Stirling
General Commissioners of Income Tax	2	Glasgow, Haddington
Immigration Appeal Tribunal	1	Glasgow
Industrial Tribunal	3	Dundee, Edinburgh, Glasgow
Medical Appeal Tribunal	2	Ayr, Edinburgh
NHS — Discipline Committee	2	Glasgow
NHS — National Appeal Panel	2	Edinburgh
Pensions Appeal Tribunal	1	Edinburgh
Rent Assessment Committee	2	Aberdeen, Glasgow
Social Security Appeal Tribunal	3	Dumbarton, Inverness, Stornoway

Traffic Commissioners	1	Edinburgh
Valuation Appeal Committees	4	Ayr, Fife, Paisley, Lanark
Value Added Tax Tribunal	1	Edinburgh
	43	

Inquiries

Public Inquiry	1	Inverness
Public Local Plan Inquiry	1	Dunblane
	2	

Training Seminars

Public Inquiries Training Seminar	1	Glasgow
Disability Appeal Tribunal	1	Edinburgh
Social Security Appeal Tribunal	1	Aberdeen
Valuation Appeal Panels	1	Edinburgh
	4	

Other visits

Meeting with officials	1	Edinburgh
	1	

Total Visits	50"	

Notes

(1) It would appear that major tribunals are always visited and attention is given to new tribunals together with those where problems have already been noted: see D. Foulkes, "The Council on Tribunals: visits policy and practice" [1994] P.L. 564. Visits are typically by arrangement, but sometimes the council has a statutory right to visit: see, for example, the Rent Assessment Committee (Scotland) Regulations 1980, reg. 4(3). **1–49**

(2) Compare the number of visits with the number of hearings of the tribunals in question. For example, in the period of the report the Criminal Injuries Compensation Appeal Panel decided 90 cases, employment tribunals a total of 1,787 cases and the immigration appeal tribunal, 40 cases. For further comparisons see the Annual Report 1997–98, Appendix B.

(3) Is the Council on Tribunals the most appropriate body for monitoring performance of tribunals? If not, what other mechanism or combination of mechanisms might be appropriate?

Annual Report of the Scottish Committee of the Council on Tribunals 1997–98

Complaints from Individuals, p. 20

"Not a Complaints Body

The Scottish Committee has no authority under the Tribunal and Inquiries Act 1992 to investigate or adjudicate on complaints about the handling of individual cases by tribunals or inquiries under our supervision. Our statutory role, and that of our parent organisation, the Council, is to advise the Government and their Departments on matters such as the composition of tribunals; the training of members; and the rules of procedure under which tribunals operate. We also provide advice on proposals to change the jurisdiction, constitution or procedures of the tribunals we supervise. **1–50**

We sometimes receive complaints from members of the public about tribunals and inquiries and we make it clear that we have no power to review or change decisions; nor do we have the resources to undertake investigations when errors in procedure are alleged to have occurred. Because we appreciate that it is sometimes difficult for the lay person to grasp the role of the Scottish Committee in relation to complaints made against tribunals, we have produced an explanatory leaflet which briefly summarises our position. However, in some instances the complainant may raise points about the procedures adopted by a tribunal which suggest that changes may be required to improve the system for those who may appeal in the future. We then take our concerns to the Department or other body with responsibility for the policy of the tribunal in question.

Those who are unhappy about the handling of an individual case should seek advice from a Citizens' Advice Bureau, legal advice centre, or solicitor. Such advice can sometimes be obtained at a reduced fee, or at no charge. In cases of alleged maladministration by the administrative staff of certain tribunals, The Parliamentary Commissioner for Administration (Ombudsman) may be able to investigate. If a complainant has a particular problem which he or she would like him to investigate, a request should be made to the local Member of Parliament to take up the complaint."

INQUIRIES

1–51   The classification of public inquiries is not a straightforward task. An inquiry might focus on a matter which is of great importance to an individual or a small group of individuals on the one hand or to a region, section of the community or nation as a whole on the other. R. E. Wraith and G. B. Lamb, *Public Inquiries as an Instrument of Government* (1971), p. 305, classify inquiries as providing an appeal or a means of objection, a form of investigation or a post-mortem. Inquiries in the form of an appeal or objection are often concerned with land use matters, such as planning or compulsory purchase. Some of the rules governing these are detailed below. Inquiries in the way of an investigation or post-mortem are often, but not always, constituted under a special statutory framework, such as the Fatal Accidents and Sudden Deaths Inquiry (Scotland) Act 1976. However, one of the most significant forms of investigative or post-mortem inquiry is that found under the Tribunals of Inquiry (Evidence) Act 1921. Inquiries under this Act are held to investigate "a definite matter of urgent public importance": section 1(1). An inquiry is chaired by a senior judge who can order documents to be produced and summon witnesses. The procedure is seen to be inquisitorial.

Notes

1–52   (1) Inquiries under the 1921 Act have included issues of major importance, such as the Aberfan disaster (1967–68 H.C. 33); the King's Cross Underground fire (1987–88 H.C. 499), the shootings at Dunblane Primary School (the Cullen Report) Cm. 3386 (1996). In earlier times, specific incidents of arguably only local importance have been subject to the procedure: see, for example, the report on the allegation of assault on John Watters (the Thurso boy case) Cmnd. 718 (1959) and for other examples see the Royal Commission on Tribunals of Inquiry (the Salmon Report) Cmnd 3121 (1966), para. 27. A case like that of the Thurso boy, raising allegations of police assault, would more likely be dealt with now under a specific inquiry mechanism such as section 29 of the Police (Scotland) Act 1967.

(2) The formal nature of inquiries under the 1921 Act has led some to conclude that it is a form of judicial process and that the procedure and safeguards found in the courts should be upheld. However, an inquiry has been judicially defined as "merely a stage in the process of arriving at an administrative decision" *per* Lord Greene M.R. in *B. Johnson & Co. (Builders) v. Ministry of Health* [1947] 2 All E.R. 395. All an inquiry under the 1921 Act can do is to make recommendations for action, which may or may not be accepted. The powers of a sheriff in relation to a fatal accident inquiry are similar: see the 1976 Act, s. 6. As inquiries under the 1921 Act are typically concerned with past events, the scope of the inquiry is to that extent predetermined. There are, however, no formal limitations on those who might appear at such an inquiry and make submissions and the practice has been to encourage the widest possible public participation in the inquiry process. While wide public participation in the inquiry process is to be welcomed, inquiries under the 1921 Act are protected by the rules on contempt of court. So in the Dunblane inquiry, the Crown Office felt compelled to issue a warning over press articles which criticised individuals whose actions might be the subject of the tribunal or who might give evidence to it: Crown Office Press Notices 0535/96 April 2, 1996. The inquiry chairman, Lord Cullen, agreed that:

> "Any further incidence of harassment of potential witnesses by the media or publication of material which might impede the investigation or interfere with the giving of evidence to the Inquiry should be referred to him."

(3) Not all inquiries into controversial issues are constituted under the 1921 Act. There is no statutory obligation on the part of Government to follow the 1921 Act procedure. The non-statutory

inquiry is rare, but it does occur. The most famous recent example was the inquiry conducted by Sir Richard Scott which produced the Report of the Inquiry into the Export of Defence Equipment and Dual-use Goods to Iraq and Related Prosecutions (1995–96 H.C. 115). Concern was expressed that unless the inquiry was held under the 1921 Act it would be "toothless' but the Government, in replying to the Opposition, indicated that if Sir Richard Scott felt that the 1921 Act procedure should be invoked, then the Government would agree to that: H.C. Deb., Vol. 214, col. 651 (November 23, 1992). A number of those appearing at the inquiry were critical of the procedure adopted by Sir Richard. Criticism was made that the principles articulated by the Salmon report were being disregarded. These principles were articulated as a response to what was perceived as being the possibility of exposure to unfair public scrutiny under the 1921 Act. In substance those principles meant that the inquisitorial nature of the procedure should be tempered by the allowance of legal representation and the ability to cross-examine witnesses. Indeed, there was some precedent for this in earlier cases.

In the Thurso boy case, the Dean of Faculty acted as counsel for the tribunal with responsibility for common witnesses to give evidence and for examining and, where necessary, cross-examining them. The two police officers involved in the allegation of police assault were called to give evidence. They both had legal representation and were told by the tribunal that they were not compelled to answer questions if the answers would incriminate them. Sir Richard, however, rejected legal representation and cross-examination. In his view, Lord Salmon's principles could not be readily applied to an inquiry, whether under the 1921 Act or otherwise. In "Procedures at Inquiries — The Duty to be Fair" (1995) 111 L.Q.R. 596 at 597 he stated:

> "There is, however, a significant and fundamental difference between litigation and Inquiries that makes procedural comparisons unsafe. Litigation in this country, whether civil or criminal, is adversarial in character. The nature of an Inquiry on the other hand is, with very rare exceptions, investigative or inquisitorial... .
>
> The overall problem, in my view, with the six Salmon 'cardinal principles' is that they are too heavily based on procedural requirements of fairness in an adversarial system... .
>
> Fairness does not, in my opinion, require that adversarial procedure such as the right to cross-examine other witnesses, the right to have an examination-in-chief or a re-examination conducted orally by a party's lawyer ... should always be incorporated into the procedure at inquisitorial Inquiries. The golden rule ... is that there should be procedural flexibility, with procedures to achieve fairness tailored to suit the circumstances of each Inquiry."

For contrary views see Lord Howe of Aberavon, "Procedure at the Scott Inquiry" [1996] P.L. 445 at 446–447, 460 and see also Sir L. Blom-Cooper, "Witnesses before public inquiries: An example of unfairness" [1996] P.L. 11.

The 1921 Act still forms a significant part of this area of law in the Irish Republic. Notwithstanding Sir Richard Scott's views the Irish Supreme Court in the case of *Haughey v. Moriarty* (Case 103/98, July 28, 1998) injected "a heavy dose of adversarial legalism into the inquisitorial process" when considering the open procedure of an inquiry into the tax affairs of the former Irish Prime Minister, Charles Haughey. Similarly, the report into the death of Stephen Lawrence, Cmnd. 4262 (1999), while noting his views, felt that the Salmon principles were of central importance. Those suspected of the killing were, therefore allowed legal representation. See Sir L. Blom-Cooper, "The role and functions of Tribunals of Inquiry — an Irish perspective" [1999] P.L. 175.

(4) For articles criticising the relative rarity of tribunals of inquiry see Z. Segal, "Tribunals of Inquiry: A British Invention Ignored in Britain" [1984] P.L. 206 and for a view predicting the increase in their use see B. K. Winetrobe, "Inquiries after Scott: the return of the tribunal of inquiry" [1997] P.L. 18. Winetrobe suggests that whether or not an inquiry is set up by the 1921 Act procedure depends on whether it can be viewed as a conventional subject meriting serious public debate, such as a disaster or a political scandal of the "arms to Iraq" type. In relation to the latter, the Government is not keen to use a 1921 Act procedure because of the wide range of powers available, but will set up a judicial inquiry as, quoting Drewry (at 28):

"deployment by politicians of the judges' status and credibility to defuse matters which those politicians feel they can neither safely ignore nor tackle by normal political and parliamentary methods".

(5) In light of some of the concerns arising from the Scott Inquiry, the Lord Chancellor's Department instigated a review of inquiry procedure. The results of the review were published in the form of advice from the Council on Tribunals. The council concluded that it would be impracticable to create a uniform procedure because of the diverse nature of inquiries. Instead it stressed core ideals of effectiveness, fairness, speed and economy. In addressing the Salmon principles against Scott's approach it suggested that any differences were "largely ones of terminology and emphasis". It also provided guidance on aspects of an inquiry from its set-up, the publication of its report, its membership, powers and procedures: see H.L. Deb., Vol. 575, cols 149–150 (1997).

(6) For further reading on inquiries under the 1921 Act and non-statutory inquiries see *Stair Memorial Encyclopaedia*, Vol. 23, paras 949–977; V. Finch and C. Ashton, pp. 206–207; and G. Drewry, "Judicial inquiries and public reassurance" [1996] P.L. 368.

Town and Country Planning (Inquiries Procedure) (Scotland) Rules 1997

1–53   "The Lord Advocate, in exercise of the powers conferred on him by section 9 of the Tribunals and Inquiries Act 1992 and of all other powers enabling him in that behalf, and after consultation with the Council on Tribunals, hereby makes the following Rules:

Citation and commencement

1. These Rules may be cited as the Town and Country Planning (Inquiries Procedure) (Scotland) Rules 1997 and shall come into force on 27th May 1997.

Application of rules

2. — (1) Subject to the provisions of this rule, these Rules apply to a local inquiry caused by the Secretary of State to be held for the purpose of any application referred to the Secretary of State or any appeal made to the Secretary of State under the Act, the Listed Buildings Act or the Hazardous Substances Act or any regulations made thereunder.

(2) These Rules shall not apply to a local inquiry held under Schedule 4 to the Act or under Schedule 3 to the Listed Buildings Act or the Schedule to the Hazardous Substances Act, except where the Secretary of State directs under paragraph 3(1) of the relevant Schedule that an appeal which, by virtue of paragraph 1 of that Schedule, falls to be determined by a person appointed by the Secretary of State, shall, instead of being determined by that person, be determined by the Secretary of State; and these Rules shall apply in relation to any step taken or thing done after the giving of the said direction, but do not affect any step taken or thing done before the giving of such direction.

(3) Where the appeal is made —
(a)   by virtue of section 130 or 169 or 180 of the Act (appeals against enforcement notices, notices requiring the replacement of trees or notices under section 179 of the Act),
(b)   under section 47 of the Act as applied to an application for consent under an order made under section 160 of the Act (appeals in relation to tree preservation orders),
(c)   by virtue of section 35 of the Listed Buildings Act (appeals against listed building enforcement notice), or
(d)   by virtue of section 19 of the Hazardous Substances Act (appeals against decisions or failure to take decisions relating to hazardous substances),
rule 4(1) below shall not apply and the references in these Rules to statutory parties shall be omitted.

Interpretation

3. — (1) In these Rules, unless the context otherwise requires —
'the Act' means the Town and Country Planning (Scotland) Act 1997;
'appeals questionnaire' means a document in the form supplied by the Secretary of State for the purpose of proceedings under these Rules;
'applicant' in the case of an appeal means the appellant;
'the application' means the application to which the inquiry relates;

'assessor' means a person appointed by the Secretary of State to sit with a reporter at an inquiry or re-opened inquiry to advise the reporter on such matters arising as the Secretary of State may specify;

'consulted person' means an authority or person consulted by the planning authority in compliance with a requirement imposed by virtue of —

(a)   section 43(1)(c) of the Act;

(b)   regulation 16 of the Town and Country Planning (Control of Advertisements) (Scotland) Regulations 1984; or

(c)   regulation 11 of the Town and Country Planning (Hazardous Substances) (Scotland) Regulations 1993;

'document' includes, in addition to a document in writing —

(a)   any map, plan, graph or drawing;

(b)   any photograph;

(c)   any disc, tape, sound track or other device in which sounds or other data (not being visual images) are recorded so as to be capable (with or without the aid of some other equipment) of being reproduced therefrom; and

(d)   any film, negative, tape, disc or other device in which one or more visual images are recorded so as to be capable (as aforesaid) of being reproduced therefrom;

'the Hazardous Substances Act' means the Planning (Hazardous Substances) (Scotland) Act 1997;

'inquiry' means a local inquiry to which these Rules apply;

'the land' means the land (including trees and buildings) to which the inquiry relates or, in the case of an inquiry relating to an advertisement, the land on which the advertisement is or is to be displayed;

'the Listed Buildings Act' means the Planning (Listed Buildings and Conservation Areas) (Scotland) Act 1997;

'listed building consent' means consent required by section 7(1) to (3) of the Listed Buildings act in respect of works for the demolition, alteration or extension of a listed building and the consent required by those subsections as applied by section 66 of the Listed Buildings Act for works for the demolition of any building in a conservation area;

'outline statement' means a written statement of the principal submissions which a person proposes to put forward at an inquiry together with a list (so far as then known) of the documents (if any) which that person intends to refer to, rely on or put in evidence;

'permission' includes consent;

'planning authority' means the council constituted under section 2 of the Local Government etc. (Scotland) Act 1994 which was responsible for dealing with the application (or in the case of a referred application would have been so responsible had it not been referred to the Secretary of State) or for service of the notice, as the case may be;

'precognition' means a written statement of the evidence which it is proposed that a witness will give to the inquiry;

'pre-inquiry meeting' means a meeting held before an inquiry to consider what may be done with a view to securing that the inquiry is conducted efficiently and expeditiously, and where two or more such meetings are held references to the conclusion of a pre-inquiry meeting are references to the conclusion of the final meeting;

'referred application' means an application referred to the Secretary of State under section 46 of the Act or that section as applied by a tree preservation order, under section 11 of the Listed Buildings Act (listed building consent), under regulations made under section 182 of the Act (control of advertisements), or under section 18 of the Hazardous Substances Act;

'relevant date' means the date of the Secretary of State's written notification to the planning authority of his intention to proceed with the consideration of the application or appeal by causing an inquiry to be held;

'relevant notice' means the Secretary of State's written notification to the planning authority of his intention to proceed with the consideration of the application or appeal by causing an inquiry to be held;

'reporter' means the person appointed by the Secretary of State to hold the inquiry and to report thereon to him;

'statement of case' means, and is comprised of —

(a)   a written statement which contains full particulars of the case which a person proposes to put forward at an inquiry; and

(b)   a list of documents (if any) which the person putting forward that case intends to refer to, rely on or put in evidence;

'statutory party' means —

(a)   any consulted person from whom representation are received whether by the planning authority or by the Secretary of State;

(b)   in relation to an application which is an application for planning permission, any person, being the owner or the agricultural tenant of land to which the application relates, from whom representations were received within the period prescribed by virtue of section 38(2) of the Act;

(c)   any other person from whom representations were received, whether by the planning authority or by the Secretary of State, before the end of the period mentioned in section 38(1) of the Act, or in the case of an application affecting a conservation area, before the end of the periods specified in section 65(3) of the Listed Buildings Act and, in the case of an application for development which does not accord with the development plan, before the end of any period prescribed by the Secretary of State in a direction given under article 18 of the Town and Country Planning (General Development Procedure) (Scotland) Order 1992;

'trees' include groups of trees and woodlands,

and other expressions have the same meaning for the purpose of these Rules as they have for the purpose of the Act.

(2) References in these Rules to section 38 of the Act shall be construed as including where appropriate references to regulations made under section 10 of the Listed Buildings Act.

(3) Where the appeal is an appeal against a notice served under the Act, any reference in these Rules to an application shall be construed as a reference to that notice.

(4) Where the appeal is made under provisions of the Act relating to a listed building, a building in a conservation area or a tree preservation order, the reference in these Rules to —

(a) development shall be construed as a reference to works for the demolition, alteration or extension of a listed building or to works for the demolition of a building in a conservation area or to the cutting down, topping or lopping of trees, as the case may be; and

(b) permission shall be construed as a reference to listed building consent, conservation area consent or consent under a tree preservation order, as the case may be.

Preliminary information and notice

4. — (1) In the case of an appeal, the planning authority shall, not later than 2 weeks after receiving notification of the appeal from the Secretary of State, send to the Secretary of State and to the appellant a completed appeals questionnaire and a copy of all documents relating to the case which are referred to in the completed appeals questionnaire (other than any written representations which the maker thereof has asked to be treated as confidential).

(2) The Secretary of State, if he determines that an inquiry is to be held, shall thereafter give written notice to that effect ('the relevant notice') to the planning authority and shall send a copy of that notice to the applicant and to any statutory party.

(3) Where —

(a)   the Secretary of State has given to the planning authority a direction restricting the grant of permission for the development for which the application was made or a direction as to how the application is to be determined; or

(b)   any government department or local authority have expressed in writing to the planning authority the view that the application should not be granted either wholly or in part, or should be granted only subject to conditions, or, in the case of an application for consent under a tree preservation order, should be granted together with a direction requiring the replanting of trees or in the case of any application that it should be granted,

the planning authority shall inform the Secretary of State, government department or local authority concerned, as the case may be, that such direction or expression of view is relevant to the application or appeal and the Secretary of State, government department or local authority, as the case may be, shall (unless they have already done so) thereupon furnish to the planning authority a statement in writing of the reasons for the direction or expression of view.

Procedure where the Secretary of State causes pre-inquiry meeting to be held

5. — (1) The Secretary of State may cause a pre-inquiry meeting to be held if it appears to him desirable and where he does so the following paragraphs apply.

(2) The Secretary of State shall serve with the relevant notice a notification of his intention to cause a meeting to be held and, in the case of a referred application, a statement of the matters about which he particularly wishes to be informed for the purposes of his consideration of the application; and in that case where any government department or local authority have expressed in writing to the Secretary of State a view which is mentioned in rule 4(3)(b), the Secretary of State shall set this out in his statement and shall supply a copy of the statement to the government department or local authority concerned.

(3) The applicant and the planning authority shall, not later than 8 weeks after the relevant date (or such other date as the person appointed for the purpose of paragraph (10) of this rule, after considering any representations from such parties as he thinks fit, may determine), each serve an outline statement on the other and on the Secretary of State.

(4) Where any direction has been given or view expressed as referred to in rule 4(3), the planning authority shall —

(a) include in or attach to their outline statement the terms of that direction or, as the case may be, that statement of view, and of the statement of reasons relating to it; and

(b) within the period mentioned in paragraph (3) of this rule, supply a copy of their statement of any such attachments to the person or body concerned.

(5) The Secretary of State may in writing require any other person who has notified him of an intention or a wish to appear at the inquiry to serve, not later than 4 weeks after being so required (or such other date as the person appointed for the purpose of paragraph (10) of this rule, after considering any representations from such parties as he thinks fit, may determine), an outline statement on him, the applicant and the planning authority.

(6) Where a person is required to serve an outline statement of case in terms of paragraph (5) of this rule, the Secretary of State may require, by such date as he may determine, service on such person by any other party of the outline statement of that other party.

(7) The meeting (or, where there is more than one, the first meeting) shall be held not later than 16 weeks after the relevant date.

(8) The Secretary of State shall give not less than 3 weeks' written notice of the meeting to the applicant, the planning authority, any person known at the date of the notice to be entitled to appear at the inquiry and any other person whose presence at the meeting seems to him to be desirable; and he may require the planning authority to take, in relation to notification of the meeting, one or more of the steps which he may under rule 15(6)(b) or (c) require them to take in relation to notification of the inquiry.

(9) The Secretary of State shall cause to be published in a newspaper circulating in the locality in which the land is situated a notice of his intention to cause a meeting to be held.

(10) A person appointed by the Secretary of State for the purpose shall preside and shall determine the matters to be discussed and the procedure to be followed at the meeting.

(11) Where a pre-inquiry meeting has been held pursuant to paragraph (1) of this rule, a further meeting may be held and, in that event, that person so appointed shall arrange for such notice to be given as appears to him necessary; and paragraph (10) of this rule shall apply to such a meeting.

Further power of reporter to hold pre-inquiry meetings

6. — (1) Where no pre-inquiry meeting is held pursuant to rule 5, the reporter may hold one if he thinks it desirable.

(2) The reporter shall arrange for not less than 2 weeks' written notice of a meeting he proposes to hold under paragraph (1) of this rule to be given to the applicant, the planning authority, any person known at the date of the notice to be entitled to appear at the inquiry and any other person whose presence at the meeting appears to him to be desirable.

(3) The reporter where he proposes to hold a meeting under paragraph (1) of this rule —

(a) may require, by such date as he may determine, the applicant, the planning authority or any other person who has notified an intention or a wish to appear at the inquiry to serve an outline statement on the applicant, the planning authority or such other person, as the case may be, and on the Secretary of State;

(b) shall preside and shall determine the matters to be discussed and the procedure to be followed at the meeting.

Service of statements of case — planning authority

7. — (1) Subject to paragraphs (3) and (4) of this rule, the planning authority shall, not later than —

(a) where no pre-inquiry meeting is held pursuant to rule 5, 8 weeks after the relevant date, or

(b) where a pre-inquiry meeting is held pursuant to rule 5, 4 weeks after the conclusion of that meeting,

and in any case not later than 4 weeks before the date fixed for the holding of the inquiry, serve a statement of case on the Secretary of State, the applicant and any statutory party.

(2) The planning authority shall include in or attach to their statement of case —

(a) except insofar as already provided, copies of all representations received by them in relation to the application or appeal;

(b) where relevant, the conditions (if any) which they presently consider should be imposed in the event that the Secretary of State decides that permission be granted; and

(c)   where a direction is given or a view expressed in terms of rule 4(3) (unless already contained in an outline statement), the terms of that direction or, as the case may be, that statement of view, and of the statement of reasons relating to it, and in that case shall serve a copy of the statement of case on the person or body concerned.

(3) Where, having regard to the number of representations received in the case of an application or appeal relating to a development to which section 34 of the Act applies, the planning authority consider it expedient, they may, instead of supplying or serving copies of all such representations as required by paragraph (2)(a) of this rule, include a summary of those representations in their statement of case.

(4) Where, having regard to the number of statutory parties and the length of the planning authority's statement of case, the Secretary of State or a reporter considers it expedient, he may, at the request of the planning authority, authorise them, instead of serving a copy of that statement of case and of the representations on all statutory parties on whom any document requires to be served in accordance with rule 13(3), to give notice to all statutory parties (whether or not that party is required to serve a statement of case in terms of rule 9(1)) stating the time and place at which the statement of case and the representations may be inspected by all statutory parties; and the authority shall afford them a reasonable opportunity to inspect and, where practicable, to take copies of the statement and the representations.

Service of statements of case — applicant

8. — (1) The applicant shall, not later than —

(a)   where no pre-inquiry meeting is held pursuant to rule 5, 8 weeks after the relevant date; or

(b)   where a pre-inquiry meeting is held pursuant to rule 5, 4 weeks after the conclusion of that meeting.

and in any case not later than 4 weeks before the date fixed for the holding of the inquiry, serve a statement of case on the Secretary of State, the planning authority and any statutory party.

(2) Rule 7(4) above shall apply, substituting references to the applicant for the references to the planning authority, in relation to the applicant's statement of case.

Service of statements of case — other persons

9. — (1) The Secretary of State or a reporter may in writing require any other persons who has notified him of an intention or a wish to appear at an inquiry to serve a statement of case, within 4 weeks of being so required, and in any event not later than 4 weeks before the date fixed for the holding of the inquiry, on the applicant, the planning authority, the Secretary of State and any statutory party.

(2) The Secretary of State or a reporter, as the case may be, shall supply any person from whom he requires a statement of case in accordance with paragraph (1) of this rule with a copy of the applicant's and the planning authority's statement of case and shall inform that person of the name and address of every person on whom his statement of case is required to be served.

(3) Rule 7(4) above shall apply, substituting references to the person required to serve a statement of case for the references to the planning authority, in relation to any statement of case required to be served under this rule.

Service of amended statements of case

10. Where prior to the commencing of the inquiry any person who has served a statement of case in accordance with rule 7, 8 or 9 —

(a)   intends to put forward at the inquiry a case materially different from the case set out in the statement of case; or

(b)   considers that conditions other than those proposed by the planning authority in accordance with rule 7(2)(b) ought to be imposed; or

(c)   is required by the Secretary of State or a reporter to provide such further information about the matters contained in the statement as may be specified,

that person shall provide the Secretary of State, or as the case may be the reporter, with an amended or additional statement and shall, at the same time, send a copy to any other person on whom the statement of case has been served.

Statement of reasons for direction by Secretary of State

11. In the case of a referred application —

(a)   the Secretary of State shall, where this has not already been done, not later than 4 weeks after the relevant date serve or cause to be served on the applicant, on the planning authority and on all statutory parties, a written statement of the reasons for his direction that the application be referred to him and of any matters which seem to him to be likely to be relevant to his consideration of the application; and

(b)   where a government department have expressed in writing to the Secretary of State the view that the application should not be granted either wholly or in part, or should be granted only subject to conditions, or, in the case of an application for consent under a tree preservation order, should be granted together with a direction requiring the replanting of trees or, in the case of any application, that it should be granted, the Secretary of State shall include this expression of view in his statement and shall supply a copy of the statement to the government department concerned.

Precognitions

12. — (1) A person entitled to appear at an inquiry who proposes to give, or to call another person to give, evidence at the inquiry by reference to a precognition shall send a copy of the precognition to the reporter together with, subject to paragraph (2) of this rule, a written summary.

(2) A written summary shall not be required in relation to a precognition which contains fewer than 2000 words.

(3) The precognition and any summary shall be sent to the reporter —

(a)   not later than 2 weeks before the date fixed for the holding of the inquiry; or

(b)   by such other date as the reporter may specify.

(4) Where the applicant or the planning authority send a copy of the precognition to a reporter in accordance with paragraph (1) of this rule they shall at the same time send a copy of that precognition and any summary to the planning authority or the applicant, as the case may be, and to any statutory party; and where any other party so sends such a copy he shall at the same time also send a copy to the applicant, the planning authority and any statutory party.

(5) Where a written summary is provided in accordance with paragraph (1) of this rule, only that summary shall be read out at the inquiry, unless the reporter permits or requires otherwise.

(6) Any person required by this rule to send a copy of a precognition to any other person shall send with it a copy of the whole, or the relevant part, of any document referred to in it, unless a copy of the document or part of the document in question is already available for inspection pursuant to rule 13 (2).

(7) The planning authority shall afford to any person who so requests a reasonable opportunity to inspect and, where practicable, take copies of any precognition, summary or document sent to or by them in accordance with this rule.

Service of statements of case, documents and precognitions

13. — (1) Any person who serves a statement of case on the planning authority shall not be obliged to serve with it a copy of any document, or of the relevant part of any document, if a copy of the document or part of the document in question is already available for inspection pursuant to paragraph (2) of this rule.

(2) The planning authority shall afford to any person who so requests a reasonable opportunity to inspect and, where practicable, take copies of any statement of case (or any part thereof) or other document which, or a copy of which, has been served on them in accordance with this rule or rule 7, 8 or 9 or of their statement of case (or any part thereof); and shall specify in their statement of case the time and place at which the opportunity will be afforded.

(3) Where under these Rules, any precognition, summary or document is required to be served by a person on a statutory party that obligation of service shall apply only in respect of a statutory party who has been required to serve a statement of case in terms of rule 9(1) and the reporter may specify the period within which the obligation must be fulfilled.

(4) Where any party intends to rely on or put in evidence any documents, that party shall, by the date 4 weeks before the day fixed for the holding of the inquiry, provide copies of those documents (or the relevant parts of those documents) to the planning authority and the Secretary of State; and where that party is the planning authority, such copies shall be provided to the Secretary of State and the planning authority shall, for the purposes of compliance by them with the duty imposed by paragraph (2) of this rule in respect of their statement of case, make such statement available by said date.

(5) The reporter, on the application of a party, may vary any time limit imposed on that party by rule 7, 8, 9 or 12 above or by paragraph (4) of this rule.

Notification of appointment of assessor

14. Where the Secretary of State appoints an assessor, he shall notify every person entitled to appear at the inquiry of the name of the assessor and of the matters on which he is to advise the reporter.

Date and notification of inquiry

15. — (1) The date fixed by the Secretary of State for the holding of an inquiry shall be, unless he considers such a date impracticable, not later than —

(a)   24 weeks after the relevant date; or

(b)   in a case where a pre-inquiry meeting is held pursuant to rule 5, 8 weeks after the conclusion of that meeting.

(2) Where the Secretary of State considers it impracticable to fix a date in accordance with paragraph (1), the date fixed shall be the earliest date which he considers to be practicable.

(3) Subject to paragraphs (1) and (2) of this rule, a date, time and place for the holding of the inquiry shall be fixed by the Secretary of State who shall give not less than 4 weeks' notice in writing of such date, time and place to —

(a)   the applicant;

(b)   the planning authority;

(c)   all statutory parties at the addresses furnished by them; and

(d)   any person to whom notification is required to be given under section 265(3) of the Act (notification of local inquiries).

(4) With the consent in writing of the applicant and of the planning authority the Secretary of State may give such lesser period of notice than that specified in paragraph (3) of this rule as may be agreed with them and in that event he may specify a date for service of the statements or other documents referred to in rule 7, 8 or 9 other than the date prescribed in those rules.

(5) The Secretary may vary the date, time and place fixed for the holding of the inquiry and he shall give such notice of the variation to the parties referred to in paragraph (3) of this rule as may appear to him to be reasonable in the circumstances.

(6) Without prejudice to the foregoing provisions of this rule and, where the Secretary of State has not already done so, he may require the planning authority to take one or more of the following steps —

(a)   not less than 2 weeks before the date fixed for the holding of the inquiry, to publish in one or more newspapers circulating in the locality in which the land is situated such notices of the inquiry as he may direct;

(b)   to serve notice of the inquiry in such form and on such persons or classes of persons as he may specify;

(c)   to post such notices of the inquiry as he may direct in a conspicuous place or places near to the land,

but the requirements as to the period of notice contained in paragraph (3) of this rule shall not apply to any such notices.

Appearances at inquiry

16. — (1) The person entitled to appear at the inquiry shall be —

(a)   the applicant;

(b)   the planning authority;

(c)   where the Secretary of State has given a direction restricting the grant of permission for the development for which the application was made or a direction as to how the application is to be determined, a representative of the Secretary of State;

(d)   where a government department have expressed a view in writing on the application and the planning authority have included this in their statement of case, a representative of that department;

(e)   any local authority;

(f)   all statutory parties;

(g)   any person on whom the Secretary of State has required notice to be served under rule 15(6)(b);

(h)   any other person to whom notification has been given under section 265(3) of the Act (notification of local inquiries).

(2) Any other person may appear at the inquiry at the discretion of the reporter.

(3) Any person entitled or permitted to appear may do so on his own behalf or be represented by counsel, solicitor or any other person.

(4) Where there are two or more persons having a similar interest in the matter under inquiry, the reporter may allow one or more persons to appear for the benefit of some or all persons so interested.

Representatives of the Secretary of State or government departments at inquiry

17. — (1) Where either —

(a)   the Secretary of State has given a direction restricting the grant of permission for the development for which the application was made or a direction as to how the application is to be determined; or

(b)   any government department have expressed in writing to the Secretary of State or to the planning authority a view on the application, any of the persons mentioned in rule 16(1) may, not later than 2 weeks before the date of the inquiry, apply in writing to the Secretary of State for a representative of the Secretary of State or government department concerned to be made available at the inquiry.

(2) Where an application is made to the Secretary of State under paragraph (1) of this rule he shall make a representative of his department available to attend the inquiry, or, as the case may be, transmit the application to the other government department concerned who shall make a representative of that department available to attend the inquiry.

(3) A representative who, in pursuance of this rule, attends an inquiry shall state the reasons for the Secretary of State's direction, or, as the case may be, the reasons for the view expressed by the department which he represents and shall give evidence and be subject to cross-examination to the same extent as any other witness.

(4) Nothing in this rule shall require a representative of the Secretary of State or a government department to answer any question which in the opinion of the reporter is directed to the merits of government policy and the reporter shall disallow any such question.

Representatives of local authorities at inquiry

18. — (1) Where any local authority have expressed in writing to the planning authority the view that the application should not be granted wholly or in part or should be granted only subject to conditions, any of the persons mentioned in rule 16(1) may, not later than 14 days before the date of the inquiry, apply in writing to the Secretary of State for a representative of the authority concerned to be made available to attend the inquiry.

(2) Where an application is made to the Secretary of State under paragraph (1) of this rule he shall transmit the application to the authority concerned, who shall make a representative of the authority available to attend the inquiry.

(3) A representative of a local authority who, in pursuance of this rule, attends an inquiry shall state the authority's reasons for the view expressed by them and shall give evidence and be subject to cross-examination to the same extent as any other witness.

Procedure at inquiry

19. — (1) Except as otherwise provided in these Rules, the procedure at the inquiry shall be such as the reporter shall in his discretion determine.

(2) The reporter shall state at or before the commencement of the inquiry the procedure which, subject to consideration of any submission by the parties, he proposes to adopt.

(3) Unless in any particular case the reporter otherwise determines, the applicant shall begin and shall have the right of final reply; and other persons entitled or permitted to appear shall be heard in such order as the reporter may determine.

(4) Subject to paragraph (5) of this rule, the applicant, the planning authority and the statutory parties shall be entitled to call evidence and to cross-examine persons giving evidence and to make closing statements but any other person appearing at the inquiry may do so only to the extent permitted by the reporter.

(5) The reporter may refuse to permit —
(a)   the giving or production of evidence;
(b)   the cross-examination of persons giving evidence; or
(c)   the presentation of any other matter,
which he considers to be irrelevant or repetitious.

(6) The reporter shall not require or permit the giving or production of any evidence whether written or oral, which would be contrary to the public interest; but save as aforesaid and without prejudice to rule 17(4) and section 265(4) to (7) of the Act (evidence at local inquiries) any evidence may be admitted at the discretion of the reporter, who may direct that documents tendered in evidence may be inspected by any person entitled or permitted to appear at the inquiry and that facilities be afforded him to take or obtain copies thereof.

(7) The reporter may at the inquiry allow any party to alter or add to the case contained in any statement served under rule 7(1), 8(1) or 9(1) or to any list of documents which accompanied such statement, so far as may be necessary for the purpose of determining the questions in dispute between the parties, but shall (if necessary by adjourning the inquiry) give the applicant or the planning authority, as the case may be, and all statutory parties an adequate opportunity of considering any such alterations or additions.

(8) If any person entitled to appear at the inquiry fails to do so, the reporter may proceed with the inquiry at his discretion.

(9) The reporter shall be entitled (subject to disclosure thereof at the inquiry) to take into account any written representations or statements received by him before or during the inquiry from any person, but shall circulate such documents in advance of the inquiry where he considers this to be practicable.

(10) The reporter may from time to time adjourn the inquiry and, if the date, time and place of the adjourned inquiry are announced before the adjournment, no further notice shall be required.

Site inspections

20. — (1) The reporter may at any time make an unaccompanied inspection of the land without giving notice of his intention to the persons entitled or permitted to appear at the inquiry.

(2) Subject to the provisions of this rule, the reporter may, and shall if so requested by the applicant or the planning authority before or during the inquiry, inspect the land during or after the close of the inquiry in the company of such of the persons entitled under paragraph (3) of this rule to accompany him as desire to do so.

(3) Where the reporter intends to make an inspection by virtue of paragraph (2) of this rule, he shall during the inquiry announce the date and time at which he proposes to do so and the applicant, the planning authority, all statutory parties and any other party to the inquiry shall be entitled to accompany him on any such inspection.

(4) The reporter shall not be bound to defer his inspection if any person entitled to accompany him is not present at the time appointed.

Procedure after inquiry

21. — (1) After the close of the inquiry, the reporter shall make a report in writing to the Secretary of State which shall include his findings of fact, his conclusions and his recommendations or his reasons for not making any recommendations.

(2) Where an assessor has been appointed, he may (and if so required by the reporter, shall), after the close of the inquiry, make a report in writing to the reporter in respect of the matters on which he was appointed to advise.

(3) Where an assessor makes a report in accordance with paragraph (2), the reporter shall append it to his own report and shall state in his own report how far he agrees or disagrees with the assessor's report and, where he disagrees with the assessor, he reasons for that disagreement.

(4) Where the Secretary of State —

(a)   differs from the reporter on a finding of fact; or

(b)   after the close of the inquiry proposes to take into consideration any new evidence (including expert opinion on a matter of fact) or any new issue of fact (not being a matter of government policy) which was not raised at the inquiry,

and by reason thereof is disposed to disagree with a recommendation made by the reporter, he shall not come to a decision which is at variance with any such recommendation without first notifying the applicant, the planning authority and all statutory parties who appeared at the inquiry of his disagreement and the reasons for it and affording them an opportunity of —

(i)   making representations thereon in writing within 3 weeks; or

(ii)   if the Secretary of State has received new evidence or taken into consideration any new issue of fact not being a matter of government policy, asking within 3 weeks for the reopening of the inquiry.

(5) The Secretary of State may in any case if he thinks fit cause the inquiry to be reopened, and shall cause it to be reopened if asked to do so in accordance with paragraph (4) of this rule, and if the inquiry is reopened, paragraph (3) to (6) of rule 15 shall apply to the reopened inquiry with the substitution in paragraph (3) of the words '3 weeks' for the words '4 weeks'.

Notification of decision

22. — (1) The Secretary of State shall notify his decision and his reasons therefor in writing to the applicant, the planning authority and the statutory parties and to any person who, having appeared or been represented at the inquiry, has asked to be notified of the decision.

(2) Where a copy of the report is not sent with the notification of the decision, the notification shall be accompanied by a summary of the reporter's conclusions and recommendations; and if any person entitled to be notified of the Secretary of State's decision under paragraph (1) of this rule has not received a copy of the report, he shall be supplied with a copy thereof on written application made to the Secretary of State within 6 weeks from the date of his decision.

(3) For the purpose of this rule 'report' means the report submitted to the Secretary of State (including the assessor's report, if any) but does not include documents appended to the report but any person entitled to be notified of the Secretary of State's decision under paragraph (1) of this rule may apply to the Secretary of State in writing within 6 weeks of the notification to him of the decision or the supply to him of the report, whichever is the later, for an opportunity of inspecting such documents, and the Secretary of State shall afford him an opportunity accordingly.

Allowing further time

23. The Secretary of State may at any time in any particular case allow further time for the taking of any step which is required or enabled to be taken by virtue of these Rules and references in these Rules to a day by which, or a period within which, any step is required or enabled to be taken shall be construed accordingly.

Service of notices by post

24. Notices or documents required or authorised to be served or sent under the provisions of any of these Rules may be sent by post.

Revocation and savings provision

25. — (1) Subject to paragraph (2) below, the Town and Country Planning (Inquiries Procedure) (Scotland) Rules 1980 are revoked.

(2) The said Rules of 1980 shall continue to apply to any application or appeal in respect of which notification by the Secretary of State of his intention to proceed by inquiry was given prior to the coming into force of these Rules."

Notes

(1) The rules amend and replace the Town and Country Planning (Inquiries Procedure)   **1–54**
(Scotland) Rules 1980 which are revoked (subject to transitional provisions contained in rule 25(2)) and are concerned with the procedures to be followed at local inquiries held for the purpose of any application referred to the Secretary of State or any appeal made to the Secretary of State under the Town and Country Planning (Scotland) Act 1997, the Planning (Listed Buildings and Conservation Areas) (Scotland) Act 1997 and the Planning (Hazardous Substances) (Scotland) Act 1997.

(2) The rules serve two purposes: to provide a means of appeal against refusal of planning permission as well as the means by which an inquiry can consider the merits of a planning application and, in particular, to consider objections made by individuals or groups to proposals for planning permission. This kind of inquiry typically involves a major development, such as the "Super Quarry Inquiry" held on Harris in 1995. Such public inquiries are relatively rare and are usually reserved for cases involving considerable controversy and where the lengthy and expensive process can be justified. Matters of national policy are typically involved: see *Bushell v. Secretary of State for the Environment* [1981] A.C. 75, extracted at para. 8–15, on the extent to which challenge to government policy could be raised at an inquiry and see generally A. R. Mowbray, "Public Inquiries and Government Policy" (1987) 137 N.L.J. 418. Other evidence exists to suggest that the utility of inquiry procedure as a means of testing policy is limited. M. Purdue, R. Kemp and T. O'Riordan, "The Government at the Sizewell B Inquiry" [1985] P.L. 475 at 488, concluded that:

> "Where Government policy is fundamental to the issues which are the subject-matter of an inquiry, a Government witness provides a useful function in explaining and elaborating this policy.... However, if Government policies are unclear or in a state of flux, the witness will be put in a difficult position.... In the case of the Sizewell B Inquiry this tendency has been increased by the length of the Inquiry...
>
> As a result, we would argue that it would be unwise to look to public inquiries as a formal mechanism for any definitive assessment of Government policy, especially in those areas which are either unclear or prone to substantial policy flux."

(3) Inquiries under these rules are therefore relatively rare, albeit the issues that tend to be raised are often of major local or national significance. Most planning appeals (90 per cent) are now dealt with by way of written submission, although both the appellant or the planning authority can request an inquiry. Set against the speed and cheapness of written submission procedure is the fact that available evidence tends to suggest that appeals which proceed by way of written representation are markedly less successful than those which to go inquiry, the ratio being 38 per cent to 52 per cent: see also the JUSTICE-All Souls Report, p. 290. Written rules on written submission procedure are contained in the Town and Country

Planning (Appeals) (Written Submissions Procedure) Regulations 1990. These rules are supplemented by a Code of Practice. At the time of writing a consultation draft has been issued and the new code is likely to be in place by June 1999. For further reading see N. Collar, *Planning* (2nd ed., 1999), paras 8.09–8.15; A. McAllister and R. McMaster, *Scottish Planning Law* (1994), pp. 141–146; and *Stair Memorial Encyclopaedia*, Vol. 23, "Town and Country Planning", para. 266.

(4) Notwithstanding the terms of the rules in the extract most appeals, whether by inquiry or written submission, are in fact dealt with by a reporter under delegated authority: (Determination by Appointed Person) (Inquiries Procedure) (Scotland) Rules 1997. The main difference between the rules governing delegated appeals and those in the extract is that, in delegated procedure, the reporter is required to draft and issue a decision letter whereas if the decision is to be taken by the Secretary of State, the reporter will make a report, which consists of his findings on fact and his recommendations along with his reasoning. Whether or not the appeal is determined by the reporter or the Secretary of State, both have to make a decision based on adequate evidence and provide reasons which are adequate, proper, clear and intelligible. For comment on this obligation to give reasons see *Wordie Property Co. Ltd v. Secretary of State for Scotland*, 1984 S.L.T. 345, noted at para. 12–36.

Although both the rules detailed in the extract and the rules dealing with delegated appeals give the right to be heard, the common law rules on natural justice still have scope. Thus although a reporter may rely on his own knowledge as well as the evidence presented to him, he cannot take into account evidence not heard at the inquiry and must inform all parties and give them the opportunity to be heard thereon. So in *City of Glasgow District Council v. Secretary of State for Scotland*, 1997 S.C.L.R. 417 a reporter (under written submissions procedure) was held not to be entitled to reach a conclusion on the lawfulness of an existing use of premises without inviting the parties to make representations thereon. There is, however, no obligation on the reporter to seek out additional information where written submissions do not cover all the points in the appeal: *City of Glasgow District Council v. Secretary of State for Scotland and William Hill (Scotland) Ltd*, 1992 S.C.L.R. 453. The Secretary of Sate is similarly bound to permit representations on any new evidence to be taken into account by him: *Wordie*, below; *Anduff Holdings Ltd v. Secretary of State for Scotland*, 1992 S.L.T. 697; and *Fairmount Investments Ltd v. Secretary of State for the Environment* [1976] 2 All E.R. 865. Matters of policy are, however, less likely to be treated as matters upon which the Secretary of State is obliged to seek representation: *Wordie*, below, and see *London & Clydeside Properties Ltd v. City of Aberdeen District Council*, 1983 S.C. 145. There is no obligation on the Secretary of State to give parties the opportunity to comment on draft National Planning Policy Guidance, since the inquiries procedure rules state there is no obligation to do so in relation to matters or government policy: *London and Midland Developments Ltd v. Secretary of State for Scotland*, 1996 S.C.L.R. 465. For further discussion see *Stair Memorial Encyclopaedia*, above, para. 266 and see also para. 6–16.

1–55   (5) The Council on Tribunals has its own role to play in relation to the work of planning inquiries. The Franks Committee concluded that inquiry procedure protected the public by giving them rights to be heard and also ensured that Ministers made decisions on the basis of the widest possible range of information. The majority of its recommendations on inquiries, unlike those for tribunals, were accepted by the Government. First, individuals should know in good time before the inquiry the case to be presented against them. Second, the line of government policy should be revealed at the inquiry. Thirdly, the reporter or report should be published at the same time as the decision letter from the Minister. Fourthly, the decision letter should contain reasons for the decision and fifthly, challenge in the Court of Session on grounds of jurisdiction procedure should be permitted. A recommendation that planning reporters or inspectors (the English term) should be under the control of the Lord Chancellor was, however, rejected. For the report's recommendations, see paras 262–277. Section 9 of the Tribunals and Inquiries Act 1992 allows the Lord Advocate, after consulting the Council on Tribunals including the Scottish Committee, to make rules for statutory inquiries, including planning inquiries, which are defined under section 16(1) as:

"(a) an inquiry or hearing held or to be held in pursuance of a duty imposed by any statutory provision, or (b) an inquiry or hearing, or an inquiry or hearing of a class, designated for the purposes of this section by an order under subsection (2) …".

Around 100 inquiries have thus far been designated. Section 1(1)(c) gives the council and its Scottish Committee power to consider and report on matters referred to it and also to instigate investigations on the administrative procedures at an inquiry if it considers that these are of special importance. On this see, for example, the role of the Scottish Committee on the formulation of the 1997 Rules on planning appeals and inquiries: Annual reports 1995–96, pp. 11–12; 1996–97, p. 19; and 1997–98, pp. 15–16.

(6) Where an appeal has been delegated to the reporter, the Secretary of State has power to "call in" the appeal and determinate it himself. This is a power that has been used sparingly and has been subject to challenge. In *London & Clydesdale Properties Ltd* the Secretary of State made a direction that he would determine an appeal personally. This was challenged by the company on the grounds that the proposed development was within the Secretary of State's own constituency and that prior to becoming Secretary of State, he had supported objections to development of the same site. The company alleged that the Secretary of State could not bring an independent mind to consideration of the appeal. Standing the high test required to succeed when such an allegation is made (on which see para. 9–7) the challenge was unsurprisingly unsuccessful.

However, in *Bryan v. United Kingdom* (1996) 21 E.H.R.R. 342 the European Court of Human Rights had to consider the issue of a recall of a planning inspector's jurisdiction. The court determined that the power of the Secretary of State to revoke an inspector's jurisdiction deprived the inspector of the appearance of independence required by Article 6(1) of the ECHR but that the appellant's right of appeal on the point of law to the High Court meant that the combined remedies of an appeal to an inspector coupled with the possibility of a further appeal to the High Court satisfied the demands of Article 6. See generally S. Crow, "Lessons from *Bryan*" [1996] J.P.L. 359.

(7) The rules in the extract were subsequently amended by the Town and Country Planning (Inquiries Procedure) (Scotland) Amendment Rules 1998, and the Town and Country Planning (Appeals) (Determination by Appointed Person) (Inquiries Procedure) (Scotland) Amendment Rules 1998. These amendments amended their respective rules by creating a new class of party at an inquiry, "the relevant person". They are entitled to receive personal copies of all statements and representations made to the inquiry. The other parties not classed as relevant persons, although retaining their status as statutory parties with the right to be notified of, and attend, the inquiry, would not be so entitled. The Scottish Committee of the Council on Tribunals expressed concern at this amendment. It felt that it did not require the reporter either to make clear how he determined that someone could be a "relevant person" or even to inform those making representations of his decision. Similarly, if a statutory party has not been classed as a "relevant person", it may no longer call evidence and cross-examine unless it has received the reporter's permission to do so. On the face of it this is a reduction in the rights available. See the 1997–98 Report, pp. 15–16.

(8) The objectives of the new rules of increasing the efficiency and effectiveness of planning appeal and inquiry procedure without affecting the Franks objectives of openness, fairness and impartiality, appear to have been met in most material respects: see J. Henderson, "Planning Inquiries and Hearings: Procedure and Good Practice" (1999) 71 S.P.E.L. 6. On planning inquiries generally see N. Collar, *Planning* (2nd ed., 1999), paras 8.18–8.33; E. Young and J. Rowan-Robinson, *Scottish Planning Law and Procedure* (1985), pp. 479–418; *Stair Memorial Encyclopaedia*, Vol. 23, paras 260–269; E. Young, *Scottish Planning Appeals* (1991); A. McMaster and R. McAllister, *Scottish Planning Law* (1994), pp. 141–153.

INSPECTION

Inspection involves examination of an activity by an officially appointed person. There are many inspectors in administration. Some may inspect private citizens — for example, school attendance officers, or commercial entities — for example, factory inspectors. Inspection may

1–56

be incidental to the main task of the inspecting party such as a planning reporter in relation to a public inquiry. Inspection can involve law enforcement, suggestions for improvement and the obtaining of information.

Report of H.M. Inspector for Scottish Constabulary 1997–98

Cmnd. 4054 (1998)

1–57   "2. The role of Her Majesty's Chief Inspector of Constabulary offers a unique opportunity to look in-depth at policing in all 8 fores and, as a result, assess the state of the Scottish police service. In every force I have found that the Inspectorate is welcomed and management receptive to ideas aimed at improving efficiency. The Inspectorate provides a conduit of good practice and during my time at Her Majesty's Inspectorate of Constabulary I am convinced of the positive influence it has on the police service. This would not be possible without the professionalism and co-operation of chief constables. ...

7. Crimes recorded by the police in Scotland continue to fall for the sixth consecutive reporting year. Current levels are now 26.5% below the peak in crimes occurring in Scotland each day than in 1991. Police performance has also improved and a 40% clearance rate has been achieved in detecting crimes, which represents a steady rise in recent years.

8. There is no room for complacency and there is still scope for improvement. There is always a concern that reductions experienced in recent years will bottom out. The general trend masks increases in recorded crime in some parts of Scotland and local circumstances have to be considered. Furthermore, the recorded crime figures do not account for all crime that is committed, not all crime is reported to and subsequently recorded by the police and, in any case, police activity is not the sole determining factor in the commission of crime. However the figures also disguise the huge increase in police activity against the misuse of drugs including a 137% increase in the number of persons reported for supply since 1991. Any uncertainties should not take away from the credit that is due to forces for tackling crime head on. Extra police officers are being used to increase the number of high profile patrols, criminals are being targeted using improved means of intelligence gathering, increased use is being made of new technology as it relates to fingerprinting and DNA and the principles of crime management are progressively being applied in a more productive fashion. I am confident that Scottish forces recognise crime reduction as a core police function. ...

12. I realise that if chief constables are to make progress in this and other matters it will demand a major cultural change, but nothing less will be required by forces to show the proper level of commitment to the Government's Best Value Regime. This already applies to local authorities and it is much more than just a welcome replacement for Compulsory Competitive Tendering. The police service is no stranger to the setting of objectives and targets in support of a strategic plan applying performance measurement to monitor achievement and inviting extensive public consultation, but Best Value will demand a rigour in terms of strategic planning which has yet to be learned and will require new skills such as benchmarking and activity costing. I have no doubt that the Scottish police service will show positive commitment to these disciplines and in time will take great satisfaction from the better understanding of their business which they will bring. ...

14. Issues of funding will be considered by the joint Study currently being conducted by Her Majesty's Inspectorate of Constabulary and the Accounts Commission. This co-operative venture breaks new ground and I am delighted with the added strength that it provides in looking at financial management, control and delegation and the arrangements for and costs of support services from local authorities and other services. The joint report is due to be published later this year and I am convinced that it will assist forces in providing strong financial management to enable them to take on fully the benefits which Best Value offers. ...

18. Society is slowly waking up to the issue of domestic violence. With the publication this year of 'Hitting Home', which made reference to good practice already being employed in some forces, I would like to think that Her Majesty's Inspectorate has made a small but significant contribution to help forces focus on the need to record statistics; arrangements for management and monitoring of domestic violence incidents; the provision, using information technology, of operational intelligence about domestic violence; the provision of follow up assistance for victims; the provision of training for officers and underlying all of these issues, the establishment of a standard definition. Since the publication of the report, which had to be reprinted because of the high level of interest generated, I have been encouraged by the general level of awareness of officers on the ground regarding the importance of this issue and the need to carry out

thorough investigations and submit comprehensive reports. We are beginning to see the incidence of recorded domestic violence increasing — it has until now been under reported — and, in the main, forces have given a very positive response to the recommendations, with a domestic violence group now established for the Scottish police service under the chairmanship of an Assistant Chief Constable. Even in forces where the response has been slower than I would have liked, there are now real signs of improvement in the approach taken towards domestic crime which encompasses a significant number of homicides where the victim is a woman, the extreme end of a form of violence which affects thousands of women each year. ...

24. Throughout the year I have paid particular attention, during inspections, to the way police forces have responded to Lord Cullen's findings on firearms licensing after the tragedy of Dunblane. I have been impressed by the effort invested in reviewing practices and procedures and the care taken by forces to ensure that relevant intelligence is made available to enquiry officers considering applications for firearm and shotgun certificates. Refusals and revocations have increased and I am pleased to see the overriding emphasis being one of public safety. The move from 3 year to 5 year certificates from 1995 will result in an opportunity for forces not faced with renewal applications to ensure that any outstanding issues which need to be resolved are addressed fully during 1998/99. During the year forces responded magnificently to the Government's 2 surrender programmes as a result of the Firearms (Amendment) Acts and the potential danger inherent in the ownership of 6,262 large-calibre and 2,764 small-calibre handguns was removed from society. ...

29. All forces have equal opportunities policies and grievance procedures and much effort has been made to train officers and staff on these issues. However, it must not end there and I have too often visited forces where publication of policy on equal opportunities is not followed through by action, e.g. where there is no record of formal grievance procedures being used. Forces must demonstrate their commitment to equal opportunities and instil in their workforces the confidence to use the procedures which are intended to safeguard them. ...

32. The Police (Health and Safety) Act 1997 was implemented in July. With its introduction, health and safety laws, previously applying only to civilian support staff, will also apply to police officers. It has been anticipated by a significant investment in effort by all forces, with the appointment of health and safety officers, the establishment of safety committees and the preparation of policy, training and awareness and generic and specific risk assessments associated with operational policing. Generally Scottish forces have responded well to the new legislation and it is an area which will be monitored closely by Her Majesty's Inspectorate for the time being.

33. The safety of police officers is a matter which is central to all operational decisions. Recent years have seen great improvement in officer safety equipment and training. It is too early to tell if these measures significantly affect the number of assaults on police officers but the additional emphasis on training ensures they are better equipped to deal with the real dangers they face. However, chief officers cannot be complacent and the testing of the use of CS incapacitant sprays, heralded in last year's report, has helped to take the issue of officer safety forward. Due to limited use in the initial trial period, the area of coverage and length of the trials have been extended and both Strathclyde Police and Tayside Police are now collecting valuable information which will help to determine the future use of this equipment in the Scottish police service. Whatever the outcome I am pleased with the sensitive approach taken and am satisfied that the issue of public safety will be of prime consideration.

34. The number of complaints against the police continues to fall and this reflects well on the time and effort committed by forces to the investigation of complaints and a willingness to apply lessons learned. In the statutory role which has been given to Her Majesty's Inspectorate, in addition to the emphasis placed on complaints during inspections, I am kept closely in tune with the way forces respond to complaints. I believe that the Inspectorate's influence, while imposing a heavy additional burden on my staff, is a positive one which has assisted in a more rigorous approach to recording complaints. The role of Her Majesty's Lay Inspector brings to the matter a strong independent element of public scrutiny."

Notes

(1) On inspection generally see O. W. Hartley, "Inspectorates in British Central Government" (1972) 50 *Public Administration* 447; B. Hutter, "An Inspector Calls: The importance of proactive enforcement in the regulatory context" (1986) 26 Brit. J. Criminol. 114; and W. Upton and R. Harwood, "The Stunning Powers of Environmental Inspectors" [1996] J.P.L. 623.   **1–58**

(2) To what extent does the implementation of an inspector's recommendation rely on the legal sanctions available to him? Consider, in the context of the police, section 33 of the Police (Scotland) Act 1967.

REGULATION

1–59 Regulation is a long-established administrative procedure. One of the most common forms of regulation is licensing, with liquor perhaps being the best-known licensed product. Planning control might also be regarded as a form of licensing. For examples of the interplay between licensing authorities and the courts in this book, see *Cinderella's Rockefalla's Ltd v. Glasgow District Licensing Board*, 1994 S.C.L.R. 591, at para. 7–6 (liquor licensing); *R. v. Gaming Board for Great Britain, ex parte Benaim and Khaida* [1970] 2 Q.B. 417, at para. 8–49, and *Laker Airways Ltd v. Department of Trade* [1977] Q.B. 643, at para. 7–21 (airlines). On whether an authority in deciding to grant, renew or revoke a licence is obliged to form procedural fairness, see *McInnes v. Onslow-Fane* [1978] 1 W.L.R. 1520, extracted at para. 8–9.

Report of the Director General of Telecommunications 1997–98

(1997–98 H.C. 652), paras 1.4–1.11, 1.19

1–60 **"Working for the customer**

1.4 There was a huge effort in the past year by our team investigating the price of calls to mobile phones. Our initial investigations led us to believe that there was scope for the mobile phone companies Cellnet and Vodaphone, and BT to make considerable price reductions. Following our reference, the Monopoly and Mergers Commission agreed with our conclusions. This allowed us to put in place a new price control, which will save £1 billion for customers over the next three years. The first results of this should be seen in consumers' bills from April 1999.

1.5 A further example of OFTEL's consumer work was the introduction, on January 1 1999, of mobile number portability. For the first time customers unhappy with their mobile provider can move to an alternative supplier and retain their original number. Customers can shop around for the best deal. The UK is the first country in the world to give customers this ability.

1.6 Junk faxes and unwanted telesales calls have been at the top of the complaints-to-OFTEL league for most of the year though there are codes of practice and other voluntary rules in place to protect customers. The sending of unwanted faxes is a particular source of irritation to many people, and others are infuriated by the interruption caused by telesales calls to their homes or businesses. People should not be harassed by telesales after clearly telling the caller they do not want to be phoned again. Last year I banned one company from making such calls. The intention was to a send a clear message to all companies involved in telesales that this behaviour will not be tolerated.

1.7 OFTEL will continue to enforce licence obligations whenever necessary. 1999 will see the introduction of a new obligatory scheme, which will be enforced by the Data Protection Registrar. Individuals can only be sent faxes with their prior consent and business can opt out from receiving junk faxes altogether. I am sure these new measures, which come into force on 1 May, will be welcomed by customers and all reputable direct marketing companies.

1.8 Last year saw the start of the publicity campaign funded by all the telephone companies to make businesses aware of the national code and number changes that will take place in 2000. Giving businesses plenty of time will help minimise their costs — for example when stationery has to be reordered, the new numbers can be included in their letterhead.

1.9 OFTEL is well aware that changing telephone numbers is never welcome, but the huge explosion in demand for faxes, mobile phones and modems for computers has meant some areas are in danger of running out of telephone numbers. OFTEL consulted on the options in 1995 and in the light of comments received, we chose the option that was most acceptable to consumers and met their requirement for clear and consistent numbering.

1.10 The changes will do two things. First, it will create a huge store of new numbers for the future. Second, it will provide a clear structure for phone services such as mobiles, pagers, and special rate services. People will know what service they are dialling and in what range the charge is likely to be.

1.11 An important part of OFTEL's work is to ensure the delivery of affordable basic telecommunications services to all consumers including those with disabilities. Last year OFTEL issued a consultation document and statement on the measures that telecommunications companies should put in place to ensure that people with disabilities have proper access to the sorts of telecommunications services which most people take for granted. These included publicising the services for people with disabilities in appropriate ways providing a free directory information service for people who cannot use a phone directory. The statement also included measures designed to improve the ease of use of textphones for people with impaired hearing, and measures to improve access to public payphones. The DTI are still considering OFTEL's proposals and should be drafting a Statutory Instrument to bring them into effect in the near future. …

Working together for the customer's benefit

1.19 There have been three important developments over the year. First, in 1998 the new competition Act received Royal Assent. OFTEL, and other regulators have been given powers concurrent with the OFT. Joint preparatory work has been started to ensure consistency in application of the new powers when they come into effect in March 2000. OFTEL is seeking to draw back from detailed prescriptive regulation whenever possible. But there are many occasions where there is a need to act to protect consumers' interests to prevent anti-competitive behaviour. It is also important that the regulators are seen to be consistent in their application of the new powers brought in by the Act."

Report of the Scottish Advisory Committee on Telecommunications (SACOT), paras 3.27–3.30

Membership and activity during 1998   **1–61**

3.27 One new member of the Committee was appointed, three including the outgoing Chairman retired, and two members resigned. The Committee held four meetings during the year, some of which were attended by senior representatives of network operators in Scotland, with which the Committee endeavours to maintain close links, and by senior officials from OFTEL. All meetings of the Committee were held at the Secretary's office in Edinburgh.

3.28 The Chairman participated in discussions with the Director General and the other Advisory Committee Chairmen, as well as attending seminars and workshops on particular topics of interest.

Major areas of work

3.29 During the year under report SACOT:

- Responded to the Department of Trade and Industry Consultative Document *A Fair Deal For Consumers: Modernising The Framework For Utility Regulation*, and also submitted comments on the subsequent phase of the consultative process concerning the establishment of statutory Consumer Councils. While giving general support to the proposals for improved representation of consumers' interests, SACOT emphasised the need to ensure that there was an effective structure for the representation of users of telecommunications services in Scotland, preferably on a statutory basis.
- Submitted views to the Director General and participated in discussion on a wide range of OFTEL consultative documents and other initiatives, including:
  - *A Better Deal for Payphone Users: OFTEL's Proposals for Payphone Regulation in the UK;*
  - *Freephone Numbers: Options for the Future;*
  - *Developing Number Administration;*
  - *Improving Accountability: Further Steps;*
  - *Proposals for Publishing Information on Complaints Received by OFTEL;*
  - *A Review of Telecommunication Licence Fees in the UK;*
  - *OFTEL's Work Programme 1998/99;*
  - *OFTEL Mobile Phone Working Group;*
  - *Carrier Preselection;*
  - *OFTEL Statement on the Principles of Affordability.*
- Reviewed the committee's strategic framework and identified a number of priorities and key objectives for action in 1999. These include:
  - Ensuring that proposed Telecommunications Consumer Council has sufficient powers and resources to do its job properly;
  - improving SACOT's own effectiveness in handling complaints and making SACOT's work better know;
  - contributing to the forthcoming review of European Union telecommunications legislation.
- Using the services of an external consultant, explored further the manner in which the Committee's profile might usefully be enhanced, and considered ways of making SACOT more accessible to consumers (with particular reference to the publication of dates of Committee meetings, agendas and papers, minutes on SACOT's section of the ACT website).
- Maintained contact with existing public telecommunications operators (PTOs) in Scotland through a series of meetings with senior managers to discuss issues of mutual interest.
- Commissioned a research study into consumers' perceptions of choice of telecommunications operator and of tariff, and into consumers' experience of getting telecommunications problems resolved.

Notes

1–62   (1) Regulation is an accepted technique for the control of privatised public utilities. The general purpose of the "Government's extensive regulation is to protect the public from harm caused by the activities of private enterprise": R. Austin, "Freedom of Information: The Constitutional Impact" in *The Changing Constitution* (J. Jowell and D. Oliver eds, 1994), p. 402. The statutes in this area include the Fair Trading Act 1973, the Restrictive Trade Practices Act 1976 and the Compensation Act 1980. More recently, the Competition and Service (Utilities) Act 1992 considerably enhanced the powers of the rail, telecommunications, gas, electricity and water industries regulators. For example, the legislation empowered the regulator to create performance standards for licensed undertakers and to consider and approve complaints handling procedures. For discussion of the Act see A. McHarg, "The Competition and Service (Utilities) Act 1992: Utility Regulation and the Charter" [1992] P.L. 385. Recently, and of major importance, is the Competition Act 1998.

From a date to be appointed the restrictive trade practices legislation (the Restrictive Trade Practices Acts 1976 and 1977, the Resale Prices Act 1976, the Restrictive Practices Court Act 1976 and the provisions on anti-competitive practices in the Competition Act 1980) are to be repealed. In their place, Part I of the Act provides for a new set of competition rules, modelled on the provisions of Articles 85 and 86 of the Treaty of Rome 1957. Of particular significance to utilities regulators is, that along with the Director General of Fair Trading in enforcing the provisions of Part I of the Act, the utility regulators can exercise those powers as well. The intention is to use the resources and specialised expertise of these regulators in tandem with the Director General's general functions. The Director General envisages that consistency of approach will be achieved by a single set of procedural rules to be adopted by the OFT and the regulators and by guidelines produced by a working party which includes the regulators. For an example of these guidelines see Oftel Press Release, January 14, 1999. Section 54 gives the regulators concurrent powers with the Director General so that a regulator can give guidance, consider complaints, impose interim measures, grant exemptions from the competition provisions, carry out investigations, impose penalties and enforce decisions. Only the Director General of Fair Trading has power to issue guidance and penalties and to make and amend the rules which set out the procedures to be followed during investigations or enforcement proceedings. For further reading see M. Grenfell and M. Coleman, *The Competition Act 1998* (1999); K. G. Middleton, "Reform of UK Competition Law", 1998 S.L.T. (News) 47; M. F. James, "The Reform of UK Competition Law: Part One" (1998) 66 S.L.G. 172; and J. Maitland-Walker, "The new U.K. competition law regime" (1999) 20 E.C.L.R. 51.

(2) The Labour Government is undertaking a major review of the regulation of utility regulation: see *A Fair Deal for Consumers: Modernising the Framework for Utility Regulation*, Cm. 3698 (1998) and *A Fair Deal for Consumers: The Response to Consultation* (London: Department of Trade and Industry, 1998). Among the proposals are:

•   Ministerial guidance should be issued on the social and environmental objectives of each utility sector and for each regulator.

•   A single primary duty should be inserted into each utility statute requiring the regulators to exercise their functions in a manner best calculated to protect the interests of consumers through the promotion of effective competition.

•   The electricity and gas regulators should be replaced as soon as possible with a single energy regulator and OFFER and OFGAS should be merged to create a single regulatory office.

•   The possibility of whether individual regulators should be supported by a statutory advisory group or replaced with a small executive board or commission is to be considered.

•   Each utility regulator should be placed under a statutory duty to consult on and publish and follow a Code of Practice and be under a duty to publish reasons for their key decisions.

Some question, however, whether the theoretical underpinning of utility regulation and models for reform, including those in the review, provide an effective regulatory structure: see, for example, T. Prosser, "Theorising Utility Regulation" (1999) 62 M.L.R. 196.

(3) Set against the growth of regulation of utilities, another government policy in recent years has been to reduce the public regulation of business. Starting initially with the White Paper, Lifting the Burden, Cmnd. 9571 (1985), the view was expressed that "too many people in central and local government spend too much of their time regulating the activities of others". Subsequently the programme was relaunched as a deregulation initiative under the Citizens Charter in 1992 and an enterprise and deregulation unit was established to promote deregulation throughout Whitehall. The Labour Government intends to continue with the programme, in particular removing burdens on the way in which *public* services are provided: see the White Paper, Modernising Government, Cm. 4301 (1999). As a consequence of this philosophy, the Deregulation and Contracting Out Act 1994 was enacted. Controversially, subordinate legislation could be made in terms of Chapter I of the Act to remove objectionable regulatory provisions, even though those provisions might be contained in primary legislation. Such a deregulation order is subject to a complex procedure. A draft of the proposed order must be laid before each House of Parliament, accompanied by an explanatory report giving details of the order and consultation with persons affected by it. A new committee, the House of Commons Deregulation Committee, and the House of Lords Delegated Powers Scrutiny Committee carry out detailed scrutiny of such orders.

(4) The courts have had little involvement to date in the affairs of major regulatory offices. In *R. v. Director General of Gas Supply, ex parte Smith*, July 31, 1989, Q.B.D., a successful action was based on natural justice. Jurisdictional control has also been exercised: *R. v. Director General of Electricity Supply, ex parte Redrow Homes (Northern) Ltd*, *The Times*, February 21, 1995. The court in *Smith* was at pains to point out that the Director General had a broad discretion in the way he carried out his duties and the court would not lightly intervene. This was confirmed in *R. v. Director General of Telecommunications, ex parte Let's Talk (UK) Ltd*, April 6, 1992, Q.B.D., where the discretion of the DGT to revoke a Code of Practice permitting the operation of a chat line was upheld. Familiar private law techniques may also have their role to play. In *Mercury Communications Ltd v. Director General of Telecommunications* [1996] 1 All E.R. 575 an action for declaration as to the proper interpretation of BT's public telecommunications operators' licence was held to be competent by the House of Lords. Concern that the vigorous application of the common law principles might conflict with the nature of a regulatory framework is sometimes expressed. In *R. v. Director General of Electricity Supply, ex parte Scottish Power plc*, Court of Appeal, February 3, 1997 a decision of the Director General not to modify the licence of Scottish Power was quashed in judicial review proceedings which alleged that the Director General had not acted rationally or fairly by allowing the modification of a licence for Hydro-Electric plc, a rival, in light of the report from the Monopolies and Mergers Commission, but not in the case of Scottish Power plc when they alleged that the factors in the MMC Report were equally applicable to their own licence.

For criticism of the case see C. Scott, "Regulatory discretion in licence modifications: the *Scottish Power* Case" [1997] P.L. 400. For general reading on intervention by the courts see A. McHarg, "Regulation as a private law function?' [1995] P.L. 539.

(5) The regulation of the water industry in Scotland is something of a hybrid. The supply of water (and sewerage provision) has not been privatised. The principal legislation is contained in Part II of the Local Government etc. (Scotland) 1994. Three water authorities have been established: East, West and North of Scotland Water. An authority must have regard to a Code of Practice in carrying out its functions, but breach of the code has no civil or criminal consequences: section 67. A Scottish Water and Sewerage Customers Council was set up to investigate complaints made against each water authority. The council cannot uphold any complaint nor can it award compensation. The council was a product of the thinking underlying the Citizens Charter initiative.

At the time of writing, a Water Authority Bill (1998–99 H.C. 1) has been presented to Parliament which will replace the council with a Water Industry Commissioner who has a general function of promoting the interest of customers of the water and sewerage authorities. A new Water Industry Consultative Committee is also to be established which will have the function of advising the commissioner on how those interests are to be promoted. The commissioner will also be obliged to comply with guidance from the Secretary of State as to how he exercises his functions. Membership of each authority is dealt with in Schedule 7 to the 1994 Act. Appointments are made by the Secretary of State. This has led to criticism that the control of water was in effect being taken outwith democratic control, paving the way to privatisation. It is clear that some of the provisions of the legislation are linked to the private finance initiative: see generally *Shaping the Future — The New Councils*, Cm. 2267 (1993).

(6) For further general readings see T. Prosser, "Regulation, Markets and Legitimacy" in *The Changing Constitution* (J. Jowell and D. Oliver eds, 1994), p. 237; R. Baldwin and C. McCrudden (eds.); *Regulation and Public Law* (1987); A. I. Ogus, *Regulation Legal Form and Economic Theory* (1994); T. Prosser, *Law and the Regulators* (1997); Finch and Ashton, p. 90–95; Harlow and Rawlings, Chap. 10; and D. Miers, "Regulation and the Public Interest: Commercial Gambling and the National Lottery" (1996) 59 M.L.R. 489.

Chapter 2

ADMINISTRATIVE TECHNIQUES 2: RULE MAKING

Administrative rule making is a significant aspect of current administrative practice. The term "rule making" has been adopted for the title of this chapter, rather than the usual delegated legislation. The latter is simply an aspect, albeit an important one, of the former. We are concerned with rule making in its broadest sense, whether formal delegated legislation, quasi-legislation such as Codes of Practice or rules made by local authorities and other public authorities, typically in the form of byelaws. The position is further complicated by the fact that one now has to consider the creation, operation and control of administrative rules in light of the creation of the Scottish Parliament and Scottish Executive.

2–1

For general reading on administrative rule making see D. R. Miers and A. C. Page, *Legislation* (2nd ed., 1990); Making the Law; The Report of the Hansard Society Commission on the Legislative Process (1993); P. P. Craig, *Administrative Law* (7th ed., 1994), Chap. 7; W. Wade, and C. Forsyth, *Administrative Law* (7th ed., 1994), Chap. 22; V. Finch and C. Ashton, *Administrative Law in Scotland* (1997), Chap. 5; *The Laws of Scotland: Stair Memorial Encyclopaedia*, Vol. 22, "Sources of Law" paras 175–201, 223–246; C. Harlow and R. Rawlings, *Law and Administration* (1997), Chaps 6–7; and M. Deans, *Scots Public Law* (1995), pp. 81–83.

Our first concern, however, is with formal delegated legislation, both at Westminster and in Edinburgh.

DELEGATED LEGISLATION: GENERAL ISSUES

Report of the Committee on Minister's Powers

Cmnd. 4060, pp. 51–52

"Necessity for Delegation

11. We have already expressed the view that the system of delegated legislation is both legitimate and constitutionally desirable for certain purposes, within certain limits, and under certain safeguards. We proceed to set out briefly — mostly by way of recapitulation — the reasons which have led us to this conclusion:

2–2

Pressure on Parliamentary time

(1) Pressure upon Parliamentary time is great, the more procedure and subordinate matters can be withdrawn from detailed Parliamentary discussion, the greater will be the time which Parliament can devote to the consideration of essential principles in legislation.

Technicality of subject matter

(2) The subject matter of modern legislation is very often of a technical nature. Apart from the broad principles involved, technical matters are difficult to include in a Bill, since they cannot be effectively discussed in Parliament... .

Unforeseen contingencies

(3) If large and complex schemes of reform are to be given technical shape, it is difficult to work out the administrative machinery in time to insert in the Bill at the provisions required; it is impossible to foresee all the contingencies and local conditions for which provision must eventually be made... .

Flexibility

(4) The practice, further, is valuable because it provides for a power of constant adaptation to unknown future conditions without the necessity of amending legislation. Flexibility is essential. The method of delegated legislation permits of the rapid utilisation of experience, and enables the results of consultation with interests affected by the operation of new Acts to be translated into practice. In matters, for example, like mechanical road transport, where technical development is rapid, and often unforeseen, delegation is essential to meet the new positions which arise.

Opportunity for experiment

(5) The practice, again, permits of experiment being made and thus affords an opportunity, otherwise difficult to ensure, of utilising the lessons of experience. The advantage of this in matters, for instance, like town planning, is too obvious to require detailed emphasis.

Emergency Powers

(6) In a modern State there are many occasions when there is a sudden need of legislative action. For many such needs delegated legislation is the only convenient or even possible remedy. No doubt, where there is time, on legislative issues of great magnitude, it is right that Parliament itself should either decide what the broad outlines of the legislation shall be, or at least indicate the general scope of the delegated powers which it considers are called for by the occasion."

J. D. B. Mitchell, Reflections on Law and Orders

1958 J.R. 19 at 23

2–3   "In the same way other shots at delegated legislation do not always hit the mark squarely. Some of the supposed faults of delegated legislation are faults of legislation in general. Delegated legislation may at times be difficult to trace, but it is hardly more so than private legislation, which may affect the innocent individual just as much. The itinerant vendor of logs who crosses the unmarked boundaries of the City of Manchester is unlikely to remember that he has come within the scope of section 38 of the Manchester Corporation Act, 1954. Again, the problem of intelligibility is a real one, but often it is no more serious in delegated legislation than elsewhere. The schedules to the Administration of Estates Act, 1925, were amended, without specific reference, by sections 91 and 115 of the Companies Act, 1948 (16th Sched.), and which themselves amended the Bankruptcy Act, 1914, which was incorporated in the Administration of Estates Act, 1925. Legislation by reference is an inconvenient and ugly device wherever it is used, yet it can be defended on the ground of legal tightness. Lawyers may seek, and courts may find, significance in slight changes of wording which are often inescapable in the process of redrafting to incorporate amendments, and it must be remembered that in many of the fields governed by delegated legislation there are as many people looking for a loophole as there are looking for one in a Finance Act. Forms of draftsmanship are often the consequences of the methods and rules of judicial interpretation. The defence cannot of course be absolute. No one can defend the device when the result is that the mysteries of a statutory instrument baffle its sponsors.

Indeed, the general problem of clarity is a major one. It is easy to say that in creating an offence the instrument should be abundantly clear. Statutes are often no more successful than statutory instruments. The apparent clarity of the definition of stealing in the Larceny Act, 1916 (s. 1), merely conceals its real obscurity. The intricacies of superannuation regulations are at least no worse than those of income tax legislation. The fault lies not with the draftsman, but with the subject-matter. Intelligibility is a relative matter. What is important is that the instrument should be clear to those who are most concerned with it and account must now be taken of the changed nature of law. In the nineteenth century law was predominantly made for lawyers. No lawyer complained, with great heat, of the unintelligibility of Conveyancing Acts. Indeed, measures which reduce general intelligibility are welcomed. There is little complaint because lawyers work the legislation and lawyers know their own language. Today, most legislation is not made for lawyers. It is made for the egg-farmer, the chemist, the engineer, and what matter is that it should be intelligible to the technician, not the lawyer. The regulations made under the Heating Appliances (Fireguards) Act, 1952, involving, as they do, references to British Standard Specifications and excursions into solid geometry, are certainly not readily appreciated by the lawyer, yet doubtless they provide clear working standards for the designer of fire-guards. Thus the criticism that consultation in the preparation of statutory instruments does not produce clarity may often be beside the point. Often the object of consultation is to secure efficiency, and efficiency for the purposes of the technicians may well be incompatible with clarity for the layman (with whom must be ranked the lawyer in this context).

There is, perhaps, in the criticisms of intelligibility some element of lament for a world that cannot return. Those regrets also influence views on 'controls.' No doubt it is easy to agree with Sir Carelton Kemp Allen that 'Far too much emphasis can be laid on the incompetence of Parliament to deal with the technical. A very great deal and perhaps the majority of legislation is of a technical character, and has always been so.' Yet agreement with the words does not always include agreement on the meaning to be given to them. Technicality has, as has been suggested, changed in its character. Debates such as that on the regulations governing margarine standards do not, on the whole, show Parliament at its best, even though the Minister concerned was technically qualified in a way that is rarely the case. The avoidance of delegation is often no happier in results. Reliance on parliamentary controls can be carried too far, particularly since they are not always used for what might be thought to be their primary purpose. Indeed, that reliance can itself be dangerous. The under-estimation of the real limits of those methods of control creates a false sense of security. Concentration upon parliamentary methods of control may not only increase present difficulties of parliamentary time and labour, but also may hinder the development of alternative forms of control. The limitations imposed upon the Scrutiny Committee by its own terms of reference could have a more general application. Parliament is perhaps best at preventing an abuse of power, and then as a last resort. The right use of power is often best controlled elsewhere. While no one would commend as a general model the elaboration and expense which have preceded the report on the egg-marketing scheme, yet the proper development of ancillary control devices such as the inquiry and of consultation is nevertheless desirable. That development is unlikely to come about if such devices are regarded as a usurpation of parliamentary functions, or if the present practical limits to parliamentary control are not fully recognised. New difficulties call for new solutions. At present, many such devices are less openly and freely used than need be, because of this concern for existing methods of parliamentary control; yet the more open use might increase the acceptability of legislation, and allay suspicion. Correspondingly, if the real limits of parliamentary control were emphasised other methods could be made more effective.

In short, it is perhaps time that we should accept the respectability of, and necessity for, delegation, seeking to live with it rather than to fight against it. Toleration need not of course amount to an uncritical acceptance. Legislation in its original as in its delegated form has uses and dangers, and the latter must be recognised. It does not, however, follow that the safeguards in the case of the delegated form need be the same, or be operated in the same forum, as those to which we are accustomed in the case of the parent legislation. The acceptance of delegated legislation might well mean that we must seek to cultivate other safeguards operated elsewhere."

Notes

(1) The committee concluded (p. 58) that delegation was "legitimate for certain purposes,   **2–4** within certain limits, and under certain safeguards. It is in fact inevitable". It countered the alarmist view of the unconstitutional nature of delegated legislation propagated by those such as Lord Hewart in his *New Despotism* (1929) and argued that while there were "dangers incidental to delegated legislation", safeguards could be built in to prevent abuse. The committee recommended that the existing Rules Publication Act 1893, which required certain categories of delegated legislation to be published, should be replaced by the many different forms in which an enabling statute required delegated legislation to be laid before Parliament should be standardised. The reform came to pass in the Statutory Instruments Act 1946. It also recommended that each House of Parliament should set up a Standing Committee for the purpose of considering and reporting on every Bill containing a proposal to confer law-making power on a Minister. The House of Commons implemented the second of these recommendations in 1994. The House of Lords already had a Scrutiny Committee. Following on the recommendations of the Joint Committee and Delegated Legislation (1972 H.L. 184; H.C. 475), a Joint Committee on Statutory Instruments was created. Concern as to the scrutiny of delegated legislation has led to further development in the form of the House of Lords Select Committee on the Scrutiny of Delegated Powers and the House of Commons Deregulation Committee.

(2) Professor Mitchell seems to suggest that in terms of form and content, delegated legislation does not differ markedly from primary legislation. Is that view justified? Consider the professor's comments again when reading the materials on control of delegated legislation.

(3) One of the difficulties identified by the committee was the drawing of a distinction between matters which were suitable for delegation and those which were not or, to put it another way, between matters of detail and matters of principle. The former but not the latter should be contained in delegated legislation: see in particular pp. 137–138. However, the distinction between these can be difficult to draw: see, for example, J. A. G. Griffith, "The Place of Parliament in the Legislative Process" (1951) 14 M.L.R. 279. This concern has been picked up more recently by the Joint Committee on Statutory Instruments and the Consultative Steering Group on the Scottish Parliament.

First Special Report from the Joint Committee on Statutory Instruments 1995–96

Report on Proceedings 1986–96 (1995–96 H.L. 103; H.C. 582), pp. 3–4

"General aspects of secondary legislation

Number of statutory instruments

2–5   4. In 1973, when the Committee was first established, 2,227 instruments came into force. In 1992 the annual total exceeded 3,000 for the first time and it has remained above 3,000 ever since. In 1995 it reached 3,345. The overall volume of statutory instruments has increased markedly over this period. In 1988 the total length of all instruments was 6,342 pages; by 1993, the last year for which figures are available, it had grown to 7,944 pages. Instruments registered in 1995 have yet to appear in bound volumes but take up approximately two feet, six inches of bookshelf.

5. The Committee does not consider all of these, local instruments not subject to any kind of parliamentary proceeding being outside its order of reference. It is difficult to compare figures for instruments considered by the Committee as parliamentary sessions vary so much in length. Nevertheless, table 2 below demonstrated clearly that the number of instruments considered by the Committee has grown over the same period... .

Scope of instruments

6. It is generally accepted that the nature of statutory instruments has also changed. Instruments have become both more complex and more far-reaching in scope. As the Committee argued in its submission to the Procedure Committee in 1985, 'secondary legislation has increasingly been used, not just to implement the "nuts and bolts" of policies laid down in primary legislation, but actually to *change* policies in ways that were sometimes not envisaged when the enabling primary legislation was passed'.

7. Recognition of this concern was one of the factors which led to the establishment of the House of Lords Delegated Powers Scrutiny Committee in Session 1992–1993. That Committee has the responsibility of examining the powers in proposed new primary legislation which will allow the making of statutory instruments in the future. The Committee's work is intended to reduce the risk that instruments change policies in a way that Parliament had not envisaged and to ensure that Parliament has appropriate control over the more wide-ranging powers. We accept that the trend towards the pursuance of measures through secondary rather than primary legislation is probably irreversible but hope that the Delegated Powers Scrutiny Committee will continue to contribute towards more effective scrutiny under these changing circumstances."

Consultative Steering Group on the Scottish Parliament

para. 29

"General

29. It is common at Westminster for detailed implementing provisions to be prescribed in secondary legislation. Such provision can have a significant impact on those affected by the provisions. Because of the volume of secondary legislation it is often difficult for interested groups and individuals to keep track of proposals, and consultation on secondary legislation is limited. There should be meaningful consultation on secondary legislation before it is laid before the Scottish Parliament. The Parliament should seek to ensure that significant provisions are included in primary rather than secondary legislation."

Notes

Note the concerns of the consultative steering group in relation to consultation. For discussion **2–6**
of consultation see Chapter 5. In many areas of decision making, the courts have been prepared
to imply into a requirement of prior consultation with affected interests as a requirement of
natural justice or where a legitimate expectation exists. However, the courts have to date been
unwilling to imply such a requirement prior to the making of delegated legislation: *Bates v.
Lord Hailsham of St Marlyebone* [1972] 1 W.L.R. 1373. Other concerns have been expressed in
relation to the use of what are known as "Henry VIII powers".

G. Ganz, "Delegated Legislation: A Necessary Evil or a Constitutional Outrage?" in
Administrative Law Facing the Future: Old Constraints and New Horizons

P. Leyland and T. Woods (eds, 1997), pp. 64–65

"Henry VIII Clauses
Probably the most objectionable type of delegated legislation, as its name implies, is the Henry VIII clause. **2–7**
This is the nickname given to clauses in Acts allowing Ministers to amend Acts of Parliament, whether the
parent Act or another statute. Again, they are not a new phenomenon but date back to the Local Government
Act 1888. The Committee on Ministers' Powers, though it did not endorse Lord Hewart's charge of a conspiracy
by the Civil Service to arrogate power to itself, recommended that they should be used only in exceptional cases
and only to bring an Act into operation subject to a one-year time limit. Such clauses were not used again till
after 1945, but it is the escalation in their use recently that has again given rise to concern. As Lord Rippon put
it, 'Ministers … take power to amend or repeal primary legislation by order almost as a matter of common
form' and without any time limit. Henry VIII clauses come in a variety of forms, some merely allowing updating
of the original Act but some provisions giving very wide powers to change the substance of policy without
limit. Matters came to a head with the Courts and Legal Services Bill 1990 in the House of Lords, when
criticism in particular by Lord Simon of Glaisdale, who castigated such clauses as a 'constitutional outrage',
forced the Lord Chancellor to give an undertaking that in the case of this Bill those clauses would be subject to
the affirmative resolution procedure. Unease about Henry VIII clauses formed part of the pressure to set up the
Delegated Powers Scrutiny Committee in the House of Lords to monitor Bills conferring such powers."

Notes

Note the views of Sir William Wade on the use of a Henry VIII clause in section 10 of the **2–8**
Human Rights Act 1998, on which see para. 11–46.

THE SCOPE OF DELEGATED LEGISLATION

Report from the Joint Committee on Delegated Legislation 1971–72

1971–1972 H.L. 184; H.C. 475

"Delegated legislation:
6. In his memorandum of evidence to Your Committee, Counsel to Mr Speaker (Sir Robert Speed) has **2–9**
defined delegated legislation thus:—
(1) Delegated legislation covers every exercise of a power to legislate conferred by or under an Act of Parliament
or which is given the force of law by virtue of an Act of Parliament. It can be expressed in a variety of forms:—
(a)   Measures passed by the General Synod of the Church of England.
(b)   Provisional orders confirmed by a Provisional Order Confirmation Act, including those made
under the Private Legislation Procedure (Scotland) Act, 1936.
(c)   Orders in Council and regulations, orders, rules, schemes or other instruments made by a Minister
or Government Department or Rule Committee or similar authority.
(d)   Orders, bye-laws or other instruments, made by public or local authorities (in some cases
confirmed by the Privy Council, a Minister or a Government Department).

(2) In some cases the power to legislate may be conferred by legislation which is itself a piece of delegated legislation, e.g. an Order in Council.

(3) The documents by which a power of delegated legislation is exercised are, in the main, statutory instruments.

(4) The definition of statutory instruments varies according to whether the Act under which the instrument is made was passed before or after January 1, 1948, the date on which the Statutory Instruments Act 1946 [below, pp. 817–821] was brought into operation.

(5) In regard to post-1947 Acts, under section 1(1) of the Statutory Instruments Act 1946 every Order in Council made in exercise of a statutory power is a statutory instrument, and every instrument made by a Minister of the Crown in exercise of a statutory power is a statutory instrument if the Act conferring the power expressly so provides.

(6) As regards pre-1948 Acts, broadly speaking, every instrument made under an Act of Parliament—

(i)   by Her Majesty in Council, or

(ii)   by a Minister of the Crown, or

(iii)   relating to any court in the United Kingdom,

is a statutory instrument if it is of a legislative and not an executive character.

(7) Measures are not statutory instruments, although in some cases the Measure does apply the Statutory Instruments Act 1946 to the subordinate legislation made thereunder. Also, as a general rule, the instruments referred to in category 1(d) above are not statutory instruments.

(8) Statutory instruments are classified as local or general according to their subject matter. Unless there are special reasons to the contrary, a statutory instrument which is in the nature of a local and personal or private Act is classified as local, and a statutory instrument which is in the nature of a public general Act is classified as general.

(9) The classification is done in the first place by the Minister responsible for the preparation of the Order in Council or the Minister by whom the instrument is made. He, when sending the instrument to the Queen's Printer, certifies it as local or general.

(10) There is a procedure under which a Committee composed of Officers of both Houses, called the Statutory Instruments Reference Committee, may determine any question referred to them regarding the classification of instruments as general or local… ."

Notes

2–10   (1) The term "statutory instrument" is not coextensive with the concept of delegated legislation. Byelaws are not statutory instruments, nor are Orders in Council made under the royal prerogative nor are Special Procedure Orders but ordinary Orders in Council, Acts of Sederunt and Acts of Adjournal are, on which see generally *Stair Memorial Encyclopaedia*, Vol. 1, para. 188 and D. M. Walker, *The Scottish Legal System* (l7th ed., 1997), pp. 254–262. The legal effect of delegated legislation other than statutory instruments depends on the provisions of the parent legislation: see, for example, Statutory Codes of Practice noted above, but the mere fact that delegated legislation is not in the form of a statutory instrument cannot of itself detract from its legislative character.

(2) Statutory instruments are almost always drafted by departmental lawyers. The Joint Committee on Statutory Instruments (First Special Report on Proceedings 1995–96, see above) at pp. 5–6 has noted that there are a number of drafting errors which often arise. It would appear that "these problems could be avoided by closer attention to the guidelines set out in Statutory Instrument Practice". Should statutory instruments, like primary legislation, be drafted by parliamentary counsel? What considerations militate against this? On this see Making the Law, below, at p. 49.

SCOPE OF DELEGATED LEGISLATION UNDER THE SCOTLAND ACT 1998

2–11   Delegated or subordinate legislation has an important role to play under the Scotland Act 1998. Delegated legislation can be made by Ministers of the U.K. or Scottish Governments. Some delegated legislation is of very great significance insofar as it is used to regulate the operation of the Scotland Act itself and can have retrospective effect or even be used to amend existing legislation, including the Scotland Act. Accordingly a distinction requires to be drawn between subordinate legislation regulating the operation of the Scottish Parliament, and the Scottish Executive and relationships between the two and U.K. institutions and subordinate legislation made in consequence of Acts of the Scottish Parliament. For commentary see C. M. G. Himsworth and C. Munro, *The Scotland Act 1998* (1999), pp. 139–147, 196–199.

Scotland Act 1998

ss. 112–114

"Subordinate legislation: general

112.—(1) Any power to make subordinate legislation conferred by this Act shall, if no other provision is made as to the person by whom the power is exercisable, be exercisable by Her Majesty by Order in Council or by a Minister of the Crown by order.

(2) But the power to make subordinate legislation under section 129(1) providing—

(a)   for the appropriation of sums forming part of the Scottish Consolidated Fund, or

(b)   for sums received by any person to be appropriated in aid of sums appropriated as mentioned in paragraph (a),

shall be exercisable only by Her Majesty by Order in Council.

(3) References in this Act to an open power are to a power to which subsection (1) applies (and include power to make subordinate legislation under section 129(1) whether or not the legislation makes provision as mentioned in subsection (2)).

(4) An Order in Council under an open power may revoke, amend or reenact an order, as well as an Order in Council, under the power; and an order under an open power may revoke, amend or re-enact an Order in Council, as well as an order, under the power.

(5) Any power to make subordinate legislation conferred by this Act shall, in relation to its exercise by a Minister of the Crown or a member of the Scottish Executive, be exercisable by statutory instrument.

Subordinate legislation: scope of powers

113.—(1) References in this section to a power are to an open power and to any other power to make subordinate legislation conferred by this Act which is exercisable by Her Majesty in Council or by a Minister of the Crown, and include a power as extended by this section.

(2) A power may be exercised so as to make different provision for different purposes.

(3) A power (as well as being exercisable in relation to all cases to which it extends) may be exercised in relation to—

(a)   those cases subject to specified exceptions, or

(b)   any particular case or class of case.

(4) A power includes power to make—

(a)   any supplementary, incidental or consequential provision, and

(b)   any transitory, transitional or saving provision,

which the person making the legislation considers necessary or expedient.

(5) A power may be exercised by modifying—

(a)   (any enactment or prerogative instrument,

(b)   any other instrument or document,

if the subordinate legislation (or a statutory instrument containing it) would be subject to any of the types of procedure referred to in Schedule 7.

(6) But a power to modify enactments does not unless otherwise stated extend to making modifications of this Act or subordinate legislation under it.

(7) A power may be exercised so as to make provision for the delegation of functions.

(8) A power includes power to make provision for sums to be payable out of the Scottish Consolidated Fund or charged on the Fund.

(9) A power includes power to make provision for the payment of sums out of money provided by Parliament or for sums to be charged on and paid out of the Consolidated Fund.

(10) A power may not be exercised so as to create any criminal offence punishable—

(a)   on summary conviction, with imprisonment for a period exceeding three months or with a fine exceeding the amount specified as level 5 on the standard scale.,

(b)   on conviction on indictment, with a period of imprisonment exceeding two years.

(11) The fact that a power is conferred does not prejudice the extent of any other power.

2–12

Subordinate legislation: particular provisions

114.—(1) A power to make subordinate legislation conferred by any of the following provisions of this Act may be exercised by modifying any enactment comprised in or made under this act (except Schedules 4 and 5): sections 89, 104, 107, 108 and 129(1).

(2) The reference in subsection (1) to a power to make subordinate legislation includes a power as extended by section 113.

(3) A power to make subordinate legislation conferred by any of the following provisions of this Act may be exercised so as to make provision having retrospective effect: sections 30, 58(4), 104 and 107."

Notes

2–13   (1) Sections 112–114 are core provisions on delegated legislation in the operation of the Scottish Parliament and the Scottish Executive. These provisions, and section 115 and Schedule 7, extracted at para. 2–19, were the subject of much debate on the Scotland Bill when it was transferred to the Delegated Powers and Deregulation Committee of the House of Lords and the amendments which resulted produced a substantially remodelled version of what is now contained in these provisions: see Twenty-Fourth Report of the Committee (1997–98) (H.L. 124) and Thirty-Second Report (1997–98 H.L. 146). Section 112(1) explicitly confirms the power to exercise many of the order-making powers contained in the Scotland Act either by way of Order in Council or other appropriate orders. Underlying this is a need to ensure flexibility in dealing with subordinate legislation which will be required from time to time: see 1997–1998 H.L. 124, Scottish Office Memorandum, para. 11.2. Section 112(3) introduces the concept of "an open power". Section 112(4), section 113 and Schedule 7 require the application of specific rules to the exercise of such an open power. Subsection (5) is significant as by section 1 of the Statutory Instruments Act 1946 an Order in Council is always made by statutory instrument. This subsection makes it clear that where a power to make subordinate legislation is conferred by the Scotland Act, whether exercised by a Minister of the Crown or by a member of the Scottish Executive, then it will be a statutory instrument and subject to the terms of the 1946 Act. It is anticipated that the 1946 Act will in due course be modified or possibly replaced to suit the particular needs of the Scottish Parliament see para. 2–20.

(2) Section 113 extends the scope of all the powers in the Act to make subordinate legislation to which it applies, that is those defined as an "open power" by section 112 and all other powers exercised by Order in Council or by a Minister of the Crown. Subsections (5) and (6) of section 113 bear comment. These confer a general power to modify enactments (and other instruments) including a Henry VIII power to amend Acts of Parliament. However, subsection (6) prohibits amendment of the Scotland Act itself or subordinate legislation thereunder and such an amendment is subject to the provisions listed in section 114 or where in case of power to amend Schedule 4 (enactments that cannot be changed by the Scottish Parliament), Schedule 5 (matters reserved for the Westminster Parliament) and section 30. Such powers are subject to para. 3 of Schedule 7 which upgrades the degree of scrutiny required for such delegated legislation, the agreement of both Parliaments being necessary.

(3) Section 114 identifies two groups of provisions to provide that the powers given by the first group in subsections (1) and (2) may be used to modify the Scotland Act itself or enactments under it and those in the second group may be used to retrospective effect in subsection (3). Both these types of provision attracted the attention of the Delegated Powers and Deregulation Committee of the House of Lords. As originally drafted sections under which other provisions of the Act could be modified were somewhat longer. Section 89 gives power to make provision in relation to cross-border public authorities. Section 104 gives power to make provision consequential on Acts of the Scottish Parliament. Section 107, which is extracted at para. 11–38, gives power to remedy *ultra vires* acts, section 108 gives power to redistribute functions by agreement. Section 129(1) gives power for transitional purposes. Note too the terms of para. 3 of Schedule 7 at para. 2–19 where relevant delegated legislation "contains provisions which add to, replace or omit any part of the text of an Act" (including this Act) the level of parliamentary control is upgraded from the use of negative procedure to affirmative procedure. The types of procedure are set out in Schedule 7 and so, for example, sections 104 and 107, which are normally type G procedure, move to type B or C.

(4) For the concept of a Scottish statutory instrument and comment thereon see para. 2–20.

PROCEDURAL REQUIREMENTS

Consultative Steering Group on the Scottish Parliament

para. 28

"Position

28. Until such time as the Scottish Parliament chooses to make its own legislation to provide   **2–14**
for the passage of subordinate legislation through the Parliament, the Statutory Instruments Act
1946, with modifications to suit the circumstances of the Scottish Parliament, will be applied.
Initially, Standing Orders will have to reflect the transitional arrangements, although such
Standing Orders may need to be adjusted should the Scottish Parliament decide to enact its own
legislation."

Statutory Instruments Act 1946

ss. 1–7, 11

"Definition of 'Statutory Instrument'

1.—(1) Where by this Act or any Act passed after the commencement of this Act to make, confirm or   **2–15**
approve orders, rules, regulations or other subordinate legislation, is conferred on His Majesty in Council
or on any Minister of the Crown then, if the power is expressed —

    (a)   in the case of a power conferred on His Majesty, to be exercisable by Order in Council;

    (b)   in the case of a power conferred on a Minister of the Crown, to be exercisable by statutory instrument,
any document by which that power is exercised shall be known as a 'statutory instrument' and the provisions
of this Act shall apply thereto accordingly.

(2) Where by any Act passed before the commencement of this Act power to make statutory rules
within the meaning of the Rules Publication act 1893, was conferred on any rule-making authority
within the meaning of that Act, any document by which that power is exercised after the commencement
of this Act, be known as a 'statutory instrument' and the provisions of this Act shall apply thereto
accordingly.

Numbering, printing, publication and citation

2.—(1) Immediately after the making of any statutory instrument, it shall be sent to the King's printer
of Acts of Parliament and numbered in accordance with regulations made under this Act, and except in
such cases as may be provided by any Act passed after the commencement of this Act or prescribed by
regulations made under this Act, copies thereof shall as soon as possible be printed and sold by [or under
the authority of] the King's printer of Acts of Parliament.

(2) Any statutory instrument may, without prejudice to any other mode of citation, be cited by the
number given to it in accordance with the provisions of this section, and the calendar year.

Supplementary provisions as to publication

3.—(1) Regulations made for the purposes of this Act shall make provision for the publication by
His Majesty's Stationery Officer of lists showing the date upon which every statutory instrument printed
and sold by [or under the authority of] the King's printer of Acts of Parliament was first issued by [or
under the authority of] that office: and in any legal proceedings a copy of any list so published […]
shall be received in evidence as a true copy, and an entry therein shall be conclusive evidence of the
date on which any statutory instrument was first issued by [or under the authority of] His Majesty's
Stationery Office.

(2) In any proceedings against any person for an offence consisting of a contravention of any
such statutory instrument, it shall be a defence to prove that the instrument had not been issued by [or
under the authority of] His Majesty's Stationery Office at the date of the alleged contravention unless
it is proved that at that date reasonable steps had been taken for the purpose of bringing the purport
of the instrument to the notice of the public, or of persons likely to be affected by it, or of the person
charged.

(3) Save as therein otherwise expressly provided, nothing in this section shall affect any enactment or
rules of law relating to the time at which any statutory instrument comes into operation.

Statutory Instruments which are required to be laid before Parliament

4.—(1) Where by this Act or any Act passed after the commencement of this Act any statutory instrument is required to be laid before Parliament after being made, a copy of the instrument shall be laid before each House of Parliament and, subject as hereinafter provided, shall be so laid before the instrument comes into operation:

Provided that if it is essential that any such instrument should come into operation before copies thereof can be so laid as aforesaid, the instrument may be made so as to come into operation before it has been so laid; and where any statutory instrument comes into operation before it is laid before Parliament, notification shall forthwith be sent to the Lord Chancellor and to the Speaker of the House of Commons drawing attention to the fact that copies of the instrument have yet to be laid before Parliament and explaining why such copies were not so laid before the instrument came into operation.

(2) Every copy of any such statutory instrument sold by the King's printer of Acts of Parliament shall bear on the face thereof:

(a)   a statement showing the date on which the statutory instrument came or will come into operation; and

(b)   either a statement showing the date on which copies thereof were laid before Parliament or a statement that such copies are to be laid before Parliament.

(3) Where any Act passed before the date of commencement of this Act contains provisions requiring that any Order in Council or other document made in exercise of any power conferred by that or any other Act be laid before Parliament after being made, any statutory instrument made in exercise of that power shall by virtue of this Act be laid before Parliament and the foregoing provisions of this section shall apply thereto accordingly in substitution for any such provisions as aforesaid contained in the Act passed before the said date.

Statutory Instruments which are subject to annulment by resolution of either House of Parliament

5.—(1) Where by this Act or any Act passed after the commencement of this Act, it is provided that any statutory instrument shall be subject to annulment in pursuance of a resolution of either House of Parliament, the instrument shall be laid before Parliament after being made and the provisions of the last foregoing section shall apply thereto accordingly, and if either House within the period of forty days beginning with the day on which a copy thereof is laid before it, resolves that an Address be presented to His Majesty praying that the instrument be annulled, no further proceedings shall be taken thereunder after the date of the resolution, and His Majesty may by Order in Council revoke the instrument, so, however, that any such resolution and revocation shall be without prejudice to the validity of anything previously done under the instrument or to the making of a new statutory instrument.

(2) Where any Act passed before the date of the commencement of this Act contains provisions requiring that any Order in Council or other document made in exercise of any power conferred by that or any other Act shall be laid before Parliament after being made and shall cease to be in force or may be annulled, as the case may be, if within a specified period either House presents an address to His Majesty or passes a resolution to that effect, then, subject to the provisions of any Order in Council made under this Act, any statutory instrument made in exercise of the said power shall by virtue of this Act be subject to annulment in pursuance of a resolution of either House of Parliament and the provisions of the last foregoing subsection shall apply thereto accordingly in substitution for any such provisions as aforesaid contained in the Act passed before the said date.

Statutory Instruments of which drafts are to be laid before Parliament

6.—(1) Where by this Act or any Act passed after the commencement of this Act it is provided that a draft of any statutory instrument shall be laid before Parliament, but the Act does not prohibit the making of the instrument without the approval of Parliament, then, in the case of an Order in Council the draft shall not be submitted to His Majesty in Council, and in any other case the statutory instrument shall not be made, until after the expiration of a period of forty days beginning with the day on which a copy of the draft is laid before each House of Parliament, or, if such copies are laid on different days, with the later of the two days, and if within that period either House resolves that the draft be not submitted to His Majesty or that the statutory instrument be not made, as the case may be, no further proceedings shall be taken thereon, but without prejudice to the laying before Parliament of a new draft.

(2) Where any Act passed before the date of the commencement of this Act contains provisions requiring that draft of any Order in Council or other document to be made in exercise of any power conferred by that or any other Act shall be laid before Parliament before being submitted to His Majesty, or before being made, as the case may be, and that it shall not be so submitted or made if within a specified period either House presents an address to His Majesty or passes a resolution to that effect, then, subject to the provisions of any Order in Council made under this Act, a draft of any statutory instrument made in exercise of the said power shall by virtue of this Act be laid before Parliament and the provisions of the last foregoing subsection shall apply thereto accordingly in substitution for any such provisions as aforesaid contained in the Act passed before the said date.

Supplementary provisions as to ss. 4, 5 and 6

7.—(1) In reckoning for the purposes of either of the last two foregoing sections any period of forty days, no account shall be taken of any time during which Parliament is dissolved or prorogued or during which both Houses are adjourned for more than four days.

(2) In relation to any instrument required by any Act, whether passed before or after the commencement of this Act, to be laid before the House of Commons only, the provisions of the last three foregoing sections shall have effect as if references to that House were therein substituted for references to Parliament and for references to either House and each House thereof.

(3) The provisions of sections four and five of this Act shall not apply to any statutory instrument being an order which is subject to special Parliamentary procedure, or to any other instrument which is required to be laid before Parliament, or before the House of Commons, for any period before it comes into operation… .

Interpretation

11.—(1) For the purposes of this Act, any power to make, confirm or approve orders, rules, regulations or other subordinate legislation conferred on the Treasury, …, the Board of Trade or any other government department shall be deemed to be conferred on the Minister of the Crown in charge of that department.

(2) If any question arises whether any board, commissioners or other body on whom any such power as aforesaid is conferred are a government department within the meaning of this section, or what Minister of the Crown is in charge of them, that question shall be referred to and determined by [the Minister for the Civil Service]."

Notes

(1) This legislation is of importance both in relation to statutory instruments whether emanating from the U.K. Government and Westminster Parliament. This Act will therefore remain significant in those areas which are not within the devolved competence of the Scottish Parliament and Scottish Executive. It will also continue to remain significant insofar as members of the U.K. Government have powers to make subordinate legislation or under the Scotland Act, for example under the provisions of section 112. As we shall see above, sections 2–8 of the Act have been set aside in relation to Scottish statutory instruments by the Scotland Act 1998 (Transitory and Transitional Provisions) (Statutory Instruments) Order 1999. Section 1 of the 1946 Act has been modified by that Order. However, given the clear similarity between the provisions of the Act and the provisions of the Order, compare for example section 3(2) of the Act and article 8(3) of the Order on the question of defence to criminal proceedings where contravention of an instrument is alleged, the practice and case law under the 1946 Act is likely to have continuing relevance under these Scottish provisions.

2–16

(2) In sections 2 and 3 the words "or under the authority of" and "purporting to be of the imprint of the King's printer" were deleted by the Statutory Instruments (Production and Sale) Act 1996. In addition section 1(1) of that Act provided that the 1946 Act "shall have effect and be taken always to have had effect" with these amendments but this does not affect the operation of section 3(2) of that Act in relation to proceedings commencing before June 21, 1996. Note that section 92 of the Scotland Act 1998 creates a new office of the Queen's Printer for Scotland who has the function of printing Acts of the Scottish Parliament and subordinate legislation: subsection (4), and who will enjoy Crown rights and privilege in relation thereto: subsection (3)(c, (d).

(3) The Statutory Instruments Regulations 1947 were made under section 8 of the 1946 Act, which enables the Minister for the Civil Service with the concurrence of the Lord Chancellor and the Speaker to have power to make regulations for the purposes of the Act. These regulations were amended by S.I. 1977 No. 641 and S.I. 1982 No. 1728. Note that regulation 2(3) provides that section 1(2) of the 1946 Act does not apply to:

"(a) any document which, although of a legislative character, applies only to a named person or premises and is not required to be laid before or subject to confirmation or approval by Parliament or the House of Commons; or

(b) any Order in Council which, being an Order for which the Lord President of the Council is the responsible authority, confirms or approves subordinate legislation in the nature of a local and personal or private Act; or

(c) any such document as is mentioned in the Schedule to these Regulations."

Regulations 3–11 deal with such matters as allocation of the instruments to the series of the year in which they are made, exemptions from the requirements as to printing and sale, temporary instruments, confidential instruments and the publication of an annual list of all instruments issued.

(4) Section 9(1) of the 1946 Act enables the Queen in Council to apply the provisions of the Act to powers in pre-1948 statutes to confirm or approve delegated legislation conferred on a Minister of the Crown which would not amount to the making of a statutory rule under the 1893 Act and accordingly would not be within section 1(2). Most of the classes to which this provision applies are no longer of any significance but one class that is still of relative importance is where a Minister has power under pre-1948 statute to confirm or approve subordinate legislation by an authority which is not a rule-making authority under the 1983 Act, which is legislative in character and which is required to be laid before Parliament or the House of Commons.

(5) Section 1 of the Laying of Documents before Parliament (Interpretation) Act 1948 provides:

"Meaning of references to laying before Parliament

1.—(1) For the removal of doubt it is hereby declared that a reference in any Act of Parliament or subordinate legislation, whether passed or made before or after the passing of this Act, to the laying of any instrument, report, account or other document before either House of Parliament is, unless the contrary intention appears, to be construed as a reference to the taking, during the existence of a Parliament, of such action as is directed by virtue of any Standing Order, Sessional Order or other direction of that House for the time being in force to constitute the laying of that document before that House, or as is accepted by virtue of the practice of that House for the time being as constituting such laying, notwithstanding that the action so directed or accepted consists in part or wholly in action capable of being taken otherwise than at or during the time of a sitting of that House; and that a reference in any such Act or subordinate legislation to the laying of any instrument, report, account or other document before Parliament is, unless the contrary intention appears, to be construed accordingly as a reference (construed in accordance with the preceding declaration) to the laying of the document before each House of Parliament.

(2) It is hereby further declared that nothing in section four of the Statutory Instruments Act 1946, is to be taken as indicating an intention that any reference in that section to the laying of copies of certain statutory instruments as therein mentioned is to be construed otherwise than in accordance with the preceding declaration."

It is not clear whether a requirement as an instrument be laid before Parliament is "mandatory" or "directory". In *Hepburn v. Wilson* (1901) 4 F. (J.) 18 it was held that a requirement in the parent Act that a regulation when made should be laid before both Houses of Parliament did not amount to an essential condition for the regulation to come into force. This case of course predates the 1946 Act but nevertheless such case law as there is since then does seem to suggest that there may be no absolute rule and much may depend on the exact wording of the instrument and the facts of the case: see A. I. L. Campbell, "Laying and Delegated Legislation" [1983] P.L. 43.

In *R. v. Secretary of State for Social Services, ex parte Camden London Borough Council*, February 26, 1986, unreported, MacPherson J. held that section 33(3)(C) of the Supplementary Benefits Act 1976 by which certain social security regulations "shall be made unless a draft of the regulation has been laid before Parliament and approved by a resolution of each House" was mandatory. The words were "clear, strong and mandatory". On appeal the Court of Appeal assumed this to be the case without deciding the point: see [1987] 1 W.L.R. 819. However, a booklet published by HMSO, which was provided for in the regulations as a means of providing information on benefits available and which was not laid before Parliament, was held not to be part of the statutory instrument and was not "a document by which the Secretary of State exercises his actual powers" for the purposes of the 1946 Act. On this case see A. I. L. Campbell, "Statutory Instruments — Laying and Legislation by Reference" [1987] P.L. 328.

R v. Sheer Metalcraft Ltd

[1954] 1 All E.R. 542

Streatfield J. "... This matter comes before the court in the form of an objection to the admissibility on **2–17** evidence of a statutory instrument known as the Iron and Steel Prices Order, 1951. It appears that part and parcel of that instrument consisted of certain deposited schedules in which maximum prices for different commodities of steel were set out. The instrument is said to have been made by the Minister of Supply on February 16, 1951; laid before Parliament on February 20, 1951; and to have come into operation on February 21, 1951. It is under that statutory instrument that the present charges are made against the two defendants in this case.

The point which has been taken is that by reason of the deposited schedules not having been printed and not having been certified by the Minister as being exempt from printing, the instrument is not a valid instrument under the Statutory Instrument Act, 1946. That point was taken in *Simmonds v. Newell* [1953] 1 W.L.R. 826, but it was expressly left open in view of a certain admission then made by the Solicitor-General, which, however, does not apply to the present case. The point arises in this way: under regulation 55AB of the Defence (General) Regulations, 1939, as amended, a competent authority, which in this case is the Minister of Supply, may by statutory instrument provide for controlling the prices to be charged for goods of any description or the charges to be made for services of any description, and for any incidental and supplementary matters for which the competent authority thinks it expedient for the purposes of the instrument to provide. It is said in the statutory instrument here that it was made in exercise of the powers conferred upon the Minister by regulations 55AB and 98 of the Defence (General) Regulations, and other statutory authorities.

The contention is that the making of that instrument is governed by the provisions of the Statutory Instruments Act, 1946... .

[His Lordship read sections 1 and 2 of the Act of 1946 and regulation 7 of the Statutory Instruments Regulations, 1947, and continued:] Section 1 visualizes the making of what is called a statutory instrument by a Minister of the Crown; section 2 visualizes that after the making of a statutory instrument it shall be sent to the King's Printer to be printed, except in so far as under regulations made under the Act it may be unnecessary to have it printed. It is said here that the Minister did not certify that the printing of these very bulky deposited schedules was unnecessary within the meaning of regulation 7. It is contended, therefore, that as he did not so certify it, it became an obligation under the Act that the deposited schedules as well as the instrument itself should be printed under section 2 of the Act of 1946, and in the absence of their having been printed as part of the instrument, the instrument cannot be regarded as being validly made.

To test that matter it is necessary to examine section 3 of the Act of 1946. By subsection (1) [see *ante* p. 295] ... There does not appear to be any definition of what is meant by 'issue,' but presumably it does mean some act by the Queen's Printer of Acts of Parliament which follows the printing of the instrument. That section, therefore, requires that the Queen's Printer shall keep lists showing the date upon which statutory instruments are printed and issued.

Subsection (2) is important and provides [see *ante* p. 295] ... It seems to follow from the wording of this subsection that the making of an instrument is one thing and the issue of it is another. If it is made it can be contravened; if it has not been issued then that provides a defence to a person charged with its contravention. It is then upon the Crown to prove that, although it has not been issued, reasonable steps have been taken for the purpose of bringing the instrument to the notice of the public or persons likely to be affected by it.

I do not think that it can be said that to make a valid statutory instrument it is required that all of these stages should be gone through; namely, the making, the laying before Parliament, the printing and the certification of that part of it which it might be unnecessary to have printed. In my judgment the making of an instrument is complete when it is first of all made by the Minister concerned and after it has been laid before Parliament. When that has been done it then becomes a valid statutory instrument, totally made under the provisions of the Act.

The remaining provisions to which my attention has been drawn, in my view, are purely procedure for the issue of an instrument validly made — namely, that in the first instance it must be printed by the Queen's Printer unless it is certified to be unnecessary to print it; it must then be included in a list published by Her Majesty's Stationery Office showing the dates when it is issued and it may be issued by the Queen's Printer of Acts of Parliament. Those matters, in my judgment, are matters of procedure. If they were not and if they were stages in the perfection of a valid statutory instrument, I cannot see that section 3(2) would be necessary, because if each one of those stages were necessary to make a statutory instrument valid, it would follow that there could be no infringement of an unissued instrument and therefore it would be quite unnecessary to provide a defence to a contravention of any such instrument. In my view the very fact that subsection (2) of section 3 refers to a defence that the instrument has not been issued postulates that the instrument must have been validly made in the first place otherwise it could never have been contravened.

In those circumstances I hold that this instrument was validly made and approved and that it was made by or signed on behalf of the Minister on its being laid before Parliament; that so appears on the fact of the instrument itself. In my view, the fact that the Minister failed to certify under regulation 7 does not invalidate the instrument as an instrument but lays the burden upon the Crown to prove that at the date of the alleged contraventions reasonable steps had been taken for bringing the instrument to the notice of the public or persons likely to be affected by it. I, therefore, rule that this is admissible... ."

Notes

2–18   (1) This case is generally accepted as stating Scots law: see *Stair Memorial Encyclopaedia*, Vol. 1, para. 300. However, does Streatfield J's analysis aid the case of legal certainty? Although it is no doubt logical to say that if the instrument was not validly made, then no law could be broken, should not publication be the only test? Moreover his judgment does not define when an instrument is "made". Arguably this would mean that one would still have to look at the parent Act. Is an instrument made when it is signed? Do you consider that it is a failing in the Act to fail to specify the effects of non-publication leaving it as a matter for the court? One also has to consider that section 2 is exclusive in its effect.

(2) Contrast with *Johnson v. Sargant and Sons* [1918] 1 K.B. 101. Under the Defence of the Realm Regulations, an Order was made requiring the requisitioning on imported beans. The Order was dated May 16, 1917 but was only made public on May 17 and did not apply to beans which "have been sold by the original consignees and paid for by the purchasers". On May 16 the plaintiff paid for and took delivery of a cargo of beans from the defendants and subsequently claimed that the contract had been cancelled by the Order. It was argued that a statute takes effect from the first moment of the day in which it is passed unless another day is named and, by analogy with this, the Order came into operation immediately after midnight on May 15 and as the beans were only paid for on May 16 the transaction was caught by the Order. However, Bailhache J. did not regard this as appropriate (at 103):

> "[T]here is about statutes a publicity even before they come into operation which is absent in the case of many Orders such as that with which we are now dealing; indeed, if certain Orders are to be effective at all, it is essential that they should not be known until they are actually published. In the absence of authority upon the point I am unable to hold that this Order came into operation before it was known, and, as I have said, it was not known until the morning of May 17."

Accordingly the transaction fell within the exemption. *Johnson v. Sargant* was not cited in *Sheer Metalcraft*. In *Simmonds v. Newell* [1953] 1 W.L.R. 826 bulky schedules relating to the Iron and Steel Prices Order 1951 were not published. Having regard to regulation 7 of the Statutory Instruments Regulations 1947, which provides for exemption from requirements as to printing and sale for *inter alia* schedules where it would be "unnecessary or undesirable having regard to the nature or bulk of the document and to any other steps taken or to be taken for bringing its substance to the notice of the public", the Ministry of Supply wrote to the editor of Statutory Instruments declaring that exemption under section 7 of the regulations had been given. The Divisional Court held that a letter did not constitute a certificate in terms of section 7 and it was accepted that the onus was therefore on the Crown to show that the defendants nevertheless were aware of terms of these schedules, as there was some evidence to show that the schedules were available for inspection and that they were well known to trade associations.

(3) In *Lim Chin Aik v. The Queen* [1963] A.C. 160 the Privy Council had to determine whether a person could be convicted of an offence of remaining in Singapore while subject to an Order prohibiting his entry if he was not aware of the Order. The Crown argued that ignorance of the law, including a statutory instrument, was no excuse. However, Lord Evershed noted (at 171):

> "[E]ven if the making of the order by the Minister be regarded as an exercise of the legislative as distinct from the executive or administrative function (as they do not concede), the maxim cannot apply to such a case as the present where it appears that there is in the State of Singapore no provision, corresponding, for example, to that contained in section 3(2) of the English Statutory Instruments Act of 1946, for the publication in any form of an order of the kind made in the present case or any other provision designed to enable a man by appropriate inquiry to find out what 'the law' is."

This suggests that ignorance of the law could be an excuse even if no express statutory defence such as section 3(2) exists.

(4) D. J. Lanham, "Delegated Legislation and Publication" (1974) 37 M.LO.R. 510 argues that *Johnson v. Sargant* should be treated as correct and that, as a matter of justice, the common law demands that delegated legislation does not come into force until it is published. For different views see A. I. L. Campbell [1982] P.L. 569 and the reply by Professor Lanham [1983] P.L. 395.

(5) Regardless of the difficulties of the case law, is section 3(2) of the 1946 Act in any event sufficiently clear? Lanham above at 521–523 notes three possibilities as to the applicability of the defence. These are:

- They apply to every statutory instrument printed and sold by the Queen's printer which would mean that the defence would be available where an instrument is issued at some time but the breach of it proceeds the date of issue.

- That the words apply to any statutory instrument and would be available wherever the instrument had not been issued when contravened.

- That the defence would only be available where the instrument had not been issued when contravened.

- That the defence would only be available where the instrument had not been issued when it was contravened and that there was also a breach of the duty to publish as in *Simmonds* and *Sheer Metalcraft*.

Consider again the terms of section 3(2) and the case law. Which interpretation appears preferable?

(6) Assuming that a statutory instrument has been validly made, then being part of the general law, they are judicially noticed and fall to be treated in the same manner as Public General Acts and so the originals need not be produced when cited; *Macmillan v. McConnell*, 1917 J.C. 43 at 47 *per* Lord Justice-Clerk (Dickson). In cases of doubt or dispute their terms are established by section 3(1) of the 1946 Act. There is also a detailed statutory provision as to alternative modes of proof: Documentary Evidence Act 1868, s. 2. As to proof of pre-1948 statutory instruments see A. G. Walker and N. M. L. Walker, *The Law of Evidence in Scotland* (1964), paras 198, 199, 201.

Scotland Act 1998

ss. 115, 118, Sched. 7

"Subordinate legislation: procedure
115.—(1) Schedule 7 (which determines the procedure which is to apply to subordinate legislation under this Act in relation to each House of Parliament and the Scottish Parliament) shall have effect.   **2–19**

(2) In spite of the fact that that Schedule provides for subordinate legislation under a particular provision of this Act (or the statutory instrument containing it) to be subject to any type of procedure in relation to the Parliament, the provision conferring the power to make that legislation may be brought into force at any time after the passing of this Act.

(3) Accordingly, any subordinate legislation (or the statutory instrument containing it) made in the exercise of the power in the period beginning with that time and ending immediately before the principal appointed day is to be subject to such other type of procedure (if any) as may be specified in subordinate legislation made under section 129(1).

Subordinate instruments
118.—(1) Subsection (2) applies in relation to the exercise by a member of the Scottish Executive within devolved competence of a function to make, confirm or approve subordinate legislation.

(2) If a pre-commencement enactment makes provision—
(a)   for any instrument or the draft of any instrument made in the exercise of such a function to be laid before Parliament or either House of Parliament,
(b)   for the annulment or approval of any such instrument or draft by or in pursuance of a resolution of either or both Houses of Parliament, or
(c)   prohibiting the making of such an instrument without that approval,

the provision shall have effect, so far as it relates to the exercise of the function by a member of the Scottish Executive within devolved competence, as if any reference in it to Parliament or either House of Parliament were a reference to the Scottish Parliament.

(3) Where—

(a) a function of making, confirming or approving subordinate legislation conferred by a pre-commencement enactment is exercisable by a Scottish public authority with mixed functions or no reserved functions, and

(b) a pre-commencement enactment makes such provision in relation to the exercise of the function as is mentioned in subsection (2),

the provision shall have effect, so far as it relates to the exercise of the function by that authority, as if any reference in it to Parliament or either House of Parliament were a reference to the Scottish Parliament.

(4) Where—

(a) a function of making, confirming or approving subordinate legislation conferred by a pre-commencement enactment is exercisable within devolved competence by a person other than a Minister of the Crown, a member of the Scottish Executive or a Scottish public authority with mixed functions or no reserved functions, and

(b) a pre-commencement enactment makes such provision in relation to the exercise of the function as is mentioned in subsection (2),

the provision shall have effect, so far as it relates to the exercise of the function by that person within devolved competence, as if any reference in it to Parliament or either House of Parliament were a reference to the Scottish Parliament.

(5) If a pre-commencement enactment applies the Statutory Instruments act 1946 as if a function of the kind mentioned in subsection (3) or (4) were exercisable by a Minister of the Crown, that Act shall apply, so far as the function is exercisable as mentioned in paragraph (a) of subsection (3) or (as the case may be) (4), as if the function were exercisable by the Scottish Ministers.

Section 115
SCHEDULE 7
Procedure for subordinate legislation

General provision

1.—(1) Subordinate legislation (or a statutory instrument containing it) under a provision listed in the left-hand column is subject to the type of procedure in the right-hand column.

(2) This paragraph is subject to paragraphs 3 and 4.

Provision of the Act	Type of procedure
Section 2(1)	Type C
Section 12(1)	Type C
Section 15	Type D
Section 18(5)	Type J
Section 30	Type A
Section 35	Type I
Section 38	Type J
Section 56(2)	Type G
Section 58	Type I
Section 60	Type G
Section 62	Type G
Section 63	Type A
Section 64(5)	Type K
Section 67(3)	Type E
Section 71(6)	Type K
Section 79	Type E
Section 88	Type I
Section 89	Type F
Section 90	Type F
Section 93	Type H
Section 97	Type A

Provision of the Act	Type of procedure
Section 103(3)(a) and (b)	Type I
Section 104	Type G
Section 105	Type G
Section 106	Type G
Section 107	Type G
Section 108	Type A
Section 109	Type H
Section 110(1)	Type C
Section 110(2)	Type I
Section 111	Type A
Section 116(9)	Type G
Section 104(1)	Type G
Section 126(2)	Type B
Section 126(8)	Type H
Section 129(1)	Type G
Schedule 2, paragraph 2	Type G
Schedule 2, paragraph 7	Type H

Notes

The entry for section 58 does not apply to an instrument containing an order merely revoking an order under subsection (1) of that section.

The entry for section 79, in relation to an instrument containing an order which makes only such provision as is mentioned in section 79(3), is to be read as referring to type K instead of type E.

Types of procedure

2. The types of procedure referred to in this Schedule are—

    Type A: No recommendation to make the legislation is to be made to Her Majesty in Council unless a draft of the instrument—

    (a) has been laid before, and approved by resolution of, each House of Parliament, and

    (b) has been laid before, and approved by resolution of, the Parliament.

    Type B: No recommendation to make the legislation is to be made to Her Majesty in Council unless a draft of the instrument has been laid before, and approved by resolution of, each House of Parliament.

    Type C: No Minister of the Crown is to make the legislation unless a draft of the instrument has been laid before, and approved by resolution of, each House of Parliament.

    Type D: No recommendation to make the legislation is to be made to Her Majesty in Council unless a draft of the instrument has been laid before, and approved by resolution of, the Parliament.

    Type E: No Minister of the Crown is to make the legislation unless a draft of the instrument has been laid before, and approved by resolution of, the House of Commons.

    Type F: The instrument containing the legislation, if made without a draft having been approved by resolution of each House of Parliament and of the Parliament, shall be subject to annulment in pursuance of —

    (a) a resolution of either House, or

    (b) a resolution of the Parliament.

    Type G: The instrument containing the legislation, if made without a draft having been approved by resolution of each House of Parliament, shall be subject to annulment in pursuance of a resolution of either House.

    Type H: The instrument containing the legislation shall be subject to annulment in pursuance of—

    (a) a resolution of either House of Parliament, or

    (b) a resolution of the Parliament.

    Type I: The instrument containing the legislation shall be subject to annulment in pursuance of a resolution of either House of Parliament.

    Type J: The instrument containing the legislation shall be subject to annulment in pursuance of a resolution of the Parliament.

    Type K: The instrument containing the legislation shall be subject to annulment in pursuance of a resolution of the House of Commons.

Special cases

3.—(1) This paragraph applies if—

(a)   the instrument containing the legislation would, apart from this paragraph, be subject to the type F, G, H, I or K procedure, and

(b)   the legislation contains provisions which add to, replace or omit any part of the text of an Act.

2. Where this paragraph applies—

(a)   instead of the type F procedure, the type A procedure shall apply.

(b)   instead of the type G procedure, the type B or (as the case may be) C procedure shall apply,

(c)   instead of the type H procedure, the type A procedure shall apply,

(d)   instead of the type I procedure, the type B or (as the case may be) C procedure shall apply,

(e)   instead of the type K procedure, the type E procedure shall apply.

4. If legislation under section 129(1) makes provision as mentioned in section 2(2) then, instead of the type G procedure, the type D procedure shall apply.

5.—(1) An instrument containing an Order in Council or order under an open power which revokes, amends or re-enacts subordinate legislation under an open power may (in spite of section 14 of the Interpretation Act 1978) be subject to a different procedure under this Schedule from the procedure to which the instrument containing the original legislation was subject.

(2) An instrument containing an Order in Council under section 89 or 90 which revokes, amends or re-enacts an Order under either section may (in spite of section 14 of the Interpretation Act 1978) be subject to a different procedure under this Schedule from the procedure to which the instrument containing the original Order was subject."

Notes

2–20   (1) The main purpose of section 115 is to give effect to Schedule 7 which specifies the procedures which apply to each provision of the Scotland Act 1998. Subsections (2) and (3) make transitional provisions to deal with order-making procedure in the period between the passing of the Scotland Act and when the Scottish Parliament acquire its powers.

(2) Section 118 applies existing provisions relating to parliamentary procedures applicable to subordinate legislation and adapts existing provisions in "pre-commencement enactments" which require the Westminster procedure referred to in subsection (2) to require instead procedures in the Scottish Parliament. The main area in which powers to make subordinate legislation will be transferred to members of the Scottish Executive are those transferred to members of the Scottish Executive by section 53 and defined within "devolved competence" by section 54, on which see para. 3–11. Subsection (3) has the same effect in respect of the kind of Scottish public authority mentioned but separate provision is made for the "cross-border" authorities detailed in sections 88 and 89. Subsection (5) is significant in relation to persons other than Ministers. This subsection applies these provisions as extended to the Scottish Ministers. On sections 115 and 118 see Himsworth and Munro, pp. 143, 146–147.

(3) Schedule 7 sets out the procedure applicable to the making of subordinate legislation made under the Scotland Act. The Schedule was added as part of the general restructuring of the Order making provisions at the House of Lords committee stage on the Scotland Bill: see *Hansard*, H.L. Vol. 593, cols 624–626, 641–642, 647–649. Some idea of the intensity of scrutiny applied to subordinate legislation under the relevant sections of the Scotland Act can be given. Subordinate legislation under section 30, which deals with the legislative competence of the Scottish Parliament, is subject to the onerous type A procedure, whereas subordinate legislation under section 15, which deals with disqualification from membership of the Scottish Parliament, simply requires the laying and the positive resolution of the Scottish Parliament to become effective. Section 107, in relation to the power to remedy *ultra vires* acts is subject to type G procedure. See generally Himsworth and Munro, pp. 196–199.

(4) Until the Parliament has the opportunity of enacting permanent legislation, the next extract which contains much of the language contained in the 1946 Act will apply to subordinate legislation made under Acts of the Scottish Parliament. The principal appointed date is July 1, 1999 and the definition of enactment under section 126(1) of the Act includes Act of the Scottish Parliament and an enactment comprised in subordinate legislation, and includes an enactment

comprised in, or in subordinate legislation under, an Act of Parliament (Westminster), whenever passed or made. With the experience of the 1946 Act, what proposals for modification or reform of the procedures for making statutory instruments should be considered by the Scottish Parliament?

The Scotland Act 1998 (Transitory and Transitional Provisions) (Statutory Instruments) Order 1999
    The Secretary of State, in exercise of the powers conferred on him by sections 112(1), 113, 114(1), 124(2) and 129(1) of the Scotland Act 1998[1] and of all other powers enabling him in that behalf, hereby makes the following Order:

Citation and commencement.
    1. This Order may be cited as the Scotland Act 1998 (Transitory and Transitional Provisions) (Statutory Instruments) Order 1999 and shall come into force —
    (a)   for the purposes of article 4(4) on 6th May 1999, and
    (b)   for all other purposes on the principal appointed day.

Interpretation
    2. (1) In this Order, unless otherwise expressly provided —
    "the Act" means the Scotland Act 1998;
    "the 1946 Act" means the Statutory Instruments Act 1946;
    "enactment" shall be construed in accordance with section 126(1) of the Act and includes any enactment comprised in this Order;
    "Queen's Printer" means the Queen's Printer for Scotland;
    "relevant Scottish public authority" means a Scottish public authority with mixed functions or no reserved functions;
    "responsible authority", in relation to a Scottish statutory instrument, means —
    (a)   where the instrument is made, confirmed or approved by a member of the Scottish Executive, that member; and
    (b)   in any other case, the person or the relevant Scottish public authority who made, confirmed or approved that instrument as mentioned in article 4(1)(b) or (c), except that, where the instrument is an Order in Council or an order made by the Privy Council, the responsible authority means the member of the Scottish Executive responsible for the preparation of the draft of the Order submitted to Her Majesty in Council or, as the case may be, to the Privy Council;
    "Scottish statutory instrument" shall be construed in accordance with article 4(2); and
    "special parliamentary procedure" means such special procedure as may be provided by or under an Act of the Scottish Parliament for the purposes of section 94(2)(b) of the Act for any provision made for the same purpose in subordinate legislation under section 129(1) of that Act.
    (2) Unless otherwise expressly provided, any reference in this Order to a numbered article is to an article bearing that number in this Order and any reference in an article in this Order to a numbered paragraph is to a paragraph bearing that number in that article.

Modification of enactments
    3. (1) Any reference in section 1 of the 1946 Act —
    (a)   to an Act passed after the commencement of the 1946 Act shall be construed as including a reference to an Act of the Scottish Parliament; and
    (b)   to a Minister of the Crown shall be construed as including a reference to the Scottish Ministers and to a relevant Scottish public authority.
    (2) In relation to a Scottish statutory instrument, the following articles of this Order shall apply (in spite of anything in the 1946 Act) in place of sections 2 to 8 of the Act.
    (3) In relation to such an instrument —
    (a)   paragraph (2) does not disapply sections 4(3), 5(2) and 6(2) of the 1946 Act, but
    (b)   the reference in each of those subsections to the foregoing provisions of the section in question shall be read as a reference to article 10, 11 or 12 (respectively).
    (4) So far as a power to make, confirm or approve subordinate legislation is conferred on the Scottish Ministers or a relevant Scottish public authority, any enactment which applies section 1 of the 1946 Act as if the power were conferred on any other person shall cease to have effect.
    (5) So far as power to make, confirm or approve subordinate legislation is exercisable within devolved competence and conferred on a person other than a Minister of the Crown, the Scottish Ministers or a

relevant Scottish public authority, section 1 of the 1946 Act shall have effect as if the power were conferred on the Scottish Ministers.

(6) Where paragraph (4) or (5) applies, section 118(5) of the Act shall not apply.

(7) References in this article to the Scottish Ministers include the First Minister and the Lord Advocate.

(8) In any enactment passed or made before the principal appointed day, any reference to section 5(1) or 7 of the 1946 Act shall, in relation to a Scottish statutory instrument, be construed as a reference to article 11 or, as the case may be, article 13(1).

Application

4. (1) This Order shall apply in relation to —

(a) the exercise by a member of the Scottish Executive of a function to make, confirm or approve subordinate legislation conferred by an enactment;

(b) the exercise by a relevant Scottish public authority of a function to make, confirm or approve subordinate legislation conferred by an enactment; or

(c) the exercise, within devolved competence, by a person other than a Minister of the Crown, a member of the Scottish Executive or a relevant Scottish public authority of a function to make, confirm or approve subordinate legislation conferred by an enactment,

where the document by which that function is exercised is (whether by virtue of this Order or otherwise) a statutory instrument and is not an excepted instrument.

(2) A statutory instrument by which such a function is so exercised and which is not an excepted instrument shall be known as a Scottish statutory instrument.

(3) An excepted instrument is one —

(a) which is made by a Minister of the Crown with the agreement of a member of the Scottish Executive or of a relevant Scottish public authority;

(b) which is made jointly by a Minister of the Crown and by a member of the Scottish Executive or by a relevant Scottish public authority; or

(c) which is an Order in Council made by Her Majesty under section 1 of the United Nations Act 1946[4].

(4) Articles 10 to 15 as they apply (or will, as from the principal appointed day, apply) to a Scottish statutory instrument shall also apply where any enactment provides, or has the effect of providing, that any other statutory instrument is —

(a) to be laid before the Scottish Parliament after being made; or

(b) to be subject to annulment in pursuance of a resolution of the Scottish Parliament,

or that any draft of any other statutory instrument is to be laid before the Scottish Parliament.

(5) Article 14 as it applies to a Scottish statutory instrument shall also apply where any enactment provides, or has the effect of providing, that any other instrument or document is to be laid before the Scottish Parliament.

(6) This article (apart from this paragraph) and the following articles shall cease to have effect on the day appointed by or under an Act of the Scottish Parliament.

Numbering and citation

5. (1) Immediately after the making of any Scottish statutory instrument, the responsible authority shall send it to the Queen's Printer who shall number it in accordance with the following provisions.

(2) All Scottish statutory instruments shall have the heading "SCOTTISH STATUTORY INSTRUMENTS" and shall be —

(a) allocated to the series of the calendar year in which they are made; and

(b) numbered in that series consecutively as nearly as possible in the order in which they are received by the Queen's Printer,

except that, where any such instrument —

(i)   will not take effect unless it is approved by the Scottish Parliament; or

(ii) is subject to special parliamentary procedure, or will become subject thereto in certain events,

the instrument may be allocated and numbered as if it had been made and received on the date on which the responsible authority notifies the Queen's Printer that the instrument has or will come into force.

(3) Any Scottish statutory instrument may, without prejudice to any other mode of citation, be cited by the letters "S.S.I." followed by the calendar year in which it was made and its number in accordance with the provisions of paragraph (2) (for example S.S.I. 1999/1).

Classification

6. (1) The responsible authority shall, on sending a Scottish statutory instrument to the Queen's Printer, certify it as local or general according to its subject matter and, unless the Presiding Officer otherwise directs, the instrument shall be classified accordingly.

(2) Unless there are special reasons to the contrary in any particular case, a Scottish statutory instrument which is in the nature of a local and personal or private Act shall be classified as local, and a Scottish statutory instrument which is in the nature of a public general Act shall be classified as general.

Printing and sale

7. (1) Subject to paragraph (2), as soon as possible after the Queen's Printer has allocated and numbered any Scottish statutory instrument in accordance with article 5(2), copies of it shall be printed and sold by, or under the authority of, the Queen's Printer.

(2) A Scottish statutory instrument which is classified as a local instrument in accordance with article 6 shall be exempt from the requirements in paragraph (1), unless —
(a)   the Presiding Officer otherwise directs in any particular case; or
(b)   the responsible authority requests the Queen's Printer, when sending her the instrument, to comply with those requirements.

Lists of Scottish statutory instruments

8. (1) The Queen's Printer shall from time to time cause to be published a list to be known as the "Scottish Statutory Instruments Issue List", showing —
(a)   the number and short title of each Scottish statutory instrument which has been issued for the first time by, or under the authority of, the Queen's Printer during the period to which that list relates; and
(b)   the date on which each such instrument was so issued.

(2) In any legal proceedings, a copy of any list so published shall be received in evidence as a true copy and an entry therein shall be conclusive evidence of the date on which any Scottish statutory instrument was first issued by, or under the authority of, the Queen's Printer.

(3) In any proceedings against any person for an offence consisting of a contravention of any Scottish statutory instrument, it shall be a defence to prove that the instrument had not been issued by, or under the authority of, the Queen's Printer at the date of the alleged contravention, unless it proved that at that date reasonable steps had been taken for the purpose of bringing the purport of the instrument to the notice of the public, or of the persons likely to be affected by it, or of the person charged.

(4) Except as otherwise expressly provided in paragraph (3), nothing in that paragraph shall affect any enactment or rule of law relating to the time at which any Scottish statutory instrument comes into force.

Annual edition

9. (1) As soon as possible after the end of each calendar year, the Queen's Printer shall cause to be prepared from the series of Scottish statutory instruments up to the end of that year an edition of Scottish statutory instruments (referred to in this article as "the annual edition") including the following matters:
(a)   a copy of so much of all Scottish statutory instruments as have, at the time of the completion of the annual edition, been printed in compliance with the requirements of article 7(1) and not been included in any previous annual edition, except that there may be omitted a copy of —
    (i)   instruments which have ceased to be in force at the time of the completion of the annual edition; and
    (ii)   local instruments;
(b)   an Annual Numerical and Issue List of Scottish Statutory Instruments showing, except for such local instruments as are exempt from the requirements of article 7(1), the numbers of all Scottish statutory instruments which during that year either were made or were issued for the first time by, or under the authority of, the Queen's Printer and, in respect of the latter, the date of such issue;
(c)   a classified list of local instruments;
(d)   tables showing the effect on enactments and previous statutory rules or statutory instruments (whether Scottish or not) of the Scottish statutory instruments included in that edition; and
(e)   an index.

(2) The annual edition shall be printed and published by, or under the authority of, the Queen's Printer.

(3) Article 8(2) shall apply to so much of the Annual Numerical and Issue List of Scottish Statutory Instruments in the annual edition as refers to the date upon which any Scottish statutory instrument was first issued by, or under the authority of, the Queen's Printer as it applies to the list mentioned in that article.

Scottish statutory instruments which are required to be laid before the Scottish Parliament

10. (1) Where any enactment provides, or has the effect of providing, that any Scottish statutory instrument is to be laid before the Scottish Parliament after being made, a copy of the instrument shall, subject to the following provisions, be laid before the Scottish Parliament before the instrument is due to come into force.

(2) Where any enactment provides, or has the effect of providing, that any Scottish statutory instrument is to be subject to annulment in pursuance of a resolution of the Scottish Parliament, a copy of the instrument shall, subject to the following provisions, be laid before the Scottish Parliament not less than 21 days before the instrument is due to come into force.

(3) Where it is necessary that an instrument of a kind mentioned in paragraph (1) or (2) should come into force at any time before —

(a)   a copy of it has been laid before the Scottish Parliament; or

(b)   in the case of an instrument mentioned in paragraph (2), the expiry of the period of 21 days mentioned in that paragraph,

the instrument may be made so as to come into force at that time but the responsible authority shall explain to the Presiding Officer why paragraph (1), (2) or (3) sold by, or under the authority of, the Queen's Printer shall bear on the face of it —

(a)   a statement showing the date on which it came or will come into force; and

(b)   either a statement showing the date on which such a copy of it was laid before the Scottish Parliament or a statement that such copy is to be laid before the Scottish Parliament.

Scottish statutory instruments which are subject to annulment by resolution of the Scottish Parliament

11. (1) Paragraphs (2) to (5) apply where any enactment provides, or has the effect of providing, that any Scottish statutory instrument is to be subject to annulment in pursuance of a resolution of the Scottish Parliament.

(2) The instrument shall be laid before the Scottish Parliament in accordance with article 10(2) and (3).

(3) If, within the period of 40 days beginning with the date on which a copy of the instrument is laid before it, the Scottish Parliament so resolves, nothing further is to be done under the instrument after the date of the resolution.

(4) Where such a resolution is made with respect to —

(a)   an instrument which is an Order in Council or an order made by the Privy Council, Her Majesty may by Order in Council revoke that instrument; and

(b)   any other instrument, the Scottish Ministers shall by order made by statutory instrument revoke the instrument.

(5) Any such resolution or revocation is without prejudice to the validity of anything previously done under the instrument or to the making of a new Scottish statutory instrument.

Scottish statutory instruments of which drafts are to be laid before the Scottish Parliament.

12. (1) Paragraphs (2) to (4) apply where any enactment —

(a)   provides, or has the effect of providing, that a draft of any Scottish statutory instrument is to be laid before the Scottish Parliament, but

(b)   does not prohibit the making of the instrument without the approval of the Scottish Parliament.

(2) The instrument shall not be made (or, in the case of a draft Order in Council, shall not be submitted to Her Majesty in Council) until after the end of the period of 40 days beginning with the day on which the draft is laid before the Scottish Parliament.

(3) No further proceedings shall be taken on the instrument if the Scottish Parliament resolves, within the period of 40 days, that the instrument be not made (or, as the case may be, be not submitted).

(4) Paragraph (3) is without prejudice to the laying of a new draft before the Scottish Parliament.

Supplementary provisions to articles 10 to 12

13. (1) In reckoning for the purposes of articles 10, 11 and 12 any period of 21 or 40 days, no account shall be taken of any time during which the Scottish Parliament is dissolved or is in recess for more than 4 days.

(2) The provisions of articles 10 and 11 shall not apply to —

(a)   any Scottish statutory instrument which is an order which is subject to special parliamentary procedure; or

(b)   any other Scottish statutory instrument which is required to be laid before the Scottish Parliament for any period before it comes into force.

Laying of Scottish statutory instruments before the Scottish Parliament

14. Any reference in any enactment to laying before the Scottish Parliament any Scottish statutory instrument is, unless the contrary intention appears, to be construed as a reference to the taking, during any time when the Scottish Parliament is not dissolved, of such action as is specified in the standing orders of the Scottish Parliament as constituting the laying of any document before the Parliament, even if the action so specified consists, in whole or in part, of action which is capable of being taken when the Parliament is in recess.

Publication in the Gazettes

15. Where any enactment requires, or has the effect of requiring, any Scottish statutory instrument to be published or notified in the London, Edinburgh or Belfast Gazette, the publication in that Gazette of a notice stating that the instrument has been made and specifying the place where copies may be purchased shall be sufficient compliance with that enactment.

Parliamentary Control

Parliament controls the making of statutory instruments in various ways. As we have seen,   **2–21** sometimes the instrument requires to be laid before Parliament. The other form of control is that through specialist committees. At Westminster these are the Joint Select Committee on Statutory Instruments and the Commons Select Committee on Statutory Instruments. The latter is composed only of House of Commons members of the Joint Committee and deals with instruments subject only to the oversight of the House of Commons. The merits of an instrument can either be dealt with in the floor of the House or in the House of Commons Standing Committee.

With regard to instruments which give effect to European Community legislation, the Select Committee on European Legislation in the House of Commons and the Select Committee on the European Communities in the House of Lords deal with delegated legislation intended to implement European Community provisions. In addition there exist two European Standing Committees to which the House of Commons Committee may refer matters. The Delegated Powers and Deregulation Committee is an important committee in the House of Lords whose work is noted above. In the context of the Scottish Parliament, it will be for the Parliament itself to decide what form of specialist committee scrutiny will be necessary. The Consultative Steering Group on the Scottish Parliament recommended that subordinate legislation which is required to be laid in the Parliament should be sent to both the relevant subject committee and a delegated legislation committee, similar in function to the Joint Committee on Statutory Instruments at Westminster.

On the face of it it would appear that the opportunity for parliamentary scrutiny of delegated legislation is wide. Is that view justified?

J. D. Hayhurst and P. Wallington, "The Parliamentary Scrutiny of Delegated Legislation"

[1988] P.L. 547 at 563

Table 3. Grounds for reporting by the Committees, 1973–83   **2–22**

Ground	Joint Committee	Commons Committee
Form or purport call for elucidation	343	30
Miscellaneous	124	18
Defective drafting	81	7
Unusual or unexpected use of statute	81	4
Vires	44	3
Delays in publication/laying	9	2
Unauthorised retrospective effect	7	1
Imposition of a charge	0	0
Made under legislation excluding judicial review	0	0
Totals	689	65

Notes

2–23   In their article the authors established that 129 instruments out of the 703 reported by the committees were in fact debated in the House. This takes account of instruments which might be debated in both Houses. The 129 instruments amount to 18.5 per cent and none of those reported were voted down by either House. For confirmation of this trend more recently, see *Making the Law*, below, at pp. 89–94 and A. Beith, "Prayers unanswered; a jaundiced view of the parliamentary scrutiny of statutory instruments" (1981) 34 Parliamentary Affairs 165.

Further concerns were examined recently by the Select Committee on Procedure.

Fourth Report from the Select Committee on Procedure 1995–96, Delegated Legislation

(1995–96 H.C. 152)

"I: Introduction

2–24   3. The House of Commons has a particular responsibility in the matter of scrutiny of delegated legislation, since the House of Lords has for a number of years operated a self-denying ordinance in this field. It neither rejects affirmative instruments nor annuls negative instruments, although it has passed technically ineffective motions calling for the amendment or withdrawal of instruments, and in July 1995 it divided on an approval Motion. In October 1994 the House of Lords formally affirmed its unfettered freedom to vote on any subordinate legislation submitted for its approval. The practice of the House of Lords may be changing. It plays a valuable role through its Delegated Powers Scrutiny Committee (see para. 14 below) and in the Joint Committee on Statutory Instruments. But for the present the onus of scrutiny and control is on the Commons.

4. Parliamentary control of delegated legislation has long been an area of concern. This is reflected in a number of select committee and other Reports over the past half century....

II: Current

Affirmative and negative

6. The current procedures for scrutinising delegated legislation differentiate between those instruments requiring a positive Resolution of the House in order to be brought into effect — 'affirmative instruments' — and those which can be annulled by a Resolution of the House if passed within 40 days of their laying — 'negative instruments'.

Affirmative instruments

As a result of the recent implementation of the Jopling proposals, an affirmative instrument stands automatically referred for debate in a Standing Committee, unless the Government agree that it be debated on the Floor of the House. Debate in Committee is on a formal and unamendable Motion, 'That the Committee has considered the draft XYZ Order 1996'. Whatever the outcome of any vote, and indeed whether or not any motion is agreed, the Chairman reports the instrument to the House. A formal approval Motion is then put forward on the Floor, usually after a few days interval. Those instruments taken on the Floor are debated on the approval Motion, which is also unamendable. In this session to May 1, 36 affirmative instruments have been taken on the Floor in 16 debates (several instruments being taken together on many occasions), compared to 47 debates in Committee on 63 instruments.

Negative instruments

Unless a Motion is tabled seeking to annul a negative instrument, it is not debated. When such a Motion has been tabled, the Government may agree either to refer the instrument to a Standing Committee upstairs, or, exceptionally, to allow the Motion to be brought forward on the Floor of the House; or it may freely disregard it. Instruments referred to a Committee are debated in the same way as are affirmative instruments, save that there are no subsequent proceedings on the Floor. Those taken on the Floor are debated on an annulment or revocation Motion. In the session to May 1, 22 negative instruments have been debated in Committee in 17 debates, and 4 prayers have been debated on the Floor.

7. As the evidence from the Clerk of the House emphasised, the distinction between affirmative and negative instruments, which determines the form of parliamentary control, is very much a matter of chance, 'grounded as often as not on the fortuitous outcome of past debate on the parent legislation'. Ministers

may concede affirmative procedure in the course of debate on a bill in committee. On other occasions Parliament may let delegation of legislative powers slip through without insisting on any parliamentary procedure. The House of Lords Delegated Powers Committee, whose terms of reference include examination of a bill to see whether it subjects the exercise of legislative powers 'to an inappropriate degree of parliamentary scrutiny', has not tried to devise any precise ground rules for determining the proper level. We question whether there is any objective means of predetermining the proper degree of scrutiny to be given to an instrument.... We have arrived at a situation where the nature of parliamentary control allowed for in legislation is being dictated by the notoriously inadequate system of scrutiny and control itself, rather than by nature of the powers to be delegated. In other words, the affirmative procedure may be insisted on as a means of attracting at least *some* form of parliamentary scrutiny, rather than as a reflection of the inherent importance of the subject matter. Were there to be a respectable means of control of negative instruments, the application of that procedure in primary legislation would be more widely acceptable, and the number of relatively insignificant affirmatives reduced accordingly.

8. It is difficult to avoid the existing dichotomy of affirmative and negative instruments, rooted as it is in past statute. There would in theory be something to be said for abolishing the distinction, and creating a uniform category of instruments, with a parliamentary mechanism for determining which required positive approval, based on their inherent significance rather than their statutory basis.... . The fact that it would require primary legislation, possibly wholesale amendment of much of statute law, must initially be a drawback. The proposals we make are less radical. Should they prove ineffective, however, we consider that serious consideration must be given to the radical proposal of a uniform category and procedure for all delegated legislation.

Super-affirmatives

9. We consider that the House would be assisted by a procedure for instruments of particular significance which went beyond the standard affirmative procedure: a 'super-affirmative' procedure, on the lines of the procedure recently established for the consideration of draft Deregulation Orders. Under such a procedure, a Minister proposing to make an order would first have to lay a proposal for a draft order. That could be examined in detail by the relevant departmental select committee, who could propose amendments to be made within the 60-day timescale used in the deregulation procedure. We doubt if the rest of the deregulation procedure is so readily transferable, since such an order is likely to be more politically controversial than deregulation orders. A Select Committee is unlikely to resolve unanimously that the subsequent draft Order be approved; nor do we consider that such orders should be exempt from debate. Such a procedure would nevertheless provide an opportunity for some detailed parliamentary examination of proposed delegated legislation of particular significance and an opportunity for effective parliamentary input. We recommend that the Government contemplate the adoption of such a procedure in appropriate forthcoming legislation.

Delegation of powers

14. There is in our view too great a readiness in Parliament to delegate wide legislative powers to Ministers, and no lack of enthusiasm on their part to take such powers. The result is an excessive volume of delegated legislation. It was partly in response to this that the House of Lords established in 1992–1993 a Delegated Powers Scrutiny Committee 'to report whether the provisions of any bill inappropriately delegate legislative power; or whether they subject the exercise of legislative power to an inappropriate degree of parliamentary scrutiny'. In response to our request, we received a very helpful memorandum on its work from the Chairman of the Committee, Lord Alexander of Weedon. It has drawn the attention of the House of Lords on several occasions to instances of inappropriate delegation of legislative power, and has also on occasions suggested the use of affirmative rather than negative procedures. The Committee is only advisory. We see no benefit in seeking to duplicate its function in the Commons. The scrutiny of powers to be delegated in primary legislation, and the procedure to be applied, are in any event already commonly part of debate on primary legislation. No procedural changes could readily influence the outcome of such debate. We have therefore concentrated on the scrutiny of the delegated legislation produced under powers granted by primary legislation, rather than on finding means of limiting the grant of such powers....

Joint Committee on Statutory Instruments

19. The Joint Committee on Statutory Instruments, and the Select Committee comprised of its Commons Members, continues to provide an expert technical legal scrutiny of all instruments laid before the House, and some not so laid. In its weekly reports, it draws attention to points arising on a number of instruments: in 1994–1995, it did so on about 1 in 10 of all the instruments it considered. Its work is painstaking, unglamorous and goes largely unregarded within the House. It nonetheless plays a vital role in policing the statutory instruments system, and it has an admirable effect on departments. Nothing should be done by way of reform which undermined its authority or diminished its standing.

20. The Chairman of the Joint Committee, Mr Andrew F. Bennett M.P., raised the question of the consideration of instruments by the House before completion of their consideration by the Joint Committee. Despite an informal agreement that this should not happen, there have been several instances in recent years of consideration by the House before completion of Joint Committee consideration. Mr Bennett revived a proposal made in earlier years that there should be a Standing Order preventing such consideration, as already exists as S.O. No. 70 in the House of Lords. He accepted that it would still be possible for such business to be proceeded with, by passage of a business motion setting aside Standing Orders: but he felt that the existence of a Standing Order in place of an informal understanding would 'push departments into being a bit fairer to all of us' in terms of the timing of debates. We have much sympathy with the principle that the House — or its Committees — should not be expected to debate instruments before the disregard of this principle on some occasions as to merit the full force of a Standing Order. We therefore recommend the passage of a Standing Order to provide that no decision on a statutory instrument should be made by the House until completion of its consideration by the Joint Committee on Statutory Instruments.

Deregulation Committee
22. We received a very detailed and informative memorandum from the Chairman of the Deregulation Committee, reporting on the first year of its work. It should be recalled from the outset that Deregulation Orders are peculiar in that they all involve amendment of primary legislation, which would require further primary legislation to amend it, were it not for the terms of the Deregulation and Contracting Out Act 1994 and the parallel establishment of the Deregulation Committee with its special powers. The degree of scrutiny given by the Committee has demanded commitment of substantial resources, which could not conceivably be extended even to all affirmative orders. It is however in our view significant that the Committee has operated smoothly and effectively; that it has used its powers to persuade government to accept nearly all the amendments it has sought; that it and its House of Lords counterpart have effectively killed off one proposal; and that the end result to date is that 17 draft Orders have been agreed to by the House without any debate, but in the full confidence that they are generally acceptable. The European Legislation Committee and the Deregulation Committee have demonstrated that scrutiny by committees can work, and can engage Members' attention and commitment."

Notes

2–25   (1) The committee made a number of other recommendations including the extension of the 40 days' prayer time to 60 days (which is the time period given for deregulation orders); that debates on instruments subject to negative resolution procedure be arranged before the expiry of the praying time: that a new committee be established to determine whether negative instruments merit debate and to examine affirmative instruments which do not; and that debates on standing committees be on motions specified classes of amendment. A comprehensive acceptance of these proposals has not been forthcoming. Reform, where it has taken place, has been piecemeal, so, for example, instruments made under section 10 of the Human Rights Act 1998, extracted at para. 11–46, require to be laid for 60 days.

(2) On the work of the House of Lords Select Committee on the Scrutiny of Delegated Powers see C. M. G. Himsworth [1995] P.L. 34 and for a review of its own work see its First Report (1992–93 H.L. 57), Twelfth Report (1993–94 H.L. 90) and Special Report (1995–96 H.L. 120).

(3) The Joint Committee on Statutory Instruments has a specific role of determining whether the House should be drawn to an instrument on any of the following grounds:

"1.   That it imposes a charge in the public revenues or contains provisions requiring payments to be made to the Exchequer or any government department or to any local or public authority in consideration of any licence or consent or of any services to be rendered, or prescribed the amount of any such charge of payment;

2.   That it is made in pursuance of any enactment containing specific provisions excluding it from challenge in the courts, either at all times or after the expiration of a specific period;

3.   That it purports to have retrospective affect where the parent statute confers no express authority so to provide;

4.   That there appears to have been unjustifiable delay in its publication or in its laying before Parliament;

5.   That there appears to have been unjustifiable delay in sending a notification under the proviso to section (1) of the Statutory Instrument Act 1946, where an instrument has come into operation before it has been laid before Parliament.

6.   That there appears to be doubt whether it is *intra vires* or that it appears to be making some unusual or unexpected use of the powers conferred by the statute under which it is made.

7.   That for any special reason it form or purport call for elucidation.

8.   That its drafting appears to be defective.

Or any other ground which does not impinge on its merits or on the policy behind it and to report its decision with the reasons thereof in any particular case."

(4) As noted above, special provisions exist in relation to deregulation orders made under Part I of the Deregulation and Contracting Out Act 1994. Such orders amend or appeal statutory provisions passed before the end of the 1993–94 session. After consultation, proposals are examined by a special Deregulation Committee of the House of Commons and the House of Lords Select Committee on the Scrutiny of Delegated Powers. These committees provide substantive scrutiny and in this area carry out the functions of the Joint Committee on Statutory Instruments. The committees cannot veto draft orders but the Government has accepted that where there is an adverse report it would normally submit a revised proposal or withdraw it altogether: see Government response (1993–94 H.C. 404) to the Fourth Report of the Select Committee on Procedure (1993–94 H.C. 238, p. viii). For further reports see the First Special Report of the Deregulation Committee (1994–95 H.C. 31) and the First Report of the Committee (1994–95 H.C. 409). The House of Lords Committee was pivotal in ensuring the procurement of amendments to the Scotland Bill in relation to clauses on subordinate legislation now contained in sections 112–115 and Schedule 7 to the Scotland Act, on which see Twenty-Fourth Report (1997–98 H.L. 124) and Thirty-Second Report (1997–98 H.L. 146).

(5) As noted above the Consultative Steering Group on the Scottish Parliament has made a number of proposals in relation to scrutiny by committee. They recommended (Rec. 30) the creation of a committee similar to the Joint Committee on Statutory Instruments to scrutinise provisions within Bills conferring powers to make subordinate legislation and also to report its concerns on any technical aspect of subordinate legislation. It would not have any role in relation to policy issues. It also recommended (Rec. 31) that all subordinate legislation should be passed to the relevant Subject Committee. Where affirmative resolution procedure was being used, it suggested that the committee would want to consider the proposed legislation and report to the Parliament with its recommendations but where negative resolution procedure was in place, the committee would have 40 days to decide whether it wished to oppose it. It was also suggested that where a member of the Scottish Parliament had concerns about subordinate legislation that such concerns be brought to the attention of the relevant committee which would consider whether it wished to debate the legislation, members would be able to explain their concerns to the committee in question, whether or not they were members of that committee (Rec. 32).

Judicial Control of Delegated Legislation

It is a long-established principle of Scots law that the jurisdiction of the courts extends to the control of delegated legislation and increasingly, it would seem, other forms of administrative rules. For a general account see *Stair Memorial Encyclopaedia*, Vol. 1, para. 298 and Finch and Ashton, pp. 120–126 and cases cited therein. Judicial control is based on *ultra vires* and can touch on either questions of substances or procedure.   **2–26**

GENERAL PRINCIPLES

Notes

(1) One of the most significant forms of control on grounds of *vires* is that of failure to relate the substance of the delegated legislation to the purpose contained in the parent Act. The clearest   **2–27**

exposition of what is sometimes known as the prescribed purpose test occurred in *Attorney General for Canada v. Hallet and Carey* [1952] A.C. 427. Here the National Emergency Transitional Powers Act 1945, s. 2(1), gave the Canadian Governor sweeping powers to legislate during wartime emergency. The relevant legislation gave the Governor broad discretion as to the subordinate legislation he could adopt. However, Lord Radcliffe explained (at 450) that:

> "That does not allow him to do whatever he may feel inclined, for what he does must be capable of being related to one of the prescribed purposes, and the court is entitled to read the Act in this way."

See also *McEldowney v. Forde*, at para. 2–29, and K. Puttick, *Challenging Delegated Legislation* (1988), pp. 118–124.

(2) The prescribed purpose test is not, however, the only test used by the courts in determining the *vires* of delegated legislation. Reference is also sometimes made to the "four corners test" referred to in the decision in *Carltona Ltd v. Commissioners of Works* [1943] 2 All E.R. 560, although Puttick is of the view that given the growth of review of the abuse of discretion, the scope of this test, which effectively limits the courts' ability to review the *vires* of an instrument to simply strict interpretation of the enabling Act, is only likely to be relevant in the context of highly subjective discretionary powers.

(3) The concept of "incidental powers" noted in Chapter 3 may be relevant in determining the *vires* of delegated legislation. In some instances an Act sets out a rule-making power and follows it with specific matters which, without prejudice to generality of that power, may be dealt with and then proceed expressly to provide that rules may deal with incidental matters. Generally speaking the courts will not regard such words as enabling provisions as adding significantly to the overall scope of the rule-making powers contained in the enabling Act: *Daymond v. South West Water Authority* [1976] A.C. 609. For incidental rule-making power to be permitted, there must be a relationship between the incidental and supplementary provisions and the regulations made: *R. v. Customs and Excise Commissioners, ex parte Hedges & Butler Ltd* [1986] 2 All E.R. 164 and generally see Puttick, pp. 124–126.

(4) Whatever method of interpretation is used, the courts will have regard to a number of principles and presumptions of interpretation, some of which might be regarded as of a fundamental constitutional nature. We have already seen in Chapter 3 that these principles are relevant in the context of the general theory of *ultra vires* and they have certainly found concrete expression in a number of cases involving substantive challenge to delegated legislation:

- *Scottish Milk Marketing Board v. Ferrier*, 1936 S.C. (H.L.) 39 (presumption against levying of tax without consent of Parliament);
- *Malloch v. Aberdeen Corporation*, 1973 S.C. 227 (removal of vested rights of class of persons) and see *Plewa v. Chief Adjudication Officer* [1994] 3 W.L.R. 317 (presumption applied in relation to new liability created under statutory régime). See generally D. Feldman, "The Presumption Against Retrospective Legislation" [1995] L.Q.R. 32. The presumption against retrospective effect is also relevant in the case law of the ECHR. In *R. v. Miah* [1974] 1 W.L.R. 683 the House of Lords referred to article 7(1) of the ECHR (which prohibits the creation of retrospective criminal offences) and rejected an argument by the Crown that the defendant could properly be convicted of an offence under regulations passed subsequent to the facts on which the offence was based. See too in relation to European Community law for a similar decision: *R. v. Kirk* [1985] 1 All E.R. 453;
- *McGregor v. Disselduff*, 1907 S.C.(J.) 21 (attempts to use instruments to subdelegate without authority unlawful on the basis of the maxim *delegatus non potest delegare*);
- *Kerr v. Hood*, 1907 S.C. 895 (attempt to exclude jurisdiction of court to decide legality of nominations at school board elections). Again, the ECHR has been used where allegations of exclusion of access to legal advice in the courts have been raised. In *Raymond v. Honey* [1983] 1 A.C. 1 it was held that section 47 of the Prison Act 1952 had to be construed in light of Article 6 of the ECHR (which protects, *inter alia*, the right of access to the courts) and accordingly prison rules concerning the interception of prisoners' correspondence to legal advisers by the governor were held to be unlawful, there being no express power or necessary implication contained in the Prison Act for this purpose: see too *R. v. Secretary of State for the Home Department, ex parte Leech* [1994] Q.B. 198;

- *Scottish General Transport Co. Ltd v. Glasgow Corporation*, 1928 S.C. 248 (power to regulate an activity used to prohibit it). For further general reading see Puttick, Chapters 4, 16 and *Stair Memorial Encyclopaedia*, Vol. 1, paras 298–301.

(5) Under the Human Rights Act 1998, subordinate legislation must be read and given effect in a way in which is compatible with Convention rights: section 3(1), and applies to subordinate legislation whenever enacted: section 3(2)(*a*). If it is not possible to construe subordinate legislation to give effect to Convention rights, this of itself does not render in *ultra vires*. For it to be held *ultra vires* one must have regard to the terms of section 6, extracted at para. 6–17. Moreover, if subordinate legislation is incompatible and, disregarding any possibility of revocation, the primary legislation under which it is made prevents removal of the incompatibility, such subordinate legislation cannot be declared *ultra vires* under section 6, but can be subject to declarator of incompatibility under section 4, on which see para. 11–41. For further analysis of section 3 see para. 3–8. For the limits on the powers of the Scottish Executive to make subordinate legislation see section 54 of the Scotland Act 1998, extracted at para. 3–11, and see sections 57(2) and 58(3) extracted at p. 000 and 000 respectively.

Moreover, standing the terms of section 6 of the Human Rights Act it will be unlawful for a public authority to issue or approve subordinate legislation which is incompatible with a Convention right.

One of the most difficult areas of challenge is alleged uncertainty.

Marshall v. Clark

1957 J.C. 68

"Anne M'Ilwain or Marshall, bus conductress, was charged in the Sheriff Court at Hawick on a summary complaint at the instance of Richard Scott Clark, Procurator-fiscal, which set forth that 'about 5.45 p.m. on 10th December 1956, you, being the conductress of a public service vehicle, registered number DSC 321, the property of Scottish Omnibuses Limited, New Street, Edinburgh, and while said motor vehicle was at the bus stop on a public road in the burgh of Hawick and county aforesaid, and at a part thereof in Slitrig Crescent and opposite Slitrig House, Slitrig Crescent aforesaid, being a road within the meaning of the Road Traffic Act, 1930, section 121, did fail to take all reasonable precautions to ensure the safety of passengers in or on or entering or alighting from said vehicle, and in particular did fail to keep a proper look-out for passengers entering by the front entrance of said vehicle and, while a passenger, viz., Sophia Entwistle or M'Gurk (69), hosiery worker, 9 Kenilworth Avenue, Hawick aforesaid, had placed her right hand on to the hand-rail at the front entrance of said vehicle, and her right foot on to the front step of said vehicle, and was entering said vehicle, you did give a bell signal to the driver of said vehicle and did cause said driver to drive the vehicle away from the bus stop, and did cause Sophia Entwistle or M'Gurk to overbalance and fall from the front entrance of said vehicle whereby her right leg and foot were crushed between the near side rear wheel of said vehicle and the kerb and said wheel passed over the right foot of said Sophia Entwistle or M'Gurk to her severe injury: Contrary to the Public Service Vehicles (Conduct of Drivers, Conductors and Passengers) Regulations, 1936, Reg. 4(*c*)."

Lord Justice General (Clyde): "This is a stated case arising out of a complaint brought against the present appellant. There are two questions in the case. The first relates to the relevancy of the complaint, and, as this involves the reconsideration of several previous decisions, the case has been remitted to a Court of five Judges. The second question is concerned with the particular facts of the present case, and raises no such general issue as does the first question.

[His Lordship quoted the terms of the complaint and of Regulation 4(*c*), and continued] — The main contention for the appellant was that the statute or regulation founded upon must itself fix what the offence is. This cannot be left to the Court to ascertain in the course of the trial, for the accused would then have no fair notice of what his alleged offence was and would therefore not be in a position to decide whether to plead guilty or not before the trial began. It was therefore contended that a failure 'to take all reasonable precautions to ensure the safety of passengers' was too indefinite to constitute a criminal offence, since no indication was given in the Regulations as to what precautions Parliament or the Minister regarded as reasonable. The contention was based mainly upon the decision in *Allan v. Howman*.

The effect of this contention, logically applied, would be very far reaching. For in effect it would mean that the incorporation of the words 'reasonable care' or 'reasonable precautions,' or similar words

2–28

of a general character, in the statutory description of a prohibition would render the prohibition so vague as to preclude the possibility of any prosecution in respect of it.

An attempt was made to avoid so far reaching a consequence by contending that there was a distinction between a statutory direction to take all reasonable steps to do something particular (which it was conceded might form the basis of a relevant charge) and a statutory direction to take all reasonable steps or precautions to achieve a general aim, as for instance the safety of bus passengers (which it was contended never could ground a relevant charge). But there is no logical justification for this distinction. If the latter type of direction is defective because of the vagueness of the word 'reasonable,' so also for the same reason must the former type be defective.

The appellant's contention, however, is in my opinion based on a fallacy. There may, of course, be regulations which are so obscurely or defectively drawn that it is impossible to tell how or where an offence against them is committed. In such cases obviously no relevant complaint for a breach could be framed. But, apart from cases of that kind, statutory prohibitions or directions in a great variety of different circumstances must necessarily incorporate words with a general signification which are incapable of rigid definition. It would be quite contrary to our law that the mere fact that such general words occur in a regulation should lead to the inference that the regulation can therefore never be effective. For instance Regulation 4(a) of the Regulation in question here provides that a driver or conductor, when acting as such, shall behave in a civil and orderly manner. There is no definition in the Regulations of what such behaviour is, and I should certainly not be prepared to say that no complaint for a breach of such a direction could be framed because the Regulation did not contain a precise list of the circumstances constituting uncivil and disorderly behaviour. So rigid a requirement could only lead to technicalities and to injustice in the particular case, and it is much fairer to an accused to leave to the Court a discretion to determine in the particular case whether the conduct amounted to what is envisaged in the Regulations as a breach. In my opinion, general words such as 'reasonable care' and 'reasonable precautions' fall into this category, and I decline to endorse the view that their presence in a regulation thereby renders the regulation so unspecific that a breach of it can never be relevantly averred.

But that is not the end of the matter. Words of a general scope in a regulation may be so unspecific that their mere repetition in a complaint may not give fair notice to an accused of what the offence with which he is charged really is. In that event it would be the duty of the prosecutor to specify in the complaint such fuller details of what he intends to prove as would give the necessary notice to the accused. For an accused is entitled to know beforehand what the charge is.

It is quite true that section 16(a) of the Summary Jurisdiction (Scotland) Act, 1954, repeating a similar provision in the 1908 Act, provides that 'the description of any offence in the words of the statute or order contravened … shall be sufficient.' But this provision has never been regarded as precluding the necessity for fair notice if the language of the statutory provision is in very general terms. As Lord Low said in *Renton v. Ramage* [6 Adam, 266] at p. 268): 'Now in this case the indictment follows exactly the words of the statute, and accordingly I think we must hold it to be sufficient. In saying that, I should like to guard myself by observing that there may be an offence framed in such general terms that it would not be fair to libel the offence in similar general terms, and in such a case it might well be necessary to give such particulars as would afford fair notice of what was charged.'

But such additional specification is not always necessary. Indeed in that case the Court was considering a complaint regarding a breach of section 15 of the Children Act, 1908. The complaint merely quoted the language of the section and gave no specification of what were 'the reasonable precautions against the risk of fire' which the prosecutor considered necessary. The complaint was none the less held to be relevant. In my opinion, that case was rightly decided, and its decision is fatal to the appellant's argument in the present case. In my opinion, therefore, an offence may be effectively created in a regulation notwithstanding the use in that regulation of general words such as 'reasonable care' or 'reasonable precautions.' But, if the scope of these general words is so wide as not to give an accused fair notice of how it is alleged that he committed the offence in a particular case, further specification may require to be embodied in the complaint to give that notice.

The fallacy in the appellant's argument consists in the failure to distinguish between two quite separate matters, (1) the effective creation of an offence in the Regulations and (2) fair notice of what the offence is in a particular case. The standard of adequate specification in the first is quite different from what is necessary in the second. Fair notice may in some cases not be given in a particular case by merely quoting in the complaint the language of the regulation. But it is quite illegitimate to conclude in such a case, as the appellant's argument does, that therefore no offence can ever be effectively created by such a regulation, and that no complaint could ever relevantly be drawn in regard to it.

This confusion between these two quite separate matters is very apparent in *Allan v. Howman*. In that case a baker was charged with a contravention of a Flour and Bread (Prices) Order which fixed a maximum price for bread and provided also that a reasonable additional charge might be made for making delivery. In the complaint the language of the Order was merely repeated, and the Court held that the complaint was irrelevant in respect that it did not state what was the reasonable additional charge for delivery which was exceeded. Had this case been decided on a question of lack of fair notice in the particular complaint, no real difficulty would have arisen in future from it. But the Court proceeded to hold that, as the regulation merely referred to the additional charge for delivery being reasonable without any further specification of what that term meant in the regulation, it was not possible to frame a relevant complaint arising out of it. This is just to confuse the efficacy of the regulation with fair notice of an alleged breach of it contained in a particular complaint. The decision in *Renton v. Ramage* was not quoted in *Allan v. Howman*, and the two decisions cannot stand together. In my opinion, *Allan v. Howman* was wrongly decided.

Allan v. Howman was followed in *Shepherd v. Howman* [1918 J.C. 78]. The Order in question in that case would appear in any event to be so vague as not to be capable of constituting an offence at all, and the decision may therefore be justified on that ground. But, in so far as it purports to proceed on the ratio of *Allan v. Howman*, it is, in my opinion, a wrong decision. The next case is *Rogers v. Howman* [1918 J.C. 88]. The ratio of *Allan v. Howman* was not applied in that case, and its decision calls for no comment. The case was concerned with a question of fair notice — see Lord Mackenzie at p. 94.

The matter next arose in *Morrison v. Ross-Taylor* [1948 J.C. 74]. In that case, where there was a strong dissent by Lord Keith, the majority of the Court followed *Allan v. Howman*. But they did so with obvious reluctance, and the Lord Justice-General (Cooper) said (at p. 78): 'I should have been willing that the precise formulation of the principle of *Allan v. Howman* should be re-examined in the light of the experience of the intervening thirty years, if we had been so moved, but we were not.' In my opinion, if *Allan v. Howman* cannot stand, the ratio of the decision in *Morrison v. Ross-Taylor* must be unsound. In *M'Fadyen v. Stewart* [1951 J.C. 164], *Allan v. Howman* and *Morrison v. Ross-Taylor* were distinguished, and the complaint, which in that case merely reproduced the general words contained in the statutory regulations, was none the less held to give fair and adequate notice of the offence and to be relevant. Finally, in *M'Ilroy v. Bell* [1952 J.C. 92], which was concerned with the same offence as in the present case, an attempt was made to present an argument similar to that presented by the appellant here. The Court refused to entertain the argument, as it had not been presented in the Court below, but the Lord Justice-General, with whom the other members of the Court concurred, said (at p. 95): 'But I think it right, in view of the argument which we have heard, to say that I am by no means satisfied that the type of criticism which prevailed in the case of *Morrison v. Ross-Taylor* can be directed against the Regulation which is here the subject of criticism. It is unnecessary for us to decide that in this case, and I formally reserve my opinion.'

It is clear therefore that, although *Allan v. Howman* and *Morrison v. Ross-Taylor* were decided some years ago, they have very rarely been followed and have more than once been adversely criticised. Their ceasing to be authoritative removes an anomaly in this branch of the law of Scotland.

The application of these considerations to the present case means that the presence of words of general signification in the Regulation in question does not prevent the Regulation from being capable of creating an offence, and the complaint in question gives more than ample notice of what the offence in this particular case was alleged to be. The Sheriff-substitute was therefore well founded in repelling the objection to relevancy, and the first question falls to be answered in the affirmative. [His Lordship then went on to consider whether on the facts the Sheriff-substitute was entitled to convict.]"

Lord Justice-Clerk (Thomson): "By virtue of section 85 of the Road Traffic Act, 1930, the Minister of Transport may make regulations as to the conduct of, *inter alia*, conductors of public service vehicles when acting as such. Subsection (2) of that section provides that, if any person to whom any such regulations apply contravenes or fails to comply with any of the provisions of the regulations, he shall be liable to a fine.

The Public Service Vehicles (Conduct of Drivers, Conductors and Passengers) Regulations, 1936, which were made by the Minister of Transport in virtue of that section and which therefore have the force of an Act of Parliament, provide, *inter alia*, that a conductor, when acting as such, shall take all reasonable precautions to ensure the safety of passengers in or on or entering or alighting from his vehicle. The appellant, a conductress, was charged with failing to comply with this regulation. The objection which she took to the relevancy of the complaint was that it is not possible for a Scots prosecutor to frame a relevant complaint based on that regulation. In other words Parliament has stultified itself and, while appearing to create an offence, has failed to do so, as the offence cannot be translated into a relevant charge.

This proposition is on the face of it somewhat startling and would appear to accuse an omnipotent parliament of legislative ineptitude. The ineptitude lies, according to the argument, in the failure of Parliament to point out a standard against which the negligence of the conductress can be measured. As there is no touchstone, there can be no offence. The foundation of this attack on the relevancy is *Allan v. Howman* which has been followed, not always with enthusiasm, in a number of cases. I am entirely in agreement with your Lordship's review of this trend of authority and with your conclusion that it should be overruled. I shall confine myself to a few observations on *Allan v. Howman* as being the *fons et origo malorum*.

The attitude of the Court is succinctly put by Lord Johnston (at p. 53): 'It is for the Order which creates the offence to leave no dubiety as to what the offence is and not to leave it to the Judge who tries the case to determine on evidence, and to a large extent according to his opinion, in what the offence consists.' The Lord Justice-General said (at p. 53): 'I seek to throw no blame upon the prosecutor for having laid before the Court an irrelevant complaint. In the circumstances it would have been impossible for him to have done otherwise.' Lord Mackenzie also said (at p. 54): 'There are not, at present, materials from which the Procurator-fiscal could construct a relevant complaint ... I cannot assent to the proposition that a man can be charged in a criminal Court on a complaint which merely tells him that he did something unreasonable.'

No doubt in 1918 regulations of this kind were something of a novelty, but since then a good deal of water — some of it pretty muddy — has flowed under Parliamentary bridges and we are now habituated not only to regulations but to legislative enactments of all sorts couched in similar general terms. For myself — quite apart from the duty which rests on both prosecutors and Courts to do what Parliament tells them — I feel no particular anxiety that the liberty of the subject will be imperilled or fair trial impeded because an enactment made by Parliament or on Parliamentary authority says that a man must take adequate care or reasonable steps and so forth and leaves it to the Judge to determine on evidence in what the offence consists. The theory of *Allan v. Howman* is that no measuring rod has been provided in advance. I see no reason why the measuring rod should not emerge at the trial. This is the only practical way to look at the matter. When a man is accused of doing something unreasonable or of failing to take adequate precautions or reasonable steps or the like, the accusation is made in regard to some particular sphere of human activity in which he is engaged and of the ordinary incidents of which he must be well aware. It may be in regard to his family, his factory, his farm, his driving of his motor car or similar activities. In some of these activities the reasonableness or adequacy of his conduct may be easily enough ascertained by the Judge. In others, the situation may be complicated and a good deal of investigation may be necessary. Where there is a complicated background, if the prosecutor does not provide material sufficient to enable the Judge to reach a proper conclusion, the case against the accused will fail. It is all a question of circumstances. But in neither class of case is there any impropriety or injustice in leaving the measuring rod to be sought at the trial. In the varied activities of modern life it would be impracticable to provide it in advance.

Once it is established that the *ratio decidendi* of *Allan v. Hownam* is unsound and that a statutory enactment does not necessarily lose its force by its failure to provide in advance a standard by which the conduct of the accused is to be measured, this stated case is plain sailing. As your Lordship has observed, there may be enactments so defectively worded that it is impossible to spell a relevant charge out of them. This particular regulation presented no such problem. There is, moreover, very full specification of the *modus* and indeed no question of relevancy in its secondary sense of lack of specification was raised. I wish, however, to reserve my opinion as to whether a complaint following literally the terms of a widely drawn and unspecific enactment might be successfully attacked on the ground of absence of fair notice, either as irrelevant in the strict sense of the word or as lacking in specification. On this aspect issues of some nicety might arise, the solution of which would turn on the precise terms of the enactment and the relative complaint."

Lord Carmont: "I agree."

Lord Patrick: "I agree."

Lord Mackintosh: "I agree."

"The Court answered the first question of law in the affirmative, and further held that on the facts stated in the case the Sheriff-substitute was entitled to find the appellant guilty."

Notes

2–29   (1) Is it clear that the test tells that the court accepts that certainty can be used as a test to establish the *vires* of statutory instrument? Whether or not the challenge will succeed depends on the balance as between the need to give the instrument a reasonable interpretation and the facts of the case to which it relates. As can be seen from the extract, prior to *Marshall* a somewhat stricter test was followed. Puttick (p. 268) describes situations where a statutory duty is imposed without identification of the steps needed to comply with that duty as being a challenge based on "insufficient particularity". As can be imagined, on the facts of the case such as *Marshall*, it will be relatively difficult to establish the sufficient degree of uncertainty required. Statutes must of necessity be general in their nature. However, in *Utah Constructions v. Pataky* [1966] A.C. 629 the Privy Council was prepared to accept that in the context of a factory legislation, there was an obligation on the relevant authority to spell out specific means by which the purpose of the rules, to prevent injury, could be carried into effect.

(2) In *McEldowney v. Forde* [1971] A.C. 632 the House of Lords had to consider the *vires* of regulations made under Northern Irish legislation which gave power to make regulations "for the preservation of peace and the maintenance of order" and specifically regulations which made unlawful membership of organisations which (at 642):

> "at the date of this regulation or at any time thereafter describing themselves as 'republican clubs' or any like organisation howsoever described".

Regulations had already been passed making specified republican authorisations unlawful. The defendant was charged with membership of a club. It was found that there was no evidence to show that he was a threat to peace or law and order and the complaint was dismissed. On appeal, the Court of Appeal in Northern Ireland held the regulations valid as did the House of Lords by a three to two majority. The majority held that there was enough to show that the regulations did relate to the purpose of maintaining peace and order in regard to both "internal" evidence — the purpose of the regulation as determined by looking at previous delegated legislation and the whole statutory context — and "external" evidence — the facts of the situation in Northern Ireland at that time. Lord Diplock in the minority, however, preferred to examine the effect of the regulations.

McEldowney v. Forde

[1971] A.C. 632

Lord Hodson: "… The proscription of present and future 'republican clubs' including 'any like organisations howsoever described' is said to be something outside the scope and meaning of the Act and so incapable of being related to the prescribed purposes of the Act. Accepting that the word 'republican' is an innocent word and need not connote anything contrary to law, I cannot escape the conclusion that in its context, added to the list of admittedly unlawful organisations of a militant type, the word 'republican' is capable of fitting the description of a club which in the opinion of the Minster should be proscribed as a subversive organisation of a type akin to those previously named in the list of admittedly unlawful organisations. The context in which the word is used shows the type of club which the Minister had in mind and there is no doubt that the mischief aimed at is an association which had subversive objects. On this matter, in my opinion, the court should not substitute its judgment for that of the Minster, on the ground that the banning of 'republican clubs' is too remote. I agree that the use of the words 'any like organisation, howsoever described' lends some support to the contention that the regulation is vague and for that reason invalid, but on consideration I do not accept the argument based on vagueness. It is not difficult to see why the Minister, in order to avoid subterfuge, was not anxious to restrict himself to the description 'republican' seeing that there might be similar clubs which he might seek to proscribe whatever they called themselves. If and when any case based on the words 'any like organisation' arises it will have to be decided, but I do not, by reason of the use of those words, condemn the regulation as being too vague or uncertain to be supported. I would dismiss the appeal."

Lord Guest: "… The final argument for the appellant related to the third category of organisations which it is said the regulation covered, namely, 'or any like organisation howsoever described.' It was submitted that this would cover any club whatever its name and whatever its objects and that such an exercise of the Minister's power was unreasonable, arbitrary and capricious. In my view this argument is not well founded. The regulation first of all embraces republican clubs eo nomine and they are caught by their very description. If they do not bear the name 'republican,' it would be a question of interpretation after evidence whether any particular club was covered by the words 'any like organisation howsoever described.' It is indeed not necessary for the purposes of this case where the organisation bore the name 'republican club' to examine this question in any great detail. But my provisional view is that the regulation would cover any organisation having similar objects to those of a republican club or of any of the named organisations or of any organisation whose objects included the absorption of Northern Ireland in the Republic of Ireland.

Having regard to all these matters I cannot say that the class of 'like organisations' is either ambiguous or arbitrary so as to invalidate the regulation. In my view this ground of attack also fails... . I would therefore dismiss the appeal."

Lord Pearce: "... Further, the 1967 regulation is too vague and ambiguous. A man may not be put in peril on an ambiguity under the criminal law. When the 1957 regulation was issued the citizen ought to have been able to know whether he could or could not remain a member of his club without being subject to a criminal prosecution. Yet I doubt if one could have said with certainty that any man or woman was safe in remaining a member of any club in Northern Ireland, however named or whatever its activities or objects.

Had the final phrase 'or any like organisation howsoever described' been absent, the regulation would have simply been an attack on the description 'republican,' however innocent the club's activities. Presumably the justification for it would have to be that the mere existence of the word republican in the name of a club was so inflammatory that its suppression was 'necessary for preserving the peace and maintaining order' and that the 'exigencies' of the need for its suppression did not permit the citizen's right in that respect to prevail. For the reasons given by the Lord Chief Justice I do not accept that such a justification could suffice. But be that as it may, the final phrase shows that this is more than an attack on nomenclature, since the club is deemed equally unlawful if it is a like organisation, whatever be the name under which it goes.

And what is the 'likeness' to a republican club which makes an organisation unlawful 'howsoever described'? Since a republican club is banned whatever may be its activities, the likeness cannot consist in its activities. And since the organisation is unlawful, howsoever described, the 'likeness' cannot consist in a likeness of nomenclature. The only possibility left seems to be that the 'likeness' may consist in the mere fact of being a club. In which case all clubs, however named, are unlawful — which is absurd.

One cannot disregard the final phrase, since that would wholly alter the meaning of the regulation. Without the final phrase it is simply an attack on nomenclature. But with the final phrase it cannot simply be an attack on nomenclature. One cannot sever the bad from the good by omitting a phrase when the omission must alter the meaning of the rest. One must take the whole sentence as it stands. And as it stands it is too vague and ambiguous to be valid.

I would therefore allow the appeal."

Lord Pearson: "... There is one further argument against the validity of this regulation, and it is the most formidable one. It is that the regulation is too vague, because it includes the words 'or any like organisation howsoever described.' I have had doubts on this point, but in the end I think the argument against the validity of the regulation ought not to prevail. The Minister's intention evidently was (if I may use a convenient short phrase) to ban republican clubs. He had to exclude in advance two subterfuges which might defeat his intention. First, an existing republican club might be dissolved, and a new one created. The words 'or at any time thereafter' would exclude that subterfuge as well as applying to new republican clubs generally. Secondly, a new club, having the characteristic object of a republican club, might be created with some other title such as 'New Constitution Group' or 'Society for the alteration of the Constitution.' The words 'or any like organisation however described' would exclude that subterfuge.

In constituting this regulation one has to bear in mind that it authorises very drastic interference with freedom of association, freedom of speech and in some circumstances the liberty of the subject. therefore it should be narrowly interpreted. Also it should if possible be so construed as to have sufficient certainty to be valid — ut res magis valeat quam pereat.

In my opinion the proper construction of the regulation is that the organisations to be deemed unlawful are —

(i)   any organisation describing itself as a 'republican club,' whatever its actual objects may be, and

(ii)   any organisation which has the characteristic object of a republican club, namely, to introduce republican government into Northern Ireland — whatever its name may be.

I would dismiss the appeal."

Lord Diplock: '... But there is another reason for rejecting this construction of the regulation which I find compelling. It is not, in my view, permissible to treat the regulation as severable in the way adopted by the majority of the Court of Appeal. To do so is to treat it as striking at more than one unrelated mischief whereas the inclusion in the description of the organisations deemed to be unlawful association of the words 'any like organisation' makes it plain that it is organisations possessing a common mischievous characteristic that are intended to be proscribed.

What then is that characteristic? Even if it were legitimate to infer that the Minister had knowledge of the objects of 'republican clubs' in existence at the date of the regulation he could not have knowledge of what would be the objects of clubs to be formed in the future which would describe themselves as 'republican clubs.' The characteristic struck at, therefore, cannot be the possession *in fact* of unlawful objects by the organisations proscribed. Nor for the reasons previously indicated can the common characteristic struck at be the use of the name 'republican club.' It is conceivable that the adoption of a particular name might of itself be so inflammatory in Northern Ireland as to endanger the preservation of peace and the maintenance of order, but the regulation proscribes 'like organisations' which do not adopt this name.

But there are no other ascertainable common characteristics of the organisations described in the regulation except that they are composed of members and possess objects of some kind or other and describe themselves by some name or other. If the Minister's intention was to proscribe all clubs and associations in Northern Ireland whatever their objects and name the regulation plainly falls outside the power delegated to him by section 1(3) of the Special Powers Act to make regulations 'for making further provision for the preservation of the peace and the maintenance of order.' It makes unlawful conduct which cannot have the effect of endangering the preservation of the peace or the maintenance of order. But if the Minister's intention was to proscribe some narrower category of organisations the suppression of which would have the effect of preserving the peace and maintaining order he has in my view failed to disclose in the regulation what the narrower category is. A regulation whose meaning is so vague that it cannot be ascertained with reasonable certainty cannot fall within the words of delegation.

It is possible to speculate that the Minister when he made the regulation now challenged bona fide believed that the sort of club which at that date described itself as a 'republican club' was likely to have unlawful objects which would endanger the preservation of the peace and the maintenance of order and by the words that he added he may have intended to do no more than to prevent such clubs from evading the regulation by dissolving and re-forming or by changing their names. If this was his intention he signally failed to express it in the regulation, for by no process of construction can it be given this limited effect. Or he may have thought it administratively convenient to insert in the regulation a description of proscribed organisations so wide as to include also those with lawful objects in order to be sure that none with unlawful objects should be omitted, and to rely upon the administrative discretion of the Attorney-General under section 3(2) of the Act not to enforce the regulation. But to do this, however, if administratively convenient, would be outside his delegated legislative powers.

But this is speculation not construction and your Lordships' function is limited to construing the words which the Minister has used. In my view the words used by the Minister in the regulation are either too wide to fall within the description of the regulations which he is empowered to make under section 1(3) of the Special Powers Act or are too vague and uncertain in their meaning to be enforceable.

I would allow this appeal."

Notes

(1) Which approach is preferable? Is it possible to detect in Lord Diplock's approach the test of proportionality? **2–30**

(2) Note the use of ambiguity or the potential for absurdity as a ground of challenge to delegated legislation. Lord Pearce, the other judge in the minority, invoked the principle that a man must "not be put in peril on an ambiguity". When the regulation was issued a member, he considered, should be able to know whether he could remain in the club without being subject to prosecution. The extension of the regulation to both "republican clubs" or "any like organisation howsoever described" clearly made club membership an uncertain proposition. Successful challenges based on ambiguity are, however, few and far between. In *Hingston v. McGugan*, 1997 S.C.C.R. 625 a woman was charged with refusing to pay a toll which she was liable to pay by virtue of the Invergarry-Kyle of Lochalsh Trunk Road (A87) Extension (Skye Bridge Crossing) Toll Order 1992 on the basis that since the toll order did not specify who was liable to pay the toll she should be acquitted. The sheriff agreed but, on appeal, the High Court held that on a proper construction of section 38(1) of the New Roads and Street Works Act 1991, the complaint was in fact relevant. It was contended by the accused that section 38(1) was ambiguous as it could justify prosecution of at least two groups of people, one of which included the accused and since the provision was penal, an interpretation more favourable to the accused should be adopted. However, as the phrase in question appeared throughout the

statute in sections which were not penal, a consistent interpretation had to be applied and the Order was upheld. Puttick (pp. 268–269) argues that ambiguity may not in fact be a basis for invalidity, but it may be relevant to construing the scope of delegated legislation: see also *Francis v. Cardle*, at para. 2–32.

(3) In *MacNeill v. Sutherland*, 1998 G.W.D. 27-1383 a person was accused of breach of regulation 3(2) of the Beef Bones Regulations 1997 made under section 53(1) of the Food Safety Act 1990. The regulation made the use of bone-in beef in the preparation of food to the ultimate consumer a criminal offence. The accused contended that the regulation was *ultra vires* in that it was manifestly absurd and uncertain. At first instance, the sheriff held that since "preparing" meat included subjecting meat to cold in terms of section 53(1), the absurd result was to make every butcher and caterer who chilled a carcass guilty of an offence and that moreover the word "preparation" was so imprecise that it could mean anything and that regulation 3(2) was *ultra vires* in singularly failing to identify permitted and prohibited conduct under reference to *Shepherd v. Howman*. The Crown appealed to the High Court who rejected the sheriff's reasoning. "Preparation" did not bear every meaning which it could have had under section 53(1) and the sheriff should have construed the regulation so as to avoid the absurd result he discerned. Lord Coulsfield observed that the fact that there may be doubtful cases at the margin did not render the regulation *ultra vires*.

Procedural Challenge

2–31   Challenge to delegated legislation can also be upheld on procedural grounds. For a discussion see generally *Stair Encyclopaedia*, Vol. 1, para. 300 and Finch and Ashton, pp. 121–125. The procedural requirements of delegated legislation have to be considered in the light of the empowering Act. Examples of procedural failure will be touched on in our examination of consultation requirements in Chapter 5. Other examples include:

- *Allied Breweries (U.K.) v. Glasgow District Licensing Board*, 1985 S.L.T. 302 (where the rubric to a statutory instrument does not correctly state the power under which it has been made);
- *Forster v. Polmaise Patent Fuel Co. Ltd*, 1947 J.C. 46 (where the wrong authority attempts to use the power);
- *Galloway v. Anderson*, 1928 J.C. 70 (where an authority seeks to use a less formal procedure than that required by the statute).

It is important to recognise, however, that not all procedural requirements are of such effect that failure to follow them leads to the instrument being struck down: see, for example, *R. v. Secretary of State for Social Services, ex parte Association of Metropolitan Authorities* [1986] 1 All E.R. 164, discussed at para. 5–18.

CIRCUMSTANCES OF CHALLENGE

Francis v. Cardle

1988 S.L.T. 578

2–32   Fifteen accused persons were charged on separate summary complaints with remaining on military lands after having being warned off by an authorised person, contrary to byelaws made by the Secretary of State under powers conferred by the Military Lands Act 1892. The accused objected to the competency of the charge on the ground that the byelaws were void because the plan referred to in the byelaws was ambiguous, the military lands were improperly defined by signs placed on the perimeter and the Secretary of State had failed to comply with certain duties to advertise the proposed byelaws locally, consult and thereafter publicise the byelaws as required by s. 17(1) of the 1892 Act. The sheriff repelled the pleas to competency and held that the validity of the byelaws was a matter of fact for proof by the Crown at the trial. The accused appealed."

Lord Justice-Clerk (Ross): "Each of the appellants was charged on a summary complaint at the instance of the respondent, and in each instance the charge was in the following terms: [his Lordship narrated the terms of the charge quoted supra, and continued:]

In the case of the appellant Alan Crawford the complaint also contained a charge of attempting to pervert the course of justice, but nothing turns upon this charge so far as the present appeals are concerned.

In the case of each of the appellants pleas to the competency of the complaint were tendered, and after sundry procedure the sheriff heard parties upon the preliminary pleas to the competency. On 31 October 1986 the sheriff repelled the preliminary pleas. On the motion of the appellants the sheriff granted leave to appeal his decision to the High Court in terms of s. 334 of the Criminal Procedure (Scotland) Act 1975 as amended. The appeals were heard together on 6 January 1987. All the appellants with the exception of Mrs Barbara Francis, Stephen William Maddiston alias Callum Freeborn, and George McCreadie Young were represented by counsel. A variety of submissions were made by counsel and on behalf of the three appellants who appeared on their own behalf.

On behalf of the appellant James Chestnut, counsel explained that although various objections were stated in the note of appeal, he proposed to argue one matter only, namely a submission that the byelaws in question were void from uncertainty. In the byelaws the military lands in the Rosneath Peninsula are defined as follows: 'The area of land shown for convenience of reference by a pecked black line on the plan hereto annexed and identified as "Plan of the Military Lands" and marked on its permitter by signs'. Counsel's submission was directed to the reference to the plan. He drew particular attention to three areas where he submitted there was ambiguity as to the boundary depicted by the pecked black line. First in the area of Garelochhead where the road appears to cross a railway line he maintained that there was confusion because there was a pecked black line on each side of the railway. Indeed he maintained that at one stage there were three pecked or broken lines and he posed the question whether the military lands included the railway line. Secondly on the west coast of Gare Loch between Mambeg and Rahane, he drew attention to the presence of two parallel pecked black lines which appeared to be on both sides of a road, and he posed the question whether the military lands included the road and the land down to high water mark on the east of the road. Thirdly he drew attention to the boundary between the protected area at Coulport (A) and the military lands (C). He pointed out that this boundary was marked only by a continuous black line and that there was no pecked black line.

He submitted that in these three respects the plan contained ambiguity and uncertainty and that accordingly the definition of the military lands was void from uncertainty. In our opinion, however, this submission was not well founded. Part of counsel's submission had been that the military lands could not be defined under reference to signs which had been fixed on the perimeter, but the Lord Advocate pointed out that the Secretary of State had a duty under s. 17(1) of the Military Lands Act 1892 to cause the boundaries of an area to which byelaws apply to be marked once byelaws have been made. In these circumstances the Lord Advocate contended that the Secretary of State was entitled to use such signs to assist in defining the area. At the end of the day, however, counsel's argument was directed to the alleged ambiguities in the plan. The Lord Advocate pointed out that the Secretary of State could only deal with Crown lands and that he could not deal with roads and railway lines which belonged to other authorities. So far as counsel's first two points were concerned he submitted that the plan made it plain that the roads and railway line were excluded. In our opinion this submission by the Lord Advocate is clearly well founded. We are satisfied that there is no ambiguity in the plan so far as these two areas are concerned. So far as the boundary between the two areas A and C is concerned we are again satisfied that there is no ambiguity. So far as that boundary is concerned, the thick black line showing the boundary of the protected area at Coulport and the pecked black line showing the boundary of the military lands (C) run on precisely the same line. Accordingly that portion of the line appears on the plan simply as a thick black line although it in fact marks the line of the pecked black line as well. In other words, the pecked black line is smothered by the thick black line.

In our opinion the description in the byelaws and the plan is perfectly intelligible and is not void from uncertainty. The sheriff expressed the view that the Secretary of State was not entitled to define the lands covered by the byelaws within the byelaws by reference to signs, but since the Secretary of State is obliged once the byelaws have been made to cause the boundaries of the area to be marked, we agree with the Lord Advocate that he is entitled when making the byelaws to make reference to signs. In any event, however, the description of the military lands which is made by reference to the pecked black line on the plan is in our opinion unambiguous and is not void from uncertainty. It follows that counsel's submission on this matter is not well founded.

Counsel who appeared for the appellant Ian Richardson adopted the submission of counsel for the third appellant.

Counsel who appeared for the appellants Alan Crawford, Ross Main, Ruth Dawes, Andrew Medley, David Bezzant, Peter Russel, and Brian Henry adopted counsel for the third appellant's argument to the effect that the byelaws were void from uncertainty. She also submitted a number of other arguments on behalf of the appellants whom she represented.

In particular counsel criticised that part of the sheriff's note where he drew a clear distinction between the first part of s. 17(1) dealing with the situation before byelaws were made, and the second part of the subsection dealing with the situation when byelaws had been made. In our opinion, however, the sheriff was correct to distinguish between the two parts of the subsection. Before making byelaws under the Act the Secretary of State requires to perform the duties imposed upon him by the first part of s. 17(1). If he fails to carry out these duties, the consequence may well be that the byelaws would be held to be invalid. Once the byelaws have been made the Secretary of State must carry out the duties imposed upon him by the second part of s. 17(1). If he fails to do so, that would not invalidate the byelaws although it might enable an accused person to have a good defence to a charge brought against him under the byelaws. However that may be, the question of whether or not the Secretary of State complied with the duties upon him under s. 17(1) raises questions of fact which can only be determined once evidence has been led.

Counsel appreciated that questions of fact did arise, but she maintained that such questions of fact should not be determined in the course of a trial but that the proper course would have been for the sheriff to hear evidence while he was hearing the debate on the competency of the complaint. She drew attention to the cases of *Tudhope v. Lawson* and *McCartney v. Tudhope*. There may be cases where it would be appropriate for a sheriff to hear evidence while hearing a debate on competency. Thus when an issue of time bar arises under s. 331 of the act of 1975, and the question is whether a warrant has been executed without undue delay, it may be appropriate and necessary for a sheriff to hear evidence upon this matter. Such evidence would come from the police and possibly the procurator fiscal's department. The situation however would be entirely different in a case like the present appeals where an issue arises as to the steps, if any, which the Secretary of State had taken both before and after making the byelaws. On this issue evidence might well be adduced not merely by the representatives of the Secretary of State but by the appellants who might wish to testify that they had been given no opportunity to object and that any steps which had been taken had been inadequate for the purposes of making the byelaws known to persons living in the vicinity. On such issues it might be necessary for the sheriff to assess the credibility of the appellants or any of them who offered evidence. It would, in our opinion, be quite undesirable that at the stage of competency the credibility of an accused person was being determined by the sheriff when the same sheriff might take the trial of that accused in the event of the complaint being held to be competent. Moreover the facts which would be relevant to the issues raised under s. 17(1) would clearly be intermingled with the facts relevant to the commission of the alleged offence, and this is a further reason for concluding that no evidence regarding the facts should be heard by the sheriff at the stage of his considering the pleas to competency.

There appeared to be some apprehension on the part of the appellants that if the pleas to competency were repelled, they would then be unable at their trial to challenge the byelaws. This would not be so. In the course of his note the sheriff has drawn attention to the provisions of ss. 312 (*q*) and 353 (2) of the Criminal Procedure (Scotland) Act 1975. The former provision makes it plain that the terms of the complaint imply inter alia that any necessary preliminary procedure had been duly gone through, and that the byelaws were duly made, published and made effectual and were in force at the time and place in question. However in terms of the latter provision it is plain that the accused would be entitled at their trial to challenge the byelaws as being ultra vires or as being incompetent upon some other ground. In all the circumstances we are satisfied that in the present cases the sheriff was well entitled to conclude that he should not hear evidence at the stage of hearing the pleas to competency but that the appellants would have the right, if so advised, to challenge the competency of the byelaws in the course of their trials.

Counsel also founded upon the provisions of s. 14 (1) of the Act of 1892. In this connection she criticised the provision of reg. 2 (2) upon the ground that these regulations appeared to govern the public use of the land and were not within the scope of byelaws which the Secretary of State was entitled to make under s. 14(1). That subsection empowers the Secretary of State to make byelaws for regulating the use of the land for the purposes to which it is appropriated and for securing the public against danger arising from that use. In our opinion this issue could not be determined until the facts had been established in the course of a trial. As already indicated the appellants will be entitled, if so advised, to challenge the byelaws as being ultra vires at their trial, and at this stage when there is no evidence before the court no opinion can be expressed upon the question of ultra vires.

[The court then dealt with matters with which this report is not concerned, and continued:]

In all the circumstances we were satisfied that the pleas to competency had not been made out at this stage and that the sheriff had arrived at the correct conclusion when he resolved to repel these pleas to competency. For these reasons we affirmed the decision of the sheriff and remitted the case to him to proceed as accords."

Notes

(1) This case is a straightforward application of the ability to challenge delegated legislation **2–33** by way of a defence to criminal proceedings. It is a specific example of the use of the defence of illegality noted in Chapter —. For other examples see *MacGillivray v. Johnston (No. 2)*, 1994 S.L.T. 1012; *H.M. Advocate v. Sutherland*, 1993 S.L.T. 404; and *Hingston v. McGuigan* below. Note that the court did not simply treat all of the byelaw as potentially invalid. A distinction was made between the Secretary of State's duty before making byelaws and after making byelaws. Although the language of mandatory/directory requirements is not used, does this underlie the court's approach? On this see para. 5–5. Sections 312(*q*) and 353(2) of the 1975 Act referred to in the judgment have been re-enacted in terms of Schedule 3, para. 12 of the Criminal Procedure (Scotland) Act 1995 as follows:

> "12. In a complaint charging a contravention of an enactment—
> (a) the statement that an act was done contrary to an enactment shall imply a statement—
>> (i) that the enactment applied to the circumstances existing at the time and place of the offence;
>> (ii) that the accused was a person bound to observe the enactment;
>> (iii) that any necessary preliminary procedure had been duly gone through; and
>> (iv) that all the circumstances necessary to a contravention existed,
> and, in the case of the contravention of a subordinate instrument, such statement shall imply a statement that the instrument was duly made, confirmed, published and generally made effectual according to the law applicable, and was in force at the time and place in question."

These provisions apply equally to indictments under solemn procedure: section 64(6). This carries with it the implication that an accused person must be careful to ensure that a plea as to the relevancy or competency is taken at the appropriate point, albeit it would appear that evidence on the matter of the validity of the instrument must be heard during the trial. Failure to take a plea will preclude later challenge. In *Macqueen v. Hingston*, 1998 S.L.T. 573 an accused person made no plea to the relevancy or competency of a violation of the Skye Bridge toll order but at the end of the Crown's case made a submission of no case to answer on the basis that the Crown had failed to prove that the necessary notice had been published and that they had also failed to prove that the toll period was running on the date of the alleged offence. Having regards to the terms of Schedule 3, the High Court held that even though the second ground of challenge appeared to be an arguable one, the absence of a plea to the relevancy having been timeously stated, the court could not now look at the *vires* of the Order.

Effect of Challenge

Challenge to delegated legislation can result in the instrument in question being struck **2–34** down in its entirety or in part. Partial invalidity is not without difficulty, as we will note at para. 000 in relation to reduction.

D.P.P. v. Hutchinson

[1990] 2 All E.R. 836

"The Secretary of State was empowered to make byelaws for land appropriated for military purposes **2–35** under the Military Lands Act 1892, s. 14(1). The power allowed for byelaws which could prohibit intrusion onto such land but did not permit any prejudicial affect on any right in common. The Secretary of State made the RAF Greenham Common Byelaws 1985 in respect of common land which had been appropriated for military purposes. Byelaw 2(b) provided that no person could enter or remain in the protected area without the permission of an authorised person. Protestors against nuclear weapons, who camped on the protected land, were charged and convicted of infringing byelaw 2(b). The Crown Court allowed the appeal on the basis that it was ultra vires as it prejudiced the rights of commoners. This decision was overturned by the Divisional Court on an appeal by case stated. The defendants appealed to the House of Lords."

Lord Bridge: "My Lords, these two appeals raise important questions as to the tests to be applied in determining whether delegated legislation which on its face exceeds the power conferred upon the legislator may nevertheless be upheld and enforced by the courts in part on the basis that the legislation is divided into good or bad parts and then the good is independent of, and untainted by, the bad.

When a legislative instrument made by a law-maker with limited powers is challenged, the only function of the court is to determine whether there has been a valid exercise of the limited legislative power in relation to the matter which is the object of disputed enforcement. If a law-maker has validly exercised his power, the court may give effect to the law validly made. But if the court sees only an invalid law made in excess of the law-maker's power, it has no jurisdiction to modify or adapt the law to bring it within the scope of the law-maker's power. These, I believe, are the basic principles which have always to be borne in mind in deciding whether legislative provision, which on their face exceed the law-maker's power may be severed so as to be upheld and enforced in part.

The application of these principles leads naturally and logically to what has traditionally been regarded as the test of severability. It is often referred to inelegantly as the 'blue pencil' test. Taking the simplest case of a single legislative instrument containing a number of separate clauses of which one exceeds the law-maker's power, if the remaining clauses enact free-standing provisions which were intended to operate and are capable of operating independently of the offending clause, there is no reason why those clauses should not be upheld and enforced. The law-maker has validly exercised his power by making the valid clauses. The invalid clause may be disregarded as unrelated to, and having no effect upon, the operation of the valid clauses, which accordingly may be allowed to take effect without the necessity of any modification or adaptation by the court. What is involved is in truth a double test. I shall refer to the two aspects of the test as textual severability and substantial severability. A legislative instrument is textually severable if a clause, a sentence, a phrase or a single word may be disregarded, as exceeding the law-maker's power, and what remains of the text is still grammatical and coherent. A legislative instrument is substantially severable if the substance of what remains after severance is essentially unchanged in its legislative purpose, operation and effect.

The early English authorities take it for granted, I think, that if byelaws are to be upheld as good in part notwithstanding that they are bad in part, they must be both textually and substantially severable... .

Our attention has been drawn to a number of more recent English authorities on the severability of provisions contained in various documents of a public law character. I doubt if these throw much light on the specific problem of severance in legislative instruments. The modern authority most directly in point and that on which the Divisional Court relied is *Dunkley v. Evans* [1981] 1 W.L.R. 1522. The West Coast Herring (Prohibition of Fishing) Order 1978 (S.I. 1978 No. 930) prohibited fishing for herring in an area defined in the Schedule to the Order as within a line drawn by reference to coordinates and coastlines. The Order was made by the Minister of Agriculture, Fisheries and Food under the Sea Fish (Conservation) Act 1967. The prohibited area included a stretch of sea adjacent to the coast of Northern Ireland, representing 0.8 per cent of the total area covered by the Order, to which the enabling power in the Act of 1967 did not extend. The defendants admitted fishing in a part of the prohibited area to which the enabling power did extend but submitted that, by including the area to which the enabling power did not extend, the Minister had acted ultra vires and, since textual severance was not possible, the whole Order was invalid. The justices accepted this submission and dismissed the informations. The Divisional Court allowed the prosecutor's appeal. Delivering the judgment of the court, Ormrod LJ cited, at pp. 1524–1525, the following passage from the judgment of Cussen J in the Supreme Court of Victoria in *Olsen v. City of Camberwell* [1926] VLR 58, 68:

> 'If the enactment, with the invalid portion omitted, is so radically or substantially different a law as to the subject matter dealt with by what remains from what it would be with the omitted portions forming part of it as to warrant a belief that the legislative body intended it as a whole only, or, in other words, to warrant a belief that if all could not be carried into effect the legislative body would not have enacted the remainder independently, then the whole must fail.'

It is to be noted that this quotation is from the judgment in a case where textual severance was possible. Following the quotation the judgment of Ormrod LJ continued:

> We respectfully agree with and adopt this statement of the law. It would be difficult to imagine a clearer example than the present case of a law which the legislative body would have enacted independently of the offending portion and which is so little affected by eliminating the invalid portion. This is clearly, therefore, an order which the court should not strive officiously to kill to any greater extent than it is compelled to do... . We can see no reason why the powers of the court to sever the invalid portion of a piece of subordinate legislation from the valid should be restricted

to cases where the text of the legislation lends itself to judicial surgery, or textual emendation by excision. It would have been competent for the court in an action for a declaration that the provisions of the Order in this case did not apply to the area of the sea off Northern Ireland reserved by section 23(1) of the Act of 1967, as amended, to make the declaration sought, without in any way affecting the validity of the Order in relation to the remaining 99.2 per cent of the area referred to in the Schedule to the Order. Such an order was made, in effect, by the House of Lords in *Hotel and Catering Industry Training Board v. Automobile Proprietary Ltd* [1969] 1 WLR 697, and by Donaldson J in *Agricultural, Horticultural and Forestry Industry Training Board v. Aylesbury Mushrooms Ltd* [1972] 1 WLR 190… .

The modern English authority to which I attach most significance is *Daymond v. Plymouth City Council* [1976] AC 609, where severability was not in issue, but where it appears to have been taken for granted without question that severance was possible. Section 30(1) of the Water Act 1973 gave power to water authorities:

to fix, and to demand, take and recover such charges for the services performed, facilities provided or rights made available by them (including separate charges for separate services, facilities or rights or combined charges for a number of services, facilities or rights) as they think fit.

The subsection was silent as to who was liable to pay the charges. The Water Authorities (Collection of Charges) Order 1974 (SI 1974 No. 448) embodied provisions which required a rating authority to collect on behalf of a water authority a 'general services charge' (article 7(2)) referable to sewerage services 'from every person who is liable to pay the general rate in respect of a hereditament… .' (article 10(1)). A householder whose property was not connected to a sewer, the nearest sewer being 400 yards away from his house, refused to pay the charge and brought an action for a declaration that the Order could not properly apply to him. This House held, by a majority of three to two, that on the true construction of the enabling legislation there was no power to impose a charge for sewerage services upon occupiers of property not connected to a sewer. As I have said, the question of severability was not raised, but there is no hint in the speeches that the invalidation of the charging provision in relation to properties not connected to sewers would affect their validity in relation to properties which were so connected.

The text of textual severability has the great merit of simplicity and certainty. When it is satisfied the court can readily see whether the omission from the legislative text of so much as exceeds the law-maker's power leaves in place a valid text which is capable of operating and was evidently intended to operate independently of the invalid text. But I have reached the conclusion, though not without hesitation, that a rigid insistence that the test of textual severability must always be satisfied if a provision is to be upheld and enforced as partially valid will in some cases, of which *Dunkley v. Evans* and *Daymond v. City Council* are good examples, have the unreasonable consequence of defeating subordinate legislation of which the substantial purpose and effect was clearly within the law-maker's power when, by some oversight or misapprehension of the scope of that power, the text, as written, has a range of application which exceeds that scope. It is important, however, that in all cases an appropriate test of substantial severability should be applied. When textual severance is possible, the test of substantial severability will be satisfied when the valid text is unaffected by, and independent of, the invalid. The law which the court may then uphold and enforce is the very law which the legislator has enacted, not a different law. But when the court must modify the text in order to achieve severance, this can only be done when the court is satisfied that it is effecting no change in the substantial purpose and effect of the impugned provision. Thus, in *Dunkley v. Evans*, the legislative purpose and effect of the prohibition of fishing in the large area of the sea in relation to which the minister was authorised to legislate was unaffected by the obviously inadvertent inclusion of the small area of sea to which his power did not extend. In *Daymond v. Plymouth City Council* the draftsman of the Order had evidently construed the enabling provision as authorising the imposition of charges for sewerage services upon occupiers of property irrespective of whether or not they were connected to sewers. In this error he was in the good company of two members of your Lordships' House. But this extension of the scope of the charging power, which, as the majority held, exceeded its proper limit, in no way affected the legislative purpose and effect of the charging power as applied to occupiers of properties which were connected to sewers.

To appreciate the full extent of the problem presented by the Greenham byelaws it is necessary to set out the full text of the prohibitions imposed by byelaw 2 which provides

No person shall (a) enter or leave or attempt to enter or leave the protected area except by way of an authorised entrance or exit; (b) enter, pass through or over or remain on or over the protected area without authority or permission given by or on behalf of one of the persons mentioned in byelaw 5(1); (c) cause or permit any vehicle, animal, aircraft or thing to enter into or upon or to pass through or over or to be or remain in or upon or over the protected area without authority or permission given by or on behalf of one of the persons mentioned in byelaw 5(1); (d) remain in the protected area after having been directed to leave by any of the persons mentioned in byelaw 4; (e) make any false statement, either orally or in writing or employ any other form of misrepresentation in order to obtain entry to any part of the protected area or to any building or premises within the protected area; (f) obstruct any constable (including a constable under the control of the Defence Council) or any other person acting in the proper exercise or execution of his duty within the protected area; (g) enter any part of the protected area which is shown by a notice as being prohibited or restricted; (h) board, attempt to board, or interfere with, or interfere with the movement of passage, of any vehicle, aircraft or other installation in the protected area; (i) distribute or display any handbill, leaflet, sign, advertisement, circular, poster, bill, notice or object within the protected area or affix the same to either side of the perimeter fences without authority or permission given by or on behalf of one of the persons mentioned in byelaw 5(1); (j) interfere with or remove from the protected area any property under the control of the Crown or the service authorities of a visiting force or, in either case, their agents or contractors; (k) wilfully damage, destroy, deface or remove any notice board or sign within the protected area; (l) wilfully damage; soil, deface or mark any wall, fence, structure, floor, pavement, or other surface within the protected area.

It is at once apparent that paragraphs (a), (b), (c), (d), (g), (j) and (l) are ultra vires as they stand. Paragraphs (e), (f), (i) and (k) appear to be valid and paragraph (h) is probably good in part and bad in part, since the exercise by a commoner of his rights may well interfere with the movement or passage of vehicles. Textual severance can achieve nothing since it is apparent that the valid provisions are merely ancillary to the invalid provisions... .

I think the proper test to be applied when textual severance is impossible, following in this respect the Australian authorities, is to abjure speculation as to what the maker of the law might have done if he had applied his mind to the relevant limitation on his powers and to ask whether the legislative instrument

> with the invalid portions omitted would be substantially a different law as to the subject matter dealt with by what remains from what it would be with the omitted portions forming part of it: *Rex v. Commonwealth Court of Conciliation and Arbitration, Ex parte Whybrow & Co.* 11 C.L.R. 1, 27.

In applying this test the purpose of the legislation can only be inferred from the term as applied to the factual situation to which its provisions relate. Considering the Greenham byelaws as a whole it is clear that the absolute prohibition which they impose upon all unauthorised access to the protected area is no less than is required to maintain the security of an establishment operated as a military airbase and wholly enclosed by a perimeter fence. Byelaws drawn in such a way as to permit free access to all parts of the base to persons exercising rights of common and their animals would be byelaws of a totally different character. They might serve some different legislative purpose in a different factual situation, as do some other byelaws to which our attention has been drawn relating to areas used as military exercise grounds or as military firing ranges. But they would be quite incapable of serving the legislative purpose which the Greenham byelaws, as drawn, are intended to serve.

For these reasons I conclude that the invalidity of byelaw 2(b) cannot be cured by severance. It follows that the appellants were wrongly convicted and I would allow their appeals, set aside the order of the Divisional Court and restore the order of the Crown Court at Reading."

[*Lords Griffith, Goff and Oliver concurred with Lord Bridge.*]

Lord Lowry: "... My Lords, the accepted view in the common law jurisdictions has been that, when construing legislation the validity of which is under challenge, the first duty of the court, in obedience to the principle that a law should, whenever possible, be interpreted ut res magis valeat quam pereat, is to see whether the impugned provision can reasonably bear a construction which renders it valid. Failing that, the court's duty, subject always to any relevant statutory provision such as the Australian section 15A, is to decide whether the whole of the challenged legislation or only part of it must be held invalid and ineffective. That problem has traditionally been resolved by applying first the textual, and then the substantial, severability test. If the legislation failed the first test, it was condemned in its entirety. If it passed that test, it had to face the next hurdle. This approach, in my opinion, has a great deal in its favour.

The basic principle is that an ultra vires enactment, such as a byelaw, is void ab initio and of no effect. The so-called blue pencil test is a concession to practicality and ought not to be extended or weakened. In its traditional form it is acceptable because, once the offending words are ignored, no word or phrase needs to be given a meaning different from, or more restrictive than, its original meaning. Therefore the court has not legislated; it merely continues to apply that part of the existing legislation which is good.

It may be argued that a policy split has developed and that it is time to show common sense and bring our thinking up to date by a further application of the ut res magis valeat quam pereat principle. I am, however, chary of yielding to this temptation for a number of reasons. 1. The blue pencil test already represents a concession to the erring law-maker, the justification for which I have tried to explain. 2. When applying the blue pencil test (which actually means ignoring the offending words, the court cannot cause the text of the instrument to be altered. It will remain as the ostensible law of the land unless and until it is replaced by something else. It is too late now to think of abandoning the blue pencil method, which has much to commend it, but the disadvantage inherent in the method ought not to be enlarged. 3. It is up to the law-maker to keep within his powers and it is in the public interest that he should take care, in order that the public may be able to rely on the written word as representing the law. Further enlargement of the court's power to validate what is partially invalid will encourage the law-maker to enact what he pleases, or at least to enact what may or may not be valid, without having to fear any worse result than merely being brought back within bounds. 4. *Dunkley v. Evans* [1981] 1 WLR, 1522 and *Thames Water Authority v. Elmbridge Borough Council* [1983] QB, 570 are very special cases. I recall in that regard what McNeill J said in *Reg. v. Secretary of State for Transport, Ex parte Greater London Council* [1986] QB 556, 582D, 5. To liberalise the test would, in my view, be anarchic, not progressive. It would tend in the wrong direction, unlike some developments in the law of negligence, which have promoted justice for physically or economically injured persons, or the sounder aspects of judicial review, which have promoted freedom and have afforded protection from power. 6. The current of decisions and relevant authority has flowed in favour of the traditional doctrine.

This last observation brings me back to *Daymond v. Plymouth City Council* [1976] AC 609, the case in which, as my noble and learned friend has said, it appears to have been taken for granted that severance was possible, and the question is, what significance should be attached to that fact when reviewing the doctrine of textual severability?

One cannot gainsay the authority of the Appellate Committee or that of the individual members of your Lordships' House of whom the committee was composed. Any indication, even if given obiter, that their Lordships, having considered the point, would have held that the Water Authorities (Collection of Charges) Order 1974 was valid and effective against occupiers of property who benefited directly from the water authority's services while inoperative against the occupiers who did not so benefit, could significantly erode the received doctrine of textual severability, since the blue pencil test could not have been used. But one must consider the way in which the case proceeded in your Lordships' House and also at first instance.

The remedy which the plaintiff sought was a declaration that the Plymouth City Council were not empowered to demand from him £4.89 or any sum on behalf of the South West Water Authority by way of a charge for sewerage and sewage disposal services. He contended that the water authority had power under section 30 of the Act of 1973 only to demand charges for services performed, facilities provided or rights made available and that, if the Order of 1974 purported to confer power to demand other charges, it was *to that event* ultra vires. The words which I have emphasised set the stage for the argument and the decision. Phillips J. made the declaration sought. On appeal direct to this House under section 12(1) of the Administration of Justice Act 1969 it was held, dismissing the appeal, Lord Wilberforce and Lord Diplock dissenting, that the plaintiff was entitled to the declaration made. The sole issue at each stage was whether section 30 empowered the water authority to charge occupiers of property who did not receive the benefit of the authority's services directly. No case was cited, and no argument was advanced, on the question whether the invalidity of the authority's demand against such occupiers as the plaintiff would nullify the Order of 1974 in relation to occupiers who were receiving the services, and both the initial judgment and their Lordships' speeches were entirely devoted to the complicated and strenuously contested issue concerning the scope of section 30. The minority took the view that section 30 authorised the proposed demand, and they had nothing to consider except the effect of the section on the plaintiff. And the majority, who reached the opposite conclusion, were concerned with the same point. The textual severability doctrine would have been of no help to either side.

It would therefore not be surprising if, having regard to the remedy sought and granted, the residual effect of the Order of 1974 on those who admittedly were liable for the charge was never mentioned.

I am therefore very reluctant to treat the case as an authority which by implication contradicts the established doctrine of textual severability for the purposes of the present appeal. Accordingly, I would allow this appeal on two grounds, (1) that there is no valid part of byelaw 2(b) which can be severed from the invalid part and stand by itself and (2) that the byelaw would not in any event survive the test of substantial severability."

Notes

2–36   There appears to be a difference in approach here. In particular, Lord Lowry appears to be taking a narrower view of the court's ability to sever the offending part of the instrument. In the view of A. W. Bradley, "Judicial Enforcement of Ultra Vires Byelaws" [1989] P.L. 1 and [1990] P.L. 293 his Lordship "had the edge in terms of the previous authorities". Underlying this approach is clearly a concern that the courts should not be carrying out the job of legislating when he stated (p. 850) that:

> "It is up to the lawmaker to keep within his powers and it is in the public interest that he should take care, in order that the public may be able to rely on the written word as representing the law."

On the facts it would certainly appear that the Ministry of Defence were aware of the limitation on their powers but appear to have acted in disregard of that. The decision in *Hutchison* was subsequently applied by the House of Lords in *R. v. Inland Revenue Commissioners, ex parte Woolwich Equitable Building Society* [1990] 1 W.L.R. 1400. Here it was contended by the Inland Revenue that even if part of the regulation in question was *ultra vires* it could be severed from the rest of the regulation. However, the fact that this could be deleted without altering the sense of what was left was insufficient to avoid total invalidity as it was "beyond argument" that the regulation without the offending part:

> "is in substance quite different from the regulation which the draftsman actually produced and intended... . What form the regulation might have taken if the invalidity of paragraph (4) had been appreciated is a matter of pure speculation" (*per* Lord Oliver at 1415).

THE SCOPE OF REVIEW

2–37   We will note in Chapter 6 that *ultra vires* can embrace not just simple cases of illegality, but also the way in which a discretion is exercised. The courts accept that this distinction is valid in the review of delegated legislation. The extent to which in practice the grounds of challenge for abuse of discretion are available in relation to an instrument laid before Parliament is considered in the next extract.

City of Edinburgh District Council v. Secretary of State

1985 S.L.T. 551

2–38   Lord Jauncey: "In this action the pursuers seek to reduce that part of the Housing Revenue Account Rate Fund Contribution Limits (Scotland) Order 1985 (S.I. No. 3) (hereinafter referred to as 'the Order') which affects the city of Edinburgh. They also petition for suspension of the Order. Both actions came before me in procedure roll when the pursuers moved for decree de plano, alternatively for a proof before answer in the action. In the former event no order would be required in the petition. The defender moved me to dismiss both actions as irrelevant. The pursuers intimated that in the event of my allowing a proof before answer they would propose to move for an interim order in the petition.

In order to understand the basis of the action it is necessary to look at the statutory and administrative history preceding the Order. In terms of s. 23(1) of the Housing (Financial Provisions) (Scotland) Act 1972 local authorities were directed to keep a 'housing revenue account' of their income and expenditure in respect of council houses for the years 1972–73 and subsequent years. Paragraph 1 of Sched. 4 to the 1972 Act provided that certain specified amounts, including income receivable from standard rates, should be carried to the credit of the housing revenue account and para. 2 provided that certain specified amounts, including loan charges, should be debited to the housing revenue account. Paragraph 11(2) of the same Schedule, which was substituted by the Housing Rents and Subsidies (Scotland) Act 1975 provided that, if for any year a deficit was shown in the housing revenue account the local authority should carry to the credit of the account a rate fund contribution of an amount equal to the deficit. The practical effect of these provisions was that a deficit in the housing revenue account in a year had to be met out of the general rate fund. A local authority could only borrow capital for housing, or indeed for any other purposes, with the consent of the Secretary of State (s. 94(1) of the Local Government (Scotland) Act 1973).

From 1980 the Secretary of State operated a system of administrative controls over rate fund contribution to the housing revenue account. That system involved specifying for each local authority's rate fund contribution for the following year, a limit known as a housing expenditure limit. If an authority included in its estimates for the following year a rate fund contribution in excess of the housing expenditure limit an amount equal to the excess was deducted from the sum which the Secretary of State would otherwise have allowed the authority to borrow for capital expenditure on housing. Thus the greater the excess the less was there capital available to the authority.

Section 8 of the Rating and Valuation (Amendment) (Scotland) Act 1984 added to the 1972 Act a new s. 23A in terms of which the Secretary of State was empowered by order to impose on a local authority a limit to the amount of rate fund contribution which could be carried to the credit of the housing revenue account for the year specified in the Order. Any such order was to be made by statutory instrument subject to annulment by either House of Parliament. In the First Scottish Standing Committee on 28 February 1984 the Under-Secretary of State for Scotland stated, in relation to any order under the proposed s. 23A that 'the Government intend there to be informal consultations with COSLA and individual authorities before the order setting limits to rate fund contributions is laid'. The order which was made in pursuance of s. 23A imposed a rate fund contribution limit for the year 1985–86 on the 56 Scottish local authorities who were under obligation to keep a housing revenue account. The limit for the pursuers was £2.824 million.

Prior to the Order coming into operation, certain events took place. On 8 October the Minister for Home Affairs and the Environment, Scottish Office, announced to the Scottish committee of COSLA (the Convention of Scottish Local Authorities), that the government proposed to exercise their powers under s. 23A of the 1972 Act. The Minister said: "Against a general climate of restraint, the Government has to decide how much the nation can afford to devote to housing… .

By letter dated 1 November to the Scottish development department, the pursuers' director of administration stated inter alia: (1) that the effect of the proposed rate fund contribution limit of £2,548 million would be to put Edinburgh in a substantially worse position than the generality of the local authorities, (2) that Edinburgh's present level of rate fund contribution was £48.77 per house or 34.4 per cent of the Scottish average of £140.07, (3) that the new administration's policy was not to increase standard rent levels so long as they were above the Scottish average (the then excess being about 28 per cent) and to increase greatly the expenditure on normal housing maintenance and management. The letter asked the Secretary of State to reconsider the limit and to receive a deputation from the pursuers. By letter dated 22 November 1984 to the pursuers' director of administration the Scottish development department inter alia asked for further information on the pursuers' estimated income and expenditure on their housing revenue account in 1985–86 and stated that the Secretary of State considered that a meeting with Ministers would be premature but suggested that a meeting should take place between officials of the pursuers and the Scottish development department. On 29 November 1984 such a meeting took place at which a number of matters were raised. Suffice it to state that officials of the Scottish development department stated that Ministers would not be prepared to concede an increase in the rate fund contribution limit of the magnitude (more than £4 million) sought by the pursuers, but that in light of the representations made by the pursuers' officials they might be prepared to increase the limit by some £25,000 to the higher of the two limits set out in the letter of 12 October. The pursuers' officials repeated the request for representatives of the pursuers to meet Minsters. No such meeting took place. On 10 December 1984, the above mentioned Scottish Office Minister met representatives of COSLA in order to discuss a number of matters including the limits on rate fund contributions. The Minister stated inter alia: (1) that representations about the provisional limits had been received from a number of authorities and that the Secretary of State had decided to make adjustment to the limits of three authorities, namely, Badenoch and Strathspey, Orkney and Edinburgh; (2) that the aggregate limit of £90 million or thereby would imply an average rent increase across Scotland of approximately £1.02 per house per week; (3) that such an increase was reasonable and would still leave Scottish rent levels a long way behind comparable levels in England and Wales. An official of the Scottish development department answering an Edinburgh councillor present at the meeting stated that Edinburgh was an exception in that its estimated rate fund contribution for 1984–85 had been more than 10 per cent below the housing expenditure limit for that year. In these circumstances the Secretary of State had raised the rate fund contribution limit to a figure 10 per cent below the housing expenditure limit. By formal letter of 21 December 1984, the Scottish development department informed the pursuers that their provisional rate fund contribution limit had been increased by £0.276 million to £2.824 million. On 4 January 1985 the Order was made and on 11 January it was laid before Parliament. ON 23 January it was debated in the House of Commons, but a prayer to annul it was not moved and it came into operation on 2 February 1985.

The grounds of reduction relied upon by the pursuers are threefold, namely, illegality, irrationality and impropriety of procedure. These are the three grounds referred to by Lord Diplock at p. 1196 in *Council of Civil Service Unions v. Minister for the Civil Service* as those on which administrative action is subject to control by judicial review. The defender challenged the application of the second and third grounds to a statutory instrument considered by Parliament and I must, therefore, first of all consider to what extent such an instrument may be the subject of judicial review. No example of a statutory instrument having been reduced or quashed on any of the foregoing grounds was cited to me. However, there appears to be no doubt that such an event could take place on the ground of illegality in what I would describe as the narrower sense. In *F. Hoffman-La Roche and Co. v. Secretary of State for Trade and Industry*, the respondent sought an injunction pending a decision in an action by the appellants claiming declarations that the procedures adopted by the monopolies commission were contrary to the rules of natural justice and that an order made by the respondent pursuant to s. 3(4) of the Monopolies and Mergers Act 1965 ordering the appellants to reduce the prices of certain drugs was ultra vires and invalid. The House of Lords held that one of the factors which had to be taken into account in determining whether the Crown should be required to give an undertaking as a condition of being granted the injunction was the likelihood of the order being held to be ultra vires. Lord Wilberforce at p. 354G said: 'That an attack can be made on a statutory instrument for want of power needs no demonstration, and I agree with your Lordships that it makes no difference, for this purpose, that the instrument has been laid before and approved by the two Houses of Parliament.' Lord Diplock at p. 365B put the matter this way: 'My Lords, in constitutional law a clear distinction can be drawn between an Act of Parliament and subordinate legislation, even though the latter is contained in an order made by statutory instrument approved by resolutions of both Houses of Parliament. Despite his indication that the majority of members of both Houses of the contemporary Parliament regard the order as being for the common weal, I entertain no doubt that the courts have jurisdiction to declare it to be invalid if they are satisfied that in making it the Minister who did so acted outwith the legislative powers conferred upon him by the previous Act of Parliament under which the order is ultra vires by reason of its contents (patent defects) or by reason of defects in the procedure followed prior to its being made (latent defects).' The pursuers argued that Lord Diplock's reference to latent defects applied not only to defects in the procedure prescribed by statute but to other illegalities and also to irrationality of approach and general impropriety in procedure such as unfairness or failure adequately to consider representation. It should here be stated that the ground of challenge of the statutory order in the *Hoffman-La Roche* case related to statutory procedure in as much as an order under s. 3(4) of the Monopolies and Mergers Act 1965 required to be preceded by a report of the monopolies commission. If the report was invalid, it would follow that any statutory order consequent thereupon would also be invalid. Thus on the face of it there are grounds for thinking that Lord Diplock only had in mind defects in statutory procedure. However, it would be unwise to consider this passage in isolation without looking at some of the other authorities on judicial review.

The appropriate starting point is the judgment of Lord Greene M.R. in *Associated Provincial Picture Houses Ltd v. Wednesbury Corporation*, where he enunciated what has become known as the *Wednesbury* doctrine in relation to judicial review of executive authority. At p. 228 the Master of the Rolls said: 'When an executive discretion is entrusted by Parliament to a body such as the local authority in this case, what appears to be an exercise of that discretion can only be challenged in the courts in a strictly limited class of case. As I have said, it must always be remembered that the court is not a court of appeal. When discretion of this kind is granted the law recognises certain principles upon which that discretion must be exercised, but within the four corners of those principles the discretion, in my opinion, is an absolute one and cannot be questioned in any court of law. What then are those principles? They are well understood. They are principles which the court looks to in considering any question of discretion of this kind. The exercise of such a discretion must be a real exercise of the discretion.' Lord Greene later summarised the position at pp. 233–4 in the following terms: 'I do not wish to repeat myself but I will summarise once again the principle applicable. The court is entitled to investigate the action of the local authority with a view to seeing whether they have taken into account matters which they ought not to take into account, or, conversely, have refused to take into account or neglected to take into account. Once that question is answered in favour of the local authority, it may be still possible to say that, although the local authority have kept within the four corners of the matters which they ought to consider, they have nevertheless come to a conclusion so unreasonable that no reasonable authority could ever have come to it. In such a case, again, I think the court can interfere. The power of the court to interfere in each case is not as an appellate authority to override a decision of the local authority, but as a judicial authority which is concerned, and concerned only, to see whether the local authority have contravened the law by acting in excess of the powers which Parliament has confided in them.'

In *Mixnam's Properties Ltd v. Chertsey Urban District Council*, Diplock L.J. at pp. 237–8 said: 'Thus, the kind of unreasonableness which invalidates a by-law is not the antonym of 'reasonableness' in the sense of which that expression is used in the common law, but such manifest arbitrariness, injustice or partiality that a court would say: "Parliament never intended to give authority to make such rules; they are unreasonable and ultra vires".' The *Wednesbury* doctrine was further considered in *Secretary of State for Education and Science v. Tameside Metropolitan Borough Council* in relation to a direction given by a Minister to an education authority under s. 68 of the Education Act 1944. In the course of his speech Lord Diplock, after referring to the *Wednesbury* case said at p. 1065: 'the question for the court is, did the Secretary of State ask himself the right question and take reasonable steps to acquaint himself with the relevant information to enable him to answer it correctly?' Lord Diplock was thus addressing himself to the first question referred to by Lord Greene M.R. in his summary at pp. 233–4 in the *Wednesbury* case (supra). In relation to the question whether the education authority were proposing to act 'unreasonably', Lord Diplock at p. 1064 said that an unreasonable exercise of discretion necessitated 'conduct which no sensible authority acting with due appreciation of its responsibilities would have decided to adopt'. This observation is of course relevant to the second matter referred to by Lord Greene M.R. in his summary (supra) and could in appropriate circumstances equally well have applied to the exercise by a Minister of his discretion to give a direction under a statutory provision. Finally in *Council of Civil Service Unions v. Minister for the Civil Service*, the House of Lords had to consider the validity of an instruction by the Minister under an article of the Civil Service Order in Council 1982. AT p. 1196 Lord Diplock classified under three heads, the grounds upon which administrative action was subject to control by judicial review. These were as I have already remarked, illegality, irrationality and procedural impropriety. Lord Diplock proceeded: 'By "illegality" as a ground for judicial review I mean that the decision-maker must understand correctly the law that regulates his decision-making power and must give effect to it. Whether he has or not is par excellence a justiciable question to be decided, in the event of dispute, by those persons, the judges, by whom the judicial power of the state is exercisable.

'By "irrationality" I mean what can by now be succinctly referred to as "*Wednesbury* unreasonableness" (*Associated Provincial Picture Houses Ltd v. Wednesbury Corporation* [1948] 1 K.B. 223). It applies to a decision which is so outrageous in its defiance of logic or of accepted moral standards that no sensible person who had applied his mind to the question to be decided could have arrived at it. Whether a decision falls within this category is a question that judges by their training and experience should be well equipped to answer, or else there would be something badly wrong with our judicial system.... I have described the third head as "procedural impropriety" rather than failure to observe basic rules of natural justice or failure to act with procedural fairness towards the person who will be affected by the decision. This is because susceptibility to judicial review under this head covers also failure by an administrative tribunal to observe procedural rules that are expressly laid down in the legislative instrument by which its jurisdiction is conferred, even where such failure does not involve any denial of natural justice. But the instant case is not concerned with the proceedings of an administrative tribunal at all.' Since Lord Diplock's head of irrationality clearly echoes the second matter referred to by Lord Greene M.R. in his summary (supra) I assume that the matters referred to by Lord Greene in his first question are embraced within Lord Diplock's head of illegality. This head thus appears to go beyond the patent and latent defects referred to by him in *Hoffman-La Roche*. Lord Roskill at p. 1200, in relation to the phrase 'principles of natural justice', said: 'But that latter phrase must not in its turn be misunderstood or misused. It is not for the courts to determine whether a particular policy or particular decision taken in fulfilment of that policy are fair. We are only concerned with the manner in which those decisions have been taken and the extent of the duty to act fairly will vary greatly from case to case as indeed the decided cases since 1950 consistently show. Many features will come into play including the nature of the decision and the relationship of those involved on either side before the decision was taken.'

In all the foregoing cases except the *Hoffman-La Roche* case the court were considering situations in which Parliament had conferred upon a Minister or a local authority a decision making power exercisable entirely at their own hand. Once the decision had been made the courts alone could stop its implementation. When Lord Greene referred to an executive discretion being entrusted by Parliament to a body such as a local authority and Lord Diplock referred to Parliament never having 'intended to give authority to make such rules' they clearly had in mind a situation in which Parliament having conferred the power had thereafter no means of controlling the exercise thereof. If Parliament could not control the exercise the courts alone could intervene to protect the subject. However, such a situation is removed from that where Parliament having entrusted the power to a Minister retains a general measure of control over the exercise of that power. In the present case Parliament not only had but made use of the opportunity of considering the exercise by the Secretary of State of the power and having so considered did not limit or control that exercise in any way. To test the matter how could the courts label as irrational or unreasonable a decision which Parliament had expressly or impliedly approved? I do not think that they could. In Wade's *Administrative Law* the following passage occurs at p. 769: 'An Act of Parliament will normally require that rules or regulations made under the Act shall be laid before both Houses of Parliament. Parliament can then keep its eye upon them and provide opportunities for criticism. Rules or regulations laid before Parliament may be attacked on any ground. The object of the system is to keep them under general political control, so that criticism in Parliament is frequently on grounds of policy.'

As I have already remarked no authority was cited to me in which *Wednesbury* principles or principles of natural justice had been applied in relation to a statutory instrument. I do not, however, find this surprising in view of the important distinction to which I have above referred. In my view when Lord Diplock in *Hoffman-La Roche* referred to defects in procedure he had in mind defects in statutory procedure laid down in the enabling Act, for example, a duty to consult before making an order such as appears in s. 108B(5) of the Local Government (Scotland) Act 1973 which was added by s. 3 of the Rating and Valuation (Amendment) (Scotland) Act 1984. This is entirely comprehensible since Parliament, having passed primary legislation, cannot lawfully authorise departure therefrom or non-compliance therewith by a Minister without amendment of that legislation. Parliament, however, is well able to determine whether a Minister's decision has been taken fairly or rationally. In these circumstances I conclude that the courts can only hold to be ultra vires a statutory instrument which has been laid before and considered by Parliament where that instrument is patently defective in that it purports to do what is not authorised by the enabling statute or where the procedure followed in making that instrument departed from the requirements of the enabling statute.

It follows that the only question in the present case is whether the Order was illegal in the sense to which I have just referred. Illegality was raised for the first time in the third speech when the pursuers' senior counsel argued that the Order was patently defective in as much as s. 23A did not empower the Secretary of State to make an order which applied to all local authorities. He could only make an order which was selective as to local authorities or classes thereof. Two reasons were advanced in support of this proposition, namely: (1) that it was not open to the Secretary of State to impose a blanket nil rate fund contribution limit; and (2) that the provisions of s. 23A relating to 'a local authority or class thereof' contrasted with those of s. 108B of the Local Government (Scotland) ACt 1973 which clearly envisaged a blanket order as the norm with selectivity the exception. I was not persuaded by this argument. If the Secretary of State, instead of making one order with a schedule appended thereto, had made an individual order in relation to each local authority, there is no doubt that he would have been entitled to do so. I see nothing in s. 23A, either looked at alone or when contrasted with s. 108B which would prevent the Secretary of State adopting the more simple course of making one order with a schedule containing an individual limit for each local authority. The pursuers' argument on illegality therefore fails."

Notes

2–39   (1) The council reclaimed against the decision of Lord Jauncey but the Second Division unanimously adopted his reasoning. The judgment of the Inner House is also reported at 1985 S.L.T. 551.

(2) It will be seen that the court had little direct authority to assist it in deciding on the effect of the annulment resolution. To that extent the court was basing its decision on an analysis of its constitutional role at the most basic level. The only authority that could assist in any real sense was the decision in *F. Hoffmann-La Roche & Co. A.G. v. Secretary of State for Trade and Industry* [1975] A.C. 295 where Lord Diplock stated (at 365):

> "My Lords, in constitutional law a clear distinction can be drawn between an Act of Parliament and subordinate legislation, even though the latter is contained in an order made by statutory instrument approved by resolutions of both Houses of Parliament. Despite this indication that the majority of members of both Houses of the contemporary Parliament regard the order as being for the common weal, I entertain no doubt that the courts have jurisdiction to declare it to be invalid if they are satisfied that in making it the Minister who did so acted outwith the legislative powers conferred upon him by the previous Act of Parliament under which the order purported to be made, and this is so whether the order is ultra vires by reason of its contents (patent defects) or by reason of defects in the procedure followed prior to its being made (latent defects)."

On one interpretation this passage can be taken as a general proposition that all instruments are subject to review on all the available grounds of review. However, it was the alternative interpretation that was fastened on to by Lord Jauncey and subsequently by the Inner House, to the effect that (at 556):

> "the courts can only hold to be ultra vires a statutory instrument which has been laid before and considered by Parliament where that instrument is patently defective in that it purports to do what is not authorised by the enabling statute or where the procedure falls in making that instrument departed from the requirements of the enabling statute."

As Lord Jauncey had earlier reasoned that *Wednesbury* amounted to "irrationality" and that the other forms of unreasonableness mentioned by Lord Greene in *Wednesbury* amounted to "illegality". Irrationality and those of illegality go beyond the patent and latent defects identified by Lord Diplock in *Hoffmann-La Roche*. This severely restricts the grounds of review that are available. The decision has been subject to criticism by C. M. G. Himsworth, "Defining the Boundaries of Judicial Review", 1985 S.L.T. (News) 369 and A. Campbell, "Approval and Statutory Instruments", 1986 S.L.T. (News) 101. While conceding that direct authority is limited, Himsworth was particularly critical of the failure to follow the line taken by Lord Keith in the Outer House in *Malloch v. Aberdeen Corporation*, 1971 S.L.T. 245 at 248 which accepted that while defects in an Order may be anything other than patent, they may be reviewable. Procedural challenge, on the approach of Lord Jauncey, would seem to be limited to failure to carry through express statutory requirements — for example, a consultation requirement. There would seem to be little room for the further development in this context of common law doctrines of procedural control, such as that of legitimate expectation.

(3) In *R. v. Secretary of State for the Environment, ex parte Nottinghamshire County Council* [1986] A.C. 240 the House of Lords had to consider a challenge to the action by the Secretary of State under the Local Government, Planning and Land Act 1980 in relation to expenditure guidance issued by him to local authorities which had a directly restraining effect on their ability to conduct their financial affairs. Such guidance required the approval by resolution of the House of Commons. The authorities in question challenged the guidance on the ground, *inter alia*, that it was unreasonable in the sense of the *Wednesbury* decision, Lord Scarman noted, however (at 247):

> "But I cannot accept that it is constitutionally appropriate, save in very exceptional circumstances, for the courts to intervene on the ground of "unreasonableness" to quash guidance framed by the Secretary of State and by necessary implication approved by the House of Commons, the guidance being concerned with the limits of public expenditure by local authorities and the incidence of the tax burden as between taxpayers and ratepayers. Unless and until a statute provides otherwise, or it has been established that the Secretary of State has abused his power, these are matters of political judgment for him and for the House of Commons. They are not for the judges or your Lordships' House in its judicial capacity.
>
> For myself, I refuse in this case to examine the detail of the guidance or its consequences. My reasons are these. Such an examination by a court would be justified only if a prima facie case were to be shown for holding that the Secretary of State had acted in bad faith, or for an improper motive, or that the consequences of his guidance were so absurd that he must have taken leave of his senses."

See also *R. v. Secretary of State for the Environment, ex parte Hammersmith and Fulham London Borough Council* [1991] 1 AC 521. Campbell, above, argues that Lord Scarman's judgment is less restrictive in theory than that of Lord Jauncey given the possibility of challenge based on bad faith, impropriety or patent unreasonableness. Do you agree? In any event, Lord Scarman's dicta came to be examined by Lord Penrose in *East Kilbride District Council v. Secretary of State for Scotland*, 1995 S.L.T. 1238 where it was held (at 1247) that:

> "These authorities appear clearly to indicate that as the law has developed in England the court has jurisdiction to consider and, if appropriate, to reduce an order subject to parliamentary procedure inter alia upon the ground of manifest absurdity. In the circumstances such a task must be demanding indeed, allowing as of necessity it does for the range of freedom available to Parliament to reach

decisions for reasons that may not generally withstand rational and objective analysis outside the political sphere. It would, of course, tend to negative the proposition by counsel for the respondent that Members of Parliament are entitled to be absurd, at least in those situations in which the absurdity is manifest on a rational consideration of their conduct. But on any view the test is exacting. There are, in my opinion, conceptual difficulties if the test is more than a recognition of the possibilities that supervening circumstances, or the identification of some order, and which had been overlooked by the minister and by Parliament alike, might undermine the making of the order and lead to its reduction. It is difficult to envisage circumstances in which this could occur other than at the instance of or with the consent of the minister. One might think that manifest absurdity must be such as to attract the common consent of the potential parties to a dispute as to the validity of the order in question. If there were scope for dispute as to the absurdity or degree of absurdity of consequences of an order, so that there was room for legitimate differences of opinion on the matter, then, on conventional constitution theory, one might expect the courts to recognise that they did not have jurisdiction to interfere with an order which had the express or implied consent of Parliament. Analysed strictly, Lord Jauncey's views might be thought too narrow. Mala fides and improper motive are recognised grounds of challenge, important in theory if seldom applied in contemporary practice. Manifest absurdity may well have a similar place in theoretical analysis. But it does not follow that Lord Jauncey omitted anything of practical application or substance in this field. Leaving aside those measures which are exclusively within the control of the House of Commons, what one has to envisage is a situation in which, at the final stage of the judicial process, members of an Appellate Committee of the House of Lords may characterise as manifestly absurd an order previously laid before that House and either expressly or impliedly approved by that House, of which at the time they, or certainly some of them, were members. Applied objectively, a test of manifest absurdity must be expected to be satisfied only in the most extreme and extraordinary of circumstances, and wholly beyond the scope for differences in matters of judgment and opinion.... It is far from clear to me that the redistribution of revenue account items could ever be a ground of challenge in circumstances such as the present. As matters stand it appears clearly from the financial statement prepared by the petitioners that council tax revenue will be diverted from East Kilbride to Eastwood District Council as an inevitable consequence of the redefinition of the local authority area in which the residents of the eastern part of Busby reside. That is an inevitable consequence of a boundary change involving an inhabited area. Further, since the setting of the council tax must take account of the expenditure of East Kilbride within its own local authority area, and since the removal was, at the material time, prospective, then given the opportunities that East Kilbride had to co-operate with other relevant authorities in selecting a date that would have fitted best the financial structure of their budgeting for expenditure and income, it is difficult to see that any substantial ground could exist for criticism of the Secretary of State in his selection of a date at the time he did with the notice he gave, and in the whole circumstances of the case. One might have expected a local authority acting reasonably to have taken account of the Secretary of State's intimated intention in budgeting for the changeover period and in determining the resources to be provided and funded in that period."

(4) Both Lords Jauncey and Lord Scarman were clearly influenced by the constitutional position of Parliament to the court. Do you consider that the Scottish Parliament will be regarded in a different light in view of its restricted legislative powers?

(5) The deferential approach in these cases was not evident in the scope of review on grounds of the reasonableness of social security regulations which were held *ultra vires* because they rendered nugatory rights of asylum seekers provided under separate asylum legislation: *R. v. Secretary of State for Social Security, ex parte Joint Council for the Welfare of Immigrants* [1996] 4 All E.R. 385. This suggests that at least where important individual rights are involved, a stricter degree of scrutiny may be applied. This of course has particular significance insofar as allegations of breach of Convention rights are made, whether under the provisions under the Human Rights Act 1998 or the Scotland Act 1998.

QUASI-LEGISLATION: GENERAL ISSUES AND CONTROL

2–40 It is accepted that administrative rule making, falling short of formal delegated legislation, is a significant part of current practice. R. Baldwin and J. Houghton, "Circular Arguments: The

Status and Legitimacy of Administrative Rules" [1986] P.L. 239 have identified eight forms of such rules including procedural rules, such as the prison rules, interpretative guides which are official statements of policy, how rules would be applied, instructions to officials such as Home Office circulars, prescriptive and evidential rules such as the HIghway Code, commendatory rules which can have the force of law such as the regulations made under the Health and Safety at Work etc. Act 1974 as simply stating desirable objectives such as guidance notes, notes issued by the Health and Safety Commission, voluntary codes such as the City Code on Takeovers and Mergers and management rules such as extra-statutory concessions issued by the Inland Revenue. Codes of Practice, circulars and guidance notes are perhaps the most significant. Such rules are almost always not subject to the Statutory Instruments Act 1946 and accordingly the various controls set down in the Act, as well as the other controls we shall examine, may only apply in part or sometimes not at all. Organisational needs, the ability to use non-technical words, flexibility compared to formal delegated legislation and a belief that such rules are not legally binding are some of the justifications underlying the use of such rules.

It will be noted that the first three justifications are in line with the justifications for formal delegated legislation. However, the last comment in relation to the legal effect of such rules needs to be examined further in light of the next extract.

R. v. Secretary of State for the Home Department, ex parte Khan

[1985] 1 All E.R. 40

"A Home Office circular letter stated that although the Immigration Rules did not permit a foreign child subject to immigration control to enter the United Kingdom for the purposes of adoption, the Secretary of State would permit such entry provided certain specified criteria were met. The criteria involved the adoption being genuine and not merely a device for obtaining entry, that the child's welfare in this country be assured, that the courts here would be likely to grant an adoption order, and that one of the intending adopters be domiciled in the United Kingdom. The letter then stated the procedure to be followed by would-be adopters. This was to obtain an entry clearance from an entry clearance officer abroad. That officer would have to be satisfied of the child's wishes and the wishes of the natural parents. The applicant and his wife wished to adopt a relative's child, living with its natural mother in Pakistan. Application for an entry clearance was made in Islamabad. All the various criteria listed above appeared to have been satisfied. However, in due course, following referral of the matter to the Home Office, entry clearance was refused. This was on the ground that there were no 'serious and compelling family and other considerations', such as would make refusal of permission to enter undesirable. The entry clearance officer's report to the Home Office had made clear the fact that the child in question was living in good conditions with his natural mother. The applicant appealed against the decision of Stephen Brown J., dismissing his application for judicial review to quash the decision to refuse clearance."

2–41

Parker L.J.: "[His Lordship noted the policy actually applied by the Home Office in coming to its decision, and continued:] … If this was the policy, the 'guidance' given in the Home Office letter is grossly misleading, as was frankly accepted by counsel on behalf of the Secretary of State. There is not a word [in the circular letter] to suggest that in exercising his discretion the Secretary of State requires to be satisfied that the natural parents are incapable of looking after the prospective adoptee, or even that their ability or inability to do so was considered relevant. Furthermore, there is no evidence that entry clearance officers were instructed to inquire as to this matter, which of course does not depend only on the standard of living enjoyed in the natural home. The whole tenor of the letter is that, if the application was genuine, if the child's welfare was assured, if a court would be likely to grant an order and if the natural parents gave a real consent, the child would be let in and its ultimate fate left to the court here. If an adoption order was made it would remain. If an order was refused it would be returned.

The applicant relies on three authorities on the basis of which he contends that the refusal of entry clearance should be quashed. The first of these cases is *R. v. Liverpool Corporation, ex p. Liverpool Taxi Fleet Operators' Association* [1972] 2 Q.B. 299. [See further, below, p. 448. His Lordship considered this decision and continued:]

In that case there was a specific undertaking, whereas here there is not; the corporation had a statutory power; and the matter complained of was a positive act, whereas here the complaint is a refusal to act. There can, however, be no doubt that the Secretary of State has a duty to exercise his common law discretion fairly. Furthermore, just as, in the case cited, the corporation was held not to be entitled to resile from an undertaking and change its policy without giving a fair hearing so, in principle, the Secretary of State, if he undertakes to allow in persons if certain conditions are satisfied, should not in my view be entitled to resile from that undertaking without affording interested persons a hearing and then only if the overriding public interest demands it.

The second of the authorities relied on by the applicant is *O'Reilly v. Mackman* [1983] 2 A.C. 237. The case is relied on solely for a statement of principle in the speech of Lord Diplock with which Lord Fraser of Tullybelton, Lord Keith of Kinkel, Lord Bridge of Harwich and Lord Brightman agreed. It is therefore necessary to state the facts only to the limited extent necessary to render that statement understandable. Four prisoners had been awarded forfeiture of remission by the board of visitors. They sought to challenge the decision of the board on the ground that there had been a failure to observe the rules of natural justice, the relief sought being declaratory only. [His Lordship set out the passage:

> 'It is not, and it could not be, contended that the decision of the board awarding him forfeiture of remission … which means no more than to act fairly towards him in carrying out their decision-making process, and I prefer so to put it' (below, p. 643).]

Here it is contended that the applicant, by virtue of the terms of the Home Office letter, had a legitimate expectation that the procedures set out in the letter would be followed and that such legitimate expectation gave him sufficient interest to challenge the admitted failure of the Secretary of State to observe such procedures. I agree and the contrary was not suggested by [counsel for the Secretary of State]. But to have a sufficient interest to afford a *locus standi* to challenge is a long way from being entitled to succeed in such challenge.

The applicant, however, contends that on the basis of the third authority on which he relies, coupled with his first which already considered, he is so entitled. That authority is a Privy Council case, *Att.-Gen. of Hong Kong v. Ng Yuen Shiu* [1983] 2 A.C. 629, which at the time of the hearing before the judge had been reported only in *The Times* newspaper. The advice of their Lordships were delivered by Lord Fraser of Tullybelton. The other members of the Judicial Committee were Lord Scarman, Lord Bridge of Harwich, Lord Brandon of Oakbrook and Sir John Megaw. For some years prior to October 23, 1980, the government of Hong Kong had adopted a policy under which illegal immigrants from China were not repatriated if they managed to reach the urban areas without being arrested. This was known as the 'reached base' policy. On October 23, 1980, the government announced that this policy would be discontinued forthwith and at the same time issued a new ordinance which, *inter alia*, gave the Director of Immigration power to make removal orders in respect of illegal immigrants. There was no statutory provision for a hearing or inquiry before a removal order was made. Subsequent to the change of policy there were a series of television announcements stating that all illegal immigrants from China would be liable to be repatriated. Mr Ng, like many others in the colony, although they had entered illegally from Macau, was of Chinese origin. They were accordingly worried and on October 28, 1980, a group, not including Mr Ng, went to Government House and submitted a petition.

There, there were read out a series of questions and answers prepared in the office of the Secretary for Security which dealt with the position of such persons and the action they should take. One of such questions, with its answer, was:

> 'Q. Will we be given identity cards? A. Those illegal immigrants from Macau will be treated in accordance with procedures for illegal immigrants from anywhere other than China. They will be interviewed in due course. No guarantee can be given that you may not subsequently be removed. Each case will be treated on its merits.'

Although Mr Ng was not present he did see a television programme on the subject on the evening of the same day.

On October 31 a removal order was made against him. This he challenged and eventually on May 13, 1981, the Court of Appeal of Hong Kong made an order of prohibition prohibiting the Director of Immigration from executing the removal order before an opportunity had been given to Mr Ng of putting all the circumstances of his case before the director. The Attorney-General appealed to the Privy Council.

The High Court and the Court of Appeal in Hong Kong had both held that Mr Ng had no general right to a fair hearing before a removal order was made against him and the Judicial Committee assumed, without deciding, that they had rightly so decided. It was concerned only with the narrow question whether what had been said outside Government House entitled Mr Ng to such a hearing. It is necessary to cite four passages from Lord Fraser's judgment:

(1) "'Legitimate expectations' in this context are capable of including expectations which go beyond enforceable legal rights, *provided they have some reasonable basis.*' (at 636E–F)

(2) 'The expectations may be based on some *statement* or undertaking by, or on behalf of, the public authority which has the duty of making the decision, if the authority has, through its officers, acted *in a way that would make it unfair or inconsistent with good administration for him to be denied such* an inquiry.' (at 637C–D)

(3) 'Their Lordships see no reason why the principle should not be applicable when the person who will be affected by the decision is an alien, just as much as when he is a British subject. The justification for it is primarily that, *when a public authority has promised to follow a certain procedure, it is in the interest of good administration that it should act fairly and should implement its promise, so long as implementation does not interfere with its statutory duty*. The principle is also justified by the further consideration that, when the promise was made, *the authority must have considered that it would be assisted in discharging its duty fairly* by any representations from interested parties and as a general rule that is correct. In the opinion of their Lordships the principle that a public authority is bound by its undertakings as to the procedure it will follow, provided they do not conflict with its duty, is applicable to the undertaking given by the government of Hong Kong to the respondent, along with other illegal immigrants from Macau, in the announcement outside Government House on October 28, 1980, that each case would be considered on its merits. The only ground on which it was argued before the Board that the undertaking had not been implemented was that the respondent had not been given an opportunity to put his case for an exercise of discretion, which the director undoubtedly possesses, in his favour before a decision was reached' (at 638E–H).

(4) 'Their Lordships consider that this is a very narrow case on its facts, but they are not disposed to differ from the view expressed by both the courts below, to the effect that the government's promise to the respondent has not been implemented. Accordingly the appeal ought to be dismissed. But in the circumstances their Lordships are of opinion that the order made by the Court of Appeal should be varied. The appropriate remedy is not the conditional order of prohibition made by the Court of Appeal, but an order of certiorari to quash the removal order made by the director on October 31, against the respondent. That order of certiorari is of course entirely without prejudice to the making of a fresh removal order by the Director of Immigration after a fair inquiry has been held at which the respondent has been given an opportunity to make such representations as he may see fit as to why he should not be removed' (at 639E–F).

The emphasis in each case is mine.

That case is, of course, not binding on this court but is of high persuasive authority. In my view it correctly sets out the law of England and should be applied.

I have no doubt that the Home Office letter afforded the applicant a reasonable expectation that the procedures it set out, which were just as certain in their terms as the question and answer in Mr Ng's case, would be followed, that if the result of the implementation of those procedures satisfied the Secretary of State of the four matters mentioned a temporary entry clearance certificate would be granted and that the ultimate fate of the child would then be decided by the adoption court of this country. I have equally no doubt that it was considered by the department at the time the letter was sent out that if those procedures were fully implemented they would be sufficient to safeguard the public interest. The letter can mean nothing else. This is not surprising. The adoption court will apply the law of this country and will thus protect all the interests which the law of this country considers should be protected. The Secretary of State is, of course, at liberty to change the policy but in my view, *vis-à-vis* the recipient of such a letter, a new policy can only be implemented after there is some overriding public interest which justifies a departure from the procedures stated in the letter... .

I would allow the appeal and quash the refusal of entry clearance. This will leave the Secretary of State free either to proceed on the basis of the letter or, if he considers it desirable to operate the new policy, to afford the applicant a full opportunity to make representations why, in his case, it should not be followed.

I would only add this. If the new policy is to continue in operation, the sooner the Home Office letter is redrafted and false hopes cease to be raised in those who may have a deep emotional need to adopt, the better it will be. To leave it in its present form is not only bad and grossly unfair administration but, in some instances at any rate, positively cruel.

[Dunn, L.J. also delivered a judgment allowing the appeal. He took the view that 'although the circular letter did not create an estoppel' it had indicated what were the relevant considerations as regards the exercise of this discretionary power, and the Secretary of State had therefore taken into account an *irrelevant* consideration. In so doing he had 'misdirected himself according to his own criteria and acted unreasonably'. Watkins L.J. dissented, taking the view that, properly construed, the circular letter only indicated factors which if not satisfied would certainly lead to refusal of clearance; it did not indicate that compliance with those factors would itself lead to grant of permission. The letter said that the Secretary 'may exercise his discretion and exceptionally allow …'. Parker L.J. had noted this formula, and had taken the view that a reader would have inferred that, provided the conditions were satisfied, permission to enter 'would be the likely result'.]"

Notes

2–42   (1) See commentary by C. Lewis, "Fairness, Legitimate Expectations and Estoppel" (1986) 49 M.L.R. 251 and A. R. Mowbray, "Administrative Guidance and Judicial Review" [1985] P.L. 558.

(2) Consider *Khan* in relation to the discussion of the scope of personal bar at para. 6–47. Do you agree with Dunn L.J. that personal bar did not arise here? On this see P. Elias in *New Directions in Judicial Review* (J. Jowell and D. Oliver eds, 1988), p. 48. For an example of the use of a circular leading to a legitimate expectation see *Rooney v. Chief Constable, Strathclyde Police*, 1997 S.L.T. 1261 where it was held that a police constable had a legitimate expectation that a Chief Constable would act according to the procedures recommended in a (non-statutory) procedures manual in relation to a decision not to accept the constable's withdrawal of a resignation letter.

(3) The judiciary have sometimes had a somewhat sceptical view of the utility and acceptability of informal administrative rules. In *Patchett v. Leatham* [1949] 65 T.L.R. 69 Streatfield J. observed:

> "Whereas ordinary legislation, by passing through both House of Parliament or, at least, lying on the table of both Houses, is thus twice blessed, this type of so called legislation is at least four times cursed. First, it has seen neither House of Parliament; secondly, it is unpublished and is inaccessible even to those whose valuable rights of property maybe affected; thirdly, it is a jumble of provisions, legislative, administrative, or directive in character, and sometimes difficult to disentangle one from the other, and fourthly, it is expressed not in the precise language of an Act of Parliament or an Order in Council but in the more colloquial language of correspondence, which is not always susceptible of the ordinary canons of construction."

Compare these views with those of Mitchell below as to the "inherent" difficulties created by administrative rule making.

(4) *Khan* is an example of the creation of a procedural right by the implication from a circular. Sometimes rights are directly and explicitly conferred. In *Palmer v. Board of Management for Inverness Hospitals*, 1963 S.C. 311 a circular issued by the Secretary of State to an NHS hospital stated that in exercising their disciplinary functions, authorities "should follow a procedure which makes it clear that each case is handled in an equitable manner" and further that "the adoption of this procedure should be made known to all concerned". A house surgeon was dismissed by a hospital and appealed against his dismissal. An initial hearing found in his favour, but a subsequent committee was convened at which the surgeon was not present or represented and which found against him. It was argued by the health authority that the circular only set forward administrative guidance and, if it was relevant at all, it only applied to the first hearing but not to the subsequent hearing which, they argued, was an appellate hearing. The Lord Ordinary (Wheatley) rejected this contention observing (at 319) that:

> "It is stated in … the circular that the procedure is designed to make it clear that an appeal against disciplinary action (actual or proposed) will be handled in an equitable manner. This, in my view, must apply to the whole procedure."

He then went on to reject the argument that as the circular left undefined the nature of such procedure, the broadest possible scope should be afforded the appellate committee. He continued:

> "As Lord Chancellor Haldane said, in *Local Government Board v. Arlidge*, [1915] A.C. 120, 'when the duty of deciding an appeal is imposed, those whose duty it is to decide must act judicially.' It would be strange if the committee appointed by the parent body was obliged to act judicially,

but the parent body, with whom the ultimate decision on the appeal lay, was not. While there is no specific provision in the circular for the procedure to be followed at the final meeting of the employing authority, and in particular no provision made for the appearance of the appellant and/ or a representative on his behalf, the basic principles of natural justice, and fair play must be carried forward into that later stage of the appeal."

(5) Judicial control at a substantive level will also be brought to bear. In *Scottish Old People's Welfare Council, Petitioners*, 1987 S.L.T. 179, extracted at para. 10–19 in relation to title and interest, the court was asked to consider whether a circular issued by the Secretary of State for Social Services in relation to the regulation of extra payments for severe weather was *ultra vires* section 3 of the Supplementary Benefits Act 1976. Referring to the decision of the House of Lords in *Gillick v. West Norfolk and Wisbech Area Health Authority* [1986] A.C. 112, which related to the *vires* of a circular relative to the provision of contraception to girls under the age of sixteen, Lord Clyde observed (at 183):

> "I must mention another line of argument advanced by counsel for the respondent. Article 7(a) of the petition states as follows: 'It is ultra vires of the respondent to issue to adjudication officers instructions as to the interpretation of regulations which is erroneous in law: *Gillick v. West Norfolk and Wisbech Area Health Authority*.' That statement is expressly admitted by the respondent in his answers. However, he submitted in argument that even if the circular was erroneous in law the advice was given on the basis of the authority of a tribunal of commissioners and, so far from acting ultra vires in giving it, the chief adjudication officer would have been acting ultra vires if he had failed to follow such authoritative guidance and was indeed bound to follow it as expressing the law at that time.... .
> The relevance of this line of argument could more readily be seen to be relevant against a case that the issuing of the circular was an exercise of an administrative discretion in a wholly unreasonable way. That was the view which Lord Scarman took of Mrs Gillick's case at p. 177 of the report. On the other hand, both Lord Bridge and Lord Templeman (although the latter was dissenting on the main point of the case) did not accept Lord Scarman's analysis and saw the case as one of the review of an error in law in a public document promulgated by a government department in a field of administration in which it exercised responsibility. The admission in pleadings seems to me to involve an acceptance of that principle of approach in the present case. On that approach the question is whether the law presented in the circular is correct and not whether the chief adjudication officer was correct in following the guidance of the tribunal."

The implication of *Gillick* and following from that, this case, is that the reasonableness of such non-statutory guidance could only be challenged by judicial review where advice was promulgated in a public document and was wrong in law. In *R. v. Code of Practice Committee of the British Pharmaceutical Industry, ex parte Professional Counselling Aids Ltd*, *The Times*, November 7, 1990 (Q.B.D.), a code of practice was subject to judicial review as it related to the performance of a public duty in relation to the promotion and advertising of medicine. See also *R. v. Secretary of State for the Home Department, ex parte Westminster Press Ltd* (1992) Admin. R.L.R. 445 where it was held that a circular issued by the Home Secretary was guidance only and, as it did not relate to the public duties of the police, was not reviewable.

This approach does not sit easily with *West v. Secretary of State for Scotland*, 1992 S.L.T. 636, extracted at para. 10–7. In *J.D.P. Investments Ltd v. Strathclyde Regional Council*, 1997 S.L.T. 408 the council sought to argue that the application of principles contained in a circular relating to how land should be sold was simply part of a decision on whether it should sell land, and did not amount to the exercise of a jurisdiction for the purposes of the test in *West*. In effect it was arguing that the matter was one of contract and did not involve public duty. However, Lord Hamilton observed (at 413H–J) that the purported application of principles contained in the circular to a case falling within its terms could be an exercise of a jurisdiction, although the issue would not be decided without first assessing what part the circular played in the decision. In *South Lanarkshire Council v. Secretary of State for Scotland*, 1998 S.L.T. 445 judicial review of a circular on how to comply with the CCT provisions of the Local Government, Planning and Land Act 1980 and the Local Government Act 1988 was sought. It was contended, *inter alia*, that the guidance was void from uncertainty and therefore irrational, but the court was not prepared to hold the circular void from uncertainty: see p. 453F–L *per* Lord Cameron of Lochbroom.

(6) Quasi-legislation can also amount to a relevant consideration for the purposes of judicial control. For example, under section 12 of the Housing (Scotland) Act 1987 housing authorities are obliged to have regard to the code of guidance which is issued from time to time by Central Government in relation to how they exercise their functions. Employment tribunals are obliged to take into account the various industrial relations Codes of Practice even if not expressly referred to by the parties: *Lock v. Cardiff Railway Co. Ltd* [1998] IRLR 358, EAT. Similarly, in *J.D.P. Investments Ltd* above it was observed that although the circular in question posed no obligation to follow its contents, its existence obliged authorities to consider its contents for making decisions affecting the land in question (at 413E–F).

The exact status of this kind of administrative rule is not always clear. The Immigration Rules, which are made under the Immigration Act 1971, s. 3(2) and which require to be laid before Parliament, have caused problems. They are published as House of Commons papers and are binding on officials. Section 19(1) gives them status in judicial proceedings. Roskill L.J. observed, "These rules have just as much delegated legislation as any other form of rule making which is empowered by Parliament" but in *R. v. Secretary of State for Home Affairs, ex parte Hosenball* [1977] 1 W.L.R. 766 this view was disputed, the rules being "a practical guide for the immigration officers ... and little more than explanatory notes in the Act itself" *per* Geoffrey Lane L.J. See too *Singh v. Immigration Appeal Tribunal* [1986] 2 All E.R. 721.

(7) Where administrative rules, of whatever degree of formality or in whatever form, exist the authority to which they relate will generally be expected to follow those rules. *Khan* is an example of that. Nevertheless, an authority cannot have regard to such rules to the exclusion of the exercise of its discretion, on which see *Minister of Technology v. British Oxygen Company* [1971] A.C. 610 at para. 7–10 and *Inglis v. British Airports Authority*, 1978 S.L.T. (Lands Tr.) 30. On guidance from Ministers generally see para. 7–21. In *South Lanarkshire Council* above an unsuccessful attempt was made to argue that the guidance in question was an improper fetter on the discretion of the council.

(8) R. Baldwin, *Rules and Government* (2nd ed., 1996) who made a detailed study of rules issued by the Factory Inspectorate, considered that rules made by Government could be divided into secondary legislation and "tertiary rules" such as administrative guidance and Codes of Practice. He argues that the legitimacy of such provisions could be evaluated according to criteria: (1) respect for due process values; (2) use of expertise in adminstration of government programmes; (3) efficient provision of public services; (4) accountability to representative bodies; and (5) achievement of legislative objectives. Are these criteria present in the models of judicial control that exist in relation to delegated legislation and tertiary rules? Is there a potential conflict between any of the criteria? Baldwin concludes (pp. 300–301) that legitimacy could be enhanced by "increasing obligations to disclose rules: by linking tertiary and secondary rules more clearly to statutory provisions, and by making the status and force of such rules more clear". See also A. R. Mowbray, "Administrative Guidance and Judicial Review" [1985] P.L. 558.

Quasi-Legislation: Creation

2–43   Flexibility is a quality found in quasi-legislation. Such rules do not fall within the provisions of the Statutory Instruments Act 1946. This is because the approach of the Act is formalistic. To be subject to the provisions of the Act and parliamentary scrutiny, the rule has to be a statutory instrument. The substantive nature of the rule in question does not determine whether and to what level scrutiny is applied. Craig (p. 273) suggests that the premise of the 1946 Act should be reversed. A general format would require to be devised which required that any rule whether delegated legislation or not should be subject to the Act.

P. P. Craig, Administrative Law

(3rd ed., 1994), p. 273

"There are two immediate difficulties with this approach.   **2–44**

The *first problem* is inherent in any substantive definition of "legislative rule". The difficulties of applying this term are legendary, and administrative law is scattered with the remnants of such efforts, some of which have given up the ghost, others of which still, despite being much maligned, retain vitality. While this point has much force it should be kept within perspective. The criticism which has been voiced of the dichotomies between legislative and executive, or legislative and administrative, has force because it is felt not just that the distinction is difficult to draw, but more because it is irrelevant as a criterion for the solution of a problem, whether it be the application of natural justice or certiorari. The position is different here. Whatever are the very real difficulties of definition, the distinction *is* important and relevant in this context. It is rules of a legislative character which our views of political theory tell us ought to be controlled by the legislative organ of government. The 1946 Act with its formalistic approach simply ducks the whole matter. More precisely, it allows the decision to reside with the executive. Since it is the latter who will frame the legislation, it will decide whether the appellation statutory instrument should be applied to delegated powers contained therein.

Whether an attempt at substantive definition is worth the candle depends ultimately on the *second problem*. How efficacious would be such control? The answer to this must be a repeat of arguments made earlier about the constraints effective on legislative scrutiny. The addition of extra weight upon an already overburdened system of legislative control, both on the floor of the House and in committee, will give cause for hope only to the most sanguine. While such scrutiny would constitute validation it is unclear that this would be anything more than a formal obeisance to democratic control."

Notes

(1) In view of the extracts on parliamentary scrutiny of delegated legislation do you feel   **2–45** that Craig's views are justified? What alternative mechanisms might be suggested? Professor Ganz has suggested that a Code of Practice be established to control the procedures followed by administrative bodies when making such rules and that a permanent agency be created

> "to advise in the creation of quasi-legal voluntary rules instead of legal rules and evolve criteria for their use. At present they seem to come into existence largely on an ad hoc basis. often as an after thought, in response to conflicting pressures to do nothing or legislate. If the rules are to be observed, rather than be political window dressing, they must be adopted for better reasons than political expediency".

In parallel with this suggestion, the House of Lords suggested that because many of the rules which took the form of Codes of Practice were in no way subject to parliamentary scrutiny, some attempt should be made to impose uniformity and a degree of control. The Government responded by producing a document entitled Guidance Codes of Practice. The full text is reproduced in [1987] Stat. L.R. 214. Ironically, as it is only a Code of Practice, its provisions have not been subject to scrutiny and, moreover, it does not have the legal effect of the Statutory Instruments Act 1946. The Citizen's Charter programme combined with the Government's Code of Practice on access to government information, on which see Chapter 00, has begun to encourage central government departments and agencies to publish the more important internal administrative guidance. For example, the Inland Revenue has now published all of its major technical guidance manuals and the Benefits Agencies publish over 50 of their internal codes and manuals. This at least provides a form of scrutiny *ex post facto*.

(2) For general reading see Lord Campbell of Alloway, "Codes of Practice as an Alternative to Legislation" [1985] Stat. L.R. 127 and A.C. Page, "Self-Regulation and Codes of Practice" [1980] J.B.L. 24. For further general reading see A. Samuels, "Codes of Practice and Legislation" [1986] Stat. L.R. 29 and see C. McCrudden, "Codes in a Cold Climate: Administrative Rule-Making by the Commission for Racial Equality" (1988) 5 M.L.R. 409; Finch and Ashton, pp. 126–132; *Stair Memorial Encyclopaedia*, Vol. 22, "Sources of Law", paras 195–201, 234–243; and G. Ganz, *Quasi-Legislation: Recent Developments in Secondary Legislation* (1987). For

the role of the Parliamentary Ombudsman, see A. R. Mowbray, "The Parliamentary Commissioner and Administrative Guidance" [1987] P.L. 570.

BYELAWS

Local Government (Scotland) Act 1973

ss. 201, 202

"**Byelaws**

Byelaws for good rule and government

2–46
201.—(1) A local authority may make byelaws for the good rule and government of the whole or any part of the region, islands area or district, as the case may be, and for the prevention and suppression of nuisances therein.

(2) The confirming authority in relation to byelaws made under this section shall be the Secretary of State.

(3) Byelaws shall not be made under this section for any purpose as respects any area if provision for that purpose as respects that area is made by, or is or may be made under, any other enactment.

Procedure, etc., for byelaws

202.—(1) The following provisions of this section shall apply to byelaws to be made by a local authority —

(a)   under this Act,

(b)   under any other enactment whenever passed, and whether local or otherwise, conferring on a local authority a power to make byelaws, or

(c)   under any enactment which incorporates or applies to any of the following enactments —

    (i)   section 57 of the Local Government (Scotland) Act 1889;

    (ii)   sections 317 to 323 of the Burgh Police (Scotland) Act 1892;

    (iii)   sections 183 to 187 of the Public Health (Scotland) Act 1897;

    (iv)   sections 301 to 303 of the 1947 Act.

(2) Unless the enactment under which the byelaws are made specifically provides otherwise, any such byelaws may apply only to a part of the area of a local authority, and different byelaws may apply to different parts of the area.

(3) The byelaws shall be authenticated by being sealed with the common seal of the local authority, and different byelaws may apply to different parts of the area.

(4) At least one month before application for confirmation of the byelaws is made, notice of the intention to apply for confirmation, of the place where a copy of the byelaws may be inspected and of the authority to whom objections may be notified shall be given in a newspaper circulating in the area to which the byelaws are to apply or in such other manner as the confirming authority on the application of the local authority may determine to be sufficient in the circumstances.

(5) For at least one month before application for confirmation is made, a copy of the byelaws shall be deposited at the offices of the local authority by whom the byelaws are made and shall at all reasonable hours be open to public inspection without payment.

(6) The local authority by whom the byelaws are made shall on application furnish to any person a copy of the byelaws or of any part thereof on payment of such sum, not exceeding 10p for every hundred words contained in the copy, as the authority may determine.

(7) Any person aggrieved by any byelaws may, within one month after notice has been published in accordance with the provisions of subsection (4) above, notify in writing his objection and the ground of his objection to the confirming authority.

(8) Before confirming byelaws, the confirming authority shall take into consideration any objections received by them and may, if they consider it necessary or desirable, hold a local inquiry or cause a local inquiry to be held.

(9) Unless the Secretary of State shall otherwise direct, every inquiry with respect to byelaws made under any provision of this Act or the Burgh Police (Scotland) Acts 1892 and 1908 shall be held by the sheriff.

(10) The confirming authority may confirm with or without modification or refuse to confirm any byelaws submitted under this section for confirmation and may fix the date on which the byelaws are to come into operation, and if no date is so fixed the byelaws shall come into operation.

(11) The local authority shall, as soon as practicable after receiving intimation of the confirmation of the byelaws by the confirming authority, cause a notice of such confirmation, of the date on which the byelaws are to come into operation, and of the place where a copy of the byelaws as confirmed may be inspected, to be given in a newspaper circulating in the area to which the byelaws are to apply or in such other manner as the confirming authority on the application of the local authority may determine to be sufficient in the circumstances.

(12) A copy of the byelaws when confirmed shall be printed and deposited at the offices of the local authority by whom the byelaws are made and shall at all reasonable hours be open to public inspection without payment, and a copy thereof shall on application be furnished to any person on payment of such sum not exceeding 20p for every copy as the authority may determine....

(14) The provisions of this section shall apply, subject to any necessary modifications, in the case of byelaws made by any authority other than a local authority under any enactment passed before the coming into force of this Act and incorporating or applying any of the enactments set out in subsection (1)(c) above.

(15) In this section "the confirming authority" means the authority or person, if any, specified in the enactment (including any enactment in this aCt) under which the byelaws are made, or in any enactment incorporated therein or applied thereby, as the authority or person by whom the byelaws are to be confirmed, or if no authority or person is so specified, means the Secretary of State:

Provided that, notwithstanding that a local Act specifies otherwise, the confirming authority in relation to byelaws made under any local Act shall be the Secretary of State."

Robert Baird and Sons Ltd v. Glasgow Corporation

1935 S.C. (H.L.) 21

Lord Tomlin: "This is an appeal from an interlocutor of the First Division of the Court of Session recalling an interlocutor of the Lord Ordinary in an action raised by the appellants, who are certain motor traders in the City of Glasgow, against the respondents, who are the Corporation of the City. The appellants sought in the action a declarator to the effect that certain bye-laws made by the respondents under section 11 of the Petroleum (Consolidation) Act, 1928, were bad, as being unreasonable or uncertain, or, alternatively, as being *ultra vires*. The Lord Ordinary held that the bye-laws in question were not bad for unreasonableness or uncertainty, but he held them to be *ultra vires*. On appeal the First Division agreed with the Lord Ordinary that the bye-laws were not bad for unreasonableness or uncertainty, but they differed from him on the question of *ultra vires*, and held that the bye-laws were *intra vires* and good.

2–47

Section 11 of the Petroleum (Consolidation) Act, 1928, so far as is material to our present purpose, reads as follows: Subsection (1). 'For the purpose of preserving for the enjoyment of the public the amenities of any rural scenery or of any place of beauty or historic interest or of any public part or pleasure promenade or of any street or place which is of interest by reason of its picturesque character, the council of any county or borough may make bye-laws — (*a*) regulating the appearance of petroleum filling stations; or (*b*) prohibiting the establishment of petroleum filling stations, in any part of their area to which the bye-laws apply; and without prejudice to the generality of the foregoing provisions, any such bye-laws regulating the appearance of petroleum filling stations may, in particular, require compliance with such provisions as may be contained in the bye-laws as to the position, design, size, colour and screening of such stations or of any parts thereof.' There then follows a number of provisos, which are not material to our present purpose.

Subsection (2) provides: 'Any part of the area of a council to which bye-laws or a draft of any bye-laws made under this section apply shall be distinctly marked and shown on plans to be signed by and deposited with the clerk of the council making the bye-laws, and the said plans shall be at all reasonable times thereafter open for the inspection of the public without charge.'

Subsection (3) provides: 'No bye-laws made under this section shall come into force until confirmed by the Secretary of State, and before submitting any such bye-laws to the Secretary of State the council by whom the bye-laws were made shall, in such manner as may be directed by the Secretary of State, publish a draft thereof, together with notice of the place where the plans marked in accordance with the provisions of this section may be inspected and of the intention of the council to apply for the confirmation of the bye-laws.'

In subsection (6) there are provisions for the recovery of penalties against any person who infringes the bye-laws.

Section 23 of the Act contains some definitions, and amongst others it defines 'Amenities' in this way: '"Amenities," in relation to any place, includes any view of or from that place.' 'Petroleum filling station' is defined as meaning 'any premises or place used or intended to be used by way of trade or for purposes of gain for fuelling motor vehicles with petroleum, and includes any building, advertisement, pump or other apparatus in, or used in connexion with, any such premises.' 'Petroleum' is also defined as including 'crude petroleum, oil made from petroleum, or from coal, shale, peat or other bituminous substances, and other products of petroleum.'

The Act of 1928, in section 11, reproduces a section of an earlier Act, and, in connexion with the provisions of that earlier section, a Departmental Committee sat and made a report by which certain model byelaws were recommended. That model form of bye-laws was subsequently, with some minor modifications, adopted and approved by the Scottish Office as appropriate for use by the authorities in Scotland exercising the powers conferred by the Act.

The respondents, having had their attention called by a letter from the Secretary of State to the advisability of considering whether they should exercise the powers of section 11 in regard to any part of their City, referred the matter to a subcommittee, which obtained a report from the three officers of the respondents most closely concerned with the matter — namely, the Master of Works, the Director of Housing, and the Petroleum Inspector. Those officers reported to the subcommittee, and their report was against any bye-law for the total prohibition of petroleum filling stations in any part of the City, but they recommended bye-laws for regulating the appearance of petroleum filling stations in certain specified areas. That report appears to have been adopted by the sub-committee, and ultimately the recommendations of the report were approved by the Corporation, and certain bye-laws were in due course framed and adopted and the proper steps were taken to bring them into operation, and they were ultimately confirmed by the Secretary of State in accordance with the provisions of the section. The bye-laws which were adopted were the model bye-laws which had been approved by the Scottish Office, with certain minor modifications.

Those bye-laws are expressed, in the first bye-law, to apply 'to the areas of the city coloured or hatched blue on the deposited maps.' I will, in a moment, indicate what those areas were. The second bye-law is as follows: 'The following provisions shall have effect with respect to every filling station within the areas aforesaid, that is to say:— (1) Except in so far as is permitted by the First Schedule to these bye-laws: (a) No visible advertisement, name or lettering used in or in connexion with a filling station shall be exhibited within the area aforesaid; (b) all visible apparatus comprised in a filling station shall, if painted or otherwise coloured, be of the same colour. (2) Every visible wall forming part of a filling station shall be constructed of or faced with' — and then a number of materials are indicated. Provision (3) is: 'Every visible roof forming part of a filling station shall be covered with natural slates, clay tiles,' and other substances mentioned.

Provision (4) deals with visible corrugated or galvanised iron, and states that it shall be painted. Provision (5) provides that 'no visible lamp giving intermittent illumination used in or in connexion with a filling station shall be exhibited in the areas aforesaid,' and by provision (6) it is provided that 'the filling station shall be kept in a tidy and orderly condition to the satisfaction of the Chief Officer of the Corporation under the Act.'

Under bye-law 3 the occupier of any filling station established at the time of the making of the bye-laws is for two years made exempt from the operation of so much of the bye-laws as requires any structural alteration of the filling station.

Bye-law 4 applies the Interpretation Act, 1889, and also contains certain definitions. It defines 'deposited maps'; it defines 'filling station' as meaning a petroleum filling station; and it defines 'standard sign' as meaning a 'sign conforming to the diagram and description set out in the Second Schedule to these bye-laws.'

Then the First Schedule, which contains the permitted deviations from the requirements of bye-law No. 2, states: 1. 'The name of any filling station and of the occupier thereof may be displayed therein once, in a position not higher than the level of the lowest part of any roof, by means of letters not exceeding twelve inches in height.' There is also a provision permitting the occupier of a filling station to display a sign of any motoring club or association which the occupier of the filling station is authorised to display. There is then a provision for the display of a standard sign 'in not more than three positions in or in connexion with any filling station.' The Second Schedule contains in Part I a diagram of the standard sign, and in Part II a description of the sign. That sign contains spaces in which certain things may be placed, some spaces with moveable panels, and some with fixed panels.

It is to be noticed in connexion with those bye-laws — because this is relevant to a point which has been made before your Lordships — that the word 'visible,' applied in the second bye-law to advertisements, apparatus, walls, roofs, corrugated or galvanised iron and lamps, has not been anywhere actually defined.

Now, the areas to which those bye-laws have been applied are considerable areas forming, in effect, a continuous belt round the central part of the City of Glasgow, and they are said to contain in all about 35 1/2 square miles. It is not disputed that they contain within themselves examples of the objects and places which are referred to in section 11 of the Act of 1928. There are to be found in each of them rural scenery, places of beauty or historic interest, public parks, pleasure promenades, and streets or places which are of interest by reason of their picturesque character. There may be considerable difference of opinion as to a number of those objects and places. There will be, no doubt, a difference of opinion as to whether some of them fall within the description of the section or whether they do not, but at any rate there are a considerable number of them present in each of the areas.

Upon the question of *ultra vires* which is the main question in the case, it is said, however, that, inasmuch as the areas include spots or tracts which cannot, it is said, be brought within any of the descriptions contained in section 11, therefore the inclusion of them in the areas is in itself improper and outside the powers of the Corporation, and that the effect of that is to make the whole of the bye-laws applied to those areas, improperly (as is alleged) including those places, bad and of no effect.

Upon the question of *ultra vires*, it is necessary, of course, for any Court adjudicating upon it, first of all, to consider the meaning of the statutory power which the Corporation are affecting to exercise by making the bye-laws; and, secondly, to consider the bye-laws themselves and to determine whether the bye-laws, when examined, contain any excess of the power as interpreted. That is the nature of the problem. Looking at the Act itself there are one or two matters which your Lordships may think are reasonably plain. The first is that, although the purpose of the section is the 'preserving for the enjoyment of the public the amenities' of certain things, the power of the authority is to make bye-laws in relation to the matters mentioned (that is, in this case, 'regulating the appearance of petroleum filling stations') 'in any part of their area to which the bye-laws apply.' That must mean, to which in the judgment of the Council the bye-laws should be made to apply in order to preserve the amenities of the things mentioned by the section which are found within their area. The moment that construction of the section is adopted it is plain that the area to which the bye-laws apply is not an area which is limited by the site of the places or objects which are mentioned in the section; it must be an area which in the judgment of the Council is an area proper to be made subject to the bye-laws in order to preserve for the enjoyment of the public the amenities of the things which are found in the area.

The next matter which may be mentioned is that many of the things described in the section are things in regard to which a judgment of some kind is necessary; for example, 'any street or place which is of interest by reason of its picturesque character.' I apprehend that the 'picturesque character' of any street or place is a matter upon which there may well be differences of opinion. The Act provides no standard by which it is to be judged, and it is an inevitable conclusion upon that construction of the section that it is the Council alone on whose judgment a matter of that sort must rest where the Council are exercising the powers of the section.

Again, it has been suggested that the word 'place' has a narrow meaning and must be confined to some spot which forms the site of a particular building, park, or other object, whereas in fact there seems no reason as a matter of language why 'place' should not be of much wider significance, and why a 'place which is of interest by reason of its picturesque character' should not include in certain circumstances a very considerable area of country. Bearing these matters in mind, on the face of the bye-laws which have been made, regarded with the deposited maps, there seems *prima facie* no reason on which there can be based a suggestion that the bye-laws are in excess of the powers of the section.

But the appellants before your Lordships have attacked the bye-laws in this way. They have said, 'Oh, but the officials of the Corporation who prepared the original report seem to have had in their minds much more the protection of the areas which were affected by the Corporation's town-planning and housing schemes than anything else,' and it suggested that, because those areas are included in the area subjected to the bye-laws, there is some ground for saying that the areas have been improperly selected. The whole argument, I think, is based on some confusion of thought, because there are two things which are quite distinct. the Corporation have not been attacked on the ground that they have made a *mala fide* use of the powers of the section. It is not said that the Corporation wanted to do one thing and, under cover of the Act and without exercising any discretion under the Act, have proceeded to do that which they wished to do, which was something outside the Act. That is not said of them. All that is said is that they have exceeded their powers. Approaching the matter in that way, it seems to me irrelevant to take into account what was in the minds of the various officers before whom the matter came in the course of its consideration before the Council themselves resolved upon the adoption of the bye-laws, because the only question here is excess or non-excess, and the motives of those who took part in the consideration of it, even if they were as alleged, seem to me to be irrelevant. But it is said that, apart from that, inasmuch as these districts contain the site of industrial works and other places which cannot be brought within the categories mentioned in section 11, therefore the application of the bye-laws to a district which contains them must necessarily be bad. It seems to me that, when once the construction of the section which I have suggested to your Lordships is approved, that argument must fail.

For these reasons I think that the attack on the bye-laws as being *ultra vires* cannot be sustained, and that in that regard the appeal fails.

There remains the question of unreasonableness and uncertainty. Upon the question of unreasonableness it is said that the opportunities of indicating what the trader does and for whom he acts as agent, and the nature of the services which he is prepared to render, are inadequate. Those are matters, no doubt, which might have been placed before those whose duty it was to consider whether the bye-laws should be adopted, or those whose duty it was to consider whether the bye-laws should be confirmed; but they can be of no avail at this time, and in this place, to support a plea of unreasonableness. Unreasonableness in regard to bye-laws of this kind is something which can never be made out except upon a case of great strength and clearness. These particular bye-laws are, in effect, in a form recommended by a Departmental Committee, approved by the Scottish Office, and ultimately adopted by the Corporation at the suggestion of the Secretary of State. Those are in themselves no grounds of course, for saying that they cannot be unreasonable, but they are some grounds for saying that any case of unreasonableness which is made against them must be made with the utmost clearness. I think that the Courts below were right in holding that unreasonableness was not made out.

That leaves only the question of uncertainty, and uncertainty has been based really upon the single word 'visible'. It is said that there is no definition of 'visible,' that nobody can tell what 'visible' means, that, inasmuch as these bye-laws lead to penalties, the trader is entitled to know clearly what he can do and what he cannot do, and that, when he reads these bye-laws and sees that 'no visible advertisement … shall be exhibited within the areas aforesaid,' he does not know what 'visible' means. If it fell to me to-day to construe these bye-laws I should feel no difficulty in construing the word 'visible.' It seems to me that the meaning is plain enough. Having regard to what the bye-laws are, and what is the Act to which they are giving effect, 'visible' plainly means visible from the outside, and I think there can be no effective argument of uncertainty based on that word. If that is right, there is nothing else to found uncertainty on, and that plea, like the other plea, must fail.

In my opinion the appeal wholly fails, and I invite your Lordships to dismiss it with the usual consequences."

Lord Thankerton: "I entirely concur with the reasons which have been expressed by my noble and learned friend on the Woolsack for dismissing this appeal, and I have nothing to add."

Lord MacMillan: "I also agree, and cannot make any useful addition."

Lord Wright: "I likewise concur."

Lord Alness: "I also agree."

Notes

2–48   (1) Byelaws are not simply issued by local authorities, although local authority byelaws are perhaps the most common and the best well known. Other authorities can issue byelaws: see, for example, the Transport Act 1962, s. 67(5) (Transport Commission); the Airports Authority Act 1975, s. 9(4) (airports authorities); the Countryside (Scotland) Act 1967, s. 58(3) (Countryside Commission for Scotland); and the Environment Act 1995, s. 31 (Scottish Environmental Protection Agency). On byelaws generally see *Stair Memorial Encyclopaedia*, Vol. 22, paras 189–193. For further discussion, including examination of management rules made under the Civic Government (Scotland) Act 1982, see J. McFadden, "Local Authority Powers: Byelaws, Management Rules and Private Legislation" (1999) 72 S.P.E.L. 34.

(2) As can be seen from section 202, the typical byelaw requires that it be confirmed by a higher authority, here the Secretary of State for Scotland. The confirming authority can confirm byelaws with or without modification or refuse to confirm them. Where the confirming authority is a judge, then matters of policy and expediency can be taken into account: *Glasgow Corporation v. Glasgow Churches' Council*, 1944 S.C. 97. The 1973 Act provides a typical framework for

the passing of byelaws. The schemes operated by other authorities are generally similar. The parent legislation will provide for the specific publicity, commencement and authenticity of byelaws. The usual model is for the authority to give public notice of its intention to apply confirmation at least one month before applying and at least one month before the application is made copies of the byelaws will be made available for inspection and purchase. Any person aggrieved or who wishes to object to the byelaws usually has one month after the giving of public notice in which to object. On procedure generally see *Stair Memorial Encyclopaedia*, Vol. 22, para. 190.

(3) *Baird* is an example of the attitude taken by the courts in relation to challenges to the *vires* of byelaws. Lord Fleming, in the Outer House, had relied on the well-known dictum of Lord Russell of Killowen C.J. in *Kruse v. Johnson* [1898] 2 Q.B. 91 where he noted (at 99) that byelaws:

> "ought to be supported if possible. They ought to be, as has been said, 'benevolently' interpreted, and credit ought to be given to those who have to administer them that they will be reasonably administered. This involves the introduction of no new canon of construction... . I think courts of justice ought to be slow to condemn as invalid any bye-law, so made under such conditions, on the ground of supposed unreasonableness."

For comments on *Kruse* see D. G. T. Williams, "The Control of Local Authorities' in *Welsh Studies in Public Law* (J. A. Andrews ed., 1970). See generally Puttick, Chapter 18. Although at one time it was thought that the test in *Kruse* was based on additional judicial deference, it is now probably better regarded as simply an example of *Wednesbury* unreasonableness. For further examples of judicial reticence in striking down a byelaw on grounds of unreasonableness see *Da Prato v. Partick Magistrates*, 1907 S.C. (H.L.) 5 and *Aldred v. Miller*, 1925 J.C. 21, although see *Dunsmore v. Lindsay* (1903) 6 F.(J.) 14 where a byelaw was struck down as being unreasonable. Note also challenge on the ground of uncertainty and see more recently *Percy v. Hall* [1996] 4 All E.R. 523 where the Court of Appeal held that the test for uncertainty of a byelaw was whether "it can be given no meaning or no sensible and ascertainable meaning, and not merely because it is ambiguous or leads to absurd results".

(4) Challenge to a byelaw on the grounds of *ultra vires* can be raised as a defence to criminal proceedings without a separate petition for judicial review: see *Francis v. Cardle* below. In England it was held that challenge to a byelaw on substantive grounds, as opposed to procedural grounds, had to be taken by way of judicial review: *Bugg v. DPP*, but see now *Boddington v. British Transport Police*.

(5) The terms of byelaws, unlike statutory instruments, require to be proved before a court can have regard to their terms: *Herkes v. Dickie*, 1958 J.C. 51 and *Donnelly v. Carmichael*, 1995 S.C.C.R. 737.

Chapter 3

SIMPLE ULTRA VIRES

An act which is *ultra vires* is an act carried out by a public or other body which it has no legal authority to perform. The term "*ultra vires*" means outwith the powers conferred. Where the act exceeds the substance of the power that has been conferred then we are concerned with substantive *ultra vires*. Where something has been done which was within the body's power, but the correct procedure has not been followed, this is procedural *ultra vires*. The *ultra vires* doctrine, when used to describe the challenge of administrative decision-making, can be used in a broad sense as the term referring to the whole body of law in which an action or a decision of a public authority can be subject to judicial review and accordingly embraces not only the principles discussed in this chapter, but jurisdictional control noted in Chapter 4, procedural *ultra vires* noted in Chapter 5 and the general grounds of legal control noted in Chapters 6, 7 and 8 embracing both abuse and retention of discretion and breach of the rules of natural justice. In this chapter we are principally concerned with the concept in its narrow sense, that of the term as an expression of legal capacity. In this sense, *ultra vires* is sometimes referred to as "simple *ultra vires*". On this area generally see V. Finch and C. Ashton, *Administrative Law in Scotland* (1997), pp. 256–260; *The Laws of Scotland: Stair Memorial Encyclopaedia*, Vol. 1, paras 214–222; W. Wade and C. Forsyth, *Administrative Law* (7th ed., 1994), pp. 41–53; P. P. Craig, *Administrative Law* (3rd ed., 1994), pp. 4–12; M. Deans, *Scots Public Law* (1995), pp. 140–141; D. Oliver, "Is the *Ultra Vires* Rule the basis of Judicial Review?" [1987] P.L. 543; C. Forsyth, "Of Fig Leaves and Fairy Tales: the Ultra Vires Doctrine, the Sovereignty of Parliament and Judicial Review" [1996] 55 C.L.J. 122; and M. Elliot, "The Ultra Vires Doctrine in a Constitutional Setting: Still the Central Principle of Administrative Law" (1999) 58 C.L.J. 129.

3–1

SIMPLE ULTRA VIRES: THE BASIC PRINCIPLES

The County Council of the County of Banff v. The Scottish Education Department

1934 S.C. 353

LORD PRESIDENT (CLYDE): "The question in this special case is one of the construction of the Education Act of 1918. Under section 4 of the that Act it is made lawful for an Education Authority — with the object of securing that no child or young person is debarred by lack of means from the benefit of attendance at an intermediate or secondary school — 'to grant assistance in the case of any such child or young person by payment of a travelling expenses, or of fees, or of the cost of residence in a hostel, or of a bursary or maintenance allowance, or any combination of these forms of assistance, or otherwise, as the authority think fit.' By a later part of the same section those powers are extended to the case of any duly qualified person resident in the education area who may otherwise be debarred from entering or attending a university, training college, or central institution.

By section 6 of the statute the Education Authority are required to submit schemes not only for the provision generally of education in their area, but also, *inter alia*, for the granting of assistance under section 4 to the two classes of people therein mentioned. In the present case the local Authority have presented a Scheme to the Education Department, which deals (in different ways) with the case of children attending or desiring to attend intermediate or secondary schools, and the case of young people attending or desiring to attend universities, central institutions, or training colleges. In the case of the children,

3–2

assistance may be given by payment (out and out) of certain charges, and no stipulations with regard to repayment are made, although a pious hope is expressed that these grants may be repaid either by the child when it grows up or by its parents or guardians. No doubt there is always a certain honourable obligation to repay assistance of this kind given out of public funds; but that is all that the Scheme says with regard to that.

In the case of the young people, however — the young students who are desirous of passing on to a university, central institution, or training college — the plan is entirely different. The sole mode of assistance provided for them is to be by way of loan, secured by the young student's personal bond, to which there may be demanded the accession of cautioners or guarantors in the shape of parents or guardians, and so on. These loans are to be without interest in the first instance, but later they are to carry interest at certain rates. The interest begins to run from the date at which the loan becomes repayable, namely, the attainment by the young student of some position which carries remuneration, or some alteration in his circumstances which, in the opinion of the Education Authority's Committee, enables him to repay the loan. There is no provision (such as in the part of the Scheme applicable to children and young persons) for direct payment of any of the expenses likely to be incurred by a young student; the sole provision of the Scheme in the case of young students is this provision by way of loan.

The Department have taken the view that the Scheme, so far as relating to the young students, is beyond the powers of the Education Authority under section 4. It is not necessary for the determination of that question to say anything about the wisdom, or expediency, or propriety of restricting the mode of assistance to young students to the granting of loans. The whole gist of the matter depends upon the determination of the question whether, on a sound construction of section 4, the assistance that may be granted by an Education Authority may be granted in the form of loans at all.

The question depends, in the first instance, on the meaning of the word 'payment' in section 4. 'Payment,' of course, is a broad term; but, when I look at the context: — 'to grant assistance … by *payment* of travelling expenses, or of fees, or of the cost of residence in a hostel, or of a bursary or maintenance allowance, or any combination of these forms' (which just means any one or more of them), I am at once made to doubt whether a power to make 'payment' of his or her travelling expenses, or of his or her fees, or of the cost of his or her residence in a hostel, and so on, can — either in the case of a child or young person, or in the case of a young student, by any fair construction be held to include a power to make loans to him or them for these purposes. *Prima facie* 'payment' means payment to the transport undertaker, or the school or college authority, or the keeper of the hostel; and I see no reason for reading the power to give assistance by making such payments as if the words used in the section had been: — 'to grant assistance by payment (of the various expenses enumerated in the statute), or by lending to the child, young person, or student, on such terms and conditions as may be fixed by the Education Authority, the sums necessary to defray such expenses.' I am not prepared to take so broad a construction of section 4 as that. Nor do I think the use of the words 'or otherwise' (at the end of the enumeration of the various methods of assistance) materially helps; for I think the Solicitor-General was right when he said that these words relate to the various kinds of payments which are authorised, and not to modes of assistance other than payment.

I am to some extent influenced by the considerations which arise from subhead (*b*) of subsection (1) of section 6, and from the general financial clauses of the statute. Even for the purpose of section 4 it is the duty of the Education Authority to provide an estimate of expenditure; and generally, with regard to the education fund, it is the business of an Education Authority under the Act to frame their budget, to fix their rates so as to meet that budget, and to carry forward from each year to the following year a surplus, if there is any, or a deficit, if there is not. I find it difficult to believe that the estimate of expenditure, or the annual budget, or the annual deficit on the school fund, was a matter which in the intention of Parliament was to be complicated by introducing into the finance of the Education Authority a block (of greater or lesser dimensions), of loans to children or young persons, or to students, on their personal security, repayment of which is dependent upon so uncertain a contingency as the success of a university student, or a young man or woman who goes through a central institution or training college, in obtaining a position which would enable him or her to repay a loan of from £50 to £150, as the case might be, with interest. I cannot believe that was the intention of Parliament; and I do not think the expressions used with regard to the accounts of the Education Authority's expenditure are consistent with that having been the true intention.

In these circumstances, while possibly it may be thought in some quarters to be a matter of regret that the Education Authority are not allowed to provide assistance in the form of loans, that is a matter of policy about which I am not qualified to say anything. It seems to me that the question of law put to us must be answered in the affirmative."

LORD BLACKBURY: "The question in this case is a comparatively short one. It depends upon the interpretation to be placed upon the powers given to local Education Authorities by section 4(1) of the Education (Scotland) Act of 1918. The section provides that it shall be lawful for the local Authority to give assistance to children or young persons, who may require assistance to enable them to attend intermediate or secondary schools, by payment of their travelling expenses, or school fees, or of a maintenance or residential allowance; and to give similar assistance to older persons to enable them to enter universities or training colleges. We are asked to say whether, in view of the terms of this section, it is within the power of a local Education Authority, instead of paying the expenses to be incurred in connexion with the further education of a young person at a university or training college, to give money on loan to such young person, and to take from him or her a bond acknowledging that the money has been advanced on loan and is repayable on certain conditions.

I do not think that the construction of the section admits of any doubt, and I have come, with some regret, to the conclusion that it contemplates that the assistance given must be by payment of the expenses alone, and that no power is given to the Local Authority to grant loans. It may be that the privilege of being able to get money required to complete their education by loan instead of in the name of charity might be very much appreciated by some members of the community, and might result in a greater use being made of the advantages which the Act offers to people of the poorer classes than is made at the present time. But I have no reasonable doubt in my mind that the question of loan is not within the contemplation of the Act at all, and that section 4 implies direct payment and nothing else; and, accordingly, the question must be answered, as your Lordship suggests, in the affirmative."

LORD MORISON: "I concur."

Notes

(1) In *Re Westminster City Council* [1986] A.C. 668 a grant of £40 million by the Greater   **3–3**
London Council in favour of ILEA was held to be *ultra vires*. The Local Government Act 1985 gave detailed provision for the financing of ILEA after their abolition of GLC. Clear but express provision would have been required to enable the GLC to make such a grant. In addition, grants to "umbrella bodies" — for example, arts and disabled centres — were also unlawful because they offended against the principle that local government finance be conducted on an annual basis: see also *Crédit Suisse v. Allerdale Borough Council* [1996] 4 All E.R. 129; *Crédit Suisse v. Waltham Forest London Borough Council* [1996] 4 All E.R. 176; *R. v. Kensington and Chelsea Royal London Borough Council, ex parte Brandt, The Times*, December 21, 1995; *R. v. Manchester City Council, ex parte Fulford* (1984) 81 L.G.R. 292; and *Rossi v. Edinburgh Magistrates* (1904) 7 F.(H.L.) 85.

(2) Simple *ultra vires* is also significant in the law on the contracts of public authorities and in relation to administrative rule making, particularly delegated legislation, on which see para. 14–14 and Chapter 2 respectively.

(3) Typically we think of *ultra vires* in administrative law as relating only to challenges to the use of statutory power. However, as *West v. Secretary of State for Scotland*, 1992 S.C. 385 held, the scope of *ultra vires* extends to decisions made under "a jurisdiction, power or authority … delegated or entrusted by statute, agreement or any other instrument" *per* the Lord President (Hope) at 650. *West* is extracted at para. 10–7.

A number of the cases referred to in *West* rested on allegations of *ultra vires* outwith a statutory context. In *Ferguson v. Scottish Football Association*, 1996 G.W.D. 11-601 a professional footballer successfully obtained judicial review of the disciplinary committee of the Scottish Football Association and its disciplinary appeals tribunal on the basis that since no action had been taken by the match referee in relation to an alleged incident, it was not open to the football authorities to seek to imply a wider power of discipline under their articles of association.

Ultra vires is limited by the fact that the scope of the doctrine is based upon the need for a statute, agreement or instrument to exist and accordingly its scope may be limited in relation to powers resting on other bases. In *Malone v. Metropolitan Police Commissioner* [1979] Ch. 344 telephone tapping was held to be lawful as it could be "carried out without committing any breach of the law, it requires no authorisation by statue or common law; it can lawfully be done simply because there is nothing to make it unlawful" and, moreover, "England, it may be said, is not a country where everything is forbidden except what is expressly permitted: it is a country where everything is permitted except what is expressly forbidden" at 381 and *per* Megarry V.-C. For comment see C. Harlow [1980] P.L. 1 and V. Bevan, "Is Anybody There?" [1980] P.L. 431. Malone subsequently went to the European Court of Human Rights where it was held that telephone tapping carried out on such a non-statutory basis was a breach of the right to respect for his private life and his home guaranteed by Article 8.1 of the European Convention on Human Rights. In particular for a restriction to be "lawful" it required to be "prescribed by law" in terms of Article 8.2 and as telephone tapping was not prescribed by or subject to any legal framework, this test was not passed. Arguably this approach was already reflected in administrative law's strong presumption against "unfettered discretion", on which see, for example, *Padfield v. Minister of Agriculture, Fisheries and Food* [1968] A.C. 997 extracted at para. 6–13; see also *Malone v. United Kingdom* (1985) 7 E.H.R.R. 14. This led to statutory reform in the Interception of Communications Act 1985. Article 8 is now a Convention right protected by the Human Rights Act 1998. Problems may, however, continue to exist in relations to actions which are founded upon prerogative power, on which see para. 10–10.

ULTRA VIRES AND IMPLIED POWERS

Piggins & Rix Ltd v. Montrose Port Authority

1995 S.L.T. 418

3–4   "A port authority acquired by statute the property, powers and responsibilities formerly vested in statutory trustees appointed to manage the harbour of Montrose. The property included lands on both banks of the River South Esk. Section 51 of the Montrose Harbour Act 1837 expressly gave the authority power to sell, feu or lease the lands on the north bank. Article 21 provided express power, in respect of the lands on the south bank, to lease or grant to others the use of or servitudes over the land. Article 2 of the 1974 Order and s. 20 of the Harbours, Docks and Piers Clauses Act 1847 provided an express power to buy adjoining lands for use for certain purposes.

The authority, having let the lands on the south bank to tenants, agreed to accept a surrender of the lease in return for the payment by them of a sum which was to be raised partly by the sale of a part of the south bank for which the authority had no need. The authority and the purchasers presented a special case for the opinion of the Court of Session on the question whether the authority had power to sell the subjects.

The purchasers argued that a statutory corporation had, in addition to their express powers, such powers as could reasonably be implied from the wording of the statutory provisions conferring express powers. In any event, such a corporation had such powers as could be implied as being reasonably incidental to the corporation's objects, which in this case were to operate the harbour, to provide lands and facilities for its users, and from time to time to improve it."

'LORD McCLUSKEY: "This is a special case presented to the Inner House under s. 27 of the Court of Session Act 1988. The agreed facts are clearly set forth in the statement of facts. The question of law submitted to the court for its opinion raises the issue as to whether or not the second parties, a statutory body, have power to dispose of certain heritable subjects to the first parties... .

Counsel for the first parties contended that a statutory corporation such as the second parties had, in addition to their express powers, such powers as could reasonably be implied from the wording of the statutory provisions conferring express powers. Furthermore, and even in the absence of express powers from which such additional powers could be inferred, the second parties possessed such powers as could be implied as being reasonably incidental to the objects of the statutory corporation. On the facts of the present case the first parties contended that the power to sell the subjects to the first parties should be regarded as within a power implied as reasonably incidental to the objects of the second parties. The express powers were those contained in the 1974 Order, notably s. 20 of the 1847 Act which was expressly incorporated therein. The objects of the second parties as a harbour authority were the provision of lands and facilities for harbour uses, the proper management and regulation of the harbour and its activities, including such matters as safety and the environment, the changing and improving of the harbour facilities as circumstances required and assorted other specific activities which were expressly specified in the governing statutes. In summary, the objects of the second parties were to operate and from time to time improve the harbour. On the matter of the implied powers counsel referred to the *Ashbury Railway Co. v. Riche*, and to the opinion of the Lord Chancellor. In *Att. Gen v. Great Eastern Railway Co.* the Lord Chancellor made it plain that the doctrine of ultra vires was to be 'reasonably', and not unreasonably, understood and applied, and that whatever might fairly be regarded as incidental to, or consequential upon, those things which the legislature has authorised, ought not (unless expressly prohibited) to be held, by judicial construction, to be ultra vires. The same doctrine was to be found in *Shiell's Trs v. Scottish Property Investment Building Society (in liquidation)*. There, the Lord Chancellor, dealing with a building society which had been created by statute, followed the *Great Eastern Railway Co.* case and stated ((1884) 12 R (HL) at p. 18): 'when you have got a main purpose expressed, and ample authority given to effectuate that main purpose, things which are incidental to it, and which may reasonably and properly be done, and against which no express prohibition is found, may and ought *prima facie* to follow from the authority for effectuating the main purpose by proper and general means ... we must ascertain first of all what the main purpose here is, then what are the general powers of the directors, then what are their special powers, and then, supposing that this is not within the natural meaning either of their general powers or of their special powers, whether it can be brought in as incidental to the main purpose and a thing reasonably to be done for effectuating it.'

Reference was also made to *London County Council v. Att. Gen., Att. Gen. v. Mersey Railway, Re Kingsbury Collieries Ltd and Moore's Contract, D. & J. Nicol v. Dundee Harbour Trs, Glasgow Tramway and Omnibus v. Magistrates of Glasgow*. The principle to be derived from these cases, and it applied not only to limited companies but also to statutory bodies other than limited companies, was that the court could look at the objects of a statutory corporation and could find that the corporation had implied powers which were reasonably incidental to and consequential upon the stated objects. That principle was still being applied as could be seen in *Rolled Steel Ltd v. British Steel Corporation*. In the present instance, it was submitted, the objects of the harbour authority were perfectly plain. Furthermore it was clear that a statutory corporation such as the second parties had to deal with land. The principle enshrined in the cases was that the court had to go from the general statement of objects to look at the particular transaction and to decide, in the circumstances of the particular case, whether or not the transaction was one which the corporation was empowered to do by reason of the fact that it was reasonably incidental to and consequential upon the achieving of their objects. It was not any part of the first parties' submission that the second parties had any wider power than the one necessary to enable them to sell this relatively small and relatively unimportant piece of land which was surplus to requirements. Such a power as the first parties contended for was in no way contrary to any express power or object of the second parties. It would not undermine or detract from the achieving of the second parties' purposes. On the contrary the sale had enabled the second parties to raise more than half the sum required to buy out the P & O lease, thus freeing what were plainly important harbour facilities and bringing them into use for the general purposes of the harbour. The sale of the subjects to the first parties was integral with that larger transaction. It was incidental to it and consequential upon it; and the larger transaction was indisputably within the powers of the second parties. With regard to the cases of *Meek v. Lothian Regional Council, Hazell v. Hammersmith Borough Council* and *McCarthy and Stone*, founded upon by the second parties and based upon the local government legislation for England and for Scotland, those cases dealt with separate questions and in particular turned upon the question as to what were to be understood as the 'functions' of local authorities. Accordingly those cases did not assist. In any event they did not contradict the line of authority seen in the cases including *D. & J. Nicol v. Dundee Harbour Trs*. Ultimately the question became one of the application of broad principles to particular facts. Here, given the small and relatively unimportant character of the land, the relationship of the sale of the subjects to the ending of the lease over the larger area of land of which the subjects had formed part, the existence of the clause of pre-emption, the payment of a fair price for land that was surplus to requirements and the fact that they had acted in good faith and after receiving professional advice, the whole transaction, including the sale or agreement to sell, could be seen to be one which fell within the implied powers of the trustees.... .

Turning to the broad proposition upon which the first parties principally founded, it was submitted that there was no principle of law to the effect that the powers of a statutory corporation could be inferred from the objects of the corporation. The law had been settled for Scotland since at least the case of *D & J Nicol v. Dundee Harbour Trs*, but it was clear in certain recent cases that the appropriate provisions of local government legislation both in England and in Scotland enshrined the settled rule. Reference was made to the obiter observations of Lord McDonald in *Meek v. Lothian Regional Council, Hazell v. Hammersmith Borough Council* and *R v. Richmond LBC, ex p McCarthy & Stone*. It was particularly to be noted that a power was not to be implied on the basis that it was incidental merely because the possession of such a power would be convenient, desirable or profitable or might help the statutory body to achieve its aims. Reference was also made to *Att. Gen. v. Manchester Corporation*. There was no dispute that the ultra vires rule had to be construed reasonably but it was submitted that once the express power had been found and construed reasonably one had to look strictly at the mater of 'incidentalness'. That was clear from *D. & J. Nicol v. Dundee Harbour Trs*. There was nothing in a case of this kind to prevent a body such as the second parties from going back to Parliament to seek additional powers if they thought they needed them. The main purpose of the legislation was to enable port and harbour facilities to be provided. The object of the trustees and their successors was to operate the harbour but only in accordance with the powers which were expressly or impliedly conferred upon the trustees. The recent cases based upon the local government legislation did indeed found upon the expression in the statute of what were the functions of the local authority. When one looked at the port authority it had no function in relation to land transactions; it had certain well defined and limited powers in relation to land transactions. Section 20 did not confer a power but a function. In the whole circumstances the question should be answered in the negative.

Given the acknowledgment that nowhere in the statutory provision which confer powers upon the second parties in there any express power to sell any part of the reclaimed land, we consider that the correct starting point for a search for implied powers is with the provisions conferring express powers. Both parties are agreed that a statutory corporation's expressly conferred powers may be so worded that other powers consequent upon or incidental to those expressly conferred powers can be implied. Thus, for example, a power to grant a lease of land forming part of the undertaking could reasonably and incidentally infer a power to renegotiate a lease of the land. Additionally, however, the principle of expressio unius est excusio alterius may be applicable in construing the enactments which constitute the statutory undertaking and confer express powers upon it. Where those enactments expressly confer several well defined, wide powers to lease the land in the undertaking or to allow the lands to be occupied by, or subject to easements or servitudes in favour of, other parties, and further confer express powers to purchase specified lands and to sell certain lands belonging to the undertaking, the sensible inference appears to be that the list of express powers in relation to transaction in land is intended to be comprehensive and exhaustive. A power to sell the land of a statutory undertaking, whether that land has been acquired by compulsory powers or by covenant, is an important power. One would not expect such a power to be left to inference. Indeed such a power was expressly conferred upon the trustee by s. 51 of the 1837 Act; the words conferring that power could hardly be clearer: [his Lordship quoted its terms and continued:]

That power to sell land related only to the harbour land on the north side of the river. When the 1974 Order was made in appears to us extremely improbable that Parliament was not conscious that the trustees already enjoyed a power of sale over the lands previously vested in them. Section 21 of that order dealt very specifically with the powers of the trustees to allow others to occupy the reclaimed land. The powers thus expressly conferred would permit the trustees, if they judged that they did not need certain lands for any proper harbour purpose for the foreseeable future, to grant a very long lease. This indeed happened when they granted the lease to P & O for nearly 50 years. No party suggested that the non-conferring of a power of sale could be treated as a casus omissus. That being so, the reasonable inference from the non-conferring of any express power of sale in relation to the newly acquired reclaimed land is that the trustees were not intended to have the power to sell it. Why such a power should have been withheld is not known to this court; the background to the making of the 1974 Order was not disclosed in the special case. It is not, however, difficult to infer that reclaimed land purchased from the Crown Estates Commissioners and bordered by land privately occupied might be seen to be in a special category. But be that as it may, the absence of any express power to sell that land or any part of it is, in our view, reasonably consistent only with a legislative intention to withhold that power. We cannot regard such a power as reasonably incidental to or consequent upon any of the express powers of the trustees, including those contained in s. 20 of the 1847 Act.

It might be said that this view is really sufficient for the disposal of the case, but we should turn to the separate and alternative submission that such a power could be inferred as reasonably incidental to and consequent upon the purposes and objects of the corporation. For the purposes of this submission we refer to the objects of the second parties as narrated in the various statutory provisions listed in the statement of facts. We can, for the purposes of considering this submission, accept the objects of the harbour authority as being broadly to provide lands and facilities for harbour users, the proper management and regulation of the harbour and its activities, including such matters as safety and the environment, the changing and improving of the harbour facilities as circumstances required and the assorted other purposes expressly specified in the governing statute. The case of *Ashbury Railway Carriage and Iron Co. v. Riche* concerned a company created a corporation under the Companies Act 1862. It was there held that the objects of a company as stated in the memorandum of association could not be departed from except insofar as permitted by s. 12 of that Act of 1862, which allowed the company to modify in the prescribed manner the conditions contained in its memorandum of association. The contract there under consideration being of a nature not included in the memorandum of association was held to be ultra vires both of the directors and of the whole company. In that context, Lord Selborne said, at (1875) LR 7 HL, pp. 693–694: 'I only repeat what Lord Cranworth, in *Hawkes v. Eastern Counties Railway Company* (when moving the judgment of this

House), stated to be settled law, when I say that a statutory corporation created by Act of Parliament for a particular purpose, is limited, as to all its powers, by the purposes of its incorporation as defined in that Act. The present and all other companies incorporated by virtue of the Companies Act of 1862 appear to me to be statutory corporations within this principle. The memorandum of association is under that Act their fundamental, and (except in certain specified particulars) their unalterable law; and they are incorporated only for the objects and purposes expressed in the memorandum ... I am unable to see any distinction for this purpose between statutory corporations under Railway Acts, and statutory corporation under the Joint Stock Companies Act of 1862.

In *Att. Gen. v. Great Eastern Railway Co.*, Lord Selborne, by then Lord Chancellor, said at (1880) 5 App Case, p 478: 'I assume that your Lordships will not now recede from anything that was determined in *The Ashbury Railway Company v. Riche*. It appears to me to be important that the doctrine of ultra vires, as it was explained in this case, should be maintained. But I agree with Lord Justice James that this doctrine ought to be reasonably, and not unreasonably, understood and applied, and that whatever may fairly be regarded as incidental to, or consequential upon, those things which the Legislature has authorised, ought not (unless expressly prohibited) to be held, by judicial construction, to be ultra vires.'

In that case it was held that the acts under scrutiny were not ultra vires but that was because they were expressly authorised by statute. At p 481 Lord Blackburn said: '*The Ashbury Railway Carriage and Iron Company v. Riche* ... appears to me to decide at all events this, that where there is an Act of Parliament creating a corporation for a particular purpose, and giving it powers for that particular purpose, what it does not expressly or impliedly authorise is to be taken to be prohibited'.

Lord Watson, at p. 486, added: 'I cannot doubt that the principle by which this House in the case of the *Ashbury Railway Company v. Riche* tested the power of a joint stock company registered (with limited liability) under the Companies Act of 1862, applies with equal force to the case of a railway company incorporated by Act of Parliament. That principle, in its application to the present case, appears to me to be this, that when a railway company has been created for public purposes, the Legislature must be held to have prohibited every act of the company which its incorporating statutes do not warrant either expressly or by fair implication. It follows that the Great Eastern Company has exceeded its statutory powers unless it can be shewn that the company has statutory authority, express or implied, to let rolling stock and plant on hire to the Southend Railway Company.'

The same general principles were applied in *Shiell's Trs v. Scottish Property Investment Building Society (in liquidation)*. In that case, Lord Selborne, at (1884) 12 R (HL), p. 18, said: 'Now, I entirely adhere to what was said in this House in the case of Attorney-General v. Great Eastern Railway Company, that when you have got a main purpose expressed, and ample authority given to effectuate the main purpose, things which are incidental to it, and which may reasonably and properly be done, and against which no express prohibition is found, may and ought *prima facie* to follow from the authority for effectuating the main purpose by proper and general means.'

The actings of the building society which were under scrutiny were there held to be intra vires. Then in *D & J Nicol v. Dundee Harbour Trs*, the same principles were applied to a body of harbour trustees, incorporated by Act of Parliament. The trustees were seeking to justify as intra vires the use of ferry steamers to carry passengers from and to places outwith the limits of the ferry as defined in the relevant private Act of Parliament of 1911. The Lord Chancellor, Viscount Haldane, in holding the activity to be ultra vires said (at 1915 SC (HL), p. 9; 1914 2 SLT, p. 418): 'It is now well settled by the judgment of this House in the appeal in that case [Ashbury Railway Carriage Company], and by subsequent decision which the House has given, that the answer to the question whether a corporation created by a statute has a particular power depends exclusively on whether that power has been expressly given to it by the statute regulating it, or can be implied from the language used. The question is simply one of construction of language, and not of presumption.'

In so saying he disapproved of what had been said by Blackburn J (as he then was), in the *Ashbury* case, that 'a general power of contracting is an incident to a corporation which it requires an indication of intention in the Legislature to take away'. Lord Dunedin, in response to the submission that the use of the vessels beyond the statutory limits of the ferry was incidental to the main purpose of the ferry said, at p. 12 (p. 420): 'This can only be so if "incidental" has such a wide interpretation as this — that any use of plant which brings in money, and so assists the main undertaking, is a use incidental to that undertaking. I cannot so hold. The appellants admit that if they went in for a regular business of excursion contractors that would be *ultra vires*. "Incidental", in my view, means incidental to the main purposes of the main business, and making excursions with the ferry boats beyond the limits of the ferry — a proceeding necessarily subjecting the boats to new and different risks from those to which they are subjected in the ordinary ferry business — can never be, in my view, a proceeding incidental to the business of the ferry just because the money so earned goes into what I may call the ferry coffers.'

Commenting on the same submission, Lord Parmoor, at p. 18 (p. 424) said: 'I think that the principle that a corporation of limited authority, if it has surplus plant, can use that plant in any way it thinks profitable, so long as such use is not in contravention of its statutory duties, is quite untenable.... . The second argument on which Mr Younger relied was based on a suggested analogy between surplus plant and surplus land, when such land had been acquired for statutory purposes, but was not being wholly used for such purposes. I regard with suspicion any argument founded on analogy; but the answer is that the possession of surplus land does not, any more than the possession of surplus plant, extend the ambit of the powers conferred on a company by statute.'

We can accept that these cases are authority for the rule that the powers of a statutory corporation are those expressly conferred upon it by the relevant statutes and also those implied from the language used as being reasonably incidental to or consequential upon the main purposes for which the corporation has been constituted. But in each of these cases, unless an *express* power was found, the actings under scrutiny were held to be ultra vires. Accordingly, it cannot be said that any of these cases is authority for the proposition that whatever is consistent with the main purposes and may be conducive to achieving them is to be taken as impliedly authorised provided only that it is not expressly forbidden. It was that error which Blackburn J fell into when the *Ashbury* case was in the lower court: *Riche v. Ashbury Railway Carriage Co* (1874) LR 9 Ex at p. 264. It is equally clear that the powers of a statutory corporation are not to be enlarged just because the activity to be engaged in appears to be sensible, convenient, and profitable. These cases also show that the court in judging of the vires of a statutory corporation must always examine and construe the language of the statutory provisions in the light of what, in the circumstances obtaining, it is claimed is impliedly authorised.

Re Kingbury Collieries Ltd and Moore's Contract is a case in which it was held that a company had an implied power to sell land which it had acquired; such a power was held to be impliedly warranted by its constitution. Kekewich J extracted from his consideration of the authorities the following: 'That seems to me to point directly to there being contained in the memorandum of association anything which is fairly incidental to the objects therein expressed, so that it can be said to be there by reasonable implication.'

But at pp. 266–267 he also founded upon the additional opinion made by Vaughan Williams LJ in *Att Gen v Mersey Railway Co* [1907] 1 Ch at p. 106: 'You ought to give a wider construction to the words of a memorandum of association creating and defining the powers of a purely commercial company having no compulsory powers and no monopoly than you would give to the words of a statute creating a company, like a railway company, having compulsory powers of land purchase and a practical monopoly.'

That statement appeared to Kekewich J 'to be extremely useful as indicating on what lines the memorandum of association of a commercial company is to be construed'. In these circumstances his decision in favour of the company's act being intra vires thus appears to rest not only upon his view of the objects of the particular company as stated in the memorandum of association but upon the nature of the company as 'a purely commercial company having no compulsory powers and no monopoly'. Lord McDonald's obiter dicta in *Meek v Lothian Regional Council* take the matter no further, although he refers to an unidentified recent expression of opinion to the effect that the words 'incidental to' should be applied with a narrow meaning and not as equivalent to 'in connection with'. The recent cases of *Hazell v. Hammersmith LBC*, concerned with the legality of swap transactions, and *R v Richmond LBC, ex p McCarthy & Stone*, concerned with the legality of a decision by a local planning authority to levy a charge on developers for inquiries relating to speculative development or redevelopment proposals, dealt with the provisions of s. 111(1) of the Local Government Act 1972, the English equivalent of s 69 of the Local Government (Scotland) Act 1973. Each section includes the words, 'Without prejudice to any powers exercisable apart from this section ... a local authority shall have power to do anything (whether or not involving the expenditure, borrowing or lending of money or the acquisition or disposal of any property or rights) which is calculated to facilitate, or is conducive or incidental to, the discharge of any of their functions'.

In the latter case Lord Lowry, delivering the principal speech, said ([1992] 2 AC at p 68): 'This provision, as both sides agree, gives statutory recognition to the common law rule governing the activities of local authorities and other statutory corporations, as recognised in such well-known authorities on the doctrine of ultra vires as *Ashbury Railway Carriage and Iron Co Ltd v Riche* (1875) LR 7 HL 653; *Attorney-General v Great EAstern Railway Co* (1880) 5 App Case 473 and *Attorney-General v Fulham Corporation* [1921] 1 Ch 440'.

In *Hazell* Lord Templeman, with whom all the other judges agreed, said ([1992] 2 AC at p 31): 'The authorities also show that a power is not incidental merely because it is convenient or desirable or profitable'.

It is thus clear that although the ultra vires doctrine is not to be applied unreasonably, the court cannot look indulgently upon the statutory provisions which constitute and regulate a statutory corporation so as to permit that corporation to do things merely upon the basis that there are perceived benefits in doing them and no obvious disadvantages. It is essential to look at the main purpose or purposes of the corporation to see whether or not the activity which it is said the corporation may indulge in is one which on a proper construction is reasonably incidental to and consequential upon those purposes.

In the present case we consider that the second parties had and have no object or purpose in relation to land transactions. It is not one of their objects or purposes to engage in land transactions. Their objects, their purposes, are all related to the provision, maintenance and operation of the harbour and its facilities. To achieve these purposes they are expressly given various powers, including well defined and limited powers in relation to land. Although these powers are limited it is difficult to think of any significant power in relation to land which is not expressly given, except that quoad the reclaimed land no power to sell is given. It cannot be said that it is in any way necessary that the second parties should possess such a power in relation to that reclaimed land. Almost anything that they could want to do with the land in relation to their harbour purposes, can be done by using the powers expressly conferred. For example, if they find part of that land to be surplus to their requirements for the foreseeable future they are free to lease it for a long period. In our view, the purposes of the second parties are to own, maintain and operate the harbour and facilities but only in accordance with the powers expressly given by statute or incidentally implied from the powers expressly given. We have not been persuaded that there is any broad principle that powers can be inferred from objects or purposes otherwise than by examining the powers expressly given for the achieving of those objects and purposes and deriving from the express powers additional powers reasonably implied as incidental to them. We cannot regard the power to sell a material part of the reclaimed land as being implied merely because it is not prohibited and, if available, would enable the second parts to raise money to achieve a desirable aim or purpose which itself lies within the objects or purposes of the second parties.

In our view, therefore, the second parties do not have power to dispone the subjects to the first parties. The question of law is answered in the negative."

Notes

(1) As will be seen from the extract, extensive reliance was placed on a series of nineteenth-   **3–5**
century cases involving statutory undertakers, particularly railway companies. This line of authority, particularly the decisions in *Riche* and *Great Eastern Railway Co.*, helped to displace the rigid application of the *ultra vires* doctrine which ruled out any exercise of power other than that which was expressly conferred. For example, in *Wakefield v. Commissioners of Supply of Renfrewshire* (1878) 6 R. 259 it was indicated by the Lord President (Inglis) (at 267) that statutory funds could only be used for purposes as expressly stated "and not a shilling of those funds can be spent for any other purpose". However, the law was not always entirely clear and there was contrary authority which suggested that activities which could be regarded as "fair and reasonable acts of administration on the part of governing body" were lawful. See here *Perth Water Commissioners v. McDonald* (1879) 6 R. 1050. This became known as the implied powers doctrine.

(2) Other applications of the doctrine of implied powers include the following:

- *Attorney General v. Manchester Corporation* [1906] 1 Ch. 643. A parcel service was regarded as ancillary to the express powers to operate a tramway service.
- *Graham v. Glasgow Corporation*, 1936 S.C. 108. The establishment of printing and book binding and stationery office incidental to performance of a local authority of an express function.
- *Ferrier v. New Monkland School Board* (1881) 9 R. 30. A parish board was held to have implied power to use poor law funds to pay the school fees of children of poor parents.
- *Cormack v. Crown Estate Commissioners*, 1983 S.L.T. 179. Power of a salmon fisheries board to execute such works as appeared to it to be expedient to protect fisheries included power to construct a barrage across the River Alness.

Implied powers were, however, held not to exist in the following cases:

- *D. & J. Nicol v. Dundee Harbour Trustees*, 1915 S.C. (H.L.) 7. Ferry boats could not be used to provide pleasure excursions under the power of harbour trustees to maintain a ferry service across the Tay.
- *McColl v. Strathclyde Regional Council*, 1983 S.L.T. 616. Held unlawful for a water authority to add fluoride to the water to improve the general dental health of users of the water. Its duty to supply wholesome water could not extend to the addition of a substance to the supply.
- *Attorney-General v. Fulham Corporation* [1921] 1 Ch. 440. Held that the power of a local authority to set up a wash-house where residents could wash their own clothes did not permit the operation to be carried out by council employees on a commercial basis.

(3) It is important to note that although the sale of land was arguably beneficial in *Piggins &* *Rix*, that in itself was not enough to justify the implication of a power to do so. Arguably the money which could have been raised by the sale of land would have gone some ways to promote the general statutory purposes provided for in the legislation, but the means, the power of sale, was not provided. This is an example of the aspect of *ultra vires* doctrine that one cannot enlarge powers, particularly where no express power is provided. On this see also *London County Council v. Attorney General* [1902] A.C. 165. Note, however, that where a choice exists as to a course of action, an authority may in general choose which course to follow and need not follow the course which was most advantageous to individuals affected by its decision. This is, however, subject to a number of exceptions. General powers in one Act may not be used to achieve a goal which is expressly authorised in another Act: *British Airports Authority v. Secretary of State for Scotland*, 1979 S.C. 200. It is an abuse of power for an authority to use one set of statutory powers to bring about purposes authorised by other legislation: *R. v. Secretary of State for Home Affairs, ex parte Soblen* [1963] 1 Q.B. 829, C.A. Special circumstances may limit a choice of action: *Westminster Bank Ltd v. Minister of Housing and Local Government* [1971] A.C. 508 at 530.

ULTRA VIRES: PRINCIPLES AND PRESUMPTIONS

3–6 Many cases of alleged *ultra vires* turn on the interpretation of the particular grant of powers. It is nevertheless possible to discern general principles which the court will use to determine whether an action or decision is *ultra vires*. Many of these indicators take the form of presumptions of interpretation but some, such as obligations to comply with European Community law are substantive legal principles. Note the reference to the principle of interpretation, *expressio unius est exclusio alterius*, in *Piggins & Rix Ltd* by way of example. For a general account see *Stair Memorial Encyclopaedia*, Vol. 1, "Administrative Law", para. 219; Vol. 12, "Interpretation of Statutes, Deeds and Other Instruments", paras. 11-1–1206; W. Twining and D. R. Miers, *How to do Things with Rules* (2nd ed., 1991), p. 335; G. Ganz, "Public Law Principles Applicable to Dismissal from Employment" (1967) 27 M.L.R. 288; and P. Robertshaw, "Unreasonableness and Judicial Control of Administrative Discretion: The Geology of the Chertsey Caravans Case" [1975] P.L. 113. Twining and Miers observe, at p. 335, that for every presumption one can find an equal and opposite presumption. Of particular note are the following:

- Recognising a taxing power without express words as in *Stirrat Park Hogg v. Dumbarton District Council*, 1994 S.C.L.R. 631 (local authority held not to have power to charge for provision of copies of planning information) and see also *Congreve v. Home Office* [1976] Q.B. 629 noted at para. 6–5.

- Deprivation of individual rights, particularly without compensation as in *Malloch v. Aberdeen Corporation*, 1973 S.C. 227 (no power on the part of the Secretary of State to make regulations and standards which purported to include power to remove a teacher's right to continue to teach) and see also *Mixnam's Properties Ltd v. Chertsey Urban District Council* [1965] A.C. 735; *Hall and Co. Ltd v. Shoreham-by-Sea Urban District Council* [1964] 1 W.L.R. in relation to property rights (caravan site licence conditions *ultra vires* in conferring effective security of tenure on occupiers of caravans when no clear words in statute providing such tenure) and for an earlier example in a similar vein see *Edinburgh Magistrates v. Warrender* (1863) 1 M. 887 (no power conferred on local authority to interrupt public right of use of golf links).

- Ousting the jurisdiction of the courts as in *Anisminic Ltd v. Foreign Compensation Commission* [1969] 2 A.C. 147 extracted at para. 4–10.

- The individual's right "to choose how to care for his own body" *McColl v. Strathclyde Regional Council*, 1983 S.L.T. 616 above at 623 *per* Lord Jauncey.

- The Crown not being bound by statute: *Lord Advocate v. Strathclyde Regional Council and Dumbarton District Council*, 1990 S.L.T. 158 extracted at para. 13–12. Other constitutional principles may be relevant as in *Officers of State v. Douglas* (1838) 1 D. 300 (George IV acted *ultra vires* purporting to appoint officers under the Crown for a period in excess of his own life).

- Obligations under European Community law as in *Watt v. Secretary of State for Scotland* [1991] 3 C.M.L.R. 429 (unsuccessful allegation that the decision of the British Government to reduce a licence to fish for various species including haddock was *ultra vires* on the basis of alleged discrimination under Article 7 of the Treaty of Rome: see also *Walkingshaw v. Marshall*, 1992 S.L.T. 1167 and *MacGillivray v. Johnston (No. 2)*, 1994 S.L.T. 1012.

- Non-compliance with international law: *Collco Dealings Ltd v. I.R.C.* [1962] A.C. 1, including obligations under treaties such as the European Convention on Human Rights, on which see *R. v. Secretary of State for the Home Department, ex parte Brind* [1991] 1 A.C. 696 extracted at para. 6–43. One of the most potentially far-reaching principles that the courts will now be able to fasten on is contained in the next extract.

Human Rights Act 1998

s. 3

"Legislation

Interpretation of legislation

    3.—(1) So far as it is possible to do so, primary legislation and subordinate legislation must be read   **3–7**
and given effect in a way which is compatible with Convention rights.
    (2) This section—
(a)   applies to primary legislation and subordinate legislation whenever enacted;
(b)   does not affect the validity, continuing operation or enforcement of any incompatible primary legislation; and
(c)   does not affect the validity, continuing operation or enforcement of any incompatible subordinate legislation if (disregarding any possibility of revocation) primary legislation prevents removal of the incompatibility."

Notes

    (1) The Human Rights Act 1998 is clearly an extremely important statute. It has as its aim   **3–8**
the furtherance of the rights and freedoms guaranteed under the European Convention on Human Rights. It is beyond the scope of this book to consider the terms of the Act in any comprehensive or detailed sense. For a general account see the Government's White Paper, *Rights Brought Home: The Human Rights Bill*, Cmnd. 3787 (1997) and the annotations by Peter Duffy Q.C., in *Current Law Statutes*; L. Betten, *The Human Rights Act 1998 — What it means* (1998); J. Coppel, *European Convention on Human Rights* (1998) and for a useful summary of the Bill from a Scots perspective, K. Campbell, "Human Rights Brought Home?", 1998 S.L.T. (News) 269. In this and other chapters, the provisions which are likely to have the most immediate impact for administrative lawyers are discussed. The Act is due to come into effect in its entirety, it is believed, over the course of 2000 and applies throughout the United Kingdom: sections 18–20, 21(5), 22 and Schedule 4 to the Act are currently in force. Its application to the Scottish Parliament and Scottish Executive differs markedly to its application to U.K. governmental institutions. One should also not overlook the fact that under the Scotland Act 1998 both the Scottish Parliament and the Executive must act in accordance with the rights protected by the Act (Convention rights) *independently* of any obligations imposed upon them by the Human Rights Act. For further comment on this see the next section on the Scotland Act.
    (2) The Act seeks to achieve incorporation of human rights while respecting the principle of parliamentary sovereignty, insofar as the Westminster Parliament is concerned. It does this by a number of routes. First, public authorities which include the Scottish Parliament and the Scottish Executive are required to act in accordance with the Convention in terms of section 6. The courts are themselves public authorities for the purpose of section 6 and are in any event obliged by section 2 of the Act to take into account, *inter alia*, jurisprudence of the European Court of Human Rights in considering the matter where allegation of breach of Convention right has arisen. The Convention rights are set out in section 1 which, with sections 2 and 6, are

noted in greater depth at para. 6–17. The next means of protection is declarator of incompatibility created by section 4 which is extracted and discussed at para. 11–41. Our present concern is, however, with the strong principle of interpretation contained in the present extract. Section 3(1) goes beyond the existing principle of interpretation that ambiguous legislation will be interpreted in accordance with the Convention, on which see, for example, *R. v. Secretary of State for the Home Department, ex parte Brind* [1991] A.C. 696 extracted at para.6–43 and *AMT, Petitioner*, 1996 S.C.L.R. 897. Section 3 effectively reverses this approach. Lord Steyn commented ("Current topic: Incorporation and Devolution" (1998) E.H.R.L.R. 153 at 155) in relation to the phrase "so far as it is possible to do so" that this means:

> "Traditionally the search has been for the one true meaning of a statute. Now this search will be for a possible meaning that would prevent the need for a declaration of incompatibility. The questions will be (i) What meanings are the words capable of yielding? (ii) And critically, can the words be made to yield a sense consistent with Convention rights? In practical effect there will be rebuttable presumption in favour of an interpretation consistent with Convention rights."

This approach parallels the doctrine of European Community law whereby national legislation is to be interpreted "so far as possible" to give effect to Community obligations, on which see, for example, *Lister v. Forth Dry Dock and Engineering Co. Ltd* [1990] 1 A.C. 546 and see also *Webb v. EMO Air Cargo (U.K.) Ltd* [1993] 1 W.L.R. 49 *per* Lord Keith at pp. 59–60; and *R. v. Secretary of State for the Environment, ex parte Greenpeace* [1994] 4 All E.R. 352 *per* Potts, J. at 365. It also follows from section 3 that where common law presumptions and principles of interpretation have developed in a manner inconsistent with Convention rights, then they will have to yield to the principle in subsection (1). Where, however, the words of a statute are clear, then it would appear that section 3 cannot assist, but the section clearly enjoins on the court an obligation to establish an alterative possible meaning before reaching such a conclusion.

(2) Subsection (2) sets out the limits to this principle of interpretation. The cumulative effect of subsections (2)(*a*)–(*c*) is to make it clear that parliamentary sovereignty will take precedence over Convention rights. Subordinate legislation which is defined in section 21(1) as including acts of the Scottish Parliament can only be set aside if it breaches the principle enshrined in section 6(1). Subsection 2(c) is necessary because if the courts had jurisdiction under section 3 to quash subordinate legislation made under primary legislation, which clearly ran contrary to the Convention, that primary legislation would be rendered unworkable. Ultimately where a court concludes that primary legislation or subordinate legislation of this kind is not compatible with Convention rights, then it has power to make a declaration of incompatibility under section 4 and thereafter to leave a remedy, if any to Parliament under section 10, on which see para. 11–45.

(3) As we have noted, Acts of the Scottish Parliament are subordinate legislation for the purpose of the Act as are the traditional categories of delegated or subordinate legislation made by a member of the Scottish Executive: section 21(1)(*b*) and (*h*). Primary legislation made at Westminster cannot be struck down as in breach of section 6. Primary legislation and of course subordinate legislation of the Scottish Parliament and the Executive can. The consequences of a finding of "inconsistent interpretation" under section 3 for such provisions therefore has a far wider reaching effect in relation to these measures than Westminster measures. In this context is it also worth comparing the principle enshrined in section 3 of the Human Rights Act 1998 with the principle contained in section 101 of the Scotland Act 1998 noted at para. 3–13.

(4) Note also the provisions of section 19. This section is in force. A Minister of the Crown in charge of a Bill in either House of Parliament must, before a second reading of the Bill either make a statement to the effect that in his view the provisions of the Bill are compatible with the Convention rights, "a statement of compatibility", or make a statement to the effect that although he is unable to make such a statement, the Government nevertheless wishes the House to proceed with the Bill: subsection (1)(*a*), (*b*). Any such statement must be in writing and published in such a manner as the Minister considers appropriate: subsection (2). The exact effect of section 19 is uncertain. The obligation to interpret legislation insofar as possible with Convention rights contained in section 3 applies whether or not such a statement is made. What is the position if

no statement is made? Declaration under section 19 can hardly have any effect on the duty imposed by section 3. The lack of such a statement may, however, indicate an intent not to comply with Convention rights and in turn could lead to a declarator of incompatibility being sought under section 4.

Similar provisions are found in section 31 of the Scotland Act 1998. Under section 31 of the Scotland Act a Member of the Scottish Executive in charge of a Bill shall, on or before introduction of the Bill in Parliament state that in his view the provisions of the Bill would be within the legislative competence of the Parliament: subsection (1). The presiding Officer of the Parliament is also obliged to make a statement as to legislative competence: subsection (2). The form of any statement and the manner in which it is to be made will be determined by the standing orders of the Parliament, which provide for any statement to be published: subsection (3). Legislative competence does of course cover, among other things, compatibility with Convention rights, on which see section 29(2) above.

(5) For further discussion on the impact of section 3 and the general policy of the Act see G. Marshall, "Interpreting interpretation in the Human Rights Bill" [1998] P.L. 167; D. Pannick, "Principles of interpretation of Convention rights under the Human Rights Act and the discretionary area of judgment" [1998] P.L. 545; Lord Hope of Craighead, "Opinion: Devolution and Human Rights" (1998) 4 E.H.R.L.R. 367; N. Bamforth, "Parliamentary sovereignty and the Human Rights Act 1998" [1998] P.L. 572; K. Campbell, "Human Rights Brought Home?" 1998 S.L.T. (News) 269; A. Miller, "Current Topic: Human Rights and the Scottish Parliament" (1998) 3 E.H.R.L.R. 260; Lord Irvine of Lairg, "The Development of Human Rights in Britain under an Incorporated Convention on Human Rights" [1998] P.L. 221; Sir A. Hooper, "Current Topic: The Impact of the Human Rights Act on Judicial Decision Making" (1998) 6 E.H.R.L.R. 666; and K. G. Ewing, "The Human Rights Act and Parliamentary Democracy" (1999) 62 M.L.R. 79.

ULTRA VIRES AND THE SCOTLAND ACT 1998

The *ultra vires* doctrine is at the heart of the scheme of legislative devolution. The Scottish Parliament is not a sovereign Parliament as the Government's White Paper, *Scotland's Parliament*, Cm. 3658 (1997) observed (para. 4.2):   **3–9**

> "The UK Parliament is and will remain sovereign in all matters … Westminster will be choosing to exercise that sovereignty by devolving legislative responsibilities to a Scottish Parliament without in any way diminishing its own powers."

For general reading see C. M. G. Himsworth and C. R. Munro, *Devolution and the Scotland Bill* (1998), Chaps 5, 6 and The Constitution Unit, "Scotland's Parliament: The Framework for a New Scotland Act" (1998), Chaps 3, 4. The powers of the Scottish Executive, with some exceptions, can only lawfully be exercised in relation to those areas of activity within the legislative competence of the Parliament. It is therefore clear that *ultra vires* in its classic or simple sense will have its role to play in the relationship between the courts, the Parliament and the Executive. The relevance of the broader grounds of *ultra vires* should not, however, be overlooked although the extent to which it is appropriate to apply these broader grounds of control is perhaps more difficult to predict.

Scotland Act 1998

s. 29

"**Legislative competence**
   29.—(1) An Act of the Scottish Parliament is not law so far as any provision of the Act is outside the   **3–10**
legislative competence of the Parliament.
   (2) A provision is outside that competence so far as any of the following paragraphs apply—
   (a)   it would form part of the law of a country or territory other than Scotland, or confer or remove functions exercisable otherwise than in or as regards Scotland,

(b)   it relates to reserved matters,
(c)   it is in breach of the restrictions in Schedule 4,
(d)   it is incompatible with any of the Convention rights or with Community law,
(e)   it would remove the Lord Advocate from his position as head of the systems of criminal prosecution and investigation of deaths in Scotland."

Scotland Act 1998

s. 54

"Devolved competence

3–11   **54.**—(1) References in this Act to the exercise of a function being within or outside devolved competence are to be read in accordance with this section.
(2) It is outside devolved competence —
(a)   to make any provision by subordinate legislation which would be outside the legislative competence of the Parliament if it were included in an Act of the Scottish Parliament, or
(b)   to confirm or approve any subordinate legislation containing such provision.
(3) In the case of any function other than a function of making, confirming or approving subordinate legislation, it is outside devolved competence to exercise the function (or exercise it in any way) so far as a provision of an Act of the Scottish Parliament conferring the function (or, as the case may be, conferring it so as to be exercisable in that way) would be outside the legislative competence of the Parliament."

Notes

3–12   (1) Unlike the previous scheme of devolution contained in the Scotland Act 1978 (on which see, for example, A. W. Bradley and D. J. Christie, *The Scotland Act 1978* (1979) the approach taken by the Government was to give general legislative competence to the Scottish Parliament under section 29, subject to the limitations contained in subsection (2) and in particular the reserved matters contained in Schedule 5 to the Act referred to in subsection (2)(*b*) and the restrictions contained in Schedule 4 referred to in subsection (2)(*c*). Detailed discussion of Schedules 4 and 5 and their inter-relationship is beyond the scope of this book, although reference is made where appropriate to further detailed comment in C. M. G. Himsworth and C. R. Munro, *The Scotland Act 1998* (1999).

For present purposes they can be summarised broadly as follows: Schedule 5 lists reserved matters included under Part I — "General reservations" under the headings: The Constitution, Political parties, Foreign affairs etc., Public service, Defence and Treason. Part II contains a far longer list of "Specific reservations" under eleven heads: Financial and Economic Matters, Home Affairs, Trade and Industry, Energy, Transport, Social Security, Regulation of the Professions, Employment, Health and Medicines, Media and Culture and Miscellaneous. As a whole, Schedule 5 is intended to give guidance to the Parliament and the Executive as well as to the courts as to the limits of legislative competence. Schedule 5 in turn requires to be read with the matters referred to in Schedule 4. As applied by subsection (2)(*c*) Schedule 4 serves to protect against modification by the Scottish Parliament, many provisions of the Scotland Act itself, as well as a list of particular enactments, many of which have constitutional significance, such as the most important provisions of the Acts of Union, para. 1(2)(*a*), the European Communities Act 1972, para. 1(2)(*c*) and the Human Rights Act 1998, para. 1(2)(*f*). Paragraph 2 of the Schedule goes on to provide that "An Act of the Scottish Parliament cannot modify, or confer power by subordinate legislation to modify, the law on reserved matters": para. 2(1). Such specific protections seems anomalous, but see Lord Clyde at *Hansard*, H.L. Vol. 592, col. 824. However, it would appear that the purpose of this paragraph is to enable the exceptions allowed by para. 2(3), (4) and para. 3 of the Schedule to have effect. For example, para. 2(3) extends the provisions made by section 29(4) for the modification of Scots private law or Scots criminal law. Where matters of Scots law were "special to a reserved matter", then they would be subject to the restrictions contained in this paragraph. Examples of a rule "special to a reserved matter" could include, for example, the Proceeds of Crime (Scotland) Act 1995 in relation to confiscation of proceeds of drug trafficking but a rule lacking such a "special" character might be a rule as to how a person may sign a document under Scots law, which may apply to both reserved and devolved areas. See *Hansard,* below, at col. 821.

While easily stated, the distinction between special and non-special areas may not always be easy to apply in practice. Matters or private law are those referred to in para. 2(3)(*a*), (*b*), (4). Of particular significance is Schedule 4, para. 3, which permits modifications on reserved matters which are "incidental to, or consequential on, provision made" and which does not relate to "reserved matters". This is intended to deal with the situation where "There is an Act of the Scottish Parliament about a devolved matter which omits to make a necessary consequential amendment to a reserved matter." It would be possible for an Act of the Scottish Parliament simply to make that "missed consequential" as "When read in the context of the prior act of the Scottish Parliament, it can be seen to be for a devolved purpose", *Hansard,* below, at col. 820. The effect of reserved matters cannot, however, be greater than "is necessary to give effect of the purpose of the provision"; para. 3(1)(*b*). Subsections (2)(*a*) and (*d*) in relation to European Community law and (3) in relation to the position of the Lord Advocate are relatively self-explanatory. Account should also be taken of section 57, noted at para. 13–9 in relation to executive functions and section 106 and Schedule 5, para. 7(2), which excepts from the general reservation of foreign affairs "observing and implementing … obligations under Community Law". In relation to Convention Rights, section 29(2)(*d*) is a reinforcement of the protection given to those rights under the Human Rights Act 1998; on this see also section 57 above, section 100, Schedule 4, paras 1(2)(*f*), 13(1)(*b*), Schedule 5, para. 7(2) and Schedule 6, para. 1 for the handling of an allegation of breach of Convention Rights as a "devolution issue". Schedule 6 is extracted at para. 10–52.

(2) From the point of view of *ultra vires* in its simplest form section 29(3) is significant. While subsection (2)(*a*), (*c*) and (*e*) gives grounds which can more or less be readily established, the extent to which a reserved matter is in issue is no less clear cut. As we have already noted, one of the most significant tools available to the courts as to whether an action is *ultra vires*, is use of the test of purpose. This subsection reflects that test in the context of reserved matters. The test is sometimes referred to as "the respection doctrine" which has its roots in the jurisprudence of Commonwealth countries and in the case law under the Government of Ireland Act 1920. As Lord Sewel observed during debate, *Hansard*, below, above at col. 818, the dictum of Lord Atkin in *Gallagher v. Lynn* [1937] A.C. 863 at 870 is illuminating in this regard:

> "It is well established that you are to look at the 'true nature and character of the legislation' … 'the pith and substance of the legislation'. If, on the view of the statute as a whole, you find that the substance of the legislation is within the express powers, then it is not invalidated if incidentally it affects matters which are outside the authorized field."

Is this a sufficiently precise test? Is the doctrine of implied powers, noted above, different from this test? For case law on some of the difficulties surrounding the application of this test see, for example, B. Hadfield, "Scotland's Parliament: a Northern Ireland perspective on the White Paper" [1997] P.L. 660; T. Jones, "Scottish Devolution and Demarcation Disputes" [1997] P.L. 283; *R. (Hume) v. Londonderry Justices* [1972] N.I. 91; B. Hadfield, *The Constitution of Northern Ireland* (1989); and H. Calvert, *Constitutional Law in Northern Ireland* (1968), Chap. 11.

What effect do you consider the phrase "in all the circumstances" to have? Subsection (4) gives guidance to the courts in assessing whether an amendment to civil or criminal law as it affects the reserved area has simply been made to ensure consistency as between devolved matters and reserved matters, although this is still not without its interpretative difficulties, on which see Himsworth and Munro (1999) at pp. 40–41.

(3) Section 29 also requires to be read along with section 30 which allows modifications of Schedules 4 and 5 by Order of Her Majesty in Council: section 30(1); section 31 (scrutiny of Bills before introduction to the Parliament); section 32 (submission of Bills for Royal assent); section 33 (scrutiny of Bills for *vires* by the Judicial Committee of the Privy Council), on which see para.10–49; section 35 (power of the Secretary of State to intervene in certain cases of possible *ultra vires* where reasonable grounds for such action exist in his eyes) and section 98 and Schedule 6 in relation to "devolution issues", on which see para.10–52. For further detailed comment on section 29 and these sections see Himsworth and Munro (1999), pp. 36–50, 166–196 and T. Prosser and T. Mullen, "Devolution and Administrative Law" (1998) 4 E.P.L. 479.

(4) Section 54, which is the main section defining the competence of the Scottish Executive, draws its limits from the definition of the legislative competence of the Parliament as defined by sections 29 and 30 and Schedules 4 and 5. For comment see Himsworth and Munro (1999), pp. 70–71.

Additional guidance to the courts as to how they will be required to interpret Acts (or in the case of the Privy Council) Bills of the Scottish Parliament or subordinate legislation by members of the Scottish Executive is contained in the next excerpt. This requires to be read with the provisions noted below.

Scotland Act 1998

s. 101

3–13   "**Interpretation of Acts of the Scottish Parliament etc.**
    101.—(1) This section applies to—
    (a)   any provision of an Act of the Scottish Parliament, or of a Bill for such an act, and
    (b)   any provision of subordinate legislation made, confirmed or approved, or purporting to be made, confirmed or approved, by a member of the Scottish Executive,
which could be read in such a way as to be outside competence.
    (2) Such a provision is to be read as narrowly as is required for it to be within competence, if such a reading is possible, and is to have effect accordingly.
    (3) In this section 'competence' —
    (a)   in relation to an Act of the Scottish Parliament, or a Bill for such an Act, means the legislative competence of the Parliament, and
    (b)   in relation to subordinate legislation, means the powers conferred by virtue of this Act."

Notes

3–14   Like the test of purpose, section 101 has as its aim the need to minimise challenge to the *vires* of legislation and subordinate legislation. The section is not without its interpretative difficulties. For example, is it appropriate to give a "narrow" reading to a Scottish measure set in breach of a Convention Right? What is the potential effect of such an approach when Convention Rights are an issue? Similarly, in the field of European community law, is it appropriate that a Scottish measure will be subject to a narrow construction when a Westminster Act or subordinate legislation will not? Note the reference to Bills in subsection (1)(a). The subsection serves as a reminder that Bills might be subject to the scrutiny of the Judicial Committee of the Privy Council prior to their enactment on questions of *vires*, on which see para. 10–49. Note also that so far as actions by the Scottish Executive are concerned, a narrow interpretation is only taken to be applied to subordinate legislation; it is therefore not applied to other forms of administrative rule.

As we have noted in Chapter 2, the distinction between formal subordinate legislation and these other forms of administrative rule is not always clear. Should an executive order, not being subordinate legislation, be subject to a different degree of scrutiny from subordinate legislation, just because of its form? Note, however, insofar as subordinate legislation is subject to narrow interpretation, its competence as such does not derive from the definition of "devolved competence" contained in section 54, but could also cover subordinate legislation made under section 53, on which see para. 13–8. As those powers are typically concerned with functions which have previously been exercised by a U.K. Minister of the Crown, is it appropriate that a different interpretative approach be adopted as compared with subordinate legislation issued by a U.K. minister? How far will this new presumption of interpretation interfere with other and possibly conflicting presumptions — for example, that statutory power should not be construed as having retrospective effect or that powers interfering with the rights of property be read narrowly as noted below? For further comment see Himsworth and Munro (1999), pp. 125–127.

LOCAL GOVERNMENT AND ULTRA VIRES

The *ultra vires* doctrine has been particularly relevant in relation to the powers of local **3–15** authorities. The powers of local authorities derive from three main sources: (1) general legislation, principally the Local Government (Scotland) Act 1973 and the Local Government etc. (Scotland) Act 1994, which establishes the council's general powers, such as the power to contract and to acquire and dispose of land; (2) legislation relating to specific services or regulatory powers such as the Civil Government (Scotland) Act 1982; and (3) private legislation, restricted in its application to the authority or the authorities that promoted it. Although the application of the *ultra vires* doctrine to local authorities was historically principally concerned with the doctrine in its narrow sense, the broader grounds of *ultra vires* are also applicable to local authority actions: for an example see *Harvey v. Strathclyde Regional Council*, 1989 S.L.T. 612, extracted at para. 6–15. For a general account see C. M. G. Himsworth, *The Local Government etc. (Scotland) Act 1994* (1995); *Stair Memorial Encyclopaedia*, Vol. 1, para. 220; Vol. 14, "Local Government", paras 128–132; and C. M. G. Himsworth, *Local Government Law in Scotland* (1995), Chap. 3. Arguments about the scope of the *ultra vires* doctrine in this area are perhaps, more than most, the legal expression matters of political controversy as the following extra shows.

Commission for Local Authority Accounts in Scotland v. Grampian Regional Council

1994 S.L.T. 1120

"Section 83(1) of the Local Government (Scotland) Act 1973 provides that 'A local authority may … **3–16** incur expenditure which in their opinion is in the interests of their area or any part of it or all or some of its inhabitants', if such expenditure is not authorised or required by any other enactment. Section 2(1) and (3) of the Local Government Act 1986 provides that 'A local authority shall not give financial … assistance to a person for the publication of material' which 'in whole or in part, appears to be designed to affect public support for a political party'.

A local authority gave money to two unincorporated associations, the Campaign for a Scottish Assembly, and the Scottish Constitutional Convention. The object of the former was the creation of a Scottish legislature; the purpose of the latter was to agree upon a scheme for such a legislature, and gain popular approval therefor. The authority stipulated that the money given to the convention was to be used for research and administration, and not for publicity.

The controller of audit submitted a special report to the Commission for Local Authority Accounts in Scotland in which he gave his opinion that the payments were contrary to law in terms of s 102(3)(a)(i) of the 1973 Act. After a hearing, the commission found that the objects of the associations were matters of political controversy, and made proposed findings in the same terms as the controller. The commission made no findings of fact as to what expenditure had been incurred by either of the associations on publicity, nor as to whether any material produced by either could be regarded as having been designed to affect public support for a political party or for persons or points of view identified with particular parties, nor as to whether such facts had been apparent when the payments had been made. On the application of the authority, the court required the commission to state a case on the questions (1) whether the payments were made within the authority's powers, and (2) whether the payments were made contrary to s 2 of the 1986 Act.

The commission argued that the payments fell outwith s 83 because they had been made to secure a general object which had no particular relationship with the area of the local authority or its inhabitants, and which related to the functions or possible functions of another level of government. They also argued that it was inevitable that material published by the associations was bound to have the effect of encouraging people to vote for and against particular political parties.…

Stated case

The Commission for Local Authority Accounts in Scotland, on a direction by the court, stated a case for the opinion of the Court of Session on two questions of law arising from findings which the commission had proposed to make, to the effect that certain payments by Grampian Regional Council were contrary to law in terms of s 102 (3) (a) (i) of the Local Government (Scotland) Act 1973.

Statutory provisions

The Local Government (Scotland) Act 1973, as amended, provides:

'83.(3) A local authority may, subject to the provisions of this section, incur expenditure which in their opinion is in the interests of their area or any part of it or all or some of its inhabitants, but a local authority shall not, by virtue of this subsection, incur any expenditure for a purpose for which they are, either unconditionally or subject to any limitation or to the satisfaction of any condition, authorised or required to make any payment by or by virtue of any other enactment.

'(2) It is hereby declared that, subject to subsection (3A) below, the power of a local authority to incur expenditure under subsection (1) above includes power to do so by contributing towards the defraying of expenditure by another local authority in or in connection with the exercise of that other authority's functions....

'(2C) A local authority may incur expenditure under subsection (1) above on publicity only by way of assistance to a public body or voluntary organisation where the publicity is incidental to the main purpose for which the assistance is given; but the following provisions of this section apply to expenditure incurred by a local authority under section 88 below on information as to the services provided by them under this section, or otherwise relating to their functions under this section, as they apply to expenditure incurred under this section....

'(3) A local authority may, subject as aforesaid, incur expenditure on contributions to any of the following funds, that is to say — (a) the funds of any charitable body in furtherance of its work in the United Kingdom; or (b) the funds of any body which provides any public service in the United Kingdom otherwise than for the purposes of gain; or (c) any fund which is raised in connection with a particular event directly affecting persons resident in the United Kingdom on behalf of whom a public appeal for contributions has been made by a chairman of a regional, islands or district council, a chairman of a community council, a lord-lieutenant or by a body of which any of these persons is a member, or by such a person or body as is referred to in section 137 (3) of the Local Government Act 1972....

'(4) The expenditure of a local authority under this section in any financial year shall not exceed the product of a rate of 2p in the pound for their area for the financial year 1988–89 or, if some other amount, whether higher or lower, is fixed by an order made by the Secretary of State, shall not exceed the product of a rate of that amount in the pound for their area for the financial year 1988–89.'

'102.—... (3) Without prejudice to subsection (1) above, if the Controller of Audit, having considered the audit under this Part of this Act of the accounts of any local authority and having made such further inquiries (if any) as he may think fit — (a) is of the opinion — (i) that any item of account is contrary to law, or (ii) that there has been a failure on the part of any person to bring into account any sum which ought to have been brought into account, or (iii) that any loss has been incurred or deficiency caused by the negligence or misconduct of any person or by the failure of the authority to carry out any duty imposed on them by any enactment; or (b) is of the opinion that any sum which ought to have been credited or debited to one account of the authority has been credited or, as the case may be, debited to another account of the authority; and (c) is not satisfied that the authority has taken or is taking such steps as may be necessary to remedy the matter; he shall make to the Commission a special report with respect to the said accounts, setting forth his opinion as aforesaid and the grounds thereof.'

The Local Government Act 1986, as amended, provides:

'2.—(1) A local authority shall not publish any material which, in whole or in part, appears to be designed to affect public support for a political party.

'(2) In determining whether material falls within the prohibition regard shall be had to the content and style of the material, the time and other circumstances of publication and the likely effect on those to whom it is directed and, in particular, to the following matters — (1) whether the material refers to a political party or to persons identified with a political party or promotes or opposes a point of view on a question of political controversy which is identifiable as the view of one political party and not of another; (b) where the material is part of a campaign, the effect which the campaign appears to be designed to achieve.

'(3) A local authority shall not give financial or other assistance to a person for the publication of material which the authority are prohibited by his section from publishing themselves....'

The commission stated a case on the following questions of law:

(1) Were the payments made by Grampian Regional Council to the Campaign for a Scottish Assembly and a Scottish Constitutional Convention within the powers of the council?

(2) Were the payments made by Grampian Regional Council to the Campaign for a Scottish Assembly and a Scottish Constitutional Convention contrary to the provisions of s 2 of the Local Government Act 1986?

The case was heard before the First Division on 8 and 9 December 1993.

On 30 December 1993 the court *answered* the first question in the *affirmative*, and the second question in the *negative*."

LORD PRESIDENT (HOPE): "This is a case which has been stated by the Commission for Local Authority Accounts in Scotland under s 103 of the Local Government (Scotland) Act 1973. The case has been stated following a direction by this court under s 103 (2) (c) of that Act on two questions of law arising on a special report by the controller of audit. The report, which was made to the commission under s 102 (3) of the 1973 Act, related to expenditure incurred by Grampian Regional Council which consisted of payments of money to the Campaign for a Scottish Assembly and the Scottish Constitutional Convention. Two questions of law have arisen in regard to these payments, namely (1) whether the payments made by the council to the Campaign and to the Convention were within the powers of the council under s 83 (1) of the 1973 Act, and (2) whether the payments were contrary to s 2 of the Local Government Act 1986... .

In the present case the controller of audit submitted a special report to the commission dated 3 September 1991. The concluding paragraph of that report was in these terms: 'I have to report that I have formed the opinion that the payment of £1,000 to the Scottish Constitutional Convention on 22nd January 1990 and each of the payments of £500 to the Campaign for a Scottish Assembly on 24th August 1988, 20th April 1989 and 28th August 1990 are items of account contrary to law in terms of section 102 (3) (a) (i) of the Local Government (Scotland) Act 1973.'

The commission then held a hearing into the matters raised in the report which took place in Aberdeen on 11 December 1991. By letters dated 1 and 29 September 1992 the council requested the commission to state a case for the opinion of the court on these matters, on the ground that they raised a substantial issue of law and were matters of considerable public interest and importance. The commission decided, on the advice of counsel, to refuse to state a case, and they went on to make proposed findings that the payments were contrary to law in terms of s 102 (3) (a) (i) of the 1973 Act. The council then presented a note to the court in terms of rule of court 278, in which they stated that matters of public importance were raised as to the proper construction of s 83 of the 1973 Act and s 2 of the 1986 Act. They sought an order on the commission to state a case under s 103 (2) (c) on the following questions: [his Lordship quoted the two questions of law and continued:]

By interlocutor dated 26 November 1992 the court directed the commission to state a case on the questions of law which the council had proposed in their note. Thereafter the commission, having considered the special report, the observations upon it by the council and the evidence given and submission made at the hearing on 11 December 1991, made the findings of fact which provide the background against which the questions of law have now been stated for our opinion.

The question whether there should be a directly elected legislative assembly or parliament for Scotland has been the subject of public debate in this country for many years. The debate has been complicated by the question whether Scotland should or should not remain part of the United Kingdom. It is not for us in this case, however, to attempt to explore or define the issues raised by this debate. Our task is to consider the question of law in the light of the facts as stated by the commission. The questions which we have to consider are questions of statutory interpretation, and we must consider them against the background of fact which has been provided for us by the commission's findings. These findings fall into two distinct chapters, one of which describes the objects and activities of the Campaign and the Convention, while the other sets out the history of the payments which were the subject of the special report by the controller.

The commission appear to have based their findings on these matters exclusively on the information which was provided to them by the controller in his report. Their findings about the Campaign for a Scottish Assembly and a Scottish Constitutional Convention are in precisely the same terms as those used by the controller, and we must assume that they contain all the information which was thought by the commission to be both relevant and available. We are told that the Campaign for a Scottish Assembly was established as an unincorporated association. The date of its inception is not stated, but we understand this to have been in or about 1986. Its object is stated to be 'the creation of a directly elected legislative Assembly or Parliament for Scotland, with such powers as may be desired by the people of Scotland'. It is stated to be 'an all-party, non-party, organisation, independent of all political parties and other organisations'. It is funded inter alia by subscriptions and has in the past sought subscriptions, described as affiliation fees, from local authorities. The Scottish Constitutional Convention was formed in 1989 at the instigation of the Campaign for a Scottish Assembly. It comprises invited representatives of certain political parties, local authorities, the Scottish Trades Union Congress, certain churches and a range of other bodies. The political parties which are said to have accepted the invitation include Labour, Social and Liberal Democrats, SDP, Greens and Communists. Other organisations including the Conservative and Scottish National Parties were invited to send representatives but declined. The purposes of the Convention are stated to be '(i) to agree a scheme for an Assembly or Parliament for Scotland; (ii) to mobilise Scottish opinion and ensure approval of the Scottish people for that scheme; (iii) to assert the right of the Scottish people to secure the implementation of that scheme'. The commission's findings on this chapter conclude with the following paragraph; 'That the desirability or otherwise of an Assembly or Parliament for Scotland is a matter of political controversy. It is supported, for example, by the Labour Party. It is opposed by the Conservative Party.'

The council's involvement in these matters began with a decision which was taken at a meeting of its policy and resources committee on 4 December 1986 to affiliate to the Campaign for a Scottish Assembly. This decision was considered and approved at a meeting of the council on 18 December 1986, but at that stage no reference was made to the payment of an affiliation fee. Subsequent to these decisions being taken, affiliation fees of £500 each were paid to the Campaign by the council on 24 August 1988, 20 April 1989 and 28 May 1990 without the matter having been referred back to a committee for deliberation, as the decision in principle to affiliate had already been taken. When the Scottish Constitutional Convention was formed in 1989 a national appeal was made for funds for the Convention. On or about 26 April 1989 the national convener of the Campaign for a Scottish Assembly sent a letter to local authorities as part of this appeal by which authorities were invited to contribute to the Campaign for a Scottish Assembly for this purpose. The letter was on notepaper bearing the heading of the Scottish Constitutional Convention. At a further meeting of the policy and resources committee on 7 September 1989 the request for a contribution to the funds of the Scottish Constitutional Convention was considered. The committee decided, after a vote, to approve a contribution of £1,000 for research and administration purposes but not publicity.

It appears that their decision was qualified in this way in the light of advice which they received from the director of law and administration, under reference inter alia to s 83 of the 1973 Act and s 2 of the 1986 Act, that it would not be within the powers of the council to make a contribution. An attempt at a meeting of the council on 21 September 1989 to suspend standing orders to enable the council to reconsider the decision of the planning and resources committee failed to obtain the necessary two thirds majority. The payment of £1,000 was then made by the council to the Scottish Constitutional Convention on 22 January 1990. No findings have been included in the stated case as to what was done with this money by the convention. But we are told that the servicing of the convention, by which is meant the task of calling meetings, issuing papers and the preparation of minutes, was undertaken by the staff of the Convention of Scottish Local Authorities on a rechargeable basis. Although the campaign and the convention are separate entities, the convener of the Campaign for a Scottish Assembly stated in his letter to all local authorities that the 'Campaign for a Scottish Assembly is acting as the funding resource of the Convention and is anxious to ensure that the funds needed are readily available'.

The controller of audit formed the view that payments to further the purposes of the Campaign and of the Convention, being intended for the purpose of changing the form of national government in Scotland, were outwith the powers of the council and were accordingly outwith the ambit of s 83 of the 1973 Act. He also formed the view that, as the purposes of the Campaign and the Convention were to promote a point of view on a question of political controversy which was identifiable with the view of one political party and not of another, and as the payments tended to facilitate publication of the aim of the Campaign and the Convention, they were struck at by the prohibition in s 2 (1) of the 1986 Act. The commission appear to have been more impressed by the latter point than by the former, as they proposed at their meeting on 13 January 1993 to make findings in these terms: '(1) The payment of £1,000 to the Scottish Constitutional Convention made on 22nd January 1990 was contrary to section 2 of the Local Government Act 196 and accordingly was an item of account contrary to the law in terms of section 102 (3) (a) (i) of the Local Government (Scotland) Act 1973; (2) Each of the payments of £500 to the Campaign for a Scottish Assembly made respectively on 24th August 1988, 20th April 1989 and 28th August 1990 were contrary to section 2 of the Local Government Act 1986 and accordingly were items of account contrary to law in terms of section 102 (3) (a) of the Local Government (Scotland) Act 1973.'

In the questions which they have stated for our opinion, however, they have asked us to consider whether the payments were within the powers of the council, which we take to be a reference to the council's powers under s 83 of the 1973 Act, and whether they were contrary to s 2 of the 1986 Act.

Section 83 of the 1973 Act enables local authorities to incur expenditure for certain purposes not otherwise authorised by that or by any other enactment. The leading provision in this section, which replaced s 339 (1) of the Local Government (Scotland) Act 1947, is set out in subs (1) which is in these terms: [his Lordship quoted the terms of s 83 (1) and continued:]

Subsection (2) declares that the power of a local authority to incur expenditure under subs (1) includes power to do so by contributing towards the defraying of expenditure by another local authority in or in connection with the exercise of that other authority's functions. Subsection (2C), which was added by s 3 (3) of the Local Government Act 1986, provides that a local authority may incur expenditure under subs (1) on publicity only by way of assistance to a public body or voluntary organisation where the publicity is incidental to the main purpose for which the assistance is given. Subsection (3), which reproduces a provision first introduced by the Local Authorities (Expenditure on Special Purposes) (Scotland) Act 1961, enables a local authority to incur expenditure on contributions to the funds of any charitable body in furtherance of its work in the United Kingdom, to the funds of any public body which provides any public service in the United Kingdom other than for the purposes of gain or to any fund raised by public appeal in connection with a particular event directly affecting persons resident in the United Kingdom. Subsection (4), as amended by s 6 of and para 27 of Sched 1 to the Abolition of Domestic Rates Etc (Scotland) Act 1987, provides that the expenditure of a local authority under the section in any financial year must not exceed the product of the rate of 2p in the pound for their area for the financial year 1988–89. Subsection (7), which was added by s 9 of the Rating and Valuation (Amendment) (Scotland) Act 1984, requires accounts to be kept by a local authority under s 96 of the 1973 Act to include a separate account of any expenditure incurred by the authority under s 83.

The section thus contains within it a number of express limitations on the way in which the power under subs (1) may be exercised. A local authority may not incur any expenditure under it for a purpose for which they are authorised or required to make any payment by or by virtue of any other enactment: subs (1). Any expenditure which they incur on publicity under that subsection may be incurred only by way of assistance to a public body or voluntary organisation where the publicity is incidental to the main purpose for which the assistance is given: subs (2C). And the amount of the expenditure in any financial year is not to exceed the product of a rate of 2p in the pound: subs (4). It is not suggested in this case that the expenditure which is under scrutiny here has breached any of these express limitations. The question then is whether it was within the power of the council to incur the expenditure on the ground that in their opinion it was 'in the interests of their area or any part of it or all or some of its inhabitants'.

Counsel for the controller recognised that these words were capable of receiving a wide interpretation, and he accepted that it had not been suggested that the opinion which the council had formed in making these payments had been arrived at in bad faith or could be said to be, in the *Wednesbury* sense, unreasonable or irrational: *Associated Picture Houses Ltd v Wednesbury Corporation; Council of Civil Service Unions v Minister for the Civil Service*. But he maintained that a local authority were not entitled, in the exercise of the power given to them by s 83 (1), to make payments for a purpose which was concerned with matters of national government. The powers of a local authority were to be understood as relating only to matters of local government. The Campaign for a Scottish Assembly was concerned with a tier of government which lay above that of local government, with which accordingly the council had no concern. He observed that a local authority had power under s 69 (1) to incur expenditure which was calculated to facilitate, or was conducive or incidental to, the discharge of any of their functions as a local authority. But they could not incur expenditure which related to the functions or possible functions of some other level of government, which was what had been done in this case.

Counsel accepted that s 83 (1) was intended to give a power to a local authority which was wider than that conferred by s 69 (1). He submitted that there had nevertheless to be a connection between the expenditure and the interests of the area of the local authority and all or some of its inhabitants. Where the expenditure was to secure some general object which had no particular relationship with that area or its inhabitants, it lay outside the power conferred by s 83 (1). He pointed out that no attempt had been made in two recently reported cases relating to the publication of information by local authorities to rely on s 83 (1) of the 1973 Act or on s 137 of the Local Government Act 1972, which is its English equivalent: *R v Inner London Education Authority, ex p Westminster City Council* [1986] 1 All E.R. 19]; *Commission for Local Authority Accounts in Scotland v City of Edinburgh District Council* [(1988) S.C.L.R. 552]. This, he said, was an indication that the power given by s 83 (1) as not unrestricted. The power had to be related, as was expressly the case in regard to s 69 (1) of the 1973 Act which dealt with the subsidiary powers of local authorities, in some way to the functions of a local authority, that is to say to the duties and functions conferred on a local authority by the Act.

As counsel for the council pointed out however, s 83 (1) confers on a local authority a general power to incur expenditure which is not otherwise authorised or required to be incurred by or by virtue of any other enactment. Where expenditure is to be incurred for functions of a local authority mentioned elsewhere in the 1973 Act or in some other legislation, the power under s 83 (1) is not available. No doubt it must be exercised within the limits and on the conditions which have been laid down for it. These set an upper limit to the amount of the expenditure in any financial year and require a separate account of the expenditure to be kept. Restrictions on the exercise of the power may be found in the provisions of some other enactment, such as in s 2 of the 196 Act which requires to be considered in the present case. But, subject only to these requirements, the power is available for use at the discretion of the local authority. The only limits to it are those set by the words used in the subsection and by the general law relating to decision taking by bodies on whom powers have been conferred by Parliament.

Since there is no suggestion in this case of bad faith or that the opinion formed by the council was unreasonable, the argument for the controller on this point came in the end to be that, as a matter of law, it could not possibly be said to be in the interests of the area or any part of it, or for all or some of its inhabitants, for the council to incur expenditure which was in any way related to the Campaign for a Scottish Assembly. We are unable, however, to find any sound basis in subs (1) or elsewhere in the Act for this submission. It seems to us that the question whether the expenditure was in the interests of the area or of its inhabitants was one of fact for the council, not one of law. In a general sense anything which relates in any way to the legitimate interests of the area or its inhabitants may be considered to fall within the words used by the subsection. It is not said here that the expenditure must be of benefit to the area or its inhabitants only and to no other area or to no one else. Nor is it said that the area or its inhabitants must benefit directly from the expenditure. A restriction to this effect is now to be found in the English legislation. Section 137 of the 1972 Act has been amended by s 36 of and Sched 2 to the Local Government and Housing act 1989, and the power may now be exercised only where the local authority are of the opinion that the expenditure will bring direct benefit to their area or any part of it or all or some of its inhabitants. A local authority are prohibited from incurring any expenditure by virtue of the subsection unless the direct benefit accruing to their area or any part of it or to all or some of the inhabitants of their area will be commensurate with the expenditure to be incurred. No such limitation has been written into s 83 (1) of the 1973 Act. The fact that Parliament thought it appropriate to restrict the wording of s 137 (1) of the 1972 Act in this way supports the view that the wording of the subsection as originally enacted is so wide that no such limitation can be implied into it.

It seems to us, therefore, that it is enough to open up the subject for consideration by the local authority that the expenditure may be in some way, although not directly or exclusively, in the interests of the area or of its inhabitants. The submission that a local authority must not concern themselves with matters relating to anything other than their own tier of government seems to us contrary to the generality of the words used here and to the place which the section occupies in the Act as a whole. There is ample provision elsewhere in the act, including the powers given by ss 69 and 88, for the incurring of expenditure relating in some way to the functions of the local authority and to general matters of local government. Section 83 (1) is designed instead to enable a local authority, within the strict financial limit which has been set for this, to take a broader look at the interests of the area and its inhabitants and to incur expenditure where this would not otherwise be authorised.

In *Re Cook and Others' Application* [1986] N.I. 242] Hutton J, as he then was, at p 255 noted that s 137 of the 1972 Act was enacted pursuant to the recommendation contained in para 323 of the 1969 *Report of the Royal Commission on Local Government in England* which stated: 'All main authorities should have a general power to spend money for the benefit of their areas and inhabitants. This is additional to their expenditure on services, for which they have statutory responsibility. A precedent exists in Section 6 of the Local Government (Financial Provisions) Act 1963. But expenditure under this section is limited to the product of a penny rate. We suggest that the only limit on the use of the new power should be the wishes of the electors and such restrictions as have to be placed on local government expenditure in the interests of national economic and financial policy.'

At p 256 he said that he considered it to be clear that a payment made pursuant to s 115 of the Local Government Act (Northern Ireland) 1972 was not subject to the ultra vires doctrine, and went on: 'Accordingly, a payment authorised to be made by a council is lawful provided that the council is of opinion that the payment is in the interests (a) of the council, or (b) of its district or of any part of its district, or (c) of the inhabitants of its district or of any parts of its district, and provided also that the decision to make the payment is not unreasonable within the *Wednesbury* case principle, and provided that the total payments made under the section by the council in any one financial year do not exceed the product of a rate of 3p in the pound on the rateable value of the district.'

Subject to the point that we do not understand Hutton J to be suggesting that the ultra vires doctrine was wholly inapplicable to the question whether expenditure had been properly incurred under s 115 but rather that it was not necessary to relate the expenditure to particular powers given elsewhere in the Act, we consider his observations to be helpful in the present case.

We note that in the *Report of the Royal Commission on Local Government in Scotland* (Cmnd 4150) (1969) under the chairmanship of the Right Honourable Lord Wheatley, paras 640 and 641, it was recommended that a local authority should not be limited by the statutory range of their functions and that they should possess a general competence making it possible for them to act outside the cover of a specific enabling statute where the circumstances seem appropriate. Reference was made to s 339 (1) of the Local Government (Scotland) Act 1974 which enabled local authorities to 'make any payment for any purpose which the opinion of the council is in the interests of the council or of the area of the council or any part thereof or of the inhabitants thereof'. It was noted that that power could be exercised only with the approval of the Secretary of State and that it was subject to a limit of a 2d rate in any one year, which it was thought virtually emptied the provision of real significance. The report then stated: 'In our opinion, a general competence power should not be restricted in financial terms, or by the need to secure approval from any higher authority. It is to the local electorate that the local council should have to answer for the use of such a power. Any restrictions should be aimed, as the Maud Committee recognised, simply at curbing any possible abuse of the powers by way of interference with private rights or the duties of other public bodies.'

This recommendation was implemented in s 83 (1) of the 1973 Act to the extent of removing the requirement to obtain the approval of the Secretary of State to the expenditure. A financial limit to the amount of the expenditure has been retained, no doubt as a precaution against too liberal a resort to a general power to incur expenditure at the discretion of the local authority.

As for the particular issue whether the payments to the Campaign for a Scottish Assembly and to the Scottish Constitutional Convention were outwith the powers given to the council by s 83 (1) of the 1973 Act, all that remains to be said on this point is that it is not self evident that the payments made to these bodies were unlawful. We do not see how the creation of a directly elected assembly or parliament for Scotland can be said to have nothing whatever to do with the interests of the council's area or of its inhabitants. The way in which the government is carried on generally, and the extent to which that will affect the functions of government to be performed locally within the area of a local authority, may indeed be a matter of legitimate concern to the inhabitants of that area. The commission have found as a fact that the desirability or otherwise of such an assembly or parliament is a matter of political controversy. But that fact in itself does not mean that it cannot be in the interests of the area or of its inhabitants for the local authority to contribute to the discussion. It is not necessary for us to go further on this matter, because unless it can be said as a matter of statutory interpretation that expenditure for this purpose was outwith the limits set by s 83 (1), the only remaining questions relate to the council's good faith and the reasonableness of the decisions, neither of which have been challenged by the controller. In our opinion the argument that, on a proper construction of s 83 (1), it was outwith the powers of the council to incur this expenditure must be rejected. We shall answer question 1 in the case in the affirmative.

We turn now to s 2 of the Local Government Act 1986. This section is in the following terms: [his Lordship quoted its terms and continued:]

The controller's view, as stated in the special report, was that each of the payments which were made by the council in this case were struck at by subs (1) of this section. But there is no question here of the council themselves having published any material of the prohibited kind by incurring this expenditure. The expenditure consisted of payments made exclusively to other bodies, and the question which arises is whether by making these payments the council were giving financial assistance to these other bodies for the publication of material which they themselves would have been prohibited from publishing by subs (1). It was to that question therefore, and to s 2 (3) in particular, that counsel for the controller addressed his argument. He conceded that neither the Campaign for a Scottish Assembly nor the Scottish Constitutional Convention could be said to be a political party. So the question is whether the payments to these bodies must be seen as financial assistance to them for the publication of material which, in whole or in part, appeared to be designed to affect support for a political party, the publication of which the council themselves were prohibited from publishing by s 2 (1) of the Act.

The commission have stated a case on this matter which is almost entirely without findings of fact. It is unfortunate that, having followed the course recommended in *Commission for Local Authority Accounts in Scotland v Stirling District Council* by holding an inquiry, the commission did not do what was recommended by Lord President Emslie in that case at 1984 SLT, p 447, which was to investigate the whole circumstances so as to enable a full disclosure of them to be made when the question of law was presented to the court. As it is, their findings are confined to a repetition of the information contained in the controller's report about the objects of the two bodies and his finding that the desirability or otherwise of an assembly or a parliament for Scotland is a matter of political controversy. They have also repeated his finding that the policy and resources committee approved of the contribution of £1,000 to the Scottish Constitutional Convention on condition that it was for research and administration purposes and not publicity. There are, however, no findings at all as to what expenditure, if any, has in fact been incurred by either of these two bodies on publicity. Nothing is said about the content or style of any such material. There has been no assessment as to whether any material produced by either body could be regarded as having been designed to affect public support for a political party, or for persons identified with any such party, or to promote or oppose a point of view on a question of political controversy which was identifiable as the view of one political party and not of another: see subs (2). Nor has there been any attempt to explore the timing of events, with particular regard to the question whether it was apparent when the payments were made that a political controversy had been generated by the activities of the Campaign. The proposition on which the controller's argument depends seems to be that any payment made to these bodies for the purposes for which they were established must be assumed to have been financial assistance for the publication of material of the kind which, if undertaken by a local authority, would be prohibited. In the way in which the case has been stated, that issue is the only issue to which we can direct our attention.

Counsel for the controller submitted that it was inevitable that material published by these two bodies would fall within the prohibition in s 2 (3) of the 1986 Act. This was because any such material was bound to be supportive of the position which the bodies were adopting on a matter which was of political controversy. He said that it was inevitable that the material which they published would be intended to influence the views of those to whom it was addressed, and to encourage them to support the idea of a Scottish Assembly or a Scottish Parliament. He accepted that it would be going too far to suggest that the bodies would be seeking to secure votes for or against any political party. But since the matter was one of political controversy this was, he said, bound to be its effect. He maintained that the findings could not be more specific on this issue, as it was clear from the outset that what these bodies were intending to do was to conduct a campaign on a matter which was bound to be both controversial and political.

In our opinion, where the prohibition in s 2 (3) is in issue, it is the purpose for which the financial or other assistance is given which must be considered. This is clear from the use of the phrase 'for the publication of material'. It is a question of fact whether the financial or other assistance was or was not given for this purpose. But there are no findings in the case which would entitle us to hold that, at the dates of the respective payments, this was the purpose for which the payments to the Campaign and the Convention were made. Such findings as there are tend to show that the purpose was to contribute in some general way to the objects for which these bodies were constituted. The subscriptions which were sought by the Campaign from local authorities were described as affiliation fees, and the single payment made to the Convention was approved for research and administration purposes, not for publicity. Money used by these bodies for research or for administration purposes cannot be assumed to have been money used for the publication of material, let alone material which was designed to affect public support for a political party.

Even if it was to be assumed that the money would be used in some way for the publication of material, the purpose which that material was designed to serve is also important here. No doubt the prohibition would be breached if the material, on examination, appeared to have been designed for the purpose described in subs (1). But we are being asked in this case to hold that any material published by these two bodies would inevitably have been so designed. In our opinion the facts found by the commission provide no real support for this argument. There is a finding that the subject is one of political controversy, but it is not stated that it is the object of either body to engage in party politics. On the contrary, the Campaign for Scottish Assembly is said to have been established as an all party, non-party organisation, independent of all political parties and other organisations. The Scottish Constitutional Convention is said to have issued invitations to representatives of all the main political parties and a number of other bodies to join in its discussions. So it does not appear from the findings that it was the intention of either body to embark upon party political controversy or publish material designed to affect public support for one political party as against another. The political controversy which has arisen appears therefore to have been the result of the differing attitudes which the various political parties have adopted to the subject. We cannot comment on what the effect of the Campaign has been, since the case lacks findings on these matters and the history of the Campaign since its inception has not been explored.

On these findings we cannot hold that, as at the date when the payments were made, all or any of such material as either body would wish to publish would inevitably be designed for the purpose prohibited by s 2 (1) of the 1986 Act.

For these reasons we shall answer question 2 in this case in the negative."

Notes

3–17   (1) Note the approach of the court in interpreting the issues as involving jurisdictional fact: on this see para.4–6. Notice also how the *Wednesbury* reasonableness is deployed as to the choice of considerations available to the local authority.

(2) Note that section 83(1) has now been amended by section 164 of the Local Government etc. (Scotland) Act 1994 as a direct result of the above decision. Under section 164(1)(c) any benefit accruing must be "direct" and also be "commensurate with the expenditure to be incurred" for it to be lawful. This is a somewhat stricter test than section 83(1). For a comment on this see G. Junor, "Changing the Rules of the Game", 1995 S.L.T. (News) 95. The equivalent English provision to section 83 is contained in section 137 of the Local Government Act 1972. In *Manchester City Council v. Greater Manchester Metropolitan County Council* (1980) 78 L.G.R. 560 the House of Lords upheld the validity of payments under this section by a county council to a trust established by the council to provide free or assisted places at independent schools for children of parents living in the local authority's area. Education was not, however, one of the county council's functions but nevertheless payment was held not to infringe the principle that local government expenditure be conducted on an annual basis; although most of the money would be held by the trustees for expenditure in future years, expenditure was properly incurred within the county council's budgets in one year. Contrast this with *Re Westminster City Council* above.

(3) Note the argument on section 2 of the Local Government Act 1986. Note the difficulty of the court in accepting the argument put forward by the Commission that the expenditure was unlawful as it was promoting the aims of the political party. In the absence of specific averments by the Commission, the court was not prepared to infer such a purpose. The doctrine of improper purpose is important in assessing whether an action is *ultra vires*, on which see para. 6–3.

(4) Note section 69 of the Local Government (Scotland) Act 1973 below which provides as follows.

Local Government (Scotland) Act 1973

s. 69

"**Part VI**

Miscellaneous Powers of Local Authorities

Subsidiary powers

Subsidiary powers of local authorities

69.—(1) Without prejudice to any powers exercisable apart from this section but subject to the provisions of this Act and any other enactment passed before or after this Act, a local authority shall have power to do any thing (whether or not involving the expenditure, borrowing or lending of money or the acquisition or disposal of any property or rights) which is calculated to facilitate, or is conducive or incidental to, the discharge of any of their functions.   **3–18**

(2) A local authority shall not by virtue of this section raise money, whether by means of rates or borrowing, or lend money except in accordance with the enactments relating to those matters respectively.

Notes

The Royal Commission on Local Government in Scotland, Cmnd. 4150 (1969), pp. 153, 154 recommended that local authorities should be granted the power of general competence making it possible for them to act without a specific enabling Act where circumstances seemed appropriate. When English local government came under the scrutiny of the Committee on the Management of Local Government (chaired by Lord Redcliffe-Maud) (HMSO, 1967) it was felt that the *ultra vires* doctrine had a   **3–19** "deleterious effect on local government because of the narrowness of the legislation governing local authority's activities. The specific nature of legislation discourages enterprise, handicaps development, robs the community of services which the Local Government might render, and encourages too rigorous oversight by the Central Government. It contributes to the excessive concern over legalities and fosters the idea that the clerk should be a lawyer" (para. 283).

As in Scotland, the committee's recommendation was not approved although section 69 of the 1973 Act was seen as a halfway house, as was section 83. The equivalent English provision to section 69 is section 111 of the Local Government Act 1972, which is in identical terms to section 69. It has been the subject of detailed judicial consideration. In *Hazell v. Hammersmith and Fulham London Borough Council* [1990] (2 Q.B. 697) the House of Lords held that swap transactions entered into on behalf of the local authority were *ultra vires*. These were speculative and entered into to make a profit. Profits were dependent on interest rates falling, but in fact they increased. In terms of the Local Government Finance Act 1982, the district auditor obtained a declaration that these transactions were contrary to law and were not authorised by Schedule 13 to the 1972 Act, which covered borrowing by local authorities. The council argued that section 111 gave adequate power. In the Divisional Court Woolf L.J. noted (at 772):

> "What is a function for the purposes of the subsection is not expressly defined but in our view there can be little doubt that in this context 'functions' refers to the multiplicity of specific statutory activities the council is expressly or impliedly under a duty to perform or has power to perform under the other provisions of the Act of 1972 or other relevant legislation. The subsection does not of itself, independently of any other provision, authorise the performance of any activity. It only confers, as the sidenote to the section indicates, a subsidiary power. A subsidiary power which authorises an activity where some other statutory provision has vested a specific function or functions in the council and the performance of the activity will assist in some way in the discharge of that function or those functions."

This was approved by the Court of Appeal [1990] 2 Q.B. 697 at 785.

In the House of Lords, Lord Templeman accepted that "borrowing" was a function for these purposes, but the transactions neither facilitated nor were conducive or incidental to borrowing. See [1991] 2 W.L.R. 372 at 383. Desirability or potential profitability did not make the power incidental. For comment on *Hazell* in relation to restitution see p. 000 and on this area generally see M. Loughlin, "Innovative Financing in Local Government: The Limits of Legal Instrumentalism" [1990] P.L. 372 and [1991] P.L. 568. In *Crédit Suisse v. Waltham Forest London Borough Council* [1996] 4 All E.R. 176 and *Crédit Suisse v. Allerdale Borough Council* [1996] 4 All E.R. 129 *Hazell* was applied to hold that power to use a part-owned company to discharge housing functions and to grant indemnities in relation to that company did not exist under section 111. In *Allsop v. North Tyneside Metropolitan Borough Council* (1992) 90 L.G.R. 462 the Court of Appeal held that section 111 did not authorise payments under a voluntary redundancy scheme if those payments were in excess of the limits permitted under statutory regulations authorising such payments. The regulations took effect by virtue of the Superannuation Act 1972, which was "other enactment" in terms of section 111. The strict logic of *Hazell* was seen in *Guinness Mahon and Co. Ltd v. Kensington and Chelsea Royal London Borough Council* [1998] 2 All E.R. 272, C.A., where although all monies under an interest rates swap transaction had been transferred and obligations on both sides fully performed, that was no bar to an action for recovery. Some attempt to limit the rigours of the *ultra vires* doctrine in local authority contracts is contained in the Local Government (Contracts) Act 1997 discussed in Chapter 14.

(2) In *Meek v. Lothian Regional Council*, 1980 S.L.T. 61 Lothian Regional Council decided to allow some of its employees nominated by their trade unions time off work without loss of pay to participate in a "national lobby of Parliament". The minority group in the Council opposed the resolution and sought to have it declared unlawful and passed in bad faith. They sought interim interdict and the court took the view that there was sufficient doubt as to the application of section 69 or 83 to the Council's resolution to make the pursuer's averments relevant and granted interim interdict. The decision in the *Great Eastern Railway Co.* case was of particular

importance here and the court accepted that "incidental" did not mean "in connection with". *Meek* is noted at para. 11–22. The functionalist approach in *Hazell* is implicit in the older Scots authorities. For example, in *Flint v. Glasgow Corporation*, 1966 S.C. 108 it was held that payments by a local authority from one of its rating accounts towards costs for installing and paying for telephones at councillors' homes was *ultra vires* in that the payments were "not incidental or consequential" on a statutory function.

In determining whether a general power such as section 69 can be the basis for lawful action one should also have regard to specific powers conferred on a local authority under other statutory provisions which can have the effect of narrowing the ability to rely on any such general or broad provision as the following extract demonstrates.

Commission for Local Authority Accounts of Scotland v. City of Edinburgh District Council

1988 S.C.L.R. 552

"Section 88(1) [of the Local Government (Scotland) Act 1973] is in the following terms: **3–20**
'A local authority may make, or assist in the making of, arrangements whereby the public may on application readily obtain, either at premises specially maintained for the purpose or otherwise, information concerning the services available within the area of the authority provided either by the authority or by other authorities or by government departments, or by charities and other voluntary organisations, and other information as to local government matters affecting the area.'
Section 88(2) provides inter alia as follows:
'A local authority may —
(a) arrange for the publication within their area of information on matters relating to local government; ...'
On 17th January 1985 the City of Edinburgh District Council ('the council') passed a motion to utilise the council's resources to publicise the effects of their budget proposals and of complying with the Secretary of State's guidelines and proposed limits on the rate fund contribution to the Housing Revenue Account. The council, in order to carry out that intention, inter alia authorised the use of the slogan 'Edinburgh District Council — Improving Services — Creating Jobs'. That slogan was used on leaflets, stickers and a variety of publicity material. The Controller of Audit appointed by the Commission for Local Authority Accounts in Scotland reported to that body that the sum of £113,281 expended on the above was unlawful. The Commission made a report to the council and held a hearing in relation to the report from the Controller of Audit. After the decision that the expenditure was unlawful the council requested the Commission to state a case for the opinion of the Court of Session and inter alia the question posed was in the following terms:

> 'Whether on the facts found by the applicants hereinbefore set out, the council's expenditure of £78,566 on the production, supply, erection and display of banners and posters, and the production and supply of lapel badges, stickers, T-shirts, paper hats, balloons and carrier bags containing only the slogan "City of Edinburgh District Council — Improving Services — Creating Jobs" in conjunction with the council crest, was contrary to law in respect that it was ultra vires of the council by virtue of the provisions of sections 69 and 88(2)(a) of the Local Government (Scotland) Act 1973".'

LORD JUSTICE-CLERK (ROSS): "This is a case stated for the opinion of the court by the Commission for Local Authority Accounts in Scotland (hereinafter referred to as 'the Commission'). The Commission are a body established under and in terms of section 97(1) of the Local Government (Scotland) Act 1973, and have the functions set out in section 97(2). In terms of section 97(4) the Commission have appointed a Controller of Audit (hereinafter referred to as 'the Controller'). Section 102(1) of the Act of 1973 provides that the Controller shall make to the Commission such reports as they may require with respect to the accounts of local authorities audited under Part VII of the Act of 1973. In particular, section 102(3) provides inter alia:

> Without prejudice to subsection (1) above, if the Controller of Audit, having considered the audit under this Part of this Act of the accounts of any local authority and having made such further enquiries (if any) as he may think fit —
> (*a*)   is of the opinion —
>   (i) that any item of account is contrary to law, ... and
> (*c*)   is not satisfied that the authority has taken or is taking such steps as may be necessary to
>   remedy the matter;
> he shall make to the Commission a special report with respect to the said accounts, setting forth his opinion as aforesaid and the grounds thereof.'

On 27th August 1986, the Controller, in the exercise of his said powers under section 102(3), made a Special Report to the Applicants (S.R. 86/4) on inter alia the City of Edinburgh District Council's expenditure of £113,281 on the production, supply, erection and display of banners and posters, and the production and supply of lapel badges, stickers, T-shirts, paper hats and carrier bags containing only the slogan 'City of Edinburgh District Council — Improving Services — Creating Jobs' in conjunction with the council crest. Reference is made in the case to the terms of that report and in particular paragraph 2.2.3. In paragraph 3.4 of said Special Report, the Controller concluded that said expenditure of £113,281 was contrary to law, in respect that it was ultra vires of the City of Edinburgh District Council.

Observations were thereafter made on the Special Report by the City of Edinburgh District Council and others. In the course of their observations the City of Edinburgh District Council requested the Commission to hold a hearing into the matters raised by the Special Report. In terms of section 103(2)(*b*) of that Act of 1973, the Commission held a hearing in the City Chambers, Edinburgh, on 8th and 9th December 1986 at which the Controller was present and the City of Edinburgh District Council and Mrs Gertrude Barton were represented.

In the course of their observations, the City of Edinburgh District Council requested the Commission to state a case to the Court of Session since they considered that the points of law arising were of such significance to them and to local authorities in general that they merited appropriate judicial consideration. The Commission duly stated this case in accordance with section 103(2)(*c*) of the Act of 1973.

So far as procedure is concerned, it should be stressed that this case has been stated after the hearing has taken place. In my opinion, it was correct for the Commission to hold the hearing first and to state their case thereafter. In following this course, the Commission have obviously had regard to what the court stated in *Commission for Local Authority Accounts in Scotland v. Stirling District Council*. In the course of his opinion the Lord President stated [at p. 447]:

'My clear impression is that the stated case was submitted prematurely. It would have been wiser to have had the whole circumstances investigated first at a hearing in order that any question to be presented to the court could have been presented upon the basis of a full disclosure of the whole circumstances.'

The Commission have made findings in fact in the case which clearly demonstrate the background to the question of law which has arisen. The starting-point is that at a meeting on 17th January 1985 the City of Edinburgh District Council resolved:

'To take whatever steps are necessary, utilising the existing resources of the Council and any additional resources required, to publicise to the maximum degree possible the effects of:
    (a) the Council's budget proposals;
    (b) complying with the Secretary of State's guidelines on general services and staying within the proposed limits on the Rate Fund contribution to the Housing Revenue Account.

'Council further agrees to co-operate and participate where possible with other local authorities and relevant bodies, who wish to preserve the rights of local government including the right to provide the level of service they believe is relevant in relation to meeting the needs of local people.

'In pursuance of the above aims, Council therefore authorises, through the Policy and Resources Committee (or in the case of emergencies the Chair of Policy and Resources), representation at any meetings or events called specifically for this purpose.'

Subsequently, at a meeting on 21st Feburary 1985, the City of Edinburgh District Council, in pursuance of the resolution of 17th January 1985

'and in order to publicise to the maximum degree possible the effect of —
    (a) the Council's budget proposals and complying with the Secretary of State's guidelines on general services; and
    (b) staying within the proposed limits on the Rate Fund contribution to the Housing Revenue Account, the Council authorises —
        (i) the adoption and use of the slogan "EDINBURGH DISTRICT COUNCIL — IMPROVING SERVICES — CREATING JOBS" in conjunction with the Council crest;
        (ii) the preparation and distribution of leaflets, stickers, badges and other items of publicity material;
        (iii) the preparation, distribution and display of banners, posters and signs;
        (iv) the taking of any action open to him by the Director of Administration to further the Council's legal position including the institution of proceedings;
        (v) such other measures as the Policy and Resources Committee (or in the case of emergencies the Chairman of the Policy and Resources Committee) may approve.'

It is further found in the case that, in pursuance of these resolutions, the City of Edinburgh District Council produced and distributed leaflets and brochures bearing the said slogan in conjunction with the council crest, but which also contained information on matters relating to local government. As I understand it no question now arises in relation to such leaflets and brochures which bore the slogan and crest but which also contained information on matters relating to local government. The question in the case arises in relation to what is referred to in finding 4. Finding 4 is in the following terms:

'That in pursuance of said resolution the council also produced, supplied, erected and displayed banners and posters, and produced and supplied lapel badges, stickers, T-shirts, paper hats, balloons and carrier bags containing only the said slogan referred to in article 3 hereof, in conjunction with the council crest.'

In the Special Report a breakdown is given of the figure of £133,281 as being the expenditure incurred by the City of Edinburgh District Council on these various items referred to above. In the case reference is made to a total figure of £78,566, in respect of expenditure on the production, supply, erection and display of the banners and other items containing only the said slogan. There is no explanation in the case as to how this figure was arrived at, but Mr Hardie for the City of Edinburgh District Council drew attention to a letter dated 15th December 1986 addressed to the Commission's secretary from the City of Edinburgh District Council which showed that expenditure amounting to £34,714.84 had been incurred in connection with banners and posters in Princes Street which contained more than the mere slogan. It appears that this matter had been raised at the hearing and that this additional information, including the figures, was sent to the Commission after the hearing had been concluded. This figure of £34,714.84 represents the difference between the Controller's figure of £113,281 and the figure of £78,566 referred to in the case.

Before this court, as in *Commission for Local Authority Accounts in Scotland v Stirling District Council* [1984 S.L.T. 442]; the Commission were represented by counsel, who adopted a neutral position. Opposing arguments were presented to us by counsel on behalf of the Controller and counsel on behalf of the City of Edinburgh District Council. The question which arose was whether the expenditure upon the items referred to in finding 4 was contrary to law. Both sides were agreed that in order to determine whether the expenditure had been legal or illegal regard had to be had to the terms of section 69 of the Act of 1973 and section 88(1) and 88(2). [His Lordship then quoted the terms of the Act as set out above and continued:]

On behalf of the Controller, Mr Martin submitted that the expenditure upon the items described in finding in fact 4 were items of account. He further submitted that these items of account were contrary to law in that they were not authorised by any of the sections of the Act of 1973 referred to above. In the first place he submitted that the expenditure could not be said to be authorised by section 88(1). This was not a situation where there was any question of arrangements having been made whereby the public might on application readily obtain at some location information as to local government matters. The exhibiting of the slogan upon banners or posters, or badges or stickers, or T-shirts or paper hats, or balloons or carrier bags could not constitute the making of arrangements of the kind described in section 88(1). He also submitted that the expenditure could not be said to be authorised by the provisions of section 69(1). That subsection referred inter alia to expenditure which was calculated to facilitate or was conducive or incidental to the discharge of any of a local authority's functions. Mr Martin maintained that this provision might be somewhat wider than section 88(2) but he contended that in the circumstances the real question must be whether the expenditure was covered by section 88(2)(*a*). In incurring expenditure on the items listed in finding in fact 4 containing only the slogan, was the City of Edinburgh District Council arranging for the publication within their area of information on matters relating to local government?

Mr Martin proceeded to consider what was meant by 'information on matters relating to local government'. He referred to *Meek v. Lothian Regional Council* [1982 S.C. 84]. In that case I stated:

'Mr Drummond Young (counsel for the pursuer) contended that "information" in this context meant factual information and not political argument. The passages complained of are set out in article 4 of the condescendence. My *prima facie* view is that what is contained in these passages can properly be regarded as "information on matters relating to local government". In my opinion to explain why the defenders have adopted a particular policy is to provide information on matters relating to local government. If Parliament had intended to restrict a local authority to the publication of purely factual information regarding decisions made, as opposed to publishing explanations or justifications for the decisions made, then Parliament would have said so. No such restriction appears in the subsection. When Parliament conferred on local authorities the power contained in section 88(2), Parliament must have appreciated that party politics do prevail in local government and that a majority group in a local authority might well select for publication information on matters relating to local government which would show or tend to show the majority group in a favourable light. The subsection contains no prohibition against such selection of information.'

What I stated in that quotation was cited with approval by Glidwell J. (as he then was) in *R. v. Inner London Education Authority*, ex parte *Westminster City Council* [[1980] 1 All E.R. 19]. In that case Glidewell J. drew a distinction between expenditure which was made for the purposes of informing and expenditure which was made for the purposes of persuading, and he expressed the view that it was necessary to determine what had been the major purpose of the council's decision to incur the expenditure in question.

Mr Martin submitted at the end of the day that the expenditure in the present case had been incurred not in the publication of information on matters relating to local government but in the adoption of a slogan as part of the campaign of the City of Edinburgh District Council in opposition to the policy being adopted by the Secretary of State.

Mr Hardie, for the City of Edinburgh District Council, pointed out that the Controller had accepted that where the slogan had been used in conjunction with other information, expenditure in that connection was not contrary to law. Even if the City of Edinburgh District Council were engaged upon a campaign, the fact of the matter is that the Controller accepted that part of their expenditure was not unlawful. Mr Hardie further contended that the slogan was informative; it conveyed either that the prime policy of the administration was to improve services and create jobs or that the administration were in fact improving services and creating jobs. He further submitted that the slogan drew the attention of the public to the fact that the City of Edinburgh District Council's policy existed, and accordingly in that sense it was conveying information. He emphasised that one must look at the matter as a 'package' and that insofar as banners containing the slogan were part of a general campaign to disseminate information, they were lawful. He submitted that the slogan was used in association with a campaign to spread information, and that expenditure upon the banners and other items bearing the slogan could be justified under section 88(1) or section 69. They could be regarded as part of the arrangements which the City of Edinburgh District Council made whereby the public could obtain information at certain premises regarding the policy of the City of Edinburgh District Council and the effect upon the public of the City of Edinburgh District Council being required to meet the Secretary of State's guidelines. In any event, the expenditure on these items could properly be regarded as incidental to the discharge by the City of Edinburgh District Council of their function of publishing information on matters relating to local government.

In limine Mr Hardie submitted that the case should be remitted back to the Commission. He reminded us that at an earlier stage we had called on the Commission to state reasons for refusing certain adjustments proposed by the City of Edinburgh District Council to the case. Reasons had been provided, but Mr Hardie contended that the reasons were unsatisfactory and inadequate. It appeared to us that the question of whether any remit was necessary could not be determined until the submissions of the parties had been fully deployed. At the end of the day I understood Mr Hardie to submit that the case should be remitted back for two reasons. In the first place he contended that the question in the case did not raise the issue of whether the expenditure in question was legal, having regard to the terms of section 88(1) of the Act of 1973. He maintained that finding 6 in the case had purported to deal with this point although it was really a matter of law. In the second place Mr Hardie contended that the terms of finding 5 made it plain that expenditure on banners flying over buildings where explanatory material might have been available was legal and that the Commission had failed to state how much of the total expenditure of £78,566 was in respect of banners flying over buildings where explanatory material might have been available.

So far as finding in fact 5 is concerned, it is certainly not expressed as clearly as it might have been. However, I am satisfied that it does not bear the meaning for which Mr Hardie contended. I do not regard the finding as indicating that the Commission were accepting that expenditure would be legal in the case of banners which flew over buildings where explanatory material might have been available. Mr Philip, for the Commission, explained that the purpose of this finding was to make it clear that even though some of the banners flew over buildings where explanatory material might have been available, there was no connection between the banners as a whole and the presence of explanatory material. In my opinion it would be reasonable to read that finding as having the meaning for which Mr Philip contended. In other words, the point which the Commission are making in finding in fact 5 is that there is no distinction between banners, balloons, stickers, badges and the other items because in no case was there any relationship between these items and the explanatory material.

So far as Mr Hardie's challenge of finding 6 is concerned, I am satisfied that his challenge is not well founded. I agree with the Commission that section 88(1) of the Act of 1973 does not authorise the expenditure in question here. I am satisfied that his challenge is not well founded. I agree with the Commission that section 88(1) of the Act of 1973 does not authorise the expenditure in question here. As the Commission say, the production, supply, erection and display of the banners and other items did not constitute arrangements whereby the public might on application readily obtain at any premises information as to local government matters. The situation might have been different if there had been any writing on the banners and other items indicating that further information could be obtained at specific addresses.

The position might also have been different if the banners or other items had borne an arrow or a sign pointing in the direction of premises where such information could be obtained. The banners and other items here, however, bore only the slogan, and that being so I am quite satisfied that there was no question of the expenditure being authorised under section 88(1) of the Act of 1973.

So far as section 69 is concerned, although it may, as Mr Martin suggested, confer a power slightly wider than that conferred by section 88(2), the essential question would still remain as to whether what the City of Edinburgh District Council were doing was arranging for the publication within their area of information on matters relating to local government. On that issue, I have come to be of opinion that the expenditure in question was not warranted by section 88(2)(a). I do not see how the words 'Edinburgh District Council — Improving Services — Creating Jobs' can be regarded as merely informative. Even Mr Hardie found it difficult to explain of what one was being informed by these words. He could not say whether the words were intended to convey what the policy of Edinburgh District Council was or whether they were intended to convey that Edinburgh District Council were in fact improving services or creating jobs. That being so, in my opinion, the words cannot be regarded as publishing information on matters relating to local government.

In my opinion, the City of Edinburgh District Council's resolution of 21st February 1985 makes it plain that what the City of Edinburgh District Council was doing was resolving to adopt and use these words as a slogan. It is clear from the terms of this resolution and the earlier resolution of 17th January 1985 that this slogan was being adopted and was to be used not as a means of publishing information on matters relating to local government but as part of a campaign being mounted by the City of Edinburgh District Council in response to guidelines laid down by the Secretary of State. The use of the word 'slogan' is significant. A slogan is a battle cry or catchword or catch-phrase. That being its purpose, it is plain that the slogan was adopted as a means of rallying support for the City of Edinburgh District Council in its opposition to the Secretary of State's guidelines. In my opinion, since the words of the slogan do not in themselves convey information nor provide the means by which information might be obtained, expenditure upon the banners and other items bearing the slogan is not lawful.

Having regard to the terms of the resolutions passed by the City of Edinburgh District Council on 17th January 1985 and 21st February 1985, I am of opinion that there is no justification for Mr Hardie's contention that the provision of banners and other articles bearing the slogan was part of a campaign to disseminate information. Although the terms of the two resolutions would suggest that there was a campaign, there is nothing in the terms of the resolution to suggest that it was a campaign to spread information. If the genuine purpose of adopting the slogan had been to convey to the public information on a matter relating to local government, I am not persuaded that displaying the slogan on banners, posters, lapel badges, stickers, T-shirts, paper hats, balloons could conceivably have that result. In any event, if that had been the true purpose of the expenditure, I would have expected to see some reference to that in the resolutions passed by the City of Edinburgh District Council on 17th January 1985 and 21st February 1985. No such reference appears in either of the resolutions.

In these circumstances I would move your Lordships to answer the question in the case in the affirmative and to remit the Commission to proceed as accords."

Lord Dunpark: "[After narrating the history and statutory references his Lordship continued:]
Thereafter banners, posters, lapel badges, stickers, T-shirts, paper hats, balloons and carrier bags were produced, issued and displayed in the city, containing the words 'CITY OF EDINBURGH DISTRICT COUNCIL — IMPROVING SERVICES — CREATING JOBS' and the council crest. Some of these articles contained no more than the above, but others had some additional information on them. The Commission deducted the sum of £34,715 from the Controller's figure of £113,281 in respect of those articles which had some additional information on them and found that the sum of £78,566 had been expended contrary to law on banners, posters, lapel badges, stickers, T-shirts, paper hats, balloons and carrier bags which contained only the name and crest of the council and the words 'IMPROVING SERVICES — CREATING JOBS', on the ground that this was merely a slogan which gave no information 'on matters relating to local government'. So the question for us is whether these articles which contained only the name, crest and the slogan fall within the terms of section 88 and 69 of the Act.

The Commission held that the money spent on the articles referred to in the question posed in the case was not authorised by section 88(1) of the Act since the production, supply, erection and display of articles containing only the name and crest of the council and the slogan did not constitute 'arrangements whereby the public may on application readily obtain ... information concerning the services available within' the council's area. Mr Hardie for the council submitted that all the articles containing only the name, crest and slogan were issued as part of an advertising campaign to bring the efforts of the council to the notice of the public and that they were therefore authorised by section 88(1). I do not agree. One has only to read section 88(1) to appreciate that the exhibition of a slogan on whatever medium cannot reasonably be construed as 'arrangements whereby the public may on application readily obtain ... information concerning the services available within the area of the authority'.

In the course of debate the question arose as to the significance of the Commission's finding 5(5), viz:

> 'That some of the said banners flew over buildings where some explanatory material may have been available but many of the said banners and posters were located where no explanatory material would be expected to be available and that there was no relationship between items such as the said balloons, stickers, badges, etc., and any explanatory material.'

It was explained to us that this finding related to an argument that a distinction might be drawn between different locations of the slogan. It was suggested that where the slogan appeared alone on or immediately outside a local authority building within which were council staff available to provide information about local government matters, the slogan should be construed as an invitation to the public to apply within for such information under section 82(1), whereas the appearance of the slogan elsewhere might not be so construed. Mr Hardie invited us to remit the case to the Commission to ascertain the amount spent on display of the slogan on or outside local authority buildings within which there were staff available to provide information and the amount spent on its display elsewhere. As I cannot construe the display of the slogan, wherever exhibited, as an invitation to the public to apply for information within any building, a remit is unnecessary, and the question of the exhibition of the slogan per se must be answered by reference to section 88(2)(a) alone because, unless the display of the name, crest and slogan falls within the function defined in section 88(2)(a), it cannot be covered as 'calculated to facilitate, or is conducive or incidental to, the discharge of any of their functions' in terms of section 69(1).

There is no dispute between the parties that 'Improving Services — Creating Jobs' is a slogan. Mr Martin, for the Controller, referred to *The Shorter Oxford English Dictionary* where the definition is given of slogan.

> 'A ... war-cry or battle-cry. The distinctive note, phrase, cry, etc. of any person or body of persons.'

He maintained that these words were no more than a slogan, containing no information; that they were part of an advertising campaign designed to win over opinion to the point of view of the party promoting the campaign and that the purpose was to persuade, not to inform (see *R. v. Inner London Education Authority*, ex parte *Westminster City Council*, per Glidewell J., at p. 33). The slogan did not inform the public of anything except the war-cry. According to the minute of 21st February one of the purposes of the campaign was to publicise the effect of the council's budget proposals, but the slogan per se did nothing to explain the effects of their budget proposals.

Mr Hardie, on the other hand, submitted that the slogan was adopted as part of an informing, not a persuasive, campaign, and that it was just part of a package of which the objective was to inform the public. He submitted that the slogan should be construed as stating two of the primary policy objectives of the council, namely, to improve services and to create jobs, and that its display was authorised by section 88(2)(a), coupled with section 69(1).

I cannot think of any sensible construction of this slogan other than as a statement of these two objections; but, assuming that it may be so construed, the question then arises whether the display of the name, crest and slogan on the various articles was 'publication ... of information on matters relating to local government' within the meaning of section 88(2)(a).

I cannot think of any sensible construction of this slogan other than a statement of these two objectives; but, assuming that it may be so construed, the question, then arises whether the display of the name, crest and slogan on the various articles was 'publication ... of information on matters relating to local government' within the meaning of section 88(2)(a).

Section 88(1) provides for the direction of citizens to places where they may on application obtain information about the services provided by a local authority and to persons there who can supply the information sought. Section 88(2)(a) relates to the publication of information on matters relating to local government. This would cover all printed material containing such information and its display for the information of the public. The other provisions of section 88(2) relate to other means of disseminating such information. However, I am of opinion that the question of whether the display of this name, crest and slogan on the relevant articles should be construed as covered by section 88(2)(a) depends upon whether it achieves the council's stated purpose. So the real question, in my opinion, is — What information about local government matters did the council intend to impart to readers of the slogan? We can only ascertain that intention by referring to the minute of the meeting of 21st February.

Mr Hardie submitted that the council's intention or purpose in authorising the use of this slogan was, as stated in the minute, in order to 'publicise to the maximum degree possible the effects of: (a) the Council's budget proposals; and (b) complying with the Secretary of State's guidelines on general services'.

Now I do not know what the council's budget proposals were nor do I know what guidelines the Secretary of State had laid down on general services. The slogan must, in my opinion, be read as confined to the purpose which the council intended it to achieve. So I ask myself another question, namely, what information does the slogan give the public about the council's budget proposals or the Secretary of State's guidelines on general services? The answer is obviously none.

I suppose that the inference from the slogan might be that the council intended spending money on improving services and creating jobs, but this case does not disclose what the council's budget proposals were or whether they complied or conflicted to any extent with the Secretary of State's guidelines on general services. Accordingly, in my opinion the display of the slogan completely fails to serve its purported purpose. It gives no information about the two matters which the council intended to publicise by its use. My concluded opinion is that the only effect that it would have upon a citizen reading the slogan would be persuasive, namely, as an invitation to support the policy of the council to improve services and create jobs.

For these reasons I answer the question of law in the affirmative."

LORD GRIEVE: "[After narrating the history and statutory references his Lordship continued:]
I did not understand counsel for the district council to maintain that the sum in question facilitated, or was incidental to, any specific function of the council so as to be covered by the terms of section 69 of the Act. He did submit, however, that the items which bore the slogan and the crest came within the provisions of both section 88(1) and 88(2)(*a*).

In my opinion none of the items in question fall within section 88(1). That subsection is concerned with the making of 'arrangements' whereby the public can obtain information as to local government matters which affect a particular matter. The display of a poster, or banner, or the wearing of a T-shirt bearing a slogan can in no sense be regarded as such an 'arrangement'.

Section 88(2)(*a*), the terms of which formed the main basis for the submissions of parties, allows a local authority to spend money on the publication of information which relates to local government matters. What information is provided by the slogan 'Improving Services — Creating Jobs'? What, one is tempted to ask, does it mean? I confess I do not know; and, by using the slogan itself, I cannot understand how anyone could have been the wiser as to the activities of the district council as a result of seeing such a slogan on a banner or a balloon.

What the district council, inter alia, resolved to do on 21st February 1985 was to spend money on a slogan which was to be displayed by a variety of means. The question for the Controller was whether the expenditure so incurred was covered by any of the provisions of the 1973 Act and, in particular, the provisions of sections 69 and 88. He concluded it was not, and in my opinion he was correct in his conclusions. The slogan neither facilitated the council's functions nor did it inform the public of any matters relating to local government. I agree with your Lordships that the question in the stated case should be answered in the affirmative, and I also agree with the reasons which your Lordships have given for so answering it."

Notes

Different approaches are evident in the judgments of the Lord Justice-Clerk and Lord **3–21** Dunpark. The former seems to take the view that because the slogan was capable of bearing two meanings, that of persuasion or provision of information, it was necessary to have regard to the terms of the resolutions passed by the council. This provided the basis upon which His Lordship concluded that the purpose of the slogan was unlawful persuasion. This is an application of the test found in the *Westminster City Council* case referred to in the extract and which is discussed further at para. 6–7 in the context of the doctrine of improper purpose. However, although the judgment of Lord Dunpark also referred to the terms of the council minute, he put more emphasis on reading the slogan in the context of whether in itself it amounted to information. In the absence of anything more than the broad purposes detailed in the council's minute, his Lordship found himself unable to conclude that any information was in fact being provided. Is it possible to interpret Lord Dunpark's judgment as suggesting that if there had been a clearer connection between the terms of the minute he referred to and the terms of the slogan, then it would have been lawful? Is it possible to interpret his judgment as accepting that the essential purpose underlying the slogan was lawful — that of providing information relating to the council's budget proposals and the impact of the Secretary of State's guidelines on general services — but that the slogan in itself failed to achieve that purpose? Is this a difference of degree or principle? Which approach is preferable? Does Lord Ross give sufficient weight to the views he expressed in *Meek* referred to in the extract?

Chapter 4

JURISDICTIONAL CONTROL

The concept of *ultra vires*, noted in Chapter 3, is easy to understand in the context of argument **4–1** that an administrative body has exceeded its powers, whether express or implied. What we are now concerned with is the way in which this matter can arise but in a rather more subtle way, that is the situation where it is accepted that the body in question can reach the decision in issue. Our concern here is that what has been done has not been in line with the required circumstances which must be held to exist before the decision may be validly made — typically the situation where power to do something only exists when certain defined circumstances also exist as contrasted with a straight grant of power.

At the heart of this matter is our concern to ensure that the judiciary control such questions of jurisdiction in a way which allows the decision maker freedom to act, but equally ensures that the decisions which are made are kept within lawful boundaries. Our primary concern is with jurisdictional control in judicial review proceedings, although some of the issues that are touched on here — for example, what is a matter of law, for the purpose of an error of law, are also of significance in appeals, on which see Chapter 12.

These boundary disputes can either arise in the context of whether or not the correct interpretation has been applied to legislation as to the circumstances in which a body has to find established before it has power to act or, alternatively, there may in fact be a dispute about whether those circumstances exist at all. The distinction is therefore between questions of law and questions of fact. The distinction is more easily stated than applied and, as noted by A. W. Bradley, *The Laws of Scotland: Stair Memorial Encyclopaedia*, Vol. 1, para. 287:

> "A full analysis of the notion of an error of law would raise difficult jurisprudential issues and also important issues of judicial policy, since the courts have not adopted uniform criteria for distinguishing between questions of law and questions of fact."

Issues of jurisdictional law are more likely to arise in the situation involving decisions by judicial bodies than by simple administrative bodies. The issues which the court may have to consider might include the composition of the body, the kind of case that has power to hear, both the procedural and substantive rules that have to be applied and the remedies that can be granted. Errors can arise in relation to all of these but that does not of itself give any guidance as to when judicial review will be permitted. Errors of jurisdictional law can be readily identified in connection with questions involving the composition of a tribunal (*Cannon v. Secretary of State for Scotland*, 1964 S.L.T. 91) or the type of case which the body has power to hear (*Cowan & Co. Ltd v. North British Railway Co.* (1901) 9 S.L.T. 296) or procedural challenge (*London and Clydeside Estates Ltd v. Aberdeen District Council*, 1980 S.C. (H.L.) 1) — the list is not exhaustive.

The real difficulty arises in connection with review of substantive decisions. There is a clear danger that an appeal can emerge. Central to this is the concept of the right of the decision maker in question to be in error whether as to law or as to fact. If challenge to all such errors must be allowed then it should be by way of appeal which is of course more widely defined. On this see Chapter 12. Given the acceptance of the distinction between appeal and review, noted in Chapter 8 this necessarily drove the courts to establish a formula by which some errors would allow a decision to be reviewed whereas others would not. As noted in *West v. Secretary of State for Scotland*, at para. 10–7, the concept of jurisdiction and in turn "excess or abuse of jurisdiction" is central to the circumstances in which judicial review can be exercised.

C. T. Emery and B. Smythe, "Error of Law in Administrative Law" (1984) 100 L.Q.R. 612 suggest that the process of decision making involves three steps:

(i)   Finding the facts, whether primary or secondary facts.
(ii)   Stating the law.
(iii)   Applying the law to the facts found.

Errors of law may arise not only at step (ii), which is the obvious area of challenge, but also at step (i) if primary facts are found for which there is no evidence or if an inference of secondary facts is based on improper legal reasoning. In connection with step (iii) an error of law may arise if the conclusion reached is one which the reviewing court cannot support.

The concept of error of law which is central to jurisdictional control may involve both the way in which a decision-making body has handled the facts before it as well as the way in which it has handled the law which it is required to apply. On jurisdictional control generally see *Stair Memorial Encyclopaedia*, Vol. 1, paras 285–289; V. Finch and C. Ashton, *Administrative Law in Scotland* (1997), pp. 278–282; and P. P. Craig, *Administrative Law* (3rd., 1994), Chap. 10.

JURISDICTION AND FACTS

R. v. Secretary of State for the Home Department, ex parte Khawaja

[1984] A.C. 74

4–2   "In this case two separate appeals to the House of Lords raising the same legal issues were heard together. The appellants, Khera and Khawaja, were both persons who, having been admitted to the United Kingdom as immigrants, had later been detained and ordered for removal as 'illegal entrants' under the Immigration Act 1971. Argument centred on two questions — (i) the meaning of the term 'illegal entrant' and (ii) the scope of review of the exercise of power to remove such persons from the United Kingdom.

These two questions had earlier been considered by the House of Lords in *Zamir v. Secretary of State for the Home Department* [1980] A.C. 930. In that case it had been held that the term 'illegal entrant' included one who had obtained permission to enter after having failed positively to disclose some matter which would have led to the refusal of permission to enter had that information been known at the time. This was so even though no request for such information may have been made by any official — in other words, *Zamir* imposed a positive duty to disclose relevant information to immigration officers, even beyond answering truthfully the various questions which might specifically have been asked by the officers. In *Khawaja* the House of Lords overruled *Zamir* on this point, holding that a person who had been admitted entry was only a 'illegal entrant' where some positive deception had been practised.

Our concern, however, is with the second of the two questions: in proceedings for judicial review is it sufficient for the Secretary of State to satisfy the court that when he exercised has power to order removal he had reasonable grounds to believe the appellant to be an illegal entrant? Or is not the critical issue whether the appellant does, or does not, in fact fall within that statutory category? *Zamir* had decided that the scope of review was of the former extent. The appellants called upon the House of Lords to reconsider the matter."

LORD FRASER: "… The second general issue relates to the function of the courts and of this House in its judicial capacity when dealing with applications for judicial review in cases of this sort: is their function limited to deciding whether there was evidence on which the immigration officer of other appropriate official in the Home Office could reasonably come to his decision (provided he acted fairly and not in breach of the rules of natural justice), or does it extend to deciding whether the decision was justified and in accordance with the evidence? On this question I agree with my noble and learned friends Lord Scarman and Lord Bridge that an immigration officer is only entitled to order the detention and removal of a person who has entered the country by virtue of an *ex facie* valid permission if the person *is* an illegal entrant. That is a 'precedent fact' which has to be established. It is not enough that the immigration officer reasonably believes him to be an illegal entrant if the evidence does not justify his belief. Accordingly, the duty of the court must be beyond inquiring only whether he had reasonable grounds for his belief. In both the present cases the immigration officers stated, in what appears to be a standard formula, that there were 'reasonable grounds to conclude, etc.'. That formula indicates, in my opinion, that they applied the wrong test... ."

LORD SCARMAN: "... [in *Zamir*] ... [t]he House approved a line of authority (beginning with *R. v. Secretary of State for the Home Department, ex p. Hussain* [1978] 1 W.L.R. 700) which put a gloss on the words of the critical provision in the 1971 Act, *i.e.* Sched. 2, para. 9 to the Act. The paragraph declares an illegal entrant to be liable to removal. It provides that where an illegal entrant is not given leave to enter or remain in the United Kingdom an immigration officer may give directions for his removal. Unless he (or the Secretary of State, para. 10) gives such directions, no power to detain him arises; for para. 16(2) provides a power to detain only in respect of a person who may be so removed....

The gloss which the House in *Zamir's* case put on the words of para. 9 was to read them as meaning not 'where a person *is* an illegal entrant' but 'where the immigration officer *has reasonable grounds for believing a person to be* an illegal entrant' he may be removed if not given leave to enter. If it be sought to justify the gloss as a proper construction of the statutory language, there is a difficulty. The gloss requires the introduction into the paragraph of words that are not there. Must they, then, be implied? This question lies at the heart of the problem.

In *Zamir's* case the House was impressed with the difficulties arising if the implication were not to be made. The House attached importance to three considerations: (1) the line of cases beginning with *Hussain*, in which the Court of Appal had held it necessary to make the implication; (2) the scheme of the Immigration Act; and, especially, (3) the nature and process of the power of decision conferred by the Act on immigration officers.

These considerations, in the view of the House, made it necessary to reject the appellant's argument based on the well-established principle that, where the exercise of an executive power depends on the precedent establishment of an objective fact, it is for the court, if there be a challenge by way of judicial review, to decide whether the precedent requirement has been satisfied. In *R. v. Governor of Pentonville Prison, ex p. Azam* [1974] A.C. 18, 34 Lord Denning M.R. (in the Court of Appeal) considered the principle applicable in the case of removal of an illegal entrant. The House recognised the existence of the principle, but, following and approving *Hussain's* case, opted for a construction of the legislation which would oust it.

In rejecting the appellant's argument based on the 'precedent fact' principle of review Lord Wilberforce said [in *Zamir*] [1980] A.C. 930, 948:

'My Lords, for the reasons I have given I am of opinion that the whole scheme of the Act is against this argument. It is true that it does not, in relation to the decisions in question, use such words as 'in the opinion of the Secretary of State' or 'the Secretary of State must be satisfied', but it is not necessary for such a formula to be used in order to take the case out of the 'precedent fact' category. The nature and process of decision conferred on immigration officers by existing legislation is incompatible with any requirement for the establishment of precedent objective facts whose existence the court may verify.'

He therefore implied into para. 9 the words needed to bring it outside the 'precedent fact' category of provision. My Lords, in most cases I would defer to a recent decision of your Lordships' House on a question of construction, even if I thought it wrong. I do not do so in this context because for reasons which I shall develop I am convinced that the *Zamir* reasoning gave insufficient weight to the important (I would say fundamental) consideration that we are here concerned with, the scope of judicial review of a power which inevitably infringes the liberty of those subjected to it. This consideration, if it be good, outweighs, in my judgment, any difficulties in the administration of immigration control to which the application of the principle might give rise. The *Zamir* construction of para. 9 deprives those subjected to the power of that degree of judicial protection which I think can be shown to have been the policy of our law to afford to persons with whose liberty the executive is seeking to interfere. It does therefore, in my view, tend to obstruct the proper development and application of the safeguards our law provides for the liberty of those within its jurisdiction... .

Accordingly, faced with the jealous care our law traditionally devotes to the protection of the liberty of those who are subject to its jurisdiction, I find it impossible to imply into the statute words the effect of which would be to take the provision, para. 9 of Sched. 2 to the 1971 Act, 'out of the "precedent fact" category' (see *Zamir* [1980] A.C. 930 at 948, *per* Lord Wilberforce). If Parliament intends to exclude effective judicial review of the exercise of a power in restraint of liberty, it must make its meaning crystal clear.'

LORD BRIDGE: "... [T]he authorities from *R. v. Secretary of State for the Home Department, ex p. Hussain* to *Zamir* have consistently affirmed the principle that the decision of an immigration officer to detain and remove a person as an illegal entrant under these provisions can only be attacked successfully on the ground that there was no evidence on which the immigration officer could reasonably conclude that he was an illegal entrant.

It will be seen at once that this principle gives to an executive officer, subject, no doubt, in reaching his conclusions of fact to a duty to act fairly, a draconian power of arrest and expulsion based on his own decision of fact.… . It will be further observed that to justify the principle important words have to be read into para. 9 of Sched. 2 by implication. That paragraph, on the face of the language used, authorises the removal of a person who is an illegal entrant. The courts have applied it as if it authorised the removal of a person whom an immigration officer on reasonable grounds believes to be an illegal entrant. The all-important question is whether such an implication can be justified.

The presently prevailing doctrine was first enunciated in *R. V. Secretary of State for the Home Department, ex p. Hussain* by Geoffrey Lane L.J. He explained the suggested basis of the doctrine rather more fully in *R. v. Secretary of State for the Home Department, ex p. Choudhary* [1978] 1 W.L.R. 1177, 1183, where he said:

> 'The whole object of this part of the Immigration Act 1971, read as a whole, is to ensure that there is a procedure, and a readily available and easy procedure, whereby the Secretary of State can detain pending removal any person such as the appellant in this case. The Secretary of State obviously, from the nature of things, has no desire to detain a man longer than is necessary to get him out of this country and back to Pakistan, or wherever it was he came from. It is conceded by [counsel for Mr Choudhary], and, if I may say so, rightly conceded, that a reasonable belief held by the Secretary of State is sufficient to justify the initial detention of the man; but it is said that, once the Secretary of State's inquiries are at an end, then one has to examine the basis of fact and, if that shows that the Secretary of State had got the factual basis wrong, then the whole of the detention from the moment the inquiries have come to an end and onwards is unlawful. With that submission I cannot agree. It seems to me that the detention in circumstances such as these is throughout a matter for the discretion of the Secretary of State; and, if he was acting on reasonable grounds and acting *bona fide* on those reasonable grounds, then he is protected.'

In *Zamir* [1980] A.C. 930, 948–949 Lord Wilberforce said:

> 'The nature and process of decision conferred on immigration officers by existing legislation is incompatible with any requirement for the establishment of precedent objective facts whose existence the court may verify.
>
> The immigration officer, whether at the stage of entry or at that of removal, has to consider a complex of statutory rules and non-statutory guidelines. He has to act on documentary evidence and such other evidence as inquiries may provide. Often there will be documents whose genuineness is doubtful, statements which cannot be verified, misunderstandings as to what was said, practices and attitudes in a foreign state which have to be estimated. There is no room for appreciation, even for discretion.'

He proceeds to contrast the disadvantageous position of the Divisional Court as a fact-finding tribunal in the relevant field.…

My Lords, we should, I submit, regard with extreme jealousy any claim by the executive to imprison a citizen without trial and allow it only if it is clearly justified by the statutory language relied on. The fact that, in the case we are considering, detention is preliminary and incidental to expulsion from the country in my view strengthens rather than weakens the case for a robust exercise of the judicial function in safeguarding the citizen's rights.

So far as I know, no case before the decisions under the Act which we are presently considering has held imprisonment without trial by executive order to be justified by anything less than the plainest statutory language, with the sole exception of the majority decision of your Lordships' House in *Liversidge v. Anderson* [1942] A.C. 206. No one needs to be reminded of the now celebrated dissenting speech of Lord Atkin in that case, or of his withering condemnation of the process of writing into the statutory language there under consideration the words which were necessary to sustain the decision of the majority. Lord Atkin's dissent now has the approval of your Lordships' House in *R. v. Inland Revenue Commissioners, ex p. Rossminster Ltd* [1980] A.C. 952.

A person who has entered the United Kingdom with leave and who is detained under Sched. 2, para. 16(2) pending removal as an illegal entrant on the ground that he obtained leave to enter by fraud is entitled to challenge the action taken and proposed to be taken against him both by application for habeas corpus and by application for judicial review. On the view I take, para. 9 of Sched. 2 must be construed as meaning no more and no less than it says. There is no room for any implication qualifying the words 'illegal entrant'. From this it would follow that, while, prima facie, the order for detention under para. 16(2) would be a sufficient return to the writ of habeas corpus, proof by the applicant that he had been granted leave to enter would shift the onus back to the immigration officer to prove that the leave had been obtained in contravention of s. 26(1)(c) of the Act, in other words by fraud... ."

LORDS WILBERFORCE and TEMPLEMAN delivered concurring speeches.

Malhi v. Secretary of State for Home Affairs

1989 S.L.T. 43

"A native of India obtained entry to the United Kingdom upon a representation that he proposed to stay for a limited period only. He stayed for several years. When investigations were made, he stated to the immigration officer that he had in fact intended to stay indefinitely at the time of his arrival. Thereupon the Secretary of State for Home Affairs determined that the petitioner was an illegal entrant to the United Kingdom and decided that he should be deported. Against that decision the petitioner appealed by judicial review contending that he had not made that admission, which contention was rejected after evidence had been heard, and that in any event there was insufficient evidence for the Secretary of State to conclude that the petitioner was an illegal entrant. It was argued against the petitioner that, not only had he admitted the deception, but also that the other evidence was consistent with that and corroborated it."

4–3

LORD WEIR: "This matter which has come before me is one of considerable urgency. If this petition does not succeed the petitioner will be removed from this country tomorrow, 16 July 1988, to India. I have heard a proof lasting two days and this opinion has been given upon the conclusion of counsel's submissions. The only question which I have to determine is whether upon the basis of the evidence which I have heard the respondent's immigration officer was justified in concluding that the petitioner gained entry to the United Kingdom by deception. It is accepted that the burden of proving that the petitioner obtained entry by this means and therefore is to be treated as an illegal entrant rests upon the respondent, and the standard of proof which is required is that of high probability (*R. v. Home Secretary, ex p. Khawaja*). The contention of the petitioner is that he obtained entry upon a representation which he maintains truthfully expressed his intentions, at the time, namely, that he proposed to stay only for a limited period.

After the immigration authorities had discovered three and a half years later that he was still in the United Kingdom, investigations were carried out and two interviews took place at the end of May 1988 in Barlinnie Prison where the petitioner had been detained. A decision was reached that the petitioner was an illegal entrant. I heard evidence from the immigration officer who carried out the interview, Mr Duguid, and from the interpreter at these interviews, Mrs Akhtar. At the first interview the petitioner gave certain information as to the reason he gave for coming to the United Kingdom and as to his employment history since arrival, some of which he admitted in evidence was lies. At the second interview the petitioner was asked to explain why he did not return to India at the end of the permitted duration of his visit. He is recorded as replying: 'When I arrived in the United Kingdom on 24 December 1984, it was my intention to stay in the United Kingdom indefinitely as I did not want to return to India on account of the family dispute.' When asked why he did not reveal his true intentions at the time of seeking entry, he is recorded as having replied: 'I thought this I would be refused entry to the United Kingdom and sent back to India.' If the statement recorded at the interview is correct, then it is clear that the petitioner all along had the intention of staying in the United Kingdom indefinitely and that he concealed this upon entry. On that state of facts the petitioner clearly gained entry by deception because it is not in dispute that if he had stated this as his true intention he would have been refused entry. However the petitioner denied ever making such a statement at the second interview. His position was that while in this country he learned of an outbreak of violence in his village affecting his family. He was afraid for his life if he returned. He changed his mind about returning there on this account only after he had been granted limited leave to enter. There was therefore no deception, it was claimed, at the time when he gained entry.

As I stated at the outset, the onus of proof rests upon the respondent. I should make it clear that having heard the evidence of what transpired at the second interview, I am prepared to accept the evidence of Mr Duguid and Mrs Akhtar that the petitioner did indeed make the critical statement. It seems to me that the interview was concluded meticulously and the petitioner well understood the questions put to him. I am also satisfied despite his protestations to the contrary that he gave the answer already quoted and that he understood what he was saying. I regarded the petitioner as an untrustworthy witness both in his demeanour in the witness box and in the content of much of what he had to say. He has admitted to telling lies at different times to the immigration authorities and if the onus of proof had rested on him, his case would have failed. However, the law is clear that no onus rests on the petitioner. Moreover the law of evidence in Scotland requires that an admission of the kind made at the second interview has to be corroborated and, in my opinion, this must necessarily be the case where the standard of proof is a relatively high one. Counsel for the respondent conceded that corroboration of the petitioner's statement was necessary, and he argued that such corroboration came from facts and circumstances. These were said to be the petitioner's originally stated intention of coming for only a short period; his sojourn despite that statement for some years in this country; his failure to tell the authorities of his prolonged stay; and the numerous evasions to the immigration authorities after his whereabouts had been discovered by them.

I accept that these facts and circumstances are consistent with the petitioner's stated intention to stay indefinitely. The question is whether the consistency of these facts and circumstances constitutes sufficient corroboration of the petitioner's statement. In this connection it has to be borne in mind that the facts and circumstances relied upon by counsel for the respondent are equally consistent with the petitioner's own account of coming originally with the intention of staying for a limited period but prolonging his stay on account of news coming from home indicating that it was unsafe for him to return there. Counsel for the respondent argued that very little was required in the way of corroboration of the petitioner's statement at the second interview. I did not have the benefit, perhaps on account of the speed at which this case had to be dealt with, of argument upon the nature and extent of what the law requires by way of corroboration of the critical statement. However, I have come to the conclusion that the evidence relied upon by the respondent does not provide sufficient confirmation of the petitioner's statement. Although, as I have already mentioned, I do not find the petitioner's evidence trustworthy, his position was supported by the evidence of three other witnesses, two of whom are related to him. These witnesses on the whole made a favourable impression upon me and, although I view what they had to say about the petitioner's intentions to stay and his alleged change of mind with some scepticism, their evidence is enough to make me pause and reflect upon where the truth of the matter may lie. In this situation, I have found it necessary to look for corroboration of the petitioner's statement at the second interview from evidence which provides an unequivocal check of that statement rather than from evidence which is consistent both with that statement and with the position maintained in court by the petitioner. Such evidence I have been unable to find. In these circumstances, but not without a feeling of some reluctance, I have come to the conclusion that the respondent has failed to discharge the onus of proving that the petitioner gained entry by deception."

Notes

4–4   (1) On *Khawaja*, see G. L. Peiris, "Judicial Review and Immigration Policy: Emerging Trends" (1988) 8 L.S. 201. Many of the problems of jurisdiction have been described as having a factual background. These extracts illustrate the basis of the court's intervention on whether a factual error has indeed arisen. Jurisdictional facts are sometimes known as "collateral facts". As Wade has recognised "there is no acid test for recognising collateral or jurisdictional facts" "Anglo-American Administrative Law: More Reflections" [1966] 82 L.Q.R. 226 at 231. Do the foregoing extracts bear this out? Arguably what was significant in both *Khawaja* and *Malhi* was the existence of an express limitation on the competence of the immigration authority, where the facts that go to that competence will probably be regarded as jurisdictional. Here the tribunal only had jurisdiction if *Khawaja* or *Malhi* were "illegal entrants". *Khawaja* is treated by the Justice-All Souls Report at p. 170 as being a rare example of the court going behind facts and inferences from facts (secondary facts). *Rae v. Criminal Injuries Compensation Board* below is perhaps more typical of the approach of the court.

Others, such as Gordon, reject the concept of jurisdictional fact as having any meaning. His view was that there is no real distinction between facts which go to the jurisdiction of the tribunal and facts which the tribunal has jurisdiction to determine. This is known as the pure theory of jurisdiction. He argued that the distinction is not logical. A fact will be jurisdictional when the reviewing court wishes to intervene and when it does not wish to intervene it will not apply that interpretation: see (1929) 45 L.Q.R. 459 and (1931) 47 L.Q.R. 386. What implications does this approach have for the scope of judicial review?

(2) *Malhi* is also a useful decision from the point of view of the way in which the court resolves disputed issues of fact in judicial review proceedings. Unlike *Khawaja*, evidence was led to establish what the petitioner actually said at the crucial interview. In *Khawaja* there appears to have been some reluctance to allow cross-examination, notwithstanding the availability of this under RSC, Ord. 53. *Malhi* does not of itself suggest when affidavits should be allowed

instead of direct examination. Some guidance is given by *Walker v. Strathclyde Regional Council (No. 2)*, 1987 S.L.T. 81 where affidavits were lodged by both petitioners and respondents in connection with a dispute over whether the respondents, an education authority, had failed in their statutory duty to secure adequate and efficient provision of school education. In the view of Lord Morison, the matter went beyond specification, noting (at 81) that:

> "The use of affidavits as a substitute for oral evidence is recognised by the acts of sederunt dealing with judicial review but it may not be appropriate to deal with contentious issues of fact or opinion even although the affidavits may be amplified, as occurred in the present case, by ex parte statements relative to matters raised at the hearing by parties or by the court. If the petitioners are right in their submission that the respondents' evidence is insufficient to prove their case in the particular respect now alleged, the proper course in the circumstances is, in my opinion, not to find that they are thereby in breach of statutory duty but to allow them an opportunity of providing further specification by oral evidence which would be subject to cross examination. On this approach I consider the evidence on the issues with which the hearing is concerned."

(3) The suggestion implicit in *Khawaja* and *Malhi*, that a body which has powers which can be exercised in certain definite situations cannot by its own decision determine conclusively that such conditions exist, needs to be qualified. There is no reason in principle why a statute should not confer powers in a body and make them exercisable in defined circumstances only, yet also make that body the conclusive judge as to whether those circumstances exist. This possibility was examined by Lord Esher M.R. in *R. v. Income Tax Special Purposes Commissioners* (1888) 21 Q.B.D. 313, C.A. Two types of case were noted. In the first type jurisdictional facts are subject to review. In the second type, however (at 319):

> "The legislation may intrust the ... body with a jurisdiction, which includes the jurisdiction to determine whether the preliminary state of facts exists as well as the jurisdiction, on finding that it does exist, to proceed further or do something more."

In determining whether grant of power is of the former or the latter kind, the words used in the legislation will be important. Here consider the reluctance of the judiciary to interpret legislation as excluding the jurisdictional control: see *Anisminic Ltd v. Foreign Compensation Corporation*, at para. 4–10 . Similarly, the nature of the decision-making body, the existence of other means of holding it accountable, and the standards which it has to apply, will also determine whether or not the facts are jurisdictional.

Ferguson v. Secretary of State for Social Services

1989 S.L.T. 117

"Hugh Ferguson appealed against a decision of the social security commissioner refusing his claim for the higher rate of supplementary benefit for heating his home under the Supplementary Benefit (Requirements) Regulations 1983 (S.I. 1983 No. 1399), Sched. 4, para. 6. The facts of the case appear from the opinion of the court.
The appeal was heard by the Second Division on 8 July 1988.

4–5

Statutory provisions

The Supplementary Benefit (Requirements) Regulations 1983 (S.I. 1983 No. 1399) provide in Sched. 4:

ADDITIONAL REQUIREMENTS
Part 1
HEATING

Items and cases applicable (1)	Weekly amount (2)
6. Person who is a householder where the home is part of an estate built with a heating system of which the Secretary of State has in his discretion recognised the running costs to be disproportionately high.	6. Where the home, excluding any bathroom, lavatory or hall, consides of — (*a*) not more than four rooms, £4.40; (*b*) five or more rooms, £8.80.

LORD DUNPARK: "This is an appeal on question of law under s. 14 of the Social Secretary Act 1980 against a decision of the social security commissioner, leave having been granted by him.

The appellant claimed the higher rate of supplementary benefit for heating his home under para. 6 of Pt. I of Sched. 4 to the Supplementary Benefit (Requirements) Regulations 1983 (S.I. 1983 No. 1399). Paragraph 6 of the Schedule provides as follows [his Lordship quoted the entry in col. (2) and continued:]

The appellant's home consists of a livingroom, two bedrooms, a kitchen and bathroom and is considered by the landlord, Glasgow District Council, to be a three apartment flat. In this flat there is also what the appellant described as 'a boxroom', measuring approximately 8 ft by 6 ft 4 in. In one corner there is a boxed-in hot water tank measuring 38 in by 25 in. The boxroom is contained entirely within the flat and does not adjoin any outside wall. It has electric light, but no power points, windows or form of ventilation.

This seems to be a test case, as the adjudication officer has noted in para. 4 of his submission as follows: 'In connection with an earlier similar claim the adjudication officer had contacted the local office of the housing management department. He was advised that the "room" in question was considered as a 'storage space' only. These "rooms" were originally designed as drying cupboards and also contained water tanks. Many of the "rooms" still had pulleys but these were no longer fitted because of an asbestos problem.'

The tribunal found in fact that 'the room has been used for drying or storage' and rejected the appellant's claim on the ground that, having no provisions for ventilation or heating, this room 'was not habitable. The size alone would restrict furniture and make it unlikely that anyone could live in it over a period of time. The tribunal agreed that the appellant's accommodation consisted of four rooms.' Against this decision the appellant appealed to the social security commissioner, who adhered to the tribunal's findings. He considered 'habitable' to be a relevant test for the purpose of this regulation, having regard to the ordinary usage of the word 'room' and found that the tribunal's conclusion was 'unassailable in an appeal on a point of law'.

Counsel for the appellant submitted to us that 'room' must be given its ordinary meaning and that the dictionary definition of 'room' must be applied. She maintained that any space enclosed by walls, a floor and ceiling was a room within the meaning of these regulations. One of a number of definitions of 'room' given in the *Oxford English Dictionary* is: 'An interior portion of a building divided off by walls or partitions; esp. a chamber or apartment in a dwellinghouse'. Counsel submitted that 'room' could only have one meaning and referred us to a number of authorities which, she maintained, supported her proposition that the word must be construed literally and that the tribunal and the commissioner had erred in qualifying 'room' by the addition of 'habitable'.

She referred to *Magor and St Mellons R.D.C. v. Newport Corporation*, for the observations of Lord Simonds at p. 191 that, in construing a statute, the court was not entitled to fill in what appeared to it to be a gap in the legislation. That case and *I.R.C. v. Collco Dealings Ltd* per Vaisey J. at p. 1002, and *Felix v. Thomas* at p. 306, are just examples of the elementary rule of statutory construction that the words used must be construed literally provided that they can only have one meaning. In *R. v. London Borough of Hillingdon, ex p. Puhlhofer*, Lord Brightman at pp. 516–517 stressed that the word 'accommodation' in the Housing (Homeless Persons) Act 1977 must be read without the qualification of 'appropriate' or 'reasonable', but he added: 'What is properly to be regarded as accommodation is a question of fact to be decided by the local authority.'

We consider that in this case the question of whether this space was a room within the meaning of the regulations was also a question of fact to be decided by the social security appeal tribunal. However, counsel for the appellant submitted that, if it was not permissible to qualify 'accommodation', it was not permissible to qualify 'room' by adding 'habitable'. She also emphasised that para. 6 of the regulations specifically excluded a 'bathroom, lavatory or hall' but did not exclude a boxroom, which is the appellant's own description of this space. However, counsel for the appellant felt compelled to concede that her literal construction of 'room' would include all walk-in cupboards and even coal cellars. It therefore appears to us that the word 'room' in these regulations is open to construction and that it was necessary for the tribunal, when construing the word, to bear in mind that the purview of the regulations was to assist householders to meet the costs of heating their homes, if the costs were disproportionately high, and to double the allowance for four rooms if the home had five or more rooms.

The literal construction only applies where the word to be construed has only one meaning. Another canon of construction requires the court to avoid a construction which would have an absurd result. It would, in our opinion, be an absurd result to make the test of whether a home had only four rooms or more, in relation to heating costs, depend upon the existence of one walk-in cupboard, which would not require to be heated even if it affected heat loss.

In our opinion the appellant's description of this space as a 'boxroom' is accurate. Since the word 'room' is open to construction, it was for the tribunal to decide how it should be construed in the context of these regulations. As Lord Reid said in *Cozens v. Brutus* at p. 861: 'The question would normally be whether their decision was unreasonable in the sense that no tribunal acquainted with the ordinary use of language could reasonably reach that decision.' In our opinion this tribunal's decision that this boxroom was not a room within the meaning of these regulations cannot possibly be said to be a decision which no reasonable tribunal, properly applying themselves to the question raised, could have reached. That leads us to the inevitable conclusion that their decision and the decision of the social security commissioner must be affirmed and this appeal refused. The tribunal was entitled to reach that decision upon a construction of the regulations and the fact that they applied the test of 'habitable' does not vitiate their decision."

Notes

(1) Where jurisdictional facts are broadly defined the court may be less likely to intervene.   **4–6** The leading example of this is the House of Lords decision in *Puhlhofer v Hillingdon London Borough Council* [1986] A.C. 484 at 517–518, referred to in *Ferguson*, where the issue of what constituted "accommodation" required to be determined. In the context of the duty of the local authority to secure accommodation for homeless persons, the court noted that "accommodation was set on a broad spectrum varying from the obvious to the debatable and just conceivable". The House went on to say (at 518) that in such cases:

> "it is the duty of the court to leave the decision of that fact to the public body to whom Parliament has entrusted the decision-making power save in a case where it is obvious that the public body, consciously or unconsciously, are acting perversely".

So long as an authority does not make a determination which demonstrates a misunderstanding of the law applicable, as based on an improper purpose or irrelevant considerations or there is some procedural flaw, then the court will not intervene with the authority's assessment of the facts even if it would have come to a different conclusion itself.

(2) Other examples of the approach in *Ferguson* and *Puhlhofer* include *Stagecoach Holdings plc v. Secretary of State for Trade and Industry*, 1997 S.L.T. 940, whether in terms of section 64 of the Fair Trading Act 1973, Dumfries and Galloway in the then Strathclyde Region amounted to a "substantial part" of the United Kingdom; *Commission for Local Authority Accounts in Scotland v. Grampian Regional Council*, 1994 S.L.T. 1120 and see para. 4–6, whether expenditure in terms of section 83(1) of the Local Government (Scotland) Act 1973 "was in the interests of the area or of its habitants"; *R. v. South Hams District Council, ex parte Gibb* [1995] 5 Q.B. 158, status as "gypsies" a question for the local authority; *Strathclyde Regional Council v. Secretary of State for Scotland*, 1991 S.L.T. 796, whether a decision as to whether or not a planning application could be held to "conform" to the structure plan in the context of an appeal to the Secretary of State under section 179(4) of the Local Government (Scotland) Act 1973 was a matter for the Secretary of State; and *Dowty Boulton Paul Ltd v. Wolverhampton Corporation (No. 2)* [1973] 2 All E.R. 491, whether or not land, the recovery of which was sought by the landlord corporation, was still being used as an "airfield" under a lease to the tenant, was a matter for the landlord.

Cases such as *Stagecoach* and *Grampian Regional Council* involved the court in considering the meaning to be given to elastic concepts. Where no statutory guidelines exist, then the role of the court in reviewing assessment of facts is even more limited. In *Bugdaycay v. Secretary of State for the Home Department* [1986] 1 All E.R. 458 at 465–466 the Court of Appeal *per* Neill L.J. noted in relation to a decision not to grant asylum to a refugee:

> "It seems to me to be clear... that Parliament has decided that all questions of leave to enter should be determined by an immigration officer or by the Secretary of State as the case might be. The court has no role to play and there is no precedent fact for the court to determine. Investigation of refugee status and the question whether an individual should be afforded asylum might involve the considerations of foreign policy and the assessment of regimes in foreign countries and other similar matters with which a court of law would be ill-equipped to deal."

A determination of the facts in this case necessarily included consideration of whether the state to which the refugee would be returned would be a country where he would reasonably fear persecution: see also *R. v. Secretary of State for the Home Department, ex parte Onibiyo* [1996] 2 All E.R. 901.

(3) Sometimes the conferral of power is couched in terms where jurisdiction is based on the existence of a belief or reasonable belief that the facts or circumstances of which jurisdiction must be exercised exist. On this see *Secretary of State for Education and Science v. Tameside Metropolitan Borough Council* [1977] A.C. 1014, at para. 6–40. How does *Tameside* compare with the statements of Lord Esher M.R. in *Income Tax Commissioners* below and the scope of control reflected in *Ferguson*?

(4) The courts, however, still find themselves in difficulty from time to time in interpreting even relatively straightforward terms. Contrast the approach of Lord Cullen in the Outer House with their Lordships in the Inner House in *Gordon v. Kirkcaldy District Council*, 1989 S.L.T. 507 and 1990 S.L.T. 644 respectively. In terms of section 124 of the Civic Government (Scotland) Act 1982 local authorities are permitted to collect "household waste" and to collect and charge for "trade waste". Section 124(5) provided that "household waste" means waste from a "dwelling house". A local authority initially collected waste free of charge from caravans in a caravan park. It changed its policy and decided to collect only from the site as a whole and to treat this as trade waste, thus being able to charge the owner of the park for this collection. The owner of the park sought to recover the sums from caravan site owners, two of whom sought judicial review of the local authority's decision seeking declarator that given that they occupied caravans which were their permanent homes their waste should be treated as "household waste". Lord Cullen stated (at 512):

> "In my view the initial argument presented by counsel for the petitioners was misconceived. It treated the question of whether the relevant waste was 'household waste' or 'trade waste' as a matter of law which it was at large for me to decide. This is most strikingly illustrated in the submission that I should grant decree of declarator that the waste arising from the petitioners' occupation of their caravans was 'household waste' within the meaning of s. 124 to be ultra vires if it proceeded upon the basis of an erroneous interpretation of law. But, if the local authority has not misdirected itself as to the law, it appears to me that the application of that law to the petitioners' case involves the assessment of matters of fact and degree from which a categorisation of the waste results. Provided that the conclusion is not one which no reasonable authority could have drawn from the facts of the case it is not open to judicial review. In my view it is of no moment that s. 124 does not in terms confer any discretion upon the local authority. It is implicit that the local authority is to reach a view as to whether the waste which it is considering falls within a particular expression or not. Otherwise this section would be unworkable. Thus within limits which I have indicated above the local authority has power to 'decide'. In these circumstances I do not consider that the cases cited by counsel from the fields of valuation and rating, taxation and rent regulation assist the petitioners in their initial argument.
>
> Accordingly, the success of the petitioners' case depends upon the later arguments which were developed by counsel. I am not satisfied that no reasonable authority could have come to any conclusion other than that the petitioners' caravans were 'dwelling-houses'....
>
> I do not require for present purposes to attempt to give an exhaustive definition of the word 'house' nor to set out what may be all the relevant considerations by means of which it may be determined whether a particular structure is a 'house'. However, it seems to me that the writer fell into error in requiring that before a structure can be a 'house' it must have 'foundations'. I do not see any reason in principle why, for example, a structure which rested by its own weight upon a hard base could not be regarded as a 'house'. A structure which was capable under certain conditions of being transported to another base might be a 'house' provided that it had in its existing location a sufficient degree of permanence and immobility. However, this is not contemplated by the writer who concentrates exclusively on the conventional elements of a 'house'.

The local authority reclaimed and the Inner House observed (at 646–649) that:

> "In my opinion, the Lord Ordinary was in error in concluding that the question of whether the relevant waste was 'household waste' or 'trade waste' was not a matter of law. In the Act of 1982 Parliament has defined what 'household waste' means and what 'trade waste' means. That being so, I am of opinion that whether waste is 'household waste' or 'trade waste' is a matter of law to be determined in the light of the established facts. I do not comsider that Parliament has conferred on

local authorities a discretion to determine whether waste falls within one or other of the definitions. If the matter were left to the discretion of local authorities, the result might be that different local authorities would arrive at different conclusions as to whether waste was 'household waste' although the waste in question came from premises which were identical in every way with one another except that one of the premises was in the jurisdiction of one local authority whereas the other premises were in the jurisdiction of a different local authority. There is nothing in the act of 1982 to suggest that Parliament intended any such result" (*per* the Lord Justice-Clerk (Ross) at 646).

LORD DUNPARK: "I agree, for the reasons given by your Lordship in the chair, that we should pronounce an interlocutor in the terms proposed by your Lordship.

The question of whether particular waste is 'household waste' or 'trade waste' is a question of mixed fact and law. In my opinion one has to know the facts which relate to the nature of the structure before one can decide whether or not the structure is a 'dwelling-house'. However, in this case senior counsel conceded that we had all the agreed facts before us to enable us to determine whether or not these caravans were 'dwelling-houses' within the meaning of s. 124(5) of the Civic Government (Scotland) Act 1982 and that the waste therefrom arose from their normal occupation as dwelling-houses. That enables us to decide, as a matter of law, that these caravans were 'dwelling-houses' within the meaning of that Act and that the waste therefrom is 'household waste' within the meaning of that section" (*per* Lord Dunpark at 648).

LORD MCLUSKEY: "The second legal issue is the main one. In the course of the debate senior counsel for the district council accepted that no fact required to be ascertained or added to enable a sound decision to be taken on the question as to whether or not these caravans fell within the description 'dwelling-house' as used in s. 124. That is to say that it was accepted on both sides that the caravans were large 'static' holiday caravans which, although mobile in the sense of having wheels, could not be towed on public roads, that they were occupied for residential purposes during the summer, that no trade or business was carried on from them, that they had remained for several years on their respective pitches, that the petitioners had no intention of removing them and that they all rested on a hard standing and were stabilised by the use of jacks at each end. It was not suggested that any additional relevant fact needed to be known or investigated. It follows that, there being no dispute on the material facts, the only question which has to be resolved is a legal question. That legal question can be put this way: 'Knowing all the relevant factual characteristics of these caravans, do they fall within the meaning of the word 'dwelling-house' contained in subs. (5)?' Putting it another way: 'Are the words "dwelling-house" apt to include these caravans?' For my part I cannot see how this can be other than a question of law. The meaning and scope of the words 'dwelling-house' in this statute is a question of law. Once all the facts are known in relation to the premises which are said to fall within the meaning of the term 'dwelling-house', the question as to whether or not they do fall within that meaning is itself a question of law. In the circumstances now before us, I do not see how the court can avoid determining whether or not these caravans fall within the meaning of the term 'dwelling-house'" (*per* Lord McCluskey at 649).

Notes

Which approach is preferable? Do you agree with the Inner House characterising the issue as one of law? Does there exist any principled distinction between the kind of issues the court had to consider in *Ferguson* and here? The distinction between issues of law and fact is examined further in Chapter 12.

4–7

JURISDICTION, FACTS AND THE ADEQUACY OF EVIDENCE

Rae v. Criminal Injuries Compensation Board

1997 S.L.T. 291

"After an oral hearing before two members of the Criminal Injuries Compensation Board a previous decision of a single member of the board, granting an inclusive award for compensation, was upheld. The applicant challenged the later decision on the grounds that the two members' assessment of the evidence was tainted by error of law, that it was vitiated by *Wednesbury* unreasonableness and that it lacked a proper basis in fact."

4–8

LORD MACFADYEN: "On 14 July 1990 the petitioner was stabbed in the chest. On 31 July 1990 he submitted an application to the Criminal Injuries Compensation Board ('the board') in respect of that incident. After sundry procedure, an award of £4,250 was confirmed by the board on 14 April 1993. The petitioner now seeks to subject the board's decision of 14 April 1993 to judicial review. He seeks reduction of the decision and an order upon the board to reconsider his application....

Before me counsel for the petitioner initially argued for reduction of the board's decision of 14 April 1993 on the two bases foreshadowed in the petition, namely (1) that it was vitiated by error in law and (2) that it was vitiated by *Wednesbury* unreasonableness. In the third speech in the debate, he also advanced an argument under reference to *Wordie Property Co Ltd v Secretary of State for Scotland*, per Lord President Emslie at 1984 SLT, p 348, that the decision should be reduced on the ground that it lacked the necessary factual basis. Counsel emphasised that the decision which he sought to bring under review was the decision of the board following the oral hearing on 14 April 1993 and expressly conceded that the decisions of the single member were not susceptible to challenge on the grounds on which he sought to challenge the ultimate decision of the board....

[C]ounsel then turned to his submission that such errors of law afforded ground for judicial review. He began this chapter of his submissions by referring to two Scottish cases in which decisions of the board were subjected to judicial review, namely *Gray v. Criminal Injuries Compensation Board* and *Craig v. Criminal Injuries Compensation Board*. In each of these cases the issue was whether the board had erred in law in holding that a particular activity did not constitute a crime of violence. Although in each case the decision was that the board had not erred in law, no doubt ws raised as to the court's entitlement to review the board's decision on the ground of the alleged error. Counsel then turned to a series of English cases in which decisions of the board were subjected to judicial review. In *R v. Criminal Injuries Compensation Board, ex p Lain* and *R v Criminal Injuries Board, ex p Tong*, the court entertained applications for certiorari to quash the board's decisions on the ground of error in law on the face of the record. In the latter case Lord Denning MR at [1976] 1 WLR, p 1242F said: 'The High Court can interfere if the board makes an error of law'. On the other hand, in *R v Criminal Injuries Compensation Board, ex p Thomstone and Crowe*, the scope for judicial review of the board's decisions in England was formulated more narrowly by Sir John Donaldson MR as follows: 'The scheme is discretionary and the discretion is that of the board. It follows that the board's decision can be reviewed if it misconstrues its mandate or, in *Wednesbury* principles, must be deemed to have done so since its decision is one which no reasonable body could have reached on the facts if it had correctly construed its mandate.'

Counsel turned from these cases which dealt specifically with review of decisions of the board to other Scottish cases on review for error of law. He referred first to *Watt v Lord Advocate*. There, in upholding a submission that the National Insurance Commissioner had made an error in law which resulted in his decision being ultra vires and therefore reducible, Lord President Emslie said (at 1979 SC, p 129; 1979 SLT, p 141): 'not every misconstruction of a statutory provision by a statutory tribunal in the course of reaching its decision will render that decision a nullity', but (at p 130 (p 142)): 'There can be no doubt that when a statutory tribunal, which quite properly enters upon an inquiry which it has jurisdiction to carry out, misconstrues the question which it is required to answer and decides some other question which was not remitted to it, its decision will be a nullity.'

At p 131 (p 143) his Lordship added, obiter: 'it seems clear that, however much this is to be regretted, the Court of Session has never had power to correct an *intra vires* error of law made by a statutory tribunal or authority exercising statutory jurisdiction'.

Counsel sought to rely also on the passage from the speech of Lord Reid in *Anisminic v Foreign Compensation Committee* at [1969] 2 AC, p 171 which is quoted by Lord President Emslie in *Watt* at p 130 (p 142), and drew attention to the fact that Lord Reid stated that he did not intend the list which he set out of circumstances which might nullify the decision of a tribunal to be exhaustive. He submitted that the board's judicial function in terms of the scheme (particularly paras 12, 25 and 26) placed it in a materially different position from a statutory tribunal. He submitted that an error which, as he contended in the present case, involved an illegitimate approach in the assessment of evidence, was sufficiently close to the type of error identified by Lord Reid in *Anisminic* to be reviewable. He argued that for the board to 'challenge' F2 in the absence of competing material was for it to 'fail to perform the duty which as been delegated or entrusted' to it (*West v Secretary State for Scotland*, per Lord President Hope at 1992 SC, p 413; 1992 SLT, p 650L), that duty being to reach its decision solely in light of the evidence brought out at the hearing (scheme, para 25). Counsel drew attention to the passage in the opinion of the court in *West* (para (c) at p 413 (p 651B)) in which it is indicated that there is no substantial difference between English law and Scots law as to the ground on which the process of decision making may be open to review, but accepted that that observation did not abrogate the distinction made in *Watt* between intra vires and ultra vires in law. Rather, counsel's submission was that the alleged error in law on which he founded came within the category of reviewable error in respect that the board had no jurisdiction to decide a case otherwise than on the evidence before it.

Counsel for the board's response to these submissions fell into two parts. In the first place, he argued that the board had not been shown to have committed an error in law. In the second place, he argued that if it had, it was an error of the non-reviewable type.

Counsel for the board formulated rather differently from counsel for the petitioner the question which was before the board. He maintained that the question was whether on the basis of the whole evidence before it, it should alter the single member's assessment of compensation. He took issue with the contention that the board was not entitled, in the absence of competing evidence, to 'challenge' the conclusions of F2, maintaining that since in terms of para 25 of the scheme the onus of making out his case at the hearing was on the applicant, the board was not obliged to accept F2 at face value but could properly subject it to critical examination. He submitted that there were grounds upon which the board was entitled to entertain doubt as to whether the wage loss claimed was attributable to the stabbing incident. Counsel for the board pointed first to what he described as the tentative language of F2. He drew attention particularly to the documents in no 14/12 of process. Accepting the first claimed period of loss of earnings, he drew attention in respect of the second period to the fact that no 14/12 of process attributed the petitioner's absence from work from 14 January to 14 February 1991 to acute asthma, and to the fact that in no 14/10 of process the petitioner himself asserted inter alia that his asthma was worse. In respect of the third period counsel referred to Dr Fennerty's expressed reservation as to why the chest pain should last so long, to the part played in that period by the further eczema attack, and, for what it was worth (albeit it was probably a mistake), to the reference in no 14/5 of process to a hand injury in June 1991. Counsel's contention was that, whatever its strength, there was some material on the basis of which the board could have taken the view that the second and third absences from work were not proved to have been caused by the stabbing incident. It was therefore not an error of law for the board to take the view it did.

In response to the argument that the board's reference to the road accident amounted to an error in law, counsel submitted that it was not clear that the board had in fact attached any weight to that factor, and pointed out that no contention in relation to the road accident was put forward in the petition.

Counsel began his submissions on the law by observing that the Inner House has warned of the need to be watchful to avoid permitting an attempt to review the merits of a decision to be 'dressed up in *Wordie* clothing'. In that connection he referred to *City of Glasgow District Council v Secretary of State for Scotland* at 1993 SLT, p 1334B. He submitted that not all errors of law opened a decision up to judicial review. He founded on the distinction made in *Watt*, and submitted that *West* did nothing to alter the rule. So far as concerned the statement in *West* (at p 413 (p 651A)) to the effect that 'failure to understand the law' would open up a decision to review, he pointed to the explanation of that passage given by Lord Cullen in *Shanks & McEwan (Contractors) Ltd v Mifflin Construction Ltd*, 1993 SLT at p 1130D, where his Lordship emphasised that the Lord President there meant a failure which was of such a character as to entail an excess or abuse of jurisdiction. Moreover, he submitted, the reference in *West* (at p 413 (0 651B)) to there being no substantial difference between English and Scots law as to the grounds on which the process of decision making may be open to review, did not involve an abrogation of the distinction discussed in *Watt*. For an alternative formulation of the type of error which would be ground for judicial review, counsel referred to *Wordie Property Co Ltd v Secretary of State for Scotland* per Lord President Emslie at 1984 SLT, p 346: 'a material error of law going to the root of the question for determination'. He accepted the formulation in *Thomstone* — 'if it misconstrues its mandate'. He identified *Gray* and *Craig* as both being cases in which the alleged error was as to the scope of the board's jurisdiction, and was therefore reviewable. With a view to explaining the apparent divergence between *Thompstone* on the one hand and *Lain* and *Tong* on the other, he cited *South East Asia Fire Bricks v Non-Metallic Mineral Products*, per Lord Fraser of Tullybelton at [1981] AC, p 370B–C. As an early example of the distinction in Scots law between reviewable and non-reviewable error of law, he cited *Leith Police Commissioners v Campbell* and, as a more recent example, *O'Neill v Scottish Joint Negotiating Committee for Teaching Staff*. He submitted that the real issue in the present case related to the soundness of the board's jurisdiction on which the board was entitled to err without subjecting itself to review.

In my opinion the board is subject to judicial review on the ground of error of law if, but only if, the error is one which involves the board in acting in a way in which it has no power to act, or in refusing to act on the ground that it has no power to do so in circumstances in which on a sound view of its powers it is entitled to act. To put the matter more briefly, ultra vires error of law is ground for review, namely *Gray* and *Craig*, are examples of the application of that rule. In each of these cases, the decision under challenge involved determination of a matter relating to the extent of the board's jurisdiction. If the board had been wrong, in these cases, in holding that the events before it did not constitute crimes of violence, it would have been wrongly refusing to exercise its jurisdiction. The same rule appears to be reflected in *Thompstone*. Insofar as *Lain* and *Tong* appear to support the proposition that in England a decision of the board may be quashed by an order of certiorari on the ground of error in law on the face of the record, without distinction between intra vires error and ultra vires error (and despite the reference in argument to *South East Asia Fire Bricks* I am not confident that I properly understand the scope of certiorari), the proposition is not in my view sound in Scots law. The references in *West* (at p 413 (p 651A–B)) to 'failure to understand the law' and to there being no substantial difference between English law and Scots law as to the grounds of review, are not in my view to be construed as a departure from the rule that review for error of law is available in Scotland only if the error involves excess or abuse of jurisdiction or erroneous refusal to exercise a jurisdiction.

The question therefore in my opinion comes to be whether the petitioner has identified an error committed by the board which had the effect that the board acted ultra vires. I accept that in terms of the scheme, and in particular paras 12, 25 and 26, the task delegated to the board is a judicial one. I do not regard as sound counsel for the petitioner's submission that that consideration has the result that in relation to decisions of the board a different approach to error of law as a ground for review is appropriate from that which would be appropriate in the case of a statutory tribunal exercising a statutory jurisdiction. Many such tribunals exercise a function which is judicial in the same sense as is that of the board. I do accept, however, that the board's jurisdiction was to assess compensation on the basis of common law damages (para 12) and to reach its decision solely in the light of evidence brought out at the hearing (para 25). (The restraint imposed on the board by para 26, not to alter the assessment made by the single member except on the same principles as the Court of Session would alter an assessment of damages made by a trial judge, has little practical effect in a case such as the present where new material is admitted at the hearing before the board, and it is therefore inevitably, as both parties accepted in argument, approaching the assessment de novo.) If the petitioner were in a position to say that the board had exceeded its jurisdiction by, for example, in contravention of para 12 making its award on a penal rather than a compensatory basis, or, in contravention of para 25 taking into account a medical report which was not put in evidence at the hearing or disclosed to the applicant, then in my view it might be said that there was an error of law which opened up its decision to review. I do not consider, however, that the circumstances relied on by the petitioner disclosed a reviewable error of law. It is said that the board misunderstood the import of F2, or 'turned it on its head'. In my view if it did so it committed an intra vires error. It was for the board, as a tribunal of fact, to consider the evidence before it, including F2, to form its own understanding of the evidence, and to reach its conclusions on the basis of its understanding of the evidence. An erroneous evaluation of the evidence by a tribunal of fact, however gross, is not in my view an error of law, still less one which involves an excess or abuse of jurisdiction. It was said that the board was not, in the absence of cross examination or conflicting medical evidence, entitled (as the board's answers put it) to 'challenge' F2 as being inconsistent with the previous medical evidence. I hesitate to place much weight on the way in which the point is expressed in the answers. In substance, I am of opinion that the board was under no obligation to accept F2 at face value and was free to examine it critically, and to compare its contents with all the other material before it, including not only the earlier medical evidence (in the narrower sense of evidence from medical practitioners) but also other evidence about the petitioner's medical condition, such as the information from the employers in no 14/12 of process and the information from the petitioner himself in no 14/10 of process. I am therefore not satisfied that it can be said that in not accepting everything that was said in the petitioner's favour in F2 the board erred in law in a way which took it out of the proper scope of its jurisdiction... .

I turn finally to the argument advanced by counsel for the petitioner in his second speech, namely that, the board's decision being one for which a factual basis was required, no proper basis in fact to support it existed (*Wordie Property Co Ltd v Secretary of State for Scotland* at p 348). I have some doubt as to whether the present case falls within the category contemplated by Lord President Emslie in that part of his opinion in *Wordie*. It seems to me that what his Lordship had in mind was a situation where a particular decision could only be validly made if a certain state of facts was held to exist, but where the tribunal purported to make the decision without first holding that that necessary state of facts existed. It is, in my view, clear that Lord Emslie was not, by his use of the phrase 'proper basis in fact', sanctioning review of the merits of a decision on a matter of fact. I therefore reject the submission that the board's decision is invalid for want of a proper basis in fact."

Notes

4–9   (1) *Rae* suggests that review on the basis of inadequate evidence appears to have restricted scope in Scots law. The only means of judicial control of the CICB is by way of judicial review. On the functional approach in *Watt v. Lord Advocate*, at para. 4–12, there was no other way by which the board's assessment of the facts could be challenged. Do you think that the court in *Rae* was in fact seeking to lay down a general proposition in relation to tribunals or fact or was it motivated more by the concerns in relation to the particular authority in question? If the latter, in what circumstances do you think it would be appropriate for the court to intervene if inadequate facts exist? Contrast *Khawaja* and *Malhi*. What difference, if any, exists between the facts in issue in those cases and those in *Rae*? Note also the recent decision of the House of Lords in *R. v. Secretary of State for Scotland*, 1999 S.L.T. 279. Here it was held by the House of Lords that a sheriff was entitled to hold on conflicting medical evidence that there existed sufficient evidence to conclude that continued treatment of a patient detained at the State Hospital was preferable to the release of the patient. They overturned the decision of the Second Division in reviewing of the sheriff's decision as having gone further than was appropriate in judicial review in disturbing the sheriff's conclusions on evidence. Lord Clyde observed (at 295):

"The statutory appeal which the respondent made to the sheriff was a summary process which is not open to the ordinary means of statutory appeal. This has been described in terms of a distinction that the sheriff in such an appeal is acting in an administrative rather than a judicial capacity ... Challenge to such a decision accordingly requires to be taken by way of judicial review....

Judicial review involves a challenge to the legal validity of the decision. It does not allow the court of review to examine the evidence with a view to forming its own view about the substantial merits of the case. It may be that the tribunal whose decision is being challenged has done something which it had no lawful authority to do. It may have abused or misused the authority which it had. It may have departed from the procedures which either by statute or at common law as matter of fairness it ought to have observed. As regards the decision itself it may be found to be perverse, or irrational, or grossly disproportionate to what was required. Or the decision may be found to be erroneous in respect of a legal deficiency, as for example, through the absence of evidence, or of sufficient evidence, to support it, or through account of being taken as an irrelevant matter, or through a failure for any reason to take account of a relevant matter, or through some misconstruction of the terms of the statutory provision which the decision maker is required to apply. But while the evidence may have to be explored in order to see if the decision is vitiated by such legal deficiencies it is perfectly clear that in a case of review, as distinct from an ordinary appeal, the court may not set about forming its own preferred view of the evidence.

[T]he judges in the Second Division went further than was appropriate in the analysis and assessment of it [the evidence]. The sheriff heard the oral evidence of seven psychiatrists as well as the respondent. He also had written reports from the psychiatrists and these were put before the Second Division. But in the summary procedure which was used there was no record made of the oral evidence beyond a brief account which the sheriff gives of the material before him. Where one only has an incomplete record of the evidence and the evidence is that of highly qualified experts dealing with the delicate matter of mental disorder, great caution ought to be taken in revisiting the substance of the decision which the sheriff reached. In the circumstances of the present case it seems to me to be particularly difficult to conclude that there was truly no evidence to support the conclusion which was reached or that the conclusion was perverse."

See too Lord Hutton at 299K–300C.

The link between the general grounds of judicial review and the attack on the adequacy of evidence is here made clear. Unless there is no evidence at all to support a decision which is of course an error of law, allegations of insufficient evidence required to be linked to these grounds of control for challenge to be competent. For a further recent example see *Campbell v. City of Edinburgh District Council*, 1989 GWD 17-877 (error of fact an irrelevant consideration). See also the discussion at note 3 below.

Compare also *Singh v. City of Glasgow Licensing Board*, 1998 G.W.D. 24-1229 where the Second Division considered an appeal by an applicant for a provisional off-sales licence. The only objector was the occupier of premises adjoining the subjects of the application. The objector alleged that the police were already called in to remove drunks from the area who were causing a nuisance. The board refused the application on the basis of section 17(1)(*b*) of the Licensing (Scotland) Act 1976 in that the premises were not suitable in view of their location within a residential area and in view of existing problems caused by drinkers and, secondly, that in terms of subsection (1)(*c*) that if the application was granted, it would be likely to cause undue public nuisance by increasing existing problems. The applicant appealed to the sheriff who found that the board had erred in relying on subsection (1)(*b*) as there was no evidence that the location of the premises was unsuitable but that subsection (1)(*c*) was sufficient to defeat the appeal as the board was entitled to take into account its local knowledge and experience and to accept the objector's view that the granting of the application would lead to an increase in problems. The applicant appealed to the Court of Session and the Second Division held that although the board was entitled to rely on and draw inferences from factual material before it, the objector's letter was insufficient in its terms to enable the board to infer that the use of the premises would materially contribute to the causing of undue public nuisance. It had erred on law. There was insufficient evidence to indicate the extent in weight of any existing problem and the possible relationship if any between that problem and the proposed use of the premises.

Singh was a statutory appeal, but a similar approach as to sufficiency of evidence as amounting to an error of law in licensing matters has also been applied in judicial review proceedings, on which see *Clark v. North Ayrshire Licensing Board*, 1998 GWD 8-397 (positive link between the existence of premises operating on an extended hours' basis and any trouble or disturbance had to be established on more than a "but for" basis).

(2) Note the dicta of Lord Reid in *R. v. Brixton Prison Governor, ex parte Armah* [1968] A.C. 192 at 234 that "Whether or not there is evidence to support a particular decision is always a question of law but it is not a question of jurisdiction." This means that although the misapplication of the technical rules of evidence might amount to an error of law, assessment of the value to be placed on evidence is essentially a question of judgment and in principle is not open to review. Typically an error in relation to the admissibility or existence of a piece of evidence might amount to such an error of law. In *Rae* it could not be said that there was a breach of this "no evidence" rule. There is a body of authority to support the view that such an error might amount to an excess of jurisdiction: *Davidson v. McLeod* (1887) 5 R. (J.) 1; *Inland Revenue Commissioners v. Fraser*, 1942 S.L.T. 280; *Mitchell v. Minister of Pensions*, 1946 S.L.T. 38; and *Edwards v. Bairstow* [1956] A.C. 14, on which see para. 12–28. Perhaps the clearest expression of the no evidence rule is found in the dissenting judgment of Lord Johnston in *McDougall v. Malcolm*, 1916 S.L.T. 33 at 37 in the context of an appeal from the then Land Court:

> "a question of law arising on ascertained facts, as, for instance, what is the sense or meaning of the statute when applied to a specific set of circumstances, that is to say, a mixed question of fact and law, is open to review. It is for the Land Court to ascertain the facts, but their legal deduction from these is not final, and may be reviewed. Such a one is the present case. But here I would add two things — (1st) that by no conceivable stretch of their functions can the Land Court make that a question of fact, by calling it a fact, which is not a question of fact but of law or of mixed fact and law; and (2nd) that neither can they make that a fact, by calling it a fact, which is not a reasonable conclusion in fact from the facts which they say have been established before them... .
>
> But the Court has also recognised that they have before them in effect a question of law where they are presented with facts and asked to determine whether on these facts [the decision-maker] was entitled to draw a conclusion in law. For this it is enough if I refer to the two cases of *Walker* (1911 S.C. 825) and *Euman* (1912 S.C. 966), in the former of which the Lord President (Dunedin) says in a considered judgment of the Court on the point: 'There is no doubt that the course of decisions, sanctioned, and indeed I may say encouraged, by the Supreme Court and the House of Lords, has quite finally fixed that, although an appeal on a case stated is only competent on a matter of law, yet it will be considered a matter of law whether a finding in fact can be reasonably supported upon the evidence adduced."

(3) What amounts to evidence for the purpose of this rule has not been given much judicial scrutiny. In *Mahon v. Air New Zealand* [1984] A.C. 808 at 821 the Privy Council noted that:

> "The technical rules of evidence applicable to civil or criminal litigation form no part of the rules of natural justice. What is required ... is that the decision to make a finding must be based upon *some* material that tends logically to show the existence of facts consistent with the finding and that the reasoning supportive of the finding, if it be disclosed, is not logically self-contradictory."

Administrative bodies are rather more free than the courts in their ability to base decisions upon information which is within their knowledge. J. A. Smillie, "The Problem of 'Official Notice': Reliance by Administrative Tribunals on the Personal Knowledge of their Members" [1975] P.L. 64 at 69 notes that such information can "*supplement* or [act as] as a *substitute for*, evidence properly and openly presented" to *evaluate and assess* the evidence properly presented."

As noted in Chapter 1 a loosening of the rules of evidence and procedure has often occurred in the creation of non-judicial administrative decision makers, especially tribunals. The approach in *Mahon* carries with it the consequence that it is only in exceptional cases that there will be a finding of no evidence and therefore error of law, but such circumstances do exist. Thus in *Mitchell v. Minister of Pensions* above, where a widow sought payment of pension based on her husband's death during wartime service under the statutory scheme involved, the onus was on the Minister to show that death was not due to such service. It was held that evidence that the cause of death was heart failure was not evidence to show that death was not due to war service.

In *Coleen Properties Ltd v. Minister of Housing and Local Government* [1971] 1 W.L.R. 433, C.A. a company which owned a building which a local authority wished to acquire compulsorily contended that the building was not "reasonably necessary for the satisfactory redevelopment of the area", which was the statutory test relied on by the council. At a local public inquiry, the objections made by the company were accepted and the inspector reported to the Minister accordingly. However, the Minister, without taking any fresh evidence, disagreed with the inspector's view and confirmed the decision. On appeal to the Court of Appeal, Lord Denning M.R. stated (at 1053):

> "Then there is the report of the inspector. He was clearly of opinion that the acquisition of Clark House was not reasonably necessary. I can see no possible justification for the Minister in overruling the inspector. There was no material whatever on which he could do so. I know that on matters of planning policy the Minister can overrule the inspector, and need not send it back to him, as happened in *Lord Luke of Pavenham v. Minister of Housing and Local Government* [[1968] 1 Q.B. 172]. But the question of what is 'reasonably necessary' is not planning policy. It is an inference of fact on which the Minister should not overrule the inspector's recommendation unless there is material sufficient for the purpose. There was none here. In my judgment the Minister was wrong and this court should intervene and overrule him."

Note the reference to planning policy in this passage. If the Minister had relied on this, then the outcome could have been different. This would seem to suggest that matters of policy are not matters of fact for the purpose of the rule. The policy in *Bushell v. Secretary of State for the Environment* above was said to be a non-factual issue. Consider also the policies in *Cinderella's Rockafella's v. Glasgow District Licensing Board* and *Sagnata Investments Ltd v. Norwich Corporation*, at paras 7–6 and 7–12. Davis has termed such policies as "legislative facts" which are normally general in effect and which do not concern the immediate parties. These are to be contrasted with "adjudicative facts" which relate to the parties. Legislative facts need not be and sometimes cannot be supported by evidence, whereas adjudicative facts must be: *Administrative Law Text* (3rd ed.), para. 15.03.

(4) Does the no evidence rule apply in the same way to (1) primary findings of fact, (2) the application of a statutory description to facts when this is regarded as a question of fact, and (3) the final decision in a case of all the relevant questions of law and fact? If a body acts on no evidence has it failed to take account of a relevant consideration or has it acted irrationally? *R. v. Secretary of State for Scotland* below, would suggest so and in *Wordie Property Co. v. Secretary of State for Scotland*, 1984 S.L.T. 345 the Lord President (Emslie) observed (at 347) that a decision:

> "will be ultra vires … if the Secretary of State has taken into account irrelevant considerations or has failed to take account of relevant and material considerations which ought to have been taken into account. Similarly [the decision] will fall to be quashed on that ground if, where it is one for which a factual basis is required, there is no proper basis in fact to support it".

This in turn raises the issue of at what point do these facts fall to be assessed for their adequacy? In *Secretary of State for Education and Science v. Tameside Metropolitan Borough Council* [1977] A.C. 1014 Lord Wilberforce observed (at 1047) that the court's power of judicial review enabled it to interfere with the exercise of discretion "on such grounds as that the minister has acted right outside his powers or outside the purpose of the Act, or unfairly, or upon an incorrect basis of fact". See too the view of Cooke J. in *Daganayasi v. Minister of Immigration* [1980] 2 N.Z.L.R. 130 that a decision could be invalid on the grounds of statement of fact.

These cases came to be considered by Lord Johnston in *Shetland Line (1984) Ltd v. Secretary of State for Scotland*, 1996 S.L.T. 653. Companies were seeking a subsidy under the Highlands and Islands Shipping Services Act 1960 from the Secretary of State for Scotland, which subsidy was based on invoices. The companies brought a petition for judicial review in which they sought, *inter alia*, reduction of the decision of the Secretary of State as to the level of subsidy to be awarded arguing that on the basis of the erroneous information, the decision was unlawful as being irrational, unfair and based on errors of fact. Lord Johnston, in rejecting the petitioner's allegations, observed (at 658):

> "irrationality may well involve an error of fact but in my opinion that error must relate to facts material to the decision in circumstances where the opportunity to appreciate the true situation was before the minister, whether personally or in the minds of his officials, at the time the decision was taken. That, in my opinion, is the true ratio of the *Tameside* case and can explain the position of Cooke J in the New Zealand case. It follows that it is not sufficient simply to point, with the benefit of hindsight, to the existence of a mistake in the mind of the decision maker at the time the decision was taken. This also accords with the dictum of Lord President Emslie in *Wordie*."

See also *R. v. London Residuary Body, ex parte Inner London Education Authority*, *The Times*, July 24, 1987, and *R. v. Secretary of State for Education, ex parte Stitt*, April 15, 1995, unreported.

(5) Under U.S. law, a reviewing court has power "to determine whether an administrative determination made after a formal hearing is supported by substantial evidence on the record taken as a whole": see B. Schwartz and H. W. R. Wade, *Legal Control of Government* (1972), pp. 228–234, 238–239. "Substantial evidence is more than a mere scintilla. It means such relevant evidence as a reasonable mind might accept as adequate to support a conclusion": *Consolidated Edison Co. v. National Labor Relations Board*, 305 U.S. 197 at 229 (1938). The "substantiality of evidence must take into account whatever in the record fairly detracts from its weight": *Universal Camera Corporation v. National Labor Relations Board*, 340 U.S. 474 at 487 (1951). An American court has greater scope in weighing evidence or choosing between the inferences in evidence or conflicting testimony. Although in British administrative practice most decisions are not supported by the full documentation found in American conditions, does that mean that something not unlike the "substantial evidence" rule should not be applied where full evidence *is* available — for example, in planning matters where perhaps an inspector's report and a ministerial decision letter are available?

JURISDICTION AND LAW: ERROR OF LAW

Anisminic Ltd v. Foreign Compensation Commission

[1969] 2 A.C. 147

4–10   Anisminic Ltd was a British company which in 1956 owned a mining property in Egypt, which they claimed was worth over £4 million. On the outbreak of hostilities between Israel and Egypt the property was occupied by Israeli forces and damaged to the extent of some £500,000. On November 1, 1956, property in Egypt belonging to British subjects had been sequestrated by the Egyptian Government. On April 29, 1957, after the Israeli forces had withdrawn, the Egyptian Government authorised a sale of the appellants' property, which was sold to an Egyptian organisation, TEDO. The appellants' property had included a large quantity of manganese ore, and they took steps to dissuade their customers from buying ore from TEDO. This apparently embarrassed the Egyptian authorities, and on November 23, 1957, an agreement was made between the appellants, TEDO and the Sequestrator General whereby the appellants purported to sell to TEDO, for £500,000, their whole business in Egypt. This was not, however, to include any claim which the appellants might "be entitled to assert against any governmental authority other than the Egyptian government, as a result of loss suffered by, or of damage to or reduction in the value of "their business or assets" during the events of October and November 1956.

In 1959 a treaty was concluded between the British and Egyptian Governments under which compensation was paid to the British Government in respect of certain properties, including the appellants', listed in Annex E to the treaty. It was accepted that at that stage the disposal of the sum was in the discretion of the British Government. The distribution of the compensation was entrusted to the Foreign Compensation Commission by the Foreign Compensation (Egypt) (Determination and Registration Claims) Order 1959 (subsequently amended), made under the Foreign Compensation Act 1950. Article 4 of the 1962 Order provided that:

> "(1) The commission shall treat a claim under this Part of the Order as established if the applicant satisfied them of the following matters: (a) that his application relates to property in Egypt which is referred to in Annex E; (b) if the property is referred to in paragraph (1)(a) or in paragraph (2) of Annex E — (i) that the applicant is the person referred to in paragraph (1)(a) or in paragraph (2), as the case may be, as the owner of the property or is the successor in title of such person; and (ii) that the person referred to as aforesaid and any person who became successor in title of such person on or before February 28, 1959, were British nationals on October 31, 1956, and February 28, 1959; ...
>
> (3) For the purposes of sub-paragraphs (b)(ii) and (c)(ii) of paragraph (1) of this article, a British national who died, or in the case of a corporation or association ceased to exist, between October 31, 1956 and February 28, 1959, shall be deemed to have been a British national on the latter date and a person who had not been born, or in the case of a corporation or association had not been constituted, on October 31, 1956, shall be deemed to have been a British national on that date if such person became a British national at birth or when constituted, as the case may be; provided that a converted company shall for the purposes of sub-paragraphs (b)(ii) and (c)(ii) of paragraph (1) of this article be deemed not to have been a British national."

The appellants submitted a claim for compensation to the Commission. After various proceedings, the Commission made a provisional determination to the effect that Anisminic Ltd had failed to establish entitlement to a claim under the Order, in respect of the sequestrated property, on the ground that TEDO, which had become the successor in title to the appellants, was not at any time a British national. Section 4(4) of the 1950 Act provided that:

> "The determination by the commission of any application made to them under this Act shall not be called in question in any court of law."

Browne J. made a declaration that the Commission's provisional determination was a nullity, and that the Commission were under a statutory duty to treat the appellants' claim as established: [1969] 2 A.C. at 223. The Court of Appeal set aside his judgment: [1968] 2 Q.B. 862. Anisminic Ltd appealed to the House of Lords.

The main questions were (1) was the nationality of a "successor in title" relevant where the claimant was the original owner of property mentioned in Annex E of the treaty? Lord Reid, Lord Pearce and Lord Wilberforce held that it was not. In their view, article 4(1) was defectively drafted. It was meant to convey (a) that if a person claimed as the original owner, he had to show that he was a British national on the dates specified, and (b) that if he claimed as the universal successor — for example, after the death of an original owner or the liquidation of an original owning company — he had to show that both he and the original owner were British nationals: see Lord Reid [1969] 2 A.C. at 173–175; Lord Pearce at 201–205; and Lord Wilberforce at 212–214. Lord Morris of Borth-y-Gest did not express a final opinion on this point. Lord Pearson at 219–223 thought the Commission correct in holding that "successor in title" meant successor in title to the claim of the owners against the Egyptian Government, and that this claim had been sold to TEDO as part of the business assets in Egypt.

(2) Did the error cause the Commission to exceed their jurisdiction, or was it an error within jurisdiction? Lord Reid, Lord Pearce and Lord Wilberforce held that there was an excess of jurisdiction. Lord Pearson (at 215) accepted that had they made such an error it would have taken them outside their jurisdiction. Lord Morris was of the opinion that it was a matter within their jurisdiction.

(3) If the determination was made in excess of jurisdiction, was it nevertheless protected by section 4(4)? All five members of the House of Lords were agreed that it was not.

LORD REID: "… The next argument was that, by reason of the provisions of section 4(4) of the 1950 Act, the courts are precluded from considering whether the respondent's determination was a nullity, and therefore it must be treated as valid whether or not inquiry would disclose that it was a nullity. Section 4(4) is in these terms:

> 'The determination by the commission by any application made to them under this Act shall not be called in question in any court of law.'

The respondent maintains that these are plain words only capable of having one meaning. Here is a determination which is apparently valid: there is nothing on the face of the document to cast any doubt on its validity. If it is a nullity, that could only be established by raising some kind of proceedings in court. But that would be calling the determination in question, and that is expressly prohibited by the statute. The appellants maintain that that is not the meaning of the words of this provision. They say that 'determination' means a real determination and does not include an apparent or purported determination which in the eyes of the law has no existence because it is a nullity. Or, putting it in another way, if you seek to show that a determination is a nullity you are not questioning the purported determination — you are maintaining that it does not exist as a determination. It is one thing to question a determination which does exist: it is quite another thing to say that there is nothing to be questioned.

Let me illustrate the matter by supposing a simple case. A statute provides that a certain order may be made by a person who holds a specified qualification or appointment, and it contains a provision, similar to section 4(4), that such an order made by such a person shall not be called in question in any court of law. A person aggrieved by an order alleges that it is a forgery or that the person who made the order did not hold that qualification or appointment. Does such a provision require the court to treat that order as a valid order? It is a well established principle that a provision ousting the ordinary jurisdiction of the court must be construed strictly — meaning, I think, that, if such a provision is reasonably capable of having two meanings, that meaning shall be taken which preserves the ordinary jurisdiction of the court.

Statutory provisions which seek to limit the ordinary jurisdiction of the court have a long history. No case has been cited in which any other form of words limiting the jurisdiction of the court has been held to protect a nullity. If the draftsman or Parliament had intended to introduce a new kind of ouster clause so as to prevent any inquiry even as to whether the document relied on was a forgery, I would have expected to find something much more specific than the bald statement that a determination shall not be called in question in any court of law. Undoubtedly such a provision protects every determination which is not a nullity. But I do not think that it is necessary or even reasonable to construe the word 'determination' as including everything which purports to be a determination but which is in fact no determination at all. And there are no degrees of nullity. There are a number of reasons why the law will hold a purported decision to be a nullity. I do not see how it could be said that such a provision protects some kinds of nullity but not others: if that were intended it would be easy to say so.

The case which gives most difficulty is *Smith v. East Elloe Rural District Council* [1956] A.C. 736 where the form of ouster clause was similar to that in the present case. But I cannot regard it as a very satisfactory case. The plaintiff was aggrieved by a compulsory purchase order. After two unsuccessful actions she tried again after six years. As this case never reached the stage of a statement of claim we do not know whether her case was that the clerk of the council had fraudulently misled the council and the Ministry, or whether it was that the council and the Ministry were parties to the fraud. The result would be quite different, in my view, for it is only if the authority which made the order had itself acted in mala fide that the order would be a nullity. I think that the case which it was intended to present must have been that the fraud was only the fraud of the clerk because almost the whole of the argument was on the question whether a time limit in the Act applied where fraud was alleged; there was no citation of the authorities on the question whether a clause ousting the jurisdiction of the court applied when nullity was in question, and there was little about this matter in the speeches. I do not therefore regard this case as a binding authority on this question. The other authorities are dealt with in the speeches of my noble and learned friends, and it is unnecessary for me to deal with them in detail. I have come without hesitation to the conclusion that in this case we are not prevented from inquiring whether the order of the commission was a nullity.

It has sometimes been said that it is only where a tribunal acts without jurisdiction that its decision is a nullity. But in such cases the word 'jurisdiction' has been used in a very wide sense, and I have come to the conclusion that it is better not to use the term except in the narrow and original sense of the tribunal being entitled to enter on the inquiry in question. But there are many cases where, although the tribunal had jurisdiction to enter on the inquiry, it has done or failed to do something in the course of the inquiry which is of such a nature that its decision is a nullity. It may have given its decision in bad faith. It may have made a decision which it had no power to make. It may have failed in the course of the inquiry to comply with the requirements of natural justice. It may in perfect good faith have misconstrued the provisions giving it power to act so that it failed to deal with the question remitted to it and decided some question which was not remitted to it. It may have refused to take into account something which it was required to take into account. Or it may have based its decision on some matter which, under the provisions setting it up, it had no right to take into account. I do not intend this list to be exhaustive. But if it decides a question remitted to it for decision without committing any of these errors it is as much entitled to decide that question wrongly as it is to decide it rightly. I understand that some confusion has been caused by my having said in *R. v. Governor of Brixton Prison, ex p. Armah* [1968] A.C. 192, 234 that if a tribunal has jurisdiction to go right it has jurisdiction to go wrong. So it has, if one uses 'jurisdiction' in the narrow original sense. If it is entitled to enter on the inquiry and does not do any of those things which I have mentioned in the course of the proceedings, then its decision is equally valid whether it is right or wrong subject only to the power of the court in certain circumstances to correct an error of law. I think that, if these views are correct, the only case cited which was plainly wrongly decided is *Davies v. Price* [1958] 1 W.L.R. 434. But in a number of other cases some of the grounds of judgment are questionable.

I can now turn to the provisions of the Order under which the commission acted, and to the way in which the commission reached their decision. It was said in the Court of Appeal that publication of their reasons was unnecessary and perhaps undesirable. Whether or not they could have been required to publish their reasons, I dissent emphatically from the view that publication may have been undesirable. In my view, the commission acted with complete propriety, as one would expect looking to its membership.

The meaning of the important parts of the Order is extremely difficult to discover, and, in my view, a main cause of this is the deplorable modern drafting practice of compressing to the point of obscurity provisions which would not be difficult to understand if written out at rather greater length.

The effect of the Order was to confer legal rights on persons who might previously have hoped or expected that in allocating any sums available discretion would be exercised in their favour. We are concerned in this case with article 4 of the Order and more particularly with para. (1)(b)(ii) of the article. Article 4 is as follows:

[His Lordship read Article 4.]

The task of the commission was to receive claims and to determine the rights of each applicant. It is enacted that they shall treat a claim as established if the applicant satisfied them of certain matters....

The main difficulty in this case springs from the fact that the draftsman did not state separately what conditions have to be satisfied (1) where the applicant is the original owner and (2) where the applicant claims as the successor in title of the original owner. It is clear that where the applicant is the original owner he must prove that he was a British national on the dates stated. And it is equally clear that where the applicant claims as being the original owner's successor in title he must prove that both he and the original owner were British nationals on those dates, subject to later provisions in the article about persons who had died or had been born within the relevant period. What is left in obscurity is whether the provisions with regard to successor in title have any application at all in cases where the applicant is himself the original owner. If this provision had been split up as it should have been, and the conditions, to be satisfied where the original owner is the applicant had been set out, there could have been no such obscurity.

This is the critical question in this case. It appears from the commission's reasons that they construed this provision as requiring them to inquire, when the applicant is himself the original owner, whether he had a successor in title. So they made that inquiry in this case and held that TEDO was the applicant's successor in title. As TEDO was not a British national they rejected the appellants' claim. But if, on a true construction of the Order, a claimant who is an original owner does not have to prove anything about successors in title, then the commission made an inquiry which the Order did not empower them to make, and they based their decision on a matter which they had no right to take into account. If one uses the word 'jurisdiction' in its wider sense, they went beyond their jurisdiction in considering this matter. It was argued that the whole matter of construing the Order was something remitted to the commission for their decision. I cannot accept that argument. I find nothing in the Order to support it. The Order requires the commission to consider whether they are satisfied with regard to the prescribed matters. That is all they have to do. It cannot be for the commission to determine the limits of its powers. Of course if one party submits to a tribunal that its powers are wider than in fact they are, then the tribunal must deal with that submission. But if they reach a wrong conclusion as to the width of their powers, the court must be able to correct that — not because the tribunal has made an error of law, but because as a result of making an error of law they have dealt with and based their decision on a matter with which, on a true construction of their powers, they had no right to deal. If they base their decision on some matter which is not prescribed for their adjudication, they are doing something which they have no right to do and, if the view which I expressed earlier is right, their decision is a nullity. So the question is whether on a true construction of the Order the applicants did or did not have to prove anything with regard to successors in title. If the commission were entitled to enter on the inquiry whether the applicants had a successor in title, then their decision as to whether TEDO was their successor in title would I think be unassailable whether it was right or wrong: it would be a decision on a matter remitted to them for their decision. The question I have to consider is not whether they made a wrong decision but whether they inquired into and decided a matter which they had no right to consider.

... In themselves the words 'successor in title' are, in my opinion, inappropriate in the circumstances of this Order to denote any person while the original owner is still in existence, and I think it most improbable that they were ever intended to denote any such person. There is no necessity to stretch them to cover any such person. I would therefore hold that the words 'and any person who became successor in title to such person' in Article 4(1)(b)(ii) have no application to a case where the applicant is the original owner. It follows that the commission rejected the appellants' claim on a ground which they had no right to take into account and that their decision was a nullity. I would allow this appeal."

Lord Morris of Borth-y-Gest: [dissenting: stated the facts and continued:] This is not a case in which there has been any sort of suggestion of irregularity either of conduct or procedure on the part of the commission. It has not been said that anything took place which disqualified the commission from making a determination. No occasion arises, therefore, to refer to decisions which have pointed to the consequences of failing to obey or of defying the rules of natural justice: nor to decisions relating to bias in a tribunal: nor to decisions in cases where bad faith has been alleged: nor to decisions in cases where a tribunal has not been properly constituted. If a case arose where bad faith was alleged the difficult case of *Smith v. East Elloe Rural District Council* [1956] A.C. 736 would need consideration: but the present case can, in my view, be approached without any examination of or reliance upon that case.

The provisions of section 4(4) of the Act do not, in my view, operate to debar any inquiry that may be necessary to decide whether the commission has acted within its authority or jurisdiction. The provisions do operate to debar contentions that the commission while acting within its jurisdiction has come to wrong or erroneous conclusions. There would be no difficulty in pursuing, and in adducing evidence in support of, an allegation such as an allegation that those who heard a claim had never been appointed or that those who had been appointed had by some irregular conduct disqualified themselves from adjudicating or continuing to adjudicate. There would be no difficulty in raising any matter that goes to the right or power of the commission to adjudicate (see *R. v. Bolton* (1841) 1 Q.B. 66). What is forbidden is to question the correctness of a decision or determination which it was within the area of their jurisdiction to make.

It is, of course, clear that no appeal is given from a determination of the commission. When Parliament sets up a tribunal and refers matters to it, it becomes a question of policy as to whether to provide for an appeal. Sometimes that is thought to be appropriate. Thus, where (by the Indemnity Act 1920), provision was made for the assessment by the War Compensation Court of certain claims for compensation for acts done in pursuance of prerogative powers it was enacted that though the decision of the tribunal (presided over by a judge) was to be final there could be an appeal by a party aggrieved by a direction or determination of the tribunal on any point of law. Sometimes, on the other hand, it is not thought appropriate to provide for an appeal. In reference to the Foreign Compensation Tribunal it was presumably thought that the advantages of securing finality of decision outweighed any disadvantages that might possibly result from having no appeal procedure. It was presumably thought that there was every prospect that right determinations would be reached if those appointed to reach them were persons in whom there could be every confidence.

I return, then, to the question as to how the appellants can justify the calling in question by them of the determination of the commission. The answer is that they boldly say that what looks like a determination was in fact no determination but was a mere nullity. That which, they say, should be disregarded as being null and void, is a determination which is signed by the chairman of the commission. There is no question here of a sham or spurious or merely purported determination. Why, then, is it said to be null and void? The answer given is that it contains errors in law which have caused the commission to exceed their jurisdiction. When analysed this really means that it is contended that when the commission considered the meaning of certain words in Article 4 of the Order in Council they gave them a wrong construction with the consequence that they had no jurisdiction to disallow the claim of the applicants.

It is not suggested that the commission were not acting within their jurisdiction when they entertained the application of the appellants and gave it their consideration nor when they heard argument and submissions for four days in regard to it. The moment when it is said that they strayed outside their allotted jurisdiction must, therefore, have been at the moment when they gave their 'determination'.

The control which is exercised by the High Court over inferior tribunals (a categorising but not a derogatory description) is of a supervisory but not of an appellate nature. It enables the High Court to correct errors of law if they are revealed on the face of the record. The control cannot, however, be exercised if there is some provision (such as a 'no certiorari' clause) which prohibits removal to the High Court. But it is well settled that even such a clause is of no avail if the inferior tribunal acts without jurisdiction or exceeds the limit of its jurisdiction.

In all cases similar to the present one it becomes necessary, therefore, to ascertain what was the question submitted for the determination of a tribunal. What were its terms of reference? What was its remit? What were the questions left to it or sent to it for its decision? What were the limits of its duties and powers? Were there any conditions precedent which had to be satisfied before its functions began? If there were, was it or was it not left to the tribunal itself to decide whether or not the conditions precedent were satisfied? If Parliament has enacted that provided a certain situation exists then a tribunal may have certain powers, it is clear that the tribunal will not have those powers unless the situation exists. The decided cases illustrate the infinite variety of the situations which may exist and the variations of statutory wording which have called for consideration. Most of the cases depend, therefore, upon an examination of their own particular facts and of particular sets of words. It is, however, abundantly clear that questions of law as well as of fact can be remitted for the determination of a tribunal.

If a tribunal while acting within its jurisdiction makes an error of law which it reveals on the face of its recorded determination, then the court, in the exercise of its supervisory function, may correct the error unless there is some provision preventing a review by a court of law. If a particular issue is left to a tribunal to decide, then even where it is shown (in cases where it is possible to show) that in deciding the issue left to it the tribunal has come to a wrong conclusion that does not involve that the tribunal has gone outside its jurisdiction. It follows that if any errors of law are made in deciding matters which are left to a tribunal for its decision such errors will be errors within jurisdiction. If issues of law as well as of fact are referred to a tribunal for its determination, then its determination cannot be asserted to be wrong if Parliament has enacted that the determination is not to be called in question in any court of law.

[His Lordship cited passages from the judgments in *R. v. Governor of Brixton Prison, ex p. Armah* [1968] A.C. 192, 234 (Lord Reid); *R. v. Northumberland C.A.T., ex p. Shaw* [1952] 1 K.B. 338, 346 (Denning L.J.); *R. v. Nat Bell Liquors Ltd* [1922] 2 A.C. 128, 156 (Lord Sumner).]

If, therefore, a tribunal while within the area of its jurisdiction committed some error of law and if such error was made apparent in the determination itself (or, as it is often expressed, on the face of the record) then the superior court could correct that error unless it was forbidden to do so. It would be so forbidden if the determination was 'not to be called in question in any court of law'. If so forbidden it could not then even hear argument which suggested that error of law had been made. It could, however, still consider whether the determination was within 'the area of the inferior jurisdiction'.

So the question is raised whether in the present case the commission went out of bounds. Did it wander outside its designated area? Did it outstep the confines of the territory of its inquiry? Did it digress away from its allotted task? Was there some preliminary inquiry upon the correct determination of which its later jurisdiction was dependent?

For the reasons which I will endeavour to explain it seems to me that at no time did the commission stray from the direct path which it was required to tread. Under Article 4 of the Order in Council the commission was under a positive duty to treat a claim under Part III as established if the applicant satisfied them of certain matters. If they had stated that they were satisfied of those matters but had then declined to treat a claim as established, there would have been a situation very different from that now under consideration and one in which the court could clearly act. So also if they had stated that they were not satisfied of the matter but had nevertheless treated the claim as established. They would have had no right to treat the claim as established unless they were satisfied of the matters. The present is a case in which, faithfully following the wording of Article 4, they stated that they were not satisfied of the matters and, therefore, did not treat the claim as established. In stating why they were not satisfied of the matters they have set out the processes of their reasoning. The more that reasoning is examined the more apparent does it, in my view, become that the members of the commission applied their minds very carefully to a consideration of the matters about which the applicant had to satisfy 'them'. To no one else were the matters remitted but to 'them'. It was for them to be satisfied and not for anyone else. The words of Article 4 state their terms of reference. In those terms were certain words and certain phrases. The commission could not possibly discharge their duty without considering those words and phrases and without reaching a decision as to their meaning. The commission could not burk that task. It seems to me that the words which stated that it was for the commission to be satisfied of certain matters, and defined those matters, inevitably involved that any necessary interpretation of words within the compass of those matters was for the commission. They could not come to a conclusion as to whether they were satisfied as to the specified matters unless and until they gave meaning to the words which they had to follow. Unless such a phrase as 'successor in title' was defined in the Order — and it was not — it was an inescapable duty of the commission to consider and to decide what the phrase signified. Doubtless they heard ample argument before forming a view. The same applies in regard to many other words and sequences of words in Article 4. But the forming of views as to these matters lay in the direct path of the commission's duties. They were duties that could not be shirked. They were central to the exercise of their jurisdiction. When their fully reasoned statement of their conclusions (which in this case can be regarded as a part of their 'determination') is studied it becomes possible for someone to contend that an alternative construction of Article 4 should be preferred to that which was thought correct by the commission. But this calling in question cannot, in my view, take place in any court of law. Parliament has forbidden it... .

In this case there has been much concentration on the question whether the commission correctly decided that the phrase 'successor in title' included an assignee. But this was but one of very many matters which might receive determination by the commission. A perusal of the Orders in Council shows that they bristle with words and phrases needing construction. For my part I cannot accept that if, in regard to any one of the many points in respect of which interpretation and construction became necessary a view can be formed that the commission made an error, the consequence follows that their determination became a nullity as being made in excess of jurisdiction... .

The claim of the applicants had to be determined by the commission and the applicants were under the obligation of satisfying the commission as to certain stated matters. They could not decide whether or not they were satisfied until they had construed the relevant parts of the Order in Council. When they were hearing argument as to the meaning of those relevant parts they were not acting without jurisdiction. They were at the very heart of their duty, their task and their jurisdiction. It cannot be that their necessary duty of deciding as to the meaning would be or could be followed by the result that if they took one view they would be within jurisdiction and if they took another view that they would be without. If at the moment of decision they were inevitably within their jurisdiction because they were doing what they had to do, I cannot think that a later view of someone else, if it differed from theirs, could involve that they trespassed from within their jurisdiction at the moment of decision.

It is sometimes the case that the jurisdiction of a tribunal is made dependent upon or subject to some condition. Parliament may enact that if a certain state of affairs exists then there will be jurisdiction. If in such case it appears that the state of affairs did not exist, then it follows that there would be no jurisdiction. Sometimes, however, a tribunal might undertake the task of considering whether the state of affairs existed. If it made error in that task such error would be in regard to a matter preliminary to the existence of jurisdiction. It would not be an error within the limited jurisdiction intended to be conferred. An illustration of this appeared in 1853 in *Bunbury v. Fuller* [1853) 9 Ex. 111.... [T]here is here no room for any suggestion that the commission failed to satisfy any condition precedent or failed to state the existence of any matter essential to their jurisdiction....

In the submissions on behalf of the appellants a phrase much used was that the commission had asked themselves wrong questions. The phrase can be employed when consideration is being given to a question whether a tribunal has correctly decided some point of construction. If, however, the point of construction is fairly and squarely within the jurisdiction of the tribunal for them to decide, then a suggestion that a wrong question has been posed is no more than a means of deploying an argument: and if construction has been left to the tribunal the argument is unavailing. The phrase is, however, valuable and relevant in cases where it can be suggested that some condition precedent has not been satisfied or where jurisdiction is related to the existence of some state of affairs.... So in some cases a tribunal may reveal that by asking some wrong question it fails to bring itself within the area of the demarcation of its jurisdiction. In *Maradana Mosque Trustees v. Mahmud* [1976] 1 A.C. 13, P.C., one part of the decision was that the rules of natural justice had been violated. The other part of the decision, relevant for present purposes, was that where statutory authority was given to a Minister to act if he was satisfied that a school *is* being administered in a certain way he was not given authority to act because he was satisfied that the school *had been* administered in that way. It could be said that the Minister had asked himself the wrong question: so he had, but the relevant result was that he never brought himself within the area of his jurisdiction... .

I would dismiss the appeal."

LORD PEARCE: "My Lords, the courts have a general jurisdiction over the administration of justice in this country. From time to time Parliament sets up special tribunals to deal with special matters and gives them jurisdiction to decide these matters without any appeal to the courts. When this happens the courts cannot hear appeals from such a tribunal or substitute their own views on any matters which have been specifically committed by Parliament to the tribunal.

Such tribunals must, however, confine themselves within the powers specially committed to them on a true construction of the relevant Acts of Parliament. It would lead to an absurd situation if a tribunal, having been given a circumscribed area of inquiry, carved out from the general jurisdiction of the courts, were entitled of its own motion to extend that area by misconstruing the limits of its mandate to inquire and decide as set out in the Act of Parliament.

If, for instance, Parliament were to carve out an area of inquiry within which an inferior domestic tribunal could give certain relief to wives against their husbands, it would not lie within the power of that tribunal to extend the area of inquiry and decision, that is, jurisdiction, thus committed to it by construing "wives" as including all women who have, without marriage, cohabited with a man for a substantial period, or by misconstruing the limits of that into which they were to inquire. It would equally not be within the power of that tribunal to reduce the area committed to it by construing 'wives' as excluding all those who, though married, have not been recently co-habiting with their husbands. Again, if it is instructed to give relief wherever on inquiry it finds that two stated conditions are satisfied, it cannot alter or restrict its jurisdiction by adding a third condition which has to be satisfied before it will give relief. It is, therefore, for the courts to decide the true construction of the statute which defines the area of a tribunal's jurisdiction. This is the only logical way of dealing with the situation and it is the way in which the courts have acted in a supervisory capacity.

Lack of jurisdiction may arise in various ways. There may be an absence of those formalities or things which are conditions precedent to the tribunal having any jurisdiction to embark on an inquiry. Or the tribunal may at the end make an order that it has no jurisdiction to make. Or in the intervening stage, while engaged on a proper inquiry, the tribunal may depart from the rules of natural justice; or it may ask itself the wrong questions; or it may take into account matters which it was not directed to take into account. Thereby it would step outside its jurisdiction. It would turn its inquiry into something not directed by Parliament and fail to make the inquiry which Parliament did direct. Any of these things would cause its purported decision to be a nullity.

Further, it is assumed, unless special provisions provide otherwise, that the tribunal will make its inquiry and decision according to the law of the land. For that reason the courts will intervene when it is manifest from the record that the tribunal, though keeping within its mandated area of jurisdiction, comes to an erroneous decision through an error of law. In such a case the courts have intervened to correct the error.

The courts have, however, always been careful to distinguish their intervention whether on excess of jurisdiction or error of law from an appellate function. Their jurisdiction over inferior tribunals is supervision, not review:

> 'That supervision goes to two points: one is the area of the inferior jurisdiction and the qualifications and conditions of its exercise; the other is the observance of the law in the course of its exercise' (*R. v. Nat Bell Liquors Ltd* [1922] 2 A.C. 128, 156).

It is simply an enforcement of Parliament's mandate to the tribunal. If the tribunal is intended on a true construction of the Act to inquire into and finally decide questions within a certain area, the courts' supervisory duty is to see that it makes the authorised inquiry according to natural justice and arrives at a decision whether right or wrong. They will intervene if the tribunal asks itself the wrong questions (that is, questions other than those which Parliament directed it to ask itself). But if it directs itself to the right inquiry, asking the right questions, they will not intervene merely because it has or may have come to the wrong answer, provided that this is an answer that lies within its jurisdiction.

It is convenient to set out the matter in broad outline because there has been evolution over the centuries and there have been many technicalities. There have also been many border-line cases. And the courts have at times taken a more robust line to see that the law is carried out and justice administered by inferior tribunals, and at times taken a more cautious and reluctant line in their anxiety not to seem to encroach or to assume an appellate function which they have not got... .

[His Lordship held that section 4(4) did not protect a purported determination made without jurisdiction.]

In my opinion, the subsequent case of *Smith v. East Elloe Rural District Council* [1956] A.C. 736 does not compel your Lordships to decide otherwise. If it seemed to do so, I would think it necessary to reconsider the case in the light of the powerful dissenting opinions of my noble and learned friends, Lord Reid and Lord Somervell. It might possibly be said that it related to an administrative or executive decision, not a judicial decision, and somewhat different considerations might have applied; certainly none of the authorities relating to absence or excess of jurisdiction were cited to the House. I agree with Browne J. that it is not a compelling authority in the present case. Again, the fact that this commission was expressly exempted from the provisions of section 11 of the Tribunals and Inquiries Act passed in 1958, though no doubt a tribute to the high standard of the commission and the fact that its chairman was a lawyer of distinction, cannot have any bearing on the construction of the Foreign Compensation Act, 1950.

If, therefore, the commission by misconstruing the Order in Council which gave them their jurisdiction and laid down the precise limit of their duty to inquire and determine, exceeded or departed from their mandate, their determination was without jurisdiction and Brown J. was right in making the order appealed from.

Pursuant to the Foreign Compensation Act 1950 the Order in Council which deals with the present claim gave a wide power to determine the amount of compensation. But with regard to the establishment of the claims under Article 4 it gave narrow powers. It gave no general discretion at all. If the applicant satisfies them of certain listed matters, the commission shall treat the claim as established. The only listed matters so far as relevant to the present claim were, the appellants argue, (1) the fact that the property referred to in Annex E was in Egypt; (2) the identify of the claimant as referred to in Annex E; and (3) the nationality of the claimant on certain dates. There is no dispute that on these matters they satisfied the commission. Therefore, on the appellants' argument, the commission had a mandatory duty to treat their claim as established. If their construction of Article 4 is correct, the appellants are right in this contention. There was no discretion in the commission, no jurisdiction to put further hurdles, other than those listed, in the path of the appellants' claim or to embark on inquiries other than those which the Order in Council directed. The commission, on the other hand, construed the Order as giving them jurisdiction to inquire and be satisfied on two further points; since they were not satisfied on these they rejected the claim. If *their* construction is correct, they were entitled to do so and have not exceeded their jurisdiction.

[His Lordship held that the commission's construction was erroneous.]"

LORD WILBERFORCE: "… In every case, whatever the character of a tribunal, however wide the range of questions remitted to it, however great the permissible margin of mistake, the essential point remains that the tribunal has a derived authority, derived, that is, from statute: at some point, and to be found from a consideration of the legislation, the field within which it operates is marked out and limited. There is always an area, narrow or wide, which is the tribunal's area; a residential area, wide or narrow, in which the legislature has previously expressed its will and into which the tribunal may not enter. Equally, though this is not something that arises in the present case, there are certain fundamental assumptions, which without explicit restatement in every case, necessarily underlie the remission of power to decide such as (I do not attempt more than a general reference, since the strength and shade of these matters will depend upon the nature of the tribunal and the kind of question it has to decide) the requirement that a decision must be made in accordance with principles of natural justice and good faith. The principle that failure to fulfil these assumptions may be equivalent to a departure from the remitted area must be taken to follow from the decision of this House in *Ridge v. Baldwin* [1964] A.C. 40. Although, in theory perhaps, it may be possible for Parliament to set up a tribunal which has full and autonomous powers to fix its own area of operation, that has, so far, not been done in this country. The question, what is the tribunal's proper area, is one which it has always been permissible to ask and to answer, and it must follow that examination of its extent is not precluded by a clause conferring conclusiveness, finality, or unquestionability upon its decisions. These clauses in their nature can only relate to decisions given within the field of operation entrusted to the tribunal. They may, according to the width and emphasis of their formulation, help to ascertain the extent of that field, to narrow it or to enlarge it, but unless one is to deny the statutory origin of the tribunal and of its powers, they cannot preclude examination of that extent… .

The courts, when they decide that a 'decision' is a 'nullity', are not disregarding the preclusive clause. For, just as it is their duty to attribute autonomy of decision of action to the tribunal within the designated area, so, as the counterpart of this autonomy, they must ensure that the limits of that area which have been laid down are observed (see the formulation of Lord Sumner in *R. v. Nat Bell Liquors Ltd* [1922] 2 A.C. 128, 156). In each task they are carrying out the intention of the legislature, and it would be misdescription to state it in terms of a struggle between the courts and the executive. What would be the purpose of defining by statute the limit of a tribunal's powers if, by means of a clause inserted in the instrument of definition, those limits could safely be passed? …

[His Lordship cited *R. v. Commissioners for Special Purposes of the Income Tax* (1888) 21 Q.B.D. 313, 319 (Lord Esher M.R.); *R. v. Shoreditch Assessment Committee, ex p. Morgan* [1910] 2 K.B. 859, 880 (Farwell L.J.); and *R. v. Northumberland C.A.T., ex p. Shaw* [1952] 1 K.B. 338, 346 (Denning L.J.).]

These passages at least answer one of the respondents' main arguments, to some extent accepted by the members of the Court of Appeal, which is that *because* the commission has (admittedly) been given power, indeed required, to decide some questions of law, arising out of the construction of the relevant Order in Council, it must necessarily have power to decide those questions which relate to the delimitation of its powers; or conversely that if the court has power to review the latter, it must also have power to review the former. But the one does not follow from the other: there is no reason why the Order in Council should not (as a matter of construction to be decided by the court) limit the tribunal's powers and at the same time (by the same process of construction) confer upon the tribunal power, in the exercise of its permitted task, to decide other questions of law, including questions of construction of the Order. I shall endeavour to show that this is what the Order has done.

The extent of the interpretatory power conferred upon the tribunal may sometimes be difficult to ascertain and argument may be possible whether this or that question of construction has been left to the tribunal, that is, is within the tribunal's field, or whether, because it pertains to the delimitation of the tribunal's area by the legislature, it is reserved for decision by the courts. Sometimes it will be possible to form a conclusion from the form and subject-matter of the legislation. In one case it may be seen that the legislature, while stating general objectives, is prepared to concede a wide area to the authority it establishes: this will often be the case where the decision involves a degree of policy-making rather than fact-finding, especially if the authority is a department of government or the Minister at its head. I think that we have reached a stage in our administrative law when we can view this question quite objectively, without any necessary predisposition towards one that questions of law, or questions of construction, are necessarily for the courts. In the kind of case I have mentioned there is no need to make this assumption. In another type of case it may be apparent that Parliament is itself directly and closely concerned with the definition and delimitation of certain matters of comparative detail and has marked by its language the intention that these shall accurately be observed. If *R. v. Minister of Health* [1939] 1 K.B. 232 was rightly decided, it must be because it was a case of the former type. The dispute related to a superannuation allowance and the statute provided that 'any dispute' should be determined by the Minister. The basis of the decision is not very clearly expressed but can, I think, be taken to be that, as the context and subject-matter showed, the Minister had a field of decision extending to the construction of the superannuation provisions of the Act. The present case, by contrast, as examination of the relevant Order in Council will show, is clearly of the latter category.

I do not think it desirable to discuss further in detail the many decisions in the reports in this field. But two points may perhaps be made. First, the cases in which a tribunal has been held to have passed outside its proper limits are not limited to those in which it had no power to enter upon its inquiry or its jurisdiction, or has not satisfied a condition precedent. Certainly such cases exist (for example *ex p. Bradlaugh* (1878) 3 Q.B.D. 509) but they do not exhaust the principle. A tribunal may quite properly validly enter upon its task and in the course of carrying it out may make a decision which is invalid — not merely erroneous. This may be described as 'asking the wrong question' or 'applying the wrong test' — expressions not wholly satisfactory since they do not, in themselves, distinguish between doing something which is not in the tribunal's area and doing something wrong within that area — a crucial distinction which the court has to make. Cases held to be of the former kind (whether, on their facts, correctly or not does not affect the principle) are *Estate and Trust Agencies (1927 Ltd v. Singapore Improvement Trust* [1937] A.C. 898, 915–917; *Seereelall Jhuggroo v. Central Arbitration and Control Board* [1953] A.C. 151, 161 ('whether [the board] took into consideration matters outside the ambit of its jurisdiction and beyond the matters which it was entitled to consider'); *R. v. Fulham, Hammersmith and Kensington Rent Tribunal, ex p. Hierowski* [1953] 2 Q.B. 147. The present case, in my opinion, and it is at this point that I respectfully differ from the Court of Appeal, is of this kind. Secondly, I find myself obliged to state that I cannot regard *Smith v. East Elloe Rural District Council* [1956] A.C. 736 as a reliable solvent of this appeal, or of any case where similar questions arise. The preclusive clause was indeed very similar to the present but, however inevitable the particular decision may have been, it was given on too narrow a basis to assist us here. I agree with my noble and learned friends, Lord Reid and Lord Pearce, on this matter."

LORD PEARSON dissented.

Notes

(1) On this case see H. W. R. Wade, "Constitutional and Administrative Aspects of the **4–11** Anisminic Case" (1969) 85 L.Q.R. 198; S. A. de Smith, "Judicial Review in Administrative Law: The Ever-Open Door?" (1969) 27 C.L.J. 161; and B. C. Gould, "Anisminic and Jurisdictional Review" [1970] P.L. 358.

(2) The question of whether or not all errors of law can be regarded as jurisdictional caused a great deal of difficulty in the English courts following *Anisminic*. In *Pearlman v. Keeper and Governors of Harrow School* [1979] Q.B. 56 Lord Denning M.R. felt that notwithstanding the difficulties in *Anisminic* in providing any clear basis for the distinction between jurisdictional and non-jurisdictional errors of law, some attempt should be made to construct a principled basis for the distinction. He founded that attempt on the concept of jurisdictional error being based on matters upon which the decision maker's decision depended, but Lane L.J. and Eveleigh L.J. adopted a more limited approach. In *Re Racal Communications* [1981] A.C. 374 Lord Diplock

based the distinction upon a functional test. *Anisminic* was applicable in the context of decisions by judicial authorities but not administrative authorities; in the latter the distinction between errors which were jurisdictional and those which were not should be regarded as at an end. Matters were taken further in *R. v. Lord President of the Privy Council, ex parte Page* [1993] 1 All E.R. 97 where in general it was held that all errors of law go to jurisdiction although there were dicta to the effect that as regards an inferior court of law, such as the county court in *Pearlman*, a statutory provision that its decision is to be "final and conclusive" will confine the remedy to abuse of power or breach of natural justice or failure to comply with a jurisdictional requirement such as proper composition of the body. *Page* made explicit the view that *Anisminic* was treated as rendering obsolete the distinction between errors of law on the face of the record and other errors of law by extending the doctrine of *ultra vires*. See also *Williams v. Bedwellty Justices* [1996] 3 All E.R. 737 at 742–743 *per* Lord Cooke of Thorndon. This train of authority has had no parallel in Scotland and in considering the following extracts you could consider the extent to which a divergence between the jurisdictions in this regard is desirable and, if not, which approach should be followed. On *Page* see H. W. R. Wade, "Visitors and Error of Law" (1993) 155 L.Q.R. 159.

Watt v. Lord Advocate

1977 S.L.T. 130

4–12   "A storeman was laid off work by his employers for three months owing to a trade dispute. The craftsmen in the factory where he worked imposed sanctions to achieve an increase in their wages which compelled the employers to lay off all the workers. Meantime at another factory belonging to the employers, wage increases for all employees were agreed with the union. The said craftsmen at the storeman's factory negotiated increases on a similar basis which were applied to all the workers there (including the storeman), and work was resumed. The storeman claimed unemployment benefit for the said period of three months which was refused by the national insurance commissioner on the ground that he was 'directly interested in the trade dispute which caused the stoppage of work' in terms of s. 22 (1) of the National Insurance Act 1965. Section 75 (1) of said Act provides that the commissioner's decision shall be final. The storeman raised an action for reduction of the commissioner's decision against the Lord Advocate for and on behalf of the Secretary of State for Social Services. The pursuer contended that the commissioner's finding was ultra vires, and even if intra vires should be reduced as erroneous in law."

LORD DUNPARK: "This case was debated before me on the procedure roll. It raises the question of the extent of the jurisdiction of the Court of Session to quash by decree of reduction a decision of a national insurance commissioner that the pursuer was not entitled to unemployment benefit for the period from 28 August to 6 December 1974. The defender pleads that the action is incompetent et separatim that the pursuer's averments are irrelevant to support the conclusion of reduction sought....

'Directly interested in'

Now the pursuer has no prospect of success in this action unless the commissioner, on the facts found by him, came to the wrong conclusion. Other commissioners in other cases have held that a person has a direct interest in a relevant trade dispute if its 'outcome is likely to affect the claimant, not at a number of removes, but virtually automatically, without further intervening contingencies'. In most cases they have had to apply a probability test, hence the use of the word 'likely' above, but in this case, in view of the known terms of the Cumbernauld settlement, it seems to me that the national insurance commissioner found that '*when* the dispute between the Dumbarton craftsmen and the employers ended, the pursuer *would* obtain the same increase in wages as had been agreed for the Cumbernauld storemen' (my italics). Does this interest then amount to a 'direct interest' in the relevant dispute, which is that between the Dumbarton craftsmen and the employers? If it does, the commissioner has not erred, and the action must be dismissed as irrelevant. If the commissioner has come to the wrong conclusion, the defender nevertheless maintains that the action is incompetent on the ground that this court has no jurisdiction to interfere with a decision of a commissioner reached within the limits of his jurisdiction or statutory powers.

Ultra and intra vires errors

It is agreed that the defender's pleas-in-law 7 and 8 put the same question in different ways. To say that he acted outwith his statutory powers is just another way of saying that he exceeded the limits of his statutory jurisdiction. The pursuer's contentions are that the commissioner did exceed his statutory powers in finding that the pursuer was directly interested in the relevant trade dispute, and that, even if he did not, the decision should be reduced by this court as erroneous in law. The distinction may be described as the distinction between an ultra vires and intra vires error. I find it convenient, first, to summarise what I believe to be the power of the Court of Session to interfere with decisions of national insurance commissioners, and then to examine the submissions of counsel in order to decide the category into which this case falls....

However, the primary argument of counsel for the pursuer was that decree of reduction should be pronounced on the ground that the commissioner's written decision disclosed an ultra vires error. There is no doubt that, if this was an ultra vires error, decree of reduction is appropriate, and I shall now examine the distinction between ultra vires and intra vires errors.

Distinction between ultra vires and intra vires errors

This distinction is easy to state, but perhaps less easy to draw. One example of how the principle may be stated is to be found in *Leith Police Commissioners v. Campbell*, at p. 252, where the Lord Justice-Clerk (Inglis) adopted a statement by Lord Alloway in the following terms: 'The great distinction is, that when this Court has previous jurisdiction, and the jurisdiction is created by the statute, the question comes to be determined on the ground, have the parties entrusted with the powers exceeded them? For while they keep within the bounds of the statute, which commits to them a discretionary power, unless excess of that power is pointed out, this Court cannot well interfere.' Ex facie that statement excludes intra vires errors from the supervisory jurisdiction of the Court of Session. It may, however, be argued that decisions in which inferior courts have been held to have exceeded their powers, by wrongly construing terms of the statutes which they were bound to apply to the facts before them, illustrate the correction by the Court of Session of intra vires errors. In my opinion this argument is unsound. There is a distinction which, in my opinion, must be drawn between misconstruction of the nature or limits of the statutory duty and misapplication of the statute to the relevant facts. The former is an ultra vires error in respect that the inferior court has wrongly defined the nature or limits of its statutory duty and, by doing something which the statute did not authorise, or by not doing something which the statute required it to do, has not acted in accordance with its statutory powers. In the latter case, the court has performed its statutory function in the manner laid down by the statute, and, acting within its statutory powers, has produced the wrong answer to a question of mixed fact and law. So long as the court asks the right question, it does not, in my opinion, necessarily make an ultra vires error by producing the wrong answer. The distinction is between 'doing wrong', which is ultra vires, and 'going wrong', which is intra vires.

I do not read any of the judicial decisions cited in this case, with the possible exception of one, as illustrating the use by the Court of Session of its supervisory powers to correct decisions of inferior courts or tribunals on the ground that they have 'gone wrong' while performing their statutory function in the manner laid down. They are, in my opinion, with the one possible exception, examples of the inferior court or tribunal having 'done wrong'. At first sight it may not be easy to separate the apparently merging shadows of 'doing wrong' and 'going wrong'. However, I think that a real distinction is to be made between those cases in which misapplication of the statutory words or phrases to the facts of the case has produced a wrong answer, and those in which the misconstruction of statutory words or phrases per se has plainly resulted in the determining body exercising a power which it did not have. The decisions, to which I shall refer, demonstrate that the Court of Session has regarded the former as intra vires errors and refused to interfere, and the latter as ultra vires errors, warranting reduction of the decisions as nullities on the ground that the determining body has ex proprio motu extended the limits of its statutory powers.

I am aware of the existence of many relevant decisions of the Court of Session which were not cited to me. I certainly do not complain of that. I mention it only to show that I have not seen fit to extend my investigations beyond the limits set for me by counsel, and that the views expressed in the immediately preceding paragraphs of this opinion are based solely on the authorities cited to me.

Examples of ultra vires error

The following cases are examples of ultra vires error, where the Court of Session has reduced the decision on the ground that the inferior court or tribunal had exceeded the bounds of its statutory jurisdiction: *Heritors of Corstorphine v. Ramsay; Young v. Milne*; *Higgins v. Heritors and Kirk Session of the Barony Parish of Glasgow*; *Edinburgh and Glasgow Railway Co. v. Meek*; and *Ashley v. Magistrates of Rothesay*. In *Lord Advocate v. Police Commissioners of Perth*, although the relevant statute provided for an appeal to the sheriff, the Court of Session held competent a petition for suspension and interdict upon the ground stated by the Lord Justice-Clerk (Moncreiff) at p. 246: 'A clause of finality cannot protect a Sheriff's judgment, when, taking an erroneous view of a statute, he either refuses to sanction a lawful act or sanctions an unlawful one.' It is clear that the Lord Justice-Clerk there refers to a sheriff 'doing wrong', not merely 'going wrong'.

A finality clause does not protect a decision which is rendered null by non-compliance with statutory procedure — see *Moss's Empires Ltd v. Assessor for Glasgow*, [also reported sub. nom. *Moss' Empires Ltd. v. Walker*] where Viscount Haldane (at 1916 2 S.L.T. p. 216) referred to the over-riding power of the Court of Session to reduce a decision on that ground. This passage was founded on by counsel for the pursuer as meaning that the power extended to the reduction of any decision which was wrong in law and which might lead to liability or deprivation of rights, but it must, in my opinion, be read secundum materiam subjectam. I read that passage as entirely consistent with the other speeches in that case and, in particular, with the following passage from Lord Shaw's speech at p. 220: 'It is within the jurisdiction of the Court of Session to keep inferior judicatories and administrative bodies right in the sense of compelling them to keep within the limits of their statutory powers, or of compelling them to obey those conditions without the fulfilment of which they have no powers whatsoever. It is within the power of the Court of Session to do that, but it is not within the power or function of the Court of Session itself to do work set by the Legislature to be performed by those administrative bodies or inferior judicatories themselves. 'Lord Paramoor, at p. 221, pointed out that the finality clause only applied to a valuation roll made up in terms of the Act, and that the roll in question had not been so made up.

In *Sinclair-Lockhart's Trustees v. Central Land Board*, Lord President Cooper emphasised that, although the determination of development charges had been confided by statute to the Central Land Board, the Court of Session had nevertheless power to reduce such a determination 'if the exercise of the Board's jurisdiction has not conformed to its statutory basis' (1951 S.L.T. at p. 126). In *Hayman v. Lord Advocate* a proof before answer was allowed on averments that a committee had not performed its statutory duty of inquiring into the adequacy of the experience of ophthalmic practitioners. The pursuers averred that no such inquiry had been conducted and that two members of the committee, who visited them, had authority only to inspect their premises and records. Lord President Cooper referred to the possibility of the committee having 'acted illegally by applying their minds to the wrong question and thus in effect acting *ultra fines compromissi*' (1952 S.L.T. at p. 216). *McDonald v. Lanarkshire Fire Brigade Joint Committee* is another example of the decision of a tribunal being reduced on the ground that, as the committee had not complied with the procedure laid down by statutory regulations, the decision was null and void. I refer to *Smeaton v. Commissioners of Police of St Andrews* because it is an early example of counsel conceding that the Court of Session had no power to review decisions of the commissioners of police acting in the exercise of their statutory powers. Suspension and interdict were refused on the ground that they had not exceeded their powers and that the question of 'necessity' was one which the legislature had committed to the sheriff for his final decision on appeal. I find the case of *Caledonian Railway Co. v. Glasgow Corporation* of particular interest. A statute directed that a register of streets in Glasgow should be prepared in which, inter alia, the width of streets might be entered, and that any proprietor aggrieved by any entry in the register might appeal to the sheriff, whose decision should be final. The pursuers appealed to the sheriff and eo die raised an action of reduction in the Court of Session on the ground that certain entries did not represent the actual widths of the streets. The defenders contended that they were not limited to entering the actual width of streets. The action was dismissed as premature, in respect that the appeal had not been heard by the sheriff, but it is clear that, if the sheriff had dismissed the appeal, the Court of Session would have reduced his decision, and all entries proved to be other than actual widths, on the ground that the defenders, by entering in the register widths which were not actual widths of streets, had not performed their statutory function. The court's decision was that the statutory power of the defenders was limited to entering the actual widths of streets, and that, if they did not exercise their power in this way, they exceeded it and acted ultra vires.

Examples of intra vires error

Against the above examples of ultra vires error, there are many cases in which the Court of Session has held applications for reduction or suspension of decisions of inferior courts and tribunals to be incompetent on the ground that, although the court or tribunal may have 'gone' wrong, i.e., come to the wrong decision by misapplying a statutory word or phrase, it had nevertheless exercised its jurisdiction in strict conformity with the terms of the statute which conferred it, and, therefore, had not 'done' wrong. The first of these is *Simpson v. Harley*, in which the court held that the application of the statutory phrase 'carried for sale' to the facts of the case was a matter which the statute had committed exclusively to the sheriff, and therefore precluded the Court of Session from examining the question of whether he had correctly applied that phrase to the facts of the case. The Lord Justice-Clerk (Boyle) said this, at p. 979: 'It is said, however, there has been excess of power. But what does the alleged excess amount to? To nothing more than that the judge has put an erroneous construction on the statute. Now, assuming that he has done so, that is merely an error in judgment, and not excess of power.' In other words the court held that the error alleged was an intra vires error, which the court had no power to correct. In *Leith Police Commissioners v. Campbell*, the Court of Session dismissed as incompetent an action for reduction of a finding, made by the sheriff in the exercise of statutory powers, that a street was not a private street. The pursuers averred that, according to the true intent and meaning of the statute, the street in question was a private street. The court held that the statute had committed to the sheriff, and to the sheriff alone, to decide whether a street was a public or private one, and that, whether or not his decision was right, he had exercised the statutory power or jurisdiction conferred upon him to decide that question. This is a very different situation from the *Caledonian Railway Company* case, in which the statute limited the power of Glasgow corporation to insert in the register of streets actual widths only. Their action involved altering the plain meaning of the statute from 'actual widths' to 'widths, which need not be the actual widths'.

In *Milne & Co. v. Aberdeen District Committee* Lord McLaren remarked (1899) 7 S.L.T. at p. 262]: 'But if … the grounds of judgment as disclosed in the interlocutor are such as to show that all the points arising in the case have been fairly considered and dealt with, then it is not a good ground of reduction that the Sheriff has not taken the view of the application of the statute which we might possibly be disposed to take'.

The decision in *Robson v. Menzies* rested upon the proper construction of statutory grounds of appeal, but *Don Brothers, Buist & Co. v. Scottish National Insurance Commissioners* seems to me to be in point. There the pursuers contended that the defenders had wrongly construed the undefined statutory phrase 'the right of remuneration per working day', but the court held that this was a question which the statute required the commissioners to determine, and that, whether they had answered it correctly or wrongly, they had not acted ultra vires. It appears from the opinion of the Lord Ordinary (Hunter), at 1913 S.C. 610, that there was more than one method of calculating the rate of remuneration for a working day, and he observed: 'Now, it appears to me that, if two constructions of the language of Part I, in the Second Schedule are possible, the Legislature has entrusted the Commissioners with the duty of interpreting the language and it is not for me to interfere even if I were of opinion that they had reached a wrong conclusion'.

Submissions by counsel for the pursuer

Counsel for the pursuer argued that the Lord Ordinary and the Lord President in *Don Brothers, Buist & Co*. had rested their decision on the fallacious analogy of arbitration, but the decision seems to me to be consistent with the earlier decisions on intra vires errors, made within the limits of the statutory jurisdiction. However, counsel for the pursuer founded on two cases which he maintained illustrated the exercise by the Court of Session of a power to correct intra vires errors. The first is *Mitchell v. Morrison*, in which the statute expressly provided for application to the Court of Session by aggrieved persons for redress by way of summary complaint. Standing the existence of this statutory power of review, the dispute was whether a bill of advocation was a competent mode of review. There is reference in the opinion of the court, at p. 232, to advocation being a mode competent at common law to review decisions of quarter-sessions, but this early 19th-century practice affords me no guidance in this case. The decision upon which counsel for the pursuer pinned their faith was *Pryde v. Heritors and Kirk-Session of Ceres*, in which a majority of the whole court held that it was competent for the Court of Session to review determinations of the heritors and kirk-session of a parish in regard to the amount of aliment awarded to paupers. I need not recite from any opinions delivered in that case, because the special nature of parochial boards is clearly illustrated by Lord Fullerton, one of the majority in the *Pryde* case in *Edinburgh and Glasgow Railway Co. v. Meek*, where he said (at pp. 158–9): '[The parochial board] form a body, who by statute are entitled to levy money from the rate-payers, on certain principles laid down in the statute, and to distribute it among persons having claims as paupers. If any one considers himself aggrieved, he proceeds against them, not as against a Court who have gone wrong, which would be absurd, but as against a party who has done wrong, and who in that character is amenable to the proper tribunal' (i.e., the Court of Session). The observations of Lord Cockburn, at p. 557 of the *Pryde* case, upon which counsel for the pursuer particularly founded, must be read in the limited context of the power to review alimentary determinations of heritors and kirk-sessions. It may be of significance that sheriffs had no power to interfere with such alimentary determinations (see Lord Fullerton at p. 574). This may explain why the Court of Session originally undertook this jurisdiction. In these circumstances I do not regard the fact that the Court of Session may have exercised a comprehensive corrective jurisdiction over determinations of parochial aid in the 18th and early 19th centuries as demonstrating that I have power to correct an intra vires error made by a national insurance commissioner in the due performance of his statutory duties. Indeed my examination of the authorities above cited leads me to the conclusion that the Court of Session has no such power. I must, therefore, consider the argument that the commissioner in this case exceeded his powers, which would render his decision, not only wrong, but null.

Before I do that, however, I would refer to the case of *Anisminic v. Foreign Compensation Commission*, in which the House of Lords, by a majority of one, held that the respondents had committed an ultra vires error which rendered their decision null. I find the ratio decidendi in a passage from the speech of Lord Wilberforce at p. 214: 'In my opinion Article 4 should be read as if it imposed three conditions only on satisfaction of which the applicant was entitled, under statutory direction, to have his claim admitted, namely — (a) that his application relates to property in Egypt referred to in Annex E; (b) that he was the person referred to in Annex E paragraph (1) (*a*) as the owner of the property; (c) that he was a British national at the specified dates. As *ex concessis*, all these conditions were fulfilled, to the satisfaction of the Commission, the appellant's claim was in law established; the Commission by seeking to impose another condition, not warranted by the Order, was acting outside its remitted powers and made no determination of that which it alone could determine. Indeed one might almost say, conversely, that having been satisfied of the three conditions, the Commission has, in law, however it described its actions, determined the claim to have been established'. At p. 171 Lord Reid cited examples of a tribunal doing or failing to do something in the course of its inquiry which is of such a nature that its decision is a nullity. 'It may have given its decision in bad faith. It may have made a decision which it had no power to make. It may have failed in the course of the inquiry to comply with the requirements of natural justice. It may in perfect good faith have misconstrued the provisions giving it power to act so that it failed to deal with the question to act so that it failed to deal with the question remitted to it and decided some question which was not remitted to it. It may have refused to take into account something which it was required to take into account. Or it may have based its decision on some matter which, under the provisions setting it up, it had no right to take into account. I do not intend this list to be exhaustive. But if it decides a question remitted to it for decision without committing any of these errors, it is as much entitled to decide that question wrongly as it is to decide it rightly'.

Counsel for the pursuer submitted that this case fell within the principles laid down in *Anisminic* in respect that (a) the commissioner had taken into account matters which he should not have taken into account, and (b) he had asked the wrong question. It is, however, to be noticed that Lord Reid does not suggest that (a) necessarily renders the decision a nullity. In this context he said: 'Or it may have based its decision on some matters which, *under the provisions setting it up*, it had no right to take into account'. The emphasis is mine. As regards (b), Lord Reid does not suggest that a decision will necessarily be rendered null by the tribunal having asked the wrong question. This results only if the question which it answers 'was not remitted to it'. In my opinion, the reference in the speech of Lord Pearce, at p. 195, to 'wrong questions' must be read subject to the same qualification, because it is only then that it steps outside its jurisdiction.

Decision of commissioner

...

As I read the commissioner's findings, the relevant trade dispute between the craftsmen at Dumbarton and the employers was settled by agreement on 6 December 1974, whereby these craftsmen received the same increase as had been granted to Cumbernauld craftsmen in October. By separate agreement between the union and employers on 12 December 1974 the storemen at Dumbarton were given the same wage increases as the storemen at Cumbernauld had received in October. The cogent argument proposed by counsel for the pursuer was that the terms of the settlement of the craftsmen's dispute at Dumbarton did not, either directly or indirectly, alter any of the pursuer's terms or conditions of employment, and that accordingly he had no direct interest in that dispute. In my opinion the point becomes confined to the proper construction of 'the trade dispute'. Is it to be read literally so that the pursuer's interest in it may be related to any aspect of it, including its termination per se, on whatever terms? If so, I should have thought that the pursuer's interest in it was a direct one. Or is to be read in what I regard as a narrower sense, so that the pursuer cannot be considered to have a direct interest in it unless its subject-matter was such that the terms of its settlement were likely to affect directly, in this case, the pursuer's wages. In s. 22 (6) 'trade dispute' is defined as 'any dispute between employers and employees ... which is connected with the employment or non-employment or the terms of employment or the conditions of employment of any persons', but this definition does not assist me to solve the point at issue.

It is plain to me that the commissioner considered that the existence of this trade dispute was the only matter which prevented the Dumbarton storemen from, not only returning to work, but also obtaining the increase in wages which the Cumbernauld storemen had been given in October. He therefore found that its existence directly affected the amount of the pursuer's wages, and that the pursuer, therefore, had a direct interest in it. In para. 13 of the decision the commissioner makes it clear that he regarded the separate agreement on 12 December about the pursuer's wages as a formality, which must inevitably follow the termination of the craftsmen's dispute. Contrary to the submission of counsel for the pursuer, I do not find in the commissioner's statement of his decision any clear indication that he confined the pursuer's direct interest in the Dumbarton dispute to its termination per se. In my opinion, the fair reading of his statement is that the Dumbarton dispute would probably be, as it in fact was, ultimately settled on the same terms as the Cumbernauld agreement, and that the pursuer had a direct interest in the Dumbarton dispute during its subsistence because, if its settlement produced the same increase of wages for the Dumbarton craftsmen as had been granted to the Cumbernauld craftsmen in October (as, on my reading of the decision, it did), that settlement would result in the pursuer obtaining the same increase in wages as had been granted to the Cumbernauld storemen in October, although that increase would have to be incorporated in a separate agreement for the storemen. If I have correctly interpreted the reasons for his decision, it is not necessarily inconsistent with his fellow commissioners' interpretation of 'direct interest'. In these circumstances I am by no means certain that the commissioner misapplied any of the terms of s. 22 of the 1965 Act to the facts which he found proved, or even that he drew a wrong inference from the facts found by him. In any event, upon the assumption that he did either of these things, I am certain that he applied his mind to the correct questions and acted in every way within his powers. It cannot be said (although it was) that 'the Commissioner did not apply his mind properly to the correct construction of "directly interested"'. He plainly did so, and, at best (or worst) for the pursuer, misapplied it to the facts, thereby committing, what Lord President Boyle described in *Simpson v. Harley*, cit. supra, as 'an error in judgment'.

The necessarily microscopic examination of the written decision of the commissioner, which was conducted in order to demonstrate where and how the commissioner had 'gone' wrong, convinced me that this action, although presented in the form of a case for the exercise of the supervisory powers of the Court of Session, was truly an appeal on a point of law. If the Court of Session were to assume jurisdiction to conduct detailed inquiry into decisions raising such a narrow issue as the one in this case, it would be tantamount to allowing appeals, not only to the Outer House of the Court of Session but ultimately to the House of Lords, against decisions which the legislature has declared to be final and excluded from the ambit of s. 9 (1) of the Tribunals and Inquiries Act 1958 (now s. 13 of the 1971 Act). The legislature might have seen fit to give to national insurance commissioners the power to state a case for the opinion of the Court of Session on a question of law, but it has not done so. Instead it has directed, in s. 70 (3) of the 1965 Act, that appeals which involved 'a question of law of special difficulty' may be dealt with by a tribunal of three commissioners, and declared in s. 75 (1) that the decision of any claim or question in accordance with the provisions of the act 'shall be final'. I am therefore of the opinion that Parliament did not intend the kind of question which has arisen in this case to be considered by the Court of Session. It is a narrow and difficult question, and, in my opinion, Parliament was content to leave the commissioners, who are I believe, all experienced lawyers, to build up their own case in law on the interpretation of the Acts within their jurisdiction. Decisions produced by exceeding or misinterpreting their statutory powers may be reduced as nullities, but decisions reached in strict accordance with their statutory powers are, in my opinion, sacrosanct, although they may have wrongly applied statutory words or phrases to the facts.

Counsel for the pursuer submitted that this view would result in the English High Court, by virtue of the prerogative writs, having wider powers of review than the Court of Session. I have not attempted to examine the scope of the English prerogative writs, because it is not within my power to do so, but I take leave to doubt the validity of counsel's submission. He submitted that, on the view which I have taken of the limited power of the Court of Session to review decisions of national insurance commissioners, the Court of Session would be unable to provide a remedy in a case such as *Punton v. Ministry of Pensions and National Insurance*, where the plaintiffs sought a declaration that, contrary to the decision of the national insurance commissioner, they were entitled to unemployment benefit as not being 'directly interested in' the relevant trade dispute. Although the court refused to grant the declaration sought, it was conceded that the plaintiffs had had the right to proceed by certiorari. If they had done so, it seems plain to me that the High Court would have confirmed the decision of the commissioner (see [1963] 1 W.L.R. per Phillimore J., at pp. 1190–1, and Sellers L.J. [1964] 1 W.L.R. at pp. 238–9). That case is not, therefore, an example of English procedure operating for the benefit of a claimant. Moreover, I am doubtful if there are many cases in which the process of certiorari would result in decisions being quashed on the ground of error on the face of the record which would not be reduced by the Court of Session in the exercise of its supervisory jurisdiction. The distinction between correcting errors which appear on the face of the record and errors in statutory construction which are held to be ultra vires may well be more apparent than real (see e.g. *R. v. Industrial Injuries Commissioner*), where reference is made to a "real" error of law. I may express the opinion that real (see e.g. *R. v. Industrial Injuries Commissioner*), where reference is made to a 'real' error of law, I may express the opinion that, on the facts of *R. v. Northumberland Compensation Appeal Tribunal*, I should have held that the tribunal had committed an ultra vires error by misinterpreting its powers. Being bound by the statutory definition of the word 'service', the tribunal in that case erroneously restricted its application to service with the hospital board, instead of including the whole period of the applicant's local government service. I consider this error to be analogous to that made by Glasgow corporation when, in construing 'widths' as including 'other than actual widths' they were held to have exceeded their statutory powers. Moreover, cases such as the *Caledonian Railway Co. v. Glasgow Corporation* and *Hayman v. Lord Advocate* suggest that the supervisory power of the Court of Session goes deeper than the law of the certiorari, if that is confined to correcting errors which appear on the face of the record, in respect that relevant averments of a body exceeding its statutory powers will warrant an inquiry by the Court of Session into all the relevant facts of the case, whether or not they appear on the record of the proceedings. The case of *Punton*, cit. supra., seems to me to illustrate that the English declaratory proceedings, as an alternative to certiorari, create difficulties which would not arise in Scotland.

Conclusions

In my opinion, the commissioner did not commit an ultra vires error. It is therefore unnecessary, and indeed incompetent, for me to decide whether or not he correctly applied the relevant terms of the statute to the facts stated by him. If there was an intra vires error, it is not one which warrants reduction in terms of the first plea-in-law for the pursuer. I shall therefore repel all three of the pursuer's pleas-in-law. I shall also repel the first, fifth and sixth pleas-in-law for the defender, but sustain the second, third, fourth, seventh and eighth pleas-in-law for the defender and dismiss the action."

The pursuer reclaimed.

Watt v. Lord Advocate

4–13

1979 S.L.T. 137

LORD PRESIDENT (EMSLIE): "In this case what is contended by the pursuer is that on a fair reading of the commissioner's decision he proceeded to find against him upon a misunderstanding of the words 'directly interested in the trade despite' and, in particular, that he laboured under a construction of these words which I have just held to be wholly erroneous. For the Lord Advocate counsel argued that it is not clear that he so construed the proviso, that the decision is not to be read as a full statement of his reasons with appeal in mind, and that, when it is fairly read, it can be seen that the commissioner appears to have found that the claimant was not only affected by the existence of the dispute but directly affected by the terms on which it was settled.

In approaching the question for his determination the commissioner does not tell us what he understood the critical words to mean. In posing the sole question he merely quoted them. It is accordingly necessary to read his answer to that question to see whether, as the pursuer contended, he understood them. I have read the decision, which was analysed with care on both sides of the Bar, many times, and I am left in no doubt that the sold ground of the decision adverse to the pursuer was that he was affected by the existence of the craftsmen's dispute in the sense that as the Lord Ordinary put it: 'the existence of this trade dispute was the only matter which prevented the Dumbarton storeman from not only returning to work but also obtaining the increase in wages which the Cumbernauld storemen had been given in October.' There is no trace anywhere in the decision of any finding that the pursuer was likely to be affected by the particular outcome of that dispute or that the attitude of the management to the question of future wages of the pursuer was depended upon the particular terms on which their dispute with the craftsmen, acting quite unofficially, was brought to an end. There is no suggestion in this case that there was only a finite sum available to the management to pay the wages of its entire work force at Dumbarton once the craftsmen's dispute had ended and I have not the slightest doubt that if the particular formula upon which the settlement of that dispute might be ended had been at all relevant to the formation of the attitude of the management to the future wage negotiations on behalf of the hourly-paid workers at Dumbarton this learned commissioner would certainly have said so in terms. He did not do so. He does not even mention precisely what it was that the craftsmen wanted, nor does he say anything about any terms upon which there was the slightest chance of the management conceding settlement, and I am quite unable and unwilling to infer from all that he has told us that his decision rested on anything other than that the mere existence of the craftsmen's dispute was the sole obstacle to the resumption of work by the Dumbarton storemen and obtaining the same wages as had been already agreed for their counterparts at Cumbernauld. If I am correct in so saying it is clear that the commissioner can only have reached his decision upon a misunderstanding of the proviso and what it was that the pursuer required to prove in order to be relieved of disqualification under s. 22 (1).

The next question is whether the decision of the commissioner was, by reason of that misconstruction, ultra vires. If it was, the finality provisions of s. 75 (1) do not in any way affect the undoubted jurisdiction of this court to reduce it and this is very properly conceded by counsel for the Lord Advocate. I approach this question on the assumption, for the moment, that if the error of construction was one which it was within his power to commit his decision would not be open to review in this or any other court. In the case of a statutory tribunal in which Parliament has conferred power and exclusive jurisdiction to carry out particular functions defined by statute it may often be far from easy, as the learned Dean of Faculty reminded us, to ascertain the extent of the interpretatory power conferred upon the tribunal and in particular to see clearly whether this question or that question of construction of statutory provisions is within the tribunal's field or whether, as Lord Wilberforce said in his speech in *Anisminic v. Foreign Compensation Commissioners* at p. 209, 'because it pertains to the delimitation of the tribunal's area by the legislature, it is reserved for decision by the courts'. As many cases show — and the Lord Ordinary has cited a number of them — not every misconstruction of a statutory provision by a statutory tribunal in the course of reaching its decision will render that decision a nullity and the answer to the question whether a particular question of construction by such a tribunal in a particular case has or has not been confided exclusively to the tribunal can in general only be determined by discovering from the statute itself the extent of the tribunal's powers and jurisdiction.

In this case, said the learned Dean of Faculty, the power of the commissioner is contained in s. 67(1) of the Act which, so far as it is relevant, provides as follows: 'Subject to the provisions of this Act any question arising under this Act: (*a*) as to the right to benefit … shall be determined … by … the National Insurance Commissioner'. Accordingly, so ran the argument, such interpretation of the provisions of the Act as is necessary to enable the commissioner to determine a question as to a right to benefit is a matter for the commissioner alone, and his decision is equally valid whether it is right or wrong on the assumption that right of review of that decision by the courts has been excluded. In the case of the particular question of construction with which this reclaiming motion is concerned I cannot agree that it was one which it was open to the commissioner to misconstrue. The general directive of the Act relating to unemployment benefit is that every person shall be entitled to it in respect of any day of unemployment if he satisfies the requirements of s. 19 (2) and (3) (as in this case the pursuer did). Section 22 (1) then proceeds to disqualify those who have lost employment by reason of a stoppage of work which was due to a trade dispute at his place of employment but, as s. 22 (1) as a whole demonstrates, it was Parliament's clear intention that this disqualification should not apply to any person who proves the particular things set out in the proviso. In the case of the pursuer it was matter of concession from the time he made his claim that he neither participated in nor financed the craftsmen's dispute and that he did not belong to a grade or class of workers of which, at the relevant time, there were members employed at his place of employment any of whom were participating in or financing or directly interested in that dispute. The only question at issue on which his right to unemployment benefit depended was whether he was able to prove that he was not 'directly interested in' the trade dispute involving the craftsmen and the management. This was the test by which alone, in this case, Parliament intended his right to benefit to be determined, and in the events which happened there came before the commissioner a single question for his determination namely, whether the pursuer had proved that he was not 'directly interested in' the trade dispute involving the craftsmen. This was the question and the only question relating to the pursuer's right to benefit which it was within the power and duty of the commissioner to determine under s. 67 (1) of the Act, and once that is clearly understood, and then it is appreciated that what is in issue in this case is a misconstruction of the only question which he commissioner had power to determine, it is as plain as plain can be that he addressed himself in the result to, and answered, the wrong question, and decided against the pursuer because he had not passed a test other than set for him by Parliament. In these circumstances, in my judgment, he clearly exceeded his powers. There can be no doubt that when a statutory tribunal, which quite properly enters upon an inquiry which it has jurisdiction to carry out, misconstrues the question which it is required to answer and decides some other question which was not remitted to it, its decision will be a nullity. If authority for this proposition is necessary it can be found in cases such as *Hayman v. Lord Advocate* and more recently in the House of Lords in the case of *Anisminic*. I content myself by quoting at this point mainly from the speech of Lord Reid, at p. 171: 'It has sometimes been said that it is only where a tribunal acts without jurisdiction that its decision is a nullity. But in such cases the word "jurisdiction" has been used in a very wide sense, and I have come to the conclusion that it is better not to use the term except in the narrow and original sense of the tribunal being entitled to enter on the inquiry in question. But there are many cases where, although the tribunal had jurisdiction to enter on the inquiry, it has done or failed to do something in the course of the inquiry which is of such a nature that its decision is a nullity. It may have given its decision in bad faith. It may have made a decision which it had no power to make. It may have failed in the course of the inquiry to comply with the requirements of natural justice. It may in perfect good faith have misconstrued the provisions giving it power to act so that it failed to deal with the question remitted to it and decided some question which was not remitted to it. It may have refused to take into account something which it was required to take into account. Or it may have based its decision on some matter which, under the provisions setting it up, it had no right to take into account. I do not intend this list to be exhaustive. But if it decides a question remitted to it for decision without committing any of these errors it is as much entitled to decide that question wrongly as it is to decide it rightly.' Lord Pearce, at p. 195, speaks to the same effect where he says: '… while engaged on a proper inquiry the tribunal … may ask itself the wrong questions; or it may take into account matters which it was not directed to take into account. Thereby it would step outside its jurisdiction. It would turn its inquiry into something not directed by Parliament and fail to make the inquiry which Parliament did direct. Any of these things would cause its purported decision to be a nullity."

This case is not one in which the commissioner misconstrued certain statutory provisions in the course of attempting to answer the right question remitted for his decision. He misconstrued that very question itself and answered a different question as a result of his error. For these reasons I am persuaded that the pursuer is well founded in his contention that the decision of the commissioner was ultra vires and that the Lord Ordinary's interlocutor cannot stand. I would accordingly allow the reclaiming motion, sustain the second and third pleas-in-law for the pursuer and grant decree of reduction in terms of the conclusions.

Although it is now unnecessary for me to express a concluded view upon the minor and alternative proposition for the pursuer I feel bound to say that if, as I have held, the commissioner's decision proceeded upon an error of law, and if that error did not render his decision a nullity, I have the gravest doubt whether this court would have had power to review it. Leaving on one side the finality provisions of s. 75 (1) it seems clear that, however much this is to be regretted, the Court of Session has never had power to correct an intra vires error of law made by a statutory tribunal or authority exercising statutory jurisdiction. As Lord Justice-Clerk Moncreiff said in *Lord Advocate v. Police Commissioners of Perth*, at p. 245: 'In the ordinary case it would now, I think, be held that where statutory powers are given, and a statutory jurisdiction is set up, all other jurisdictions are excluded …'. There is no indication in any subsequent authority that this view has been doubted or even questioned and I entirely agree with the Lord Ordinary for the reasons which he gives that the fact that the Court of Session may have exercised a comprehensive corrective jurisdiction over determinations of parochial aid in the 18th and early 19th centuries does not in any way support the existence of a jurisdiction in this court to correct errors by a statutory tribunal in the due performance of its statutory duties.

I cannot leave this case without expressing my regret that whereas it appears that the High Court in England still has, in spite of the provisions of s. 75 (1) of the National Insurance Act 1965, jurisdiction in procedure by way of the prerogative writ of certiorari to correct errors of law by National Insurance Commissioners which appear on the face of the record, the Court of Session has no such power. It can hardly be suggested that it is in the best interests of statutory tribunals themselves that recourse to the appellant courts of the United Kingdom to determine difficult questions of law authoritatively should not be available in both of the great jurisdictions."

R. J. Reed, "Judicial Review of Error of Law"

1979 S.L.T. (News) 241 at 243

"The Scottish background

4–14   In Scots law the courts have no power to review a decision made intra vires, even if it involves an error of law. This is clearly established by the authorities (e.g. *Don Brothers, Buist & Co. Ltd v. Scottish National Insurance Commissioners*, 1913 1 S.L.T. 221; *Smeaton v. Commissioners of Police of St Andrews* (1865) 3 M. 816), despite speculative arguments based on *Pryde v. Heritors and Kirk-Session of Ceres* (1843) 5 D. 552 (a decision whose ratio depends on the special nature of parochial boards, as explained by Lord Fullerton in *Edinburgh & Glasgow Railway Co. v. Meek* (1849) 12 D. 153).

Some examples of intervention may be given. In *Caledonian Railway Co. v. Glasgow Corporation* (1905) 7 F. 1020 the corporation was empowered to enter the width of streets on a register. Planning permission would not be granted without special consent where the building would reduce the width of the street. The corporation entered target widths greater than the actual widths. It was held to be doing something quite different from what the statue directed. In *Bennett v. Scottish Board of Health*, 1921 S.C. 772 the court was willing to determine whether a committee set up to hear complaints about 'medical attendance and treatment' could hear a complaint about a doctor's abusive language during a visit: the committee's jurisdiction depended on the meaning of the statutory phrase. Finally, in *Hayman v. Lord Advocate*, 1952 S.L.T. 209 the approval of opticians depended (a) on their holding prescribed diplomas or being on an older approved list, and (b) on a finding by a committee that they had 'adequate, including recent experience'. Lord Cooper said that if the committee had investigated the pursuer's professional rectitude and the nature of his premises, instead of investigating whether he had recently utilised the prescribed qualifications so as to be a sufficiently experienced practitioner, then they had 'acted illegally by applying their minds to the wrong question and thus in effect acting *ultra vires compromissi*' ... .

The Watt decision

The facts of the case were as follows. All the staff at a factory were laid off for some months because of an unofficial dispute between skilled craftsmen and the management. Throughout this period the union had been negotiating a wage increase for all the employees, but this could not be accepted until work had been resumed. A settlement was eventually reached between the craftsmen and the management, everyone went back to work, and a few days later the increase offered to all the staff was accepted. The pursuer, an unskilled worker, was refused unemployment benefit for the period he was laid off, on the ground that he was 'directly interested in the trade dispute which caused the stoppage of work', since the sooner the dispute ended the sooner he would get a wage increase.

In the Outer House (1977 S.L.T. 130) Lord Dunpark distinguished between cases where 'misapplication of the statutory words or phrases to the facts of the case has produced a wrong answer' and cases where 'the misconstruction of statutory words or phrases per se has plainly resulted in the determining body exercising a power which it did not have'. The latter was a question of law which the court might review; but the former was a question of mixed fact and law in which the court had no power to intervene. It is difficult to see how this test is to be applied. If the committee in *Bennett* had decided that the complaint did not relate to 'treatment', did its error arise from the misapplication of the word to the facts, or from the misconstruction of the word per se? The distinction is arguably non-existent (the separability of meaning and use being one of the unresolved problems of linguistic philosophy) and certainly unhelpful.

Lord Dunpark purported to apply *Anisminic*, which he interpreted in a similar way to Geoffrey Lane L.J. in *Pearlman*. Referring to the speech of Lord Reid, he emphasised that for a decision to be invalid the tribunal must have based the decision on matters which 'under the provisions setting it up' it had no right to take into account, or must have answered not merely the wrong question but a question which 'was not remitted to it'. This seems to mean that if the statute poses a certain question, then the tribunal can interpret that question however it likes, so long as it does not answer another question. The *Caledonian Railway* case indicates that this is a question of degree, the test perhaps being that it could not reasonably be adopted by a tribunal acquainted with the ordinary use of language. Lord Dunpark gave another reason for his decision. The case raised such a narrow and difficult question that it was not truly an application for review, but an appeal on a point of law.

On appeal, this decision was reversed. Unlike Lord Dunpark, the First Division were in no doubt that the legislation had been misconstrued. This meant that the commissioner's decision was inconsistent with those of other commissioners — again, a finding not made by Lord Dunpark. The question then was whether the error went to jurisdiction. The court held that it did: 'once ... it is appreciated that what is in issue in this case is a misconstruction of the only question which the commissioner had power to determine, it is as plain as plain can be that he addressed himself in the result to, and answered, the wrong question, and decided against the pursuer because he had not passed a test other than that set for him by Parliament' (per Lord Emslie).

At the same time, Lord Emslie reaffirmed that the Court of Session had no power to correct an error of law within jurisdiction, and distinguished between cases in which the commissioner misconstrued statutory provisions in the course of answering the question remitted to him and cases where the question itself had been misconstrued so that a different question had been answered. This raises the same problem as the judgment of Eveleigh L.J. in *Pearlman*: any error of law, it appears, can be treated as jurisdictional by manipulating phraseology. In practice a distinction will be drawn; and one returns to Lord Wilberforce's dictum that it will be a functional distinction grounded in the nature of the tribunal's task. As Lord Dunpark emphasised, the jurisdiction of the courts is supervisory. They must not become courts of appeal from specialised tribunals whose decisions Parliament has declared final. It is perhaps inevitable that Lord Emslie's test should hover between the circumspect and the unsurprising: 'The answer to the question whether a particular question of construction by such a tribunal in a particular case has or has not been confided exclusively to the tribunal can in general only be determined by discovering from the statute itself the extent of the tribunal's powers and jurisdiction.'

Differences between the jurisdictions

Lord Emslie expressed his regret in *Watt* that the Court of Session had no power to correct intra vires errors of law. However, an examination of both jurisdictions suggests that Lord Dunpark was correct in doubting whether there are many situations in which decisions would be quashed in England for error on the face of the record and yet be beyond the intervention of the Court of Session. Lord Dunpark said that if the *Northumberland* case (*R. v. Northumberland Compensation Appeal Tribunal ex parte Shaw* [1952] 1 K.B. 338, in which this ground of review was established) had come before him he would have held that the tribunal had made an ultra vires error by misinterpreting its powers; and there can be little doubt that if the case had come up after *Anisminic* it would have been treated in the same way without having to resurrect peculiarities of certiorari. If the (discretionary) power to quash errors on the face of the record is to be used to supervise specialised tribunals only where the error is clear and important or has led to inconsistent decisions, then it adds little if anything to the powers possessed by the Court of Session."

Notes

4–15   (1) The views of Lord Dunpark are particularly helpful insofar as they provide a useful summary of situations which have held to amount to error of law and those which have not. For further examples see *Stair Memorial Encyclopaedia*, Vol. 1, para. 288.

(2) Note Reed's comment that "any error of law, it appears, can be treated as jurisdictional by manipulating phraseology".

Do you agree with this? What seems to have been a particular concern to the Inner House was the failure of the Commissioner to exercise properly his jurisdiction delegated to him. He did not ask the question set by the legislation as to whether or not the pursuer was "directly interested in a trade dispute". What seems to underlie the approach adopted by both Lord Dunpark and the Inner House is a view of the function of both the decision-making body and the court. In Lord Dunpark's view, not only was the Commissioner entitled to reach a wrong decision, but the pursuer was not entitled to convert judicial review proceedings into appellate proceedings. (Note now that section 15 of the Social Security Act 1998, which is to replace its predecessor, section 14 of the Social Security Act 1980, provides a right of appeal from a decision of a Social Security Commissioner on a point of law). The Inner House did not accept that it was being asked to exercise an appellate function. That this was so was borne out by the finding of the court that the Commissioner had misconstrued the only question which he was required to consider. The complex issues detected by Lord Dunpark and which in his view converted the proceedings into an appeal, were not present in the view of the Inner House. This echoes the approach of L.Jaffe in his 1957 article, "Judicial Review: Constitutional and Jurisdictional Fact", in 70 Harv.L.Rev. 953 and also his *Judicial Control of Administrative Action* (1958), pp. 631–633. This was equally applicable to questions of jurisdictional facts and those of law and recognised that, typically, a grant of power is specific at some points but less so at others. The specific grant of power can be regarded as jurisdictional, the latter cannot. The line between the two is itself blurred and depends on the interpretation of the statute granting the power. In turn this depends on the legal structure and status of the administrative body being considered, the context in which the issue arises or the nature of the remedy sought. Jurisdiction is regarded as functional, that is it is "used to validate review when review is felt to be necessary"; see above at 963 and p. 633. See also by the same author, "Judicial Review: Questions of Law" 69 Harv.L.Rev. 239 (1955) and "Judicial Review: Questions of Fact" 69 Harv.L.R. 1020 (1956).

The question of "direct interest" might be regarded as a specific matter, the need for consistency detected by the Inner House, but not by Lord Dunpark, as a matter of context, and the lack of an alternative remedy by way of an appeal, a question of structure and status requiring a remedy, namely judicial review. This may assist in deciding in what circumstances a court would be prepared to interfere. *Watt* itself is an example of the use of an ouster clause. Consider also *Anisminic* in this connection and the cases noted in Chapter 10 in relation to ineffective alternative remedies and *London and Clydeside Estates Ltd v. Aberdeen District Council*, at para. 11–17, in relation to the remedy of reduction. Consider too those cases where the court was not prepared to interfere, such as *Council of Civil Service Unions v. Minister for the Civil Service*, at para. 10–10, on grounds of justiciability and *Martin v. Bearsden and Milngavie District Council*, at para. 10–40, another ouster clause case. This seems to suggest that a degree of autonomy is granted to administrative action which in its context is a reasonable attempt to exercise the power or jurisdiction conferred and that reasonableness rather than correctness is made the criterion by which judicial intervention is measured.

(3) Lord Emslie had cause to reconsider his approach in *Wordie Property Co. v. Secretary of State for Scotland*, 1984 S.L.T. 345 at 347–438 where jurisdictional control was expressed as being reliant "upon a material error of law going to the root of the question for determination". This seems to be another way of emphasising that error of law in itself it is not enough to justify judicial intervention, even in the context of the statutory appeal which was being determined in *Wordie*. Both *Watt* and *Wordie* came to be considered by the court in *West v. Secretary of State for Scotland*, at para. 10–7. The basis of judicial intervention in *West* is that of "excess or abuse of jurisdiction". An error of law must amount to one of these for it to be reviewable. Lord Emslie had seemed to suggest in *Wordie* that the concept of error of law was based on exclusive categories — for example, taking into account irrelevant considerations or leaving out of account relevant considerations, or there being no proper basis of fact for a decision or a decision being unreasonable; see above. As the Lord President (Hope) observed in *West*, however (at 651):

> "The categories of what may amount to an excess of abuse of jurisdiction are not closed, and they are capable of being adapted in accordance with the development of administrative law."

P. Gilmore, "Judicial Review of Errors of Law", 1993 S.L.T. (News) 371 at 375 notes:

> "This makes sense. To require a petitioner in a judicial review or a pursuer in a statutory appeal, where statute does not require him to do so, to slot his case into the categories of error in law, procedural impropriety or unreasonableness can have some strange results. For example, Lord Emslie's formula in *Wordie* can lead to a decision being attacked on the ground that the decision maker took irrelevant matters into account. But that 'error' may not necessarily lead to the decision being one so unreasonable that no reasonable decision maker properly directing himself to the matter before him would have reached."

4–16

By way of an example he refers to the decision in *Gordon* below and notes that:

> "by concentrating overmuch on 'error in law' the court failed properly to address the argument that the waste was perfectly capable of being treated as 'trade waste' under s 124 on the facts before the court — namely, that the waste arose through the presence of a commercially owned caravan site being operated in a normal commercial manner."

(4) The approach in *Watt* has been followed in a number of cases:

- In *Re EK v. Secretary of State for the Home Department*, March 11, 1988, unreported it was held that an immigration tribunal had applied the wrong test in deciding whether or not a person was under fear of persecution in his own country. The tribunal had asked itself whether the petitioner was "personally marked out for persecution", rather than the test set out in para. 165 of the then Immigration Rules which provided, *inter alia* that:

> "A deportation order will not be made against a person if the only country to which he can be removed is one to which he is unwilling to go to owing to a well founded fear of being persecuted for reasons of race, religion, nationality, membership of a particular group or political opinion."

- In *Wilson v. Nithsdale District Council*, 1992 S.L.T. 1131 judicial review was sought of the decision of a local authority in deciding that an 18-year-old girl, unable to live at the family home, who had left college and who had been sexually assaulted, had a difficult pregnancy and psychological problems, was not "vulnerable" in terms of section 25(1) of the Housing (Scotland) Act 1987 as she was not at "great risk". The proper test should have been a comparison with the vulnerability of the average homeless person.

- In *Henderson v. Cumnock and Doon Valley District Council*, 1992 S.C.L.R. 489 a planning application was made to the planning authority to reopen a disused quarry which bounded on the petitioner's farm. It was suggested that planning permission for the quarry had already been granted in 1951 but, as no official record was found, it was impossible to state with certainty what area was covered by the original permission or what schemes of work were authorised. The petitioners argued that the planning authority in entertaining the second application had erred in law as, under section 26(1) of the Town and Country Planning (Scotland) Act 1972, they were bound to have regard to all considerations material to the application which included whether or not a grant of permission for the quarry already existed. The court held that no error of law was present. It was for the planning authority to take into account this matter and what weight should be given to it. Provided they did so "they are as much entitled to decide that question wrongly as they are to decide it rightly" (at 496).

*   In *O'Neill v. Scottish Joint Negotiating Committee for Teaching Staff*, 1987 S.L.T. 648 it was contended that a committee, which was in effect an arbitration committee, had erred in its interpretation of one of the conditions of the petitioner's employment. It was observed by Lord Jauncey that by taking into account earlier conditions in determining the present question that "It may be that they misdirected themselves in law in construing condition 29(a) by reference to these matters, but that is not the same as misdirecting themselves as to the question addressed to them."

*   In *Milton v. Argyll and Clyde Health Board*, 1996 S.C.L.R. 1072 it was alleged that the failure of a sheriff to award expenses after a hearing (which was characterised as administrative) because he was unable to find a special circumstance to do so, was an error of law. Lord Gill considered that while the approach taken by the sheriff was not one that he would have followed had he been asked to decide the question, nevertheless the sheriff was still acting within the jurisdiction conferred on him and if there was an error, it was an *intra vires* one.

*   In *Murray v. Social Fund Inspector*, 1996 S.L.T. 38 it was alleged that a social fund inspector had erred in law in failing to consider, on an individual basis, claims from the social fund for payment for specific items of furniture, but instead had relied on a general assessment of need. It was held that no reviewable error of law existed on her interpretation of the relevant sections of the Social Security Contributions and Benefits Act 1992.

(5) In *Morgan Guaranty Trust Co. of New York v. Lothian Regional Council*, 1995 S.L.T. 299 the Lord President (Hope) noted that it was important to ensure that there was consistency as between Scotland and England in the approach to be adopted on the matter of recovery of payments made under an error of law as to the meaning of a general public statute. He noted (at 315) that:

"we will be achieving the same result by reference to the principles of Scots law. I regard that as satisfactory, because it would be inequitable that a remedy which is now available in England in this important field of transactions between the citizen and a public authority should be denied here on the ground that it was not permitted by our law."

One of the reasons the decision at first instance in *Watt* was reclaimed was that it appeared to mean that in Scotland the citizen had fewer rights than his English counterpart. The Lord President in *Watt* expressed regret that the Court of Session had no power to correct *intra vires* errors of law. Although it may be that in many areas in practice, similar results will in any event be reached on either side of the border, so long as the Scottish courts do not follow the approach in *Page*, some meaning must be given to the error of law test. An attempt was made to argue in *Rae* below that in view of *West*, any distinction should no longer be maintained. However, Lord Macfadyen observed (at 295):

"The references in *West* (at p 413 (p 651A–B)) to 'failure to understand the law' and to there being no substantial difference between English law and Scots law as to the grounds of review, are not in my view to be construed as a departure from the rule that review for error of law is available in Scotland only if the error involves excess or abuse of jurisdiction or erroneous refusal to exercise a jurisdiction."

Chapter 5

PROCEDURAL ULTRA VIRES

Action by a public authority which may be substantively valid may nevertheless still be held **5–1** to be invalid if some aspect of that action offends the principles governing procedural challenge. Procedural issues can arise in many ways. For example, a statute may specify the way in which a decision is taken, the time-limits which apply to the decision-making process, the forms of evidence that might be admitted, or the nature of the person or body to whom the decision is ultimately entrusted. The list is not exhaustive but illustrates that the areas in which procedural challenge can arise are very varied indeed. In this chapter we consider the approach taken by the courts in determining whether or not a challenge to a procedural flaw should be upheld. We will go on to examine some of the most important areas in which procedural challenge arises, namely in the area of delegation of authority and consultation procedure.

GENERAL PRINCIPLES

Historically, a distinction has been drawn between breaches of procedural conditions which are **5–2** mandatory and those which are directory. In the former case, breach entails the decision being found to be *ultra vires*; in the latter, any flaw at most is an *intra vires* error. As we shall see, that distinction has been regarded as having less weight in recent case law and at most might be regarded as a convenient way of labelling flaws which have or have not, led to successful procedural challenge. The following extract is illustrative of the circumstances in which procedural challenge might arise.

Moss's Empires Ltd v. Assessor for Glasgow

1917 S.C. (H.L.) 1

EARL LOREBURN: "In this case the facts are extremely short and simple. A property in Glasgow **5–3** was valued at £950 a year, and in the Valuation-roll of the succeeding year it was raised to £1300, but no notice was given by the Assessor to the persons affected, the result of which was they had not a reminder that they could appeal. They did not appeal, and they lost the benefit of the statutory right. Those facts are to be assumed, and the question is whether the parties are to be admitted to proof.

Now, upon that the aggrieved parties come to the Court and ask for two things — in the first place, that the entry should be reduced, and in the second place, that the pre-existing figure should be substituted for the figure of £1300. Those are two quite separate questions, and I deal with the first.

It is said that there is a statutory finality in this Valuation-roll. Whatever finality there be is not created by the general principles of law, but is dependent upon the Act of Parliament in order to see what the nature of this Valuation-roll is, and I shall refer to them a little at length because the question arises as to the meaning of some words that are there used.

The Act says that the magistrates shall annually cause to be made up a Valuation-roll; that they may take the assistance of the officers of Inland Revenue; that in order to making up of such valuation they shall appoint Assessors; that the duty of the Assessors is to ascertain and assess and to make up such Valuation-roll; that a new Valuation-roll is to be made up by the Assessors every year; that the magistrates shall hold a Court for hearing appeals against it, and their deliverances upon such appeals shall be final and conclusive; that all persons who are entered by the Assessor in the Valuation-roll shall be entitled to appeal; that the Valuation-roll when made up by the Assessor is to be retained by him for a certain time; that as soon as the appeals have been heard and the valuation thereby completed, the Valuation-roll shall then be in force; that after the completion of each Valuation-roll the magistrates to cause an account to be made out of the costs; and then there is a provision in regard to mistakes to which I shall have again to refer.

Now, as I understand it, under this Act the making up of the Valuation-roll is the duty of the Assessor; it is the duty of the magistrates to cause a Valuation-roll to be made up. The duty of the Assessor relates to value and entry; the Valuation-roll is completed when the appeals have been disposed of; it then is to be authenticated, and then the Valuation-roll is in force.

Valuation consists in the ascertaining of the rent or value, which is a matter to be determined by evidence, by opinion, by comparison of values, and it is a question of fact. One would expect that a Court of law would not be permitted to inquire into such matters. One would expect also that technical difficulties would not be allowed to interfere with the validity of the Valuation-roll. That is the character of the finality described, in my opinion, by this statute. One would expect that informalities or errors should be declared to be innocuous and to be disregarded, and also that a Court of law should not be permitted to take the duty of valuation upon itself. As a matter of general principle I certainly consider that unless a Court of law is precluded by statute it may reduce any order or assessment which imposes a liability to pay, unless it is made pursuant to the Act of Parliament conferring the right to make it upon those who do make it. But here there is, as one would expect, a provision for finality — that is to say, the provision contained in section 30 of this Act of 1854.

The part of section 30 of this Act which is material says that 'no Valuation-roll which shall be made up and authenticated in terms of this Act, and no valuation which shall be contained therein, shall be challengeable, or be capable of being set aside or rendered ineffectual, by reason of any informality, or of any want of compliance with the provisions of this Act, in the proceedings for making up such valuation or Valuation-roll.'

Now here there has been a non-compliance with the provisions of this Act, because notice has not been given. Was that a non-compliance in the proceeding for making up such valuation or Valuation-roll? I do not think that it was. The making up of the Valuation-roll was the duty of the Assessor, and the non-compliance with the Act was not connected with the duty of the Assessor in making up that Valuation-roll, and therefore, in my opinion, this non-compliance is not protected by the 30th section. It seems to me that if, for example, no Assessor were appointed, or no Court of Appeal were appointed, or no notice were given to the persons entitled to notice, the power of the Court to interpose and to reduce the entry has not been taken away. But the failure to comply with the Act in making up the Roll — that is to say, in the Assessor discharging his duty in that respect — could not be considered by the Court.

That seems to me to support entirely the decision of the Inner House in reducing this entry. I do not deal with the ulterior question whether the assessment of the previous year ought to be restored, because that question may never arise; it may appear upon the trial that notice was given, and we ought not to adjudicate upon a hypothesis which may never be realised. The argument of the Dean of Faculty was that we could not reduce an unlawful entry because we are not able to put anything in its place. I hope it may appear that something can be put in its place if necessary but, whether that be so or be not so, it is not right that an unlawful entry should be permitted to remain upon the Roll."

VISCOUNT HALDANE: "I have arrived at the same conclusion as my noble and learned friend on the woolsack. The question before us is a more narrow one than might be gathered from some expressions which occur in the judgments; it is simply and solely whether the pursuer has stated a case sufficiently relevant to allow him to bring his action to proof.

Two objections are taken to the case going further. The first is an objection based on the ground of want of jurisdiction in the Court of Session; the second is an objection based upon the terms of the statute.

Now, dealing with the first point, it seems to me plain that, whenever an inferior tribunal has done something contrary to law which may lead to liability or deprivation of rights, then, unless Parliament has stepped in and prevented the Court of Session declaring that to be a nullity and a noxious nullity which is a nullity and a noxious nullity, the Court of Session has the power to make a declaration to that effect. That is of the very essence of the power of suspension and reduction. Parliament may have taken away the right, but, if Parliament has not taken away the right to invoke the Court of Session for assistance, then no consideration of inconvenient consequence can affect the mere question of the jurisdiction of the Court of Session to deal with the matter. I am therefore of opinion that the first of the conclusions sought for by the summons — a conclusion for reduction, either in terms as there stated or in some modified terms — is a proper conclusion for invoking the jurisdiction of the Court, and that the question of relevancy is not affected by the considerations to which I have referred.

I pass to the second question, which is whether the statute has taken away the power to invoke the jurisdiction of the Court in this case by enacting that no actionable wrong has been suffered, and this turns on the terms of section 30. As the case comes before this House only on the footing of relevancy, it must be taken that the averment in paragraph 9 of the condescendence is for present purposes admitted — an averment which alleges that the present appellants, the defenders in the action, failed to transmit to the pursuers the notice to which they were entitled under the Act of Parliament.

Now the structure of the Act of Parliament is this. A Valuation-roll is to be made up in which the valuing authority, the magistrates or Commissioners of Supply, may invoke the assistance of an Assessor and direct the Assessor to make up a Valuation-roll. The Assessor makes up the Roll, but if he makes an alteration in any entry of value which occurred in the previous year, then he is by the terms of the statute to give notice to the person affected in order to enable that person to object to the entry proposed to be made; and, if that person does object, then the question goes to a tribunal of review on which is imposed the duty of dealing with the question by way of review of the Assessor's decision.

Now, in the present case that notice was not given. That such notice ought to have been given is quite clear, because section 5 says that the Assessor is to transmit a copy of the entry to the person included in his valuation along with a notice to such person that, if he considers himself aggrieved by such valuation, that is to say, by the entry which is proposed to be put in, he may appeal to the Commissioners of Supply or the magistrates, as the case may be, under the terms of the Act, or may obtain redress without the necessity of such appeal by satisfying the Assessor that the Assessor was wrong. The material consideration is that the Assessor, if the valuation which he makes is confirmed and authenticated, has taken a step which may very materially affect the civil rights of the person whose property is entered in the Valuation-roll for the new figure, and consequently the statute has imposed upon the Assessor duty of giving that person notice before his rights are interfered with.

The Act of Parliament is not a very carefully drawn Act, and I think that the expression about which there has been so much argument, 'making up the Valuation-roll,' is an expression that is used with a certain amount of ambiguity. But it is quite clear to my mind that in section 1, where the Valuation-roll is spoken of as something which the magistrates or Commissioners are to cause to be made up by the Assessor, and in sections 3, 4, 5, 8 and 11, and in section 12 which expressly distinguishes authentication from the making up of the Roll, it is shown that 'making up' is an expression which belongs to the stage at which the Assessor is himself dealing with the Valuation-roll. On the other hand it is quite true that in sections 18 and 35 'making up' is used in a wider sense which may well extend to some things which other parts of the Act appear to regard as belonging to authentication.

Now, if that be so, the utmost result is that the expression 'making up' is used in section 30 in an ambiguous form. I am not going to read section 30 again. What it says is in substance that mere mistake or variances in names or designations in the Valuation-roll are not to render it void, and that, where the Valuation-roll has been made up and authenticated in terms of the Act, neither the Roll nor any valuation therein is to be set aside or rendered ineffectual by reason of any informality or want of compliance with the provisions of the Act in the proceedings for making up such valuation or Valuation-roll. Your Lordships will observe that making up and authentication are in that very section distinguished, and the concluding words with which we are dealing here are confined to making up.

I think it is a sound rule of construction in dealing with an Act of Parliament that, where the Act as a whole contains a scheme which expressly confers a definite right on the person concerned, then you are not to treat the definite language of that Act in an earlier section as repealed by language which is not precise, and which occurs in a merely general form, in a later section, only because the later language is capable of that construction. If the language is ambiguous, if a phrase like 'making up' is used in two senses, then you ought, in my view of the rule of construction, to interpret the statute, not as destroying the right previously given, or as abrogating it, and accordingly, applying that rule, I have come to the conclusion that the expression 'making up' is, to put the case at its very highest, an ambiguous expression which is not sufficient to take away the right conferred in definite terms by section 5.

Other arguments have been relied upon in the judgments in the Court below, and the rule of *ejusdem generis* has been invited. I think that rule is very often — more often perhaps than is commonly realised — a difficult rule to apply. As I understand the principle, it applies when there is an enumeration of particular instances, every one of which illustrates a species which makes up a class. Then when you have general words following the enumeration of the individual cases you confine these general words by the species which is the dominant factor in the enumeration. It is difficult to say what the species is here, but I think that, without invoking the rule of *ejusdem generis*, you may properly say that, looking at section 30 as a whole, the kind of mistakes and omissions which are intended are mistakes and omissions not of a substantive character, and that the only possible exception to that is the expression at the end relating to want of compliance with the provisions of the Act in the proceedings for making up such valuation or Valuation-roll. It appears to me that the natural construction of these words is to regard them as, at all events, not covering anything more important, or much more important, than the specific and rather trivial cases which are referred to in the earlier part of the section. And I am the more impressed with the necessity of that construction by the circumstances that I can see no limit to what might be included in these words if the Dean of Faculty's contention were right. It may well be that the magistrates might sit in a fashion which made the case absolutely *coram non judice*, or that there might be no proper sittings of the magistrates at all. The provisions of the statute would be violated, and, if the provisions of the statute as referred to in the concluding words of section 30 are to have no limits set as to the cases which are there included, then I can see no corresponding limit to what the Dean of Faculty's argument would cover.

Under these circumstances I have come to the conclusion that the judgment of the majority of the Inner House was right, and that this appeal ought to be dismissed."

Lord Kinnear: "I agree entirely with my noble and learned friends, and I shall endeavour to state very shortly what is the view of the case which strikes me.

I confess that I have found only one serious difficulty in considering it, and that is because I find myself differing so widely from three learned Judges for whose opinions I have great respect; but when I think that the dissentient Judges have been misled by an entire misapprehension of the pursuers' case, as if this were an action for obtaining a review in the Court of Session of the erroneous decision of a Valuation Court whereby the value of the pursuers' property has been overstated in the Roll. If that were so, then I should agree with the dissentient Judges, and with a great part of the argument which has been addressed to your Lordships, that the Court of Session had no jurisdiction to do anything of the kind. That Court is not a Valuation Court, it is not a Valuation Appeal Court, and I take it to be perfectly certain that it has no jurisdiction to determine the annual value of lands and heritages in Scotland. But, then, this is not a process of review; on the contrary, it is an action brought in the Supreme Court for the purpose of setting aside as incompetent and illegal a valuation made by the Assessor in excess of the power committed to him by the statute.

Now I apprehend that there can be no question at all of the jurisdiction of the Court of Session to entertain an action of that kind. Wherever any inferior tribunal or any administrative body has exceeded the powers conferred upon it by statute to the prejudice of the subject, the jurisdiction of the Court to set aside such excess of power as incompetent and illegal is not open to dispute.

I think that is what the Court is asked to do in this case. They are not asked to consider whether the Assessor has not made an erroneous valuation, or to substitute a different value of their own in place of his. The complaint is that, by the Assessor's failure to perform his statutory duty, the pursuers have been deprived of their right of appeal, and upon that the Court is not invited to consider any question of valuation whatever, but solely to determine whether the Assessor's proceeding is conform to the statute or not, and if not, to set aside his valuation as null. That consideration seems to me to dispose entirely of the argument of the learned Judges in the minority as to the exclusive jurisdiction of the Valuation Court. It is nothing to the purpose to say that in matters of valuation the jurisdiction of the Valuation Court is exclusive, and when the pursuers complain that they were prevented from appealing, it is futile to answer that if they were aggrieved by a valuation their remedy was to go the Valuation Appeal Courts and not to the Court of Session. The whole ground of complaint is that they were not allowed to do what it is said they ought to have done. The Lord Justice-Clerk cites the language of Lord President Inglis in the case of *Stirling v. Holm* [(1873) 11 Macph. 2 480], but, with very great deference, there is nothing in that language which touches the question in hand. The Lord President says that the Judges of the Valuation Appeal Court are just as much a supreme tribunal as the Judges of the Court of Session, but the point of that observation is this — that, assuming that the Court of Session had no jurisdiction to interfere with decisions of the Valuation Appeal Court on the merits, it had been argued that, on the principle I have already suggested, they might interfere if the procedure of the Valuation Appeal Court were *ultra vires*; and it is upon that point that the Lord President says they are not an inferior Court, they are a supreme Court; and we do not interfere with it any more than we interfere with the Court of Justiciary or the Court of Teinds. But that does not affect in the slightest degree the doctrine that the Court will correct the proceedings, not of a supreme Court but of an inferior Court, or, as I have said, of an administrative body, in so far as they are *ultra vires*. It seems, however, to be suggested in the judgment to which I have referred that the Valuation

Appeal Judges are the only competent Court even for this purpose, and it may be that the Dean of Faculty is right in saying that it would be within their power to decide any such question if it were brought before them in any competent form. But they are excluded by exactly the same cause as has excluded the Appeal Court of the magistrates. No attempt has been made to show that they have any jurisdiction whatever except by way of appeal from the magistrates, and a complaint against the unlawful proceedings of an Assessor which have never been considered by the magistrates at all cannot in any form be brought before the Appeal Judges.

If there is no doubt as to jurisdiction — and I think there is none — the only question is whether this action is excluded by the condition in the 30th section of the Act that no Valuation-roll and no valuation contained therein 'shall be challengeable or be capable of being set aside or rendered ineffectual by reason of any informality or of any want of compliance with the provisions of this Act in the proceedings for making up such valuation or Valuation-roll.'

Now I agree entirely with, and I do not desire to repeat, what has been said upon that section by both my noble and learned friends. I entirely assent to the observation of my noble friend near me (Viscount Haldane), which I think was also made by the noble Earl on the woolsack in the course of the discussion, that the argument derives no aid from the doctrine of *ejusdem generis*. But taking the words as they stand, I apprehend that they are to be construed, not as an isolated enactment, but as part of a statute which is to be read as one consistent whole. I cannot assent to the doctrine laid down by the Lord Justice-Clerk that you are to treat this single Act of Parliament as if it were two separate statutes, so that a later clause may be held as by implication repealing an earlier one. The rule is that you must construe an Act of Parliament as a whole; and, so reading it, I apprehend that it is a very startling proposition to say that, when the Act has begun by conferring a substantial right upon the subject which is necessary for his protection, it is to be assumed that that right has been destroyed or nullified by an ambiguous clause in a later part of the same statute. One thing that is clear is that Parliament thought it necessary that the owner or occupant of premises that were to be valued should have an opportunity of appealing to the Valuation Court if he were aggrieved by any valuation. Now that is a valuable substantive right. I do not consider whether it would have been at all reasonable or just to subject the owners and occupiers of land to the individual judgment or individual caprice of an Assessor or valuing expert without appeal, because that was a question for Parliament and is plainly decided by the provisions of the Act, and I cannot hold that the right so given is taken away by any subsequent ambiguous clause. But, taking the clause as it stands, I am of opinion, for the reasons already given by my noble and learned friends, that the ground of the pursuer's complaint is not a departure from, or non-compliance with, provisions in the proceedings for making up the valuation. His complaint is that a valuation has been fixed upon him under conditions which the Assessor was not empowered by the Act to impose upon him. The Assessor is called upon to value his land and to give him an opportunity of appealing if he is aggrieved, and there is nothing in the statute which would enable him to substitute for that appealable deliverance a final peremptory decision of his own, and that is in fact what has been done.

Now the true objection of the pursuer is that what has been done is in excess of power — it goes beyond any power contained in the Act — and I think it is no answer to say that you cannot find fault with a departure from the provisions of the Act as regards procedure. Whether you can or not, the Assessor has still to show under what clause in the Act he has power to do what he has done. There is no affirmative power which will enable the Assessor to value lands subject to any other condition than those which the Act has imposed. The appellants' argument comes to this, that any stretch of authority, however oppressive, will be unchallengeable provided only it involves a breach of some express provision of the statute. But this reduces the point to an absurdity. The only secure basis of valuation must be found in a positive enactment. I think that if the facts averred are proved, the Act has been distinctly violated, and for that reason I agree entirely with the course proposed by my noble and learned friends."

Lord Shaw of Dunfermline: "There has been such an elaboration of pleadings in this case, and the summons contained such a variety of conclusions, that it might have been supposed that a much larger question was before the House than there actually is. The actual question before this House is whether a certain very limited proof allowed in the Court of Session should proceed, to which question the appellants reply that the action as laid should at the present stage be dismissed, a Court of law not having jurisdiction to entertain it.

With regard to that order for proof, what is asked by the pursuer of the case is that he should be allowed to establish that the Corporation of Glasgow did not, in terms of the Act of 1854, transmit to him a notice which would have warned him that, as compared with the preceding year, the current year's Valuation-roll was to contain an altered figure with reference to his property. That is the sole subject of probation — a probation which presumably would have been simple and brief. I feel some regret that the appeal has reached this House at this stage.

On this and on other grounds it is highly undesirable that this House should now be led into a discussion of what remedies would be open as between the parties if the entry of £1300 in the Valuation-roll should have to be deleted as unlawful. When, if ever, that discussion is reached the problem it presents will have to be solved. But it is inexpedient to enter upon it upon a basis of hypothesis and at a stage which is premature.

My own view with regard to the Valuation Act of 1854 is largely in accord with those of your Lordships, but is most nearly expressed by the noble and learned Earl on the woolsack, because I think that when the statute deals with the making up of a valuation and a Valuation-roll it deals with it, in the first place, as the work of the appointed officer, the Assessor; and, in the second place, as having to be substantially finished by, I think, the 25th of August in each year; while, in the third place, it deals with the ascertainment and statement of a figure of money.

If that be the true view of the expression 'making up of the roll,' viz., as the work of a certain man, done by a certain date, and resulting in a certain figure, it appears to me that, that being accomplished, we are then asked to look at the other provisions of the statute as to what is to be done, it may be concomitant with, but generally in many cases subsequent to, that operation of making up.

Thus comes the stage of appeal, and the decisions of Appeal Courts, or of private applications made to the Assessor, and the substitution of a new figure. All these things may result in certain corrections or alterations made upon the Roll which the Assessor made up, and the Roll which he has made up, plus the corrections and alterations made as the result of these proceedings to which I have referred, is then treated in the statute, not as a 'made up' Roll, but as a completed Roll, and it is to the completed Roll, first made up, then corrected or altered, that the final mark of authentication is attached.

That being the proceeding, I ask myself now what is the construction to be placed upon section 30 of this statute. Upon that topic I have to observe that I respectfully dissent from some of the learned Judges in the Court below in holding that section 30 does not in itself, by one expression as the context of another, limit and define what are the possible applications of the section. Your Lordships will forgive me for citing again that in section 30 what cannot be assailed is not 'any want of compliance with the provisions of this Act.' There are more than one of the judgments in the Court below which treat it not only as merely that, but say that that is not in any way affected by the context. That is not what the statute says. The statute refers to 'any want of compliance with the provisions of this Act in the proceedings for making up such valuation of Valuation-roll.' For the reasons that I have given it appears to me clear that the want of compliance there referred to applies, and applies solely, to that first stage of making up the Roll by the Assessor at the fixed date to which I have referred. It would be sufficient, therefore, to say that section 30 of the statute does not apply to the stage of error or fault or defect which is referred to in this record, viz., an omission to give the appellant the statutory notice which would have warned him of the increased valuation and opened the way for an appeal against it.

But I do not think it would be right or doing justice to this case to treat it merely upon that ground, because in the view which I take of this statute, or of any statute affecting the liberty or the pecuniary rights of the subject, I think it would be the very last resort of construction to give a clause such as section 30 — namely, an absolvitor from defects as to compliance with certain conditions — the effect of entirely wiping out the careful and detailed provisions set forth in the statute for the protection of the subject's rights. I cannot hold that that is the correct construction. For instance I find myself confronted by section 5, and section 5 is a plain provision to the effect that, if in making up the Roll for this year the Assessor finds that he has to vary the figure which is in the Roll of last year, he shall give intimation of that fact to the ratepayer, or assumed ratepayer, so as to permit him to make that appeal to the judgment of the Appeal Court under which he will obtain justice. It would require the very plainest language in the Act of Parliament itself, or in a subsequent Act, to wipe that section out of existence. For myself I have the greatest doubt of the possibility, apart from a most clear and express provision to that effect, of wiping out a series of protective clauses of a statute by a reference to a general provision at the end with regard, it may be, to procedure.

It is upon that view of the case that I listened with much interest to the argument upon jurisdiction. Your Lordships have dealt with it in a manner to which I entirely assent, but I trust my noble and learned friend Lord Kinnear will permit me to say that I agree particularly with him that none of the judgments of the Court of Session in regard to valuation cases are invaded in substance or effect by the judgment which this House is now pronouncing. I would, however, except from that category the case of *Sharp v. Latheron Parochial Board* [(1883) 10 R. 1163] in this sense, that I am not quite able to follow the grounds of the judgment of the Second Division in that case. But I am consoled by the reflection that that decision was ultimately come to after a judgment had been pronounced by my noble and learned friend Lord Kinnear, and I take this opportunity of appending in this House my adhesion to what he said with regard to the function of the Court of Session even in valuation cases. As a Court for keeping the administrative bodies in the country right in regard to obedience to, or compliance with, the statute, his Lordship says [20 S.L.R. at p. 773]: 'The complainer has been twice assessed, and will require to pay a double poor-rate for the subjects in question unless he can obtain redress in this process. If his statement is correct, he was, in my opinion, entitled to rely upon the assessor having followed the course prescribed by the statute, and to assume that no entry affecting him would appear in the valuation roll except those which had been sent to him, and of which he had approved. As he had no notice of the entries he had no opportunity of appealing against them. But he cannot be precluded by the statutory finality of the valuation roll if the conditions upon which it is made conclusive have not been satisfied.' ...

I would put my view as to jurisdiction thus: It is within the jurisdiction of the Court of Session to keep inferior judicatories and administrative bodies right, in the sense of compelling them to keep within the limits of their statutory powers or of compelling them to obey those conditions without the fulfilment of which they have no powers whatsoever. It is within the power of the Court of Session to do that, but it is not within the power or function of the Court of Session itself to do work set by the Legislature to be performed by those administrative bodies or inferior judicatories themselves... ."

LORD PARMOOR: "I agree. The question appears to me to be a simple one of statutory construction... ."

Notes

(1) It perhaps seems odd that it required a decision of the House of Lords to determine **5–4** whether or not the failure complained of was sufficiently serious as to invalidate the whole decision. Nevertheless, this illustrates one of the most common problems in relation to breach of statutory conditions, that of failure to specify the effect in law of such a breach. Similarly, the onus of establishing that procedural irregularity has occurred will always lie with the party alleging irregularity. In effect this amounts to a presumption, sometimes described as *omnia praesumuntur rite et solemniter acta esse* (all proper procedures have been followed). This is only a presumption and the appropriateness of the application of the maxim depends on many factors including lapse of time: *Scottish Milk Marketing Board v. Paris*, 1935 S.C. 287; nor does it apply where there is definite evidence of irregularity: *Murray v. Arbuthnot* (1870) 9 M. 198. On the apparently conclusive provisions of the legislation, the presumption was applicable to the facts of this case. For the application of the presumption in the context of interim remedies see Chapter 00 and on this generally see *The Laws of Scotland: Stair Memorial Encyclopaedia*, Vol. 1, para. 232.

(2) The case is also significant as it involved a clause which purported to exclude the jurisdiction of the court. On this see also *McDaid v. Clydebank District Council*, 1984 S.L.T. 162, noted at para. 10–41. Both *Moss Empires Ltd* and *McDaid* illustrate the fact that in the field of procedural challenge, as in substantive challenge, the courts are more likely to supply closer scrutiny to failures which impact on the property rights or financial position of a litigant, although that approach has not always been consistently maintained: see *Hamilton v. Fyfe*, 1907 S.C. (J.) 79.

(3) Other examples of flaws in procedure which led to a decision being held to be invalid and, to that extent, are illustrative of breaches of "mandatory" provisions, include:

- *Cadder Local Authority v. Lang* (1879) 6 R. 1242 — failure to provide a property owner with an opportunity of remedying a property before statutory action was taken.
- *Stakis v. Boyd*, 1989 S.L.T. 333 — failure to provide information in the form of a sworn affidavit under section 9(3) of the Food and Drugs (Scotland) Act 1956 in proceedings relating to the destruction of food alleged to be unfit for human consumption.
- *Arcari v. Dunbartonshire County Council*, 1948 S.C. 62 — failure by a local authority to adopt a resolution required by statute.
- *McDonald v. Lanarkshire Fire Brigade Joint Committee*, 1959 S.C. 141 — failure to serve required notice on firemen subject to disciplinary proceedings.
  By way of contrast, decisions which have involved flaws which have been considered to be insufficiently serious and therefore "directory" in effect only include:
- *National Commercial Bank of Scotland Ltd v. Fife Assessor*, 1963 S.C. 197 — appeal against entry in the valuation role arriving one day after time-limit for lodgment of appeal.

- *Tait v. City of Glasgow District Licensing Board*, 1987 S.L.T. 340 — time-limit in section 13 of the Licensing (Scotland) Act 1976 for lodging of renewal or liquor licence "directory" only.
- *Hepburn v. Wilson* (1901) 4 F. (J.) 18 — requirement of the regulation to be laid before both Houses of Parliament, although see now para. 2–16.

Relative uncertainty as to the scope of procedural challenge persisted until 1980 when the House of Lords had the opportunity of considering the matter again.

London and Clydeside Estates Ltd v. Aberdeen District Council

1980 S.C. (H.L.) 1

5–5   "Sec. 25 of the Land Compensation (Scotland) Act 1963 enables a person whose interest in land is proposed to be acquired by an authority possessing compulsory purchase powers to apply to the local planning authority for a Certificate of Alternative Development as to the nature of the development for which planning permission might reasonably have been expected to be granted on the hypothesis that the land in question was not to be acquired compulsorily for another purpose. Such a certificate is relevant to the amount of compensation to be paid to the applicant in respect of compulsory acquisition. Art. 3(3) of the Town and Country Planning (General Development) (Scotland) Order 1959 provides that if such a certificate is issued it shall include a statement in writing of the rights of appeal to the Secretary of State given by [sec. 26 of the Land Compensation (Scotland) Act 1963] and by the Order. By art. 4 (1) the time for giving notice of an appeal is one month from the date of receipt of the certificate.

The owners of three areas of ground at Bridge of Don applied to Aberdeen County Council for a Certificate of Alternative Development in respect of the land, which the council proposed to acquire for educational purposes. The applicants submitted that an appropriate class of development would be residential with associated commercial purposes. The council granted a certificate stating *inter alia* that planning permission could not reasonably be expected to be granted other than for educational purposes, but the certificate omitted any mention of the applicants' right of appeal to the Secretary of State. An appeal against the certificate was rejected by the council on the ground that the one-month time period set by art. 4 (1) had expired. The applicants raised an action against (1) the district council of the City of Aberdeen as statutory successors of Aberdeen County Council and (2) the Secretary of State for Scotland, concluding (first) for reduction of the Certificate of Alternative Development, and (second) for declarator that the first defenders were bound on the application of the pursuers to issue a fresh Certificate of Alternative Development in respect of the said three areas of ground; and for decree ordaining the first defenders to issue such certificate within two months after the date of the decree to follow thereon.

After sundry procedure the Lord Ordinary dismissed the action so far as directed against the Secretary of State and granted decree for reduction and for declarator against the first defenders in terms of the first and second conclusions of the summons the grounds that the certificate was voidable. The Second Division affirmed the Lord Ordinary's decision that the certificate was invalid and should be reduced, but refused as incompetent decree ordaining the first defenders to issue an amended certificate."

LORD HAILSHAM OF ST MARYLEBONE (LORD CHANCELLOR): "My Lords, my task in this case is rendered considerably lighter by reason of the fact that I have had the advantage of reading in draft the opinions prepared by my noble and learned friends Lord Fraser of Tullybelton and Lord Keith of Kinkel. With them I agree, and accordingly I am of the opinion that this appeal should succeed, the cross-appeal be dismissed, and that the appellants should be allowed their expenses throughout these proceedings, including those of the proceedings before your Lordships' House, other than the expenses relating to the joinder of the second defender as to which it is not now sought to disturb the order of the Second Division of the Court of Session. Nevertheless I wish to frame my reasons for coming to this conclusion....

It will be convenient to deal with the points raised in what I conceive to be their logical order rather than the order in which they were argued by the respective counsel.

On this basis, the first question for consideration is the consequence of what was admitted to be a defect in the purported certificate of 22nd October 1974, namely the failure by the predecessors of the respondents to include in the certificate information in writing as to the appellants' rights of appeal to the Secretary of State. Was this requirement, which has the authority of Parliament behind it, mandatory or was it in some sense directory only? I have no doubt that it was mandatory, and that the failure to include this information was fatal to the certificate. In the course of argument counsel for the respondents candidly conceded that the only purpose of the requirement was to inform the applicant of his rights of appeal, including the time limit within which they should be exercised. The present appellants aver that they were misled by this defect and that it was as a result of this that their appeal was out of time. The averment has never been put to the proof, and one of the respondents' alternative arguments was that, in the event of otherwise total failure, the appellants should be put to the proof of this. But in my view this argument is without foundation. The validity of the certificate itself is in question, and if, as I believe, the requirement is mandatory, the certificate falls independently of whether the appellants were in fact misled. I find it impossible to accept that a requirement by an instrument of statutory force designed for the very purpose of compelling a public authority to inform the subject of his legal rights can be treated as simply regulatory if the requirement is not complied with. If I required authority for this proposition I would refer to *Agricultural Horticultural and Forestry Industry Training Board v. Kent* [1970] 2 Q.B. 19 C.A., *Rayner v. Stepney Corporation*, [1911] 2 Ch. 312, and *Brayhead (Ascot) Ltd v. Berkshire C.C.*, [1964] 2 Q.B. 203, D.C. notwithstanding that it relied on *Edwick v. Sunbury U.D.C.*, [1962] 1 Q.B. 229 which was disapproved in *James v. Secretary of State for Wales*, [1968] A.C. 409, which was decided on an argument irrelevant to the present appeal. However I am content to assert a general principle to the effect that where Parliament prescribes that an authority with compulsory powers should inform the subject of his right to question those powers, *prima facie* the requirement must be treated as mandatory. For the reasons which follow, however, this does not dispose the matter in the appellants' favour.

If the requirement that the subject should be informed of his legal rights was mandatory, what follows? The respondents attempted, as I thought, at one time, to argue that it thereupon became a nullity, and that therefore a decree of reduction was inappropriate because there was nothing upon which it could operate. But I do not accept this argument. The certificate was effective until it was struck down by a competent authority (cf. *Brayhead (Ascot) Ltd v. Berkshire C.C. (supra)*; *James v. Secretary of State for Wales (supra)*. In the course of argument I ventured to draw attention to the passage at p. 445 of the opinion of the Judicial Committee in *Calvin v. Carr*, [1979] 2 All E.R. 440 in which Lord Wilberforce says of a contention that a decision of the stewards of the Australian Jockey Club was void for breach of natural justice: 'This argument led necessarily into the difficult area of what is void and what is voidable, as to which some confusion exists in the authorities. Their Lordships' opinion would be, as if it became necessary to fix on one or other of those expressions, that a decision made contrary to natural justice is void, but that, until it is so declared by a competent body or court, it may have some effect, or existence, in law. This condition might be better expressed by saying that the decision is invalid or vitiated. In the present context, where the question is whether an appeal lies, the impugned decision cannot be considered as totally void, in the sense of being legally non-existent. So to hold would be wholly unreal.'

The subject matter of that case was wholly different from the present, but my opinion is that the thinking behind it is applicable. The certificate was vitiated in the sense that it failed to comply with a mandatory requirement. But the subject could not safely disregard it as not having been issued. Had he done so, he might well have fallen into the very trap of losing his right to complain of the vitiating factor which has caught other subjects in the reported decisions, and, in my view, he was not only wise but bound to seek a decree of reduction or some other appropriate remedy striking down the offending certificate.

A similar line of reasoning disposes of the next contention of the respondents, also rejected in the Second Division, to the effect that, if the certificate is vitiated, the position is the same as if no certificate had been issued and that section 26 (4) of the Land Compensation (Scotland) Act 1963 then operates in such a way that, no certificate having been issued under section 25, the preceding provisions of the section as to appeals should apply at the expiry of the prescribed period 'as if' the local planning authority had issued a certificate 'containing such a statement as is mentioned in' section 25 (4) (*b*) of the Act. The effect of this read with articles 3 and 4 of the Order would have put the appellants out of time for appeal on the expiry of one month after the expiry of the prescribed (2 months) for the due issue of the certificate by the respondents. The fallacy in this argument lies in the assumption (for it is no more) that the issue by an authority of a certificate vitiated by failure to comply with a mandatory requirement is the same thing as the failure by that authority to issue any purported certificate at all....

At this stage I should notice a contention on the part of the respondents, which, though, as will be seen, I partly agree with it, does not seem to me to be relevant to the disposal of the cross-appeal.

The contention was that in the categorisation of statutory requirements into 'mandatory' and 'directory,' there was a subdivision of the category 'directory' into two classes composed (i) of those directory requirements 'substantial compliance' with which satisfied the requirement to the point at which a minor defect of trivial irregularity could be ignored by the court and (ii) those requirements so purely regulatory in character that failure to comply could in no circumstances affect the validity of what was done. The contention of the respondents was that, even on the assumption against themselves that the requirement of the Order that the certificate should include a notification of the appellants' rights to appeal to the Secretary of State, the rest of the certificate was so exactly in accordance with the provisions of the order that the remaining defect could be safely ignored.

I do not consider that this argument assists the respondents in the present appeal. I have already held that the requirement relating to notification of the appellants' right of appeal was mandatory and not directory in either sense contended for by the respondents. But on the assumption that I am wrong about this, a total failure to comply with a significant part of a requirement cannot in any circumstances be regarded as 'substantial compliance' with the total requirement in such a way as to bring the respondents' contention into effect.

Nevertheless I wish to examine the contention itself. In this appeal we are in the field of the rapidly developing jurisprudence of administrative law, and we are considering the effect of non-compliance by a statutory authority with the statutory requirements affecting the discharge of one of its functions. In the reported decisions there is much language presupposing the existence of stark categories such as 'mandatory' and 'directory,' 'void' and 'voidable,' a 'nullity,' and 'purely regulatory.'

Such language is useful; indeed, in the course of this opinion I have used some of it myself. But I wish to say that I am not at all clear that the language itself may not be misleading in so far as it may be supposed to present a court with the necessity of fitting a particular case into one or other of mutually exclusive and starkly contrasted compartments, compartments which in some cases (*e.g.* 'void' and 'voidable') are borrowed form the language of contract or status, and are not easily fitted to the requirements of administrative law.

When Parliament lays down a statutory requirement for the exercise of legal authority it expects its authority to be obeyed down to the minutest detail. But what the courts have to decide in a particular case is the legal consequence of non-compliance on the rights of the subject viewed in the light of a concrete state of facts and a continuing chain of events. It may be that what the courts are faced with is not so much stark choice of alternatives but a spectrum of possibilities in which one compartment or description fades gradually into another. At one end of its spectrum there may be cases in which a fundamental obligation may have been so outrageously and flagrantly ignored or defied that the subject may safely ignore what has been done and treat it as having no legal consequences upon himself. In such a case if the defaulting authority seek to rely on its action it may be that the subject is entitled to use the defect in procedure simply as a shield or defence without having taken any positive action of his own. At the other end of the spectrum the defect in procedure may be so nugatory or trivial that the authority can safely proceed without remedial action, confident that, if the subject is so misguided as to rely on the fault, the courts will decline to listen to his complaint. But in a very great number of cases, it may be in a majority of them, it may be necessary for a subject, in order to safeguard himself, to go to the court for declaration of his rights, the grant of which may well be discretionary, and by the like token it may be wise for an authority (as it certainly would have been here) to do everything in its power to remedy the fault in its procedure so as not to deprive the subject of his due or themselves of their power to act. In such cases, though language like 'mandatory,' 'directory,' 'void,' 'voidable,' 'nullity' and so forth may be helpful in argument, it may be misleading in effect if relied on to show that the courts, in deciding the consequences of a defect in the exercise of power, are necessarily bound to fit the facts of a particular case and a developing chain of events into rigid legal categories or to stretch or cramp them on a bed of Procrustes invented by lawyers for the purposes of convenient exposition. As I have said, the case does not really arise here, since we are in the presence of total non-compliance with a requirement which I have held to be mandatory. Nevertheless I do not wish to be understood in the field of administrative law and in the domain where the courts apply a supervisory jurisdiction over the acts of subordinate authority purporting to exercise statutory powers, to encourage the use of rigid legal classifications. The jurisdiction is inherently discretionary and the court is frequently in the presence of differences of degree which merge almost imperceptibly into differences of kind.

There was only one other argument for the respondents on their cross-appeal that I need notice. This was that the requirement not complied with was separable from the rest of the requirements as to the certificate. I do not read it as such. It was an integral part of the requirement that the certificate should 'include' a written notification of the rights of appeal.

Once the cross-appeal is disposed of, I do not find much difficulty in stating my reasons for allowing the appeal. In my view the Second Division only refused the second conclusion of the summons because in their view of article 3(2) of the Order the respondents had no power to issue the new certificate demanded. Again, I do not so read the Order. The duty under section 25 is a continuing duty. The fact that article 3(2) of the Order is not complied with in time does not put an end to the obligation of the authority to comply. That this is so is apparent from a construction of section 25 (as amended) in the light of section 26 which expressly allows the parties to agree an extension of time, which would not be possible if an extension of time was *ultra vires* the authority.

In my view, therefore, the appeal succeeds, and the cross-appeal fails with the results indicated in the first paragraphs of this opinion."

Notes

(1) Lord Hailsham's speech represents a more flexible approach than was found in earlier case **5–6** law. In *Tullis v. Macdouall* (1847) 10 D. 261 it was stated by the Lord President (Boyle) (at 273) that:

> "Procedural requirements may be mandatory 'if the words be clear and positive, though there be no declaration of nullity'."

However, given the difficulties illustrated by *Moss Empires Ltd*, it is clear that that approach could only have been treated as a very general guide. Although the mandatory/directory distinction occasionally still appears in judgments — see, for example, *Inverclyde District Council v. Lord Advocate* [1982] J.P.L. 313 and *Ryrie (Blingery) Wick v. Secretary of State for Scotland*, below — the more flexible approach in *London and Clydeside Estates Ltd* has found favour. In *Main v. Swansea City Council* (1985) 49 P. & C.R. 26, it was held by the Court of Appeal that the grant of outline planning permission for residential development of certain land was in effect invalid because of a failure in the necessary certification that all other owners of the land in question had been notified. This was required in terms of article 10 of the Town and Country Planning General Development Order 1973. Citing *London and Clydeside Estates Ltd* Lord Parker L.J. said (at 37):

> "In our judgment, the most significant observation in Lord Hailsham's speech, indeed in the whole of the [*Clydeside*] case, is that the court must consider the consequences in the light of a concrete state of facts and a continuing chain of events. This recognises that the court looks not only at the nature of the failure but also at such matters as the identity of the applicant for relief, the lapse of time, the effect on other parties and on the public and so on."

Nevertheless on the facts of the case, and in particular owing to the delays involved, the planning permission was not in fact quashed. Another consequence of Lord Hailsham's approach is that the language of the statute in question can only be an indicator, albeit a strong one, of the consequences of procedural failure. Thus an apparently permissive expression such as "may" may in fact be held to be obligatory: *Mecca Bookmakers (Scotland) Ltd v. East Lothian District Licensing Board*, 1988 S.L.T. 520.

(2) In *Ryrie (Blingery) Wick v. Secretary of State for Scotland*, 1988 S.L.T. 806 Lord Cullen was asked to consider the terms of section 29(4) of the Agriculture Act 1970. The petitioners argued that the failure of the Secretary of State to furnish them with the report on which the decision to revoke a grant paid to the petitioners under the Act was based amounted to a material procedural failure. The Minister adopted the language of the mandatory/directory distinction and argued that the requirement to provide a report was simply a directory one and that in any event no prejudice had been caused to them as there was no right to further representation when shown the report and, in any event, the Minister would still have adhered to his decision. Lord Cullen stated (at 809):

> "In approaching the arguments addressed before me I consider that it is important to bear in mind the context of the provisions in which the requirement under para. (iii) is set. It is provided that 'before revoking an approval in whole or in part under this subjection the appropriate Minister … (iii) shall consider the report by any person so appointed and supply a copy of that report to the applicant.' This indicates that it was intended by Parliament that the minister should not revoke an approval unless he had already supplied a copy of the report to the applicant. It is true that no provision is made as to the making of representations. However I do not consider that this was necessary. The plain implication of the requirement is that the supplying of the report was one of the prerequisites of a decision in accordance with s. 29(4). If a purpose for this requirement is to be found it lies in the opportunity which it gives to the applicant to make any further representations in regard to the report. Para. (iii) can be seen in its context to be one of a number of safeguards enacted for the protection of the legitimate interests of the applicant. In these circumstances the legislative provisions favour the interpretation that the requirement of para. (iii) which was not carried out in the present case was a mandatory one.'

Here His Lordship was referring to the fact that para. (iii) was hedged by other requirements allowing for the provision of a statement of reasons and the right to be heard and indeed represented. The provision of a report was seen to be an integral part of that process.

In considering the argument by the Secretary of State that in any event no prejudice arose, he went on to say (at 810) that:

> 'I do not consider that the submissions by counsel for the respondent dispose of the petitioners' case for reduction. The matters which I have mentioned above appear to have relevance in some degree to the exercise of the Secretary of State's discretion. I am not satisfied that I can safely affirm that if these points had been put to the respondent in representations made by the petitioners after receiving a copy of the report, they would have made no difference to the decision of the respondent in the proper exercise of the discretion conferred on him by s. 29(4). The petitioners were denied the opportunity of inviting the respondent to consider the cumulative effect of these points. As counsel for the petitioners pointed out, the respondent had a discretion not merely as to whether or not he should revoke but also as to whether or not he should revoke in whole or in part. The respondent might have been persuaded to confine his revocation to part only of the grant. It is not of course for me to say what value the respondent would or should have attached to any of these points. That would have been a matter for the respondent."

His Lordship clearly felt that the question of prejudice could not be treated as separate from the question of procedural failure. In his view they were linked. The inability to rely on the terms of the report led in his view to at least the possibility of the Secretary of State failing properly to exercise his discretion. Although many cases involving successful procedural challenge will involve an element of prejudice, Lord Hailsham's approach does not require this. *London and Clydeside Estates Ltd* is an example of a case where it could not be said that the petitioner had been positively misled by the procedural failure.

(3) The question of prejudice is, however, significant in the context of statutory applications to quash — for example, under the Acquisition of Land (Authorisation Procedure) (Scotland) Act 1974, s. 1(1), Sched. 1, para. 15(1)(*b*) and under the Town and Country Planning (Scotland) Act 1997, s. 239(5)(*b*): see para. 12–18.

(4) In certain situations substantial compliance with a statutory requirement will be accepted as sufficient. In *London and Clydeside Properties Ltd v. City of Aberdeen District Council*, 1984 S.L.T. 50 it was held that although a reporter should have provided a more detailed report in the context of an appeal under section 233 of the Town and Country Planning (Scotland) Act 1972 (now section 239 of the Town and Country Planning (Scotland) Act 1997) nevertheless the report contained enough to comply substantially with the requirements of the legislation. The acceptance of substantial compliance demonstrates that procedural *vires* is not concerned with ensuring the very highest standards in administrative procedures: see *Black v. Grangemouth Magistrates* (1907) 14 S.L.T. 548 and *R. v. Dacorum Gaming Licensing Committee, ex parte E.M.I. Cinemas and Lesiure Ltd* [1971] 3 All E.R. 666.

(5) The question of public interest is an important consideration in determining whether or not the flaw is so serious that a decision should be set aside. In *Johnston v. Secretary of State for Scotland*, 1992 S.L.T. 387 it was argued that a decision by the Secretary of State for Scotland to accept the late lodgment (by three days) of appeal papers on behalf of the Chief Constable under the Police Appeals (Scotland) Rules 1969 in the context of an appeal by a constable against a finding of assault amounted to an *ultra vires* flaw. It was contended by counsel for the petitioner that where a procedural flaw was alleged, such a flaw could only be ignored if there was a reasonable excuse for the breach and the innocent party had suffered no prejudice. If those conditions could not be fulfilled then the decision could not be allowed to stand. In delivering the opinion of an Extra Division of the Inner House, Lord McCluskey referred to the speech of Lord Hailsham, and noted (at 392) that:

> "[T]he real point was not the choice of adjective to describe the character of the rule, but the consequences of any failure to obtemper it to the letter. In the present instance, the rules were part of a quasi-judicial procedure. They were not conceived in the interests of the chief constable; they were made to enable the Secretary of State to consider in a quasi-judicial way both the interests of the parties and the public interest. The public interest was relevant to the court's assessment of what were the consequences of non-compliance with the prescriptions such as rule 3(1) contained. The proviso to rule 3(1) was there because, once the appeal process had been started, it was really desirable to avoid delay; but the rule did not really contemplate the possibility that the chief constable would neither submit a statement within 21 days nor seek an extension of that period."

Similarly, in *Wang v. Commissioner of Inland Revenue* [1995] 1 All E.R. 367 the Privy Council rejected an argument by a Hong Kong taxpayer that tax assessments had not been confirmed by the Depute Commissioner of Inland Revenue for Hong Kong "within a reasonable time", as required by section 64 of the Hong Kong Inland Revenue Ordinance. As in *Johnston*, the question was regarded as being one of statutory purpose. Their Lordships could find nothing in the statute which would permit the deprivation of income tax due and which would lead to an increased tax burden on other taxpayers. The question of public interest in the validity or otherwise of decision-making procedures will always of course be a matter of degree and will involve a balancing of the rights and interests of the party seeking relief as well as the wider public interests.

(6) Considerations of public interest underlie section 27(5) of the Scotland Act 1998, which provides that the validity of any proceedings leading to the enactment of an Act of the Scottish Parliament may not be called in question in any legal proceedings. This is a statutory expression of the common law of rule relating to Acts of the Westminster Parliament as laid down in *Edinburgh and Dalkeith Railway v. Wauchope* (1842) 8 Cl. & F. 710 and reaffirmed in *Pickin v. British Railways Board* [1974] A.C. 765. This provision does not of course affect questions of substantive *ultra vires*. For similar provisions concerning the procedure relating to the appointment of Scottish Ministers and other persons see section 17(5) (Members of the Scottish Parliament), section 19(7) (Presiding Officer), section 50 (Scottish Ministers) and section 69(3) (Advocate General for Scotland).

DELEGATION

Accountability demands that there be a readily identifiable person to whom both political and legal remedies can be directed. In the modern State it is not always easy to determine who is accountable for a decision. The Latin maxim, *delegatus non potest delegare*, which is to the effect that a delegate may not himself delegate, expresses a classic method of ensuring legal accountability. As with many concepts in Scots administrative law, it has its roots in general common law, particularly in the law of agency. The following extracts are concerned with the application of the rule in the context of the function of administrative bodies.

5–7

J. Willis, "Delegatus non potest delegare"

(1943) 21 Can. Bar Rev. 257

"When is delegation permissible? The answer to this question depends entirely on the interpretation of the statute which confers the discretion. A discretion conferred by statute is prima facie intended to be exercised by the authority on which the statute has conferred it and by no other authority, but this intention may be negatived by any contrary indications found in the language, scope or object of the statute; to put the matter in another way, the word 'personally' is to be read into the statute after the name of the authority on which the discretion is conferred unless the language, scope or object of the statute shows that the words 'or any person authorized by it' are to be read thereinto in its place. This prima facie rule of construction dealing with delegation is derived in part from the 'literal' rule of construction, in part from the political theory known as 'the rule of law,' and in part from the presumption that the naming of a person to exercise some discretion indicates that he was deliberately selected because of some aptitude peculiar to himself. The literal rule of construction prescribes that nothing is to be added to a statute unless there are adequate grounds to justify the inference that the legislature intended something which it omitted to express; to read in the word 'personally' adds nothing to the statute, to read in the words 'or any person authorized by it' does. The 'rule of law' says that, since the common law recognizes no distinction between government officials and private citizens, all being equal before the law, no official can justify interference with the common law rights of the citizen unless he can point to some statutory provision which expressly or impliedly permits him to do so; to point to a provision justifying interference by A does not, of course, justify interference by B. The presumption that the person named was selected because of some aptitude peculiar to himself requires the authority named in the statute to use its own peculiar aptitude and forbids it to entrust its statutory discretion to another who may be less apt than it, unless it is clear from the circumstances that some reason other than its aptitude dictated the naming of it to exercise the discretion.

5–8

Because, however, the courts will readily mould the literal words of a statute to such a construction as will best achieve its object; because they will, recognizing the facts of modern government, readily imply in an authority such powers as it would normally be expected to possess; because the presumption of deliberate selection, strong when applied to the case of a principal who appoints an agent or a testator who selects a trustee, wears thin when applied to a statute which authorizes some governmental authority, sometimes with a fictitious name such as 'Governor-in-Council' or 'Minister of Justice', to exercise a discretion which everyone, even the legislature, knows will in fact be exercised by an unknown underling in the employ of the authority, the prima facie rule of *delegatus non potest delegare* will readily give way, like the principles on which it rests, to slight indications of a contrary intent.

What are these indications? The prima facie rule is displaced, of course, by a section in the statute which expressly permits the authority entrusted with a discretion to delegate it to another. In the absence of such a provision, how does the court decide whether the rule is or is not intended to apply; how does it decide whether to read in the word 'personally' or the words 'or any person authorized by it'? The language of the statute does not, ex hypothesi, help it; it is driven therefore to the scope and object of the statute. Is there anything in the nature of the authority to which the discretion is entrusted, in the situation in which the discretion is to be exercised, in the object which its exercise is expected to achieve to suggest that the legislature did not intend to confine the authority to the personal exercise of its discretion? This question is answered in practice by comparing the prima facie rule with the known practices or the apprehended needs of the authority in doing its work; the court inquires whether the policy-scheme of the statute is such as could not readily be realized unless the policy which requires that a discretion be exercised by the authority named thereto be displaced; it weighs the presumed desire of the legislature for the judgment of the authority it has named against the presumed desire of the legislature that the process of government shall go on in its accustomed and most effective manner and where there is a conflict between the two policies it determines which, under all the circumstances, is the more important."

Young v. Fife Regional Council

1986 S.L.T. 331

5–9　　　The Scottish Teachers Salaries Memorandum 1973, as amended by the Remuneration of Teachers (Scotland) Amendment Order 1975, provided that where, in prescribed circumstances, a dispute between an education authority and a teacher employed by them remained unresolved the authority was to refer the matter to the Scottish Teachers Salaries Committee for determination. The committee was constituted in terms of the Remuneration of Teachers (Scotland) Act 1967. A dispute between a teacher and his local authority employer about the grading of his post was referred to the committee for determination. The teacher claimed the dispute was referred by agreement; the local authority claimed the referral was by virtue of the provisions of the memorandum. It appeared from the averments for the teacher that the decision on the dispute in favour of the teacher was made by a sub-committee of the committee and was subsequently confirmed by a decision of the committee. The teacher also contended that in any event the matter in dispute was one of procedure and the local authority accordingly were personally barred from denying the validity of the decision because of their participation in this and other procedures before a sub-committee, and also claimed that they had waived their right to attack its validity."

LORD ROSS: "Having concluded that the pursuer's pleadings and the relevant documents showed that the matter was determined by the sub-committee and not by the Scottish Teachers Salaries Committee, the question arises as to whether the sub-committee were entitled to decide such an issue.

For the pursuer, counsel contended that power to delegate here arose by necessary implication. A study of the documents, including the 1973 memorandum, showed that there were 36 members of the Scottish Teachers Salaries Committee, and it was thus plainly to be implied that the committee could delegate to the sub-committee. Counsel stated that much would depend on whether the delegation was of a judicial or an administrative function. In this connection, they referred to *R. v. Race Relations Board, ex p. Selvarajan* and to *Vine v. National Dock Labour Board*.

It is not disputed that there is no express power given to the Scottish Teachers Salaries Committee to delegate any of its functions to a sub-committee. The general rule is that where statutory powers are given to a body, exercise of their powers and functions may not be delegated unless there is express provision in the statute or where the power to delegate can be necessarily implied. As already indicated, the contention of the pursuer here is that power to delegate arises by necessary implication.

It is also clear from the authorities that it is easier to delegate in an administrative function than a judicial function. In *Barnard v. National Dock Labour Board*, Denning L.J. (as he then was) said: 'While an administrative function can often be delegated, a judicial function rarely can be. No judicial tribunal can delegate its functions unless it is enabled to do so expressly or by necessary implication. In *Local Government Board v. Arlidge*, the power to delegate was given by necessary implication; but there is nothing in this scheme authorising the board to delegate this function, and it cannot be implied.' In the same case, Singleton L.J. expressed the view that the powers in question were of a judicial or certainly of a quasi-judicial nature. In my opinion, the same is true in this case. Having regard to the way in which the committee is composed and the consequences which their determination may have, I am of opinion that the functions which they require to exercise should be regarded as at least of a quasi-judicial nature. In this connection I refer also to *Vine v. National Dock Labour Board* and *Jeffs v. New Zealand Dairy Production and Marketing Board*. In all the circumstances, I am not persuaded that power to delegate here can have arisen by necessary implication.

If the sub-committee had no authority to exercise this function, then their decision is a nullity. If it is a nullity, the Scottish Teachers Salaries Committee cannot give it validity by purporting to confirm it.

As already indicated, it was suggested by the pursuer that the Scottish Teachers Salaries Committee had delegated to the sub-committee the function of fact-finding. In *Vine v. National Dock Labour Board*, Lord Somervell having expressed the view that judicial authority normally cannot be delegated, went on to say that the appointment of a committee to take evidence and report is not in itself a delegation of authority. It does not however appear from no. 17 of process (being the document dealing with the functions of the disputes sub-committee) that the sub-committee was a committee appointed to take evidence and to report. To the contrary, para. 5 of the letter (no. 17 of process) shows that the dispute sub-committee will not merely report back to the Scottish Teachers Salaries Committee but will make a decision and intimate it in writing to the parties.

In any event, even if the disputes sub-committee could be regarded as a committee appointed to receive evidence, there is nothing to indicate that that evidence was ever transmitted to the Scottish Teachers Salaries Committee. In *Jeffs v. New Zealand Dairy Production and Marketing Board* Viscount Dilhorne stated: 'Unfortunately no such procedure was followed in this case. The committee was not appointed by the board, nor was it asked by the board to receive evidence for transmission to it. The committee's report did not state what the evidence was and the board reached its decision without consideration of and in ignorance of the evidence.

'The board thus failed to hear the interested parties as it was under an obligation to do in order to discharge its duty to act judicially in the determination of zoning applications.' Likewise in the present case, the disputes sub-committed were not asked to transmit evidence or a report of submissions to the Scottish Teachers Salaries Committee, and they never sent to the Scottish Teachers Salaries Committee any report containing any summary of the evidence or of the submissions. In *R. v. Race Relations Board, ex p. Selvarajan* Lord Denning M.R. said of *Jeffs v. New Zealand Dairy Production and Marketing Board*: 'It was necessary, therefore, for the board at least to have an accurate summary of the evidence and of the submissions.' Number 16 of process is the minute of the meeting of the Scottish Teachers Salaries Committee on 22 December 1981. It is true that a number of those present at that meeting were also present at the meeting of the disputes sub-committee held on 18 September 1980, but there is nothing to indicate that these individuals or anyone else ever communicated to the Scottish Teachers Salaries Committee an accurate summary of the evidence and submissions which the disputes sub-committee had heard. It follows that, even if the Scottish Teachers Salaries Committee can be regarded as having delegated to the sub-committee the duty of fact-finding, the Scottish Teachers Salaries Committee had never received an accurate sub-committee with the consequence that the Scottish Teachers Salaries Committee were precluded from discharging their duty to act judicially in this matter.

Before leaving the matter of delegation, I would mention that counsel drew attention to the Education (Scotland) Act 1981 which by Sched. 5 now enables the Scottish Teachers Salaries Committee to appoint a sub-committee to discharge such of the functions of the Scottish Teachers Salaries Committee as that committee may specify. The relevant portion of the Act came into force on 1 January 1982. Counsel for the defenders pointed out that if the pursuer were right, there would have been no need for this amendment to the powers of the Scottish Teachers Salaries Committee.

So far as personal bar and waiver are concerned, the matter can be disposed of fairly shortly. In art. 4 of the condescendence, the pursuer refers to previous occasions when the defenders had referred cases for a hearing by the sub-committee, and to a number of occasions when the defenders had participated in proceedings before the sub-committee. In art. 3 of the condescendence the pursuer also refers to the fact that the defenders had agreed to the procedure laid down in the letter of 12 January 1976 (no. 17 of process). The pursuer has also made averments of waiver. In the light of these averments, the pursuer has the seventh and eighth pleas in law which are in the following terms: '7. The defenders, in the circumstances condescended upon, being personally barred from denying the validity of the said decision, decree should be pronounced in terms of the conclusions. 8. The defenders, in the circumstances condescended upon, having waived any right to object to the validity or regularity of the proceedings by which the said decision was reached, the said decision is binding upon them and decree should be pronounced in terms of the conclusions.'

Counsel for the defenders submitted that these averments were irrelevant because no amount of personal bar or waiver could validate acts of a body empowered to act by statute which were done without statutory authority, and were thus ultra vires and fundamentally null.

In my opinion, that submission is well founded, and I understood junior counsel for the pursuer to accept the soundness of the proposition contended for by the defenders. However, he drew a distinction between procedural matters and matters of substance. He submitted that personal bar or waiver could set up a procedural matter and that the matter here was one of procedure. I do not agree. A power to act and a power to delegate are not matters of mere procedure but are matters of vires or jurisdiction. Accordingly, I agree that the averments regarding personal bar and waiver are irrelevant, and that the pursuer's seventh and eighth pleas in law should be repelled. [His Lordship then dealt with matters with which this report is not concerned.]

Notes

5–10   (1) See also C. Weir, "The Principles of Unlawful Delegation", 1998 J.R. 3(4), 211–216. Willis and Lord Ross adopt slightly different approaches. Willis emphasises the interpretative approach to deciding whether or not delegation is permitted. Of particular relevance to Willis are the legislation in question, the function in question and the nature of the decision-making body. Of essential importance to Lord Ross, it would appear, is the nature of the body. Here he classes the Scottish Teachers Salaries Committee — perhaps controversially — as carrying out a judicial function and to that extent arguably narrows the ambit of the maxim. In any event, given the apparent necessity under the regulations for the board to make the decision in question, it would appear that by applying the interpretative analysis, the same result would, in any event, have been achieved. In a judicial or quasi-judicial context, even officials exercising a partisan role have not escaped the ambit of the doctrine. In *McMurdo v. McCracken* (1907) 14 S.L.T. 418 a law agent appointed by a school board to prosecute offences under the then education legislation relating to non-attendance was held not to have power to delegate the preparation of conduct of any prosecution to another law agent.

(2) Note the decision in *Barnard v. National Dock Labour Board* [1953] 1 All E.R. 1113, which considered whether the board had power to delegate its disciplinary functions to a manager. Denning L.J. considered such a function to be a judicial one. This carried particular weight with Lord Ross. Contrast *Barnard* with *Vine v. National Dock Labour Board* [1957] A.C. 488. Although nevertheless regarding the function of discipline as a judicial one, the House of Lords doubted whether or not the fact that a function was administrative would of itself permit the latitude suggested by Lord Denning on the question of legislation. Lord Cohen (at 505) doubted the conclusive nature of "the mere fact that it was an administrative act" and Lord Somervell said (at 512):

> "In deciding whether a 'person' has power to delegate one has to consider the nature of the duty and the character of the person. Judicial authority normally cannot, of course, be delegated, though no one doubted in *Arlidge's* case that the Local Government Board, which consisted of the President, the Lord President and the Council, the Secretaries of State, the Lord Privy Seal and the Chancellor of the Exchequer (Local Government Board Act, 1871), could act by officials duly deputed for the purpose, whether or not the act to be done had judicial ingredients. There are, on the other hand, many administrative duties which cannot be delegated. Appointment to an office or position is plainly an administrative act. If under a statute a duty to appoint is placed on the holder of an office, whether under the Crown or not, he would, normally, have no authority to delegate. He could take advice, of course, but he could not by a minute authorize someone else to make the appointment without further reference to him. I do not, therefore, find it necessary to consider what judicial requirements might be held implicit in the local board's proceedings under clause 16. I am, however, clear that the disciplinary powers, whether 'judicial' or not, cannot be delegated. The non-entitlement to pay, the suspension, the notice or the dismissal must be a step taken by the

board and not by a delegate. The penalties, in some cases, may be slight but, in some cases, very great. A man who has worked all his life in the docks may find himself precluded altogether from doing so. Today it may be easy for him to get other work, but that has not always been so. The constitution of the board also supports the conclusion. It is clearly constituted so as to inspire confidence and weigh fairly the interests of the employers and employed. The purported delegation in the present case was to a representative of each side, but it is impossible to imply a limited right of delegation. *Osgood v. Nelson* [(1872) L.R. 5 H.L. 636] decides that in somewhat similar circumstances the appointment of a committee to take evidence and report is not in itself a delegation of authority. If there are administrative difficulties, this may be an answer to them."

It would therefore appear that the formal classification of a function as "judicial" or "administrative" is but one aspect of considering whether or not the power to delegate exists and is of equal or perhaps more importance in the terms of the relevant legislation or empowering instruments and the impact the decision is likely to have on the person subject to it. For a decision turning on the terms of the instrument in question see *Rooney v. Chief Constable, Strathclyde Police*, 1997 S.L.T. 1261 (Chief Constable entitled to delegate power to accept or decline resignation of probationer constable under police procedures manual). It is also evident from this approach that where it can be shown what has occurred was simply the provision of assistance, that of itself is not improper provided that the assistant body stays within its assisting or investigatory role. That did not occur in *Young*. Note also *Wheelan v. Seed Crushers (Scotland) Ltd*, 1998 S.L.T. 1308 which held that SEPA were entitled to delegate investigatory power to an official in relation to an alleged breach of section 23 of the Environment Act 1995, but not the power to impose conditions under the section. However, note that in light of *Jeffs v. New Zealand Dairy Production and Marketing Board* [1967] 1 A.C. 551, even when proper delegation does occur, a body such as the committee of inquiry will still be bound by the rules of natural justice.

(3) In *R. v. Race Relations Board, ex parte Selvarajan* [1975] 1 W.L.R. 1686 Selvarajan complained of unlawful discrimination. This complaint was investigated by a committee appointed under section 15(2)(a) of the Race Relations Act 1968 and then reinvestigated by the full board under section 15(5). Under section 14(4) the board could act by a group of members elected by the chairman and the reinvestigation was undertaken by the board's employment committee of seven. Each committee member was given a copy of the conciliation committee's report and some other notes. However, further information was collected by one of the board's conciliation officers and when the committee met to consider the case only three of the members had seen the full papers. The other four had seen only the officer's summary. Lord Denning M.R. suggested (at 1695) that these four

"were not in a position to form an opinion of their own. They must have gone by the opinion of the other three ...

If this had been a judicial body, I do not think this would be right. Every member of a judicial body must have access to all the evidence and papers in the case, he must have heard all the arguments, and he must come to his own conclusion. The maxim delegatus non potest delegare applies strictly to judicial functions. But it is different with a body which is exercising administrative functions or which is making an investigation or conducting preliminary inquiries, especially when it is a numerous body".

See also *Attorney General, ex rel. McWhirter v. Independent Broadcasting Authority* [1973] 1 Q.B. 629.

(4) Note also the views expressed in *Young* as to whether or not the existence of personal bar or waiver could cure improper delegation. On personal bar see Chapter 6. In jurisdictional terms this may be a question of degree. Failure to carry out appointment procedure will often lead to a decision thereby made being challenged: see, for example, *McGregor v. Cox* (1895) 5 S.L.T. 215. Sometimes there is statutory warrant for this: see the Local Government (Scotland) Act 1973, s. 33. If the failure can be characterised as fundamental, then the flaw will go to jurisdiction: *Cannon v. Secretary of State for Scotland*, 1964 S.L.T. 91.

DELEGATION WITHIN CENTRAL GOVERNMENT

School Board of the Parish of Dalziel v. The Scotch Education Department

1915 S.C. 234

5–11   "In March 1913 the School Board of the parish of Dalziel in the county of Lanark, being a body corporate under the Education (Scotland) Act, 1872, brought an action against the Scotch Education Department, constituted under the Education (Scotland) Act, 1872, and the Secretary for Scotland Act, 1885. The conclusions of the action were for declarator that three letters from the Scotch Education Department, of date 15th May 1912, 20th July 1912, and 10th September 1912, did not proceed upon and were not authorised by any decision or resolution or direction of the defenders, and were null and void and in no way binding upon the defenders, and should, if necessary, be reduced. There was also an alternative conclusion that the alleged resolution of the defenders communicated by these letters to the pursuers was in any case *ultra vires*. This alternative conclusion was abandoned when the case came before the Inner House.

The facts of the case were thus narrated by the Lord Ordinary in his opinion:—'On 18th March 1912 the School Board of the parish of Dalziel dismissed from service Miss Marshall, an assistant teacher in the Knowetop Public School, Motherwell, the dismissal to take effect on 30th April 1912. The reason for this action on the part of the School Board was that Miss Marshall, shortly before, had, in their opinion, on account of her having been admitted to the membership of the Roman Catholic Church, become unsuited to discharge the whole duties which her position as assistant teacher entailed and which included the giving of religious instruction. Against this decision Miss Marshall appealed to the Scotch Education Department under section 21 of the Education (Scotland) Act, 1908. Following upon this appeal certain communications were sent by the secretary and assistant secretary of the Department to the School Board. On 20th July 1912 the secretary intimated that, as a result of inquiries made, the Department were of opinion that the dismissal of Miss Marshall was not reasonably justifiable, and that it was their intention, in the event of further action on their part being necessary, to attach to the resolution of dismissal the condition that the Board pay Miss Marshall a sum equivalent to three months' salary, at the rate of remuneration due to her while in the service of the Board. In reply to this communication the Board intimated that they adhered to their resolution of 18th March 1912 dismissing Miss Marshall. On 10th September 1912 the assistant secretary of the Department wrote to the Board that the Department, in virtue of their powers under section 21 of the Education (Scotland) Act, 1908 and otherwise, "attach to the resolution dismissing Miss Marshall the condition that the School Board shall pay to her a sum equivalent to three months' salary at the rate of remuneration due to her while in the service of the Board'."

LORD DUNDAS: "We had the benefit of a full debate in this interesting case; but the grounds on which my own opinion is based can be stated within comparatively brief limits.

Since the case was before the Lord Ordinary, two changes have been made as regards the conditions of the pleadings. In the first place, the pursuers definitely abandoned at our bar the alternative conclusion of their summons, with the relative averments (cond. 10) and plea in law (3), founded upon alleged *ultra vires* acting by the Department. In the second place, it appeared to us at an early stage in the debate that there might be an awkwardness, to put it no higher, in our deciding the case while the only person, viz., the teacher, Miss Marshall, referred to on record, whose individual rights and interests were liable to be affected by our decision, was no party to the cause and, so far as appeared, might be in ignorance of its dependence. The pursuers' counsel, following a suggestion from the bench, asked and obtained leave to amend his record by adding Miss Marshall as a party defender. The action was accordingly served upon that lady — now Mrs Graham — and her husband. They have not, I understand, entered appearance.

The facts of the case are sufficiently summarised by the Lord Ordinary and I need not resume them. By their summons, the pursuers ask for declarator that three letters libelled, signed by the secretary and assistant secretary respectively of the Department, did not proceed upon and were not authorised by any decision or resolution of the Department; that the Department had not deliberated or formed any opinion upon the subject-matter of the letters of made any finding, resolution, or decision thereanent; and that the letters were therefore not binding upon the pursuers, but are null and void; and they conclude for reduction accordingly. The substantive counter case made on record by the Department is thus stated:—'The duties of the Department are to administer education in Scotland under the Education (Scotland) Acts, 1872 to 1908; and in accordance with the practice invariably followed since 1885, the business of the Department is conducted by the secretary of the Department acting by and under the directions of the Vice-President. The letters mentioned in the condescendence were written by the directions and under the authority of the

Vice-President, and the decisions taken in the case of Miss Marshall were taken by the Vice-President and were intimated to the pursuers in accordance with the directions of the Vice-President.' We must decide, in the fist place, whether or not the averments quoted, assuming them to be true, form a relevant defence to the pursuers' case. I have come to the conclusion that they do.

One must look at the principal statutory enactments relating to the Scotch Education Department. By section 1 of the Education (Scotland) Act, 1872, '"Scotch Education Department" shall mean the Lords of any Committee of the Privy Council appointed by Her Majesty on Education in Scotland'—a definition which was verbally altered by the Interpretation Act, 1889, section 12(7), to 'the Lords of the Committee for the time being of the Privy Council appointed for Education in Scotland.' In 1885 the Secretary for Scotland Act was passed. By section 5, various statutory powers and duties were transferred to, vested in, and imposed upon the Secretary for Scotland, who by section 6 was appointed Vice-President of the Scotch Education Department, and by section 7 the whole powers and duties of that Department constituted under the Education (Scotland) Act, 1872, were, from and after the appointment of the Vice-President, transferred to, vested in, and imposed upon the Scotch Education Department constituted under the Act of 1885. It is common ground between the parties that the members of the Committee of the Privy Council appointed by the King and forming the Scotch Education Department during the period referred to in this action were the Lord President of the Council, the Secretary for Scotland (Vice-President), the First Lord of the Treasury, the Lord Advocate, Lord Haldane, Lord Shaw, Lord Reay, and Lord Elgin. It is plain from the tenor of the Education (Scotland) Act, 1872, that the policy of Parliament was to leave to the Department a very free hand indeed as to the methods by which they might think fit to conduct their business. The Department is made directly responsible to Parliament, *e.g.* (by section 75) it is bound to lay before both Houses in each year a report of its proceedings during the preceding year, containing a special report upon each school erected after the passing of the Act, not being a public school which, in the opinion of the Department, is entitled to receive a Parliamentary grant. On the other hand, there is nowhere any provision as to the holding of meetings, or as to the chairmanship, or the quorum, or any rules of procedure to be followed, if a meeting were held. We were told that it is not the practice of the Department to hold formal meetings; and it is averred by the pursuers, and not denied, that no meeting has in fact been held since 1909, when the Committee above named was appointed. The duties of the Department involve, no doubt, the consideration and decision of important matters of various kinds. The Department are, of course, bound to act honestly and fairly in dealing with all such matters; but I think that they are entitled to deal with them in such manner as they may consider best, not only as regards formal procedure, but as regards the whole conduct of their business, and that their methods are not subject to challenge and investigation in the law Courts, provided they are not contrary to the statutory powers of the Department or to the inherent principles of justice and fair dealing. It seems to me, therefore, to be reasonably clear that the Department might, if they thought fit, competently leave the general conduct of their business to their secretary acting by and under the direction and authority of the Vice-President, and, if this had been formally done, *e.g.*, by a minute or resolution of the whole members, I do not think such a step could have been challenged as being contrary to the intent or the letter of the statutes. The defenders aver that, in accordance with their uniform practice since 1885, the business of the Department has been conducted in this way. The pursuers' counsel argued, and I agree, that no practice could make that legal which was illegal as being contrary to the statutes; but I do not see that this method of conducting the business, if it might competently have been authorised by a formal resolution, could not with equal competency be sanctioned informally by the tacit practice of the Board. I think that the defenders' averments in stat. 2 form a relevant defence to the action.

The pursuers, however, contend that, assuming the relevancy of the defence, there must be a proof as to its accuracy in fact. I think it is out of the question to allow such a proof. The Department, appearing as defenders, make a deliberate statement on record as to their 'practice invariably followed since 1885,' and the learned Solicitor-General, appearing for them at our bar, endorsed that statement. I think it is one which, in the absence of specific denial, we are bound to accept. For the rest, the averments by the Department in stat. 2 may not be absolutely clear and unambiguous as matter of verbal composition; but the Solicitor-General expressly stated on behalf of the Department that they are intended to mean (as I think they may reasonably be read to mean) that the Vice-President did apply his mind to, and did duly consider and decide upon, the subject-matter of the three letters, and that these express the results of his decision, and were written and intimated to the pursuers by his authority and direction. If the statement thus made and supported were not to be accepted, it could, I think, only be in respect of very distinct and specific counter averments on record. I do not say that a case might not be figured where such averments were so precise and specific as to be entitled to probation. But I am clear that the present pursuers' record is quite insufficient in these respects. It does not meet and counter the defenders' statement that the letters express the result of consideration and decision by the Vice-President; and it amounts to no more than that the pursuers 'believe and aver' that the alleged decisions were those of 'the Secretary only or of some other official.' The defenders' statements, therefore, seem to me to stand practically uncontradicted, and must, in the absence of ny relevant counter averment, be accepted as true... .

On the whole matter, I have come to the same conclusion as the Lord Ordinary, though not precisely and at all points upon the same grounds; and I am for adhering to his interlocutor."

LORD MACKENZIE: "The pursuers are the School Board of Dalziel, and the defenders the Scotch Education Department. The object of the action is to have it found that certain decisions which purport to have been pronounced by the defenders under section 21 of the Education (Scotland) Act, 1908, are not decisions of the Department.

The main question argued upon the reclaiming note and before the Lord Ordinary was whether the decision of the Vice-President of the Board is, or is not, the decision of the Department within the meaning of the Education Acts. It was also contended by the defenders that the terms of section 65 of the Education (Scotland) Act, 1872, are such that, once it is admitted(as here) that the orders complained of were signed by the secretary or assistant secretary, it is incompetent to prove that they were not made by the Department.

One of the difficulties in the case arises from the state of the record. The defenders maintained that the pursuers' averments are irrelevant. The argument of the Solicitor-General in support of this view was as follows:—The Scotch Education Department means the Lords of any Committee of the Privy Council appointed by His Majesty on Education in Scotland (35 and 36 Vict., cap. 62, sec. 1; 48 and 49 Vict. cap. 61, sec. 6; 52 and 53 Vict. cap. 63, sec. 12(7)); the Committee at present is composed of those persons whose names are set out on record, viz., Lord Morley (President), the Secretary for Scotland, the First Lord of the Treasury, the Lord Advocate, Lord Haldane, Lord Shaw, Lord Reay, and Lord Elgin; they were appointed in 1909; the pursuers' case, and their only case, is that the whole of the defenders did not adjudicate upon the matter in dispute, though the duty they had to discharge under section 21 of the Act of 1908 is of a judicial character. The Solicitor-General's comment upon this was that it was out of the question to maintain that it was necessary under the statute that all the members of the Department should be convened to pronounce a decision under section 21, and that, unless the pursuers were prepared to put forward a tenable theory as to what constitutes a quorum of the Department, their averments are irrelevant. In the view I take of the case, it is not necessary to discuss the question raised by this contention. It is sufficient to note, before passing to the defenders' statement of facts, that the pursuers do not expressly aver that the Vice-President of the Department did not apply his mind to the matter in dispute, and come to a decision upon it.

Coming to the defenders' statement of facts their averment in stat. 2 is that 'in accordance with the practice invariably followed since 1885, the business of the Department is conducted by the Secretary of the Department acting by and under the directions of the Vice-President.' In 1885 the Secretary for Scotland Act was passed, under section 6 of which the Secretary for Scotland was appointed Vice-President of the Department. The same section enacted that the Scotch Education Department shall mean the Lords of any Committee of the Privy Council appointed by His Majesty on Education in Scotland. Section 7 provided for the transference of the powers and duties vested in or imposed on the Scotch Education Department constituted under the Education (Scotland) Act, 1872, to the Scotch Education Department constituted under the Act of 1885, Stat. 2 then goes on 'The letters mentioned in the condescendence were written by the directions and under the authority of the Vice-President, and the decisions taken in the case of Miss Marshall were taken by the Vice-President and were intimated to the pursuers in accordance with the directions of the Vice-President.' This averment is not unambiguous. It might mean that all the Vice-President had done was to put his hand to a minute prepared by the secretary or other subordinate official without having gone into the matter himself. The Court were however informed by counsel for the Education Department that the meaning of the statement is that the Vice-President had applied his mind to all the facts of the case, and that the decisions are the result of his deliberation. This being the situation, it would, in my opinion, have needed some very specific averment in reply to have entitled the Court to inquire into the matter. All that the pursuers say in reply is 'Not known and not admitted.' The pursuers' side of the record being in such a position, both on their answer to stat. 2 and on the substantive averment in their own condescendence, there is enough, in my opinion, to warrant us in holding that the decision was that of the Vice-President.

The next and the important question is whether the act of the Vice-President alone is the act of the Department. The argument upon this (apart from the point founded on section 65 of the 1872 Act) was that the decision of the Vice-President, as head of the Department, is equivalent to the decision of the Department, and that the responsibility of the Department is to Parliament and not to the Court. This argument has been given effect to by the Lord Ordinary, and reference is made in his opinion to writers on constitutional history in support of it. For myself, I am unable to find, within the four corners of the record, that a question of constitutional law is properly raised. The essential feature of a plea in law to formulate the legal proposition is wanting. The difficulty is to find out how upon record the defenders bridge over the hiatus between section 21 which speaks of the Department doing something, and uses such language as 'if as the result of such inquiry they are of opinion that the dismissal is not reasonably justifiable, they shall communicate such opinion to the School Board,' and the defenders' statement 2, which sets out that the opinion complained of is the result of the labours of a single individual.

I have come to the conclusion that the only feasible way, in this case, of getting over the difficulty, is to hold that there has been tacit delegation by the Department to one of their number. The defences are defences for the Department, and the statement as to the practice since 1885 is the statement of all its members. Counsel for the Department were careful to disclaim any intention of arguing the case on the ground of ratification. The act of the Department, according to their contention, being valid, requires no ratification. The Court, as it appears to me, is bound to accept the defenders' statement as to what the practice has been. The question is whether it is legal. In my opinion it would have been competent for the members of the Department to have delegated in express terms, by minute or otherwise, the duty entrusted to them by section 21 of the Act of 1908 to the Vice-President. If they could have done so expressly, then, in my opinion, they could by practice impliedly sanction such a delegation. As the practice must be taken to be in accordance with the defenders' averment, I am of opinion that the act of the Vice-President was, in this case, the act of the Department.

This is sufficient for the determination of the case, and it is, therefore, not necessary to express an opinion upon the proper construction to be put upon section 65 of the Act of 1872. In my opinion, the Lord Ordinary is clearly right in the view he takes.

Miss Marshall has now been added as a party to the case, which obviates any difficulty as to our giving judgment in the case.

I am of opinion that the Lord Ordinary's interlocutor is right."

LORD CULLEN: "I have had an opportunity of reading, and I concur in, the opinion of Lord Dundas. I desire entirely to reserve my opinion as to the construction of section 65 of the Act of 1872."

Air 2000 v. Secretary of State for Transport (No. 2)

1990 S.L.T. 335

"A company which held a licence to operate chartered air flights from Glasgow to Orlando, Florida,   **5–12**
and which was 'contemplating the possibility of operating charter flights from Edinburgh to Orlando' during the following year, presented a petition for judicial review seeking to challenge the validity of two sets of regulations made by the Secretary of State for Transport. The regulations were the Traffic Distribution Rules 1989 for Prestwick and Glasgow and for Prestwick and Edinburgh, which forced transatlantic flights from Glasgow and Edinburgh airports to stop at Prestwick airport. The company argued that they had sufficient title and interest to pursue the application and that the rules were invalid as they failed to come within the scope of s. 31 of the Airports Act 1986, in that they did not seek to distribute the traffic between two or more airports. They further argued that the rules were invalid as the Secretary of State had not complied with s. 31 (4) of the 1986 Act which required him to obtain advice from the Civil Aviation Authority before making any rules, in that nothing which had been given to him constituted advice, that even if it was advice, it had not been given to the Secretary of State but only to an interdepartmental working party, and that even if it was advice given to him as Secretary of State the advice did not relate to the particular rules in issue. The Secretary of State argued that, in respect of the Edinburgh rules, the petitioners had no title or interest to sue since they had not yet made an application for a licence to fly from Edinburgh airport. The Secretary of State further contended that the regulation did distribute traffic and that, the Secretary of State having taken advice in relation to the subject matter of the rules within the requirements of s. 31 (4) of the 1986 Act, the petition should be dismissed."

LORD CLYDE: "This application for judicial review has been brought to challenge the validity of two sets of regulations made by the Secretary of State for Transport. The regulations are described as the Traffic Distribution Rules 1989 for Prestwick and Glasgow and the Traffic Distribution Rules 1989 for Prestwick and Edinburgh. The rules relate to the kind of air traffic which may or may not use the respective airports. The petitioner is an operator of charter flights. It has aircraft based at Glasgow airport and presently operates charter flights between Glasgow airport and Orlando airport, Florida, USA. It does so under an existing licence issued by the Civil Aviation Authority to which I hereinafter refer to as the 'C.A.A.'. The only compearing respondent is the Secretary of State for Transport. The petition came before me for a first hearing. Parties were agreed that I should dispose of the case at this stage under reference to the pleadings, certain productions which were agreed in terms of a joint minute and the submissions which were presented by each side.

In April of this year a somewhat similar application was presented to challenge the validity of an earlier rule which appeared as rule 3 (Glasgow and Edinburgh rule 1) of the Traffic Distribution Rules 1986 for Scotland. That application came before Lord Dervaird for a hearing and on 27 April 1989 his Lordship held the rule to be ultra vires [1989 S.L.T. 698]. On 9 May 1989 the Secretary of State for Transport issued the rules which are the subject of the present application. Each of the rules states that they are to come into force immediately. The two sets of rules are in substantially similar terms. They each start with a brief preamble. Rule 1 contains some definitions. Rule 2 relates to situations of emergency and other special circumstances. Rule 3 which is in identical terms in each set of rules is in the following terms: [his Lordship quoted the terms of rules 3, 4 and 5 of the Rules for Prestwick and Glasgow and continued:]

The Edinburgh rules 4 and 5 are in the same terms subject to the substitution of the word 'Edinburgh' for 'Glasgow'. The Glasgow rules have an express revocation of the Traffic Distribution Rules 1986 for Scotland. Both sets of rules conclude with the provision that the respective rules shall come into force immediately.

The rules bear to have been made by the Secretary of State in accordance with s. 31 of the Airports Act 1986. Much of the debate before me was concerned with the terms of that section and it is convenient to set out here the first five subsections of s. 31 of that Act. [His Lordship quoted the terms of s. 31(1) to (5) and continued:]

It will be observed at the outset that the rules are curiously convoluted. While the statute provides in s. 31 (3) for the rules to make permissions, prohibitions or restrictions on the use of particular airports in relation to classes of air traffic and no more, other than the provision of an effective date for the rules, these rules are framed with a degree of complexity which requires care in the unravelling. For example rule 3 permits traffic engaged on general or business aviation to use Prestwick airport. General or business aviation is defined in rule 1 to mean air traffic not falling into any of six specified categories. Rule 3 however also positively specifies some of those specified categories as categories which are permitted to use Prestwick. Again in rules 4 and 5 what may be conveniently referred to as intercontinental traffic is prohibited from using in the case of one set of rules Glasgow and in the other case Edinburgh. But there is excepted from that class of traffic inter alia engaged on general or business aviation which as I have already mentioned is defined as meaning any air traffic not falling into the six specified categories, so that the double exception has to be worked through in order to discover the scope of rules 4 and 5. The elaborate style of their formulation does not ease the task of considering their validity.

The concern of the petitioner is with long haul or intercontinental flights, that is to say flights extending beyond Europe and in particular with flights to the USA. The effect of rules 4 (b) and (c) and 5 (b) and (c) is to prohibit the use of Glasgow or Edinburgh airports for intercontinental flights unless the flight lands at Prestwick immediately before landing at Glasgow or Edinburgh or immediately after taking off from Glasgow or Edinburgh as the case may be. All outgoing and incoming aircraft require to make a compulsory stop at Prestwick.

The respondent has tabled in his answers a plea of no title or interest. That plea however is restricted to the extent that the application relates to the rules for Prestwick and Edinburgh. The respondent thus recognises and accepts that the petitioner has both title and interest to challenge the rules for both Prestwick and Glasgow. I shall turn immediately to a consideration of this plea.

It was accepted by junior counsel for the respondent that the issue before me was a justiciable one. The validity of the rules in question is a matter perfectly open to competent challenge and review. The problem is whether the issue is justiciable at the instance of the petitioner. It is not always easy to distinguish questions of title and questions of interest and the point becomes all the more fine in the present case when the objection both to title and to interest was taken on one and the same ground. It was submitted that the petitioner had not yet made an application for a licence to fly to Orlando from Edinburgh and that is admitted to be the factual position. On that ground alone it was said that the petitioner has no title and no interest to challenge the validity of the Edinburgh rules. The petitioner holds a licence to make such flights from Glasgow and it is accepted that he has title and interest to challenge the Glasgow rules. It was indeed accepted by the respondent that even if he did not hold a licence, if he had applied for one relating to Edinburgh, that would be sufficient to give him title and interest.

On the matter of title I was referred to *D. & J. Nicol v. Trustees of the Harbour of Dundee* and *Scottish Old People's Welfare Council, Petrs.* It was pointed out that s. 31 (2) of the 1986 Act obliged the C.A.A. in performing its licensing functions to secure that any traffic distribution rules in force were complied with. It was then argued by the respondent that until an application was made to the C.A.A. no legal relationship would exist such as would enable a title to be created. The legislation did not in its own terms lay express duties on the respondent which created any entitlement to the petitioner, nor did the C.A.A. have any duties to the petitioner until an application for a licence was made. The Solicitor-General elaborated on the argument by exploring the well known dictum of Lord Dunedin in *D. & J. Nicol* (1914 2 S.L.T. at p. 421), where he said that for a person to have a title to sue 'he must be a party (using the word in its widest sense) to some legal relation which gives him some right which the person against whom he raises the action either infringes or denies'.

It must be noted that that dictum does not pretend to be a definition of title. Lord Dunedin expressly disowned the intention to formulate a definition. Nevertheless it provides a convenient starting point for any consideration of title. The Solicitor-General argued that there has to be a legal relationship giving rise to a legal right which is being infringed. The dictum did not specify with whom the relationship required to be nor against whom the right might be enforceable. He argued that only when an application was made to the C.A.A. would a legal relationship with the C.A.A. be created giving a right which might then be infringed by the Secretary of State. But it seems to me that even without the actual making of an application, there is a relationship between the petitioner and the Secretary of State such as creates in the petitioner the necessary title to sue.

I do not find it necessary to explore the wider analysis of Lord Dunedin's dictum which the Solicitor-General's argument invites because I accept the petitioner's contention that there is a relationship between the petitioner and the Secretary of State which suffices in the present case whatever may be the position between the petitioner and the C.A.A. The petitioner is an established air traffic operator who uses the airports at Glasgow and Edinburgh and operates flights between Glasgow and the U.S.A. The petitioner is one of those who may be closely affected by the performance of the Secretary of State's duties under s. 31 in the conduct of its business. The Dean of Faculty pointed to s. 31 (4) (*b*) to suggest that the petitioner would be a person who would be consulted by the C.A.A. in anticipation of the making of traffic rules. It was argued in reply that if, as the averments in the petition indicate, the petitioner was merely contemplating the possibility of operating flights to the USA he would not qualify as a person to be consulted under that subsection. But I am not persuaded that the petitioner would not fall within the category in question. I should have thought that an established operator already using Glasgow and contemplating the possibility of using Edinburgh might well appear to the C.A.A. to be likely to be affected by traffic rules relating to Edinburgh and Prestwick.

The respondent argued that there was no real issue raised in connection with the validity of the Edinburgh rules. No question of licensing had yet arisen. The matter was only one of a future possibility. The Solicitor-General argued that all kinds of circumstances could change between now and the time when any licence was applied for: administrations, policies, rules could change in the meantime. That consideration seems to me to belong more to the matter of interest than of title and I have yet to consider that aspect of the problem. But in the present context at least the nature of the petitioner's business seems to me to be sufficient to give the petitioner at least a title to challenge the validity of air traffic rules which have been made by the Secretary of State. The Secretary of State has a duty properly to exercise his statutory powers and it seems to me that the petitioner is among the people who have at least a title to see that that duty is performed and to challenge it if it is not. There is in my view a relationship between the petitioner and the Secretary of State such as to create in the former a title to sue the latter in respect of an alleged illegality in the performance of the latter's duties under s. 31.

The argument on interest turned solely on the same point that the petitioner was only contemplating the possibility of operating charter flights from Edinburgh to Orlando airport. I am quite satisfied that the petitioner has pled an interest sufficient to complete his locus standi. The matter is essentially one depending on the circumstances of the particular case. The necessity to make a stop at Prestwick is averred to involve extra cost and I heard no reason to doubt the soundness of that averment. It appears from the adjustments added by the petitioner to its averments that it would receive no earnings from the extra landing at Prestwick. The granting of a licence by the C.A.A. for air traffic services between Edinburgh an Orlando is affected by the provision of the rules complained of because the C.A.A. are bound by s. 31 (2) of the Act of 1986 in performing their licensing functions to secure compliance with any traffic distribution rules. As Lord Dervaird recognised in the case before him, the exercise of their discretion is limited by the rules complained of. They would be bound to refuse to grant a licence for a service between Orlando and Edinburgh which did not stop at Prestwick. It is true that the petitioner has not yet applied for a licence in respect of flights between Edinburgh and Orlando and that is the basis of the respondent's plea. The petitioner is making plans for the routes to be operated in 1990 and is contemplating the possibility of operating charter flights from Edinburgh to Orlando commencing in May 1990. The Solicitor-General argued that merely thinking about what they might do did not suffice to constitute an interest and there was no live issue. The application ought under the relevant regulations to be made six months in advance but it seems in practice that late applications are entertained. There is thus ample time for an application yet to be made. But it seems to me that the validity of the rules is not an academic or theoretical issue so far as the petitioner is concerned. While there may yet be several months before it requires to make an application it obviously needs to engage now upon planning for its operations next year and there would be no purpose served in making an application which under the present rules would be doomed to failure. That the circumstances might change between now and the time of any application, as the Solicitor-General suggested in the course of his argument under the question of title to sue, seems to me too speculative a consideration to be taken realistically. The issue of the validity of the Edinburgh regulations as well as those relating to Glasgow seems to me to be a matter of immediate and real concern to the petitioner. For the purpose of present planning it is obviously important to know whether and under what conditions licences may be granted. The petitioner's concern about the Edinburgh rules seems to me to be sufficient to constitute the interest which the law requires.

I was referred to the opinion of Lord Cullen in *Shaw v. Strathclyde Regional Council*, where a petitioner was held not to have a sufficient interest in circumstances where she believed that the relevant authority would fail properly to consider an application for a clothing grant which she had yet to make. The case is clearly distinguishable from the present both in respect that it concerned the validity of a policy and not existing regulations and raised what was in the circumstances of the case a hypothetical or future issue. But Lord Cullen observed that it would not always be necessary for a person to have made an application before he or she could be regarded as having a sufficient interest to litigate in a matter which was pertinent to the application. The observation is, as junior counsel for the respondent pointed out, obiter but it accords with what seems to me to be the correct approach and to the view which I have taken in the albeit different circumstances of the present case.

So far as the merits of the application are concerned the petitioner's first attack was that the two sets of rules both failed to come within the scope of s. 31 of the Act of 1986. I have already quoted the terms of that Act and the terms of the rules. Rule 3 is purely permissive. By itself it achieves no distribution of traffic. In the context which was accepted by both parties before me of a basic freedom for aircraft to land at any airport it is not immediately obvious what purpose the rule serves. It was explained by the Solicitor-General that if an express prohibition on some traffic at one airport was provided it was desirable expressly to permit such traffic at the other and permission was extended beyond the cases of intercontinental flights lest an argument on the basis of the principle of construction expressio unius might be made to the effect that certain categories were impliedly excluded. Some question arose on that score with regard to the precise scope of rule 3 in relation to official flights but that matter is not critical so far as the present case is concerned. It is sufficient to note that the scope of rule 3 extends beyond intercontinental flights. It is with rules 4 and 5 that the present case is more particularly concerned. Each of these rules is framed in terms of a prohibition and I have already quoted them.

Section 31 (1) and (3) of the Act of 1986 both refer to classes or descriptions of air traffic. Section 29 (2) of the act provides that any class or description may be framed by reference to any matters or circumstances whatever. Thus the circumstance of landing at a named airport may suffice as the criterion of a class or description. Counsel for the petitioner indeed did not suggest otherwise. But they submitted that the use of that criterion does not achieve any distribution of traffic and for that reason the rules were invalid.

Counsel for the petitioner submitted that to be valid the rules must be such as to distribute traffic between two or more airports. They can achieve that in the methods laid down in subs. (3) (*a*) and (*b*) and by those methods alone. But the rules in question do not do that. What they do is to impose a condition upon intercontinental traffic flying to or from Glasgow or Edinburgh. So far from distributing the intercontinental traffic so as to allot it to one or other of the two airports in each case, as for example by requiring all intercontinental traffic serving central Scotland to fly to and from Prestwick, they forbid such traffic to fly to and from Glasgow or Edinburgh unless it stops at Prestwick. That is not a distribution of traffic between Prestwick and Glasgow or between Prestwick and Edinburgh.

The Dean of Faculty sought to develop the argument by illustrating the operation of the rule in relation particularly to chartered aeroplanes. He pointed out that the rules do not require any actual taking on board or discharging of passengers or cargo at Prestwick. All that is required is that facilities are afforded for such operations. A charter plane would in practice be fully loaded in Edinburgh or Glasgow. But the plane would require to stop at Prestwick for no practical purpose. He did not present this as an argument on any unreasonableness of the rules. Indeed the Solicitor-General took immediate objection when it appeared that such an argument might be being contemplated because no such argument is anticipated in the pleadings. The illustration however was merely presented in order to demonstrate the absence of any element of distribution effected by the rule. The Solicitor-General however argued that the Dean of Faculty's argument was wholly irrelevant because the issue was not concerned with passengers or cargo but with aeroplanes. Whether passengers boarded or alighted or not at Prestwick was irrelevant to the question whether there was a distribution of the flights of the aircraft.

The expression 'air traffic' is not defined in the Act. I consider it would be wrong to consider solely the passengers and the cargo although on the other hand one cannot leave out of account the reality that the aeroplanes contain passengers or cargo. But it is primarily the flights of the aeroplanes which are the things to be distributed under the rules and while the Dean of Faculty's illustration shows that in some respects there may not be a distribution between the airports I consider that I have principally to concern myself with the aeroplanes themselves and not simply their contents. In the course of his reply the Solicitor-General observed that planes do stop at Prestwick in the course of intercontinental flights and passengers may board and disembark there which demonstrated a distribution. But again it seems to me that it is the distribution of the aircraft to which I have to have regard and not simply passengers....

The petitioner also submitted that the rules were invalid because the Secretary of State had not complied with s. 31 (4) which I have quoted earlier. The respondent admits that he did not comply with that subsection but he founds upon the terms of s. 31 (5) which he submits applies in the present case and which I have also quoted. The advice on which the respondent relies for this argument is contained in a document from the C.A.A. dated 5 October 1984. That is plain from the preamble to the rules which expressly states that the C.A.A. has given advice to the Secretary of State in relation to the subject matter of the rules on 5 October 1984. It appears that in December 1983 the C.A.A. granted an application to British Midland Airways Ltd. for a licence to operate on a route Manchester/Abbotsinch/New York. The Secretary of State however upheld an appeal against that grant. A letter of 4 May 1984 setting out his considerations in that regard was produced. That letter was signed by a Mr Blanks. Following upon that in May 1984 the Secretary of State set up a review of the Scottish lowland airports policy to be carried out by an interdepartmental working group. A consultation document was sent out to among others the C.A.A. in July 1984 seeking comments on the document. These were to be sent to a Mr McInnes whose address was given in the consultation document as 'Civil Aviation Policy Directorate, Department of Transport, Room 57/10, 2 Marsham Street, London'. The covering letter sent with the document was dated 17 July 1984 and was signed by Mr Blanks. On 5 October 1984 the C.A.A. sent to Mr McInnes a statement of their comments. This appears to have been circulated to the working group. In the statement the C.A.A. adhered to their reasoning in the British Midlands application. They expressed their view that long haul services should be permitted from Abbotsinch despite the effect which that would have on Prestwick. They concluded in the last paragraph: 'Thus the advice of the Civil Aviation Authority would be to amend airports policy in such a way as to allow long haul flights both charter and scheduled, to operate from Abbotsinch. The Authority recognises however that such a policy would involve other considerations, such as employment, which it is proper for the government to take into account and which are not matters on which the Authority feels able to comment.'

There was some question whether the document of 5 October 1984 qualified as 'advice' within the meaning of that word in s. 31 (5). Reference was made to s. 16 of the Civil Aviation Act 1983 whereby the Secretary of State may require advice and the advice may be given to him or to others. An illustration of advice by the C.A.A. given in response to a requirement under s. 31 (4) was produced in no. 9 of process. But as the Solicitor-General submitted, the advice which may be given under s. 31 (5) does not require to be so handsomely presented as is achieved in that production. Indeed I would agree that there are no requirements as to its form. It might be oral or written. Nor does it seem to me necessary that the word 'advice' should be used, although that word does in fact occur in the final paragraph of the comments by the C.A.A. of 5 October 1984. Further, it does not seem to me necessary that the advice should have been given in response to an invitation. It was not argued that the advice was restricted to advice already given under s. 31 (4) because of the express reference to the possibility of it having been given before the Act was passed. Further, as the Solicitor-General pointed out, the five year period between the giving of advice and the making of rules would have extended back prior to the coming into effect of s. 16 of the Civil Aviation Act 1982 and accordingly the advice referred to cannot be limited to advice given under that section. It seems to me that the word is to be taken quite generally and would include gratuitous advice given without request. But the more generous the interpretation here, the more careful in my view must one be to secure that the advice related to the relevant subject matter.

The next line of attack here however, was that even if the document of 5 October 1984 was advice it was not advice given to the Secretary of State. It was pointed out that in terms of s. 31 (5) the advice required to be given to the Secretary of State. In the present case the advice had been required for and had been given to an interdepartmental working party and there was nothing to show that the Secretary of State had ever seen it. The view of the C.A.A. appeared in the eventual report of the working party but that is not relevant to the question whether the original advice of 5 October 1984 was given to the Secretary of State.

The proposition that a minister is unable to perform each and all of his functions personally and that what is done by his responsible official may be taken to be done by him was accepted as sound in principle by both parties. It is vouched by a line of authority from *Carltona Ltd. v. Commissioners of Works*. Reference was also made to *H.M. Advocate v. Copeland*. In the present case it is not a question of the acting of the minister but whether the minister was the recipient of advice. Counsel for the respondent submitted that the delivery of a letter of advice into the office of the minister was sufficient to establish the giving of advice to him. It seems to me that may be too extreme a position. It may not be reasonable to hold that advice in a letter which is delivered to his department without regard to who if anyone has actually seen it or read it has been given to a minister. On the other hand if it is given to an official who has responsibility for the matter in question that should suffice. The problem in the present case is then whether the recipient of the advice was an officer with the relevant responsibility. The facts here are somewhat sparse. The advice was sent to Mr McInnes. It appears that his office was within the offices of the Department of Trade. There is nothing to show what function or responsibility he had in relation to the Secretary of State's statutory duties in relation to the control or regulation of air traffic. He served at least as the agent for distributing among the working group any advice received in response to the consultation paper but beyond that the extent and nature of his responsibilities are not evident. On the other hand, as the Solicitor-General pointed out, he was employed in the Department of Transport and the working group had been set up under the instructions of the Secretary of State for Transport. It is evident that the working group was comprised of civil servants and the Solicitor-General pointed out, under reference to s. 5 of and Sched. 1 to the Interpretation Act 1978, that any Secretary of State would satisfy the terms of s. 31 and advice given to the working group would constitute advice given to officers acting under some Secretary of State or other. I also note that Mr Blanks was on the working group. It would have been helpful to have had further factual information on Mr McInnes' status and responsibilities and I would have instructed evidence on the matter if it was critical for the decision of the case. On the material before me I am not persuaded that the advice was not given to the Secretary of State and to that extent the terms of s. 31 (5) seem to me to be satisfied."

Notes

5–13   (1) Underpinning the decisions in *Dalziel* and *Air 2000* is the doctrine of ministerial responsibility, both for the decisions of the Minister himself and for those of his officials, whether those officials are comprised in a formally constituted body, such as the Scottish Education Department, or, as in the case of *Air 2000*, a more informal working party. The doctrine of ministerial responsibility will continue to remain an important constitutional principle in the workings of the devolved Scottish Parliament and, for a specific example, in relation to the working of agency arrangements as between central government and the Scottish Executive and responsibility therefor, see section 93(2) of the Scotland Act. Generally, see V. Finch and C. Ashton, *Administrative Law in Scotland* (1997), Chap. 3. The issue of title and interest is examined further at para. 10–22.

(2) In *Carltona Ltd v. Commissioners of Works* [1943] 2 All E.R. 560 Lord Greene M.R. said (at 563):

> "In the administration of government in this country the functions which are given to ministers (and constitutionally properly given to ministers because they are constitutionally responsible) are functions so multifarious that no minister could ever personally attend to them. To take the example of the present case no doubt there have been thousands of requisitions in this country by individual ministries. It cannot be supposed that this regulation meant that, in each case, the minister in person should direct his mind to the matter. The duties imposed upon ministers and the powers given to ministers are normally exercised under the authority of the ministers by responsible officials of the department. Public business could not be carried on if that were not the case. Constitutionally, the decision of such an official is, of course the decision of the minister. The minister is responsible. It is he who must answer before Parliament for anything that his officials have done under his authority, and if for an important matter he selected an official of such junior standing that he could not be expected competently to perform the work, the minister would have to answer for that in Parliament. The whole system of departmental organisation and administration is based on the view that ministers, being responsible to Parliament, will see that important duties are committed to experienced officials. If they do not do that, Parliament is the place where complaint must be made against them."

The approach in *Carltona* was reaffirmed in *R. v. Secretary of State for the Home Department, ex parte Doody* [1993] 1 All E.R. 151 where it was held the length of a sentence for life prisoners could properly be delegated by the Home Secretary to a junior minister. See also *R. v. Skinner* [1968] 2 Q.B. 700 where it was held that approval of a breath testing device in terms of section 7(1) of the Road Safety Act 1967 could be given by an assistant's secretary in the police department of the Home Office, acting in the name of the Home Secretary. See also *Re Golden Chemical Products Ltd* [1976] Ch. 300 and on the *Carltona* principle generally, see D. Lanham, "Delegation and the Alter Ego Principle" (1984) 100 L.Q.R. 587.

(3) In deciding to devolve the Ministers' discretion, the deference shown in *Carltona* to the exercise of that discretion is perhaps a reflection of the way the courts' approach government decisions in wartime. Even so, the scope for challenge under the *Carltona* principle in more settled times is still relatively limited. In *R. v. Secretary of State for the Home Department, ex parte Oladehinde* [1990] 3 All E.R. 393, H.L. the Divisional Court, the Court of Appeal and the House of Lords had to consider the lawfulness of a practice by which the Home Secretary delegated to immigration inspectors and senior civil servants, his power under the Immigration Act 1971 to authorise service of notices of intention to deport persons from the United Kingdom. These inspectors made decisions in light of reports from immigration officers. After a notice was served a right of appeal in certain cases existed to an independent immigration adjudicator or to the Immigration Appeal Tribunal. Such appeals were restricted by the terms of the Immigration Act 1988. The practice meant that following an unsuccessful appeal, or if an appeal was not competent, the deportation department at the Home Office would examine each case before a final decision as to confirmation of deportation was made by the Secretary of State.

The Divisional Court and the Court of Appeal accepted that express limitations on the power to devolve decision making might exist, such as sections 13(5), 14(3) and 15(3) and (4) of the 1971 Act. The scope of challenge on implied grounds, such as that of *Wednesbury* unreasonableness, which had the support of Woolf J. in the Divisional Court, appears to have been given narrower scope in the Court of Appeal, particularly given the emphasis of Lord Donaldson M.R. on the advantages of relying on readily available civil servants possessed of suitable expertise in making the provisional decision to report. In the House of Lords the approach taken by the Court of Appeal was endorsed and a number of other observations were made which assist in determining challenge based on grounds other than express limitations. Lord Griffiths indicated (at 402) that given the explicit limitations contained in the 1971 Act the court

> "should be very slow to read into the statute a further implicit limitation... .
>
> [Moreover] the immigration service is comprised of Home Office civil servants for whom the Home Secretary is responsible and I can for myself see no reason why he should not authorise members of that service to take decisions under the *Carltona* principle providing they do not conflict with or embarrass them in the discharge of their specific statutory duties under the Act and that the decisions are suitable to their grading and experience.
>
> [In particular] it would not be right to authorise an inspector to take a decision ... in any case on which he had been engaged as an immigration officer, for to do so would be too much like asking a prosecutor to be judge in the same cause."

Here Lord Griffiths has in mind the rule of natural justice discussed in Chapter 9. It is clear from his speech that the categories of potential challenge are not closed and are undoubtedly linked to the grounds of challenge discussed in Chapter 6. Given the volume of decisions involved and the consequent demands on resources and efficiency, it is perhaps not surprising that in the immigration field at least, inroads on the *Carltona* principle based on *Wednesbury* grounds are not likely to be successful. Whether there is room for further development of the approach found in this case in other fields where the legislative structure and policy and resource implications differ, remains to be seen.

(4) The *Carltona* principle does not apply, however, to delegation to persons or bodies outwith the government department in question. Specific authorisation is required. In *Allingham v. Minister of Agriculture and Fisheries* [1948] 1 All E.R. 780 a Minister delegated his power to

give directions as to the way in which land was to be cultivated to a committee. The committee made a decision to part of the land owned by Allingham but left the exact location of the land in question to a civil servant. Allingham contravened the direction given by the civil servant and was fined. He successfully challenged the decision on the basis that no power to issue such direction existed. The decision might also be seen as an example of the presumption against sub-delegation. See too *Nelms v. Roe* [1969] 3 All E.R. 1379.

(5) Statute can make a difference. Sections 69–72 of the Deregulation and Contracting Out Act 1994 provide that in certain circumstances decisions contracted out to a private person or body are in law deemed to be the decisions of the Minister. These provisions bolster the power of a Minister or office holder to authorise another person to undertake statutory or common law functions.

DELEGATION IN LOCAL GOVERNMENT

Local Government (Scotland) Act 1973

s. 56

"Arrangements for discharge of functions by local authorities

5–14   56.—(1) Subject to any express provision contained in this Act or any Act passed after this Act, a local authority may arrange for the discharge of any of their functions by a committee of the authority, a sub-committee, an officer of the authority or by any other local authority in Scotland.

(2) Where by virtue of this section any functions of a local authority may be discharged by a committee of theirs, then, unless the local authority otherwise direct, the committee may arrange for the discharge of any of those functions by a sub-committee or an officer of the authority.

(3) Where by virtue of this section any functions of a local authority may be discharged by another local authority, subsections (1) and (2) above shall apply in relation to those functions as they apply in relation to the functions of that other authority, except that —

(*a*)   the foregoing provision shall have effect subject to the terms of the arrangement relating to the functions; and

(*b*)   that other authority shall not, by virtue of this subsection, arrange for the discharge of those functions by some other local authority.

(4) Any arrangement made by a local authority or committee under this section for the discharge of any functions by a committee, sub-committee, officer or local authority shall not prevent the authority or committee by whom the arrangement is made from exercising those functions.

(5) Two or more local authorities may discharge any of their functions jointly and, where arrangements are in force for them to do so,—

(*a*)   they may also arrange for the discharge of those functions by a joint committee of theirs or by an officer of one of them, and subsection (2) above shall apply in relation to those functions as it applies in relation to the functions of the individual authorities; and

(*b*)   any enactment relating to those functions or the authorities by whom or the areas in respect of which they are to be discharged shall have effect subject to all necessary modifications in its application in relation to those functions and the authorities by whom and the areas in respect of which (whether in pursuance of the arrangements or otherwise) they are to be discharged.

(6) A local authority's functions with respect to —

(a)   determining a rate;

(b)   setting an amount of council tax in accordance with section 93(1) of the Local Government Finance Act 1992, or setting a reduced amount of council tax under section 94 of that Act or paragraph 3 of Schedule 7 to that Act;

(c)   setting an amount of council water charge in accordance with paragraph 9 of Schedule 11 to the Local Government Finance Act 1992; or

(d)   borrowing money.

shall be discharged only by the authority

. . .

(8) Any enactment, except one mentioned in subsection (9) below, which contains any provision—

(*a*)   which empowers or requires local authorities or any class of local authorities to establish committees (including joint committees) for any purpose or enables a Minister to make an instrument establishing committees of local authorities for any purpose, or empowering or requiring a local authority or any class of local authorities to establish committees for any purpose; or

(b)   which empowers or requires local authorities or any class of local authorities to arrange or to join with other authorities in arranging for the exercise by committees so established or by officers of theirs of any of their functions or provides that any specified functions of theirs shall be discharged by such committees or officers, or enables any Minister to make an instrument conferring such a power, imposing such a requirement or containing such a provision;

shall, to the extent that it makes any such provision, cease to have effect.

(9) The following enactments are exempted from subsection (8) above—

(a)   section 36 of the Fire Service Act 1947 so far as relating to administration schemes;

(b)   sections 19, 20 and 21 of the Police (Scotland) Act 1967 (amalgamation schemes);

(c)   ...

(d)   paragraph 3 of Schedule 3 to the said Act of 1968 (children's panel advisory committees);

(e)   section 7 of the Superannuation Act 1972 (superannuation of persons employed in local government service, etc.);

(f)   section 9 of the said Act of 1972 (superannuation of teachers).

(10) This section shall not authorise a local authority to arrange for the discharge by any committee, sub-committee or local authority of any functions which, by any enactment mentioned in subsection (9) above, are required or authorised to be discharged by a specified committee, but the foregoing provision shall not prevent a local authority who are required by or under any such enactment to establish, or delegate functions to, a committee established by or under any such enactment from arranging under this section for the discharge of their functions by an officer of the local authority or committee, as the case may be.

...

(14) References in this section and section 57 below to the discharge of any of the functions of a local authority include references to the doing of anything which is calculated to facilitate, or is conducive or incidental to, the discharge of any of those functions.

Notes

Section 56 clearly provides extensive power to delegate. However, the underlying philosophy of section 56 is that delegation should not undermine the status of the local authority.

5–15

Wheatley Commission on Local Government in Scotland

Cmnd. 9797 (1969), para. 495

"The first thing to get clear in the organisation of an authority is the position of the council itself, because that is the hub of the whole machine. In the entire body of elected members, meeting as a council, resides a constitutional status and independence of each authority from which all other parts derive, whatever status and powers they enjoy. No form of internal organisation can be acceptable if it treats the council as a mere talking shop, assembly or show place, while the real business is done elsewhere."

5–16

Notes

(1) Delegation of functions to committees has a long history in Scottish local government law. Prior to the Local Government (Scotland) Act 1973 there were a number of pieces of legislation given specific authority to delegate decision making: see, for example, the Police (Scotland) Act 1967 concerning certain appointments. It will be seen that very wide powers indeed exist in relation to the discharge of local authority functions. Sub-delegation is specifically allowed in terms of section 56(2). Prior to this, on the authority of *Thomson v. Dundee Police*

5–17

Commissioners (1887) 15 R. 164, such sub-delegation was not permitted. However, sub-delegation must be genuine and, in particular, sub-delegation to a committee means just that. A committee of one is not permissible. See *R. v. Secretary of State for the Environment, ex parte Hillingdon London Borough Council* [1986] 1 W.L.R. 192 interpreting the parallel English legislation in the Local Government Act 1972, s. 101(1). Committees and sub-committees have a clearly defined status in law. A "group" or "working party" are not the equivalent of committees or sub-committees: *Moffat v. Eden District Council*, Court of Appeal, November 8, 1988, unreported.

(2) Note also the terms of the Local Government and Housing Act 1989, s. 4(5), which provides that in addition to the prohibition of delegation of certain functions contained in section 56, any formal reports by the council head of its paid service or by its monitoring officer have to be considered by the full council. The same requirement is imposed in relation to the consideration of further reports from the Ombudsman and for certain audit reports. The equivalent English provision of section 56(14) has been interpreted to the effect that although the power to borrow money is not delegable, functions incidental to the borrowing of money can be: see para. 3–19.

(3) No particular model of delegation of function is prescribed by section 56 and, in particular, there is no regulation of what committee or sub-committees might be formed or what the relationship is to be between them. It is not clear whether something approaching the *Carltona* principle applies in local government. There appears to be no direct Scots authority. In *Provident Mutual Life Assurance Association v. Derby City Council* (1981) 79 L.G.R. 297 the House of Lords held that "administrative matters" in connection with the collection of rates could be dealt with by members of the council treasury staff where the power to collect rates had been delegated to the treasurer. See also *Cheshire County Council v. Secretary of State for the Environment* [1988] J.P.L. 30 and *R. v. Southern London Borough Council, ex parte Bannerman* (1990) 22 H.L.R. 459.

However, C. M. G. Himsworth, *Local Government Law in Scotland* (1995), pp. 56–57, without referring to these English cases, doubts whether the *Carltona* principle would be applied in a Scottish context.

(4) A decision once taken under a valid scheme of delegation is binding on the parent body: *Bettelley v. Findsbury Borough Council* (1958) 56 L.G.R. 165 and, moreover, will have no effect on any remedy that is sought, as in *Lord Advocate v. Glasgow Corporation*, 1973 S.L.T. 33 (H.L.), where a default order was made and enforced against a local authority even though its powers in the relevant area had been delegated to another authority.

(5) In situations where an official acts outwith the authority delegated to him, the doctrine of personal bar may be relevant. On this see generally para. 6–47.

CONSULTATION PROCEDURES

5–18   Consultation can be regarded as an aspect of good administration, by providing a mechanism by which decision makers may take account of, and benefit from, a broad range of experience and opinion in reaching a decision. For example, section 63(1)(*c*) of the Scotland Act 1998 provides that Order in Council may be passed in relation to a function of a Minister of the Crown in or as regards Scotland only with the agreement of, and after consultation with, the Scottish Ministers. New consultation obligations can be imposed by virtue of such an Order: s. 63(3). The result of consultation might amount to a relevant consideration, on which see Chapter 6. Consultation which in effect amounts to dictation is unlawful: see Chapter 7. Here we are concerned with failings in consultation procedure and the effect of such failure. Consultation obligations are particularly relevant in relation to the making of administrative rules, particularly statutory instruments. A body making an instrument may be required to consult specific persons or more commonly, it has a discretion to decide who should be consulted, a discretion which must be exercised reasonably. Further aspects of consultation as a procedural control of administrative rules can be found in Chapter 2.

Agricultural, Horticultural and Forestry Industry Training Board v. Aylesbury Mushrooms Ltd

[1972] 1 All E.R. 280

"The Industrial Training Act 1964 provided for the establishment by Order of industrial training boards. **5–19** Each board arranged training for those employed in the industry concerned, and was supported by levies imposed on the employers in those industries. Section 1(4) of the Act provided:

'Before making an industrial training order the Minister shall consult any organisation or association of organisations appearing to him to be representative of substantial numbers of employers engaging in the activities concerned and any organisation or association of organisations appearing to him to be representative of substantial numbers of persons employed in those activities; and if those activities are carried on to a substantial extent by a body established for the purpose of carrying on under national ownership any industry or part of an industry or undertaking, shall consult that body.

In 1965, the Ministry of Labour was minded to set up the plaintiff board. Consultations were held between Ministry officials and the largest representative body concerned, the National Farmers' Union. By April 1966 a draft order had been prepared. An advance copy of the schedule to the Order, which defined the industry to which the order related, was sent to the National Farmers' Union on April 15, 1966. On April 26, 1966, copies of this document were circulated to a large number of addresses, including the Mushroom Growers' Association, inviting comments. Simultaneously there was a press notice summarising the activities which it was proposed should be covered by the new board and advising any organisation which considered that it had an interest in the draft schedule and which had not received a copy to apply to the Ministry of Labour. No comments were received from the Mushroom Growers' Association and no application was made by them for a copy of the schedule.

The Order was made on August 2, 1966, laid before Parliament on August 11, and came into operation on August 15. The Mushroom Growers' Association applied in May 1968 for complete exemption from the Order on various grounds. They had never received a copy of the draft schedule, and had no knowledge of the consultations between the Ministry and the National Farmers' Union, or of the press notice. The Mushroom Growers' Association was a specialist branch of the National Farmers' Union, although largely autonomous. It represented about 85 per cent of all mushroom growers in England and Wales, who were responsible for about 80 per cent of mushroom production.

The Board sought a determination as to whether the Minister had complied with his duty of consultation, and if not, what were the consequences. The real defendants were the Mushroom Growers' Association, but as that was an unincorporated association, it was thought more convenient that the nominal defendants should be Aylesbury Mushrooms Ltd, who were representative of the mushroom Growers' Association membership."

DONALDSON J.: "Both parties are agreed that under the terms of section 1(4) of the Act, some consultation by the Minister is mandatory and that in the absence of any particular consultation which is so required, the persons who should have been but were not consulted are not bound by the Order, although the Order remains effective in relation to all others who were in fact consulted or whom there was no need to consult. Both parties are further agreed that if consultation with the Mushroom Growers' Association was mandatory and there was no sufficient consultation the Order takes effect according to its terms subject to a rider that it does not apply to the growing of mushrooms or to persons engaged in this activity solely by reason of their being so engaged. They may, of course, come within the scope of the Order in some other capacity.

Both parties are also agreed that the organisations required to be consulted are those which appear to the Minister, or to his alter ago who in this case was a Mr Devey, to be representative of substantial numbers of employers engaging in the activities concerned or persons employed therein and nationalised industries which engage in those activities to a substantial extent. Thus whether any particular organisation has to be consulted depends upon a subjective test, subject always to *bona fides* and reasonableness which are not in question.

Against this background Mr Bradburn, for the association, submits that the court must see what organisations appeared to the Minister to fall into the specified categories, and that the Minister clearly sought to consult the Mushroom Growers' Association thereby showing that he regarded it as being within the class of organisation which had to be consulted. It follows, as he submits, that neither the board nor the Minister can now turn round and say that consultation with the National Farmers' Union constituted a sufficient discharge of his duties. Mr Bradburn goes on to submit that there can be no consultation without at least unilateral communication and that no such communication occurred.

Mr Gettleson for the board submitted that 'any' in the phrase 'the Minister shall consult any organisation' imposed a duty to consult not more than one organisation, that posting the letter of April 26, 1966, constituted consultation with the Mushroom Growers' Association despite the fact that it was never received, that the Mushroom Growers' Association was not an organisation which had to be consulted and that consultation with the National Farmers' Union involved consultation with all its branches including the Mushroom Growers' Association.

I have no doubt that Mr Gettleson's first point is without foundation. 'Any' must mean 'every' in the context of section 1(4). There is a little more to be said for his submission that the mere sending of the letter of April 26, 1966, constituted consultation in that the Shorter Oxford English Dictionary gives as one definition of the verb 'to consult' to ask advice of, seek counsel from; to have recourse to for instruction or professional advice'. However, in truth the mere sending of a letter constitutes but an attempt to consult and this does not suffice. The essence of consultation is the communication of a genuine invitation, extended with a receptive mind, to give advice: see *per* Bucknill L.J. approving a dictum of Morris J. in *Rollo v. Minister of Town and Country Planning* [1948] 1 All E.R. 13, 17. If the invitation is once received, it matters not that it is not accepted and no advice is proferred. Were it otherwise organisations with a right to be consulted could, in effect, veto the making of any order by simply failing to respond to the invitation. But without communication and consequent opportunity of responding, there can be no consultation.

This leaves only the related questions of whether the Mushroom Growers' Association did in fact appear to the Minister to be an organisation falling within the categories set out in section 1(4) with the consequence that he as under an obligation to consult them and whether in any event his consultations with the National Farmers' Union constituted consultation with the Mushroom Growers' Association as a branch of the N.F.U. This is the heart of the problem.

Mr Devey has deposed in paragraph 5 of his affidavit:

'In accordance with practice the circulation of the draft schedule was not restricted to organisations that appeared to me to be representative of substantial numbers of employers engaging in activities specified in the draft schedule. This will appear sufficiently from a perusal of the document. In particular the Mushroom Growers' Association was listed, although it was, and remains, a specialist branch of the National Farmer's Union. The listed address of the association is the same as that of the union which is Agriculture House, Knightsbridge, London, S.W.1.'

In each case he sent a covering letter in one of three forms. The addresses on the first list, such as the National Farmers' Union, the Trades Union Congress, the Confederation of British Industry, and major government departments received special letters from Mr Devey. Those on the second list received letters which were in standard form but were sent personally to named officials of the organisation concerned. These included the Local Government Examinations Board which clearly is an organisation which should have been consulted, but not one which in the terms of the Act had to be consulted. Those on the third list, including the Mushroom Growers' Association, received or should have received letters in standard form addressed to the organisation impersonally. I can find no clue in the form of the covering letter to whether any particular addressee appeared to the Minister to be a section 1(4) organisation and examples can be found in each list of organisation which plainly fall outside this category. I am thus thrown back on Mr Devey's affidavit coupled with a letter dated January 20, 1969, signed by a Mr Thomson of the Department of Employment and Productivity which states that a copy of the draft schedule was sent to the National Farmers' Union of which it is understood that the Mushroom Growers' Association is a specialist branch 'and also as a matter of courtesy to that association'. Bearing in mind the importance which attaches to consultation in the scheme of the Industrial Training Act 1964, which seems to be based upon the healthy principle of 'no taxation without consultation', and the fact that Mr Devey has not in terms said that the association did not appear to him to fall within the scope of section 1(4), I feel obliged to conclude that it was an organisation which had to be consulted, although its small membership in the context of the number of persons employed in agriculture, horticulture and forestry, and the specialised nature of their activities could well have led the Minister to take a different view.

This only leaves the question of whether it was consulted vicariously, and it may be accidentally, by means of the consultations with the National Farmers' Union. This is a nice point. *Prima facie* consultation with the parent body undoubtedly constitutes consultation with its constituent parts, but I think that this general rule is subject to an exception where, as here, the Minister has also attempted and intended direct consultation with a branch. The association's complaint has very little merit, because it seems to have been completely blind to all that was going on around it. Nevertheless it is important that statutory powers which involve taxation shall be strictly construed and, so construed, I consider that the association should have been consulted and was not consulted.

I therefore answer the questions in the originating summons as follows: 'Whether before making an order establishing a training board for the agricultural, horticultural and forestry industry, the Minister was under a duty to consult the Mushroom Growers' Association' — yes.

'Whether the consultations held by the Minister with the National Farmers' Union constituted a sufficient consultation with an organisation or association of organisations representative of those engaged in the activity of horticulture' — no.

'If it be held that the Minister was under a duty to consult the Mushroom Growers' Association, whether on the facts such consultation took place' — no.

'If it be held that the Minister was under a duty to consult the Mushroom Growers' Association and failed to do so, what effect such failure had upon the provisions of the Industrial Training (Agricultural, Horticultural and Forestry Board) Order 1966 (S.I. 1966 No. 969)' — the Order has no application to mushroom growers as such."

Notes

(1) See case notes by D. Foulkes (1972) 35 M.L.R. 647.   **5–20**

(2) Arguably, what was significant in *Aylesbury Mushrooms Ltd* was the fact that a power to tax was involved. As noted in Chapter 3 where there is the levying of a charge, the courts are more likely to take a stricter view of the legality of such a power. Also of significance is the overall context in which the decision is made and this may be relevant to both the level and nature of consultation. For example, in *R. v. Secretary of State for Health, ex parte United States Tobacco International Inc.* [1992] 1 Q.B. 353 regulations were quashed on the grounds of inadequate consultation. Under the Consumer Protection Act 1987, section 11(5)(*a*) provided that before making safety regulations, the Secretary of State was under a duty to consult "such organisations as appear to him to be representative of interests substantially affected by the proposal". Taylor L.J. stated that there were three reasons why consultation under this section in the present case required "a high degree of fairness". These included the history of the relationship between the company and the Government and that although the applicants "cannot successfully rely on the doctrine of legitimate expectation, the fact is that they were led up the garden path"; although the regulations were general of their application, they were almost exclusively effective on the company as they were the sole manufacturers of the product in the United Kingdom; finally, the effect of the regulations was likely to be devastating to the company's U.K. business. The Secretary of State refused to disclose the text of professional advice received from his advisory committee. This refusal did not square with the court's finding (370) that:

> "it was important that the Secretary of State ... should give the applicants a full opportunity to know and respond to the material and valuations which led him to such a striking change of policy".

(3) Consultation in both *Aylesbury Mushrooms Ltd* and *United States Tobacco International Inc.* was discretionary. Provided that the authority making the statutory instrument did not act in a manner which could be regarded as *Wednesbury* unreasonable, then it was free to decide whom it should consult. See also *R. v. Secretary of State for Trade and Industry, ex parte Garman (t/a Celebration of Fireworks)*, October 19, 1997, Q.B.D. and contrast with *R. v. Fairoaks Airport Ltd., ex parte Roads*, November 3, 1998, Q.B.D. where fairness, in preference to the *Wednesbury* test, was held to be the criterion upon which a local community group had the right to be consulted by the airport's consultative committee in relation to possible aircraft noise under the Civil Aviation Act 1982, s. 35(2). Consultation is sometimes required with specific bodies by statute. The Council on Tribunals must be consulted before procedural rules are drawn up for a large number of statutory tribunals: Tribunals and Inquiries Act 1992, s. 8, Sched. 1. Under the Social Security Act 1980, the social security advisory committee was set up. One of its functions was to consider regulations regarding social security benefits other than industrial injuries benefits, war pensions and occupational pensions. Regulations and draft require to be sent to it unless it appears to the Secretary of State that "by reason of the urgency

of the matter it is inexpedient so to refer them" or the committee otherwise agrees: Social Security Administration Act 1992, s. 173(1)(*a*). When laying regulations before Parliament, the Secretary of State must also supply to the committee's report a comment confirming the extent to which any recommendations have been implemented or if not, why not: s. 174. Where urgency applies, and draft regulations have not been submitted, the final regulations must be submitted to the committee unless the committee otherwise agrees. Moreover, in urgent cases the Secretary of State may refer drafts to the committee to make regulations before receiving its advice: s. 173(3). It is sufficient for proposed amendments to the regulations to be summarised: see *R. v. Secretary of State for Social Services, ex parte Cotton, The Times*, December 14, 1985.

(4) Clearly the facts in *United States Tobacco International Inc.* were somewhat unusual, but nevertheless the case can be regarded as a specific example of proposition that consultation must be meaningful. In this context, the dictum of Webster J. in *R. v. Secretary of State for Social Services, ex parte Association of Metropolitan Authorities* [1986] 1 W.L.R. 1 is illuminating. This case concerned the Housing Benefits Act 1982. In terms of section 36(1), before making regulations relating to housing benefit, "the Secretary of State shall consult with organisations appearing to him to be representative of the authorities concerned". It was the practice to consult local authority associations including AMA before making the regulations and it was accepted that AMA was one of the organisations that would have been consulted. On November 16, 1984 the DHSS wrote to them asking for their views and proposals to make some amendments to regulations. This was received on November 22 and a response was sought by November 30. AMA requested an extension of time but when no answer was forthcoming the further proposed amendments were summarised in a letter of December 4 which sought a response by December 12. No draft of the amendments was enclosed and AMA replied on December 13 with brief comments. The amending regulations were made on December 17 and became law on December 19. Declarator to the effect that they had failed to comply with section 36(1) was granted. Declarator to the effect that they had failed to comply with section 36(1) was granted. Webster J. noted (at 4):

> "There is no general principle to be extracted from the case law to what kind or amount of consultation is required before delegated legislation, of which consultation is a precondition, can validly be made. But in any context the essence of consultation is the communication of a genuine invitation to give advice and a genuine receipt of that advice. In my view it must go without saying that to achieve consultation sufficient information must be supplied by the consulting to the consulted party to enable it to tender helpful advice. Sufficient time must be given by the consulting to the consulted party to enable it to do that, and sufficient time must be available for such advice to be considered by the consulting party. Sufficient, in that context, does not mean ample, but at least enough to enable the relevant purpose to be fulfilled. By helpful advice, in this context, I mean sufficiently informed and considered information or advice about aspects of the form or substance of the proposals, or their implications for the consulted party, being aspects material to the implementation of the proposal as to which the Secretary of State might not be fully informed or advised and as to which the party consulted might have relevant information or advice to offer.
>
> These propositions, as it seems to me, can partly be derived from, and are wholly consistent with, the decision in various dicta, which I need not enumerate, in *Rollo v. Minister of Town and Country Planning* [1948] 1 All E.R. 13 and *Port Louis Corporation v. Attorney-General of Mauritius* [1965] A.C. 1111.

To determine whether consultation in substance had occurred the court:

> "should have regard not so much to the actual facts which preceded the making of the regulations as to the material before the Secretary of State when he made the regulations, that material including facts or information as it appeared or must have appeared to him acting in good faith, and any judgments made or opinions expressed to him before the making of the regulations about those facts which appeared ... to him to be reasonable".

Webster J. concluded that although the department could expect a quick response the situation was not so urgent as to justify views within such a short period that the response might well amount to insufficient information or consultation. Note, however, that the regulations were not quashed as revocation would mean applicants for housing benefits would be placed in an uncertain position. A Scottish court may not have been able to exercise the same discretion in granting declarator, on which see para. 11–5.

(5) The dictum of Webster J. was quoted with approval in *MacGillivray v. Johnston (No. 2)*, 1994 S.L.T. 1012. A person was accused of a breach of article 3 of the Inshore Fishing (Prohibition of Carriage of Monofilament Gill Nets) (Scotland) Order 1986. Prior to his trial he took a plea to the competency of the charge arguing that the Order was *ultra vires* owing to the Secretary of State's failure to carry out consultation. Evidence was led to the effect that interested bodies had been invited to submit their comments on the Order to the Scottish Office and that a meeting had been requested with the Secretary of State prior to the Order being promulgated but that no meeting had been held, despite a previous practice of doing so. At first instance the sheriff held that the lack of meeting was fatal to there being adequate consultation. On successful appeal by the Crown to the High Court Lord Sutherland observed (at 1022) that:

> "The important features of that test [the Webster dictum] are that the consultee should be given sufficient information to enable him to provide meaningful comment should he so desire, that he should be given time to prepare adequately his response and that when his response is received it should be adequately considered by the appropriate minister.... It may well be that on previous occasions he had decided that such meetings would be useful and such meetings had been arranged.... It is not for this court to examine in detail everything that took place during the consultation procedure and decide whether or not this court would have taken any further steps. All that we can decide is whether or not a genuine consultation procedure has been carried out rather than something which could be described as a sham or a fiction."

Note that, unlike *United States Tobacco International Inc.*, no question of legitimate expectation arose. The expectation of the accused was that they be consulted, but that the form which that consultation took was a matter within the discretion of the Minister. On legitimate expectation see paras 8–31 to 8–36.

(6) The court may also be asked to determine whether in substance the party seeking consultation has received adequate information. In *Air 2000* above, the petitioners sought to argue that the Secretary of State for Transport had failed in his duty under section 31(4) of the Airports Act 1986 to consult with the CAA in relation to air traffic distribution regulations. The petitioners contended that the information provided by the CAA did not amount to "advice" within the meaning of the Act. As a matter of statutory construction, Lord Clyde held that advice had been provided.

Chapter 6

GROUNDS OF LEGAL CONTROL 1: ABUSE OF DISCRETION

In this chapter we are concerned, not if whether or not discretion exists — the subject matter of jurisdictional control discussed in Chapter 00... — but whether or not discretion has been exercised properly. Although we are primarily concerned with the grounds of control in judicial review proceedings, some of the grounds of control such as that of reasonableness have parallels in the context of statutory appeals. A common theme running through the decisions which follow is the emphasis on the distinction between review and appeal, which distinction should be borne in mind when considering the extracts. Has that distinction always been maintained?   **6–1**

    The grounds of control fall into two categories. First, where it is alleged that there has been an abuse of power by the decision maker. Typically we are concerned with allegations that power has been used for an improper purpose or that a relevant consideration has been left out of account or an irrelevant consideration taken into account, or that the power has been used maliciously or has been exercised in an unreasonable manner. Of growing importance is challenge based on the grounds of inconsistency and proportionality. While the former might simply be regarded as an extension of concept of reasonableness, proportionality as a ground of challenge may have profound implications for the scope and nature of judicial review itself.

    The second category is concerned with challenge based on an allegation that a decision maker has fettered his discretion by adherence to rigid policy or acted under dictation. This category is discussed in the next chapter on retention of discretion.

    It is important to bear in mind that these two categories are not watertight. Thus adherence to a rigid policy might amount to taking into account an irrelevant consideration. Similarly, allegations that a decision maker has acted in an inconsistent manner could be met with the defence that the decision maker cannot fetter his discretion. Equally, the case law discussed in Chapter 5 on improper delegation can be regarded as an expression of the concern to ensure that discretion is properly and freely exercised. Other parallels can be drawn and the connections between the various grounds of challenge should be kept in view. On grounds of control generally, see V. Finch and C. Ashton, *Administrative Law in Scotland* (1997), Chap. 10; *The Laws of Scotland: Stair Memorial Encyclopaedia*, Vol. 1, paras 235–240; P.P. Craig, *Administrative Law* (3rd ed., 1994), Chap. 11; and W. Wade and C. Forsyth, *Administrative Law* (7th ed., 1994), Chap. 12.

IMPROPER PURPOSES

Macbeth v. Ashley

(1874) 1 R. (H.L.) 14

    The Public Houses Acts (Amendment) Act 1862 declared the opening and closing times of public houses to be 8 a.m. and 11 p.m. respectively, with the qualification that the times could be reduced by up to two hours within any area by the local magistrate. The Magistrates of Rothesay resolved to set a closing time of 10 p.m. for an area that included all public houses,   **6–2** inns and hotels in Rothesay. Ashley and other hotel keepers raised an action seeking reduction, declarator and damages, together with the substitution of 11 pm for 10 pm in their licensing certificates.

LORD CHANCELLOR: "My Lords, the question, and the only question, to be determined in this case is, whether an order made by the Magistrates of the burgh of Rothesay was within the powers conferred upon them by the Act of Parliament under which they were proceeding; for if the order was within these powers it was not for the Court of Session, and it is not for your Lordships, to examine into the discretion exercised by the Magistrates. The exercise of that discretion is entirely for them, and for them alone.

The question, in the view which I should submit of it to your Lordships, turns really upon one Act of Parliament — the 25 and 26 Vict. c. 35. It is true that before that Act, another Act, that of the 16 and 17 Vict., had been passed upon this subject; but if your Lordships will turn to the Act of the 16 and 17 Vict. you will observe that the form in which that enactment is couched is this — it gives in a schedule a form of certificate of licence to be granted to a hotel or public house, and in that form there occurs the condition that the house is not to be opened before eight o'clock in the morning, or to be kept open later than eleven o'clock at night. And then the 11th section of the Act provides, after declaring that the Magistrates may grant a licence in the form to which I have referred, that 'in localities requiring other hours for opening and closing public houses, &c. than those contained in the schedule, it shall be lawful for the Justices or Magistrates to insert in the schedule such other hours, not being earlier than six or later than eight o'clock in the morning for opening, or earlier than nine o'clock or later than eleven o'clock in the evening for closing the same.'

The proviso therefore is a power given to alter or modify the particular form of licence which is contained in the schedule to that Act.

But when your Lordships turn to the Act of the 25 and 26 Vict., upon which I shall have immediately to comment, you will find that the form of certificate given by the earlier Act is entirely swept away, and another form substituted for it. Therefore the proviso in the earlier Act, which was to operate upon the form of certificate given in that Act, of necessity comes to an end when the certificate given by the earlier Act is removed out of the way. Without stopping to consider what may have been the meaning of the proviso in the earlier statute, it appears to me sufficient to say that the certificate given in the earlier statute being now at an end, and being a certificate which cannot be granted, the earlier statute itself is no longer to be considered.

In this case the Magistrates of Rothesay have made an order substituting a different hour — an earlier hour — for closing, for the hour specified in the later statute to which I have referred. They have done that, not for the whole burgh in point of form, but for a portion of the burgh, so far as regards metes and bounds. But the portion of the burgh for which their order has been made is admitted to contain all the hotels and inns and public-houses which exist in the burgh; and therefore though in form the order does not extend to every square yard of the burgh, for the purposes of licensing it really does comprise the whole of the burgh, because it comprises the whole of the hotels and public-houses in the burgh. This indeed was not denied at the bar. It was very properly assumed to be an order which practically did affect, and (what is more important) which was meant to affect, the whole of the houses within the burgh which were to be licensed.

Now, bearing that in mind, let me direct your Lordships' attention to the provisions contained in the later statute, the 25 and 26 Vict. That later statute provides three forms of certificates in the schedule. Each of these forms contains a condition that the house to which a certificate is to be granted shall not be opened earlier in the morning than eight o'clock, or later in the evening than eleven o'clock. These hours therefore are taken by the Legislature to be the hours which, as a general rule, are to be applied to all licensed houses. The 2d section of the Act provides that these forms of certificates to which I have referred shall come in place of the forms of certificates provided by the earlier Acts, and that it shall be lawful for the Justices, 'where they shall deem it inexpedient to grant to any person a certificate in the form applied for, to grant him a certificate in any other of the forms contained in the schedule.' And then come these words, — 'Provided always that in any particular locality within any county or district or burgh, requiring other hours for opening and closing inns and hotels and public-houses than those specified in the forms of certificates in said schedule applicable thereto, it shall be lawful for such Justices or Magistrates respectively to insert in such certificates such other hours, not being earlier than six of the clock or later than eight of the clock for opening, or earlier than nine of the clock or later than eleven of the clock in the evening for closing the same, as they shall think fit.'

Now, if your Lordships take these words in the proviso as they are to be literally interpreted, it appears to me to be beyond all doubt that they point to a discretion reposed in the Magistrates, which is to be exercised not with reference to the whole county, district, or burgh within their jurisdiction, but, as the words expressly bear, with reference to a particular locality within (that is, inside of) the county, or district or burgh; and I think your Lordships will easily see how reasonable and intelligible this provision of the Legislature was. The subject of the general hours for opening and closing public-houses is a matter, and has always been treated as being a matter, of great public moment. It has been treated as a matter to be reserved for and determined by the consideration of the Imperial Parliament. It has accordingly been a subject upon which Parliament has in this Act expressed its opinion with regard to what should be the general rule as to the hours mentioned in the certificate. But then the Act takes notice that in any particular district over which the licensing authority shall exercise its power there may be some reason why a portion of the district, or a locality within the district, should have applied to it a different rule from that which is to be the rule of the district at large; in other words, that there should be a power of making an exception from that which is to be the general rule. But that is to be the form in which the discretion is to be exercised. There is to be a general rule, and there may be an exception; but if the exception is to swallow up the rule it ceases of course to be an exception at all; and that which might fairly have been an exercise of discretion becomes no exercise of the kind of discretion mentioned in this Act. That, my Lords, appears to me to be the obvious and literal meaning of the words, and the only way in which the literal meaning of the words was attempted to be met was in the very clear argument of the Lord Advocate, who said: — 'Here is a power, a discretion, given to the Magistrates to take a particular locality within their district, — that is, a discretion which they may exercise not only once, but again and again. They may first take one locality, and they may afterwards take another locality, and in that way they may traverse the whole of their district, and, in fine, by taking a number of localities they may ultimately take the whole district. Why, therefore, should they not take the whole of the district at once?' Now, my Lords, I will assume, though it is not for your Lordships now to decide, as the question has not arisen, that this may be a discretion which may be exercised more than once. That may be so, and upon that I express no opinion; but of this I am quite certain, that if Magistrates under the guise of exercising a discretion had taken portion after portion of the district, not with reference to the view of the particular wants or requirements of each portion they selected, but in order by degrees to take possession of the whole of their district, and, under pretence of exercising a discretion for each portion, virtually to subvert and change the general rule laid down by the Legislature, — if, I say, your Lordships were to find, which I cannot imagine or suppose you ever would find, Magistrates adopting that course for the purpose of doing what I must describe as evading an Act of Parliament, your Lordships would not be prepared to sanction, but would discountenance and prevent the exercise of a power which was used in that way. That, however, has not been done by the Magistrates in this case. They have done that which they believed was within their power. They have, once for all, attempted, with regard to all the public-houses in the district, to change the rule laid down by the Act. That, in my opinion, is a power which has not been entrusted to them by the Legislature; and I therefore submit to your Lordships that the view taken by the Court of Session was correct, in reducing the order which was thus made by the Magistrates.

I therefore propose to your Lordships that the interlocutors appealed against should be affirmed, and the appeal dismissed, with costs."

Notes

(1) This case is one of the clearest examples of the long-established rule of Scots law that a **6–3** power may not be used except for the purpose for which it was conferred: see generally *Stair Memorial Encyclopaedia*, Vol. 1, para. 238 and Finch and Ashton, pp. 282–286. It also illustrates the way in which the court establishes whether an improper purpose exists. The court inferred such a purpose from the consideration of the whole circumstances in the case, including of course the statutory framework. It is not always easy to reach such a conclusion. In *Lawson v. St Andrews Senatus Academicus* (1898) 5 S.L.T. 269 it was alleged that the actions of the university court in preventing Lawson taking up the chair of English Literature at the university were motivated by a wish to hinder the procedure to establish the University of Dundee. In the absence of clear and weighty evidence tending to support such an argument, the court was not prepared to infer an improper purpose.

(2) Where a statutory obligation exists to lay out on record the factual basis upon which another party's actions are said to be based, it is incumbent on the person making any allegation of improper purpose to provide a relevant and specific case, on which see *Commission for*

Local Authority Accounts in Scotland v. Grampian Regional Council, 1994 S.L.T. 1120 at 1126–1127. This case is extracted at para. 3–16. Consider also the potential difficulties in establishing improper purpose if questions of public interest immunity arise, on which see Chapter 15 above. *Macbeth* is an example of an attempt to use a statutory power in a way which took the use beyond the scope of the statute. The doctrine of improper purpose is, however, equally applicable to the use of one statutory power to promote an outcome which is separately provided for in terms of another statutory power. The following excerpt illustrates this.

Wheeler v. Leicester City Council

[1985] A.C. 1054

6–4   "The local authority purported to terminate the use which Leicester [Rugby] Football Club made of a recreation ground owned by the council. This action was taken following the club's refusal to comply fully with a number of requirements made of it by the local authority. The requirements were the council's response to the decision of three of the club's players to take part in a rugby tour of South Africa. The club was willing to condemn the tour but was not willing, and indeed doubted its powers, to put pressure on the players to induce them not to take part in the tour. The club applied for certiorari to quash the council's decision. In the proceedings the council argued that its policy was in accordance with its obligations under section 71 of the Race Relations Act 1976 — 'it shall be the duty of every local authority to make appropriate arrangements with a view to securing their various functions are carried out with due regard to the need — (a) to eliminate unlawful racial discrimination; and (b) to promote equality of opportunity, and good relations, between persons of different racial groups.' The council was acting, it argued, in the interests of its local population, which consisted of 25 per cent persons of Asian or Afro-Caribbean origin.

The club was unsuccessful at first instance and in the Court of Appeal ([1985] 2 All E.R. 151). It then appealed to the House of Lords."

LORD ROSKILL: "… None of the judges in the courts below have felt able to hold that the action of the club was unreasonable or perverse in the *Wednesbury* sense. They do not appear to have been invited to consider whether those actions, even if not unreasonable on *Wednesbury* principles, were assailable on the grounds of procedural impropriety or unfairness by the council in the manner in which… they took their decision to suspend for 12 months the use by the club of the Welford Road recreation ground.

I would greatly hesitate to differ from four learned judges on the *Wednesbury* issue but for myself I would have been disposed respectfully to do this and to say that the actions of the council were unreasonable in the *Wednesbury* sense. But even if I am wrong in this view, I am clearly of the opinion that the manner in which the council took that decision was in all the circumstances unfair within the third of the principles stated in *Council of Civil Service Unions v. Minister for the Civil Service*. [Editor's note: *i.e.* 'procedural impropriety'.] The council formulated those four questions in the manner of which I have spoken and indicated that only such affirmative answers would be acceptable. They received reasoned and reasonable answers which went a long way in support of the policy which the council had accepted and desired to see accepted. The views expressed in these reasoned and reasonable answers were lawful views and the views which, as the evidence shows, many people sincerely hold and believe to be correct. If the club had adopted a different and hostile attitude, different considerations might well have arisen. But the club did not adopt any such attitude.

In my view, therefore, this is a case in which the court should interfere because of the unfair manner in which the council set about obtaining its objective. I would not, with profound respect, rest my decision upon the somewhat wider ground which appealed to Browne-Wilkinson L.J. in his dissenting judgment. Since preparing this speech I have had the advantage of reading in draft the speech of my noble and learned friend Lord Templeman with which I find myself in complete agreement …"

LORD TEMPLEMAN: "My Lords, in my opinion the Leicester City Council were not entitled to withdraw from the Leicester Football Club the facilities for training and playing enjoyed by the club for many years on the council's recreation ground for one simple and good reason. The club could not be punished because the club had done nothing wrong.

The 1984 Rugby Tour of South Africa was organised by the Rugby Football Union which invited individuals, including three members of the club, to join the tour. There were two views about the tour amongst the opponents of apartheid. The view taken by the council, a view which I share, was that the tour would endorse the racist policies of the South African Government. The opposite view was expressed by

Mr Dodge, who was one of the three members of the club who participated in the tour and who gave sworn evidence in these proceedings as follows:

> 'I personally deplore apartheid as being morally wrong. It is nevertheless my genuine belief that maintaining sporting links with South Africa does help break down the evil social barriers of apartheid, a personal belief which has been strengthened by observing in 1984 the improvement since 1980.'

The council agreed that this belief was sincerely held not only by Mr Dodge but by other opponents of apartheid. The Government had subscribed to the Gleneagles agreement but did not take steps to ban the tour, leaving the decision to each individual invited to take part. The club does not practise racial discrimination, does not support apartheid, has not been guilty of any infringement of the Race Relations Act 1976, did not support the decision of the three members to join the tour and sought to discourage them from joining the tour by sending them copies of the reasoned memorandum published by the opponents of the tour. The council does not contend that the club should have threatened or punished the three club members who participated in the tour or that the club could properly have done so. Nevertheless, the club has been punished by the council according to Mr Soulsby for 'failing to condemn the tour and to discourage its members from playing'. My Lords, the laws of this country are not like the laws of Nazi Germany. A private individual or a private organisation cannot be obliged to display zeal in the pursuit of an object sought by a public authority and cannot be obliged to publish views dictated by a public authority.

The club having committed no wrong, the council could not use their statutory powers in the management of their property or any other statutory powers in order to punish the club. There is no doubt that the council intended to punish and have punished the club. When the club were presented by the council with four questions it was made clear that the club's response would only be acceptable if, in effect, all four questions were answered in the affirmative . . .

. . . In my opinion, this use by the council of its statutory powers was a misuse of power. The council could not properly seek to use its statutory powers of management or any other statutory powers for the purposes of punishing the club when the club had done no wrong.

In *Congreve v. Home Office* [1976] Q.B. 629, the Home Secretary had a statutory power to revoke television licences. In exercise of that statutory power he revoked the television licences of individuals who had lawfully surrendered an existing licence and taken out a new licence before an increase in the licence fee was due to take effect. Lord Denning M.R. said, at 651:

> 'If the licence is to be revoked — and his money forfeited — the Minister would have to give good reasons to justify it. Of course, if the licensee had done anything wrong — if he had given a cheque for £12 which was dishonoured, or if he had broken the conditions of the licence — the Minister could revoke it. But when the licensee has done nothing wrong at all, I do not think the Minister can lawfully revoke the licence, at any rate, not without offering him his money back, and not even then except for good cause. If he should revoke it without giving reasons, or for no good reason, the courts can set aside his revocation and restore the licence. It would be a misuse of the power conferred on him by Parliament: and these courts have the authority — and, I would add, the duty — to correct a misuse of power by a Minister or his department, no matter how much he may resent it or warn us of the consequences if we do.'

Similar considerations apply, in my opinion, to the present case. Of course this does not mean that the council is bound to allow its property to be used by a racist organisation or by any organisation which, by its actions or its words, infringes the letter or the spirit of the Race Relations Act 1976. But the attitude of the club and of the committee of the club was a perfectly proper attitude, caught as they were in a political controversy which was not of their making.

For these reasons and the reasons given by my noble and learned friend Lord Roskill, I would allow the appeal."

Lords Bridge, Brightman and Griffiths expressed their agreement with both Lord Roskill and Lord Templeman.

Notes

(1) For comments on *Wheeler*, see C. Turpin, "Race relations, rugby football and the law"   **6–5** [1985] 44 C.L.J. 333 and case notes by T.R.S. Allan (1985) 48 M.L.R. 448 and (1986) 49 M.L.R. 121 where the dissenting judgment of Browne-Wilkinson L.J. in the Court of Appeal,

based on the view that the council's action violated the fundamental human right of free speech and that Parliament could not have intended this under section 71 of the Race Relations Act 1976, is fully discussed.

(2) The use of planning control to achieve non-planning ends has frequently been before the courts. In *David Lowe & Sons Ltd v. Musselburgh Town Council*, 1973 S.C. 130 an attempt was made by the planning authority to link the development of a residential site to its general responsibilities to provide housing in terms of local government legislation. A condition was imposed which provided that (at 137):

> "The sites are approved for the Burgh's estimated future Local Authority and private housing needs over the next twenty years which cannot be accommodated within the existing burgh boundaries, in the proportion of one private house to four local authority houses."

The Inner House drew a distinction between the use of land and the user of the land. The Lord President (Emslie) quoted the statutory definition of "development" and stated (at 142) that the planning legislation

> "is concerned with the control of development thus defined, and for the purposes of planning permission is not concerned with ownership or occupation of land or buildings".

On this case see E. Young, "Planning Condition apportioning Land between Private and Local Authority Housing" [1975] J.P.L. 139. See also *R. v. Hillingdon London Borough Council, ex parte Royco Homes Ltd* [1974] Q.B. 720 where a condition providing that the first occupiers of a residential development should be persons on the housing waiting list for a period in excess of 10 years be given security of tenure under the Rent Acts was held by Lord Widgery CJ. (at 732) to be

> "the equivalent of requiring the applicants to take on at their own expense a significant part of the duty of the council as housing authority. However well intentioned and however sensible such a desire on the part of the council may have been [it was] ultra vires."

Moral considerations cannot relate to a proper planning purpose, although in *Marie Finlay v. Secretary of State for the Environment and London Borough of Islington* [1983] J.P.L. 802 the showing of sexually explicit films in premises could be regarded as detrimental to the character of the area. On this area generally see E. Young and J. Rowan-Robinson, *Scottish Planning Law and Procedure* (1985), Chap. 9; *Stair Memorial Encyclopaedia*, Vol. 23, "Town and Country Planning," paras 240–241; and N. Collar, *Planning* (1994), p. 304.

6–6 (3) Not all exercises of power for an improper purpose are necessarily well intentioned. In *Congreve v. Home Office* [1976] Q.B. 629, cited in *Wheeler*, was an example of misuse of power which was clearly intended to be to the benefit of the public authority and not for the public benefit. *Wheeler* and *David Lowe* could be viewed as situations in which public authority believed that it was acting in the public interest as there was at least some statutory warrant for its action, contained either in the statute itself as in *David Lowe* or in some other statute, as in *Wheeler*.

Congreve was one of over 20,000 people who took out a second television licence before the expiry of the existing licence. There was an anticipation of an increase in the licence fee by £6 from April 1, 1975. In terms of section 1(2) of the Wireless Telegraphy Act 1949, "A licence… may be issued subject to such terms, provisions and limitations as the [Minister] may think fit." Section 1 (4) provided that a licence "may be revoked… by a notice in writing… served on the holder…". No other limitations existed in the statute. The Home Office feared a loss in revenue and threatened revocation of the existing licence unless a new licence was taken out at the higher fee. The Court of Appeal declared that any such revocation was unlawful. The reasoning of Geoffrey Lane L.J., which was approved by Lord Templeman in *Wheeler*, was as follows (at 662):

> "The licence was a valid one at the time of its issue. At that time the new regulation increasing the fee to £18 had not come into operation and therefore did not in law exist. There was no power to demand the extra £6 nor to receive it.

[The revocation] is illegal for two reasons. First, it is coupled with an illegal demand which taints the revocation and makes that illegal too. Secondly, or possibly putting the same matter in a different way, it is an improper exercise of a discretionary power to use a threat to exercise that power as a means of extracting money which Parliament has given the executive no mandate to demand: see *Attorney-General v. Wilts United Dairies Ltd.* [(1922) 91 L.J. K.B. 897]."

Note also the old Scots case of *William Reid* (1765) Mor. 7361. It was alleged that Excise Officers had entered a snuff mill on the pretence of searching for smuggled goods but in reality to discover a secret process. It was alleged that the power for which the right of entry was conferred was being used to confer a benefit on those who wished to know the nature of the process.

(4) It is important to understand that a purpose can only be regarded as improper and so unlawful if it is beyond the powers of the body promoting that purpose. To that extent, the concept of improper purpose is inextricably linked to the concept of simple *ultra vires*, discussed in Chapter 3. This point fell to be considered in *Highland Regional Council v. British Railways Board*, 1996 S.L.T. 274. In terms of the Railways Act 1993, s. 37, a railway company wishing to close a railway passenger service required to submit itself to closure procedure which of necessity would involve further delay in closing this service and in particular required public consultation. British Railways Board, the party responsible for the provision of this service, sought to avoid closure procedure by maintaining three substitute services. On the facts, the Inner House held that those substitute services could not be regarded as railway passenger services and were a device to avoid initiating the closure procedure. If those services had on the facts been held to be genuine railway services then no matter how undesirable the removal of a sleeper service was and no matter that that was in fact the ulterior motive then that of itself would not render the decision unlawful. The Lord President (Hope) noted (at 281):

"As for the complaint that the decision was in bad faith because of the ulterior motive, we do not think that it is open to this criticism so long as all the steps taken by the board were within their powers under the Act. In *Gerry Cottle's Circus Ltd v City of Edinburgh District Council*, 1990 S.L.T. 235 at p 240C Lord Dervaird said that he did not consider that if the policy of the district council was within its powers as a licensing authority, the application of that policy could properly have been invalidated as a use of licensing powers for an ulterior motive. Applying that reasoning to the present case, we do not think that if the board were acting within their powers in treating the substitute services as railway passenger services for these lines for the purposes of s 37 (1) of the Act, the decision to close the sleeper service without initiating the closure procedure could be invalidated on the ground of an improper motive. The board on this view would simply be giving effect to the provisions of s 37 (1) which do not require the closure procedure to be initiated until the decision is taken to discontinue all the railway passenger services on the line.

These observations do however show how important it is to examine very closely the purpose for which s 37 (1) was enacted and the intention of Parliament as to what services can properly be taken into account for the purposes of that subsection as railway passenger services. In our opinion it is on the ground of illegality that the board's decision can be seen to have been an improper one. We agree with the Lord Ordinary that, if the provision of the substitute services would have had the effect in law of preventing closure of the three sections of line within the meaning of the subsection, the board's decision could not be regarded as being either irrational or unreasonable. As we agree with him also that the substitute services did not have this effect in law, the result that the decision to discontinue the sleeper service falls to be reduced on the ground of illegality."

We now turn to consider the situation in which a decision may have been motivated by a number of purposes, some lawful, some not. How does the court deal with this?

Westminster Corporation v. London and North Western Railway Company

[1905] A.C. 426

"The Corporation, a sanitary authority, constructed public lavatories underground in the middle of   **6–7**
Parliament Street. In the words of Lord Macnaghten:
'The plan of the construction is this: On each aside of the roadway there is an entrance, five feet nine inches wide, protected by railings and leading by a staircase of the same width to a passage or subway, ten

feet wide and eight feet high, which runs the whole way across on a level with the underground conveniences. Out of this subway there are openings — two for men and one for women — into spacious chambers, where the usual accommodation (politely described as lavatories and cloak-rooms) is provided on a large and liberal scale. All the arrangements seem to have been designed and carried out with due regard to decency, and with every possible consideration for the comfort of wayfarers in need of such accommodations.'

The Railway Company owned a large block of buildings on the east side of Parliament Street. They objected to the sanitary works, and sought to have them removed, basing their claim alternatively on trespass, or obstruction to the highway causing special damage. The Corporation relied on their powers under the Public Health (London) Act 1891 to provide, make and maintain public lavatories and sanitary conveniences. The Company pointed out that both the Corporation and its predecessor, the Vestry of St Margaret's, Westminster, had exhibited a wish to have a subway constructed at that site. In September 1900 the Vestry's surveyor wrote to the Company referring to the construction of a 'subway', and making no mention of the construction of the convenience. In December the acting town clerk of Westminster wrote that 'the intention is the construction of a subway to facilitate pedestrians crossing… a thoroughfare of great width and very considerable traffic…. Admission to the conveniences, which will be accessible from the subways, could otherwise have been provided from refuges above them.'

The railway company claimed an injunction to prevent the corporation from continuing to trespass on their premises and to obstruct the footway opposite the premises and damages. When the parties came to trial, it was found that owing to some mistake, the corporation's works had encroached upon the footway. The trial judge, Joyce J. ([1902] 1 Ch. 269), ordered the corporation to remove the encroachment. On appeal, the Court of Appeal (Vaughan Williams, Stirling and Cozens-Hardy L.JJ. [1904] 1 Ch. 759) ordered the corporation to 'pull down and remove the whole of the staircase, railings, and other works placed by the defendants upon the lands of the plaintiffs other than the conveniences in the pleadings mentioned, and such further portion of the construction as the court [might], upon application, sanction as a proper approach to the said conveniences'. The order was suspended pending an appeal to the House of Lords. On appeal the corporation acquiesced in the order of Joyce J. but contended that the order of the Court of Appeal was wrong."

LORD MACNAGHTEN: "… There can be no question as to the law applicable to the case. It is well settled that a public body invested with statutory powers such as those conferred upon the corporation must take care not to exceed or abuse its powers. It must keep within the limits of the authority committed to it. It must act in good faith. And it must act reasonably. The last proposition is involved in the second, if not in the first. But in the present case I think it will be convenient to take it separately.

Now, looking merely at what has been done — at the work as designed and actually constructed — it seems to me that, apart from the encroachment on the footway, it is impossible to contend that the work is in excess of what was authorized by the Act of 1891. The conveniences themselves, extensive as the accommodation is, have not been condemned by the Court of Appeal or even attacked in the evidence.

[His Lordship then held that the entrance from the roadway was not excessively wide.]

Then I come to the question of want of good faith. That is a very serious charge. It is not enough to shew that the corporation contemplated that the public might use the subway as a means of crossing the street. That was an obvious possibility. It cannot be otherwise if you have an entrance on each side and the communication is not interrupted by a wall or a barrier of some sort. In order to make out a case of bad faith it must be shewn that the corporation constructed this subway as a means of crossing the street under colour and pretence of providing public conveniences which were not really wanted at that particular place. That was the view of their conduct taken by the Court of Appeal. 'In my judgment,' says Vaughan Williams L.J., 'it is not true to say that the corporation have taken this land which they have taken with the object of using it for the purposes authorized by the Legislature.' 'You are acting *mala fide*,' he added, 'if you are seeking to acquire and acquiring lands for a purpose not authorized by the Act of Parliament.' So you are; there can be no doubt of that. The other learned Lord Justices seem to take the same view of the conduct of the corporation. Now this, as I have said, is a very serious charge. A gross breach of public duty, and all for a mere fad! The learned judge who tried the case had before him the chairman of the works committee. That gentleman declared that his committee considered with very great care for a couple of years or more the question of these conveniences in Parliament Street. He asserted on oath that 'the primary object of the committee was to provide these conveniences'. Why is this gentleman not to be believed? The learned judge who saw and heard him believed his statement. The learned judges of the Court of Appeal have discredited his testimony, mainly, if not entirely, on the ground of two letters about which he was not asked a single question…. The letter of the surveyor was a foolish letter, which the writer seems to have thought clever. The letter of the temporary representative of the acting town clerk, if you compare the two letters, seems to have derived its inspiration from the same source. I cannot conceive why the solemn statement of the chairman of the committee should be discredited on such a ground. I do not think there is anything in the minutes tending to disprove his testimony. I entirely agree with Joyce J. that the primary object of the council was the construction of the conveniences with the requisite and proper means of approach thereto and exit therefrom…"

LORD JAMES (dissenting): "… [T]he question to be solved seems to be thus formulated: Was the so-called tunnel an approach to the conveniences only, or was it something more? (1) Was it a subway distinct from the approach, or (2) was it a subway in combination with the approach used for two distinct purposes?

In my judgment the construction in question comes within one or other of the two latter alternatives. Possibly within the first, certainly within the second.

If this finding on the facts is correct, the works, so far as they constitute the subway, are constructed without legal authority. The Legislature has not thought it right to confer on local bodies the power to compulsorily take land or impose rates for the purpose of constructing subways. In this case some land has been taken which would not have been required if the approach had not been enlarged into a subway, and an unauthorized burthen has been imposed upon the ratepayers in consequence of this enlargement.

Thus it is, in my opinion, that the appellants have acted beyond their powers and without justification."

THE EARL OF HALSBURY L.C. and LORD LINDLEY delivered speeches in favour of dismissing the appeal.

R. v. Inner London Education Authority, ex parte Westminster City Council

[1986] 1 All E.R. 19

"The ILEA, being opposed to central government public expenditure limitation policies, commenced a programme by which they sought to raise public awareness of those policies and of their implications. Under section 142(2) of the Local Government Act 1972 the ILEA had power to incur expenditure on publishing within its area 'information on matters relating to local government'. In July 1984 a sub-committee of the ILEA resolved to retain an advertising agency to mount a media and poster campaign, at a cost of some £651,000. The ILEA acknowledged that the purpose of the campaign was both to 'inform' the public about government proposals and their effects (a lawful purpose) and to 'persuade' the public to support the ILEA's stance on this matter (an unlawful purpose). The applicant council argued that the resolution was *ultra vires* the power in section 142(2), *inter alia*, because of the unlawful purpose and because the ILEA had taken into account an irrelevant consideration — its desire to persuade the public to oppose government policy."

6–8

GLIDEWELL J. [outlined the facts, reviewed the terms of section 142(2), and continued:]… "[T]he decision of July 23, 1984, was made with the two purposes of informing and persuading.

Two purposes
This brings me to what I regard as being the most difficult point in the case, namely: if a local authority resolves to expend its ratepayers' money in order to achieve two purposes, one of which it is authorised to achieve by statute but for the other of which it has no authority, is that decision invalid?

I was referred to the following authorities.

(i) *Westminster Corp. v. London and North Western Ry Co.* [1905] A.C. 426…

[His Lordship summarised this decision and concluded:]… this suggests that a test for answering the question is, if the authorised purpose is the primary purpose, the resolution is within the power.

(ii) *Sydney Municipal Council v. Campbell* [1925] A.C. 338. This… decision of the Privy Council… does not really deal with the question that confronts me of a resolution passed with two purposes in mind.

(iii) More recently in *Hanks v. Minister of Housing and Local Government* [1963] 1 Q.B. 999, Megaw J. did have to deal with a case in which it was alleged that a compulsory purchase order had been made for two purposes, one of which did not fall within the empowering Act. At 1019, he quoted part of the dissenting judgment of Denning L.J. in *Earl Fitzwilliam's Wentworth Estates Co. Ltd v. Minister of Town and Country Planning* [1951] 2 K.B.284, 307:

> 'If Parliament grants to a government department a power to be used for an authorised purpose, then the power is only validly exercised when it is used by the department genuinely for that purpose as its dominant purpose. If that purpose is not the main purpose, but is subordinated to some other purpose which is not authorised by law, then the department exceeds its powers and the action is invalid.'

It had been submitted to Megaw J. that, although Denning L.J. had dissented from the decision of the majority, this passage in his judgment did not differ from the view of the majority.
Megaw J. went on ([1963] 1 Q.B. 999, 1020):

> 'I confess that I think confusion can arise from the multiplicity of words which have been used in this case as suggested criteria for the testing of the validity of the exercise of a statutory power. The words used have included "objects", "purposes", "motives", "motivation", "reasons", "grounds" and "considerations". In the end, it seems to me, the simplest and clearest way to state the matter is by reference to "considerations". A "consideration", I apprehend, is something which one takes into account as a factor in arriving at a decision. I am prepared to assume, for the purposes of this case, that, if it be shown that an authority exercising a power has taken into account as a relevant factor something which it could not properly take into account in deciding whether or not to exercise the power, then the exercise of the power, normally at least, is bad. Similarly, if the authority fails to take into account as a relevant factor something which is relevant, and which is or ought to be known to it, and which it ought to have taken into account, the exercise of the power is normally bad. I say "normally", because I can conceive that there may be cases where the factor wrongly taken into account, or omitted, is insignificant, or where the wrong taking-into-account, or omission, actually operated in favour of the person who later claims to be aggrieved by the decision...'

I have considered also the views of the learned authors of textbooks on this. Professor Wade in *Administrative Law* (5th ed., 1982), p. 388 under the heading 'Duality of Purpose' says:

> 'Sometimes an act may serve two or more purposes, some authorised and some not, and it may be a question whether the public authority may kill two birds with one stone. The general rule is that its action will be lawful provided the permitted purpose is the true and dominant purpose behind the act, even though some secondary or incidental advantage may be gained for some purpose which is outside the authority's powers.'

Professor Evans, in *de Smith's Judicial Review of Administrative Action* (4th ed., 1980), pp. 329–332, comforts me by describing the general problem of plurality of purpose as 'a legal porcupine which bristles with difficulties as soon as it is touched'. He distils from the decisions of the courts five different tests on which reliance has been placed at one time or another, including —

> '(1) What was the *true purpose* for which the power was exercised? If the actor has in truth used his power for the purposes for which it was conferred, it is immaterial that he was thus enabled to achieve a subsidiary object... (5) Was any of the purposes pursued an unauthorised purpose? If so, and if the unauthorised purpose has materially influenced the actor's conduct, the power had been invalidly exercised because irrelevant considerations have been taken into account.'

These two tests, and Professor Evans' comment on them, seem to me to achieve much the same result and to be similar to that put forward by Megaw J. in *Hanks v. Minister of Housing and Local Government* [1963] 1 Q.B. 999 in the first paragraph of the passage I have quoted from his judgment. That is the part that includes the sentence: 'In the end, it seems to me, the simplest and clearest way to state the matter is by reference to "considerations".' I gratefully adopt the guidance of Megaw J., and the two tests I have referred to from *de Smith*.

It thus becomes a question of fact for me to decide, on the material before me, whether, in reaching its decision of July 23, 1984, the staff and general sub-committee of I.L.E.A. was pursuing an unauthorised purpose, namely that of persuasion, which has materially influenced the making of its decision. I have already said that I find that one of the sub-committee's purposes was the giving of information. But I also find that it had the purpose of seeking to persuade members of the public to a view identical with that of the authority itself, and indeed I believe that this was a, if not the, major purpose of the decision...

Adopting the test referred to above, I thus hold that I.L.E.A.'s sub-committee did, when making its decision of July 23, 1984, take into account an irrelevant consideration, and thus that decision was not validly reached.

If I am wrong on this, there would remain for consideration the last two arguments advanced by counsel for the city council. I will deal with these shortly. As to the alleged breach of fiduciary duty to the ratepayers, it is true that the cost of employing AMV was very substantially greater than the sums which I.L.E.A. had already authorised to be expended on the 'campaign'. But this is a matter of discretion for the authority, which was advised that it had to take into account its duty to the ratepayers. It would be for Westminster City Council to show, if they could, that I.L.E.A. had disregarded that duty. In my view,

Westminster City Council have failed to do this. Similarly, I cannot say on the material before me that I.L.E.A.'s decision was so unreasonable as to be perverse. If therefore the matter depended on either of these two grounds, Westminster City Council's challenge would fail."

Notes

(1) The second case was referred to in *The Commission for Local Authority Accounts in Scotland*   **6–9**
v. City of Edinburgh District Council, 1988 S.C.L.R. 552, which is extracted at para. 3–20.

(2) In *R. v. Broadcasting Complaints Commission, ex parte Owen* [1985] 2 All E.R. 522 Dr David Owen alleged that the Broadcasting Complaints Commission had failed in their duty under section 54 of the Broadcasting Act 1981 to consider and adjudicate upon complaints of "unjust or unfair treatment" in radio or television programmes. Dr Owen alleged that the air time given to the Social Democratic Party was unjust and unfair, given their share of the vote in the 1983 General Election, as compared to the radio and television coverage given to the Labour Party. It was argued for Dr Owen that if any one of the five reasons given by the Commission for declining to entertain the complaint was unlawful, then the presence of one unlawful reason was sufficient to vitiate the whole of the decision. In giving his judgment May L.J. stated (at 533):

> "Where the reasons given by a statutory body for taking or not taking a particular course of action are not mixed and can clearly be disentangled, but where the court is quite satisfied that even though one reason may be bad in law, nevertheless the statutory body would have reached precisely the same decision on the other valid reasons, then this court will not interfere by way of judicial review. In such a case, looked at realistically and with justice, such a decision of such a body ought not to be disturbed."

On this case see H.F. Rawlings, "Impartiality in Television Coverage of Politics" (1985) 48 M.L.R. 584. In *Grieve v. Douglas-Home*, 1965 S.L.T. (Notes) 21, electoral impropriety of another kind was alleged. An unsuccessful candidate for the Perth and Kinross seat at the 1964 General Election alleged that the successful candidate, Sir Alex Douglas-Home, leader of the Conservative Party, and also the Prime Minister had, by appearing in party political broadcasts, breached sections 63 and 64 of the Representation of the People Act 1949. It was alleged that he had benefited from expenditure on these party political broadcasts and that in turn helped to promote his election as local MP. It was, however, held that on the facts, the proper motivation behind the expenditure was not to promote the election of one MP, but to provide information for the public in a general sense. Contrast these cases with *R. v. Lewisham London Borough Council, ex parte Shell UK Ltd* [1988] 1 All E.R. 938 where the council passed a resolution to boycott Shell products. The Divisional Court found that the resolution had two purposes: a lawful one to promote good race relations in terms of section 71 of the Race Relations Act 1976 and an unlawful one to put pressure on Shell to withdraw from South Africa. Where two reasons or purposes could not be disentangled, and one was bad and the bad reason demonstrably exerted a substantial influence, the court would quash the decision in its entirety. Here the two purposes were deemed to be inextricably mixed up thus vitiating the decision as a whole: see on this T.R.S. Allan, "Abuse of Statutory Powers — Apartheid, Disinvestment and Coercion" [1988] 47 C.L.J. 334.

In *Blair v. Smith*, 1924 J.C. 24 it was alleged that a statutory power had been used unlawfully to compel Sunday observance. Blair hired boats in Saltcoats. He was convicted of hiring out a boat on a Sunday in contravention of the condition imposed on his licence and was duly fined. He contended that such a condition was *ultra vires* the Burgh Police (Scotland) Act 1892. The High Court of Justiciary, however, held that a proper purpose could be found on grounds of public safety as fewer rescue facilities were available on Sundays. Contrast this with *Western Isles Islands Council v. Caledonian MacBrayne Ltd*, 1990 S.L.T. (Sh.Ct) 97. Here a byelaw prohibiting the unloading of goods or vehicles at Lochmaddy pier on Sundays was held to be *ultra vires* as no other ground other than Sunday observance could be discerned as the basis for the byelaw.

(3) Older authorities suggest that purposes not authorised by legislation may nevertheless be used as a basis to support a decision not otherwise justified by statutory purpose on grounds of the public interest: see *West v. Aberdeen Harbour Commissioners* (1876) 4 R. 207 and, *Fleming v. Liddesdale District Committee* (1897) 5 S.L.T. 191. It is doubtful whether these cases would represent good law now. They would probably be confined to their own facts.

MALICE AND BAD FAITH

Innes v. Royal Burgh of Kirkcaldy

1963 S.L.T. 325

6–10   Lord Cameron: "This is an application for recall of an interim interdict which was granted *ex parte* on 26th March. The interdict is sought in an action of declarator and interdict in which the summons was signeted on 16th March. The declarator is to the effect that a pretended resolution of the defenders of 11th March 1963, whereby they resolved to approve a recommendation of their finance committee of 4th March 1963 that the rents of all council houses including miscellaneous houses owned by the defenders should be reduced by 25 per cent, was passed in *mala fide* and is null and void. The consequential conclusions are for production and reduction of the pretended resolution and for interdict against the defenders acting upon it, and also for interim interdict....

Now the pursuer avers that in agreeing to the resolution to reduce rents the defenders did not act in good faith, did not make an assessment of the whole relevant factors, but acted upon utterly irrelevant considerations. It is said specifically by the pursuer that the majority of the defenders who voted in favour of the pretended resolution constitute a group who, in or about May 1962, pledged themselves to oppose all rent increases and to have the decision of January 1962 revoked. It is also averred, and is matter of admission, that group meetings took place to discuss the defenders' affairs on occasions antecedent to formal meetings of the defenders, and the pursuer avers that at such meetings persons who are not members of the defenders are in the habit of attending and discussing, *inter alia*, the defenders' affairs. The pursuer further believes and avers that in the course of meetings of this kind, prior to the defenders' meeting on 11th March, the members of the group bound themselves to vote as a group at this coming meeting in favour of the resolution to reduce rents irrespective of any consideration that might be advanced at that meeting. He further avers that there was no material before the defenders on 11th March upon which they could honestly reach the opinion that a reduction of municipal rents was justified and goes on to say that the majority voted in favour of the resolution in respect of irrelevant considerations, such as the large subsidies paid by the legislature to farmers, the high rates of interest and the high rents for privately-owned houses permitted by the legislature, the increases in the cost of rent permitted by the central government, and the necessity to reimburse tenants of corporation houses for alleged subsidies made by them in the years 1925 to 1960 to owner-occupiers of property in the Burgh of Kirkcaldy. It is said that the majority group put forward these considerations at the meeting of 11th March as their reasons why rents should be reduced, and the pursuer goes on to aver that the defenders, in agreeing to this pretended resolution, paid no regard to the interests of the general body of ratepayers such as the pursuer, who are not tenants of corporation houses, notwithstanding that the effect of the pretended resolution, if acted upon, will be to place upon the general body of ratepayers a further burden of £91,000 per annum or 1s. 6d. per £ of the rateable value in Kirkcaldy. The pursuer makes a further general averment of his belief that having regard to the consideration specified by him on which the majority purported to act, the defenders, in reaching their decision, were attempting thereby to usurp the functions of the legislature and to redress what they consider to be a nationwide grievance by local administrative methods designed to bring pressure to bear upon the central government. The defenders admit the course of events, but deny that the majority were actuated by the considerations tabulated by the pursuer. They also admit that one effect of the resolution of 11th March, if put into operation, will be to increase the rates by approximately 1s. 6d. in the £ of rateable value. It is explained by the defenders that they acted in good faith and upon a consideration of all factors which they say are relevant. They deny that the majority of the defenders, whom they admit constitute a group, are opposed to all rent increases, but admit that at the meeting of the group, which took place prior to the defenders' council meeting on 11th March, agreement was reached on the view which should be put forward at the meeting on the former date. It is said that the reasons which prompted the majority of the defenders to vote in favour of the resolution under reduction were, *inter alia*, that the wages paid in the Kirkcaldy area were on average low, that the rents in Kirkcaldy for municipal houses were the highest rents for municipal houses in Scotland, and that the defenders were not able at that time to sustain the position of charging highest rents for municipal houses in Scotland, that the increase of rents on 15th January 1962 was too severe, having regard to the circumstances prevailing, and that further consideration of all the relevant circumstances show that the decision of 15th January 1962 could not now be justified. It was considered, said the defenders, that the effect of the decision of January 1962 was that a fair balance had not been preserved between council house tenants on the one hand and the general body of ratepayers on the other. In these circumstances, the defenders resolved that a further review of rents was necessary and the resolution of 11th March was passed in good faith....

For the pursuer, counsel... maintained that it is always open to the court to intervene and give a remedy if it can be shown that an authority has acted on dishonest, plainly irrelevant or improper considerations. He referred in that connection to the observations of Lord Sumner in the case of *Roberts v. Hopwood* [1925] A.C. 578, in particular at page 603, where Lord Sumner said this: 'The respondents conceded that for wages fixed *mala fide* no exemption from review could be claimed and that the mere magnitude of the wages paid, relatively to the wages for which the same service was procurable, might be enough in itself to establish bad faith. This admission, I am sure, was rightly made, but it leads to two conclusions. Firstly, the final words of the section are not absolute, but are subject to an implied qualification of good faith — "as the board may bona fide think fit." Is the implication of good faith all? That is a qualification drawn from the general legal doctrine, that persons who hold public office have a legal responsibility towards those whom they represent — not merely towards those who vote for them — to the discharge of which they must honestly apply their minds. Bona fide here cannot simply mean that they are not making a profit out of their office or acting in it from private spite, nor is bona fide a short way of saying that the council has acted within the ambit of its powers and, therefore, not contrary to law. It must mean that they are giving their minds to the comprehension and their wills to the discharge of their duty towards that public, whose money and local business they administer.' He also referred to the judgment of the Master of the Rolls in *Associated Provincial Picture Houses Ltd. v. Wednesbury Corporation* [1948] 1 K.B. 223. Now Lord Greene in that case, at page 228, said this: — 'The courts must always, I think, remember this: first, we are dealing with not a judicial act, but an executive act; secondly, the conditions which, under the exercise of that executive act, may be imposed are in terms, so far as language goes, put within the discretion of the local authority without limitation. Thirdly, the statute provides no appeal from the decision of the local authority. What, then, is the power of the courts? They can only interfere with an act of executive authority if it be shown that the authority has contravened the law. It is for those who assert that the local authority has contravened the law to establish that proposition... It is not to be assumed *prima facie* that responsible bodies like the local authority in this case will exceed their powers; but the court, whenever it is alleged that the local authority have contravened the law, must not substitute itself for that authority. It is only concerned with seeing whether or not the proposition is made good. When an executive discretion is entrusted by Parliament to a body such as the local authority in this case, what appears to be an exercise of that discretion can only be challenged in the courts in a strictly limited class of case. As I have said, it must always be remembered that the court is not a court of appeal. When discretion of this kind is granted the law recognises certain principles upon which the discretion must be exercised, but within the four corners of those principles the discretion, in my opinion, is an absolute one and cannot be questioned in any court of law. What then are those principles? They are well understood. They are principles which the court looks to in considering any question of discretion of this kind. The exercise of such a discretion must be a real exercise of the discretion. If, in the statute conferring the discretion, there is to be found expressly or by implication matters which the authority exercising the discretion ought to have regard to, then in exercising the discretion it must have regard to those matters. Conversely, if the nature of the subject-matter and the general interpretation of the Act make it clear that certain matters would not be germane to the matter in question, the authority must disregard those irrelevant collateral matters. There have been in the cases expressions used relating to the sort of things that authorities must not do, not merely in cases under the Cinematograph Act but, generally speaking, under other cases where the powers of local authorities came to be considered. I am not sure myself whether the permissible grounds of attack cannot be defined under a single head. It has been perhaps a little bit confusing to find a series of grounds set out. Bad faith, dishonesty — those of course, stand by themselves — unreasonableness, attention given to extraneous circumstances, disregard of public policy and things like that have all been referred to, according to the facts of individual cases, as being matters which are relevant to the question. If they cannot all be confined under one head, they at any rate, I think, overlap to a very great extent. For instance, we have heard in this case a great deal about the meaning of the word "unreasonable".

'It is true the discretion must be exercised reasonably. Now what does that mean? Lawyers familiar with the phraseology commonly used in relation to exercise of statutory discretions often use the word "unreasonable" in a rather comprehensive sense. It has frequently been used and is frequently used as a general description of the things that must not be done. For instance, a person entrusted with a discretion must, so to speak, direct himself properly in law. He must call his own attention to the matters which he is bound to consider. He must exclude from his consideration matters which are irrelevant to what he has to consider. If he does not obey those rules, he may truly be said, and often is said, to be acting "unreasonably". Similarly, there may be something so absurd that no sensible person could ever dream that it lay within the powers of the authority. Warrington, L.J., in *Short v. Poole Corporation* [1926] Ch. 66, at pages 90, 91, gave the example of the red-haired teacher dismissed because she had red hair. That is unreasonable in one sense. In another sense it is taking into consideration extraneous matters. It is so unreasonable that it might almost be described as being done in bad faith; and, in fact, all these things run into one another.' That passage which I have just quoted from the judgment of the Master of the Rolls was concurred in by the other members of the Court of Appeal....

The issues raised sharply at this stage are of considerable moment. In my opinion, counsel for the defenders' argument goes too far when it seeks to deny any right to a ratepayer to challenge acts or decisions which are prima facie *intra vires* of local authorities. I think that if it can be shown that an authority clothed with discretionary power, has exercised it for reasons which are corrupt or wholly unrelated to the matters in issue or for purposes entirely dissociated from the function or duty in respect of which the power is exercised, then its exercise of that power can be restrained. Equally, if it can be shown that an authority or a majority of its members has deliberately closed its mind to matters which in the exercise of its discretion it would require to take into account, so also in that case its action or position can be subject to successful challenge on record. This, of course, is something very different from mere disagreement with the grounds of action taken by an authority acting prima facie *intra vires*, grounds which are objected to for personal or political reasons, or because it is felt that the grounds, though proper for consideration, appear to the party aggrieved to be of insufficient weight to warrant the decision arrived at.

I respectfully agree with and adopt as my own the passage which I have already quoted from the judgment of Lord Greene in the *Provincial Cinematograph* case....

The question at this stage, therefore, is whether the pursuer has here made any relevant averments which, if established, would entitle him to restrain the defenders from putting their resolution into effect and justifying his reductive conclusion. Now what does he say? First, he refers to the pledge of May 1962 and I must take his averments *pro veritate*. The only meaning I can give to that averment is that the majority group in the council entered on consideration of this case with their minds closed at least to one side of the matter, determined not to apply their unaffected judgment to the issue before them. In addition, he makes further serious charges against them. On the negative side he alleges, as I have indicated, that the majority group determined to exercise the discretion in one way only and that they came to the meeting of 11th March with that resolution in their minds. On the positive side he alleges that they openly professed as the justification of their action to be influenced by considerations which on the face of them are wholly extraneous to the problem which they were purporting to solve in the exercise of the discretion given to them by Parliament. In addition, it is at least matter of implied admission by the defenders that there had been no change of factual circumstances between the date of the determination to increase rents and the date when the decision was taken to reduce them, which appeared on the face of it to affect the issue of increase or decrease. If these averments can be proved and these reasons shown to be those on which the decision to reduce rents was taken, then I am far from thinking that the resolution under attack could stand. As at present advised, if these allegations were established I should regard them as wholly irrelevant and indeed improper considerations for the defenders to take into account and as being in no way related to the powers which the defenders were entitled to exercise in this particular regard. In any event, none of them appear to have any bearing on the extent of the reduction made, which prima facie appears to have been wholly arbitrary....

Having regard to the interest of parties on both sides and to the administrative and financial difficulties referred to, I think that the balance of convenience in this case lies in the preservation of the *status quo*. Being of the opinion which I have expressed on the issues of relevancy and title which were debated before me I shall, therefore, refuse the defenders' motion for recall of the interim interdict *in hoc statu*."

Notes

6–11   (1) See also *Pollok School Co. Ltd v. Glasgow Town Clerk*, 1946 S.C. 373. Challenge on the ground of malice or bad faith has long been recognised by Scots law. In the case of *Dawson v. Allardyce*, February 18, 1809 F.C. the Court of Session held that, with reference to a decision of the Magistrates:

> "If it appeared, that in their judicial capacity their proceedings were dictated by injurious and oppressive motives... or if... a malversation of duty were committed, it would be competent for the Court of Session to apply a remedy to this wrong, but entertain in an action of damages at the instance of [the victim] against them, and by decreeing damages to such an amount as should effectually relieve [the victim] from any inconvenience originating from so great an abusive power and violation of duty."

Allegations of malice and bad faith are highly important in the context of actions in delict against public authorities, including actions for misfeasance or abuse of public office, on which see para.14–59 and generally Finch and Ashton, pp. 286–287 and *Stair Memorial Encyclopaedia*, Vol. 1, para. 239.

(2) It is not sufficient to infer malice or bad faith from a decision simply because it appears to the petitioner or the pursuer to be unfair. Malice and bad faith require to be specifically averred and supported in evidence. In *Micosta S.A. v. Shetland Islands Council*, 1986 S.L.T. 193 Lord Ross observed (at 198):

> "In my opinion, deliberate misuse of statutory powers by a public body would be actionable under the law of Scotland. at the instance of a third party who has suffered loss and damage in consequence of the misuse of statutory powers, provided that there was proof of malice or proof that the action had been taken by the public authority in the full knowledge that it did not possess the power which it purported to exercise."

(3) As with the question of improper purpose, mixed motives in relation to allegations of bad faith and malice raise difficult questions. In *Pollok School Co. Ltd* above it was alleged that the local authority had requisitioned a building which belonged to a private, fee-paying school to house homeless families evacuated under emergency powers during the last war. The school alleged that the authority's motive was based on a dislike of private education. The allegations were sufficiently relevant to go to proof. Even if true, what if there had also been a proper motivation to secure the property for homeless families under the emergency powers?

In *Macfarlane v. Mochrum School Board* (1875) 3 R. 88 the Lord President (Inglis) stated: (at 101):

> "But it is quite possible, and not a thing... unknown in practice, that parties should perform... what would be an unpleasant duty to impartial persons, with a great zest and liking for the duty ... They may have been gratifying their own private malice at the same time that they were performing an obvious act of public duty. But will that invalidate the act of public duty? Most certainly not. If the thing ought to be done, the circumstance that the person who did it has the greatest rancour and hatred against the object of that resolution will not make the resolution invalid if it is well-founded in itself."

This view was echoed more recently by the Privy Council in *David v. Abdul Cader* [1963] 1 W.L.R. 834 where it was held (at 840) that:

> "The presence of spite or ill-will may be insufficient in itself to render actionable a decision which has been based on unexceptionable grounds of consideration and has not been vitiated by the badness of the motive."

A.W. Bradley, *Stair Memorial Encyclopaedia*, Vol. 1, para. 239, submits that the court should be prepared to set aside a decision materially affected by elements of malice or bad faith, notwithstanding the views expressed in *Macfarlane* and *David*. As his authority, he uses the dictum of Lord Deas in *Philip v. Forfar Building Investment Co.* (1868) S.J. 102 where it was stated (at 102):

> "What was done might be so grossly unjustifiable that the law should hold equivalent to personal malice."

This was in the context of enforcement of a debt decree. Do you think that the court should give more weight to ensuring that administration is only motivated by good faith? Allegations of bad faith will not be sufficient to overcome a statutory time-limit restricting judicial control: see *R. v. Secretary of State for the Environment, exp. Ostler* [1977] Q.B. 122, on which see para.10–41.

(4) In *Highland Regional Council v. British Railways Board*, above, it was argued for the board that an ulterior motive might amount to bad faith. On the facts, this was held not to be so but it is at least possible that one might be able to characterise malice or bad faith as an improper purpose and argue that it is inextricably linked to proper purposes. On the latter point see *R. v. Lewisham Borough Council, ex p. Shell UK Ltd*, above.

RELEVANT AND IRRELEVANT CONSIDERATIONS

6–12   On the face of it, this ground of challenge should not be any different in substance from that of improper purpose. An irrelevant consideration will of necessity involve regard to an improper purpose. Nevertheless, the case law shows that a distinction is drawn. As with the concept of "improper purpose", sometimes statutes are explicit as to the considerations which need to be taken into account in coming to a decision in the exercise of a power, but more usually, the courts are left to determine in terms of the legislation as a whole matters which are relevant or irrelevant. Moreover, even where a statute sets out matters which must or must not be taken into account, that does not mean to say that other matters may not be relevant or irrelevant. One of the most significant developments in relation to this area of challenge is likely to come under the provisions of the Human Rights Act 1998. Under section 6, public authorities are obliged to act in accordance with the rights secured by the Act in section 1, and by virtue of section 2, courts and tribunals which are themselves public authorities are obliged to take into account Convention rights and in particular the case law of the European Court of Human Rights in assessing the legality of the actions of, among others, those public authorities. Section 6 is yet to be brought into force. These sections are discussed above. Our first concern is, however, with the application of this ground in a more traditional context.

Padfield v. Minister of Agriculture, Fisheries and Food

[1968] 1 All E.R. 694

6–13   Section 19(3) of the Agriculture Marketing Act 1958 provides that:

> "A committee of investigation shall… be charged with the duty, if the Minister in any case so directs, of considering, and reporting to the Minister on… any complaint made to the Minister as to the operation of any scheme which, in the opinion of the Minister, could not be considered by a consumer's committee…"

England and Wales were divided into 11 regions for the purpose of the Milk Marketing Board. Producers had to sell their milk to the board at prices which differed from region to region to reflect varying costs of transportation from producer to consumer. Transport costs had altered and the south east region wished the differential to be altered. The constitution of the board made it impossible for the south east producers to get a majority for their proposals and they asked the Minister to appoint a committee of investigations. When the Minister refused he applied for an order of mandamus (broadly the equivalent of an action for performance of statutory duty in Scots law, on which see para.11–11) directing him to refer the complaint to the committee of investigations or to deal with it according to law, that is on relevant considerations only, to the exclusion of irrelevant considerations. At first instance this was granted but the Court of Appeal allowed an appeal by the Minister and the producers appealed to the House of Lords.

LORD REID: "… The respondent contends that his only duty is to consider a complaint fairly and that he is given an unfettered discretion with regard to every complaint either to refer it or not to refer it to the committee as he may think fit. The appellants contend that it is his duty to refer every genuine and substantial complaint, or alternatively that his discretion is not unfettered and that in this case he failed to exercise his discretion according to law because his refusal was caused or influenced by his having misdirected himself in law or by his having taken into account extraneous or irrelevant considerations.

In my view, the appellants' first contention goes too far. There are a number of reasons which would justify the Minister in refusing to refer a complaint. For example, he might consider it more suitable for arbitration, or he might consider that in an earlier case the committee of investigation had already rejected a substantially similar complaint, or he might think the complaint to be frivolous or vexatious. So he must have at least some measure of discretion. But is it unfettered?

It is implicit in the argument for the Minister that there are only two possible interpretations of this provision — either he must refer every complaint or he has an unfettered discretion to refuse to refer in any case. I do not think that is right. Parliament must have conferred the discretion with the intention that it should be used to promote the policy and objects of the Act; the policy and objects of the Act must be determined by construing the Act as a whole and construction is always a matter of law for the court. In a matter of this kind it is not possible to draw a hard and fast line, but if the Minister, by reason of his having misconstrued the Act or for any other reason, so uses his discretion as to thwart or run counter to the policy and objects of the Act, then our law would be very defective if persons aggrieved were not entitled to the protection of the court. So it is necessary first to construe the Act.

When these provisions were first enacted in 1931 it was unusual for Parliament to compel people to sell their commodities in a way to which they objected and it was easily foreseeable that any such scheme would cause loss to some producers. Moreover, if the operation of the scheme was put in the hands of the majority of the producers, it was obvious that they might use their power to the detriment of consumers, distributors or a minority of the producers. So it is not surprising that Parliament enacted safeguards.

The approval of Parliament shows that this scheme was thought to be in the public interest, and in so far as it necessarily involved detriment to some persons, it must have been thought to be in the public interest that they should suffer it. But in sections 19 and 20 Parliament drew a line. They provide machinery for investigating and determining whether the scheme is operating or the board is acting in a manner contrary to the public interest.

The effect of these sections is that if, but only if, the Minister and the committee of investigation concur in the view that something is being done contrary to the public interest the Minister can step in. Section 20 enables the Minister to take the initiative. Section 19 deals with complaints by individuals who are aggrieved. I need not deal with the provisions which apply to consumers. We are concerned with other persons who may be distributors or producers. If the Minister directs that a complaint by any of them shall be referred to the committee of investigation, that committee will make a report which must be published. If they report that any provision of this scheme or any act or omission of the board is contrary to the interests of the complainers *and* is not in the public interest, then the Minister is empowered to take action, but not otherwise. He may disagree with the view of the committee as to public interest, and, if he thinks that there are other public interests which outweigh the public interest that justice should be done to the complainers, he would be not only entitled but bound to refuse to take action. Whether he takes action or not, he may be criticised and held accountable in Parliament but the court cannot interfere.

I must now examine the Minister's reasons for refusing to refer the appellants' complaint to the committee. I have already set out the letters of March 23 and May 3, 1965. I think it is right also to refer to a letter sent from the Ministry on May 1, 1964, because in his affidavit the Minister says he has read this letter and there is no indication that he disagrees with any part of it. It is as follows: [His Lordship read the letter and continued:]

The first reason which the Minister gave in his letter of March 23, 1965, was that this complaint was unsuitable for investigation because it raised wide issues. Here it appears to me that the Minister has clearly misdirected himself. Section 19(6) contemplates the raising of issues so wide that it may be necessary for the Minister to amend a scheme or even to revoke it. Narrower issues may be suitable for arbitration but section 19 affords the only method of investigating wide issues. In my view it is plainly the intention of the Act that even the widest issues should be investigated if the complaint is genuine and substantial, as this complaint certainly is.

Then it is said that this issue should be 'resolved through the arrangements available to producers and the board within the framework of the scheme itself'. This restates in a condensed form the reasons given in paragraph 4 of the letter of May 1, 1964, where it is said 'the Minister owes no duty to producers in any particular region', and reference is made to the 'status of the Milk Marketing Scheme as an instrument for the self-government of the industry', and to the Minister 'assuming an inappropriate degree of responsibility'. But, as I have already pointed out, the Act imposes on the Minister a responsibility whenever there is a relevant and substantial complaint that the board are acting in a manner inconsistent with the public interest, and that has been relevantly alleged in this case. I can find nothing in the Act to limit this responsibility or to justify the statement that the Minister owes no duty to producers in a particular region. The Minister is, I think, correct in saying that the board is an instrument for the self-government of the industry. So long as it does not act contrary to the public interest the Minister cannot interfere. But if it does act contrary to what both the committee of investigation and the Minister hold to be the public interest the Minister has a duty to act. And if a complaint relevantly alleges that the board has so acted, as this complaint does, then it appears to me that the Act does impose a duty on the Minister to have it investigated. If he does not do that he is rendering nugatory a safeguard provided by the Act and depriving complainers of a remedy which I am satisfied that Parliament intended them to have.

Paragraph 3 of the letter of May 1, 1964, refers to the possibility that, if the complaint were referred and the committee were to uphold it, the Minister 'would be expected to make a statutory Order to give effect to the committee's recommendations'. If this means that he is entitled to refuse to refer a complaint because, if he did so, he might later find himself in an embarrassing situation, that would plainly be a bad reason. I can see an argument to the effect that if, on receipt of a complaint, the Minister can satisfy himself from information in his possession as to the merits of the complaint, and he then chooses to say that, whatever the committee might recommend, he would hold it to be contrary to the public interest to take any action, it would be a waste of time and money to refer the complaint to the committee. I do not intend to express any opinion about that because that is not this case. In the first place it appears that the Minister has come to no decision as to the merits of the appellants' case and, secondly, the Minister has carefully avoided saying what he would do if the committee were to uphold the complaint.

It was argued that the Minister is not bound to give any reasons for refusing to refer a complaint to the committee, that if he gives no reasons his decision cannot be questioned, and that it would be very unfortunate if giving reasons were to put him in a worse position. But I do not agree that a decision cannot be questioned if no reasons are given. If it is the Minister's duty not to act so as to frustrate the policy and objects of the Act, and if it were to appear from all the circumstances of the case that that has been the effect of the Minister's refusal, then it appears to me that the court must be entitled to act....

I have found no authority to support the unreasonable proposition that it must be all or nothing — either no discretion at all or an unfettered discretion. Here the words 'if the Minister in any case so directs' are sufficient to show that he has some discretion but they give no guide as to its nature or extent. That must be inferred from a construction of the Act read as a whole, and for the reasons I have given I would infer that the discretion is not unlimited, and that it has been used by the Minister in a manner which is not in accord with the intention of the statute which conferred it.

As the Minister's discretion has never been properly exercised according to law, I would allow this appeal."

LORD HODSON: "... The reasons disclosed are not, in my opinion, good reasons for refusing to refer the complaint seeing that they leave out of account altogether the merits of the complaint itself. The complaint is, as the Lord Chief Justice pointed out, made by persons affected by the scheme and is not one for the consumer committee as opposed to the committee of investigation and it was eligible for reference to the latter. It has never been suggested that the complaint was not a genuine one. It is no objection to the exercise of the discretion to refer that wide issues will be raised and the interests of other regions and the regional price structure as a whole would be affected. It is likely that the removal of a grievance will, in any event, have a wide effect and the Minister cannot lawfully say in advance that he will not refer the matter to the committee to ascertain the facts because, as he says in effect, although not in so many words, 'I would not regard it as right to give effect to the report if it were favourable to the appellants.'

It has been suggested that the reasons given by the Minister need not and should not be examined closely for he need give no reason at all in the exercise of his discretion. True it is that the Minister is not bound to give his reasons for refusing to exercise his discretion in a particular manner, but when, as here, the circumstances indicate a genuine complaint for which the appropriate remedy is provided, if the Minister in the case in question so directs, he would not escape from the possibility of control by mandamus through adopting a negative attitude without explanation. As the guardian of the public interest he has a duty to protect the interests of those who claim to have been treated contrary to the public interest.

I would allow the appeal accordingly..."

LORD PEARCE: "... It is quite clear from the Act in question that the Minister is intended to have *some* duty in the matter. It is conceded that he must properly consider the complaint. He cannot throw it unread into the waste-paper basket. He cannot simply say (albeit honestly) 'I think that in general the investigation of complaints has a disruptive effect on the scheme and leads to more trouble than (on balance) it is worth; I shall therefore never refer anything to the committee of investigation.' To allow him to do so would be to give him power to set aside for his period as Minister the obvious intention of Parliament, namely, that an independent committee set up for the purpose should investigate grievances and that their report should be available to Parliament. This was clearly never intended by the Act. Nor was it intended that he could silently thwart its intention by failing to carry out its purposes. I do not regard a Minister's failure or refusal to give any reasons as a sufficient exclusion of the court's surveillance. If all the *prima facie* reasons seem to point in favour of his taking a certain course to carry out the intentions of Parliament in respect of a power which it has given him in that regard, and he gives no reason whatever for taking a contrary course, the court may infer that he has no good reason and that he is not using the power given by Parliament to carry out its intentions. In the present case, however, the Minister has given reasons which show that he was not exercising his discretion in accordance with the intentions of the Act."

LORD UPJOHN: "… My Lords, I would only add this: that without throwing any doubt upon what are well known as the club expulsion cases, where the absence of reasons has not proved fatal to the decision of expulsion by a club committee, a decision of the Minister stands on quite a different basis; he is a public officer charged by Parliament with the discharge of a public discretion affecting Her Majesty's subjects; if he does not give any reason for his decision it may be, if circumstances warrant it, that a court may be at liberty to come to the conclusion that he had no good reason for reaching that conclusion and order a prerogative writ to issue accordingly.

The Minister in my opinion has not given a single valid reason for refusing to order an inquiry into the legitimate complaint (be it well founded or not) of the South-Eastern Region; all his disclosed reasons for refusing to do so are bad in law."

LORD MORRIS OF BORTH-Y-GEST dissented.

Notes

(1) For comments on this case see case notes by J. F. Garner (1968) 31 M.L.R. 446 and H.W.R. Wade (1968) 84 L.Q.R. 166; and see also R.C. Austin, "Judicial Review of Subjective Discretion — at the Rubicon; Whither Now?" (1975) 28 C.L.P. 150 at 167–173 in particular. **6–14**

(2) Notice how the decision might also be interpreted as a failure to carry through the exercise of a power in accordance with statutory purpose. The dicta of Lord Upjohn (at 719), that if a "Minister… does not give any reason for his decision it may be, if circumstances warrant it, that a court may be at liberty to come to the conclusion that he had no good reason for reaching that conclusion…", have been used as a positive basis for the development of common law duty to give reasons, on which see paras 8.37–8.42.

(3) The Minister did in fact decide to refer the complaint back to the committee of investigation, which reported on January 7, 1969 "that the Acts and/or admissions of the board in prescribing the terms on, and the prices at which, milk should be sold to the board were contrary to the reasonable interests of the complainants and were not in the public interest". See H.C. 423, Session 1967–68, p. 10; H.C. 445, Session 1968–69; and 780 H.C. Deb., cols 46–47, March 31, 1969. Note the view of C. Harlow, "Administrative Reaction to Judicial Review" [1976] P.L. 116 at 120 that:

> "The remedy had proved illusory; the same decision could be reached with only nominal deference to the court, and the waste of time and money entailed is a deterrent to future complainants."

(4) Lord Upjohn, in considering an argument by the Secretary of State that regard must be had to the political context of decision making, made the trenchant observation (at 717) that "political considerations… are pre-eminently extraneous". Do you agree? Compare *Secretary of State for Education and Science v. Tameside Metropolitan Borough Council* [1977] A.C. 1014 extracted at para. 6–40.

(5) Many decisions on relevance involve consideration as to the extent to which a duty to act or to do something exists. In *Padfield* the apparently unfettered discretion of the Minister was nevertheless found to be subject to a duty which limited the manner in which that discretion could be exercised. This is consistent with older Scots law. In *Young v. Milne*, June 23, 1814 F.C. road trustees in Banff were empowered to take private land for making a road under the power of a local Act. The procedure involved a jury being appointed to set a value in any land which had been taken to estimate any compensation payable. The jury were required to "take under consideration all circumstances". In Milne's case the jury refused to consider evidence brought by Milne regarding the value of the land and awarded only a nominal sum in compensation. The Inner House held that the broad requirement to take into account all

circumstances meant that evidence should have been allowed; see also *Corstorphine Heritors v. Ramsay*, March 10, 1812 F.C.

(6) The wording of the relevant statute or instruments creating the power to decide is not always helpful in determining whether or not a duty exists to which regard should be had. In *Julius v. Bishop of Oxford* (1885) 5 App. Cas. 214, House of Lords, Earl Cairns L.C. (at 225) stated that where a power to act vested in a public office could benefit a class of persons, subject to conditions on which those persons could be called, in order for the power to be used the words "may" and "it shall be lawful" could in fact impose a duty to act.

In *Lord Advocate v. Glasgow Corporation*, 1973 S.C. (H.L.) 1 the existence of such permissive words did not preclude the court holding that the Secretary of State for Scotland had no discretion in deciding whether or not to exercise a default power in relation to failure of Glasgow Corporation as education authority to comply with a direction as to provision of local schools. Contrast this with *Hallett v. Nicholson*, 1979 S.C. 1, extracted at para. 14–23, where permissive words did not impose a duty on a fire authority which required to be taken into account in deciding whether or not it had to advise a local hotel of fire risks. For other examples see *Stair Memorial Encyclopaedia*, Vol. 1, para. 302.

(7) Compare the extract with *British Oxygen Co. Ltd v. Minister of Technology* [1971] A.C. 610, extracted at para. 7–10, where it was held that Parliament had not given any guidance as to how the ministry's power to give grants to eligible applicants was to be exercised.

Once the range of relevant determinations has been determined it is a matter for the decision maker to decide what weight should be attached to each of those considerations. This is another expression of the distinction between appeal and review.

Harvey v. Strathclyde Regional Council

1989 S.L.T. 25; 1989 S.L.T. 612, H.L.

6–15   "An education authority made certain decisions as regards the closure and amalgamation of schools in their area. A parent of a pupil at one of the three schools proposed for closure presented a petition for judicial review seeking reduction of a decision to close the school. As at the hearing before the Lord Ordinary the question of the authority's right to implement their decisions insofar as they involved two of the schools had been referred to the Secretary of State. The petitioner averred that it was probable that the Secretary of State would refuse consent to the closure of one of those schools (Paisley Grammar) and were that to arise the authority would be bound to reconsider all their other decisions as to secondary education in light of the Secretary of State's decision. Therefore, to proceed to close down the school attended by the petitioner's child in advance of the other decisions was an unreasonable exercise of the authority's discretion. The Lord Ordinary granted decree of reduction but stated that, had it been necessary, he would have granted decree of suspension. Before the education authority there had been argument as to whether the authority, for the future of education in their area, should adopt any of a number of 'four school' solutions (each including the retention of the school of the petitioner's child) or a 'three school' solution.

By the time of the hearing on the respondents' reclaiming motion the Secretary of State had refused his consent to the closure of Paisley Grammar School. As a result of this decision the petitioner argued that a four school solution was probably in prospect once more because of certain pronouncements by two influential members of the authority reported in the press which suggested that in respect of one particular 1,200 pupil school the authority would still insist on preserving it even though there were only 297 pupils on its roll. The petitioner accordingly argued that in these circumstances any reasonable education authority, considering the educational area covered by it as a whole, would reconsider the entire scheme and would not restrict its available options. The First Division refused to grant suspension. The petitioner appealed... On 29 June 1989 the House *dismissed* the appeal."

1989 S.L.T. 25 (First Division)

Lord President (Emslie): "... 'As later refined however, the proposition for the petitioner came to be this: having demonstrated that the overwhelming majority of parents in the review area had expressed a wish that their children be educated under a four school non-denominational secondary school system (and in particular that the parents at Stanely Green High School had done so), and that the education authority had arrived at a decision which entailed that henceforth pupils would. be educated in a manner contrary to the wishes of those parents, the petitioners had done enough to give rise to the inference that the respondents in arriving at that decision had failed to fulfil their obligation under s. 28 (1), and the onus passed to the respondents to demonstrate that they had fulfilled their statutory duty in this respect and that the general principle mentioned in the subsection did not prevail for appropriate reasons. The respondents contended that the statutory requirement is to have regard to the general principle that pupils are to be educated in accordance with the wishes of their parents, and not to secure that particular wishes are implemented. That contention is, in my opinion, sound so far as it goes, and the cases relied upon in that respect (*Keeney v. Strathclyde Regional Council* and *Watt v. Kesteven County Council*) amply support it. That there is a difference between a duty to have regard to a general principle that children are educated in accordance with the wishes of their parents and a duty to secure that they are so educated is obvious. There is however equally a difference which I consider to be critical in the present case between a duty to have regard to the wishes of parents as to the education of their children and a duty to have regard to the general principle that pupils are to be educated in accordance with the wishes of their parents. The latter, but not the former, appears to me to emphasise the importance of parental wishes and it is the latter which is the duty incumbent on the respondents. That is not of course to say that the general principle (which is itself qualified in relation to the compatibility of such education with the provision of suitable instruction and training and the avoidance of unreasonable public expenditure) is to be treated as necessarily paramount. Other considerations may justify the education authority in departing from that general principle. But the critical issue is whether it is enough in the first instance for a party complaining of a breach of s. 28 (1) to establish the facts as mentioned at least when as in the present case it is also clear that the qualifications stated internally to s. 28 (1) itself do not arise. After considerable hesitation I have come to the view that by establishing those factors, the petitioners have done enough to give rise to the inference that there has been a failure to fulfil the statutory obligation by the respondents in the absence of adequate explanation from them.'...

In our opinion the Lord Ordinary's approach and conclusion over which he felt considerable hesitation is entirely wrong. There is no real difficulty in construing s. 28 (1) if full weight is given to its entire language, and in particular to the words 'have regard to', the words 'general principle' and the qualifications expressed in the subsection itself. The subsection only lays down that there is a general principle to which an education authority must have regard so far as it is compatible with the provision of suitable instruction and training and the avoidance of unreasonable public expenditure. It is obvious, too, that in the performance of its duties and in the exercise of its powers an education authority will be entitled to have regard to other relevant considerations apart from those expressly mentioned and, indeed, that there may be exceptions to the general principle. Since the language of s. 76 of the Education Act 1944 is for all practical purposes identical to that of s. 28 (1), it is instructive to notice with approval what Denning L.J. (as he then was) and Parker L.J. had to say about it in *Watt v. Kesteven County Council*. Denning L.J. at p. 424 said this: 'Even if it was the duty of the county council to make available all the independent schools in the country, nevertheless I do not think that section 76 means that every parent has a right to choose any of them he likes. Section 76 does not say that pupils must in all cases be educated in accordance with the wishes of their parents. It only lays down a general principle to which the county council must have regard. This leaves it open to the county council to have regard to other things as well, and also to make exceptions to the general principle if it thinks fit to do so. It cannot therefore be said that a county council is at fault simply because it does not see fit to comply with the parent's wishes.' Parker L.J. at p. 429 said this: 'It was, I think, at one time contended on behalf of the plaintiff that the obligation to "have regard to the general principle that..." meant that the authority must have exclusive regard to that general principle and, accordingly, that if and in so far as the parent's wishes were not incompatible with the two matters referred to, effect has to be given to these wishes. This, it seems to me, is plainly wrong, and indeed it was in the end admitted that there might be other matters which an authority could take into consideration.

'I say that it is plainly wrong because there must be a number of administrative matters — and the authority in exercising its powers and performing its duties is acting administratively — which one would expect it to be in a position to consider, and the wording used, and in particular the words "general principle", contemplating as it does exceptions, point to the obligation meaning no more than that the authority must take into account the general principle, weighing it in the balance together with and against other considerations. Provided that the authority has regard to the general principle in this sense, I think that it fulfils its obligation.' In *Keeney v. Strathclyde Regional Council*, Lord Ross in construing s. 28 (1) agreed with Denning L.J. in *Watt*.

Precisely the same argument which the Lord Ordinary accepted in this case was presented to Lord Cullen in the case of *Neil McIntyre and Another v. Western Isles Islands Council*. In his opinion delivered on 1 July 1988 Lord Cullen had this to say — and we agree with him entirely — 'I find myself unable to agree with Lord Dervaird that a duty to have regard to the general principle that pupils are to be educated in accordance with the wishes of their parents emphasises the importance of parental wishes, whereas a duty to have regard to the wishes of parents as to the education of their children does not. It seems to me that, if anything, the former underlines the possibility that an education authority may take a different view from the parents, by its reference to a "general principle", especially if the general principle is inherently qualified by two out of a number of possible exceptions. Further I am unable to agree that the adverse decision of an education authority in face of the opposition of parents creates an onus on the education authority to show that there has not been after all a failure on their part to fulfil their duty under s. 28 (1). It is true that the education authority are bound to apply their minds to the wishes of the parents in question and to take into consideration the objective which is enshrined in the general principle. Incidentally, although the point is not material in the present case, it appears to be correct to treat the general principle as referring to the wishes of particular parents in respect of their own particular children: cf. *Wood v. Ealing London Borough Council*, per Goff J. at p. 383. However, the wishes of those parents are only one of a number of factors which the education authority are entitled to take into account. As counsel for the respondents pointed out, the decision on the part of the education authority which is not in agreement with the wishes of the parents can arise, on a strict analysis of s. 28 (1), in a number of ways. For example, it could arise from the education authority giving greater weight to one of the stated qualifications which are inherent in the general principle. It could arise from the fact that, after taking the wishes of the parent and the objective of the general principle into consideration, they gave greater weight to other matters which were available for their consideration. However, the fact that the education authority have made such a decision does not, in my view, create a presumption that they have failed to have regard to the general principle in accordance with s. 28 (1).'

For the foregoing reasons and upon a proper understanding of s. 28 (1) there can be no logical justification for the view that proof or admission of a divergence between the wishes of parents and an administrative decision by an education authority gives rise to a rebuttable presumption that the education authority has failed to have regard to the general principle mentioned in that subsection. It follows, accordingly, that the Lord Ordinary was not entitled, for the reasons which he gives, to sustain the first plea in law for the petitioner and to reduce the decision complained of. We have only to add that even if we had agreed with the Lord Ordinary's approach in this case, we would not have supported his conclusion that the respondents had failed to provide the 'adequate explanation' which he expected of them. Consideration of the respondents' averments and the documentary productions before us leaves us in no doubt that in reaching their decision the respondents did have regard to the general principle in the sense described by Parker L.J. in *Watt*. Many other relevant considerations came into play including the objective of avoiding unreasonable public expenditure."

1989 S.L.T. 612, H.L.

LORD KEITH OF KINKEL: "… By the time the case came before the First Division the Secretary of State had reached his decision on the proposed closures of John Neilson and Paisley Grammar School. He consented to the former but not to the latter. In that situation it was contended for the applicant that the decision to close Stanely Green should be suspended until such time as the respondent council had reconsidered the whole of the matter of non-denominational secondary education in Paisley in the light of the Secretary of State's decision. It was argued on the principle of *Associated Provincial Picture Houses Ltd. v. Wednesbury Corporation* that to proceed with the closure of Stanely Green under the prevailing circumstances would be so obviously unreasonable that no reasonable education authority could properly do so. That argument was rejected, and suspension was refused.

The applicant now appeals to your Lordships' House, and advances the arguments in favour of the correctness of the Lord Ordinary's opinion which were rejected by the First Division. It is maintained in the first place that the reference in s. 28 (1) to the 'general principle' there enunciated has the effect that this general principle must be treated as the primary consideration of any education authority in the discharge of its functions under the Act. The effect of so treating it was not made clear either in the applicant's written case or in her counsel's argument, though counsel appeared to accept that other considerations might be capable of outweighing the general principle.

In order to succeed in securing judicial review the applicant must show either that the respondents paid no regard at all to the general principle embodied in s. 28(1), or that they paid to it a degree of regard lesser than any reasonable education authority would have paid. It is clear that the mere fact that the decision of the respondents to close Stanely Green was in conflict with the desire of most of the parents of children there to keep it open goes no distance at all to establish the applicant's case. It certainly does not raise any presumption that the respondents failed to have regard to s. 28 (1), and the applicant's written case appears to disclaim any suggestion that the Lord Ordinary said that it did."

Notes

(1) Note the emphasis in the House of Lords to the effect that even if a consideration were **6–16**
taken into account, if in all the circumstances the weight given to it was unreasonable in the
Wednesbury sense then that could provide a ground for challenge.

(2) As to the issue of what is a relevant consideration, the question of what weight should
be attached to it can be a controversial one, as the extract shows. The issue also arose in sharp
focus in *Bromley London Borough Council v. Greater London Council* [1983] 1 A.C. 768.
The House of Lords held, inter alia, that the GLC had acted unlawfully, in their Lordships'
view, by treating themselves bound to honour an election pledged to implement a subsidised
public transport scheme without giving due weight to a "fiduciary duty" owed to ratepayers,
who in part would be paying for the scheme. The case has been subject to much criticism:
see, for example, J. Dignan, "Policy-Making, Local Authorities and the Courts: The 'G.L.C.
Fares' Case" (1983) 99 L.Q.R. 605; J.A.G. Griffith, "Judicial Decision-Making in Public
Law" [1985] P.L. 564 at 575–579; and analysis by J.L. Yelland [1982] P.L. 171. For earlier
case law recognising the importance accorded to "fiduciary duty" see *Roberts v. Hopwood*
[1925] A.C. 578 and *Prescott v. Birmingham Corporation* [1955] 1 Ch. 210. In *Commission
for Local Authority Accounts in Scotland v. Stirling District Council*, 1984 S.L.T. 442 it was
argued by the Controller of Audit that a local authority owed a duty to ratepayers and if it had
reasonable regard for the interests of ratepayers it would have reduced the rate set in response
to an earlier request from central government to do so, thus avoiding the loss of some £700,000
in rates support grant. *Roberts*, *Prescott* and *Bromley* were cited in argument to that effect.
While on the facts, the court felt that there was insufficient information in the stated case
presented by the Commission to determine whether there had been a breach of fiduciary
duty, the Lord President (Emslie) accepted that such a duty existed (at 446). Lord Cameron
was unhappy about the use of the phrase "fiduciary duty" in the narrow sense of a duty owed
to ratepayers, which he regarded the English cases as authorities for, and suggested that a
duty might also be owed to the total body of constituents for whom a local authority is required
to provide services (at 447). This alternative formulation echoes some of the argument used
in *Bromley* that relevant duties were owed to those who used the transport in question, some,
but by no means all, of whom were ratepayers. For discussion see C.M.G. Himsworth,
"Fiduciary Duties of Local Authorities", 1982 S.L.T. (News) 241 and 249; C. Crawford, "A
Distinctly Scottish Fiduciary Duty", 1984 S.L.T. (News) 333; and *Stair Memorial
Encyclopaedia*, Vol. 14, "Local Government", para. 132.

(3) In *London and Midland Developments v. Secretary of State for Scotland*, 1996 S.C.L.R. 465
in an appeal under section 233 of the Town and Country Planning (Scotland) Act 1972, the
appellants sought to argue, inter alia, that the Secretary of State had acted unreasonably in
determining on an appeal from the inquiry reporter that more weight should be given to
considerations of environmental impact rather than economic regeneration, which in effect
reversed the decision of the reporter. The appellants also sought to argue that in differing from
the reporter, insufficient reasons had been given in the decision letter. The court rejected the
appeal stating (at 473):

> "We are satisfied that the submissions for the Secretary of State and the second respondents are to
> be preferred. In the first place, we are satisfied that the Secretary of State did give a reason for his
> decision. It is quite clear from paragraph 9 of the decision letter that the Secretary of State differed
> from the reporter because he attached more weight to environmental benefits and less weight to
> the potential for economic regeneration than the reporter had done. The Secretary of State in his
> decision letter accepted what the reporter had said regarding what were the material planning
> considerations. But the Secretary of State was entitled to determine, as a matter of planning
> judgment, what weight should be attached to the material planning factors identified by the reporter.
> In our opinion, the Secretary of State was not exceeding his powers when he determined that
> environmental impact was a factor which merited more weight than the potential for economic
> regeneration. That was plainly a matter for planning judgment and the Secretary of State was not
> acting unreasonably in differing from the reporter on this matter."

The decision letter itself did not indicate why environmental impact was given greater weight than economic regeneration. On that basis do you think it complied with the test set out in *Wordie Property Co. Ltd v. Secretary of State for Scotland*, 1984 S.L.T. 345 noted at para.12–36 that the reasons should "leave the informed reader in the court in no real and substantial doubt"? Should there be an obligation to explain why more weight was given to one consideration than another? Consider here *Seddon Properties Ltd v. Secretary of State for the Environment and Macclesfield Borough Council* (1978) 248 E.G. 951 where, on similar facts, the decision was quashed, on which see para. 12–23.

(4) Other recent, and important cases on what are or are not relevant considerations include *R. v. Somerset County Council, ex parte Fewings* [1995] 1 W.L.R. 1037 (local authority, empowered to manage land for the benefit and improvement of an area, banned deer hunting for ethical reasons, held benefit or improvement related to physical improvement of the land, and did not include ethical considerations); *Safeway Stores plc v. National Appeal Panel (No. 2)*, 1997 S.C. 189 (decision of the panel quashed on the ground that it failed to take into account the desirability of the provision of pharmacy services by Safeway in its premises under the National Health Service (General Medical and Pharmaceutical Services) (Scotland) Regulations 1974; and *R. v. Gloucestershire County Council, ex parte Barry* [1996] 4 All E.R. 421, C.A. (local authority could not take into account its financial resources when deciding whether or not it owed a duty to make provision for the needs of a disabled person under the Chronically Sick and Disabled Persons Act 1970. Once it was decided that provision should be made, the level of resources was relevant as regards the level and nature of provision. The difficulty of what is or is not a relevant consideration is made clear by the fact that on appeal to the House of Lords, the decision that "cost of provision" was not a relevant consideration, was reversed by a majority of three to two, on which see [1997] 2 All E.R. 1).

(5) For further reading see Finch and Ashton, pp. 270–278; P.P. Craig, *Administrative Law* (3rd ed., 1994), pp. 400–432; and W. Wade and C. Forsyth, *Administrative Law* (7th ed., 1994), pp. 379–387.

As noted above, one of the most significant developments in this aspect of the grounds of legal control is the impact that the provisions of the Human Rights Act 1998 will have.

Human Rights Act 1998

ss. 1, 2, 6

"The Convention Rights

6–17   **1.** — (1) In this Act "the Convention rights" means the rights and fundamental freedoms set out in —

(a)   Articles 2 to 12 and 14 of the Convention,
(b)   Articles 1 to 3 of the First Protocol, and
(c)   Articles 1 and 2 of the Sixth Protocol.

as read with Articles 16 to 18 of the Convention.

(2) Those Articles are to have effect for the purposes of this Act subject to any designated derogation or reservation (as to which see sections 14 and 15).

(3) The Articles are set out in Schedule 1.

(4) The Secretary of State may by order make such amendments to this Act as he considers appropriate to reflect the effect, in relation to the United Kingdom, of a protocol.

(5) In subsection (4) "protocol" means a protocol to the Convention —

(a)   which the United Kingdom has ratified; or
(b)   which the United Kingdom has signed with a view to ratification.

(6) No amendment may be made by an order under subsection (4) so as to come into force before the protocol concerned is in force in relation to the United Kingdom.

Interpretation of Convention rights

2. — (1) A court or tribunal determining a question which has arisen in connection with a Convention right must take into account any —

(a)   judgment, decision, declaration or advisory opinion of the European Court of Human Rights,

(b)   opinion of the Commission given in a report adopted under Article 31 of the Convention,

(c)   decision of the Commission in connection with Article 26 or 27(2) of the convention, or

(d)   decision of the Committee of Ministers taken under Article 46 of the Convention

whenever made or given, so far as, in the opinion of the court or tribunal, it is relevant to the proceedings in which that question has arisen.

(2) Evidence of any judgment, decision, declaration or opinion of which account may have to be taken under this section is to be given in proceedings before any court or tribunal in such manner as may be provided by rules.

(3) In this section 'rules' means rules of court or, in the case of proceedings before a tribunal, rules made for the purposes of this section —

(a)   by the Lord Chancellor or the Secretary of State, in relation to any proceedings outside Scotland;

(b)   by the Secretary of State, in relation to proceedings in Scotland; or

(c)   by a Northern Ireland department, in relation to proceedings before a tribunal in Northern Ireland —
(i)   which deals with transferred matters; and
(ii)   for which no rules made under paragraph (a) are in force.

Acts of public authorities

6. — (1) It is unlawful for a public authority to act in a way which is incompatible with a Convention right.

(2) Subsection (1) does not apply to an act if —

(a)   as the result of one or more provisions of primary legislation, the authority could not have acted differently; or

(b)   in the case of one or more provisions of, or made under, primary legislation which cannot be read or given effect in a way which is compatible with the Convention rights, the authority was acting so as to give effect to or enforce those provisions.

(3) In this section "public authority" includes —

(a)   a court or tribunal, and

(b)   any person certain of whose functions are functions of a public nature, but does not include either House of Parliament or a person exercising functions in connection with proceedings in Parliament.

(4) In subsection (3) 'Parliament' does not include the House of Lords in its judicial capacity.

(5) In relation to a particular act, a person is not a public authority by virtue only of subsection (3)(b) if the nature of the act is private.

(6) 'An act' includes a failure to act but does not include a failure to —

(a)   introduce in, or lay before, Parliament a proposal for legislation; or

(b)   make any primary legislation or remedial order."

Notes

(1) Sections 1, 2 and 6 are not yet in force but will of course be very significant when they are. Section 1 defines the rights and fundamental freedoms protected as Convention rights. Not included is Article 13 which guarantees that where the rights and freedoms in the Convention are violated then the victim "shall have an effective remedy before a national authority…". For discussion of this omission see para. 11–40.   **6–18**

Article 2 guarantees the right to life; Article 3, prohibits torture; Article 4 prohibits slavery and forced labour; Article 5 guarantees the right to liberty and security of the person and covers in particular, the procedures upon which a person can be detained; Article 6 guarantees, inter alia, a fair and public hearing in the determination of civil rights and obligations or of any criminal charge; Article 7, inter alia, guarantees that no one shall be punished by virtue of a retrospective criminal law; Article 8 guarantees the right to respect for private and family life, home and correspondence; Article 9 guarantees freedom of thought, conscience or religion; Article 10 guarantees freedom of expression; Article 11 guarantees freedom of assembly and association; and Article 12, the right to marry. Article 14 secures that the freedoms guaranteed by the Convention shall exist without discrimination on grounds, including, but not limited to, sex, race, religion and politics. The Articles in the first and sixth protocols respectively extend protection to peaceful enjoyment of possessions, the right to education, the right to free elections, and the abolition of the death penalty except in time of war. Article 16 permits the freedoms guaranteed by Articles 10, 11 and 14 to be restricted in relation to the political activity of aliens; Article 17 is a general prohibition on the abuse of rights protected by the Convention; and Article 18 limits any restriction on rights and freedoms permitted by the Convention to purposes which are only permitted by the Convention. Section 14(1) defines "designated derogation" as meaning the current derogation from Article 5(3) of the Convention (requiring prompt judicial scrutiny after arrest) to legitimise the Prevention of Terrorism (Temporary Provisions) Act 1989, Sched. III, Part 1, by subsection (1)(*a*) or any derogation made by the United Kingdom from an Article or protocol of the Convention designated as such by order of the Secretary, section (1)(*b*). Section 15 sets out the extent of "designated reservations" in similar terms to section 14. The only current designated reservation is a minor one, part of Article 2 of the first protocol (restricting the right for parents to ensure education and teaching in conformity with their own religious and philosophical convictions only insofar as is compatible with the provision of efficient instruction and training and the avoidance of unreasonable public expenditure). For a general account of the rights and freedoms guaranteed by the Convention see *Stair Memorial Encyclopaedia* Vol. 12, "Human Rights in Europe", paras 24–78, 85–87 and J. Coppel, *European Convention on Human Rights* (1998).

(2) The provisions in section 2 require courts and tribunals to take into account decisions of the bodies mentioned in subsection (1)(*a*)–(*d*). Subsection (1)(*a*) is self-explanatory. Subsection (1)(*b*) relates to reports of the Commission on the merits of cases *after which* they have been declared admissible. Subsection (1)(*c*) relates to admissability decisions of the Commission. Subsection (1)(*d*) concerns reports prepared by the Committee of Ministers in connection with its role in supervising the execution of judgments under Article 46. Opinions under (*b*) and decisions under (*c*) will no longer be produced with the entry into force of Protocol 11. Obviously decisions of the European Court of Human Rights itself are likely to be the most influential in fashioning domestic human rights jurisprudence. However, the combined effect of the section is that while courts in the United Kingdom are obliged to consider relevant Convention decisions, they are not binding. Accordingly, while such decisions are clearly very important and will certainly be highly persuasive, it is not necessarily the case that domestic case law will mirror that of Strasbourg: Various reasons have been given for this. First of all, the Court of Human Rights does not operate a rigid system of precedent. The court has frequently stated the view that the Convention is "a living instrument" to be interpreted in light of modern conditions. Second, the role of national judges and those in Strasbourg are not identical. This is reflected in the "margin of appreciation" doctrine noted below which envisages relatively restrained scrutiny of national law. Finally, decisions made by Convention institutions might simply be regarded as unpersuasive. See, generally, Lord Irvine of Lairg, *Hansard*, H.L., Vol. 513, col. 514. Subsections (2) and (3) have the combined effect of rendering decisions or opinions "judicially noticed", notwithstanding that such decisions and opinions do not form part of Scots or English law.

(3) Section 6 is one of the key provisions in ensuring respect for Convention rights. The others are the strong principle of interpretation contained in section 3, on which see para. 3–7 and the combination of declarator of incompatibility under section 4 and remedial order under section 10, on which see paras 11–41 and 11–45 respectively. What is a public authority for the purposes of this section has been left deliberately vague, though subsections (3), (4) and (5) give some guidance. Some authorities are obviously public such as local authorities, the police or statutory regulatory authorities and government Ministers and departments. Section 3(*a*) makes it clear that the definition includes a court or tribunal but what is a court or tribunal? It would appear, for example, that the Professional Practice Committee of the GMC is not a court even though it exercises a judicial function in relation to disciplinary matters in the public interest and within a statutory context and its procedures are modelled on court procedure:see *General Medical Council v. BBC* [1998] 3 All E.R. 426. The committee was held not to be a court by a Court of Appeal as "it was not part of the judicial system of the state" (at 434). Tribunal is, however, defined in the act as "any tribunal in which legal proceedings may be brought": section 21(1). This is somewhat wider than "judicial system of the state" and arguably

this would be apt to cover tribunals subject to the supervisory jurisdiction of the Court of Session, as noted by Lord President (Hope) in *West v. Secretary of State for Scotland*, 1992 S.L.T. 636, extracted at para. 10–7. Thus statutory tribunals could be included but equally and more controversially so could disciplinary proceedings of any kind in the sense that they have proceedings to vindicate rights and obligations arising out of a legal relationship. This would be consistent with the views expressed in *West* and *McDonald v. Burns*, 1940 S.C. 376, extracted at para. 8–2. See also *Lally, Petitioner*, February 27, 1998 Outer House, unreported. Subsection (3) (*b*) raises rather different issues by clearly accepting that some bodies of persons can exercise both private and public functions. The test of "functions of a public nature" suggests that even where the means of performing those functions is a "private mechanism", such as a contract concluded by a local authority or a regulator, the purpose of the act could remain the furtherance of a public function. Where a body genuinely has a mix of public and private functions, such as combining the regulation of its members (a public function) with other activities on behalf of its members such as promotion of its activities (a private function), such a body is only a public authority in connection with its public function.

As we will note in relation to the discussion in *West*, tests based upon public function as the basis of judicial review have found little favour. On one analysis, the need to identify a public function might well drive one to the conclusion in judicial review proceedings at least, that the guidance in *West* must now be read subject to this new requirement, at least insofar as an allegation of breach of section 6 is made. It should of course be remembered that not all allegations of unlawful action under section 6 will necessarily be brought by way of judicial review, on which see section 7, extracted and discussed at para. 10–59. Equally, could one suggest that given the importance of the test of "function", what is important is not the formal source of a body's power — such as a bilateral relationship in contract — but rather the substance, nature and purpose of the function in question? Whatever difficulties arise on the boundaries of the definition, it is clear that the obvious public authorities such as government Ministers and departments, local authorities, the police and statutory regulatory authorities will be public authorities for the purpose of the section, as will of course the Scottish Executive and administration and the Scottish Parliament. Subsection (3)(*b*) makes it clear that either of the Houses of Parliament at Westminster is not covered by the definition, thus preserving ultimate power of this Parliament to enact legislation which infringes Convention rights. Also note subsection (2)(*a*) and (*b*), which ensures the general principle of the Act contained in section 3(2)(*b*) and 4(6)(*a*), on which see paras 3–8 and 11–41 respectively, that incompatible primary legislation will remain fully effective unless and until repealed or modified. Note also subsection (6). Primary legislation does not include Acts of the Scottish Parliament: section 21(1). For further discussion see N. Bamforth, "The Application of the Human Rights Act 1998 to Public Authorities and Private Bodies" (1999) 58 C.L.J. 159.

(4) Until this Act, the status of the Convention in Scots and English law was difficult to state with certainty. Certainly the English courts had been prepared to have regard for the provisions of the Convention where a statute was ambiguous: *R. v. Home Secretary, ex parte Brind* [1991] 1 A.C. 696, extracted at para. 6–43 or where the law was uncertain: *Derbyshire County Council v. Times Newspapers Ltd* [1993] A.C. 534 and *R. v. Secretary of State for the Home Department, ex parte Norney* (1995) 7 Admin. L.R. 681; and see also *R. v. Secretary of State for Defence, ex parte Smith* [1996] 1 All E.R. 257, extracted at para. 6–31. In Scotland, however, the initial reaction was that no regard could be had to the European Convention on Human Rights either as an aid to construction or otherwise: *Kaur v. Lord Advocate*, 1980 S.C. 319; and see also *Moore v. Secretary of State for Scotland*, 1985 S.L.T. 38; *Hamilton v. Secretary of State for Scotland*, 1991 G.W.D. 10–624; and *Re Budh Singh*, July 13, 1988, Outer House, unreported. However, subsequently in *A.M.T., Petitioner*, 1996 S.C.L.R. 897 the Lord President (Hope) in considering whether a homosexual man should be allowed to adopt a child observed (at 910):

> "It is now clearly established as part of the law of England and Wales, as a result of decisions in the House of Lords, that in construing any provision in domestic legislation which is ambiguous in the sense that it is capable of a meaning which either conforms to or conflicts with the Convention, the courts will presume that Parliament intended to legislate in conformity with the Convention, not in conflict with it."

See also *Anderson v. H.M. Advocate*, 1996 S.C.L.R. 114 at 121 and generally J.L. Murdoch, "The European Convention on Human Rights in Scots Law" [1991] P.L. 40; A. Brown, "The European Convention on Human Rights in Scottish Courts", 1996 S.L.T. (News) 267; and Finch and Ashton, pp. 274–278.

6–19   (5) Paradoxically, given the hitherto cautious approach to Convention rights, these now have potentially greater scope for impact in Scots law than ever before. This is because regard must not only be had to section 6 but also to the provisions of the Scotland Act 1998. Under section 29(2)(*d*) of the Act a provision of an Act of the Scottish Parliament is outwith its competence and hence unlawful insofar as it is incompatible with Convention rights or with European Community law, on which see para. 3–10. Note also section 57(2) in relation to actions by the Scottish Executive, on which see para. 3–9 and note also section 54 extracted at para. 3–11 in relation to subordinate legislation. By contrast, primary legislation of the Westminster Parliament, including legislation on those areas not devolved to the Scottish Parliament, is only subject to the interpretative obligation placed on the courts by section 3 of the Human Rights Act 1998, on which see para. 3–8. As noted, where that obligation cannot be adhered to, it will ultimately be a matter for a Minister of the Crown to decide whether or not to amend the offending provision and whether or not to give such an amendment retrospective effect. Such is not the position under the Scotland Act 1998. The Scottish courts will be required to strike down Scottish legislation that is found to contravene the incorporated Convention rights. It is important to realise that the Convention rights to which the Scottish Parliament and the Executive are subject are the same as the rights set out in section 1 of the Human Rights Act 1998, but that the obligation to comply with those rights has its source in both the relevant provisions of the Scotland Act itself and the Human Rights Act. This is a complex area and for further discussion see para. 10–63. For further reading see A. Miller, "Human Rights and The Scottish Parliament" (1998) 1 Scotland Forum 7 and C. Gane, "Human Rights Bill: Impact on the Law of Scotland" (1998) 43(5) J.L.S.S. 16, "Human Rights Bill: The domain of Convention rights" (1998) 43(6) J.L.S.S. 28 and "Human Rights Bill: Bound to have a profound effect" (1998) 43(7) J.L.S.S. 22.

(6) One of the most intriguing aspects of the scheme of the Human Rights Act is the extent to which the question of weight to be given to a Convention right by a public authority will be dealt with by a reviewing court when asked to decide if there has been a breach of a Convention right. We have already seen that the matter of weight to which relevant consideration is given is a matter for the decision maker. This has parallels in the jurisprudence of the doctrine of the "margin of appreciation" of the European Court of Human Rights. The doctrine is a reflection of the fact that state authorities are in a better position than the Court of Human Rights to assess the needs of a particular country and recognises a degree of latitude or deference in recognition of this relative advantage. On this see for example D. O'Sullivan, "The allocation of scarce resources and the right to life under the European Convention on Human Rights" [1998] P.L. 389; P. Mahoney, "Marvellous Richness of Diversity or Invidious Cultural Relativism" (1998) 19 H.R.L.J. 1; and T. Jones, "The Devaluation of Human Rights Under the European Convention" [1995] P.L. 430. The doctrine exists because "the machinery of protection established by the capital Convention is subsidiary to the national systems safeguarding human rights": *Handyside v. The United Kingdom* (1976) 1 E.H.R.R. 737 at 753, para. 48. National authorities "are in principle better placed than an international court to evaluate local needs and conditions": *Buckley v. United Kingdom* (1997) 23 E.H.R.R. 101 at 129, para. 75. Although there is no express warrant for the operation of a similar doctrine under the Human Rights Act, D. Pannick in "Principles of interpretation of Convention rights under the Human Rights Act and the discretionary area of judgement" [1998] P.L. 545 at 549 speculates:

> "Just as there are circumstances in which an international court will recognise that national institutions are better placed to assess the needs of society, and to make difficult choices between competing considerations, so national courts will accept that there are circumstances in which the legislature and the executive are better placed to perform those functions."

6–20   He goes on to suggest a tentative list of factors which the court might take into account in deciding whether or not sufficient weight has been given to a Convention right. These are as follows (at 549):

"(1) The nature of the Convention right. Many of the rights are protected by the Convention (for example Articles 8–11 and Article 1 of Protocol No. 1) require a balance to be struck between competing considerations. [For example, Article 8.2 permits interference by a public authority in accordance with law provided the interference is necessary in a democratic society in the interests of national security, public safety or the economic well-being of the country, for the prevention of disorder or crime, for the protection of health or morals, or for the protection of the rights and freedoms of others.] Other rights (such as Article 3) are absolute.

(2) The extent to which the issues require consideration of social, economic or political factors. [In this connection he goes on to note that the Supreme Court of Canada in interpreting its Canadian Charter of Rights and Freedoms has observed that:] courts are not specialists in the realm of policy-making, nor should they be. This is a role properly assigned to the elected representatives of the people, who have at their disposal the necessary institutional resources to enable them to compile and assess social science evidence, to mediate between competing social interests and to reach out and protect vulnerable groups.

(3) The extent to which the court has special expertise, for example in relation to criminal matters.

(4) Where the rights claimed are of especial importance, 'a high degree of constitutional protection' will be appropriate [*Libman v. Attorney General of Quebec* (1998) 3 B.H.R.C. 269 at 289–290, para. 60 (Supreme Court of Canada]. The European Court of Human Rights has recognised as being of especial importance rights to freedom of expression (especially in relation to political speech), access to the courts, and protection of intimate aspects of private life. In such contexts, judicial deference is far less appropriate, and the courts will carry out particularly strict scrutiny of State conduct."

Note that in relation to the last point sections 12 and 13 of the Human Rights Act require the court to have particular regard to the importance of the Convention right to freedom of expression: section 12(4), and any question arising under the Act which might affect the exercise by a religious organisation, the Convention right to freedom of thought, conscience and religion: section 13(1). As courts and tribunals are themselves public authorities bound by the Act, any domestic doctrine margin of appreciation must still be consistent with the obligation on the court or tribunal to take into account the decisions of the bodies detailed in section 2(1)(*a*)–(*d*). Sections 12 and 13 are not yet in force.   **6–21**

REASONABLENESS

Challenge on this ground is rather different from the grounds we have been considering already. Challenge based on improper purpose or relevant consideration is essentially based on there being objective proof, whether in the form of affidavits or direct evidence or the way in which a decision has been reached. Unreasonableness focuses on the substantive outcome of the decision-making process.   **6–22**

As we have already seen, in judicial review, the court is keen to ensure that the distinction between the legality and the merits of a decision is maintained. The reasonableness of the merits of a decision might be open to challenge on an appeal, but not in judicial review proceedings. Reasonableness is a test of the legality of a decision based on the constitutional assumption that any body which gives powers to another in terms of a jurisdiction, confers those powers on the basis that they will be exercised reasonably. For general reading see Finch and Ashton, pp. 290–297; *Stair Memorial Encyclopaedia*, Vol. 1, para. 240; Craig, pp. 400–409; and Wade and Forsyth, pp. 387–411.

Donaldson's Hospital v. Educational Endowments Commissioners

1932 S.C. 585

The Commissioners who were appointed under the Educational Endowments (Scotland) Act 1928 put forward a scheme amalgamating Donaldson's Hospital, Edinburgh and the Edinburgh Royal Institution for the Education of Deaf and Dumb Children and so affecting the former that its governors decided that its character and identity were destroyed. The   **6–23**

Commissioners contended that even though the scheme was radical, it was within their powers and a case under section 25 of the Act was presented to the Court of Session for an opinion on the legality of the proposed move.

LORD PRESIDENT CLYDE: "… The Commissioners rest their case on the width and discretionary character of their powers. There is no doubt that the preparation of schemes is a matter committed to the discretion of the Commissioners, and no doubt that the discretion is as wide as it could be made. But the proposition which lies at the foundation of the Commissioners' argument, namely, that the protection given to their acts by the conferment upon them of discretionary powers renders these acts invulnerable at law, will not hold — however wide the discretion may be. For all discretionary powers, without exception, must be used both reasonably and according to law. Were it otherwise, there would be no difference between a discretionary power and an arbitrary one; and, if those upon whom a discretion is conferred exercise it, not reasonably or according to law, but arbitrarily, they are not using, but abusing, their discretion. Whenever this can be established as a matter of fact, their acts become liable to be interfered with by a Court of law."

Notes

6–24   See too *Dundee General Hospitals v. Bell's Trustees*, 1950 S.C. 406 and 1952 S.C. (H.L.) 78. In older law there are observations to the effect that discretionary powers, particularly statutory powers, must receive a reasonable interpretation: *Yeats v. Taylor* (1863) 1 M. 221 at 224 *per* the Lord President (McNeil.) See also *School Board of Perth v. Henderson* (1917) 1 S.L.T. 92 at 95 *per* Lord Salvesen. However, the most recent formulation of this test was found in an English decision, the celebrated *Wednesbury* case.

Associated Provincial Picture Houses Ltd v. Wednesbury Corporation

[1948] 1 K.B. 223

6–25   The plaintiff applied for permission to give Sunday performances at its cinema. The local authority was empowered to allow cinemas to be opened and used on Sundays "subject to such conditions as the authority think fit to impose": Sunday Entertainments Act 1932, s. 2(1). The authority gave the plaintiff permission on the condition that no children under the age of 15 should be admitted to Sunday performances. The plaintiff sought a declaration that the condition was *ultra vires*.

LORD GREENE M.R.: "… Mr Gallop, for the plaintiffs, argued that it was not competent for the Wednesbury Corporation to impose any such condition and he said that if they were entitled to impose a condition prohibiting the admission of children, they should at least have limited it to cases where the children were not accompanied by their parents or a guardian or some adult. His argument was that the imposition of that condition was unreasonable and that in consequence it was *ultra vires* the corporation. The plaintiffs' contention is based, in my opinion, on a misconception as to the effect of this Act in granting this discretionary power to local authorities. The courts must always, I think, remember this: first, we are dealing with not a judicial act, but an executive act; secondly, the conditions which, under the exercise of that executive act, may be imposed are in terms, so far as language goes, put within the discretion of the local authority without limitation. Thirdly, the statute provides no appeal from the decision of the local authority.
     What, then, is the power of the courts? They can only interfere with an act of executive authority if it be shown that the authority has contravened the law. It is for those who assert that the local authority has contravened the law to establish that proposition. On the face of it, a condition of the kind imposed in this case is perfectly lawful. It is not to be assumed prima facie that responsible bodies, like the local authority in this case will exceed their powers; but the court, whenever it is alleged that the local authority have contravened the law, must not substitute itself for that authority. It is only concerned with seeing whether or not the proposition is made good. When an executive discretion is entrusted by Parliament to a body such as the local authority in this case, what appears to be an exercise of that discretion can only be challenged in the courts in a strictly limited class of case. As I have said, it must always be remembered that the court is not a court of appeal. When discretion of this kind is granted the law recognizes certain

principles upon which that discretion must be exercised, but within the four corners of those principles the discretion, in my opinion, is an absolute one and cannot be questioned in any court of law. What then are those principles? They are well understood. They are principles which the court looks to in considering any question of discretion of this kind. The exercise of such a discretion must be a real exercise of discretion. If, in the statute conferring the discretion, there is to be found expressly or by implication matters which the authority exercising the discretion ought to have regard to, then in exercising the discretion it must have regard to those matters. Conversely, if the nature of the subject-matter and the general interpretation of the Act make it clear that certain matters would not be germane to the matter in question, the authority must disregard those irrelevant collateral matters. There have been in the cases expressions used relating to the sort of thing that authorities must not do, not merely in cases under the Cinematograph Act but, generally speaking, under the other cases where the powers of local authorities came to be considered. I am not sure myself whether the permissible grounds of attack cannot be defined under a single head. It has been perhaps a little bit confusing to find a series of grounds set out. Bad faith, dishonesty — those of course, stand by themselves — unreasonableness, attention given to extraneous circumstances, disregard of public policy and things like that have all been referred to, according to the facts of individual cases, as being matters which are relevant to the question. If they cannot all be confined under one head, they at any rate, I think, overlap to a very great extent. For instance, we have heard in this case a great deal about the meaning of the word 'unreasonable'.

It is true the discretion must be exercised reasonably. Now what does that mean? Lawyers familiar with the phraseology commonly used in relation to exercise of statutory discretions often use the word 'unreasonable' in a rather comprehensive sense. It has frequently been used and is frequently used as a general description of the things that must not be done. For instance, a person entrusted with a discretion must, so to speak, direct himself properly in law. He must call his own attention to the matters which he is bound to consider. He must exclude from his consideration matters which are irrelevant to what he has to consider. If he does not obey those rules, he may truly be said, and often is said, to be acting 'unreasonably'. Similarly, there may be something so absurd that no sensible person could ever dream that it lay within the powers of the authority. Warrington L.J. in *Short v. Poole Corporation* [1926] Ch. 66, 90, 91, gave the example of the red-haired teacher, dismissed because she had red hair. That is unreasonable in one sense. In another sense it is taking into consideration extraneous matters. It is so unreasonable that it might almost be described as being done in bad faith; and, in fact, all these things run into one another.

In the present case, it is said by Mr Gallop that the authority acted unreasonably in imposing this condition. It appears to me quite clear that the matter dealt with by this condition was a matter which a reasonable authority would be justified in considering when they were making up their mind what condition should be attached to the grant of this licence. Nobody, at this time of day, could say that the well-being and the physical and moral health of children is not a matter which a local authority, in exercising their powers, can properly have in mind when those questions are germane to what they have to consider. Here Mr Gallop did not, I think, suggest that the council were directing their mind to a purely extraneous and irrelevant matter, but he based his argument on the word 'unreasonable', which he treated as an independent ground for attacking the decision of the authority; but once it is conceded, as it must be conceded in this case, that the particular subject-matter dealt with by this condition was one which it was competent for the authority to consider, there, in my opinion, is an end of the case. Once that is granted, Mr Gallop is bound to say that the decision of the authority is wrong because it is unreasonable, and in saying that he is really saying that the ultimate arbiter of what is and is not reasonable is the court and not the local authority. It is just there, it seems to me, that the argument breaks down. It is clear that the local authority are entrusted by Parliament with the decision on a matter which the knowledge and experience of that authority can best be trusted to deal with. The subject-matter with which the condition deals is one relevant for its consideration. They have considered it and come to a decision upon it. It is true to say that, if a decision on a competent matter is so unreasonable that no reasonable authority could ever have come to it, then the courts can interfere. That I think, is quite right; but to prove a case of that kind would require something overwhelming, and, in this case, the facts do not come anywhere near anything of that kind. I think Mr Gallop in the end agreed that his proposition that the decision of the local authority can be upset if it is proved to be unreasonable, really meant that it must be proved to be unreasonable in the sense that the court considers it to be a decision that no reasonable body could have come to. It is not what the court considers unreasonable, a different thing altogether. If it is what the court considers unreasonable, the court may very well have different views to that of a local authority on matters of high public policy of this kind. Some courts might think that no children ought to be admitted on Sundays at all, some courts might think the reverse, and all over the country I have no doubt on a thing of that sort honest and sincere people hold different views. The effect of the legislation is not to set up the court as an arbiter of the correctness of one view over another. It is the local authority that are set in that position and, provided they act, as they have acted, within the four corners of their jurisdiction, this court, in my opinion, cannot interfere.

This case, in my opinion, does not really require reference to authority when once the simple and well known principles are understood on which alone a court can interfere with something prima facie within the powers of the executive authority, but reference has been made to a number of cases... [His Lordship referred to *Harman v. Butt* [1944] K.B. 491; *R. v. Burnley JJ.*, 85 L.J. (K.B.) 1565; and *Ellis v. Dubowski* [1921] 3 K.B. 621, the latter two being cases of unlawful delegation of powers.] Another case on which Mr Gallop relied is *Roberts v. Hopwood* [1925] A.C. 578, [above, p. 321]. That was a totally different class of case. The district auditor had surcharged the members of a council who had made payments of a minimum wage of 4*l.* a week to their lowest grade of workers. That particular sum had been fixed by the local authority not by reference to any of the factors which go to determine a scale of wages, but by reference to some other principle altogether, and the substance of the decision was that they had not fixed 4*l.* a week as wages at all and that they had acted unreasonably. When the case is examined, the word 'unreasonable' is found to be used rather in the sense that I mentioned a short while ago, namely, that in fixing 4*l.* they had fixed it by reference to a matter which they ought not to have taken into account and to the exclusion of those elements which they ought to have taken into consideration in fixing a sum which could fairly be called a wage. That is no authority whatsoever to support the proposition that the court has power, a sort of overriding power, to decide what is reasonable and what is unreasonable. The court has nothing of the kind...

In the result, this appeal must be dismissed. I do not wish to repeat myself but I will summarize once again the principle applicable. The court is entitled to investigate the action of the local authority with a view to seeing whether they have taken into account matters which they ought not to take into account, or, conversely, have refused to take into account or neglected to take into account matters which they ought to take into account. Once that question is answered in favour of the local authority, it may still be possible to say that, although the local authority have kept within the four corners of the matters which they ought to consider, they have nevertheless come to a conclusion so unreasonable that no reasonable authority could ever have come to it. In such a case, again, I think the court can interfere. The power of the court to interfere in each case is not as an appellate authority to override a decision of the local authority, but as a judicial authority which is concerned, and concerned only, to see whether the local authority have contravened the law by acting in excess of the powers which Parliament has confided in them. The appeal must be dismissed with costs."

SOMERVELL L.J. and SINGLETON L.J. agreed.

Notes

6–26   (1) The formulation of Lord Greene M.R. of the test is the *locus classicus*. Notwithstanding this, the case law shows a number of other formulations. In *Council of Civil Service Unions v. Minister for the Civil Service* [1985] A.C. 374 Lord Diplock, having described the basis of challenge of "irrationality", commented (at 410):

> "It applies to a decision which is so outrageous in its defiance of logic or of accepted moral standards that no sensible person who had applied his mind to the question to be decided could have arrived at it."

This formulation was followed by the Inner House in *McTear v. Scottish Legal Aid Board*, 1997 S.L.T. 108. In *Nottinghamshire County Council v. Secretary of State for the Environment* [1986] A.C. 240 Lord Scarman explained that although reasonableness would be a ground of challenge a decision must be so absurd that the decision maker "must have taken leave of his senses" (at 247).

(2) It has been suggested that the ground of reasonableness may often be available more in theory than in practice. Thus, reasonableness was invoked but rejected as a ground of challenge in the following cases: *S. v. Criminal Injuries Compensation Board*, 1997 G.W.D 5–172, (decision not to reopen application for criminal injuries compensation in respect of sexual abuse as a child based on serious change of condition, not unreasonable, it being stated that where a qualification is a matter of degree then challenge based on unreasonableness would be particularly difficult to satisfy); *City of Aberdeen Council v. Local Government Boundary Commission for*

Scotland, 1997 G.W.D. 5–212 (held not to be unreasonable to reduce electoral representation from 50 to 43 seats within a local government boundary); *Bonelle v. West Lothian Council*, 1997 G.W.D. 26–1332 (held not unreasonable to refuse grant for improvement of domestic property as work commenced before grant approved in view of the need to conserve resources and to properly regulate the statutory scheme under section 240(1)(*b*) of the Housing (Scotland) Act 1987); *Francois v. Secretary of State for the Home Department*, 1999 S.L.T. 79 (not unreasonable to reject refugee's evidence that he had sustained injury from persons in the country he had left, even though supported by a medical report); *Jones v. City of Glasgow Council Housing Benefit Review Board*, 1997 G.W.D. 28–1453 (not unreasonable to refuse housing benefit where sufficient facts existed to justify the view of the review board that the petitioner's liability to pay rent appeared simply to have been created to take advantage of the housing benefit scheme); *Banks v. Scottish Legal Aid Board*, 1996 G.W.D. 17–1008 (not unreasonable to refuse legal aid to permit representation for the husband of a woman whose death was the subject of a fatal accident inquiry, as it was likely that the procurator fiscal would be in a position to produce all relevant evidence which would have had a bearing on the husband's interest); *Saini v. Secretary of State for the Home Department*, 1999 G.W.D. 12–567 (held not irrational or unreasonable to refuse leave to remain in United Kingdom when it had not been established that the petitioner, an illegal immigrant, would be permanently separated from his wife if leave to remain was refused). For further examples, particularly in the context of English decisions, see G.L. Peiris, "*Wednesbury* Unreasonableness: the Expanding Canvas" [1987] C.L.G. 53.

(3) Notwithstanding the apparently residual basis of challenge, reasonableness or irrationality has been successfully utilised in the following circumstances. As successful challenge on this ground is relatively unusual, it is worth detailing the facts in these cases.   **6–27**

In *Imperial Chemical Industries plc v. Central Region Valuation Appeal Committee*, 1988 S.L.T. 106 a decision was quashed as being unreasonable because of procedural flaw. The Rating and Valuation (Amendment) (Scotland) Act 1984, s. 12(1) gives the Lands Tribunal for Scotland power to determine appeals referred to them by a local valuation appeal committee. In deciding whether or not to refer the matter to the Lands Tribunal, the valuation appeal committee was required to have regard to any representations made by the parties. Regulation 4(3) of the Valuation Appeal Committee Procedure (Scotland) Regulations 1984 provides that if it appears to the committee that the case is highly technical or that the law is uncertain then the committee is to refer the appeal to the Lands Tribunal. The local committee in this case refused to hear representations to the effect that the matter did fall within regulation 4(3). Judicial review was sought. The court held that the law was indeed uncertain and, in view of the conflicting positions of the parties, it was in "defiance of logic" to conclude that the matter was not one which should have been referred to the Lands Tribunal.

In *Woods v. Secretary of State for Scotland*, 1991 S.L.T. 197 the petitioner sought judicial review of a decision of the Scottish Education Department to refuse payment of a postgraduate student's allowance. Closing date for applications in the guide issued by the department was December 31, 1988. The department had no record of a form having been received by it by that date. In May 1989 the petitioner was notified of non-payment of his fees by the department. On July 26, 1989 the department wrote to the petitioner confirming refusal of the payment. The petitioner contended that the refusal was unreasonable because of the rigid adherence by the department to its policy of only accepting applications received by it by the closing date, which in turn was based on the department's concern to appear fair to those to whom grants had been refused originally. Lord Morton of Shuna stated (at 199) that:

> "In the circumstances, when the petitioner wrote saying that he had sent in the application form I do not consider that it was right to rely rigidly on the guide which has no statutory force. If the decision was based on the minister of state's letter, the decision appears wholly irrational. An analogy would be that if a person sentenced for a crime was discovered to be innocent he could not be released from prison because it would be unjust to those who had served their whole sentence before establishing their innocence."

Moreover, he accepted that the petitioner was in good faith and that the department were in effect seeking to hold on to a windfall profit for a sum of money which it had already budgeted on paying. He went on to say:

> "It appears to me that it is on the face of it unreasonable to refuse to pay fees which the department had budgeted to pay and when the student has attended the course, merely because the petitioner did not notice that he had not received an acknowledgment."

Local authority policy was found to be irrational in *Gerry Cottle's Circus Ltd v. City of Edinburgh District Council*, 1990 S.L.T. 235. A circus company sought judicial review of the decision of the council of its refusal of a temporary public entertainment licence. The council had a policy that it would not permit in terms of such a licence "performances featuring live animals on the premises, exhibit performing live animals on the premises, or use live animals to promote the premises". The policy was modified to the effect that it would not apply to "brief appearances by cats, dogs, horses, ponies and the like so long as the Council is satisfied that adequate arrangements have been made for their welfare, and [also that it did] not apply to displays by working animals, e.g. sheep dog trials or service or police dog displays".

Lord Dervaird observed (at 240) that:

> "I would have been in favour of the petitioners' further argument that the decision was vitiated by irrationality in the sense in which that word has been used in past cases . . . it seems to me that if a local authority has moved from a policy which (however obnoxious it may have been to other concepts of administrative law) had the merit of consistency, to a policy subject to exceptions, then if the exceptions are such as to destroy the basis of the original policy and (worse) are or bear to be expressly at variance with the stated policy upon which the authority has subsequently proceeded, then the decision reached upon so flawed a basis cannot, it appears to me, stand... I repeatedly asked counsel for the respondents upon what rational basis the provisos attached by the counsel were held entitled to permit a public entertainment involving certain types of animals and not others. At one time he stated the distinction was between wild animals and domestic animals. But that does not apply or does not apply adversely to the petitioners in the instant case unless 'domestic' is confined to those animals which as matter of history form part of the animals ordinarily in use to be treated as domestic animals in Scotland some considerable time ago. Nor was it clear what was intended to relate to 'working animals', however they might be categorised, and whether cruelty was involved in the training or performance by such animals. I should also record that I was not able to obtain from him any satisfactory explanation as to what was involved in displays by working animals, nor as to whether or not there was meant to be any distinction between a performance by an animal and an appearance by an animal. I could find no rational basis therefore for the distinctions in the manner put forward by the respondents between those which apparently they were prepared to permit, and the cases in which they were utterly opposed to the appearance of the animal in question; in any event the whole effect of the proviso appeared to me to be destructive of the basis upon which the policy as stated in the grounds of reasons allegedly proceeded. I would, had it been necessary, have considered that this decision failed to pass the test of rationality in the circumstances outlined above."

For a further example of inconsistency as irrationality see *Cashley v. City of Dundee District Council*, 1994 S.C.L.R. 6, extracted at para. 6–55.

6–28   In *James Aitken & Sons (Meat Producers) v. City of Edinburgh District Council*, 1990 S.L.T. 241 the petitioners sought judicial review of a decision by Edinburgh District Council to grant planning permission to Link Housing who were applicants for planning permission for housing development for land next to the petitioners' premises. The local authority had failed to reach a decision within the time set out by the planning legislation to reach a decision on the application and appealed to the Secretary of State who appointed a reporter to determine the appeal. Prior to the reporter's decision being issued, Link Housing submitted an amended application for planning permission. The petitioners objected to that application also. Prior to the reporter issuing his decision the local authority granted the amended application. The petitioners argued, *inter alia*, that for the planning authority to come to a view on the second application notwithstanding that the first application still required to be determined was plainly unreasonable. They were effectively depriving themselves of the benefit of the views of the

Secretary of State on the very issue of principle involved, whether housing in the locality was desirable at all. The amendments made to the application did not deal with that basic principle. Lord Dervaird agreed (at 243):

> "to dispose of the second application while the appeal in relation to the first application was as yet undecided, was unreasonable in the sense in which that word is used in the *Wednesbury* case... To say that the first respondents had regard to the material consideration that the matter was before the Secretary of State on appeal, is in my opinion, a travesty. That the appeal on the first application was before the Secretary of State could only be a material fact in relation to the second if the outcome of that appeal was material to the deliberations of the district council in relation to the application before them. Otherwise it had and could have no materiality in relation to this matter at all. In these circumstances, to come to a determination in, what I was invited to hold was, the knowledge that a material matter was not yet available for their consideration which would focus on the issue of principle raised by both applications (see *Alexander Russell v. Secretary of State for Scotland* [1984 S.L.T. 81]) was, in my opinion, to act in a manner in which no reasonable authority charged with the duties under the planning Acts would have acted."

See also *Trusthouse Forte (U.K.) Ltd v. Perth and Kinross District Council*, 1990 S.L.T. 737 and *Ladbroke Racing (Strathclyde) Ltd v. William Hill (Scotland) Ltd*, 1995 S.L.T. 134. Contrast with *Henderson v. Argyll and Bute Council*, 1998 S.L.T. 1224 and *Asda Stores Ltd v. Secretary of State for Scotland*, 1999 S.L.T. 503.

(4) It is difficult to escape the court's conclusion in these cases that the decision was taken **6–29** when the decision maker "must have taken leave of his senses". The decisions do seem to fall foul of the wide area of discretion permitted by Lord Greene's analysis. There are observations from time to time to the effect that the threshold of unreasonableness or irrationality may be lower, where there is merit in competing positions.

In *West Glamorgan County Council v. Rafferty* [1987] 1 W.L.R. 457 the Court of Appeal decided that a local authority had acted unreasonably on the basis of *Wednesbury* unreasonableness in seeking an order for possession against gypsies occupying a site owned by the council. The council believed that the gypsies were creating a nuisance. Set against that was the fact that the council itself had been in breach of its duty under section 6 of the Caravan Sites Act 1968 to provide accommodation for the gypsies for a period of over 10 years. Ralph Gibson L.J. said (at 477):

> "The court is not, as I understand the law, precluded from finding a decision to be void for unreasonableness merely because there are admissible factors on both sides of the question. If the weight of the factors against eviction must be recognised by a reasonable council, properly aware of its duties and its powers, to be overwhelming, then a decision the other way cannot be upheld if challenged. The decision on eviction was a decision which required the weighing of the factors according to the personal judgment of the councillors but the law does not permit complete freedom of choice or assessment because legal duty must be given proper weight."

For commentary on the case see R. Ward, "The Romany in Briton" (1987) 46 C.L.J. 374. *Rafferty* was considered in *William Forrest & Son (Paisley) Ltd v. Scottish Environment Protection Agency*, 1997 G.W.D. 28–1434. Here, the largest meat-rendering facility in Scotland, William Forrest & Son (Paisley) Ltd sought judicial review of a notice served on them by the Scottish Environment Protection Agency requiring them to carry out modifications to plant and machinery at the premises no later than April 1, 1996 as a consequence of government policy in respect of the BSE crisis. The petitioners contended that the agency had failed to take account of the economic impact these modifications would have on their business and the impact on the public interest in the meat-rendering industry, the petitioners having a different view of what steps should be taken in light of the BSE crisis. The court considered that the agency's conduct was not so outrageous in substance that it went beyond what was to be reasonably expected of a rationally operating decision maker. Adequate notice had already been given to the petitioners about the nuisance caused by the plant and they had already been given an opportunity to address the matter and had intimated that they were unlikely to enforce the notice if progress and the modifications required were made. The agency's action could not be irrational since they had responsibilities for monitoring the petitioners' conduct and withdrawal of the notice would have meant that the petitioners would have complied with the agency's requirements. Lord Johnston considered that the approach in *Rafferty* was unique on its own facts and that a case for irrationality could only be made out if the balance of factors was overwhelmingly against the decision under attack. See also *Guthrie v. Scottish Environment Protection Agency*, 1997 G.W.D. 6–244.

(5) Unreasonableness constitutes a ground upon which the validity of byelaws may be challenged: *Robert Baird & Sons Ltd v. Glasgow Corporation*, 1935 S.C. (H.L.) 21, extracted at para. 2–47.

6–30 (6) "Irrationality" is not available as a ground of challenge where the decision has been approved by either or both Houses of Parliament and quite possibly the Scottish Parliament. On which see *City of Edinburgh District Council v. Secretary of State for Scotland*, 1985 S.L.T. 551, extracted at para. 2–38.

(7) J. Jowell and A. Lester, "Beyond *Wednesbury*: Substantive Principles of Administrative Law" [1987] P.L. 368 argue that "*Wednesbury* unreasonableness" is unsatisfactory. It is "confusing, because it is tautologous". It is "unrealistic", because the courts in practice are "willing to impugn decisions that are far from absurd and are indeed often coldly rational" and in particular that (at 371):

> "Intellectual honesty requires a further and better explanation as to *why* the act is unreasonable. The reluctance to articulate a principled justification naturally encourages suspicion that prejudice or policy considerations may be hiding underneath *Wednesbury's* ample cloak."

They argue that the courts should develop substantive principles of review based upon standards of administrative integrity such as the doctrine of bad faith, or good practice such as consistency and proportionality, or violation of objectively defined fundamental rights or freedoms, such as the European Convention on Human Rights. On proportionality see paras 6–42 to 6–46.

The next extract is regarded as possibly the leading modern discussion of *Wednesbury* unreasonableness and is perhaps of particular significance given the subject matter of fundamental human rights.

R. v. Ministry of Defence, ex p. Smith

[1996] 1 All E.R. 257, C.A.

6–31 "The four appellants, a lesbian and three homosexual men, were administratively discharged from service in the armed forces pursuant to a Ministry of Defence policy. The policy related to sexual orientation. It mandated discharge even without there being any evidence of overt sexual conduct; nor any evidence of an individual's ability to discharge responsibilities having been impaired. In fact all four servicemen were accepted to have exemplary service records. The appellants sought judicial review of the Ministry of Defence policy. The Divisional Court held the Ministry policy to be lawful. The appellants appealed to the Court of Appeal."

SIR THOMAS BINGHAM M.R.: "... The appellants challenge the lawfulness of their discharge and thus, indirectly, of the policy which required them to be discharged. They say that the policy is irrational, and in breach of the European Convention for the Protection of Human Rights and Fundamental Freedoms (Rome, November 4, 1950; T.S. 71 (1953); Cmd. 8969) and contrary to Council Directive (EEC) 76/207 on the implementation of the principle of equal treatment for men and women as regards access to employment, vocational training and promotion, and working conditions. They accept without reservation that any member of the armed services who acts inappropriately towards any other member, or who is guilty of any harassment, or who commits any offence or breach of service discipline, may be discharged administratively, if not on disciplinary grounds. So too, if a member's sexual orientation undermines that member's efficiency as a member of the service or is shown to cause demonstrable damage to the service. They claim no right or liberty to commit homosexual acts or to make homosexual advances on the mess-deck or in the barrack-room or in any other service setting. The accept that membership of a disciplined fighting force involves a curtailment of freedoms enjoyed by others in civilian employments, and recognise that the exigencies of service life may properly justify restrictions on homosexual activity and manifestations of homosexual orientation. Their challenge is, and is only, to the blanket, non-discretionary, unspecific nature of the existing policy.

Background

There can be no doubt that public attitudes to homosexuals and homosexuality have in the past varied widely from country to country, and within the same country at different times, and among different social groups in the same country. Almost any generalisation can be faulted. But there has in this country been a discernible trend, over the last half century or so, towards greater understanding and greater tolerance of homosexuals by heterosexuals, and towards greater openness and honesty by homosexuals. In part this trend has prompted, in part it may have been a result of, legislative change.

Section 1(1) of the Sexual Offences Act 1967 decriminalised homosexual acts between consenting adults in private. It only applied to males, since homosexual acts between women were not criminal anyway. This legislative change, now nearly 30 years ago, followed and gave effect to the *Report of the Committee on Homosexual Offences and Prostitution* (Cmnd. 247) (the Wolfenden Committee) in 1957. At that time very few European countries took cognisance of homosexual behaviour between consenting parties in private (see para. 59 and App III of the report). It does not appear that that committee addressed the issues with specific reference to the armed forces. But it is important to note that s.1(1) of the Act did not, by virtue of s.1(5), prevent a homosexual act being an offence (other than a civil offence) under the statutes governing the three services. Any person subject to those statutes remained liable to punishment of homosexual acts. So, by s.2 of the 1967 Act, did the crew of British merchant ships. Plainly, the view was then taken that to permit homosexual acts by or between members of the armed services, or in the special conditions pertaining aboard ship, would be subversive of discipline, efficiency and good order.

The routine quinquennial review of the statutes governing the armed forces has the effect that issues such as the treatment of homosexuals are reconsidered periodically. In 1986 a Select Committee of the House of Commons, despite argument that service law should be brought into line with civilian law, concluded that the law should remain as it then stood. But opinion did not stand still. In 1991 another House of Commons Select Committee returned to the subject. Submissions were then made that service law should be brought into line with civilian law and that homosexual orientation *alone* should not be a bar to membership of the armed forces. The Select Committee accepted the first of these submissions, seeing 'no reason why Service personnel should be liable to prosecution under Service law for homosexual activity which would be legal in civilian law' (see *Special Report from the Select Committee on the Armed Forces Bill* (H.C. Paper (1990–1991) No. 179, para. 41). But they rejected the second submission, concluding that there was 'considerable force to MoD's argument that the presence of people known to be homosexual can cause tension in a group of people required to live and work sometimes under great stress and physically at very close quarters, and thus damage its cohesion and fighting effectiveness' (see para. 40). The Select Committee were not persuaded in 1991 that the time had yet come to permit the armed forces to accept homosexuals or homosexual activity.

In 1992 the responsible minister announced that in future individuals who engaged in homosexual activity that was legal in civilian law would not be prosecuted under service law. For want of parliamentary time, legislative effect was not given to this change until 1994, when s.146(1) of the Criminal Justice and Public Order Act 1994 was enacted. But s.146(4) provided that this change should not prevent a homosexual act (with or without other acts or circumstances) from constituting a ground for discharging a member of the armed forces.

In upholding the existing policy that homosexual activity or orientation should be an absolute bar to membership of the armed forces, the 1991 Select Committee undoubtedly reflected the overwhelming consensus of service and official opinion in this country. It does not appear that the Select Committee required or received any evidence of actual harm done by sexual orientation alone or by private homosexual activity outside the context of service life. Nor does the Select Committee appear to have considered whether the objectives of the existing policy could be met by a rule less absolute in its effect than that which was then applied.

In other areas of national life opinion has shifted. In July 1991 the Prime Minister announced that neither homosexual orientation nor private homosexual activity should henceforth preclude appointment even to sensitive posts in the home civil service and the diplomatic service. Lord Mackay of Clashfern L.C. has made similar announcements in relation to judicial office. In July 1994 the Royal Fleet Auxiliary introduced an equal opportunities policy stating that it did not discriminate on grounds of homosexuality. A majority of police forces now follow the same policy.

Outside the United Kingdom also, opinion has not stood still. Very few NATO countries bar homosexuals from their armed forces. This practice does not appear to have precluded the closest co-operation between such forces and our own. In the course of 1992–1993 Australia, New Zealand and

Canada relaxed their ban on homosexuals in their armed services but, importantly, introduced codes of conduct which defined the forms of homosexual conduct which were judged to be unacceptable. In the United States, on the other hand, as an authoritative report in 1993 made plain, military opinion remained overwhelmingly against allowing homosexuals to serve. The lawfulness of the legislative compromise adopted in that country is in doubt (see *Able v. U.S.* (1995) 880 F. Supp 968 at 975). In arguing that case the U.S. government 'recognized that a policy mandating discharge of homosexuals merely because they have a homosexual orientation or status could not withstand judicial scrutiny'.

I regard the progressive development and refinement of public and professional opinion at home and abroad, here very briefly described, as an important feature of this case. A belief which represented unquestioned orthodoxy in Year X may have become questionable by Year Y, and unsustainable by Year Z. Public and professional opinion are a continuum. The four appellants were discharged towards the end of 1994. The lawfulness of their discharge falls to be judged as of that date.

Irrationality

(1) The test

Mr Davick Pannick Q.C. (who represented three of the appellants, and whose arguments were adopted by the fourth) submitted that the court should adopt the following approach to the issue of irrationality:

> 'The court may not interfere with the exercise of an administrative discretion on substantive grounds save where the court is satisfied that the decision is unreasonable in the sense that it is beyond the range of responses open to a reasonable decision-maker. But in judging whether the decision-maker has exceeded this margin of appreciation the human rights context is important. The more substantial the interference with human rights, the more the court will require by way of justification before it is satisfied that the decision is reasonable in the sense outlined above.'

This submission is in my judgment an accurate distillation of the principles laid down by the House of Lords in *Bugdaycay v. Secretary of State for the Home Dept* [1987] 1 All E.R. 940; [1987] A.C. 514 and *Brind v. Secretary of State for the Home Dept* [1991] 1 All E.R. 720, [1991] 1 AC 696. In the first of these cases Lord Bridge of Harwich said ([1987] 1 All E.R. 940 at 952; [1987] A.C. 514 at 531):

> 'I approach the question raised by the challenge to the Secretary of State's decision on the basis of the law stated earlier in this opinion, *viz.* that the resolution of any issue of fact and the exercise of any discretion in relation to an application for asylum as a refugee lie exclusively within the jurisdiction of the Secretary of State subject only to the court's power of review. The limitations on the scope of that power are well known and need not be restated here. Within those limitations the court must, I think, be entitled to subject an administrative decision to the more rigorous examination, to ensure that it is in no way flawed, according to the gravity of the issue which the decision determines. The most fundamental of all human rights is the individual's right to life and, when an administrative decision under challenge is said to be one which may put the applicant's life at risk, the basis of the decision must surely call for the most anxious scrutiny.'

Lord Templeman spoke to similar effect (see [1987] 1 All E.R. 940 at 956; [1987] A.C. 514 at 537). In the second case, having concluded that it was not open to an English court to apply the European Convention on Human Rights, Lord Bridge said ([1991] 1 All E.R. 720 at 723; [1991] 1 A.C. 696 at 748–749):

> 'But I do not accept that this conclusion means that the courts are powerless to prevent the exercise by the executive of administrative discretions, even when conferred, as in the instant case, in terms which are on their face unlimited, in a way which infringes fundamental human rights. Most of the rights spelled out in terms in the convention, including the right to freedom of expression, are less than absolute and must in some cases yield to the claims of competing public interests. Thus, art. 10(2) of the convention spells out and categories the competing public interests by reference to which the right to freedom of expression may have to be curtailed. In exercising the power of judicial review we have neither the advantages nor the disadvantages of any comparable code to which we may refer or by which we are bound. But again, this surely does not

mean that in deciding whether the Secretary of State, in the exercise of his discretion, could reasonably impose the restriction he has imposed on the broadcasting organisations, we are not perfectly entitled to start from the premise that any restriction of the right to freedom of expression requires to be justified and that nothing less than an important competing public interest will be sufficient to justify it. The primary judgment as to whether the particular competing public interest justifies the particular restriction imposed falls to be made by the Secretary of State to whom Parliament has entrusted the discretion. But we are entitled to exercise a secondary judgment by asking whether a reasonable Secretary of State, on the material before him, could reasonably make that primary judgment.'

Again, Lord Templeman spoke to similar effect ([1991] 1 All E.R. 720 at 726; [1991] 1 A.C. 696 at 751):

'It seems to me that the courts cannot escape from asking themselves only whether a reasonable Secretary of State, on the material before him, could reasonably conclude that the interference with freedom of expression which he determined to impose was justifiable.'

It was argued for the ministry, in reliance on *Nottinghamshire C.C. v. Secretary of State for the Environment* [1986] 1 All E.R. 199; [1986] A.C. 240 and *Hammersmith and Fulbam London B.C. v. Secretary of State for the Environment* [1990] 3 All E.R. 589; [1991] 1 A.C. 521, that a test more exacting than *Wednesbury* was appropriate in this case (see *Associated Provincial Picture Houses Ltd v. Wednesbury Corp.* [1947] 2 All E.R. 680; [1948] 1 K.B. 223). The Divisional Court rejected this argument and so do I. The greater the policy content of a decision, and the more remote the subject matter of a decision from ordinary judicial experience, the more hesitant the court must necessarily be in holding a decision to be irrational. That is good law and, like most good law, common sense. Where decisions of a policy-laden, esoteric or security-based nature are in issue, even greater caution than normal must be shown in applying the test, but the test itself is sufficiently flexible to cover all situations.

The present cases do not affect the lives or liberty of those involved. But they do concern innate qualities of a very personal kind and the decisions of which the appellants complain have had a profound effect on their careers and prospects. The appellants' right as human beings are very much in issue. It is now accepted that this issue is justiciable. This does not of course mean that the court is thrust into the position of the primary decision-maker. It is not the constitutional role of the court to regulate the conditions of service in the armed forces of the Crown, nor has it the expertise to do so. But it has the constitutional role and duty of ensuring that the rights of citizens are not abused by the unlawful exercise of executive power. While the court must properly defer to the expertise of responsible decision-makers, it must not shrink from its fundamental duty to 'do right to all manner of people'.

(b) The facts

The reasons underlying the present policy were given in an affidavit sworn by Air Chief Marshal Sir John Willis K.C.B. C.B.E., the vice-chief of the defence staff, an officer of great seniority and experience. The relevant paragraphs of his affidavit have been recited in full by Simon Brown L.J. in his judgment in the Divisional Court, and it is unnecessary to duplicate that recital. Sir John advanced three reasons. The first related to morale and unit effectiveness, the second to the role of the services as guardian of recruits under the age of 18, and the third to the requirement of communal living in many service situations. Sir John described the ministry's policy as based not on a moral judgment but on a practical assessment of the implications of homosexual orientation on military life. By 'a practical assessment' Sir John may have meant an assessment of past experience in practice, or he may have meant an assessment of what would be likely to happen in practice if the present policy were varied. His affidavit makes no reference to any specific past experience, despite the fact that over the years very many homosexuals must have served in the armed forces. He does, however, make clear the apprehension of senior service authorities as to what could happen if the existing policy were revoked or varied, and the grounds upon which he relies were the subject of consideration by the House of Commons Select Committees to which reference has already been made.

The first factor relied on by Sir John, morale and unit effectiveness, was the subject of searing criticism by Mr Pannick. He submitted that the effect of a homosexual member of any military unit would depend on the character, ability and personality of the member involved. He pointed out that many homosexuals had successfully served in the services over the years. He drew attention to the experience of other disciplined forces such as the police. He submitted that inappropriate behaviour by homosexual members of the armed forces could be effectively regulated. He submitted that the ministry should not be deterred from doing what fairness and good sense demanded by apprehensions of irrational and prejudiced behaviour on the part of others.

Mr Pannick also criticised the second factor relied on by Sir John. He pointed out that any service member behaving inappropriately towards an under-age member of the service could be disciplined and punished in the same way as in society at large. He rejected the suggestion that homosexuals were less able to control their sexual impulses than heterosexuals. Again he suggested that the policy of the ministry was pandering to ignorant prejudice.

Mr Pannick accepted, of course, that members of the services could in many situations find themselves living together in conditions of very close proximity, although he pointed out that one of the appellants (by reason of his seniority) and another of the appellants (by reason of her particular occupation) were in no foreseeable situation likely to share accommodation with anyone. The lack of privacy in service life was, he suggested, a reason for imposing strict rules and discipline, but not a reason for banning the membership of any homosexual. He drew attention to the experience of other disciplined services. He pointed out that each of the appellants had worked in the armed forces for a number of years without any concern being expressed or complaints made about inappropriate behaviour. Each of them had earned very favourable reports. The same, it was said, was true of many other homosexual members of the services.

Above all, Mr Pannick criticised the blanket nature of the existing rule. He placed great emphasis on the practice of other nations whose rules were framed so as to counter the particular mischiefs to which homosexual orientation or activity might give rise. He pointed out that other personal problems such as addiction to alcohol, or compulsive gambling, or marital infidelity were dealt with by the service authorities on a case by case basis and not on the basis of a rule which permitted no account to be taken of the peculiar features of the case under consideration.

The arguments advanced by Mr Pannick are in my opinion of very considerable cogency. They call to be considered in depth, with particular reference to specific evidence of past experience in this country, to the developing experience of other countries, and to the potential effectiveness or otherwise of a detailed prescriptive code along the lines adopted elsewhere in place of the present blanket ban. Such a reassessment of the existing policy is already, as I have noted, in train, and I note that the next Select Committee quinquennial review of the policy is to receive a departmental paper of evidence covering all the matters canvassed on this appeal. What the outcome of that review will be, I do not know.

The existing policy cannot in my judgment be stigmatised as irrational at the time when these appellants were discharged. It was supported by both Houses of Parliament and by those to whom the ministry properly looked for professional advice. There was, to my knowledge, no evidence before the ministry which plainly invalidated that advice. Changes made by other countries were in some cases very recent. The Australian, New Zealand and Canadian codes had been adopted too recently to yield much valuable experience. The ministry did not have the opportunity to consider the full range of arguments developed before us. Major policy changes should be the product of mature reflection, not instant reaction. The threshold of irrationality is a high one. It was not crossed in this case.

The European Convention
Article 8 of the European Convention on Human Rights provides:
'1. Everyone has the right to respect for his private and family life, his home and his correspondence.
2. There shall be no interference by a public authority with the exercise of this right except such as is in accordance with the law and is necessary in a democratic society in the interests of national security, public safety or the economic well-being of the country, for the prevention of disorder or crime, for the protection of health or morals, or for the protection of the rights and freedoms of others.'
It is, inevitably, common ground that the United Kingdom's obligation, binding in international law, to respect and secure compliance with this article is not one that is enforceable by domestic courts. The relevance of the convention in the present context is as background to the complaint of irrationality. The fact that a decision-maker failed to take account of convention obligations when exercising an administrative discretion is not of itself a ground for impugning that exercise of discretion. ... I would dismiss these appeals."

HENRY L.J.: "... I agree with the judgment of Sir Thomas Bingham M.R.I will add some words of my own on the first and second topics.

Irrationality
On the evidence before us, our armed forces have had a long-standing absolute prohibition on those known to be homosexual joining or, once discovered, remaining in the armed forces. We are told that that policy existed throughout the years of conscription (1939 to 1960). This fact may surprise post-war national servicemen, whom I believe to have been generally unaware that a genuine homosexual orientation would

have rendered them exempt from compulsory national service, but their ignorance is explained before us on the basis that the policy did not need to be publicised, committed to paper, or indeed specifically addressed until some time after male homosexual acts between consenting adults in private were decriminalised in civilian life (though not under military law) in 1967.

Despite this ban (and in the early years, perhaps as a result of ignorance of it) it seems to be realistically accepted on all sides that the reality is that many more homosexuals served in the armed forces than the relatively small numbers dismissed for it either on disciplinary grounds relating to their conduct (the minority) or on administrative grounds based on their status as homosexuals (the vast majority, at any rate in recent years). This suggests that the majority of serving homosexuals were undetected and had a useful and productive service life and that there had been nothing in their conduct which either disclosed their sexual orientation or threatened the cohesion of their units. This experience clearly should not be disregarded when considering the necessity for an absolute ban, especially as that experience is replicated in the case histories of the appellants before us.

Additionally, over the years since the passing of the Sexual Offences Act 1967, there can be no doubt that public opinion has moved a very long way towards toleration and acceptance of homosexuals (as Lord Wolfenden himself commented as long ago as 1976 in his autobiography *Turning Points*, pp. 144–146). We have seen a greater and greater public awareness and acceptance of homosexuality, together with a greater personal openness in acknowledging it. Consequently there has been a growing recognition of the specific human rights of homosexuals, including rights in the workplace.

But both sides of the argument as to acceptance of homosexuals in the armed forces accept first that the armed forces are quite unlike any other employer, that military life is quite different from civilian life, and second that the forces can properly demand (and those serving must unquestioningly accept) restriction on their liberty and behaviour that would not be acceptable if imposed on a citizen in civilian life. It is accepted that these personal sacrifices can be demanded and must be made in the interests of the overall goal of military effectiveness, based on high morale, good discipline and unit cohesion. It is accepted that certain conduct, whether homosexual or heterosexual, can threaten military effectiveness, and so can reasonably be proscribed by the armed forces where a civilian employer could not lawfully do so. For example, in America in 1993 the National Defense Research Institute (RAND), given by the Secretary of Defense the task of preparing a draft of an executive order 'ending discrimination on the basis of sexual orientation in determining who may serve in the Armed Forces' in a way which was 'practical and realistic, and consistent with the high standards of combat effectiveness and unit cohesion our Armed Forces must maintain', found that the only policy option to achieve that result was one conduct-based, commenting, 'all personnel, including acknowledged homosexuals, must understand that the military environment is no place to advertise one's sexual orientation'. (To like effect is the Australian Defence Force which in Annex B to its statement of policy on 'Unacceptable Sexual Behaviour by Members of the Australian Defence Force' which may threaten operational effectiveness includes, for example 'public flaunting and advocacy of a particular sexual proclivity'.)

So the plaintiffs here accept the legitimacy of the armed forces achieving their aim by a non-discriminatory, conduct-based code restricting expression or other manifestation of their sexual orientation. What they challenge is the legitimacy of a status-based absolute proscription of all homosexuals in the armed forces, however exemplary their service conduct.

The sole question on the irrationality issue is, accepting the formulation as proposed by Mr Pannick Q.C. and accepted by Sir Thomas Bingham M.R., whether it was irrational at the end of 1994, when these appellants were discharged, for the defendants still to have in place an absolute proscription of all homosexuals.

I agree with Sir Thomas Bingham M.R. it was not. I would add only these remarks to his reasons. On the evidence before us, the issue between a conduct-based code or status-based ban was a relatively new one. It does not seem to have been raised before the Select Committee in 1986. It was raised in broad terms by the Stonewall Group in 1991. The Select Committee recognised that there was much more tolerance of differences in sexual orientation both without and (possibly) within the armed forces. But they were not persuaded that the time had yet come to require the armed forces to accept homosexuals. But the clock did not stop there. Since then Canada, Australia and New Zealand all (in 1992 or 1993) moved away from an absolute ban, and the American middle position of 'Don't ask, don't tell' is under powerful legal attack, with the last appellate word probably not yet said (see *Able v. U.S.* (1995) 880 F. Supp 968). All these were matters to be taken into consideration when the individual decision in these cases were taken.

It would seem that the movement in public opinion recognised by the Select Committee is continuing, and it might be that positions within the armed forces of Canada, Australia and New Zealand have shifted also — though the evidence does not make this clear. But the advice received from those with experience in our armed forces remained the same: that the absolute ban was necessary for the reasons stated. We know from the material before us the substance of that advice and the assertions contained in it, but we do not know details of the experience which informed that advice. Hence the lawyers' criticism that the advice is not based on evidence. I would not at this stage of the debate assume that the views of the armed forces are not based on evidence, though that evidence is not before us.

Those responsible for the policy were faced with a rapidly changing scene on a highly charged issue of great importance to both the armed forces and the individuals. That combination of circumstances points against precipitate action both by the policy maker with primary responsibility and, a fortiori, by the reviewing court in its secondary role. At the end of 1994 it could not be said that reasonable decision-makers must inevitably conclude that the existing policy was unlawful and so must be changed. It was not legally irrational to continue the policy. What was needed is what has now been set up — namely the ministry preparing a paper of evidence to assist the Select Committee. I am pleased to see that there are to be visits to overseas armed forces, as I was not persuaed by the bald submission in evidence that 'comparison with other countries does not assist'. In the balance, proper appreciation will have to be given both to the impact of a total ban on the human rights of the affected individuals, and to any practical justification for that ban and the evidence supporting it."

THORPE L.J.: "I agree with both the preceding judgments . . ."

Notes

6–32   (1) The case is noted by C.R. Munro, "Fundamental Rights in National Law", 1997 S.L.T. (News) 221 at 224 where, in reviewing this case and the others cited in the article, he comments:

> "As things stand, it is reasonable to conclude . . . that 'the courts will look significantly harder at cases involving infringements of human rights, but without reversing the onus or burden of proofs or necessarily abandoning all of the *Wednesbury* reserve'."

He goes on:

> "There is, admittedly, rather scant evidence of this development in judicial review cases in Scotland, but there is at least some evidence of the courts using fundamental rights as a yardstick for scrutiny of executive actions. In *Singh, Petr*, . . . (1988 GWD 32–1377). Lord Morison in considering deportation policy, said that 'if the policy of the Home Office is one which ignores the obvious humanitarian principle of respect for family life, it would in my view be unreasonable and subject to the court's review' . . . And in a prison administration case, an Extra Division did acknowledge (without referring specifically to the ECHR) that there was a 'basic civil right . . . that access to the courts should be unimpeded; (*Leech v Secretary of State for Scotland*, 1993 SLT 365 at p 370K). In the new juridical and governmental climate which obtains, there is every reason for Scottish courts to follow developments in England in this respect."

Equally one can point to dicta in the opposite direction: In *McRae v. Parole Board for Scotland*, 1996 G.W.D. 14–852, it was observed that challenge of decisions of the Parole Board could only be challengeable on grounds of irrationality if a very strong case could be made out. See *Holmes v. Secretary of State for Scotland*, 1998 G.W.D. 27–1351, again a parole case and requiring that the decision be "outrageous". In *A.B. v. Scottish Legal Aid Board*, 1991 S.C.L.R. 702 it was stated that the test of reasonableness in the context of refusal of a legal aid application was "an exacting one".

6–33   (2) The Human Rights Act 1998 will have a significant impact in this area. In particular, the courts will now have available to them a list of rights to which they and the decision maker, whose decision they are reviewing, must have regard to in assessing the rationality of that decision. To that extent, there may be less scope for controversy in determining what fundamental or human rights are recognised by Scots law. Moreover, it will no longer be sufficient for a decision such as that in *Smith* to meet the test of rationality. Smith, if he had been able to bring this case under the Act, would have been entitled to argue that the test of proportionality should also have been applied to the decision to discharge him. He would have been entitled to argue that on the basis of Article 8.2 the test of the restriction being "necessary" had not been met. It would not be sufficient that a State exercises its discretion reasonably, as the act is subject "to the court's control as regards to compatibility of its conduct with the engagements it has undertaken under the Convention": *The Sunday Times v. The United Kingdom* (1979–80) 2 E.H.R.R. 245 at 276, para. 59. Moreover, even if the Government had been able to demonstrate that the test of necessity had been met in response to one of the grounds of restriction referred to in Article 8.2 (commonly referred to as a "pressing social need" in the jurisprudence of the European Court of Human Rights), it would still be required to demonstrate that the restriction was "proportionate to the legitimate aim pursued", *The Sunday Times* at para. 62 and see also *Dudgeon v. United Kingdom* (1982) 4 E.H.R.R. 149. ECHR.This means that a restriction with the prima facie appearance of legitimacy will only be held to be lawful under the Convention if it is proportionate to the aim being pursued and is the least onerous means of attaining that stated aim. Mr Smith's counsel was David Pannick, author of the article on the question of the margin of appreciation available under the Human Rights Act, noted above. If that doctrine had been applied here, how might it have been handled?

(3) Note also the rejection of the Ministry of Defence's attempt to invoke "super *Wednesbury*" standard of increased deference to the decision maker (based on the *Nottinghamshire* and *Hammersmith* cases and arguably also found in even more advanced form in *City of Edinburgh District Council v. Secretary of State for Scotland*, 1985 S.L.T. 551 and *East Kilbride District Council v. Secretary of State for Scotland*. 1995 S.L.T. 1238, which cases are discussed at para. 2–39). Sir Thomas Bingham M.R. seems to accept that there is a sliding scale of reasonableness and in particular that:

> "The greater the policy content of a decision, and the more remote the subject matter of a decision from the ordinary judicial experience, the more hesitant the court must necessarily be in holding the decision to be irrational."

For similar views see also Sir John Laws, "Is the High Court the Guardian of Fundamental Constitutional Rights?" [1993] P.L. 59 and generally M. Fordham, "Surveying the Grounds: Key Themes in Judicial Intervention" in *Administrative Law Facing the Future: Old Constraints and New Horizons* (P. Leyland and T. Woods eds 1997), p. 184.

Is a sliding scale of reasonableness permissible? Should the policy content of a decision be relevant in any event given the courts' implicit acceptance of the greater justification needed where there is substantial interference with human rights? Lord Irvine of Lairg, "Judges and Decision-Makers: The Theory and Practice of *Wednesbury* Review" [1996] P.L. 59 at 65, does not believe that it should for:

> "This is to stray far beyond the limits laid down in *Brind*, and to lead the judges into dangerous territory. In practice, few cases which touch upon the protection of fundamental rights reflect the beguiling simplicity of the legal slogan. The political and legal choices which import consideration of fundamental rights protection are among the most difficult and the most subjective, and offer immense scope for political and philosophical disagreement. It cannot be right that such questions should be regarded as more rather than less suitable to judicial determination. The approach adopted in *Brind*, which states conclusively that the *Wednesbury* threshold of unreasonableness is not lowered in fundamental rights cases, must prevail."

The decision in *Brind* is noted below.

Lord Irvine's comments were of course written before the advent of the Human Rights Act. On the face of it his rejection of substantive review in human rights cases seems to have been overtaken by events. One should not be too ready to dismiss Lord Irvine's comments as no longer relevant. It may be some time into the operation of the new legislation before one can readily state that the courts have fully embraced the implications of substantive review. Much will also depend on the extent to which the courts create a domestic margin of appreciation. For a general survey of the issues see F. Donson, "Civil Liberties and Judicial Review: Can the Common Law Really Protect Rights?" in Leyland and Woods (eds), p. 347 and below.

(4) Lord Irvine's cautious approach may still have relevance in relation to rights not protected **6–34** by the Human Rights Act. An alleged "social" right to housing or an "economic" right to work

might be regarded by many as of fundamental importance along with freedom of expression or the right to privacy, but on the face of it these rights are not guaranteed by the ECHR or the Human Rights Act. In response to the Labour Government's consultation document, *Bringing Rights Home*, Professor K. Ewing and Professor C. Gearty pointed out in "Rocky Foundations for Labour's New Rights" [1997] 2 E.H.R.L.R. 146 that:

> "Despite carefully fostered appearances to the contrary, the European Convention is a deeply ideological document. Incorporation would guarantee supremacy to its narrowly individualistic view of society and would then make it impossible or extremely difficult to undermine or overthrow this ideology through the ordinary process. As such it represents a triumph of liberalism over socialism and as such fixes its triumph irrevocably into the Constitution."

For a possible models for reform see W. Finnie, "Rewriting the European Convention on Human Rights", 1994 S.L.T. (News) 389 and K. Ewing, "Social Rights and Constitutional Law" [1999] P.L. 104.

It is therefore perhaps tempting to conclude that even if the courts do adopt a robust approach to the protection of the rights guaranteed by the Act, social or economic rights certainly offer the kind of scope for disagreement noted by Lord Irvine. In these areas, *Wednesbury* reserve may still remain the mark of judicial scrutiny of decisions impacting on such rights.

REASONABLENESS AS A SPECIFIC DUTY

6–35 Here we are concerned with the existence of a positive requirement of reasonableness. The courts are required to consider whether such a requirement has been met and to that extent are not necessarily restricted to the formulation found in *Wednesbury*. However, the extent to which the courts are prepared to utilise the potentially greater freedom that such a positive requirement entails depends greatly on the statutory context under consideration. Also under consideration may be questions of fact.

Nakkuda Ali v. M.F. de S. Jayaratne

[1951] A.C. 66

6–36 The Controller of Textiles in Ceylon, the respondent, used his power to cancel a textile dealer's licence "where the Controller has reasonable grounds to believe that any dealer is unfit to be allowed to continue as a dealer". The appellant sought to have the decision quashed on the ground of breach of natural justice. This aspect of the case is discussed by Lord Reid in *Ridge v. Baldwin*, extracted at para. 8–4. One specific point dealt with by the Privy Council was whether the requirement that the Controller had "reasonable grounds" indicated that he was acting judicially, which was the view of the Supreme Court of Ceylon.

LORD RADCLIFFE delivered the opinion of the Privy Council (LORDS PORTER, OAKSEY and RADCLIFFE, SIR JOHN BEAUMONT and SIR LIONEL LEACH): "… It would be impossible to consider the significance of such words as 'Where the Controller has reasonable grounds to believe…' without taking account of the decision of the House of Lords in *Liversidge v. Sir John Anderson* [1942] A.C. 206. That decision related to a claim for damages for false imprisonment, the imprisonment having been brought about by an order made by the Home Secretary under the Defence (General) Regulations, 1939, reg. 18B, of the United Kingdom. It was not a case that had any direct bearing on the court's power to issue a writ of certiorari to the Home Secretary in respect of action taken under that regulation: but it did directly involve a question as to the meaning of the words 'If the Secretary of State has reasonable cause to believe any person to be of hostile origin or associations…' which appeared at the opening of the regulation in question. And the decision of the majority of the House did lay down that those words in that context meant no more than that the Secretary of State had honestly to suppose that he had reasonable cause to believe the required thing. On that basis, granted good faith, the maker of the order appears to be the only possible judge of the conditions of his own jurisdiction.

Their Lordships do not adopt a similar construction of the words in reg. 62 which are now before them. Indeed, it would be a very unfortunate thing if the decision of *Liversidge's* case came to be regarded as laying down any general rule as to the construction of such phrases when they appear in statutory enactments. It is an authority for the proposition that the words 'if A.B. has reasonable cause to believe' are capable of meaning 'if A.B. honestly thinks that he has reasonable cause to believe' and that in the context and attendant circumstances of Defence Regulation 18B they did in fact mean just that. But the elaborate consideration which the majority of the House gave to the context and circumstances before adopting that construction itself shows that there is no general principle that such words are to be so understood; and the dissenting speech of Lord Atkin at least serves as a reminder of the many occasions when they have been treated as meaning 'if there is in fact reasonable cause for A.B. so to believe'. After all, words such as these are commonly found when a legislature or law-making authority confers powers on a minister or official. However read, they must be intended to serve in some sense as a condition limiting the exercise of an otherwise arbitrary power. But if the question whether the condition has been satisfied is to be conclusively decided by the man who yields the power the value of the intended restraint is in effect nothing. No doubt he must not exercise the power in bad faith: but the field in which this kind of question arises is such that the reservation for the case of bad faith is hardly more than a formality. Their Lordships therefore treat the words in reg. 62, 'where the Controller has reasonable grounds to believe that any dealer is unfit to be allowed to continue as a dealer' as imposing a condition that there must in fact exist such reasonable grounds, known to the Controller, before he can validly exercise the power of cancellation . . ."

Notes

(1) The case was subsequently approved in *Ridge v. Baldwin* and in *Inland Revenue Commissioners v. Rossminster Ltd* [1980] AC 952. *Liversidge v. Anderson* [1942] A.C. 206 is arguably an exceptional case: see on this R.F.V. Heuston, "*Liversidge v. Anderson* in Retrospect" (1970) 86 L.Q.R. 33, and "*Liversidge v. Anderson*: Two Footnotes" (1971) 87 L.Q.R. 161.

6–37

(2) Under the Licensing (Scotland) Act 1976, s. 39 (4)(*d*), the sheriff may uphold an appeal if a licensing board in arriving at its decision "exercised its discretion in an unreasonable manner". Parallel provision is found in the Civic Government (Scotland) Act 1982, Sched. 1, para. 18(7) in relation to the activities under that Act which require local authority licences. It is important to recall that the circumstances of the statutory appeal are somewhat different from judicial review proceedings in that in the context of appellate proceedings, the court has a wider discretion as to what decision it can reach and in particular, in the context of appeals under section 39(4), the court has the ability to "reverse or modify the decision of the licensing board": section 39(6). In an early case, *Kieran v. Adams*, Glasgow Sheriff Court, February 7, 1978, unreported, it was observed that this ground of appeal exists to "enable a sheriff to correct decisions which are on the face of them arbitrary, capricious or perverse". This echoes the test of "irrationality" articulated by Lord Diplock in the GCHQ case. Concern as to the limitations placed on the sheriff by this test were expressed in *Loosefoot Entertainment Ltd v. Glasgow District Licensing Board*, 1990 S.C.L.R. 584 at 587. This approach has now fallen out of favour. In *The Noble Organisation Ltd v. City of Glasgow District Council (No. 3)*, 1991 S.C.L.R. 380, an appeal under the Civic Government (Scotland) Act 1982, it was argued for the council (at 387):

"on the basis of the familiar dicta contained in cases such as *Associated Provincial Picture Houses v Wednesbury Corporation* and *Wordie Property Co. Ltd v Secretary of State for Scotland*, that the court's entitlement to intervene in a decision based on the exercise of an authority's discretion could only be justified if the decision was 'so unreasonable that no reasonable tribunal could have reached it' ".

The relevance of these dicta was doubted by Lord Morison (at 387):

"accepting that these authorities may indicate that, in order to justify the court's intervention on the ground that a tribunal has exceeded its jurisdiction, something more is required than merely to show that a decision is unreasonable, they do not in my view apply in this respect to the appellate function of the sheriff... That function is the subject of express statutory provision in paragraph 18(7) of Schedule 1 to the 1982 Act, which provides inter alia that the sheriff may uphold an appeal if he considers that the licensing authority '...exercised their discretion in an unreasonable manner. "No further definition of the basis upon which the sheriff is entitled to intervene is required."

This approach was subsequently followed in *Latif v. Motherwell District Licensing Board*, 1994 S.L.T. 414, in the context of an appeal under section 39(4) of the Licensing (Scotland) Act 1976, where it was observed (at 415) that notwithstanding the apparent freedom afforded the sheriff in determining an appeal he must nevertheless act objectively and in particular could not act

"subjectively and [leave] out of account the very important fact that a licensing board has had the advantage of hearing many such applications, knows its own area and may be assumed to have developed some expertise in assessing problems such as the overprovision of licensed premises".

See also *Caledonian Nightclubs Ltd v. City of Glasgow District Licensing Board*, 1996 S.L.T. 451, where the House of Lords approved this line of reasoning.

6–38   (3) An unreasonable exercise of the board's discretion has been held to exist where there are defects in a statement of reasons: *R.W. Cairns Ltd v. Busby East Church Kirk Session*, 1985 S.L.T. 493; a rigid application of a policy: *Aitken v. City of Glasgow District Council*, 1988 S.C.L.R. 287; and inconsistency of approach: *Cashley v. City of Dundee District Council*, 1994 S.L.T. 1111, extracted at para. 6–55. These cases represent situations in which it was easier to stigmatise a decision as being unreasonable as they all appear to offend against other principles on which a decision can be attacked, thus *R.W. Cairns Ltd* can be regarded as a failure to follow procedure by not providing an appropriate statement of reasons; *Aitken*, as an example of the fettering of discretion and *Cashley*, as misapplication of a policy.

(4) Some licensing decisions, such as the refusal of a regular extension of permitted hours, can only be challenged by way of judicial review. The dividing line between reasonableness in a statutory appeal and in judicial review proceedings is difficult to state with any accuracy, as noted by J.C. Cummins, *Licensing Law In Scotland* (1993), commenting on the decision in *Noble* (at p. 308):

"In the result, the standard of 'unreasonableness' required for judicial review purposes is now well-settled but probably falls to be distinguished from the 'reasonable board' test applied in statutory appeals, in a manner which has yet to be clearly focused".

(5) For further reading see Cummins, above, pp. 295–299, 307–308: C. Agnew, Q.C. and H.M. Baillie, *The Licensing (Scotland) Act 1976* (4th ed., 1996), pp. 117–119; A. Hajducki, Q.C. and S. Stuart, *Scottish Civic Government Licensing Law* (1994), pp. 119–120; and Finch and Ashton, pp. 299–301.

(6) A number of provisions in the Scotland Act 1998 fall to be noted. Under section 35 (1) (*a*), (*b*) the Secretary of State can make an order prohibiting the Presiding Officer of the Scottish Parliament from submitting a Bill for Royal Assent where:

"(*a*) [he] has reasonable grounds to believe it would be incompatible with any international obligations or the interests of defence or national security or, (*b*) which make modifications of the law as it applies to reserved matters and which the Secretary of State has reasonable grounds to believe would have an adverse effect on the operation of the law as it applies to reserved matters".

The power can be exercised by any UK Secretary of State, not just the Secretary of State for Scotland. Any such order must state the reasons for its making, subsection (2). See also the provisions of section 58, extracted at para.13–10, and for comment on sections 35 and 58 generally see C.M.G. Himsworth and C.R. Munro, *The Scotland Act 1998* (1999), pp. 48–50, 75–76.

REASONABLENESS AND SUBJECTIVE POWERS

6–39   Here we are concerned with the review of powers where the powers expressed in subjective form, typically the power to act in circumstances which are "believed" to exist, or to do something that the person holding the power thinks fit. On the face of it, it is difficult to see how such subjective expressions of power could be open to review, save perhaps on the limited ground of good faith. However, as the following extract shows reasonableness can be applied with effect.

Secretary of State for Education and Science v. Tameside Metropolitan Borough Council

[1977] A.C. 1014

A local education authority's scheme for introducing comprehensive education was approved **6–40** by the Secretary of State in November 1975 and was due to be implemented at the beginning of the school year in September 1976. In May 1976 control of the council and the education authority changed as a result of local elections and the new majority, which had promised to reconsider the question of comprehensive education in its election literature, proposed to postpone plans to convert a number of grammar schools. The authority informed the Secretary of State that the schools in the area were not ready for the changes which, if made then, would, in its view, disrupt children's education. It proposed to retain 240 selective places for 11-year-olds and planned to select them by a combination of reports, records and interviews. In the event, 783 applications (in response to the letters sent to 3,200 parents) were made for these places. Section 68 of the Education Act 1944 gives the Secretary of State power to give such directions as to the exercise of any power or duty given to or imposed on any local education authority "as appear to him to be expedient" provided that he

> "is satisfied, either on complaint by any person or otherwise, that any local education authority … have acted or are proposing to act unreasonably with respect to the exercise of any power conferred or the performance of any duty imposed by or under this Act".

Using this section, he directed the authority to implement the scheme approved by him in 1975 including the arrangement previously made of the allocation of 11-year-olds on a non-selective basis. He then applied for an order of mandamus (the equivalent of an action for performance of statutory duty in Scots law, on which see para. 11–13) to compel compliance with the direction. The Divisional Court made the order but their decision was reversed by the Court of Appeal. The Secretary of State appealed to the House of Lords.

[IN THE COURT OF APPEAL]

LORD DENNING M.R.: "…. It was suggested in one place in the papers — on June 21, 1976 by the chief officers of the council — that once the Secretary of State said he was 'satisfied', his decision could not be challenged in the courts unless it was shown to be made in bad faith. We were referred by counsel for the Secretary of State to *Liversidge v. Anderson* ([1942] A.C. 206, at 233) where Lord Atkin drew attention to cases where the Defence Regulations required the Secretary of State to be 'satisfied' of something or other. Lord Atkin said: 'In all these cases, it is plain that unlimited discretion is given to the Secretary of State assuming, as everyone does, that he acts in good faith' to which I would add a similar passage by Somervell L.J. in *Robinson v. Minister of Town and Country Planning* ([1947] K.B. 702, at 721). Those statements were made, however, in regard to regulations in war time or immediately after the war when the decisions of the executive had to be implemented speedily and without question. That was pointed out by Lord Radcliffe in *Nakkuda Ali v. M.F. de S. Jayaratne* ([1951] A.C. 66 at 77) and by Lord Reid in *Ridge v. Baldwin* ([1964] A.C. 40 at 73). Those statements do not apply today. Much depends on the matter about which the Secretary of State has to be satisfied. If he is to be satisfied on the matter of opinion, that is one thing. But if he has to be satisfied that someone has been guilty of some discreditable or unworthy or unreasonable conduct, that is another. To my mind, if a statute gives a Minister power to take drastic action if he is satisfied that a local authority have acted or are proposing to act improperly or unreasonably, then the Minister should obey all the elementary rules of fairness before he finds that the local authority are guilty or before he takes drastic action overruling them. He should give the party affected notice of the charge of impropriety or unreasonableness and a fair opportunity of dealing with it. I am glad to see that the Secretary of State did so in this case. He had before him the written proposals of the new council and he met their leaders. In addition, however, the Minister must direct himself properly in law. He must call his own attention to the matters he is bound to consider. He must exclude from his consideration matters which are irrelevant to that which he has to consider. And the decision to which he comes must be one which is reasonable in this sense, that it is, or can be, supported with good reasons or at, any rate be a decision which a reasonable person might reasonably reach. Such is, I think, plain from *Padfield v. Minister of Agriculture, Fisheries and Food* ([1968] A.C. 997), which is a landmark in our administrative law and which we had in mind in *Secretary of State for Employment v. Associated Society of Locomotive Engineers and Firemen* (No. 2) ([1972] 2 Q.B. 455). So much for the requirements if the Minister is to be 'satisfied'…

[His Lordship held that the Secretary of State must have misdirected himself on the interpretation of 'unreasonableness', and that there was no evidence on which the Secretary of State could declare himself satisfied that the council were proposing to act unreasonably.]"

Scarman L.J. [delivered a concurring judgment, which included the following passage]: "... I do not accept that the scope of judicial review is limited to quite the extent suggested by counsel for Secretary of State [*i.e.* to bad faith, misdirection in law, taking account of irrelevant matters, omitting to consider relevant matters, taking a view that no reasonable man could take]. I would add a further situation to those specified by him; misunderstanding or ignorance of an established and relevant fact. Let me give two examples. The fact may be either physical, something which existed or occurred or did not, or it may be mental, an opinion. Suppose that, contrary to the Secretary of State's belief, it was the fact that there was in the area of the authority adequate school accommodation for the pupils to be educated, and the Secretary of State acted under the section believing that there was not. If it were plainly established that the Secretary of State were mistaken, I do not think that the could substantiate the lawfulness of his direction under this section. Now, more closely to the facts of this case, taking a matter of expert professional opinion. Suppose that, contrary to the understanding of the Secretary of State, there does in fact exist a respectable body of professional or expert opinion to the effect that the selection procedures for school entry proposed are adequate and acceptable. If that body of opinion be proved to exist, and if that body of opinion proves to be available both to the authority and to the Secretary of State, then again I would have thought it quite impossible for the Secretary of State to invoke his powers under section 68. By adding this situation to situations more commonly described as occasions for judicial review, I can find no objection in principle. Lord Denning M.R. has briefly referred to some of the case law on the matter; and in the short time available I have looked to see if there is authority which would belie what I believe to be the law, and there is none."

Geoffrey Lane L.J. delivered a concurring judgment.

[IN THE HOUSE OF LORDS]

Lord Wilberforce: "... This section (s.68 of the Education Act 1944) does not say what the consequences of the giving of directions are to be, but I accept, for the purposes of the appeal, that the consequences are to impose on the authority a statutory duty to comply with them which can be enforced by an order of mandamus.

Analysis of the section brings out three cardinal points. 1. The matters with which the section is concerned are primarily matters of educational administration. The action, which the Secretary of State is entitled to stop, is unreasonable action with respect to the exercise of a power or the performance of a duty; the power and the duty of the authority are presupposed and cannot be interfered with. Local education authorities are entitled under the 1944 Act to have a policy, and this section does not enable the Secretary of State to require them to abandon or reverse a policy just because the Secretary of State disagrees with it. Specifically, the Secretary of State cannot use power under this section to impose a general policy of comprehensive education on a local education authority which does not agree with the policy. He cannot direct it to bring in a scheme for total comprehensive education in its area, and if it has done so he cannot direct it to implement it. If he tries to use a direction under section 68 for this purpose, his direction would be clearly invalid. A direction under section 68 must be justified on the ground of unreasonable action in doing what under the 1944 Act the local authority is entitled to do, and under the Act it has a freedom of choice. I do not think that there is any controversy on these propositions.

The critical question in this case, and it is not an easy one, is whether, on a matter which appears to be one of educational administration, namely whether the change of course proposed by the authority in May 1976 would lead to educational chaos or undue disruption, the Secretary of State's judgment can be challenged.

2. The section is framed in a subjective form — if the Secretary of State 'is satisfied'. This form of section is quite well known, and at first sight might seem to exclude judicial review. Sections in this form may, no doubt, exclude judicial review on what is or has become a matter of pure judgment. But I do not think that they go further than that. If a judgment requires, before it can be made, the existence of some facts, then, although the evaluation of those facts is for the Secretary of State alone, the court must enquire whether those facts exist, and have been taken into account, whether the judgment has been made on a proper self direction as to those facts, whether the judgment has not been made on other facts which ought not to have been taken into account. If these requirements are not met, then the exercise of judgment, however bona fide it may be, becomes capable of challenge: see *Secretary of State for Employment v. Associated Society of Locomotive Engineers and Firemen* (No. 2) ([1972] 2 Q.B. 455 at 493), *per* Lord Denning M.R.

3. The section has to be considered within the structure of the 1944 Act. In many statutes a Minister or other authority is given a discretionary power and in these cases the court's power to review any exercise of the discretion, though still real, is limited. In these cases it is said that the courts cannot substitute their opinion for that of the Minister; they can interfere on such grounds as that the Minister has acted right outside his powers or outside the purpose of the Act, or unfairly, or on an incorrect basis of fact. But there is no universal rule as to the principles on which the exercise of a discretion may be reviewed: each statute or type of statute must be individually looked at. This Act of 1944, is quite different from those which simply create a ministerial discretion. The Secretary of State, under section 68, is not merely exercising a discretion; he is reviewing the action of another public body which itself has discretionary powers and duties. He, by contrast with the courts in the normal case, may substitute his opinion for that of the authority: this is what the section allows, but he must take account of what the authority, under the statute, is entitled to do. The authority — this is vital — is itself elected, and is given specific powers as to the kind of schools it wants in its area. Therefore two situations may arise. One is that there may be a difference of policy between the Secretary of State (under Parliament) and the local authority: the section gives no power to the Secretary of State to make his policy prevail. The other is that, owing to the democratic process involving periodic elections, abrupt reversals of policy may take place, particularly where there are only two parties and the winner takes all. Any reversal of policy if at all substantial must cause some administrative disruption; this was as true of the 1975 proposals as of those of Tameside. So the mere possibility, or probability, of disruption cannot be a ground for issuing a direction to abandon the policy. What the Secretary of State is entitled, by a direction if necessary, to ensure is that such disruptions are not 'unreasonable', *i.e.* greater than a body, elected to carry out a new programme, with which the Secretary of State may disagree, ought to impose on those for whom it is responsible. After all, those who voted for the new programme, involving a change of course, must also be taken to have accepted some degree of disruption in implementing it.

The ultimate question in this case, in my opinion, is whether the Secretary of State has given sufficient, or any, weight to this particular factor in the exercise of the judgment.

I must now enquire what were the facts on which the Secretary of State expressed himself as satisfied that the council were acting or proposing to act unreasonably. The Secretary of State did not give oral evidence in the courts, and the facts on which he acted must be taken from the department's letters at the relevant time — *i.e.* on or about June 11, 1976 — and from affidavits sworn by its officers. These documents are to be read fairly and in *bonam partem*, if reasons are given in general terms, the court should not exclude reasons which fairly fall within them: allowance must be fairly made for difficulties in expression. The Secretary of State must be given credit for having the background to this actual situation well in mind, and must be taken to be properly and professionally informed as to education practices used in the area and as to resources available to the local education authority. His opinion based as it must be on that of a strong and expert department, is not to be lightly overridden.

On June 11 the direction under section 68 was given in a letter of that date. The letter stated that the Secretary of State was satisfied that the authority was proposing to act unreasonably according to the formula used in section 68. A change of plan designed to come into effect in less than three months must, in the opinion of the Secretary of State, give rise to 'considerable difficulties'. It pointed out that over 3,000 pupils transferring from primary schools had already been allocated and allotted places. Then followed this paragraph (which I shall call 'para. A'):

> 'The Authority's revised proposals *confront* the parents of children due to transfer in September *with the dilemma* of either adhering to secondary school allocations for their children which they may no longer regard as appropriate, or else *submitting* to an improvised selection procedure (the precise form of which the Secretary of State understands, has even now not been settled) carried out in circumstances and under a timetable which raise substantial doubts about its educational validity.'

A further objection was taken to the proposed possible reallocation during or after the first year... The change of plan at this time in the educational year threatened to give rise to practical difficulties in relation to the appointments of staff already made and the construction of buildings for the new comprehensive schools and to create a degree of confusion and uncertainty which could impair the efficient working of the schools.

These arguments were re-stated and expanded in the affidavit sworn on behalf of the Secretary of State in support of the application for mandamus. The affidavit stated three points. Point (i): that 653 of the 802 transfers, promotions and other appointments (of teachers) required to implement the reorganisation had been made. Point (ii): that contracts had been entered into for building work directly related to the change in character of two of the schools and work had started under the contracts. In the case of a third school, the authority had entered into commitments for such building work. Point (iii): that preparations were made for courses on the basis that the proposals communicated to the Secretary of State would be put into effect.

These points (i), (ii) and (iii) were dealt with fully by the authority and I need say no more about them than that they were completely exploded. They were held to have no substance in them by five of the six learned judges who have considered this matter: the sixth indicated general agreement without specific discussion and indeed point (ii) was criticised with some severity by one of the learned Lords Justices in the Court of Appeal.

Some attempt was made to rehabilitate these points in this House, but learned counsel decided, no doubt wisely, to concentrate on the allocation issue. But these three points cannot just be discarded as if they had never been made. They form part of a composite set of facts relied on as showing unreasonable conduct, and I am not at all sure that the disappearance of so many planks does not fatally weaken the stability of the platform. At the least — and I will give the department the benefit of this assumption — the remaining factual basis would need to be strong and clear if it alone were to be the basis for the Secretary of State's 'satisfaction' as to unreasonable conduct.

So I come to the question of allocation, which was at the centre of the case as argued and it can best be approached via 'para. A' above, a paragraph which I regard as revealing. It shows a very strange attitude toward the decision taken by the authority. After the electorate, including no doubt a large number of parents, had voted the new authority into office on the platform that some selective basis would be preserved, to say that this created 'a dilemma' for the parents, with the undertone that this was something unreasonable, appears to me curious and paradoxical. Parents desired to have a chance of selective places. The new authority were giving it them. If they did not want selective places, they had no need and no obligation to apply for them. Unless the creation of freedom of choice, where no such freedom existed previously, is intrinsically an evil, it seems hard to understand how this so-called dilemma could be something unreasonably created. The impression which it gives of upsetting 3,000 places is entirely a false one since over 90 per cent of these would remain unaltered. Then, to refer to 'submitting to an improvised selection procedure' hardly does justice to the authority's plan. Some selection procedure was inherent in what the electorate had voted for, a choice which, if it meant anything, must involve some change in allocation for the forthcoming school year and, unless exactly 240 parents applied for the 240 places, some selection. It would seem likely that in voting for this change in May 1976 the electors must have accepted, if not favoured, some degree of improvisation. The whole paragraph forces the conclusion that the Secretary of State was operating under a misconception as to what would be reasonable for a newly elected council to do, and that he failed to take into account that it was entitled — indeed in a sense bound — to carry out the policy on which it was elected, and failed to give weight to the fact that the limited degree of selection (for 240 places out of some 3,000), which was involved, though less than perfect, was something which a reasonable authority might accept and which the parents concerned clearly did accept.

What the Secretary of State was entitled to do, under his residual powers, was to say something to the effect that: 'the election has taken place; the new authority may be entitled to postpone the comprehensive scheme: this may involve some degree of selection and apparently the parents desire it. Nevertheless from an educational point of view, whatever some parents may think, I am satisfied that in the time available this, or some part of it, cannot be carried out, and that no reasonable authority would attempt to carry it out.' Let us judge him by this test, though I do not think that this was the test he himself applied. Was the procedure to be followed for choosing which of the applicants were to be allotted the 240 selective places such that no reasonable authority could adopt it? The authority's letter of June 7 said that selection would be by 'a combination of reports, records and interviews'. They had about three months in which to carry it out. The plan was lacking in specification, but it must have conveyed sufficient to the experts at the department to enable them to understand what was proposed. Selection by 11-plus examination was not the only selection procedure available. Lancashire, part of which was taken over by Tameside, had evolved and operated a method of selection by head teacher recommendation, ranking of pupils, reports and records, and standardised verbal reasoning tests. The Tameside authority had set up in May a panel of selection to operate a procedure of this kind, the chairman of which was experienced in the Lancashire method. He was, as he deposed in an affidavit before the Court of Appeal, of opinion that even though a verbal reasoning test might not be practicable in the time there would be no difficulty in selecting the number of places required. There were other opinions, expressed with varying degrees of confidence by experts, and no doubt the procedure could not be said to be perfect, but I do not think that such defects as there were could possibly, in the circumstances, having regard to the comparatively small number of places involved, enable it to be said that the whole of the authority's programme of which this was a part was such that no reasonable authority would carry it out.

But there is a further complication. The authority's selection plans were opposed by a number of the teachers' unions, and there was the likelihood of non-cooperation by some of the head teachers in the primary schools in production of records and reports. The department letters and affidavits do not rely on this matter, for understandable reasons, but they must be assumed to have had it in mind. Is this a fact on which the Secretary of State might legitimately form the judgment that the authority were acting unreasonably?

To rephrase the question: on June 11, 1976 (this is the date of the direction, and we are not entitled to see what happened thereafter) could it be said that the authority were acting unreasonably in proceeding with the selection procedure which was otherwise workable, in face of the possibility of persistent opposition by teachers' unions and individual teachers, or would *the only* (not 'the more') reasonable course have been for the authority to abandon their plans? This is I think the ultimate factual question in the case. And I think that it must be answered in the negative, *i.e.* that it could not be unreasonable, in June 1976, and assuming that the Secretary of State did not interfere, for the authority to put forward a plan to act on their approved procedure. The teachers, after all, are public servants, with responsibility for their pupils. They were under a duty to produce reports. These reports and the records in the primary schools are public property. I do not think that it could be unreasonable (not 'was unreasonable') for the authority to take the view that if the Secretary of State did not intervene under his statutory power, the teachers would cooperate in working the authority's procedure — a procedure which had, in similar form, been operated in part of this very area.

On the whole case, I come to the conclusion that the Secretary of State, real though his difficulties were, fundamentally misconceived and misdirected himself as to the proper manner in which to regard the proposed action of the authority after the local election of May 1976; that if he had exercised his judgment on the basis of the factual situation in which this newly elected authority were placed — with a policy approved by their electorate, and massively supported by the parents — there was no ground, however much he might disagree with the new policy, and regret such administrative dislocation as was brought about by the change, on which he could find that the authority were acting or proposing to act unreasonably. In my opinion, the judgments in the Court of Appeal were right and the appeal must be dismissed."

LORD DIPLOCK: "... A relevant question to which the Secretary of State should have directed his mind was the extent to which head teachers would be likely to persist in a policy of non-cooperation if he himself was known to have declined to stop the council from proceeding with their plan. There is no suggestion in the letter, nor in either of the affidavits sworn on his behalf by Mr Jenkins, that the Secretary of State ever directed his mind to this particular question or formed any view about it. Indeed, it is not until the second affidavit that it is disclosed that the teachers' trade unions had been writing directly to the department on the matter at all. It is not for a court of law to speculate how the Secretary of State would have answered that question had he directed his mind to it, although like others of your Lordships and members of the Court of Appeal, I find it difficult to believe that responsible head teachers, regardful of the interests of their pupils, would have persisted in a refusal to do their best to make the selection procedure work fairly and effectively if the Secretary of State had made it clear to them by his decision that he was not prepared himself to interfere with the council's proceeding with its plans. Assuming, however, that he had formed the view that cooperation by head teachers, was likely to be only partial so that the selection process would be liable to greater possibility of error than where full cooperation could be obtained, the Secretary of State would have to consider whether the existence of such a degree of imperfection in the selection system as he thought would be involved was so great as to make it unreasonable conduct for the council to attempt to fulfil the mandate which they had so recently received from the electors. Again, there is no indication that the Secretary of State weighed these two considerations against one another.

Like all your Lordships, I would dismiss this appeal, although I prefer to put it on the ground that, in my view, the council have succeeded in establishing in these proceedings that the Secretary of State did not direct his mind to the right question: and so, since his good faith is not in question, he cannot have directed himself properly in law."

LORD SALMON: "... In my opinion, section 68, on its true construction, means that before the Secretary of State could lawfully issue directions under it, he must satisfy himself not only that he does not agree with the way in which the authority have acted or are proposing to act nor even that the authority are mistaken or wrong; the question he must ask himself is, could any reasonable local authority act in the way in which this authority have acted or are proposing to act? If, but only if, he is satisfied on any material capable of satisfying a reasonable man that the answer to the crucial question is No, he may lawfully issue directions under section 68...

I find it impossible... to accept that any reasonable man could be satisfied that no reasonable authority on the evidence could take the view that a satisfactory selection of candidates for the 240 places in the grammar schools could have been made between June 11 and September 1, 1976. Therefore, either the Secretary of State must have erred in law by misconstruing s.68 and failing to ask himself the right question, or he asked himself that question and answered it No without any valid ground for doing so."

Viscount Dilhorne and Lord Russell of Killowen delivered concurring speeches.

Notes

6–41   (1) The case is discussed by H.W.R. Wade [1977] 93 L.Q.R. 4 and D.G.T. Williams (1977) 36 C.L.J. 1. For an account of the factual background see D. Bull *"Tameside* Revisited" (1987) 50 M.L.R. 307.

(2) Section 1 of the Education Act 1944 required of the Secretary of State that he adhere to the duty to:

> "promote the education of the people of England and Wales and the progressive development of institutions devoted to that purpose, and to secure the effective execution by local authorities, under his control and direction, of the national policy for providing a varied and comprehensive educational service in every area".

Was sufficient emphasis given to this section in the decision?

(3) As originally drafted section 68 included the following:

> "Where the performance of any duty imposed by or for the purposes of this Act or a local education authority or in the managers or governors of any county school or auxiliary school is thereby made contingent upon the opinion of the authority or of their managers or governors, the minister may nevertheless require the authority, managers or governors to perform that duty if an opinion or circumstances are such as to require the performance thereof."

This clause was withdrawn after a debate in the House of Lords where it was replaced by what became section 68: see H.L. Deb., cols 540–552, June 29, 1944 and H.L. Deb. cols 862–864, July 12, 1944 and cols 954–966 July 18, 1944. The Lord Chancellor (Viscount Simon) explained that section 68 would mean that the Minister could act to prevent "monstrous abuses" of discretion or "utterly" unreasonable exercise of discretion. Do you consider that the court has sufficient regard to the reasoning behind this section? While the courts now have the power to have regard to parliamentary proceedings in interpreting statute, given it appears to be confined to provisions which are ambiguous, obscure or absurd if the words are given their natural meaning, it is not clear that even standing the decision in *Pepper v. Hart* [1993] A.C. 593 a different approach would in any event have resulted.

(4) *Tameside* is also significant in view of the observations that it contains in relation to the extent to which a court can review questions of fact and evidence. First, the court appears to be in agreement that the decision made by the Secretary of State had to be judged on the basis of circumstances as of June 11, 1976. In particular, Lord Russell of Killowen did not (at 1076)

> "subscribe to the view that facts subsequently brought forward as then existing can properly be relied upon as showing that the proposals were not unreasonable unless those facts are of such a character that they can be taken… within the knowledge of the department".

The Scottish courts are equally reluctant to allow "new evidence" to support the reasonableness of a decision already taken: *Shetland Line (1984) Ltd v. Secretary of State for Scotland*, 1996 S.L.T. 653 noted at para. 4–9. Is this appropriate in the context of administrative law?

(5) For comments on the speech of Lord Wilberforce in the context of jurisdictional control see para. 4–9.

PROPORTIONALITY

6–42   As the Lord President noted in *West*, the categories of judicial review are never closed and are apt to be expanded as administrative law develops. In this regard there is a real degree of uncertainty as to the extent of which the concept of "proportionality" is or should be considered as a ground of review. It is an accepted principle both in European Community law and in the jurisprudence of the European Court of Human Rights. In substance, proportionality allows the court to intervene if it considers that the harm attendant on a particular use of power is disproportionate to the benefit sought by its use. The most authoritative discussion of the status of proportionality in a domestic context to date arose in the next extract.

R v. Secretary of State for the Home Department, ex parte Brind

[1991] 1 A.C. 696

In October 1988 the Home Secretary, using powers under the Broadcasting Act 1981 (in relation to independent broadcasting) and the BBC's licence and agreement, issued a directive prohibiting the broadcasting of "words spoken" by any person representing or purporting to represent certain organisations. The organisations were those banned under the Northern Ireland (Emergency Provisions) Act 1978, the Prevention of Terrorism (Temporary Provisions) Act 1984, and Sinn Féin, Republican Sinn Féin and the Ulster Defence Association. Under the directive, the Secretary of State admitted to require broadcasting authorities to "refrain from broadcasting any matter or classes of matter specified in the notice". A group of journalists applied for judicial review of the Home Secretary's decision and were unsuccessful in both the Divisional Court and the Court of Appeal, on which see [1990] 1 A.C. 700. They appealed to the House of Lords.

6–43

LORD BRIDGE OF HARWICH: "My Lords, this appeal has been argued primarily on the basis that the power of the Secretary of State... to impose restrictions... may only be lawfully exercised in accordance with art. 10 of the European Convention on Human Rights... Any exercise by the Secretary of State of the power in question necessarily imposes some restriction on freedom of expression. The obligations of the United Kingdom, as a party to the convention, are to secure to every one within its jurisdiction the rights which the convention defines, including both the right to freedom of expression under art. 10 and the right under art. 13 to 'an effective remedy before a national authority' for any violation of the other rights secured by the convention. It is accepted, of course, by the appellants that, like any other treaty obligations which have not been embodied in the law by statute, the convention is not part of the domestic law, that the courts accordingly have no power to enforce convention rights directly and that, if domestic legislation conflicts with the convention, the courts must nevertheless enforce it. But it is already well settled that, in construing any provision in domestic legislation which is ambiguous in the sense that it is capable of a meaning which either conforms to or conflicts with the convention, the courts will presume that Parliament intended to legislate in conformity with the convention, not in conflict with it. Hence, it is submitted, when a statute confers upon an administrative authority a discretion capable of being exercised in a way which infringes any basic human right protected by the convention, it may similarly be presumed that the legislative intention was that the discretion should be exercised within the limitations which the convention imposes. In confess that I found considerable persuasive force in this submission. But in the end I have been convinced that the logic of it is flawed. When confronted with a simple choice between two possible interpretations of some specific statutory provision, the presumption whereby the courts prefer that which avoids conflict between our domestic legislation and our international treaty obligations is a mere canon of construction which involves no importation of international law into the domestic field. But where Parliament has conferred on the executive an administrative discretion without indicating the precise limits within which it must be exercised, to presume that it must be exercised within convention limits would be to go far beyond the resolution of an ambiguity. It would be to impute to Parliament an intention not only that the executive should exercise the discretion in conformity with the convention, but also that the domestic courts should enforce that conformity by the importation into domestic administrative law of the text of the convention and the jurisprudence of the European Court of Human Rights in the interpretation and application of it. If such a presumption is to apply to the statutory discretion exercised by the Secretary of State... in the instant case, it must also apply to any other statutory discretion exercised by the executive which is capable of involving an infringement of convention rights. When Parliament has been content for so long to leave those who complain that their convention rights have been infringed to seek their remedy in Strasbourg, it would be surprising suddenly to find that the judiciary had, without Parliament's aid, the means to incorporate the convention into such an important area of domestic law and I cannot escape the conclusion that this would be a judicial usurpation of the legislative function.

But I do not accept that this conclusion means that the courts are powerless to prevent the exercise by the executive of administrative discretions, even when conferred, as in the instant case, in terms which are on their face unlimited, in a way which infringes fundamental human rights. Most of the rights spelled out in terms in the convention, including the right to freedom of expression, are less than absolute and must in some cases yield to the claims of competing public interests. Thus, art. 10(2) of the convention spells out and categorises the competing public interests by reference to which the right to freedom of expression may have to be curtailed. In exercising the power of judicial review we have neither the advantages nor the disadvantages of any comparable code to which we may refer or by which we are bound. But again, this surely does not mean that in deciding whether the Secretary of State, in the exercise of his discretion, could reasonably impose the restriction he has imposed on the broadcasting organisations, we are not perfectly entitled to start from the premise that any restriction of the right to freedom of expression requires to be justified and that nothing less than an important competing public interest will be sufficient to justify it. The primary judgment as to whether the particular competing public interest justifies the particular restriction imposed falls to be made by the Secretary of State to whom Parliament has entrusted the discretion. But we are entitled to exercise a secondary judgment by asking whether a reasonable Secretary of State, on the material before him, could reasonably make that primary judgment.

Applying these principles to the circumstances of the case... I find it impossible to say that the Secretary of State exceeded the limits of his discretion. In any civilised and law-abiding society the defeat of the terrorist is a public interest of the first importance. That some restriction on the freedom of the terrorist and his supporters to propagate his cause may well be justified in support of that public interest is a proposition which I apprehend the appellants hardly dispute. Their real case is that they, in the exercise of their editorial judgment, may and must be trusted to ensure that the broadcasting media are not used in such a way as will afford any encouragement or support to terrorism and that any interference with that editorial judgment is necessarily an unjustifiable restriction on the right to freedom of expression. Accepting, as I do, their complete good faith, I nevertheless cannot accept this proposition. The Secretary of State, for the reasons he made so clear in Parliament, decided that it was necessary to deny to the terrorist and his supporters the opportunity to speak directly to the public through the most influential of all the media of communication and that this justified some interference with editorial freedom. I do not see how this judgment can be categorised as unreasonable. What is perhaps surprising is that the restriction imposed is of such limited scope. There is no restriction at all on the matter which may be broadcast, only on the manner of its presentation. The viewer may see the terrorist's face and hear his words provided only that they are not spoken in his own voice. I well understand the broadcast journalist's complaint that to put him to the trouble of dubbing the voice of the speaker he has interviewed before the television camera is an irritant which the difference in effect between the speaker's voice and the actor's voice hardly justifies. I well understand the political complaint that the restriction may be counter-productive in the sense that the adverse criticism it provokes outweighs any benefit it achieves. But these complaints fall very far short of demonstrating that a reasonable Secretary of State could not reasonably conclude that the restriction was justified by the important public interest of combating terrorism. I should add that I do not see how reliance on the doctrine of 'proportionality' can here advance the appellants' case. But I agree with what my noble and learned friend, Lord Roskill, says in his speech about the possible future development of the law in that respect.

I would dismiss the appeal."

LORD TEMPLEMAN: "... The English courts must, in conformity with the *Wednesbury* principles ... consider whether the Home Secretary has taken into account all relevant matters and has ignored irrelevant matters. These conditions are satisfied by the evidence in this case, including evidence by the Home Secretary that he took the convention into account. If these conditions are satisfied, then it is said on *Wednesbury* principles the court can only interfere by way of judicial review if the decision of the Home Secretary is 'irrational' or 'perverse'.

The subject-matter and date of the *Wednesbury* principles cannot in my opinion make it either necessary or appropriate for the courts to judge the validity of an interference with human rights by asking themselves whether the Home Secretary has acted irrationally or perversely. It seems to me that the courts cannot escape from asking themselves only whether a reasonable Secretary of State, on the material before him, could reasonably conclude that the interference with freedom of expression which he determined to impose was justifiable. In terms of the convention, as construed by the European Court of Human Rights, the interference with freedom of expression must be necessary and proportionate to the damage which the restriction is designed to prevent.

My Lords, applying these principles I do not consider that the court can conclude that the Home Secretary has abused or exceeded his powers. The broadcasting authorities and journalists are naturally resentful of any limitation on their right to present a programme in such manner as they think fit. But the interference with freedom of expression is minimal and the reasons given by the Home Secretary are compelling.

I, too, would dismiss this appeal."

LORD ACKNER: "... The Secretary of State's reasons for taking the action complained of are set out in the Hansard Reports of those debates and were before your Lordships. The four matters which influenced the Secretary of State were ... (1) offence had been caused to viewers and listeners by the appearance of the apologists for terrorism, particularly after a terrorist outrage; (2) such appearances had afforded terrorists undeserved publicity which was contrary to the public interest; (3) these appearances had tended to increase the standing of terrorist organisations and to create a false impression that support for terrorism is itself a legitimate political opinion; (4) broadcast statements were intended to have, and did in some cases have, the effect of intimidating some of those at whom they were directed.

The Challenge

I now turn to the bases upon which it is contended that the Secretary of State exceeded his statutory powers.

(1)...

(2) The directives were unlawful on 'Wednesbury' grounds

Save only in one respect, namely the European Convention for the Protection of Human Rights and Fundamental Freedoms ... which is the subject-matter of a later heading, it is not suggested that the minister failed to call his attention to matters which he was bound to consider, nor that he included in his considerations matters which were irrelevant. In neither of those senses can it be said that the minister acted unreasonably. The failure to mount such a challenge in this appeal is important. In a field which concerns a fundamental human right, namely that of free speech, close scrutiny must be given to the reasons provided as justification for interference with that right. Your Lordships' attention was drawn to *R. v. Secretary of State for Transport, ex p. de Rothschild* [1989] 1 All E.R. 933, a case which concerned compulsory purchase and therefore involved, albeit somewhat indirectly, another fundamental human right — the peaceful enjoyment of one's possessions: see art. 1 of the First Protocol to the Convention. In that case Slade L.J. said, at 939:

> 'Given the obvious importance and value to land owners of their property rights, the abrogation of those rights in the exercise of his discretionary power to confirm a compulsory purchase order would, in the absence of what he perceived to be a sufficient justification on the merits, be a course which surely no reasonable Secretary of State would take.'

Slade L.J. was in no sense increasing the severity of the *Wednesbury* test ... He was applying that part of it which requires the decision-maker to call his attention to matters that he is obliged to consider. He was emphasising the Secretary of State's obligation to identify the factors which had motivated his decision so as to ensure that he had overlooked none which a reasonable Secretary of State should have considered.

There remains however the potential criticism under the *Wednesbury* grounds... that the conclusion was 'so unreasonable that no reasonable authority could ever have come to it'. This standard of unreasonableness, often referred to as 'the irrationality test', has been criticised as being too high. But it has to be expressed in terms that confine the jurisdiction exercised by the judiciary to a supervisory, as opposed to an appellate, jurisdiction. Where Parliament has given to a minister or other person or body a discretion, the court's jurisdiction is limited, in the absence of a statutory right of appeal, to the supervision of the exercise of that discretionary power, so as to ensure that it has been exercised lawfully. It would be a wrongful usurpation of power by the judiciary to substitute its view, the judicial view, on the merits and on that basis to quash the decision. If no reasonable minister properly directing himself would have reached the impugned decision, the minister has exceeded his powers and thus acted unlawfully and the court, in the exercise of its supervisory role, will quash that decision. Such a decision is correctly, though unattractively, described as a 'perverse' decision. To seek the court's intervention on the basis that the correct or objectively reasonable decision is other than the decision which the minister has made, is to invite the court to adjudicate as if Parliament had provided a right of appeal against the decision, that is to invite an abuse of power by the judiciary.

So far as the facts of this case are concerned it is only necessary to read the speeches in the Houses of Parliament, ... to reach the conclusion, that whether the Secretary of State was right or wrong to decide to issue the directives, there was clearly material which would justify a reasonable minister making the same decision. In the words of Lord Diplock in *Secretary of State for Education and Science v. Tameside Metropolitan Borough* [1977] A.C. 1014, 1064:

'The very concept of administrative discretion involves a right to choose between more than one possible course of action on which there is room for reasonable people to hold differing opinions as to which is to be preferred.'

… I entirely agree with McCowan L.J. [in the Court of Appeal] when he said that he found it quite impossible to hold that the Secretary of State's political judgment that the appearance of terrorists on programmes increases their standing and lends them political legitimacy is one that no reasonable Home Secretary could hold…

Mr Lester has contended that in issuing these directives the Secretary of State has used a sledgehammer to crack a nut. Of course that is a picturesque way of describing the *Wednesbury* "irrational" test. The Secretary of State has in my judgment used no sledgehammer. Quite the contrary is the case.

I agree with Lord Donaldson M.R. who, when commenting on how limited the restrictions were, said in his judgment …:

'They have no application in the circumstances mentioned in para. 3 (proceedings in the United Kingdom Parliament and elections) and, by allowing reported speech either verbatim or in paraphrase, in effect put those affected in no worse a position than they would be if they had access to newspaper publicity with a circulation equal to the listening and viewing audiences of the programmes concerned. Furthermore, on the applicants' own evidence, if the directives had been in force during the previous 12 months, the effect would have been minimal in terms of air time. Thus, [ITN] say that 8 minutes 20 seconds (including repeats) out of 1,200 hours, or 0.01%, of air time would have been affected. Furthermore, it would not have been necessary to omit these items. They could have been recast into a form which complied with the directives.'

Thus the extent of the interference with the right to freedom of speech is a very modest one…

(3) The minister failed to have proper regard to the European Convention for the Protection of Human Rights and Fundamental Freedoms and in particular art. 10

Article 10 reads as follows:

'(1) Everyone has the right to freedom of expression. This right shall include freedom to hold opinions and to receive and impart information and ideas without interference by public authority and regardless of frontiers. This Article shall not prevent States from requiring the licensing of broadcasting, television or cinema enterprises.

(2) The exercise of these freedoms, since it carries with it duties and responsibilities, may be subject to such formalities, conditions, restrictions or penalties as are prescribed by law and are necessary in a democratic society, in the interests of national security, territorial integrity or public safety, for the prevention of disorder or crime, for the protection of health or morals, for the protection of the reputation or rights of others, for preventing the disclosure of information received in confidence, or for maintaining the authority and impartiality of the judiciary.'

[His Lordship noted that the Convention is a treaty to which the United Kingdom is a party but which has not been incorporated by legislation into English domestic law. He also noted that the terms of a treaty may be used to resolve an ambiguity in an Act, but held that there was no such ambiguity in the terms of the 1981 Act. He then referred to a further argument of counsel for the applicants, and continued:]

… Mr Lester … claims that the Secretary of State before issuing his directives should have considered not only the convention (it is accepted that he in fact did so) but that he should have properly construed it and correctly taken it into consideration. It was therefore a relevant, indeed a vital, factor to which he was obliged to have proper regard pursuant to the *Wednesbury* doctrine, with the result that his failure to do so rendered his decision unlawful. The fallacy of this submission is, however, plain. If the Secretary of State was obliged to have proper regard to the convention, *i.e.* to conform with art. 10, this inevitably would result in incorporating the convention into English domestic law by the back door. It would oblige the courts to police the operation of the convention and to ask itself in each case, where there was a challenge, whether the restrictions were 'necessary in a democratic society…' applying the principles enunciated in the decisions of the European Court of Human Rights. The treaty, not having been incorporated in English law, cannot be a source of rights and obligations and the question — did the Secretary of State act in breach of art. 10? — does not therefore arise…

(4) The Secretary of State has acted ultra vires because he has acted 'in a disproportionate manner'

This attack is not a repetition of the *Wednesbury* 'irrational' test under another guise. Clearly a decision by a minister which suffers from a total lack of proportionality will qualify for the '*Wednesbury* unreasonable' epithet. It is, ex hypothesi, a decision which no reasonable minister could make. This is, however, a different and severer test.

Mr Lester is asking your Lordships to adopt a different principle: the principle of 'proportionality' which is recognised in the administrative law of several members of the European Economic Community. What is urged is a further development in English administrative law, which Lord Diplock viewed as a possibility in *Council of Civil Service Unions v. Minister for the Civil Service* [1985] A.C. 374, 410.

In his written submissions, Mr Lester was at pains to record 'that there is a clear distinction between an appeal on the merits and a review based on whether the principle of proportionality has been satisfied'. He was prepared to accept that to stray into the realms of appellate jurisdiction involves the courts in a wrongful usurpation of power. Yet in order to invest the proportionality test with a higher status than the *Wednesbury* test, an inquiry into and a decision upon the merits cannot be avoided. Mr Pannick's (Mr Lester's junior) formulation — could the minister reasonably conclude that his direction was necessary? — must involve balancing the reasons, pro and con, for his decision, albeit allowing him 'a margin of appreciation' to use the European concept of the tolerance accorded to the decision-maker in whom a discretion has been vested. The European test of 'whether the "interference" complained of corresponds to a "pressing social need" ' (*The Sunday Times v. United Kingdom* (1979) 2 E.H.R.R. 245 at 277) must ultimately result in the question — is the particular decision acceptable? — and this must involve a review of the merits of the decision. Unless and until Parliament incorporates the convention into domestic law, a course which it is well known has a strong body of support, there appears to me to be at present no basis upon which the proportionality doctrine applied by the European Court can be followed by the courts of this country.

I would accordingly dismiss this appeal..."

LORD ROSKILL: "My Lords, I agree that this appeal must be dismissed for the reasons given in the speech of my noble and learned friend Lord Bridge which I have had the advantage of reading in draft and with which I entirely agree. I add some observations of my own only on one matter, namely the principle of 'proportionality'. Reliance was placed on behalf of the appellants upon a passage in the speech of my noble and learned friend Lord Diplock in *Council of Civil Service Unions v. Minister for the Civil Service* [1984] 3 All ER 935 at 950, [1985] AC 374 at 410 where, after establishing his triple categorisation of the fields in which judicial review might operate, he added:

> 'That is not to say that further development on a case by case basis may not in course of time add further grounds. I have in mind particularly the possible adoption in future of the principle of "proportionality" which is recognised in the administrative law of several of our fellow members of the European Economic Community; but to dispose of the instant case the three already well-established heads that I have mentioned will suffice'

In that passage my noble and learned friend was concerned to make plain, first, that his triple categorisation was not exhaustive and, secondly, that the time might come when further grounds might require to be added notably by reason of the 'possible adoption' of that principle in this country. He clearly had in mind the likely increasing influence of Community law upon our domestic law which might in time lead to the further adoption of this principle as a separate category and not merely as a possible reinforcement of one or more of these three stated categories such as irrationality. My noble and learned friend emphasised that any such development would be likely to be on a case by case basis. I am clearly of the view that the present is not a case in which the first step can be taken for the reason that to apply that principle in the present case would be for the court to substitute its own judgment of what was needed to achieve a particular objective for the judgment of the Secretary of State upon whom that duty has been laid by Parliament. But so to hold in the present case is not to exclude the possible future development of the law in this respect, a possibility which has already been canvassed in some academic writings."

LORD LOWRY: "My Lords, I agree with your Lordships that this appeal should be dismissed. In particular I agree with the observations of my noble and learned friend Lord Ackner, whose speech relieves me from the need to consider the matter in detail and, taken in conjunction with the other observations which have fallen from your Lordships, could well be thought to render unnecessary any contribution by me to the debate....

Because they are of general importance, I will mention just two points, which are closely related, the test of unreasonableness in judicial review and the doctrine of proportionality.

The kind of unreasonableness for which a court can set aside an administrative act or decision is popularly called '*Wednesbury* unreasonableness" from the name of the famous case, *Associated Provincial Picture Houses Ltd v Wednesbury Corp* [1947] 2 All ER 680, [1948] 1 KB 223, in which Lord Greene MR spoke of a decision 'so absurd that no sensible person could ever dream that it lay within the powers of the authority' (see [1947] 2 All ER 680 at 683, [1948] 1 KB 223 at 229). In *Secretary of State for Education and Science v Tameside Metropolitan Borough* [1976] 3 All ER 665 at 671, [1977] AC 1014 at 1026

Lord Denning MR referred to decisions 'so wrong that no reasonable person could sensibly take that view'. In *Council of Civil Service Unions v Minister for the Civil Service* [1984] 3 All ER 935 at 951, [1985] AC 374 at 410 Lord Diplock, having used irrationality as a synonym of *Wednesbury* unreasonableness, said that 'It applies to a decision which is so outrageous in its defiance of logic or of accepted moral standards that no sensible person who had applied his mind to the question to be decided could have arrived at it', while in *Nottinghamshire CC v Secretary of State for the Environment* [1986] 1 All ER 199 at 202, [1986] AC 240 at 247 Lord Scarman, when invited to examine the detail and consequences of guidance given by the Secretary of State, said:

> 'Such an examination by a court would be justified only if a prima facie case were to be shown for holding that the Secretary of State had acted in bad faith, or for an improper motive, or that the consequences of his guidance were so absurd that he must have taken leave of his senses.'

These colourful statements emphasise the legal principle that judicial review of administrative action is a supervisory and not an appellate jurisdiction. I recall that in *R v Nat Bell Liquors Ltd* [1922] 2 AC 128 at 156, [1922] All ER Rep 335 at 351 Lord Sumner, admittedly speaking of an attempted challenge to the validity of court proceedings, said that the superior court's jurisdiction was one 'of supervision, not of review'....

Of course, whichever kind of jurisdiction is being exercised on the subject of reasonableness, there is bound to be a subjective element in the decision. There is no objective standard in either case which would allow the result to be foretold with certainty. The important requirement, however, is to ask the right question.

The appellants have relied on the doctrine of proportionality. That is, in one sense of the word, a deeply rooted and well understood idea in English law. In a claim for damages for personal injuries suffered by a workman allegedly through his employer's negligent system of work the court has to weigh the risk of an accident, the likely severity of the consequences, the expense and difficulty of taking precautions and the resources of the employer with a view to deciding whether the employer failed to take reasonable care for the safety of the workman. In another field, as counsel once contended in *R v Secretary of State for Transport, ex p Pegasus Holdings (London) Ltd* (1987) [1989] 2 All ER 481 at 490, [1988] 1 WLR 990 at 1001, proportionality is simply a way of approaching the *Wednesbury* formula: was the administrative act or decision *so much* out of proportion to the needs of the situation as to be 'unreasonable' in the *Wednesbury* sense?

Mr Lester, however, frankly relied on proportionality, a well-known concept of European law, as a doctrine calculated to advance his cause further than *Wednesbury* unreasonableness, but conceded that there was a clear distinction between an appeal on the merits and a review based on the principle of proportionality. Mr Pannick equally frankly drew the same distinction and posed the test: 'Could the minister reasonably conclude that his direction was necessary?' Here, of course, one comes back to the word 'reasonably'. I shall try to avoid repeating what has been said by my noble and learned friend Lord Ackner who has already referred to such phrases as 'margin of appreciation' and 'pressing social need'.

In my opinion proportionality and the other phrases are simply intended to move the focus of discussion away from the hitherto accepted criteria for deciding whether the decision-maker has abused his power and into an area in which the court will feel more at liberty to interfere.

The first observation I would make is that there is *no* authority for saying that proportionality in the sense in which the appellants have used it is part of the English common law and a great deal of authority the other way. This, so far as I am concerned, is not a cause for regret for several reasons. (1) The decision-makers, very often elected, are those to whom Parliament has entrusted the discretion and to interfere with that discretion beyond the limits as hitherto defined would itself be an abuse of the judges' supervisory jurisdiction. (2) The judges are not, generally speaking, equipped by training or experience, or furnished with the requisite knowledge and advice, to decide the answer to an administrative problem where the scales are evenly balanced, but they have a much better chance of reaching the right answer where the question is put in a *Wednesbury* form. The same applies if the judges' decision is appealed. (3) Stability and relative certainty would be jeopardised if the new doctrine held sway, because there is nearly always something to be said against any administrative decision and parties who felt aggrieved would be even more likely than at present to try their luck with a judicial review application both at first instance and on appeal. (4) The increase in applications for judicial review of administrative action (inevitable if the threshold of unreasonableness is lowered) will lead to the expenditure of time and money by litigants, not to speak of the prolongation of uncertainty for all concerned with the decisions in question, and the taking up of court time which could otherwise be devoted to other matters. The losers in this respect will be members of the public, for whom the courts provide a service.

1(1) *Halsbury's Laws* (4th edn reissue) para 78 recognises proportionality in the context of administrative law as follows:

'**78. Proportionality.** The courts will quash exercise of discretionary powers in which there is not a reasonable relationship between the objective which is sought to be achieved and the means used to that end, or where punishments imposed by administrative bodies or inferior courts are wholly out of proportion to the relevant misconduct. The principle of proportionality is well established in European law, and will be applied by English courts where European law is enforceable in the domestic courts. The principle of proportionality is still at a stage of development in English law; lack of proportionality is not usually treated as a separate ground of review in English law, but is regarded as one indication of manifest unreasonableness.'

(The High Court's decision in the instant case (see (1989) Times, 30 May) is cited in the copious footnotes to this paragraph as the authority for the concluding statement.)

It finally occurs to me that there can be very little room for judges to operate an independent judicial review proportionality doctrine in the space which is left between the conventional judicial review doctrine and the admittedly forbidden appellate approach. To introduce an intermediate area of deliberation for the court seems scarcely a practical idea, quite apart from the other disadvantages by which, in my opinion, such a course would be attended."

Notes

(1) For discussion of *Brind* see C. Lewis, "The European Convention, Proportionality and the Broadcasting Ban" (1991) 50 C.L.J. 211; B. Thompson, "Broadcasting and Terrorism" [1989] P.L. 527 (Divisional Court Hearing) and [1991] P.L. 346; J. Jowell [1990] P.L. 149 (Court of Appeal); and M. Halliwell, "Judicial Review and Broadcasting Freedom: The Route to Europe" (1991) 42 N.I.L.Q. 246.

6–44

(2) Note the views of Lord Bridge and Lord Roskill that proportionality may be appropriate in terms of future development in administrative law, but that it would not be appropriate to endorse it in the instant case because it would take the court to the area of review of merits. Is it made clear why that would not be the case in areas not in issue in this case? Does the context of national security perhaps explain this? What factors were influential in the judgment of Lord Lowry in his outright rejection of proportionality? Note his Lordship's concern that proportionality may well serve to create a lower threshold for review than *Wednesbury* unreasonableness. Compare that with the views of Jowell and Lester below and see also the discussion of *Smith* below. Lord Ackner's judgment may well be the most significant for the future development of the doctrine. He emphasises the role of the doctrine in the context of the decisions of the European Court of Human Rights and suggests that the case of that court cannot be followed until the Convention is incorporated into domestic law and, moreover, he seems to accept that proportionality involves some consideration of merits. The judgments of Lord Templeman and Lord Bridge appear to be based on reformulations of the *Wednesbury* test given the extreme conduct needed to challenge successfully a decision on this basis, "the use of a sledgehammer to crack a nut". There may not be any great difference between those formulations of the *Wednesbury* test and those cases following within the doctrine of proportionality involving a penalty which may be too extreme for the infringement in question. Where the difficulty does arise, it is noted by Lord Ackner as being in those areas where proportionality requires the court to go beyond the limited scope of review provided by *Wednesbury* and into the realm of "second guessing" the legislature. Such an approach would require an assessment of the appropriateness and necessity of a decision not only with regard to whether or nor an act achieves its objective, but also whether there are other measures which may better secure that objective. The legitimacy of such an approach would require a fundamental change in the constitutional relationship between the courts and the legislature. The Human Rights Act 1998 may well now represent the basis upon which such a new relationship can be developed. Note, though, that decisions which do not fall within the ambit of the new Act may well still be subject to the more restricted form of review noted in *Brind* and discussed below in relation to *Smith* at para. 6–34.

(3) J. Jowell and A. Lester, Q.C., "Proportionality: Neither Novel Nor Dangerous" in *New Directions in Judicial Review* (J. Jowell and D. Oliver eds, 1988), pp. 51–69 conclude that the concept exists not only in European Community law and in the law of the European Convention

on Human Rights but is implicit in the reasoning found in such diverse areas of English law as the law of restrictive covenants (*Herbert Morris Ltd v. Saxelby* [1916] A.C. 688); the legality of planning condition (*Hall & Co. Ltd v. Shoreham-by-Sea Urban District Council* [1964] 1 All E.R. 1); the area of penalities (*R. v. Barnsley Metropolitan Borough Council, ex parte Hook* [1976] 1 W.L.R. 1052); and human rights (*Wheeler v. Leicester City Council* [1985] A.C. 1054 at para. 6–4).

They go on to argue that proportionality should be lifted from being an implicit aspect of existing grounds of challenge — for example, improper purpose in *Wheeler*, relevant consideration in *Hall* and unreasonableness in *Morris* and *Hook* to an independent ground of review. Anticipating the views of the House of Lords in *Brind* three years later they

> "stress that we do not see proportionality as permitting intervention in the merits of the decisions of public officials to an extent greater than the *Wednesbury* test already allows. Like the *Wednesbury* test, proportionality is designed to guide the exercise of discretionary powers, and allows the court to interfere with the substance of official decisions as well as the procedures by which they are reached. However it by no means releases judges from their proper reserve in interfering with decisions on the ground of policy, or assessment of fact or merits. Indeed, because proportionality advances a relatively specific legal principle — one that is at any rate far more specific than 'unreasonableness' or 'irrationality' — it focuses more clearly than those vaguer standards on the precise conduct it seeks to prevent. By concentrating on the specific it is more effective in excluding general considerations based on policy rather than principle."

6–45   (4) A number of the areas mentioned by the authors have direct parallels in Scots law. *Woods* above might be regarded as a case involving an excessive penalty. Equally cases such as *Hall* in the field of planning and *Morris* in employment are regarded as authorities in Scots law. Jowell and Lester also note that one of the aspects of proportionality is the idea that the value of a benefit must by set against the cost of obtaining that benefit. This is known as cost/benefit analysis. If the cost of a particular outcome is disproportionate to the benefit arising then a decision which prefers cost to benefit will be lawful. In *McTear v. Scottish Legal Aid Board*, 1997 S.L.T. 108 Lord Kirkwood, under reference to the decision in *R. v. Legal Aid Committee No. 8, exparte Megarry*, July 1, 1994, Queen's Bench Division, unreported, used cost/benefit analysis in judicial review proceedings seeking to quash a decision of the Scottish Legal Aid Board to refuse legal aid to the widow of a man who had died from lung cancer allegedly arising from tobacco use. The board had argued that the cost of granting of legal aid would far outstrip any benefit that would accrue to the widow. Although the decision ultimately rested on a finding that the board had not exercised its discretion in an unreasonable or irrational manner, it is perhaps tempting to conclude that the explicit use of proportionality would have led to the same outcome. More recently there has been explicit reference to the concept of "disproportionality". For example, in *Abdadou v. Secretary of State for the Home Department*, 1998 S.C. 504 the petitioner sought reduction of a decision of the Home Secretary refusing application made on October 21, 1996 for leave to remain in the United Kingdom by reason of his marriage in August of that year to a Scottish woman. It was argued on behalf of the petitioner that the decision was not only unreasonable and irrational in the *Wednesbury* sense but that it constituted a breach of Article 8 of the ECHR (respect for family and private life). The Lord Ordinary, while accepting the treatment of proportionality in *Brind*, acknowledged however that in the context of immigration and family life there is a measure of overlap between proportionality and irrationality and went on to suggest (at 518) that:

> "a decision may thus be so disproportionate as also to be unreasonable in the *Wednesbury* sense. If a decision fails the test of proportionality with the consequence that it is in breach of art 8, that may well support the view that the decision is unreasonable."

This approach suggests in the first place an assessment of whether the measure under review breaches any ECHR provision followed by an evaluation of whether a finding of such a breach supports a finding of irrationality. The Lord Ordinary reduced the decision as disproportionate and irrational. See also *Saini v. Secretary of State for the Home Department* at para. 6–26 (no likelihood that husband would be permanently separated from wife by virtue of refusal to remain in the United Kingdom and so decision not so disproportionate as to be unreasonable). Note also the dictum of Lord Clyde in the House of Lords in *R v. Secretary of State for Scotland*, 1999 S.L.T. 279 where, in reviewing the grounds of review available to challenge the decision of a hospital authority not to release a patient from the state hospital observed (at 295) that the decision "may be found to be perverse, or irrational, or grossly disproportionate to what was required". This should not be taken too far. Subject to the implications of incorporation of the Convention in domestic law a finding of disproportionality serves merely as a way of establishing whether a decision "falls outwith the range on span of decisions open to a reasonable decision taker" (*Abdadou* at 518). For comment see J. Larkin, "Proportionality and irrationality — two recent cases" (1998) 256 SCOLAG 163.

(5) As noted in *Brind*, proportionality is well established in European Community Law. On this see D. Wyatt and A. Dashwood, *The Substantive Law of the E.E.C.* (3rd ed., 1993), pp. 89–91; F. Stroink, "*Judicial Control: Comparative Essays on Judicial Review* (1995), pp. 81–100; *Stair Memorial Encyclopaedia*, Vol. 10, "European Community Law", para. 97; and *Halsbury's Laws of England* (4th ed., Vol. 1(1) reissue, 1989). Indeed, it has now been written into the EC Treaty as by the Treaty on European Union (1992) it is a formal principle of community law that "any action by the Community shall not go beyond what is necessary to achieve the objectives of this Treaty": EC Treaty, art 3 b, 3rd para. **6–46**

In *State v. Watson and Bellmann* (Case 118/75) proportionality was used to challenge a restriction in freedom of movement of persons. Watson was claiming rights of residence in Italy. The right of the free movement of workers expressed in Article 48 of the Treaty of Rome is regarded as a fundamental right, subject only to limitations which are justified on the grounds of public policy, public security or public health (Article 48(3)). The Italian authorities sought to invoke these exceptions to expel Watson from Italy on the basis that she had failed to comply with certain administrative procedures required under Italian law to record and monitor her movements in Italy. The European Court of Justice, held that, while States were entitled to impose penalties for non-compliance with their administrative formalities, these must not be disproportionate and could never provide a ground for deportation.

Similarly in Case 181/84, *R. v. Intervention Board for Agricultural Produce, ex parte E.D. & F. Man (Sugar) Ltd*, [1985] 3 C.M.L.R. 759; [1986] 2 All E.R. 115, the European Court of Justice stated that:

> "in order to establish whether a provision of Community law is in conformity with the principle of proportionality it is necessary to ascertain whether the means which it employs are appropriate and necessary to attain the objective sought."

See also *R. v. The Minister of Agriculture, Fisheries and Food in the Secretary of State for Health, ex parte Fedesa* [1990] E.C.R. I-4023.

Issues of community law have arisen in proceedings in Scotland where proportionality has been used. In *Scotch Premier Meat Ltd v. Secretary of State for Scotland*, 1997 S.L.T. 1080 where in considering a petition for judicial review, including a crave for interim interdict preventing the implementation of a scheme implemented by the Government to carry through E.C. Commission Regulation 716/96 to protect against BSE, the court held that the means by which implementation of the regulation was to be achieved were subject to, *inter alia*, the test of proportionality. Provided that the means used in the scheme bore a *reasonable proportion to* the objective sought by the regulation, then the court would not interfere. See also *Walkingshaw v. Marshall*, 1992 S.L.T. 1167; *Thomas v. Adjudication Officer* [1991] 3 All E.R. 315, *Stoke-on-Trent City Council v. B & Q Plc* [1991] 4 All E.R. 221; *NALGO v. Secretary of State of the Environment* [1992] T.L.R. 576; and *R. v. Manchester Metropolitan University, ex parte Nolan* [1994] E.L. Rev 380.

CONSISTENCY

In this section we are concerned with the extent to which the courts can use methods based on the idea of consistency to control administrative action. This is a difficult area. We will note in **6–47**

Chapter 7 that where a body exercises discretion, it cannot do so in a way which fetters that discretion. Moreover, the concept of simple *ultra vires* carries with it the implication that a body cannot by its own act enlarge its powers beyond those conferred. Set against this is the basic idea of fairness, that an administrative body should act consistently and with regard to the rights and interests that might be affected by its action. The cases seem to fall into two broad categories. In the first, we will look at the extent to which the concept of personal bar can apply in administrative action, particularly with reference to delegation of authority to agents. Here we are typically concerned with the situation where an administrative body has led the citizen to expect something different from the course of action or decision actually taken, and that loss or harm based on that reliance has resulted. In the second category of case, we are concerned with a body with discretion to act in a variety of ways or not to act at all, whether it could commit itself to a particular course of action because it had previously acted so as to engender in the citizen a legitimate expectation that it would exercise its discretion in that way, even though no loss of prejudice in the sense of the first class of cases has arisen. The following extract examines the issues raised by the first category.

Western Fish Products Ltd v. Penwith District Council

[1981] 2 All E.R. 204

6–48   "In April 1976 W.F.P. bought an industrial site at Stable Hobba which included the buildings of a disused factory. The factory had previously been used for the production of fertiliser from fish and fishmeal. This use had ceased in 1975. W.F.P. wanted to use the site for the manufacture of fish oil and fishmeal, and for the preparation and packaging of fresh fish for human consumption. The company intended to spend considerable sums of money, demolishing some of the old buildings, repairing others, and building new buildings. On April 7, 1976, a meeting took place between the Chairman of W.P.F. (Mr. de Savary) and an official (Mr. Giddens) of the district council, deputy to and representing the council's chief planning officer. De S. asserted that because of the previous factory use of the site there existed an 'established user right' which entitled his company to carry on their intended processes without needing to obtain planning permission from the council. G. said that W.F.P. should satisfy him of such entitlement in writing; and that if he was so satisfied, the council would do everything they could to assist the project.

W.F.P. then wrote two letters supplying G. with information. G. replied, on behalf of the chief planning officer. This letter included a statement which 'confirmed that the limits of the various component parts of the commercial undertaking as now existing appear to be established.' On the strength of this letter, which W.F.P. later stated they regarded as confirmation that planning permission for their proposed use of the land was not needed, the company began to demolish, renovate, repair, build, and install equipment. This work was carried out to the knowledge of the council's officials. Then, on July 6, G. contacted W.F.P. and asked that it submit applications for planning permission in respect of the building operations, and for an 'established use certificate' under section 94 of the Town and Country Planning Act 1971. G. explained that the application for this certificate was purely a formality.

W.F.P. submitted applications for planning permission and for the certificate. On August 26 a full meeting of the council refused all the applications, and authorised the service of enforcement and stop notices in respect of the work in progress. In September the enforcement notices were issued and all work at the site stopped.

W.F.P. brought an action seeking declarations that they were entitled to existing use rights entitling them to use the factory for their intended purpose, or that they were entitled to be treated as having planning permission for that purpose. W.F.P. also claimed injunctions to prevent the enforcement of the notices, and damages. Walton J. dismissed the claims. The company appealed to the Court of Appeal."

MEGAW L.J. delivered the judgment of the Court (MEGAW, LAWTON and BROWNE L.JJ):

"Outline of issues
This appeal raises points which may, very broadly, be stated as follows.
(A) Did the defendant council make representations to the plaintiffs as to what the plaintiffs were permitted to do on the Stable Hobba site in such circumstances that the defendant council became estopped from making decisions contrary to the representations, and so that, the defendant council having made or purported to make such decisions, the plaintiffs are entitled to damages and other relief?

(B) Did the defendant council make any determination under s.53 [see below, p. 331] or s.94 of the Town and Country Planning Act 1971, and, if so, what is the effect?

(C) Did the defendant council act in abuse of their statutory powers, or act negligently, so as to give the plaintiffs the right by action in a court of law to claim damages or any other remedy?

[His Lordship considered whether the company had existing use rights in respect of its proposed processes, and, concluding that it did not, held that planning permission was therefore required for such development. His Lordship then addressed the question whether by process of estoppel the company should be treated as having been given such permission:]

...Here arise various issues which we shall consider later, such as whether any oral statements which were made could be treated as giving rise to an estoppel, and if so, an estoppel as to what, whether the letter of April 26, 1976, from Mr. Giddens constitutes a relevant representation of anything, and if so, what, and whether the plaintiffs did rely on any representation which may be contained, or which they thought was contained, in that letter...

Was the letter of April 26, a representation and, if so, of what?

...We are unable to accept that a person familiar with the relevant facts known to both the writer and the recipient of the letter, reading the letter with reasonable care, could reasonably have read it as giving the plaintiffs confirmation that there was an existing use right which would cover the uses contemplated by the plaintiffs' scheme without the necessity for planning permission in respect of use. Whether Mr. de Savary's belief that the letter contained that confirmation was because he was so firmly convinced of the 'incontrovertible right' that he did not read the letter with due care, or whether it was for some other reason, we are unable to see how, taking full account of the relevant circumstances and of the context of the letter itself and of the letters and conversations which had led up to it, the words 'Accordingly it is confirmed that the limits of the component parts of the commercial undertaking as now existing appear to be established' could reasonably be understood to be a confirmation of that which the plaintiffs allege it did confirm.

At the most the letter means that Mr. Giddens on behalf of the defendant council was satisfied that the buildings on the site had been used previously for the purposes written on the plan and that the dimensions of the respective buildings used for those various purposes were correctly shown. If and in so far as it could be interpreted as confirming any use right, it was no more than a use right for the purposes for which the site had previously been used.

It follows that no relevant estoppel, 'proprietary' or otherwise, can be founded on any representation contained in that letter.

Did the plaintiffs rely on such representation as they allege?

Even if it were to be construed as having the meaning which the plaintiffs placed on it, it would still, in our judgment, not avail the plaintiffs as an estoppel. They did not act on it to their detriment.

The judge, as we understand his judgment, has held that the plaintiffs, through Mr. de Savary, did rely on what he understood to be the representation. 'I think,' says the judge, 'he acted on that assurance, by going ahead with his projects as a whole'; and again. 'He regarded it as all important, and considered that, having obtained that confirmation, all his troubles were over...'

We regard the evidence provided by the contemporary documents and by Mr. de Savary himself in the witness box as being overwhelmingly in support of the conclusion that, if the plaintiffs had not received the letter of April 26, or had not construed it as they did, they would have gone ahead with their planned project as they did go ahead with it, both in timing and other respects. Mr. de Savary's absolute conviction of the incontrovertible status of his user rights in respect of his planned operations was such that he would not have been deterred by the absence of a confirmation from Mr. Giddens ...

Even if we had been satisfied that the defendant council through their officers had represented to the plaintiffs that all they wanted to do on the Stable Hobba site could be done because of the existing uses, planning permission being required only for new buildings and structures, and that they had acted to their detriment to the knowledge of the defendant council because of their representations, their claim would still have failed. There are two reasons for this; first, because they did not have the equitable right which has come to be called proprietary estoppel; and, second, because in law the defendant council could not be estopped from performing their statutory duties under the 1971 Act.

[His Lordship considered the doctrine of *proprietary estoppel*: 'when A to the knowledge of B acts to his detriment in relation to his own land in the expectation, encouraged by B, of acquiring a right over B's land, such expectation arising from what B has said or done, the court will order B to grant A that right on such terms as may be just.' His Lordship noted that 'there was no question of [W.F.P.] acquiring any rights in relation to any other person's land, which is what proprietary estoppel is concerned with,' and so held this argument inapplicable. His Lordship then proceeded to explain why the argument that the council could be estopped from the performance of its statutory duties failed:]

...The defendant council's officers, even when acting within the apparent scope of their authority, could not do what the 1971 Act required the defendant council to do; and if their officers did or said anything which purported to determine in advance what the defendant council themselves would have to determine in pursuance of their statutory duties, they would not be inhibited from doing what they had to do. An estoppel cannot be raised to prevent the exercise of a statutory discretion or to prevent or excuse the performance of a statutory duty (see *Spencer Bower and Turner on Estoppel by Representation* (3rd ed., 1977, p. 141) and the cases there cited). The application of this principle can be illustrated on the facts of this case: under section 29 of the 1971 Act the defendant council as the planning authority had to determine applications for planning permission, and when doing so had to have regard to the provision of the development plan and 'to any other material considerations.' The plaintiffs made an application for planning permission to erect a tail chimney on the site. When considering this application the defendant council had to 'take into account any representations relating to that application' which were received by them following the publishing and posting of notices: see sections 26 and 29(2). This requirement was in the interests of the public generally. If any representation made by the defendant council's officers before the publication or posting of notices bound the council to act in a particular way, the statutory provision which gave the public opportunities of making representations would have been thwarted and the defendant council would have been dispensed from their statutory obligation of taking into account any representation made to them. The officers were appointed by the defendant council but the council's members were elected by the inhabitants of their area. Parliament by the 1971 Act entrusted the defendant council, acting through their elected members, not their officers, to perform various statutory duties. If their officers were allowed to determine that which Parliament had enacted the defendant council should determine there would be no need for elected members to consider planning applications. This cannot be. Under section 101(1) of the Local Government Act 1972 (which repealed section 4 of the 1971 Act, which re-enacted in an amended from section 64 of the Town and Country Planning Act 1968), a local authority may arrange for the discharge of any of their functions by an officer of the authority. This has to be done formally by the authority acting as such. In this case the defendant council issued standing orders authorising designated officers to perform specified functions including those arising under sections 53 and 94 of the 1971 Act. Their officers had no authority to make any other determinations under the 1971 Act. We can see no reason why Mr. de Savary, acting on behalf of the plaintiffs, and having available the advice of lawyers and architects, should have assumed, if he ever did, that Mr. Giddens could bind the defendant council generally by anything he wrote or said.

Counsel for the plaintiffs submitted that, notwithstanding the general principle that a statutory body could not be estopped from performing its statutory duties, there are exceptions recognised by this court. This case, he asserted, came within the exceptions.

There seem to be two kinds of exceptions. If a planning authority, acting as such, delegates to its officers powers to determine specific questions, such as applications under sections 53 and 94 of the 1971 Act, any decisions they make cannot be revoked. This kind of estoppel, if it be estoppel at all, is akin to *judicata*. Counsel for the Department of the Environment accepted that there was this exception, as did counsel for the defendant council in his final submissions. *Lever (Finance) Ltd. v. Westminster Corpn.* [1970] 3 All E.R. 496, [1971] 1 Q.B. 222 can, we think, be considered as an application of this exception. The trial judge had found that it was a common practice amongst planning authorities, including the defendants, for planning officers to sanction immaterial modifications to plans sent with successful applications for planning permission. This is what one of the defendants' planning officers thought he was doing when he agreed with the plaintiffs' architect that they could make a modification to the plans of some houses which were being erected; but Lord Denning M.R. thought that what he had agreed to was not an immaterial modification: it was a material one. He should have told the plaintiffs that they required planning permission to make it. When the defendants found out what had happened as a result of complaints made by members of the public who were likely to be affected by the modification, they suggested to the plaintiffs that they should apply for planning permission. They did; and their application was refused. This court affirmed the declaration made by the trial judge that there was a valid planning permission for the modification. The members of this court gave different reasons for finding as they did. Sachs L.J. stated that the combined effect of the past practice, taken with the powers of delegation under section 64 of the 1968 Act, was that the oral agreement made between the plaintiffs' architect and the defendants' planning officer operated as if all the formalities of section 43 of the Town and Country Planning Act 1962 (now section 53 of the 1971 Act) had been complied with. The other members of the court (Lord Denning M.R. and Megaw L.J.) made no mention of this reasoning. It follows that it was not the *ratio decidendi* of the judgment. We do not agree with it, as appears later in this judgement. Lord Denning M.R. rested his judgment on estoppel and delegation. After referring to the authorities setting out the general rule that planning authorities cannot be estopped from doing their public duty, he went on as follows ([1970] 3 All E.R. 496 at 500, [1971] 1 Q.B. 222 at 230):

'But those statements must now be taken with considerable reserve. There are many matters which public authorities can now delegate to their officers. If an officer, acting within the scope of his ostensible authority, makes a representation on which another acts, then a public authority may be bound by it, just as much as a private concern would be.'

He went on to refer by way of illustration to *Wells v. Minister of Housing and Local Government* [1967] 2 All E.R. 1041, [1967] 1 W.L.R. 1000, which was concerned with what this court adjudged to be an informal application made under section 43 of the 1962 Act. It is pertinent to note too that Lord Denning M.R. used the words 'may be bound.' Megaw L.J. said that he agreed with the reasons for judgment given by Lord Denning M.R. This case, of course, binds us unless there is in the reasoning an element which can be said to be '*per incuriam*'. In our judgment it is not an authority for the proposition that every representation made by a planning officer within his ostensible authority binds the planning authority which employs him. For an estoppel to arise there must be some evidence justifying the person dealing with the planning officer for thinking that what the officer said would bind the planning authority. Holding an office, however senior, cannot, in our judgment, be enough by itself. In the *Lever (Finance) Ltd.* case there was evidence of a widespread practice amongst planning authorities of allowing their planning officers to make immaterial modifications to the plans produced when planning permission was given. Lever (Finance) Ltd.'s architect presumably knew of this practice and was entitled to assume that the practice had been authorised by the planning authorities in whose areas it was followed. The need for some evidence of delegation of authority can be illustrated in this way. Had Lever (Finance) Ltd.'s architect produced plans showing material and substantial modifications to the planning permission for a large development in Piccadilly Circus already granted, he could not sensibly have assumed that the planning officer with whom he was dealing had authority to approve the proposed modifications without putting them before the planning authority. Whether anyone dealing with a planning officer can safely assume that the officer can bind his authority by anything he says must depend on all the circumstances. In the *Lever (Finance) Ltd.* case [1970] 3 All E.R. 496 at 501, [1971] 1 Q.B. 222 at 231 Lord Denning M.R. said: 'Any person dealing with them (*i.e.* officers of a planning authority] is entitled to assume that all necessary resolutions have been passed.' This statement was not necessary for the conclusion he had reached and purported to be an addendum. We consider it to be *obiter*; with all respect, it stated the law too widely.

In this case there was no evidence of any relevant delegations of authority save in relation to applications under sections 53 and 94. We deal later in this judgment with the plaintiffs' submissions about the operation of those sections.

We can deal with the second exception shortly. If a planning authority waives a procedural requirement relating to any application made to it for the exercise of its statutory powers, it may be estopped from relying on lack of formality. Much, however, will turn on the construction of any statutory provisions setting out what the procedure is to be. *Wells v. Minister of Housing and Local Government* is an example of the exception. Both counsel for the Department of the Environment and counsel for the defendant council submitted that this case was wrongly decided. Counsel for the Department of the Environment said that the dissenting judgment of Russel L.J. was to be preferred and both he and counsel for the defendant council reserved the right to argue this point elsewhere. Save in relation to the plaintiffs' submissions as to the operation of sections 53 and 94 on the facts of this case, this exception cannot have any application to this case.

The extension of the concept of estoppel beyond these two exceptions, in our judgment, would not be justified. A further extension would erode the general principle as set out in a long line of cases of which the decision of the Privy Council in *Maritime Electric Co. Ltd. v. General Dairies Ltd.* [1937] 1 All E.R. 748, [1937] A.C. 610 and the judgment of the Divisional Court in *Southend-on-Sea Corpn. v. Hodgson (Wickford) Ltd.* [1961] 2 All E.R. 46, [1962] 1 Q.B. 416 are not notable examples. Parliament has given those who are aggrieved by refusals of planning permission or the serving of enforcement notices a right of appeal to the Secretary of State: see sections 36 and 88 of the 1971 Act. He can hear evidence as to the merits and take into account policy considerations. The courts can do neither. The application of the concept of estoppel because of what a planning officer had represented could result in a court adjudging that a planning authority was bound to allow a development which flouted its planning policy, with which the courts are not concerned.

There is another objection to any extension of the concept of estoppel which is illustrated by the facts of the *Lever (Finance) Ltd.* case. If the modifications which were permitted by the planning officer in that case had been properly to be regarded as immaterial, no problem of general principle would arise. But the court regarded itself as competent to decide as to the materiality and, despite the submission to the contrary by the successful plaintiffs, held that the modifications were material. On what basis of evidence or judicial notice the court reached that conclusion, we need not stay to consider. We assume both that the court had jurisdiction to decide that question, and that, on the facts of that case, their decision as to materiality was right. But then comes the difficulty, and the real danger of injustice. To permit the estoppel no doubt avoided an injustice to the plaintiffs. But it also may fairly be regarded as having caused an injustice to one or more members of the public, the owners of adjacent houses who would be adversely affected by this wrong and careless decision of the planning officer that the modifications were not material. Yet they were not, and it would seem could not, be heard. How, in their absence, could the court balance the respective injustices according as the court did or did not hold that there was an estoppel in favour of the plaintiffs? What 'equity' is there in holding, if such be the effect of the decision, that the potential injustice to a third party, as a result of the granting of the estoppel is irrelevant? At least it can be said that the less frequently this situation arises the better for justice.

In *Brooks and Burton Ltd. v. Secretary of State for the Environment* (1976) 75 L.G.R. 285 at 296 Lord Widgery C.J. adverted to extending the concept of estoppel. He said:

> 'There has been some advance in recent years of this doctrine, of estoppel as applied to local authorities through their officers, and the most advanced case is the one referred to by the inspector, namely *Lever Finance Ltd. v. Westminster (City) London Borough Council.* I do not propose to read it. It no doubt is correct on its facts, but I would deprecate any attempt to expand this doctrine because it seems to me, as I said a few minutes ago, extremely important that local government officers should feel free to help applicants who come and ask them questions without all the time having the shadow of estoppel hanging over them and without the possibility of their immobilising their authorities by some careless remark which produces such an estoppel.'

We agree with what he said.

The statutory position

We turn now to 'the statutory position.' Counsel for the plaintiffs submits that besides their claims based on estoppel the plaintiffs have rights and remedies arising from the planning legislation and the decisions of the courts as to the exercise by statutory authorities of their powers and duties. The consideration of these rights and remedies over-laps at one point with the estoppel claim, but the plaintiffs could succeed on the 'statutory position' even if they fail on estoppel. The essence of this part of the plaintiffs' case is that the decisions made by the defendant council on August 26, were invalid, a 'nullity,' an 'abuse of their powers' and 'unlawful.' We have already said that there was no fraud or malice on the part of the defendant council or their officers. In this part of the case, therefore, the phrase 'abuse of powers' means no more than that the defendant council have mistakenly acted in a way which was not permitted by their powers.

Sections 53 and 94 of the 1971 Act

In addition or in the alternative to their contention that the letter of April 26, is the foundation of an estoppel, the plaintiffs contend that it was a 'determination' under section 53 of the 1971 Act, or alternatively an 'established use certificate' under section 94 of that Act. Counsel for the defendant council accepts that if it was such a determination or certificate the council would be bound by it; under their standing orders the power to make such decisions is delegated to their officers.

Section 53(1) provides as follows:

> 'If any person who proposes to carry out any operations on land, or to make any change in the use of land, wishes to have it determined whether the carrying out of those operations, or the making of that change, would constitute or involve development of the land, and, if so, whether an application for planning permission in respect thereof is required under this Part of this Act, having regard to the provisions of the development order, he may, either as part of an application for planning permission, or without any such application, apply to the local planning authority to determine that question.'

Section 53(2) applies in relation to applications and determinations under this section a number of other provisions of the 1971 Act, relating to development orders (ss.24 and 31(1)), determinations by local planning authorities (s.29(1)), the power of the Secretary of State to give directions to local planning authorities (s.31(1)), the keeping of registers of applications which are open for inspection by the public (s.34(1) and (3)), the powers of the Secretary of State to call in applications (s.35) and the right of appeal to the Secretary of State (ss.35 and 36).

The Town and Country Planning General Development Order 1973 ... makes provision for the procedure to be followed on section 53 applications and determinations. Articles 6(2) and 7(2), (3) and (4) provide for the steps to be taken, the provision in each case being governed by the word 'shall.'

... Counsel for the plaintiffs does not contend that the letter of April 26, amounted to a determination that no planning permission was required in respect of the plaintiffs' building operations, but he contends that it was a determination either that the user contemplated by the plaintiffs' project did not constitute development or that no planning permission was required for such development.

It seems to us that section 53(2) of the 1971 Act and articles 6(2) and 7(2), (3) and (4) of the 1973 order contemplate a considerable degree of formality in applications and determinations under section 53. But counsel for the plaintiffs relied on the decision of the majority of this court in *Wells v. Minister of Housing and Local Government* [1967] 2 All E.R. 1041, [1967] 1 W.L.R. 1000 and on the judgment of Sachs L.J. in *Lever (Finance) Ltd. v. Westminster Corpn.* [1970] 3 All E.R. 496, [1971] 1 Q.B. 222 as establishing that no particular formalities are required.

In the *Wells* case the plaintiffs had applied for planning permission for the erection of a concrete batching plant 27' 6" in height. The council engineer and surveyor replied by letter saying: 'I am now instructed to inform you that the works proposed can be regarded as "permitted development" under Class VIII of the... Development Order... and it is therefore not proposed to take any further action on your application.' The plaintiffs then changed their minds and decided to build a plant 48' high. Their architect assumed that this new proposal would be covered by the council's letter in respect of the 27′ 6" plant and applied for byelaw consent in respect of the 48′ plant. The council granted byelaw consent on a form which contained the words: 'No action should be taken hereunder till the approval of the town planning and licensing authority have been obtained' (*sic*); these words had been struck out but were still legible. The majority of the court (Lord Denning M.R. and Davies L.J., Russell L.J. dissenting) held that there had been a valid application and determination under section 43 of the 1962 Act (now s.53) that planning permission was not required for the 27' 6" plant, but the court held unanimously that there had been no application for planning permission, nor any application or determination under section 43 in respect of the 48′ plant.

In the *Lever (Finance) Ltd.* case (the facts of which have already been stated) Sachs L.J. took the view that what had happened could and should be treated as a valid application and determination under section 43 of the 1962 Act that no further planning permission was needed for the change in the position of the house (see [1970] 3 All E.R. 496 at 503–504, [1971] 1 Q.B. 222 at 234). But the majority of the court (Lord Denning M.R. and Megaw L.J.) put their decision on different grounds, which have been considered earlier in this judgment.

This court is, of course, bound by the ratio of the decision of the majority in the *Wells* case, though if we may respectfully say so we find the dissenting judgment of Russell L.J. very powerful. In our view, the ratio on which Lord Denning M.R. and Davies L.J. were agreed was that a formal written application for a determination under section 43 (now s. 53) was not necessary and that an application for planning permission impliedly contains an invitation to determine under section 43 that planning permission is not required (see [1967] 2 All E.R. 1041 at 1045, 1046, [1967] 1 W.L.R. 1000 at 1008, 1010, *per* Lord Denning M.R. and Davies L.J.). But all three members of the court held that there was no application or determination under section 43 in respect of the 48' plant, Lord Denning M.R. saying [1967] 2 All E.R. 1041 at 1045, [1967] 1 W.L.R. 1000 at 1008):

> 'Ready as I am to waive irregularities and procedural defects, I think that to satisfy section 43 there must be at least a positive statement in writing by or on behalf of the planning authority that no planning permission is necessary.'

If we are right in our understanding of the ratio of the majority in the *Wells* case, it does not bind us to hold that there was in the present case an application under section 53: there was in April 1976 no application for planning permission. Although the judgment of Sachs L.J. in the *Lever (Finance) Ltd.* case would, we think, greatly extend beyond the *Wells* case the permitted degree of informality in applications and determinations under section 53, it is, as we have already said, not binding on this court. In our judgment, the decision of the majority in the *Wells* case as to the 27' 6" plant should not be extended beyond cases in which there has been an application for planning permission; we feel supported in this view by the unanimous decision as to the 48′ plant.

But even if this is wrong, and some communications from a proposed developer to a planning authority other than an application for planning permission can constitute an application under section 53, we should find it impossible to hold as a matter of construction of the letters of April 8 and 26, that they constituted an application or a determination under section 53...

We also reject the alternative contention that the letter of April 26, was an established use certificate under section 94 of the 1971 Act ... The purpose and effect of a section 94 certificate is that it is conclusive evidence 'as respects any matters stated therein' for the purposes of an appeal to the Secretary of State against an enforcement notice served in respect of any land to which it relates (s.94(7)); the benefit of the certificate runs with the land. One would therefore expect that it would be required to be a formal document, and Sched. 14 to the 1971 Act and Article 18 of the Town and Country Planning General Development Order 1973 contain provisions to that effect as to the application and the certificate. We do not think we need refer to them in detail. But they include provisions that an application 'shall not be entertained' unless it is accompanied by a certificate containing the prescribed particulars (see para. 3(1) of Sched. 14 and art. 18(2)), which the letter of April 26, was not, and that established use certificates 'shall be issued' in the form set out in Part II of Schedule 6 to the 1973 order, which of course does not bear the slightest resemblance to the letter of April 26. Even if these formal defects are not in themselves a complete answer to this contention, as in our view they are, we think it is impossible to construe the letter of April 26, as a certificate under section 94. We cannot see that it is capable of being conclusive evidence of anything…"

Notes

6–49   (1) In *Robertson v. Minister of Pensions* [1949] 1 K.B. 227 at 232 Lord Denning M.R. observed:

> "In my opinion if a government department in its dealings with a subject takes it upon itself to assume authority upon a matter which with he is concerned, he is entitled to reply upon it having the authority which it assumes. He does not know, and cannot be expected to know, the limits of its authority."

See too *Howell v. Falmouth Boat Construction Co. Ltd* [1950] 2 K.B. 16 and *Wells v. Minister of Housing and Local Government* [1967] 1 W.L.R. 1000. This robust approach was however, disavowed by the House of Lords in *Howell* when Lord Simonds stated ([1951] A.C. 837 at 845) that:

> "The illegality of an act is the same whether or not the actor has been misled by an assumption of authority on the part of a government officer however high or low in the hierarchy."

For further comment on *Robertson* see N. Bamforth, "Legitimate Expectation and Estoppel" (1998) 3 (4) J.R. 196–204.

(2) The concept of estoppel is broadly equivalent to personal bar in Scots law and the issues raised by it have been particularly acute in the field of planning law as the extract all too clearly shows. The question of delegation of authority has assumed particular importance. At one level Megaw L.J's judgment might be looked at as simply one of the interpretation of the letter from Mr Giddens. Nevertheless, the two exceptions mentioned by his Lordship make it clear that there is real concern about extending the ambit of estoppel or personal bar to issues of substantive discretion. Contrast this with Craig (2nd ed., 1989), p. 481 who argues that it would be preferable if instead of adopting a general rule (either applying the estoppel principle to public authorities, or denying its applicability) the courts were to develop a balancing approach in which the court would enquire on the facts of the case whether:

> "The disadvantages to the public interest by allowing estoppel to be pleaded really do outweigh the injustice to the individual."

There is no direct modern authority in Scots law in the issues raised by the extract, although most academic commentators appear to accept that the approach in the case would be followed here: see *Stair Memorial Encyclopaedia*, Vol. 1, paras 294–296 and see also C. Crawford and C.T. Reid, "Planning Officers' Advice and Undertakings: Estoppel and Personal Bar in Public Law" (1982) Occasional Paper No. 3, Scottish Planning Law and Practice. Consider also J. Rankine, *The Law of Personal Bar in Scotland* (1921), pp. 179–184 where he distinguishes acts outwith the power of a corporation (including a public authority) and acts within their powers but carried out by the inappropriate person without regard to proper procedure. In his view the latter, but not the former, are capable of giving rise to personal bar, since "No corporate body can be bound by estoppel to do something beyond their powers", here quoting the dictum of Fry L.J. in *The British Mutual Banking Co. Ltd v. The Charnwood Forest Railway Co.*

[1887] 18 Q.B.D. 714 at 719. Would this approach be an adequate way of resolving the difficulties identified in the extract? Consider also *Clyde Port Authority v. Firth of Clyde Dry Dock Co. Ltd*, 1971 S.L.T. (Sh.Ct) 22.

(3) For other examples of personal bar or estoppel in the field of planning law see *Graham v.*   **6–50**
Secretary of State for the Environment and East Hampshire District Council [1993] J.P.L. 353 where it was held that a council could not be estopped by its officers from its duty to exercise unfettered discretion as regards to enforcement of planning control. See also *Garner v. Secretary of State for the Environment*, December 12, 1996, Queen's Bench Division and *Norfolk County Council v. Secretary of State for the Environment* [1973] 1 W.L.R. 1400.

(4) Personal bar cannot cure actings which are *ultra vires* in the sense of there being a complete lack of underlying power. That much is apparent from the extract. Older Scots law is consistent with this. In *Crawford v. Beattie* (1860) 22 D. 1064 it was held that a parish board was not bound by agreement entered into by the board's inspector which was *ultra vires* the board's power to award poor relief. No question of authority or ostensible authority could arise. Similarly in *McGroarty v. Stirling District Council*, 1987 S.L.T. 85 it was held that a contract for sale of a council house was void because terms of the missive between the purchaser and the local authority were contrary to the terms of the Tenants' Rights, Etc. (Scotland) Act 1980, on which now see Housing (Scotland) Act 1987. Similarly in *Rhyl Urban District Council v. Rhyl Amusements Ltd* [1959] 1 All E.R. 257 it was held that it was competent for a local authority to plead that it was not bound by the terms of a lease which it had entered into and which was *ultra vires* the authority. See also *Young v. Fife Regional Council*, extracted at para. 5–9. For further examples of the inability to enlarge power by the operation of personal bar see *Stair Memorial Encyclopaedia*, Vol. 1, para. 294. The converse of the foregoing is that it is not possible to argue that personal bar can be set up so as to prevent the exercise of statutory duty. So in *Maritime Electric Co. Ltd. v. General Dairies Ltd* [1937] A.C. 610, P.C. Maritime, who supplied electricity in terms of the then utilities legislation to General Dairies, had only charged for 10 per cent of the electricity supplied. General Dairies had incorporated electricity charges into the price they in turn levied on farmers processing milk. Lord Maugham observed (at 620) that:

> "Where, as here, the statute imposes a duty of a positive kind, not avoidable by the performance of any formality, for the doing of the very act which the plaintiff seeks to do, it is not open to the defendant to set up an estoppel to prevent it . . . an estoppel is only a rule of evidence which under certain special circumstances can be invoked by a party to an action; it cannot therefore avail in such a case to release the plaintiff from an obligation to obey such a statute . . ."

See also *Rush v. Fife Regional Council*, 1985 S.L.T. 451.

(5) Matters might be different with regard to the Crown. Many of its powers derive from it having personality at common law rather than statutory power. On Scots law in relation to personal bar as it affects the Crown see generally *Stair Memorial Encyclopaedia*, Vol. 1, para. 296 and J.D.B. Mitchell, "The Royal Prerogative in Modern Scots Law" [1957] P.L. 304, where he notes that on the authority of *Clarke v. Brodie*, 1801 Hume 548 and *McKay v. Brodie*, 1801 Hume 549, on similar facts to *Robertson*, a plea of personal bar was allowed against the Crown. Later Scots law seems to suggest a watering down of this approach, perhaps more consistent with a view of Lord Simonds. See here *Somerville v. Lord Advocate* (1893) 20 R. 1050 and *McKay v. Board of Admiralty* (1924) 13 S.L.R. 48 citing Erskine, Institute, I,II,27 Mitchell's view was that these cases only contain *obiter dicta* to the effect that the Crown is not bound by the errors of its officers, and that the general proposition is better expounded in the older case law, which seems to suggest that the importance of the issue in question and the relative position of the parties should determine the issue. This reflects the balancing test suggested by Craig and Rankine. Consider also *R. v. Inland Revenue Commissioners, ex parte Preston*, at para. 6–35, as reflecting the current position of the Crown in Inland Revenue matters.

(6) For consideration of the position of the Crown in relation to criminal matters see Finch and Ashton, p. 312; C.T. Reid, "Renouncing the Right to Prosecute" (1998) 43 J.L.S.S. 117; and *H.M. Advocate v. Waddell*, 1976 S.L.T. (Notes) 61.

6-51   It will be seen that the courts are not keen to bind a public authority in terms of personal bar or estoppel unless the kind of exceptional circumstances envisaged in *Western Fish Products* arise. The courts have developed other ways of reconciling the conflicting interests of public authorities with the interests and expectations of those affected by agreements or representations. The doctrine of relevant considerations might mean that a failure to take account of such a consideration might amount to an abuse of discretion: see para. 6–16. Inconsistent acting might also amount to *Wednesbury* unreasonableness and the concept of legitimate expectation might mean that a representation or undertaking might be protected by allowing the person affected an opportunity to make representations before an authority can lawfully decide to act inconsistently, on which see para. 8–32. A non-judicial remedy might also be available, such as in an application to the relevant ombudsman as a result of maladministration, on which see Chapter 16.

Notes

6-52   (1) In *Rootkin v. Kent County Council* [1981] 1 W.L.R. 1186 the plaintiff's daughter was given a place at a school more than three miles from her home. In terms of the Education Act 1944 the authority could either provide transport or reimburse the cost of transport. It decided to reimburse the cost by providing a bus pass in terms of the same Act. It then discovered that she lived less than three miles from the school. The pass was withdrawn. *Rootkin* argued that the authority was not entitled to change its mind and in any event was subject to estoppel. The Court of Appeal, *per* Lawton L.J. at 1195, held that there was a distinction between circumstances where

> "a citizen is entitled to payment in certain circumstances and a local authority is given the duty of deciding whether the circumstances exist and if they do exist of making the payment, then there is a determination which the local authority cannot rescind . . . But that . . . does not apply . . . to a case where the citizen has no right to a determination on certain facts being established; but only to the benefit of the exercise of a discretion by the local authority."

On estoppel, there was a conflict with statutory discretion and moreover there were no exceptional circumstances as contemplated in *Western Fish* and that, in any event, the plaintiff had not altered her position to entitle her to rely on the doctrine anyway, on which see Lawton L.J. at 1196. Note that the plaintiff sought to argue that estoppel was separate from whether or not the decision could be revoked. This would be because it would appear that within the class of decisions identified by the Court of Appeal as binding the authority, once a decision is made and communicated to the individual affected, the function of the authority has ceased and the individual does not require to show that he has acted to his detriment on a decision being communicated. The question of whether or not the decision amounts to such a binding determination appears to be essentially one of statutory construction: *Livingstone v. Westminster Corporation* [1904] 2 K.B. 109; *Re 56, Denton Road, Twickenham, Middlesex*, [1952] 2 All E.R. 799; and *Matchett v. Dunfermline District Council*, 1993 S.L.T. 537.

(2) In view of the interpretation of the statutory scheme in *Rootkin*, a decision based on a material mistake of fact could be revoked. There is also some authority that reconsideration on policy grounds might also permit revocation: *Coull v. Fife Education Authority*, 1925 S.C. 240 where discretionary conferment of graduate status upon a head teacher which was withdrawn was held to be competent in view of a change of policy. Note though the more recent case law on legitimate expectation below. The informal release of a decision or leak cannot create a decision that cannot be revoked even if in other circumstances it would be binding: *R. v. Secretary of State for Education and Science, ex parte Hardy, The Times*, July 28, 1988. As the scope of the doctrine of permissible revocation is somewhat uncertain, quite often statute has intervened to create schemes providing for the detailed provision of the review of revocation of earlier decisions, including the grounds upon which review might take place and the conditions to which a revised decision must conform and any relevant rights of appeal — for example, the Town and Country Planning (Scotland) Act 1997, ss. 65–67, 76–82 regarding revocation and

modification of planning permission and the Social Security Administration Act 1992, ss. 25–29, 35 and see now the Social Security Act 1998, s. 9 in relation to review of decisions given in ignorance or mistake as to material fact, or where a relevant change of circumstances exists. See also *Gilbertson v. Department of Health for Scotland*, 1933 S.C. 707, decided under earlier social security legislation. On this area generally see *Stair Memorial Encyclopaedia*, Vol. 1, para. 297; G. Ganz, "Estoppel and Res Judicata in Administrative Law" [1965] P.L. 237; M. Akehurst, "Revocation of Administrative Decisions" [1982] P.L. 613; J.A. Andrews, "Estoppels against Statutes" (1966) 29 M.L.R. 1; and A.W. Bradley, "Administrative Justice and the Binding Effect of Official Acts" (1981) 34 C.L.P. 1.

Re Preston

[1985] A.C. 835, H.L.

An inspector of the Inland Revenue sought a meeting with the applicant taxpayer in May 1978 to discuss his tax returns for the years 1975–77, and in particular to discuss certain claims for reliefs in respect of losses and certain share transactions. The inspector sought full details of these transactions but only bare details were given by the applicant. In subsequent correspondence the applicant offered to withdraw his claim to release if the Inland Revenue would settle his tax affairs for those years and raise no further questions about the share transactions. This was agreed in July 1978 in a letter from the inspector to the applicant. The taxpayer withdrew the claims and paid the capital gains tax in respect of the shares but in October 1979 the Inland Revenue received information which led them to believe that the sale of the shares had been used as part of a tax avoidance scheme. In July 1982, by which time it was too late for the applicant to make his claim for relief, the Inland Revenue issued a notice under section 465 of the Income and Corporation Taxes Act 1970 requiring the applicant to provide information about the sale of the shares. This information was provided and in September 1982, the Inland Revenue issued a further notice under section 460 cancelling the tax advantage gained by the applicant through the sale of the shares.

    At first instance, Woolf J. held that the Revenue had failed to consider facts (the 1978 agreement) relevant to the exercise of its discretion to issue the section 460 notice and that it had exercised its discretion unreasonably, on which see [1983] 2 All E.R. 300. The Court of Appeal allowed the Revenue's appeal as it differed from the trial judge on the question of reasonableness. The taxpayer appealed to the House of Lords.

6–53

LORD TEMPLEMAN: ". . . The court can only intervene by judicial review to direct the commissioners to abstain from performing their statutory duties or from exercising their statutory powers if the court is satisfied that 'the unfairness' of which the applicant complains renders the insistence by the commissioners on performing their duties or exercising their powers an abuse of power by the commissioners.
In most cases in which the court has granted judicial review on grounds of 'unfairness' amounting to abuse of power there has been some proven element of improper motive. In the leading case of *Padfield v. Minister of Agriculture, Fisheries and Food* [1968] A.C. 997 the Minister abstained from exercising his statutory discretion to order an investigation because he feared the consequences of the investigation might be politically embarrassing. In *Congreve v. Home Office* [1976] Q.B. 629 the Minister exercised his power to revoke television licences because he disapproved of the conduct of the licence holders, albeit they had acted lawfully. In *Laker Airways Ltd. v. Department of Trade* [1977] Q.B. 643 the Minister exercised his statutory discretion to give directions with regard to civil airways with the ulterior motive of making it impossible for one of the airlines to pursue a course of which the Minister disapproved. In these case judicial review was granted because the Ministers acted 'unfairly' when they abused their powers by exercising or declining to exercise those powers in order to achieve objectives which were not the objectives for which the powers had been conferred. The question of 'fairness' was considered in *H.T.V. Ltd. v. Price Commission* [1976] I.C.R. 170.
    In that case the Price Commission misconstrued the counter inflation price code and changed its mind as to the treatment of exchequer levy as an item in the costs of television companies allowable for the purpose of increasing their advertising charges within the limits prescribed by the code. The effect of the change of mind of the Price Commission was to deprive the companies of an increase of advertising

charges which they were plainly intended to enjoy and which they badly needed in order to remain financially viable. Lord Denning M.R. said, at pp. 185–186:

> 'It has been often said, I know, that a public body, which is entrusted by Parliament with the exercise of powers for the public good, cannot fetter itself in the exercise of them. It cannot be estopped from doing its public duty. But that is subject to the qualification that it must not misuse its powers: and it is a misuse of power for it to act unfairly or unjustly towards a private citizen when there is no overriding public interest to warrant it…'

In the *H.T.V.* case [1976] I.C.R. 170 my noble and learned friend, then Scarman L.J., … after considering the Price Commission's change of mind, said, at p. 192, that 'the commission's inconsistency has already resulted in unfairness, and, unless corrected, could cause further injustice. Firstly, it gives rise to a real possibility of an erosion of profit margin…' Next, if, as the Price Commission contended, the Exchequer levy was excluded in 1976 but included in 1973 then the television companies would be unable to obtain a fair increase in advertising charges corresponding to increase in costs between 1973 and 1976:

> 'The commission, to avoid being unfair, must either include or exclude Exchequer levy as a cost upon both sides of the comparison. Since it has made clear that, in the absence of a ruling to the contrary, it intends to exclude it when calculating current profit margins, the commission must also exclude it when calculating the profit margin at April 30, 1973. I am not completely sure that it intends so to do if it succeeds in this litigation… The commission has acted inconsistently and unfairly; and on this ground, were it necessary, I would think H.T.V. are also entitled to declaratory relief.'

In the *H.T.V.* case [1976] I.C.R. 170, the 'unfairness' of the decision was due not to improper motive on the part of the Price Commission but to an error of law whereby the Price Commission misconstrued the code they were intending to enforce. If the Price Commission had not misconstrued the code, they would not have acted 'inconsistently and unfairly.' Of course the inconsistent and unfair results to which Scarman L.J. drew attention were themselves powerful support for the contention that the Price Commission must have misconstrued the code.

In the present case, the appellant does not allege that the commissioners invoked section 460 for improper purposes or motives or that the commissioners misconstrued their powers and duties. However, the *H.T.V.* case and the authorities there cited suggest that the commissioners are guilty of 'unfairness' amounting to an abuse of power if by taking action under section 460 their conduct would, in the case of an authority other than Crown authority, entitle the appellant to an injunction or damages based on breach of contract or estoppel by representation. In principle I see no reason why the appellant should not be entitled to judicial review of a decision taken by the commissioners if that decision is unfair to the appellant because the conduct of the commissioners is equivalent to a breach of contract or a breach of representation. Such a decision falls within the ambit of an abuse of power for which in the present case judicial review is the sole remedy and an appropriate remedy. There may be cases in which conduct which savours of breach of conduct or breach of representation does not constitute an abuse of power; there may be circumstances in which the court in its discretion might not grant relief by judicial review notwithstanding conduct which savours of breach of contract or breach of representation. In the present case, however, I consider that the appellant is entitled to relief by way of judicial review for 'unfairness' amounting to abuse of power if the commissioners have been guilty of conduct equivalent to a breach of contract or breach of representations on their part.

[His Lordship reviewed the facts of the case and concluded that there had been no abuse of power in the above sense. In particular, the correspondence did not support the applicant's contention that the Revenue had agreed that there would be no further inquiries into the share transactions even on the Revenue becoming aware that the assessments, made in the light of the incomplete information supplied by the applicant, did not represent his full tax liability.]"

LORD SCARMAN, agreeing with the reasons given by LORD TEMPLEMAN, said: "It was the appellant's case that upon the true construction of the correspondence in 1978 … the commissioners purported to contract or to represent that they would not thereafter re-open the tax assessments … if he withdrew his claims for interest relief and capital loss. Had he made good this case, I do not doubt that he would have been entitled to relief by way of judicial review for unfairness amounting to abuse of the power… But he failed upon the construction of the correspondence…"

LORDS EDMUND-DAVIES, KEITH OF KINKEL and BRIGHTMAN also agreed with the reasons given by LORD TEMPLEMAN.

Notes

Representations have also been held to be insufficient to create legitimate expectations in *R. v. Jockey Club, ex parte RAM Racecourses Ltd* [1993] 2 All E.R. 225; *R. v. Inland Revenue Commissioners, ex parte Matrix-Securities Ltd* [1994] 1 W.L.R. 334; and *R. v. Secretary of State for the Home Department, ex parte Briggs*, *The Independent*, September 26, 1995. On *Preston* see C. Lewis "Fairness, Legitimate Expectations and Estoppel" (1986) 49 M.L.R. 251.

6–54

Cashley v. City of Dundee District Council

1994 S.L.T. 111

LORD MCCLUSKEY: "In October 1990 the pursuer and appellant applied to the City of Dundee District Council for a taxi licence. Such a licence may be granted by the licensing authority under section 10 of the Civic Government (Scotland) Act 1982 and the procedures in relation to the disposal of the application are contained in Schedule 1 to that Act. On 17th November 1990 the Chief Constable of Tayside Police, to whom intimation had been made under paragraph 2(1) of Schedule 1, formally objected to the application by letter in terms of paragraph 2(1). The ground of the objection was that the applicant was not a fit and proper person to hold such a licence. This was an objection relating to paragraph 5(3)(*a*)(ii) of the Schedule; in terms of that paragraph, the licensing authority must refuse such an application if, in their opinion, the applicant is not 'a fit and proper person to be the holder of the licence'. The chief constable's letter of objection drew the attention of the licensing authority to three convictions recorded against the applicant. They were listed in an annexation to the letter as follows: (1) on 20.9.79 in Dundee Sheriff Court he was convicted of theft and fined £75; (2) on 7.8.80 at Glasgow Sheriff Court he was convicted of 'theft H.B.' and fined £100; and (3) on 7.7.81 in Dundee District Court he was convicted of theft and fined £35. The licensing committee, which was empowered to exercise the functions of the authority in relation to such applications, met at Dundee on 6th December 1990. The committee considered the objection along with the application and after hearing an agent on the applicant's behalf and having considered all the objections voted on a motion to approve the application. The votes for and against were equal but the motion was defeated by the casting vote of the convener. It is not in dispute that although other objectors took objections on different grounds against the application, the refusal was not based to any extent upon those other objections but was related entirely to the objection made by the chief constable. The applicant did not request the licensing authority to give reasons in writing for arriving at that decision, although it was open to him to do so under paragraph 17 of the Schedule. However, he did exercise his right of appeal to the sheriff under paragraph 18. The appeal was by way of summary application and the sheriff exercised his power under paragraph 18(6) of Schedule 1 to require the authority to give reasons for the decision. That was duly done and the written reasons are contained in a letter dated 9th July 1991. It is not necessary to refer to the whole letter, but the material part reads as follows.

6–55

> 'At the said meeting of the Licensing Committee on 6th December 1990 the Chief Constable's representative on the Committee reiterated his objection and drew attention to the previous convictions of Mr Cashley, as listed in the annexation to his… letter. The Committee, being of the opinion that the applicant's previous convictions would have a bearing on his fitness to be the holder of a licence, considered the convictions contained in the said annexation. Mr Cashley's agent, i.e., your Mr McMichael, made representations on Mr Cashley's behalf to the effect that Mr Cashley's last conviction was nine years ago and that the convictions as a whole were old and should not be a bar to his obtaining a licence. Having considered the contents of the said letter by the Chief Constable together with representations on Mr Cashley's behalf, the Committee felt that Mr Cashley was not a fit and proper person to be the holder of a taxi licence. The Committee considered that the nature of the previous convictions, i.e., offences of dishonesty, and in one case also involving a violation of privacy, was such that in all the circumstances Mr Cashley could not be considered to be a fit and proper person in terms of paragraph 5(3)(*a*)(ii) of Schedule 1 to the said 1982 Act, the Committee being of the opinion that these considerations outweighed the fact that the convictions were some nine/ten years ago and also taking into account his recent clean record. For these reasons, the Committee decided to refuse his application for a taxi licence.'

The pleadings and the hearing before the sheriff disclose the full background to this application. The basis of the appeal, as recorded by the sheriff, was that the authority

> 'had refused the appellant's application because he had a criminal record while, at the same sitting of the committee, many other applications had been granted where the applicants also had criminal records'.

It was argued to the sheriff that in the case of several of the other applicants, to whom the chief constable had also lodged objection upon the same ground based upon their previous convictions, the relevant convictions were much more serious than those of the appellant; and this demonstrated a failure on the part of the committee to exercise its discretion reasonably. The agent for the authority, however, submitted to the sheriff that the court could look only at the individual case which was the subject of the appeal and the circumstances pertaining to that case; the committee, it was submitted, was clearly entitled to reach the decision it did on the facts of this particular case. The sheriff accepted the latter submission and refused the appeal. He did so, however, with clearly expressed reluctance because, looking at the details of some of the other applications which were granted (he lists details of nine of them) he found it quite extraordinary that some of them were granted, given the applicants' criminal records'. He noted that the chief constable has also objected to these other applicants and by reference to the same statutory provision. His conclusion in relation to the appeal was expressed in the following terms.

'I find it equally difficult to understand how the committee could reach the conclusion that the appellant, a person with three convictions for dishonesty, the most recent of which is nearly ten years old, was less fit to hold a taxi licence than the other persons whose convictions I have listed above. However, the fact that the committee acted in an almost incomprehensible way in other cases avails the appellant nothing as, in my opinion, when adjudicating on an exercise of discretion, it is necessary to look at each individual case separately and not compare one with another. Had the appeal been on the ground of acting contrary to natural justice other considerations might well have applied, and a different result might have been achieved.'

From the decision the applicant has appealed to this court on a point of law under paragraph 18(12) of the Schedule. There are four grounds of appeal but we need quote only the two expressly founded upon. They are:

'1. That the learned sheriff erred in law in not holding that, in the circumstances of the case, the first-named defenders and respondents unreasonably exercised their discretion in refusing the pursuer and appellant's application for a taxi licence.

3. Separatim, that in the circumstances of the case, the first-named defenders and respondent erred in law by breaching the rules of natural justice.'

Mr Jones, for the pursuer and appellant, drew our attention to the fact that in 1987 the applicant had obtained a taxi-driver's licence under section 13 of the 1982 Act. That licence had been granted by the same authority and was renewed by them in 1990 before the applicant applied for the taxi licence under section 10. Thus it was clear that, for the purpose of the section 13 taxi-driver's licence, the licensing authority could not have formed the opinion that the appellant was not a fit and proper person to be the holder of a section 13 licence. The character of a taxi licence, to which section 10 related, was admittedly different from that of a taxi-driver's licence regulated by section 13 and the question of fitness fell to be considered in relation to the particular licence for which application was made; but it was clear from section 10 that the main considerations in relation to a taxi licence related to the suitability of the vehicle to be operated under the licence. That was made plain in *McDowall v Cunninghame District Council*. In that case the court had also held that different considerations could apply to the two types of licence. The court had concluded that the respondent authority in that case had erred in proceeding upon the basis that a criminal record which rendered a person not 'fit and proper' to drive a taxi also automatically rendered him not 'fit and proper' to have a taxi licence. The court had also treated convictions which bore upon the fitness of an applicant under section 13 as having relatively less importance in relation to the fitness of an applicant for a section 10 licence. When one examined the other cases which were before the committee at the meeting of 6th December 1990, all detailed in the minute of that meeting contained in the appendix, it was clear that a number of applicants had been successful despite having criminal records which were comparable to or worse than that of the applicant. These criminal records were disclosed in the annexations to the relevant letters of objection by the chief constable. Some of the records disclosed were worse, in the sense that they were more recent of the penalties were more severe or the offences were more pertinent to the holding of the taxi licence. In particular, he referred to the cases of Bain (pp. 39–40 of the appendix), Menzies (pp. 45–46), Colligan (pp. 49–50), Anderson (pp. 51–52), Cullen (pp. 59–60) and Black (pp. 55–56). The [last] had been fined £1,000 for reset in Dundee Sheriff Court in July 1981 and also had driving convictions. Anderson had eight previous convictions between 1983 and 1985 for assorted charges, including Road Traffic Act charges resulting in his being disqualified from driving for life. It was thus clear that the licensing authority were operating a policy of some sort in relation to the effect and significance of a criminal record, but it was plainly not a policy that one or several convictions for dishonesty were sufficient to render a person not fit and proper for the holding of such a licence. Equally they were not making such a judgment purely on the basis of how recent the last convictions were or how severely they were regarded by the court. In these circumstances, the decision arrived at by the committee in relation to the appellant's application was one which no reasonable committee could have arrived at; they had exercised their discretion in a capricious and unreasonable manner and had acted contrary to natural justice, these being grounds for upholding an appeal under paragraph 18(7). Looking at the appellant's case on its own, the interested bystander would not be able to understand what the appellant's criminal record had to do with the business of operating a taxi licence. Further and in any event the committee had had no warrant whatsoever for the assertion contained in the statement of reasons that one of the appellant's convictions involved 'a violation of privacy'. Presumably that related to the theft by housebreaking; but there was no explanation by the committee as to why it had reached such a view, given that it had been explained that this conviction related to a theft of some lead from an unoccupied house between the date when it had been sold and vacated by one owner and the date when it was to be occupied by the new owner. Having regard to this error, to the type of licence sought, to the age and minor character of the convictions and to the fact that the appellant had held a taxi-driver's licence and had not been objected to as not fit and proper to do so for over three years, the decision could not possibly be justified. He accepted that the committee were entitled, despite the terms of the Rehabilitation of Offenders Act 1974, to take the appellant's previous convictions into account. But, in doing so, they could only do so in a way that was reasonable and fair. It was plain that by treating the appellant as not fit and proper by reason of convictions which, on any objective view, were less serious than the convictions of some of those who had been successful, the committee had not acted fairly and reasonably. The appeal should therefore be allowed and the court should direct the sheriff to grant the application in terms of paragraph 18(9)(*b*).

Sir Crispin Agnew for the licensing authority explained that following the decision in *Francey v Cunninghame District Council*, which indicated that convictions which were 'spent' under the Rehabilitation of Offenders Act 1974 might be considered by the licensing authority, the respondent authority had introduced a policy of considering such convictions in relation to applications in respect of taxi licences. He was unable to inform the court if the authority, in renewing the appellant's taxi-driver's licence in 1990, had then given consideration to his spent convictions. He submitted that the Court of Session, like the sheriff, had to consider each case on its own merits. The result of the appellant's application before the committee could not be criticised upon the basis that other applicants, with different circumstances, had achieved success while the appellant had failed. In *Loosefoot Entertainment Ltd v City of Glasgow District Licensing Board* the court, in refusing the appeal, approved of the approach of Sheriff Gordon who, in explaining that approach, had adopted a dictum from the Sheriff Principal's note in *Kieran v Adams*, namely:

> 'I think it quite clear that it is no part of the court's duty to exercise a general supervision over the decisions of the Board to ensure that they are uniform' [1990 S.C.L.R. at p. 587E].

As a matter of law, the Court of Session in an appeal under the 1982 Act could look only at each individual case on its own. In *Walsh v Magistrates of Pollokshaws* at p. 1018 the Lord President had pointed out that an authority of this kind had to give 'personal consideration' to each case 'in the sense of not mixing it up with other cases'. Accordingly, even if it were true, as the sheriff had thought, that the committee had erred in allowing others to have a licence, it did not follow that they were obliged to grant the appellant a licence when they considered him not to be a fit and proper person to hold one. Reference was made both to *Ranachan v Renfrew District Council* and to *Hughes v Hamilton District Council*: these cases demonstrated that it was for the committee to make its own assessment on the basis of the material before it and its judgment was not to be characterised as unreasonable simply because the court might have taken a different view. It was accepted that the question of fitness of the applicant might be assessed differently in a section 10 application and in a section 13 application; but an applicant for a section 10 taxi licence still had to satisfy the committee that he was fit and proper and that raised questions which went beyond the character and features of the vehicle in respect of which the licence was to be held. In short, this court could not properly look at the other cases to which the sheriff and the appellant had referred. Looking at the case on its merits as disclosed in the statement of reasons, it could not be said that the licensing authority had taken a decision which was so unreasonable that no properly directed licensing authority could have arrived at it.

There was no challenge by either party to the decision or the opinions in the cases of *Ranachan* and *Hughes* to which reference has been made. We proceed upon the basis that where the authority have before them relevant material relating to the fitness of the applicant for a licence then it is for the licensing authority to determine what weight falls to be attached to that material and to assess the importance and significance of any convictions recorded against the applicant. It is the function of the authority, not of this court, to judge that material in the light of their view as to the public interest. For ourselves, we are not entirely clear why the relatively elderly spent convictions recorded against the appellant should have been judged to render him not to be a fit and proper person to hold a taxi licence ...

That, however, is not an end of the matter. We agree entirely with the surprise expressed by the sheriff at the fact that certain other applications, some fourteen in number, from people who had comparable, or even in some cases worse, criminal records were granted. We note indeed that they were all granted without any adverse vote. For reasons which are not apparent, the only application (out of a total of seventy-six) on which a vote was taken was that of the present appellant. We do not disagree with the respondents' submission that each individual case must be judged on its own merits and that it is not a proper basis for criticising the authority in relation to one refusal to say that they should also have refused other applications. But, even accepting that approach, we are still faced with a situation in which it is clear, and indeed is conceded, that, despite the terms of section 7(3) of the Rehabilitation of Offenders Act 1974, the committee, as a matter of policy, decided that they would have regard to all the convictions of the applicants, including spent convictions. In terms of the section, the authority had to be satisfied that justice could not be done unless evidence relating to the spent convictions was admitted. In deciding to have regard to spent convictions they were deliberately adopting a policy and we have no doubt that justice required that that policy be applied fairly and evenly in all cases where the applicants had spent convictions. No criticism was made of the licensing authority for deciding to look at all the convictions, even very old ones, and we make no such criticism ourselves. It can hardly be disputed, however, given the terms of section 7(3), that the authority were not entitled to adopt a policy of having regard to the convictions of some applicants while ignoring those of others. We observe that in fact they appear to have had regard to all the convictions placed before them, even in one case to a spent conviction which, at the date of the hearing, was nearly twenty-eight years old. As Sir Crispin Agnew explained, they were treating *Francey* as providing authoritative guidance in this regard and as necessitating their having a policy on previous convictions. When one observes, however, that the convictions recorded against the present appellant were no worse and no more recent than those recorded against several of the successful applicants and also that, in some cases, the successful applicants had criminal records which appeared to be significantly more serious and more relevant to the fitness of a person to hold a section 10 licence, it appears to us to be clear that, in applying the policy of attaching weight to convictions, including spent convictions, this licensing authority did not act consistently. We do not wish it to be thought that the court requires an inflexible uniformity of approach in relation to such a matter. But where the difference in approach from one case to another suggests, as it does here, that the policy has been applied in an arbitrary fashion, and where the statement of reasons gives no satisfactory explanation for the different application of the policy in the only case where it appears to have been applied severely, namely that of the applicant, it appears to us that the licensing authority must be held to have exercised their discretion in an unreasonable manner. It might also be that they acted contrary to natural justice, but it is not necessary to form any separate view on that as in this case, these two matters, though separate in paragraph 18(7) of the Schedule, are bound up very closely together. In essence, our view is that when the licensing authority came to consider the application by the appellant and decided to apply to it the same general policy on previous convictions as they were applying to all applications by persons with such convictions, it was their duty to apply that policy fairly and even-handedly. In our opinion, it is not clear that that happened in this case. On the contrary, it appears not to have happened. Accordingly the authority in considering the appellant's application, appear to have failed to apply to that consideration the same policy that they applied to other cases to which the policy also fell to be applied. Thus the consideration of the appellant's case was flawed by that failure. In these circumstances, the authority have not exercised their discretion in a reasonable manner. Accordingly we shall recall the interlocutors complained of."

Notes

6–56   (1) *Cashley* does not use the language of legitimate expectation found in *Preston*, but could it have? Here inconsistency was equated with irrationality. As *Cashley* was decided in the context of a statutory appeal under the Civic Government (Scotland) Act 1982 where reasonableness and natural justice are separate grounds of appeal, the court was in a position to treat natural justice as a separate matter, which in turn gave the question of consistency as irrationality independent content regardless of whether or not *Cashley* had been denied a hearing. *Cashley* would also appear to be authority for the view that the extent to which one can rely on policy depends on the form that policy takes, particularly with regard to its application.

This was also borne out in *R. v. Inland Revenue Commissioners, ex parte MFK Underwriting Agents Ltd* [1990] 1 All E.R. 91. MFK founded on assurances given by the Inland Revenue that they would treat a particular element payable in relation to financial securities as capital and not income. The Revenue taxed on that basis until October 1988, the practice having lasted nearly two years. It then changed its view. The decision in *Preston* was considered by the Queen's Bench Division. It was observed by Bingham L.J. that:

"I am, however, of opinion that in assessing the meaning, weight and effect reasonably to be given to statements of the Revenue the factual context, including the position of the Revenue itself, is all important. Every ordinarily sophisicated taxpayer knows that the Revenue is a tax-collecting agency, not a tax-imposing authority. The taxpayers' only legitimate expectation is, prima facie, that he will be taxed according to statute, not concession or a wrong view of the law (see *R. v. Attorney-General, ex p. Imperial Chemical Industries plc* (1986) 60 T.C. 1, 64 *per* Lord Oliver). Such taxpayers would appreciate, if they could not so pithily express, the truth of the aphorism of 'One should be taxed by law, and not be untaxed by concession'. See *Vestey v. Inland Revenue Commissioners, per* Walton J. [1979] Ch. 177, 197. No doubt a statement formally published by the Revenue to the world might safely be regarded as binding, subject to its terms, in any case falling clearly within them. But where the approach to the Revenue is of a less formal nature a more detailed inquiry is, in my view, necessary. If it is to be successfully said that as a result of such an approach the Revenue has agreed to forgo, or has represented that it will forgo, tax which might arguably be payable on a proper construction of the relevant legislation it would in my judgment, be ordinarily necessary for the taxpayer to show that certain conditions had been fulfilled. I say 'ordinarily' to allow for the exceptional case where different rules might be appropriate, but the necessity in my view exists here. First, it is necessary that the taxpayer should have put all his cards face upwards on the table. This means that he must give full details of the specific transaction on which he seeks the Revenue's ruling, unless it is the same as an earlier transaction on which a ruling has already been given. It means that he must indicate to the Revenue the ruling sought. It is one thing to ask an official of the Revenue whether he shares the taxpayer's view of a legislative provision, quite another to ask whether the Revenue will forgo any claim to tax on any other basis. It means that the taxpayer must make plain that a fully considered ruling is sought. It means, I think, that the taxpayer should indicate the use he intends to make of any ruling given. This is not because the Revenue would wish to favour one class of taxpayers at the expense of another but because knowledge that a ruling is to be publicised in a large and important market could affect the person by whom and the level at which a problem is considered and, indeed, whether it is appropriate to give a ruling at all. Second, it is necessary that the ruling or statement relied on should be clear, unambiguous and devoid of relevant qualification.

In so stating these requirements I do not, I hope, diminish or emasculate the valuable developing doctrine of legitimate expectation. If a public authority so conducts itself as to create a legitimate expectation that a certain course will be followed it would often be unfair if the authority were permitted to follow a different course to the detriment of one who entertained the expectation, particularly if he acted on it. If in private law a body would be in breach of contract in so acting or estopped from so acting a public authority should generally be in no better position. The doctrine of legitimate expectation is rooted in fairness. But fairness is not a one-way street. It imports the notion of equitableness, of fair and open dealing, to which the authority is as much entitled as the citizen. The Revenue's discretion, while it exists, is limited. Fairness requires that its exercise should be on a basis of full disclosure. Counsel for the applicants accepted that it would not be reasonable for a representee to rely on an unclear or equivocal representation. Nor, I think, on facts such as the present, would it be fair to hold the Revenue bound by anything less than a clear, unambiguous and unqualified representation."

On this case see A.R. Mowbray, "Legitimate Expectations and Departmental Representations" (1990) 106 L.Q.R. 568 and W. Hinds, "Estopping The Tax Man" [1991] B.T.R. 191. Contrast *MFK* with the decision in *R. v. Secretary of State for the Home Department, ex parte Khan* [1985] 1 All E.R. 40, extracted at para. 2–41. Was there a case of personal bar or estoppel in substance, even if not in form made out in that case? On this see P. Elias, "Legitimate Expectation and Judicial Review" in *New Directions in Judicial Review* J. Jowell and D. Oliver, eds, (1988), p. 45.

(2) The concept of legitimate expectation is central to challenge based on consistency. Initially it emerged as a procedural tool, used to provide a hearing in situations where the traditional

rules of natural justice would not normally have been permitted, on which see Chapter 8. Here our concern, however, is the extent to which there is a link between the existence of legitimate expectation and the extent to which legitimate expectation can give rise to substantive rights. We are concerned with the extent to which, in addition to giving a right to a hearing, inconsistency would prohibit a decision being taken which defeats an expectation which the body in question has created or stops a decision being taken unless the public interest demands it to be taken.

6–57   (3) In *Laker Airways Ltd v. Department of Trade* [1977] Q.B. 643, C.A. Laker were given a licence by the Civil Aviation Authority for a cheap passenger air service between London and New York. The Government in power at the time was the Conservative Government and they, together with Laker, thought to persuade the American Government to grant a permit for operations over U.S. territory "without undue delay", provided Laker came up to prescribed standards. Some £6 million was spent on the project. However, in 1975, three years after the initial decision, a Labour Government was in power and it reversed the previous Government's policy and decided that not more than one U.K. airline should be licensed for this particular route. The CAA was instructed to revoke Laker's licence. In the Divisional Court it was held that the Government was estopped from withdrawing the licence by its previous conduct. However on appeal it was held by Lawton L.J. (at p. 728) that:

> "Whatever representations the Secretary of State in office between 1972 and 1974 may have made to Laker Airways Ltd. he made them pursuant to his public duty and in good faith. If in 1976 his successor was of the opinion that the public interest required him to go back on those representations, he was in duty bound to go back on them. The fact that Laker Airways Ltd. suffered loss as a result of the change is unfortunate: they have been the victims of a change of government policy. This often happens. Estoppel cannot be allowed to hinder the formation of government policy."

Lord Denning M.R. observed (at p. 707):

> "The underlying principle is that the Crown cannot be estopped from exercising its powers, whether given in a statute or by common law, when it is doing so in the proper exercise of its duty to act for the public good, even though this may work some injustice or unfairness to a private individual: see *Maritime Electric Co. Ltd.* v. *General Dairies Ltd.* ... where the Privy Council, unfortunately. I think, reversed the Supreme Court of Canada [1935] S.C.R. 519. It can, however, be estopped when it is not properly exercising its powers, but is misusing them: and it does misuse them if it exercises them in circumstances which work injustice or unfairness to the individual without any countervailing benefit for the public ..."

6–58   (4) There are further authorities which support the view that a legitimate expectation can create substantive rights. In *R. v. Secretary of State for the Home Department, ex parte Ruddock* [1987] 2 All E.R. 518 the Vice President of CND sought judicial review of a warrant issued by the Secretary of State authorising the tapping of her telephone, arguing that it fell outwith the criteria for such action. It was alleged that those criteria required reasonable cause to believe that major subversive activity was being carried out and interception was not to be used for purely party political purposes. What was significant was that these criteria had been published and adhered to by successive Governments. It was argued by the Secretary of State that legitimate expectation only related to cases where there was an expectation of the rights to be consulted or to give representations before a decision was made, and that given the very nature of the operation in question, there could be no question of these rights being generated. Taylor J. (at 531) accepted that most of the cases involving legitimate expectation would involve procedural rights, but not all:

> "Indeed, in a case where ex hypothesi there is no right to be heard, it may be thought the more important to fair dealing that a promise or undertaking by a minister as to how he will proceed should be kept. Of course such promise or undertaking must not conflict with his statutory duty or his duty, as here, in the exercise of a prerogative power. I accept ... that the respondent cannot fetter his discretion. By declaring a policy he does not preclude any possible need to change it. But then if the practice has been to publish the current policy, it would be incumbent on him in dealing fairly to publish the new policy, unless again that would conflict with his duties."

The expectation here arose from an express promise that a practice had been adhered to, and the fact of that practice itself. The Secretary of State did not argue that the criteria had been changed or that an exception had been made. His argument was that the intercept fell within those criteria and on the facts Taylor J. accepted that the Secretary of State had not flouted the criteria and the decision to grant the warrant was not irrational. *Ruddock* was considered in *Pirie v. City of Aberdeen District Council*, 1993 S.L.T. 1155. Here, an applicant for a place in the district council's housing waiting list sought judicial review for reduction of a decision to refuse the application. In terms of the Housing (Scotland) Act 1987, s. 21(1), (4), the local authority was under a duty to publish rules governing the criteria upon which admissions to the housing list would be made and which would be available to the public. The rules stated that applications would not normally be accepted from former tenants of the local authority or any other authority who had been unsatisfactory. The council decided that in view of the applicant's wife's previous poor history as a tenant, the applicant be refused a place on the waiting list. The petitioner argued that he had a legitimate expectation that the council would conform to the rules which it was under a duty to publish and moreover, on the basis of *Ruddock*, unless the council could show a legitimate reason for deviating from those rules, that a legitimate expectation of a substantive nature would exist. In view of the terms of the rules, Lord Cullen did not have to consider whether a legitimate expectation had been created, as the rules were clearly mandatory in their terms, allowing of no exception. The competence of the argument did not appear to have been doubted though: see also *Walsh v. Secretary of State for Scotland*, 1990 S.L.T. 526.

(5) Legitimate expectation will not always prevent a change in policy. In *Re Findlay* [1985] A.C. 318 the Home Secretary announced a change to parole policy in respect of prisoners sentenced to life for certain kinds of murder. They would normally now serve at least 20 years and those serving determinate sentences of over five years for offences of violence or drug dealing would, save in exceptional circumstances, be granted parole only when under supervision for a few months before the end of the sentence when there was likely to be a reduced risk to the public. Prisoners who were affected by the changes sought judicial review on a number of grounds. One ground was that two life sentence prisoners argued that they had good reason to expect release under the old policy much earlier than under the new policy. Lord Scarman observed (at 338):

6–59

> "The doctrine of legitimate expectation has an important place in the developing law of judicial review. It is however, not necessary to explore the doctrine in this case, it is enough merely to note that a legitimate expectation can provide a sufficient interest to enable one who cannot point to the existence of a substantive right to obtain the leave of the court to apply for judicial review. These two appellants obtained leave. But their submission goes further. It is said that the refusal to except them from the new policy was an unlawful act on the part of the Secretary of State in that his decision frustrated their expectation. But what was their *legitimate* expectation? Given the substance and purpose of the legislative provisions governing parole, the most that a convicted prisoner can legitimately expect is that his case will be examined individually in the light of whatever policy the Secretary of State sees fit to adopt provided always that the adopted policy is a lawful exercise of the discretion conferred upon him by the statue. Any other view would entail the conclusion that the unfettered discretion conferred by the statute upon the minister and in some cases be restricted so as to hamper, or even to prevent, changes of policy. Bearing in mind the complexity of the issues which the Secretary of State has to consider and the importance of the public interest in the administration of parole I cannot think that Parliament intended the discretion to be restricted in this way."

See also *Rea v. Parole Board for Scotland*, 1993 S.L.T. 1074, for application of the approach in *Findlay* in Scottish proceedings.

The requirement of leave is of course unnecessary in judicial review proceedings in Scotland. Similarly in *R. v. Secretary of State for Health, ex parte United States Tobacco International Inc.* [1992] 1 Q.B. 353 the Divisional Court considered a challenge to the Secretary of State's change of policy in deciding to make regulations banning oral snuff (a tobacco product). In 1985 United States Tobacco International Inc. opened a factory in Scotland to manufacture the product on the basis that the Government permitted them to do so provided they agreed not to sell the product to persons under the age of 18. A government grant was given to create the factory. In 1986 the Government received advice from scientific advisers to ban the product and in February 1988 the Secretary of State announced that such a ban was in fact being proposed. The regulations were quashed on the ground of a lack of consultation, on which see para. 5–20. Legitimate expectation of a substantive nature was, however, rejected. Taylor L.J. noted the passages from Lord Scarman's judgment in *Findlay* and his own judgment in *Ruddock* and observed (at 369):

> "In the present case, if the Secretary of State concluded on rational grounds that a policy change was required and oral snuff should be banned in the public interest, his discretion could not be fettered by moral obligations to the applicants deriving from his earlier favourable treatment of them. It would be absurd to suggest that some moral commitment to a single company should prevail over the public interest."

See also Morland J. at 372.

B. Schwehr and P. Brown, "Legitimate Expectation — Snuffed Out?" [1991] P.L. 163 criticise this case. They argue that the court did not distinguish between whether or not a legitimate expectation existed and if it did, whether there was sufficient public interest in overriding it. They suggest (at 166) that the correct formulation for a court to adopt in such circumstances is not "is there a legitimate expectation?" but "has the minister shown a good reason for changing his mind?" See also P.P. Craig, "Legitimate expectations: a conceptual analysis" (1992) 108 L.Q.R. 79 at 97.

6–60   (6) In the cases we have been considering so far we have generally been looking at situations where some form of representation or practice existed upon which legitimate expectation could be found. However, in *R. v. Inland Revenue Commissioners, ex parte Unilever plc* [1996] S.T.C. 681 the Court of Appeal held that an abuse of a power amounting to unfairness could exist in the absence of a "unqualified and unambiguous representation". For 20 years tax calculations by Unilever had been accepted by the Revenue even though relief in respect of trading losses was not expressly sought and such an express claim was in fact required by the Income and Corporation Taxes Act 1988, s. 393. The Court of Appeal held that on these "unique facts" the Revenue's actions in rejecting the claims in reliance on the fact that they were outwith the two-year time-limit generally permitted, without general advance notice, was unfair as to be an abuse of power and irrational. Sir Thomas Bingham M.R. stated (at 690):

> "The categories of unfairness are not closed, and precedent should act as a guide not a cage."

It was also observed by Simon Brown L.J. (at 695) that he regarded the

> "*MFK* category of legitimate expectation as essentially but a head of *Wednesbury* unreasonableness, not necessarily exhaustive of the grounds upon which a successful substantive unfairness challenge may be based."

On this case see N. Bamforth, "Fairness and Legitimate Expectation in Judicial Review" [1997] 56 C.L.J. 1 and R. Gordon and T. Ward, "The billowing fog" [1996] 146 N.L.J. 1663.

(7) It will be apparent from the foregoing that the question of public interest in overcoming a legitimate expectation assumed particular significance. How is the public interest assessed? How are the competing interests balanced? In *R. v. Secretary of State for the Home Department, ex parte Hargreaves* [1997] 1 W.L.R. 906 the Court of Appeal overruled *R. v. Ministry of Agriculture, Fisheries and Food, ex parte Hamble (Offshore) Fisheries Ltd* [1995] 2 All E.R. 714 where Sedley J. indicated that it was for the reviewing court to assess whether there was sufficient public interest in allowing a change of policy to override an expectation. Hirst L.J. criticised the approach in *Hargreaves* (at 921):

> "Mr Beloff characterised Sedley J.'s approach as heresy, and in my judgment he was right to do so. On matters of substance (as contrasted with procedure) *Wednesbury* provides the correct test. It follows that while Sedley J.'s actual decision in [the *Hamble* case] stands, his ratio in so far as he propounds a balancing exercise to be undertaken by the court should in my judgment be overruled."

See also *R. v. Secretary of State for Transport, ex parte Richmond-upon-Thames London Borough Council* [1994] 1 W.L.R. 74 at 94 and C.F. Forsyth, "*Wednesbury* protection of substantive legitimate expectations" [1997] P.L. 375.

(8) It is possible that there may be a negative aspect to legitimate expectation. This point is illustrated by the decision of the European Court of Human Rights in *National & Provincial Building Society v. United Kingdom* [1997] S.T.C. 1466. A year before judgment was delivered in *Woolwich Equitable Building Society v. Inland Revenue Commissioners* [1990] 1 W.L.R. 1400, H.L., on which see para. 14–65, a number of the building societies, including the National & Provincial Building Society (the N & P), commenced proceedings to recover a sum that they had paid under the regulations which were ultimately held to be *ultra vires*. Writs were issued after the Government had announced its intention to legislate to validate the original regulations. After judgment was given in the *Woolwich* case, the Government presented legislation to Parliament which retrospectively validated the *ultra vires* regulations and thus deprived the N & P and others of a right to restitution. The N & P thereafter went to the European Court of Human Rights alleging, *inter alia*, that the introduction of retrospective legislation amounted to unjustifiable interference with a right to peaceful enjoyment of their "possessions", namely their claim for restitution under Article 1 of Protocol 1 to the European Convention on Human Rights. While the Court did not accept that claims to restitution were "possessions" within the meaning of Article 1 of Protocol 1, in any event, the Court did not accept that there had been any deprivation of legitimate expectation. The N & P had argued that they had a sufficiently established right to constitute "possessions" and that this gave them a clearly legitimate expectation that they would be treated similarly to the Woolwich. The court reasoned as follows:

"The House of Lords judgment in the Woolwich 2 case, which is central to their claim to have an established right amounting to possessions, was in fact delivered one year after the writs had been issued. Furthermore, while it may be the case that the authorities did not intimate to the applicant societies in the course of the Woolwich I litigation that they would seek to restore with retroactive effect the original intention of Parliament should that case go against the Inland Revenue, it is reasonable to question whether these two building societies could have had a "legitimate expectation" that the Government would not have reacted as they did to the outcome of the litigation. As the Government have pointed out, the writs were issued after the decision had been taken to rectify with retrospective effect the inadvertent defects in the 1986 Regulations and in the days immediately preceding the official announcement by the Government of this course of action.

While noting that the Leeds and the National & Provincial may be considered to have at best a precarious basis on which to assert a right amounting to "possessions", the Court is of the view that the claims asserted in the judicial review proceedings and the second set of restitution proceedings brought by all three applicant societies in May and June 1992 respectively could not be said to be sufficiently established or based on any "legitimate expectation" that those claims would be determined on the basis of the law as it stood.

Having regard to a Contracting State's margin of appreciation in the tax field and to the public-interest considerations at stake, it could not be said that the decisions taken by Parliament to enact these measures with retrospective effect were manifestly without reasonable foundation or failed to strike a fair balance between the demands of the general interest of the community and the protection of the rights of the applicant societies. The latter were in fact seeking by means of opportunistic legal proceedings to exploit technical defects in the 1986 Regulations and to frustrate the original intention of Parliament. They clearly understood what that intention was and they could not have had any legitimate expectations following the Woolwich 1 litigation that Parliament would be content to leave the law as it then stood and allow them to retain a windfall."

Is this convincing? Assuming that the N & P had been able to establish a right, should they also have been required to establish a legitimate expectation or continuation of that right? There are, however, parallels with this analysis in European Community law, on which see *Firma A. Racke v. Hauptzollamt Mainz* [1979] E.C.R. 69 at 86 and generally J. Schwarze, *European Administrative Law* (1992). On the N & P case see D. Oliver, "A negative aspect to legitimate expectations" [1998] P.L. 558.

As will be seen from the foregoing, case law in Scotland is relatively scant. The next extract is therefore perhaps the most detailed survey of the issues occurring in a Scottish case to date.

6–61

McPhee v. North Lanarkshire Council

1998 S.L.T. 1317

6–62   LADY COSGROVE: "The factual background as it appears from the averments in the petition is as follows. The petitioner is a travelling person with four dependent children who is permanently separated from her husband. In or around 1994 she resided with her mother at a pitch on the site in question and at that time the respondents cleared the site to allow for modernisation. In about October 1994 the respondents raised proceedings in the sheriff court for recovery of the pitch occupied by the petitioner. On or around 8 November 1994 the petitioner met with officials of the respondents housing department with responsibility for managing the site and asked for confirmation that if she voluntarily removed herself she would, on completion of the refurbishment works, be offered the tenancy of a pitch on the site. An unconditional representation was then made by the respondents' officers that once the site had been modernised, the petitioner would be offered the tenancy of a pitch and she then agreed that she would vacate the site upon receipt of written confirmation of the said unconditional representation. Thereafter the pursuer received a letter from the respondents' director of housing dated 28 November 1994 which is in the following terms:
'Dear Mrs McPhee,
'I refer to our meeting on Tuesday 8 November 1994 and am to confirm that you will be offered accommodation at Kirklee Road, Mossend, after completion of refurbishment works to the site subject to the same terms and conditions as any other travelling family seeking accommodation from the Council.'
It is averred that thereafter, and in reliance on the respondents' said representation, the petitioner vacated the site. The refurbishment works were completed and the site reopened in or around March 1996. By letter of 12 November 1996 the petitioner made an application for allocation of the tenancy of a pitch on the site and by letter dated 3 December 1996 the respondents refused her application. By letter of 20 December 1996 the petitioner sought written reasons for the said refusal. While it is averred in the petition that no such reasons have been provided, the respondents' letter dated 8 May 1998, to which reference has already been made and which follows on their reconsideration of the application on the first day of this hearing, includes the reasons for the continued rejection of her application, which are said to be (a) that it is considered that the application form contained a false declaration as to the petitioner being separated from her husband, and (b) that her husband has a known record of anti-social behaviour. It is said that these considerations outweigh the assurances previously given and that the application is rejected in the interests of maintaining the site in a satisfactory condition for other travellers.
It is averred on behalf of the petitioner that the respondents' decision to refuse to allocate her the tenancy of a pitch on the site was unreasonable and contrary to law and in particular that their said offer, verbally and in writing, raised a legitimate expectation that she would be made such an offer and that that was breached by the respondents' conduct. It is averred further that esto she had no such legitimate expectation, she had at least an expectation that her application would not be refused without adequate and comprehensible reasons being given therefore and an opportunity afforded to her to be heard in reply.
The respondents, in their answers, admit the factual basis as averred in the petition. They explain that the refurbishment works which were carried out at the site were at a cost of more than £300,000 and were substantially funded by Government grant. It is admitted that they have declined to give the petitioner reasons for their decision and they aver that in the past when reasons have been provided there have been incidents of violence and verbal abuse directed against site managers. It is also averred that when her application was refused, the petitioner had outstanding arrears in respect of her previous occupancy of the site and that at or about the time the application form was completed her husband was, contrary to the petitioner's assertion, cohabiting with her. It is further averred that the allocation of pitches on a site such as this is an important factor in the success of the site; this is particularly so in the case of a new site or one which is being reopened after refurbishment. If persons with a record of anti-social behaviour are permitted to reside in a site this deters other travelling people from applying for pitches there; the petitioner's husband has such a record and other members of the travelling community are reluctant to seek pitches on sites inhabited by members of the McPhee family.
On behalf of the petitioner it was submitted that the respondents, on their own admission, having given a particular promise of a quasi-contractual nature were, as a matter of law, bound by it unless it could be shown that to keep it would be inconsistent with their duty or that there was an overriding public interest in refusing to do so. The promise given by the respondents was of such a nature as to give rise to a substantive expectation, that is to say an expectation of the particular benefit promised which required to be achieved unless the respondents could demonstrate sufficient cause for their failure. The averments upon which the respondents rely were not sufficient to support the proposition that offering the tenancy would be either inconsistent with their duty or with the public interest, bearing in mind that the onus is, as a matter of law, on the respondents.

Reference was made by both counsel to the analysis of the concept of legitimate expectation by Simon Brown LJ in the case of *R v Devon County Council, ex p Baker* [1995] 1 All ER at pp 88–89. While it was common ground that the assurance with which the present case is concerned was one which fell within the first of the four categories described by his Lordship, that is to say was a promise of a substantive right, competing contentions were advanced as to the effect of that assurance. The issue which is focused in this case is whether a public authority is entitled to take a decision which differs from such an earlier assurance or promise given by them; that is to say, does such an assurance when it relates to a substantive right constitute a legitimate expectation which gives rise to a remedy, as distinct from a hope that a benefit might be extended, which does not.

The proposition advanced by counsel for the respondents was that while a public body must have regard to the legitimate expectations which arise from an assurance it has given, it may depart from such an earlier assurance when it comes to take a decision in the exercise of its statutory discretion but in doing so it will be tested by reference to whether or not the decision in question was one which was reasonable in the *Wednesbury* sense (*Associated Provincial Picture Houses Ltd v Wednesbury Corporation*). It was important to bear in mind that the expectation said to have been raised in the present case was in respect of a matter of substance rather than of procedure. Reference was made in this connection to the opinion of Hirst LJ in *R v Home Secretary, ex p Hargreaves* at [1997] 1 WLR, p. 921: 'On matters of substance (as contrasted with procedure) *Wednesbury* provides the correct test.' His Lordship characterised as heresy the rejection by Sedley J in *R v Ministry of Agriculture, Fisheries and Food, ex p Hamble (Offshore) Fisheries Ltd* of the proposition that neither precedent nor principle goes further than the enforcement of legitimate procedural expectations. The basis of the attack on Sedley J's approach was that the authorities cited by him dealt only with alleged procedural irregularities on the part of a minister in respect of which it was appropriate for the court to conduct an inquiry into the fairness of the procedure followed, but not with decisions on matters of substance.

Reference was also made by counsel to *R v Beatrix Potter School, ex p K* as a recent example of the application of the proposition advanced by him. In that case the applicant, K, was a pupil attending the Beatrix Potter nursery school. The headmaster of the main school confirmed that a place was available for her by letter to her parents dated 19 July 1996 stating that K would enter school on the morning of 9 September 1996. On receipt, the applicant's mother bought her a school uniform but later that day the head teacher rang up and told her that the offer was withdrawn. It was argued that the offer gave rise to a legitimate expectation based on an express promise which was relied on and gave rise to some detriment. The court dismissed the application and held that while all the factors necessary to give rise to legitimate expectation existed, that was only a factor to be taken into account in deciding whether the respondent had acted *Wednesbury* unreasonably. In considering the *Wednesbury* principle and whether the withdrawal of the offer was unreasonable, the court came to the clearest conclusion that it was impossible to categorise the decision to withdraw the offer as *Wednesbury* unreasonable. In relation to legitimate expectation Popplewell J said (at [1997] ELR, p 476): 'Legitimate expectation is in my view a factor to be taken into account in deciding whether the respondents have acted *Wednesbury* unreasonably. In some cases it might be the only factor and would therefore be wholly decisive in an applicant's claim. In other cases it may be no more than one of the matters to be taken into account. It is really an aspect of the general public law obligation and the obligation on the respondents not to act unreasonably'.

References was also made to *R v London Borough of Brent, ex p McDonagh*, a case in which the applicant who was a traveller was furnished with a letter stating inter alia that the respondents, the local authority council, intended to take action to limit the number of travellers on the site she was then occupying but that in the meantime no action would be taken against the recipients of the letter pending the availability of a proper site. The applicant was subsequently evicted and sought judicial review on the basis that she had a legitimate expectation arising from the letter sent to her by the respondents that she would not be evicted from the site without either being offered an alternative pitch or at the very least without being informed of the proposal to be evicted and being given the chance to make representations. It was held that the said letter from the respondents did give rise to such a legitimate expectation and the respondents' decision was quashed with the effect that it was open to them to reconsider the matter and to reach a fresh decision taking into account the representations of the applicant.

Counsel submitted that it was implicit from that decision that an authority was not prevented from withdrawing from an earlier assurance. The court in quashing the existing decision acknowledged (at (1989) 21 HLR, p 503) that the effect of that may be no more than some temporary relief for the applicant prior to the respondents reconsidering the matter, it being clearly recognised that they may then reach the same view. That decision was thus entirely in accordance with the general proposition posited on behalf of the respondents, namely that where an assurance is given by a public authority it may, when it comes to take its decision in the exercise of its discretion, depart from that assurance but in doing so it will be tested by reference to the well known principles of judicial review. In the present case a procedural mechanism was now being offered to the petitioner whereby she would be given the opportunity to make representations in relation to the respondents' decision which no doubt they would take into account. It was submitted that since there is an issue of disputed fact between the parties the order sought could not be granted as it was impossible for the court to affirm on the information available that no reasonable authority could do other than grant this order. The effect of granting the order would be to pre-empt the respondents' exercise of their discretion in terms of their statutory powers. Where the existence or non-existence of a fact is left to the judgment and discretion of a public body, it is the duty of the court to leave the decision of that fact to the public body to whom Parliament has entrusted the decision making power save where it is obvious that the public body are acting perversely (*Puhlhofer v Hillingdon London Borough Council*) ....

Counsel contended that the two factors set out in the answers to the petition were matters to which a reasonable authority was entitled to have regard. In the first place, it was incumbent upon the applicant to list in the application form all intended occupants of the site, whereas the petitioner had described herself as married but separated with no indication that her husband was an intended occupant. The affidavit from the respondents' accommodation manager indicates that inquiries made by him and his officers disclosed that the petitioner's husband was indeed living with her at the site in Glasgow which she gave as her current address at the time of completing the application. That affidavit also indicates that the applicant had outstanding rent arrears and other charges in respect of a previous tenancy with the respondents, that there were criminal proceedings pending against her husband in respect of his assault on a member of the council's staff and that the travelling persons' community is afraid of the petitioner's family. The respondents' position was put no higher than that they have information which raises a question as to whether or not the petitioner is cohabiting with her husband, and it would be open to her now to make representations on this matter and the authority would then reach a considered view as to the appropriate factual basis.

Senior counsel for the petitioner submitted that the proposition that the existence of a legitimate expectation gave rise to a remedy only in respect of procedural rights was ill founded. The courts have recognised that legitimate expectation can constitute a substantive right to be relied upon. Reference was made in this connection to *R v. Inland Revenue Commissioners, ex p Preston*, a case in which an inspector of the Inland Revenue informed a taxpayer that he did not intend to raise any further inquiries on his tax affairs if the taxpayer withdrew certain claims for interest relief and capital loss. The taxpayer did so but thereafter was issued with a formal notification by the revenue initiating a procedure for the cancellation of a tax advantage and he then sought judicial review of the revenue's decision. The decision of the House of Lords turned on the fact that the appellant had not made a full disclosure to the respondent's inspector which it was held he had a right to expect and on which he plainly relied, and in that situation the inhibitory effect of the respondent's inspector's letter was held to have been lost to the appellant. While the House of Lords did not in the circumstances require to decide whether the appellant was entitled to relief by judicial review for conduct which amounted to breach of representation. Lord Templeman observed (at [1985] 1 AC, pp 866–867): 'In principle I see no reason why the appellant should not be entitled to judicial review of a decision taken by the commissioners if that decision is unfair to the appellant because the conduct of the commissioners is equivalent to a breach of contract or a breach of representation. Such a decision falls within the ambit of an abuse of power for which in the present case judicial review is the sole remedy and an appropriate remedy. There may be cases in which conduct which savours of breach of conduct [sic] or breach of representation does not constitute an abuse of power there may be circumstance in which the court in its discretion might not grant relief by judicial review notwithstanding conduct which savours of breach of contract or breach of representation. In the present case, however, I consider that the appellant is entitled to relief by way of judicial review for 'unfairness' amounting to abuse of power if the commissioners have been guilty of conduct equivalent to a breach of contract or breach of representations on their part.'

Reference was also made to *R. v Inland Revenue Commissioners, ex p Matrix Securities Ltd.* a case in which a company which had constructed a tax avoidance scheme sought a declaration that the Inland Revenue were not entitled to revoke tax clearances given by them in a letter from the inspector of taxes. The House of Lords, in holding that the taxpayer must put all his cards face upwards on the table and having found that the applicant had not done so, refused his application. Once again the decision turned on its particular facts, but I observe that the court's discretion to grant or refuse relief appears to have been confirmed. As Lord Jauncey, in commenting upon the passage in the opinion of Lord Templeman in the *Preston* case to which reference has already been made, observed (at [1994] 1 WLR, p 352): 'I take from these passages (i) that the court may properly review a decision of the revenue to exercise its statutory powers if the decision is so unfair as to amount to an abuse of power although the court has a discretion to refuse relief even if such decision does savour of such abuse.'

Counsel sought to distinguish the case of Hargreaves relied upon by counsel for the respondents on the ground that the expectation there involved a declaration as to the respondents policy and different considerations must clearly apply where an attempt is being made to hold a public authority to a previously declared policy as distinct from a previous promise to an individual in the present case all the factors necessary to give rise to legitimate expectation existed and the respondents were thus bound by their earlier assurance. The petitioner was accordingly entitled to the remedy she seeks unless the court was satisfied that to provide this would be inconsistent with the respondents duty or with an overriding contrary public interest. It was for the respondents to put these matters in issue and if they failed to do so the petitioner was entitled to succeed. Further, the respondents should appropriately be regarded as having made their decision in November 1994 when they offered the petitioner accommodation. While the two factors now put in issue by them were both highly relevant to the proposition that the promise need not have been given at that time, neither was a fresh factor which could logically be regarded as relevant to their refusal to keep their promise.

It is clear that the notion of a legitimate expectation which gives rise to a prima facie entitlement to procedural fairness in the exercise of a statutory power or authority is well established in law. What is not clear in my view is whether legitimate expectation can constitute a substantive right. I do not read the authorities relied upon by counsel for the petitioner in this connection as unequivocally vouching the proposition advanced by him. I observe that the view has been expressed by Sedley J in *ex p Hamble (Offshore) Fisheries Ltd.* at [1995] 2 All ER, p 724) that there is no reason in principle why it might be less unfair to frustrate an expectation that something will or will not be done rather than an expectation that an applicant will be listened to before a particular decision is taken. While that view may be justified, the consequence of raising the expectation of obtaining a benefit to the level enjoyed by the expectation of discussion prior to the taking of a decision would be to extend the supervisory jurisdiction of the court into situations beyond those in which it has habitually been exercised. While the courts have always been alive to the need to intervene to ensure that a fair procedure is followed, it is clear that in such cases the court is not in any way pre-empting the decision making power of the public authority. In cases involving substantive benefit, on the other hand, intervention by the court to impose on the authority a particular result would inevitably trespass upon the proper authority's decision making function. I consider that the approach which is adopted should recognise and give effect to the undoubtedly delicate balance which requires to be struck between intervention by the court and allowing the decision maker to take those decisions allocated to it.

With these considerations in mind, I have reached the view that the respondents' submission as to the law to be applied prevails. I consider that in cases such as the present involving an assurance as to a substantive right, the authority providing the assurance may depart from it but if it chooses to do so it will fall to be scrutinised by reference to the *Wednesbury* test of unreasonableness and that in applying that test the fact that the assurance or promise has been given will be an important factor to be taken into consideration.

I turn therefore to consider whether the withdrawal by the respondents of their offer was *Wednesbury* unreasonable. That is to say, whether the decision was 'so outrageous in its defiance of logic or of accepted moral standards that no sensible person who had applied his mind to the question to be decided could have arrived at it' (*CGSU v Minister for the Civil Service*, per Lord Diplock at [1985] AC, p 410). As has already been observed, the respondents have now consented to the reduction of their decision of 3 December 1996 to refuse the application of the petitioner for a pitch on the site. I observe in this connection that while the basis for this concession was never specified it seems reasonable to assume recognition on the part of the respondents that they had, in arriving at their decision, acted in some way unreasonably. A further decision was taken by the respondents following the adjournment granted on the first day of the hearing and that is contained in their letter of 8 May 1998. There was however no motion on behalf of the petitioner for the reduction of that recent decision which thus remains extant and the only order I was invited to make was to grant a declarator in terms of crave 3 (c) of the petition that the petitioner is entitled to be allocated a pitch on the site. Had the decision of 8 May been under challenge, it seems to me that it would have been difficult to do other than categories it as unreasonable in the *Wednesbury* sense inasmuch as it was arrived at without affording the petitioner a chance to make representations in a situation where it was acknowledged by the respondents that their earlier decision was vitiated and that the dispute on matters of fact remained unresolved. Had I been asked to quash that decision I would have been prepared to do so. The effect of that may of course have been no more than some temporary relief for the petitioner because it would then have been open to the respondents to reconsider the matter, and having given the petitioner the opportunity to make representations, to make a fresh decision which may or may not have differed from that of 8 May.

The particular remedy now sought by the petitioner does not involve any reference to the decision making authority and, in effect, asks the court to declare that it is outrageous to consider that any authority, having provided the earlier assurance, could do other than grant her application. The question which arises, in my view, is whether or not there are present factors which would entitle an authority such as the respondents to depart from their earlier assurance. In this connection I consider that there are matters to which a public authority could reasonably have regard in deciding whether or not to grant this application, including their belief that the petitioner has not been candid in the information provided on her application form, the potential of anti-social behaviour in the event of the petitioner's husband joining her on the site and the sensitive nature of the decision as to whether or not to grant or refuse a pitch. I find it impossible to hold in the circumstances that these three factors could not outweigh the assurance given by the respondents notwithstanding that they may have been known to them at the time the assurance was given. Finding as I do that the existence of disputed issues of fact makes it impossible to affirm that no reasonable authority could do other than grant the petitioner's application, I shall sustain the respondents' fifth plea in law and refuse to pronounce decree in terms of crave 3(c) of the petition.

I am conscious that the effect of a refusal to grant the declarator sought will, in the circumstances, result in a situation where the petitioner is not afforded a remedy despite the recognition by the respondents that their initial decision was unreasonable and notwithstanding the view that I have reached as to the fairness of the procedure adopted by them in respect of their recent decision. The respondents have now given an assurance that the petitioner will be afforded the opportunity to make representations and it seems to me to be unfortunate that this recognition of their responsibilities in the proper exercise of their statutory function has come at such a late stage in these proceedings."

Notes

6–63   For further discussion of the issues see G. Junor, "What Did You Expect?", 1998 S.L.T. (News) 123; G. Ganz, "Legitimate Expectation" in *Public Law and Politics* (C. Harlow ed., 1986) Chap. 8; P. Elias, "Legitimate Expectation and Judicial Review" in *New Directions in Judicial Review* (J. Jowell and D. Oliver eds, 1988), p. 37; B. Hadfield, "Judicial Review and the Concept of Legitimate Expectation" (1988) 39 N.I.L.Q. 103; P.P. Craig, "Substantive Legitimate Expectations in Domestic and Community Law" (1996) 55 C.L.J. 289; R. Baldwin and D. Horne, "Expectations in a Joyless Landscape" (1986) 49 M.L.R. 685; and P.P. Craig, "Legitimate Expectations: A Conceptual Analysis" (1992) 108 L.Q.R. 79.

Chapter 7

GROUNDS OF LEGAL CONTROL 2: THE RETENTION OF DISCRETION

The very essence of a discretion is that it confers flexibility and can be contrasted with the relative rigidity of rules being used as the basis for a decision. For practical reasons of administrative need, some attempt to structure discretion often occurs most typically in the form of a policy as to the way in which a discretion will be exercised. Our concern is confined to examining challenge to policies which do not offend any of the other principles of legal control, such as irrationality, relevancy, consistency, etc. Our concern here is in relation to challenge to the way in which such policies are applied.

7–1

In addition we go on to examine the situation in which a discretion is not properly exercised because the person on whom the discretion is vested is in effect prevented from exercising that discretion because of the actions of another person or institution. This ground of challenge is sometimes known as acting under dictation and it, together with challenge based on the argument that a policy has been followed in an overly rigid manner, are sometimes known as grounds of control based on the fettering or retention of discretion. As we have noted in the immediately preceding chapter, the overlap between these grounds of control and other grounds of control should not be forgotten. Thus the decision in *Lavender (H.) & Son Ltd v. Minister of Housing and Local Government* [1970] 3 All E.R. 871 at para. 7–19 can be viewed not just as a decision on acting under dictation but also as having relevance in the field of consultation obligations in procedural *ultra vires*, on which see para. 5–20. Similarly, there is an inherent tension on the one hand between an expectation created by the existence of a policy… other hand might be defeated by the principle that a policy cannot in the final analysis fetter the discretion to which it relates: see, for example, *Re Findlay* [1985] A.C. 318, noted at para. 6–53. The relationship between fettering or the retention of discretion and personal bar or estoppel in *Western Fish Products Ltd. v. Penwith District Council* [1981] 2 All E.R. 204, extracted at para. 6–48, is also apparent. Other examples can be given and one should not overlook the context in the field of the contracts of public authorities, on which see Chapter 14. Our first concern, however, is with the relationship between policy and discretion and in particular where it is alleged that there has been an overly rigid application of a policy.

POLICY: CREATION AND CHALLENGE

The first extract by Galligan provides an analysis of the function of policy within a discretionary power. The next extract, that of the case of *Kilmarnock Magistrates v. Secretary of State for Scotland*, provides an insight into the way in which the courts accept the function of policy as an aspect of modern administration.

7–2

D. Galligan, "The Nature and Function of Policies within Discretionary Power"

[1976] P. L. 332

"INTRODUCTION

7–3   THERE is an idea buried deep in the hearts of various constitutional theorists and judges that 'to discipline administrative discretion by rule and rote is somehow to denature it.' According to this idea, there is something about the nature of discretionary power which requires each decision to be made according to the circumstances of the particular situation, free from the constraints of preconceived policies as to the ends and goals to be achieved by such power. The circumstances of the situation will indicate the proper decision and policy choices must remain in the background. An alternative view is to recognise that discretion entails a power in the decision-maker to make policy choices, not just to deal with the individual case, but to develop a coherent and consistent set of guidelines which seek to achieve ends and goals within the scope of powers and which determine particular decisions. It will be argued that an analysis of the role of policies within discretion shows that the latter view reflects more realistically how policies function in practice. Then it is necessary to show that this role of policies can be accommodated within a coherent and satisfactory concept of discretion and that the courts in judicial review have begun constructing a framework of principles for full realisation of this concept.

A. POLICIES IN DISCRETIONARY DECISION-MAKING
(i) Individuation of discretionary power
One of the central tasks of an authority exercising discretion is to translate a grant of general power to a specific decision. To do this, an authority must make choices as to the ends to be achieved and the actions to be pursued within the terms of its power. Discretionary power by its nature entails a capacity to choose amongst alternative courses of action in order to achieve desired ends and goals. An authority, for example, given discretion to make welfare payments according to 'need' must give some content and definition to such a vague and variable concept; it must decide what factors will determine need and their respective weights. By such policy decisions an authority can develop guidelines to bridge the gap between the general power and the particular case.

      Thus a policy represents a choice by a decision-maker, acting within the scope of his discretionary powers, to adopt or pursue a course of action where such course of action embodies or contributes towards achieving a goal or end which the decision-maker considers desirable, advantageous or expedient. The extent of an authority's power to choose policies will depend on the terms of the statutory power. It may be couched in such wide terms that the range of choices open to the authority is almost unlimited; in other cases choices may be closely restricted to implementing powers conferred in clear and specific terms. Within the varying degrees between these extremes it may be necessary to make a number of policy decisions, of varying specificity, before a power may be translated to a particular case. For example, the decision of the Minister pursuant to his extensive planning powers to preserve a green belt around towns provides a broad guide to planning decisions. But such a policy itself uses concepts so open-textured that a network of subordinate policy decisions will be necessary before a particular decision can be made.

      In some cases each exercise of discretion is made afresh according to policies that seem appropriate to the moment and the exigencies of the particular case, but without regard to past or future decisions. But this is the exception rather than the rule. In vast areas of welfare, licensing and planning, similar discretionary powers are exercised repeatedly and usually by busy officials, boards, and tribunals. There is a tendency in such areas to generalise policies so that they serve not merely to decide one particular case, but to guide decisions in all cases to which they are relevant. This can be seen clearly from the way policies are made. Often they are chosen deliberately in advance of an initial exercise of power; for example, the green belt policy which significantly determines the use of planning powers for the future. When policy choices are made merely to deal with the case in hand, they may be unexpressed and quite difficult to extract; but even in such cases, after a number of decisions, it may be possible to identify consistent policies that are implicit in such decisions and to generalise them for use in future cases. Indeed one may be able to show that the decision-maker himself, expressly or impliedly, is generalising from past decisions to assist in deciding future cases. The observation of L. L. Fuller that 'in actual systems for controlling and directing human conduct, a total failure to achieve anything like a general rule is rare,' seems quite accurate. Even where polices are chosen in advance, circumstances in individual cases may prompt their modification, extension or even abandonment.

      The tendency to generalise policies may be expressed by saying that an authority makes policy choices which are used as guides in making particular decisions in the future. This process of adopting or developing guides by generalising policies to give content to discretionary power, which is constant from one decision to another, may be called 'individuation,' and the guides that result 'principles of individuation.' One may identify characteristics of coherence amongst these principles, of generality in their application, and of continuity and consistency from one application to another. The common characteristic of all principles of individuation is that they guide and condition the choice of the decision-maker in the particular case. At one extreme the principles of individuation may operate as broad, flexible guides which the decision-maker takes into account but which do not determine a particular result; at the other extreme the principles may operate as norms, whose terms are clear and specific, and which determine the decision in particular cases. Between these extremes the degree of choice left in applying any principle of individuation to a particular situation will vary. Thus to the extent that discretion is individuated by policy choices, the elements of choice in a particular case are reduced.

The central issue in the legal control of policies is now clear: it is the resolution of the apparent conflict between the interest of the decision-maker in developing policies which determine particular decisions and the interest of the individual in obtaining discretionary decisions which take proper account of the special features of his claim. A resolution of this conflict is central to the present study.

(ii) Merits of individuation

The tendency to individuate discretionary power is a natural and inevitable aspect of decision-making which must be taken into account in an analysis of discretion. Not only is individuation natural and inevitable, but it is also highly desirable. By adopting principles of individuation and making them known an authority is able to satisfy demands of fairness by decisions which are both consistent from one exercise to another and reasonably predictable. To individuate is to recognise that, except in rare cases, decisions are made not in splendid isolation from each other, but in a context of continuity where criteria and categories are generalised to influence and even determine the outcome of the particular decision, while allowing for proper account of its unique characteristics. It may even be that the formulation of generalisations and their application to individual cases will foster a more critical reflective attitude in the decision-maker in that he will be conscious of fitting each decision into a coherent pattern.

Nonetheless often it is argued that some decisions are made more appropriately according to the exigencies of the particular case, rather than in a context of predetermined principles. Clearly there are types of discretion where this is so, but it will be shown that in general the peculiarities of the particular case can be accommodated by individuation provided that the principles function in some way short of rules.

A more fundamental limitation on individuation derives from the idea that some questions are inherently unsuited to determination by generalised criteria. The central characteristics of such questions are unique in that they are non-recurring and so incapable of classification into categories for general use. An example suggested is the highly individualistic concept of 'need' in social security claims. The recognition of such questions when they occur will demand skilled and sensitive decision-makers to distinguish areas suitable for individuation from areas that are not. But in practice it may be realistic to recognise that in vast areas of decision-making such people are lacking so that there is great pressure to develop categories, to make policy choices and to mould the particular decision accordingly. This may mean that highly variable considerations are forced a little crudely into categories which neglect some of the subtleties of the particular case. If this is so one has to accept that decision-making on a large scale by people of varying perception and responsibility is a rather blunt instrument. The only consolation is that the disadvantages to the individual are offset to some extent by the advantages of a system of decision-making which is generalised, consistent and predictable."

Kilmarnock Magistrates v. Secretary of State for Scotland

1961 S.C. 350

"The Police (Scotland) Act, 1956, enacts: 'Section 6 (1) Subject to any regulations made under section 11 of this Act... a person shall be appointed to the office of chief constable... by the police authority with the approval of the Secretary of State.' Section 11 of the Act conferred upon the Secretary of State for Scotland power to make regulations as to the government and administration of police forces. Such regulations were made by the Secretary of State. No prohibition was contained in these regulations of the appointment of a Chief Constable from within a police force. On the leet selected by a police authority for appointment to the office of Chief Constable of a burgh police force was the Deputy Chief Constable. The representatives of the police authority were convened to a meeting with the representative of the Secretary of State to discuss the inclusion of the Deputy Chief Constable's name. They were then informed that the Secretary of State had decided as a matter of policy that, in normal circumstances, appointments to the rank of Chief Constable of a police force should not be made from within that force. After considering the persons on the leet and interviewing them, the police authority decided that their own Deputy Chief Constable was the best qualified and most suitable candidate and unanimously resolved to appoint him. The Secretary of State refused to approve his appointment. The police authority brought an action to have it declared that,

7–4

in exercising his powers under the Police (Scotland) Act, 1956, the Secretary of State was bound to have regard only to the qualifications for appointment of Chief Constable prescribed in the regulations and to no other qualifications of general application, and for declarator that the defender was not entitled to withhold his approval of their appointee. Counsel for the pursuers contended that, in professedly following a 'general policy' which was not reflected in the statutory regulations in relation to the approval of an appointment, the defender was acting in breach of his statutory powers."

LORD CAMERON: "The pursuers in this action are the Provost, Magistrates and Councillors of the Burgh of Kilmarnock in their capacity as the police authority for the burgh in terms of sections 1 and 2 of the Police (Scotland) Act, 1956, and the defender is the Secretary of State for Scotland against whom the pursuers seek certain declarators in respect of the discharge of his functions and powers under that Act in the matter of the appointment of a chief constable. The pursuers ask, first, for declarator that the defender is bound, in exercising the power conferred upon him by section 6 (1) of the Police (Scotland) Act, 1956, to have regard to the qualifications for appointment of chief constables laid down in Regulation 4 of the Police (Scotland) Regulations, 1956, as amended by the Police (Scotland) Amendment Regulations, 1957, and to no other qualifications of general application, and second, for a declarator that the defender is not entitled to withhold his approval of appointment as Chief Constable made by the pursuers in conformity with the said regulations, on the general ground that immediately before his appointment the candidate was serving in the local police force. The second conclusion, in its original form, was challenged by the defender in argument as incompetent, in view of the terms of the Crown Proceedings Act, 1947, but counsel for the pursuer sought and obtained leave during the debate to amend that conclusion to its present shape. The Police (Scotland) Act, 1956, provides, *inter alia*, as follows: [His Lordship quoted the Act and Regulations.]

The pursuers plead in their first plea-in-law that the defender is bound in terms of the Act and Regulations, and in the absence of special qualifications, to have regard only to the qualifications laid down in the Regulations and they also plead that the defences are irrelevant. The defender also states a plea to relevancy (as well as one to the competency of the action in relation to the pursuers' original second conclusion). In addition, the defender pleads that he is not bound to approve the appointment, and that, being entitled to withhold his approval of the appointment of the pursuers' candidate although he may be qualified for appointment in terms of Regulation 4 of the Regulations, he should be assoilzied from the declaratory conclusions of the summons.

The question which is raised by this action is, therefore, one of general importance and of principle extending beyond the limits of the particular case, as, indeed, is clear from a consideration of the language of the declaratory conclusions of the summons, which are not specifically directed to the particular circumstances of the appointment of a Chief Constable of Kilmarnock, but are set out in terms of general application.

The parties were agreed in asking me to dispose of the case on the pleadings, and neither sought proof of their averments of fact. They were also agreed that I should consider the terms of the letter of 19th May 1960, referred to on record. This means that not only is there no challenge of the accuracy of the pursuer's averment as to the state of the Kilmarnock police force, or the qualifications of the officer whom they have selected for the post of Chief Constable, but also that the pursuers do not challenge the accuracy of the defender's statements as to the reasons which, in this case, have led him to refuse approval of the pursuers' selection. Now, it is to be noted that, in addition to a reference to his so-called general policy, the defender goes on to give particular reasons for his action, reasons which are special to the case of the burgh and to the pursuers' appointee in relation to the burgh police force and its recent history. The pursuers did not suggest that these particular reasons — which are purely administrative — were not such as the defender was entitled to take into account or act upon. Nor did I understand them to maintain that these might not properly be regarded as in themselves special circumstances. Equally, the defender has not argued that his decision in this case can be justified on these particular grounds alone, leaving on one side any question of general policy. I was thus relieved of the difficulty of considering how far an exercise of administrative discretion (assuming the defender to have a discretion) that was professedly based on a number of reasons both particular and general, but all of administrative character, would be vitiated and held to be *ultra vires* because one of the reasons or grounds was incompetent and such as the defender was not entitled to take into account. Both parties argued the case as one of general principle, and directed their contentions solely to the question of whether the Secretary of State was acting in breach of his statutory powers in professedly following what was called a 'general policy' in relation to the approval of the appointment of a chief constable. The conclusions, as originally drawn and upon which parties went to debate, raised an initial difficulty, in that, taken together, they seemed to suggest that, if the defender was found to have acted in excess of his powers, the remedy which the pursuers might obtain thereunder would be one which in effect required him to approve the appointment already made by them. Counsel for the pursuers' amendment of his second conclusions, however, seems to me to have removed this difficulty, as well as to meet the point of competency which the defender raised, and to which his plea (also added by way of amendment) was directed. The general issue which the parties raise is of importance, not only to themselves, but also, it may well be, to other police authorities throughout the country. But, of course, a decision on this issue is not, and cannot be, a decision on the merits, either of the question of policy to which parties refer or of the particular case. These are essentially matters of administration and I have neither the jurisdiction nor the material to express any opinion on such matters. I would venture to say only this; that they are obviously matters on which divergent views may be held by responsible persons and supported by substantial and respectable reasons. I would also, at this stage, again emphasise that there is nothing in the pleadings which in any way reflects on the personal capacity of the officer whose appointment to the post of chief constable has given rise to this litigation...

The pursuers' positive and simple contention was that the Secretary of State, by announcing in speech and letter what he calls his general policy, has exceeded his statutory power, and has in effect and in substance made and sought to act upon a general regulation affecting qualifications for office, which contradicts those laid down in the relevant statutory Regulations. There is only one competent way (they said) in which a general qualification can be prescribed, and that is by Regulation made in terms of the Act and after such consultation as the Act lays down. The success of the pursuers' argument thus turns upon whether they can show what the defender has done is in substance to make a non-statutory Regulation. On this critical point the defender takes issue with the pursuers. He denies the accusations levelled against him by the pursuers of unconstitutional conduct and maintains that the pursuers' action is irrelevant, because what he is doing is nothing more than to follow a certain line of administrative policy, which is flexible and subject to exception in its operation when the particular circumstances of the case make its application inappropriate or undesirable. Such action he maintains to be well within his administrative competence and in no way partakes of extra statutory regulation. A number of authorities were cited in the course of the debate, but I doubt if much help is got from them, as the principles of law which are applicable in a case of this kind are not in serious dispute. If Parliament has laid down the manner in which Regulations prescribing qualification for a particular office are to be made by a minister, then any purported Regulation not so made is illegal and the action of the minister *ultra vires*. In considering an issue of this kind, the substance of what a minister has done is to be regarded, as well as the form in which he has done it. Therefore, the defence of administrative policy will not protect a minister from successful attack, if what he has really done is to make and operate a Regulation which can only be legally made in accordance with the procedure laid down by Parliament. The area of dispute, as so often, lies not in the ascertainment but in the application of the law. It was at one stage, however, suggested by junior counsel for the defender that, as the opening words of section 11 of the Police Act contained the word 'shall' as requiring the Secretary of State to make regulations, and as the provision as to the content of these Regulations was merely permissive as evidenced by the use of the word 'may' in subsection (2) of that section, therefore the defender did not require to set out all or any of the qualifications for office in the Regulations made by him. But whether the language of section 11 (2) be mandatory or merely permissive, and on this point I express no opinion, the issue is academic because, in fact, the Secretary of State has made Regulations prescribing the qualification for appointment and, by admission of the Solicitor-General, if he does so, he must prescribe all the requisite qualifications *uno flatu* in the Regulations so made. Thus the familiar trend of authority cited by counsel for the defender beginning with *Julius* v. *Bishop of Oxford* (1880) 4 Q.B.D. 245, 5 App.Cas. 214, becomes irrelevant to the only live issue in the case. That issue was succinctly stated by counsel for the pursuers in his admirable argument for the pursuers. He maintained that the Secretary of State's action showed that he had misunderstood the scope and limit of his powers and he had thereby flouted the Act of Parliament because, by the express terms of section 40 of the Act, he can only prescribe qualifications for appointment as chief constable in the manner laid down by the Act, and that is by Regulations made in conformity with the Act, after appropriate consultation and laid before Parliament. Counsel for the pursuers maintained that the practical result which followed from this action was that the defender had deprived both the pursuers and potential appointees of a right which had been secured to them by Regulation, because the defender's avowed policy meant that, in practice, service in a particular force disqualified a candidate from appointment as Chief Constable of that force, although the properly made Regulation declared him qualified for this office. If this was to be done it could, and should, be done openly and properly by way of amending Regulation, which would have to run the gauntlet of statutory consultation and be subject to Parliamentary scrutiny. The pursuers' consequential argument was that, as the Secretary of State had thus acted *ultra vires*, his refusal to approve the appointment made by them was vitiated and ineffectual, because it was avowedly founded upon this improperly prescribed and unauthorised regulation. Therefore, the pursuers claimed they are entitled to the declarators which (as now amended) they ask me to pronounce.

The pursuers argued that the accuracy of their contention as to the real nature of what the defender had done was not susceptible of contradiction by him, because they pointed to the defender's admissions in his pleadings and particularly to what is averred on record in his answer 5, where the defender explains that 'In these circumstances the defender considers it generally undesirable that appointment to the office of chief constable of a police force should be made from within that force, unless specialties exist sufficient to out-weigh these considerations'. This, say the pursuers, is nothing more or less than an admission of prescribing a general disqualification, subject to relaxation in particular cases by the exercise of a retained but unlimited dispensing power, and the position is made worse because there is no guide as to the nature of the specialties which will be regarded by the defender as sufficient to take a case out of his general rule. Thus, he legislates without the authority of Parliament and, at the same time, endows himself with a prerogative power of dispensing with his own legislation. The defender stoutly denies the accuracy of the pursuers' analysis of his action, and maintains that he is doing no more than he is entitled, because his administrative function necessarily involves questions of policy, and, therefore, he is entitled to have and to make known, if he so determines, the lines of that policy, cf. *General Poster & Publicity Co.* v. *Secretary of State for Scotland*, 1960 S.C. 266 (1961 S.L.T. 62), at page 275, per the Lord Justice-Clerk. It is clear enough that, if the Secretary of State's approval is to be anything more than the impress of a rubber stamp on a public authority's choice, he must have a power of rejection. That power must be exerciseable in case of appointees who, it is to be assumed, will possess the requisite qualifications as laid down in the Regulations, and whose possession of these qualifications has already been affirmed by the police authority. So much was conceded by pursuers' counsel, and necessarily so, in my opinion. Now, if the Secretary of State is to exercise a discretion in determining whether to give or withhold his approval, he must necessarily have regard to some considerations bearing on the particular choice he is asked to approve. These considerations may, and probably will, in every case involve both the personal qualities of the candidate as well as the nature and quality of the particular post he is to occupy. But a police force does not exist in a void, each force is geographically linked with its immediate neighbour and there are special statutory provisions in the Police Act itself for mutual aid of police forces. This being so, I do not see how it could be argued that, in considering the immediate question of approval of a particular appointment, the Secretary of State is not entitled to look beyond the boundaries of a particular force and take into account such possible external consequences of a particular appointment as, for example, the extent to which a particular appointee might be ready to co-operate with or seek assistance from another police force, or to have regard to the importance of experience gained outwith a particular force, as assisting an officer to be chosen for the office of Chief Constable in the important duty of maintaining a high degree of efficiency in the force. These are matters on which different minds may place greater or less weight, but I do not think (nor indeed was it suggested) that they are illegitimate or improper considerations for a Secretary of State to have in mind or to give such weight as he thinks fit. But may the Secretary of State not go further, and in a particular case apply a general rule or principle of administration, especially where that rule or principle is professedly subject to discretion and exception in its exercise according to circumstances, or, to put it another way, may he only have regard to particular considerations affecting a particular appointment, without regard to other or wider or even general administrative considerations? I should have thought that, as a general rule, in the words of the Lord Justice-Clerk, 'administrative function… necessarily involves questions of policy', i.e. of general policy. If he has a discretion in the discharge of his statutory duty, the limits of which are not defined by statute, in my opinion this discretion is not exercised *ultra vires*, if exercised by reference to general administrative considerations in the true sense. This is just to say that he is entitled to have regard to and to follow a policy. Indeed, I do not understand the pursuers' pleas or conclusions to traverse this as a general proposition and even if they had, I would have been against them. But the dividing line between the legitimate pursuit of a general policy in a matter of administration and the enforcement of an extra statutory Regulation may be narrow and sometimes difficult to draw, and it is here that the kernel of the case is reached. I do not see how it could be maintained that if an administrative discretion is to be properly exercised in recurrent instances, it should be improper, far less illegal, for the authority exercising that discretion to have regard to considerations of general character affecting that recurrent exercise, as well as particular circumstances affecting the particular instance of its exercise. What the pursuers say, of course, is that what the defender calls 'general policy' in this particular aspect of his administrative function, when applied to the considerations governing the appointment of a Chief Constable, is just another way of saying Regulation of qualification or disqualification, and I think that counsel for the pursuers' formidable catalogue of errors, which he alleged have been committed by the defender, would be true, if the assumption on which his argument is based were sound. But counsel for the defender argued forcefully that to lay down and operate a flexible administrative policy in this matter of the approval of an appointment to the office of Chief Constable was not to prescribe a qualification, and that, therefore, what was done by the defender was not the promulgation of an illegitimate Regulation. In support of this, argument he cited the definition of 'qualification' contained in the *Shorter Oxford, English Dictionary* as 'a necessary condition, which must be fulfilled before a certain right can be acquired, an office held, or the like.' As he paraphrased the matter, 'qualifications are those *sine quibus non* that are indispensible for consideration for appointment.' Further, the language in which the policy was expressed showed that it did not aim at bringing about a qualification or disqualification of general or universal application. In any event, if it were practicable to embody such a policy into a Regulation (which he submitted would be impracticable), it would have to be operated by the appointing authority, and thus the discretionary control would pass from the hands of the Secretary of State into those of the appointing authority. Counsel for the defender urged that if the substance of what the defender has done and has not done should be considered, and it was the substance of the matter which had to be regarded, it was plain that he had not fallen into the catalogue of error of which he stood accused by counsel for the pursuers. In the first place, he has not limited the field in which his discretion can be exercised: he has not deprived himself of the power in any particular case to approve the appointment of a chief constable appointed from the ranks of the force he is to command, nor has he defined or attempted to delimit what he will regard as special circumstances justifying his departure from the 'normal' policy in any particular case. Now counsel for the pursuers did not deny that the defender would be entitled to have regard, for example, to the quality as well as the prescribed length of police experience of any candidate for office as chief constable. Thus, he might well regard experience in a small rural force as a disabling factor in considering whether to give approval to the appointment of a candidate of such limited experience to the charge of a large urban force in an area where crime was rife. This being so, counsel for the defender argued that if, therefore, the Secretary of State has left himself and is free in any given case to exercise a choice between an appointee from within a force and one from outside, each of whom possesses the requisite qualifications as laid down in the Regulations, how can it be said that in expressing a general intention to prefer candidates from outside he is legislating or prescribing a general disqualification for appointments? As the defender has not attempted to describe or define what are the special considerations which, in any particular case, will weigh with him so as to lead him to depart from his general policy, in the result nothing more is left than a rule of practice subject to exception in any circumstances which, in the unfettered discretionary judgment of the defender, warrant departure from that rule. Certainly it cannot be said that in any case has the Secretary of State professed to insist that his approval will only be given to an appointee from an outside police force. Counsel for the defender founded strongly on the moderation of the language of the Scottish Home Department letter of 19th May 1960 and, in particular, the passage where — referring to the Secretary of State's address at Tulliallan in October 1958 — it is stated that 'the Secretary of State therefore asked police authorities to consider very carefully whether appointment to the office of Chief Constable of an officer who has spent all or most of his service in the force was in general desirable; and he suggested that in normal course the width of experience and open and fresh approach, which are necessary are more likely to be found in candidates from other forces than in an officer with long service in the force with the vacancy'. In these circumstances, according to the counsel for the defender's argument, the defender has neither prescribed a qualification nor a disqualification in the proper sense of the word. The pursuers have consequently lost nothing which was secured to them by the Regulations nor have prospective appointees, and the pursuers' action is therefore irrelevant. Against this view of the matter, in the final speech for the pursuers, counsel argued that the terms of the letter of 19th May 1960 showed that there was no exercise of discretion at all in the present case, no consideration of personal issues — as nothing could be said against the appointee personally — but solely the blind application of a policy of disqualification laid down eighteen months before, in effect, the operation of a Regulation. According to him, the defender has rendered nugatory the Regulation that specifically admits local appointment — but the defender has not refused to consider local candidates; the defender is said 'to have gone through the provisions of section 11 (6), and 36 (2) of the 1956 Act with the bulldozer of administrative discretion' — but this begs the question, which is whether, in fact, the defender has added a non-statutory disqualification. Equally fallacious, in my opinion, is the argument that the defender is guilty of the constitutional sin of attempting to legislate by proclamation without the sanction of statutory authority. This contention also begs the question whether, in fact, the defender has attempted to legislate by proclamation. In introducing his new policy, counsel for the pursuers said the defender has purported to alter the law which had recognised that local men can be appointed Chief Constable of their own forces, but the answer to this is that he has not done anything of the kind — local men can still be so appointed and their appointments approved, and, therefore, it is wrong for the pursuers to say, as counsel for the pursuers argued, that the defender has deprived the pursuers and their Deputy Chief Constable of a right hitherto unquestioned. It seems to me that here is the crux of the matter. What right, hitherto secured by Regulations, has the defender's policy taken away? In my opinion, the pursuers have lost no right. They never had the right to insist on approval of any appointment made by them, nor under the Regulations have they the right to demand to know the defender's reasons for refusing his approval of an appointment made by them. As regards the candidates for appointment, I think it is equally true to say that they have been deprived of none of the legal rights secured to them by Regulations. The Regulations, in prescribing qualifications, do not at the same time tabulate the weight to be given to each qualification either by the appointing or the approving authority.

If a candidate for office possesses the qualifications set out in the Statutory Regulations, he has the right and is entitled to be considered for appointment and, if appointed by the police authority, is entitled to have his appointment considered for approval by the Secretary of State. But neither candidate nor police authority could compel approval of a qualified and selected appointee, nor is the Secretary of State bound to give his reasons to the disappointed appointee if he refuses to approve. All that the candidate possessed as of right, if otherwise qualified under the Regulations, was to have his name considered by the police authority and, if appointed, by them, to have it submitted for approval by the Secretary of State in the exercise of his statutory discretion. In my judgment the pursuers' rights, as secured to them by Parliament and Regulations, have not been infringed, nor has the defender refused consideration of the merits of their case, nor has he taken into account considerations that he could not legally bring into balance. The rights of candidates for appointment, as secured to them by the Regulations, remain unaffected, because the qualification for consideration for appointment remain unchanged. In my opinion, the defender, in the exercise of an administrative discretion, is entitled to pursue a course of action in line with a policy determined by him, and in doing so here he has not exceeded his powers or sought *ultra vires* to make a new Regulation of disqualification under the guise of following a general policy in discharge of his administrative duty. That being so, I think that the pursuers' contentions fail and that their action should be dismissed."

Notes

7–5 For further analysis of the relationship between policy and discretion see H.L. Molot, "The Self-Created Rule of Policy and Other Ways of Exercising Administrative Discretion" (1972) 18 McGill L.J. 310; P.P. Craig, *Administrative Law* (3rd ed., 1994), pp. 391–400; H.W.R. Wade and C. Forsyth, *Administrative Law* (7th ed., 1994), pp. 360–366; V. Finch and C. Ashton, *Administrative Law in Scotland* (1997), pp. 287–290; *The Laws of Scotland Stair Memorial Encyclopaedia*, Vol. 1, para. 241.

One of the most recent and well-known challenges to administrative policy occurred in the following extract.

Cinderella's Rockafella's Ltd v. Glasgow District Licensing Board

1994 S.C.L.R. 591

7–6 LORD PROSSER. "The petitioners are the holders of an entertainment licence in respect of Tuxedo Princess, Broomielaw, Glasgow. The respondents are the Glasgow [District] Licensing Board, who granted that entertainment licence. The petitioners had applied, in terms of the Licensing (Scotland) Act 1976, for a regular extension of permitted hours, from 11 p.m. until 3 a.m., Monday to Sunday, for one year from the end of June 1993. On 8th June 1993 the respondents granted the application for the year in question, Monday to Sunday, but (*a*) they restricted the hours to the period from 11 p.m. to 2 a.m. and (*b*) they applied a condition to the grant that 'there shall be no entry or re-entry by patrons to the premises after 12 midnight on each night'. On 29th June 1993 they issued a statement of reasons.

The petitioners contend that the respondents acted ultra vires and erred in law, (*a*) in refusing the application in respect of the period from 2 a.m. to 3 a.m. and (*b*) by applying the condition to the grant. If this contention is sound, the question of remedy arises; but it is convenient to leave that matter aside at this stage.

The issue between the parties centres upon a change of policy, adopted by the respondents in May 1993. It was then agreed that:

> 'The following policy… will apply with regard to opening hours: — for liquor-licensed premises, regular extensions of permitted hours if approved in all other respects would be granted for premises having an entertainment licence… throughout the city until 2 a.m…. In addition, it was agreed that a condition should be attached to regular extensions granted in respect of entertainment licences throughout the city… such that patrons would not be permitted to enter or re-enter the licensed premises after 12 midnight.'

Both the time-limit and the entry condition constituted change in policy. A policy document was prepared and was intimated to the petitioners on 19th May, when they were informed that their application would be heard on 7th June.

The background to these changes in policy is of some significance. In August 1992 Strathclyde Police wrote to the respondents, saying that it had been necessary over the past few weeks to draft into the city-centre area additional uniformed personnel to deal with the levels of violence and disorder occurring in the late evening and early morning. Overall statistics were given relating to the period between 11 p.m. and 7 a.m. There had been a dramatic decrease in the number of incidents and apprehensions due to the increased presence of uniformed police; but it was indicated that this could only be a temporary solution and that a more permanent answer would be required. It was observed that because the incidence of violence and disorder was spread out over eight hours, this made it difficult for the police to maintain an effective presence in the area throughout the period. The opinion was expressed that if the permitted hours for entertainment and fast-food premises were to be 'unified within a shorter time scale', the police would be enabled to deploy their personnel to the maximum effect and thereby reduce the level of violence and disorder. Certain options on these lines were suggested for discussion. It was in consequence of this that a joint working party was set up in October 1992 to consider the problems associated with the late licensing of premises, particularly in the city-centre area. The working party considered matters and in February 1993 a report to the working party by the respondents' clerk led to an agreement by the working party that regular extensions of permitted hours until 2 a.m. were likely to be the most appropriate in all the circumstances and could be recommended for acceptance by the respondents. It was also agreed that a condition would be attached to regular extensions granted for entertainment licences, such that patrons would not be permitted to enter or re-enter the premises after twelve midnight. In April a consultation statement was issued on behalf of the joint working party containing these proposals and various responses were received. It was against this background that the changes of policy were adopted in May.

The restriction on time and the 'curfew' condition which the respondents imposed in granting the petitioners' application can thus be seen to constitute a direct application of the new policies. In their statement of reasons the respondents set out certain matters to which they had regard in reaching their decision and go on to say that the board decided that, in the particular circumstances of this application, 'there was no reason to depart from its revised policy'. They accordingly agreed to grant extended hours 'in terms of the revised policy' from 11 p.m. to 2 a.m., Monday to Sunday. Additionally it is stated that the board agreed 'in accordance with the revised policy' to apply what has been called the curfew condition.

In contending that the respondents had acted ultra vires and had erred in law counsel for the petitioners advanced a number of separate submissions. First, it was submitted that the respondents had not been entitled to adopt the new policy. It was accepted that a licensing board were entitled to have general policies. But these must be policies which conformed to their own function and were consistent with the statutory scheme for handling applications and objections. Moreover, the policies must have a sound factual basis, if they were to be regarded as rational. It was submitted that the respondents' new policy document did not meet these requirements. The time-limit and curfew condition were not being imposed in fulfilment of the board's function: they were an attempt to make use of the board's powers for what were essentially police purposes, because the police had a manpower problem in fulfilling their general responsibility for public order. It was acknowledged that if disorder on the streets could be identified as having been caused by the way in which the licensed premises were operated, or if it could be related to specific premises, the board could use their powers in particular cases for the purpose of reducing or eliminating such disorder. That being so, they could have general policies as a basis for such ad hoc action. But that was not the nature of the policies here in question. The violence and disorder which had been identified by the police related to a long, eight-hour period and were not connected either to the operation of premises such as the petitioners' or to patrons of such premises. They were wholly unrelated to the particular premises or their patrons. The police simply wanted to have far fewer people on the streets in the early hours of the morning, because they lacked the manpower to cope with such numbers of people and the violence and disorder which might be incidental to such numbers. Because they could not cope themselves, they had effectively instigated a purported use of the board's licensing powers as a means of clearing the streets. In any event, it was submitted that the policy was inconsistent with the statutory framework for objections. In terms of the Act, the chief constable had the right to object in relation to an application such as the petitioners'. If he did object, the statute required that he should make his objection in a given way, so that the applicants would have notice of the nature of his objection. The policy effectively accepted the chief constable's view that the time restriction and curfew condition should be imposed and, by doing so, freed him of the need to lodge objections in particular cases and deprived applicants of the opportunity to respond to, and rebut, any specific objection by the chief constable. The statutory scheme was being bypassed. It was to be noted that the chief constable had not in fact objected to the application made by the petitioners. Finally, in relation to the policy itself, it was submitted that it had no proper factual basis. It was not apparent that the time restriction and curfew condition had any proper factual basis. In relation to the validity of the respondents' policy counsel for the petitioners referred to *Sagnata Investments Ltd* v *Norwich Corporation*; *Elder* v *Ross and Cromarty Licensing Board*; and *Freeland* v *City of Glasgow District Licensing Board*.

Secondly, it was submitted that even if the policy itself could be seen as a valid one, the respondents had not been entitled to apply it in the present case as they did. They had not applied it merely as a general policy, in relation to which there would be exceptions justified by particular circumstances. They had treated it as a common or universal policy, to which there would be no exceptions. They had thus effectively treated it as fettering their exercise of discretion in individual cases. Reference was made to *Holt* v *Watson*. Since the purpose of the policy was to produce a universal close-down of entertainment premises at one selected time, any departure from it might be seen as destructive of it. While I think this line of attack might be seen as an attack on the adoption of the policy rather than its application, the argument remains that the board, in considering the particular application, had effectively fettered their use of discretion in advance.

Thirdly, it was submitted that the respondents had acted unfairly, and thus ultra vires, in dealing with the application as they did. In giving notice to the petitioners of the new policies, what had been said on behalf of the respondents was that if the board were satisfied in respect of all other relevant matters,

> 'then thereafter it will have regard to the attached policy statement in the course of considering what extended hours are to be granted and whether the relevant condition should be imposed'.

It had also been expressly stated that the board

> 'of course will in the case of all applications for the regular extension of permitted hours have regard to the individual merits of each application and submissions made in support thereof before reaching their final decision'.

The petitioners had appreciated that the new policy would be a factor in the respondents' consideration of matters. But the respondents had in fact treated the policy not merely as a factor. They had effectively treated the policy as a presumption against granting applications free of the time restriction or curfew condition, and imposed an onus on applicants (which it would be extremely difficult to discharge) of satisfying the respondents that an exception to the policy could be justified in the particular case, notwithstanding its universal nature. As a matter of notice and procedural fairness, what had been said about the policy misdescribed the weight which it would have in the board's mind when dealing with applications such as this. Reference was made to *Lakin* v *Secretary of State for Scotland*. There was procedural unfairness, rendering the decision unsound.

Fourthly, it was submitted that the respondents' statement of reasons was insufficient: it gave no clear indication of the basis upon which the respondents had decided to impose the time restriction and curfew condition. The final passage in the statement of reasons (to which I have already referred) portrayed the decision as simply an application of policy, there having been no reason to depart from it. But if one looked at the list of matters to which the respondents expressly said they had had regard, it was impossible to disover what the true basis of their decision had been. That list began with a simple reference to the board's discretion in terms of section 64(3) of the Act and a reference to the revision of their policy (with an apparent assertion that the revision of the policy had proceeded upon some of the matters subsequently referred to as the basis of the present decision). The list then referred to the fact that the policy had been intimated to applicants and went on to mention the submissions which had been made to the board, with a general reference to the shorthand notes of the submissions. And, finally, the list referred to the fact that the 1976 Act imposed a duty on the board to assess a number of factors, particular reference being made to section 64(8) of that Act. Reference was also made to the requirements of section 47(1)(*b*) of the Law Reform (Miscellaneous Provisions) (Scotland) Act 1990. While the time restriction and curfew condition had been imposed, it was to be noted that the respondents had in fact granted an extension of permitted hours until 2 a.m. It was not at all clear what view if any they had taken in relation to either of the two sections mentioned. Moreover, there was no mention at all of the fundamental considerations to which the board must have regard in terms of section 64(3) of the 1976 Act. It was submitted that without making it clear what their views were on the matters covered by these statutory provisions, the board could not be said to have provided an appropriately clear explanation of the basis of their decision.

Finally, it was submitted that the decision was ultra vires as being unreasonable in relation to the curfew condition. Whatever might be said about time-limits, the curfew condition had no genuine licensing purpose: the purpose of section 64 was to licence the sale of alcohol during whatever period of extended hours might be granted and it was no part of this to control movement on the streets, by forcing patrons who wanted to use premises during permitted hours to opt for one set of premises two hours before they closed and to deprive them thereafter of the choice between those premises and other premises where the permitted hours were still running. A particular example of the effects of the veto upon entry during the last two permitted hours was said to arise in relation to section 58 of the 1976 Act. It was submitted that, where a notice under that section had been given, the effect of the curfew condition was to prevent entry and thus to negate the effect which the statute intended such a notice to have.

It is convenient to deal with the petitioners' submissions in an order different from that in which they were presented. I consider first whether the board have given sufficiently clear reasons for their decision. While I think that the statement of reasons might have been clearer, I am none the less satisfied that it is clear enough. As counsel for the respondents submitted, I think that a fair reading of the statement reveals that the board had had regard to the general statutory requirements when considering and adopting the policy. They plainly accepted that, having regard to these general requirements, it would be legitimate for them to grant extended hours up to 2 a.m., unless there were particular reasons in relation to particular premises for refusing to do so. Moreover, it appears to me to be clear that they saw no reason to refuse extended hours, up to 2 a.m., in terms of section 64(8), provided that the curfew condition was imposed. They were thus not in a position of regarding violence or disorder, as a matter of general policy, as a reason for refusing extended hours. So far as the particular decision is concerned, it appears to me that the board were quite simply considering whether there was any reason in this particular case for departing from the general policy and decided that there was not. They make it clear that they considered the submissions made on behalf of the petitioners and I was informed that these were essentially concerned with the merits of the policy as such and had not contained particular submissions to the effect that these particular premises should be treated as an exception. Upon the hypothesis, at this stage, that the policy itself was a legitimate one, I can see nothing wrong with the board's reasons in this particular case.

I am also satisfied that no procedural unfairness arose as a result of the form of notice which was given. As counsel for the respondents submitted, the petitioners could not be entitled to some specific notice of how much weight the policy would be given in the particular case. The board themselves could not know that in advance. I shall come to the underlying question of whether the policy was such that it would be impossible, or very difficult, for a particular applicant to persuade the board not to apply it to particular premises. But I am satisfied that the notice which was given made it plain that the policy would be of great significance and that, if the present applicants wanted their application to be granted up to 3 a.m. and free of the curfew condition, they would have to find specific and positive reasons for such a departure from policy. One may sympathise with the impossibility or difficulty of this task; but I do not think that as a matter of notice there was any procedural unfairness.

On the basis that the decision is not invalidated by the form of either the prior notice or the subsequent statement of reasons, the most specific attack upon what the board have done may be seen as that based upon section 58 of the Act. However, no very full argument was presented upon that matter and it appears to me, in the absence of full submissions, that the extension of time obtained, for the purpose of that section, by notice under that section, would run from the end of permitted hours, including any extension of permitted hours already granted. In the present case, the section 58 notice was given at a time when the permitted hours had already been extended to 2 a.m. I am not persuaded that there is any inconsistency between the limitations imposed by the curfew condition, affecting the period up to 2 a.m. and any extension thereafter, by virtue of the section 58 notice. From what was said by counsel on either side, I think that this may not be the view which is taken by either party; but neither of them appeared to me to advance a more satisfactory interpretation of the effect of the section.

I come to the fundamental attack upon the policy itself. Counsel for the respondents acknowledged that the board's powers extended only to the regulation of the supply of liquor. But he submitted that, in deciding how to regulate this matter, the board were obliged, on behalf of the community, to have regard not only to the manner of supply, but to such consequences as they thought there might be from any permitted supply, including any adverse consequences in terms of general public order. If they took steps to ameliorate possible adverse consequences of this kind, that remained a part of their licensing function. It was a matter for their judgment whether such adverse consequences could be reduced by trying to ensure that movement into or out of licensed premises would occur at times when the police would be able to deploy their forces more effectively. The fact that the time-limit and curfew conditions had originated as a result of a police initiative, and had been based upon police advice, did not mean that the board were departing from their own proper functions, or misusing their powers to achieve police ends. It was quite accepted that the hour between two and three was not the peak hour or a crisis hour. But the combination of the curfew condition and the 2 a.m. limit to extended hours was judged by the board, when they adopted the new policy, as likely to reduce the adverse consequences of the supply of liquor and this restriction and condition therefore met not merely the wishes of the police, in terms of their public responsibilities, but also the wishes of the board, for their own purposes and in terms of their own responsibility for limiting the adverse consequences of the supply of liquor. Taking the time-limit in isolation, I am satisfied that the approach of counsel for the respondents is sound. As a matter of general policy, I am satisfied that a board are well entitled to decide that one particular time-limit should in general be applied when extended hours are being granted. I do not think that any such general policy is rendered unsound by being based upon a wish for a single common 'closing time' rather than upon some view that things will be worse if a later hour is adopted. As regards the curfew condition, I had initially some misgivings. The general aim of preventing movement between premises after midnight, and the underlying aim of simply reducing the population on the streets between those hours, appeared to me to be very different from the ordinary 'adverse consequences in terms of public order', such as drunken brawls in the immediate vicinity of particular premises. Moreover, I was disposed to see some force in the petitioners' final submission on unreasonableness, emphasising the way in which the curfew condition ruled out access to premises during hours when the supply of liquor was ex hypothesi permitted. But I have come to the view that just as adverse consequences may flow from general rather than particular causes, so also the steps which are required to limit or control these adverse consequences may be general rather than particular. It is not for me to judge whether disorder is more or less likely if everyone who wishes to attend premises of this kind has to get in just before midnight; nor is it for me to balance the advantage of relatively quieter streets thereafter against the restrictions on choice and patrons' reactions to these restrictions. It is for the police, for their purposes, and the board, for their purposes, to assess these matters and, no doubt, to monitor them carefully. And I am satisfied that in adopting this policy the board were indeed attempting to take general steps which in their judgment would help to limit or reduce the incidence of violence or disorder, which could not of course be attributed solely to the supply of liquor or the way in which licensed premises are operated, but which none the less could properly be seen as consequential upon, or exacerbated by, longer permitted hours, or free movement between premises in the early hours of the morning. Some of the consequences of the policy and, in particular, of the curfew conditions may be regrettable, but I am satisfied that its aims and purposes are within the powers of the board. The control of violence is not merely a police responsibility. It is the responsibility of any body which has power to regulate situations which give rise to violence.

I am also satisfied that in adopting the new policy the board had a proper basis in fact and advice for doing so. These are matters for judgment and I am not persuaded that the policy required any more precise basis than it had. The remaining criticism of the policy itself has given me more anxiety. The statutory provisions, whereby the chief constable can object and notice is received of his objections, are explicit and plainly important. For the chief constable to have his wishes on a particular matter included in a general policy and thereafter to abstain from making particular objections might, at least at first sight, be seen as a device for depriving an applicant of a proper explanation for the objection, open to direct scrutiny and a direct response. On the other hand, where the chief constable's 'objection' relates not to particular premises, but to the general length of permitted hours and the freedom of movement within them, I am satisfied that he is entitled to bring this to the board's notice at the level of policy and that they are entitled to adopt his view as their own and incorporate it in their policy. In the present case, the advice was recent and the board would be well entitled, in the absence of any indication from the police that they have changed their view, to maintain the policy which was derived from that advice. As counsel for the respondents submitted, where a board have taken advice before formulating a policy, it cannot be necessary for those who gave the advice to object to every application individually merely to support the policy and oppose applications in conflict with it. Treating the policy as one which the board have adopted for their own purposes, and not merely in support of police purposes, I am satisfied that the policy is not in substitution for, or in conflict with, the statutory mechanisms of objection. I am satisfied that, in adopting the new policy, the board were not acting ultra vires or unreasonably. The policy is a valid one.

It is trite that an authority vested with a discretion must not merely apply a general policy in all cases, without considering whether it is right in particular cases to do so. Have the board in the present case fettered their discretion in this way, by acting as if they were committed in advance to imposing the time-limit and curfew condition contained in the policy? Counsel for the respondents rejected the suggestion that the restriction and condition had been universally applied and cited two applications where they had not been applied. Neither of these appeared to me to be what one might call an ordinary disco and I think they were not so much exceptions as an indication that the policy has been refined, with the category of premises to which the policy will be applied being more precisely defined. Such a refinement had been suggested when the policy was agreed. Even so, and assuming that the policy had been universally applied to the category in question, I am not persuaded that the board applied the policy in such a way as to eliminate the proper exercise of their discretion. The problem is, I think, that the policy itself is designed to make this restriction and condition universal in their application. It is difficult to imagine what circumstances would be seen as justifying an exception, since even a few, or perhaps one, departure might be seen as destroying the policy itself. None the less, I see no grounds for holding that the board shut their mind to the possibility of an exception; and whether the matter is considered in relation to the terms of the policy, or its application, I am satisfied that they acted intra vires. Parties were agreed that I could dispose of the petition either way at this stage. I shall sustain the respondents' plea to relevancy and dismiss the petition."

Notes

(1) This case is a useful illustration of the current attitude of the courts to the question of formulation of policies by licensing authorities. On this generally see J.C. Cummins, *Licensing Law In Scotland* (1993), pp. 296–299 and C. Agnew, Q.C. and H.M. Baillie, *The Licensing (Scotland) Act 1976* (4th ed., 1996), pp. 117–120 and in the context of civic government licensing see A. Hajducki, Q.C. and S. Stuart, *Scottish Civic Government Licensing Law* (1994), pp. 76–78.

7–7

(2) Note the reference to the use of the reasonableness of the policy being a basis of challenge and the concern as to whether or not the policy was promoting an improper purpose, namely a general policing power. This amply demonstrates what was noted in the introduction to this section, that the other grounds of judicial review may be relevant to challenge of a policy. Equally, one may have to show that in acting in accordance with a policy one has acted fairly by giving prior notice of the policy and having indicated that representations to changes of policy would be considered. This is an aspect of the duty to act fairly, on which see *City of Glasgow District Council v. Doyle*, 1993 S.L.T. 604, extracted at para. 8–29.

(3) Failure to follow a policy without good reason may also give rise to successful challenge on the basis of inconsistency or irrationality, on which see *Cashley v. City of Dundee District Council*, 1994 S.C.L.R. 6, extracted at para. 6–55. See also *R. v. Director of Public Prosecutions, exparte Chaudhary* (1995) 159 J.P. 227 (failure of Crown Prosecution Service to follow its code for prosecutors); *Morbaine Ltd v. Secretary of State for the Environment and South Northampton District Council* (1994) 68 P. & C.R. 525 (facts pointing to one decision following on an announced policy with a different decision reached, the court was willing to infer irrationality); and *Texaco Ltd v. West Fife Divisional Licensing Board*, 1998 S.C. 470 (reference to application of policy in statement of reasons given by licensing board when policy in fact not applied to the application when heard, irrational).

(4) Note the court's apparent concern that the policy may have been general in effect rather than particular in its application and in particular the passage at 599G–600A where it stated that it was difficult to conceive circumstances in which the policy would not be applied.

Do you think that this suggests a concern that if one exception to the policy is made, then the basis of the policy is destroyed? Does that not suggest that the policy was in fact a relatively rigid one? The court obviously took the view that in the absence of any clear statement from the licensing authority that the policy would always be applied, regardless of the merits of an application, the appeal must fail. Do you consider that reliance on the establishing of such a statement is overly formalistic? Compare the circumstances here with those found in *R. v. Port of London Authority, ex parte Kynoch Ltd* [1919] 1 K.B. 176, extracted at para. 7–8.

(5) It has been suggested that in the absence of a clear intent to fetter discretion, one would require to aver bad faith to found a challenge. On this see Cummins, pp. 184–185. Do you agree? Would such an averment have been likely to meet with any more success?

(6) In *Holt v. Watson*, 1983 S.L.T. 588 referred to in the extract, the applicant for a taxicab operator's taxi licence was advised that applicants were required to state to the committee that they would have no other employment outwith running a taxi. The applicant signed such an assurance but in any event continued to operate other business interests. His licence was revoked "on the grounds that he failed to comply with the assurance given by him to the committee". In giving the judgment of the court the Lord Justice-Clerk (Wheatley) noted that while the licensing committee might consider a policy which would (at 591):

"involve a restriction in other forms of employment or other interests but there would require to be a relationship between the two… Inherent in this concept would be the right on the part of the applicant to demonstrate that these other interests would not in any way affect the proper operation of the taxicab operator's licence. Then the exercise of the committee's discretion would come into play. Here the total exclusion of other employment, and in due course other business interests, of any nature whatsoever, irrespective of the circumstances and without any right to the applicant to make representations… clearly represents an unreasonable condition and constitutes a policy which does not square with the purposes of the Act. In its rigid application it left no scope for the exercise of discretion."

Successful challenge to the application of a policy came in the next extract.

R v. Port of London Authority, ex parte Kynoch Ltd

[1919] 1 K.B. 176

7–8   Kynoch Ltd owned land at Canvey Island on the north bank of the Thames. They applied to the port of London authority for a licence to construct a deep-water wharf and other works. In November 1917 the authority rejected the application "on the ground that the accommodation applied for is of the character of that which Parliament has charged the Authority with the duty of providing in the port". Kynoch applied for a licence under the Port of London Act 1908, s. 7, and the Thames Conservancy Act 1894, s. 109. Under the 1908 Act, the authority was under a duty "to take into consideration the state of the river and the accommodation and facilities afforded in the Port of London, and, subject to the provisions of this Act to take such steps as they may consider necessary for the improvement thereof." Under section 2(2) they had power to "construct, equip, maintain, or manage any docks, quays, wharves . . . and other works in connexion there with". In April 1918 Kynoch gave notice of an appeal to the Board of Trade under the 1918 Act but in September of that year they withdrew the appeal and applied instead to the court to compel the authority to exercise its discretion according to law. An affidavit from the Secretary to the authority made it clear that the merits of the application had been fully considered by two committees and the authority itself. At first instance Kynoch lost but they appealed to the Court of Appeal.

BANKES L.J.: "The main ground [upon which the appellants sought mandamus] was that the Port authority had not heard and determined the application of June 8, 1917, for permission to carry out works of a very important character with a very extensive frontage to the river…

Every case must depend on its own particular circumstances; but decided cases furnish some rules which ought to govern the court in the exercise of its discretion to grant or refuse the prerogative writ of mandamus. There must be something in the nature of a refusal to exercise jurisdiction by the tribunal or authority to whom the writ is to be directed. A refusal may be conveyed in one of two ways: there may be an absolute refusal in terms, or there may be conduct amounting to a refusal. In the latter case it is often difficult to draw the line between those cases where the tribunal or authority has heard and determined erroneously upon grounds which it was entitled to take into consideration and those cases where it has heard and determined upon grounds outside and beyond its jurisdiction; but this conclusion may be drawn from decided cases, that there is no refusal to hear and determine unless the tribunal or authority has in substance shut its ears to the application which was made to it, and has determined upon an application which was not made to it. On this point I would refer to the words of Farwell L.J. in *R. v. Board of Education* [1910] 2 K.B. 165, 179: 'If the tribunal has exercised the discretion entrusted to it *bona fide*, not influenced by extraneous or irrelevant considerations, and not arbitrarily or illegally, the courts cannot interfere; they are not a Court of Appeal from the tribunal, but they have power to prevent the intentional usurpation or mistaken assumption of a jurisdiction beyond that given to the tribunal by law, and also the refusal of their true jurisdiction by the adoption of extraneous considerations in arriving at their conclusion or deciding a point other than that brought before them, in which cases the courts have regarded them as declining jurisdiction.' Again, in *R. v. Bowman* [1898] 1 Q.B. 663, 667, where licensing justices had allowed their decision to be influenced by extraneous considerations, Wills J. said: 'There has been no real hearing, and the mandamus must therefore go.' Those two cases furnish a rough test for deciding when a tribunal, in considering matters outside its jurisdiction, has refused to exercise its true and proper jurisdiction.

In the present case there is another matter to be borne in mind. There are on the one hand cases where a tribunal in the honest exercise of its discretion has adopted a policy, and, without refusing to hear an applicant, intimates to him what its policy is, and that after hearing him it will in accordance with its policy decide against him, unless there is something exceptional in his case. I think counsel for the applicants would admit that, if the policy has been adopted for reasons which the tribunal may legitimately entertain, no objection could be taken to such a course. On the other hand there are cases where a tribunal has passed a rule, or come to a determination, not to hear any application of a particular character by whomsoever made. There is a wide distinction to be drawn between these two classes . . . [His Lordship referred to *R. v. Sylvester* (1862) 31 L.J.M.C. 93, and *R. v. L.C.C., ex p. Corrie* [1918] 1 K.B. 68.]

Now to apply these principles to the facts of this case. There is the letter of November 2 written on behalf of the Port authority by their secretary . . . and there is his affidavit. It negatives the suggestion that the only matter considered by the Port authority was that specified in the letter. We must decide this case upon the affidavit. Read carefully and fairly it amounts to a statement that the Port authority did nothing which could be properly described as a refusal to hear and determine. But I go a step further. Even assuming that the letter contains the only ground on which the application was refused, I think, considering the position of the Port authority, that the matters involved in that decision were rightly and properly considered by them, and warrant the adoption of a general policy in granting licences for works of this particular class. Therefore on the main point the rule must be discharged…"

WARRINGTON L.J. agreed.

SCRUTTON L.J. delivered a concurring judgment.

Notes

(1) The case was followed in *R. v. Canterbury City Council, ex p. Gillespie* (1987) 19 H.L.R. 7 (over-rigid application of statutorily required general policy as to allocation of council accommodation); *Sopwith v. Cruickshank*, 1959 S.L.T. (Notes) 50 (policy of automatic sentence of 12-month driving ban on conviction of use of vehicle with defective steering gear unlawful); and *Merchandise Transport Ltd v. British Transport Commission* [1961] 3 All E.R. 495 (transport tribunal not bound to follow precedents in issuing public carriage licences). In *Stringer v. Minister of Housing and Local Government* [1970] 1 W.L.R. 1281 the issue of the policy of the Minister to discourage development which had interfered with the Jodrell Bank radio telescope came to be considered. It was held that the Minister was entitled to rely on this policy in refusing an application for planning permission, Cooke J. noted (at 1298):

> "It seems to me that the general effect of the many relevant authorities is that a Minister charged with the duty of making individual administrative decisions in a fair and impartial manner may nevertheless have a general policy in regard to matters which are relevant to those decisions, provided that the existence of that general policy does not preclude him from fairly judging all the issues which are relevant to each individual case as it comes up for decision.
>
> I think that in this case the Minister was entitled to have a policy in regard to Jodrell Bank, and I think that his policy is not such as to preclude him from fairly considering a planning appeal on its merits. I do not think that it precluded him from fairly considering Mr. Stringer's appeal. I do not think that the Minister has prejudged the case, or tied his own hands, or abdicated any of his functions."

(2) Where an appeal lies to a Minister against a decision, then a Minister may take account of decisions on earlier appeals but cannot use those decisions as a way of creating a policy to be followed without having sufficient regard to the scheme under which the appeal is made: *Alexander & Sons Ltd v. Minister of Transport*, 1936 S.L.T. 553.

(3) Contrast the statement of how the policy was to operate with that found in *Cinderella's Rockafella's*. What distinguishes the policy in *Kynoch*? Consider the application of *Kynoch* in the next case.

7–9

British Oxygen Co. Ltd v. Minister of Technology

[1971] A.C. 610

7–10   Section 1(1) of the Industrial Development Act 1966 provides that the Board of Trade "may make to any person carrying on a business in Great Britain a grant towards approved capital expenditure incurred by that person in providing new machinery or plant". The board adopted a policy of denying grants for any item or plant costing less than £25 and, further to that policy, rejected an application for a grant in respect of gas cylinders costing just under £20 each. In proceedings for a declaration the court was asked, *inter alia*, to determine the extent of the board's discretion.

Lord Reid: "[I]t is necessary to consider what is the duty of the respondent in administering the Act and what rights, if any, the Act confers on those eligible for grants.

Section 1 of the Act provides that the Board of Trade 'may' make grants… But how were the Board intended to operate that discretion? Does the Act read as a whole indicate any policy which the Board is to follow or even give any guidance to the Board? If it does then the Board must exercise its discretion in accordance with such policy or guidance (*Padfield v. Minister of Agriculture, Fisheries and Food* [below, p. 303]). One generally expects to find that Parliament has given some indication as to how public money is to be distributed. In this Act Parliament has clearly laid down the conditions for eligibility for grants and it has clearly given to the Board a discretion so that the Board is not bound to pay to every person who is eligible to receive a grant. But I can find nothing to guide the Board as to the circumstances in which they should pay or the circumstances in which they should not pay grants to such persons.

[His Lordship referred to the long title, section 1(6) and sections 2 to 8 of the 1966 Act.]

Sections 11 and 12 are perhaps more relevant. Section 11 provides for the appointment of committees to advise the Board on the administration of the Act and it could be taken as an indication that otherwise the Board's discretion is unlimited. Section 12 provides for an annual report to Parliament so that Parliament can *ex post facto* consider the way in which this discretion has been exercised…

I cannot find that these provisions give any right to any person to get a grant. It was argued that the object of the Act is to promote the modernisation of machinery and plant and that the Board were bound to pay grants to all who are eligible unless, in their view, particular eligible expenditure would not promote that object. That might be good advice for an advisory committee to give but I find nothing in the Act to require the Board to act in that way. If the Minister who now administers the Act, acting on behalf of the Government, should decide not to give grants in respect of certain kinds of expenditure, I can find nothing to prevent him… [I]f the Minister thinks that policy or good administration requires the operation of some limiting rule, I find nothing to stop him.

[His Lordship cited *R. v. Port of London Authority, ex p. Kynoch*, in particular the passage from the judgment of Bankes L.J. beginning — 'There are on the one hand… ', and ending — 'between these two classes'.]

I see nothing wrong with that. But the circumstances in which discretions are exercised vary enormously and that passage cannot be applied literally in every case. The general rule is that anyone who has to exercise a statutory discretion must not 'shut his ears to an application' (to adapt from Bankes L.J.). I do not think there is any great difference between a policy and a rule. There may be cases where an officer or authority ought to listen to a substantial argument reasonably presented urging a change of policy. What the authority must not do is to refuse to listen at all. But a Ministry or large authority may have had to deal already with a multitude of similar applications and then they will almost certainly have evolved a policy so precise that it could well be called a rule. There can be no objection to that, provided the authority is always willing to listen to anyone with something new to say — of course I do not mean to say that there need be an oral hearing. In the present case the respondent's officers have carefully considered all that the appellants have had to say and I have no doubt that they will continue to do so…"

Viscount Dilhorne: "[His Lordship read the passage from *ex p. Kynoch* quoted by Lord Reid above.]

Bankes L.J. clearly meant that in the latter case there is a refusal to exercise the discretion entrusted to the authority or tribunal but the distinction between a policy decision and a rule may not be easy to draw. In this case it was not challenged that it was within the power of the Board to adopt a policy not to make a grant in respect of such an item. That policy might equally well be described as a rule. It was both reasonable and right that the Board should make known to those interested the policy it was going to follow. By doing so fruitless applications involving expense and expenditure of time might be avoided.

The Board says that it has not refused to consider any application. It considered the appellants'. In these circumstances it is not necessary to decide in this case whether, if it had refused to consider an application on the ground that it related to an item costing less than £25, it would have acted wrongly.

I must confess that I feel some doubt whether the words used by Bankes L.J. in the passage cited above are really applicable to a case of this kind. It seems somewhat pointless and a waste of time that the Board should have to consider applications which are bound as a result of its policy decision to fail. Representations could of course be made that the policy should be changed.

I cannot see any ground on which it could be said that it was *ultra vires* of the Board to decide not to make grants on items costing less that £25 . . . In my opinion, this appeal should be dismissed."

LORD MORRIS OF BORTH-Y-GEST, LORD WILBERFORCE and LORD DIPLOCK concurred with LORD REID.

Notes

(1) The underlying approach in this case seems to be to allow a policy to be treated effectively   **7–11** as a rule allowing an applicant the right to seek change of the policy. Is this logical? Contrast with the decision in *Kilmarnock Magistrates*. The approach was arguably justified because of the complex administrative issues involved and the processing of a large number of applications. Were those considerations present in *Cinderella's Rockafella's?* The approach in *British Oxygen* has particular significance in the context of decisions relating to the allocation of resources. One only has to think of policies operating in the fields of social security or housing. There is at least some authority, albeit from the sheriff court, that seems to suggest that complexity of subject matter should not of itself allow greater scope for an authority to adopt a relatively inflexible policy. In *Aitken v. City of Glasgow District Council*, 1988 S.C.L.R. 287 the sheriff (Mowat) had to consider an appeal against refusal of a taxi licence. The appellant contended that the council had failed to exercise its discretion and had therefore acted unreasonably in adhering to the application of a policy requiring a maximum number of permitted licences. The licence in question, if granted, would have exceeded that number. In construing section 10(3) of the Civic Government (Scotland) Act 1982 the sheriff observed (at 293):

> " '(3) Without prejudice to paragraph 5 of Schedule 1 to this Act the grant of a taxi licence may be refused by a licensing authority for the purpose of limiting the number of taxis in respect of which licences are granted by them if, but only if, they are satisfied that there is no significant demand for the services of taxis in their area which is unmet.'
>
> This seems to me to indicate that if an optimum number had been decided upon in advance it can only be a guideline and the authority must satisfy itself at the time of considering the application whether it is still applicable as being sufficient to meet the demand.
>
> Such a view of the right of a licensing authority to decide on an optimum figure in advance seems to be in line with the passages from De Smith referred to by Mr Kelly and the cases cited therein. At p. 285 De Smith says:
>
> 'The authority in which a discretion is vested can be compelled to exercise that discretion, but not to exercise it in any particular manner. In general, a discretion must be exercised only by the authority to which it is committed. That authority must genuinely address itself to the matter before it: it must not act under the dictation of another body or disable itself from exercising its discretion in each individual case.'
>
> I recognise that this passage is directed at the situation where a body allows outside forces to fetter its discretion and not at the voluntary fettering of its discretion by its own previous decision, but the principle that each case must have the discretion exercised in deciding it may be relevant. Again at p. 311, De Smith says:
>
> 'A tribunal trusted with a discretion must not, by the adoption of a fixed rule of policy, disable itself from exercising its discretion in individual cases... . A body to which discretion has been entrusted may also, of course, have been expressly authorised to make regulations that in some way affect its exercise of discretion. To the extent that it has exercised its statutory rule-making power it must decide individual cases by reference to any relevant provision in its regulations, rather than by applying the terms of the empowering Act. But otherwise discretion may not generally be validly exercised by a public body solely on the basis of some policy or rule that it had informally previously adopted.' "

Kynoch was cited in argument. This approach implicitly accepts that an authority is obliged to consider whether or not a policy should be adopted at all and thereafter to give careful consideration as to the weight to be given to it: see also *Douglas v. City of Glasgow District Council*, 1996 S.L.T. 713. Moreover, it would appear that there is a continuing duty on a licensing authority to consider whether its policy requires to be updated, on which see *Coyle v. City of Glasgow Council*, 1998 S.L.T. 453 (policy decision as to number of taxi licences necessary to meet demand made in 1991, when application for a new taxi operator's licence was made in 1996).

One of the underlying considerations in the reviewing or appellate court accepting a challenge to the application of a policy, is that it may involve a court becoming involved in assessing the factual basis and therefore, implicitly, the rationale for such a policy having been adopted in the first place. This touches on issues of jurisdictional control noted in Chapter 4. The next extract is illuminating.

Sagnata Investments Ltd v. Norwich Corporation

[1971] 2. Q.B. 614

7–12   "The Betting, Gaming and Lotteries Act 1963, Sched. 6, para. 2 provided that the grant of a permit for amusements with prizes should be 'at the discretion of the local authority'. Schedule 6, para. 6, provided that where a local authority refused an application for a permit, the applicant could 'appeal in accordance with the provisions of the Quarter Sessions Act 1849' to quarter sessions. Section 1 of the 1849 Act provided that 'In every case of appeal... to any court of quarter sessions 14 clear days' notice of appeal... shall be given... and such notice of appeal shall be in writing,... and the grounds of appeal shall be specified in every such notice: Provided always, that it shall not be lawful for the appellant or appellants, on the trial of any such appeal, to go into or give evidence of any other ground of appeal besides those set forth in such notice.'

In March 1969, Sagnata Investments Ltd applied under the Act of 1963 for a permit for amusements with prizes at an amusement arcade to be built at a site known as Old Post Office Court in Norwich. That application was in due course refused by the Fire Service and Licensing Committee of Norwich Corporation, and their written grounds of refusal were in the following terms:

> '(a) The use of these premises as an amusement place would be likely to have undesirable social effects on the young people expected to frequent them; (b) the making available of gaming facilities in Norwich which could be used by children was something which the committee are not prepared to permit; (c) the number of amusements with prizes machines legally available elsewhere in Norwich for the use of adults was sufficient to meet all reasonable needs.'

The unsuccessful applicants appealed from that refusal to Norwich City Quarter Sessions, their stated ground of appeal being, 'that the decision... was unreasonable, having regard to the information available to the committee and contrary to natural justice'.

The recorder, Michael Havers Q.C., found the following facts to be either proved or admitted: that no objection was made to the company, the premises or the site, the last named being particularly suitable; that the council as a whole had by an overwhelming majority of 41 to 1 taken a general policy decision not to grant permits for amusements with prizes for any such amusement places in Norwich and that decision had been applied to the application by the committee; that whilst it was likely that a certain number of children and young people would use the amusement arcade there was no evidence either way as to whether or not they would do so to a considerable extent and/or whether or not such a use would be socially undesirable. In that respect evidence was called before the recorder in the form of the committee chairman — a Norwich city councillor since 1934 and a former Lord Mayor who expressed his fears in that matter. Whilst accepting his evidence, the recorder did not find that it amounted to anything more than the expression of a realistic and honest opinion; that the committee's decision was reached fairly and honestly with a genuine belief in the socially harmful result of setting up such an amusement arcade; that there were not sufficient facilities of that nature in Norwich at the present time.

The recorder was of the opinion that the committee had so fettered its discretion by following the policy decisions of the council that no application for such a permit could succeed before it and the committee had therefore failed to exercise its discretion at all; that it was for the corporation to prove that the provision of an amusement arcade would be socially undesirable; that having regard to the exclusion of amusement places from section 3 of the Betting, Gaming and Lotteries Act 1964 neither the committee nor quarter sessions were entitled to take into consideration the fact that by reason of the purpose for which or the persons by whom the premises were to be used ti was undesirable that such a permit be granted; that the *obiter dictum* of Lord Parker C.J. in *R. v. Essex Quarter Sessions, ex p. Thomas* [1966] 1 W.L.R. 359, 362, that:

> 'Speaking for myself, I would hesitate, and I would expect any chairman of quarter sessions to hesitate, long before differing from the local justices who had dealt with the matter in their locality with the greatest care,'

had no bearing on such an appeal as the recorder was hearing. In the result the recorder felt he had no alternative but to allow the appeal.

The Corporation appealed unsuccessfully to the Divisional Court, and then to the Court of Appeal. The grounds of appeal were that the recorder (1) misdirected himself that his appellate discretion was absolute and unfettered, with the result that he substituted his own discretion for that of the Fire Service and Licensing Committee notwithstanding the fact that the committee were not shown to have erred in fact or law; (2) misdirected himself in holding as a matter of law and/or fact that the committee had fettered its own discretion by implementing a general policy decision of the whole council; (3) misdirected himself in holding that the views of the councillors who sat on the committee were irrelevant and/or of no evidential value to him as appellate tribunal in deciding the issue as to the desirability and need for the provision of such an amusement arcade; (4) failed to take into consideration the evidence of the chairman of the committee; (5) erred in fact and in law in holding that there was no sufficient evidence before him to establish that the provision of such facilities in the locality was socially undesirable or harmful; (6) failed to deal adequately or at all with the third and final ground on which the committee based its refusal, namely, that such new facilities were not required since there were adequate amusement with prizes machines already available elsewhere in Norwich."

LORD DENNING M.R.: "(dissenting) [His Lordship summarised the facts, the legislative history and the relevant statutory provisions, and continued:]
4. The Hearing by the Local Authority
On May 2, 1969, the licensing committee of the City of Norwich heard the application. The applicants were represented by a solicitor, who put their case fully. The committee asked pertinent questions which the solicitor answered. At the end of the committee thanked him for presenting a clear case and he, in his turn, thanked the committee for listening to him. We were given a note of the proceedings before the committee. I append it herewith (*post*, p. 628G). It shows that the committee acted with the utmost fairness and discretion. They explored questions of policy and of detail, and, at the end, reserved their decision...
5. The Appeal to the Recorder
[His Lordship summarised the reasons of the recorder in allowing the appeal, and pointed out that no evidence was given in support of the stated ground of appeal.] The recorder was not even told of the 'information available to the committee'. And I see no possible justification for the assertion that the decision was 'unreasonable' or 'contrary to natural justice...'.
6. The General Policy Decision
There has been much discussion lately on the right of a licensing body to lay down for itself a general policy to guide its decisions. In the past, recourse has been had to the words of Bankes L.J. in *R. v. Port of London Authority, ex p. Kynoch Ltd* [1919] 1 K.B. 176, 182–186, and to the judgment of Lord Goddard C.J. in *R. v. Torquay Licensing Justices, ex p. Brockman* [1951] 2 K.B. 784, 788–792; but these cases have now to be read in the light of the decisions of Cooke J. in *Stringer v. Minister of Housing and Local Government* [1970] 1 W.L.R. 1281, 1297–1298 and of the House of Lords in *British Oxygen Co. Ltd v. Board of Trade* [1971] A.C. 610, and of this court in *Cumings v. Birkenhead Corporation* [1971] 2 W.L.R. 1458. I take it to be perfectly clear now that an administrative body, including a licensing body, which may have to consider numerous applications of a similar kind, is entitled to lay down a general policy which it proposes to follow in coming to its individual decisions, provided always that it is a reasonable policy which it is fair and just to apply. Once laid down, the administrative body is entitled to apply the policy in the individual cases which come before it. The only qualification is that the administrative body must not apply the policy so rigidly as to reject an applicant without hearing what he has to say. It must not 'shut its ears to an application': see [1971] A.C. 610, 625, *per* Lord Reid. The applicant is entitled to put forward reasons urging that the policy should be changed, or saying that in any case it should not be applied to him. But, so long as the administrative body is ready to hear him and consider what he has to say, it is entitled to apply its general policy to him as to others.

The local authority at Norwich fulfilled every one of these requirements. If you read the note of the proceedings before the committee, it is apparent that, although the city council laid down a general policy, the licensing committee did not regard that policy as inflexible or as binding on them: that they listened to everything that the applicants had to say: and yet decided against them.

The recorder seems to have thought that the local authority were not entitled to have a general policy at all: or, at any rate, not to be able to apply it in any individual case. He said:

> 'I have sympathy with the committee who feel that the well-being and protection of the young people of this city is part of their general responsibility, and I am absolutely certain that they have acted fairly, honestly and fearlessly in forming their policy. It may be that their policy is right, but unless and until Parliament provides for a local authority in this type of application the right to make the kind of policy rule that does exist in respect of other premises, each application must be treated on its merits...'

I think that, in these words, the recorder misdirected himself in law. By his very words, he acknowledges that the policy was fairly and honestly formed and was a reasonable policy. If so, the local authority were entitled to have the policy and to apply it in this individual case, provided that they listened to all the applicant had to say — which they most clearly did.

7. Evidence de Novo

The recorder said:

> '... this being an appeal to quarter sessions, I must consider the matter de novo... I must now approach the matter afresh with a complete and unfettered discretion. What is the evidence? As I have said, no objection is taken to the applicant, the premises or the site. The objection for which I have some sympathy is really the risk of providing easily accessible gambling facilities to children and young persons. On the facts there seems to be very little evidence of this;... I would require some evidence not only that such a place would be used to a considerable extent by young people, but also that such a use would be socially undesirable.'

Those were the grounds of the recorder's judgment.

Mr Boreham Q.C. [counsel for the company] supported this view. He submitted that the recorder ought to hear the evidence afresh, and exercise his own discretion, quite uninfluenced by what the local authority had done. He relied on *Godfrey v. Bournemouth Corporation* [1969] 1 W.L.R. 47, 52. I do not think this is correct. It is plain from the Act of 1849 that the recorder must hear evidence on all matters raised by the notice of appeal: and is not to travel outside on to other matters, because that might prejudice the respondent. It is also plain that the recorder ought to give great weight to the decision of the local authority. Lord Parker C.J. said so in *R. v. Essex Quarter Sessions, ex p. Thomas* [1966] 1 W.L.R. 359, 361–362, and repeated it in this very case.

In this case the local authority formed the opinion that it was socially undesirable to have amusement arcades in Norwich. That is why they laid down their general policy. But the recorder put their views on one side. He was not prepared, he said, to act on 'unproved general principles of social undesirability and potential danger to young people', but wanted evidence on it.

I think that, in so holding, the recorder misdirected himself in law. Seeing that Parliament has entrusted the discretion to the local authority, it must intend then that their views should carry great weight. They are elected by the people to do all things proper to be done for the good administration of their city. They know their locality. They know its needs. They respond to the feelings of the citizens. If they think that an amusement arcade is socially undesirable, they are entitled to say so. They do not require evidence for the purpose. It is a matter of opinion on which their views are worth as much as those of any other person: and, indeed, worth more than those of a stranger. In any case, their views coincide with those of the Churches' Committee on Gambling: and that goes a long way. Their views should not be pushed on one side by the courts as worth nothing. Just as with their power to make by-laws, so also with their power to grant licences for amusement arcades. Their decision 'ought to be supported if possible': see *Kruse v. Johnson* [1898] 2 Q.B. 91, 99, *per* Lord Russell C.J. In rejecting their views, the recorder was in error.

8. Conclusion

In my opinion the recorder erred in law in the two respects which I have stated. I would therefore allow the appeal and uphold the decision of the local authority.

My brethren disagree. Together with the recorder, and all the other judges, they hold that the views of the citizens of Norwich must be overruled. They must grant the freedom of their city to this amusement arcade, even though they believe it to be socially undesirable. I do not think this is right. This, in my opinion, is a matter for local self-government. Parliament intentionally made this a matter for the discretion of the local authority and there is no good reason for overruling their decision."

EDMUND DAVIES L.J.: "... This litigation is said to raise in an acute form the question as to the nature of appeals to quarter sessions in such cases as the present. At one stage, Lord Denning M.R. summarised the issue in this way:

> 'Is the hearing to be treated as a new trial to be determined on evidence de novo, without being influenced by what the local authority has done? Or is the hearing to be treated as an appeal proper, in which the local authority's decision is to be regarded as of considerable weight, and is not to be reversed unless their decision is shown to be wrong?'

With profound respect, however, I do not think that this is the proper antithesis, and I shall seek to show that there is a half-way house between these two approaches.

It is well established that no right of appeal exists apart from statute. As already observed, the only statutory provision relevant to the present case is that 'the applicant may appeal in accordance with the provisions of the Quarter Sessions Act 1849'. In *Drover v. Rugman* [1951] 1 K.B. 380, dealing with a case stated by quarter sessions on an appeal from the juvenile court, Lord Goddard C.J. said, at 382:

> 'When a case goes to a quarter sessions it is reheard; the person seeking an order proves his case over again. That only means that quarter sessions are taking the place, as it may be expressed, of petty sessions; but the proceedings are none the less an appeal.'

This, he explained, was due to the fact that there was no formal record of proceedings before justices, an observation equally true of proceedings before the licensing committee of this local authority, which (as Lord Denning M.R. has observed) are wholly dissimilar to those conducted by a body exercising judicial functions.

For my part, I cannot see how it is practicable in cases such as the present for an appeal to quarter sessions to be other than by way of a complete rehearing. Having no record before him of what transpired before the local authority, how could the recorder otherwise begin to judge the cogency of the written reasons placed before him?...

As it appears to me, Mr Tapp [counsel for the corporation] has attached excessive weight to the fact that the granting or renewal of a permit under the Act of 1963 is expressed to be 'at the discretion of the local authority' when he concludes therefrom that quarter sessions are bound by the decision of the local authority and its stated reasons unless it can be demonstrated that they were wrong. A similar contention was raised — and rejected — in *Stepney Borough Council v. Joffe* [1949] 1 K.B. 599, where street traders' licences to trade were revoked by the borough council. This they had done pursuant to a statutory provision where 'the applicant or licensee is on account of misconduct or for any other sufficient reason in their opinion unsuitable to hold such licence...'. Section 25(1) of the London County Council (General Powers) Act 1947 provided that persons aggrieved by such refusal 'may appeal to a petty sessional court and on any such appeal the court may confirm, reverse or vary the decision of the borough council...'. The traders accordingly appealed to a magistrate, whereupon the council contended (1) that the magistrate was not entitled to substitute his own opinion as to the suitability of the traders to hold licences for that of the council; (2) that he was not empowered to review the merits; and (3) that his jurisdiction was limited to considering whether or not there was any material on which the council could reasonably have arrived at their decisions to revoke the licences. (One may note, in parenthesis, the close similarity of those submissions to that advanced by the present appellant.) But the magistrate would have none of this. He held that he was bound to consider the whole matter de novo, and he allowed the appeals. Upholding that decision in the Divisional Court, and referring to the submission that the magistrate had not been entitled to substitute his opinion for that of the borough council and that all he could decide was whether there was evidence upon which the council could arrive at their conclusion, Lord Goddard C.J. said, at 602:

> 'If that argument be right, the right of appeal,... would be purely illusory. Such an appeal would... really be only an appeal on the question of law whether there was any evidence upon which the borough council could have formed an opinion. If their decision were a mere matter of opinion and that opinion were to be conclusive, I do not know that the borough council would be obliged to have any evidence. They could simply say: "In our opinion this person is unsuitable to hold a licence." It is true that they must give a sufficient reason, but they could give any reason they liked and say: "That is sufficient in our opinion." I do not know how a court could then say on appeal that that was not a sufficient reason. If the reason need only be one which is sufficient in the opinion of the borough council, it is difficult to see how any court of appeal could set aside their decision. It seems to me that [section 25(1)] gives an unrestricted right of appeal, and if there is an unrestricted right of appeal, it is for the court of appeal to substitute its opinion for the opinion of the borough council.'

I would apply those words in full measure to the present case. The provision for an appeal to quarter sessions seems to me largely, if not entirely, 'illusory' if the contention of the appellant council is right. If it is, I am at a loss to follow how the recorder would set about discharging his appellate function. Lacking all information as to what had happened before the local authority, save the bare knowledge that they had refused the application and their written grounds for refusal, he would be powerless, as I think, to make any effective examination of the validity of those reasons. Furthermore, unless he is free to embark on a complete consideration of all the relevant material presented to him, how can he in due course proceed to state a case for the Divisional Court if called upon to do so? The customary (and preferable) way of doing this is *inter alia* to set out in separate paragraphs those facts found by the lower court to have been 'proved or admitted', and indeed we were shown a copy of the draft case prepared (but ultimately not used) by the local authority in the present case which was in that form. But how could the recorder proceed to state what *his* findings of fact were if he was not free to receive evidence and assess it? No satisfactory answer to this question has, in my judgment, been advanced, and for this reason, among others, I am forced to the conclusion that the appellants are wrong in their main contention. I hold that the proceedings before this recorder were by way of a complete rehearing.

But, contrary to what has been contended, this conclusion does *not* involve that the views earlier formed by the local authority have to be entirely disregarded by quarter sessions. It is true that in *Godfrey v. Bournemouth Corporation* [1969] 1 W.L.R. 47, after observing that an appeal to quarter sessions under Schedule 6 to this same Act was by way of a complete rehearing, Lord Parker C.J. said, at 52, 'the discretion is a discretion which the recorder in the present case had to arrive at himself uninfluenced by what the local authority had done'. But with respect, I do not accept this. It went much too far, it was in direct conflict with the view which Lord Parker C.J. had earlier expressed in *R. v. Essex Quarter Sessions, ex p. Thomas* [1966] 1 W.L.R. 359, 363, it was contrary to the approach adopted both by the recorder and by Lord Parker C.J. himself in the instant case, and it was, with deference, an uncalled-for observation. Here again, *Stepney Borough Council v. Joffe* [1949] 1 K.B. 599 establishes what I regard as the proper approach, for, having made the point that there was in that case an unrestricted appeal, Lord Goddard C.J. continued, at 602, 603:

> 'That does not mean to say that the court of appeal, in this case the metropolitan magistrate, ought not to pay great attention to the fact that the duly constituted and elected local authority have come to an opinion on the matter, and ought not lightly, of course, to reverse their opinion. It is constantly said (although I am not sure that it is always sufficiently remembered) that the function of a court of appeal is to exercise its powers when it is satisfied that the judgment below is wrong, not merely because it is not satisfied that the judgment was right.'

I find no reason for thinking that the recorder in the present case failed in any degree to pay proper regard to the decision arrived at by an overwhelming majority of the local authority. On the contrary, he manifestly entertained considerable sympathy with their attitude. But, as he said, he was ultimately obliged to act on the totality of the material placed before him, balancing that called for the appellants against that presented by the local authority and paying due regard to the existing decision being appealed from. Having done so, he concluded that the appellants had made out their case, the Divisional Court in its turn have upheld him, and for my part I have to say that it was not established to my satisfaction that either erred in law. I therefore find myself compelled to hold that this appeal should be dismissed and that the order of the recorder granting the permit be upheld."

PHILLIMORE L.J.: '...[T]here is no need for authority for the proposition that a council and its committees are entitled to agree on a policy provided always that they do not impose it inflexibly. In this case, however, we were told that the chairman of the committee — a former Mayor of Norwich — gave evidence before the recorder to the effect that they had rejected the application solely on the basis of the policy decision taken by the General Purposes Committee...
[The recorder said:]

> 'I am forced to the conclusion that in this case, where the application met with all the ordinary requirements as to suitability of site, premises and management, the general policy must have been applied. In other words, no application to the local authority, however suitable, would succeed.'

In other words the council had *not* exercised any form of discretion. They had simply dismissed this application after going through the necessary motions without regard to its individual merits or demerits. I take this to be a finding of fact with which this court is in no position to interfere.

Incidentally, I cannot see that the recorder could avoid this decision. Apparently no evidence was called to support either ground (a) or ground (b). Nobody came forward to say that this sort of arcade had resulted in disastrous damage to the morality of the young in Great Yarmouth or any other seaside place or was likely to prove particularly harmful to the young of Norwich. Indeed, as I think, the Act of 1964 by section 3 tends to suggest that in regard to premises such as this it is wrong to refuse a licence on the ground that some particular class such as young persons may be injuriously affected...

I think that the recorder was clearly right and that his judgment should not be disturbed. This is a case where he was satisfied that the council's committee had failed to keep an open mind and had applied their policy without regard to the facts of the individual case.

[His Lordship agreed with EDMUND DAVIES L.J. that the appeal to Quarter Sessions was by way of rehearing.]"

Notes

(1) Galligan, above, commenting on this case, observed: **7–13**

"The problem facing the court in the *Sagnata* case can be seen. There was a policy decision of the council based on stated reasons; there was also a finding by the Recorder that there was no evidence to support these reasons. The problem becomes more acute with the developing tendency in the courts and the legislature to require the statement of reasons. When reasons are stated, the court may ensure they are within the scope of the statute; but when the reasons stated are expressed as policies, the courts may be tempted to require supporting evidence. However to require evidence to support policies entails two basic difficulties.

First, the majority requirement in the *Sagnata* case is the very kind of irruption into the discretionary sphere that traditionally has been avoided. The decision that amusement centres were socially undesirable because children might be adversely affected was a policy decision within the discretion of the licensing authority; it was clearly not a matter of fact capable of determination in an objective way, nor is it a question for which the statute specifies criteria. Only Lord Denning M.R. wished to maintain the traditional distinction; he looked into the legislative history of the Act, and concluded that Parliament clearly intended that the local authority should finally decide whether amusement centres were to be allowed...

It is submitted that this is the better view; it recognises that a policy represents a choice of social goals and values, for which reasons may be given, but which often cannot be reduced to questions of fact for objective determination."

(2) Contrast with the evaluation of the factual basis of the policy in *Cinderella's Rockafella's*.   **7–14** *Sagnata* was referred to in that case but does not appear to have been relied on by the court in reaching its conclusions as to the factual basis of the policy adopted. What appears to have been of particular significance to the court in that case was the fact that the aspects of the policy relating to the imposition of a curfew and standard closing time were based on the conclusions of a working party, which in turn had drawn on extensive research into the link between levels of violence and disorder in the early morning in relation to the licensed premises. It is not clear from the judgment whether or not licensees were invited to make representations to the working party. Nevertheless Lord Prosser concluded (at 599) that he was:

> "satisfied that in adopting the new policy the board had a proper basis in fact and advice for doing so. These are matters for judgment and I am not persuaded that the policy required any more precise basis than it had."

To what extent do you think the court should be influenced by whether or not affected persons were consulted in relation to the adoption of policy? Were the facts in *Cinderella's Rockafella's* of the same character as the facts in the preceding extract? Galligan, commenting on the point made by Phillimore L.J. that "Nobody came forward to say that this sort of arcade had resulted in disastrous damage to the morality of the young in Great Yarmouth", expressed doubt as to the utility of any test based upon availability of evidence (at p. 342):

> "It is difficult to see what inferences could be drawn from evidence of this kind... The reasons behind such policies are a combination of facts and interpretation, evaluation and speculation

about them. The sort of evidence that might be useful would depend upon the criteria of 'social harmfulness,' this criteria is itself a matter for policy choices by the decision-maker. Reasons, based upon policy choices, can be coherent and persuasive without necessarily attempting to invoke objective evidence in their support."

(3) The grant of permits in respect of provision of amusements with prizes is now governed by Part III of the Gaming Act 1968 and the Lotteries and Amusements Act 1976, on which generally see Cummins, Chapter 12. Note the power in Part III of the 1968 Act which gives considerable policy-making powers. Subject to the exemption in respect of "any premises used or to be used wholly or mainly for the provision of amusements by means of machines to which Part III of this Act applies" (Sched. 9, para. 4(2)), the local authority may pass a resolution that it will not grant or renew permits in respect of certain classes of premises and may also resolve to limit the number of machines in respect of which a permit may be granted. The view was formerly expressed that such blanket resolutions purporting to affect all premises except those protected by para. 4 of Schedule 9 were probably invalid: *Walker v. Leeds City Council* [1976] 3 All E.R. 709 but this approach has in fact been approved in *R. v. London Borough of Barnet, ex parte Ellina and Hawrylczak* [1992] 10 L.R. 15. Cummins has expressed the view that it is doubtful whether the latter case would in fact be followed in Scotland and this may be a reflection of the long-held view in Scots law that power to regulate an activity does not imply power to ban it: see *Cadenhead v. Smart* (1894) 22 R. (J.) 1 and *Gerry Cottle's Circus Ltd v. City of Edinburgh District Council*, 1990 S.L.T. 235.

7–15   (4) Dawn Oliver argues that in assessing the factual basis of a policy the courts adopt essentially a rationalistic point of view. If facts are self-evident then the courts will be slow to intervene. In *Cinderella's Rockafella's* Lord Prosser appeared to be treating the facts as self-evident but his reliance on the assessment of the facts "being matters for judgment" perhaps suggests that where the facts in issue are in reality simply assumptions or indeed value judgments then the role of the court is severely curtailed in questioning the legitimacy of the policy: see "The Courts and the Policy-making Process" in *New Directions in Judicial Review* (J. Jowell and D. Oliver eds, 1988), p. 97. Echoes are arguably found in the judgment of Lord Scarman in *Re Findlay* [1985] A.C. 318, noted at para. 6–59. Consider also the discussion of the relationship between matters of jurisdiction and matters of fact in Chapter 4.

(5) In some circumstances, particularly where the statutory criteria for exercise of administrative power are perhaps tighter than those found in cases such as *Findlay* and *Cinderella's Rockafella's*, the court may characterise policies based on value judgments as irrelevant considerations. On that basis the court is effectively precluding consideration of such matters based not on a test of questioning the legitimacy of such policies and their factual bases, but rather conformity with the requirement of legality. Consider in this connection *Gerry Cottle's Circus Ltd v. Edinburgh District Council*, noted at para. 6–27 and *R. v. Somerset County Council, ex parte Fewings* [1995] 1 WLR 1037 noted at para. 6–16.

ACTING UNDER DICTATION

R v. Children's Hearing for the Borders Region

1984 S.L.T. 65

7–16   "Following the birth of a child, whose brother (a battered baby) had already been adopted, the local authority passed supervision orders and in March 1982, the social work committee made a resolution for the assumption of parental rights of the child with a view to placing her for adoption with the same persons as had adopted her brother. On 31 May 1982, the sheriff dismissed an application by the local authority for an order that the March resolution should not lapse, and thereafter the local authority required the children's hearing to review the supervision requirements imposed under s. 44(1) of the Social Work (Scotland) Act 1968. The hearing did this on 8 July 1982, when they purported to vary the supervision requirement by ordering that the child 'should reside in a pre-adoptive home chosen by the local authority'. The mother appealed to the sheriff against this requirement who... upheld the appeal.... The children's hearing appealed to the Court of Session by way of stated case. The question for the court was: 'Was it ultra vires of the panel to include in a supervision requirement, a condition to the effect that the child should reside in a pre-adoptive home chosen by the local authority?' "

LORD JUSTICE-CLERK (WHEATLEY): "[His Lordship referred to the facts and continued:] For convenience I shall refer to the children's hearing as the appellants and to Mrs R. as the respondent.

7–17

The question for the opinion of the court is: 'Was it ultra vires of the panel to include in a supervision requirement, a condition to the effect that the child should reside in a pre-adoptive home chosen by the local authority?'

In my opinion the straightforward answer to that issue was clouded by the introduction of the matter of the contemplated action by the local authority to initiate proceedings to have the child M. adopted by the people who had adopted her brother. To determine the question posed the first thing to do is to examine the relevant statutory provisions and see whether what was done conformed to them. If it did not and something not in accord with the appellants' statutory powers was included, then that body acted ultra vires and the condition attached to the supervision requirement was bad and invalid.

[Having recited the provisions of the Social Work (Scotland) Act 1968, s. 44 (1), his Lordship continued:] The report of proceedings at the children's hearing on 8 July 1982 at which the condition now under consideration was adjected to the supervision requirement simply records that the decision proceeded under and in terms of s. 47 (1) of the Act, but the condition was obviously a s. 44 (1) (a) one. It is clear from the records as a whole and the statement of reasons by the appellants for their decision to adject a condition in these terms that they were complying with the desire of the local authority to pave the way for the child's subsequent adoption. But did the form which the condition took square with the provisions of s. 44 (1) (a) read as a whole? I have no doubt that the power under s. 44 (1) (a) to make a condition specifying where the child is to reside confers a wide discretion on the children's hearing as to where the child should reside, provided that the selected place is within the geographical limits specified and is not a residential establishment. I do not consider, however, that this discretion extends to the children's hearing divesting itself of the responsibility of specifying where that residence has to be, and delegating the selection to a third party subject to a restriction on the type of home, such as was prescribed here. A supervision requirement does not supersede the rights of the natural parents, and while it results in the child being in the care of the local authority for certain statutory purposes (s. 44 (5)) the natural parents still have parental rights in relation to the child. That being so, the word 'place' in s. 44 (1) (a) has to be given a narrow rather than an expansive meaning. The condition must accordingly specify precisely where that supervision will be taking place, so that parties with an interest in and title to the child may know where to look for it. In my view the delegation of choice to a third party and the lack of specification take the condition in this case beyond the permissible bounds of statutory competence into the category of ultra vires. On that short ground I consider that the question of law falls to be answered in the affirmative and that the appeal should be dismissed.

I have already indicated that the debate before us was clouded by various arguments in relation to the purpose of the local authority to arrange for the child's adoption. In view of the decision which I have reached supra I do not consider it necessary to go into all these arguments in detail, and I confine myself to one which in my view is also supportive of the respondent's case. It is quite clear from what was said to the sheriff by the representative of the local authority that what the local authority was concerned with in this review was the furthering of its purpose to place the child for adoption and that with the couple who had already adopted the child's brother.

The argument revolved round whether in terms of s. 57 (2) of the Adoption Act 1958 the appellants, in adjecting the said condition, had done something which they were not entitled to do, and had so acted ultra vires. [Having outlined the provisions of ss. 29 (1) and 57 (2) of the Adoption Act 1958, his Lordship continued:]

It was submitted by counsel for the respondent that, in giving effect to the local authority's submission to them by imposing the said condition for the clear purpose of having the way for the adoption of the child, the appellants were 'causing another to do so' in terms of the last part of that subsection, and thereby infringing the provisions of s. 29 (1) when read with the opening paragraph of s. 57 (2). Counsel for the appellants argued that they were not a 'person' within the meaning of s. 29 (1) supra. In my opinion that submission is not tenable, and I accept the submission by counsel for the respondent that in acting as they did in imposing the said condition the appellants were in contravention of s. 29 (1) and accordingly acted invalidly and ultra vires. Had it been necessary I would have found in favour of the respondent on that ground too."

Notes

7–18   (1) This is an example of the doctrine of acting under dictation. The children's hearing had simply delegated its authority to act to another entity but did so in a way in which the substantive discretion which in fact it should have exercised was lost.

(2) When R. was decided, the children's hearing or children's panel system was a sub-department of the authority's Social Work Department. This is no longer the case. See now the Local Government etc. (Scotland) Act 1994, Pt III, ss. 127–138 which established a separate Children's Hearings Administration. However, the doctrine of acting under dictation is equally applicable in situations where power is exercised by quite distinct bodies, vested with different common law and statutory powers as the following extract illustrates.

Lavender H. & Son Ltd v. Minister of Housing and Local Government

[1970] 3 All E.R. 871

7–19   Lavender & Son Ltd sought to use a farm belonging to them for gravel extraction. Permission was refused by the local authority. They appealed to the Minister of Housing and Local Government and an inquiry was held. The Minister stated that it was policy to apply the recommendations of the report on gravel working on agricultural land which stated that such land should be protected against disturbance by gravel working, that he would not deviate from these "unless the Minister of Agriculture, Fisheries and Food is not opposed to working" and that as in this case the Minister of Agriculture, Fisheries and Food had not consented, planning permission would not be granted. The company sought to quash the Minister's decision.

WILLIS J.: "... It is those last two sentences in the decision letter which lie at the heart of the matter in issue; and it is submitted, first of all, by counsel for the applicants, that they show, in this case, that the Minister had so fettered his own discretion to decide the appeal by the policy which he had adopted that the decisive matter was not the exercise of his own discretion on a consideration of the report and other material considerations, but the sustained objection of the Minister of Agriculture. In effect, he says that the decision was not that of the Minister of Housing and Local Government, the tribunal entrusted with the duty to decide, but the Minister of Agriculture, who had no status save perhaps in a consultative capacity and certainly no status to make the effective decision...

... In general support of his main submission, counsel for the applicants has referred me to Professor de Smith's well-known work, *Judicial Review of Administrative Action* ((2nd ed., 1968), pp. 292–297) and to certain of the cases cited therein. He really puts his argument in two ways: (1) that the Minister has fettered his discretion by a self-created rule of policy; and (2) that the Minister, who has a duty to exercise his own discretion in determining an appeal, has in this case delegated that duty to the Minister of Agriculture, who has no such duty and is, statutorily, a stranger to any decision. It is, of course, common ground that the Minister is entitled to have a policy and to decide an appeal in the context of that policy. He can also differ from the inspector on any question of fact, and disagree with the inspector's conclusion and recommendations. He can, and no doubt should, reject any recommendation of an inspector which runs counter to his policy, since, as counsel for the Minister points out, it is of the very essence of the duties laid on the Minister by section 1 of the Minister of Town and Country Planning Act 1943 that he should secure consistency and continuity in the framing and execution of a national policy with respect to the use and development of land.

The courts have no authority to interfere with the way in which the Minister carries out his planning policy (see *per* Lord Denning M.R., *Lord Luke of Pavenham v. Minister of Housing and Local Government* [1968] 1 Q.B. 172 at 192). There is also no question but that the Minister, before making a decision whether or not to allow an appeal, may obtain the views of other government departments (see *Darlassis v. Minister of Education* (1954) 52 L.G.R. 304 at 318, *per* Barry J.). The duties of the Minister and their extent in relation to a matter such as the appeal in the present case, comprising in a hybrid form both administrative and quasi-judicial functions, were enunciated by Lord Greene M.R. in a well-known passage in *B. Johnson & Co. (Builders) Ltd v. Minister of Health* [1947] 2 All E.R. 395, at 397 and 399:

> 'The duty placed on the Minister with regard to objections is to consider them before confirming the order. He is also to consider the report of the person who held the inquiry. Having done that, his functions are laid down by the last words of the paragraph (*i.e.* para. 4 of Sched. 1 to the Housing Act 1936), *viz.*, "and may then confirm the order either with or without modification".

Those words are important, because they make it clear that it is to the Minister that Parliament has committed the decision whether he will or will not confirm the order after he has done all that the statute requires him to do. There is nothing in that paragraph, or anywhere else in the Act, which imposes on the Minister any obligation with regard to the objections, save the obligation to consider them. He is not bound to base his decision on any conclusion that he comes to with regard to the objections, and that must be so when one gives a moment's thought to the situation. The decision whether to confirm or not must be made in relation to questions of policy, and the Minister, in deciding whether to confirm or not, will, like every Minister entrusted with administrative duties, weigh up the considerations which are to affect his mind, the preponderating factor in many, if not all, cases being that of public policy, having regard to all the facts of the case.... That decision must be an administrative decision, because it is not to be based purely on the view that he forms of the objections, *vis-à-vis* the desires of the local authority, but is to be guided by his view as to the policy which in the circumstances he ought to pursue.'

Can there, nevertheless, come a point in this hybrid process when the court can interfere with a Ministerial decision which, *ex facie*, proceeds on a consideration of the inspector's report and concludes by applying Ministerial policy?

Counsel for the applicants submits that such a point can be reached and has been reached in this case. It is reached, he says, adopting the words of Professor de Smith (see p. 294), if a tribunal, entrusted with a discretion as the Minister was in the present case, disables itself from exercising that discretion in a particular case by the prior adoption of a general policy. In *R. v. Port of London Authority, ex p. Kynoch Ltd*, Bankes L.J. said:... [His Lordship cited the passage 'In the present case... by whomsoever made' (above, p. 257)].

In another licensing case, *R. v. County Licensing (Stage Plays) Committee of Flint County Council, ex p. Barrett* [1957] 1 All E.R. 112 at 122, where the decision was given in the interests of consistency, Jenkins L.J. said:

'Then they went on... to conclude... that the Queen's Theatre licence must follow the fate of the Pavilion Theatre licence, because it was essential that the same rule should be applied in all cases or, in other words, that the committee should be consistent. I cannot think that that method of approach fulfils the requirement that the matter should be heard and determined according to law... It seems to me that it wrongly pursues consistency at the expense of the merits of individual cases.'

I have referred to these two cases since they were relied on by counsel for the applicants, but I am inclined to agree with counsel for the Minister that the considerations applicable to licensing cases are not of much assistance when considering the scope of a Minister's duties within a statutory framework...

It is, of course, clear that if the Minister has prejudged any genuine consideration of the matter before him, or has failed to give genuine consideration (*inter alia*) the inspector's report, he has failed to carry out his statutory duties properly (see *Franklin v. Minister of Town and Country Planning* [1948] A.C. 87 [below, p. 526]).

In the present case counsel for the applicants does not shrink from submitting that the decision letter shows that no genuine consideration was given to the question whether planning permission could, in the circumstances, be granted. I have carefully considered the authorities cited by counsel, but I have not found any clear guide to what my decision should be in this case. I have said enough to make it clear that I recognise that in the field of policy, and in relation to Ministerial decisions coloured or dictated by policy, the courts will interfere only within a strictly circumscribed field (see *per* Lord Greene M.R. in *Associated Provincial Picture Houses Ltd v. Wednesbury Corp.* [see below, p. 349]). It is also clear, and is conceded by counsel for the Minister, that where a Minister is entrusted by Parliament with the decision of any particular case he must keep that actual decision in the last resort in his own hands (see *R. v. Minister of Transport, ex p. Grey Coaches* (1933) 77 S.J. 301). I return, therefore, to the words used by the Minister. It seems to me that he has said in language which admits of no doubt that his decision to refuse permission was solely in pursuance of a policy not to permit minerals in the Waters agricultural reserves to be worked unless the Minister of Agriculture was not opposed to their working. Counsel for the Minister submits that, read as a whole, the decision letter should be taken as implying some such words as 'I have gone through the exercise of taking all material consideration into account, but you have not persuaded me that this is such an exceptional case as would justify me in relaxing my policy; therefore I stick to it and apply it.' If that were the right construction perhaps counsel for the Minister would be justified in saying that there was no error in law. But in my judgment the language used is not open to any such implication. There is no indication that this might be an exceptional case such as would or could induce the Minister to change his policy. It is common ground that the Minister must be open to persuasion that the land should not remain in the Waters reservation. How can his mind be open to persuasion, how can an applicant establish an 'exceptional case' in the case of an inflexible attitude by the Minister of Agriculture? That attitude was well known before the inquiry, it was maintained during the inquiry, and presumably thereafter. The inquiry was no doubt, in a sense, into the Minister of Agriculture's objection, since, apart from that objection, it might well have been that no inquiry would have been necessary, but I do not think that the Minister, after the inquiry, can be said in any real sense to have given genuine consideration to whether, on planning (including agricultural) grounds, this land could be worked. It seems to me that by adopting and applying his stated policy he has in effect inhibited himself from exercising a proper discretion (which would of course be guided by policy considerations) in any case where the Minister of Agriculture has made and maintained an objection to mineral working in an agricultural reservation. Everything else might point to the desirability of granting permission, but by applying and acting on his stated policy I think that the Minister has fettered himself in such a way that in this case it was not he who made the decision for which Parliament made him responsible. It was the decision of the Minister of Agriculture not to waive his objection which was decisive in this case, and while that might properly prove to be the decisive factor for the Minister when taking into account all material considerations, it seems to me quite wrong for a policy to be applied which in reality eliminates all the material considerations save only the consideration, when that is the case, that the Minister of Agriculture objects. That means, as I think, that the Minister has by his stated policy delegated to the Minister of Agriculture the effective decision on any appeal within the agricultural reservations where the latter objects to the working...

If the Minister was intending to follow his stated policy, I think that it was very undesirable that it should not have been made known in advance. It is possible to imagine great hardship falling on appellants who, all unawares, embark on an expensive appeal foredoomed to failure by reason of a strict though unannounced policy. However, I agree with counsel for the Minister that the failure to publicise the policy is not a ground for questioning the decision...

On the main ground on which this case has been argued, however, I am satisfied that the applicants should succeed. I think that the Minister failed to exercise a proper or indeed any discretion by reason of the fetter which he imposed on his exercise in acting solely in accordance with his stated policy; and further that on the true construction of the Minister's letter the decision to dismiss the appeal, while purporting to be that of the Minister, was in fact, and improperly, that of the Minister of Agriculture."

Notes

7–20   (1) See case note by D.G.T. Williams (1971) 29 C.L.J. 6. It is important to realise that this decision does not mean that an authority is not entitled to consult with another authority or other persons and bodies and take its views into account. Nor does it mean that one Minister may not consult with another: see, for example, *Kent County Council v. Secretary of State for the Environment* (1976) 75 L.G.R. 452. Indeed in some instances planning legislation actually requires planning authorities to consult with specified persons and authorities. On this generally see C.T. Reid, "A Planning Authority's Duty to Consult" (1982) S.P.L. 4.

We have noted already in Chapter 5 that it is quite usual, when granting power, to impose obligations to consult those affected by a decision. Often a failure to consult will be a mandatory failure of procedure, on which see... below. Equally, the expanding canvas of natural justice may impose obligations to consult by virtue of the doctrine of legitimate expectations: see paras 8–31 to 8–36. *Lavender* seeks to give guidance as to when the line between proper consultation and improper dictation is drawn. Is the guidance sufficiently clear?

7–21   (2) In some instances, legislation may expressly empower one body to issue "guidance" to another as to the way in which the latter power should be exercised. Perhaps the most famous example of this arose in *Laker Airways Ltd v. Department of Trade* [1977] Q.B. 643. In terms of the Civil Aviation Act 1971 the Secretary of State was empowered to give "guidance" to the Civil Aviation Authority, which in turn imposed an obligation on the authority to "perform those functions in such a manner as it considers is in accordance with the guidance": section 3(2). The Court of Appeal considered that this did not mean that guidance could be issued which contradicted the general policy objectives contained in the 1971 Act. Guidance was limited to power to explain or supplement those objectives. Lord Denning M.R. explained (at 699):

"So long as the 'guidance' given by the Secretary of State keeps within the due bounds of guidance, the Authority is under a duty to follow his guidance. Even so, the Authority is allowed some degree of flexibility. It is to perform its function 'in such a manner as it considers is in accordance with the guidance.' So, while it is obliged to follow the guidance, the manner of doing so is for the Authority itself."

Contrast the foregoing with the National Health Service and Community Care Act 1990, s. 51, which provides as follows:

"Power of Secretary of State to give directions

51. After subsection (1) of section 5 (powers of Secretary of State) of the Social Work (Scotland) Act 1968... there shall be inserted the following subsection-

'(1A) Without prejudice to subsection (1) above, the Secretary of State may issue directions to local authorities, either individually or collectively, as to the manner in which they are to exercise any of their functions under this Act or any of the enactments mentioned in section 2(2) of this Act; and a local authority shall comply with any direction made under this subsection.' "

In *Laker* the CAA was required to follow directions given by the Secretary of State but had a discretion as to the way in which those directions were implemented. That flexibility does not exist in section 51. There is no restriction as to the form the directions might take and while the power potentially puts social work departments under the control of the Secretary of State, the Government stressed that it is a reserved power to be used sparingly (*Hansard*, H.L. Vol. 520, col. 687). The Under-Secretary of State stated that the clause provides for powers that may be necessary to ensure that the Government's policy on the mixed economy of care is carried out. However, the direction-making power is not restricted to community care issues but extends to all social work functions.

(3) In the absence of any compelling legal authority, there is, however, no obligation to follow such directions: on which see *Inglis v. British Airports Authority*, 1978 S.L.T. (Lands Tr.) 30. Indeed, *R. v. Police Complaints Board, ex parte Madden* [1983] 1 W.L.R. 447 demonstrates that there may be dangers in following guidance which is not obligatory. Here the Police Complaints Board was required by the Police Act 1976 to 'have regard" to guidance given to it by the Secretary of State. The board adopted a policy of always following the guidance. It was held by McNeill J. that the board had failed properly to exercise its discretion as to its powers and in regard to its obligation to "have regard" to guidance as an obligation to "comply with" it. The board "ought to [have been] asserting its independence" (at 470). The guidance was a relevant consideration but no more than that: see also *Daymond v. South West Water Authority* [1976] A.C. 609 and *R. v. Secretary of State for the Environment, ex parte Lancashire County Council* [1994] 4 All E.R. 165.

(4) Acting under dictation has proven to be a particularly difficult area in the context of party politics. In *R. v. Waltham Forest London Borough Council, ex parte Baxter* [1988] Q.B. 419 a private party meeting was held by members of the ruling group where the policy of the group as to the setting of the domestic and non-domestic rate to be considered at the forthcoming council meeting was discussed. A rate increase of 62 per cent for the domestic rate and 56.6 per cent for the non-domestic rate was agreed. The ruling group standing orders provided that members were required to refrain from voting in opposition to group decisions, the sanction being withdrawal of the party whip. Some members voted against the level of increase at the group meeting but in favour of it at the council meeting and the increase in rate was duly agreed to by a majority of five. Baxter and a number of other ratepayers sought judicial review on a number of grounds, including their argument that six or seven of the councillors had voted contrary to their personal views. The Court of Appeal held that the resolution was approved not because they were in favour of it but because they had fettered their discretion at the group meeting. However, on the facts the court held that this was not so and that the councillors were entitled to take into account party political loyalty as a relevant consideration provided that this was not the only consideration. Withdrawal of the party whip did not mean that a councillor could not

7–22

continue to act: he could do so as an independent. Is this consistent with the views expressed by Lord Reid and Lord Upjohn in *Padfield v. Minister of Agriculture, Fisheries and Food*, extracted at para. 6–13?

Some attempt to inject balance into party politics is contained in sections 15–17 of the Local Government and Housing Act 1989 which requires political balance on committees and on a number of other bodies. This legislation has not, however, yet been extended to Scotland. Similarly, section 14 of the same Act provides that it is possible to co-opt on to local authority committees persons who are not members of the local authority, or in the case of sub-committees, members of the appointing committee by removing the numerical restrictions on such appointments. It is no longer required that two-thirds, or in the case of education committees, half of the membership, be members of the appointing authority. Although such persons would have the advantages of other members in terms of their rights to receive papers and access to information and to attend meetings, they would not be entitled to vote other than at advisory committees. These provisions too have not yet been extended to Scotland. There is some authority for the view that an overly rigid application of the party line could lead to a decision being stigmatised as having been taken in bad faith: on this see *Innes v. Royal Burgh of Kirkcaldy*, 1963 S.L.T. 325, extracted at para.6–10.

(5) For further reading see Craig, pp. 386–390; Wade and Forsyth, pp. 358–360; Finch and Ashton, pp. 308–309; and *Stair Memorial Encyclopaedia*, Vol. 1, para. 41.

Chapter 8

Natural Justice 1: The Right To A Hearing

In administrative law the "rules of natural justice" have been regarded as comprising the **8–1** rules *audi alteram partem* and *nemo judex in causa sua*. Under the first rule, a decision maker requires to gives notice of the decision to the person affected by it and an opportunity to make representations in relation to it. The second rule, which is concerned with preserving the impartiality of decision makers, is considered in the next chapter. The rules might also be regarded as specific aspects of the concept of procedural *ultra vires* examined in Chapter …Historically speaking, the rules are tied into judicial decision making in the ordinary courts but they have been applied to a wide range of administrative functions and decision makers. It is not clear, however, how far the traditional rules of natural justice should apply to such decisions and there has been a tendency to use the expression that there is a duty to act "fairly" in such cases. For general reading see *The Laws of Scotland: Stair Memorial Encyclopaedia*, Vol. 1, paras 259–284; V. Finch and C. Ashton, *Administrative Law in Scotland* (1997), pp. 313–315, 324–362; P.P. Craig, *Administrative Law* (3rd ed., 1994), pp. 281–324; W. Wade and C. Forsyth, *Administrative Law* (7th ed., 1994), pp. 494–570; C. Harlow and R. Rawlings, *Law and Administration* (2nd ed., 1997, Chap. 15; M. Deans, *Scots Public Law* (1995), pp. 154–160.

The right to a hearing is recognised by the ECHR and protected by the Human Rights Act 1998. This Convention right is of course also protected from lawful interference by the Scottish Parliament and the Scottish Executive and Administration under the Scotland Act 1998. Article 6(1) of the Convention provides:

"**Article 6**
Right to a Fair Trial
   1. In the determination of his civil rights and obligations or of any criminal charge against him, everyone is entitled to a fair and public nearing within a reasonable time by an independent and impartial tribunal established by law. Judgment shall be pronounced publicly but the press and public may be excluded from all or part of the trial in the interest of morals, public order or national security in a democratic society, where the interests of juveniles or the protection of the private life of the parties so require, or to the extent strictly necessary in the opinion of the court in special circumstances where publicity would prejudice the interests of justice."

Articles 6.2 and 6.3 go on to provide specific protections in the field of criminal law, such as guarantees to the rights to legal assistance and notice of the accusation made. For a helpful review of the case law under Article 6 and for suggestions on how the law might develop in light of incorporation of the Article in domestic law, see Sir R. Walker, "The Impact of the European Standards on the Right to a Fair Trial in Civil Proceedings in United Kingdom Domestic Law" [1999] 1 E.H.R.L.R. 4.

In considering the extent to which the right to a hearing applies, one must consider first, does the rule apply to a decision maker and secondly, if it does, what is the exact content of the rule in that situation? The following excerpt gives some idea as to the scope of its application.

THE RIGHT TO A HEARING: SCOPE

McDonald v. Burns

1940 S.C. 376

8–2   LORD JUSTICE-CLERK (AITCHISON): "In this action the pursuers seek a declarator against five extern sisters of the convent of Poor Clares (Colettines), Mount Alvernia, Liberton, Edinburgh, that they have no longer a right of residence in the convent or in any part thereof, and ask the Court to decree their removal therefrom. There are two bodies of pursuers, first, the trustees who *ex officio* are heritably vested in the convent under a feu-charter dated in 1896 constituting the foundation. Of these pursuers Miss Susan Henry and Miss Emma Atherton are admittedly without title, their tenure of the offices of abbess and vicaress respectively of the convent having lapsed through failure of re-election in June 1937. The alternative branch of plea 1 for the defenders that these two pursuers have no title to sue will therefore fall to be sustained. The second body of pursuers comprise the Archbishop of the Roman Catholic Archdiocese of St Andrews and Edinburgh as Local Ordinary, designated as being charged with the duty of executing the judgments of the Sacred Congregation of Religious in Rome, and the said Miss Susan Henry and Miss Emma Atherton, designated as having as abbess and vicaress control over, and as representing, the said convent. This second instance is unnecessary.

The defenders claim that they have a right to continue to reside in the convent in virtue of their membership of the religious order or community of Poor Clares, which membership they assert has not been validly terminated in accordance with the law and constitution of the Roman Catholic Church. If it has been validly terminated, their status as extern sisters comes to an end, and all rights flowing from that status cease and determine including the right of residence. The Lord Ordinary has held that it is sufficiently instructed by the pleadings, and particularly by the admissions of the defenders, that there was ground, in the refusal of the defenders to renew their vows in the manner enjoined on them, that might warrant their dismissal from religion, and that they had not alleged relevant ground for reducing the judgment of dismissal. Accordingly, he granted decree of removal *de plano*. The question is whether the case can be disposed of without inquiry.

It was not contended by the pursuers that membership of a religious order, which carries with it as an inherent ingredient of that membership the right of residence in a religious house, was not a patrimonial interest that would be within the cognisance of the Courts of law. But the limits within which the Courts will interfere with the judgments of ecclesiastical bodies are strictly defined, and should not be incautiously extended. Where civil rights are concerned, appeal may be made to the Courts of law for their protection, or for some form of redress, but the mere fact that a civil right is affected by itself forms no justification for interference by the Court, for civil consequences may often result from decisions of ecclesiastical Courts in matters that lie properly within their own jurisdiction. Even in those cases in which the Court will interfere, the remedy to be afforded is not necessarily the restoration of the civil right, where there has been deprivation of it, or an interdict against interference where it is threatened. In many cases the only suitable remedy, owing to the intimate and special nature of the relationship arising from membership within a religious communion, may be an award of damages.

The right of the Courts, in suitable circumstances, to give a remedy for the violation, actual or threatened, of a patrimonial interest connected with a religious office was affirmed in the House of Lords in the case of *Forbes v. Eden* [5 Macph. (H.L.) 36, L.R., 1 H.L. Sc. 568]. That was a case brought by a clergyman of the Episcopal Church of Scotland against the members of the General Synod of the Church, concluding, *inter alia*, for the reduction of certain canons enacted by them which the pursuer alleged to be in violation of the previous canons in force when he was ordained, and injurious to him, as rendering him liable to deprivation of office for want of conformity thereto. The action also concluded for damages for injury done to the pursuer through his bishop refusing to license a curate, engaged by the pursuer, who would not subscribe the new canons. The action was dismissed upon the ground that the pursuer had not made a relevant averment of damage arising out of the violation of a civil right, sufficient to sustain the petitory conclusion.

In dismissing the action the Lord Chancellor (Lord Chelmsford) said (at p. 47): 'The appellant, in this case, has not been disturbed, either in his charge of the congregation at Burntisland, or in his legal position as a minister of the Scotch Episcopal Church. If he had been, though in this latter respect only, I should have considered with the Lord Justice-Clerk, that "the possession of a particular status, meaning by that term the capacity to perform certain functions, or to hold certain offices, is a thing which the law will recognise as a patrimonial interest, and that no one can be deprived of its possession by the unauthorised or illegal act of another without having a legal remedy." ' And Lord Cranworth said (at p. 51): 'If connected with any office in a voluntary association there is the right to the enjoyment of any pecuniary benefit, including under that term the right to the use of a house, or land, or chapel, or a school, then incidentally the Court may have imposed on it the duty of inquiring as to the regularity affecting the status in the society of any individual member of it.'

But while this principle has been generally affirmed, and was undisputed by the pursuers, the intervention of the Court in disputes arising out of the decisions of religious associations, and affecting the relations between them and their members, has always been regarded as subject to certain very clearly defined limitations. The judicatories of religious bodies in Scotland are not in the position of ordinary civil judicatories whose decisions are reviewable by appeal or suspension. They have their own exclusive jurisdictions, and their decisions, within their own sphere and in matters pertaining to their own life and discipline, are final and binding upon their own members, and are not open to review unless in exceptional circumstances...

In what circumstances, then, will the Courts entertain actions arising out of the judgments of ecclesiastical bodies? Speaking generally, in either of two situations — (first) where the religious association through its agencies has acted clearly and demonstrably beyond its own constitution, and in a manner calculated to affect the civil rights and patrimonial interests of any of its members, and (secondly) where, although acting within its constitution, the procedure of its judicial or *quasi*-judicial tribunals has been marked by gross irregularity, such fundamental irregularity as would, in the case of an ordinary civil tribunal, be sufficient to vitiate the proceedings. But a mere irregularity in procedure is not enough. It must be so fundamental an irregularity that it goes beyond a mere matter of procedure, and becomes something so prejudicial to a fair and impartial investigation of the question to be decided as to amount to a denial of natural justice, as, for example, if a conviction of an ecclesiastical offence were to take place without an accusation being made, or without allowing the person accused to be heard in his defence. In short, the irregularity alleged must not be simply a point of form, or a departure from prescribed regulation, but must go to the honesty and integrity of the proceedings complained of.

Thus, if there has been 'such a gross and wilful violation of the rules of the body, in order to effect a purpose which could not be attained without it, as shall amount to an entire breaking up of the contract, on the faith of which any jurisdiction was committed to these Courts' there may be a point 'not undeserving the consideration of the Court,' *per* Lord Moncreiff (at p. 671) in *Smith v. Galbraith* [5 D. 665]. It is perhaps unnecessary that the violation should be wilful, but, at least, it must be fundamental. There must be some vital disconformity to the law and constitution of the religious association whose decision is being impugned, or some flagrant departure from elementary justice in the conduct of its proceedings, or some usurpation of jurisdiction, or, to put it generally, something against the essential faith of the contract by which the members of the body by entering into association have expressly or impliedly agreed that they shall be bound.

The question is — Do the facts alleged by the defenders in the present case satisfy this standard? Broadly speaking, the allegations are these: In the first place it is said that the investigation of the conduct of the defenders said to justify their dismissal was a mere pretence, carried out by a 'pretended tribunal' arranged in order 'to frame a report prejudicial to the defenders and forward it to the Sacred Congregation of Religious in Rome.' It is plain that what the pursuers describe as a tribunal was really an investigating committee, appointed by the Archbishop as Local Ordinary to inquire into the disobedience of the defenders. We were not referred to any rule or statute of the Roman Catholic Church which requires a tribunal of investigation to be constituted in any particular way. No doubt the Vicar-General and the other members of the tribunal were subordinates of the Local Ordinary holding office or faculties at his pleasure, but it has not been shown, nor is it averred, that their appointment as an investigating committee was in any way contrary to the law of the Church. If the report of the Archbishop to the Sacred Congregation, which alone has power to dismiss the defenders, was based on the report of this committee, the position may be anomalous, but, as Lord Neaves pointed out in *Wight v. Presbytery of Dunkeld* [8 Macph. 921, at p. 927] 'ecclesiastical proceedings are in many respects anomalous... all church Courts are more or less inquisitorial.' Apart from criticism of the personnel of the tribunal, the defenders' averments that the proceedings were a pretence, carried through with the ulterior purpose of securing the dismissal of the defenders, are vague, unsatisfactory and wanting in adequate specification. If they had stood alone, I should have had hesitation in thinking that they were sufficient to justify inquiry.

The second ground alleged by the defenders as bearing upon the validity of their dismissal raises a much more serious issue. The defenders allege that they had no notice of any charges to be brought against them, apart from vague generalisations as to 'disobedience' and 'contumaciousness,' that no specific accusations were ever made, and no formal charge preferred against them at any time. The Lord Ordinary in considering these averments has laid stress upon the word 'formal,' and has said that 'it is impossible to read the defenders' averments as a whole without concluding that, on their own admissions, they knew the purpose of the inquiry by the "tribunal," and the substance of the subject-matter for inquiry — namely, their alleged disobedience in the culminating question of the renewal of their religious vows.' The averments are over-elaborated, and it is not easy to bring them into clear focus, but I am not satisfied that the refusal to renew their vows was the real cause of the defenders' dismissal. The averment of the pursuers is 'that the conduct of the defenders in fact afforded ample grounds' (for dismissal) 'amounting to grave external motives with incorrigibility.' But there is no statement as to what the grave external motives were, and the defenders aver that 'even yet they are in ignorance of what the ground of complaint against them is.' The refusal of the defenders to renew their vows, in the manner in which they were required to renew them, may have been a sufficient ground for their dismissal as being conduct in breach of their solemn obligation of obedience to the authority of the Church, but it does not appear upon any admission of the defenders, nor is it clear upon the averments of the pursuers themselves, that this disobedience was the true ground of their dismissal from religion.

The dismissal of sisters in perpetual vows is regulated by express enactment contained in the statutes for extern sisters promulgated by the authority of the Sacred Congregation in Rome. Statute 119 is as follows: — 'For the dismissal of a sister in perpetual vows grave external motives are required, together with incorrigibility, experience having proved that, after two admonitions, suitable corrections and penances having been given in vain, there is no hope of amendment. If, in the judgment of the abbess and in the judgment of her council, which must be made manifest by a majority of votes in a secret ballot, all this is clearly established, the Local Ordinary, having manifested to the sister the motives for her dismissal and given her full freedom to reply, and having faithfully recorded her reply in the Acts, shall transmit to the Sacred Congregation of Religious all the Acts and documents with a statement of his own judgment on the case, and that of the Regular Superior, if the monastery be subject to Regulars.' It is thus expressly prescribed by the constitution of the Church with reference to nuns of any order, that grave external motives are required for dismissal of a sister in perpetual vows, and it is expressly required that the motives for dismissal shall be manifested to the sister, who shall be given full freedom to reply.

It was thus essential that, after the abbess and her council had decided grave external motives to exist, these should be made manifest to the defenders, that is to say the actual motives upon which the dismissal was to proceed had to be made clear to the sisters concerned. It is averred by the defenders that this was not done. On a *prima facie* construction of statute 119, the duty of making manifest the motives would appear to rest on the Local Ordinary, which would seem to be a reasonable provision in a matter affecting a deprivation of status with the civil consequences which it must entail. I do not find in the pursuers' averments anything to indicate that in the present case this duty was discharged personally by the Local Ordinary. The practice of the Church may permit that it be regarded as a duty which is capable of being delegated by the Local Ordinary, and in fact it may have been so delegated in the present case. On the other hand, if the duty is incapable of delegation on the true meaning of the statute, and in conformity with the practice of the Church, then it would follow that this protective direction of the statute was not complied with, and, if this should happen to be so, that might amount to an irregularity of a kind sufficient to invalidate the decree of dismissal. I have come therefore to the conclusion that without evidence whether in fact grave external motives existed for the dismissal of the defenders, and were made manifest to them, and, if so, whether the practice of the Church did not require that they should have been made manifest by the Local Ordinary, it would be unsafe to decide upon the pleadings that the dismissal of the defenders was not invalidated by irregularity. The only satisfactory course is to allow inquiry.

There is a further ground to support inquiry. The Rescript of the Sacred Congregation, dated 5th April 1937, intimated that it was decided that —

'(2) the dismissal of the extern sister Clare Harris is to be carried out forthwith;

'(3) the dismissal of the other extern sisters, unless they give signs of true amendment, is to be effected gradually.'

The dismissal of sister Clare Harris was absolute, but the dismissal of the other extern sisters was conditional upon their not giving signs of true amendment. The terms of this conditional dismissal were at no time intimated to the extern sisters. The Rescript of 5th April 1937 was notified to sister Clare Harris on 24th May, but the first intimation of dismissal was made to the other extern sisters on 10th January 1938, when in a communication of that date from the Vicar-General and the Diocesan Notary they were informed that by decree of the Sacred Congregation dated 5th April 1937 it had been decerned that they be 'dismissed from religion.' They were not notified of the qualifying condition.

It was maintained by counsel for the pursuers that the effect of the condition 'unless they gave signs of true amendment' was simply to leave it to the discretion of the ecclesiastical superiors to observe the conduct and behaviour of the extern sisters, and that there was no obligation to give them any intimation of the condition. It may be so, but I am not satisfied that it is so. *Prima facie* I should have thought that, when the Supreme Court of the Church had adjected to the dismissal a suspensive or resolutive condition, it would only have been reasonable to communicate that condition to the sisters concerned. If that was the intention of the direction of the Sacred Congregation, then it was not complied with, and I am not prepared to say, without inquiry, and without knowing what is the practice of the Church in a disciplinary matter of this kind, that there was not such a departure from regularity as might be fatal to the proceedings. In a matter so grave in its consequences to the defenders, affecting not only their status but also their livelihood, it is very necessary to avoid hasty conclusions that might result in irremediable injustice."

Notes

(1) *McDonald* was of course referred to in *West* (at para. 10–7) as one of the cases which **8–3** justified the application of the supervisory jurisdiction to domestic tribunals. See also *Gunstone v. Scottish Women's Amateur Athletic Association*, 1987 S.L.T. 611 and *St Johnstone Football Club Ltd v. Scottish Football Association Ltd*, 1965 S.L.T. 171 in relation to the right to a hearing in membership decisions affecting other domestic tribunals, here sporting bodies.

(2) The right to he heard has been permitted in a wide range of situations:

- General Commissioners of Income Tax may not decide issues adverse to either the tax authority or the taxpayer without giving a fair opportunity to both sides of correcting or challenging any relevant statements: *Inland Revenue v. Barrs*, 1961 S.C. (H.L.) 22.
- A local valuation appeal committee requires to ensure that parties are informed of the relevant facts on which the decision is to be based and given the opportunity to deal with them: *Moss' Empires Ltd v. Glasgow Assessor*, 1917 S.C. (H.L.) 1, extracted at para. 5–3.
- The Crofters Commission cannot bind the landlord by a decision upon which the landlord was not invited to make representations: *Dalgleish v. Livingston* (1895) 2 S.L.T. 564.
- Trade unions, in the context of disciplinary proceedings against a member, must give that member a right to be heard: *Breen v. Amalgamated Engineering Union* [1971] 1 All E.R. 1148.
- A police Chief Constable, when exercising his statutory powers to discharge a probationer constable, must give adequate notice with the charge against the constable and the right to be heard in relation to it: *Chief Constable of North Wales v. Evans* [1982] 1 W.L.R. 1155.

For further examples see *Stair Memorial Encyclopaedia*, Vol. 1, para. 259.

The most significant restatement of the application of the right to be heard to date arose in the next extract.

Ridge v. Baldwin

[1964] A.C. 40

"The Municipal Corporations Act 1882 provided by section 191: '(4) The Watch Committee, …may **8–4** at any time dismiss, any borough constable whom they think negligent in the discharge of his duty, or otherwise unfit for the same.' The Police Act 1919 provided by section 4(1): 'It shall be lawful for the Secretary of State to make regulations as to the …conditions of service of the members of all police forces within England and Wales, and every police authority shall comply with the regulations so made.' It was accepted that the 1919 Act did not impliedly repeal the relevant provisions of the 1882 Act. The relevant regulations contained detailed provisions as to the procedure to be followed where a report or allegation was received by the police authority from which it appeared that a chief constable might have committed an offence against the 'Discipline Code' (set out in the regulations).

According to the regulations, the detailed procedure, which involved a formal hearing before a specially constituted tribunal, could only be dispensed with if the chief constable admitted that he had committed an offence against the code.

Charles Ridge was appointed chief constable of the County Borough of Brighton in 1956. The appointment was 'subject to the Police Act and Regulations'. In 1957, Ridge, two police officers and two others were indicted for conspiracy to obstruct the course of justice between 1949 and 1957. Ridge was acquitted, but the other two police officers were convicted. On February 28, in passing sentence, the trial judge, Donovan J., made certain observations as to the chief constable's conduct. In the words of Lord Evershed: 'As I understand the language of Donovan J. …the appellant had been shown not to possess a sense of probity or of responsibility sufficient for the office which he held, and so had been unable to provide the essential leadership and example to the police force under his control which his office properly required.' On March 6, no evidence was offered against R on a further charge of corruption. Here Donovan J. referred to the police force's need for a leader 'who will be a new influence and who will set a different example from that which had lately obtained.' The following day, the Watch Committee, purporting to act under section 191(4) of the 1882 Act summarily dismissed R on the ground that in their opinion he had been negligent in the discharge of his duty, and was unfit for the same. He was given neither any notice of the meeting, nor any opportunity to make representations. The regulations were in no way operated. On March 18, the committee heard representations from R's solicitor, but gave no further particulars of the case against him. On July 5, the Home Secretary dismissed R's appeal under the Police (Appeals) Act 1927 (as amended), holding 'that there was sufficient material on which the Watch Committee could properly exercise their power of dismissal under section 191(4)'. The appeal had been made expressly without prejudice to any rights to contend that the purported dismissal was bad in law as being contrary to natural justice and not in accordance with the regulations.

R then brought an action in the High Court for a declaration that the dismissal was illegal, *ultra vires* and void, and for damages. His main purpose was to obtain the opportunity to resign voluntarily, his pension rights thus being preserved.

Eight significant issues arose:

1. Did the regulations apply? If they did, there had been a clear non-compliance.
2. If they did not, did the *audi alteram partem* rule of natural justice nevertheless apply?
3. If it applied, was it complied with?
4. If the decision to dismiss was bad under either of the foregoing heads, was it void or voidable?
5. If the initial dismissal was bad, was it cured by the second meeting of the committee on March 18?
6. Did the exercise of the right of appeal cure any invalidity?
7. Was the invalidity cured by the Police (Appeals) Act 1927, s.2(3), which stated that the Secretary of State's decision should be final and binding on all parties?
8. Should the invalidity be ignored, on the ground that the case was 'as plain as a pikestaff?'

Streatfeild J. at first instance ([1961] 2 W.L.R. 1054), held that natural justice had to be observed, and that the Watch Committee had done so. The Court of Appeal ([1963] 1 Q.B. 539) held that natural justice did not have to be observed as the action of the committee was 'administrative' or 'executive'. They were not deciding a question between two contending parties. Ridge's appeal to the House of Lords was allowed. The leading speeches were those of Lord Reid, who dealt mainly with natural justice at common law, and Lord Morris of Borth-y-Gest, who dealt mainly with the regulations. Lord Hodson came to the same conclusions as both Lord Reid and Lord Morris. Lord Devlin's speech was based solely on the regulations. Lord Evershed dissented."

LORD REID: "…The appellant's case is that in proceeding under the Act of 1882 the watch committee were bound to observe what are commonly called the principles of natural justice. Before attempting to reach any decision they were bound to inform him of the grounds on which they proposed to act and give him a fair opportunity of being heard in his own defence. The authorities on the applicability of the principles of natural justice are in some confusion, and so I find it necessary to examine this matter in some detail. The principle *audi alteram partem* goes back many centuries in our law and appears in a multitude of judgments of judges of the highest authority. In modern time opinions have sometimes been expressed to the effect that natural justice is so vague as to be practically meaningless. But I would regard these as tainted by the perennial fallacy that because something cannot be cut and dried or nicely weighed or measured therefore it does not exist. The idea of negligence is equally insusceptible to exact definition, but what a reasonable man would regard as fair procedure in particular circumstances and what he would regard as negligence in particular circumstances are equally capable of serving as tests in law, and natural justice as it has been interpreted in the courts is much more definite than that. It appears to me that one reason why the authorities on natural justice have been found difficult to reconcile is that insufficient attention has been paid to the great difference between various kinds of cases in which it has been sought to apply the principle. What a minister ought to do in considering objections to a scheme may be very different from what a watch committee ought to do in considering whether to dismiss a chief constable. So I shall deal first with cases of dismissal. These appear to fall into three classes: dismissal of a servant by his master, dismissal from an office held during pleasure, and dismissal from an office where there must be something against a man to warrant his dismissal.

The law regarding master and servant is not in doubt. There cannot be specific performance of a contract of service, and the master can terminate the contract with his servant at any time and for any reason or for none. But if he does so in a manner not warranted by the contract he must pay damages for breach of contract. So the question in a pure case of master and servant does not at all depend on whether the master has heard the servant in his own defence: it depends on whether the facts emerging at the trial prove breach of contract. But this kind of case can resemble dismissal from an office where the body employing the man is under some statutory or other restriction as to the kind of contract which it can make with its servants, or the grounds on which it can dismiss them. The present case does not fall within this class because a chief constable is not the servant of the watch committee or indeed of anyone else.

Then there are many cases where a man holds an office at pleasure. Apart from judges and others whose tenure of office is governed by statute, all servants and officers of the Crown hold office at pleasure, and this has been held even to apply to a colonial judge (*Terrell v. Secretary of State for the Colonies* [1953] 2 Q.B. 482). It has always been held, I think rightly, that such an officer has no right to be heard before he is dismissed, and the reason is clear. As a person having the power of dismissal need not have anything against the officer, he need not give any reason. That was stated as long ago as 1670 in *R. v. Stratford-on-Avon Corporation* (1809) 11 East 176 where the corporation dismissed a town clerk who held office *durante bene placito*. The leading case on this matter appears to be *R. v. Darlington School Governors* (1844) 6 Q.B. 682 although that decision was doubted by Lord Hatherley L.C. in *Dean v. Bennett* (1870) L.R. 6 Ch. 489 and distinguished on narrow grounds in *Willis v. Childe* (1851) 13 Beav. 117. I fully accept that where an office is simply held at pleasure the person having power of dismissal cannot be bound to disclose his reasons. No doubt he would in many cases tell the officer and hear his explanation before deciding to dismiss him. But if he is not bound to disclose his reason and does not do so, then, if the court cannot require him to do so, it cannot determine whether it would be fair to hear the officer's case before taking action. But again that is not this case. In this case the Act of 1882 only permits the watch committee to take action on the grounds of negligence or unfitness. Let me illustrate the difference by supposing that a watch committee who had no complaint against their present chief constable heard of a man with quite outstanding qualifications who would like to be appointed. They might think it in the public interest to make the change, but they would have no right to do it. But there could be no legal objection to dismissal of an officer holding office at pleasure in order to put a better man in his place.

So I come to the third class, which includes the present case. There I find an unbroken line of authority to the effect that an officer cannot lawfully be dismissed without first telling him what is alleged against him and hearing his defence or explanation. An early example is *Bagg's Case* (1615) 11 Co.Rep. 93b though it is more properly deprivation of the privilege of being a burgess of Plymouth. *R. v. Gaskin* (1799) 8 Term Rep. 209 arose out of the dismissal of a parish clerk, and Lord Kenyon C.J. referred to *audi alteram partem* as one of the first principles of justice. *R. v. Smith* (1844) 5 Q.B. 614 was another case of dismissal of a parish clerk, and Lord Denman C.J. held that even personal knowledge of the offence was no substitute for hearing the officer: his explanation might disprove criminal motive or intent and bring forward other facts in mitigation, and in any event delaying to hear him would prevent yielding too hastily to first impressions. *Ex parte Ramshay* (1852) 18 Q.B. 173 is important. It dealt with the removal from office of a county court judge, and the form of the legislation which authorised the Lord Chancellor to act is hardly distinguishable from the form of section 191, which confers powers on the watch committee. The Lord Chancellor was empowered if he should think fit to remove on the ground of inability or misbehaviour, but Lord Campbell C.J. said (*ibid.*, 190) that this was 'only on the implied condition prescribed by the principles of eternal justice'. In *Osgood v. Nelson* (1872) L.R. 5 H.L. 636 at 649, H.L., objection was taken to the way in which the Corporation of the City of London had removed the clerk to the Sheriff's Court, and Lord Hatherley L.C. said: 'I apprehend, my Lords, that, as has been stated by the learned Baron who has delivered, in the name of the judges, their unanimous opinion, the Court of Queen's Bench has always considered that it has been open to that court, as in this case it appears to have considered, to correct any court, or tribunal, or body of men who may have a power of this description, a power of removing from office, if it should be found that such persons have disregarded any of the essentials of justice in the course of their inquiry, before making that removal, or if it should be found that in the place of reasonable cause those persons have acted obviously upon mere individual caprice.'

That citation of authority might seem sufficient, but I had better proceed further. In *Fisher v. Jackson* [1891] 2 Ch. 84 three vicars had power to remove the master of an endowed school. But, unlike the *Darlington* case, 6 Q.B. 682 the trust deed set out the grounds on which he could be removed — briefly, inefficiency or failing to set a good example. So it was held that they could not remove him without affording him an opportunity of being heard in his own defence. Only two other cases of this class were cited in argument, *Cooper v. Wilson* [1937] 2 K.B. 309 and *Hogg v. Scott* [1947] K.B. 759. Both dealt with the dismissal of police officers and both were complicated by consideration of regulations made under the Police Acts. In the former the majority at least recognised that the principles of natural justice applied, and in deciding the latter Cassels J. in deciding that a chief constable could dismiss without hearing him an officer who had been convicted of felony, appears to have proceeded on a construction of the regulations.

Of course, if the regulations authorised him to do that and were *intra vires* in doing so, there would be no more to be said. I do not think it necessary to consider whether the learned judge rightly construed the regulations, for he did not expressly or, I think, by implication question the general principle that a man is not to be dismissed for misconduct without being heard.

Stopping there, I would think that authority was wholly in favour of the appellant, but the respondent's argument was mainly based on what has been said in a number of fairly recent cases dealing with different subject-matter. Those cases deal with decisions by ministers, officials and bodies of various kinds which adversely affected property rights or privileges of persons who had had no opportunity or no proper opportunity of presenting their cases before the decisions were given. And it is necessary to examine those cases for another reason. The question which was or ought to have been considered by the watch committee on March 7, 1958, was not a simple question whether or not the appellant should be dismissed. There were three possible courses open to the watch committee — reinstating the appellant as chief constable, dismissing him, or requiring him to resign. The difference between the latter two is that dismissal involved forfeiture of pension rights, whereas requiring him to resign did not. Indeed, it is now clear that the appellant's real interest in this appeal is to try to save his pension rights.

It may be convenient at this point to deal with an argument that, even if as a general rule a watch committee must hear a constable in his own defence before dismissing him, that case was so clear that nothing that the appellant could have said could have made any difference. It is at least very doubtful whether that could be accepted as an excuse. But, even if it could, the respondents would, in my view, fail on the facts. It may well be that no reasonable body of men could have reinstated the appellant. But as between the other two courses open to the watch committee the case is not so clear. Certainly on the facts, as we know them, the watch committee could reasonably have decided to forfeit the appellant's pension rights, but I could not hold that they would have acted wrongly or wholly unreasonably if they had in the exercise of their discretion decided to take a more lenient course.

I would start an examination of the authorities dealing with property rights and privileges with *Cooper v. Wandsworth Board of Works* (1863) 14 C.B.(N.S.) 180.

[His Lordship summarised this case, and *Hopkins v. Smethwick Local Board of Health* (1890) 24 Q.B.D. 712; *Smith v. The Queen* (1878) L.R. 3 App.Cas. 614, P.C.; and *De Verteuil v. Knaggs* [1918] A.C. 557.]

I shall now turn to a different class of case — deprivation of membership of a professional or social body. In *Wood v. Woad* (1874) L.R. 9 Ex. 190 the committee purported to expel a member of a mutual insurance society without hearing him, and it was held that their action was void, and so he was still a member. Kelly C.B. said of *audi alteram partem (ibid.* 196): 'This rule is not confined to the conduct of strictly legal tribunals but is applicable to every tribunal or body of persons invested with authority to adjudicate upon matters involving civil consequences to individuals.' This was expressly approved by Lord Macnaghten giving the judgment of the Board in *Lapointe v. L'Association de Bienfaisance et de Retraite de la Police de Montréal* [1906] A.C. 535, P.C. In that case the board of directors of the association had to decide whether to give a pension to a dismissed constable — the very point the watch committee had to decide in this case — and it was held *(ibid.* p. 539) that they had to observe 'the elementary principles of justice'.

Then there are the club cases, *Fisher v. Keane* (1878) 11 Ch.D. 353 and *Dawkins v. Antrobus* (1879) 17 Ch.D. 615, C.A. In the former, Jessel M.R. said of the committee, 11 Ch.D. 353 at 362–363: 'They ought not, as I understand it, according to the ordinary rules by which justice should be administered by committees of clubs; or by any other body of persons who decide upon the conduct of others, to blast a man's reputation for ever — perhaps to ruin his prospects for life, without giving him an opportunity of either defending or palliating his conduct.' In the latter case it was held that nothing had been done contrary to natural justice. In *Weinberger v. Inglis* [1919] A.C. 606, H.L., a member of enemy birth was excluded from the Stock Exchange, and it was held that the committee had heard him before acting. Lord Birken-head L.C. said *(ibid.* at 616): '...if I took the view that the appellant was condemned upon grounds never brought to his notice, I should not assent to the legality of this course, unless compelled by authority'. He said this although the rule under which the committee acted was in the widest possible terms — that the committee should each year re-elect such members as they should deem eligible as members of the Stock Exchange.

I shall not at present advert to the various trade union cases because I am deliberately considering the state of the law before difficulties were introduced by statements in various fairly recent cases. It appears to me that if the present case had arisen 30 or 40 years ago the courts would have had no difficulty in deciding this issue in favour of the appellant on the authorities which I have cited. So far as I am aware none of these authorities has ever been disapproved or even doubted. Yet the Court of Appeal have decided this issue against the appellant on more recent authorities which apparently justify that result. How has this come about?

At least three things appear to me to have contributed. In the first place there have been many cases where it has been sought to apply the principles of natural justice to the wider duties imposed on Ministers and other organs of government by modern legislation. For reasons which I shall attempt to state in a moment, it has been held that those principles have a limited application in such cases and those limitations have tended to be reflected in other decisions on matters to which in principle they do not appear to me to apply. Secondly, again for reasons which I shall attempt to state, those principles have been held to have a limited application in cases arising out of war-time legislation; and again such limitations have tended to be reflected in other cases. And, thirdly, there has, I think, been a misunderstanding of the judgment of Atkin L.J. in *R. v. Electricity Commissioners, ex p. London Electricity Joint Committee Co.* [1924] 1 K.B. 171.

In cases of the kind I have been dealing with the Board of Works or the Governor or the club committee was dealing with a single isolated case. It was not deciding, like a judge in a lawsuit, what were the rights of the person before it. But it was deciding how he should be treated — something analogous to a judge's duty in imposing a penalty. No doubt policy would play some part in the decision — but so it might when a judge is imposing a sentence. So it was easy to say that such a body is performing a quasi-judicial task in considering and deciding such a matter, and to require it to observe the essentials of all proceedings of a judicial character — the principles of natural justice.

Sometimes the functions of a minister or department may also be of that character, and then the rules of natural justice can apply in much the same way. But more often their functions are of a very different character. If a minister is considering whether to make a scheme for, say, an important new road, his primary concern will not be with the damage which its construction will do to the rights of individual owners of land. He will have to consider all manner of questions of public interest and, it may be, a number of alternative schemes. He cannot be prevented from attaching more importance to the fulfillment of his policy than to the fate of individual objectors, and it would be quite wrong for the courts to say that the minister should or could act in the same kind of way as a board of works deciding whether a house should be pulled down. And there is another important difference. As explained in *Local Government Board v. Arlidge* [1915] A.C. 120 a minister cannot do everything himself. His officers will have to gather and sift all the facts, including objections by individuals, and no individual can complain if the ordinary accepted methods of carrying on public business do not give him as good protection as would be given by the principles of natural justice in a different kind of case.

We do not have a developed system of administrative law — perhaps because until fairly recently we did not need it. So it is not surprising that in dealing with new types of cases the courts have had to grope for solutions, and have found that old powers, rules and procedure are largely inapplicable to cases which they were never designed or intended to deal with. But I see nothing in that to justify our thinking that our old methods are any less applicable today than ever they were to the older types of case. And if there are any dicta in modern authorities which point in that direction, then, in my judgment, they should not be followed.

And now I must say something regarding war-time legislation. The older authorities clearly show how the courts engrafted the principles of natural justice on to a host of provisions authorising administrative interference with private rights. Parliament knew quite well that the courts had an inveterate habit of doing that and must therefore be held to have authorised them to do it unless a particular Act showed a contrary intention. And such an intention could appear as a reasonable inference as well as from express words. It seems to me to be a reasonable and almost an inevitable inference from the circumstances in which Defence Regulations were made and from their subject-matter that, at least in many cases, the intention must have been to exclude the principles of natural justice. War-time secrecy alone would often require that, and the need for speed and general pressure of work were other factors. But it was not to be expected that anyone would state in so many words that a temporary abandonment of the rules of natural justice was one of the sacrifices which war conditions required — that would have been almost calculated to create the alarm and despondency against which one of the regulations was specifically directed. And I would draw the same conclusion from another fact. In many regulations there was set out an alternative safeguard more practicable in war time — the objective test that the officer must have reasonable cause to believe whatever was the crucial matter. (I leave out of account the very peculiar decision of this House in *Liversidge v. Anderson* [1942] A.C. 206.) So I would not think that any decision that the rules of natural justice were excluded from war-time legislation should be regarded as of any great weight in dealing with a case such as this case, which is of the older type, and which involves the interpretation of an Act passed long before modern modifications of the principles of natural justice became necessary, and at a time when, as Parliament was well aware, the courts habitually applied the principles of natural justice to provisions like section 191(4) of the Act of 1882.

The matter has been further complicated by what I believe to be a misunderstanding of a much-quoted passage in the judgment of Atkin L.J. in *R. v. Electricity Commissioners, ex p. London Electricity Joint*

Committee Co. [1924] 1 K.B. 171 at 205. He said: '...the operation of the writs [of prohibition and certiorari] has extended to control the proceedings of bodies which do not claim to be, and would not be recognised as, courts of justice. Wherever any body of persons having legal authority to determine questions affecting the rights of subjects, and having the duty to act judicially, act in excess of their legal authority, they are subject to the controlling jurisdiction of the King's Bench Division exercised in these writs.'

A gloss was put on this by Lord Hewart C.J. in *R. v. Legislative Committee of the Church Assembly, ex p. Haynes-Smith* [1928] 1 K. B. 411. There it was sought to prohibit the Assembly from proceeding further with the Prayer Book Measure 1927. That seems to me to have no resemblance to a question whether a person should be deprived of his rights or privileges, and the case was decided on the ground that this was a deliberative or legislative body and not a judicial body. Salter J. put it in a few lines (*ibid.* at 419): 'The person or body to whom these writs are to go must be a judicial body in this sense, that it has power to determine and to decide; and the power carries with it, of necessity, the duty to act judicially. I think that the Church Assembly has no such power, and therefore no such duty.' But Lord Hewart said (*ibid.* at 415) having quoted the passage from Atkin L.J.'s judgment: 'The question, therefore, which we have to ask ourselves in this case is whether it is true to say in this matter, either of the Church Assembly as a whole, or of the Legislative Committee of the Church Assembly, that it is a body of persons having legal authority to determine questions affecting the rights of subjects, and having the duty to act judicially. It is to be observed that in the last sentence which I have quoted from the judgment of Atkin L.J. the word is not "or", but "and". In order that a body may satisfy the required test it is not enough that it should have legal authority to determine questions affecting the rights of subjects; there must be superadded to that characteristic the further characteristic that the body has the duty to act judicially. The duty to act judicially is an ingredient which, if the test is to be satisfied, must be present. As these writs in the earlier days were issued only to bodies which without any harshness of construction could be called, and naturally would be called courts, so also today these writs do not issue except to bodies which act or are under the duty to act in a judicial capacity.'

I have quoted the whole of this passage because it is typical of what has been said in several subsequent cases. If Lord Hewart meant that it is never enough that a body simply has a duty to determine what the rights of an individual should be, but that there must always be something more to impose on it a duty to act judicially before it can be found to observe the principles of natural justice, then that appears to me impossible to reconcile with the earlier authorities ...And, as I shall try to show, it cannot be what Atkin L.J. meant.

In *R. v. Electricity Commissioners, ex p. London Electricity Joint Committee Co.* [1924] 1 K.B. 171, the commissioners had a statutory duty to make schemes with regard to electricity districts and to hold local inquiries before making them. They made a draft scheme which in effect allocated duties to one body which the Act required should be allocated to a different kind of body. This was held to be *ultra vires*, and the question was whether prohibition would lie. It was argued that the proceedings of the commissioners were purely executive and controllable by Parliament alone. Bankes L.J. said (*ibid.* at 198): 'On principle and on authority it is in my opinion open to this court to hold, and I consider that it should hold, that powers so far-reaching, affecting as they do individuals as well as property, are powers to be exercised judicially, and not ministerially or merely, to use the language of Palles C.B., as proceedings towards legislation.' So he inferred the judicial element from the nature of the power. And I think that Atkin L.J. did the same. Immediately after the passage which I said has been misunderstood, he cited a variety of cases and in most of them I can see nothing 'superadded' (to use Lord Hewart's word) to the duty itself. Certainly Atkin L.J. did not say that anything was superadded. And a later passage in his judgment convinces me that he, like Bankes L.J., inferred the judicial character of the duty from the nature of the duty itself. Although it is long I am afraid I must quote it [1924] 1 K.B. 171 at 206–207: 'In the present case the Electricity Commissioners have to decide whether they will constitute a joint authority in a district in accordance with law, and with what powers they will invest that body. The question necessarily involves the withdrawal from existing bodies of undertakers of some of their existing rights, and imposing upon them of new duties, including their subjection to the control of the new body, and new financial obligations. It also provides in the new body a person to whom may be transferred rights of purchase which at present are vested in another authority. The commissioners are proposing to create such a new body in violation of the Act of Parliament, and are proposing to hold a possibly long and expensive inquiry into the expediency of such a scheme, in respect of which they have the power to compel representatives of the prosecutors at attend and produce papers. I think that in deciding upon the scheme, and in holding the inquiry, they are acting judicially in the sense of the authorities I have cited.'

There is not a word in Atkin L.J.'s judgment to suggest disapproval of the earlier line of authority which I have cited. On the contrary, he goes further than those authorities. I have already stated my view that it is more difficult for the courts to control an exercise of power on a large scale where the treatment to be meted out to a particular individual is only one of many matters to be considered. This was a case of that kind, and, if Atkin L.J. was prepared to infer a judicial element from the nature of the power in this case, he could hardly disapprove such an inference when the power relates solely to the treatment of a particular individual.

The authority chiefly relied on by the Court of Appeal in holding that the watch committee were not bound to observe the principles of natural justice was *Nakkuda Ali v. Jayaratne* [1951] A.C. 66. In that case the Controller of Textiles in Ceylon made an order cancelling the appellant's licence to act as a dealer, and the appellant sought to have that order quashed. The controller acted under a Defence Regulation which empowered him to cancel a licence 'where the controller has reasonable grounds to believe that any dealer is unfit to be allowed to continue as a dealer'.

The Privy Council regarded that (*ibid.* at 77) as 'imposing a condition that there must in fact exist such reasonable grounds, known to the controller, before he can validly exercise the power of cancellation.' But according to their judgment certiorari did not lie, and no other means was suggested whereby the appellant or anyone else in his position could obtain redress even if the controller acted without a shred of evidence. It is quite true that the judgment went on, admittedly unnecessarily, to find that the controller had reasonable grounds and did observe the principles of natural justice, but the result would have been just the same if he had not. This House is not bound by decisions of the Privy Council, and for my own part nothing short of a decision of this House directly in point would induce me to accept the position that, although an enactment expressly requires an official to have reasonable grounds for his decision, our law is so defective that a subject cannot bring up such a decision for review however seriously he may be affected and however obvious it may be that the official acted in breach of his statutory obligation.

The judgment proceeds: 'But it does not seem to follow necessarily from this that the controller must be acting judicially in exercising the power. Can one not act reasonably without acting judicially? It is not difficult to think of circumstances in which the controller might, in any ordinary sense of the words, have reasonable grounds of belief without having ever confronted the licence holder with the information which is the source of his belief. It is a long step in the argument to say that because a man is enjoined that he must not take action unless he has reasonable ground for believing something he can only arrive at that belief by a course of conduct analogous to the judicial process. And yet, unless that proposition is valid, there is really no ground for holding that the controller is acting judicially or quasi-judicially when he acts under this regulation. If he is not under a duty so to act then it would not be according to law that his decision should be amenable to review and, if necessary, to avoidance by the procedure of certiorari.'

I would agree that in this and other Defence Regulation cases the legislature has submitted an obligation not to act without reasonable grounds for the ordinary obligation to afford to the person affected an opportunity to submit his defence. It is not necessary in this case to consider whether by so doing he has deprived the courts of the power to intervene if the officer acts contrary to his duty. The question in the present case is not whether Parliament substituted a different safeguard for that afforded by natural justice, but whether in the Act of 1882 it excluded the safeguard of natural justice and put nothing in its place.

So far there is nothing in the judgment of the Privy Council directly relevant to the present case. It is the next paragraph which causes the difficulty and I must quote the crucial passage (*ibid.* at 78): 'But the basis of the jurisdiction of the courts by way of certiorari has been so exhaustively analysed in recent years that individual instances are now only of importance as illustrating a general principle that is beyond dispute. That principle is most precisely stated in the words of Atkin L.J. in *R. v. Electricity Commissioners, ex p. London Electricity Joint Committee Co.* [1924] 1 K.B. 171 at 205' — and then follows the passage with which I have already dealt at length. And then there follows the quotation from Lord Hewart, which I have already commented on, ending with the words — 'there must be superadded to that characteristic the further characteristic that the body has the duty to act judicially'. and then it is pointed out: 'It is that characteristic that the controller lacks in acting under regulation 62.'

Of course, if it were right to say that Lord Hewart's gloss of Atkin L.J. stated 'a general principle that is beyond dispute', the rest would follow. But I have given my reasons for holding that it does no such thing, and in my judgment the older cases certainly do not 'illustrate' any such general principle — they contradict it. No case older than 1911 was cited in *Nakkuda's* case on this question, and this question was only one of several difficult questions which were argued and decided. So I am forced to the conclusion that this part of the judgment in *Nakkuda's* case was given under a serious misapprehension of the effect of the older authorities and therefore cannot be regarded as authoritative.

I would sum up my opinion in this way. Between 1882 and the making of police regulations in 1920 section 191(4) had to be applied to every kind of case. The respondents' contention is that, even where there was a doubtful question whether a constable was guilty of a particular act of misconduct, the watch committee were under no obligation to hear his defence before dismissing him. In my judgment it is abundantly clear from the authorities I have quoted that at that time the courts would have rejected any such contention. In later cases dealing with different subject-matter, opinions have been expressed in wide terms so as to appear to conflict with those earlier authorities. But learned judges who expressed those opinions generally had no power to overrule those authorities, and in any event it is a salutary rule that a judge is not to be assumed to have intended to overrule or disapprove of an authority which has not been cited to him and which he does not even mention. So I would hold that the power of dismissal in the Act of 1882 could not then have been exercised and cannot now be exercised until the watch committee have informed the constable of the grounds on which they propose to proceed and have given him a proper opportunity to present his case in defence.

Next comes the question whether the respondents' failure to follow the rules of natural justice on March 7 was made good by the meeting on March 18. I do not doubt that if an officer or body realises that it has acted hastily and reconsiders the whole matter afresh, after affording to the person affected a proper opportunity to present his case, then its later decision will be valid. An example is *De Verteuil's* case. But here the appellant's solicitor was not fully informed of the charges against the appellant and the watch committee did not annul the decision which they had already published and proceed to make a new decision. In my judgment, what was done on that day was a very inadequate substitute for a full rehearing. Even so, three members of the committee changed their minds, and it is impossible to say what the decision of the committee would have been if there had been a full hearing after disclosure to the appellant of the whole case against him. I agree with those of your Lordships who hold that this meeting of March 18 cannot affect the result of this appeal.

The other ground on which some of your Lordships prefer to proceed is the respondents' failure to act in accordance with the Police Regulations. I have had an opportunity of reading the speech about to be delivered by my noble and learned friend, Lord Morris of Borth-y-Gest, and I agree with his view about this.

Then there was considerable argument whether in the result the watch committee's decision is void or merely voidable. Time and again in the cases I have cited it has been stated that a decision given without regard to the principles of natural justice is void, and that was expressly decided in *Wood v. Woad*. I see no reason to doubt these authorities. The body with the power to decide cannot lawfully proceed to make a decision until it has afforded to the person affected a proper opportunity to state his case.

Finally, there is the question whether by appealing to the Secretary of State the appellant is in some way prevented from now asserting the nullity of the respondents' decision. A person may be prevented from asserting the truth by estoppel, but it is not seriously argued that that doctrine applies here. Then it is said that the appellant elected to go to the Secretary of State and thereby waived his right to come to the court. That appears to me to be an attempt to set up what is in effect estoppel where the essential elements for estoppel are not present. There are many cases where two remedies are open to an aggrieved person, but there is no general rule that by going to some other tribunal he puts it out of his power thereafter to assert his right in court; and there was no express waiver because in appealing to the Secretary of State the appellant reserved his right to maintain that the decision was a nullity.

But then it was argued that this case is special because by statute the decision of the Secretary of State is made final and binding. I need not consider what the result would have been if the Secretary of State had heard the case for the appellant and then given his own independent decision that the appellant should be dismissed. But the Secretary of State did not do that. He merely decided 'that there was sufficient material on which the watch committee could properly exercise their power of dismissal under section 191(4)'. So the only operative decision is that of the watch committee, and, if it was a nullity, I do not see how this statement by the Secretary of State can make it valid.

Accordingly, in my judgment, this appeal must be allowed. There appears to have been no discussion in the courts below as to remedies which may now be open to the appellant, and I do not think that this House should do more than declare that the dismissal of the appellant is null and void and remit the case to the Queen's Bench Division for further procedure. But it is right to put on record that the appellant does not seek to be reinstated as chief constable: his whole concern is to avoid the serious financial consequences involved in dismissal as against being required or allowed to resign."

LORD EVERSHED (dissenting) held that:

"(1) the shortcomings of the appellant as chief constable' did not fall within the Discipline Code;

(2) therefore, the Watch Committee were entitled to exercise their residual powers under section 191(4) of the 1882 Act without observing the regulations;

(3) there was no 'report or allegation' before the Watch Committee. Those words suggested 'something in the nature of an accusation as distinct from a conclusion reached after proper inquiry' (*i.e.* Donovan J.'s conclusion);

(4) that 'this was a special and entirely exceptional case outside the scope of the regulations, and, as a matter of public notoriety, requiring instant action by the Watch Committee';

(5) that if natural justice ought to have been observed, a decision in breach of natural justice would normally be voidable, not void, in that the body would be 'acting within its jurisdiction.' A decision would only be void if based on 'frivolous or futile' grounds or if there had been 'a real substantial miscarriage of justice';

(6) that apart from the prejudice to pension rights, the Watch Committee need not have given the plaintiff any opportunity to state points he had already made before Donovan J. The committee also had to act urgently. However, his Lordship was prepared to assume that the plaintiff should have had an opportunity to state his case for being allowed to resign;

(7) that justice had been done as representations had been made to the Watch Committee on March 18;

(8) that if he (his Lordship) was wrong on the last point, any defect was cured by the appeal to the Secretary of State, whose decision was rendered 'final and binding' by section 2(3) of the Police (Appeals) Act 1927.

Therefore his Lordship would have dismissed the appeal."

LORD MORRIS OF BORTH-Y-GEST held that:

"(1) there was a 'report or allegation' before the Watch Committee. There were, for example, a transcript of the judge's remarks, and 'certain statements made ...by members of the committee and the town clerk';

(2) the regulations should have been applied. As there was no admission of the commission of an offence, the regulations required a hearing;

(3) as the regulations had been ignored, the dismissal was void. (*Andrews v. Mitchell* [1905] A.C. 78, *Lapointe v. L'Association de Bienfaisance et de Retraite de la Police de Montréal* [1906] A.C. 535, and *Annamunthodo v. Oilfield Workers' Trade Union* [1961] A.C. 945 applied);

(4) the defect was not cured by the second hearing on March 18, as the plaintiff was never given notice of the allegations against him;

(5) the defect was not cured by the appeal to the Secretary of State as the original decision was a nullity, and the plaintiff so maintained during the appeal;

(6) apart from the regulations, natural justice should have been observed. The dismissal was not an 'executive or administrative act' as it was based on a 'suggestion of neglect of duty';

(7) a decision in breach of natural justice was void not voidable."

LORD HODSON delivered a speech concurring substantially with LORD REID and LORD MORRIS.

LORD DEVLIN held that the regulations applied and should have been observed. Any decision in breach of the regulations would be voidable unless any regulation laid down a "condition precedent to the conferment of authority on the committee which had not been fulfilled". Article 11(1) of the 1882 regulations allowed the police authority to act only on receipt of a report from the tribunal set up under the regulations to hear the evidence and make recommendations. The committee's decision was therefore void *ab initio*.

His Lordship held that a decision in breach of natural justice was voidable only.

Notes

(1) The scope of natural justice, the curing of a defective decision, whether such decisions are void or simply voidable, the nature of the procedural requirements and the issue of action taken in an emergency situation are all raised by this case. Unsurprisingly, it has been widely followed and cited in subsequent cases and discussed in a number of articles: see A.W. Bradley, "A Failure of Justice and Defect of Police" [1964] C.L.J. 83; A.L. Goodhart, "Ridge v. Baldwin: Administration and Natural Justice" (1964) 80 L.Q.R. 105; S.A. de Smith, "The House of Lords on Natural Justice" (1963) 26 M.L.R. 543; case notes by G.H.L. Friedman (1963) 113 L.J. 716; and D. Paterson, "Lord Reid and the Writ of Certiorari" [1966] N.Z.L.J. 107.

8–5

(2) Lord Reid was of course a Scottish judge, and arguably the approach he expounded here was of less significance in Scots, than in English, law. Certainly, the classificatory approach criticised by Lord Reid appears to have had a less sure footing in Scots law. J. Bennett Miller, "The Place of the Quasi-Judicial Decision in Scots Law" (1958) 3 J.R. 39 argued that the distinction between judicial, quasi-judicial and administrative decisions referred to in authorities prior to *Ridge* was based on the concerns of the English system of prerogative orders and the failure to understand the limitations of the concept of *lis inter partes* (essentially, a dispute

requiring judicial resolution). In particular, he denies the validity of the concept of the quasi-judicial decision, central to the classificatory approach as having any place in Scots law:

> "If, after this protracted survey the quasi-judicial is evaluated in reference to Scots law, it appears that the term serves no useful purpose in that legal system either (a) as to the type of remedy available to the citizen adversely affected by the decision in question, or (b) as a guide to the proper circumstances in which the rules of Natural Justice must be observed. On the latter point, Lord Somervell of Harrow [*Vine v. National Dock Labour Board* [1957] 2 W.L.R. 106 at 121] observed, 'The court has to consider whether a Minister, tribunal or board has to act "judicially" in some respect and has failed to do so. The respect in which he has to observe judicial procedure will depend on the statutory or other provisions under which the matter arises.' This eschewal of conceptual thinking upon judicial and quasi-judicial powers closely approaches the attitude hitherto adopted by the Scottish courts to such problems. It is the approach adopted by Lord Birnam in *Secretary of State for Scotland v. Burgh of Ayr* [1950 S.C. 102, S.L.T. 257] and by the court in *Hayman v. Lord Advocate* [1951 S.C. 621, 1952 S.L.T. 209] and in *Barrs v. British Wool Marketing Board* [1957 S.C. 72, S.L.T. 153]. In the two last-mentioned cases, the appearance of the term 'quasi-judicial' has in no way done violence to that approach, and it is not criticised on any other ground than that in it there is introduced into Scots law a term of no clear significance, and of uneasy history for which there appears to be no necessity in our legal system.
>
> Its introduction is particularly unwelcome at a stage when English lawyers appear to be at last shaking off the trammels of the conceptualists and when the recently published Report of the Committee on Administrative Tribunals and Enquiries [(1957) Cmnd. 218, para. 276] has, with a refreshing air of realism, discarded the shibboleths of judicial, quasi-judicial and administrative and has addressed itself directly 'to the task of finding a reasonable balance between the conflicting interests.' "

On quasi-judicial functions generally see *Stair Memorial Encyclopaedia*, Vol. 1, para. 212. In its focus on the nature of the interest at stake, *Ridge* is certainly consistent with *McDonald* and has been cited with approval in a number of further leading Scottish decisions: see *Malloch v. Aberdeen Corporation*, 1971 S.C. (H.L.) 85 and *Errington v. Wilson*, 1995 S.L.T. 1193. Classification of function is not wholly redundant. It may still be relevant to determine the nature of a function for other purposes within administrative law, such as whether a body may delegate its functions to some of its members or whether its functions are judicial and thus non-delegable, on which see, for example, *Young v. Fife Regional Council*, 1986 S.L.T. 331, extracted at para. 5–9, or if a decision-making body has power to award expenses, on which see *Milton v. Argyll and Clyde Health Board*, 1997 S.L.T. 565, or whether an action has been taken in the exercise of an administrative function and is within the jurisdiction of the Parliamentary Commissioner for Administration, on which see Chapter 16, or whether a function of a sheriff is truly administrative or judicial for the purpose of an appeal on a point of law to the Court of Session, on which see *Rodenhurst v. Chief Constable, Grampian Police*, 1992 S.L.T. 104, noted at para.12–15; see generally *Stair Memorial Encyclopaedia*, Vol. 1, paras 209–211.

8–6   (3) *Ridge* came to be considered in *Durayappah v. Fernando* [1967] 2 AC 337. A Minister had power to order the dissolution of a municipal council if it appeared to him that (at 350):

> "it is not competent to perform …or persistently makes a default in the performance of any duty or duties imposed upon it; or…persistently refuses or neglects to comply with any provision of law".

Such an order was made in relation to Jaffna Municipal Council in Ceylon and challenged on the ground that no hearing had been given. The Supreme Court of Ceylon held that the subject and wording of the provisions of the order automatically excluded a duty to act judicially. The Privy Council rejected this. Lord Upjohn observed (at 349):

> "Outside the well-known classes of cases, no general rule can be laid down as to the application of the general principle in addition to the language of the provision. In their Lordships' opinion there are three matters which must always be borne in mind when considering whether the principle should be applied or not. These three matters are: first, what is the nature of the property, the office held, status enjoyed or services to be performed by the complainant of injustice. Secondly, in what circumstances or upon what occasions is the person claiming to be entitled to exercise the

measure of control entitled to intervene. Thirdly, when a right to intervene is proved, what sanctions in fact is the latter entitled to impose upon the other. It is only upon a consideration of all these matters that the question of the application of the principle can properly be determined."

Here, the Privy Council observed that the council was first, by statute a public corporation with important duties. Secondly, the charge was a serious one. Thirdly, the sanction imposed was absolute. In the circumstances, the Minister should have observed natural justice and given a hearing. The appellant, the mayor, was refused a remedy as he lacked title to sue: see case note by J.M. Eekelaar. "Breach of Natural Justice: Void or Voidable?" (1967) 30 M.L.R. 701.

(4) In *Malloch v. Aberdeen Corporation*, 1971 S.C. (H.L.) 85, Lord Reid had cause to consider further the tri-partite classification of employment situations propounded by him in *Ridge*. Under the Education (Scotland) Act 1946, Malloch was a teacher employed by the corporation. Subsequently, regulations were made in terms of that Act requiring all teachers to register with a new statutory body, the General Teaching Council for Scotland. Malloch could register but on a point of principle refused to do so. He was advised by the corporation that they could no longer employ him. In terms of their duty under the Education (Scotland) Act 1962 they had to convene a meeting to pass a resolution for his dismissal. He was allowed to attend the meeting but not to address it. The committee resolved to dismiss him. He sought judicial review of the decision arguing that there had been a breach of the rules of natural justice. Lord Reid observed (at 104):

> "An elected public body is in a very different position from a private employer. Many of its servants in the lower grades are in the same position as servants of a private employer. But many in higher grades or 'offices' are given special statutory status or protection. The right of a man to be heard in his own defence is the most elementary protection of all and, where a statutory form of protection would be less effective if it did not carry with it a right to be heard, I would not find it difficult to imply this right."

Accordingly, notwithstanding that he was held to be an office holder subject to dismissal at pleasure, the legislation was held to imply the right to a hearing. See, however, the dissent of Lord Guest and Lord Morris of Borth-y-Gest; see too *Chief Constable of North Wales v. Evans* noted by J. McMullen, "Dismissal, Natural Justice and Judicial Review" (1984) 47 M.L.R. 234.

(5) It will be noted in addition that the categories mentioned by Lord Reid are not necessarily exhaustive. A case of master and servant may resemble dismissal from office when the body in question is subject to statutory restrictions as to the decisions that it can make in relation to its servants or on the grounds for which it can dismiss them. When is a decision more than simply a pure employment one and involving the exercise of a jurisdiction, thus potentially attracting judicial review? *Malloch* was not regarded as a case involving considerations purely of employment law. A house surgeon employed by the hospital board was entitled to a fair hearing under procedures for his dismissal approved by the Secretary of State as an inherent condition of his contract of service: *Palmer v. Inverness Hospitals Board of Management*, 1963 S.C. 311. See in particular the opinion of the Lord Justice-Clerk (Wheatley), extracted at para. 2–42, where a fireman was subject to a statutory code of discipline, then a decision leading to his dismissal, in breach of the code, was held to be ineffective in judicial review proceedings: *McDonald v. Lanarkshire Fire Brigade Joint Committee*, 1959 S.C. 141 and on disciplinary proceedings in the prison service see *R. v. Secretary of State for the Home Department, ex parte Benwell* [1985] Q.B. 554.

The existence of a claim to the right to be heard is different from the procedure by which this can be vindicated. Thus, in view of *West v. Secretary of State for Scotland*, 1992 S.C. 385, extracted at para. 10–7, and *Tehrani v. Argyll and Clyde Health Board (No. 2)*, 1990 S.L.T. 118, which distinguished *Malloch*, extracted at para. 10–5, it is no longer clear that the procedure that *Palmer* invoked, that of judicial review, would be competent. Compare also the decision in *Blair v. Lochaber District Council*, 1995 S.L.T. 407, extracted at para. 10–14. Similarly, a "servant" like McDonald may now require to take proceedings against his employer for unfair dismissal or wrongful dismissal as a breach of contract, under the Employment Rights Act 1996, rather than invoking judicial review. Even though use of judicial review for breach of natural justice in an employment situation has been somewhat restricted, the courts have increasingly been prepared to imply an obligation to observe natural justice in contracts of employment and grant remedies accordingly: see, for example, *Stevenson v. United Road Transport Union* [1977] I.C.R. 893 (trade union official); *R. v. British Broadcasting Corporation, ex parte Lavelle* [1983] 1 W.L.R. 23 (BBC employee); and on this generally see F.P. Davidson, "Judicial Review of Decisions to Dismiss" (1984) 35 N.I.L.Q. 121; and *Stair Memorial Encyclopaedia*, Vol. 1, para. 269.

8–7   (6) The argument that nothing that the Chief Constable in *Ridge* could have said would have made any difference also arose in *Malloch*. The Corporation argued that the hearing contended for by Malloch was unnecessary as they were bound by the regulations to dismiss him. Lord Reid observed (at 104):

> "Then it was argued that to have afforded a hearing to the appellant before dismissing him would have been a useless formality, because whatever he might have said could have made no difference. If that could clearly be demonstrated, it might be a good answer. But I need not decide that, because there was here, I think, a substantial possibility that a sufficient number of the committee might have been persuaded not to vote for the appellant's dismissal. The motion for dismissal had to be carried by a two-thirds majority of those present, and at the previous meeting of the committee there was not a sufficient majority carrying a similar motion. Between these meetings the committee had received a strong letter from the Secretary of State urging them to dismiss the teachers who refused to register. And it appears that they had received some advice which might have been taken by them to mean that those who failed to vote for dismissal might incur personal liability. The appellant might have been able to persuade them that they need not have any such fear.
>
> Then the appellant might have argued that on their true construction the Regulations did not require the committee to dismiss him and that, if they did require that, they were *ultra vires*. The question of *ultra vires* was not argued before us and on that I shall say no more than that it is not obvious that the Secretary of State had power under any statute to make Regulations requiring the dismissal of teachers who failed to acquire and pay for a new qualification such as registration. But the question of the proper construction of the Regulations was argued and there I think that the appellant had at least an arguable case."

See also the speech of Lord Wilberforce, particularly at p. 118. The court appears to accept that it might be possible in some circumstances to argue that a hearing would make no difference, but guidance as to what those circumstances might be is a little lacking. On the one hand, it could be that no breach of natural justice has occurred unless something of substance has been lost. For example, in *Glynn v. Keele University* [1971] 2 All E.R. 89 a student who appeared naked on campus was dismissed by his university without notice of the charge and without the opportunity to state his case. The offence was seen as being so serious that the courts could find no ground to disturb a decision which, it accepted, had been taken in breach of natural justice. In *George v. Secretary of State for the Environment* (1979) 77 L.G.R. 689 Lord Denning M.R. stated (at 695) in the context of a statutory application to quash (on which see para. 12–22), that:

> "There is no such thing as a technical breach of natural justice …the position under the first limb is almost indistinguishable from that under the second limb. You should not find a breach of natural justice unless there has been substantial prejudice to the applicant as a result of the mistake or error which has been made."

The second limb referred to was that the applicant has been substantially prejudiced by failure to comply with the procedural requirement, on which see para. 12–22: see also *Scott v. Aberdeen Corporation*, 1976 S.L.T. 141 at 147 *per* Lord Avonside and *Cinnamond v. British Airports Authority* [1980] 2 All E.R. 368 at 377 *per* Brandon L.J. However, the observation in *Barrs v. British Wool Marketing Board*, 1957 S.C. 72, extracted at para. 9–11, that "Justice should not only be done but should also be seen to be done" and the acceptance in *Errington v. Wilson*, 1995 S.L.T. 1193 above that where there is an allegation of breach of natural justice prejudice did not require to be established, seems to cast doubt on this approach: see also *Tait v. Central Radio Taxis (Tollcross) Ltd*, 1987 S.L.T. 506 at 510 and *Kanda v. Government of Malaya* [1962] A.C. 322 at 337 *per* Lord Denning. Note, too, the view of A.W. Bradley, that the decision in *Glynn* would not necessarily be followed in Scotland and the court may not have the same discretion to refuse relief if a breach of natural justice has occurred: *Stair Memorial Encyclopaedia*, Vol. 1, para. 270, and see generally D.H. Clark, "Natural Justice: Substance and Shadow" [1975] P.L. 27 and H.W.R. Wade, "Nudism and Natural Justice" (1971) 87 L.Q.R. 320.

THE DUTY TO ACT FAIRLY

Re HK (an infant)

[1967] 2 Q.B. 617

"Until the Commonwealth Immigrants Act 1962 came into force, Commonwealth subjects were entitled as of right to come to the United Kingdom. Thereafter, under section 2(1) of that Act, an immigration officer had a discretion to refuse admission to Commonwealth citizens, or to admit them subject to conditions. However, under section 2(2), that discretion could not be exercised in respect of 'any person who satisfies an immigration officer that he ...(a) is ordinarily resident in the United Kingdom or was so resident at any time within the past two years; or (b) is the ...child under 16 years of age, of a Commonwealth citizen who is resident in the United Kingdom...'. Paragraph 2(4) of Schedule 1 to that Act gave an immigration officer power to cancel a notice refusing a person admission.

Abdul Rehman Khan, a native of Pakistan, settled in Bradford in 1961. He claimed that he had left in Pakistan a wife and five children. In 1966, he went to Pakistan and returned with H.K., whom he said was his son aged 15 ½. On arrival at London Airport they were interviewed by an immigration officer. Abdul Rehman appeared to be within s.2(2)(a). However, the officer's suspicions were aroused because H.K. appeared to be well over 15. The officer sent H.K. to the port medical officer, who estimated the boy's age at '17 years'. The officer then interviewed A.R. and H.K. separately, with the aid of interpreters. His suspicions were increased, and he referred the matter to the Chief Immigration Officer, Mr Collison. As a result of further interviews Mr Collison made up his mind that he was not satisfied that H.K. was under 16, and a notice refusing admission was served on November 21. H.K. was to be removed at noon on the following day. The following morning, further inquiries were made concerning a school certificate which gave as a date of birth February 29, 1951 (a non-existent date). Abdul Rehman applied for a writ of habeas corpus, and H.K.'s departure was delayed. During the course of the hearing by the Divisional Court he was given leave to move also for an order of certiorari to quash the decision to refuse H.K. admission."

LORD PARKER C.J.: "...Mr Gratiaen [counsel] submits that in deciding whether or not he is satisfied as to the matter set out in the subsection — in this case whether he is satisfied that the boy is under 16 — an immigration officer is acting in a judicial or quasi-judicial capacity and must conform to the rules of natural justice. Subject to there being due compliance with those rules, Mr Gratiaen admits that the decision of the immigration officer cannot be challenged and that this court could not interfere. He does, however, maintain that the rules of natural justice require that before reaching his decision the immigration officer must give the immigrant an opportunity to satisfy him and if, as in this case, he has formed an impression that the immigrant is 16 or more, he must give the immigrant an opportunity to remove that impression. He claims that if that opportunity had been given, evidence would have been provided such as has been produced before us in these proceedings and that such evidence would have satisfied the officer. Having regard to the course which these proceedings have taken, it is unnecessary and, I think, indeed inadvisable to comment on that further evidence ...One thing I myself am quite clear on and that is that even if an immigration officer is required to act judicially or quasi-judicially, even if that is so, he is not under any duty to hold a full-scale inquiry or to adopt judicial process and procedure. The burden here under the Act is on the immigrant to satisfy the immigration officer and the provisions of the Schedule to which I have referred quite clearly show that it is impossible and therefore not contemplated that an immigration officer should hold any inquiry of that sort ...I doubt whether it can be said that the immigration authorities are acting in a judicial or quasi-judicial capacity as those terms are generally understood. But at the same time, I myself think that even if an immigration officer is not in a judicial or quasi-judicial capacity, he must at any rate give the immigrant an opportunity of satisfying him of the matters in the subsection, and for that purpose let the immigrant know what his immediate impression is so that the immigrant can disabuse him. That is not, as I see it, a question of acting or being required to act judicially, but of being required to act fairly. Good administration and an honest or bona fide decision must, as it seems to me, require not merely impartiality, nor merely bringing one's mind to bear on the problem, but acting fairly; and to the limited extent that the circumstances of any particular case allow, and within the legislative

8–8

framework under which the administrator is working, only to that limited extent do the so-called rules of natural justice apply, which in a case such as this is merely a duty to act fairly. I appreciate that in saying that it may be said that one is going further than is permitted on the decided cases because heretofore at any rate the decisions of the courts do seem to have drawn a strict line in these matters according to whether there is or is not a duty to act judicially or quasi-judicially. It has sometimes been said that if there is no duty to act judicially or quasi-judicially there is no power in the court whatever to interfere. I observe that in the well-known case of *Nakkuda Ali v. M.F. de S. Jayaratne* [1951] A.C. 66 again a decision of the Privy Council, the court were considering this kind of case. There the Controller of Textiles in Ceylon was empowered to revoke licences where the controller had reasonable grounds to believe that any dealer was unfit to be allowed to continue as a dealer. Those were the words to be considered in that case which are of course different in the present case. But Lord Radcliffe, when giving the advice of the Judicial Committee, began by distinguishing that case from the well-known case of *Liversidge* [1942] A.C. 206 and went on to consider the position of the controller in law. He said [1951] A.C. 66 at 78:

> 'In truth, when he cancels a licence he is not determining a question: he is taking executive action to withdraw a privilege because he believes, and has reasonable grounds to believe, that the holder is unfit to retain it.'

He goes on to say that:

> 'the power conferred on the controller …stands by itself on the bare words of the regulation and, if the mere requirement that the controller must have reasonable grounds of belief is insufficient to oblige him to act judicially, there is nothing else in the context or conditions of his jurisdiction that suggests that he must regulate his action by analogy to judicial rules.'

Having come to that decision, Lord Radcliffe then went on in effect to deal with the position if that was wrong, and if the controller was acting in a judicial capacity. He said (*ibid.* at 81):

> 'It is impossible to see in this any departure from natural justice. The respondent had before him ample material that would warrant a belief that the appellant had been instrumental in getting the interpolations made and securing for himself a larger credit at the bank than he was entitled to. Nor did the procedure adopted fail to give the appellant the essentials that justice would require, assuming the respondent to have been under a duty to act judicially.'

That might be understood as saying that if there was no duty to act judicially, then it would be impossible to interfere, even if the applicant had not been given the essentials that justice requires. I very much doubt, however, whether it was intended to say any more than that there is no duty to invoke judicial process unless there is a duty to act judicially. I do not understand him to be saying that if there is no duty to act judicially, then there is no duty even to be fair.

When, however, that has been said, it seems to me impossible in the present case to say that the decision made on the evening of November 21, 1966, was not arrived at, as I put it, fairly. It is impossible to believe other than that both father and son knew full well of what they had to satisfy the authorities. They were, as it seems to me, given ample opportunity to do so, and the fact that the officer was not satisfied is not, as is admitted, a matter for this court.

[His Lordship then held that any question as to whether the authorities should have taken any further steps in the light of evidence adduced after the decision had been taken was not a matter for certiorari or habeas corpus. Furthermore the matter was now having the personal attention of the Home Secretary. 'Accordingly, it seems to me that Mr Gratiaen has had even more that he hoped for, and that there is no reason why this court should retain any further control over it …I would dismiss both the application for habeas corpus and the application for certiorari.']"

SALMON L.J.: "…I have no doubt at all that …the immigration officer is obliged to act in accordance with the principles of natural justice. That does not of course mean that he has to adopt judicial procedures or hold a formal inquiry, still less than he has to hold anything in the nature of a trial, but he must act, as Lord Parker C.J. has said, fairly in accordance with the ordinary principles of natural justice. If, for example, and this I am sure would never arise, it could be shown that when he made an order refusing admission he was biased or had acted capriciously or dishonestly, this court would have power to intervene by the prerogative writ. There are, as my Lord has said, a good many cases in which the view has been expressed that unless a person exercising a power is acting in a judicial or quasi-judicial capacity the courts cannot intervene. Of course, an immigration officer is acting in an administrative rather than in a judicial capacity. What, however, is a quasi-judicial capacity has, so far as I know, never been exhaustively defined. It seems to me to cover at any rate a case where the circumstances in which a person who is called upon to exercise a statutory power and make a decision affecting basic rights of others are such that the law impliedly imposes upon him a duty to act fairly. When Parliament passed the Commonwealth Immigrants Act 1962, it deprived Commonwealth citizens of their right of unrestricted entry into the United Kingdom. It laid down conditions under which they might enter and left it to the immigration officers to decide whether such conditions existed. Their decision is of vital importance to the immigrants since their whole future may depend upon it. In my judgment it is implicit in the statute that the authorities in exercising these powers and making decisions must act in accordance with the principles of natural justice.

Mr Gratiaen has not suggested, nor would it be possible to suggest on the evidence before this court, that when on November 21, 1966, the immigration officer refused admission to H.K. to enter the United Kingdom, he acted otherwise than in accordance with the rules of natural justice. It is quite plain that no one could say that on the material then before him as a fair man he must have been satisfied that this boy was under 16 years of age. The material before him did not satisfy him and I for one am not at all surprised. Therefore the refusal made and the notice served on November 21, 1966, are unimpeachable. It follows that the boy's detention pending his removal abroad was lawful.
Accordingly, the application in this case is quite hopeless.

BLAIN J.: "...I would only say that an immigration officer having assumed the jurisdiction granted by those provisions [*i.e.* to cancel a notice refusing admission, under Sched. 1, para. 2(4)] is in a position where it is his duty to exercise that assumed jurisdiction, whether it be administrative, executive or quasi-judicial, fairly, by which I mean applying his mind dispassionately to a fair analysis of the particular problem and the information available to him in analysing it. If in any hypothetical case, and in any real case, this court was satisfied that an immigration officer was not so doing, then in my view mandamus would lie. That is not the position in this case, nor indeed is the court in this case moved for leave to issue a writ of mandamus.

I need say no more other than that I agree with what has fallen from my Lords."

McInnes v. Onslow Fane

[1978] 3 All E.R. 211

"The plaintiff had held a promoter's licence for boxing matches issued in the 1950s by the British   **8–9** Boxing Board of Control (a voluntary self-regulatory organisation). In 1971 the board granted him a trainer's licence and in 1973 a master of ceremonies' licence. After an incident at a boxing match in 1973, the Board withdrew all the plaintiff's licences. Subsequently, he applied to the Board for a manager's licence on five occasions, but his applications were rejected. The plaintiff sought a declaration against the Board (represented by two of its members) that it had acted contrary to the rules of natural justice/or unfairly by (1) failing to inform the plaintiff of the case against him so that he could answer those concerns and (2) by not granting him an oral hearing prior to rejecting his last licence application."

MEGARRY V.-C.: "...It was common ground between Mr Beloff [counsel for the plaintiff] and Mr Moses [counsel for the defendants] that the points before me was the subject of no direct authority: although expulsion from clubs and other bodies is the subject of an ample range of authorities, the refusal of applications for membership is much less richly endowed. It was also accepted that the point is of considerable general importance. There are many bodies which, though not established or operating under the authority of statute, exercise control, often on a national scale, over many activities which are important to many people, both as providing a means of livelihood and for other reasons. Sometimes that control is exercised, as by the board, by means of a system of granting or refusing licences, and sometimes it is operated by means of accepting or rejecting applications for membership. One particular aspect of this is membership of a trade union, without which it is impossible to obtain many important forms of work. In such cases it is plainly important, both to the body and the applicant, for them to know whether, before the application is rejected, the applicant is entitled to prior notice of any case against granting him a licence or admitting him to membership, and whether he is entitled to an oral hearing.

I think that I should take the matter by stages. First, there is the question of whether the grant or refusal of a licence by the board is subject to any requirements of natural justice or fairness which will be enforced by the courts. The question is not one that is governed by statute or contract, with questions of their true construction or the implication of terms; for there is no statute, and there is no contract between the plaintiff and the board. Nevertheless, in recent years there has been a marked expansion of the ambit of the requirements of natural justice and fairness reaching beyond statute and contract. A striking example is *Nagle v. Feilden* [1966] 2 Q.B. 633. There, a woman sought a declaration and injunctions against the Jockey Club to enforce her claim that she ought not to be refused a trainer's licence for horse-racing merely because she was a woman. At first instance her claim had been struck out, but the Court of Appeal reversed this decision. Lord Denning M.R. accepted that social clubs could refuse to admit an applicant for membership as they wished; but the Jockey Club exercised 'a virtual monopoly in an important field of human activity', and what gave the courts jurisdiction was 'a man's right to work': see 644, 646. In reaching his conclusion, Lord Denning M.R. observed that being a jockey could be regarded as being an unsuitable occupation for a woman, whereas being a trainer could not: see 647.

...[W]here the court is entitled to intervene, I think it must be considered what type of decision is in question. I do not suggest that there is any clear or exhaustive classification; but I think that at least three categories may be discerned. First, there are what may be called the forfeiture cases. In these, there is a decision which takes away some existing right or position, as where a member of an organisation is expelled or a licence is revoked. Second, at the other extreme there are what may be called the application cases. These are cases where the decision merely refuses to grant the applicant the right or position that he seeks, such as membership of the organisation, or a licence to do certain acts. Third, there is an intermediate category, which may be called the expectation cases, which differ from the application cases only in that the applicant has some legitimate expectation from what has already happened that his application will be granted. This head includes cases where an existing licence-holder applies for a renewal of his licence, or a person already elected or appointed to some position seeks confirmation from some confirming authority: see, for instance, *Weinberger v. Inglis* [1919] A.C. 606; *Breen v. Amalgamated Engineering Union* [1971] 2 Q.B. 175; and see *Schmidt v. Secretary of State for Home Affairs* [1969] 2 Ch. 149, 170, 173 and *R. v. Barnsley Metropolitan Borough Council, ex p. Hook* [1976] 1 W.L.R. 1052, 1058.

It seems plain that there is a substantial distinction between the forfeiture cases and the application cases. In the forfeiture cases, there is a threat to take something away for some reason: and in such cases, the right to an unbiased tribunal, the right to notice of the charges and the right to be heard in answer to the charges (which in *Ridge v. Baldwin* [1964] A.C. 40, 132, Lord Hodson said were three features of natural justice which stood out) are plainly apt. In the application cases, on the other hand, nothing is being taken away, and in all normal circumstances there are no charges, and so no requirement of an opportunity of being heard in answer to the charges. Instead, there is the far wider and less defined question of the general suitability of the applicant for membership or a licence. The distinction is well-recognised, for in general it is clear that the courts will require natural justice to be observed for expulsion from a social club, but not on an application for admission to it. The intermediate category, that of the expectation cases, may at least in some respects be regarded as being more akin to the forfeiture cases than the application cases; for although in form there is no forfeiture but merely an attempt at acquisition that fails, the legitimate expectation of a renewal of the licence or confirmation of the membership is one which raises the question of what it is that has happened to make the applicant unsuitable for the membership or licence for which he was previously thought suitable.

I pause there. I do not think that I need pursue the expectation cases, for in the present case I can see nothing that would bring the plaintiff within them...

...In my judgment, the case is plainly an application case in which the plaintiff is seeking to obtain a licence that he has never held and had no legitimate expectation of holding; he had only the hope (which may be confident or faint or anything between) which any applicant for anything may always have.

...[T]here is the question of the requirements of natural justice or fairness that have to be applied in an application case such as this. What are the requirements where there are no provisions of any statute or contract either conferring a right to the licence in certain circumstances, or laying down the procedure to be observed, and the applicant is seeking from an unofficial body the grant of a type of licence that he has never held before, and, though hoping to obtain it, has no legitimate expectation of receiving?

I do not think that much help is to be obtained from discussing whether 'natural justice' or 'fairness' is the more appropriate term. It one accepts that 'natural justice' is a flexible term which imposes different requirements in different cases, it is capable of applying appropriately to the whole range of situations indicated by terms such as 'judicial', 'quasi-judicial' and 'administrative'. Nevertheless, the further the situation is away from anything that resembles a judicial or quasi-judicial situation, and the further the question is removed from what may reasonably be called a justiciable question, the more appropriate it is to reject an expression which includes the word 'justice' and to use instead terms such as 'fairness', or 'the duty to act fairly': see *Re H.K. (An Infant)* [1967] 2 Q.B. 617, 630, *per* Lord Parker C.J.; *Re Pergamon Press Ltd* [1971] Ch. 388, 399, *per* Lord Denning M.R.; *Breen's* case [1971] 2 Q.B. 175, 195, *per* Edmund Davies L.J. ('fairly exercised'); *Pearlberg v. Varty* [1972] 1 W.L.R. 534, 545, *per* Viscount Dilhorne, and at 547, *per* Lord Pearson. The suitability of the term 'fairness' in such cases is increased by the curiosities of the expression 'natural justice'. Justice is far from being a 'natural' concept. The closer one goes to a state of nature, the less justice does one find. Justice, and with it 'natural justice', is in truth an elaborate and artificial product of civilisation which varies with different civilisations: see *Maclean v. Workers' Union* [1929] 1 Ch. 602, 624, *per* Maugham J. To Black J., 'natural justice' understandably meant no more than 'justice' without the adjective: see *Green v. Blake* [1948] I.R. 242, 268. However, be that as it may, the question before me is that of the content of 'the duty to act fairly' (or of 'natural justice') in this particular case. What does it entail? In particular, does it require the board to afford the plaintiff not only information of the 'case against him' but also an oral hearing?…

I think it is clear that there is no general obligation to give reasons for a decision. Certainly in an application case, where there are no statutory or contractual requirements but a simple discretion in the licensing body, there is no obligation on that body to give their reasons…

As I have said, Mr Moses accepted that the board were under a duty to reach an honest conclusion without bias and not in pursuance of any capricious policy. That, I think, is right: and if the plaintiff showed that any of these requirements had not been complied with, I think the court would intervene. Mr Beloff accepted that the burden of proof would have been on him if any such questions had arisen. But assume a board acting honestly and without bias or caprice: why should a duty to act fairly require them to tell an applicant the gist of the reasons (which may vary from member to member) why they think he ought not to be given a licence? Is a college or university, when selecting candidates for admission or awarding scholarships, or a charity when making grants to the needy, acting 'unfairly' when it gives no reason to the unsuccessful? Are editors and publishers 'unfair' when they send out unreasoned rejection slips? Assume that they are under no enforceable duty to act fairly, and it may still be a matter of concern to them if they are to be told that they are acting 'unfairly' in not giving the gist of their reasons to the rejected. Again, do judges act unfairly when, without any indication of their reasons, they refuse leave to appeal, or decide questions of costs?…

Looking at the case as whole, in my judgment there is no obligation on the board to give the plaintiff even the gist of the reasons why they refused his application, or proposed to do so. This is not a case in which there has been any suggestion of the board considering any alleged dishonesty or morally culpable conduct of the plaintiff. A man free from any moral blemish may nevertheless be wholly unsuitable for a particular type of work. The refusal of the plaintiff's application by no means necessarily puts any slur on his character, nor does it deprive him of any statutory right. There is no mere narrow issue as to his character, but the wide and general issue whether it is right to grant this licence to this applicant. In such circumstances, in the absence of anything to suggest that the board have been affected by dishonesty or bias or caprice, or that there is any other impropriety, I think that the board are fully entitled to give no reasons for their decision, and to decide the application without any preliminary indication to the plaintiff of those reasons. The board are the best judges of the desirability of granting the licence, and in the absence of any impropriety the court ought not to interfere.

There is a more general consideration. I think that the courts must be slow to allow any implied obligation to be fair to be used as a means of bringing before the courts for review honest decisions of bodies exercising jurisdiction over sporting and other activities which those bodies are far better fitted to judge than the courts. This is so even where those bodies are concerned with the means of livelihood of those who take part in those activities. The concepts of natural justice and the duty to be fair must not be allowed to discredit themselves by making unreasonable requirements and imposing undue burdens. Bodies such as the board which promote a public interest by seeking to maintain high standards in a field of activity which otherwise might easily become degraded and corrupt ought not to be hampered in their work without good cause. Such bodies should not be tempted or coerced into granting licences that otherwise they would refuse by reason of the courts having imposed on them a procedure for refusal which facilitates litigation against them. As Lord Denning M.R. said in *Re Pergamon Press Ltd* [1971] Ch. 388, 400, 'No one likes to have an action brought against him, however unfounded.' The individual must indeed be protected against impropriety; but any claim of his for anything more must be balanced against what the public interest requires.

That brings me to the fifth point, the contention that the board are obliged to afford the plaintiff a hearing. This, I think, has in large part been disposed of by what I have said in rejecting the contention that the plaintiff has a right to be told the gist of the reasons for proposing to reject his application. The contention that the plaintiff ought to be given a hearing seems to have been put forward mainly as an ancillary to the alleged obligation to inform him of the gist of the reasons for provisionally deciding not to grant him the licence, and so as to enable him to meet what is said. However, if one treats the right to a hearing as an independent requirement, I would say that I cannot see how the obligation to be fair can be said in a case of this type to require a hearing. I do not see why the board should not be fully capable of dealing fairly with the plaintiff's application without any hearing. The case is not an expulsion case where natural justice confers the right to know the charge and to have an opportunity of meeting it at a hearing.

I cannot think that there is or should be any rule that an application for a licence of this sort cannot properly be refused without giving the applicant the opportunity of a hearing, however hopeless the application, and whether it is the first or the fifth or the fiftieth application that he has made. Certainly Mr Beloff has not referred me to any authority which appears to me to give any real support to such a proposition in a case such as this. I therefore reject the contention that the board should be required to give the plaintiff a hearing or interview.

In my judgment, therefore, the plaintiff's claim fails. It is easy to understand a very natural curiosity and, doubtless, anxiety on his part to know what it is that stands between him and the grant of the licence that he seeks. He may wonder whether it is something that endeavour on his part may put right, or whether it is something beyond cure. It may be that it would be considerate of the board if they were to give him at least some indication of what stands in his way. I for one would not be surprised if his previous career as a licence-holder had played a substantial part in this, although no details of the various episodes have been put before me. At the same time, I can well see that the board would be reluctant to adopt a more elaborate and time-consuming procedure for determining applications for licences, and even more reluctant to be required to give reasons (whether in full or in outline) which might provide ammunition for litigation against the board. The board's regulations seem to me to make fair and reasonable provisions for disciplinary cases which may lead to the suspension or withdrawal of a licence and so on, and the distinction under the regulations between such cases and applications for the grant of licences seems to me to be proper and generally in accordance with the law. Furthermore, the offer of a hearing made by the board's solicitors after the originating summons had been issued seems to me to have been reasonable and benign; I regret that the plaintiff's solicitors should have been insistent upon the board paying the plaintiff's costs. My duty, however, is simply to apply the law as I understand it; and for the reasons that I have given, I hold that on the questions that are before me the plaintiff's claims fail and will be dismissed."

D.J. Mullan, "Fairness: The New Natural Justice?"

(1975) 25 U.T.L.J. 281 At 300

8–10   "It is the ultimate thrust of this article that the development of the doctrine of procedural fairness is a most desirable advance in the common law relating to judicial review of administrative action. It is desirable primarily because it allows the courts to ask what kind of procedural protections are necessary for a particular decision-making process unburdened by the traditional classification process. In other words, it enables the asking of the real questions which the classification process has hidden artificially for many years. It recognizes that there is a very broad spectrum of decision-making functions for which varying procedural requirements are necessary and rejects the notion that such functions can be categorized satisfactorily into either one of two categories. The classification process was essentially accepted at a time when the administrative process was far less sophisticated. Its deceptive simplicity was perhaps adequate initially but it rapidly ceased to be realistic. If 'fairness' enables the courts to move away from this approach much will have been achieved in that an effective functional approach will have been substituted for a superficially attractive but actually inappropriate functional approach."

Notes

8–11   (1) "The duty to act fairly" is said to originate in *Re HK*. There are dicta in earlier cases which indicate that certain decisions must be taken in a fair manner. In *Moore v. Clyde Pilotage Authority*, 1944 S.L.T. 111 the authority was obliged to act according to the "ordinary principles of fairplay" *per* Lord Fleming at 115. In *Board of Education v. Rice* [1911] A.C. 179 the board was under a duty "to act in good faith and fairly listen to both sides" *per* Lord Loreburn L.C. In *Lithgow v. Secretary of State for Scotland*, 1973 S.L.T. 81 Lord Dunpark observed that the common law imposed a duty upon a person or body making a decision after a planning inquiry in the following terms (at 87):

> "Even if there is a set statutory procedure, it is not enough for him [the decision maker] to comply with it; he must exercise all his powers fairly in relation to those who object to their exercise. He must always give all interested parties the opportunity of adequately stating their case."

See too *R. v. Birmingham City Justice, ex parte Chris Foreign Foods (Wholesalers) Ltd* [1970] 1 W.L.R. 1428 (proceedings for the condemnation of unfit food) and *Cinnamond v. British Airports Authority* [1980] 2 All E.R. 368 (power to ban taxi drivers from stance at Heathrow airport).

(2) What is the relationship between the duty to act fairly and the right to a hearing under natural justice? Lord Parker appears to use the concepts interchangeably, but in *Pearlberg v. Varty* [1972] 1 WLR 534 at 547, H.L. Lord Pearson seemed to suggest that there was a distinction: see also *R v. Secretary of State for the Home Department, ex parte Mughal* [1974] QB 313, C.A. *per* Lord Denning M.R. and Scarman L.J. In *Errington v. Wilson*, 1995 S.L.T. 1193 (for the facts see para. 8–13) the following observations were made:

> LORD HOPE: "In view of the nature of these proceedings I consider that the justice was under a duty to have regard to the principles of natural justice, and that in the circumstances of this case this is simply another way of expressing the broad proposition that she was under a duty to act fairly. As Harman LJ said in the Court of Appeal in *Ridge v Baldwin* at [1963] 1 QB, p 578, natural justice is after all only fair play in action. In *Furnell v Whangarei High Schools Board* at [1973] AC, p 679G Lord Morris of Borth-y-Gest, delivering the majority judgment of the board, said that natural justice is but fairness writ large and juridically. He also noted that the conceptions which are indicated when natural justice is invoked or referred to are not to be confined within hard and fast and rigid rules. These observations were anticipated by Lord President Clyde in *Barrs v British Wool Marketing Board* at 1957 SC, pp 82–83; 1957 SLT, p 157 when he said that, where a tribunal had not dealt fairly and equally with the parties, its conduct of the proceedings had been at variance with the principles of natural justice. In *Breen v Amalgamated Engineering Union* [1971] 2 QB at p 190G, Lord Denning MR said that even though the functions of a domestic body are not judicial or quasi-judicial, but only administrative, the body must still act fairly. Edmund Davies LJ at p 195B and Megaw LJ at p 200C treated the expressions "acting unfairly' and 'acting contrary to natural justice' as interchangeable. In my opinion it is sufficient for the purposes of the present case to say that the duty to act fairly, which the second and third respondents admit, and the duty to act in accordance with the principles of natural justice, which the petitioner avers, are different ways of expressing the same thing. The point which is at issue is whether, in the exercise of this duty, the justice was bound to allow the petitioner's counsel to cross examine the second respondents' witnesses."

> LORD CLYDE: "It was argued on behalf of the reclaimers that the petitioner's formulation of his challenge was misconceived because the only duty on the justice was to act fairly and that that duty was in some way different from the duty to observe the principles of natural justice. But that is a fallacious approach. The observation made by Lord Morris of Borth-y-Gest in the case of *Furnell v Whangarei High Schools Board* [1973] AC at p 679 seems to me entirely applicable to the present case. His Lordship there said: 'Natural justice is but fairness writ large and juridically. It has been described as "fair play in action". Nor is it a leaven to be associated only with judicial or quasijudicial occasions. But ...the requirements of natural justice must depend on the circumstances of each particular case and the subject matter under consideration.'

> As I understand it the term 'natural justice' is used where attention is to be directed to those aspects of fairness which apply to what may be described as the constitutional and procedural aspects of the task of decision making. The term 'fairness' may be particularly appropriate where the issue is further removed from what may reasonably be called a justiciable question (*McInnes v Onslow-Fane* [1978] 1 WLR at p 1530). The cross examination of witnesses is a matter falling within the procedural aspects of the decision making and the petitioner was in my view correct in focusing attention on matters of natural justice and not simply raising the point as one of fairness.

> The excerpt from the speech of Lord Morris of Borth-y-Gest which I have just quoted is also relevant to another distinction which the reclaimers sought to raise and found upon before us, namely a distinction between administrative and judicial or quasi-judicial decisions. The purpose of this argument was to enable the proposition to be advanced that any right to cross examination would belong to judicial or quasi-judicial proceedings and not to administrative proceedings, that the proceedings in question in the present case were administrative in character and accordingly that no right to cross examination should arise in the present case. The first leg of this argument relates in part to the alleged distinction between fairness and the principles of natural justice, but just as those labels are useful in particular contexts to focus attention on particular areas of inquiry but may not be determinative, so also the categorisation of functions as administrative or judicial or quasi-judicial, while often useful as an element in the decision whether particular acts or omissions were or were not lawful as falling or not falling within the scope of what in the circumstances was required under the general principle of fairness, nevertheless should not be seen as determinative of that issue. As Sir William Wade expressed it (*Administrative Law* (7th ed), p 511) the 'judicial' fallacy was repudiated in *Ridge v Baldwin*. An approach along the lines of such categorisation was held to be unnecessary by Parker LJ in *R v Birmingham City Justices* [1970] 1 WLR at p 1432, and the duty to act fairly in both administrative and judicial decisions was recognised in *Breen v Amalgamated Engineering Union*."

More recent English case law appears to have abandoned this distinction in this context: see *R. v. Commission for Racial Equality, ex parte Hillingdon London Borough Council* [1982] A.C. 779. Even if one abandons any distinction between natural justice and the duty to act fairly, the fact that a court is concerned with an "administrative" decision may still make it possible that an oral hearing will not be required: *Young v. Criminal Injuries Compensation Board*, 1997 S.L.T. 297, extracted at para. 8–24. If a decision can still be held "fair", as in *Young* or *McInnes*, does that suggest that there might be a danger that the court will hold that the duty to act fairly will involve very little or nothing? Is that implied by Megarry V.-C. in *McInnes*? What are the implications of this for cases where in the past natural justice would have applied? On this see *Dunlop v. Woollahra M.C.* [1975] 2 N.S.W.L.R. 446 at 467–71 and see D. Clark [1975] P.L. 27 at 28–36.

8–12   (3) Mullan above notes three criticisms of the duty to act fairly discussed in earlier academic literature as follows:

1.   Different judges see the duty to act fairly as meaning different things and that the boundaries of the duty to act fairly are unclear.
2.   That the concept of the duty to act fairly is so unpredictable, as opposed to the question of the content of natural justice, lawyers cannot tell the relevant parties what it involves.
3.   That it will impose "entirely inappropriate procedural requirements" on statutory bodies which will in turn have an adverse effect on the efficiency and effectiveness of the decision-making process.

How would you assess these criticisms? Do you think that the concept of acting fairly should develop rules which do not reflect on adjudicative framework? Would this deal with the points raised by Mullan? On fairness generally see *Stair Memorial Encyclopaedia*, Vol. 1, para. 283; M. Loughlin, "Procedural Fairness: A Study of the Crisis in Administrative Law Theory" (1978) 28 U.T. L.J. 215; and D.J. Mullan, "Natural Justice and Fairness — Substantive as well as Procedural Standards for the Review of Administrative Decision-Making?" (1981) 27 McGill L.J. 250.

(4) Even if a decision maker is subject to the duty to act fairly, that duty does not apply to each and every decision that the body is called on to make. In *Stannifer Developments Ltd v. Glasgow Development Agency*, 1998 S.C.L.R. 870 in judicial review proceedings, it was argued that the Agency were under a duty to act fairly in relation to the consideration to be given to a tender to undertake work made by Stannifer. Stannifer had alleged that notwithstanding that offers were to be put in a sealed envelope, another party was given the opportunity of offering a higher price after the envelopes were opened. They had not been given an opportunity to increase their offer and they contended that they had been treated unequally and unfairly and that their legitimate expectation as to the procedure which would be adopted had been defeated. On legitimate expectation see para. 8–32 above. This formed the ground (*c*) of their petition. They relied in particular on the English decision of *R. v. Lord Chancellor, ex parte Hibbit and Saunders* [1993] C.O.D. 326. Lord Macfadyen, in rejecting such a "blanket approach", observed:

"It is therefore, in my view, necessary to examine separately the relevancy of the averments in support of each ground of challenge founded upon. To illustrate the point by reference to one of the petitioners' grounds of challenge, ground (*c*), it is not to be assumed, from the fact that the respondents are amenable to judicial review, that in making their every decision they are subject to a duty to act fairly. It is necessary to consider first whether circumstances have been averred from which the existence of a duty on the part of the respondents to act fairly may be inferred; and it is only if that is decided in the affirmative that it is necessary to consider whether it has relevantly been averred that the respondents acted unfairly in breach of that duty."

He went on to consider the factors which might lead to the imposition of a duty to be fair in the circumstances of a particular case as follows:

"I am of opinion that care must be taken in placing reliance on the dicta in *R. v Lord Chancellor*, ex parte *Hibbit and Saunders* which were relied upon in the course of the debate. A number of factors can, in my view, be regarded as gateways on the path leading towards the conclusion that a duty of procedural fairness was incumbent on a decision-maker in the process leading up to a particular decision. That the decision-maker is a body constituted by statute for a public administrative purpose, as the respondents in the present case are, is in my view one such gateway, although (because of the broader basis of the supervisory jurisdiction in Scotland) there may be other parallel gateways which give admission to the same stage of the path. That the decision is one made in exercise of a statutory power, or circumscribed by a statutory duty, gains admission to a further stage of the path. As Waller J. said in *R. v Lord Chancellor*, ex parte *Hibbit and Saunders* (transcript p. 13):

The fact that a body is exercising a statutory power will entitle the court to consider whether there must be implied an obligation, for example, to act fairly.'

In other words, the presence of statutory underpinning is not per se a sufficient condition for the presence of a duty to act fairly. Waller J. (earlier on the same page) made the point that the mere fact that a governmental body entered into a contract in the course of carrying out governmental functions did not necessarily give rise to obligations over and above those constituted under the contract, and added that there was no justification for distinguishing pre-contract negotiations from the contract itself. He said:

'A governmental body is free to negotiate contracts, and it would need something additional to the simple fact that the governmental body was negotiating the contract to impose on that authority any public law obligation in addition to any private law obligations or duties there might be.'

Although that dictum is expressed in terms of the public law/private law dichotomy, it seems to me to be making broadly the same distinction as was made in *West v Scottish Prison Service* at [p. 526D–E;] p. 651B.

'(*d*) Contractual rights and obligations, such as those between employer and employee, are not as such amenable to judicial review. The cases in which the exercise of the supervisory jurisdiction is appropriate involve a tripartite relationship, between the person or body to whom the jurisdiction, power or authority has been delegated or entrusted, the person or body by whom it has been delegated or entrusted and the person or persons in respect of or for whose benefit that jurisdiction, power or authority is to be exercised.' "

His Lordship went on to observe that while the decision to dispose of the property under the relevant statute (the Enterprise and New Towns (Scotland) Act 1990) might amount to the exercise of a jurisdiction, the manner in which offers were dealt with did not and there was no duty to accord offerors equal treatment throughout the decision-making process (at 890).

THE RIGHT TO A HEARING: CONTENT

THE RIGHT TO CROSS-EXAMINE

Errington v. Wilson

1995 S.L.T. 1193

LORD PRESIDENT (HOPE): "This is a reclaiming motion by the second and third respondents against an **8–13** interlocutor which the Lord Ordinary pronounced after the first hearing in a petition for judicial review. The petitioner carries on business near Carnwath under the name H J Errington & Co. His business consists in the manufacture and sale of various products including a blue veined semi-hard cheese known as Lanark Blue. He sought judicial review of a decision by the first respondent, who is a justice of the peace, that 44 batches of his Lanark Blue cheese were contaminated with listeria monocytogenes, were unfit for human consumption and should be disposed of or destroyed. The second respondents are the food authority for the District of Clydesdale in terms of s 5 of the Food Safety Act 1990. The third respondent is an authorised officer of the second respondents for the purposes of that Act.

The decision was issued on 3 March 1995 after a hearing which took place before the justice on 24 February 1995. The petitioner sought its reduction on three grounds. The first was that there had been communings before the hearing between the justice and the solicitor for the second respondents. But nothing was made of this point at the first hearing, as the facts are still in dispute. The second was the refusal by the justice to allow the cross examination of witnesses. The third was that the justice had failed to give reasons for her decision. The Lord Ordinary held that in refusing senior counsel for the petitioner the opportunity of cross examining the second respondents' witnesses there had been a denial of natural justice. On this ground he sustained the petitioner's first plea in law and pronounced decree of reduction.

He was inclined to the view, in regard to the third ground, that the justice should have given proper and adequate reasons for her decision. He also said that it would be highly desirable, in view of the complex issues involved in this case, that the services of an experienced sheriff should be sought rather than those of a lay person. The second and third respondents have challenged the Lord Ordinary on all these points in this reclaiming motion. But the principal issue is whether the justice was under a duty to allow the petitioner's counsel to cross examine the second respondents' witnesses.

Among the provisions which the 1990 Act contains in regard to food safety is the power given by s 9 to an authorised officer of a food authority to inspect any food intended for human consumption. If it appears to him that any food fails to comply with the food safety requirements, he has power under subs (3) of that section to seize the food and remove it in order to have it dealt with by a justice of the peace. In Scotland the expression 'justice of the peace' includes a reference to the sheriff and to a magistrate: see s 9 (9) (a). Although these expressions are not further defined in the 1990 Act, it is clear that the references to a justice of the peace and to a magistrate in Scotland are references to a justice of the peace appointed under s 9 of the District Courts (Scotland) Act 1971 and to a stipendiary magistrate appointed under s 5 of that Act. The expression 'sheriff' in relation to Scotland includes the sheriff principal: see s 5 of and Sched 1 to the Interpretation Act 1978. Thus there is in Scotland a wide choice of persons by whom the matter may be dealt with on the application of the authorised officer.

Subsections (5) and (6) of s 9 of the 1990 Act are in these terms: [his Lordship quoted the terms of s 9 (5) and (6) and continued:]

When the hearing took place on 24 February 1995 the petitioner was represented by senior counsel. He had with him as his witness Richard North of Leeds Metropolitan University, a food safety adviser. The second respondents were represented by a solicitor. She had with her as witnesses the third respondent, Dr J McLauchlin of the Central Public Health Laboratory, London, and Dr Ahmed, a consultant in public health medicine with Lanarkshire Health Board.

The precise sequence of events at the hearing is not agreed. There is a dispute in fact between the parties as to when it was that the justice said that there was to be no cross examination of the witnesses. The petitioner avers that she commenced the proceedings by saying that she would not allow cross examination. The second and third respondents aver that she adjourned to consider the parties' submissions on this point and that, having done this, she intimated that cross examination was not appropriate but that she would ensure that everyone would be given an opportunity to speak and to answer questions through her. It is however agreed that the dispute on this point of detail does not matter if, as the petitioner avers, the justice was obliged to allow both parties to cross examine each other's witnesses. Her decision not to allow cross examination had clearly been taken by the time the second respondents' witnesses gave evidence. It is also agreed that the justice said that any questions to witnesses would have to be put through her. The petitioner's senior counsel declined to put any questions in this way to the second respondents' witnesses. The respondents aver that the solicitor for the second respondents put a few questions to the petitioner's witness Mr North through the justice.

After hearing submissions for both parties the justice reserved her decision. On 3 March 1995 she issued her decision, which was in these terms:

'The following decision has been made after the hearing held on Friday 24th February 1995 and on the basis of relevant evidence presented and in the absence of any statutory provision at the present time, regarding contamination of cheese with listeria monocytogenes.

'I am of the opinion that the contaminated batches of Lanark Blue cheese are potentially hazardous to public health and are therefore unfit for human consumption and should be disposed of or destroyed.

'Any reasonable expenses in connection with the destruction or disposal of the cheese to be defrayed by the owner, H J Errington & Co.'

The Lord Ordinary held that the justice was under a duty to exercise her powers under s 9 (6) of the 1990 Act in accordance with the principles of natural justice, especially as she was obliged by the statute to reach her decision in this case on the basis of evidence. As to whether her refusal to allow cross examination was a breach of these requirements, he was not willing to affirm that failure to allow cross examination would necessarily be unfair in all circumstances. In his opinion regard had to be paid to the scheme of the legislation, to the circumstances of each case and to the extent to which prejudice may have resulted when cross examination has been disallowed. Having examined all these factors, he was of the opinion that there was a denial of natural justice in this case because the petitioner's counsel was denied the opportunity, by cross examining the second respondents' witnesses, of testing the strength of their evidence...

The argument for the second and third respondents was that it was a matter for the discretion of the justice whether or not cross examination should be allowed. It was said that, as it was for her to decide in terms of s 9 (6) what evidence was appropriate in the circumstances, it was for her to decide how witnesses were to give their evidence, and that as the petitioner did not attack the exercise by her of a discretion, that was an end of the case. Counsel also submitted that her decision was a sound one because cross examination was peculiar to judicial and certain kinds of quasi-judicial proceedings. He said that it was not a normal incident of administrative proceedings such as those on which she was engaged in this case. Any suggestion that there was a presumption in favour of allowing cross examination would be based neither on reason nor on precedent. This argument was forcefully presented, but in my opinion it overlooks the point that the duty to act fairly may include other duties according to the circumstances. Thus if fairness requires that something be done, not to do that thing will be a breach of the duty to act fairly. If it is necessary to permit cross examination in order to perform the duty to act fairly, then there is a duty to permit cross examination. It is not a matter of discretion, as the duty to act fairly does not leave it to the discretion of the decision maker to decide what is and what is not fair. That is a matter to be decided in the light of the circumstances, and any view which the decision maker may take on it is subject to review by the court…

We were referred to a number of cases to illustrate the circumstances in which cross examination might or might not be appropriate. In *Cowe v McDougall* the pursuer had obtained a decree in the small debt court. It was held that there had been oppression within the meaning of s 31 of the Small Debt (Scotland) Act 1837 because the sheriff substitute had refused to allow the defender to cross examine the pursuer or to lead evidence on the question of damages. Lord Low described the procedure in that case as amounting to a refusal to hear parties, and Lord Ardwall said that there had been a departure from the principles of natural justice. I do not think that that case has any direct bearing on the circumstances with which the justice was faced in the present case. But the observations of Lord Low and Lord Ardwall indicate the importance of allowing cross examination in a case where a party has a right to be heard and where it would be unfair not to permit him to cross examine the other party's witnesses. In *R v Deputy Industrial Injuries Commissioner, ex p Moore* [1965] 1 QB at p 488A, Diplock LJ said that the rules of natural justice which the deputy commissioner had to observe could be reduced to two, of which the second was that, if a hearing was requested, he must fairly listen to the contentions of all persons who were entitled to be represented at the hearing. At p 490C-F he went on to say this: 'Where, however, there is a hearing, whether requested or not, the second rule requires the deputy commissioner (a) to consider such "evidence" relevant to the question to be decided as any person entitled to be represented wishes to put before him, (b) to inform every person represented of any "evidence" which the deputy commissioner proposes to take into consideration, whether such "evidence" be proferred by another person represented at the hearing, or is discovered by the deputy commissioner as a result of his own investigation; (c) to allow each person represented to comment upon any such "evidence" and, where the "evidence" is given orally by witnesses, to put questions to those witnesses; and (d) to allow each person represented to address argument to him on the whole of the case. This in the context of the Act and the regulations fulfils the requirement of the second rule of natural justice to listen fairly to all sides.'

Counsel submitted that the requirement mentioned in head (c) of this passage to allow each person represented 'to put questions to those witnesses' was satisfied in this case, because the justice said that she was willing to allow questions to be put through her to the witnesses. But I understand the requirement which was being described here by Lord Diplock as being to allow each person to put his own questions to the witnesses, by questioning the witness himself directly, not putting questions through the deputy commissioner or any other intermediary. In my opinion this passage provides strong support for the view that the justice was obliged in the present case to allow the petitioner's counsel to put questions to the second respondents' witnesses — that is, to cross examine them on their evidence.

In *R v Board of Visitors of Hull Prison, ex p St Germain (No 2)* it was held that the board of visitors were not bound by the technical rules of evidence, but that the admission by them of hearsay evidence was subject to the overriding obligation to provide the accused with a fair hearing. Geoffrey Lane LJ said at [1979] 1 WLR, p 1409F that, depending upon the nature of the evidence and the particular circumstances of the case, the sufficient opportunity to deal with the hearsay evidence might well involve the cross examination of the witness whose evidence was initially before the board in the form of hearsay. I do not see this case or the other cases to which we were referred as indicating that there is a presumption that cross examination should be allowed, as junior counsel for the petitioner suggested. But in my opinion they show that a failure to allow cross examination may amount to a failure to give a fair hearing to a party who wishes to challenge the evidence on which the other party seeks to rely…

In *R v Birmingham City Justices, ex p Chris Foreign Foods (Wholesalers) Ltd* it was held that a justice acting under s 9 of the Food and Drugs Act 1955, although acting in an administrative or executive capacity, was obliged to act fairly and impartially. James J said at [1970] 1 WLR, p 1434C that the exercise of that duty should be seen to be carried out openly, impartially and with fairness. This echoes Donovan J's observation in *Kerley* [[1956] 1 W.L.R. 910] at p 911 that the justice has to bring qualities of impartiality and fairness to bear upon the problem. While these dicta are helpful to the petitioner, it seems to me that neither of these cases has a direct bearing on the point which is at issue here. They do not address the crucial question which is whether the refusal to allow cross examination was a breach of the duty to act fairly.

The answer to that question must in the end depend upon the circumstances. In my opinion it is clear from the facts in this case that the justice could not decide whether the cheese failed to comply with food safety requirements without examining the evidence of the expert witnesses. We were not referred in detail to their evidence, but the documents which were shown to us indicate that important questions were raised by the petitioner's expert about the reliability of the evidence of the second respondents' witnesses. The nature of these questions was such that they could not be answered without a detailed study and understanding of the witnesses' evidence. Counsel for the second and third respondents submitted that the point which was being made by these witnesses was a simple one. There were no statutory guidelines, but they said that the matter could be decided by the application of the PHLS Guidelines which did not give rise to any questions of difficulty. But the application of those guidelines to this case was disputed, and the justice could not decide that issue fairly between the parties without examining the detail of their evidence.

In a case of this difficulty there was an obvious risk of unfairness if the second respondents' witnesses were not open to cross examination on the detail of their evidence. There was a risk that defects in that evidence would lie undetected, and that the justice would not be informed about the issues which she had to decide. It is no answer to this point to say that she put both parties on an equal footing by denying to both of them the opportunity of cross examining each other's witnesses. Nor is it an answer to say that the public have an interest in food safety. The consequences for the petitioner and his business were likely to be very serious if the case went against him, and he had a right under the statute to attend and to call witnesses. The issues which the petitioner's representative wished to raise in cross examination were issues on which the petitioner wished to be heard. These were issues which he wished to raise by way of challenge to the evidence of the second respondents' expert witnesses. The unfairness to him lay in the denial to him of the opportunity of opening up these issues by putting questions about them directly to the second respondents' expert witnesses.

Counsel for the second and third respondents also submitted that, in order to plead a successful case on an alleged breach of the rules of natural justice, a petitioner had to aver prejudice and that as there were no averments of prejudice in this case the petitioner's averments were irrelevant. This submission appeared to be based on a statement in the rubric in *Cigaro Ltd v City of Glasgow District Licensing Board* at 1982 SC, p 105 that it was observed in that case that "a breach of the rules of natural justice cannot relevantly be averred in the absence of averments of prejudice". But it is clear from an examination of the opinion at p 112 (1983 SLT, p 553) that this part of the rubric is inaccurate. Lord President Emslie's observations were directed to the averments in that case only, which he described as speculative. He did not say that an averment of prejudice was required in all cases where a breach of the rules of natural justice was alleged. In *Barrs v British Wool Marketing Board* at p 82 (p 157) Lord President Clyde said that the question was whether the tribunal had dealt fairly and equally with the parties before it in arriving at its result. It was sufficient in that case that the conduct of the proceedings was at variance with the principles of natural justice, and there was no discussion as to whether the result of that unfairness had been to create prejudice. In most cases it can be assumed that prejudice will result from a failure in the duty to act fairly.

In the present case the prejudice which resulted from the refusal to allow cross examination is self evident. There was a difference of opinion between experts on points which were crucial to a sound determination of the questions which the justice had to decide. The result of her refusal to allow cross examination was that the evidence of the second respondents' witnesses could not be challenged in the only manner which was likely to be effective in a case of such difficulty. So I consider that the Lord Ordinary was well founded in his decision that by refusing to allow cross examination in these circumstances the justice disabled herself from reaching a fully informed conclusion upon the evidence. This amounted to a denial of natural justice to the petitioner, as her duty to act fairly in this case required her to permit cross examination of the second respondents' witnesses...

For these reasons I would refuse this reclaiming motion and adhere to the interlocutor of the Lord Ordinary."

LORD ALLANBRIDGE: "I have read the opinion of your Lordship in the chair and, for the reasons stated therein, I agree this reclaiming motion should be refused."

The reclaimers then came to argue that the matter of a right to cross examine was a matter of discretion for the justice in the exercise of her general duty to act fairly. This was linked in argument to the proposition that she was bound only by principles of fairness and not bound by principles of natural justice. But I have already sought to displace the distinction sought to be made between these concepts. It is certainly correct that the petitioner does not present his case as a challenge to the exercise of a discretion and in the submission made on his behalf in the reclaiming motion there was no attempt to argue that the matter was one of discretion. What the respondent argued was that it was a matter of obligation on the justice in the circumstances of the case.

In my view it is evident from the authorities to which we were referred that the existence of a duty to allow cross examination in the context of a statutory hearing such as in the present instance depends upon the circumstances of the case. If there is no duty to allow it there may be circumstances where it may be allowed as a matter of discretion, and then the exercise of that discretion could be a potential matter for review. But that is not the position in the present case. Here the matter is one of a duty in the circumstances. In *Bushell v Secretary of State for the Environment* [1981] AC at p 97 Lord Diplock stated that a refusal to allow cross examination of a witness who had given evidence at a local inquiry was not unfair per se. The circumstances there were those of an inquiry attended by many parties who wished to make representations without incurring the cost of legal representation and without the ability to attend throughout the whole length of the proceedings. Lord Diplock regarded it as unfair to "over-judicialise" such an inquiry by insisting on the observance of court procedures. He stated (at p 97E): "Whether fairness requires an inspector to permit a person who has made statements on matters of fact or opinion, whether expert or otherwise, to be cross-examined by a party to the enquiry who wishes to dispute a particular statement must depend on all the circumstances".

On the other hand, as was noticed in the case of *R v Board of Visitors of Hull Prison* at [1979] 1 WLR, p 409, in some circumstances to deprive a party of the opportunity of cross examination would be to deprive him of a fair hearing.

In the circumstances of this case I consider that it was part of the duty of affording a fair hearing to the petitioner that he should have been given a right to cross examine. This was in terms of the Act a hearing before either a justice or a sheriff. The person in charge of the food, who may be liable to prosecution under the Act, is entitled under s 9(5) to be heard and to call witnesses. The justice or sheriff may be the person who is sitting in the court before whom the alleged offender is charged. The justice or sheriff must proceed upon such evidence as he considers appropriate, but these words cannot be construed so as to cut across the duty to act fairly or in accordance with natural justice. I also note, although counsel were not concerned to put much weight on the point, that if an order is made it is to be at least sufficient evidence for the purpose of a criminal prosecution (s 9 (9)). The matter in the present case was not a dispute about an isolated incident affecting one piece of food but related to a whole brand of product. It had direct consequences of the gravest importance for the petitioner, his business and his workforce. It involved the possible destruction of his property. Furthermore, despite the attempts of counsel for the reclaimers to suggest that the issue was a simple one, it was to my mind one of considerable technical complexity calling for expert witnesses on both sides in an area where no clear guidance was available. To my mind a fair hearing in these circumstances required the giving of a right to cross examine the witnesses led on behalf of the food authority. As in the cases of *R v Deputy Industrial Injuries Commissioner, ex p Moore* and *Cowe v McDougall*, so also here the duty to listen fairly to the contentions of all parties entitled to be represented at the hearing required the justice to allow the petitioner to put questions to the witnesses who gave oral evidence and in this case at least that involved the right to cross examine. The ground on which the justice evidently proceeded in refusing cross examination was that she considered it sufficient that the parties should "set out their positions". In so understanding what the purpose of the hearing was she failed to appreciate that fairness required that the respective positions of the parties should be tested by cross examination. In my view she erred in law and her decision was rightly quashed by the Lord Ordinary.

It was suggested that the readiness of the justice in the present case to have questions asked through her was sufficient. Reference here was made to the propriety recognised in the case of *R v Board of Visitors of Hull Prison, ex p St Germain (No 2)* of requiring questions to be channelled through the chairman where direct questioning could lead to the proceedings becoming out of control. But that situation is far removed from the situation of a cross examination of expert witnesses by senior counsel. In the circumstances of this case such channelling was no substitute for cross examination. It was accepted by counsel for the reclaimers that it would give the justice a freedom to decide whether or not any question should be asked and in the circumstances of this case in my view that would amount to a denial of a fair hearing. While it was argued that both parties were treated equally in respect that both were denied the right to cross examine, the fact was that only the petitioner wished to cross examine. The deprivation of the right for both parties thus still created an inequality between them.

It was also argued for the reclaimers that the petitioner's case was not relevant in the absence of averments of prejudice to the petitioner. This was sought to be supported by reference to the case of *Cigaro Ltd v City of Glasgow District Licensing Board*. In my view that case is not authority for the proposition that in every case a petitioner seeking judicial review must be able to aver and establish some particular prejudice beyond the fact that the decision of which he complains has been tainted by some breach of the principles of natural justice. The case of *Barrs v British Wool Marketing Board*, which was referred to in the decision in *Cigaro*, is a clear authority to the converse. In my view the decision of the Lord Ordinary was correct on this point and I agree also with his observation that the petitioner was prejudiced by the very fact of being denied the opportunity to test the strength of his opponent's experts…

On the whole matter I agree that the reclaiming motion should be refused."

Notes

8–14   Is it possible to discern differing approaches by the members of the court? In what circumstances do you consider that cross-examination will not be necessary to fulfil the needs of fairness? Consider the following extract.

Bushell v. Secretary of State for the Environment

[1981] A.C. 75

8–15   "The Department had proposed the construction of two adjoining stretches of motorway in the West Midlands. Local residents, and other amenity groups, objected to the proposals. Under the terms of the Highways Act 1959, the Secretary of State was obliged to hold a local public inquiry into such objections. One local inquiry was convened to hear the above objections (100 different parties were present at the inquiry which lasted for 100 working days). The respondents were objectors who sought to challenge the statistical methods used by the department to predict future traffic needs. The inspector allowed the respondents to criticise the department's methodology (contained in the 'Red Book') and to call expert witnesses to support their criticisms, but he would not permit them to cross-examine the department's representatives upon this matter. The inspector noted the respondents' criticisms in his report which was generally favourable to the department's proposals. The Secretary of State accepted the inspector's recommendations and made schemes for the construction of these sections of motorway. The respondents applied, under Schedule 2 to the 1959 Act, to the High Court to quash the schemes on the ground, *inter alia*, that the inspector had been wrong in law to disallow them from cross-examining departmental representatives on the 'Red Book'. The High Court dismissed their application, but the Court of Appeal (Templeman L.J. dissenting) allowed their appeal. The Secretary of State appealed to the House of Lords."

LORD DIPLOCK: "The provision and improvement of a national system of routes for through traffic for which a government department and not a local authority should be the highway authority has formed a part of national transport policy since the passing of the Trunk Roads Act in 1936. As part of this national network, or superimposed upon it, there have been constructed by stages during the course of the last 30 years special roads familiarly known as motorways which were first authorised by the Special Roads Act 1949. The construction of motorways is a lengthy and expensive process and it has been the policy of successive governments, which would in any event have been dictated by necessity, to construct the network by stages. The order in which the various portions of the network are to be constructed thus becomes as much a matter of government transport policy as the total extent and configuration of the motorway network itself. It also has the consequence that schemes for the provision of special roads which the Minister proposes to make under section 11 of the Highways Act 1959 deal with comparatively short stretches in a particular locality of what, when the other stretches are completed, will be integral parts of the national network. It follows, therefore, that there will be a whole series of schemes relating to successive stretches of the national network of motorways each of which may be the subject of separate local inquiries under Schedule 1, paragraph 9, to the Act.

…So from the publication of the draft scheme to the actual construction of the stretch of motorway which is authorised the process is necessarily a long one in the course of which circumstances may alter and even government policy may change.

Where it is proposed that land should be acquired by a government department or local authority and works constructed on it for the benefit of the public either as a whole or in a particular locality, the holding of a public inquiry before the acquisition of the land and the construction of the works are authorised has formed a familiar part of the administrative process ever since authorisation by ministerial order of compulsory acquisition of land for public purposes began to be used to replace parliamentary authorisation by Private Bill procedure in the nineteenth century. The essential characteristics of a 'local inquiry', an expression which when appearing in a statute has by now acquired a special meaning as a term of legal art, are that it is held in public in the locality in which the works that are the subject of the proposed scheme are situated by a person appointed by the Minister upon whom the statute has conferred the power in his administrative discretion to decide whether to confirm the scheme. The subject-matter of the inquiry is the objections to the proposed scheme that have been received by the Minister from local authorities and from private persons in the vicinity of the proposed stretch of motorway whose interests may be adversely affected, and in consequence of which he is required by Schedule 1, paragraph 9, to hold the inquiry. The purpose of the inquiry is to provide the Minister with as much information about those objections as will ensure that in reaching his decision he will have weighed the harm to local interests and private persons who may be adversely affected by the scheme against the public benefit which the scheme is likely to achieve and will not have failed to take into consideration any matters which he ought to have taken into consideration.

...The Highways Act 1959 being itself silent as to the procedure to be followed at the inquiry, that procedure, within such limits as are necessarily imposed by its qualifying for the description 'local inquiry', must necessarily be left to the discretion of the Minister or the inspector appointed by him to hold the inquiry on his behalf, or partly to one and partly to the other. In exercising that discretion, as in exercising any other administrative function, they owe a constitutional duty to perform it fairly and honestly and to the best of their ability, as Lord Greene M.R. pointed out in his neglected but luminous analysis of the quasi-judicial and administrative functions of a Minister as confirming authority of a compulsory purchase order made by a local authority, which is to be found in *B. Johnson & Co. (Builders) Ltd v. Minister of Health* [1947] 2 All E.R. 395, 399–400. That judgment contains a salutary warning against applying to procedures involved in the making of administrative decisions concepts that are appropriate to the conduct of ordinary civil litigation between private parties. So rather than use such phrases as 'natural justice' which may suggest that the prototype is only to be found in procedures followed by English courts of law, I prefer to put it that in the absence of any rules made under the Tribunals and Inquiries Act 1971, the only requirement of the Highways Act 1959, as to the procedure to be followed at a local inquiry held pursuant to Schedule 1, paragraph 9, is that it must be fair to all those who have an interest in the decision that will follow it whether they have been represented at the inquiry or not. What is a fair procedure to be adopted at a particular inquiry will depend upon the nature of its subject-matter.

What is fair procedure is to be judged not in the light of constitutional fictions as to the relationship between the Minister and the other servants of the Crown who serve in the government department of which he is the head, but in the light of the practical realities as to the way in which administrative decisions involving forming judgments based on technical considerations are reached. To treat the Minister in his decision-making capacity as someone separate and distinct from the department of government of which he is the political head and for whose actions he alone in constitutional theory is accountable to Parliament is to ignore not only practical realities but also Parliament's intention. Ministers come and go; departments, though their names may change from time to time, remain. Discretion in making administrative decisions is conferred upon a Minister not as an individual but as the holder of an office in which he will have available to him in arriving at his decision the collective knowledge, experience and expertise of all those who serve the Crown in the department of which, for the time being, he is the political head. The collective knowledge, technical as well as factual, of the civil servants in the department and their collective expertise is to be treated as the Minister's own knowledge, his own expertise. It is they who in reality will have prepared the draft scheme for his approval; it is they who will in the first instance consider the objections to the scheme and the report of the inspector by whom any local inquiry has been held and it is they who will give to the Minister the benefit of their combined experience, technical knowledge and expert opinion on all matters raised in the objections and the report. This is an integral part of the decision-making process itself; it is not to be equiparated with the Minister receiving evidence, expert opinion or advice from sources outside the department after the local inquiry has been closed...

It is evident that an inquiry of this kind and magnitude is quite unlike any civil litigation and that the inspector conducting it must have a wide discretion as to the procedure to be followed in order to achieve its objectives. These are to enable him to ascertain the facts that are relevant to each of the objections, to understand the arguments for and against them and, if he feels qualified to do so, to weigh their respective merits, so that he may provide the Minister with a fair, accurate and adequate report on these matters.

Proceedings at a local inquiry at which many parties wish to make representations without incurring the expense of legal representation and cannot attend the inquiry throughout its length ought to be as informal as is consistent with achieving those objectives. To 'over-judicialise' the inquiry by insisting on observance of the procedures of a court of justice which professional lawyers alone are competent to operate effectively in the interests of their clients would not be fair. It would, in my view, be quite fallacious to suppose that at an inquiry of this kind the only fair way of ascertaining matters of fact and expert opinion is by the oral testimony of witnesses who are subjected to cross-examination on behalf of parties who disagree with what they have said. Such procedure is peculiar to litigation conducted in courts that follow the common law system of procedure; it plays no part in the procedure of courts of justice under legal systems based upon the civil law, including the majority of our fellow Member States of the European Community; even in our own Admiralty Court it is not availed of for the purpose of ascertaining expert opinion on questions of navigation — the judge acquires information about this by private inquiry from assessors who are not subject to cross-examination by the parties. So refusal by an inspector to allow a party to cross-examine orally at a local inquiry a person who has made statements of facts or has expressed expert opinions is not unfair *per se*.

Whether fairness requires an inspector to permit a person who has made statements on matters of fact or opinion, whether expert or otherwise, to be cross-examined by a party to the inquiry who wishes to dispute a particular statement must depend on all the circumstances. In the instant case, the question arises in connection with expert opinion upon a technical matter. Here the relevant circumstances in considering whether fairness requires that cross-examination should be allowed include the nature of the topic upon which the opinion is expressed, the qualifications of the maker of the statement to deal with that topic, the forensic competence of the proposed cross-examiner, and, most important, the inspector's own views as to whether the likelihood that cross-examination will enable him to make a report which will be more useful to the Minister in reaching his decision than it otherwise would be is sufficient to justify any expense and inconvenience to other parties to the inquiry which would be caused by any resulting prolongation of it.

The circumstances in which the question of cross-examination arose in the instant case were the following. Before the inquiry opened each objector had received a document containing a statement of the Minister's reasons for proposing the draft scheme. It was itself a long and detailed document, and was accompanied by an even longer and more detailed one called 'Strategic Studies Information', which gave an account of various traffic studies that had been undertaken between 1964 and 1973 in the area to be served by M42 Bromsgrove and M40 Warwick, the methodology used for those studies and the conclusions reached. The second paragraph of the Minister's statement of reasons said: 'The Government's policy to build these new motorways' (*sc.* for which the two schemes provided) 'will not be open to debate at the forth-coming inquiries [*sic*]: the Secretary of State is answerable to Parliament for this policy.'

'Policy' as descriptive of departmental decisions to pursue a particular course of conduct is a protean word and much confusion in the instant case has, in my view, been caused by a failure to define the sense in which it can properly be used to describe a topic which is unsuitable to be the subject of an investigation as to its merits at an inquiry at which only persons with local interests affected by the scheme are entitled to be represented. A decision to construct a nationwide network of motorways is clearly one of government policy in the widest sense of the term. Any proposal to alter it is appropriate to be the subject of debate in Parliament, not of separate investigations in each of scores of local inquiries before individual inspectors up and down the country upon whatever material happens to be presented to them at the particular inquiry over which they preside. So much the respondents readily concede.

At the other extreme the selection of the exact line to be followed through a particular locality by a motorway designed to carry traffic between the destinations that it is intended to serve would not be described as involving government policy in the ordinary sense of that term. It affects particular local interests only and normally does not affect the interests of any wider section of the public, unless a suggested variation of the line would involve exorbitant expenditure of money raised by taxation. It is an appropriate subject for full investigation at a local inquiry and is one on which the inspector by whom the investigation is to be conducted can form a judgment on which to base a recommendation which deserves to carry weight with the Minister in reaching a final decision as to the line the motorway should follow.

Between the black and white of these two extremes, however, there is what my noble and learned friend, Lord Lane, in the course of the hearing described as a 'grey area'. Because of the time that must elapse between the preparation of any scheme and the completion of the stretch of motorway that it authorises, the department, in deciding in what order new stretches of the national network ought to be constructed, has adopted a uniform practice throughout the country of making a major factor in its decision the likelihood that there will be a traffic need for that particular stretch of motorway in 15 years from the date when the scheme was prepared. This is known as the 'design year' of the scheme. Priorities as between one stretch of motorway and another have got to be determined somehow. Semasiologists may argue whether the adoption by the department of a uniform practice for doing this is most appropriately described as government policy or as something else. But the propriety of adopting it is clearly a matter fit to be debated in a wider forum and with the assistance of a wider range of relevant material than any investigation at an individual local inquiry is likely to provide; and in that sense at least, which is the relevant sense for present purposes, its adoption forms part of government policy.

The 'need' for a new road to carry traffic between given destinations is an imprecise concept. If it is to be used as an important factor in comparing one situation with another for the purpose of determining priorities, there must be uniform criteria by which that need in each locality is to be measured. The test of future needs in the design year which the department has adopted is: whether, if the new stretch of motorway is not constructed, there will be undue congestion of traffic on existing roads, either in the locality or forming other parts of the national network of motorways, for which the new stretch of motorway would provide an alternative route. To apply this test of need to a design year 15 years ahead involves, among other things, estimating (1) the amount of traffic that the existing roads in the locality are capable of bearing without becoming so congested as to involve unacceptable delays; and (2) the amount of traffic that in the absence of the new stretch of motorway would in the design year be using those existing roads which the motorway is intended to relieve.

The methods used by the department for arriving at these estimates are very complicated. So far as I am capable of understanding them as one who is by now (I hope) a reasonably well-informed layman, it is obvious to me that no one who is not an expert in this esoteric subject could form a useful judgment as to their merits. The methods used are kept under periodical review by the department's own experts as a result of which they are revised from time to time. They are described in published documents. One which it will be necessary to mention dealt with the capacity of rural roads; but that which is most relevant to the respondents' complaint about refusal to permit cross-examination in the instant case has been referred to as 'Red Book'. It was published in 1968 under the title *Traffic Prediction for Rural Roads (Advisory Manual on)* and described the method that had been used for predicting the growth of traffic up to the design year on the roads which the M42 Bromsgrove and M40 Warwick were intended to relieve. Important features of the method set out in the Red Book for predicting traffic that will be using the roads in a particular locality are the assumptions (1) that in general, traffic on rural roads throughout the country will grow at the same rate in all areas, except where exceptional changes can be foreseen as likely to take place in a particular locality; and (2) that the annual rate of growth will fall off as vehicle ownership in the country approaches saturation point; and that the best way of predicting what the growth will have been up to a particular design year is by assuming that it can be graphically represented by a curve that is asymptotic (*i.e.* broadly 'S'-shaped) and whose shape where it represents future years can be extrapolated (*i.e.* predicted) from the shape of the curve which represents the observed annual increase in vehicle registrations over past years. It was recognised that predictions as applied to individual roads could only be very approximate and were subject to margins of error as high as 10 per cent to 20 per cent.

The decisions to make these two assumptions for the purpose of calculating and comparing what traffic needs will be in all localities throughout the country in which it is proposed to construct future stretches of the national network of motorway might not, in a general context, be most naturally described as being government policy; but if a decision to determine priorities in the construction of future stretches of the national network of motorways by reference to their respective traffic needs in a design year 15 years ahead can properly be described as government policy, as I think it can, the definition of 'traffic needs' to be used for the purposes of applying the policy, *viz.* traffic needs as assessed by methods described in the Red Book and the departmental publication on the capacity of rural roads, may well be regarded as an essential element in the policy. But whether the uniform adoption of particular methods of assessment is described as policy or methodology, the merits of the methods adopted are, in my view, clearly not appropriate for investigation at individual local inquiries by an inspector whose consideration of the matter is necessarily limited by the material which happens to be presented to him at the particular inquiry which he is holding. It would be a rash inspector who based on that kind of material a positive recommendation to the Minister that the method of predicting traffic needs throughout the country should be changed and it would be an unwise Minister who acted in reliance on it.

At the local inquiry into the M42 Bromsgrove and the M40 Warwick, objectors including the respondents, whose property would be affected by the scheme, and the M42 Action Committee, a 'pressure group' which supported them primarily upon environmental grounds, had studied in advance the Minister's reasons for the schemes, the 'Strategic Studies Information' and the Red Book. They came to the inquiry prepared to criticise the methods used to predict the traffic needs in the design year on local roads in the localities of the M42 Bromsgrove and M40 Warwick and to call evidence of witnesses with professional qualifications to testify to their unreliability. The circumstances in which the inspector was induced to give an early ruling as to what evidence he would admit and what cross-examination he would allow are recounted in the speeches of my noble and learned friends. In the result — and when one is considering natural justice it is the result that matters — the objectors were allowed to voice their criticisms of the methods used to predict traffic needs for the purposes of the two schemes and to call such expert evidence as they wanted to in support of their criticisms. What they were not allowed to do was to cross-examine the department's representatives upon the reliability and statistical validity of the methods of traffic prediction described in the Red Book and applied by the department for the purpose of calculating and comparing traffic needs in all localities throughout the country. This is the only matter in relation to the conduct of the inquiry by the inspector of which complaint is made.

Was this unfair to the objectors? For the reasons I have already given and in full agreement with the minority judgment of Templeman L.J. in the Court of Appeal, I do not think it was. I think that the inspector was right in saying that the use of the concept of traffic needs in the design year *assessed by a particular method* as the yardstick by which to determine the order in which particular stretches of the national network of motorways should be constructed was government policy in the relevant sense of being a topic unsuitable for investigation by individual inspectors upon whatever material happens to be presented to them at local inquiries held throughout the country…"

VISCOUNT DILHORNE: "…It is clear that the objectors at this inquiry had every opportunity of putting forward their case. An inspector at an inquiry has a wide discretion as to its conduct. He may, in my view, properly disallow a particular line of cross-examination if it is not likely to serve any useful purpose. An admission or expression of view in the course of cross-examination at a trial may well affect the result, but the views of departmental witnesses as to the comparative merits of different methods of forecasting traffic elicited in the course of cross-examination are not likely to affect the ultimate outcome.

In the lengthy and detailed report of the inspector the evidence of the expert witnesses called by objectors was faithfully recorded. It was there for the Secretary of State to see and consider, no doubt in the light of advice he received from the civil servants in his department. I cannot think that the expression of views at the inquiry by civil servants as to methods of forecasting traffic would have assisted him or have served any useful purpose.

In my opinion the inspector was fully entitled in the exercise of his discretion to refuse to allow that cross-examination and only if one treats proceedings at an inquiry as a trial — which they are not — can any ground be found for saying that in disallowing this cross-examination there was a denial of natural justice or unfairness. In my opinion there was not…"

LORD EDMUND-DAVIES (dissenting): "…My Lords, for the present I defer considering whether the outcome of the inquiry would, or might have been, different had cross-examination been allowed. The topic now under consideration relates solely to the propriety of its refusal. I have natural diffidence in differing from your Lordships in regarding that refusal as clearly wrong, but such is my considered view. It is beyond doubt that the inspector could — and should — disallow questions relating to the merits of government policy. But matters of policy are matters which involve the exercise of political judgment, and matters of fact and expertise do not become 'policy' merely because a department of government relies on them. And, as the Franks committee had put it in 1957: 'We see no reason why the factual basis for a departmental view should not be explained and its validity tested in cross-examination.' (*Report of the Committee on Administrative Tribunals and Inquiries* (Cmnd. 218), para. 316.)

Then, if the Red Book is not 'government policy,' on what basis can the cross-examination of departmental witnesses relying on its methodology be properly refused? Sir Douglas Frank Q.C. surprisingly asserted, 76 L.G.R. 460, 472–473 (a) that its *authors* 'were the only persons competent to answer questions on it', and (b) that 'it seems to me necessarily to follow that the inspector was entitled to disallow cross-examination on it of a person who had had nothing to do with its preparation'. But expert witnesses frequently quote and rely upon the publications of others and are regularly cross-examined upon the works so relied upon even though they played no part in their preparation. Nor, my Lords, is it right to assume, as was suggested in the course of the inquiry and as some of your Lordships appear to accept, that Mr Brooks, the highly qualified and experienced traffic engineer, would have been incompetent to deal in cross-examination with questions directed to establishing the unreliability of the Red Book methodology upon which he himself heavily relied, albeit not without some emendations. Indeed, in paragraph 567 of this report the inspector described the witness as 'thoroughly competent'.

Pausing there, I conclude that the grounds hitherto considered for refusing cross-examination are unacceptable. But is it the case that, in an inquiry such as that with which this House is presently concerned, some special rule prevails which renders regular a procedure which in other circumstances would undoubtedly have been condemned as irregular? The general law may, I think, be summarised in this way: (a) In holding an administrative inquiry (such as that presently being considered), the inspector was performing quasi-judicial duties. (b) He must therefore discharge them in accordance with the rules of natural justice. (c) Natural justice requires that objectors (no less than departmental representatives) be allowed to cross-examine witnesses called for the other side on all relevant matters, be they matters of fact or matters of expert opinion. (d) In the exercise of jurisdiction outside the field of criminal law, the only restrictions on cross-examination are those general and well-defined exclusionary rules which govern the admissibility of relevant evidence (as to which reference may conveniently be had to *Cross on Evidence*, (5th ed., 1979), p. 17); beyond those restrictions there is *no* discretion on the civil side to exclude cross-examination on relevant matters.

There is ample authority for the view that, as Professor H.W.R. Wade Q.C. puts it (*Administrative Law* (4th ed., 1977), p. 418): '…it is once again quite clear that the principles of natural justice apply to administrative acts generally.' And there is a massive body of accepted decisions establishing that natural justice requires that a party be given an opportunity of challenging by cross-examination witnesses called by another party on relevant issues; see, for example, *Marriott v. Minister of Health* (1935) 52 T.L.R. 63, *per* Swift J., at 67 — compulsory purchase orders inquiry; *Errington v. Minister of Health* [1935] 1 K.B. 249, *per* Maugham L.J., at 272 — clearance order; *R. v. Deputy Industrial Injuries Commissioner, ex p. Moore* [1965] 1 Q.B. 465, *per* Diplock L.J., at 488A, 490E — G; and *Wednesbury Corporation v. Ministry of Housing and Local Government (No. 2)* [1966] 2 Q.B. 275, *per* Diplock L.J., at 302G–303A — local government inquiry.

Then is there any reason why those general rules should have been departed from in the present case? We have already seen that the parameters of the inquiry, as agreed to by the department representatives, embraced *need* as a topic relevant to be canvassed and reported upon. We have already considered the unacceptable submission that the Red Book was 'government policy'. And, while I am alive to the inconvenience of different inspectors arriving at different conclusions regarding different sections of a proposed trunk road, the risk of that happening cannot, in my judgment, have any bearing upon the question whether justice was done at this particular inquiry, which I have already explained was, in an important respect, unique of its kind.

There remains to be considered the wholly novel suggestion, which has found favour with your Lordships, that there is a 'grey area' — existing, as I understand, somewhere between government policy (which admittedly may not be subjected to cross-examination) and the exact 'line' of a section of a motorway (which may be) — and that in relation to topics falling within the 'grey area' cross-examination is a matter of discretion. I find that suggestion to be too nebulous to be grasped. Furthermore, *why* such an area should exist has not been demonstrated — certainly not to my satisfaction — nor have its boundaries been defined, unlike those existing restrictions on cross-examination to which I have already referred. And I confess to abhorrence of the notion that any such area exists. For the present case demonstrates that its adoption is capable of resulting in an individual citizen denied justice nevertheless finding himself with no remedy to right the wrong done to him.

My Lords, it is for the foregoing reasons that I find myself driven to the conclusion that the refusal in the instant case to permit cross-examination on what, by common agreement, was evidence of cardinal importance was indefensible and unfair and, as such, a denial of natural justice…"

LORD LANE: "…The objectors submit that by depriving them of the opportunity of cross-examining the department's witnesses as to how they came to the conclusion that the motorway was necessary the inspector in short did not accord them a fair hearing.

There can be no doubt that the obligation to hold an inquiry comprises the requirement that the inquiry should be fair. If the inquiry is not fair then there has been a 'failure to comply' within the terms of paragraph 3 of Schedule 2 to the Act of 1959. If that failure has resulted in the objectors' interests being substantially prejudiced, then the court may quash the order…

It is clear that all the material was before the Secretary of State and his staff. The only things missing were the replies which Mr Brooks might have made to questions put to him by the objectors and their representatives. I find it difficult to see how in the circumstances the inability to cross-examine can be described as unfair. There are some occasions when cross-examination may be vital, for example, when at trial a witness's accuracy of recollection or observation is in question. But this was not a trial, nor was the witness's accuracy being challenged. It was a local inquiry convened because there had been objections to proposals in respect of one stretch of a proposed motorway. The obligation on the Secretary of State under paragraph 10 of Schedule 1 to the Act of 1959 was simply to consider any objections which were not withdrawn and to consider the report of the person holding the inquiry before coming to his conclusion about the scheme. To say, as the objectors do, that because cross-examination would have been allowed at a trial it was wrong to disallow it here is to misunderstand the nature of the inquiry. The refusal of cross-examination did not *ipso facto* result in unfairness. If cross-examination had been permitted, the result would have been, as is apparent from the extract from the report I have quoted, an even lengthier hearing without any appreciable advantage…"

Notes

(1) Is there any significance in the fact that Lord Diplock appears to rely on fairness, but **8–16** Lord Edmund-Davies on natural justice?

(2) The equivalent statutory provisions to those in *Bushell* in Scotland are contained in the Town and Country Planning (Inquiries Procedure) (Scotland) Rules 1997, on which see para. 1–53. In

Lithgow v. Secretary of State for Scotland, 1973 S.C. 1 Lord Dunpark (at 11) drew a distinction between matters of fact and matters of policy. In relation to the former, the Secretary of State was

> "not entitled to obtain relevant and material factual information from one of the parties without giving opposing parties the opportunity to answer this. Failure in this respect is so great an infringement of the right of every person with a legal interest to a fair hearing that it invalidates the decision."

Why do you consider such a strict approach is not applied in relation to matters of policy? (3) Writing in 1980 in "Fairness and Natural Justice" (96 L.Q.R. 497), Professor Jackson observed (at 499):

> "Dicta abound for, and against the view that natural justice (or fairness) requires a right to cross-examine. To take them out of context as authority for an absolute rule is misleading. *Bushell* demonstrates, in an unusually full discussion of the problem, that the answer depends on a number of factors including the purpose of the hearing, the issue involved, and the nature of the evidence."

For similar comments on cross-examination in the judicial forum, see *Mahon v. Air New Zealand Ltd* [1984] A.C. 808 at 821 *per* Lord Diplock. The issue to the right to cross-examine is clearly bound up with the form and nature of the evidence being examined. If a witness is called, the right to cross-examine would more readily be implied: *Ayr Magistrates v. Lord Advocate*, 1950 S.C. 102. However, given the contextual approach noted by Professor Jackson, does it always follow that presence of a factual dispute will more readily imply this? Was that what *Errington* decided?

THE RIGHT TO LEAD EVIDENCE

J.A.E. (Glasgow) Ltd v. City of Glasgow District Licensing Board

1994 S.L.T. 1164

8–17   "The holders of an entertainment licence applied unsuccessfully to a licensing board for the grant of a regular extension of permitted hours. In terms of s 5 (2) (c) and (7) of the Licensing (Scotland) Act 1976 the proceedings in regard to such an application required to be held in public. The chief constable intimated objection on the grounds that the sale and supply of alcoholic liquor during the period after 11 pm was the cause of undue public nuisance or a threat to public order or safety. Eleven incidents had been referred to by him as having occurred since October 1992 either within the premises or outwith the premises but which could be attributed to the premises. The licence holders had disputed the material facts of at least four of the 11 alleged incidents and, in their application for judicial review of the licensing board's refusal to grant the extension, submitted that the board had been bound, as a matter of natural justice, to hear evidence, failing which they should have disregarded those incidents since, by refusing to hear evidence, and by denying the licence holders the opportunity to challenge the incidents in evidence, the board had treated the opposing parties unequally. They further argued that, even if the board had a discretion rather than a duty to hear evidence, the refusal in the circumstances was unreasonable; and additionally that no reasons had been given for the refusal to hear evidence, contrary to s 18 (1) of the 1976 Act."

LORD CULLEN: "On 25 August 1993 the first petitioners as the holders of an entertainment licence in respect of premises known as 'Framptons', 1236 Maryhill Road, Glasgow, applied under s 64 of the Licensing (Scotland) Act 1976 for the grant of a regular extension of permitted hours. The second petitioner was shown in the application as the person responsible for the day to day running of the premises which were used for a variety of purposes including the provision of snooker, bars, live entertainment and social gatherings. The extension which was sought was from 11 pm to 2 am every Monday to Sunday and from 11 am to 12.30 pm and from 2.30 pm to 6.30 pm every Sunday, for one year from the date of the quarterly meeting of the first respondents in October 1993.

By letter dated 28 September the second respondent intimated to the first petitioners that he intended to object to the application as specified in the attached copy of his letter to the first respondents' clerk dated 29 September. In that letter he stated that objection was taken on the grounds that the sale and supply of alcoholic liquor during the period after 11 pm in the evening was the cause of undue public nuisance or a threat to public order or safety. He stated that since October 1992 11 incidents had occurred either within the premises or outwith the premises but which could be attributed to them. I will refer to the details of these alleged incidents later in this opinion.

Section 64 of the 1976 Act provides by subs (3) that after considering the application and any objections made thereto, a licensing board may grant an application for the regular extension of permitted hours if, having regard to the social circumstances of the locality in which the premises in respect of which the application is made are situated or to activities taking place in that locality, the board considers it desirable to do so. It is provided by subs (8) that: 'A licensing board shall not grant an extension of permitted hours under this section if it considers that the extension is likely to cause undue public nuisance or to be a threat to public order or safety.' [Lord Cullen narrated the alleged incidents.]

During the course of the hearing Superintendent Gray said that the information which he was using was based on information from police officers and civilian witnesses; and that he was satisfied as to the accuracy of that information. The petitioners' solicitor was accompanied by the director of the petitioners to whom I have referred above. He drew attention to the fact that there appeared to be a cluster of incidents in August and stated that the director believed that certain individuals had been engaged to cause disruption at the premises. He emphasised that the loss of extended hours would be tragic for the petitioners. They did not permit entry after midnight or when the premises were full. Occupancy had been limited to 325. They did not permit queueing outside the premises. They had installed panic devices, video-taping and an intercom. The police were called at the first sign of trouble. The petitioners had done a great deal to avoid trouble occurring.

I turn now to the submissions made by counsel in regard to the first and second grounds upon which the first respondents' decision was challenged.

Counsel for the petitioners submitted that since there was a dispute in regard to the material facts of at least four of the alleged incidents, namely nos 5, 6, 7 and 10, the first respondents were bound as a matter of natural justice to hear evidence. If they did not do so they should have disregarded those allegations and had plainly not done so. In accepting what was said on behalf of the second respondent and denying the petitioners the opportunity to challenge it in evidence, the first respondents had created an unequal treatment of the opposing parties. The first respondents knew that the granting of the application was of fundamental importance to the petitioners. If, contrary to his primary position, the first respondents were not bound to hear evidence, their decision to refuse to do so was unreasonable. The lack of any stated reason for refusal was of significance as indicating the lack of any reasonable basis for that refusal. Counsel added that if the first respondents had decided to hear evidence it would have been for each party to decide what evidence, oral or written, should be put before them. Administrative inconvenience was irrelevant on the question of whether evidence should be heard; but it might be relevant in regard to how far evidence should be allowed to extend.

The submissions made by counsel on behalf of the first respondents were adopted by counsel for the second respondent. He submitted that under the 1976 Act the licensing board were not empowered to hear evidence, and in particular evidence on oath. He contracted this with the position of the licensing board under para 17 of Sched 2 to the Gaming Act 1968. In any event the hearing of evidence was a matter within the discretion of the licensing board. They were not required to make findings in fact; and it was sufficient for the purposes of subs (8) of s 64 that they 'considered' that the extension was likely to cause either result mentioned in that provision. The scheme of the Act was designed to give an informal hearing to the applicant and any objector, at which it was for the objector to substantiate his objection. It was inappropriate that one party should be regarded as entitled to insist that the form of hearing should be changed. In the event the first respondents had heard the submissions of both parties before coming to a decision. There had been a large measure of agreement that incidents had taken place. The weight to be attached to them was a matter for the first respondents. It was enough if there was a link between the premises and the incident. The objector did not have to show that the result was due to the way in which the premises had been managed. As regards the reasons given by the first respondents for their decision, they had stated that they were satisfied that they were entitled to rely upon and have regard to the information provided by the second respondent; and that there were 'sufficient grounds' to find that the extension was likely to cause undue public nuisance or to be a threat to public order or safety. It had not been shown that the refusal to hear evidence was unreasonable. The mere absence of reasons for such refusal did not show this. Counsel for the first respondents also made a submission, which was elaborated upon by counsel for the second respondent, that while administrative inconvenience could not be decisive on the question of whether oral evidence should be heard it was a factor for consideration by a licensing board in the exercise of their discretion.

It was not in dispute that in dealing with an application under s 64 or other applications under the Act, the first respondents fell to be treated as an administrative body exercising quasi-judicial functions. It was also not in dispute that in exercising those functions they were under a duty to observe the principles of natural justice and in particular the principle of audi alteram partem. That particular principle can be expressed in other words as the principle that no person against whom an adverse decision may be taken should be denied a fair hearing. While this is the general principle, the specific application of that principle depends upon the circumstances of the case such as the character of the decision making body, the kind of decision it has to make and the statutory framework in which it operates.

I begin by considering the 1976 Act. It makes no explicit provision for the hearing of evidence or even the consideration of written evidence apart from the information contained in the application and any objection. In the case of s 64 provision is made for the application and any objection to be in writing. In terms of s 5 (2) (e) and (7) the proceedings in regard to such an application require to be in public. In terms of s 15 (1) a licensing board may decline to consider an application if the applicant or his representative does not attend the meeting at which the application is to be considered. As I have already noted there is no appeal to the sheriff against the refusal of an application under s 64, but the licensing board are required by s 18 (1) to give reasons for arriving at their decision on such an application. Counsel for the first respondents submitted that in the case of other applications an appeal to the sheriff provided an adequate safeguard against a licensing board proceeding on any incorrect material fact since this was a ground on which an appeal could be taken under s 39. He also drew a distinction between the language of s 64 (8) and other provisions of the 1976 Act in respect that it used the word 'considers' rather than the words 'finds' or 'is satisfied'. The first of those expressions is used in s 17 which deals with the grounds for refusal of applications for new licences and the permanent transfer of a licence. The latter expression is used in ss 31 and 65 which deal respectively with the suspension of a licence and the making of a restriction order.

In a number of the cases to which I was referred reference is made to the words of Lord Loreburn LC in *Board of Education v Rice* where in dealing with the decision of an administrative body he said at [1911] AC, p 182 that in ascertaining the law and the facts 'they must act in good faith and fairly listen to both sides, for that is a duty lying upon every one who decides anything. But I do not think they are bound to treat such a question as though it were a trial. They have no power to administer an oath, and need not examine witnesses. They can obtain information in any way they think best, always giving a fair opportunity to those who are parties in the controversy for correcting or contradicting any relevant statement prejudicial to their view'.

In *General Medical Council v Spackman* it was held that the council was bound to hear evidence tendered by a registered medical practitioner where it had to decide whether his name should be removed from the register for infamous conduct in a professional respect following upon a divorce case in which it was held that he had committed adultery. It may be noted that at [1943] AC, pp 635–636 Viscount Simon LC stated that the form in which the duty of adjudication was discharged, for example whether by hearing evidence viva voce or otherwise, was for the rules of the tribunal to decide. However, in the circumstances of that case the House of Lords considered that fairness entailed that the practitioner should have an opportunity to rebut the evidence which had been given in the divorce case by tendering additional evidence on his own behalf.

In *R v Deputy Industrial Injuries Commissioner, ex p Moore* the question at issue was whether the deputy commissioner was entitled to treat medical opinions given in previous cases as independent evidence in the case before him. At [1965] 1 QB, p 476 Willmer LJ pointed out that there was a considerable latitude before the deputy commissioner. If there was a hearing witnesses might or might not be called, might or might not be sworn. It was to his mind abundantly clear that Parliament intended that there should be a minimum of formality. He went on to say: 'Where so much is left to the discretion of the commissioner, the only real limitation, as I see it, is that the procedure must be in accordance with natural justice. This involves that any information on which the commissioner acts, whatever its source, must be at least of some probative value. It also involves that the commissioner must be prepared to hear both sides, assuming that he has been requested to grant a hearing, and that on such hearing he must allow both sides to comment on or contradict any information that he has obtained.'

This was, he said, in conformity with the statement of principle by Lord Loreburn in *Board of Education v Rice*. At pp 487–488 Diplock LJ said: 'Where, as in the present case, a personal bias or mala fides on the part of the deputy commissioner is not in question, the rules of natural justice which he must observe can, in my view, be reduced to two. First, he must base his decision on evidence, whether a hearing is requested or not. Secondly, if a hearing is requested, he must fairly listen to the contentions of all persons who are entitled to be represented at the hearing.

'In the context of the first rule, "evidence" is not restricted to evidence which would be admissible in a court of law. For historical reasons, based on the fear that juries who might be illiterate would be incapable of differentiating between the probative values of different methods of proof, the practice of the common law courts has been to admit only what the judges then regarded as the best evidence of any disputed fact, and thereby to exclude much material which, as a matter of common sense, would assist a fact-finding tribunal to reach a correct conclusion: cf. *Myers v. Director of Public Prosecutions* [1964] 3 WLR 145.

'These technical rules of evidence, however, form no part of the rules of natural justice. The requirement that a person exercising quasi-judicial functions must base his decision on evidence means no more than it must be based upon material which tends logically to show the existence or non-existence of facts relevant to the issue to be determined, or to show the likelihood or unlikelihood of the occurrence of some future event, the occurrence of which would be relevant. It means that he must not spin a coin or consult an astrologer, but he may take into account any material which, as a matter of reason, has some probative value in the sense mentioned above. If it is capable of having any probative value, the weight to be attached to it is a matter for the person to whom Parliament has entrusted the responsibility of deciding the issue.'

Diplock LJ went on to state that the medical opinions were put to the expert witnesses who were called by the claimant and the insurance officer. They were invited to comment on them and were cross examined about them. At p 491 he said that the deputy commissioner was entitled to treat those opinions as 'evidence' in their own right even if neither medical witness who was actually called had adopted them. If both those witnesses had disputed them, this would have gone not to their admissibility but to their weight, and would, no doubt, have reduced their probative value in the eyes of the deputy commissioner to practically nothing. Before me counsel were in dispute as to whether the submissions of a party could be regarded as having 'probative value' in the sense of that expression as it was used by Diplock LJ. I was satisfied that they could.

This last case may be compared with *R v Board of Visitors of Hull Prison, ex p St Germain*. This case was concerned with the board's hearing of certain charges against prisoners of breach of prison discipline. Two points arose. First, it was held that the rules of natural justice required that the prisoners should have the opportunity of calling evidence in their exculpation, subject to a discretion on the part of the chairman, which had to be exercised reasonably and in good faith. It may be noted that at [1979] 1 WLR, p 1405, Geoffrey Lane LJ said that the procedure before the board followed essentially that which would occur in any magistrate's court on summary trial. At p 1407 he expressed the opinion that a fair chance of exculpation could not in many cases be given without hearing the accused's witness, e g in a case of alibi defence. As regards the chairman's discretion, mere administrative difficulties simpliciter were not in his view enough. 'Convenience and justice are often not on speaking terms: see Lord Atkin in *General Medical Council v Spackman*'.

Secondly, it was held that while the technical rules of evidence were not applicable to proceedings before the board, the admission of hearsay evidence was subject to the overriding obligation to provide the prisoner with a fair hearing and a fair opportunity to controvert the charges. A sufficient opportunity to deal with hearsay evidence might well involve the cross examination of the witness whose evidence was initially before the board in the form of hearsay.

I turn next to examine the decision in *Cigaro (Glasgow) Ltd v City of Glasgow District Licensing Board*. In this case a company applied to the licensing board for a gaming licence which was refused after a hearing of the applicants and objectors. While the main question in the appeal was concerned with the question of the proper scope of an appeal to the sheriff, the opinion of Lord President Emslie contained observations on the applicant's claim that the procedure adopted by the board involved a breach of the rules of natural justice. It was claimed that because of their established practice the board would have refused a motion by the applicants to allow evidence to be led. At 1982 SC, pp 111–112; 1983 SLT, p 553, the Lord President said: 'For Cigaro, counsel conceded that this practice affects both or all parties to any application so it can scarcely be maintained that in following it the Board does not treat parties equally, or that it does not act fairly as between them. In this case it is not averred that the Board did not act in good faith or that they did not fairly listen to all that was presented to them on both sides of the argument. No motion to allow evidence to be led was made to the Board and counsel for Cigaro was quite unable to say that his clients had been in any way prejudiced in the presentation of their application because no evidence had been led. He could not, in particular, identify any particular matter which in the absence of evidence could not be, and was not, fully developed before the Board.

'There is no magic in the words "natural justice". The substance of their meaning was put succinctly by the Lord President (Clyde) in *Hood Barrs v. British Wool Marketing Board*, 1957 S.C. 72 at p. 82 [1957 SLT at p 157] when he said: "The question is whether the Tribunal has dealt fairly and equally with the parties before it in arriving at its result." Here the statute makes it clear that the Board is not bound to hear evidence. It may do so, but this is entirely a matter within their discretion, and a refusal to hear evidence, whatever else it may amount to, is not in itself an act contrary to natural justice.'

Counsel for the first respondents submitted that these remarks were applicable to the present case although they were obiter. Counsel for the petitioners, on the other hand, sought to distinguish this case in respect that there had been no motion for the hearing of evidence. Further in the present case it could be seen from the existence of a substantial factual dispute that the effect of the board not hearing evidence was to prejudice the position of the petitioners.

Counsel for the petitioners also founded on two decisions in the sheriff court as supporting the two grounds on which the first respondents' decision was challenged. The decision of Sheriff Macphail in *Lorimer's Breweries Ltd v City of Glasgow District Licensing Board*, 20 October 1980, unreported, arose out of the refusal of an application for renewal of a public house licence. It may be noted that in this case the board refused a motion on behalf of the applicant that evidence be heard before hearing ex parte statements made to them on behalf of the applicants and the objectors. It was not clear to the sheriff what was the effect of the statements made on behalf of the applicants, and in particular whether they admitted or denied the allegations made by the objectors. The sheriff was, in his own words, left with a strong impression that they were content to take their stand on the motion that matters should be explored in evidence. He criticised the board for not ascertaining the extent to which the allegations were admitted and then considering whether they had before them sufficient undisputed material to enable them to dispose of the application. If they considered that they did not have sufficient, they should have gone on to consider how the remaining disputed issues of fact were to be resolved. The board's view that they were entitled to resolve such issues without hearing evidence, and that there was nothing in the 1976 Act which required them to hear cases by way of evidence was unsound. The sheriff went on to say that at least in the vast majority of cases in which matters of fact were in issue a board could not properly adjudicate thereon without hearing evidence. After considering a number of authorities in regard to the opportunity to lead evidence and cross examine he expressed the view that the board were bound to take these requirements of natural justice into account. In what appears to be the ratio of his decision he stated that the board had been 'labouring under a misapprehension as to the nature of their duties in regard to the determination of disputed questions of fact when adjudicating upon applications for licences such as that which was sought in the present case. In this case their erroneous view of their duties deflected them from ascertaining the extent of the undisputed facts and then, if necessary, properly enquiring into the matters in dispute'.

I must say that I did not find this process of reasoning to be satisfactory. If it was unclear to what extent the allegations were admitted or denied it was difficult to see to what extent there was a need for correction or contradiction of information which was put before the board by the objectors. If on the other hand, the board were regarded as at fault in the procedure which they adopted in dealing with the applicants' motion, this raised a serious question as to whether this could amount to a breach of the rules of natural justice. None of the authorities considered by the sheriff or drawn to my attention appeared to deal with such a point. Further I did not consider that the sheriff's decision could be reconciled with that in *Cigaro (Glasgow) Ltd v City of Glasgow District Licensing Board*, at least in view of the absence of any basis for the view that the applicants were prejudiced.

The second case was that of *Devana Investments Ltd v City of Aberdeen Licensing Board*. This was concerned with an application under s 65 of the 1976 Act for a restriction order in the case of an entertainment licence. The chief constable who applied for the order founded on 47 incidents of alleged disorder associated with the premises. At the hearing the licence holders indicated that they did not agree with a substantial number of allegations and submitted that the only way of resolving these disputes would be by hearing evidence. The licensing board refused to allow evidence to be heard and ruled that their procedure should be by way of ex parte statements. Following the hearing of the statements the board made the restriction order. In the statement of reasons for their decision the board found as fact incidents which had been challenged by the licence holders. Sheriff A M G Russell expressed the view that unless there were a sufficient number of incidents which were to be admitted and the board considered these to be sufficient to establish a case, evidence would have to be heard in relation to the disputed incidents if justice was to be done. 'To do otherwise would be to ignore that fundamental rule that a party should not be precluded from being allowed to lead relevant evidence in disputed matters which are essential to his cause' (1992 SCLR, p 619).

As it was, the board based their conclusion on incidents which had been challenged. At p 622 he expressed the view that to reach a decision on facts in such circumstances was to act contrary to natural justice. He also said that while the question whether evidence was to be allowed or not was a discretionary matter in the hands of the board, 'Discretion must be exercised and must be seen to be exercised properly and in the present case I can find no reason advanced for the basis of the defenders' decision to refuse to allow the pursuers to lead evidence. There is no material upon which I can examine the basis of their discretion.' In these circumstances he held that he was satisfied that the board's discretion had not been shown to have been properly exercised…

It has, of course, to be recognised that the licensing board's discretion is subject to any overriding requirement of natural justice. The mere fact that the board decide to proceed upon one type of material and not upon another would not of itself indicate a failure to comply with natural justice. What matters is whether they have denied a party that equality of treatment which is involved in the right to a fair hearing.

The cases of *General Medical Council v Spackman* and *R v Board of Visitors of Hull Prison, ex p St Germain* are cases in which considerations of natural justice led the court to conclude that a party should not be denied the opportunity to lead evidence or to cross examine witnesses. However, in each case it was held in effect that it would be unfair if that party was not able to meet evidence with evidence; and it was held, rightly in my opinion, that administrative inconvenience was no answer, although there was a discretion in the body hearing the case to determine how far that opportunity should be allowed to be exercised. It may be noted that in each case the body was dealing with a charge against an individual of conduct which, if established, could give rise to a penalty.

The context of applications under the 1976 Act is somewhat different, being concerned with the granting, removal or modification of the various forms of authority for which the Act provides. I do not doubt that a licence holder should have a fair opportunity to correct or contradict information which is put before the board by an objector, but I do not accept that this means that he has the right to insist that he do so by leading evidence. The observation by Sheriff Russell in *Devana Investments Ltd* that there was a 'fundamental rule that a party should not be precluded from being allowed to lead relevant evidence in disputed matters which are essential to his cause' appeared to me to be without support from authority and to be too widely expressed, at least in the case of an administrative body exercising quasi-judicial functions. I have already expressed my reservations as to the soundness of the reasoning of Sheriff Macphail in the case of *Lorimer's Breweries v City of Glasgow District Licensing Board*. I should add that in any event there are significant differences between the present case and the two sheriff court cases. In each of the latter the board refused a motion to hear evidence before hearing to what extent the allegations made by the objector were admitted or denied.

As regards the present case the lack of equality of treatment of which counsel for the petitioners complained was that the first respondents accepted what was said on behalf of the second respondent and denied the petitioners the opportunity to challenge it in evidence. However, each party had and took the opportunity to make submissions in regard to what was alleged; and in that sense there was equality of treatment. The complaint came close to a complaint that the first respondents awarded the palm of victory to the second respondent. However, lack of success is not the test of unfairness. Further I did not regard the reasons for the first respondents' decision as indicating that they had found as fact the entirety of each allegation on behalf of the second respondent. They held that in view of the serious nature of the police objections 'there were sufficient grounds' to find that the extension was likely to cause undue public nuisance or to be a threat to public order or safety. To the extent that there was a material dispute of fact as between the petitioners and the first respondents, this would have tended to reduce the 'probative value' of the second respondent's submission. I should add that the value which the first respondents attached to the different pieces of information given to them by the second respondent is not under challenge in this petition. Any attack on that ground would require to show that their evaluation was unreasonable. There is nothing which would show that this was the case...

In these circumstances I dismissed the petition."

Notes

(1) The concept of equality of treatment is clearly present in the court's analysis. If the   **8–18**
procedure is flawed or unfair does it matter if there is equality of opportunity? Does this approach give sufficient weight to the wider public interest in decisions being taken on a fully informed basis?

(2) Contrast the extract with the views of the sheriff (A.M.G. Russell, C.B.E., Q.C.) in *Devana Investments Ltd v. City of Aberdeen Licensing Board*, 1992 S.C.L.R. 616 where licence holders who were the subject of a complaint by the Chief Constable were denied the opportunity to lead evidence in relation to 10 out of 20 alleged incidents found to be "established" by the board that (at 622):

> "To accept a disputed version of the material and vital facts in the teeth of a motion to be allowed to lead evidence is courting disaster and disregarding the natural laws of justice."

(3) It will be apparent that as with the right to cross-examine, the right to lead evidence in support of one's depends on the nature, procedure and function of the body determining it. The closer a body resembles the judicial model, arguably the stronger the right is to lead evidence in support of one's case and in contradiction of the opponents. Even so, the idea of equality of treatment has been extended to situations which do not conform to the judicial model. Thus, after a public inquiry into a clearance order, a government department which received further

evidence from a local authority without informing the owners of the affected property of the new evidence was held to be acting in breach of natural justice: *Hamilton v. Roxburghshire County Council*, 1970 S.C. 248; see also *Fairmount Investments Ltd v. Secretary of State for the Environment* [1976] 2 All E.R. 865, H.L. However, a person appointed to conduct a public inquiry is not required to reveal material he has received from a department concerning the scope or nature of the inquiry: *Wednesbury Corporation v. Ministry of Housing and Local Government (No. 2)* [1965] 3 All E.R. 571, C.A. Similarly, a domestic committee, looking into a complaint in relation to a taxi driver's conduct, was not entitled to rely on minutes of a previous meeting not put to the driver in question during the current hearing: *Tait v. Central Radio Taxis (Tollcross) Ltd*, 1989 S.C. 4.

(4) It is an accepted part of the law of evidence that a court is entitled to bring its own knowledge to bear on a matter before it to supplement any evidence led provided that knowledge falls within the accepted ambit of judicial knowledge. See *Stair Memorial Encyclopaedia*, Vol. 10, "Evidence", paras 510–512. It is accepted that administrative bodies are entitled to bring their own knowledge and expertise to bear on a decision and it will always be a question of circumstance as to what extent such knowledge requires to be disclosed to parties appearing before it. Thus a tribunal member can use specialist knowledge in evaluating evidence given by parties, but may not introduce additional evidence himself: *Taylor v. Minister of Pensions*, 1946 S.C. 99. A licensing board is entitled to rely on its knowledge of the area it is responsible for, but the extent to which it requires to disclose that knowledge to those appearing before it varies, on which see para. 8–30. On this area generally see *Stair Memorial Encyclopaedia*, Vol. 1, para. 276.

CAN A BREACH OF NATURAL JUSTICE BE CURED BY AN APPEAL?

Calvin v. Carr

[1980] A.C. 574

8–19   "The appellant was the part-owner of a racehorse which competed in a race organised under the auspices of the Australian Jockey Club. The horse did not run as well as expected and his performance was subject to a stewards' inquiry. The stewards interviewed, inter alios, the jockey, the trainer and the appellant. They also saw film of the horse running in other races. 13 days after the race, the stewards determined that the jockey was guilty of an offence under the Club's Rules of Racing (namely not running a horse on its merits) and that the appellant was a party to that breach. They disqualified the appellant from membership of the Club for one year, which prevented him from entering any horse in a race organised by the Club for that period. The appellant exercised his right, under the Rules, to appeal against the stewards' decision to a committee of the Club. Before the committee he was represented by counsel and had full opportunity to call witnesses and subject others to cross-examination. The committee dismissed his appeal. The appellant then brought an action in the Supreme Court of New South Wales for a declaration that his disqualification from the Club was unlawful and an injunction to restrain the Club from acting on the purported disqualification. The major argument advanced by the appellant was that the stewards had acted in breach of the right to a fair hearing, consequently their decision was invalid, and this defect could not be cured by a lawful hearing before the appellate committee. The action was dismissed by the Australian court, so the appellant brought this appeal before the Privy Council"

LORD WILBERFORCE: "...The plaintiff's second argument can be stated, for purposes of description, as being that such defects of natural justice as may have existed as regards the proceedings before the stewards were not capable of being cured by the appeal proceedings before the committee, even though, as was not contested before this Board, these were correctly and fairly conducted. The defendants contend the contrary. This part of the argument involved consideration of a wide range of authorities of this Board, and in Australia, Canada, England and New Zealand. As regards decisions of this Board a conflict was said to exist between *Annamunthodo v. Oilfields Workers' Trade Union* [1961] A.C. 945 and *Pillai v. Singapore City Council* [1968] 1 W.L.R. 1278, each of which has been followed by other decisions. There was also said to be a conflict between *Annamunthodo's* case, and the High Court in *Australian Workers' Union v. Bowen*: (No. 2) (1948) 77 C.L.R. 601, a conflict giving rise to difficulties for Australian state courts. Other individual decisions were cited which it appears difficult to reconcile.

Although, as will appear, some of the suggested inconsistencies of decisions disappear, or at least diminish, on analysis, their Lordships recognise and indeed assert that no clear and absolute rule can be laid down on the question whether defects in natural justice appearing at an original hearing, whether administrative or quasi-judicial, can be 'cured' through appeal proceedings. The situations in which this issue arises are too diverse, and the rules by which they are governed so various, that this must be so. There are, however, a number of typical situations as to which some general principle can be stated. First there are cases where the rules provide for a rehearing by the original body, or some fuller or enlarged form of it. This situation may be found in relation to social clubs. It is not difficult in such cases to reach the conclusion that the first hearing is superseded by the second, or, putting it in contractual terms, the parties are taken to have agreed to accept the decision of the hearing body, whether original or adjourned. Examples of this are *De Verteuil v. Knaggs* [1918] A.C. 557, 563; *Posluns v. Toronto Stock Exchange and Gardiner* (1965) 53 D.L.R. (2d) 193; *Re Clark and Ontario Securities Commission* (1966) 56 D.L.R. (2d) 585; *Re Chromex Nickel Mines Ltd* (1970) 16 D.L.R. (3d) 273; and see also *Ridge v. Baldwin* [1964] A.C. 40, 79, *per* Lord Reid.

At the other extreme are cases, where, after examination of the whole hearing structure, in the context of the particular activity to which it relates (trade union membership, planning, employment, etc.) the conclusion is reached that a complainant has the right to nothing less than a fair hearing both at the original and at the appeal stage. This was the result reached by Megarry J. in *Leary v. National Union of Vehicle Builders* [1971] Ch. 34. In his judgment in that case the judge seems to have elevated the conclusion thought proper in that case into a rule of general application. In an eloquent passage he said, at 49:

'If the rules and the law combine to give the member the right to a fair trial and the right of appeal, why should he be told that he ought to be satisfied with an unjust trial and a fair appeal? ...As a general rule ...I hold that a failure of natural justice in the trial body cannot be cured by a sufficiency of natural justice in an appellate body.'

In their Lordships' opinion this is too broadly stated. It affirms a principle which may be found correct in a category of cases: these may very well include trade union cases, where movement solidarity and dislike of the rebel, or renegade, may make it difficult for appeals to be conducted in an atmosphere of detached impartiality and so make a fair trial at the first — probably branch — level an essential condition of justice. But to seek to apply it generally over-looks, in their Lordships' respectful opinion, both the existence of the first category, and the possibility that, intermediately, the conclusion to be reached, on the rules and on the contractual context, is that those who have joined in an organisation, or contract, should be taken to have agreed to accept what in the end is a fair decision, notwithstanding some initial defect.

In their Lordship's judgment such intermediate cases exist. In them it is for the court, in the light of the agreements made, and in addition having regard to the course of proceedings, to decide whether, at the end of the day, there has been a fair result, reached by fair methods, such as the parties should fairly be taken to have accepted when they joined the association. Naturally there may be instances when the defect is so flagrant, the consequences so severe, that the most perfect of appeals or rehearings will not be sufficient to produce a just result. Many rules (including those now in question) anticipate that such a situation may arise by giving power to remit for a new hearing. There may also be cases when the appeal process is itself less than perfect: it may be vitiated by the same defect as the original proceedings: or short of that there may be doubts whether the appeal body embarked on its task without predisposition or whether it had the means to make a fair and full inquiry, for example where it has no material but a transcript of what was before the original body. In such cases it would no doubt be right to quash the original decision. These are all matters (and no doubt there are others) which the court must consider. Whether these intermediate cases are to be regarded as exceptions from a general rule, as stated by Megarry J., or as a parallel category covered by a rule of equal status, is not in their Lordships' judgment necessary to state, or indeed a matter of great importance. What is important is the recognition that such cases exist, and that it is undesirable in many cases of domestic disputes, particularly in which an inquiry and appeal process has been established, to introduce too great a measure of formal judicialisation. While flagrant cases of injustice, including corruption or bias, must always be firmly dealt with by the courts, the tendency in their Lordships' opinion in matters of domestic disputes should be to leave these to be settled by the agreed methods without requiring the formalities of judicial processes to be introduced...

It remains to apply the principles above stated to the facts of the present case. In the first place, their Lordships are clearly of the view that the proceedings before the committee were in the nature of an appeal, not by way of an invocation, or use, of whatever original jurisdiction the committee may have had...

In addition to these formal requirements, a reviewing court must take account of the reality behind them. Races are run at short intervals; bets must be disposed of according to the result. Stewards are there in order to take rapid decisions as to such matters as the running of horses, being entitled to use the evidence of their eyes and their experience. As well as acting inquisitorially at the stage of deciding the result of a race, they may have to consider disciplinary action: at this point rules of natural justice become relevant. These require, at the least, that persons should be formally charged, heard in their own defence, and know the evidence against them. These essentials must always be observed but it is inevitable, and must be taken to be accepted, that there may not be time for procedural refinements. It is in order to enable decisions reached in this way to be reviewed at leisure that the appeal procedure exists. Those concerned know that they are entitled to a full hearing with opportunities to bring evidence and have it heard. But they know also that this appeal hearing is governed by the Rules of Racing, and that it remains an essentially domestic proceeding, in which experience and opinions as to what is in the interest of racing as a whole play a large part, and in which the standards are those which have come to be accepted over the history of this sporting activity. All those who partake in it have accepted the Rules of Racing, and the standards which lie behind them: they must also have accepted to be bound by the decisions of the bodies set up under those rules so long as when the process of reaching these decisions has been terminated, they can be said, by an objective observer, to have had fair treatment and consideration of their case on its merits.

In their Lordships' opinion precisely this can, indeed must, be said of the present case. The plaintiff's case has received, overall, full and fair consideration, and a decision, possibly a hard one, reached against him. There is no basis on which the court ought to interfere, and his appeal must fail…"

Notes

8–20   (1) It will be seen that there is no hard and fast rule as to whether or not an appeal can cure an earlier breach of natural justice. The approach must of necessity be a pragmatic one. For comment on this case see M. Elliott, "Appeals, Principles and Pragmatism in Natural Justice" (1980) 43 M.L.R. 66. Consider the passage in the context of a typical administrative scheme: how helpful would the speech be to an administrator asked to devise procedural rules for a two-tier system of appeal and disciplinary proceedings in an organisation falling within the "intermediate category"?

(2) The approach of Lord Wilberforce has been applied in a number of subsequent decisions. In *R. v. Brent London Borough Council, ex p. Gunning* (1985) 84 L.G.R. 168 it was argued that any defects in the local council's consultation process in relation to closure of schools under the Education Act 1980, s. 6 was cured by the further procedure of objection to the Secretary of State under section 12 of the Act. Hodgson J. doubted whether the principles of fairness "developed in the quasi-judicial field of domestic disciplinary proceedings", could apply to "purely administrative procedures of a sort with which we are concerned". In any event he was satisfied that the failure to consult was sufficiently serious in itself as an example of procedural *ultra vires*, that no further procedure could cure it. Similarly in *Brown v. Executive Committee of the Edinburgh District Labour Party*, 1995 S.L.T. 985, extracted at para. 11–7, at a hearing on interim interdict and ssuspension, the court was asked to treat *Calvin* as authority for the view that alleged breaches of natural justice which were about to take place would be remedied by appeal procedure. Lord Osborne observed (at 990):

> "I know nothing of any appeal which might follow the determination of those proceedings …It appears to me therefore that I cannot, at this stage, reach any conclusion as to whether such an appeal might or might not 'cure' the apprehended defect in natural justice in the original contemplated hearing."

The lesson here would appear to be that for the court to make any assessment of whether or not an appeal is likely to cure a previous defect, those arguing the point will have to provide sufficient information to the court for it to make assessment of whether or not the appeal would be an adequate method of resolving any difficulties. Note the view expressed in *Ahmed v. Stirling District Licensing Board*, 1980 S.L.T. (Sh. Ct) 51 that it could amount to an unreasonable exercise of discretion on the part of a licensing board to assume that an appeal could cure a defect.

RIGHT TO LEGAL REPRESENTATION

Tait v. Central Radio Taxis (Tollcross) Ltd

1987 S.L.T. 506

"A taxi driver, a member of a radio taxi company, was subjected to disciplinary procedure as a result **8–21** of which he was requested to resign his membership or be barred from membership. The disciplinary proceedings were before a disciplinary committee and were subject to appeal. No direct evidence of the complaint was led. The taxi driver appealed. He wished to be represented by a solicitor. The solicitor was told that no such representation would be permitted. The appeal was conducted without the presence of the solicitor and without the taxi driver and was refused. The taxi driver sought damages from the company, claiming that the decision was wrongful and that there had been breaches of natural justice in that (1) he had been given insufficient specification of the charges to be made against him, (2) no proper evidence had been before the committee since no direct evidence on which the taxi driver could cross examine had been led, (3) the taxi driver's past disciplinary record had been before the committee and he had not been heard in mitigation upon it, and (4) he had not been allowed representation in the appeal."

LORD WYLIE: "The basis of the pursuer's case, as focused in the second plea in law, is that these proceedings were in breach of the rules of natural justice and having sustained patrimonial loss as a consequence the pursuer is entitled to reparation. The question as to whether or not the requirements of natural justice have or have not been satisfied by the procedure adopted in any given case must depend to a very large extent on the circumstances of the case. As Tucker L.J. said in *Russell v. Duke of Norfolk* at p. 118: 'There are, in my view, no words which are of universal application to every kind of inquiry and every kind of domestic tribunal. The requirements of natural justice must depend on the circumstances of the case, the nature of the inquiry, the rules under which the tribunal is acting, the subject-matter that is being dealt with, and so forth.' Accepting that reservations must apply to the utility of general definitions in this branch of the law, there are certain accepted features which do emerge from the decided cases. It was put in these terms by Harman J. in *Byrne v. Kinematograph Renters Society Ltd.* at p. 784, cited with approval by Lord Jenkins in *Ceylon University v. Fernando* at p. 231: 'What then are the requirements of natural justice in a case of this kind. First, I think that the person accused should know the nature of the accusation made; secondly, that he should be given an opportunity to state his case; and, thirdly, of course, that the tribunal should act in good faith. I do not myself think that there really is anything more.' Almost identical language was used by Lord Hodson in *Ridge v. Baldwin* at p. 132. The courts will interfere with the decision of any judicial or quasi-judicial tribunal if these requirements are not met, provided always that the irregularity is so fundamental 'that it goes beyond a mere matter of procedure, and becomes something so prejudicial to a fair and impartial investigation of the question to be decided as to amount to a denial of natural justice, as, for example, if a conviction ...were to take place without an accusation being made, or without allowing the person accused to be heard in his defence. In short, the irregularity alleged must not be simply a point of form, or a departure from prescribed regulation, but must go to the honesty and integrity of the proceedings complained of' (per Lord Justice-Clerk Aitchison in *McDonald v. Burns*, 1940 S.L.T. at pp. 331–332)...

The final attack was directed towards the proceedings before the appeal committee. It was argued in the first place that no reasons were given for the initial decision and that, since no reasons had been put to him by the committee, the pursuer was not in a position to formulate his own grounds of appeal. This is not an issue which is focused in the pleadings and I do not consider that there is substance in it. The issue for the committee was a narrow one. The pursuer was made aware of the allegation which had been made, and had been given the opportunity to meet it. He intimated his dissatisfaction with the decision immediately and his intention to appeal against it.

The primary complaint in relation to the appeal proceedings was the refusal to allow the pursuer to be represented by his solicitor, whose request to do so was refused. A supplementary complaint was the refusal by the defenders to postpone the appeal proceedings, which the pursuer's solicitor had like-wise requested. It is the case that the appeal in this instance was conducted with unusual expedition, but Mr Ford explained that the reason for this was the imminence of the next annual meeting, at which he was to stand down as disciplinary convener. He was anxious in these circumstances to 'clear the books' so far as his participation in disciplinary matters was concerned. The object of a postponement, as the pursuer himself conceded, was to resolve the issue of professional representation on which he was insisting although he had never known of this being done in the past.

Counsel for the pursuer referred me to Lord Stott's decision in *Walker v. Amalgamated Union of Engineers and Foundry Workers* and the decision of the Court of Appeal in *Pett v. Greyhound Racing*

Association. After considering the provisions in the defenders' rules in relation to the right of an appellant to be accompanied at the hearing by one other person, which in his Lordship's view did not exclude a right to legal representation, he went on to say (1969 S.L.T. at p. 153): 'In any event, what I am concerned with is not a right of audience in the abstract but what was reasonable and fair in the circumstances of this case. In my opinion it was inconsistent with any reasonable idea of fairness that the pursuer should, at the last moment, be compelled to present his own case when he had been led to suppose that his lawyer would speak for him and when he must be presumed to have made no preparation for conducting his case himself.' To a material extent the facts and circumstances were of course special to the case, but his Lordship was clearly influenced by the decision in *Pett*, 'which decided that at a hearing on matters which might affect reputation by counsel or solicitor should be permitted if the accused person so wished'. This is a reference to a passage by Lord Denning M.R. in *Pett* at pp. 132–133 where, after considering the dictum of Maugham J. in *McLean v. Workers Union*, Lord Denning went on to say: 'The dictum may be correct when confined to tribunals dealing with minor matters where the rules may properly exclude legal representation ...But the dictum does not apply to tribunals dealing with matters which affect a man's reputation or livelihood or any matters of serious import. Natural justice then requires that he can be defended, if he wishes, by counsel or solicitor.'

The case of *Pett* was a decision on appeal against the granting of an interlocutory injunction restraining an organisation from holding an inquiry unless the person involved was allowed legal representation, and it was held, dismissing the appeal, that a prima facie case had been made out to support the injunction. Although Russell L.J. made reference to the requirements of natural justice, he was more guarded in his observations (at p. 135): 'As at present advised, I think a sufficient prima facie case is made out to support this interlocutory injunction; and the balance of convenience is certainly in favour of the injunction, for no sort of case is made out yet that legal representation on an occasion such as this will make the system unworkable. ...How the case may ultimately turn out, I know not, but as an interlocutory matter, I too would dismiss the appeal.' Subsequently, in *Pett v. Greyhound Racing Association*, Lyall J. held that the defendants had not acted contrary to the rules of natural justice in refusing to allow legal representation and applied *Ceylon University v. Fernando*, but when this decision came before the Court of Appeal the court was informed that the rules had been revised and that legal representation would be allowed at the proposed inquiry.

This line of authority was considered in *Enderby Town Football Club Ltd. v. Football Association Ltd.*, in which it was held that a rule which excluded legal representation except where the lawyer was chairman or secretary of the club was not invalid as being contrary to natural justice. At p. 605 Lord Denning M.R. posed the question: 'Is a party who is charged before a domestic tribunal entitled *as of right* to be legally represented?' and answered it thus: 'Much depends on what the rules say about it. When the rules say nothing, then the party has no absolute right to be legally represented. It is a matter for the *discretion* of the tribunal. They are masters of their own procedure: and, if they, in the proper exercise of their discretion, decline to allow legal representation, the courts will not interfere.' His Lordship went on to explain that the court intervened in *Pett* because the tribunal had fettered itself with an absolute rule against legal representation. No such qualification is to be found in the other judgments. Fenton Atkinson L.J. observed that the rule applied to both parties, that it enabled a decision to be taken speedily without heavy costs being incurred, and by persons familiar with the issues involved and the rules in question. Any delicate questions of law could still be resolved by recourse to the courts, and his Lordship concluded (at p. 609) by observing that, if a rule against legal representation was contrary to the principles of natural justice 'a very large number of persons, including our legislators, must have been very insensitive over a long period of years to what natural justice requires'. Cairns L.J. considered that those responsible for drafting such rules were entitled to take the view that justice as well as convenience would be served by a rule exluding legal representation and there was no need to make any exceptions. See also *Maynard v. Osmond*, a decision involving a consideration of the Police (Discipline) Regulations 1965.

In the present case there was no provision for legal representation, nor was there any provision precluding such representation. It was never the practice to involve such representation, and when the request was made in this instance it was refused. Having regard to the subject matter of the investigation and the composition of the appeal committee it cannot be said, in my view, that the denial of legal representation constituted a breach of the principles of natural justice. On the non-appearance of the pursuer the committee could simply have dismissed the appeal. Instead, according to the evidence, they waited some time for the pursuer to appear, they attempted to contact him and, having considered the complaint and the pursuer's version of events as recorded in the minutes of the disciplinary committee, they decided to uphold the decision of that committee.

For these reasons I am satisfied that the pursuer's case must fail, and that the second plea in law for the pursuer falls to be repelled."

Notes

(1) In principle, the citizen has a right to seek legal advice and be legally represented if he so **8–22** wishes. In *Enderby Town Football Club Ltd v. Football Association Ltd* [1971] Ch. 591 a contract existed which specifically excluded legal representation, a limitation accepted by the individual in question. *Tait* is closer to *Pett v. Greyhound Racing Association* [1970] 1 Q.B. 46 on the issue of whether or not to allow legal representation as being a question of the exercise of discretion, and therefore one of the extent to which that discretion has been abused. The view that a rule which prevented the exercise of legal representation as amounting to an abuse of the discretion was endorsed by the Outer House in *Abbas v. Secretary of State for the Home Department*, 1993 S.L.T. 502 at 504: see generally *Stair Memorial Encyclopaedia*, Vol. 1, para. 279.

(2) Notwithstanding the apparent certainty attaching to the kind of clause found in *Enderby* there is some doubt as to whether or not the absolute effect claimed for it is correct. In *Enderby* Lord Denning thought that such a clause was directory only and exceptions to it could be allowed. However, in *Maynard v. Osmond* [1977] Q.B. 240 at 252 he noted, *obiter*: "it is permissible for [a domestic body] to decree otherwise. "*Maynard* was an example of the exclusion of legal representation based on (English) police regulations. It would seem odd if a higher standard was expected of domestic tribunals simply because of the form of prohibition. On *Maynard* see W. McKean, "Representation Before a Police Tribunal" (1977) 36 C.L.J. 205 and for the current Scottish police regulations see Police (Discipline) (Scotland) Regulations 1967, regulation 7(2) of which excludes legal representation in certain proceedings.

(3) The issue of legal representation has been sharply focused in the context of prison regulations. In *R. v. Secretary of State for the Home Department, ex parte Tarrant* [1985] Q.B. 251 a prisoner charged with a disciplinary offence was held to have no right to legal representation although the board of visitors had a discretion to grant representation. In the exercise of that discretion, Webster J. thought that the following criteria should be considered:

1. The seriousness of the charge and of the potential penalty.
2. Whether any points of law are likely to arise in the proceedings.
3. The capacity of a prisoner to present his own case.
4. Procedural difficulties — for example, whether the prisoner had been able to interview witnesses prior to the hearing.
5. The need for reasonable speed in making a decision.
6. The need for fairness between prisoners and between prisoners and prison officers.

These criteria were quoted with approval in *R. v. Board of Visitors of H.M. Prison, The Maze, ex parte Hone* [1988] 1 AC 379 where a prisoner serving a life sentence in Northern Ireland was charged with an assault of a prison officer in breach of the Prison Rules (Northern Ireland) 1982. The board of visitors found the charge proved and sentenced him to 30 days' solitary confinement and loss of privileges for 60 days. He sought, but was denied, legal representation. Notwithstanding the seriousness of the offence, and the substantial penalty imposed, the House of Lords held that there had been no breach of natural justice by the board's denial of legal representation. Particular emphasis was placed on there being no issue of law at stake and the pressing need to make a quick decision in difficult circumstances. M.J. Dixon, "Public Law and Prison Inmates — Two Part Disharmony" (1989) 40 N.I.L.Q. 71, is particularly critical of *Hone*, and argues that it pays lip-service to the criteria stated in *Tarrant*, with undue weight being given to the needs of the administration.

The Scottish Board of Visitors has not exercised its disciplinary jurisdiction since 1991 and the current prison disciplinary regulations are contained in the Prisons and Young Offenders Institutions (Scotland) Rules 1994. Rule 97(7) provides that in relation to disciplinary matters, the governor may allow legal representation "where in exceptional circumstances he considers such representation is necessary". To what extent could the criteria in *Tarrant* be applied to other contexts?

(3) When representation is permitted, discretion as to the choice of representative may exist. **8–23** In *R. v. Supplementary Benefits Commission, ex parte Donlan* [1977] S.B. 12 the commission was held entitled to refuse to interview an applicant for benefit in the presence of a friend who

was not acceptable to the commission and in *Templeton v. Criminal Injuries Compensation Board*, 1997 S.L.T. 953 the board was held entitled to refuse to allow representation by a solicitor who had been struck off the roll of solicitors is Scotland. Compare *R. v. Leicester City Justices, ex parte Barrow* [1991] 2 Q.B. 260.

(4) Sometimes a statutory right to representation is permitted. Under the Town and Country Planning (Inquiries Procedure) (Scotland) Rules 1997, r. 16(3), those entitled to be heard at an inquiry can be represented by a lawyer or by another person with the permission of the inquiry; see too the Social Security (Adjudication) Regulations 1995, reg. 2(1)(*b*).

(5) Article 6 of the ECHR only confers a *right* to legal representation in the context of criminal offences: see *Granger v. United Kingdom* (1990) 12 E.H.R.R. 469; *Boner v. United Kingdom*, 1995 S.C.C.R. 1; and generally S. Naismith, "European Court of Human Rights" (1995) 40 J.L.S.S. 32.

ORAL OR WRITTEN REPRESENTATIONS?

Young v. Criminal Injuries Compensation Board

1997 S.L.T. 297

8–24   LORD GILL: "The petitioner applied unsuccessfully to the Criminal Injuries Compensation Board ('the respondents') for compensation under the Criminal Injuries Compensation Scheme 1990 ('the scheme') in respect of injuries suffered by him when he was assaulted and stabbed in a club in Dunoon in April 1992. The application followed the normal course. In October 1992 the petitioner completed a medical questionnaire at the request of the respondents. Thereafter his solicitors received from the respondents a formal notification of determination dated 17 November 1992. It stated, inter alia:

'I am writing to inform you that I have considered this application and have concluded that the applicant is not eligible for an award.

'Under Paragraph 6 (c) of the Scheme, compensation may be withheld if it seems inappropriate that an award should be made from public funds on account of the appellant's character as shown by his criminal convictions. Having regard to the applicant's list of convictions I have concluded that no award can be made'.

The petitioner then submitted a formal request dated 30 November 1992 for a hearing before the respondents in accordance with para 22 of the scheme. The request was made on the respondents' official form in accordance with para 23 of the scheme. The request was in the following terms:

'I …do not accept the decision of the Board on my application for an ex-gratia payment of compensation. My reasons are as follows: The locus was my work place. I had been employed there for approximately one month prior to being attacked. Although I was off duty I could not stand back and watch my employer being robbed. My assailant had been trying to steal money from the till. The fact that I tried to stop him was deemed sufficient "provocation".

'Although I do have a previous conviction for assault, this was several years ago. There were absolutely no knives involved on that occasion. I do not have any previous convictions for offences reflecting the gravity of the injury I sustained. I therefore request a Hearing before the Board in accordance with the provisions of Paragraph 22 of the Scheme.'

Although the petitioner's request for an oral hearing does not make the matter entirely clear, I understand from counsel for the petitioner that the schedule of previous convictions that was before the respondents was accurate and that it included two convictions in respect of which the petitioner had received custodial sentences.

The respondents sent a letter dated 2 December 1992 to the petitioner's solicitors, acknowledging receipt of the petitioner's request and stating that they would contact his solicitors in due course to inform them of the decision concerning the procedure to be adopted in his case.

The respondents thereafter sent to the petitioner's solicitors a letter dated 5 February 1993 in the following terms:

'I am writing to inform you that your [client's] application for an oral hearing was reviewed by the Board under the terms of Paragraph 24 (c) of the Scheme and refused.

'A decision to refuse an application for a hearing is final.'

The petitioner seeks judicial review of the decision which this letter communicated to him. Counsel agreed that if I were minded to grant the petition the appropriate order would be to reduce the decision and to remit the petitioner's application to the respondents for them to convene a hearing.

The Scheme and the Guide

The key texts in this case are paras 22 to 24 of the scheme and paras 37 to 39 of the February 1990 edition of the respondents' document 'Victims of Crimes of Violence: A Guide to the Criminal Injuries Compensation Scheme' ('the guide') which was in force at the relevant date.

Paragraphs 22 to 24 of the scheme set out the procedure for the determination of applications for compensation.

Paragraph 22 provides first for the making of the application for compensation and of the decision upon it. It then provides that: [his Lordship quoted the terms of para 22 and then para 23 set out supra and continued:]

Paragraph 24, so far as it is relevant to this case, provides as follows: [his Lordship quoted the terms of para 24 set out supra and continued:]

Paragraphs 37 to 39 of the guide are as follows: [his Lordship quoted paras 37–39 and continued:]

The Case for the Petitioner

Counsel for the petitioner argued (1) that the decision to refuse the request for an oral hearing contravened the scheme; (2) that the decision was vitiated by a failure to give reasons, and (3) that the provision in the scheme which enabled the respondents to deny the petitioner an oral hearing was contrary to natural justice. I think that counsel for the respondents was right in saying that the third argument has no proper foundation: on record but I need not reject it on that technicality since I have decided that it is not a good argument anyhow.

The Refusal of a Hearing

The starting point in the first argument for the petitioner is the letter of 17 November 1992 containing the notification of determination. In that letter the writer stated that he had 'concluded' that the petitioner was not eligible for an award and that having regard to the petitioner's list of convictions he had 'concluded' that no award could be made. Counsel for the petitioner argued that in his request for an oral hearing the petitioner had made clear that conclusion. Therefore, she argued, there was at once a dispute as to the conclusion upon which the decision was based. That being so, it followed that in terms of para 24 (c) of the scheme the respondents were obliged to grant an oral hearing.

In my opinion, this argument is flawed. The flaw lies in the misinterpretation of the word 'conclusions' in para 24 (c) of the scheme. In making a decision under para 24 (c) the respondents had to ask themselves two questions, namely, whether there was a dispute as to the material facts or conclusions on which the decision to refuse compensation was based, and whether it appeared that the decision to refuse compensation might have been wrong in law or in principle. Counsel for the petitioner accepted that in this case only the first of these questions was in issue.

In my opinion, it cannot be said that there was a dispute as to the material facts or conclusions on which the decision to refuse compensation was based. The references in para 24 (c) to 'material facts' and to 'conclusions' are references, in my view, to the primary facts and to the conclusions of a factual nature which fall to be drawn from such primary facts. For example, the injuries suffered by an applicant are material facts. A conclusion might be drawn from those facts as to the degree of disfigurement or disability resulting from the injuries. The facts and the surrounding circumstances of an assault would be material facts. A conclusion might be drawn from those facts that the victim provoked the assault or that the victim was acting in self defence.

In the present case compensation was refused by reason of the petitioner's character as shown by his previous convictions. The convictions constituted the material facts on which the decision was based.

The petitioner did not dispute these material facts. He disputed the decision itself. Accordingly the requirements of para 24 (c) were not made out. It follows therefore that the petitioner was not entitled to an oral hearing.

The argument for the petitioner is founded on the unfortunate use of the expression 'I have concluded' in the notification of determination dated 17 November 1992. In my opinion, the words 'I have concluded' mean in that context, 'I have decided'. That is to say, these words do not set out a conclusion of the kind which para 24 (c) contemplates. The petitioner's argument fails to distinguish between the conclusions on which a decision is based and the decision itself. This distinction becomes clear in the latter part of para 24 which provides, inter alia, that the application for a hearing will be refused 'if it is considered on review that if any facts or conclusions which are disputed were resolved in the applicant's favour it would have made no difference to the initial or reconsidered decision'…

Natural Justice

The third ground on which the petitioner seeks judicial review is that the scheme itself, in making it possible for the respondents to refuse an application for review without giving the applicant a hearing, is contrary to natural justice. In support of this ground, counsel for the petitioner argued that paras 37 to 39 of the guide demonstrate that previous convictions are not per se a bar to compensation. It followed therefore that as soon as it became clear that the applicant's previous convictions were a decisive consideration, it was the duty of the respondents to give the petitioner a hearing so that he could have an opportunity to explain why the convictions should not count against him. Since the scheme entitled the respondents to decline such a hearing, it was unfair on that account.

This ground implies that there is a structural unfairness in the scheme itself. If that were so, the scheme would contravene natural justice no matter how reasonably the respondents attempted to apply it.

In my opinion, the argument for the petitioner on this ground too is flawed. It fails to distinguish between a right to a hearing and a right to be heard.

In administrative procedures such as this, the refusal of a hearing is not per se a denial of natural justice (cf *Pearlberg v Varty; Furnell v Whangarei High Schools Board*) and in my view there is nothing in the scheme that would have that effect.

The scheme is non-adversarial throughout. When applying for an award the applicant has the opportunity to give the respondents all relevant information (para 22). He may even have a positive obligation to do so (paras 6 (b), 14; cf guide, paras 49, 53, 54). If he is dissatisfied with the initial decision he is entitled to apply for an oral hearing. His application for an oral hearing should be supported by reasons and by any additional evidence on which he may rely (scheme, para 23). In submitting his reasons and any additional evidence he can take account of the reasons for the initial decision, which the respondents are obliged to give (para 22).

It follows, in my view, that nothing in the scheme deprives the applicant of a reasonable opportunity of presenting his case (cf *Russell v Duke of Norfolk*, Tucker LJ at [1949] 1 All ER, p 118). The scheme therefore involves no denial of natural justice.

Decision

I conclude therefore that the petitioner has failed to make out a relevant ground of challenge to the decision complained of.

I shall therefore repel the petitioner's plea in law, sustain the respondents first and third pleas in law and refuse the prayer of the petition."

Notes

8–25   (1) Contrast *Young* with *Malloch* above, and see *McIndoe v. Glasgow District Licensing Board*, 1989 S.C.L.R. 325.

(2) The issue of the context in which a decision is made and the function of the decision-making body has long been relevant in this area: see, for example, the comments of Lord Shaw of Dunfermline in *Local Government Board v. Arlidge* [1915] A.C. 120, H.L.

(3) In *Lloyd v. McMahon* [1987] A.C. 625 the district auditor had to consider whether or not to surcharge councillors in Liverpool Council for wilful failure to discharge their duty to set the local authority rate. They were informed that they could make a written representation to the auditor before a decision was reached. They made a written response to the auditor and did not ask for an oral hearing. The auditor found that the councillors were jointly and severally liable for the sum in question, just over £100,000. The councillors appealed to the High Court under section 20(3) of the Local Government Finance Act 1982 and the matter ultimately came before the House of Lords, the councillors arguing that the district auditor should have proceeded by way of an oral hearing relying in particular on the Code of Local Government Audit Practice for England and Wales made under section 14 of the 1982 Act. In considering this argument, Lord Keith of Kinkel observed:

> "The argument by counsel for the appellants did not invite your Lordships to enter deeply into the merits of the question whether or not they had been guilty of wilful misconduct, nor was attention drawn to any details of the affidavits and other material placed before the Divisional Court. The substance of the argument was that the district auditor's decision had been vitiated by his failure to offer the appellants an oral hearing before reaching it, and should therefore have been quashed. The argument was supported by an examination of earlier legislation in regard to local government audits, starting with the Poor Law Amendment Act 1844 (7 & 8 Vict. c. 101), where oral hearings were the order of the day, and by reference to the Code of

Local Government Audit Practice for England and Wales, made under section 14 of the Act of 1982 and approved by resolution of both Houses of Parliament. The code, by paragraphs 16 to 20, contemplates that an oral hearing will be held where the auditor is dealing with a notice of objection given under section 17(3) of the Act of 1982, which itself refers to the objector attending before the auditor. The code does not deal with the procedure to be followed where the auditor takes action under section 20(1). Counsel produced a list of all instances since 1972 where a district auditor had occasion to consider an issue of wilful misconduct, indicating that in all but one of them an oral hearing had been offered. This had the effect, so it was maintained, of creating a legitimate expectation on the part of the appellants that they would be offered an oral hearing before the district auditor arrived at his decision.

My Lords, if the district auditor had reached a decision adverse to the appellants without giving them any opportunity at all of making representations to him, there can be no doubt that his procedure would have been contrary to the rules of natural justice and that, subject to the question whether the defect was capable of being cured on appeal to the Divisional Court, the decision would fall to be quashed. In the event, written representations alone were asked for. These were duly furnished, in very considerable detail, and an oral hearing was not requested, though that could very easily have been done, and there is no reason to suppose that the request would not have been granted. None of the appellants stated, in his or her affidavit before the Divisional Court, that they had an expectation that an oral hearing, though not asked for, would be offered. The true question is whether the district auditor acted fairly in all the circumstances. It is easy to envisage cases where an oral hearing would clearly be essential in the interests of fairness, for example where an objector states that he has personal knowledge of some facts indicative of wilful misconduct on the part of a councillor. In that situation justice would demand that the councillor be given an opportunity to depone to his own version of the facts. In the present case the district auditor had arrived at his provisional view upon the basis of the contents of documents, minutes of meetings and reports submitted to the council from the auditor's department and their own officers. All these documents were appended to or referred to in the notice of June 26 sent by the district auditor to the appellants. Their response referred to other documents, which were duly considered by the district auditor, as is shown by his statement of reasons dated September 6, 1985. No facts contradictory of or supplementary to the contents of the documents were or are relied on by either side. If the appellants had attended an oral hearing they would no doubt have reiterated the sincerity of their motives from the point of view of advancing the interests of the inhabitants of Liverpool. It seems unlikely, having regard to the position adopted by their counsel on this matter before the Divisional Court, that they would have been willing to reveal or answer questions about the proceedings of their political caucus. The sincerity of the appellants' motives is not something capable of justifying or excusing failure to carry out a statutory duty, or of making reasonable what is otherwise an unreasonable delay in carrying out such a duty. In all the circumstances I am of opinion that the district auditor did not act unfairly, and that the procedure which he followed did not involve any prejudice to the appellants...

Upon the view which I take, that the district auditor's decision was not vitiated by procedural unfairness, the question whether such unfairness, had it existed, was capable of being cured by the appeal to the High Court does not arise directly for decision. It is, however, my opinion that the particular appeal mechanism provided for by section 20(3) of the Act of 1982, considered in its context, is apt to enable the court, notwithstanding that it finds some procedural defect in the conduct of an audit which has resulted in a certificate based on wilful misconduct, to inquire into the merits of the case and arrive at its own decision thereon. Section 20(3)(b) empowers the court to 'confirm the decision or quash it and give any certificate which the auditor could have given'. The relevant rules of court enable a rehearing of the broadest possible scope to take place. Evidence may be given on oath, which is not possible before the auditor, and there is no limit to the further material which may be introduced so as to enable the whole merits to be fully examined. There is no question of the court being confined to a review of the evidence which was available to the auditor...

I may add that I agree entirely with all that is said upon this aspect of the appeal in the speech of my noble and learned friend Lord Bridge of Harwich."

For the equivalent Scottish provision see sections 101–104 of the Local Government (Scotland) Act 1973. Lord Keith's approach is contextual and he placed particular emphasis on the fact that the councillors did not seek an oral hearing. Should special weight have been placed on this?

8–26   (4) The question of whether or not a hearing should be an oral one also arose in *R. v. Army Board of the Defence Council, ex parte Anderson* [1992] 1 Q.B. 169. Anderson, a black soldier, made a formal complaint of racial discrimination under the Race Relations Act 1976. He had gone absent without leave from his unit and was arrested. He justified his absence by complaining that he was subject to racial harassment. He was not happy with the action taken by his commanding officer in relation to the complaint and complained to the Army Board. He sought disclosure of an internal report and sought an oral hearing on his complaint. This was rejected and he sought judicial review. The Court of Appeal quashed the board's decision on the grounds, inter alia, that it had fettered its discretion on the matter of an oral hearing. Referring to Lloyd, Taylor L.J. observed (at 187):

> "Whether an oral hearing is necessary will depend upon the subject matter and circumstances of the particular case and upon the nature of the decision to be made. It will also depend upon whether there are substantial issues of fact which cannot be satisfactorily resolved on the available written evidence. This does not mean that whenever there is a conflict of evidence in statements taken, an oral hearing must be held to resolve it. Sometimes such a conflict can be resolved merely by the inherent unlikelihood of one version or the other. Sometimes the conflict is not central to the issue for determination and would not justify an oral hearing. Even when such a hearing is necessary, it may only require one or two witnesses to be called and cross-examined."

See also *R. v. Department of Health, ex parte Gandhi* [1991] 4 All E.R. 547; and see *R. v. Secretary of State for Wales, ex parte Emery* [1996] 4 All E.R. 1 (Secretary of State required to hold a public inquiry into conflicting evidence on the status of a footpath when fairness demanded it, notwithstanding that there was no statutory obligation to do so under the Wildlife and Countryside Act 1981).

SUPPLEMENTATION OF PROCEDURE

Durayappah v. Fernando

[1967] 2 A.C. 337

8–27   "This was an appeal from the Supreme Court of Ceylon. Section 277 (1) of the Municipal Councils Ordinance (c. 252), as amended, provided:

> 'If at any time, upon representation made or otherwise, it appears to the Minister [of Local Government] that a municipal council is not competent to perform, or persistently makes default in the performance of, any duty or duties, imposed upon it, or persistently refuses or neglects to comply with any provision of law, the Minister may, by Order published in the Gazette, direct that the council shall be dissolved and superseded, and thereupon such council shall …be dissolved, and cease to have, exercise, perform and discharge any of the rights, privileges, powers, duties, and functions conferred or imposed upon it, or vested in it'….

The Minister had received a number of complaints about the Jaffna Municipal Council. The Commissioner of Local Government, who was sent to investigate these matters, reported to the Minister, who, acting under s. 277, dissolved the Council on the ground that it appeared to him that the Council was not competent to perform its duties: see further p. 333 *infra*, where it will be seen that the Privy Council decided the Minister had acted in breach of natural justice. This extract is concerned with the status of the Minister's order dissolving the Council of which the appellant had been the Mayor at the time of its dissolution."

LORD UPJOHN [delivering the judgment of their Lordships]: "…[I]t is not in doubt that if [the Minister] was bound to observe the principle audi alteram partem he failed to do so…

Upon the question of audi alteram partem the Supreme Court [of Ceylon] followed and agreed with the earlier decision of *Sugathadasa v. Jayasinghe*, [(1958) 59 N.L.R 457] a decision of three judges of the Supreme Court upon the same section and upon the same issue, namely, whether a council was not competent to perform its duties. That decision laid down [(1958) 59 N.L.R. 471] 'as a general rule that words such as "where it appears to . . ." or "if it appears to the satisfaction of …" or "if the …considers it expedient that …" or "if the …is satisfied that…" standing by themselves without other words or circumstances of qualification, exclude a duty to act judicially.'

Their Lordships disagree with this approach. These various formulae are introductory of the matter to be considered and [give] little guidance upon the question of audi alteram partem. The statute can make itself clear upon this point and if it does cadit quaestio. If it does not then the principle stated by Byles J. in *Cooper v. Wandsworth Board of Works* [(1863) 14 C.B.N.S. 180, 194] must be applied. He said:

'A long course of decisions, beginning with *Dr. Bentley's* case, [(1723) 1 Stra. 557] and ending with some very recent cases, establish, that, although there are no positive words in the statute requiring that the party shall be heard, yet the justice of the common law will supply the omission of the legislature.'

…The solution to this case is not to be found merely upon a consideration of the opening words of section 277. A deeper investigation is necessary. Their Lordships were of course referred to the recent case of *Ridge v. Baldwin* [1964] A.C. 40] where this principle was very closely and carefully examined. In that case no attempt was made to give an exhaustive classification of the cases where the principle audi alteram partem should be applied. In their Lordships' opinion it would be wrong to do so. Outside well-known cases such as dismissal from office, deprivation of property and expulsion from clubs, there is a vast area where the principle can only be applied upon most general considerations. For example, as Lord Reid [1964] A.C. 40, 76] when examining *Rex* v. *Electricity Commissioners* [1924] 1 K.B. 171] pointed out, Bankes L.J. [1924] 1 K.B. 171, 198] inferred the judicial element from the nature of the power and Atkin L.J. [1924] 1 K.B. 171, 206–207] did the same. Pausing there, however, it should not be assumed that their Lordships necessarily agree with Lord Reid's analysis of that case or with his criticism of *Nakuda Ali v. Jayaratne* [1951] A.C. 66]. Outside the well-known classes of cases, no general rule can be laid down as to the application of the general principle in addition to the language of the provision. In their Lordships' opinion there are three matters which must always be borne in mind when considering whether the principle should be applied or not. These three matters are: first, what is the nature of the property, the office held, status enjoyed or services to be performed by the complainant of injustice. Secondly, in what circumstances or upon what occasions is the person claiming to be entitled to exercise the measure of control entitled to intervene. Thirdly, when a right to intervene is proved, what sanctions in fact is the latter entitled to impose upon the other. It is only upon a consideration of all these matters that the question of the application of the principle can properly be determined. Their Lordships therefore proceed to examine the facts of this case upon these considerations.

As to the first matter it cannot be doubted that the Council of Jaffna was by statute a public corporation entrusted like all other municipal councils with the administration of a large area and the discharge of important duties. No one would consider that its activities should be lightly interfered with …The legislature has enacted a statute setting up municipal authorities with a considerable measure of independence from the central government within defined local areas and fields of government. No Minister should have the right to dissolve such an authority without allowing it the right to be heard upon that matter unless the statute is so clear that it is plain it has no right of self-defence. However, this consideration is perhaps one of approach only. The second and third matters are decisive.

Upon the second matter it is clear that the Minister can dissolve the council on one of three grounds: that it (*a*) is not competent to perform any duty or duties imposed upon it (for brevity their Lordships will refer to this head as incompetence); or (*b*) persistently makes default in the performance of any duty or duties imposed upon it; or (*c*) persistently refuses or neglects to comply with any provisions of law…

While their Lordships are only concerned with the question of incompetence, the true construction of the section must be considered as a whole and its necessary intendment in the light of the common law principles already stated. It seems clear to their Lordships that it is a most serious charge to allege that the council, entrusted with these very important duties, persistently makes default in the performance of any duty or duties imposed upon it. No authority is required to support the view that in such circumstances it is plain and obvious that the principle audi alteram partem must apply.

Equally it is clear that if a council is alleged persistently to refuse or neglect to comply with a provision of law it must be entitled (as a matter of the most elementary justice) to be heard in its defence. Again this proposition requires no authority to support it. If, therefore, it is clear that in two of the three cases, the Minister must act judicially, then it seems to their Lordships, looking at the section as a whole, that it is not possible to single out for different treatment the third case, namely incompetence. Grammatically, too, any differentiation is impossible. Section 277 confers upon the Minister a single power to act in the event of one or more closely allied failures and he can only do so after observing the principle audi alteram partem. Had the Minister been empowered to dissolve the council only for incompetence and on no other ground it might have been argued that as 'incompetence' is very vague and difficult to define Parliament did not intend the principle audi alteram partem to apply, in the circumstances, but their Lordships would point out that charges of inefficiency or failing to be diligent or to set a good example have been held subject to the principle: see *Fisher v. Jackson* [1891] 2 Ch. 84.

The third matter can be dealt with quite shortly. The sanction which the Minister can impose and indeed, if he is satisfied of the necessary premise, must impose upon the erring council is as complete as could be imagined; it involves the dissolution of the council and therefore the confiscation of all its properties ...The council owned large areas of land, had a municipal fund and was empowered to levy rates from its inhabitants though it was bound to apply them in accordance with its constitution. In their Lordships' opinion this case falls within the principle of *Cooper* v. *Wandsworth Board of Works* where it was held that no man is to be deprived of his property without having an opportunity of being heard. For the purposes of the application of the principle it seems to their Lordships that this must apply equally to a statutory body having statutory powers, authorities and duties just as it does to an individual. Accordingly on this ground too the Minister should have observed the principle.

For these reasons their Lordships have no doubt that in the circumstances of this case the Minister should have observed the principle audi alteram partem. *Sugathadasa* v. *Jayasinghe* was wrongly decided..."

Notes

8–28   (1) Where a procedure provides for some form of hearing, it is always a question of interpretation as to the extent to which the court will imply further safeguards. Sometimes the task of the courts is made easier in that the statute will sometimes enjoin the decision maker to adhere to the rules of natural justice thus broadening the scope of potential challenge; see, for example, the Licensing (Scotland) Act 1976, s. 39(4) and the Civic Government (Scotland) 1982, s. 4, Sched. 1, para. 18(7). In the absence of such positive indications, the extent to which the court can apply additional safeguards is subject to limits. In *Wiseman v. Borneman* [1971] A.C. 297 at 308 Lord Reid noted that:

> "before this unusual kind of power is exercised it must be clear that the statutory procedure is insufficient to achieve justice and that to require additional steps would not frustrate the apparent purpose of the legislation".

Sometimes the conclusion must be that an omission was deliberate as in *Kennedy v. A.*, 1986 S.L.T. 358 which held that in a children's hearing, reports need not be revealed to a child's parents where this would not be in the interests of the child. The practical effect of this decision has now been reversed by the European Court of Human Rights: *McMichael v. United Kingdom* (1995) 20 E.H.R.R. 205 and see now the Children's Hearings (Scotland) (Amendment) Rules 1996. Sometimes there is a positive indication that an aspect of the right to be heard is excluded; see, for example, the Town and Country Planning (Scotland) Act 1997, s. 10 (6) and the Social Security Act 1998, s. 16, Sched. 5.

(2) Where some form of procedural protection is afforded, the initial question for the court is to determine whether or not that procedure has been complied with, that is whether or not there is a question of procedural *ultra vires*, on which see Chapter 5. The more detailed the procedure, the less likely will the court be to imply additional protection. Thus in *Furnell v. Whangarei High School Board* [1973] A.C. 660 the Privy Council considered a procedural code set out in regulations made by the Governor-General of New Zealand on the advice of a government Minister and on a joint recommendation of two advisory organisations. In such a situation the Privy Council stated that it was "not likely to be affirmed" that such a regulation was unfair; see too *Bates v. Lord Hailsham of St. Marylebone* [1972] 1 W.L.R. 1373 at 1378 and on this area generally see P. Jackson, "A Maxim to be Watched" (1984) 100 L.Q.R. 367: J.M. Evans, "Some Limits to the Scope of Natural Justice" (1973) 36 M.L.R. 439; and *Stair Memorial Encyclopedia*, Vol. 1, para. 271.

NOTICE OF THE CASE TO BE MET

City of Glasgow District Council v. Doyle

1995 S.L.T. 327

"Three holders of taxi (operators') licences had their applications for renewal refused by the licensing sub-committee. The committee had previously determined the number of taxi licences it considered necessary to meet local demand. All but three of this quota had been allocated at the time that the applicants' cases, together with seven further applications, were considered by the committee. The committee granted one licence on the basis that the application had special merit. It did not give consideration to the fact that the applicants were previously holders of taxi licences, but in its reasons stated that regard had been had to experience that the various applicants had had as holders of taxi drivers' licences. On this basis it awarded the two remaining licences to two of the other applicants. The three appealed to the sheriff, who held that in granting the one application on its special merit the committee had failed to specify the reasons for its success and consequently the reasons for failure of the others. He also held that in having regard to the experience of the various applicants as taxi drivers, without giving previous notice of this criterion, the committee had acted in breach of natural justice. In allowing the applicants' appeals he declined to grant the licence applications but remitted the appeals back to the committee for further consideration.

The licensing authority appealed to the Court of Session, arguing that the sheriff had erred in holding that experience as a taxi driver was irrelevant, and that there was no duty on an administrative body to tell applicants what facts to put forward in support of their applications. The applicants lodged cross appeals, arguing that the sheriff had interpreted the grounds for reversing the committee's decision too narrowly and that he had been wrong to remit the cases for reconsideration."

8–29

LORD COULSFIELD: "The appellants in these three appeals are the City of Glasgow District Council in their capacity as the authority responsible for the licensing of taxis and taxi drivers in Glasgow. At a meeting held on 22 January 1992, the appellants refused applications for the grant of taxi licences made by the three respondents to the present appeals. In one of the cases, the application was made for the grant of two taxi licences, so that four licences in all were the subject of the applications by these respondents.

The material circumstances affecting all three appeals are identical and it is not necessary to draw distinctions between the position of the various respondents. At the meeting of the appellants' sub-committee on licensing applications, the four applications in question were presented on behalf of the respondents by one solicitor and the submissions in respect of the four were heard together. In a statement of reasons for the decision to refuse the applications, dated 3 February 1992, the appellants stated, inter alia, that in reaching their decision they had taken into account a decision taken by the licensing committee on 12 February 1991 that, without prejudice to the consideration of all taxi licence applications on their merits, 1,428 was the number of taxi licences considered necessary to meet the demand for the services of taxis in Glasgow, the fact that by the time the applications came to be considered at the meeting 1,425 licences had already been issued and the fact that a further seven applications for the grant of a taxi licence fell to be considered at the same meeting. The subcommittee state that they also considered objections from and submissions on behalf of persons interested in taxi operation in Glasgow. The statement of reasons for the decision recorded that it had been submitted that all the four applicants had recently been holders of taxi licences but had forgotten to submit timeous applications for renewal, that as a result they had suffered prejudice in certain respects, and that their business had been operated in an impeccable manner while the licences were in force.

The reasons for the decision of the committee then state: 'The sub-committee, at said meeting, were required to consider these four applications along with other applications for the grant of a taxi licence as aforesaid. In view of the fact, therefore, that in total 11 applications now fell to be considered and that, at most, in terms of the policy on limitation on numbers as aforesaid, only three licences were available to be issued, the sub-committee considered that the fairest way to proceed would be to hear all applications individually and then determine which, if any, merited the grant of a taxi licence. Having considered the applications individually the sub-committee determined that one had particular/outstanding merit and it was decided that this application should be approved. The sub-committee were then left with ten applications but only two licences remaining available for issue. Having considered each application carefully and the circumstances prevailing in each case, the sub-committee considered that the appropriate way to proceed was to distinguish between them on the basis of the number of years service/experience the applicants had in the trade, generally as holders of taxi driver's licences. The sub-committee were not prepared to give favourable consideration to applications simply because the applicants were previously holders of taxi licences which they had forgotten to renew timeously. Therefore, having determined the criteria by which they would distinguish between the applicants, the sub-committee determined that two of the other applicants had considerably more years experience in the trade in the capacity of taxi drivers, and the sub-committee considered that, on that basis, the applications for those two should be approved. Therefore the four applications submitted by your clients were refused at that stage as, having taken the said decisions in favour of the other applicants, no licences were then available as all 1,428 as aforesaid had been granted/ issued. This decision was taken in light of said policy decision, as the sub-committee determined that, in terms of section 10 (3) of the above Act, there was no significant demand for the services of taxis in their area which is unmet with all said 1,428 licences granted/issued.'

The respondents appealed to the sheriff. The crave in each appeal requested the court to reverse the decision of 22 January 1992 to refuse to grant the application for a taxi licence and failing such reversal to modify said decision or remit the case to the respondents with a recommendation that the licence be granted with or without such conditions as the court might deem appropriate. In each case, the first plea in law was that as the appellants had exercised their discretion in an unreasonable manner decree should be granted as craved, and secondly that the authoirty having acted contrary to natural justice decree should be granted in trerms of the first crave. There was also a plea in law that the answers being lacking in specification and irrelevant decree should be granted in terms of the first crave.

On 16 November 1992, the sheriff sustained the third plea in law for each of the respondents to the extent of remitting the applications to the district council for reconsideration....

The present appeal was put foward on three grounds which are dealt with in the order in which they were presented. The first ground of appeal was that the sheriff had erred in holding that experience as a taxi driver was irrelevant. It was submitted that it was legitimate, under s 10 (3) of the Civic Government (Scotland) Act 1982, to adopt a policy limiting the number of licences, to inform applicants about the policy to hear the applications and to decide in accordance with the policy. Reference was made to *R v Port of London Authority, ex p Kynoch*. In the present case, the authority had had 11 applicants and three licences to grant in accordance with the policy. One of these was granted to an application of exceptional merit and, as regard the other applicants, reference to experience as taxi drivers was a legitimate means of distinguishing between the applicants. It was true that it was possible to get a taxi operator's licence without driving experience, but driving experience remained a relevant factor and therefore a useful criterion to adopt in such a situation. For the respondents, it was submitted that it was clear that taxi operator's licences, which fell under s 10 of the 1982 Act, were different from taxi driver's licences which fell under s 13. The policy adopted by the appellants might be sound in general but the number had remained fixed at 1,428 for a long time and never exceeded. From the statement of reasons it could be inferred that the committee had come to the decision with a fixed determination to grant no more than three licences as in fact they had done. It was not, however, rational to give weight to driving experience as opposed to operating experience or indeed general business experience. Before the sheriff, the only ground put forward to justify the use of this criterion had been its objectivity but that was of no significance in itself. At best, experience as a driver could become a relevant consideration only when all other considerations were equal, including that of experience as an operator.

In our view, this issue can be disposed of quite briefly. We see no reason to regard experience as a taxi driver as necessarily being an irrelevant consideration in relation to an application for an operator's licence. According to the particular circumstances, it might be a consideration which would bear greater or less weight, and it appears unlikely that it would ever be the sole consideration to which regard might be had in determining applications. Nevertheless, it is, in our view, easy to see that experience of the actual driving of a taxi in the area could well be relevant to undertaking the responsibilities of a taxi operator. Accordingly, we consider that the appellants could not be said to be in error in the present case merely because they took experience as a taxi driver into account in considering the various applications.

The second ground of appeal was that the sheriff was in error in suggesting that an opportunity should have been given to each of the applicants to comment upon the question of experience and upon what was said on behalf of the other applicants. When dealing with a number of applications, as in this case, it was not part of the role of an administrative body to tell the applicants what facts to put forward in support of their applications. It might be more difficult for the authority if the test adopted was one on which no information was given at all and in that case they might have to reconvene their meeting. But where it was obvious that there was a relevant factor such as driving experience, there was no need for the authority so to proceed. The case was to be distinguished from the case where the local authority relied on knowledge of its own which had not been put to an applicant. There would have to be a lack of notice of the facts relied on in relation to refusal and in the present case the criticism, if any, was not reliance on facts but a failure to explain the criteria being applied. It was accepted that the consequence of that position was that the appellants said that it was fair in this context to leave it to the applicants to put up whatever arguments they wished and to reach a decision on that basis and it was accepted that that meant that the applicants, to an extent, presented their applications blind, but any other view would place an excessive burden upon the authority. The respondents had not been deprived of the chance of putting forward their own experience as a relevant consideration although they were not alerted to the fact that the authority would apply the particular criterion in question. For the respondents, it was submitted that the sheriff had been entitled to conclude that the district council acted in a way inconsistent with natural justice in that the respondents had been denied the opportunity to address themselves both to the validity of the use of experience as a taxi driver as a criterion and as to the application of that criterion in their own cases, as compared with the cases of other applicants.

In our opinion, the sheriff reached a correct conclusion on this point. It may be that on an occasion when applications are made for licences and there is no ceiling on the number of licences that may be granted, it will be sufficient for the authority to leave it to the individual applicants to put themselves forward in the best light that they can and to submit those facts and circumstances which they think will advance their application. The position must, however, alter when a ceiling, whether precisely fixed or containing some degree of flexibility, is imposed upon the number of licences that may be granted. By imposing such a ceiling, the authority necessarily require that an element of competition will enter into the presentation of applications and it follows, in our view, that the authority can act fairly among applicants only if they give the applicants some warning, either in advance of the submission of applications, or in advance of the decision to grant particular selected applications, of the grounds which they propose to use to discriminate between the applications submitted to them. In the present case, although, for the reasons given above, it is accepted that experience as a taxi driver is or may be a relevant consideration in the type of application with which we are concerned, it is not by any means so obvious that it is one which should be treated as the determining consideration among a group of applicants unless, as was submitted on behalf of the respondents, all other considerations are equal in every respect. It follows that the importance and indeed the relevance of driving experience were not so obvious that it was unnecessary to give notice to applicants that the length of driving experience might be treated as decisive of the competition. Accordingly, if the appellants proposed to proceed upon that basis notice should have been given. The need for such notice is emphasised in the present case by the circumstance that the appellants themselves did not proceed upon that condition alone in deciding which applicants should receive the three licences available. They relied upon other circumstances, the nature of which is not disclosed, to select one particular application as particularly meritorious. These two considerations, lack of notice and the use of undisclosed criteria, amount, in our view, to a departure from natural justice. It was, at one stage of the appellants' argument, submitted that the provisions of the Local Government: (Access to Information) Act 1985, and of s 50A of the Local Government (Scotland) Act 1973 and Sched 7A to that Act, prevented the appellants from disclosing information relevant to applications, but counsel for the appellants eventually accepted that he was not able to argue that these provisions had any application to meetings of the district council acting as licensing authority. In all the circumstances, therefore, the sheriff was correct in holding that the appellants' decision was vitiated by a failure in natural justice.

The third ground argued was that the sheriff had been incorrect in regarding the appellants' reasons for their decision as being insufficiently specific insofar as they proceeded upon the ground of special merit in a particular application. That argument depended upon the considerations relating to the confidentiality of information to which we have just referred and in view of the concession which has been mentioned does not require to be further dealt with."

Note

(1) Note the emphasis placed by the court and the fact that the criteria relied upon by the **8–30** licensing authority were undisclosed. What appears to have been particularly significant to the court is that the applicant was competing for a limited resource, a licence, and that appeared to place a higher onus on the authority to emphasise its reliance on this criteria and the weight which would be given to it.

(2) The issue of the extent to which knowledge of a decision maker should be disclosed to the person affected by a decision has been particularly important in licensing and planning law. Thus in relation to licensing boards, there appears to be a distinction between private specific knowledge of the board which must be put to an individual, *Freeland v. City of Glasgow District Licensing Board*, 1979 S.C. 226; local knowledge of a substantial nature openly before the

board and on which inferences can be drawn, *Richmond Inns Ltd v. City of Aberdeen District Council District Licensing Board*, 1991 S.C.L.R. 204, and finally knowledge which is really just expertise or acquaintance with the area in question and which does not require to be brought to the notice of the applicant, *Latif v. Motherwell District Licensing Board*, 1994 S.L.T. 414 and also *Mirza v. City of Glasgow Licensing Board*, 1996 S.L.T. 1029.

In planning law, in *City of Glasgow District Council v. Secretary of State for Scotland*, 1998 S.L.T. 283 a decision of a reporter was quashed because he took into account a matter of law upon which the parties had not been asked to comment and in *Dunfermline District Council v. Secretary of State for Scotland*, 1996 S.L.T. 89 a decision of the reporter was quashed when he decided to impose a planning condition, the basis of which again had not been the subject of any representation to him. For further discussion see E. Young and J. Rowan-Robinson, *Scottish Planning Law and Procedure* (1985), pp. 483–484, 510–511.

(3) Contrast *Doyle* with *Cinderella's Rockafella's Ltd v. Glasgow District Licensing Board*, 1994 S.C.L.R. 591, extracted at para. 6–14, where the board's policy was disclosed. Was sufficient notice of the *weight* given to that policy disclosed? Should there be an obligation to emphasis the weight to be given to one of a number of relevant considerations? Consider this point in light of the discussion of relevant considerations at para.7–6.

(4) In *R. v. Secretary of State for the Home Department, ex parte Fayed* [1997] 1 All E.R. 228, C.A. the Secretary of State was held to be under a duty to act fairly in making a decision to refuse Fayed's application for naturalisation under the British Nationality Act 1981. Section 44(2) of the Act states that the Secretary of State was not obliged to provide reasons for decisions on naturalisation. No reasons were given. It was held, however, that he was under a duty to give an applicant sufficient information as to the nature of any possible objections that might be made to his application to ensure that any representations by the applicant were meaningful. Although section 44 (2) also provided that a decision was not to be subject to appeal or review in any court, this did not exclude the need for notice to be given. The duty to give notice in these circumstances was, however, limited to complex cases where the applicant would have difficulty making out his case without some indication of the nature of the objections to the applications. See particularly the judgment of Woolf M.R. and compare the dissenting judgment of Kennedy L.J. Contrast *Clyde Cablevision Ltd v. The Cable Authority*, 1990 S.C.L.R. 28 (authority not obliged to raise with petitioners matters about which they were in doubt in relation to the petitioners' application for a cable television licence under section 1 of the Cable and Broadcasting Act 1984) and *Buchanan v. Secretary of State for Trade and Industry, The Times*, March 1, 1995 (no obligation on the part of the Secretary of State to disclose to petitioner detailed information relating to basis of notice of objection under section 60(1) of the Insurance Companies Act 1982 to the petitioners' agreement to take up position of chief executive of a life assurance company on basis that he was not a fit and proper person to be appointed). On *Fayed* and *Clyde Cablevision Ltd* see S.C. Smith, "The Comprehensive Approach to Fairness", 1997 S.L.T. (News) 265.

PROCEDURAL LEGITIMATE EXPECTATION

Council of Civil Service Unions v. Minister for the Civil Service

[1985] A.C. 374

8–31   "The main functions of Government Communications Headquarters ('GCHQ') were to ensure the security of military and official communications and to provide the Government with signals intelligence; they involved the handling of secret information vital to national security. Since 1947, staff employed at GCHQ had been permitted to belong to national trade unions, and most had done so. There was a well-established practice of consultation between the official and trade union sides about important alterations in the terms and conditions of service of the staff. On December 22, 1983, the Minister for the Civil Service gave an instruction, purportedly under article 4 of the Civil Service Order in Council 1982, for the immediate variation of the terms and conditions of service of the staff with the effect that they would no longer be permitted to belong to national trade unions. There had been no consultation with the trade unions or with the staff at GCHQ prior to the issuing of that instruction. The applicants, a trade union and six individuals, sought judicial review of the minister's instruction on the ground that she had been under a duty to act fairly by consulting those concerned before issuing it. In an affidavit, the Secretary to the Cabinet deposed to disruptive industrial action in support of national trade unions that had taken place at GCHQ as part of a national campaign by the unions designed to damage government agencies and that it had been considered that prior consultation about the minister's instruction would have involved a risk of precipitating further disruption and would moreover have indicated vulnerable areas of GCHQ's operations. Glidewell J. granted the applicants a declaration that the instruction was invalid and of no effect. The Court of Appeal allowed an appeal by the minister, and a further appeal was dismissed.

The House of Lords held (1) that the Government's action was not immune from judicial review merely because it was in pursuance of a common law or a prerogative power; (2) that the applicants would apart from national security considerations have had a legitimate expectation that unions and employees would have been consulted before the instruction was issued; but (3) that the Minister had shown that her decision had in fact been based on considerations of national security that outweighed the applicant's legitimate expectation.

The following extracts concern the second issue:"

LORD FRASER OF TULLYBELTON:...
"The Duty to Consult
Mr Blom-Cooper submitted that the Minister had a duty to consult the CCSU, on behalf of employees at GCHQ, before giving the instruction on December 22, 1983, for making an important change in their conditions of service. His main reason for so submitting was that the employees had a legitimate, or reasonable, expectation that there would be such prior consultation before any important change was made in their conditions.

It is clear that the employees did not have legal right to prior consultation. The Order in Council confers no such right, and article 4 makes no reference at all to consultation. The Civil Service handbook (*Handbook for the New Civil Servant*, 1973 ed. as amended 1983) which explains the normal method of consultation through the departmental Whitley Council, does not suggest that there is any legal right to consultation; indeed it is careful to recognise that, in the operational field, considerations of urgency may make prior consultation impracticable. The Civil Service Pay and Conditions of Service Code expressly states:

> 'The following terms and conditions also apply to your appointment in the Civil Service. It should be understood, however, that in consequence of the constitutional position of the Crown, the Crown has the right to change its employees' conditions of service at any time, and that they hold their appointments at the pleasure of the Crown.'

But even where a person claiming some benefit or privilege has no legal right to it, as a matter of private law, he may have a legitimate expectation of receiving the benefit or privilege, and, if so, the courts will protect his expectation of judicial review as a matter of public law. This subject has been fully explained by my noble and learned friend, Lord Diplock, in *O'Reilly v. Mackman* [1983] 2 A.C. 237 and I need not repeat what he has so recently said. Legitimate, or reasonable, expectation may arise either from an express promise given on behalf of a public authority or from the existence of a regular practice which the claimant can reasonably expect to continue. Examples of the former type of expectation are *R. v. Liverpool Corporation, ex p. Liverpool Taxi Fleet Operators' Association* [1972] 2 Q.B. 299 and *Attorney-General of Hong Kong v. Ng Yuen Shiu* [1983] 2 A.C. 629. (I agree with Lord Diplock's view, expressed in the speech in this appeal, that 'legitimate' is to be preferred to 'reasonable' in this context. I was responsible for using the word 'reasonable' for the reason explained in *Ng Yuen Shiu*, but it was intended only to be exegetical of 'legitimate') An example of the latter is *R. v. Board of Visitors of Hull Prison, ex p. St Germain* [1979] Q.B. 425 approved by this House in *O'Reilly*, at 274D. The submission on behalf of the appellants is that the present case is of the latter type. The test of that is whether the practice of prior consultation of the staff on significant changes in their conditions of service was so well established by 1983 that it would be unfair or inconsistent with good administration for the Government to depart from the practice in this case. Legitimate expectations such as are now under consideration will always relate to a benefit or privilege to which the claimant has no right in private law, and it may even be to one which conflicts with his private law rights. In the present case the evidence shows that, ever since GCHQ began in 1947, prior consultation has been the invariable rule when conditions of service were to be significantly altered. Accordingly in my opinion if there had been no question of national security involved, the appellants would have had a legitimate expectation that the minister would consult them before issuing the instruction of December 22, 1983."

Lord Diplock "...Judicial review, now regulated by R.S.C., Ord. 53, provides the means by which judicial control of administrative action is exercised. The subject-matter of every judicial review is a decision made by some person (or body of persons) whom I will call the 'decision-maker' or else a refusal by him to make a decision.

To qualify as a subject for judicial review the decision must have consequences which affect some person (or body of persons) other than the decision-maker, although it may affect him too. It must affect such other person either:

(a) by altering rights or obligations of that person which are enforceable by or against him in private law; or

(b) by depriving him of some benefit or advantage which either (i) he had in the past been permitted by the decision-maker to enjoy and which he can legitimately expect to be permitted to continue to do until there has been communicated to him some rational grounds for withdrawing it on which he has been given an opportunity to comment; or (ii) he has received assurance from the decision-maker will not be withdrawn without giving him first an opportunity of advancing reasons for contending that they should not be withdrawn. (I prefer to continue to call the kind of expectation that qualifies a decision for inclusion in class (b) a 'legitimate expectation' rather than a 'reasonable expectation,' in order thereby to indicate that it has consequences to which effect will be given in public law, whereas an expectation or hope that some benefit or advantage would continue to be enjoyed, although it might well be entertained by a 'reasonable' man, would not necessarily have such consequences. The recent decision of this House in *Re Findlay* [1985] A.C. 318 presents an example of the latter kind of expectation. 'Reasonable' furthermore bears different meanings according to whether the context in which it is being used is that of private law or of public law. To eliminate confusion it is best avoided in the latter.)

For a decision to be susceptible to judicial review the decision-maker must be empowered by public law (and not merely, as in arbitration, by agreement between private parties) to make decisions that, if validly made, will lead to administrative action or abstention from action by an authority endowed by law with executive powers, which have one or other of the consequences mentioned in the preceding paragraph. The ultimate source of the decision-making power is nearly always nowadays a statute or subordinate legislation made under the statute; but in the absence of any statute regulating the subject-matter of the decision the source of the decision-making power may still be the common law itself, *i.e.* that part of the common law that is given by lawyers the label of 'the prerogative'. Where this is the source of decision-making power, the power is confined to executive officers of central as distinct from local government and in constitutional practice is generally exercised by those holding ministerial rank.

It was the prerogative that was relied on as the source of the power of the Minister for the Civil Service in reaching her decision of December 22, 1983, that membership of national trade unions should in future be barred to all members of the home civil service employed at GCHQ...

My Lords, I see no reason why simply because a decision-making power is derived from a common law and not a statutory source, it should *for that reason only* be immune from judicial review. Judicial review has I think developed to a stage today when without reiterating any analysis of the steps by which the development has come about, one can conveniently classify under three heads the grounds upon which administrative action is subject to control by judicial review. The first ground I would call 'illegality', the second 'irrationality' and the third 'procedural impropriety'. That is not to say that further development on a case by case basis may not in course of time add further grounds. I have in mind particularly the possible adoption in the future of the principle of 'proportionality' which is recognised in the administrative law of several of our fellow members of the European Economic Community; but to dispose of the instant case the three already well-established heads that I have mentioned will suffice.

By 'illegality' as a ground for judicial review I mean that the decision-maker must understand correctly the law that regulates his decision-making power and must give effect to it. Whether he has or not is par excellence a justiciable question to be decided, in the event of dispute, by those persons, the judges, by whom the judicial power of the state is exercisable.

By 'irrationality' I mean what can by now be succinctly referred to as '*Wednesbury* unreasonableness' (*Associated Provincial Picture Houses Ltd v. Wednesbury Corporation* [1948] 1 K.B. 223). It applies to a decision which is so outrageous in its defiance of logic or of accepted moral standards that no sensible person who had applied his mind to the question to be decided could have arrived at it. Whether a decision falls within this category is a question that judges by their training and experience should be well equipped to answer, or else there would be something badly wrong with our judicial system. To justify the court's exercise of this role, resort I think is today no longer needed to Viscount Radcliffe's ingenious explanation in *Edwards v. Bairstow* [1956] A.C. 14 of irrationality as a ground for a court's reversal of a decision by ascribing it to an inferred though unidentifiable mistake of law by the decision-maker. 'Irrationality' by now can stand upon its own feet as an accepted ground on which a decision may be attacked by judicial review.

I have described the third head as 'procedural impropriety' rather than failure to observe basic rules of natural justice or failure to act with procedural fairness towards the person who will be affected by the decision. This is because susceptibility to judicial review under this head covers also failure by an administrative tribunal to observe procedural rules that are expressly laid down in the legislative instrument by which its jurisdiction is conferred, even where such failure does not involve any denial of natural justice. But the instant case is not concered with the proceedings of an administrative tribunal at all...

His Lordship concluded that it was well established that decisions whose ultimate source of power was the common law (whether or not labelled as 'the prerogative') could be the subject of judicial review on the grounds of illegality or procedural impropriety. There was no *a priori* reason to rule out challenge on the ground of irrationality, he found it difficult to envisage cases where such a challenge would be justifiable.]

Prima facie ...civil servants employed at GCHQ who were members of national trade unions had, at best, in December 1983, a legitimate expectation that they would continue to enjoy the benefits of such membership and of representation by those trade unions in any consultations and negotiations with representatives of the management of that government department as to changes in any term of their employment. So, but again *prima facie* only, they were entitled, as a matter of public law under the head of 'procedural propriety', before administrative action was taken on a decision to withdraw that benefit, to have communicated to the national trade unions by which they had theretofore been represented the reason for such withdrawal, and for such unions to be given an opportunity to comment on it..."

LORD ROSKILL "...The particular manifestation of the duty to act fairly which is presently involved is that part of the recent evolution of our administrative law which may enable an aggrieved party to evoke judicial review if he can show that he has 'a reasonable expectation' of some occurrence or action preceding the decision complained of and that that 'reasonable expectation' was not in the event fulfilled.

The introduction of the phrase 'reasonable expectation' into this branch of our administrative law appears to show its origin to Lord Denning M.R. in *Schmidt v. Secretary of State for Home Affairs* [1969] 2 Ch. 149, 170 (when he used the phrase 'legitimate expectation'). Its judicial evolution is traced in the opinion of the Judicial Committee delivered by my noble and learned friend, Lord Fraser of Tullybelton, in *Attorney-General of Hong Kong v. Ng Yuen Shiu* [1983] 2 A.C. 629, 636–638. Though the two phrases can. I think, now safely be treated as synonymous for the reasons there given by my noble and learned friend, I prefer the use of the adjective 'legitimate' in this context and use it in this speech even though in argument it was the adjective 'reasonable' which was generally used. The principle may now be said to be firmly entrenched in this branch of the law. As the cases show, the principle is closely connected with 'a right to be heard'. Such an expectation may take many forms. One may be an expectation of prior consultation. Another may be an expectation of being allowed time to make representations especially where the aggrieved party is seeking to persuade an authority to depart from a lawfully established policy adopted in connection with the exercise of a particular power because of some suggested exceptional reasons justifying such a departure...

My Lords, if no question of national security were involved I cannot doubt that the evidence and the whole history of the relationship between management and staff since 1919 shows that there was a legitimate expectation of consultation before important alterations in the conditions of service of civil servants were made. No doubt in strict theory civil servants are dismissible at will and the various documents shown to your Lordships seek to preserve the strict constitutional position. But in reality the management-staff relationship is governed by an elaborate code to which it is unnecessary to refer in detail. I have little doubt that were management to seek to alter without prior consultation the terms and conditions of civil servants in a field which had no connection whatever with national security or perhaps, though the matter does not arise in this appeal, with urgent fiscal emergency, such action would in principle be amenable to judicial review."

LORDS SCARMAN and BRIGHTMAN delivered concurring speeches.

Notes

(1) For a summary of *Attorney-General of Hong Kong v. Ng Yuen Shiu* [1983] 2 A.C. 629, see **8–32** *R v. Secretary of State for the Home Department, ex parte Khan* [1984] 1 W.L.R. 1337, extracted at para. 2–41.

(2) The first Scottish reaction to this case came in *Strathkelvin District Council v. Secretary of State for the Environment*, 1987 G.W.D. 9–258. Strathkelvin District Council sought to rely on the dicta of Lord Diplock to argue that it had a right to be consulted by the Scottish

Development Department (SDD) in relation to the sale of Crown land basing the claim for such a right on a memorandum addressed to all district councils from the SDD that the SDD would endeavour to ensure that the future use of such land would be in line with local authority planning policies and any conflicting use would be drawn to the local authority's planning department. The council sought judicial review, arguing that as the disposal here did in fact conflict with those policies, it had legitimate expectation of being heard. Lord Jauncey, however, interpreted Lord Diplock's dicta as applying to the legitimate expectation relating to the continuation of a benefit currently enjoyed and the procedural impropriety of the manner in which it was terminated. On the facts here, the memorandum conferred upon the council neither benefit nor advantage nor powers which it did not already have. To treat the expectation of discussion and the expectation of the continued enjoyment of benefits, such as trade union membership, would have extended the supervisory jurisdiction of the court beyond its proper bounds.

(3) Legitimate expectation had developed somewhat since the decision in the extract and the first Scottish reaction to it in *Strathkelvin District Council*. The most recent cogent analysis was made by Simon Brown L.J. in *R. v. Devon County Council, ex parte Baker* [1995] 1 All E.R. 73 at 88–89

"(1) Sometimes the phrase is used to denote a substantive right: an entitlement that the claimant asserts cannot be denied him. It was used in this sense and the assertion upheld in cases such as *R. v. Secretary of State for the Home Dept, ex p. Khan* [1985] 1 All E.R. 40; [1984] 1 W.L.R. 1337 and *R. v. Secretary of State for the Home Dept, ex p. Ruddock* [1987] 2 All E.R. 518; [1987] 2 All E.R. 518; [1987] 1 W.L.R. 1482. It was used in the same sense but unsuccessfully in, for instance, *R. v. Board of Inland Revenue, ex p. MFK Underwriting Agencies Ltd* [1990] 1 All E.R. 91; [1990] 1 W.L.R. 1545 and *R. v. Jockey Club, ex p. RAM Racecourses Ltd* (1990) [1993] 2 All ER 225. These various authorities show that the claimant's right will only be found established when there is a clear and unambiguous representation upon which it was reasonable for him to rely. Then the administrator or other public body will be held bound in fairness by the representation made unless only its promise or undertaking as to how its power would be exercised is inconsistent with the statutory duties imposed upon it. The doctrine employed in this sense is akin to an estoppel. In so far as the public body's representation is communicated by way of a stated policy. this type of legitimate expectation falls into two distinct sub-categories: cases in which the authority are led entitled to change their policy even so as to affect the claimant, and those in which they are not. An illustration of the former is *R. v. Torbay B.C., ex p. Cleasby* [1991] C.O.D. 142; of the latter, *ex p. Khan*.

(2) Perhaps more conventionally the concept of legitimate expectation is used to refer to the claimant's interest in some ultimate benefit which he hopes to retain (or, some would argue, attain). Here, therefore, it is the interest itself rather than the benefit that is the substance of the expectation. In other words the expectation arises not because the claimant asserts any specific right to a benefit but rather because his interest in it is one that the law holds protected by the requirements of procedural fairness; the law recognises that the interest cannot properly be withdrawn (or denied) without the claimant being given an opportunity to comment and without the authority communicating rational grounds for any adverse decision. Of the various authorities drawn to our attention, *Schmidt v. Secretary of State for Home Affairs* [1969] 1 All E.R. 904; [1969] 2 Ch. 149, *O'Reilly v. Mackman* [1982] 3 All E.R. 1124; [1983] 2 A.C. 237 and the recent decision of Roch J. in *R. v. Rochdale Metropolitan B.C., ex p. Schemet* [1993] 1 F.C.R. 306 are clear examples of this head of legitimate expectation.

(3) Frequently, however, the concept of legitimate expectation is used to refer to the fair procedure itself. In other words it is contended that the claimant has a legitimate expectation that the public body will act fairly towards him. As was pointed out by Dawson J. in *Att.-Gen. for New South Wales v. Quin* (1990) 93 A.L.R. 1 at 39 this use of the term is superfluous and unhelpful: it confuses the interest which is the basis of the requirement of procedural fairness with the requirement itself:

'No doubt people expect fairness in their dealings with those who make decisions affecting their interests, but it is to my mind quite artificial to say that this is the reason why, if the expectation is legitimate in the sense of well founded, the law imposes a duty to observe procedural fairness. Such a duty arises, if at all, because the circumstances call for a fair procedure and it adds nothing to say that they also are such as to lead to a legitimate expectation that a fair procedure will be adopted.'

(4) The final category of legitimate expectation encompasses those cases in which it is held that a particular procedure, not otherwise required by law in the protection of an interest, must be followed consequent upon some specific promise or practice. Fairness requires that the public authority be held to it. The authority is bound by its assurance, whether expressly given by way of a promise or implied by way of established practice. *Re Liverpool Taxi Owners' Association* [1972] 2 All E.R. 589; [1972] 2 Q.B. 299 and *Att.-Gen. of Hong Kong v. Ng Yuen Shiu* [1983] 2 All E.R. 346; [1983] 2 A.C. 629 are illustrations of the court giving effect to legitimate expectations based upon express promises; *Council of Civil Service Unions v. Minister for the Civil Service* an illustration of a legitimate expectation founded upon practice albeit one denied on the facts by virtue of the national security implications."

(4) A legitimate expectation to be heard was found to exist in *Perfect Leisure Ltd v. City of Edinburgh District Licensing Board*, 1996 S.L.T. 1267. Here an application was made to obtain extended hours for the sale of alcohol. In terms of section 47 of the Law Reform (Miscellaneous Provisions) (Scotland) Act 1990, a licensing board requires to ensure such an extension will not be granted unless it is satisfied that there is a need in the locality and that the granting of the extension is likely to be of more benefit than detriment to the local community. The licensees of a public house applied for a regular extension from Monday to Saturday between 5.30 a.m. and 11.30 a.m. There were objections and so immediately prior to the hearing of the application it was amended to restrict the extension to 8 a.m. and 11 a.m. which had been permitted in the previous five years. Objections were, however, maintained. The board was addressed by the objectors and the solicitor for the licensees who did not argue a case of need or benefit to the community. The board refused the early morning extension stating that it was not satisfied that need had been made out or benefit. In the petition for judicial review it was argued that the practice of the board was only to seek submissions where the hours were contentious in the sense of never having been granted before. The petitioner relied on the decision in the extract. The board denied such a practice and argued that the onus was on the petitioner to satisfy the board as to need and benefit. Lord Penrose held, however, that it could not be right to require of applicants that they addressed every issue so as to ensure that nothing was left uncovered which might form the basis for refusal of an application. This is significant, because on the face of it, the onus under section 47 seems to require treatment of each case on its merits, but it would seem that the approach in the extract was extended to allow a legitimate expectation to exist on the basis of practice and interpretation which differed from the underlying statutory basis for a decision. Does the extract support such an extension? Moreover, what are the potential implications of such an approach? For a recent case where practice in the field of planning was alleged to found legitimate expectation, albeit unsuccessfully, see *Campbell v. City of Edinburgh Council*, 1998 G.W.D. 17–877.

(5) A legitimate expectation of being heard or consulted may arise simply from the nature of the applicant's interests, as distinct from past practice or an express undertaking. This is illustrated by the following excerpt.

8–33

Lakin Ltd v. Secretary of State for Scotland

1988 S.L.T. 780

Lakin Ltd presented a petition for judicial review of a decision of the Secretary of State for Scotland, calling as respondents the Secretary of State and Central Regional Council. They sought reduction of a letter issued by the Secretary of State dated March 19, 1987, declining to call in a certain planning application, and declarator that in all the circumstances he was bound and obliged to call in the application in terms of section 32 of the Town and Country Planning (Scotland) Act 1972 (see now section 46 of the Town and Country Planning (Scotland) Act 1997) and interdict against Central Regional Council from granting certain planning applications relating to a site at Broadleys Farm, Stirling. At first instance, the Lord Ordinary (Davidson) sustained the petitioners' contention that the Secretary of State had adopted an unfair procedure and granted the prayer of the petition. The respondents reclaimed. The

8–34

decisions in *CCSU v. Minister for the Civil Service* [1985] 1 A.C. 374; *R. v. Inland Revenue Commissioners, ex parte Preston* [1985] 1 A.C. 835 and *Wheeler v. Leicester City Council* [1985] 1 A.C. 1054 are reproduced at paras 6–53 and 6–4. The decision in *D. & J. Nicol v. Dundee Harbour Trustees*, 1915 S.C. (H.L.) 7 is reproduced at para. 10–19. The facts and circumstances of the case are set out at length in the opinion of the Lord Justice-Clerk (Ross).

LORD DAVIDSON: "The petitioners in this application for judicial review are a company called Lakin Ltd. For some time now they have been attempting to obtain planning permission for the development of one major superstore and related development on a site at Corbiewood, Stirling. In September 1985 the petitioners lodged an application with Stirling District Council for outline planning permission in respect of a proposed superstore and other facilities at the Corbiewood site. That application was later called in by Central Regional Council, the second respondents, together with 18 other major retail proposals concerning other sites within the region, in terms of s. 179 of the Local Government (Scotland) Act 1973. The most significant of the rival planning applications was one submitted by three developers for a Tesco superstore to be developed at Broadleys Farm, Stirling. The regional council own the land upon which it is proposed to develop the Tesco superstore.

In November 1985 the regional council refused the petitioners' application relating to the Corbiewood site on the grounds of shopping and countryside policy at regional and local level, prematurity, and the need for public expenditure to implement the proposals. In terms of s. 33 of the Town and Country Planning (Scotland) Act 1972 (the 1972 Act) the petitioners appealed against that refusal to the Secretary of State for Scotland, who is the first respondent. The Secretary of State appointed a reporter to determine that appeal and a public local inquiry was conducted during four days in September 1986. On 28 October 1986 the reporter determined that the petitioners' appeal should be dismissed. In the course of an extensive report the reporter made the following points. Looked at purely in relation to the shopping policies contained in the approved Stirling-Alloa structure plan he found that the petitioners' proposal would be contrary to the provisions of that plan, principally because the plan encouraged the consolidation of existing shopping centres and did not provide for any new major shopping development in the Stirling area, nor for developments outwith existing centres unless these were appropriately placed and served a purely local function. He considered that the proposed superstore at Corbiewood would be a major addition to the shopping facilities, that it would be outwith the existing hierarchy of centres and that it would clearly serve a wide area which the petitioners' consultant had identified as the primary catchment area. In addition the proposal would not conform to the 1978 national planning guideline on the location of major shopping developments, principally because it would be an out of town site detached from existing shopping centres. A short time before the inquiry was held the regional council had published revised structure plan shopping policies, one of the provisions of which was that in Stirling the council were prepared to support the development, in an off centre location, of one new superstore for essential shopping. Although these revised shopping policies had not been formally incorporated in the structure plan at the time of the inquiry, the reporter allowed evidence to be led on the assumption that one new superstore for essential shopping would be allowed in an off centre location in Stirling. He recognised that the competing sites in Stirling effectively represented mutually exclusive options, and be heard evidence about the comparative merits of the Corbiewood and Broadleys Farm sites. On a consideration of that evidence the reporter came to the conclusion that he had insufficient information to draw any firm conclusion on the comparative merits of Corbiewood and Broadleys Farm. The reporter's decision to refuse the petitioners' appeal was based upon the following grounds: (1) The proposal would be contrary to existing policies. (2) It had not been demonstrated that it would be a suitable exception to those policies, both in relation to the status of the emerging revised structure plan shopping policies, and in relation to the selection from competing alternative sites at which any additional superstore might be located. In the reporter's view it would be undesirable and inappropriate to grant planning permission for a development which would involve serious disadvantages, and which would pre-empt the imminent completion of planning studies initiated by the regional council.

In January 1986 the petitioners lodged a duplicate outline planning application with Stirling District Council in relation to the Corbiewood site. This second application was called in by the regional council for determination. The regional council issued a refusal of consent in November 1986. In January 1987 the petitioners lodged an appeal in terms of s. 33 of the 1972 Act against the regional council's refusal of outline planning permission. That appeal has not yet been determined by the Secretary of State. On 5 November 1986 the regional council's planning and development committee decided that the Broadleys Farm applications should be granted. By granting these applications the regional council would depart from the terms of the approved structure plan. Accordingly in terms of the Town and Country Planning (Notification of Applications) (Scotland) Direction 1981 the regional council were obliged to notify the Secretary of State of their intention to grant the consent. On 12 December 1986 the regional council formally intimated to the Secretary of State their intention to grant the Broadleys Farm applications. In terms of s. 32 of the 1972 Act the Secretary of State was empowered to call in these applications for planning permission. On 19 March 1987 the Secretary of State issued a letter containing his decision not to call in from the regional council in terms of s. 32 of the 1972 Act the planning applications relating to Broadleys Farm ('the decision letter').

In this application for judicial review the petitioners seek reduction of the decision letter and a declarator that in the circumstances the Secretary of State is bound and obliged to call in the Broadleys Farm applications in terms of s. 32 of the 1972 Act.

Before I turn to the merits I have to deal with two preliminary points which arose, the first concerning the competency of the application and the second the petitioners' title to sue. Neither of the respondents sought to have their plea to competency sustained. I shall repel these pleas, being satisfied that the application is competent. I refer to and follow my own decision in *London and Clydeside Estates Ltd v. Secretary of State for Scotland*. I also note the concession made by counsel for the Secretary of State that the appeal procedure allowed under s. 233 of the 1972 Act would not afford the petitioners the remedy which they seek. I am also of opinion that the petitioners have set forth sufficient title to sue. The petitioners made no attempt to derive their title from s. 32 of the 1972 Act. I refer to *Simpson v. Edinburgh Corporation*. Instead the petitioners based their title upon the fact that they are appellants in an appeal under s. 33 of the 1972 Act.

Counsel for the petitioners submitted that the decision letter was unreasonable, contrary to natural justice and procedurally unfair. In developing that submission counsel placed his main emphasis upon procedural unfairness. This submission was to the following effect. The regional council were prepared to support the development of one superstore in an off centre location in Stirling. Although several developers had applied for planning permission, realistically the choice was restricted to one between two sites, Corbiewood and Broadleys Farm. The regional council favoured Broadleys Farm and had intimated their intention to grant consent. Before that could be done the Secretary of State had to be informed so that he might consider whether he should direct a reference to himself. At the time when the decision letter was issued the Secretary of State had pending before him an appeal lodged by the petitioners against a refusal of planning permission relating to the Corbiewood site. By virtue of s. 33(4) of the 1972 Act the petitioners would be entitled to have their appeal heard by a person to be appointed by the Secretary of State before that appeal was determined. The central issue on the petitioners' appeal would be whether the Corbiewood site should be preferred to the Broadleys Farm site. The effect of the Secretary of State's decision letter was to remove the sole obstacle to grant of planning permission in relation to the Broadleys Farm site. Once that consent was granted, then any comparison of the merits of the two rival sites would no longer have any purpose, and the decision in the petitioners' appeal would be pre-empted. Hence by issuing the decision letter when he did the Secretary of State precluded himself from dealing fairly with the petitioners' appeal. Reference was made to *Stringer v. Minister of Housing* at p. 1297 B–C, per Cooke J.; *Att. Gen. of Hong Kong v. Ng Yuen Shiu*, at p. 636, per Lord Fraser of Tullybelton. The decision letter amounted not merely to a denial of natural justice. In addition, the decision was wholly unreasonable. Resolution of the main planning issue involved a comparison of the merits of the two sites. It was unreasonable on the part of the Secretary of State to deny himself the opportunity of examining that issue at a public inquiry at which the merits of each site could be compared. If the petitioners' argument was sound, then the decision letter could not stand and should be reduced. In addition the court should pronounce a declarator to the effect that the Secretary of State was bound to call in the Broadleys Farm application in terms of s. 32 of the 1972 Act.

In my opinion the main argument advanced on behalf of the petitioners is too broadly stated, and to a certain extent is based upon a misconception of the rights and responsibilities vested in the Secretary of State under the planning legislation. The powers of the Secretary of State under s. 32 of the 1972 Act are not expressly qualified. In addition the section contains no criteria to which the Secretary of State must have regard in the application of his powers under that section. I refer to *Williams v. Secretary of State for Wales* at p. 33, per Kerr L.J. Consequently the Secretary of State has a discretion as to when he decides upon an application notified to him. By virtue of the 1981 direction the regional council were obliged to intimate the Broadleys Farm application to the Secretary of State. That was because the application would, if granted, involve a departure from the structure plan. Had the structure plan previously been amended so as to admit of one off centre superstore in Stirling, then the regional council would not have been bound to intimate the application to the Secretary of State. They would have been entitled to refuse the petitioners' application for Corbiewood and to grant consent for the Broadleys Farm development. Had the council done that, then, while the petitioners would have had their right of appeal under s. 33 of the 1972 Act against the refusal of their application, they would have had no right to challenge the grant of planning consent in respect of the Broadleys Farm development. In that situation the petitioners would effectively have failed in their attempt to obtain planning permission.

In an affidavit sworn on 16 April 1987 Mr J. S. Graham, the present head of the planning division of the Scottish Development Department, explained the reasoning and working of the 1981 direction.

According to Mr Graham the various categories of case which under the direction have to be notified all potentially raise a national issue of some sort. In the case of applications notified because they are departures from an approved structure plan the potential national issue arises because the structure plan itself has been approved by the Secretary of State, with the implication that there is a national interest in the policies in the plan. The Secretary of State therefore has to consider whether each application notified to him actually raises a national issue of sufficient importance for the case to be further examined and determined by him, rather than being determined by the planning authority. In the present case the Secretary of State had considered whether the Broadleys Farm application raised an issue of sufficient national importance to justify his directing a reference in terms of s. 32 of the 1972 Act.

In this connection I quote the following passage from the decision letter: 'The Secretary of State recognises that the Regional Council's decision to approve these applications is based on the revised shopping policies adopted by the Council last summer after a comprehensive review. He has therefore considered how far the revised policies in so far as they affect these applications, and the applications themselves are consistent with the National Planning Guidelines on the Location of Major Retail Developments issued in December. He has concluded that the applications are unlikely to have a substantial impact on shopping centres outwith Central Region, and that the applications generally meet the siting criteria set out in the Guidelines. In his view the impact of the applications on existing centres within the Region is difficult to assess with precision, but is unlikely to lead in the longer term to a substantial decline in the vitality and viability of the main existing centres.'

One effect of the decision letter was to enable the regional council to sanction the proposed development at Broadleys Farm. Once that happened the petitioners' appeal, while still competent, would no longer be worthwhile pursuing. But in my opinion the petitioners are not entitled to say that once the Broadleys Farm planning application had been notified to the Secretary of State in terms of the 1981 direction, the existence of the petitioners' appeal left the Secretary of State with no choice but to direct a reference to himself under s. 32. The passage which I have quoted from the decision letter reveals that on a consideration of the potential national issue raised by the application the Secretary of State was not satisfied that a case had been made out for a reference to him under s. 32. That conclusion appears to have been based upon a consideration of the likely impact of the proposed development on shopping centres outwith Central Region. In my opinion the intimation procedure under the 1981 direction of itself does not confer upon appellants such as the petitioners an advantage which they would not enjoy if that procedure did not require to be complied with. In particular, I am not satisfied that in a situation such as that disclosed in the present case parties in the position of the petitioners can by the mere lodging of an appeal under s. 33 require the Secretary of State to direct that another planning application should be referred to him. Consequently if the issue in the present application depended solely upon an examination of the decision letter, I would have no hesitation in holding that the petitioners are not entitled to the remedy which they seek.

A more difficult question is posed by the following passage contained in Mr Graham's affidavit: 'The Secretary of State, in considering whether to call in the applications notified to him by Central Region, certainly gave consideration to the information which was available to him as to whether a better alternative site might be available for a development of the proposed nature. In particular, of course, he considered the information as to the Corbiewood site which was available to him.' Mr Graham then goes on to detail the various sources of information that were available to him about the Corbiewood site, including the decision letter issued on 28 October 1986 in relation to the petitioners' first appeal. Mr Graham then continues as follows: 'The Secretary of State considered all that information in reaching his decision about Broadleys, because the main respect in which the Broadleys' proposals were out of accord with the approved structure plan was in their off centre location, and the Secretary of State therefore had to consider the merits of the proposed location with some care. Having considered the information, the Secretary of State formed the view that he did not require further evidence before reaching a decision on Broadleys. In the circumstances he did not regard it as reasonable to delay issuing his decision on Broadleys until the process of appeal on Corbiewood and other sites had been completed or to call in the Broadleys and other applications so that the sites could have been considered simultaneously. In view of the amount of information available to him, the Secretary of State did not think it reasonable to delay reaching a conclusion merely because a second appeal relating to Corbiewood was outstanding. He was of course aware that, since the regional council's revised policies provide for only one off centre superstore in the Stirling area and the Secretary of State's own guidelines lay careful stress on the importance of weighing up the effects of off centre development proposals on town centres, the granting of approval for the Broadleys proposal by the regional council which is likely to follow his decision not to call in the application, would affect other comparable proposals including Corbiewood.'

In my view the passage which I have quoted reveals that, once the application had been notified to him, the Secretary of State did not restrict his inquiries to a consideration of the likely effect of a superstore at Broadleys Farm on shopping patterns outside Central Region. He went on to inquire whether, assuming that an off centre superstore were to be sanctioned in Stirling, there were other sites, including Corbiewood, that might be more appropriate. Had the Secretary of State chosen to leave the claims of the Corbiewood site out of account altogether, and had he rested his decision not to direct a reference upon the absence of any national issue in the proposal, in my view the petitioners would have had no cause to complain merely because one consequence of his decision was to deprive their appeal of any value. The petitioners would have had no cause for complaint because the decision which rendered their appeal worthless was one made by the Secretary of State in relation to another application on a consideration of evidence which was pertinent to that application alone. In other words, I think that by taking a blinkered view of the merits of the Broadleys Farm application the Secretary of State would be entitled to ignore any prejudice that his decision might have on an appeal relating to a rival site. But it appears to me that the Secretary of State was not content to take such a blinkered view. He thought it relevant to a decision whether or not to direct a reference that he appraise the merits of alternative sites, including Corbiewood. Once he had decided to embark on this wider inquiry, I consider that the Secretary of State should have appreciated that his discretion, otherwise unrestricted, was limited by his duty to act fairly in relation to the merits of the petitioners' appeal under s. 33 of the 1972 Act, especially having regard to the fact that the prime issue in the petitioners' appeal was whether Corbiewood should be preferred to Broadleys Farm. In the situation which developed I do not think it was fair for the Secretary of State to take advantage of the notification to him of the Broadleys Farm application to decide the main issue raised by the petitioners' appeal and to use that decision as one of his reasons for declining to direct a reference. In the present case I consider that the petitioners' complaint is a substantial one, because there is no reason to suppose that at an inquiry into their second appeal the reporter would hear no more than a recapitulation of the evidence that had been led at the first inquiry. The reporter in the first inquiry stated that he had insufficient information to enable him to reach a conclusion on the comparative merits of Broadleys Farm and Corbiewood. It is therefore reasonable to suppose that the petitioners would take the opportunity of remedying this defect in the course of the second appeal.

If the conclusion which I have reached on an examination of Mr Graham's affidavit is sound, it follows that the decision letter, being tainted with unfairness, cannot stand and must be reduced. In addition I think that the passage quoted indicates that a comparison of the alternative sites influenced the Secretary of State's decision not to direct a reference. In that state of affairs I consider that the petitioners are also entitled to the declarator that they seek. That is because in my view the only fair way of appraising the merits of the rival sites is by affording the competing developers an opportunity to lead evidence and submit arguments to a reporter.

In the result I repel the first two pleas in law for each of the respondents. I sustain the first plea in law for the petitioners in so far as it challenges the decision letter on the grounds that it is contrary to natural justice. I also sustain the second plea in law for the petitioners and will grant declarator accordingly.

The respondents reclaimed."

Reclaiming Motion

The reclaiming motion was heard by the Second Division on 23 and 24 February 1988.

On 11 March 1988 the court *refused* the reclaiming motion.

LORD JUSTICE-CLERK (ROSS): "In this petition the petitioners seek judicial review of a decision of the first respondent who is the Secretary of State for Scotland. Certain powers are conferred and duties imposed on the first respondent in terms of the Town and Country Planning (Scotland) Act 1972. Section 32 of the Act of 1972 deals with the procedure for 'calling in' by the first respondent applications for planning permission which would otherwise be dealt with by a planning authority. Section 33 of the Act of 1972 deals with appeals against planning decisions. The second respondents are Central Regional Council who are the regional planning authority. In terms of s. 179 of the Local Government (Scotland) Act 1973 the second respondents are empowered to call in an application for planning permission in certain circumstances.

The petitioners seek reduction of the decision of the first respondent dated 19 March 1987, declarator that in the circumstances the first respondent is bound and obliged to call in certain specific planning applications in terms of s. 32 of the Act of 1972, and interdict against the second respondents from granting certain planning applications relating to a site at Broadleys Farm, Stirling. On 1 and 6 May 1987 the Lord Ordinary pronounced decrees of reduction, declarator and interdict, and it is against these two interlocutors that the first and second respondents have now reclaimed.

The background to this petition is that in September 1985 the petitioners lodged an application with Stirling District Council for outline planning permission in respect of a proposed superstore, shops, restaurant, petrol filling station and car park at Corbiewood, Stirling. This application was subsequently called in by the second respondents together with 18 other major retail proposals elsewhere in Central Region in terms of s. 179 of the Act of 1973. In November 1985 the application of the petitioners was refused. The petitioner appealed against that decision to the first respondent in terms of s. 33 of the Act of 1972. The first respondent appointed a reporter to determine the appeal. A public local inquiry into the appeal was held between 16 and 19 September 1986. On 28 October 1986 the reporter determined that the appeal should be dismissed. In January 1986 a duplicate application for outline planning permission was lodged by the petitioners with Stirling District Council. This application was again called in by the second respondents for determination by them. In November 1986 a refusal of consent for this application was issued by the second respondents. In January 1987 the petitioners appealed to the first respondent against the refusal of outline planning permission. That appeal has still to be determined by the first respondent.

Among the applications called in by the second respondents are three outline planning applications for developments at Broadleys Farm, Stirling of which land the second respondents are the heritable proprietors. These three applications are (a) an outline planning application for a superstore and related development at Broadleys Farm submitted by Tesco Stores Ltd. (ref. no. E86/452); (b) an outline planning application for a non-food retail warehouse plus garden centre at Broadleys Farm submitted by Dunedin Property Development Co. (Retail) Ltd. (ref. no. E86/427); and (c) an outline planning application for a superstore and related development at Broadleys Farm submitted by Norfolk House (London) Ltd. (ref. no. E86/443).

In his decision letter relating to the refusal of the first appeal, the reporter expressed the view that the petitioners' proposals would be contrary to the provisions of the Stirling-Alloa structure plan, principally because the plan encourages the consolidation of existing shopping centres and does not provide for any new major shopping development in the Stirling area, nor for developments outwith existing centres unless they are appropriately placed and serve a purely local function. He expressed the view that the petitioners' proposed superstore would be a major addition to the shopping facilities, would be outwith the existing hierarchy of centres, and would clearly serve a wide area. He also expressed the view that the petitioners' proposal would not conform to the 1978 national planning guideline on the location of major shopping developments, principally because it would be an out of town site detached from existing shopping centres. The second respondents have adopted revised structure plan shopping policies; these have not yet been submitted for approval by the first respondent. In terms of these revised shopping policies, the second respondents have recognised that there is scope for the development of one major superstore and related development in Stirling district. The second respondents favour Broadleys Farm site for the said developments. Since the revised shopping policies have not yet been submitted for the formal approval of the first respondent, if the second respondents wished to grant an application for outline planning permission which was consistent with the revised plan but contrary to the approved structure plan, it would be necessary for them to inform the first respondent of such an application. This is a consequence of the provisions of the Town and Country Planning (Notification of Applications) (Scotland) Direction 1981 and Amendment Direction 1984.

As already indicated, the outline planning applications at the instance of Tesco Stores Ltd., Dunedin Property Development Co. (Retail) Ltd. and Norfolk House (London) Ltd. were called in by the second respondents, as was the petitioners' duplicate outline application. In November 1986 as well as refusing the petitioners' duplicate outline application, the second respondents determined that the planning applications by Tesco Stores Ltd., Dunedin Property Development Co. (Retail) Ltd. and Norfolk House (London) Ltd. in respect of the site at Broadleys Farm, Stirling should be granted, but subject to notifying the first respondent of the intention to grant consent as required by the 1981 direction. On 12 December 1986 the second respondents advised the first respondent of their intention to grant the said applications for planning permission.

In terms of s. 32 of the Act of 1972 the first respondent is empowered to call in the said applications for planning permission. Section 32 provides as follows: [his Lordship narrated the provisions of s. 32 and continued:]

In the petition, the petitioners explain that their grounds of appeal against the refusal of outline planning permission for the proposed superstore and related development at Corbiewood, Stirling are inter alia that their proposal is not in conflict with currently revised structure or local plan policies. They also contend that the policy and strategic planning issues in respect of the proposed development at Corbiewood are identical with and indeed inseparable from the policy and strategic planning issues in respect of the proposed development at Broadleys Farm. That being so, they maintain that the granting of planning permission for a superstore and related development at Corbiewood would directly and adversely affect an application for planning permission for a superstore and related development at Broadleys Farm and vice versa. In these circumstances the petitioners submitted to the first respondent that he should call in the planning applications by Tesco Stores Ltd., Dunedin Property Development Co. (Retail) Ltd. and Norfolk House (London) Ltd. in order that the applications in respect of Corbiewood and Broadleys Farm could be determined at the same time.

On 19 March 1987, the first respondent determined that the planning applications in respect of Broadleys Farm notified to him by the second respondents in terms of the 1981 direction should not be called in in terms of s. 32 of the Act of 1972. It is matter of admission that it is the intention of the second respondents to grant these applications. The petitioners maintain that the granting of the said applications would effectively determine the petitioners' appeal in respect of Corbiewood since such appeal is almost certainly bound to fail upon the granting of permission in respect of Broadleys Farm. They contend that the petitioners' appeal can only properly and fairly be determined on a comparison of the relative advantages or disadvantages of the Corbiewood site and the Broadleys Farm site for a food superstore as potential sites for that purpose. In particular they aver in art. 11 of the petition: 'If planning permission were granted for Broadleys Farm site pending the appeal, it would cease to be a potential site, such comparison would no longer have any purpose, and the decision of said appeal would be effectively pre-empted.'

In the foregoing circumstances, the petitioners contend in this petition that the decision of the first respondent of 19 March 1987 is perverse and unreasonable. They also contend that the decision is contrary to natural justice in respect that it is procedurally unfair. It is on these grounds that the petitioners are seeking reduction, declarator and interdict.

Before the Lord Ordinary it appears to have been contended both that the decision of the first respondent was perverse and unreasonable, and that it was procedurally unfair. As I read the Lord Ordinary's opinion he did not uphold the contention that the first respondent's decision was perverse and unreasonable, but he did sustain the argument that it was procedurally unfair. This was confirmed by counsel for the respondents who accepted that no point on unreasonableness arose in this case, and that what was in issue was whether there had been procedural unfairness. Since the allegation that the first respondent's decision was perverse and unreasonable is no longer being insisted in, it is unnecessary to review all the cases which counsel for the first respondent cited in opening the reclaiming motion. It is now well recognised that procedural impropriety or procedural irregularity may be a ground for challenging a decision of this kind. It is plain that this ground of challenge is related to the manner in which the decision has been reached. There have been a number of recent authorities dealing with judicial review which is the means by which judicial control of administrative action is exercised. In *C.C.S.U. v. Minister for Civil Service* at p. 410 Lord Diplock said: 'Judicial review has I think developed to a stage today when without reiterating any analysis of the steps by which the development has come about, one can conveniently classify under three heads the grounds upon which administrative action is subject to control by judicial review. The first ground I would call "illegality", the second "irrationality" and the third "procedural impropriety". That is not to say that further development on a case by case basis may not in course of time add further grounds.' Subsequently at p. 411 Lord Diplock added: 'I have described the third head as "procedural impropriety" rather than failure to observe basic rules of natural justice or failure to act with procedural fairness towards the person who will be affected by the decision. This is because susceptibility to judicial review under this head covers also failure by an administrative tribunal to observe procedural rules that are expressly laid down in the legislative instrument by which its jurisdiction is conferred, even where such failure does not involve any denial of natural justice. But the instant case is not concerned with the proceedings of an administrative tribunal at all.' Lord Roskill agreed with Lord Diplock's classification of the three grounds upon which administrative action might be controlled by judicial review. He observed that in this regard reference is sometimes made to acting in a manner contrary to the 'principles of natural justice'. He observed at p. 414: 'As to this last, the use of this phrase is no doubt hallowed by time and much judicial repetition, but it is a phrase often widely misunderstood and therefore as often misused. That phrase perhaps might now be allowed to find a permanent resting-place and be better replaced by speaking of a duty to act fairly. But that latter phrase must not in its turn be misunderstood or misused. It is not for the courts to determine whether a particular policy or particular decisions taken in fulfilment of that policy are fair. They are only concerned with the manner in which those decisions have been taken and the extent of the duty to act fairly will vary greatly from case to case as, indeed, the decided cases since 1950 consistently show. Many features will come into play including the nature of the decision and the relationship of those involved on either side before the decision was taken.'

In *R. v. Inland Revenue Commissioners, ex p. Preston*, Lord Scarman observed that unfairness in the purported exercise of a power can be such that it is an abuse or excess of power. A similar view was expressed by Lord Templeman. He also pointed out at p. 864 that in most cases in which the court has granted judicial review on grounds of 'unfairness' amounting to abuse of power there has been some proven element of improper motive. The matter is taken further in *Wheeler v. Leicester City Council*.

At p. 1078 Lord Roskill observed: 'None of the learned judges in the courts below have felt able to hold that the action of the club was unreasonable or perverse in the *Wednesbury* sense. They do not appear to have been invited to consider whether those actions, even if not unreasonable on *Wednesbury* principles, were assailable on the grounds of procedural impropriety or unfairness by the council in the manner in which, in the light of the facts which I have outlined, they took their decision to suspend for 12 months the use by the club of the Welford Road recreation ground.'

In *Nottinghamshire County Council v. Secretary of State for the Environment* at p. 249, Lord Scarman said: 'The ground upon which the courts will review the exercise of an administrative discretion by a public officer is abuse of power. Power can be abused in a number of ways: by a mistake of law in misconstruing the limits imposed by statute (or by common law in the case of a common law power) upon the scope of the power; by procedural irregularity; by unreasonableness in the *Wednesbury* sense; or by bad faith or an improper motive in its exercise. A valuable, and already "classical", but certainly not exhaustive analysis of the grounds upon which courts will embark on the judicial review of an administrative power exercised by a public officer is now to be found in Lord Diplock's speech in *Council of Civil Service Unions v. Minister for the Civil Service.*'

That Lord Diplock's classification of the three grounds upon which judicial review may be sought is accepted to be part of the law of Scotland is made clear in *City of Edinburgh District Council v. Secretary of State for Scotland*. Counsel for the first respondents also drew attention to *R. v. Secretary of State for the Environment, ex p. London Borough of Southwark*. That was a case where allegations were made of unfairness and Lloyd L.J. observed that there was no such thing as a technical breach of natural justice. He added: 'This means that nobody can be held to complain unless there is a risk of substantial prejudice'.

In my opinion, it is clear from these authorities that when the court is being invited to review an administrative decision, it is not for the court to determine whether the decision was fair or unfair. The court is, however, entitled to consider whether the manner in which the decision was taken was fair or unfair. 'Procedural propriety' or 'procedural irregularity' covers that sort of situation; the person making the administrative decision has a duty to act fairly in the manner in which he arrives at his decision. 'Procedural impropriety' or 'procedural irregularity' may arise where there has been a failure to comply with procedural rules; but it may also arise where there has simply been unfairness in the manner in which a decision has been arrived at. This will be so particularly if an individual who has the legitimate expectation of a hearing is denied any hearing before a decision affecting him is taken (*Att. Gen. of Hong Kong v. Ng Yuen Shiu; C.C.S.U. v. Minister for Civil Service*).

In this reclaiming motion the critical question is whether the petitioners have made out a case of procedural impropriety or procedural irregularity. On behalf of the first respondent counsel submitted that there had been no procedural impropriety in relation to either the s. 32 process or in relation to the second appeal at the instance of the petitioners. Counsel submitted that what the petitioners here were complaining of was not procedural unfairness but that the decision arrived at by the Secretary of State was unfair. In any event, counsel submitted that esto there had been procedural unfairness, the petitioners had not shown that they would suffer any substantial prejudice. Counsel further emphasised that planning was essentially the responsibility of a planning authority and that the first respondent exercised a supervisory role only. In determining whether or not to call in an application, the first respondent had an unlimited and unfettered discretion. Under the planning procedures, a third party had no right to appeal against the granting of planning permission to another, and accordingly any unfairness in the present case was a result of the planning legislation and not a consequence of any procedural impropriety on the part of the first respondent.

Counsel for the first respondent further contended that in any event the petitioners had no right to challenge the decision of the first respondent; that being so they sought to support their plea of no title to sue.

In all the circumstances counsel for the first respondent moved the court to recall the interlocutors of the Lord Ordinary of 1 May and 6 May 1987.

A similar motion was made by counsel on behalf of the second respondents. Counsel contended that the Secretary of State had been fully entitled to consider the detailed representations made to him regarding inter alia alternative sites. He stressed that if there had been no question of the calling in procedure being operated, the petitioners would have had no means of protecting their position once the second respondents resolved to grant the applications at the instance of those who wished to develop the Broadleys Farm site. Counsel also stressed that it was not the purpose of the planning legislation to preserve the status quo, but that what was behind the call-in procedure was to ensure that national planning objectives were maintained. The first respondent should therefore exercise his discretion with that in mind. Reference was made to *Padfield v. Minister of Agriculture, Fisheries and Food* at p. 1030. Under reference to the legislation then being considered, Lord Reid said: 'Parliament must have conferred the discretion with the intention that it should be used to promote the policy and objects of the Act; the policy and objects of the Act must be determined by construing the Act as a whole and construction is always a matter of law for the court.' In these circumstances counsel submitted that the call-in procedure which had been triggered by the notification procedure fell to be used in order to achieve the proper planning objectives and not to be used to confer upon the petitioner in a different process a benefit to which he was not otherwise entitled.

On behalf of the petitioners counsel contended that the Lord Ordinary had reached the correct conclusion. They stressed that over recent years the authorities showed an increasing emphasis on procedural unfairness as opposed to unreasonableness as a ground of judicial review. Counsel contended that there was a duty to act fairly in carrying out an administrative act where the rights of third parties were affected, and that merely to say that the Secretary of State was exercising an unfettered administrative discretion was not sufficient to excuse unfairness. It was accepted that the duty was to act fairly in the manner in which the decision was arrived at, and that it was not the fairness of the decision itself that was in issue. It was further emphasised that the petitioners having appealed and having indicated that they wished to have the appeal decided by public local inquiry, they had the legitimate expectation of a hearing; in that situation the Secretary of State would be acting unfairly if he arrived at a decision without affording the petitioners the opportunity of a meaningful hearing. Counsel accepted that the requirement of procedural fairness depended upon the circumstances of the case, and they contended that the circumstances here were such that for the first respondent to decline to call in the Broadleys Farm applications meant that the he had pre-empted the appeal at the instance of the petitioners in relation to Corbiewood. The contention of the first and second respondents had been that the purpose of call-in procedure was to enable the first respondent to determine national issues, but it was plain that in this case he had gone much further than merely considering national issues and had considered the merits of the two competing sites at Corbiewood and Broadleys Farm. This meant that he had not acted fairly in the manner in which he had arrived at his decision not to call in. Counsel further contended that it was quite unrealistic to suggest that the appeal at the instance of the petitioners might still succeed. They contended that the petitioners should have been afforded an opportunity to lead evidence at an inquiry against the refusal of planning permission for Corbiewood before the Secretary of State reached any conclusion upon the merits of the alternative sites. They contended that the petitioners had clearly demonstrated prejudice in the present case because the decision of the Secretary of State not to call in the Broadleys Farm applications affected the petitioners' appeal in relation to Corbiewood. Under reference to *D. & J. Nicol v. Dundee Harbour Trustees* they submitted that the petitioners had a title and interest to present this petition for judicial review.

I entirely accept that if there had been no question of the call-in procedure applying, the second respondents could have granted the applications relating to Broadleys Farm and the petitioners would have had no ground upon which to object to that course being followed. What is important, however, is that the call-in procedure did operate. Because the applications in relation to Broadleys Farm were contrary to the approved structure plan it was necessary for the second respondents to notify the first respondent and to send him the information detailed in the 1981 direction. Once that has been done, the Secretary of State must within a period of 28 days (or such longer period as he may notify) decide that the application should be referred to him instead of being dealt with by the planning authority or that it may be left to the planning authority to proceed to determine the application. In other words the Secretary of State has to decide whether or not to call in the application. There is no doubt that s. 32 confers upon the Secretary of State what appears to be an unfettered discretion. In his affidavit, Mr Graham, an assistant secretary in the Scottish Office who is presently head of the planning division of the Scottish Development Department, states that the Secretary of State has not published any guidance explaining the manner in which he exercises this discretion. However, he goes on to explain that the various categories of case which have to be so notified to the Secretary of State all potentially raise a national issue of some sort. As regards cases like the present where an application has been notified because it is contrary to the approved structure plan Mr Graham says: 'In the case of applications notified because they are departures from an approved structure plan the potential national issue arises because the structure plan itself has been approved by the Secretary of State, with the implication that there is a national interest in the policies in the plan. The Secretary of State therefore has to consider whether each application notified to him actually raises a national issue of sufficient importance for the case to be further examined and determined by him rather than being determined by the planning authority.'

It is thus clear from the affidavit that in deciding whether or not to call in an application notified to him, the Secretary of State regards himself as requiring to consider whether there are national issues raised by the application. The decision of the Secretary of State not to call in the applications notified to him, is contained in the letter dated 19 March 1987. The terms of that letter would suggest that the Secretary of State had indeed approached the matter in that way. In para. 3 of the letter it is stated: '3. The Secretary of State recognises that the Regional Council's decision to approve these applications is based on the revised shopping policies adopted by the Council last summer after a comprehensive review. He has therefore considered how far the revised policies in so far as they affect these applications, and the applications themselves are consistent with the National Planning Guidelines on the Location of Major Retail Developments issued in December. He has concluded that the applications are unlikely to have a substantial impact on shopping centers outwith Central Region, and that the applications generally meet the siting criteria set out in the Guidelines. In his view the impact of the applications on existing centers within the Region is difficult to assess with precision, but is unlikely to lead in the longer term to a substantial decline in the vitality and viability of the main existing centres. The Secretary of State has noted the steps being taken by the Regional Council to restrict the range of goods to be sold in the proposed new developments and the measures to protect and strengthen the main existing centres which are included in your Council's revised policies'.

The letter then goes on to explain that the Secretary of State has concluded that the applications do not raise issues of sufficient importance to make it necessary for him to call them in for his determination. If the matter had ended there, it would, in my opinion have been extremely difficult for the petitioners to suggest that there had been any procedural impropriety or unfairness in this case. Ex facie of the letter there is nothing to suggest that there had been anything unfair in the manner in which the first respondent had arrived at his decision not to call in the applications. The terms of the letter of decision of 19 March 1987 strongly suggest that the first respondent approached the matter from the point of view of considering whether there were any national issues raised in these applications, in the sense that there is a national interest in policies which have been approved by planning authorities. The Secretary of State recognised that the second respondents had adopted revised shopping policies and he proceeded to consider how far these revised policies in so far as they affected the applications were or were not consistent with the national planning guidelines. He then proceeded to consider what impact, if any, the applications would have on shopping centres both within and outwith Central Region.

What, however, has given rise to the principal argument presented to this court has been what is stated in later paragraphs of Mr Graham's affidavit where a full and commendably frank description is given of the manner in which the first respondent arrived at his decision not to call in the applications. Before considering what is stated in these later paragraphs of the affidavit, it is useful first to identify the issues which are raised in the pending planning appeal in relation to the Corbiewood site.

The terms of the appeal lodged by the petitioners in relation to the second refusal of planning permission for Corbiewood contain a number of grounds of appeal. The fourth ground of appeal is in the following terms: 'It is not accepted that the appeal site is inferior in terms of retail planning criteria to the preferred site of the Regional Council. In fact, it is considered that the merits outlined above mean that it would be preferred on any rational comparison of the two sites.' It is thus plain that one of the issues raised in the pending appeal is the relative merits of the competing sites at Broadleys Farm and Corbiewood. That this should be so is even clearer when regard is had to the terms of the report of the reporter into the first appeal in relation to the Corbiewood site. In para. 14 of the report the reporter makes it plain that one of the main matters which was at issue was 'the relationship of the present appeal to the decisions to be taken by the Regional Council on other major shopping proposals in the Stirling area'. Subsequently in para. 45 of his report, having said something regarding alternative sites, the reporter states: 'For this reason, I attempted to obtain information at the public local inquiry on the merits of the alternative sites. The witnesses were able to offer preliminary personal judgments on this (see paragraph 72–77 below), but there had been no systematic comparative assessment of the sites, and the detailed analysis of the trading implications of the various options had not yet taken place.' More important, however, is what the reporter says in para. 71: 'The final element requiring consideration is that of alternative sites. In many planning situations, these have limited relevance. However it is clear that the prospects for a fourth superstore in Stirling would be greatly reduced by the approval of a third superstore, both from a commercial and planning policy point of view. Thus the competing sites in Stirling effectively represent mutually exclusive options. They are being compared in a systematic way by the Regional Council who hope to make their choice on 5 November 1986. Approval of the Corbiewood site prior to then would jeopardise that procedure unless it is clear that the appeal site is better, or at least no worse, than the possible alternatives.' Subsequently in para. 79, the reporter states that he considers that he has insufficient information to draw any firm conclusion on the comparative merits of Corbiewood and Broadleys. He goes on to refer to particular advantages and disadvantages of the two sites.

In my opinion it is luce clarius that in the pending planning appeal one of the principal issues to be raised will be a comparison between the Broadleys Farm site and the Corbiewood site as the location for a superstore. The contention of the petitioners is that the first respondent's decision not to call in the applications leaves the second respondents free to grant the applications in relation to Broadleys Farm and that the necessary consequence of that is that the decision in the petitioners' appeal will be effectively pre-empted.

Bearing that in mind, I turn to examine in greater detail Mr Graham's affidavit. As already indicated, the earlier paragraphs of the affidavit are entirely consistent with the first respondent's having applied his mind to the national issues involved. However, it is quite clear from the later paragraphs of the affidavit that the first respondent in fact considered much more than merely the national issues involved. In para. 5 it is stated that the first respondent gave consideration to the information which was available to him as to whether a better alternative site might be available for a development of the proposed nature. Reference is then made to various documents which were before him dealing with the comparative merits of the two sites. In para. 6 it is stated that the first respondent considered all this information in reaching his decision about Broadleys because the first respondent had to consider the merits of the proposed location with some care. It is also stated that the first respondent was aware inter alia of the fact that the granting of approval for the Broadleys proposal by the regional council which is likely to follow the first respondent's decision not to call in the application would affect other comparable proposals including Corbiewood. In para. 8 the point is made that like the second respondents the first respondent was obliged to consider the Broadleys Farm case 'on its planning merits'.

Having regard to what Mr Graham says in these later paragraphs of his affidavit, I am clearly of opinion that the procedure which the first respondent adopted in deciding not to call in the Broadleys Farm applications involved unfairness; there was unfairness in the manner in which he arrived at his decision. Indeed it appears to me that the approach described by Mr Graham is misconceived. What the first respondent required to decide was whether to call in the applications under s. 32 and not how the applications should be determined. On reading the affidavit, it is plain that what was being done was determining the merits of the Broadleys Farm applications. There are, in the affidavit, repeated references to 'the merits' of the applications. In my opinion it was no part of the first respondent's duty at this stage to consider the merits of the applications at all. What he ought to have been considering was whether the applications should be called in by him so that he could then proceed to determine the merits of the applications. When considering whether to call in the applications, the first respondent should not have been considering the merits of the applications at all. The fact that the first respondent approached the question of calling in the applications in the wrong manner, in my opinion, amounts to procedural impropriety or unfairness. This is particularly so in the present case where the first respondent deliberately considered the question of whether a better alternative site might be available for the proposed development in the knowledge that he had pending an appeal at the instance of the petitioners which raised this very issue of alternative sites. The petitioners who had appealed against the refusal of planning permission for Corbiewood and had stated that they wished their appeal to be decided by public local inquiry, had the legitimate expectation of a hearing being held into the matter of alternative sites. In my opinion the first respondent followed an unfair procedure when he considered at his own hand the issue of alternative sites and arrived at a decision upon the merits of the Broadleys Farm application without affording the petitioners an opportunity of having the matter of alternative sites fully investigated at a public local inquiry.

On behalf of the first respondent it was suggested that the first respondent had before him all the relevant information bearing upon the matter of alternative sites. It was said under reference to para. 5 of the affidavit that he had considered the information as to the Corbiewood site which was available to him, and that there was a considerable amount of information upon this matter. Reference was made to the documents lodged by the second respondents along with the notification; in particular reference was made to the minute of the second respondents' planning and development committee dated 5 November 1987, and to various papers referred to therein. It was also said that the first respondent's attention was drawn to the decision letter issued in respect of the first appeal, and that he also had regard to representations made to him by the agents acting on behalf of the petitioners who enclosed a report on the comparative merits of the Corbiewood and Broadleys Farm sites commissioned from consultants. The first respondent also had regard to representations received from Stirling and Falkirk District Councils; he thus was aware that as between the two sites Stirling District Council favoured Corbiewood as the site for a superstore. All this may well be so, but, in my opinion, taking all that written material into account was not a substitute for allowing the petitioners to have these matters fully investigated at a public local inquiry. It is well recognised that matters made the subject of written representations may appear rather different once they have been subjected to cross examination at a public local inquiry. Moreover it was made clear by the reporter in the first appeal that the considered that he had insufficient information to draw any firm conclusion on the comparative merits of Corbiewood and Broadleys. Likewise, the consultants for the petitioners whose report was referred to in the affidavit expressly stated in their report that the arguments put forward for or against the two sites should be subjected to further legal and/or planning scrutiny before any decision was taken. They also stated in the report that the supporting information which formed part of the submission to the planning and development committee on 5 November 1986 was partially inaccurate and incomplete. In their findings they stated that further evidence would seem to be necessary before a decision could be made as to whether Broadleys or Corbiewood is the better site. The reasonable assumption must be that at a public inquiry into their appeal, the petitioners would lead additional evidence, i.e. evidence of which the first respondent is not yet aware.

Despite these limitations in the written material which he considered, the first respondent proceeded to consider the merits of the two sites, and to conclude that he did not require further evidence before reaching a decision on the Broadleys Farm site. He did this although he was aware that the granting of approval for the Broadleys Farm site by the second respondents which was likely to follow his decision not to call in the application 'would affect other comparable proposals including Corbiewood' (para. 6 of affidavit). Moreover, in ans. 10 for the first respondent it is averred: 'The granting of planning permission for one of the sites could affect the other site.' In ans. 11 for the first respondent it is stated: 'Believed to be true that the second respondent intends to grant planning permission in respect of the Broadleys Farm applications and that the granting of planning permission for that site could diminish the possibility of planning permission being granted in respect of an alternative site at Corbiewood. The Secretary of State was aware that the granting of planning permission for the Broadleys Farm site would affect other comparable proposals.'

It is accordingly clear that the first respondent when considering whether to call in the Broadleys Farm applications proceeded to consider the merits of the competing sites in the full knowledge that if he did not call in the applications the second respondents intended to grant planning permission which would then have an adverse affect upon the appeal at the instance of the petitioners. This appears to me to be the adoption of improper or unfair procedure on the part of the first respondent in the manner in which he took his decision not to call in the Broadleys Farm applications. In my opinion, if that is so, then in principle this is the sort of situation where the court is entitled to interfere. In *Wheeler v. Leicester City Council* the court interfered because of the unfair manner in which the council set about obtaining its objective. There was no suggestion in the present case that the first respondent had adopted this procedure in order to attain a particular objective prejudicial to the petitioners, but, in my opinion, the ground of procedural impropriety or unfairness is available even though there may have been no ulterior motive on the part of the decision maker. If a decision complained of has been arrived at through the adoption of procedure which is improper or unfair, then the decision is subject to control by judicial review.

Counsel for the first respondent maintained that there had not in fact been any competition between the two sites, but having regard to the terms of the documents to which I have already referred, it is perfectly plain that there was indeed competition between the sites. Counsel also contended that there had been no identifiable procedure in this instance and accordingly no room for the court holding that there had been any unfairness procedurally. In my opinion, however, it is plain that the procedure which the first respondent chose to follow involving a consideration of alternative sites was a procedure which was unfair in the circumstances of this case. Counsel for the first respondent submitted that it was entirely proper for the first respondent to consider the alternative sites since, if he concluded that there was a better alternative site, it might then be less damaging to the structure plan than the Broadleys Farm sites. I do not agree. It was no part of the first respondent's duty at this stage to consider the merits of the sites at all; accordingly there was no need for him to consider the impact of Corbiewood at all. At one stage, I understood counsel to submit that the Secretary of State required to form a prima facie view on the merits of the sites, but, in my opinion at this stage of proceedings when he was considering only the question of the possible calling in of the Broadleys Farm applications, there was no need for him to form any view on the merits of the alternative sites.

It was also contended on behalf of the first respondent that even though the Broadleys Farm applications should be granted by the second respondents, the appeal at the instance of the petitioners for Corbiewood might still succeed. In my opinion, such a submission goes in the face of what is stated by Mr Graham in his affidavit and what is stated on the first respondent's behalf in his pleadings. Since the first respondent had already considered and acted upon his view on the question of alternative sites, that necessarily prejudges the petitioners appeal. The reporter on the first appeal recognised that the competing sites in Stirling effectively represented mutually exclusive options, and in my opinion he was well entitled to express that view. Standing the second respondents' revised shopping policies to which the first respondent had regard as evidenced by the decision letter of 19 March, the competing sites are mutually exclusive, and it follows that if one of them has received planning permission, there is no real prospect of planning permission for the other being granted. In my opinion counsel for the petitioners was well founded when he submitted that if Broadleys Farm had received planning permission his appeal for Corbiewood would, in any real sense, be without any hope. The first respondent's decision not to call in the Broadleys Farm applications is, in my opinion, clearly prejudicial to the petitioners, and means that their appeal has in effect been pre-empted.

So far as title to sue is concerned, I am of opinion that the petitioners have a title to sue. As Lord Dunedin pointed out in *D. & J. Nicol v. Dundee Harbour Trustees*, a party has a title to sue if he is a party to some legal relation which gives him some right which the person against whom he raises the action either infringes or denies. There is a legal relation between the petitioners and the Secretary of State in that the petitioners are appellants to the Secretary of State in relation to the Corbiewood site. They have a right to have their appeal determined at a public local inquiry, and if the first respondent has prejudged the issue and pre-empted the appeal then he has plainly infringed a right belonging to the petitioners.

In seeking to challenge the decision of the Lord Ordinary, counsel for the first respondent pointed out that if the planning applications were called in, the first respondent had no power to order a joint inquiry into these applications and the planning appeal relating to Corbiewood. Thus it was said the first respondent could not force there to be any simultaneous consideration of the two sites. Therefore, they contended, calling in of the applications in relation to Broadleys Farm would not produce the result desired by the petitioners. Counsel for the petitioners, on the other hand, accepted that the first respondent could not insist on a joint inquiry, but they reminded us that a joint inquiry might be held of consent of parties. In any event, the first respondent required to hold an inquiry into the planning appeal since the petitioners had exercised their right to insist on a public local inquiry. So far as the called in applications were concerned, an inquiry could be insisted upon by either the applicants for planning permission or the second respondents. If neither the applicants for Broadleys Farm nor the second respondents express any desire for a public inquiry, the Secretary of State himself has power to order an inquiry to be held.

It follows that in the event of there being no agreement to a joint inquiry the first respondent could order two separate inquiries to be held into Broadleys Farm on the one hand and Corbiewood on the other. No doubt in each of these inquiries evidence would be led about the merits of alternative sites. As regards the appeal, in exercise of his powers under para. 3 (1) of Sched. 7 to the Act of 1972 the first respondent could direct that he himself would determine the appeal instead of the person appointed by him. This would enable him to consider the appeal along with the report on the inquiry into the called in applications. In this way he could arrive as a decision on the competing sites at one and the same time. No one could then complain that the decision in one process pre-empted the decision in the other...

In the whole matter I have reached the conclusion that the Lord Ordinary was well founded in concluding that a case had been made for judicial review. The Lord Ordinary, however, has not made it entirely clear in his opinion that he was proceeding upon the basis of procedural impropriety or procedural unfairness and not upon the view that the decision itself was unfair. I would stress that I am in favour of the petitioners not upon the view that the decision was unfair because that is not a matter upon which the court is entitled to have a view. My reason for favouring the petitioners is that I am satisfied that there was procedural impropriety or unfairness. This clearly emerges from a perusal of Mr Graham's affidavit.

Since there was procedural impropriety or unfairness, I am of opinion that the petitioners are entitled to the reduction on which they seek. It was not contended on behalf of either of the respondents that if decree of reduction were pronounced decree of declarator and interdict should not follow. Accordingly I am of opinion that the petitioners are entitled to the remedies which the Lord Ordinary gave them.

I would accordingly move your Lordships to refuse this reclaiming motion and adhere to the interlocutor of the Lord Ordinary."

LORD DUNPARK and LORD MAYFIELD delivered concurring opinions.

Notes

(1) For another example of this approach albeit on rather different facts in the context of **8–35** planning law see *Castelow v. Stirling District Council*, 1992 G.W.D. 19–1139 and contrast and an similar facts *Asda Stores Ltd v. Secretary of State for Scotland*, 1997 S.C.L.R. 661 and *Asda Stores Ltd v. Secretary of State for Scotland*, 1999 S.L.T. 503; see also *Campbell* above.

(2) In *R. v. Brent London Borough Council, ex p. Gunning* [1985] 84 L.G.R. 168 it was held by Hodgson J. that while there was no statutory duty placed on a local education authority to consult parents or pupils before making proposals for closure or amalgamation, parents nevertheless had a legitimate expectation that they would be consulted. That parents had an interest was implied by the whole statutory scheme. In terms of section 6 of the Education Act 1980, that interest is recognised and moreover, there were also duties on parents in relation to their child's education. Some of the authorities in any event had a practice of consultation with parents and as the proposals adopted were substantially different from those upon which some consultation had taken place, parents should have been given the further opportunity to be consulted. Controversially, it was stated (at 187) that legitimate expectation could be ...the same right as if it had been given by statute. However, in *R. v. Gwent County Council, ex p. Bryant, The Independent*, April 19, 1998, Hodgson J. accepted that he had gone too far and in the former case a defect in consultation could be rectified by the Secretary of State, and in the latter it could not; see also *Devon County Council, ex parte Baker* above and on this area generally see P. Meredith, "Legitimate Expectations and School Closures" [1988] P.L. 4.

(3) The conduct of the party claiming the expectation can be relevant in determining whether an expectation will be upheld. This takes a number of forms. First, where the circumstances giving rise to the expectation have been created by the person founding on them, then even though in other circumstances the expectation would be upheld, here it would not. In *Butt v. Secretary of State for the Home Department*, 1995 G.W.D. 16–905 Butt was detained under the Immigration Act 1971 under a deportation order. The order had been made some years earlier but to date had not been enforced. At the same time, ministerial guidance was issued to the effect that leave to rémain should be allowed where it was accepted that a genuine marriage had been entered into which had lasted for at least five years or that one or more children of the marriage had the right to stay in the United Kingdom. In 1994 Butt married and had a child who was born in 1995 in the United Kingdom. Towards the end of 1994, he applied to remain in the United Kingdom on the basis of the guidance. The Secretary of State refused that application. In early 1995 his wife gave birth. The child had the right to stay in the United Kingdom. He argued that the guidance gave him a legitimate expectation that he would be allowed to remain in the United Kingdom. When he had applied for leave to remain, he did not meet either of the qualifying conditions. When the guidance was announced in June 1992 he was not one of those to whom it applied but he thought himself to be within the circumstances covered by the guidance. It was not possible to create ones own expectation and, moreover, the legitimacy of it was in doubt given the existence of a deportation order.

8–36   (4) The second circumstance in which conduct might be relevant in determining whether a legitimate expectation exists or not is where a person's misconduct may deprive him of legitimate expectation. In *Cinnamond v. British Airports Authority* [1980] 1 WLR 582 the authority exercised its power under byelaws to stop six car-hire drivers from entering Heathrow airport until further notice. The drivers had convictions for loitering, an offence under the byelaws, and also had fines outstanding. The drivers argued that the notices were invalid and sought judicial review, arguing on the ground that they had not been given an opportunity to make out their case. Lord Denning M.R. observed (at 590) that the drivers had no legitimate expectation.

> "suppose that these car-hire drivers were of good character and had for years been coming into the airport under an implied licence to do so. If in that case there was suddenly a prohibition order preventing them from entering, then it would seem only fair that they should be given a hearing and a chance to put their case. But that is not this case. These men have a long record of convictions. They have large fines outstanding. They are continuing to engage in conduct which they must know is unlawful and contrary to the byelaws. When they were summoned for past offences, they put their case, no doubt, to the justices and to the Crown Court. Now when the patience of the authority is exhausted, it seems to me that the authority can properly suspend them until further notice — just like the police officer I mentioned. In the circumstances they had no legitimate expectation of being heard. It is not a necessary preliminary that they should have a hearing or be given a further chance to explain. Remembering always this: that it must have been apparent to them why the prohibition was ordered: and equally apparent that, if they had a change of heart and were ready to comply with the rules, no doubt the prohibition would be withdrawn. They could have made representations immediately, if they wished, in answer to the prohibition order. That they did not do."

See also Lord Shaw L.J. at 592 and Brandon L.J. at 593. S. de Smith, H. Woolf and J. Jowell, *Judicial Review of Administrative Action* (5th ed., 1995) doubt the validity of Lord Denning's approach (at p. 429):

> "it is wrong to suggest that a legitimate expectation can be forfeited, for example by unmeritorious conduct on the part of the applicant. Unless the expectation were expressly made conditional upon the applicant's 'good behaviour', the decision whether to rely on the expectation or to waive it lies with the applicant alone. It would also seem wrong to pre judge the merits of the applicant's present case on his previous wrong doing."

(5) The relationship between procedural legitimate expectation and consultation procedures and in particular administrative rule making should not be overlooked. On this see para. 5–18 and paras 2–6 and 2–42 respectively.

THE PROVISION OF REASONS

P.P. Craig, "The Common Law, Reasons and Administrative Justice"

1994 C.L.J. 283

"II. THE IMPORTANCE OF REASONS

Before examining the extent to which the common law presently insists upon the provision of reasons it may be helpful to review briefly why such an obligation is of importance. There are a number of specific advantages to be secured by insisting upon reasons for decisions.

First, reasons can assist the courts in performing their supervisory function. This supervisory function is often based on criteria such as whether the agency took account of relevant considerations or acted for improper purposes, and these criteria are much easier to apply if the agency's reasons are actually made evident.

Secondly, an obligation to provide reasons will often help to ensure that the decision has been thought through by the agency. This is particularly so where the agency in question deals with a large number of applications, or where the decision in question is of generalised importance for the functioning of that administrative system.

Thirdly, the provision of reasons can be of real significance in ensuring that other objectives of administrative law are not frustrated. If, for example, we decided to grant consultation rights in certain areas, then a duty to furnish reasons will make it more difficult for the decision-maker merely to go through the motions of hearing interested parties without actually taking their views into account.

Finally, a duty to give reasons can also perform a more general function. As Rabin has stated, the 'very essence of arbitrariness is to have one's status redefined by the state without an adequate explanation of its reasons for doing so'. By way of contrast the provision of reasons can increase public confidence in, and the legitimacy of, the administrative process.

A duty to provide reasons can, therefore, help to attain both the instrumental and non-instrumental objectives which underly process rights. The instrumental justification is based upon a causal connection between the presence of process rights and the accuracy of the outcome on the substance of the case: the substantive rule which is being applied will, it is thought, be more likely to be applied correctly if the individual is afforded the opportunity of being heard. The non-instrumental rationale for procedural rights has a rather different orientation. One basic aspect of this rationale is that it is part of what is owed to one as a person that one should be told what one is thought to have done and have some opportunity to respond. The Kafkaesque world is so nightmarish and dehumanising precisely because this is absent: the power of the state is brought to bear without the individual having any idea of what he or she is alleged to have done, and without any real possibility of responding to the 'charges'.

These foundational ideas have been recognised by the courts, and the important recent decision in *R. v. Secretary of State for the Home Department, ex p. Doody* [[1993] 3 All E.R. 92]succinctly captures the role which reasons can play in attaining both of these objectives. The case will be examined in detail below. Suffice to say for the present that the applicants were mandatory life prisoners who sought information as to why a penal element of a certain period of time had been chosen for their sentences. Lord Mustill gave the judgment of the House of Lords and indicated why this information was so important to the applicants. Having stated that the prisoners could deduce the length of the penal element Lord Mustill continued as follows [[1993] 3 All E.R. 92 at 98].

> So much each prisoner knows, but what he does not know is why the particular term was selected, and he is now trying to find out, partly from an obvious human desire to be told the reason for a decision so gravely affecting his future and partly because he hopes that once the information is obtained he may be able to point out errors of fact or reasoning and thereby persuade the Home Secretary to change his mind, or if he fails in this to challenge the decision in the courts.

The twin rationales behind the applicants' claim mentioned in this quotation reflect the non-instrumental and instrumental justifications for being accorded process rights. As Lord Mustill states, the information is desired in part on non-instrumental grounds: the applicants simply wish to know something which has such a marked impact upon their lives. The other reason for seeking the information is instrumental: they hope thereby to be able to show that the Home Secretary has made some error of fact or reasoning in applying the substantive rule to their particular cases."

Notes

(1) Other arguments in favour of the duty to give reasons are contained in the Justice-All Souls Report (at pp. 69–71). They include better informed decision making and public confidence

8–37

8–38

in the decision-making process. The main arguments against provision of reasons noted by the report included the need for free and uninhibited discussion, increased burden on the administration, delay and expense, the possibility of excessive challenge to decisions and the view that the existence of a duty would not necessarily mean that accurate or complete reasons would be given. The statutory, as opposed to any common law, duty to give reasons, is discussed at paras 12–33 to 12–37.

(2) Notwithstanding the arguments in favour of a general duty to give reasons, the basic position in both Scots and English law might be stated in the proposition that there is no general duty at common law for a decision maker to provide reasons for any decision made: see *Thomson, Petitioner*, 1989 S.L.T. 343 and *Purdon v. City of Glasgow District Licensing Board*, 1989 S.L.T. 201. However, based on some of the dicta in *Padfield v. Minister of Agriculture, Fisheries and Food* [1968] A.C. 997, extracted at para. 6–13, the absence of reasons for a decision might infer that only bad and undisclosed reasons existed.

The idea that silence as to reasons might infer improper reasons for a decision has been used in a number of cases. In *R. v. Civil Service Appeal Board, ex parte Cunningham* [1991] 4 All E.R. 310 Cunningham, a prison officer, was dismissed from the prison service after an alleged assault on a prisoner. The Civil Service Appeal Board held the dismissal to be unfair and recommended reinstatement but the Home Office refused to do so. The board assessed compensation at £6,500 but an industrial tribunal would have assessed the compensation at nearer £15,000. The board refused to give any reasons for its award, citing the justification that the simple procedure adopted would become cumbersome if reasons had to be provided. Cunningham sought judicial review. Lord Donaldson M.R., although rejecting any suggestion that there was a general duty to provide reasons at common law, observed (at 319) that if justice required reasons to be given then a duty would be imposed. The board was required to state its reasons:

> "to show to what they were directing their mind and thereby indirectly showing not whether their decision was right or wrong, which is a matter solely for them, but whether their decision was lawful. Any other conclusion would reduce the board to the status of a free-wheeling palm tree."

In *Dumbarton District Council v. Commission for Local Authority Accounts in Scotland*, 1993 G.W.D. 34–2160 Lord Marnoch reduced a recommendation by the commission on surcharge on the ground of its irrationality, considering that its findings were not properly explained and justified. See also *R.v. Penwith District Council, ex parte May*, November, 22, 1985, unreported where a decision to prevent CND from selling literature and badges by a local authority, which now required the activity to be licensed when before it was unlicensed, without reasons being given, was held to be irrational and unlawful.

8–39   (3) *Padfield* has its limitations. In *R.v. Secretary of State for Trade and Industry, ex parte Lonrho plc* [1989] 2 All E.R. 609 Lonrho plc sought disclosure of a report prepared by the Department of Trade and Industry into the acquisition of the House of Fraser group. The Serious Fraud Office was also investigating and the Secretary of State announced that the DTI report would not be released until the investigations of the SFO were concluded. Lonrho, which for years had been attempting to obtain a controlling interest in the Harrods store owned by the House of Fraser, sought disclosure of the DTI report and at first instance judicial review of the refusal to do so was granted. This was overturned by the Court of Appeal and the matter came to be considered by the House of Lords per Lord Keith of Kinkel:

> "*Padfield v. Minister of Agriculture, Fisheries and Food* [1968] A.C.997 was relied upon by Lonrho to support two limbs of their argument. First it was said to support a construction of the Act that imposed a duty on the Secretary of State to make a reference to the M.M.C., and secondly, the fact that the Secretary of State had given no reason for his decision not to make a reference led to the conclusion that no rational reason existed for his decision. In my view that case does not support either limb of the argument. The decision in *Padfield* turned on the construction of the Agricultural Marketing Act 1958...
> Although reference was made to the judgment of Sir John Donaldson M.R. in *R.v. Lancashire Country Council, ex p. Huddleston* [1986] 2 All E.R. 941 in which he referred to the desirability

of proceedings for judicial review being conducted with the cards face up on the table, it was not submitted to your Lordships that there was any general duty to give reasons for a decision in all cases, nor was it submitted that this Act imposed a particular duty on the Secretary of State to give reasons for his refusal to make a reference to the M.M.C.; and it is not the practice of the Secretary of State to give reasons when he decides not to make a reference to the M.M.C.

The absence of reasons for a decision where there is no duty to give them cannot of itself provide any support for the suggested irrationality of the decision. The only significance of the absence of reasons is that if all other known facts and circumstances appear to point overwhelmingly in favour of a different decision, the decision-maker who has given no reasons cannot complain if the court draws the inference that he had no rational reason for his decision."

On this see D.G.T. Williams, "Unfettered Discretion" (1989) 48 C.L.J. 161 and see also *R.v. Inland Revenue Commissioners, ex parte T.C. Coombs & Co.* [1991] 2 A.C. 283, H.L., reversing the Court of Appeal, Lord Lowry stated (at 301) that "If ...a strong case" was made for quashing a notice under the Taxes Management Act 1970, s. 20(3) which required the production of documents "it may be the duty of the revenue to meet that case with something more cogent than silence, however understandable or justifiable". Lonrho was in turn followed in *Bass Taverns Ltd v. Clydebank District Licensing Board*, 1995 S.L.T. 1275. Licence holders who had previously been granted a regular extension of permitted hours on certain mornings, evenings and Sunday afternoons, sought a further application for regular extension in respect of morning periods on a Monday to Saturday but this was refused as a result of change of board policy. The applicant contended that the decision was irrational where there was no suggestion of any change of circumstances since the earlier application had been granted, particularly as no reasons had been given for refusal. In relation to that argument, Lord Sutherland observed (at 1277):

"I accept entirely the test laid down by Lord Keith in the case of *R v Trade and Industry Secretary, ex p Lonrho plc* when his Lordship points out that the absence of reasons for a decision when there is no duty to give them cannot of itself provide any support for the suggested irrationality of the decisions. The only significance of the absence of reasons it that if all other known facts and circumstances appear to point overwhelmingly in favour of a different decision, the decision maker who has given no reasons cannot complain if the court draws the inference that he had no rational reason for his decision. As I have pointed out ...the decision taken by the respondents in this case cannot be said to be plainly irrational simply because they have changed their view as to whether or not it is desirable for early morning extensions to be granted. That was the policy which they were entitled to make and which is not said to be unreasonable..."

See also *Atherton v. Strathclyde Regional Council*, 1994 G.W.D. 1-1 and *Martin v. City of Dundee District Licensing Board*, 1994 G.W.D. 2–108.

Another basis upon which a duty to give reasons might be founded, that of the requirement of fairness, is considered in the next extract.

R. v. Secretary of State for the Home Department, ex parte Doody

[1994] 1 A.C. 531

"The respondents, Doody and three others, were prisoners who had been convicted of murder and sentenced to a mandatory term of life imprisonment. After consulting the trial judge and the Lord Chief Justice, the Home Secretary (or another Minister at the Home Office) determined the period of imprisonment (the tariff or penal element) that the respondents should serve before the Parole Board would consider whether to recommend, to the Home Secretary, that the prisoner could be released on life licence. The respondents sought judicial review of the Home Secretary's decisions regarding the penal elements of their sentences on the ground that he had followed an unfair procedure. One significant element in the respondents' challenge was their argument that fairness required the Home Secretary to give reasons where he decided to impose a different penalty element from that recommended by the judiciary. The High Court dismissed the application, but on appeal the Court of Appeal decided in part in favour of the respondents. The Home Secretary appealed to the House of Lords."

8–40

LORD MUSTILL: "My Lords, the sentencing of a convicted murderer according to English law is a unique formality. Although it is a very grave occasion it is a formality in this sense, that the task of the judge is entirely mechanical. Once a verdict of guilty is returned the outcome is preordained. No matter what the opinion of the judge on the moral quality of the act, no matter what circumstances there may be of mitigation or aggravation, there is only one course for him to take, namely to pass a sentence of life imprisonment.

This purely formal character of the sentencing proces is unique in more than one respect. Thus, whilst it is true that there are other, comparatively unimportant, offences where a particular sentence, or component of a sentence, is prescribed by law, there is in practice no other offence besides murder for which a custodial sentence is mandatory. This singularity is not to be accounted for by the fact that the crime has resulted in the death of the victim, since although the offence of manslaughter carries a maximum penalty of life imprisonment the sentence is discretionary and the maximum is rarely imposed; and other offences in which the death of the victim is an element are subject to maximum fixed terms. Nor can the uniqueness of the mandatory sentence of murder be ascribed to the uniquely wicked quality of the intent which accompanies the fatal act, since as every law student knows, although many who speak in public on the subject appear to overlook, it is possible to commit murder without intending to kill, and many of those convicted of murder have intended to do no more than commit grievous bodily harm. In truth the mandatory life sentence for murder is symbolic.

The sentence of life imprisonment is also unique in that the words which the judge is required to pronounce do not mean what they say. Whilst in a very small minority of cases the prisoner is in the event confined for the rest of his natural life, this is not the usual or the intended effect of a sentence of life imprisonment, as a judge faced with a hard case will take pains to explain to the offender before sentence is passed. But although everyone knows what the words do not mean, nobody knows what they do mean, since the duration of the prisoner's detention depends on a series of recommendations to, and executive decisions by, the Home Secretary, some made at an early stage and others much later, none of which can be accurately forecast at the time when the offender is sent to prison.

There is, however, another form of life sentence, of which the philosophy, statutory framework and executive practice are quite different even though the words pronounced by the judge are the same. This is the discretionary life sentence...

The discretionary life sentence may thus be regarded as the sum of two sentences, to be served consecutively. First, a determinate number of years appropriate to the nature and gravity of the offence. This is often called the 'tariff' element of the sentence. For my part, although I recognise that this is not inappropriate in the context of a discretionary life sentence, I consider that for reasons which I will later develop it is illogical and misleading when the usage is transferred to a mandatory sentence. I therefore prefer to avoid this terminology and will instead call the first component of the life sentence the 'penal element'. The second component is an undeterminate period, which the offender begins to serve when the penal element is exhausted. I will call this the 'risk element'...

My Lords, I believe that this summary has shown how, in contrast with the position as regards discretionary life sentences, the theory and the practice for convicted murderers are out of tune. The theory — and it is the only theory which can justify the retention of the mandatory life sentence — was restated by Mrs Rumbold, Minister of State at the Home Office in 1991 less than two years ago. It posits that murder is an offence so grave that the proper 'tariff' sentence is invariably detention for life, although as a measure of leniency it may be mitigated by release on licence. Yet the practice established by Mr Brittan, Home Secretary in 1983 and still in force founds on the proposition that there is concealed within the life term a fixed period of years, apt to reflect not only the requirements of deterrence, but also the moral quality of the individual act (retribution). These two philosophies of sentencing are inconsistent. Either may be defensible, but they cannot both be applied at the same time.

I make this point, not to argue for one regime rather than another, nor to suggest that each of them is unsatisfactory. This is a question for Parliament and we must take the law as it stands. The importance of the inconsistency for present purposes is that the choice of the theory goes a long way towards determining the requirements of fairness with which the practice should conform...

For this reason I believe it impossible to proceed any distance towards determining the present appeal without deciding which of the two competing philosophies is to form the starting point. As it seems to me, the only possible choice is the regime installed by Mr Brittan, as later modified. This is the regime by which successive Home Secretaries have chosen to exercise the wide powers conferred by Parliament, and the arguments have throughout assumed that the regime is faimly in place, and that the task of the courts is to decide what the elements of fairness demand as to the working out of that regime, in the light of the sentencing philosophy which is expressed to underlie it. This being so, I think it essential not to cloud the discussion by introducing the inconsistent theory enunciated by the Minister of State, and I shall leave this entirely out of account...

What does fairness require in the present case? My Lords, I think it unnecessary to refer by name or to quote from, any of the often-cited authorities in which the courts have explained what is essentially an intuitive judgment. They are far too well known. From them, I derive the following. (1) Where an Act of Parliament confers an administrative power there is a presumption that it will be exercised in a manner which is fair in all the circumstances. (2) The standards of fairness are not immutable. They may change with the passage of time, both in the general and in their application to decisions of a particular type. (3) The principles of fairness are not to be applied by rote identically in every situation. What fairness demands is dependent on the context of the decision, and this is to be taken into account in all its aspects. (4) An essential feature of the context is the statute which creates the discretion, as regards both its language and the shape of the legal and administrative system within which the decision is taken. (5) Fairness will very often require that a person who may be adversely affected by the decision will have an opportunity to make representations on his own behalf either before the decision is taken with a view to producing a favourable result, or after it is taken, with a view to procuring its modification, or both. (6) Since the person affected usually cannot make worthwhile representations without knowing what factors may weigh against his interests fairness will very often require that he is informed of the gist of the case which he has to answer.

My Lords, the Secretary of State properly accepts that whatever the position may have been in the past these principles apply in their generality to prisoners, including persons serving life sentences for murder, although their particular situation and the particular statutory regime under which they are detained may require the principles to be applied in a special way. Convesely, the respondents acknowledge that it is not enough for them to persuade the court that some procedure other than the one adopted by the decision-maker would be better or more fair. Rather, they must show that the procedure is actually unfair. The court must constantly bear in mind that it is to the decision-maker, not the court, that Parliament has entrusted not only the making of the decision but also the choice as to how the decision is made.

I accept without hesitation, and mention it only to avoid misunderstanding, that the law does not at present recognise a general duty to give reasons for an administrative decision. Nevertheless, it is equally beyond question that such a duty may in appropriate circumstances be implied, and I agree with the analyses by the Court of Appeal in *R. v. Civil Service Appeal Board, ex p. Cunningham* [1991] 4 All E.R. 310 of the factors which will often be material to such an implication.

Turning to the present dispute I doubt the wisdom of discussing the problem in the contempoary vocabulary of "prisoner's rights", given that as a result of his own act the position of the prisoner is so forcibly distanced from that of the ordinary citizen, nor is it very helpful to say that the Home Secretary should out of simple humanity provide reasons for the prisoner, since any society which operates a penal system is bound to treat some of its citizens in a way which would, in the general, be thought inhumane. I prefer simply to assert that within the inevitable constraints imposed by the statutory framework, the general shape of the administrative regime which ministers have lawfully built around it, and the imperatives of the public interest, the Secretary of State ought to implement the scheme as fairly as he can. The giving of reasons may be inconvenient, but I can see no ground at all why it should be against the public interest: indeed, rather the reverse. This being so, I would ask simply: is a refusal to give reasons fair? I would answer without hesitation that it is not. As soon as the jury returns its verdict the offender knows that he will be locked up for a very long time. For just how long immediately becomes the most important thing in the prisoner's life. When looking at statistics it is easy to fall into the way of thinking that there is not really very much difference between one extremely long sentence and another: and there may not be, in percentage terms. But the percentage reflects a difference of a year or years: a long time for anybody, and longer still for a prisoner. Where a defendant is convicted of, say, several armed robberies he knows that he faces a stiff sentence: he can be advised by reference to a public tariff of the range of sentences he must expect; he hears counsel address the judge on the relationship between his offences and the tariff; he will often hear the judge give an indication during exchanges with counsel of how his mind is working; and when sentence is pronounced he will always be told the reasons for it. So also when a discretionary life sentence is imposed, coupled with an order under s.34. Contrast this with the position of the prisoner sentenced for murder. He never sees the Home Secretary; he has no dialogue with him: he cannot fathom how his mind is working. There is no true tariff, or at least no tariff exposed to public view which might give the prisoner an idea of what to expect. The announcement of his first review date arrives out of thin air, wholly without explanation. The distant oracle has spoken, and that is that.

My Lords, I am not aware that there still exists anywhere else in the penal system a procedure remotely resembling this. The beginnings of an explanation for its unique character might perhaps be found if the Executive had still been putting into practice the theory that the tariff sentence for murder is confinement for life, subject only to a wholly discretionary release on licence: although even in such a case I doubt whether in the modern climate of administrative law such an entirely secret process could be justified. As I hope to have shown, however, this is no longer the practice, and can hardly be sustained any longer as the theory. I therefore simply ask, is it fair that the mandatory life prisoner should be wholly deprived of the information which all other prisoners receive as a matter of course? I am clearly of the opinion that it is not.

My Lords, I can moreover arrive at the same conclusion by a different and more familiar route, of which *ex p. Cunningham* [1991] 4 All E.R. 310 provides a recent example. It is not, as I understand it, questioned that the decision of the Home Secretary on the penal element is susceptible to judicial review. To mount an effective attack on the decision, given no more material than the facts of the offence and the length of the penal element, the prisoner has virtually no means of ascertaining whether this is an instance where the decision-making process has gone astray. I think it important that there should be an effective means of detecting the kind of error which would entitle the court to intervene, and in practice I regard it as necessary for this purpose that the reasoning of the Home Secretary should be disclosed. If there is any difference between the penal element recommended by the judges and actually imposed by the Home Secretary, this reasoning is bound to include, either explicitly or implicitly, a reason why the Home Secretary has taken a different view. Accordingly, I consider that the respondents are entitled to an affirmative answer on the third issue...

'It is declared that: (1) The Secretary of State is required to afford to a prisoner serving a mandatory life sentence the opportunity to submit in writing representations as to the period he should serve for the purposes of retribution and deterrence before the Secretary of State sets the date of the first review of the prisoner's sentence. (2) Before giving the prisoner the opportunity to make such representations, the Secretary of State is required to inform him of the period recommended by the judiciary as the period he should serve for the purposes of retribution and deterrence, and of any other opinion expressed by the judiciary which is relevant to the Secretary of State's decision as to the appropriate period to be served for these purposes. (3) Secretary of State is obliged to give reasons for departing from the period recommended by the judiciary as the period which he should serve for the purposes of retribution and deterrence.' "

LORDS KEITH, LANE, TEMPLEMAN and BROWNE-WILKINSON agreed with the speech given by Lord Mustill.

Notes

8–41   (1) While restating the lack of a general duty to give reasons, Lord Mustill provides a broad basis upon which a duty to provide reasons in specific circumstances might well be found. The significance of the approach in *Doody* is apparent when one considers the grounds upon which allegations of illegality or irrationality in administrative decision making might be made. Consider, for example, the cases where it is alleged that a body acted for an improper purpose or on an irrelevant consideration. Unless one can establish the reasons for a decision, then review will be difficult. For commentary see N.R. Campbell "The duty to give reasons in administrative law" [1994] P.L. 184 and Craig above.

(2) The ambit of the duty to give reasons was considered in *R. v. Higher Education Funding Council, ex p. Institute of Dental Surgery* [1994] 1 All E.R. 651. The institute had its output assessed by a funding council. The council awarded a lower grade to the institute's work compared to its previous grade and as a result it lost £270,000 in funding. No reasons were given on the basis that the matter was one of professional judgment. The institute sought judicial review of the decision on the basis of the violation of a duty to give reasons based on the obligation of fairness. Sedley J. observed (at 666):

"each case will come to rest between two poles, or possibly at one of them: the decision which cries out for reasons, and the decision for which reasons are entirely inapposite. Somewhere between the two poles comes the dividing line separating those cases in which the balance of factors calls for reasons from those where it does not. At present there is no sure indication of where the division comes. ...No doubt the common law will develop, as the common law does, case by case. It is not entirely satisfactory that this should be so, not least because experience suggests that in the absence of a prior principle irreconcilable or inconsistent decisions will emerge ...At present, however, this court cannot go beyond the proposition that, there being no general obligation to give reasons, there will be decisions for which fairness does not demand reasons."

Commenting on *Doody* he concluded (at 672):

"1. There is no general duty to give reasons for a decision, but there are classes of case where there is such a duty.

2. One such class is where the subject matter is an interest so highly regarded by the law — for example personal liberty — that fairness requires that reasons, at least for particular decisions, be given as of right.

3. (a) Another such class is where the decision appears aberrant. Here fairness may require reasons so that the recipient may know whether the aberration is in the legal sense real (and so challengeable) or apparent. (b) It follows that this class does not include decisions which are themselves challengeable by reference only to the reasons for them. A pure exercise of academic judgment is such a decision."

If the criterion of fairness had been adopted in *Bass Taverns* above would be decision have been different? Could the petitioner have argued that a legitimate expectation existed? If so, would it have made a difference?

(3) Subsequent to *Doody*, in a number of cases, fairness has obliged the Home Secretary to give reasons for refusal of entry clearance for an alien to enter the United Kingdom: *R. v. Secretary of State for the Home Department, ex parte Moon, The Times*, December 8, 1995 and at common law the Home Secretary is obliged to give reasons for a refusal to accept an application for naturalisation as a British citizen: *R. v. Secretary of State for the Home Department, ex p. Fayed* [1997] 1 All E.R. 228 above, although section 44 (2) of the British Nationality Act 1981 overrode that duty. Fairness does not, however, require the local authority to give reasons for refusing housing renovation grant: *R. v. Bristol County Council, exp. Bailey* [1994] 27 H.L.R. 307, nor does it oblige a planning authority to give reasons for the grant of planning permission or where permission is granted after an earlier refusal: *R. v. Aylesbury Vale District Council, ex p. Chaplin, The Times*, July 23, 1996.

8–42

(4) The extent to which fairness obliges the giving of reasons in Scots law is yet to be authoritatively determined, although there has been evidence in recent cases that the general approach found in the English case law might be followed here as well. For discussion see C.R. Munro, "The Duty to Give Reasons for Decisions", 1995 S.L.T. (News) 5.

In *Lawrie v. Commission for Local Authority Accounts in Scotland*, 1994 S.L.T. 1185 the commission investigated the affairs of a certain local authority and found that a loss of around £24 million had been sustained. Under section 103(3) of the Local Government (Scotland) Act 1973 the commission recommended to the Secretary of State that an order be made requiring the persons responsible to repay the money to the authority. These persons were officers of the local authority who petitioned for judicial review of the commission's findings arguing that, on the basis of *Lonrho*, no good reasons existed as the decision was patently irrational and, alternatively, that fairness required reasons to be given where the facts established by the commission did not appear to support its findings. Lord Prosser had regard to *Cunningham* and *Doody* and concluded that *Cunningham* was authority for the view that the duty to give reasons might exist where the decision maker was acting in a judicial, as opposed to an administrative, manner. He concluded that the commission was acting in an administrative manner.

This seems to be at odds with the broader reading of *Cunningham* given in *Doody* and moreover, classification of function has never been much favoured in Scots law in assessing the applicability of the right to a hearing. *Lawrie* is perhaps an unsatisfactory case, although some support for Lord Prosser's position was expressed recently in *Swan v. Secretary of State for Scotland (No. 2)*, 1999 G.W.D. 16–761. Lord Prosser was perhaps influenced by the fact that there was in his view sufficient in the commissioner's report in any event to infer proper reasons. A classificatory approach was used in *W. v. Criminal Injuries Compensation Board*, 1999 G.W.D. 14–631 to hold that the board as a quasi-judicial body was required to allow a claimant to know why a decision refusing compensation was made.

(5) In *Ritchie v. Secretary of State for Scotland*, 1999 S.L.T. 55, *Doody* was relied upon to argue that the Secretary of State was obliged by fairness to invite a prisoner to make representations on a decision by the Secretary of State to change a review of sentence and eligibility to every two years instead of every one year. He was entitled to know why this change had occurred and to make representations as to why it should not apply in his case. *Ritchie* clearly falls within the second of the categories identified by Sedley J. The argument identified by Craig, that a right of appeal will more readily infer a right to reasons, was examined

in *Dundee United Football Co. Ltd v. Scottish Football Association*, 1998 S.L.T. (Notes) 1244. Here, judicial review was sought by Dundee United Football Club of a decision of the Scottish Football League appeals committee, including inter alia, a decision not to provide reasons for upholding an appeal against the decision of the club to terminate the contract of one of its players. Lord Bonomy stated (at 1244):

> "In my opinion the existence of a right of appeal is a factor strongly indicative of an obligation on the decision maker to give reasons for his decision. Whether or not there is a duty to give reasons will depend on the particular circumstances of the decision being made.
>
> ...It is my opinion that in general the issues before the appellate body, viz, the association, would be more clearly identified, and the arguments presented would be more focused, were reasons for the decision appealed against given ...in the absence of written reasons for a decision affecting the livelihood or major commercial interest of a party, the failure of the league to give written reasons for the decision or to explain the position at the appeal hearing before the association could lead the court to conclude that the association were acting unfairly by adjudicating on the appeal without insisting on the reasons for the original decision being made known to the appellant."

(5) Where fairness requires reasons to be given, the adequacy of those reasons will be examined. In *R. v. Secretary of State for Transport, ex parte Richmond upon Thames London Borough Council (No. 4)* [1996] 4 All E.R. 903 the Court of Appeal observed per Brooke L.J. at 919:

> "The question the court has to decide, therefore, is whether the reasons in fact given by the minister enable the reader to know what conclusions he has reached on the principal important controversial issues."

LIMITS ON THE RIGHT TO A HEARING

NATIONAL SECURITY

R. v. Secretary of State for Home Affairs, ex parte Hosenball

[1977] 1 W.L.R. 766

8–43   "The appellant was a United States citizen who worked as a journalist in the United Kingdom. At first he worked for the weekly journal *Time Out* and was responsible for an article entitled 'The Eavesdroppers' about communications monitoring by the Government, which appeared in May 1976. During July 1976, Hosenball moved to the *Evening Standard* as a general news reporter. In November 1976, he was informed that the Home Secretary had decided to deport him on the grounds that Hosenball's 'departure from the United Kingdom would be conducive to the public good as being in the interests of national security'. The Home Secretary considered that Hosenball had sought and obtained for publication information harmful to the security of the United Kingdom and prejudicial to the safety of Crown servants. Hosenball had no right of appeal against the decision under the terms of the Immigration Act 1971. However, he was given a non-statutory hearing before 'three advisers' (appointed by the Home Secretary) who reported back in confidence to the Secretary of State. The Home Secretary later made a deportation against Hosenball. Hosenball then applied for an order of cèrtiorari to quash the deportation order on the ground, inter alia, that the principle of audi alteram partem had been breached by the failure to supply him with details of the case against him prior to his appearance before the 'three advisers'. The High Court dismissed Hosenball's application and he then appealed to the Court of Appeal."

LORD DENNING M.R.: "...Now I would like to say at once that if this were a case in which the ordinary rules of natural justice were to be observed, some criticism could be directed upon it. For one thing, the Home Secretary himself, and I expect the advisory panel also, had a good deal of confidential information before them of which Mr Hosenball knew nothing and was told nothing: and which he had no opportunity of correcting or contradicting; or of testing by cross-examination. In addition, he was not given sufficient information of the charges against him so as to be able effectively to deal with them or answer them. All this could be urged as a ground for upsetting any ordinary decision of a court of law or of any tribunal, statutory or domestic: see *Kanda v. Government of Malaya* [1962] A.C. 322, 337.

But this is no ordinary case. It is a case in which national security is involved: and our history shows that, when the state itself is endangered, our cherished freedoms may have to take second place. Even natural justice itself may suffer a set-back. Time after time Parliament has so enacted and the courts have loyalty followed. In the first world war in *R. v. Halliday* [1917] A.C. 260, 270 Lord Finlay L.C. said: 'The danger of espionage and of damage by secret agents …had to be guarded against.' In the second world war in *Liversidge v. Sir John Anderson* [1942] A.C. 206, 219 Lord Maugham said:

> '…there may be certain persons against whom no offence is proved nor any charge formulated, but as regards whom it may be expedient to authorise the Secretary of State to make an order for detention.'

That was said in time of war. But times of peace hold their dangers too. Spies, subverters and saboteurs may be mingling amongst us, putting on a most innocent exterior. They may be endangering the lives of the men in our secret service, as Mr Hosenball is said to do.

If they are British subjects, we must deal with them here. If they are foreigners, they can be deported. The rules of natural justice have to be modified in regard to foreigners here who prove themselves unwelcome and ought to be deported…

So it seems to me that when the national security is at stake even the rules of natural justice may have to be modified to meet the position. I would refer in this regard to the speech of Lord Reid in *R. v. Lewes JJ., ex p. Secretary of State for the Home Department* [1973] A.C. 388, 402…

The information supplied to the Home Secretary by the Security Service is, and must be, highly confidential. The public interest in the security of the realm is so great that the sources of the information must not be disclosed — not should the nature of the information itself be disclosed — if there is any risk that it would lead to the sources being discovered. The reason is because, in this very secretive field, our enemies might try to eliminate the sources of information. So the sources must not be disclosed. Not even to the House of Commons. Nor to any tribunal or court of inquiry or body of advisers, statutory or non-statutory. Save to the extent that the Home Secretary thinks safe. Great as is the public interest in the freedom of the individual and the doing of justice to him, nevertheless in the last resort it must take second place to the security of the country itself…

There is a conflict here between the interests of national security on the one hand and the freedom of the individual on the other. The balance between these two is not for a court of law. It is for the Home Secretary. He is the person entrusted by Parliament with the task. In some parts of the world national security has on occasions been used as an excuse for all sorts of infringements of individual liberty. But not in England. Both during the wars and after them, successive ministers have discharged their duties to the complete satisfaction of the people at large. They have set up advisory committees to help them, usually with a chairman who has done everything he can to ensure that justice is done. They have never interfered with the liberty or the freedom of movement of any individual except where it is absolutely necessary for the safety of the state. In this case we are assured that the Home Secretary himself gave it his personal consideration, and I have no reason whatever to doubt the care with which he considered the whole matter. He is answerable to Parliament as to the way in which he did it and not to the courts here.

I would dismiss the appeal."

GEOFFREY LANE L.J.: "There are occasions, though they are rare, when what are more generally the rights of an individual must be subordinated to the protection of the realm. When an alien visitor to this country is believed to have used the hospitality extended to him so as to present a danger to security, the Secretary of State has the right and, in many cases, has the duty of ensuring that the alien no longer remains here to threaten our security. It may be that the alien has been in the country for many years. It may be that he has built a career here in this country, and that consequently a deportation order made against him may result in great hardship to him. It may be that he protests that he has done nothing wrong so far as this country's security is concerned. It may be that he protests that he cannot understand why any action of this sort is being taken against him. In ordinary circumstances common fairness — you can call it natural justice if you wish — would demand that he be given particulars of the charges made against him; that he be given the names of the witnesses who are prepared to testify against him and, indeed, probably the nature of the evidence which those witnesses are prepared to give should also be delivered to him. But there are counter-balancing factors…

It may well be that if an alien is told with particularity what it is said he has done it will become quite obvious to him from whence that information has been received. The only person who can judge whether such a result is likely is the person who has in his possession all the information available. That, in this case, is the Secretary of State himself. If he comes to the conclusion that for reasons such as those which I have just endeavoured to outline he cannot afford to give the alien more than the general charge against him, there one has the dilemma. The alien certainly has inadequate information upon which to prepare or direct his defence to the various charges which are made against him, and the only way that could be remedied would be to disclose information to him which might probably have an adverse effect on the national security. The choice is regrettably clear: the alien must suffer, if suffering there be, and this is so on whichever basis of argument one chooses…

Different principles and strict principles apply where matters of the safety of the realm are at stake. What is fair cannot be decided in a vacuum: it has to be determined against the whole background of any particular case. The advisory panel system is an effort to ensure fairness as far as possible in these difficult circumstances, but in the end it is the Secretary of State who must in those circumstances be trusted to speak the last word…

I would dismiss the appeal."

CUMMING-BRUCE L.J. "I agree with all that has fallen from Lord Denning M.R. and Geoffrey Lane L.J.…."

Notes

8–44   (1) Claims of national security have, however, been more closely scrutinised where the European Court of Human Rights has been asked to examine whether a breach of the Convention has occurred. In *Chahal v. United Kingdom* (1997) 23 E.H.R.R. 413 the European Court of Human Rights held that the limited review offered by the (English) High Court and panel of three advisers in relation to a potential national security deportee did not comply with Article 5 (4) of the Convention, which provides for the right to seek review by a court of the lawfulness of detention. During the 1991 Gulf War the Home Secretary deported a number of Iraqis and other Arabs living in Britain on the ground of national security. A Lebanese who had lived here for 15 years sought judicial review. He argued that the denial of legal representation and the lack of detailed allegations against him amounted to a breach of natural justice. Lord Donaldson M.R., rejecting this, observed (at 335): "natural justice has to take account of realities and something which would otherwise constitute a breach it was not to be so considered if it is avoidable"; see also *R. v. Secretary of State for the Home Department, ex parte Cheblak* [1991] 2 All E.R. 319 and I. Leigh, "The Gulf War Departations and the Courts" [1991] P.L. 331. The Government's legislative response was the Special Immigration Appeals Commission Act 1997 which creates, inter alia, a special commission to deal with circumstances like those in *Chahal*, with the membership consisting of one person who has held judicial office, one who must have served as a chief adjudicator under the Immigration Act 1971 and a third member, who will in practice have experience of national security matters. On this see I. Dickinson "The Sequel to *Chahal v UK*", 1998 S.L.T. (News) 31.

(2) In *Hewitt and Harman v. United Kingdom* (1989) 67 D.R. 88 the European Commission on Human Rights rejected the analysis of Lord Denning in *Hosenball* in reaching its opinion that the security service had violated the right to privacy guaranteed under Article 8 of the convention by secret information gathering. The Government's response was the Security Service Act 1989 which placed the security service on a statutory basis and created a tribunal to deal with complaints against the organisation. Further reforms are contained in the Intelligence Services Act 1994.

(3) European Community law is also a source of challenge to judicial conservatism. In *Johnston v. Chief Constable of the Royal Ulster Constabulary* (Case 222/84) [1986] E.C.R. 1651; [1987] 1 Q.B. 129 a woman police constable in Northern Ireland challenged a rule of the RUC which discriminated between male and female police officers as being in breach of the Equal Treatment Directive. The Secretary of State certified the rule as made for the purpose of safeguarding national security and for protecting public safety and further, under Northern Ireland statute, the certificate was deemed to be conclusive evidence of all matters stated therein. The European Court of Justice held that this rule could not exclude judicial review of the matter totally since this would deprive the court of effective control and the court required to examine whether the rule had been properly made for safeguarding national security in public safety. See too *R. v. Secretary of State for the Home Department, ex parte Gallagher, The Times,*

February 16, 1994 (Court of Appeal) and *The Times*, December 12, 1995 (European Court of Justice), which held that before the right in European Community law to freedom of movement could be denied to a community national by an exclusion order under the terms of the Prevention of Terrorism (Temporary Provisions) Act 1989, the Government was required to show that the person appointed by the Government to listen to arguments why exclusion should not be implemented was able to act in an independent manner and, except in cases of urgency, this authority should also be able to give an opinion on the proposed expulsion before it was confirmed by the Government: see too *R. v. Secretary of State for the Home Department, ex parte McQuillan* [1995] 4 All E.R. 400. For further discussion of arguments based on national security or public interest, see Finch and Ashton, pp. 359–362.

EMERGENCY ACTION

R. v. Secretary of State for Transport, ex parte Pegasus Holdings (London) Ltd

[1988] 1 W.L.R. 990

"The applicant companies provided foreign holidays from the United Kingdom and used aircraft chartered from a Romanian organisation and flown by a Romanian crew. In order for the Romanian aircraft and crew to be allowed to operate such holiday flights from the United Kingdom they had received a permit from the Secretary of State granted under the authority of the Air Navigation Order 1985, Article 83. Article 62 of the Order empowered the Transport Secretary to provisionally suspend permits if he thought fit, pending a full investigation of the matter. During the middle of July 1987, five Romanian pilots voluntarily undertook flying tests conducted by the British Civil Aviation Authority; all these pilots failed the test (four displayed an inability to manoeuvre the aircraft). On July 29 at midday, the Department of Transport received a letter from the CAA, informing them of these test results. During the ensuing afternoon the Department alerted the applicants to the concerns of the CAA. On July 30 the Secretary of State signed provisional suspension orders (made under Article 62) regarding the Romanians' permit to operate the holiday charter flights from the United Kingdom. This decision caused the applicant package holiday company great difficulties in transporting its customers. The applicants sought a judicial review of the decision of the Transport Secretary, claiming, inter alia, that the suspension orders had been made in breach of the requirements of natural justice."

8–45

SCHIEMANN J.: "…So far as the law is concerned, I do not think that there is anything between the parties as to the principles to be applied. These are conveniently set out in the leading case of *Wiseman v. Borneman* [1971] A.C. 297, where Lord Guest, at 311, cites an earlier judgment by Tucker L.J. in *Russell v. Duke of Norfolk* [1949] 1 All E.R. 109, 118 in which Tucker L.J. opined:

'There are, in my view, no words which are of universal application to every kind of inquiry and every kind of domestic tribunal. The requirements of natural justice must depend on the circumstances of the case, the nature of the inquiry, the rules under which the tribunal is acting, the subject-matter that is being dealt with, and so forth. Accordingly, I do not derive much assistance from the definitions of natural justice which have been from time to time used, but, whatever standard is adopted, one essential is that the person concerned should have a reasonable opportunity of presenting his case.'

Mr Flint accepts that the opportunity to state a case can in certain circumstances be excluded in relation to such provisional matters as those with which I am concerned but says that they should not be excluded unless the situation genuinely demands it.

Mr Pannick referred me to a Court of Appeal case, *Lewis v. Heffer* [1978] 1 W.L.R. 1061, where there are discussions in the various unreserved judgments delivered by the court that are not precisely to the same effect in what they say. In particular, he drew my attention to the following comments of Lord Denning M.R., at 1073. After having quoted Megarry J. in *John v. Rees* [1970] Ch. 345 where he had said, at 397:

'suspension is merely expulsion pro tanto. Each is penal, and each deprives the member concerned of the enjoyment of his rights of membership or office. Accordingly, in my judgment the rules of natural justice prima facie apply to any such process of suspension in the same way that they apply to expulsion.'

Lord Denning M.R. went on to say:

'Those words apply, no doubt, to suspensions which are inflicted by way of punishment: as for instance when a member of the Bar is suspended from practice for six months, or when a solicitor is suspended from practice. But they do not apply to suspensions which are made, as a holding operation, pending inquiries. Very often irregularities are disclosed in a government department or in a business house: and a man may be suspended on full pay pending inquiries. Suspicion may rest on him: and so he is suspended until he is cleared of it. No one, so far as I know, has ever questioned such a suspension on the ground that it could not be done unless he is given notice of the charge and an opportunity of defending himself and so forth. The suspension in such a case is merely done by way of good administration. A situation has arisen in which something must be done at once. The work of the department or the office is being affected by rumours and suspicions. The others will not trust the man. In order to get back to proper work, the man is suspended. At that stage the rules of natural justice do not apply:...'

It is right to point out that the other Lords Justices tend not to go quite as far as Lord Denning M.R. in that formulation.

In the present case, I am content to proceed on the basis that the rules of natural justice do apply but that, in the words chosen by Mr Pannick, in such an emergency as the present, with a provisional suspension being all that one is concerned with, one is at the low end of the duties of fairness. Mr Pannick referred me in the course of his submissions on this point to *R. v. Civil Aviation Authority, ex p. Northern Air Taxis Ltd* [1976] 1 Lloyd's Rep. 344. That case, which was a Divisional Court case, was concerned with matters not dissimilar in some ways to the present. Natural justice as such was not argued; the matters were dealt with on the basis of the statutory requirements, but undoubtedly the result does lend some support to the view that, when one is dealing with this type of situation, not much is required of the Secretary of State in order to act fairly.

The way the case is put by Mr Flint is this. He says that in the present case the Secretary of State could not reasonably decline to afford Tarom a short period to put its case as to why the permit should not be suspended, having regard to a number of matters that Mr Flint identified. One of these is the lack of action on the letter of July 14, which I have read. As I have indicated, I regard that letter as irrelevant. A second matter to which Mr Flint drew my attention in this context was the time that the CAA took to refer the matter, which he said was some indication as to its view of the urgency. I have set out the relevant dates. It is clear that the failing of the tests took place on July 17, and the Secretary of State was not informed until July 29. That may or may not be a legitimate criticism of the CAA, but in my judgment, so far as the action of the Secretary of State is concerned, it cannot be regarded as unfair in the circumstances of this case that he acted in the speedy way in which he did act. One has in the context of unfairness to bear in mind, on the one hand, the no doubt substantial economic damage to the applicants and perhaps the irritation and inconvenience that I do not doubt the passengers suffered. On the other hand, one has to bear in mind the magnitude of the risk, by which I mean not so much the high percentage chance of it happening but the disastrous consequences of what would happen if something did happen. It is the old problem that one has with installations of nuclear power, or vehicles such as aeroplanes carrying a large number of people, that, if something goes wrong, then very many lives will be lost. While I do not doubt that different people, and maybe different Secretaries of State, would react differently to the same basic material, I am not prepared to say that the failure of the Secretary of State to permit more by way of representations than I have indicated took place was a breach of the rules of natural justice..."

Notes

8–46   (1) How far should emergency action be used to justify the limitation of natural justice? Does the excerpt provide a principled basis for such a justification? Was it relevant that the decision was a provisional one? It seems that where a provisional decision is made, the full weight of the right to a hearing has limited scope: *Pearlberg v. Varty* [1972] 1 W.L.R. 534. Here, a taxpayer contended that the Inland Revenue were obliged to give him a fair hearing prior to making a tax assessment on him. There was a suggestion of fraud on the part of the taxpayer. The House of Lords rejected the argument, Lord Hailsham L.C. observing that his remedy was to appeal against the decision once made (at 540). See too *Wiseman v. Borneman* [1971] A.C. 297 at 308 per Lord Reid holding that an individual has no right to be heard before a decision that he should be prosecuted is made.

(2) Regard should also be paid to the view sometimes expressed that some procedural safeguard may be required in a preliminary decision, quite often a decision that is taken in an emergency. There is perhaps a danger that a preliminary decision may tend to persist in colouring the view of the later reviewing body. The weight given to the preliminary decision in the consideration of the final decision would obviously be of importance. For example, would the onus of proof now be on the person affected by the decision or would matters be considered de novo? On this see *Herring v. Templeman* [1973] 3 All E.R. 569. Where a preliminary decision is merely a part of a wider decision, and is of itself not open to question in later proceedings, procedural protection would seem to be strengthened, on which see *R. v. Kent Police Authority, ex parte Godden* [1971] 3 All E.R. 20, noted at para. 9–6, and *Lockhart v. Irving*, 1936 S.L.T. 567, extracted at para. 9–5. See also *McDonald v. Burns* below in relation to review of an initial investigation. Do you think it was relevant that the investigation and decision was being made by a "private" organisation in that case?

(3) There would appear to be no general obligation for regulatory authorities to advise those about to be affected by the decision to make representation that a decision is about to be made and that representations are to be entertained: see *R. v. Birmingham City Council, ex p. Ferrero Ltd* [1993] 1 All E.R. 530 (trading standards officers) and *R. v. Life Assurance and Unit Trust Regulatory Organisation Ltd, ex p. Ross* [1993] 1 All E.R. 545 (the regulatory body, LAUTRO).

(4) Article 15 of the European Convention on Human Rights permits derogation from Convention rights, including the rights guaranteed under Articles 5 and 6 in the event "of war or other public emergency threatening the life of the nation …to the extent strictly required by the exigencies of the situation". Note too the possibility of derogation or reservation from Convention rights guaranteed by the Human Rights Act 1998, ss. 14–17.

FAILING OF ADVISERS

Al-Mehdawi v. Secretary of State for the Home Department

[1990] 1 A.C. 876

"The respondent was an Iraqi citizen who was refused a further extension of his leave to remain in the   **8–47** United Kingdom during May 1984. In March 1985 the respondent was notified that the Home Secretary had decided to make a deportation order against him. The respondent instructed solicitors to appeal against the deportation decision. The solicitors were notified of the hearing date for the appeal before an immigration adjudicator; however, neither they nor the respondent attended the appeal. Consequently, the adjudicator determined the appeal on the basis of the documents before him and dismissed the appeal. There was no appeal lodged against the adjudicator's decision within the statutory time limits. Subsequently, it emerged that the respondent's solicitors had sent notice of the hearing date and the adjudicator's decision to a previous address of the respondent (even though they knew his current one) with the result that he had received no information regarding the appellate proceedings. The respondent sought judicial review of the adjudicator's decision on the ground that there had been a breach of the rules of natural justice in that he had been denied a hearing. The High Court granted his application and the Court of Appeal affirmed that decision. The Home Secretary appealed to the House of Lords."

LORD BRIDGE OF HARWICH: "…The appeal raises a question of great importance with respect to the scope of the remedy by order of certiorari to quash the decision of an inferior tribunal. Does certiorari lie to quash a decision given without hearing the applicant for certiorari when the tribunal giving the decision has acted correctly in the procedure adopted but the applicant was deprived of the opportunity to put his case by the negligence of his own legal advisers or otherwise without personal fault on the part of the applicant. This question had been considered once before by the Court of Appeal in *R. v. Diggines, ex p. Rahmani* [1985] 1 Q.B. 1109. That was another case relating to the decision of an adjudicator under the Act of 1971 who was mistakenly informed by the United Kingdom Immigrants Advisory Service ('U.K.I.A.S.'), acting for the appellant, that they had no instructions. The Court of Appeal quashed the decision on the ground of a denial of natural justice to the appellant arising from the fault of the U.K.I.A.S. The Court of Appeal proceeded on the assumption that there had been no error of procedure by the adjudicator. However, when *ex p. Rahmani* came before your Lordships' House on appeal the House held that the question decided by the Court of Appeal did not arise and dismissed the appeal on the ground that the adjudicator had erred in determining the appeal without a hearing in reliance on rule 12(c) of the Immigration Appeals (Procedure) Rules 1972 (S.I. 1972 No. 1684), the rules then in force, since there was no material before the adjudicator which justified him in finding under that sub-rule that no person was authorised to represent the appellant at the hearing. In the instant case, by contrast, no criticism is, nor could be, made of the procedure adopted by the adjudicator in hearing and determining the appeal in the absence of the appellant in the exercise of the express discretion conferred on him by rule 34(2) of the Rules of 1984…

The central submission made by Mr Laws, for the Secretary of State, is that the so-called rules of natural justice are concerned solely with the propriety of the procedure adopted by the decision maker. In particular, the rule expressed in the Latin maxim audi alteram partem requires no more than that the decision maker should afford to any party to a dispute an opportunity to present his case. This view certainly receives support from many classic statements of the doctrine. The duty 'fairly to hear both sides' is described by Lord Loreburn L.C. in *Board of Education v. Rice* [1911] A.C. 179, 182 as 'a duty lying upon every one who decides anything'. In *Ridge v. Baldwin* [1964] A.C. 41, 64, Lord Reid said of the watch committee who had dismissed the chief constable without a hearing:

> 'Before attempting to reach any decision they were bound to inform him of the grounds on which they proposed to act and give him a fair opportunity of being heard in his own defence.'

…Mr Laws submits that the very concept of impropriety in the procedure by which a decision is reached necessarily connotes an irregularity in the conduct of the proceedings by the decision maker. Conversely, a failure by the legal adviser or any other agent to whom a party to any proceedings has entrusted the conduct of his case, being beyond the knowledge and control of the decision maker, cannot involve either any procedural impropriety or the breach of any duty which the decision maker owes to that party.

However, the authority on which Sir Charles Fletcher-Cooke [counsel for the respondent] relies, and which persuaded the Court of Appeal that the procedural impropriety involved in a breach of the rules of natural justice could not be confined to errors on the part of the decision-making body, is *R. v. Leyland Justices, ex p. Hawthorn* [1979] Q.B. 283. In that case the driver of one of two cars involved in a collision had been prosecuted and convicted for driving without due care and attention. The police had taken statements from two witnesses of the accident, but these witnesses were not called by the prosecution and their existence was not disclosed to the defence. The driver successfully applied for an order of certiorari to quash the conviction. Delivering the first judgment Lord Widgery C.J. said, at 286:

> 'There is no doubt that an application can be made by certiorari to set aside an order on the basis that the tribunal failed to observe the rules of natural justice. Certainly if it were the fault of the justices that this additional evidentiary information was not passed on, no difficulty would arise. But the problem — and one can put it in a sentence — is that certiorari in respect of breach of the rules of natural justice is primarily a remedy sought on account of an error of the tribunal, and here, of course, we are not concerned with an error of the tribunal; we are concerned with an error of the police prosecutors. Consequently, amongst the arguments to which we have listened an argument has been that this is not a certiorari case at all on any of the accepted grounds.
>
> 'We have given this careful thought over the short adjournment because it is a difficult case in that the consequences of the decision either way have their unattractive features. However, if fraud, collusion, perjury and such-like matters not affecting the tribunal themselves justify an application for certiorari to quash the conviction, if all those matters are to have that effect, then we cannot say that the failure of the prosecution which in this case has prevented the tribunal from giving the defendant a fair trial should not rank in the same category.
>
> 'We have come to the conclusion that there was here a clear denial of natural justice. Fully recognising the fact that the blame falls on the prosecutor and not on the tribunal, we think that it is a matter which should result in the conviction being quashed. In my judgment, that is the result to which we should adhere.'

This decision was followed in *R. v. Blundeston Prison Board of Visitors, ex p. Fox-Taylor* [1982] 1 All E.R. 646.

Though I do not question the correctness of the decision in *ex p. Hawthorn* [1979] Q.B. 283, I do question whether it is correctly classified as a case depending on either procedural impropriety or a breach of the rules of natural justice. Certainly there was unfairness in the conduct of the proceedings, but this was because of a failure by the prosecutor, in breach of a duty owed to the court and to the defence, to disclose the existence of witnesses who could have given evidence favourable to the defence. Although no dishonesty was suggested, it was this *suppressio veri* which had the same effect as a *suggestio falsi* in distorting and vitiating the process leading to conviction, and it was, in my opinion, the analogy which Lord Widgery C.J. drew between the case before him and the cases of fraud, collusion and perjury which had been relied on in counsel's argument, which identified the true principle on which the decision could be justified.

In any event, *ex p. Hawthorn*, if it is relied on as an authority to support the conclusion of the Court of Appeal in *ex p. Rahmani* [1985] Q.B. 1109 and the instant case, proves too much. If unfairness resulting from a failure by the prosecutor to disclose the names of witnesses, so that the defence is deprived of their evidence, is taken as a precedent for allowing certiorari on the ground of a failure in the conduct of proceedings by the defendant's own legal advisers, the logic of the argument would lead to the conclusion that a negligent failure by the defendant's own legal advisers to secure the attendance of necessary defence witnesses would entitle the defendant to have his conviction quashed if he was personally free of blame for the failure. But this was a conclusion which Sir Charles Fletcher-Cooke rightly declined to support...

But there are many familiar situations where one party to litigation will effectively lose the opportunity to have his case heard through the failure of his own legal advisers, but will be left with no remedy at all except against those legal advisers. I need only instance judgments signed in default, actions dismissed for want of a prosecution and claims which are not made within a fixed time limit which the tribunal has no power to extend. In each of these situations a litigant who wishes his case to be heard and who has fully instructed his solicitor to take the necessary steps may never in fact be heard because of his solicitor's neglect and through no fault of his own. But in any of these cases it would surely be fanciful to say that there had been a breach of the *audi alteram partem* rule. Again, take the case of a county court action where a litigant fails to appear at the hearing because his solicitor has neglected to inform him of the date and consequently judgment is given against him. He can at best invite the court in its discretion to set aside the judgment and it is likely to do so only on the terms that he should pay the costs thrown away. Yet, if it can be said that he has been denied natural justice, he ought in principle to be able to apply for certiorari to quash the judgment which, if he is personally blameless, should be granted as a matter of course.

These considerations lead me to the conclusion that a party to a dispute who has lost the opportunity to have his case heard through the default of his own advisers to whom he had entrusted the conduct of the dispute on his behalf cannot complain that he has been the victim of a procedural impropriety or that natural justice has been denied to him, at all events when the subject-matter of the dispute raises issues of private law between citizens. Is there any principle which can be invoked to lead to a different conclusion where the issue is one of public law and where the decision taken is of an administrative character rather than the resolution of a *lis inter partes*? I cannot discover any such principle and none has been suggested in the course of argument...

But I would add that, if once unfairness suffered by one party to a dispute in consequence of some failure by his own advisers in relation to the conduct of the relevant proceedings was admitted as a ground on which the High Court in the exercise of its supervisory jurisdiction over inferior tribunals could quash the relevant decision, I can discern no principle which could be invoked to distinguish between a "fundamental unfairness", which would justify the exercise of the jurisdiction, and a less than fundamental unfairness, which would not. Indeed, Sir Charles Fletcher-Cooke was constrained to rest on the proposition that, in the last analysis, it was all a matter of discretion and the court could be trusted only to exercise its discretion in extreme cases where justice demanded a remedy. I am of the opinion that the decision of the Court of Appeal can only be supported at the cost of opening such a wide door which would indeed seriously undermine the principle of finality in decision making.

The effect of this conclusion in a deportation case may appear harsh, though no harsher than the perhaps more common case when an immigrant's solicitor fails to give notice of appeal under section 15 within the time limited by rule 4 of the Rules of 1984. But it is perhaps worth pointing out that in neither case is the immigrant left wholly without a remedy. In the case of a notice of appeal served out of time, the Secretary of State has a discretion under rule 5 to extend the time 'if he is of the opinion that, by reason of special circumstances, it is just and right so to do'. In the case where the immigrant has failed to attend the hearing of his appeal to the adjudicator and the appeal has been heard and dismissed in his absence, the Secretary of State has the discretion conferred on him by section 21 of the Act whereby the 'may at any time refer for consideration under this section any matter relating to the case which was not before the adjudicator'. If such a reference is made, the adjudicator is required by section 21(2) to 'consider the matter which is the subject of the reference and report to the Secretary of State the opinion of the adjudicator ...thereon'. It would, as it seems to me, certainly be open to the Secretary of State, if persuaded that the merits of a case required it, to invite an adjudicator to hear the oral evidence of an appellant whose appeal had, through no fault of his own, been dismissed in his absence, and to report his opinion whether this evidence would have affected the outcome of the appeal.

I would allow the appeal, set aside the orders of MacPherson J. and the Court of Appeal and restore the determination of the adjudicator."

LORDS ROSKILL, BRANDON OF OAKBROOK, OLIVER OF AYLMERTON and GOFF OF CHIEVELEY agreed with the speech given by LORD BRIDGE.

Notes

8–48   (1) Does the approach here give adequate weight to the public interest in ensuring that the decisions are being made on the basis of proper argument? Is the remedy of damages in an action for professional negligence against an adviser an adequate remedy for someone in the position of Al-Mehdawi? For comment and criticism of this decision see J. Herberg, "The Right to a Hearing: Breach Without Fault? [1990] P.L. 467.

(2) There is no recent authority on Scots law on the issues raised in the extract. It would appear that anything done by an advocate or solicitor in the course of conducting litigation (as opposed to preparatory work) will be binding on the client and the client's only remedy will be either an action for negligence or a complaint to the appropriate professional body: *Batchelor v. Pattison and Mackersy* (1876) 3 R. 914.

(3) In criminal law the position may be different. In *Anderson v. H.M. Advocate*, 1996 S.C.C.R. 114 the Court of Criminal Appeal heard an argument that the appellant's legal adviser had not properly presented the appellant's case at trial and as a result he was denied the right to be heard. The court considered that Scots law was consistent with the provisions of Articles 6.1–6.3 of the ECHR and that if it could be shown that the appellant suffered a miscarriage of justice in terms of section 228(1) of the Criminal Procedure (Scotland) Act 1995 then an appeal could succeed. On Anderson see the contributed article, "Miscarriages of Justice and Legal Practice" (1996) 41 JLSS 5. It remains to be seen whether this concept of a fair trial based on Article 6.1 of the Convention will be extended to failings of legal advisers in civil or administrative proceedings in cases under the Human Rights Act 1998.

(4) The inadequacy of a legal adviser may be relevant in arguing that there is an "exceptional circumstance" justifying an exception to the obligation to exhaust alternative remedies before seeking judicial review of a decision, on which see para. 10–3.

CONFIDENTIAL INFORMATION

R v. Gaming Board for Great Britain, ex parte Benaim and Khaida

[1970] 2 All E.R. 528, C.A.

8–49   "The Gaming Act 1968 prohibited gaming except in premises licensed for this purpose by the justices. Before any person could apply for a licence he had to obtain a 'certificate of consent' from the Gaming Board, a body set up by the 1968 Act. The present applicants, the joint managing directors of Crockford's gaming club, applied unsuccessfully for a certificate. The board declined to give reasons for the refusal. In particular they refused to specify the matters which troubled them. The applicants sought certiorari to quash the refusal, and mandamus to compel the board to give sufficient information to enable them to answer the case against them."

LORD DENNING M.R.: "…To what extent are the board bound by the rules of natural justice? That is the root question before us. Their jurisdiction is country wide. They have to keep under review the extent and character of gaming in Great Britain: see s. 10(3). Their particular task in regard to Crockford's is to see if the applicants are fit to run a gaming club: and if so, to give a certificate of consent.

Their duty is set out in Schedule 2, para 4(5) and (6):

'…(5) …the board shall have regard only to the question whether, in their opinion, the applicant is likely to be capable of, and diligent in, securing that the provisions of this Act and of any regulations made under it will be complied with, that gaming on those premises will be fairly and properly conducted, and that the premises will be conducted without disorder or disturbance.

(6) For the purposes of sub-paragraph (5) …the board shall in particular take into consideration the character, reputation and financial standing — (a) of the applicant, and (b) of any person (other than the applicant) by whom …the club …would be managed, or for whose benefit …that club would be carried on, but may also take into consideration any other circumstances appearing to them to be relevant in determining whether the applicant is likely to be capable of, and diligent in, securing the matters mentioned in that sub-paragraph.'

Note also that Schedule 1, paragraph 7, gives the board power to regulate their own procedure. Accordingly the board have laid down an outline procedure which they put before us. It is too long to read in full. So I will just summarise it. It says that the board will give the applicant an opportunity of making representations to the board, and will give him the best indications possible of the matters that are troubling them. Then there are these two important sentences:

'In cases where the *source* or *content* of this *information is confidential*, the board accept that they are obliged to withhold particulars of the disclosure of which would be a breach of confidence inconsistent with their statutory duty and the public interest…'

'In the course of the interview the applicant will be made aware, to the greatest extent to which this is consistent with the board's statutory duty and the public interest, of the matters that are troubling the board.'

Mr Quintin Hogg criticised that outline procedure severely. He spoke as if Crockford's were being deprived of a right of property or of a right to make a living. He read his client's affidavit saying that 'Crockford's has been established for over a century and is a gaming club with a worldwide reputation for integrity and respectability', with assets and goodwill valued at £185,000. He said that they ought not to be deprived of this business without knowing the case they had to meet. He criticised especially the way in which the board proposed to keep that confidential information. He relied on some words of mine in *Kanda v. Government of Malaya* [1962] A.C. 322, 337, when I said 'that the judge or whoever has to adjudicate must not hear evidence or receive representations from one side behind the back of the other'.

Mr Hogg put his case, I think, too high. It is an error to regard Crockford's as having any right of which, they are being deprived. They have not had in the past, and they have not now, any right to play these games of chance — roulette, chemin-de-fer, baccarat and the like — for their own profit. What they are really seeking is a privilege — almost, I might say, a franchise — to carry on gaming for profit, a thing never hitherto allowed in this country. It is for them to show that they are fit to be trusted with it.

If Mr Hogg went too far on his side, I think Mr Kidwell went too far on the other. He submitted that the Gaming Board are free to grant or refuse a certificate as they please. They are not bound, he says, to obey the rules of natural justice any more than any other executive body, such as, I suppose, the Board of Trade, which grant industrial development certificates, or the Television Authority, which awards television programme contracts. I cannot accept this view. I think the Gaming Board are bound to observe the rules of natural justice. The question is: What are those rules?

It is not possible to lay down rigid rules as to when the principles of natural justice are to apply: nor as to their scope and extent. Everything depends on the subject-matter: see what Tucker L.J. said in *Russell v. Norfolk (Duke of)* [1949] 1 All E.R. 109, 118 and Lord Upjohn in *Durayappah v. Fernando* [1967] 2 A.C. 337, 349. At one time it was said that the principles only apply to judicial proceedings and not to administrative proceedings. That heresy was scotched in *Ridge v. Baldwin* [1964] A.C. 40. At another time it was said that the principles do not apply to the grant or revocation of licences. That too is wrong. *R. v. Metropolitan Police Commissioner, ex p. Parker* [1953] 1 W.L.R. 1150 and *Nakkuda Ali v. Jayaratne* [1951] A.C. 66 are no longer authority for any such proposition. See what Lord Reid and Lord Hodson said about them in *Ridge v. Baldwin* [1964] A.C. 40, 77–79, 133.

So let us sheer away from those distinctions and consider the task of this Gaming Board and what they should do. The best guidance is, I think, to be found by reference to the cases of immigrants. They have no right to come in, but they have a right to be heard. The principle in that regard was well laid, down by Lord Parker C.J. in *Re H.K. (An Infant)* [1967] 2 Q.B. 617. He said, at 630:

'…even if an immigration officer is not in a judicial or quasi-judicial capacity, he must at any rate give the immigrant an opportunity of satisfying him of the matters in the subsection, and for that purpose let the immigrant know what his immediate impression is so that the immigrant can disabuse him. That is not, as I see it, a question of acting or being required to act judicially, but of being required to act fairly.'

Those words seem to me to apply to the Gaming Board. The statute says in terms that in determining whether to grant a certificate, the board 'shall have regard only' to the matters specified. It follows,

I think, that the board have a duty to act fairly. They must give the applicant an opportunity of satisfying them of the matters specified in the subsection. They must let him know what their impressions are so that he can disabuse them. But I do not think that they need quote chapter and verse against him as if they were dismissing him from an office, as in *Ridge v. Baldwin* [1964] A.C. 40; or depriving him of his property, as in *Cooper v. Wandsworth Board of Works* (1863) 14 C.B.N.S. 180. After all, they are not charging him with doing anything wrong. They are simply inquiring as to his capability and diligence and are having regard to his character, reputation and financial standing. They are there to protect the public interest, to see that persons running the gaming clubs are fit to be trusted.

Seeing the evils that have led to this legislation, the board can and should investigate the credentials of those who make application to them. They can and should receive information from the police in this country or abroad who know something of them. They can, and should, receive information from any other reliable source. Much of it will be confidential. But that does not mean that the applicants are not to be given a chance of answering it. They must be given the chance, subject to this qualification: I do not think they need tell the applicant the source of their information, if that would put their informant in peril or otherwise be contrary to the public interest. Even in a criminal trial, a witness cannot be asked who is his informer. The reason was well given by Lord Eyre C.J. in Hardy's case [R. v. Hardy] 24 State Trials 199, 808:

> '…there is a rule which has universally obtained on account of its importance to the public for the detection of crimes, that those persons who are the channel by means of which that detection is made, should not be unnecessarily disclosed.'

And Buller J. added, at 818: '…if you call for the name of the informer in such cases, no man will make a discovery, and public justice will be defeated.' That rule was emphatically reaffirmed in *Attorney-General v. Briant* (1846) 15 M. & W. 169 and *Marks v. Beyfus* (1890) 25 Q.B.D. 494. That reasoning applies with equal force to the inquiries made by the Gaming Board. That board was set up by Parliament to cope with disreputable gaming clubs and to bring them under control. By bitter experience it was learned that these clubs had a close connection with organised crime, often violent crime, with protection rackets and with strong-arm methods. If the Gaming Board were bound to disclose their sources of information, no one would 'tell' on those clubs, for fear of reprisals. Likewise with the details of the information. If the board were bound to disclose every detail, that might itself give the informer away and put him in peril. But, without disclosing every detail, I should have thought that the board ought in every case to be able to give to the applicant sufficient indication of the objections raised against him such as to enable him to answer them. That is only fair. And the board must at all costs be fair. If they are not, these courts will not hesitate to interfere.

Accepting that the board ought to do all this when they come to give their decision, the question arises, are they bound to give their reasons? I think not. Magistrates are not bound to give reasons for their decisions: see *R. v. Northumberland Compensation Appeal Tribunal, ex p. Shaw* [1952] 1 K.B. 338, at 352. Nor should the Gaming Board be bound. After all, the only thing that they have to give is their opinion as to the capability and diligence of the applicant. If they were asked by the applicant to give their reasons, they could answer quite sufficiently: 'In our opinion, you are not likely to be capable of or diligent in the respects required of you.' Their opinion would be an end of the matter.

Tested by those rules, applying them to this case, I think that the Gaming Board acted with complete fairness. They put before the applicants all the information which led them to doubt their suitability. They kept the sources secret, but disclosed all the information. Sir Stanley Raymond said so in his affidavit: and it was not challenged to any effect. The board gave the applicants full opportunity to deal with the information. And they came to their decision. There was nothing whatever at fault with their decision of January 9, 1970. They did not give their reasons. But they were not bound to do so.

But then complaint is made as to what happened afterwards. It was said that the board did not pin-point the matters on which they thought the explanations were not satisfactory. They did not say which of the matters (a) to (e) they were not satisfied about. But I do not see anything unfair in that respect. It is not as if they were making any charges against the applicants. They were only saying they were not satisfied. They were not bound to give any reasons for their misgivings. And when they did give some reasons, they were not bound to submit to cross-examination on them.

Finally, complaint was made that the board refused to consider a new or amended application in respect of these premises of Crockford's in the current round. They refused to consider applications in other names or in new names. But here again I see nothing unfair. Crockford's had full opportunity of putting their application in the first instance. If there had been a technical defect in it, I feel sure that the board would have allowed an amendment. But if the application fails in matters of substance, that should be the end of it. There must be an end to the claim to 'cut and come again'.

In all the circumstances I think that all the criticisms of the board's conduct fail, and in my opinion the application should be dismissed."

LORD WILBERFORCE and PHILLIMORE L.J. agreed.

Notes

(1) Confidentiality was used as a reason for not revealing information in *R. v. Joint Higher Committee on Surgical Training, ex parte Milner* [1995] 7 Admin. L.R. 454. Milner applied for accreditation as a surgeon with the joint committee on surgical training but his application was rejected, partly on the basis of references from senior surgeons. He sought judicial review to basis that the substance of the references should have been disclosed to him. The court drew a distinction between matters of opinion and matters of fact and in connection with the former, natural justice did not require an opportunity of challenge and in the interests of confidentiality outweighed the interests in disclosure. Is this approach too broadly stated? Does it give sufficient weight to the issue of the accuracy of the facts on which an opinion might be based? Compare *Clyde Cablevision Ltd v. The Cable Authority*, above.

(2) Public interest immunity may also be relevant in limiting the right to information on in which see Chapter 15 and for application of the doctrine to the gaming board, see *R. v. Lewes Justices, ex parte Secretary of State for the Home Department* [1973] A.C. 388.

8–50

Chapter 9

NATURAL JUSTICE 2: THE RULE AGAINST BIAS

In the view of Erskine, "it is a rule founded in nature itself, that no man ought to be a judge in **9–1** his own cause" (An Institute of the Law of Scotland, i, 2, 25). See also Stair, *The Institutions of the Law of Scotland*, iv, 1, 35 and iv, 39, 14.

When Erskine was writing, his concern was to ensure that confidence was maintained in the judicial system. However, with the growth of the administrative state the rule has been extended to a great range of other forms of decision-making, many far removed from the judicial arena.

The concerns identified by Erskine are found in Article 6(1) of the European Convention on Human Rights which provides:

> "In the determination of his civil rights and obligations or of any criminal charge against him, everyone is entitled to a fair and public hearing …by an independent and impartial tribunal…"

For a general account of this area see *Stair Memorial Encyclopaedia*, *The Laws of Scotland*: Vol. 1, paras 251–258; P. P. Craig, Chap. 9; *S. Administrative Law* (3rd ed., 1994) W. Wade and C. Forsyth, de Smith, H. Woolf and J. Jowell, *Judicial Review of Administrative Action* (5th ed., 1995) 2 Chap. 12; V. Finch and C. Ashton, *Administrative Law in Scotland* (1997) pp. 316–324.

GENERAL PRINCIPLES

Wildridge v. Anderson

(1897) 25 R. (J) 27

"On 24th June 1897 Thomas Wildridge, apprentice joiner, Port-Glasgow, was charged in the Police **9–2** Court at Port-Glasgow, before Mr John Niven, one of the magistrates of the burgh, on a complaint, under the Burgh Police (Scotland) Act, 1892, at the instance of the Burgh Prosecutor, setting forth that the accused 'did, on the 12th day of June 1897 years, within the Moffat Library, situated in King Street, Port-Glasgow, wickedly, wilfully, maliciously, and mischievously tear, damage, and destroy a cushion of one of the forms in the billiard-room there, the property or in the lawful possession of the trustees of the said Moffat Library, and to their loss and damage.'

The accused pleaded not guilty, but after evidence had been led was convicted and fined 7s. 6d., with the alternative of five days' imprisonment.

He brought a suspension, in which he stated, *inter alia*; — (Stat. 8) 'At the time of said trial the complainer was not aware, but he has since learned, that the said John Niven [the presiding Magistrate] was long before and at the time of said trial, and is still, one of the trustees of the said Moffat Library, the alleged damage to whose property is the subject of the complaint, and that the said John Niven was thus personally interested in the matter of the complaint. At all events, the said John Niven being one of the said trustees, it was incompetent for him to preside at said trial and pronounce judgment therein.'

He pleaded, *inter alia*; — (1) The conviction and sentence complained of should be suspended, in respect they were pronounced by a magistrate who was personally interested in the property said to have been damaged, and who was one of the said trustees, and the complainer should be found entitled to repetition of the sum paid by way of fine, and to expenses."

LORD MONCREIFF: "On 24th June 1897 the complainer was convicted by Mr John Niven, one of the magistrates of Port-Glasgow, on a charge of malicious mischief at common law, she charge being that he wilfully, maliciously, and mischievously tore, damaged, or destroyed a cushion on one of the forms in a billiard-room in the Moffat Library, Port-Glasgow, 'the property or in the lawful possession of the trustees of the said Moffat Library and to their loss and damage.' The complainer was fined 7s, 6d., or five days in default of payment.

The sole ground of suspension, baldly stated, is that since conviction the complainer has ascertained that at the date of the trial Mr John Niven was one of the trustees of the Moffat Library, and thus one of the proprietors of the cushion which is said to have been damaged; and therefore, the complainer maintains, was disqualified by interest from presiding at the trial.

We were informed at the hearing that by the settlement of the founder of the library the Provost, Magistrates, and Council of Port-Glasgow were named as *ex officio* trustees of the library, and it was assumed in argument that Mr Niven at the date of the trial was an accepting and acting trustee.

The general and salutary rule is that no man can be a judge in his own cause, and that rule within certain limits is rigorously applied. The reason of it is obvious, viz., to ensure not merely that the administration of justice shall be free of bias but that it shall be beyond suspicion. It is subject, however, to qualifications and exceptions. The result of the authorities which were cited to us may be stated as follows:-

1. As a general rule a pecuniary interest, if direct and individual, will disqualify, however small it may be.
2. An interest although not pecuniary may also disqualify, but the interest in that case must be substantial.
3. Where the interest which is said to disqualify is not pecuniary, and is neither substantial nor calculated to cause bias in the mind of the Judge, it will be disregarded, especially if to disqualify the Judge would be productive of grave public inconvenience.

In the present case the presiding magistrate had no pecuniary interest in the case; he had no appreciable personal interest in it. Under the 454th section of the Burgh Police (Scotland) Act, 1892, he had jurisdiction, and was bound to take cognisance of all crimes and offences committed within the burgh which were within the jurisdiction of the magistrates of any royal burgh. If he was disqualified to try the case, so were his colleagues. If the complainer is right, in the event of any petty offence being committed in connection with any of the burgh property vested in the Commissioners of Police, the whole of the magistrates would be disqualified, and the Sheriff would have to be brought in each case from Greenock to sit in the Police Court.

On those grounds I am of opinion that the ground of suspension is not well founded, and that the suspension should be refused."

Notes

9–3   (1) This case must still be taken as a starting-point of any examination of the rule against bias where interest is alleged. S McMurtrie, "The Principle of *nemo judex in causa sua* in Scots Law" 1996 J.R. 304, at 305, states that *Wildridge*

> "can only serve as a basic guide, as it does not explore the subtleties or divisions. Nor does it account for the differing approach when dealing with interest derived from a public office or function. This is one of the factors which affect the application of the maxim.... There are, however, three other factors which additionally influence the workings of the doctrine: necessity; the remoteness of the interest; and the actual function of the decision-maker."

This analysis should be borne in mind in considering the extracts. Nevertheless the three rules stated by Lord Moncreiff provide the basis for examining allegations of bias.

(2) Under the first rule it has been held that a judge may not hear a case if he owns shares in a company which is a party to the litigation in question. In *Sellar v. Highland Railway Co.*, 1919 S.C. (H.L.) 19 ownership of bank shares in the defender company by the judge presiding over the case was a ground for his declining to preside over the proceedings further. See also *Dimes v. The Proprietors of the Grand Junction Canal* (1852) 3 H.L.C. 759; *Blaikie's Trustee v. Scottish Widows Fund* (1864) 2 M. 595; and for comment generally see R. Lamond, "Of Interest as a Disqualification in Judges" (1907) 23 S.L.R. 152. For a form of the rule for judges of the Court of Session see section 103 of the Court of Session Act 1868.

The concept of pecuniary interest is read subject to the requirement that it should not be "too remote". In *R. v. Rand* (1866) L.R. 1 Q.B. 230 Bradford Corporation were empowered by statute to take water flowing into a river and could do so without the consent of the owners of the river if they provided a certificate from a local justice of the peace that this was required. Two such certificates were granted from justices who were trustees of institutions which held bonds in Bradford Corporation. This interest did not disqualify them even though it could be argued that "the security of the trusts would be improved by anything improving the borough fund, and anything improving the waterworks ...would produce that effect". However, it was observed that they may have been disqualified by interest had they been "liable to costs, or to other pecuniary in loss or gain" in consequence of an office as trustees (*per* Blackburn J. at 232).

It appears that a more relaxed approach has recently been adopted in England at least. An Old Bailey judge, who owned 1,600 shares in a bank, did not have a prohibited interest which prevented him from presiding over the trial of persons accused of robbing a branch of that bank: *R. v. Mulvihill* [1990] 1 All E.R. 436. See also *Eves v. Hambros Bank (Jersey) Ltd* [1996] 1 W.L.R. 251. It is doubtful, standing *Wildridge* and *Sellar*, whether such a direct and personal interest would not provide a ground for declinature in Scotland.

(3) Under the second rule, personal relationship to one of the parties could be grounds for disqualification. In former times, legislation prevented a judge from sitting in cases involving relatives: see the Declinature Acts 1594 and 1681. However, personal relationship could still be a ground for disqualification at common law: S.L.C. Report No. 111. **9–4**

One particular non-pecuniary interest is that of a clash of capacity. In *Jex-Blake v. Edinburgh University Senatus* (1873) 11 M. 784 the Lord President (Inglis) declined to preside over a case involving the university, of which he was Chancellor. However, the declinature of the Lord Justice-Clerk (Moncreiff) was not felt necessary as he was simply a member of the university court. Here, too, remoteness seems to have its role to play in determining whether a challenge will succeed. See too *Forrest's Trustees v. Commissioners on Educational Endowments* (1884) 11 R. 719. Note too the recent decision of the House of Lords in *R. v. Bow Street Metropolitan Stipendiary Magistrate, ex p. Pinochet Ugarte (No. 2)* [1999] 1 All E.R. 577. The principle that a judge who would be automatically disqualified from hearing a matter on which he has an interest was held to include a directorship in a charity with close links to Amnesty International, which was represented in proceedings to extradite the former Chilean dictator, General Pinochet, to Spain.

Clash of capacity has been followed in relation to officers of the court. In *Smith v. East Dunbartonshire Council*, 1997 S.L.T. 997 it was alleged that there had been a breach of natural justice in that the chairman of the Lands Tribunal for Scotland was a consultant to and a former partner in a firm of solicitors with two brothers of the council's solicitor and that he had an interest in the outcome of an application by the pursuer to vary a land obligation. It was alleged that the council's solicitor might have faced a claim for professional negligence in relation to the way in which the land had been disposed of. It was held that the link between the council's solicitor and the tribunal's chairman was so tenuous as to be non-existent and in any event the chairman had no financial interest in the outcome of any action for negligence against the council's solicitor: see also *Laughland v. Galloway*, 1968 S.L.T. 272. Contrast with *Low v. Kincardineshire Licensing Court*, 1974 S.L.T. (Sh.Ct) 54 where proceedings, which were partly held in private, were invalidated because the solicitor for one party was appearing before his father, the clerk to the licensing board, who was also a partner in the same firm as the solicitor: see also *R. v. Sussex Justices, ex p. McCarthy* [1924] 1 K.B. 256.

Wildridge and many of the cases referred to above took place in the familiar context of a court of similar forum. However, the ambit of the principles relating to the bias has grown with the administrative state, as the following extract shows.

Lockhart v. Irving

1936 S.L.T. 567

"On 11th May 1936 Inspector Lockhart, Constables Gordon Mitchell, Henry Matthew, Robert A. Bruce, William Rankin, William M'Donald, and William Dey, all of Coatbridge Police Force, presented a petition for suspension and interdict against James Irving, Chief Constable, Coatbridge. **9–5**

The Court, on 11th May 1936, granted interim interdict, and ordained the respondent to lodge answers within seven days after 'service.' Answers were lodged and a record made up."

LORD ROBERTSON: "This case arises out of the actings of certain members of the Coatbridge Burgh Police Force in submitting to the Town Council of the burgh, as the Police Authority, a statement containing allegations against the Chief Constable of the burgh. The substance of the principal allegation was that the Chief Constable repeatedly made use of an official police car for his own private purposes. The respondent, who is the Chief Constable, explains in his answers that the statement prepared by the petitioners (which was lodged on 25th April with the Town-Clerk for submission to the Provost, Magistrates, and Councillors, and was accompanied by supporting documents) was handed by the Town-Clerk to the Provost of the burgh, who, as Chief Magistrate and head of the Police Authority, instructed the respondent to arrange for a parade of the officers and men concerned in making the statement. This parade took place on 27th April, and the respondent's averment is that at the parade the Provost 'intimated to the officers and men present that, as Provost and Chief Magistrate, he looked to the Chief Constable to maintain the discipline of the Burgh Police Force, and said that, having carefully considered the complaints, he had handed them to the respondent with a request that he would examine the documents, take any disciplinary action that he might consider necessary, and thereafter report to him as to the action taken and give his observations on the complaints made.' It will be observed that while the Provost is alleged to have stated that he had carefully considered the complaints, there is no averment that he had instituted any enquiry into them, or that, without enquiry and upon consideration of the statement and documents alone, together with explanations from the Chief Constable, he had decided that the complaints were ill-founded, or that he had decided that they were frivolous or unworthy of enquiry. On the contrary, the procedure adopted by the Provost, according to my understanding of the respondent's own averments, was to submit the complaints against the respondent to the respondent himself so that he might decide whether they were well- or ill-founded, and take such action as might be appropriate by way of disciplinary measures. This situation is somewhat veiled by the language used in the answers, but I think that the position plainly was what I have stated it to be. I cannot understand a request to the Chief Constable to 'take such disciplinary action as he might consider necessary' following upon an 'examination' to be made by him of the documents, and thereafter to 'give his observations on the complaints made,' to mean anything other than that he was to enquire into and decide upon the complaints made against himself. In plain language, the procedure adopted was to institute an investigation by the Chief Constable into charges of misconduct brought by his subordinates against himself. Such an investigation, in which the Chief Constable is made judge in his own cause, is repugnant to justice. It makes a fair trial impossible — in a sense favourable to the accused but unfavourable (with possible serious consequences) to the accusers. It led directly to accusations by the accused against the accusers, in which the accused was to be the judge of his accusers. The present petition is in substance for interdict against the original accused acting as judge of his own accusations against the original accusers; and, in substance, these accusations are that the original accusers made false accusations against him. I cannot conceive of any proceedings more gravely fraught with injustice than these — or more likely in fact to give rise to injustice — or more certain, in any event, to result in convincing those who are now accused, and the public at large, that injustice and not justice had been done. In my opinion it is not only against justice to the officers and men concerned, but also against the public interest that any such investigation should proceed, and unless I am driven to an opposite result by statutory injunction I am prepared, if I have the power, to prevent it from proceeding.

Following upon the instructions given at the parade to which I have referred, the Chief Constable suspended the men concerned, and they remain suspended. Further, he served upon them a complaint that they had been guilty of offences against discipline. It was maintained in argument for the respondent that as he was tied down in the enquiry which he proposed to conduct (and against which interim interdict is at present standing) to the matters set forth in the complaint, he would not truly be acting as judge in his own cause. In my opinion there is no substance in this argument. The first item in the complaint is that the accused did commit an offence against discipline by wilfully and negligently making a false, misleading, or inaccurate statement, 'and this you did at the time and place aforesaid by stating in a report signed by you …that …the car was seldom seen unless with the Chief Constable sitting in it, which statement is false.' In an inverted form this raises for judgment by the Chief Constable the very complaint against himself out of which the whole matter originated.

I note that after the Provost had issued his instructions at the parade of the men concerned the matter came before a meeting of his Committee on 4th May, and the Committee approved of his action; and that, on 7th May, a special meeting of the Town Council was held at which the minute of the Provost's Committee and the procedure to be followed were unanimously approved. The complaints against discipline formulated against the present petitioners were served upon them by the respondent on 4th May, and the enquiry which he proposed to hold was to have taken place on 12th May. Interim interdict was granted on 11th May. The minute of the special meeting of 7th May bears that the Council unanimously endorsed the action which had been taken, 'being satisfied that the complaints were frivolous and did not justify their going further into the matter.' When this minute came up for confirmation at the monthly meeting of the Town Council held on 21st May, approval of it was moved by the Provost, but Treasurer Tennant, seconded by Baillie Bruce, thereupon moved, as an amendment, approval of the minute subject to deletion of the words quoted above. There was no seconder to the Provost's motion, and, after discussion, the amendment became the finding of the meeting. It was explained to me at the debate that the deletion of the quoted words proceeded on the view that the Town Council ought only to register their decision and not their reasons, and that it did not carry the inference that the complaints were not considered to be frivolous or unworthy of enquiry. Accepting that to be so, the result is that there is now no finding of the Council affirming that the complaints against the Chief Constable were either frivolous or unworthy of enquiry. I regard a finding upon that matter — failing a definite decision that the complaints were ill-founded — as a preliminary essential to the propriety of a decision to remit to the Chief Constable to make investigations and take action of a disciplinary character against his subordinates in relation to these very complaints. The opposite view, upon which the Town Council apparently proceeded, involves that in their view there was no impropriety in remitting to the Chief Constable to be the judge of complaints made against himself, which were neither held to be ill-founded nor frivolous nor unworthy of enquiry. I disagree with that view, and I think it can only be explained by a failure to appreciate the true situation. If the Town Council had appreciated that they were placing the Chief Constable in the indefensible position of being judge in his own cause, I cannot but think that they would have seen the necessity for deciding, in the first place, upon the complaints made against him, and would have made and minuted their decision — not as a 'reason' for remitting the subsequent enquiry to him, but as an essential clearing of the ground, without which any subsequent disciplinary enquiry by him could not in common fairness take place. Unless the charges brought against the Chief Constable are definitely held and stated to be either ill-founded or else frivolous and unworthy of enquiry, my view is that an enquiry into them and a decision upon them by some person or body other than the Chief Constable is necessarily antecedent, or principles fundamental to the administration of justice, to any disciplinary enquiry by the Chief Constable into the conduct of his subordinates in formulating and making the charges against him. I think that the present situation has arisen out of a failure to appreciate the foregoing considerations. I have no materials to enable me to decide, and do not profess to decide, whether the complaints made against the Chief Constable were either well-founded or ill-founded, or were either substantial or frivolous. But I am of opinion that unless and until a decision on one or other of these matters has been made by a third party it is against principle that the disciplinary enquiry by the Chief Constable should be allowed to proceed. That enquiry might issue in grave consequences for the petitioners. If they should be dismissed or required to resign they would have a right of appeal to the Secretary of State under section 1 of the Police (Appeals) Act, 1927. But if a lesser punishment should be inflicted upon them they would have no appeal, and their 'misconduct' in the matter would be permanently recorded against them individually. There are therefore, in my view, strong reasons against allowing the disciplinary enquiry to proceed while the charges made against the Chief Constable remain in abeyance...

But the respondent maintained, as he was entitled to do, that, whatever might be the intentions of the Police Authority as to future proceedings, he was entitled to a judicial decision on the question whether the standing interdict ought not to be recalled. It was argued for him that the Police (Scotland) Regulations had statutory effect in view of section 4 of the Police Act, 1919, and that under these Regulations it was imperative that an enquiry into discipline relating to the Police Force under him must be held by the Chief Constable. This was denied by the petitioners, but, on a construction of the Regulations, I am of opinion that it is well-founded. The Chief Constable is not himself within the ambit of these Regulations, which make no provision for any enquiry into his own conduct. In my view they assume that he is himself above suspicion in relation to the matters in which he is designated as judge. If he is not above suspicion (as appears from the fact that there are charges against him standing undisposed of), then he cannot be the judge of these very matters and charges unless principles upon which the administration of justice is founded are violated, and in my view the Regulations, and the statute authorising them, must be read in the light of that fundamental consideration. So regarding the matter, I think that the solution is this — that if there is to be disciplinary enquiry, then it may be that the Chief Constable must be the judge, unless some special *ad hoc* procedure can be followed; but that, since the Chief Constable cannot be judge in his own cause, it is in any event premature to institute a disciplinary enquiry until the correlated charges against him have been disposed of. I am asked by the respondent here and now to recall the interim interdict. The ultimate and absolute position may be different, and in relation to it the statutory provisions may disable the Court from interfering. I do not see that they disable the Court from here and now deciding *ad interim* that the disciplinary enquiry, being at all events premature in the circumstances, should not be allowed to proceed in the meantime. That is all that is involved in a continuance of the interim interdict, and I shall continue it accordingly."

Notes

9–6   (1) In *R. v. Kent Police Authority, ex p. Godden* [1971] 3 All E.R. 20 a police chief inspector was subject to investigation by a police authority. He was examined by a Dr Crosbie Brown, acting for the police authority as Chief Medical Officer, who regarded him as suffering from "a mental disorder of a paranoid type". He was certified as unfit for police duty and was put on sick leave. The inspector then saw his own doctor who referred him to a consultant psychiatrist who concluded that he was "psychiatrically completely normal". The police would not allow the psychiatrist to see the earlier report. The police authority then took steps to retire him compulsorily and notified him that he had been selected to attend Dr Crosbie Brown once more as their "duly qualified practitioner" to determine whether the applicant was "permanently disabled" under regulation 70(2) of the Police Pensions Regulations 1971. The inspector sought relief in the Divisional Court, which dismissed his application. He appealed. Lord Denning M.R. noted (at 25):

> "I am clearly of opinion that the decisions leading to compulsory retirement are of a judicial character and must conform to the rules of natural justice ...Dr Crosbie Brown had said that the chief inspector was suffering from a mental disorder. Dr Crosbie Brown acted on that opinion by putting him on sick leave. He has put his opinion on affidavit. He has committed himself to a view in advance of the enquiry. I think it would be impossible for Dr Crosbie Brown — who is just a general medical practitioner and not a consultant — to bring a completely impartial mind to bear upon the matter. In any event, to the person affected by it, Chief Inspector Godden, it must inevitably appear that Dr Crosbie Brown cannot bring an impartial judgment to bear on the matter."

(2) Other decision makers caught by the rule include specialised judicial procedures, *Glass v. Smith*, 1941 S.L.T. 78; administrative tribunals, *Barrs v. British Wool Marketing Board*, 1957 S.L.T. 153 below; arbiters, *Edinburgh Magistrates v. Lownie* (1903) 10 S.L.T. 752; the disciplinary proceedings of a political party, *Brown v. Executive Committee of the Edinburgh District Labour Party*, 1995 S.L.T. 985; and the proceedings of a professional disciplinary committee, *Murphy v. General Teaching Council for Scotland*, 1997 S.L.T. 1152.

Particular difficulties have arisen in the context of decisions being made which touch on matters in which the decision maker's function means a prior involvement in, or active support for, a particular outcome. Planning law has provided much material.

London and Clydeside Estates Ltd v. Secretary of State for Scotland

1987 S.C.L.R. 195

9–7   "The petitioners made an application for planning consent for an area of ground within the Pentlands constituency in Edinburgh. A public local enquiry was held and a constituent of Mr Malcolm Rifkind, the Member of Parliament for the Pentlands constituency, wrote a letter objecting to the grant of planning consent. He enlisted Mr Rifkind's support to his objection. Mr Rifkind entered into correspondence with the then Secretary of State (Mr George Younger) supporting his constituent's objections. Edinburgh District Council failed to give timeous notice of their decision on the planning application and in terms of s. 34 of the Town and Country Planning (Scotland) Act 1972 it was deemed to be refused. The petitioners subsequently appealed to the Secretary of State, which post by this time was held by Mr Rifkind. On 14th April 1986 the Secretary of State decided to determine the appeal himself. He appointed a reporter to hold a public local enquiry and submit a report to him. At the opening of the enquiry counsel for the petitioners drew the reporter's attention to the terms of the correspondence between the objector at the initial enquiry and Mr Rifkind. The reporter adjourned the enquiry to enable the matter to be resolved. The Secretary of State indicated to the reporter by letter that having considered his preliminary report of the objections taken at the enquiry, there were no grounds for recalling his appointment and directing him to reopen the enquiry.

The petitioners sought a declarator that the Secretary of State was disqualified from determining the appeal, an order quashing the direction of 14th April 1986 and reduction of the reporter's appointment."

LORD DAVIDSON: "In this application for judicial review the petitioners, London and Clydeside Estates Limited, seek, among other things, a declarator that the present Secretary of State for Scotland, the Right Honourable Malcolm Rifkind, Q.C., M.P., is disqualified from determining himself an appeal which they are pursuing against a planning decision made by Edinburgh District Council in respect of subjects at Woodhall Mains Farm, Colinton, Edinburgh. The application is opposed by the Secretary of State and by Mr Thomas Peattie, the reporter who was appointed to hold an enquiry into the appeal. At the first hearing counsel for the parties represented were agreed that, although answers have not been lodged, there is no dispute about the facts averred in the petition, and that, assuming that the application is a competent one in terms of Rule of Court 260B, the issue on the merits can be resolved as one of relevancy.

The petitioners' appeal relates to two fields at Woodhall Mains Farm extending to approximately 31.4 acres. In October 1985 the petitioners submitted an application to Edinburgh District Council for outline planning consent to develop these two fields for residential and ancillary purposes. There is, however, an earlier planning history relating to these two fields. In July 1982 a company called Hermiston Homes Limited applied for outline planning permission to develop for residential purposes a seventy-acre site at Woodhall Mains Farm which included the two fields. After that application was refused by Edinburgh District Council, Hermiston Homes appealed to the Secretary of State, the Right Honourable George Younger, M.P. In the exercise of his powers under paragraph 3(1) of Schedule 7 to the Town and Country Planning (Scotland) Act 1972 ("the 1972 Act"), the Secretary of State directed that he would determine the appeal himself on the ground that it related to a substantial area of good-quality agricultural land. A public and local enquiry was held into that appeal in December 1983. Following submission to him of the enquiry report, Mr Younger, by letter dated 24th July 1984, dismissed the appeal.

Woodhall Mains Farm lies in the Parliamentary constituency of Pentlands, for which Mr Rifkind has been the sitting member since 1974. One of the objectors at the enquiry was Mr Archibald J. C. Clark of 33 Lanark Road West, Edinburgh, who, in a letter dated 22nd August 1983 addressed to the Planning Appeals Branch of the Scottish Development Department, set out his reasons for objecting to the proposed development in the form of a commentary. Mr Clark sent a copy of that letter to Mr Rifkind. On 31st August 1983 Mr Rifkind wrote a personal letter to Mr Younger in the following terms.

'Dear George,
'My constituent, Mr Archibald J. C. Clark of Millbank, 33 Lanark Road West, Currie, Midlothian, has sent me a copy of his letter addressed to the Planning Appeals Branch of the Scottish Development Department indicating his objections to the proposed development at Woodhall Mains Farm, which is now the subject of an appeal to you.
'I would be grateful if you would note my support for my constituent's objections to this application, as I do not believe the development proposed at Woodhall Mains Farm would be desirable, due to the loss of amenity which would result and particularly the pressure that would be involved for existing facilities.
"For convenience I enclose copies of correspondence sent to me by Mr Clark.
'Yours ever,
'Malcolm."

On 30th July 1984 Mr Rifkind, in his capacity as Member of Parliament for the Pentlands constituency, wrote a letter to Mr Clark in the following terms. [His Lordship quoted the letter as set out above.] Edinburgh District Council as local planning authority failed to give timeous notice of their decision on the petitioners' planning application, which was accordingly deemed to be refused in terms of section 34 of the 1972 Act. The petitioners subsequently appealed to the Secretary of State in terms of section 33 of the Act against the deemed refusal. By letter dated 14th April 1986 the Scottish Development Department wrote to the petitioners' estates director, inter alia, as follows. [His Lordship quoted the letter as set out above.]

The Secretary of State referred to in the letter of 14th April 1986 was Mr Rifkind. In furtherance of that direction the Secretary of State appointed Mr Peattie to conduct a public local enquiry into the appeal and to report thereon to him. On the opening day of the enquiry, which was 21st July 1986, counsel for the petitioners drew attention to a written submission, dated 4th July 1986, which had been tendered in connection with the enquiry by Mr Clark. Mr Rifkind's letter to Mr Clark dated 30th July 1984 was attached to the submission. Counsel for the petitioners then invited Mr Peattie to adjourn the enquiry to enable the question as to who should decide the appeal to be resolved by negotiation, or, if necessary, by the court in judicial review proceedings. After hearing submissions, Mr Peattie adjourned the enquiry indefinitely to enable the matter to be considered.

On 12th August 1986 the Private Secretary to the Secretary of State wrote to Mr Peattie, inter alia, as follows.

"The Secretary of State has carefully considered your report of the circumstances contained in your letter and the arguments put forward by the appellants' solicitors. He is, however, not persuaded that any valid legal grounds have been put forward to justify the highly unusual step of:

(*a*) revoking his direction recalling the delegation of this case for decision by the Secretary of State, and

(*b*) recalling your appointment and nominating instead as reporter for this case a person who is not a member of the panel of full-time reporters.

"In the opinion of the Secretary of State these are matters firmly within the exercise of his discretion and not matters for negotiation with the parties to an enquiry. The Secretary of State's reason for recalling the delegation was given to parties in the Department's letter of 14th April and that reason has not been shown to be untrue, invalid or improper in any way. The choice of reporter for an enquiry is also clearly a matter for the Secretary of State's exercise of discretion. The Secretary of State's involvement as a constituency M.P. in relation to a previous appeal has no bearing on his consideration of the present appeal. Any such considerations are irrelevant in relation to his statutory duty to decide in the light of a report on the evidence and the submission of parties whether or not planning permission for the development now proposed should be granted.

"Accordingly he has decided that there is no good ground on which he should recall your appointment and modify your remits. Please proceed to reopen the enquiry after consultation with the parties."

In addition to the declarator sought, the petitioners seek an order quashing the direction of 14th April 1986 and reduction of Mr Peattie's appointment as reporter...

On the merits of the application, counsel for the petitioners submitted that the issue was focused by the letter dated 12th August 1986 from the Private Secretary of the Secretary of State to Mr Peattie. The petitioners accepted that the reason given for the direction dated 14th April 1986 had not been shown to be untrue, invalid or improper in any way. The petitioners also conceded that the choice of reporter for an enquiry was clearly a matter for the exercise of the Secretary of State's discretion. But the petitioners did not agree that the Secretary of State's involvement as a constituency M.P. in relation to the previous appeal had no bearing on his consideration of the present appeal. Nor did they accept that any such considerations were irrelevant in relation to his statutory duty to decide in the light of the report on the evidence and the submissions of parties whether or not planning permission for the development now proposed should be granted. On the contrary, counsel for the petitioners maintained that Mr Rifkind's letter to Mr Clark dated 30th July 1984 revealed that he had associated himself actively with the latter's objections to the extent of taking some credit for the outcome of the appeal. In addition, in his personal letter to Mr Younger, dated 31st August 1983, Mr Rifkind had indicated his support for the detailed written objections submitted by Mr Clark in opposition to the earlier appeal. In discharging his statutory duty in the present appeal, Mr Rifkind, as Secretary of State, had to exercise a quasi-judicial function, especially at the stage of considering the report of the enquiry. In exercising his quasi-judicial function, the Secretary of State had to observe the rules of natural justice. That meant that he must bring an unbiased and independent mind to consideration of the appeal. The history of Mr Rifkind's involvement with the previous appeal was calculated to raise a suspicion in the mind of a reasonable man that Mr Rifkind would not be impartial in his consideration of the present appeals. Counsel for the petitioners also submitted that if his main argument about bias were to be accepted, the result would not be an impasse. If that main argument was sound, then the Secretary of State should not have issued his direction in terms of paragraph 3(1) of Schedule 7, and thereafter appointed Mr Peattie as reporter. If, as should happen, the direction were to be quashed and Mr Peattie's appointment reduced, then the way would be clear for the appeal to be determined by a person appointed by the Secretary of State in terms of paragraph 1 of Schedule 7.

Counsel for the petitioners cited extensive authority to the proposition that in determining the appeal, the Secretary of State exercised a quasi-judicial function, and that in relation to alleged bias the appropriate test was that of suspicion of bias in the mind of a reasonable man. I do not find it necessary to summarise these authorities or to reach a concluded view upon the submissions which were based upon them. Counsel for the respondents as a generality did not quarrel the main proposition advanced by counsel for the petitioners. But counsel for the respondents qualified his position in two important respects. In the first place he submitted that support for a particular department or other policy could not be regarded as disqualifying bias. Secondly, counsel for the respondents submitted a separate argument to the effect that in issuing the direction dated 14th April 1986 the Secretary of State did not act in a quasi-judicial capacity. The petitioners had conceded that, taken by itself, that direction was not improper. Accordingly, the rules of natural justice had to yield to necessity, because once a direction had been properly given in terms of paragraph 3(1) of Schedule 7, the appeal had to be determined by the Secretary of State and by no other person.

I am not satisfied that the respondents' separate argument is sound. The argument proceeds on the footing that if as Secretary of State Mr Rifkind is entitled to, and does, direct that an appeal shall be determined by the Secretary of State, then it follows that Mr Rifkind as Secretary of State must go on to determine the appeal. I am not persuaded that that consequence necessarily follows. "Secretary of State" means one of Her Majesty's Principal Secretaries of State — Interpretation Act 1978, Schedule 1. Accordingly, if after a direction has been issued in relation to a planning appeal under paragraph 3(1) of Schedule 7 it appears that the Secretary of State for Scotland is disqualified on the ground of, for example, pecuniary interest from bringing an independent mind to bear on a planning appeal, I see no reason why the decision should not be entrusted to another Secretary of State. I refer to Secretaries of State Act 1926, section 1, and *Agee* v *Lord Advocate*.

If I am right in refusing to uphold the respondents' separate argument based upon the direction of 14th April 1986, there remains no obstacle to a consideration of the main argument on the merits. Upon an examination of Mr Rifkind's letters to Mr Younger and Mr Clark and of Mr Clark's written commentary dated 22nd August 1983 I have come without hesitation to the conclusion that Mr Rifkind is not disqualified on the ground of bias from determining the present appeal. The present appeal raises issues of fact and of policy. So far as policy is concerned I did not understand counsel for the petitioners to contend that Mr Rifkind would be disqualified merely because he had previously expressed public support for the policy of the planning authority or of central government so far as it related to the land at Woodhall Mains Farm. In any event, I do not consider that such a contention would be a tenable one. I refer to, and respectfully adopt, Professor H. W. R. Wade's treatment of this subject in *Administrative Law*, fifth edition, at pp. 435–438. Counsel for the petitioners did, however, maintain that it is one thing for a constituency M.P. to express general approval for a policy and another thing for him to ally himself actively with a constituent who supports that policy to the extent of appearing as an objector at a planning appeal enquiry. While conceding that, if the test of the reasonable man is applied, questions of degree may arise, counsel submitted that in the present case Mr Rifkind's active support for Mr Clark's objections was such as to justify suspicion of partiality in the mind of a reasonable man.

One can envisage the possibility of a Minister expressing support for a particular policy with such a degree of intransigence and intemperance as to betray a mind not only closed against reasoned argument but unable to weigh up proved facts in a fair way. If subsequently such a Minister were charged with the duty of exercising a quasi-judicial function in relation to an appeal to which that policy related, there would be obvious force in the argument that he had disqualified himself by bias from so acting. I am, however, satisfied that so far as his support for Mr Clark's objection endorsed planning policy Mr Rifkind's letters are far removed from the extreme scenario which I have outlined. Were I to accede to the petitioners' contention on the material put before me, one result would be that a Minister's impartiality would be in inverse proportion to his efficiency, a point which, as Professor Wade has noted, was made as long ago as 1932 by the Committee on Minister's Powers.

I turn finally to consider that part of Mr Rifkind's letter to Mr Younger in which he expressed support for Mr Clark's written objection. I have read with care Mr Clark's commentary dated 22nd August 1983, which extends to three pages. Assuming that Mr Rifkind's stated support for Mr Clark's objections implied that he had studied the commentary and formed a view on each of the points raised, I am not satisfied that as a result Mr Rifkind would have disqualified himself from fairly evaluating evidence that may be led at the enquiry in the present appeal. On several matters of fact Mr Clark's commentary was a plea for further information. On other matters of fact Mr Clark made assertions based upon information available at that time and designed to criticise an outline scheme to develop a seventy-acre site. The present appeal, on the other hand, relates to an area of 31.4 acres. In my view it is reasonable to suppose that further information has become available during the period which has elapsed since December 1983, and that the evidence led at the enquiry in the present appeal will differ in content and emphasis from that led in 1983. In any event, putting myself in the position of a reasonable man, on a detailed, as well as an overall, consideration of Mr Rifkind's letters, I find no basis for suspecting that he has disqualified himself from discharging his quasi-judicial function properly and giving a fair consideration to the petitioners' appeal. I shall therefore determine the application by refusing the petitioners the remedies which they seek."

Notes

(1) What factors were of crucial significance in determining whether or not a question of interest arose? Does it seem paradoxical that if a small pecuniary interest had been established that that may have been enough to create a ground of challenge, but that an obvious political

9–8

interest may not? For an example of a Minister having been found to have a pecuniary interest, see *R v. Secretary of State for Trade, ex parte Anderson Strathclyde plc* [1983] 2 All E.R. 233.

(2) Do you think that an approach based on demonstrating "intransigence" sets too high a burden on the party alleging an interest? Is this test stricter than that found in the case law dealing with fettering of discretion noted in Chapter 6? Are the considerations underlying an allegation of bias in this context and fettering of discretion different?

(3) The extract is an example of a planning decision which did not involve the Minister as initiating authority. It is perhaps difficult to escape the conclusion that what influenced Lord Davidson was that the support expressed by Mr Rifkind was in the context of support for a general policy made when he was constituency M.P. and that this was distinct from his role as a decision maker determining a specific appeal. Is this distinction tenable? What is the position where the decision maker is responsible for the initiation of the planning proposals?

In *Franklin v. Minister of Town and Country Planning* [1948] A.C. 87 objection was taken to the confirmation of the Stevenage New Town (Designation) Order 1946. Franklin was opposed to the development of the new town and sought to challenge confirmation of the Order on a number of grounds including comments made by the Minister at a public meeting prior to the making of the Order. It was apparent from the meeting that there was a real body of public opinion opposed to the plan. The Court of Appeal decided that the Minister had prejudged the issue at the time of the meeting and quashed the Order. The Minister appealed to the House of Lords. Lord Thankerton observed (at 103):

> "My Lords, I could wish that the use of the word 'bias' should be confined to its proper sphere. Its proper significance, in my opinion, is to denote a departure from the standard of even-handed justice which the law requires from those who occupy judicial office, or those who are commonly regarded as holding a quasi-judicial office, such as an arbitrator. The reason for this clearly is that, having to adjudicate as between two or more parties, he must come to his adjudication with an independent mind, without any inclination or bias towards one side or another in the dispute ...in the present case, the respondent having no judicial duty, the only question is what the respondent actually did, that is, whether in fact he did genuinely consider the report and the objections."

On one interpretation this approach would seem to preclude the possibility of a challenge on the ground of bias in the context of decisions in which the decision maker, whether Minister or other public authority, has direct involvement from an early stage. By extension it must be taken also to include decisions outwith the planning sphere. In *R.v. City of London Corporation, ex parte Allan* (1980) 79 L.G.R. 223 Woolf J. treated *Franklin* as "the low water mark of administrative law". To the extent that Lord Thankerton's decision was based on classification of functions, that may well be correct. However, in terms of its broader ratio, a more sensitive approach is now evident. In *R v. Amber Valley District Council ex parte Jackson* [1985] 1 W.L.R. 298 the question of the effect of party policy at local government level in favour of a development was considered. Woolf J. noted (at 307):

> "The rules of fairness or natural justice cannot be regarded as being rigid. They must alter in accordance with the context. Thus in the case of highways, the department can be both the promoting authority and the determining authority. When this happens, of course any reasonable man would regard the department as being pre-disposed towards the outcome of the inquiry. The department is under an obligation to be fair and carefully to consider the evidence given before the inquiry but the fact that it has a policy in the matter does not entitle a court to intervene. So in this case I do not consider the fact that there is a declaration of policy by the majorities group can disqualify a district council from adjudicating on a planning application. It may mean that the outcome of the planning application is likely to be favourable to an applicant and therefore unfavourable to objectors. However Parliament has seen fit to lay down that it is the local authority which has the power to make the decision and an applicant for planning permission in the normal way is entitled to have a decision from the local authority if the Secretary of State decides not to intervene...
>
>   I do not say that the court can never intervene. ...However in this case, while the Labour majority undoubtedly had a policy, there is no evidence before me on which it would be right to hold that they would not (despite the policy) consider the objections to the planning application on their merits. I would make it absolutely clear that they are under a duty to do so."

See also *R. v. Sevenoaks District Council, ex parte Terry* [1985] 3 All E.R. 226; *R. v. Secretary of State for the Environment, ex parte Kirkstall Valley Campaign Ltd* [1996] 3 All E.R. 304; and see now also *Lothian, Borders and Angus Co-operative Society Ltd v. Scottish Borders Council, The Times*, March 10, 1999.

(4) In *City of Glasgow District Council v. Secretary of State for Scotland (No. 1)*, 1993 **9–9** S.L.T. 198 a district planning authority contended that since the Secretary of State determined an appeal against refusal by the authority of planning consent (a situation in which ordinarily the appeal would have been determined by a Reporter), there was sufficient evidence to create in the mind of a reasonable man a suspicion of bias. Part of the planning application had related to construction of a section of road. The Secretary of State had been the promoter of that road outwith the appellant's area. Lord McCluskey, in giving the decision, observed (at 201):

> "The planning appeal came into a class of appeal to be determined by a person appointed by the Secretary of State rather than by the Secretary of State himself: it was accepted that the first respondent had powers to direct that he would in fact determine the appeal himself and it was not suggested that it was itself improper for him to do so. Nonetheless that factor, taken along with others, was likely to induce in the mind of a reasonable man a suspicion as to his impartiality in determining this particular planning appeal. The other factors included the circumstances that the decision on the appeal was announced on the newspaper of the Scottish Development Department and that the decision of the Secretary of State was contrary to the recommendations of the reporter in the two important respects mentioned.
>
> In reply, counsel for both respondents accepted that the principles of natural justice applied generally to the exercise by the first respondent of his planning functions under the 1972 Act, notably in relation to determining planning appeals. However it was obvious that that Act, like the Roads Act itself, contemplated that the Secretary of State might frequently have to determine matters in which he had an interest. Accordingly, the principle that no man should be the judge in his own case had to yield to necessity derived from the provisions of the legislation (*London and Clydeside Estates Ltd v Secretary of State for Scotland*). The Secretary of State, in determining a planning appeal such as the present, was acting in an executive or administrative capacity (*Lithgow v Secretary of State for Scotland*). Any planning authority, including the appellants themselves when the issue was before them as a planning authority, might have a responsibility to determine a planning appeal in which they had an interest. A planning authority might have an interest, for example as the partners of a developer making a planning application to them. The appellants were not suggesting, and it could not be suggested, that the first respondent had acted incompetently or improperly in exercising his powers under para 3 (1) of Sched 7 to the Town and Country Planning (Scotland) Act 1972 and deciding to determine the appeal himself. It was not disputed that there was a proximity of interest between the first and second respondents in relation to the Ayr Road route. The Ayr route was part of government policy, as had been explained at the public local inquiry. It was perfectly appropriate that the same counsel should appear for both respondents at the public local inquiry; indeed the appellants were not suggesting otherwise. It was very usual for decisions of the Secretary of State to be issued by the Scottish Development Department in such a case. It was entirely appropriate that in considering no fewer than 10 schemes and orders the Secretary of State should decide to determine these himself. The fact that he differed from the reporter in two relatively minor respects could not be prayed in aid as a factor which would lead a reasonable man to suppose that he had not acted impartially in determining the planning appeal."

See also *Strathclyde Regional Council v. Secretary of State for Scotland*, 1991 S.L.T. 796.

(5) Where, however, an authority has an interest in a matter which does not fall within the **9–10** ambit of existing or fixed and pre-determined administrative procedures, then it would appear that the authority is subject to the duty to be fair and in particular is required to appoint an independent person to conduct any inquiry which is needed.

In *Edinburgh University v. Craik*, 1954 S.C. 190 a person was appointed to hear representations in relation to the future of the Centre for Rural Economy. This person was a civil servant in the Department of Agriculture who part-managed the centre. It was observed by the Lord President (Cooper) (at 195):

> "that the inquiry should in this case have been taken by a wholly independent person, and that the utilisation of officials of the Department [of Agriculture] for the purpose in hand might well have led to a challenge of the proceedings".

The assistance of a technical assessor from a government department in the context of an inquiry into a local authority's proposal on a property in which the department has no special interest, would not, however, fall within the ambit of this rule, as the assessor's report did not disclose any matter on which objectors had not had the opportunity to be heard: see *General Poster & Publicity Co. Ltd v. Secretary of State for Scotland and East Lothian County Council*, 1960 S.C. 266 and compare *Anduff Holdings Ltd v. Secretary of State for Scotland*, 1991 S.C. 385 at 390.

HOW IS BIAS ESTABLISHED?

Barrs v. British Wool Marketing Board

1957 S.C. 72

9–11   LORD PRESIDENT (CLYDE): "The pursuer in this case has brought an action for the reduction of a decision given on 19th March 1954 by a valuation appeal tribunal appointed under the British Wool Marketing Scheme (Approval) Order, 1950, [S.I. 1950, No. 1326]. The Lord Ordinary after a proof has assoilzied the defenders, and, against his interlocutor so doing, the pursuer has presented a reclaiming motion.

The pursuer is a sheep farmer and a registered producer of wool under the British Wool Marketing Scheme, 1950, in terms of which he is required to sell his wool to, or through the agency of, the marketing Board. The price which he gets for his wool is not the price which it obtains in the market, but a figure fixed in terms of provisions in the Scheme, which is designed to secure something in the nature of a guaranteed price for the producer. Under paragraph 72 (4) of the Scheme the Board is required at the beginning of each year to publish a schedule of maximum prices at which wool of each class specified in the schedule will be valued. This price is fixed in the light of the guaranteed wool price adjusted under statutory powers by the Minister of Agriculture and Fisheries and the Secretary of State for Scotland. Paragraph 72 (5) provides that "as soon as practicable after any wool has been duly tendered by any registered producer or accepted for or by way of sale by the Board during the year the Board shall cause it to be valued having regard to the prescribed schedule of maximum prices and to the class or classes and the quality and condition of the wool and thereupon the Board shall notify the registered producer of the result of such valuation." In practice this valuation involves fixing the appropriate deduction from the maximum price in respect of defects of quality or condition of the particular wool. Paragraph 72 (6) further provides that "the said valuation shall be conclusive as to the value of the wool unless within ten days after the receipt of the said notification the registered producer shall give notice of appeal against the valuation in such manner as the Board may prescribe and in that case the matter shall be referred to a tribunal constituted in the manner described in paragraph 91 of the Scheme. The tribunal shall thereupon decide the value and this decision shall be conclusive as to the value of the wool." Paragraph 72 (7) provides that "when the value of the wool is finally decided the Board shall pay that amount to the producer." Paragraph 91 provides that a valuation appeal tribunal is to be constituted from three panels of persons for each region, the first consisting of persons nominated, so far as Scotland is concerned, by Area Executives of the National Farmers' Union of Scotland which are within the region: the second panel consisting of persons nominated by such body or bodies as the Board may think best fitted to represent the views of wool merchants; and the third panel consisting of persons nominated by the Board. The tribunal consists of five persons nominated by the Board from the panels for the region in which the wool is to be valued: one person from the panel nominated by the Board and two persons from each of the other two panels.

The wool with which this case is concerned was duly transmitted by the pursuer to the premises of wool merchants in Greenock on directions to that effect given by the Board. It was there valued under paragraph 72 (5) of the Scheme by two appraisers employed by the Board for that purpose at 53³/₄d. per lb., being 3d. per lb. below the prescribed maximum price. The pursuer was dissatisfied with this valuation and appealed under paragraph 72 (6) to the valuation appeal tribunal. That tribunal, consisting of five persons nominated in terms of paragraph 91 of the Scheme, duly assembled at the wool merchants' premise in Greenock on 19th March 1954. The pursuer was represented there by his manager, Mr M'Sporran, and the two appraisers from whose valuation the appeal had been taken were also present. The regional officer of the Board (a Mr M'Cullough) and a representative of the wool merchants were also there.

There persons all went to the store where the wool was lying, and the tribunal opened every bale and examined the wool. During the discussion at the store one of the appraisers drew a few staples of wool, which he showed to the others and took away. After scouring them, he brought them back and showed to the tribunal the result of the scouring and the extent of the tinting of the wool, even after scouring. The pursuer's manager was present and had a full opportunity of examining and stating his views about the staples in question and the effect of the scouring. The tribunal then retired to deliberate on the matter, and one of its members instructed the appraiser to put the samples of tinted wool on the table in the room where the tribunal was to deliberate.

So far, in my opinion, no exception could be taken to the propriety of what had been done, but the real issue in the case arises out of the next stage in the proceedings. When the tribunal retired to deliberate, the chairman told Mr M'Sporran and the wool merchants' representative that they were not to be present during the deliberations of the tribunal, and they consequently did not enter the room. The two appraisers, however, and Mr M'Cullough went into the room with the members of the tribunal and remained with them while the deliberations were going on. After about half an hour Mr M'Sporran was summoned to the room and informed of the decision of the tribunal, the value fixed by them being $52^3/_4$d. per lb., *i.e.*, one penny lower than the value against which the appeal was taken. This is the decision, which is sought to be reduced in the present case.

The basis in law upon which the pursuer's case is laid is that the decision of the tribunal was reached in circumstances contrary to natural justice. The main allegation in fact upon which this contention was based was that the two appraisers and Mr M'Cullough took part in the deliberations of the tribunal out with the presence of any representative of the pursuer. After a proof, however, the Lord Ordinary had no hesitation in rejecting this allegation, and in holding that in fact the three individuals in question said nothing at all while the tribunal was deliberating. This conclusion in fact was not challenged before us, and indeed on the evidence there was ample warrant for it.

Two incidental matters were referred to in argument which I can conveniently dispose of at this stage. In the first place, one of the appraisers brought the scoured staples to the room where the deliberation took place and laid them on the table there. But there is no significance in this, one way or the other, since it is clear that he did so at the request of a member of the tribunal, and neither he nor anyone else subsequently made any reference to the staples. The other matter was the discrepancies in the evidence regarding exactly where the two appraisers and Mr M'Cullough sat while the tribunal was deliberating. But the discrepancies are not really material. It is clear that these three did not sit in among the members of the tribunal, as appears at one time to have been suggested by the pursuer. Moreover, it seems to be established in the evidence that the two appraisers sat at one end of the room, and were further back from the table than the members of the tribunal, who were sitting, roughly, round it.

The question therefore comes to be whether this Court will reduce a decision of this tribunal as being contrary to natural justice when it appears that, while the tribunal was deliberating on what its decision was to be, the two appraisers and Mr M'Cullough were present in the room, although silent, and no representative of the pursuer was there.

Before dealing with this question, it is necessary in the first place to consider the nature of the valuation appeal tribunal. It was constituted in virtue of the statutory Scheme and was designed to play an important function in the statutory operation of the Scheme. For the payments which wool producers could secure from the Board, if determined by the tribunal, were, under the Scheme, to be finally fixed. Moreover, the tribunal was to perform the functions of an appellate Court, as appears from its name and from the provision in the Scheme for a notice of appeal to it. Further, "the matter" which is referred to it under paragraph 72 (6) of the Scheme. I read as meaning not merely the valuing of the wool but as including also the soundness or otherwise of the appraisers valuation. Finally, this tribunal is not a mere servant or committee of the Board, but a separate body including persons upon it who may be nominated by outside interests, the object no doubt being to arrive at as fair a decision on the appeal as is practicable. The tribunal in these circumstances was in my opinion, something much more important than a mere administrative hand of the Board. It was a separate and independent body of a quasi-judicial character with quasi-judicial, powers which it was contemplated would act judicially. It is true that there is nothing in the Scheme laying down what procedure the tribunal is to adopt, but this in no way removes it from that wide category of semi-judicial bodies which are so common a feature nowadays.

I am quite unable to accept the defenders contention that this tribunal was just performing the function of an appraiser, and, in effect, revaluing the wool. Under the Scheme it was to conduct an appeal against the appraisers' valuation. And, in fact, that was how it performed its task in this case. For, at the preliminary hearing at the warehouse, the appraisers took up the rôle of criticising the quality of the pursuer's wool, and thereby impliedly justifying their own valuation, while the pursuer's representative sought to minimise their criticisms and to point to the merits of the wool in question. This conduct on the part of both parties was, in my view, perfectly correct.

The consequence, however, of the provisions of the Scheme, and of the way in which it inevitably operates in practice, is to equate the Board in some respects to a respondent in the appeal, and to give them an interest not merely to support and justify the appraisers' valuation when the matter is appealed to the tribunal, but also to ensure, in the interests of other producers as a whole, that the appellant's valuation is not unduly high. But for these considerations the appraisers had no right to be present before the tribunal at all, and it was, in my opinion, these considerations which alone warranted their taking part in the proceedings before the tribunal prior to its retiring to deliberate. But, if so, they were in effect representing the Board and were parties to the appeal in a real and substantial sense.

I turn, then, to consider the standards which a body of this kind must adopt, and the circumstances in which a Court of law will interfere with its decisions. Although quasi-judicial bodies such as this tribunal are not Courts of law in the full sense, it has always been the law of Scotland that they must conform to certain standards of fair play, and their failure to do so entitles a Court of law to reduce their decisions. Were this not so, such tribunals would soon fall into public disrepute, and confidence in them would evaporate. Fair and equal opportunity afforded to all interests before the tribunal is the fundamental basis upon which the tribunal must operate, and, in the absence of such fair play to all, it is right and proper that a Court of law should reduce the tribunal's decision. The principle is well illustrated in reference to arbitrations, which are at least as much judicial proceedings as those of this tribunal. In *Mitchell* v. *Cable* [(1848) 10 D. 1297] Lord Jeffrey says of an arbiter (at p. 1309): "The true principle is, that his decree-arbitral can stand only when he has done his duty *fairly*. I do not mean *fairly*, in reference to his moral dispositions; but he is bound to show this Supreme Court that he has dealt *fairly*, that is *equally*, with both parties. Otherwise it must be held that he has violated the contract of submission, and acted *ultra vires compromissi*." (Compare Lord Dunedin in *Black* v. *John Williams & Co. (Wishaw), Limited* [1924 S.C. (H.L.) 22], at p. 27.)

It is important to observe the width of this principle. It is not a question of whether the tribunal has arrived at a fair result; for in most cases that would involve an examination into the merits of the case, upon which the tribunal is final. The question is whether the tribunal has dealt fairly and equally with the parties before it in arriving at that result. The test is not "Has an unjust result been reached? "but" Was there an opportunity afforded for injustice to be done?" If there was such an opportunity, the decision cannot stand. Hence, if one party is allowed to give evidence, and this is denied to another, the decision would be reduced, not because the evidence led had convinced the tribunal, for this could hardly ever be established, but because the standards of fair play which underlie all such proceedings had not been satisfied. Similarly, in the present case, the real test for the validity of the decision of the tribunal is not "Did the appraisers put forward arguments to the tribunal outwith the presence of the pursuer's representative?" The real test is "Did the tribunal create a situation in which they gave an opportunity to the appraisers to put forward arguments without giving an equal opportunity to the pursuer's representative?" Judged by that standard, there can only be one answer. The tribunal did so, and the decision therefore cannot stand. For the conduct of the proceedings was at variance with the principles of natural justice and the presence of the appraisers at the deliberations of the tribunal in the absence of any representative of the pursuer is fatal to the validity of the decision.

The Lord Ordinary's ground of judgment is, in my opinion, fallacious. He says: "As I hold that the two appraisers and the regional officer said nothing at all and that they in no way influenced the tribunal during the deliberations. I reach the conclusion that in fact no injustice was done." This was why he assoilzied the defenders. But his conclusion by no means follows from his premises. It does not necessarily follow from the fact that the three persons said nothing that the tribunal was not influenced by their presence in the room or that the result would necessarily have been the same had they not been there. It is just because no one can tell about this that the Courts have always rejected the Lord Ordinary's test — whether the members of the tribunal were proved to have been influenced in fact by the presence of the extraneous persons — and have taken as the true test whether all the parties were treated equally and fairly by the tribunal in the course of the proceedings, regardless of what influence in fact any of the parties may have had on the tribunal.

But, apart from this aspect of the matter altogether, the tribunal were engaged in the final deliberation prior to their decision. It is quite contrary to British principles of fair play that any person outside the members of the tribunal itself (with the possible exception of their clerk in certain circumstances) should be present when the members are deliberating. As Lord Wright, M. R., said in *Middlesex County Valuation Committee* v. *West Middlesex Assessment Committee* [[1937] Ch. 361], at p. 376: "It would be most improper on general principles of law that extraneous persons, who may or may not have independent interests of their own, should be present at the formulation of that judicial decision." Upon this view both the appraisers and Mr M'Cullough were extraneous persons who should not have been present, and the presence of any one of the three of them during these deliberations is fatal. Mr M'Cullough's presence cannot be justified on the ground that he was acting merely as clerk to the tribunal.

For these reasons, in my opinion, the principles of natural justice which must be observed by all tribunals such as this were not complied with in the present case, and the decision in question cannot therefore stand. It is only right that I should make it clear that in adopting the course which they took the members of the tribunal were quite clearly not actuated by malice or by any intention to create an unfair advantage. The appraisers and Mr M'Cullough were brought into the room where the deliberations were to take place because in the past it had been the custom to have them there at that stage. No other reason is suggested for this having been done. But the custom is a bad one and should be permanently discontinued. The surest way to discredit the proceedings of such a tribunal is to pursue such a custom, for it inevitably leads to an inference that some injustice may either be contemplated or carried out. That is just why the Courts have taken, as the test for reducing the decisions of such bodies, not "Has injustice been committed?" but "Has fair play been exercised?"

I am confirmed in this conclusion by a consideration of a series of cases in England where a similar approach has been made to the question. The circumstances of these cases are, of course different, although all the bodies in question were in that judicial or quasi-judicial category into which, in my opinion, the tribunal in the present case falls. In *Rex* v. *Essex Justices* [[1927] 2 K.B. 475] (at p. 488) Avory, J., quotes from Lord Hewart, C.J., in *Rex* v. *Sussex Justices* [1924] 1 K.B. 256] (at p. 259), as follows: "The question therefore is not whether in this case the deputy clerk made any observation or offered any criticism which he might not properly have made or offered, the question is whether he was so related to the case in its civil aspect as to be unfit to act as clerk to the justices in the criminal matter. The answer to that question depends not upon what actually was done, but upon what might appear to be done. Nothing is to be done which creates even a suspicion that there had been an improper interference with the course of justice." This same principle was applied as the test for the validity of a decision by an assessment committee in *Rex* v. *Salford Assessment Committee* [[1937] 2 K.B. 1]. A similar criterion was applied in *Cooper* v. *Wilson* [[1937] 2 K.B. 309], which was concerned with the dismissal of a police constable by a watch committee. The Chief Constable in that case had adopted a course analogous to that taken in the present case by the appraisers. He presented the arguments before the Committee, upon which he submitted that they should dismiss the constable, and he sat with them while they deliberated. Greer, L.J., at p. 323 said: "I think he [the plaintiff] is fairly entitled to complain that the presence of one of the respondents to his appeal on the Bench when they were deliberating as to whether they would or would not affirm his sentence was contrary to natural justice." In the same case Scott, L.J., at p. 344 says: "The fact that he remained with them [*i.e.*, the Committee] when the Court was cleared for the Committee to consider its decision, is fatal to the validity of the proceedings. It makes no difference whether he then discussed the case with them or not: the risk that a respondent may influence the Court is so abhorrent to English notions of justice that the possibility of it or even the appearance of such a possibility is sufficient to deprive the decision of all judicial force, and to render it a nullity." In the course of the argument before us two other English cases were referred to, but they do not in any way, in my opinion, assist the defenders in the present case. The decision in *Rex* v. *Brixton Income Tax Commissioners* [29 T.L.R. 712] is of little value, as it proceeded largely on an admission. The case of *In re Lauson*. [57 T.L.R. 315] where the Court refused to interfere with the decision of the tribunal, is of no help to the defenders, since the Court's decision was based upon the conclusion that there was no possibility of bias on the part of the clerk whose presence during the deliberations of the Committee was the subject-matter of complaint by the plaintiff. The Lord Chief Justice, at p. 318, said: "I accept the view …that if anyone by his conduct, or necessarily by his position, might be suspected of bias, he is disqualified from …attending the Committee when they deliberate on the matter in private." But he held in fact that there was no possibility of any such bias. The possibility of bias on the part of the appraisers — a bias against increasing the value and in favour of their own figure — cannot be excluded in the present case, which therefore is clearly distinguishable from *In re Lauson* [57 T.L.R. 315].

On the whole matter, in my opinion, the interlocutor of the Lord Ordinary should be recalled and decree granted."

Notes

(1) Where pecuniary interest exists, there is no need for a test to demonstrate a basis for challenge. Such an interest can be established objectively. Where the interest is non-pecuniary or where there is a concern as to the procedure adopted, as in *Barrs*, then one has to determine if a case of bias has been made out. This requires a test. *Barrs* was followed in *McDonnell, Petitioner*, 1987 S.L.T. 486. Here an applicant for housing benefit from Cumbernauld

9–12

Development Corporation appealed under the Housing Benefits Regulations 1985 to Cumbernauld Development Corporation Review Board. At the hearing the applicant's representatives left the room after the parties' submissions but the representatives of the corporation remained with the members. It was not alleged that the representatives had taken part in any aspect of the deliberating but a petition for judicial review succeeded in having the decision reduced. See also *R. v. Barnsley Metropolitan Borough Council, ex p. Hook* [1976] 1 W.L.R. 1052, C.A.

(2) It is apparent from the extract that it is not necessary to demonstrate that the party alleging bias needs to show prejudice. In *Mahmood v. West Dunbartonshire Licensing Board*, 1998 S.C.L.R. 843 it was alleged that the chairman of a licensing board had acted in a way which created a suspicion of bias. It was established that during a site visit to the premises in question, he had had a private conversation with a person who objected to the licence being granted. The applicant for the licence appealed to the sheriff under section 39(4) of the Licensing (Scotland) Act 1976, which provides that a sheriff may uphold an appeal if he considers that the board, in arriving at their decision, "acted contrary to natural justice". The sheriff accepted that a case for bias had been made out on the basis of the test set out in the extract, but the board appealed to the Inner House. It was argued for the board, *inter alia*, that the fact that other members of the board had not been tainted with this suspicion of bias by not having been involved in that conversation would be sufficient to reverse the sheriff's finding. This was rejected by Lord McCluskey (at 847):

> "It was also submitted, under reference to *Piper v Kyle and Carrick: District Council*, that the collective decision of the board was not vitiated by a finding of possible bias on the part of one member. *Piper* is, however, a very different type of case. All the proceedings there took place in public and no one suggested that there had been the slightest possibility of any clandestine departure from the principles of natural justice. That was no doubt why cases such as *Barrs v British Wool Marketing Board* were not even referred to in the opinion in that case. In any event, it is plain that, after his private conversation with the objector inside the objector's premises and before the board formally reconvened at the adjourned meeting to hear the applicant and the objectors, there must have been an opportunity for the chairman to influence other members of the board. We should make it abundantly clear that there is no suggestion that in fact any such influence was exerted or was sought to be exerted. That, however, is not the point, as the opinions, notably that of the Lord President, in *Barrs v British Wool Marketing Board* make clear. The point is that the opportunity was afforded for injustice to be done. In *R. v Gough* (just as in *Barrs*) no attempt was made to justify what happened on the basis that the collective decision of the deciding body, the jury, could survive a departure from the rules of natural justice relating to a single member of it."

(3) The test for bias in *Barrs* appears to have been based on a reasonable suspicion of bias. *Wildridge* can be viewed in a similar light. The test has been applied not just in circumstances like those in *Barrs*, but also where personal interest or preconceived opinion might exist as the next extract demonstrates. See also *Harper v. Heywood*, 1998 S.L.T. 644 (rudeness of the sheriff to counsel) and compare *Black v. Scott Lithgow Ltd*, 1990 S.L.T. 612 (no case of interest made out where the sheriff heard a proof in relation to circumstances arising from a matter he required to consider at an earlier fatal accident inquiry). See also *Dumfries and Galloway Regional Council v. O*, 1994 S.C.L.R. 661.

Bradford v. McLeod

1986 S.L.T. 244

9–13   "During the miners' strike in 1984 a conversation took place at a social function in Ayr at which the strike was discussed. A sheriff and a solicitor were both present during the conversation. At one point the sheriff made certain remarks to the effect that he 'would not grant legal aid to miners'. The solicitor understood this observation to be seriously made. Subsequently a miner represented by that solicitor appeared for trial before the same sheriff on a summary complaint alleging breach of the peace at a picket line. The solicitor moved the sheriff to disqualify himself from hearing that case in the light of the views he had expressed at the social function. The sheriff refused, saying that he did not propose to disregard his judicial oath. The trial proceeded. The same solicitor renewed his motion on a number of subsequent occasions at the start of other trials in which miners came before the sheriff charged with picket line offences. In each case the sheriff refused the motion and heard each trial. Fourteen miners who had been convicted by the sheriff in these circumstances sought to have their respective convictions and sentences suspended on the grounds that in each case there had been a miscarriage of justice. It was argued that the sheriff, in refusing to disqualify himself, had applied the wrong test: the question was not whether the sheriff was biased or had disregarded his judicial oath, but whether the circumstances were such as to create in the mind of a reasonable man a suspicion of the sheriff's impartiality."

LORD JUSTICE-CLERK (ROSS): "In these 14 bills of suspension, each of the complainers contends that his conviction by the sheriff and the following sentence should be suspended simpliciter. The ground for seeking suspension in each case is that the actings of the sheriff amounted to a miscarriage of justice.

Each of the complainers was charged at the instance of the respondent that he did on 7 May 1984 at the entrance to British Steel Terminal, Hunterston, Cunninghame District, Strathclyde, conduct himself in a disorderly manner, form part of a disorderly crowd, shout and swear, throw material at passing lorries and commit a breach of the peace.

The background to the charges was that there was a miners strike, and that each of the complainers was a striking miner who was said to have been involved in picketing at the British Steel Terminal at Hunterston.

In all 14 bills, the point raised is the same. However, the cases were not all heard by the sheriff on the same day, and there are some differences of detail between the cases and the allegations made therein. It was agreed, however, that the same result should follow in each case.

Put shortly, it is averred in each bill that at the trial diet, the agent for the complainer moved the sheriff to disqualify himself from considering the case in the light of certain views which he had expressed when present at a function in Ayr on 22 June 1984.

When the bills first came before this court on 11 June 1985, this court remitted to the sheriff principal to inquire and report on certain matters relating to the bills. The sheriff principal has now reported, and on 23 October 1985, counsel for the complainers moved us in each instance to pass the bill and to suspend the conviction and sentence pronounced on each complainer.

In each bill, it is averred that the sheriff had attended a social function organised by Ayr Curling Club at Ayr Ice Rink on 22 June 1984. The sheriff was a member of the committee of the club as was Mr. J. R. B. Penny, solicitor, who acted for some of the complainers. A committee photograph was to be taken and prior to that being done some discussion took place in the course of which the sheriff made certain remarks. It is not necessary to go into the matter in detail, since the sheriff principal has done that in his report. More than one statement regarding miners is attributed to the sheriff in the bills, and the sheriff principal has made it clear in his report that there were discrepancies between the witnesses whom he interviewed. However the sheriff principal's conclusion on the matter is that at some point during the evening, either before or after the photographs, two gentlemen who were present expressed views hostile to certain miners arising from what they considered was happening on the picket lines. The sheriff and Mr. Penny were present during this conversation although neither initiated it. At some point in the conversation the sheriff observed that he would not grant legal aid to miners. The sheriff principal states that it is not clear whether he meant miners in general or miners who had been engaged in particular activities; nor is it clear whether he specifically addressed his observation to Mr. Penny or whether Mr Penny just happened to hear it. The sheriff principal adds "Beyond what may be inferred from anything he said about legal aid I cannot be satisfied that Sheriff Smith gave vent to any expression of prejudice towards miners or any group of them".

At this stage I would only refer to two other observations of the sheriff principal. He interviewed the sheriff and states that the sheriff simply cannot remember any detail of the various social conversations he had at the function. It is thus clear, that the sheriff did not deny that he made the observation quoted above regarding legal aid. The other point is this. According to the sheriff principal, both Mr Penny and one of the other two gentlemen who heard the remark, understood the observation about legal aid to be seriously made.

The first trials of any of the complainers took place on 11 September 1984. At no time prior thereto had any hint been given by Mr Penny or anyone else that Sheriff Smith was unacceptable to Mr Penny's clients as a trial judge. The first case to call was one involving a client of Mr Penny who is not one of the complainers. Before the trial began Mr Penny made a submission to the effect that Sheriff Smith should disqualify himself from hearing the miners' cases in the light of the views which he had expressed on 22 June 1984. He stated that the views which the sheriff had expressed with regard to miners clearly indicated that he had made up his mind with regard to the miners and the accused who were appearing before him.

When this motion was made to him, the sheriff expressed himself as being flabbergasted that what had passed between two members of the committee of the curling club at a social gathering late in the evening should form the basis of such a submission in court. No doubt the sheriff considered on 22 June 1984 that he was conversing with friends on a private occasion. It may be that he was confident that others present would treat his remarks on the same basis, but if so, his confidence in Mr Penny appears to have been misplaced. However that may be, on 11 September 1984, Mr Penny referred to the conversation in open court, and the sheriff had then to rule upon the motion which had been made.

The sheriff adjourned the court for approximately 20 minutes. Apparently he regarded the allegation which had been made as reflecting on his judicial competence and integrity. He consulted the sheriff clerk. We are informed by the sheriff principal that the sheriff clerk was in no doubt that the sheriff gave the motion anxious and judicial consideration. In the event, when he returned to court, he stated that he did not propose to disregard the judicial oath which he had taken, and he refused to decline jurisdiction. Three trials took place that day, and on subsequent dates in September and October 1984 the trials took place of the remaining complainers. Before each trial the sheriff was moved to disqualify himself from hearing the case on grounds similar to those advanced before the first trial, and in each case he refused to decline jurisdiction. In the result each of the complainers was convicted and sentenced.

For the complainers, senior counsel put at the forefront of his submissions the following proposition in the form of a question — whether there were circumstances affecting the sheriff which would create in the mind of a reasonable person a suspicion of his impartiality? If that question fell to be answered in the affirmative, senior counsel submitted that that would disqualify the sheriff even though no bias in fact existed.

I am entirely satisfied that what are commonly referred to as the rules of natural justice apply to criminal trials in this country. In the unreported case of *Stewart* v. *Agnew*, the Lord Justice-General said: "But it is vital in every criminal prosecution not only that justice should be done but that justice should be visibly done." In the same case, Lord Russell stated: "By tradition and practice it is fundamental to the proper conduct and proceedings in our criminal courts that justice should not only be done but should also be seen to be done."

This principle which applies to criminal trials also applies to persons performing judicial duties in a domestic forum. The rule was well expressed by Eve J. In *Law* v. *Chartered Institute of Patent Agents* at p. 289 where he said: "Each member of the council in adjudicating on a complaint thereunder is performing a judicial duty, and he must bring to the discharge of that duty an unbiassed and impartial mind. If he has a bias which renders him otherwise than an impartial judge he is disqualified from performing his duty. Nay, more (so jealous is the policy of our law of the purity of the administration of justice), if there are circumstances so affecting a person acting in a judicial capacity as to be calculated to create in the mind of a reasonable man a suspicion of that person's impartiality, those circumstances are themselves sufficient to disqualify although in fact no bias exists." That dictum, in my opinion, also represents the law in Scotland upon this matter.

Applying that dictum to the present case, I am clearly of opinion that the contentions of the complainers must prevail. When the solicitor for the complainers moved the sheriff to disqualify himself from considering the case, I am of opinion that the sheriff misdirected himself as to the test to be applied. The sheriff regarded the motion as reflecting on his judicial competence, and emphasised that he would observe his judicial oath. For myself, I am quite satisfied that the sheriff, in trying the various complainers, did not disregard his judicial oath. Investigations have been carried out by the sheriff principal, and there is nothing in his report to suggest that at the trials the sheriff acted unfairly. What the sheriff failed to note, however, when the motion was made that he should decline jurisdiction was that the interest of justice required not merely that he should not display bias but that the circumstances should not be such as to create in the mind of a reasonable man a suspicion of the sheriff's impartiality.

It could hardly be suggested that a sheriff who had refused an applicant legal aid, was thereby precluded from taking the trial of that applicant. But that was not the situation here. The effect of s. 1 (7) (*a*) (ii) of the Legal Aid (Scotland) Act 1967 is that a person shall not be given legal aid in connection with summary criminal proceedings unless the court considers that in all the circumstances of the case it is in the interests of justice that legal aid should be available to the accused and grants a legal aid certificate. In his report, the sheriff principal explains that at Kilmarnock the sheriffs have a policy, under reference to the foregoing subsection, that legal aid should only be granted in summary criminal proceedings if the accused can satisfy the sheriff that he has a serious defense in advance. In that situation, the effect of the sheriff's observation on 22 June 1984 to the effect that he personally would not grant legal aid to miners is that irrespective of the circumstances his view was that no miners should receive legal aid as they had no answer to the charges. He was indicating ab ante that without considering the merits of an application for legal aid at the instance of any miner, he would refuse it.

In my opinion, a reasonable person on hearing that the sheriff had made that observation would be likely to conclude that the sheriff was biased so far as cases involving miners were concerned. Indeed the generality of the observation is such as to create in the mind of a reasonable man a definite suspicion that the sheriff may have such a bias. As explained by Eve J. in the passage quoted above, that is sufficient to disqualify a judge from performing his duty even though as matter of fact the judge is not biased. I appreciate that at the time when the sheriff made the observation about legal aid, he had no reason to suppose that he personally would be involved in the determination of legal aid applications by any miners as he was not the nominated legal aid sheriff at Kiimarnock for the year in question. In my opinion, that does not matter since the important question is the effect that hearing the observation would have on a reasonable person. I should add for the sake of completeness that, in the absence on leave of the nominated legal aid sheriff and the other permanent sheriff at Kilmarnock. Sheriff Smith did in fact deal with and refuse legal aid applications lodged by the seven complainers represented by Mr Penny. The seven complainers subsequently made second applications for legal aid which were refused by the nominated legal aid sheriff. The remaining seven complainers (not represented by Mr Penny) had their legal aid applications dealt with and refused by the nominated legal aid sheriff who also refused second applications at the instance. It is thus clear that as regards the seven complainers represented by Mr Penny, Sheriff Smith duly acted as he had said he would when he made the observation on 22 June 1984.

In my opinion, in refusing the motion to decline jurisdiction, the sheriff acted in error. He mistakenly thought that the sole issue was whether he was prepared to act fairly and in accordance with his judicial oath; he failed to realise that it was not enough that justice should be done, but that justice must also be seen to be done. Regrettably, because of the observations which it is established that the sheriff made on 22 June 1984, justice could not be seen to be done when he conducted the trials of the complainers.

I can readily appreciate, as the sheriff principal observes, that the sheriff was naturally concerned about the impact which this matter could have on the conduct of court business. There were many trials to be taken involving miners, and if the motion made to him was well founded, then he would be disabled from carrying out part of the business of the court. None the less, once Mr Penny had made public what the sheriff had said on 22 June 1984, the inevitable consequence was that the sheriff was disabled from dealing with any case involving a miner.

As I have already indicated, having read the sheriff principal's report, I have no reason to think that the complainers did not in fact receive fair trials. Indeed we were informed by the advocate-depute that in three other instances Sheriff Smith had acquitted miners who had been charged with similar offences. That would certainly go some way towards negativing the suggestion that the sheriff was in fact biased against miners. However, as already explained, that was not the sole issue raised by the motion.

It follows that the convictions cannot stand. It is a tribute to the law in Scotland that there are so few recorded cases where it has been alleged that justice has not been seen to be done. This case may serve as a reminder that the law in Scotland is jealous of its reputation for doing justice and for ensuring that justice is seen to be done; it may also serve to remind judges that if justice is not merely to be done but is to be visibly done, they like Caesar's wife must be above suspicion.

In all the circumstances I move your Lordships to pass these bills, and to suspend the convictions and sentences passed".

LORD HUNTER: "I am in complete agreement with the opinion of your Lordship in the chair. The proposition that it is fundamental to the proper conduct of proceedings in the criminal courts of Scotland that justice should not only be done but should be seen to be done is a salutary one. The principle derived from that proposition, which is particularly applicable to the circumstances of the present cases, was well stated in the concluding words of the passage from the judgment of Eve J. in *Law* v. *Chartered Institute of Patent Agents* at p. 289, quoted by your Lordship. That statement of principle merits repetition: 'If there are circumstances so affecting a person acting in a judicial capacity as to be calculated to create in the mind of a reasonable man a suspicion of that person's impartiality, those circumstances are themselves sufficient to disqualify although in fact no bias exists'."

LORD DUNPARK: "I agree with the comprehensive opinion of your Lordship in the chair. The fact that the sheriff acquitted three other miners charged with a similar offence satisfies me that he had not prejudged the issue in these cases. Nevertheless, as your Lordship has demonstrated, the question for us is not whether the complainers received fair trials but is whether what the sheriff said socially was sufficient to create in the minds of reasonable men the suspicion that he *might* not be impartial. In my opinion the sheriff cannot be blamed for applying the wrong test after hearing a submission at a trial diet without advance warning and without, apparently any citation of authority. I cannot understand why the solicitor in question gave no intimation to anyone of his intention to make this submission until after the calling of the trial diets. The sensible course for him to take was to notify the sheriff clerk in good time before the trial diets that he intended to submit that the sheriff had disqualified himself from presiding at these trials. Had he done that, there would have been time for arrangements to be made for another sheriff to take these trials and thus to avoid the undesirable publicity which these cases have attracted. I trust that this advice will be followed if ever a similar situation arises in future."

Notes

9–14   (1) The reference to the English civil case of *Law v. Chartered Institute of Patent Agents* [1919] 2 Ch. 276 suggests that where an issue of prejudgment or preconceived opinion arises, the test of reasonable suspicion might be of universal application, although there is yet to be an authoritative ruling by the Scottish courts. In *Donald v. Marquetty*, 1986 G.W.D. 4-83 *Bradford* was considered in the context of administrative proceedings, but no ruling was made as to whether or not it provided the correct test. It has certainly been followed in a number of subsequent criminal cases. For example, in *Tennant v. Houston*, 1987 S.L.T. 317 objection was taken to the fact that a councillor sat beside a fellow justice hearing a case concerning an enforcement notice served by the council and in *Bassi v. Normand*, 1992 S.L.T. 341 the imposition of a fine was quashed where it had been imposed without a plea in mitigation. Although an opportunity for a plea in mitigation was given later, the fine remained. See too *Hawthorn v. McLeod*, 1986 S.L.T. 657 and contrast *Beattie v. Scott*, 1991 S.L.T. 110 (not oppressive for the accused to be asked to stand up to assist with identification).

Indeed, it is not apparent that a universal test can in fact be constructed. For example, in *Docherty v. Strathkelvin District Council*, 1994 S.L.T. 1064 it was noted that the test to be applied in connection with the conduct of a member of an industrial tribunal was "that there be a real likelihood of bias". Both *Barrs* and *Mahmood* suggest that administrative tribunals and courts are subject to the test of reasonable suspicion. Where the court is considering a criminal matter that test might be easier to satisfy: see *Mahmood*, p. 847C. Reasonable suspicion was applied in *Brown v. Executive Committee of the Edinburgh District Labour Party*, 1995 S.L.T. 985. Similarly, in *London and Clydeside Estates* above, it appears as if something approaching "real likelihood" was necessary to make out a relevant challenge in the circumstances of that case.

(2) Doubts in England as to whether there was a unitary test for bias fell to be considered by the House of Lords in *R. v. Gough* [1993] A.C. 646. Gough had been indicted on a count of conspiracy to rob a betting shop. The co-accused was his brother but proceedings against his brother had been dropped at the committal hearing. During the trial, his brother's name had been given in a police photograph of him which had been presented to the jury. Gough was convicted and sent to jail for 15 years. The brother then began shouting in protest from the public gallery of the court whereupon one of the jurors realised that the brother was in fact her next-door neighbour. She swore an affidavit that she had never seen the appellant before the trial and the fact that his brother was her neighbour did not influence her thinking as a juror. Nevertheless, Gough appealed arguing that the presence of his brother's neighbour on the jury amounted to a sufficiently serious irregularity in the conduct of the trial as to have it quashed. In delivering the judgment of the House Lord Goff of Chieveley set out a unitary test (at 670):

> "I think it possible, and desirable, that the same test should be applicable in all cases of apparent bias, whether concerned with justices or members of other inferior tribunals, or with jurors, or with arbitrators. Likewise I consider that, in cases concerned with jurors, the same test should be applied by a judge to whose attention the possibility of bias on the part of a juror has been drawn in the course of a trial, and by the Court of Appeal when it considers such a question on appeal. Furthermore, I think it unnecessary, in formulating the appropriate test, to require that the court should look at the matter through the eyes of a reasonable man, because the court in cases such as these personifies the reasonable man; and in any event the court has first to ascertain the relevant circumstances from the available evidence, knowledge of which would not necessarily be available to an observer in court at the relevant time. Finally, for the avoidance of doubt, I prefer to state the test in terms of real danger rather than real likelihood, to ensure that the court is thinking in terms

of possibility rather than probability of bias. Accordingly, having ascertained the relevant circumstances, the court should ask itself whether, having regard to those circumstances, there was a real danger of bias on the part of the relevant member of the tribunal in question, in the sense that he might unfairly regard (or have unfairly regarded) with favour, or disfavour, the case of a party to the issue under consideration by him…"

Gough was subsequently applied in *Reid v. Chief Constable of Merseyside, The Times,* February 5, 1996 where the use of the phrase "the niggers in the wood pile", which was a reference to certain police officers in the context of a civil action by a black person for malicious prosecution, did not meet the test of real danger. The judge had immediately made it clear that she realised her error and apologised to the plaintiff.

Similarly, in *R. v. Inner West London Coroner, ex parte Dallaglio* [1994] 4 All E.R. 139 a coroner, in the course of a lengthy inquest into the 51 deaths arising from the *Marchioness* sinking, referred to one of the parents of the deceased as being "unhinged" in the context of an interview with journalists. The parents sought judicial review of the coroner's refusal to remove himself on the grounds of alleged bias. Real danger was established. The comment was "injudicious and insensitive but bound to be interpreted as a gratuitous insult" *per* Simon Brown L.J. at 153. For a recent and controversial example of the application of *Gough* see *Re Pinochet* [1999] 1 All E.R. 577, H.L.

Do you consider that the difficulties identified by the court in *Gough* relating to the question of reasonableness of suspicion were valid? Does it matter if the question of suspicion is being determined by the court or by the reasonable bystander? Is it desirable or realistic to create a unitary test to cover all forms of decision making? *Gough* was considered in *Mahmood* but the test in *Barrs* was accepted as representing the law of Scotland, as least insofar as administrative tribunals are concerned.

(3) Craig (2nd ed.), p. 237, in considering the choice between a reasonable suspicion and a real risk of bias, observed:

> "How high the second part of the hurdle should be pitched, suspicion or likelihood, will depend again on value judgments. It is unlikely that the presence of the higher hurdle will prevent reviewing courts from quashing a decision should they feel that this is warranted. The tendency within more recent authority is to pitch the second part of the hurdle at varying levels depending upon the nature of the decision-maker in question. Thus where the body is judicial in nature the lower test of reasonable suspicion should suffice, reflecting the importance of the idea that justice should be seen to be done. Administrative decisions should only be overturned if the higher hurdle of real likelihood of bias could be overcome, and there are suggestions that the test should be further modified when the administrative body, such as a local authority, necessarily has an interest in the outcome of a decision. In such situations its decision should only be overturned for bias when it acted in such a way prior to its decision that it could not properly have exercised its discretion, taking due account of its interest in the proceedings."

Does this, written prior to *Gough*, provide a coherent analysis of why a unitary test is not desirable? In terms of value judgments, does it seem that the same standard should be applied to cases involving serious crime and, in the context of highly judicial proceedings, to matters of a more routine, and often considerably less serious, moment in administrative procedures? McMurtrie above at 320 has gone further in suggesting that no particular test exists in Scots law. The test for bias is essentially one of the circumstances of each case. Relevant considerations include the nature of the interest and whether the relationship, monetary or non-pecuniary interest is set against the necessity of the decision being made, the remoteness of the interest, the subject matter of the decision and the function of the decision-maker. While that view does not seem to be justified on the authorities, which after all do seem to seek to establish some form of test, it may be the case that these circumstances are relevant to the value judgments referred to by Craig.

(4) Under the jurisprudence of the European Court of Human Rights, in assessing the **9–15** independence and impartiality of a decision maker from the parties seeking a decision and government, regard is had to the way in which its members are appointed and on what terms, the presence or otherwise of guarantees against outside pressures and also whether a body

appears to be independent. The test that applies is partly subjective and partly objective. In subjective terms the test is "on the basis of the personal conviction of a particular judge in a given case" and in objective terms whether the judge "offered guarantees sufficient to exclude any legitimate doubt in this respect": see *Hauschildt v. Denmark* (1990) 12 E.H.R.R. 266 at 279. The subjective test is primarily concerned with the decision marker's conduct. The objective test is concerned to ascertain facts independent of that conduct which creates a legitimate concern as to impartiality. Whether or not such a fact existed depends on whether "it can be held objectively justified" and concern by the party appearing before the decision maker would be relevant but not decisive (at 280). Although *Hauschildt* involved the criminal courts, the same test has been applied to administrative proceedings.

In *De Haan v. Netherlands* (1998) 26 E.H.R.R. 417 De Haan had been claiming a social security benefit for being absent from work owing to illness. She was thereafter examined by a doctor who decided that she was in fact fit for work and her entitlement to the benefit ceased. She appealed to the appeals tribunal and the expert attached to the tribunal agreed with the first doctor as to her fitness for work. The president of the appeals tribunal, relying on that report, dismissed De Haan's appeal. She thereafter lodged an appeal against that decision. The same judge who had heard that appeal was to officiate again. Although De Haan's lawyer took exception to this, the objection was rejected. An appeal was made to the European Court of Human Rights. Although, on the facts, there is nothing to suggest any bias on the part of the judge, the decisive feature was that he presided over a tribunal called upon to decide on an objection to a decision for which he himself had been responsible. In the circumstances, De Haan's fears about the impartiality of the tribunal were objectively justified. There had therefore been a violation of Article 6(1). Under this test, the United Kingdom system of courts martial was found to be in breach of Article 6(1) of the European Convention on Human Rights: see *Findlay v. United Kingdom* (1997) 24 E.H.R.R. 221. and *Cable v. United Kingdom*, February 4, 1999; see too *Campbell and Fell v. United Kingdom* (1985) 7 E.H.R.R. 165; *Langborger v. Sweden* (1990) 12 E.H.R.R. 416; and *Thomann v. Switzerland* (1997) 24 E.H.R.R. 553.

BIAS: STATUTORY RULES

Local Government (Scotland) Act 1973, ss. 38–42

Restrictions on voting

Disability of members of authorities for voting on account of interest in contracts, etc.

9–16   **38.** — (1) Subject to the provisions of section 60 of this Act, if a member of a local authority has any pecuniary interest, direct or indirect, in any contract, proposed contract or other matter, and is present at a meeting of the local authority at which the contract or other matter is the subject of consideration, he shall at the meeting, and as soon as practicable after its commencement, disclose the fact and shall not take part in the consideration or discussion of the contract or other matter or vote on any question with respect to it.

(2) If any person fails to comply with the provisions of subsection (1) above, he shall for each offence be liable on summary conviction to a fine not exceeding £200 unless he proves that he did not know that the contract, proposed contract or other matter in which he had a pecuniary interest was the subject of consideration at that meeting.

(3) A local authority may, by standing orders, provide for the exclusion of a member of the authority from a meeting of the authority while any contract, proposed contract or other matter in which he has a pecuniary interest, direct or indirect, is under consideration.

(4) The following, that is to say —

(a)   the receipt by the convener or vice-convener of a council of an allowance to meet the expenses of his office or his right to receive, or the possibility of his receiving, such an allowance;

(b)   the receipt by a member of a local authority of an allowance or other payment under any provision of sections 45 to 48 of this Act or his right to receive, or the possibility of his receiving, any such payment;

shall not be treated as a pecuniary interest for the purposes of this section.

Pecuniary interests for purposes of section 38

39. — (1) For the purposes of section 38 of this Act, a person shall be treated, subject to the following provisions of this section and to section 41 of this Act, as having indirectly a pecuniary interest in a contract proposed contract or other matter, if —

(a)   he or any nominee of his is a member of a company or other body with which the contract was made or is proposed to be made or which has a direct pecuniary interest in the other matter under consideration; or

(b)   he is a partner, or is in the employment, of a person with whom the contract was made or is proposed to be made or who has a direct pecuniary interest in the other matter under consideration.

(2) Subsection (1) above does not apply to membership of or employment under any public body, and a member of a company or other body shall not by reason only of his membership be treated as having an interest in any contract, proposed contract or other matter if he has no beneficial interest in any securities of that company or other body.

(3) In the case of married persons living together, the interest of one spouse shall, if known to the other, be deemed for the purpose of section 38 of this Act to be also an interest of the other.

General notices and recording of disclosures for purposes of section 38

40. — (1) A general notice, given in writing to the proper officer of the authority by a member thereof, to the effect that he or his spouse is a member or in the employment of a specified company or other body, or that he or his spouse is a partner or in the employment of a specified person, or that he or his spouse is the tenant of any premises owned by the authority, shall, unless and until the notice is withdrawn, be deemed to be a sufficient disclosure of his interest in any contract, proposed contract or other matter relating to that company or other body or to that person or to those premises which may be the subject of consideration after the date of the notice.

(2) The proper officer of the authority shall record, in a book to be kept for the purpose, particulars, of any disclosure made under section 38 of this Act and of any notice given under this section, and the book shall be open at all reasonable hours to the inspection of any local government elector for the area of the local authority.

Removal or exclusion of disability, etc.

41. — (1) The Secretary of State, as respects a member of any local authority, may, subject to such conditions as he may think fit to impose, remove any disability imposed by section 38 of this Act in any case in which the number of members of a local authority disabled by that section at any one time would be so great a proportion of the whole as to impede the transaction of business, or in any other case in which it appears to the Secretary of State in the interests of the inhabitants of the area that the disability should be removed.

(2) The power of the Secretary of State under subsection (1) above includes power to remove, either indefinitely or for any period, any such disability which would otherwise attach to any member, or any class or description of member, by reason of such interests, and in respect of such matters, as may be specified by the Secretary of State.

(3) Nothing in section 38 of this Act precludes any person from taking part in the consideration or discussion of, or voting on, any question whether an application should be made to the Secretary of State for the exercise of the powers conferred by subsections (1) and (2) above.

(4) Section 38 of this Act does not apply to an interest in a contract, proposed contract or other matter which a member of a local authority has as a council tax payer or inhabitant of the area, or as an ordinary consumer of water or to an interest in any matter relating to the terms on which the right to participate in any service, including the supply of goods, is offered to the public.

(5) For the purposes of section 38 of this Act, a member shall not be treated as having a pecuniary interest in any contract, proposed contract or other matter by reason only of an interest of his or of any company, body or person with which he is connected, as mentioned in section 39 of this Act, which is so remote or insignificant that it cannot reasonably be regarded as likely to influence a member in the consideration or discussion of, or in voting on, any question with respect to that contract or matter.

(6) Where a member of a local authority has an indirect pecuniary interest in a contract, proposed contract or other matter by reason only of a beneficial interest in securities of a company or other body, and the total nominal value of those securities does not exceed £1,000 or one-hundredth of the total nominal value of the issued share capital of the company or body, whichever is the less, and if the share capital is of more than one class, the total nominal value of shares of any one class in which he has a beneficial interest does not exceed one-hundredth of the total issued share capital of that class, sections 38 and 39 of this Act shall not prohibit him from taking part in the consideration or discussion of the contract or other matter or from voting on any question with respect to it, without prejudice, however, to his duty to disclose his interest.

Interpretation of sections 39 and 41

42. — (1) In sections 39 and 41 of this Act, 'securities' and 'shares' have the same meaning respectively as in the Prevention of Fraud (Investments) Act 1958.

(2) In section 39 of this Act, 'public body' includes any body established for the purpose of carrying on under national ownership any industry or part of an industry or undertaking, the governing body of any university, or college, school or hall of a university, college of education or central institution or of any institution established under section 81 (2) of the Education (Scotland) Act 1962, and the National Trust for Scotland for Places of Historic Interest or Natural Beauty incorporated by the Order confirmed by the National Trust for Scotland Order Confirmation Act 1935.

In this subsection, 'college of education' and 'central institution' have the meanings assigned to them by section 145 of the said Act of 1962."

Notes

9–17   (1) For discussion of the above generally see C.M.G. Himsworth, *Local Government Law in Scotland* (1995), pp. 266–270 and *Stair Memorial Encyclopaedia*, Vol. 14, paras 213–217. The term "or any other matter" has received a broad interpretation in England: see *Rands v. Oldroyd* [1958] 3 All E.R. 344.

(2) Note the power given to the Secretary of State to remove any disability. This power has been exercised individually and also by way of reference to a class description of members — for example, in relation to tenants of local authority houses: Scottish Office Environment Department Circular 15/92, para. 20. Note that notwithstanding the terms of section 41(4), members who are in arrears of community charge or council tax are restricted from voting in matters relating to these taxes: the Local Government Finance Act 1992, s. 112(2) and see J. McFadden, "New Restrictions on Voting", 1993 S.L.T. (News) 9.

(3) The statutory rules on disclosure of interest are not exhaustive. The common law rules on bias still operate in areas not governed by statute and, moreover, sometimes specific statute also buttresses sections 38–42: see, for example, section 20(3) of the Housing (Scotland) Act 1987 in relation to housing allocation decisions which excludes from such decisions a member of an authority whenever (*a*) the house in question is situated in, or (*b*) the applicant for the house in question resides in, the member's ward. See also section 19 of the Local Government and Housing Act 1989, which provides that within a month of making a declaration of office, a councillor is obliged to disclose matters on which he or she has an interest.

(4) Councillors are also subject to a National Code of Local Government Conduct. This originated in a proposal of the Redcliffe-Maud Committee, Cmnd. 5636 (1974). The current code was issued in terms of section 31 of the Local Government and Housing Act 1989. Its text may be found in the Scottish Development Department Circular 11/90, April 10, 1990. The code emphasises that on admission to office an adherence to specific rules and disclosure of interest, and a general obligation to "at all times avoid any occasion for suspicion and any appearance of improper conduct": paras 6–7. Although there is no specific enforcement mechanism for the code, the Local Ombudsman may have regard to its terms investigating maladministration, on which see Chapter 16. On taking office, councillors are required to make a formal declaration of acceptance of the terms of the code: Local Authorities (Councillors) (Declaration of Acceptance of Office) (Scotland) Order 1990.

9–18   (5) Notwithstanding the provisions of sections 38–42 and the code, there has been growing concern as to the adequacy of existing controls on the interests of councillors. The Third Report of the Committee on Standards in Public Life: Standards of Conduct of Local Government in England, Scotland and Wales, July 1997, Cmnd. 3702 (the Nolan Report), concluded that there was a profusion of rules resulting in a growing lack of clarity over standards of conduct and that a new start be made on an ethical framework for local government. The Government's response for Scotland came in a consultation paper, "A New Ethical Framework for Local Government in Scotland". On the proposal for a new Code of Conduct, the Nolan Report set out 18 principles of personal conduct, one of which, "honesty", obliges councillors to declare private interests. As with the existing code, each councillor will be required to declare an obligation to observe the code. In relation to the councillor's personal interests, the general principle of "honesty" asks councillors to declare any private interest relating to their public duties. The Nolan Report was critical of the present approach to councillors as being unnecessarily complex. It recommended a new system of registration of personal interest, whether pecuniary or non-pecuniary, interest which might relate closely to the activities of the council or which members of the public might reasonably think could influence a councillor's judgment. This would include pecuniary interests of close family members and people living in the same household as the councillor. It would no longer be a criminal offence to fail to register a pecuniary interest, but failure to do so would be enforced through a new local government tribunal. In relation to direct pecuniary and other interests, the proposals of the Nolan Report were accepted by the Government in the consultation paper as providing an acceptable basis for both statutory reform and inclusion in the new Code of Conduct. As for the new code, the government proposes that a Minister of the Scottish Executive, will, after consultation with COSLA, the Accounts Commission for Scotland and the Local Ombudsman Statement of General Principles of Conduct for Local Councils in Scotland and their draft Code. Each councillor would be required to adopt a Code and the Code would be enforced through a new independent body, the Standards Commission, rather than the proposed Local Government Tribunal. Legal action to enforce the code in the courts, particularly in a criminal context, would be available in certain circumstances. In summary these are as follows:

- Unless they have a dispensation, councillors who have a direct pecuniary interest in the matter under consideration should have to declare that interest, withdraw from the meeting or discussion, and take no further part in the business in question.
- Councillors should have to declare any interest which is not of a pecuniary kind, which members of the public could reasonably think could influence their actions, speeches or votes.
- Unless they have a dispensation, councillors should withdraw from consideration of matters where they have an interest whose existence creates a real danger of bias, that is where they or their close family are likely to be affected more than the generality of those affected by the decision in question.
- All the existing primary legislation or conflicts of interest in local government should be repealed and be replaced by a provision giving effect to the common law principle set out above.
- Regulations under the statute should be confined to requiring councils to have rules covering declaration, withdrawal and disciplinary procedures.

Note the use of both the suspicion of a reasonable person and a real danger of bias. The Government accepted the Nolan Report's categorisation of interest as between direct pecuniary interest, which required declaration and withdrawal from any further participation in the matter under consideration and "other interests" which required only declaration. The Government, however, did not accept the Nolan Report as to whether a councillor was affected more than the generality of those affected by the decision in question. The Nolan Report advocated a test which would have required a sub-division of the "other interest category". The Government preferred a twofold test asking first, is the councillor, or his or her close family, affected more than the generality of those affected by the decision? And, secondly, would an ordinary member of the public, being aware of the facts of the case and the general principles of conduct, think it wrong for the councillor to take part in the decision in question? If the answer to either limb of the test is yes the councillor concerned would have a declarable interest debarring him or her from participating in the decision concerned. In relation to dispensations, the Nolan Report again criticises their complexity. The Government proposes that dispensations be governed by the Code of Conduct and that the Standards Commission would have a role to play in granting or refusing such a dispensation, rather than the Secretary of State as under the present structure.

A failure to declare a direct pecuniary interest and to withdraw from the meeting would continue to be a criminal offence by way of a new statutory offence of misuse of public office. The Nolan Report recommended that breaches of the Code of Conduct would first be dealt with by the council's own Standards Committee, but the Government and the Scottish Committee of the Council on Tribunals expressed concern that the council should have any input in determining if councillors breached the Code: see the Scottish Committee Annual Report 1997–98, pp. 5–6. Instead, they propose that the Standards Committee has a role in promoting the principles of good conduct, but not in disciplining councillors for breach of the code. The Government proposes that a Standards Commission be established both to investigate allegations of breach of the Code of Conduct and to discipline those found to be in breach. The Scottish Committee of the Council on Tribunals has, however, expressed concern that the Commission will have both an investigative and an adjudicative rule and observed "care will have to be taken that the adjudicative rule is not compromised by the investigative process". It also proposes that the Commission be brought under its supervision as a tribunal: see the 1997–98 Report, pp. 5–6.

(6) For other formulations of the rule see for example the Licensing (Scotland) Act 1976, s. 2 (grounds of disqualification from sitting on licensing board). In addition, the decisions of licensing boards and civic government licensing committees can be appealed to the sheriff on the grounds that there has been a breach of natural justice, including allegations of bias and impartiality: see the 1976 Act, s. 39(4)(c); *Mahmood*; and generally see, Sir C. Agnew and H. M. Baillie, *Licensing (Scotland) Act 1976* (4th ed., 1996), pp. 50–53, at 116–118 and in relation to civic government licensing the Civic Government (Scotland) Act 1982, Sched. 1, para. 18, on which see *Piper v. Kyle and Carrick District Council*, 1988 S.L.T. 267 and generally A. Hajducki and S. L. Stuart, *Civic Government Licensing Law*, pp. 116 119.

(7) For the role of the Local Ombudsman in relation to enforcement of the Code of Conduct, see p. 000. The Scottish Executive has announced that as part of its first legislative programme, there will be a Bill on Ethical Standards in Local Government. Details of the Bill are awaited.

Chapter 10

Judicial Control of Administrative Action

The growth in government in the twentieth century in both scale and complexity has seen with it growing concern to ensure that government and administration in all their forms are accountable. While democratic control is primarily aimed at securing political accountability, through the parliamentary process whether at Westminster or in Edinburgh, or through local government, attempts to hold government and administration to account often occur at a far lower and more direct level. The focus for such challenge often arises when the courts are called upon to determine the scope of governmental power and whether it has been lawfully exercised. There is a long tradition in Scots law which recognises the need to ensure accountability through law. One only has to consider the words of Lord Kames, quoted with approval by the Lord President in *West v. Secretary of State for Scotland*, 1992 S.C. 385 to see the strength of that tradition.

The forms of control available vary from procedures which have their parallels in familiar areas of private law such as actions for breach of contract to negligence. Some of the issues in those areas are examined in Chapter 14. Sometimes Parliament has created specialised remedies to ensure that the needs of the citizen are not ignored in new, as well as established, areas of administrative action, such as actions to enforce performance of a statutory duty or the quashing of ministerial orders, or appeals to special tribunals or the sheriff, examined in Chapters 11 and 12 respectively.

Our concern in this chapter is, however, mainly with judicial review procedure in the Court of Session. We also go on to examine the special forms of judicial control created by the Scotland Act 1998 and the Human Rights Act 1998. These are examined later in the chapter.

JUDICIAL REVIEW: THE PROCEDURE

Act of Sederunt (Rules of the Court of Session) 1994

58.1–58.3, 58.5–58.10

"Applications for Judicial Review

Application and Interpretation of This Chapter

58.1. — (1) This Chapter applies to an application to the supervisory jurisdiction of the court.
(2) In this Chapter —
'the first hearing' means a hearing under rule 58.9:
'the second hearing' means a hearing under rule 58.10.

Disapplication of Certain Rules to this Chapter

58.2. The following rules shall not apply to a petition to which this Chapter applies:
rule 14.4 (form of petitions),
rule 14.5 (first order in petitions),
rule 14.9 (unopposed petitions).

Applications for judicial review

58.3. — (1) Subject to paragraph (2), an application to the supervisory jurisdiction of the court, including an application under section 45(b) of the Act of 1988 (specific performance of statutory duty), shall be made by petition for judicial review.

(2) An application may not be made under paragraph (1) if that application is made, or could be made, by appeal or review under or by virtue of any enactment.

Nominated Judge

58.5. A petition for judicial review shall be heard by a judge nominated by the Lord President for the purposes of this Chapter or, where such a judge is not available, any other judge of the court (including the vacation judge).

Form of Petition

58.6. — (1) A petition for judicial review shall be in Form 58.6.

(2) The petitioner shall lodge with the petition all relevant documents in his possession and within his control.

(3) Where the petitioner founds in the petition on a document not in his possession or within his control, he shall append to the petition a schedule specifying the document and the person who possesses or has control over the document.

(4) Where the decision, act or omission in question and the basis on which it is complained of is not apparent from the documents lodged with the petition, an affidavit shall be lodged stating the terms of the decision, act or omission and the basis on which it is complained of.

First order

58.7. On being lodged, the petition shall, without appearing in the Motion Roll, be presented forthwith to the Lord Ordinary in court or in chambers for —

(a)   an order specifying —
        (i)   such intimation, service and advertisement as may be necessary;
        (ii)   any documents to be served with the petition;
        (iii)   a date for the first hearing, being a date not earlier than seven days after the expiry of the period specified for intimation and service; or
(b)   any interim order; and, having heard counsel or other person having a right of audience, the Lord Ordinary may grant such an order.

Compearing Parties

58.8. — (1) A person to whom intimation of the first hearing has been made and who intends to appear —

(a)   shall intimate his intention to do so to —
        (i)   the agent for the petitioner, and
        (ii)   the Keeper of the Rolls,

not less than 48 hours before the date of the hearing; and

(b)   may lodge answers and any relevant documents.

(2) Any person not specified in the first order made under rule 58.7 as a person on whom service requires to be made may apply by motion for leave to enter the process; and if the motion is granted, the provisions of this Chapter shall apply to that person as they apply to a person specified in the first order.

First Hearing

58.9. — (1) At the first hearing, the Lord Ordinary shall —

(a)   satisfy himself that the petitioner has duly complied with the first order made under rule 58.7; and
(b)   hear the parties.

(2) After hearing the parties, the Lord Ordinary may —

(a)   determine the petition; or
(b)   make such order for further procedure as he thinks fit, and in particular may —
        (i)   adjourn or continue the first hearing to another date;
        (ii)   order service on a person not specified in the first order made under rule 58.7;
        (iii)   make any interim order;
        (iv)   order answers to be lodged within such period as he shall specify;
        (v)   order further specification in the petition or answers in relation to such matters as he shall specify;
        (vi)   order any fact founded on by a party at the hearing to be supported by evidence on affidavit to be lodged within such period as he shall specify;

(vii)   order any party who appears to lodge such documents relating to the petition within such period as the Lord Ordinary shall specify;

(viii) appoint a reporter to report to him on such matters of fact *as* the Lord Ordinary shall specify; or

(ix)   order a second hearing on such issues as he shall specify.

Second Hearing

58.10 — (1) Where the Lord Ordinary orders a second hearing under rule 58.9(2)(b)(ix), the Keeper of the Rolls shall, in consultation with the Lord Ordinary and the parties, fix a date for the second hearing as soon as reasonably practicable.

(2) Subject to the terms of any order for further procedure made under rule 58.9(2)(b), the parties shall, not less than seven days before the date of the second hearing, lodge all documents and affidavits to be founded on by them at the second hearing with copies for use by the court.

(3) At any time before the date of the second hearing, the Lord Ordinary may cause the petition to be put out for hearing on the By Order Roll for the purpose of obtaining such information from the parties as he considers necessary for the proper disposal of the petition at the hearing.

(4) At a hearing on the By Order Roll under paragraph (3), the Lord Ordinary may make such order as he thinks fit, having regard to all the circumstances, including an order appointing a commissioner to recover a document or take the evidence of a witness.

(5) At the second hearing, the Lord Ordinary may —

(a)   adjourn the hearing;

(b)   continue the hearing for such further procedure as he thinks fit; or

(c)   determine the petition."

Notes

(1) Rule 58 was originally enacted in rule 260B of the Act of Sederunt (Rules of Court Amendment No. 2) (Judicial Review) 1985. The current rules governing judicial review procedure have their basis in the report of the working party chaired by the late Lord Dunpark whose remit was: **10–3**

> "To devise and recommend for consideration a simple form of procedure, capable of being operated with reasonable expedition, for bringing before the court, for such relief as is appropriate, complaints by aggrieved persons (1) against Acts or decisions of inferior courts, tribunals, public bodies, authorities, or officers, in respect of which no right of appeal is available alleging that the Acts or decisions are *ultra vires*, or that they have been done or taken without compliance with particular statutory procedural requirements; and (2) a failure of any body or person to perform statutory duty, which it or he could be compelled to perform in terms of section 91 of the Court of Session Act 1868."

This procedural reform was prompted by the fact that since 1977 the procedure known as an application for judicial review had existed in England and, in light of the existence of that procedure, the comments of the late Lord Fraser of Tullybelton in *Brown v. Hamilton District Council*, 1983 S.L.T. 397 (H.L.) at 418 and *Stevenson v. Midlothian District Council*, 1983 S.L.T. 433 at 437 on the need for Scottish reforms. On *Brown* and *Stevenson* see P.Q. Watchman, "No Recourse for the Homeless in Scotland?", 1983 S.L.T. (News) 33.

The report of the working party was published in June 1984. For discussion see A.C. Page, "Just and Reasonable", 1984 S.L.T. (News) 290. As a procedural reform it could not affect questions of substantive law and this, as we shall see, has had significance in relation to certain matters.

(2) Note the terms of rule 58.3 (2). The most significant exclusions are the procedures contained in section 238 (validity of structure plans) and section 239 (the validity of other orders, decisions and directions) of the Town and Country Planning (Scotland) Act 1997; applications under para. 15 of Schedule 1 to the Acquisition of Land (Authorisation Procedure) (Scotland) Act 1947 (validity of compulsory purchase order). These procedures are examined in Chapter 12. The working party had in fact recommended that such proceedings should be taken under the new judicial review procedure. What considerations do you think underlay the

rejection of this proposal? Compare and contrast the procedures discussed in Chapter 12. Is it desirable to have such "specialised" forms of review as well as general judicial review procedure? Rule 58.4, which relates to remedies, is extracted at para.11–12.

Judicial review is meant to be a speedy procedure and the provisions of rules 58.6–58.10 are geared towards that end. Writing in 1996, the authors of a major empirical study of judicial review in Scotland concluded that the serious delays associated with the English judicial review case load have not been repeated in Scotland, that cases appeared to progress much more quickly under the Scottish procedure than the English procedure, and that judicial review procedure is quicker than ordinary civil procedure in the Court of Session: see T. Mullen, K. Pick and T. Prosser, "Judicial Review in Scotland Part I" (1996) 1 S.L.P.Q. 366 at 379.

Note rule 58.5. The working party had recommended that there should be available a panel of nominated judges who had expertise. Notwithstanding the apparently mandatory word "shall", other judges still have substantial involvement in judicial review proceedings. Mullen, Pick and Prosser noted that in the years of their study, almost half of first hearings were before judges other than nominated judges, albeit that they go on to note that this did not appear to affect the actual outcome of petitions: at 379.

(3) The following give a useful outline of the way in which the procedure works in practice: V. Finch and C. Ashton, *Administrative Law in Scotland* (1997), Chap 12; M. Deans, *Scots Public Law* (1995), pp. 171–174; *Laws of Scotland: Stair Memorial Encyclopaedia*, Vol. 1, paras 346–347; C.M.G. Himsworth, "Judicial Review in Scotland" in *Judicial Review: A Thematic Approach* (B. Hadfield ed. 1995); A.W. Bradley, "Applications for Judicial Review — The Scottish Model" [1987] P.L. 313; W. Wolffe, "The Scope of Judicial Review in Scots Law" [1992] P.L. 625; and T. Mullen and T. Prosser, "Judicial review in practice" (1997) 3 E.P.L. 322. For a major analytical account of the operation of judicial review in practice see T. Mullen, T. Prosser, K. Pick, *Judicial Review in Scotland* (1996) and also the earlier work of M. Deans and A. Page, Economic and Social Research Council Paper (Reference 00232187) (1996).

One has to determine in advance whether or not the subject matter of the petition is governed by rule 58. If it is not, then another form of legal control needs to be used. This means that one has to have regard to the scope of judicial review in determining whether or not the correct procedure is being adopted. What then is the basis of the scope of judicial review in Scots law?

Tehrani v. Argyll and Clyde Health Board (No. 2)

1989 S.C. 342

10–4   The petitioner was a surgeon employed by the NHS at a hospital in Greenock. He was suspended from duty following a complaint about his treatment of a patient who had died. A committee of inquiry was set up by the local Health Board to investigate. The board dismissed the petitioner who sought judicial review of the decision. At first instance, the Lord Ordinary (Weir) held that the manner in which the dismissal had been carried out was unreasonable and granted decree of reduction. The board reclaimed on the basis that the petition for judicial review had been incompetent, no matter of public law having been raised.

10–5   LORD JUSTICE-CLERK (ROSS): "... After hearing parties on the petition and answers, the Lord Ordinary sustained the first plea in law for the petitioner under deletion of the words 'and/or an abuse of the respondents' power' and proceeded to reduce the decision of the respondents dated 11 January 1989. It is against that decision of the Lord Ordinary that the reclaiming motion has now been taken.

On behalf of the respondents it was contended that the decision of the respondents was not amenable to judicial review under Rule of Court 260B and that the petition was accordingly incompetent. Alternatively it was submitted that, if the decision was susceptible to judicial review the Lord Ordinary had applied the wrong tests and in particular had failed to recognise that the proper test was whether in the circumstances a reasonable health board could reasonably have concluded that the petitioner was in material breach of his contract so that they were entitled to dismiss him summarily. They submitted that the Lord Ordinary had misdirected himself both as to the test to be applied in relation to summary dismissal, and also as to the test of unreasonableness if that indeed arose. Counsel intimated that they were no longer to argue that the petition was incompetent on the ground that the petitioner had failed to exhaust other remedies available to him.

The petitioner on the other hand maintained that the decision was amenable to judicial review since a matter of public law was present in the contract of service between the respondents and the petitioner. Counsel for the petitioner made it clear that the real complaint of the petitioner was that he had been dismissed summarily. They pointed out that what was sought was reduction of the respondents' decision to that effect; if reduction were granted it would then be open to the respondents to dismiss the petitioner upon notice, and if that course were followed the petitioner would then have a right of appeal to the Secretary of State in terms of para. 190 of the National Health Service Hospital Medical and Dental Staff Scotland — Terms and Conditions of Service (February 1987) (Revised). It should be observed that the petitioner does not aver bad faith on the part of the respondents.

The first matter to be determined is whether the petition is in the circumstances competent. In holding that the dismissal of the petitioner by the respondents was amenable to judicial review, the Lord Ordinary relied upon the terms of Rule of Court 260B and *Malloch* v. *Aberdeen Corporation*. He was also referred to *R.* v. *East Berkshire Health Authority, ex p. Walsh* and to two Outer House cases in Scotland where that decision was applied. The Lord Ordinary expressed the view that the distinction in English law between public law and private law in this context did not necessarily apply in Scotland.

Rule of Court 260B contains inter alia the following provisions: [his Lordship quoted rule 260B (1) and (4) and continued:] We were reminded that the origin of this rule is to be found in the speech of Lord Fraser of Tullybelton in *Brown* v. *Hamilton District Council*. Our attention was also drawn to the *Report by the Working Party on Procedure for Judicial Review of Administrative Action* under the chairmanship of Lord Dunpark. Counsel for the respondents suggested that it was legitimate to look at the report of the working party in order to identify the mischief to which the new Rule of Court was addressed. In my opinion, however, it is sufficient to have regard to what Lord Fraser of Tullybelton said in his speech in *Brown* v. *Hamilton District Council*. We were also referred, as was the Lord Ordinary to *Forbes* v. *Underwood*, and to what Lord President Inglis said at p. 467 regarding the supereminent jurisdiction of the Court of Session. In my opinion, however, what is stated by Lord Fraser of Tullybelton is a sufficient explanation of what is meant by 'the supervisory jurisdiction of the court': 'The supervisory jurisdiction over inferior courts and tribunals is vested exclusively in the Court of Session, as supreme court' (p. 414). Under reference to *Forbes* v. *Underwood* Lord Fraser of Tullybelton added (at p. 415): 'I accordingly regard the passage that I have quoted as authority for two propositions relevant to this appeal; first, the Court of Session has a supervisory jurisdiction over decisions of administrative bodies such as local authorities, whether the decisions are administrative, judicial or quasi-judicial; and secondly, that supervisory jurisdiction is private to the Court of Session and is not shared by the sheriff court.'

Subsequently in his speech, Lord Fraser said (at p. 418): 'Secondly, it is for consideration whether there might not be advantages in developing special procedure in Scotland for dealing with questions in the public law area, comparable to the English prerogative orders. Now that the technical restrictions which previously applied to the prerogative orders have been removed by amendment of the rules of court in 1977, and by s. 31 of the Supreme Court Act 1981, they have advantages over ordinary procedure such as declaration, particularly by making available remedies which are speedy and cheap and which protect public authorities from unreasonable actions, as explained by Lord Diplock in *O'Reilly*. Similar advantage might possibly be derived in Scotland from reviving what Lord President Cooper in *J. and J.* v. *C's Tutor* referred to (1948 S.L.T. at p. 481) as 'obsolete advocation and obsolescent suspension' as methods of review of decisions in the public law field, which are not subject to appeal to the court.'

In the event, the remedy provided by Rule of Court 260B was not to revive advocation and suspension, but to utilise existing remedies such as reduction and declarator in an accelerated procedure. It is plain from the speech of Lord Fraser of Tullybelton that what he envisaged being introduced was a special procedure to deal with questions in the public law area.

Counsel for the respondents pointed out that in some cases stress has been laid upon the distinction between public and private law. It was pointed out that the supervisory jurisdiction of the Court of Session which enables it to provide certain remedies in the area of public law may also under private law enable it to review decisions taken by voluntary associations (*McDonald* v. *Burns*; *St Johnstone Football Club Ltd.* v. *Scottish Football Association Ltd.*; and *Brentnall* v. *Free Presbyterian Church of Scotland*). Although there was some discussion upon it, I am satisfied that in the present case it is not necessary to determine in any comprehensive way the scope of the Scottish procedure of judicial review under Rule of Court 260B. So far as the present case is concerned, counsel for the petitioner accepted that in order for the petitioner to succeed in this application he must be able to focus upon a matter of public law. In this context he regarded public law as synonymous with administrative law: 'Administrative law is concerned with the composition, procedures, powers, duties, rights and liabilities of the organs of central and local government and of other public authorities. More concisely, administrative law regulates the organisation, functions and powers of administrative officials and departments' (*Stair Memorial Encyclopaedia*, Vol. 1, para. 201).

Accordingly, in determining whether or not the present petition is competent, the question is whether a matter of public law is raised in the application. Counsel for the respondents maintained that no issue of public law arose. The dismissal of the petitioner arose out of the private contractual relationship between him and the respondents as his employers. On the other hand, counsel for the petitioner maintained that there was a public law element in this case. They contended that a number of public law elements could be detected in this case, and the principal of these was that the appellant under the Hospital and Medical Dental Staff Scotland — Terms and Conditions of Service had a right to appeal against his dismissal to the Secretary of State, but that, by dismissing him, the respondents had effectively eliminated this. This it was said, injected the necessary public element into the situation to make the dismissal of the petitioner by the respondents susceptible to judicial review.

In the light of these submissions it is critical to examine the provisions of the National Health Service — Hospital Medical and Dental Staff Scotland — Terms and Conditions of Service. It is matter of agreement between the parties that the petitioner's employment with the respondents is governed by inter alia para. 190 of the terms and conditions of service. (Article 5 (vii) and Answer 5 (vii) of the Petition and Answers.) Paragraph 190 provides as follows: [his Lordship quoted the terms of para. 190 and continued:] This right of appeal under para. 190 is to be contrasted with the right to appeal under s. 40–10 of the Whitley Council conditions of service since action on the latter is at the discretion of the Secretary of State.

The committee of inquiry were appointed by the respondents to conduct an inquiry into the professional conduct of the petitioner at Inverclyde Royal hospital with a view to possible disciplinary action by the respondents against him. Their terms of reference required them to make findings on all relevant facts of the case in relation to certain specified matters, and to make a finding as to whether or not the petitioner was at fault in respect of all or any of these specified matters, and to explain the basis upon which their finding was reached. The committee of inquiry was set up in accordance with the guidance on the procedure to be followed in disciplinary cases contained in Scottish Hospital Memorandum No. 49/1968. In terms of para. 16 of the memorandum, it is provided that the terms of reference of a committee of inquiry should normally request that the report of the committee should contain recommendations as to disciplinary action but that the report should not contain such recommendations unless they have been specifically requested. In para. 18 it is provided that the report of the committee of inquiry should, if requested by the disciplinary authority, contain recommendations to the disciplinary authority as to disciplinary action but in no circumstances should the committee of inquiry itself be given disciplinary powers. The memorandum also makes it plain that 'disciplinary authority' means the regional hospital board or board of management. In the present case the terms of reference did not request the committee of inquiry to include any recommendations as to disciplinary action in their report and accordingly the report contained no such recommendations. The Lord Ordinary in his opinion regarded para. 16 as of importance because the respondents had not asked the committee of inquiry to make recommendations, but before this court it was accepted that the respondents were fully entitled to refrain from requesting the committee of inquiry to make recommendations.

It is unnecessary in this opinion to narrate in detail the findings of the committee of inquiry. The Lord Ordinary has dealt with these in sufficient detail. However, the particular matters concerning the management of the case of Mrs Clarke upon which they were requested to make findings were: '(a) that Mr Tehrani failed to attend the patient to examine her and to decide on clinical grounds whether the offer from Glasgow Royal Infirmary's vascular unit to take the patient should be accepted; (b) that he instructed that a laparotomy should be performed without any justifiable plan of action, knowing that a leaking aneurysm was likely to be found and that Mr Wishart would be unable to deal with this; (c) that if he felt that he himself was unable to deal with this lesion, he failed to ascertain whether a suitably qualified local colleague was available to operate on his behalf; (d) that by instructing the Surgical Registrar to close the abdomen he thus either (1) decided not to operate on a potentially remediable lesion; or (2) decided to subject the patient to a second laparotomy'.

In their report, the committee of inquiry expressed their position in relation to these sub-heads as follows: '(a) In the particular circumstances of this case it was a failure of professional duty by Mr Tehrani not to attend Inverclyde with a view to making a clinical examination in person of Mrs Clarke when considering how he should respond to the conditional offer by Glasgow Royal Infirmary's Vascular Unit; (b) While the instruction by Mr Tehrani that Mr Wishart perform a diagnostic laparotomy was part of a plan designed to satisfy the condition apparently though remarkably laid by Glasgow, it was not in the circumstances a justifiable plan of action. On the contrary, it was a wholly unjustifiable instruction which fell seriously below the standard to be expected of a Consultant Surgeon; (c) This sub-head is truly an element of the situation which has been considered under sub-head (b). It was unacceptable that in the circumstances a laparotomy be performed on Mrs Clarke at Inverclyde without the presence of a Consultant Surgeon. The presence of Mr Morrice was an alternative to the presence of Mr Tehrani. No assessment of fault separate from that made in (b) falls to be made; (d) Alternative (2) is simply a consequence of the matter described in (b) and requires no separate assessment. Alternative (1) has not been established and Mr Tehrani has not been found to be at fault on this aspect.'

The committee of inquiry also made findings upon the matter of the petitioner's poor working relationships with consultant surgeon colleagues and upon steps which he had taken on the day following the death of Mrs Clarke to persuade a junior doctor to sign a statement. The committee of inquiry concluded that the petitioner must accept a significant degree of responsibility for the poor working relationships in the hospital, and they also held that he was wholly to blame for the exacerbation of the working relationship with Mr Morrice due to his then solicitor having made at the fatal accident inquiry an unfounded allegation against Mr Morrice. In addition they held that he was guilty of serious misconduct as regards the attempt to persuade his junior colleague to sign this statement.

Counsel for the petitioner made it clear throughout that his attack on the decision of the tribunal was not on the fact of dismissal as such but upon the mode of dismissal which was chosen. In particular, as already explained, counsel maintained that what was objectionable was that the dismissal was summary dismissal instead of dismissal after notice. The question then arises as to when an employer is entitled to dismiss a servant summarily without notice. In his opinion, the Lord Ordinary stated that there was no fixed rule of law which defined the degree of conduct which would justify dismissal or summary dismissal. Reference was made to *Laws* v. *London Chronicle (Indicator Newspapers) Ltd*. The Lord Ordinary then stated: 'Summary dismissal is dismissal on the spot and in my view it means that in the mind of the employers the conduct of the employee has been such as to make it intolerable for him to remain one moment longer at work.'

Counsel for the respondents challenged that statement and maintained that the Lord Ordinary had misdirected himself as to the conditions which required to be present before summary dismissal could be justified. In my opinion, their criticism of the Lord Ordinary on this point is well founded. Before this court counsel for both parties accepted that the true test which fell to be applied in the present case was whether a reasonable hospital board could reasonably have concluded that the petitioner was in material breach of his contract so that they were entitled to dismiss him summarily. Reference was made to *Blyth* v. *Scottish Liberal Club*. In that case at 1983 S.L.T., p. 265 Lord Dunpark said: 'If by words or deed one party to a contract demonstrates that he will no longer be bound by his contract, that is actual repudiation which entitles the other party at once to cancel or rescind the contract. But the remedy of cancellation is also given to a party who is not in breach of contract whenever the other party is in breach of an essential condition going to the root of the contract, even if the party in breach is willing to fulfil all his other contractual obligations. In such a case the innocent party may treat the breach of one essential condition as if the party in breach had repudiated all his unperformed contractual duties. He has not actually repudiated these but he is deemed to have done so because he is in breach of one material term or condition of his contract.' In all the circumstances, I am of opinion that the true test of whether summary dismissal is justifiable is not that expressed by the Lord Ordinary but is the test for which the respondents have contended in this reclaiming motion.

Counsel for the respondents then proceeded to maintain that the next question was whether the respondents were entitled to hold that the breaches of contract on the part of the petitioner were material breaches entitling them to rescind. In my opinion having regard to what the committee of inquiry held, and in particular what they found in (a) and (b) as set out above, they were clearly entitled to regard the petitioner as in material breach of his contract so as to entitle them to dismiss him summarily. As I understood it counsel for the petitioner did not dispute that this was so. But for the existence of para. 190, I understood counsel to accept that in the light of these findings the respondents would have been entitled to dismiss the appellant summarily. They further submitted however that they were not entitled to do so since the effect of doing so would be to eliminate the petitioner's right of appeal to the Secretary of State under para. 190. It was this loss of his right of appeal which counsel maintained introduced the necessary public element which rendered the decision reviewable by judicial review.

In my opinion, counsel for the petitioner were not well founded when they contended that the respondents were not entitled to dismiss the appellant summarily since this would deny him his right of appeal to the Secretary of State under para. 190. In my opinion para. 197 expressly recognises the right of the respondents to terminate the petitioner's employment without notice provided that his conduct has been such as would enable them to dismiss him summarily at common law. Counsel for the petitioner recognised that the findings of the committee of inquiry were such as to entitle the respondents to treat the petitioner as in material breach of contract so as to entitle them to dismiss him summarily. In my opinion, since this right is expressly recognised in para. 197, it cannot be maintained that the effect of para. 190 is to prevent the respondents from exercising a power conferred upon them by para. 197.

Counsel for the petitioner founded strongly upon *Malloch* v. *Aberdeen Corporation*, as authority for the proposition that there was a public law element in this case. They contended that the relationship between the petitioner and respondents was not merely one of servant and master. That case concerned the need to observe the rules of natural justice. In his speech, Lord Wilberforce said: 'A comparative list of situations in which persons have been held entitled or not entitled to a hearing, or to observation of rules of natural justice, according to the master and servant test, looks illogical and even bizarre. A specialist surgeon is denied protection which is given to a hospital doctor; a university professor, as a servant, has been denied the right to be heard, a dock labourer and an undergraduate have been granted it; examples can be multiplied (see *Barber* v. *Manchester Regional Hospital Board*; *Palmer* v. *Inverness Hospitals Board*; *Vidyodaya University Council* v. *Silva*; *Vine* v. *National Dock Labour Board*; *Glynn* v. *Keele University*). One may accept that if there are relationships in which all requirements of the observance of rules of natural justice are excluded (and I do not wish to assume that this is inevitably so), these must be confined to what have been called "pure master and servant cases", which I take to mean cases in which there is no element of public employment or service, no support by statute, nothing in the nature of an office or a status which is capable of protection. If any of these elements exist, then, in my opinion, whatever the terminology used, and even though in some inter partes aspects the relationship may be called that of master and servant, there may be essential procedural requirements to be observed, and failure to observe them may result in a dismissal being declared to be void.'

Counsel for the petitioner submitted that in the present case there was an element of public employment or service, and that the Scottish Hospital Memorandum No. 49/1968, although not a statute, is a document within the administrative process. Counsel relied upon what the Lord Ordinary said in his opinion where he identified six features as supporting the proposition that there was a public element in this case. The Lord Ordinary observed (1) that the respondents are constituted by Act of Parliament; (2) the board members are appointed by the Secretary of State; (3) the method of appointment of officers or servants of a health board and the qualification, remuneration and conditions of service of such persons are to be prescribed by regulation; (4) reg. 3 (2) of the National Health Service (Remuneration and Conditions of Service) (Scotland) Regulations 1974 deals with the situation where conditions of service have been the subject of negotiations by a negotiating body; (5) the respondents are a disciplinary authority operating under the Scottish Hospital Memorandum No. 49/1968; and (6) the memorandum is a circular laying down procedural requirements as does para. 190 of the conditions of service. The Lord Ordinary concluded that the fact that the conditions of service were not formally prescribed by statute or regulation did not affect the matter. He also observed that the court in England has held that it is prepared to take note of such circulars either for any legal effect they may have or as being subject to judicial review (*Gillick* v. *West Norfolk and Wisbech Area Health Authority*).

I agree with counsel for the respondents that merely to hold that a particular case is one where the principles of natural justice must be observed does not mean that the case is thereby elevated into the domain of public administrative law. In *Malloch* v. *Aberdeen Corporation* the power of dismissal was conferred by statute. The case was accordingly different to the present case. In my opinion the present case on its facts is much closer to *R.* v. *East Berkshire Health Authority, ex p. Walsh*. That case concerned the dismissal of a senior nursing officer for misconduct. The senior nursing officer was employed by a health authority under a contract which incorporated the Whitley Council agreement on conditions of service in the health service. He was dismissed by a district nursing officer for misconduct and applied for judicial review. The Court of Appeal held that the decision was not susceptible to judicial review. After considering the dictum of Lord Wilberforce in *Malloch* v. *Aberdeen Corporation* Sir John Donaldson M.R. stated at p. 164: 'Employment by a public authority does not per se inject any element of public law. Nor does the fact that the employee is in a "higher grade" or is an "officer." This only makes it more likely that there will be special statutory restrictions upon dismissal, or other underpinning of his employment: see per Lord Reid in *Malloch* v. *Aberdeen Corporation* [[1971] 1 W.L.R.] at p. 1582. It will be this underpinning and not the seniority which injects the element of public law. Still less can I find any warrant for equating public law with the interest of the public. If the public through Parliament gives effect to that interest by means of statutory provisions, that is quite different, but the interest of the public per se is not sufficient.'

Subsequently the Master of the Rolls said: 'The ordinary employer is free to act in breach of his contracts of employment and if he does so his employee will acquire certain private law rights and remedies in damages for wrongful dismissal, compensation for unfair dismissal, an order for reinstatement or re-engagement and so on. Parliament can underpin the position of public authority employees by directly restricting the freedom of the public authority to dismiss, thus giving the employee "public law" rights and at least making him a potential candidate for administrative law remedies. Alternatively it can require the authority to contract with its employees on specified terms with a view to the employee acquiring "private law" rights under the terms of the contract of employment. If the authority fails or refuses to thus create "private law" rights for the employee, the employee will have "public law" rights to compel compliance, the remedy being mandamus requiring the authority so to contract or a declaration that the employee has those rights. If, however, the authority gives the employee the required contractual protection, a breach of that contract is not a matter of "public law" and gives rise to no administrative law remedies.'

I respectfully agree with the foregoing reasoning of the Master of the Rolls. He concluded that there was no public law element in the applicant's complaints which could give rise to any entitlement to administrative law remedies. In the same way, and for the same reasons, I am satisfied in the present case that there are no public law elements in the petitioner's case which could give rise to any entitlement to a public law remedy such as judicial review. I do not regard the six features identified by the Lord Ordinary as justifying the conclusion that there is a public element in this case. I would accept that in dealing with the petitioner the respondents required to observe the rules of natural justice. However I agree with counsel for the respondents that that consideration is insufficient to elevate the contract into one within the domain of public administrative law. In my opinion despite the fact that the respondents are a board established by statute, the issue between them and the petitioner regarding his employment was essentially a matter of private law. If the petitioner is aggrieved by the decision of the respondents, he can pursue any remedies which are open to him under private law. He has the remedies described by the Master of the Rolls in *Walsh*. He is not, however, entitled to seek to have their decision reviewed by judicial review since the case does not fall within the ambit of public administrative law. Senior counsel for the petitioner sought to distinguish the case of *Walsh* upon the ground that the applicant there was seeking to quash his dismissal whereas the petitioner here was challenging only the fact that the dismissal was summary. I do not, however, regard that consideration as any justification for not adopting the reasoning of the Master of the Rolls in the passages cited. *Walsh* was in fact very similar to the present case; both were instances of contractual issues arising out of very similar contracts of employment.

I do not find it necessary to review all the cases which were cited to the court in argument. The petitioner relied to some extent upon *Council of Civil Service Unions* v. *Minister for the Civil Service*. Counsel for the petitioner maintained that that was a case of employer and employee, but it must be remembered that civil servants have no proper contract of employment; they hold their appointments at the pleasure of the Crown (per Lord Fraser of Tullybelton at p. 400). We were also referred to [the Outer House opinion in] *Bank of Scotland* v. *Investment Management Regulatory Organisation Ltd*. This was a decision of Lord Cullen. The case was a very special one but meantime I would wish to reserve my opinion upon the question of whether that case was correctly decided.

For the foregoing reasons I am of opinion that the Lord Ordinary erred in concluding that the decision of the respondents was amenable to judicial review under Rule of Court 260B. Accordingly in my opinion the petition was incompetent..."

LORD WYLIE: "... The petition was brought to challenge this decision by way of judicial review. Reduction of the decision was sought, in terms of the pleas in law for the petitioner on the grounds that: (1) the decision was 'unreasonable and/or an abuse of the respondents' power', and (2) that 'The petitioner having had a legitimate expectation in the circumstances that the termination of his appointment would be considered by the Secretary of State for Scotland and said consideration being denied him by the respondents' decision.... said decision should be reduced'...

There is no question of course but that the parties were in the contractual relationship of employer and employee. In this situation the normal remedy open to an employee who has been dismissed is either an action of damages at common law for breach of contract, where this can be demonstrated, or proceedings under the Employment Protection Act 1978 which contemplates the broader concept of 'unfair dismissal'. The principles of public administrative law have no part to play because the issues raised are essentially matters of private law. In this instance however, so it was argued, there were elements of public law in the contract of employment and it was accepted by counsel for the petitioner that such elements had to be traced before a public administrative law remedy could be available.

Certainly there is a statutory background to the contract, and the Lord Ordinary lists these provisions in the course of his opinion in support of his decision to reject the argument that the petitioner's dismissal was not amenable to judicial review. The employers were constituted by Act of Parliament and the board members were appointed by the Secretary of State (National Health Service (Scotland) Act 1978, s. 2 (1)). The method of appointment of officers or servants of a health board and the qualification, remuneration and conditions of service of such person (who included the petitioner) were to be prescribed by regulations.

In terms of reg. 3 (2) of the National Health Service (Remuneration and Conditions of Service) (Scotland) Regulations 1974 (S.I. 1974 No. 276) where conditions of service have been the subject of negotiation by a negotiating body, or have been approved by the Secretary of State, the conditions of service of any officer belonging to that class shall include the conditions so approved. The board was a disciplinary authority which operated under a circular emanating from the Scottish Home and Health Department which laid down procedural requirements and, in relation to the matter of an appeal to the Secretary of State, para. 190 of the conditions of service applied. It was on this last mentioned requirement that counsel laid most stress. The provision falls under the general heading 'Termination of Employment' and the subheading 'Representations against dismissal'. It provides, read short, as follows: [his Lordship quoted extensively from para. 190 and continued:] These provisions clearly relate to the situation where a decision to terminate the employment on notice has been made and in terms of para. 196 the contractual minimum period of notice, so far as the petitioner is concerned, was three months. It was this provision in particular which, it was submitted, introduced the element of public law which justified invoking review of the decision by judicial review procedure. Likewise, it was the conscious elimination of this right of appeal in the circumstances of the case which satisfied the test laid down by Lord Greene M.R. in the well known passage in *Associated Provincial Picture Houses Ltd.* v. *Wednesbury Corporation* at p. 229. The formidable nature of this test is described by Lord Diplock as 'a decision which is so outrageous in its defiance of logic or of accepted moral standards that no sensible person who had applied his mind to the question to be decided could have arrived at it' *Council of Civil Service Unions* v. *Minister for the Civil Service* at p. 410). Having quoted the provisions of paras. 190 and 196 it would only be appropriate to refer to the further qualifying provisions of para. 197, under the heading 'Application of Minimum Periods', which is in these terms: [his Lordship quoted para. 197 as set out supra and continued:] This last mentioned provision is highly significant in the context of the board's alternative submission.

The Lord Ordinary drew support for his view that the petitioner's dismissal was amenable to judicial review from a passage in the speech of Lord Wilberforce in *Malloch* v. *Aberdeen Corporation*, 1971 S.L.T. at p. 255. In the relevant passage, his Lordship makes reference to the 'risk of a compartmental approach which, though convenient as a solvent, may lead to narrower distinctions than are appropriate to the broader issues of administrative law'. After citing examples of the apparently 'illogical and even bizarre' situations which could result according to the master and servant test, his Lordship went on to say: 'One may accept that if there are relationships in which all requirements of the observance of rules of natural justice are excluded (and I do not wish to assume that this is inevitably so), these must be confined to what have been called 'pure master and servant cases', which I take to mean cases in which there is no element of public employment or service, no support by statute, nothing in the nature of an office or a status which is capable of protection. If any of these elements exist, then in my opinion, whatever the terminology used, and even though in some inter partes aspects the relationship may be called that of master and servant, there may be essential procedural requirements to be observed, and failure to observe them may result in a dismissal being declared to be void'. Counsel for the petitioner accordingly submitted that the presence of a contractual relationship did not per se preclude procedure by judicial review provided that a public law element arose.

The fact that the employer is a public body does not per se inject an element of public law into the contract of service, nor does the fact that the employee has the benefit of statutory provisions in relation to conditions of service. As Sir John Donaldson M.R. observed in *R.* v. *East Berkshire Health Authority, ex p. Walsh* at p. 166, it would otherwise be open to all National Health Service employees to whom the Whitley Council agreement on conditions of service applied to seek judicial review. The facts in *Walsh* bear a close resemblance to those in the present case. It concerned the dismissal of a senior nursing officer employed by a health authority in terms of a contract which likewise incorporated the Whitley Council agreement on conditions and service, and the Court of Appeal held that the decision to dismiss was not amenable to judicial review. The applicant was seeking to enforce private contractual rights and accordingly his application was a misuse of the procedure for judicial review. The decision in *Malloch's* case was distinguished on the basis that the ratio of that decision was the fact that his entitlement to a hearing was a statutory provision implied in the principal statute regulating the relationship between education authorities and the teachers in their employment. It requires a particular statutory provision, expressly stated or plainly implied, to inject the element of public law which attracts the administrative law remedy. Purchase L.J. observed, at p. 176: 'There is a danger of confusing the rights with their appropriate remedies enjoyed by an employee arising out of a private contract of employment with the performance by a public body of the duties imposed upon it as part of the statutory terms under which it exercises its powers.' In the present case, after considering the various factors to which I have already referred, and under reference to para. 190 of the conditions of service, the Lord Ordinary concluded: 'The fact that the conditions of service and in particular the provisions governing dismissal procedure are not formally and directly prescribed by statute or regulation does not seem to me, in principle, to affect the matter.'

With all respect to the Lord Ordinary it seems to me that he has confused the two quite distinct issues to which Purchas L.J. referred, although to be fair to the Lord Ordinary he expressly stated that he was declining to follow English authority in this field of law having regard to what he described as the distinctive origins and development of the remedies covered by judicial review in both countries. I think however that he was wrong to do so. The two procedures and the distinctive remedies provided are of course different but their purposes and the mischief for which they seek to provide remedies are the same in both jurisdictions. Judicial review procedure in Scotland springs from the observations in the speech of Lord Fraser of Tullybelton in *Brown* v. *Hamilton District Council*, 1983 S.L.T. at p. 418, where his Lordship suggested: 'it is for consideration whether there might not be advantages in developing special procedure in Scotland for dealing with questions in the public law area, comparable to the English prerogative orders'. Its purpose is to provide a simple form of procedure, capable of being operated expeditiously, for bringing before the court complaints in relation to the exercise of statutory or prerogative powers by the executive and public bodies. It is not concerned with private contractual rights and obligations. I agree with counsel for the respondents that there is no good reason for differences between the two jurisdictions to develop in this field and indeed that it would be regrettable if they did.

I have reached the conclusion that when the decision was taken to dismiss the petitioner the board was exercising rights arising out of a private contract of employment, and, notwithstanding the statutory background, it was not an exercise of powers conferred by statute. In such circumstances the issue is essentially a matter of private law and it is accordingly in my opinion not open to judicial review. It follows that I would allow the reclaiming motion..."

LORD MURRAY: delivered a concurring opinion.

Notes

(1) The creation of the procedure under rule 260B led to the confusion which was of critical importance in *Tehrani*. Prior to the case the concept of public law as the basis for the exercise of the court's supervisory or judicial review jurisdiction appears not to have had any substantive meaning or existence as a term of art: see Wolffe above at 626. Concern over the development of a test of competence based on a public law element being present was expressed by Lord Clyde, both extrajudicially in "The Nature of the Supervisory Jurisdiction and the Public/Private Distinction in Scots Administrative Law" in *Edinburgh Essays in Public Law* (W. Finnie, C.M.G. Himsworth and N. Walker eds, 1991), pp. 281–293 and judicially in *Watt* v. *Strathclyde Regional Council*, 1992 S.L.T. 324. The concept of public law certainly had relevance in England. In *O'Reilly* v. *Mackman* [1983] 2 A.C. 237 the House of Lords held that the equivalent English procedure for judicial review, R.S.C. Ord. 53 and the Supreme Court Act 1981, sections 29–31 required a matter of public law to be present before judicial review was competent. Notwithstanding reservations, the concept of public law was applied in various guises by different judges. In *Darroch* v. *Strathclyde Regional Council*, 1992 S.C.L.R. 465 Lord McLean held that a decision by a local authority to designate an official as a deputy chief officer was a matter of public law and was subject to judicial review. In *Connor* v. *Strathclyde Regional Council*, 1986 S.L.T. 530 review of a decision of the Council Selection Board for an assistant head teacher was held to be incompetent as no matter of public law was raised. In *Safeway Food Stores* v. *Scottish Provident Institution*, 1989 S.L.T. 131 an ordinary action to reduce an arbitral decree was held competent notwithstanding the terms of rule 260B, because the case did not involve a statutory or public law element. Equally, in *Kyle and Carrick District Council* v. *A.R. Kerr & Sons*, 1992 S.L.T. 629 Lord Penrose accepted that an application to reduce an arbitral award could be pursued by way of judicial review and he found enough of a "public law element" present to justify his decision. Clearly public law was present if one gave it an elastic definition. Unease over the proper basis of the scope of judicial review ultimately required to be examined by the Inner House.

10–6

West v. Secretary of State for Scotland

1992 S.C. 385

10–7   Lord President (Hope): "This is a petition for judicial review of a decision taken by the Scottish Prison Service. The petitioner is a serving prison officer, who holds his appointment as a civil servant in the Scottish Home and Health Department. This is the government department for the Scottish Prison Service, by which his letter of appointment was issued on 13 December 1982. In terms of their conditions of service all prison officers are designed as mobile staff and they are liable to be transferred to any prison service establishment in Scotland. Provisions are made for the reimbursement of certain expenses incurred as a result of the transfer, but it was provided that not all types of transfer qualified for reimbursement of home removal expenses. The decision which the petitioner seeks to challenge was a refusal by the Scottish Prison Service to reimburse him for the expenses of moving house when he was transferred from H.M. Young Offenders Institution, Polmont, to H.M. Prison, Edinburgh, following a compulsory permanent transfer in March 1989. He was granted permission to live outwith official quarters at his new posting, and he purchased a house in Edinburgh to which he moved from his previous residence near Falkirk. He avers that shortly before he was due to take up his new post he was informed by the Scottish Prison Service that he would not be reimbursed the expenses of his removal. His contention is that that decision was an unreasonable exercise of the discretion available to them in respect of the terms for his compulsory transfer. He seeks reduction of the decision together with a declaration that he is entitled to be reimbursed for the expenses of his removal and damages.

The petition was served on the Scottish Prison Service, and answers were then lodged on their behalf in the name of the Secretary of State for Scotland who is responsible for the administration of the Scottish Prison Service and for the decisions such as that complained of. He sought dismissal of the petition on the grounds of both competency and relevancy. When the matter came before the Lord Ordinary the argument was confined to the matter of competency. It was understood that if the plea to the competency were to be repelled it would then be open to the respondent to argue his plea to relevancy. In the event the Lord Ordinary sustained the plea to competency, and it is his decision on this matter which is now before us in this reclaiming motion.

Counsel for both parties were agreed before the Lord Ordinary that the plea to the competency of the petition raised an important question about the extent of the jurisdiction of the court in proceedings for judicial review. The Lord Ordinary has endorsed this view. He regarded the submissions to which he listened as raising important issues which have far reaching implications for the future development of this branch of the law. It was indicated to him that his decision would be the subject of a reclaiming motion whichever way he decided the case. He made it clear at the end of his opinion that he would welcome the opportunity which a reclaiming motion might give for a comprehensive consideration and statement of the scope of the court's supervisory jurisdiction under Rule of Court 260B.

We accept that it is now necessary for guidance to be given as to the scope of this procedure. Having listened to a full and careful argument on the matter, we propose in this opinion to examine the history of the supervisory jurisdiction of the Court of Session prior to the introduction of the new procedure by Rule of Court 260B. We shall then comment on some of the cases which have been decided since that rule was introduced. One issue of particular importance is the extent to which it is relevant, in determining the limits of the new procedure, to have regard to the development of judicial review in England and to employ the terminology of English law. We shall examine the origins of this usage and the extent to which it can be reconciled with the Scottish cases. In conclusion we shall set out what we consider to be the principles which may be used to define the limits of the supervisory jurisdiction of this court. But in order to set the context for this discussion it is first necessary to explain in a little more detail the circumstances of the present case.

The nature of the relationship between the petitioner and the Scottish Prison Service has been described by the Lord Ordinary. The petitioner is a civil servant, and for constitutional reasons he is said to hold his appointment at the pleasure of the Crown. Accordingly he has no formal contract of employment, but this does not mean that the relationship between him and the Scottish Prison Service is without any mutual rights or obligations. On the contrary, his letter of appointment made reference to conditions of service applicable to his appointment in terms which indicated clearly that there were to be rights and obligations on both sides. The Lord Ordinary was satisfied from a study of the petitioner's terms of service that they gave rise to rights and duties of a contractual nature which might be enforceable by law. Counsel for the petitioner did not challenge that conclusion, nor did he challenge the Lord Ordinary's statement that the petitioner's position in respect of these matters was indistinguishable from that of a person holding a contract of employment with a private employer.

The decision which is challenged in this case was taken under para. 80 of the petitioner's conditions of service, the first sentence of which is in these terms: 'Not all types of transfer qualify for reimbursement of home removal expenses and it is a matter for Personnel Services Division's discretion in all cases whether the distance between the old and new stations justifies the payment of expenses.'

It should be noted that, although there is a reference here to the personnel services division, no attempt has been made by the petitioner to present the decision as being that of any particular officer or body which can be seen to have a separate identity from the Scottish Prison Service itself. This is important, because from the pleadings in this case it appears that it was for the Scottish Prison Service, and not some third party to whose jurisdiction the matter was committed, to decide whether or not the petitioner was to be reimbursed for his expenses. Had this been a case where the decision was one to be taken by a third party, the point to be decided in this case would have been different for reasons to which we shall return. As it is, the issue appeared to the Lord Ordinary to be of the nature of a private dispute between the petitioner and the Scottish Prison Service arising from his terms of service. We agree with that analysis, and we regard this case as indistinguishable in that respect from any other dispute of a similar nature between an employer and an employee. It is for that reason that the respondent maintains that the petition is incompetent, on the ground that the only issue is a pure matter of contract between the parties and as such is not amenable to judicial review.

The Supervisory Jurisdiction Prior to Rule of Court 260B

We turn now to our examination of the history of the supervisory jurisdiction of the Court of Session prior to the introduction of the new procedure by Rule of Court 260B. In his submissions for the petitioner, counsel invited us to consider the early history of the Court of Session from its institution in 1532, and he drew our attention to the significance for its development of the abolition of the Scots Privy Council in 1708.

There is no doubt that this act of the new Parliament at Westminster left a significant gap in the administration of justice in Scotland. Prior to the union the Privy Council had exercised a wide equitable jurisdiction of a kind which was not enjoyed by the Court of Session at that time. As Sheriff McNeill has explained in 'The Passing of the Scottish Privy Council', 1965 J.R. 263, the contrast was between the Court of Session, whose functions were essentially that of a court of law, and the Privy Council as the chief executive organ of the state which dispensed the extraordinary power of the Crown. In the words of Hill Burton, in his introduction to Vol. I of the Privy Council Register, it was 'as if the Court of Session were bound by the strict doctrines of the law, while the Privy Council could administer abstract justice by its innate prerogative, and was bound in duty to interfere if the strict rule of law should inflict a wrong'. As McNeill has pointed out, however, no statute, Act of Sederunt or Act of Adjournal was passed in 1708 to distribute the jurisdiction formerly enjoyed by the Scots Privy Council, so it was left to the Court of Session itself to develop its own jurisdiction in order to provide an extraordinary equitable remedy where none was available within the strict limits of the law. This development was described by Lord Kames in his *Principles of Equity* (3rd ed., 1778), Vol. I, pp. 30–31: 'In Scotland, as well as in other civilized countries, the King's council was originally the only court that had power to remedy defects or redress injustices in common law. To this extraordinary power the court of session naturally succeeded, as being the supreme court in civil matters; for in every well-regulated society, some one court must be trusted with this power, and no court more properly than that which is supreme.'

But a more cautious approach to the limits of this initiative is evident from this passage in Lord Kames' *Historical Law Tracts* (4th ed., 1778) at pp. 228–229: 'Under the cognisance of the privy council in Scotland came many injuries, which, by the abolition of that court, are left without any peculiar remedy; and the court of session have with reluctance been obliged to listen to complaints of various kinds that belonged properly to the privy council while it had a being. A new branch of jurisdiction has thus sprung up in the court of session, which daily increasing by new matter, will probably in time produce a general maxim. That it is the province of this court, to redress all wrongs for which no other remedy is provided. We are, however, as yet far from being ripe for adopting this maxim. The utility of it is indeed perceived, but perceived too obscurely to have any steady influence on the practice of the court; and for that reason their proceedings in such matters are far from being uniform.'

These comments were referred to with approval by Erskine, I.iii.23 where he said: 'The author of Historical Law Tracts reasonably conjectures that it will soon be considered as part of the province of the Court of Session to redress all wrongs for which a peculiar remedy is not otherwise provided.' But these predictions are an imperfect guide to what in fact took place, and in order to identify the limits of this supereminent jurisdiction in the exercise of the court's supervisory role it is necessary to examine the cases which, as the court entered the 19th century, were beginning to establish a consistent pattern for the next 200 years.

As Lord Fraser of Tullybelton pointed out in *Brown* v. *Hamilton District Council*, 1983 S.L.T. at p. 414, the principle upon which the supervisory jurisdiction has been exercised was stated in terms which, so far as they go, would be perfectly appropriate at the present day in *Magistrates of Perth* v. *Trustees on the Road from Queensferry to Perth* at p. 319. A statute had provided that the justices should 'finally determine' questions between the road trustees and other persons. Lord Kilkerran held that the provision did not exclude the supreme jurisdiction of the Court of Session 'to determine what it is that falls within their powers; but whatever matter is found to be within their power, this court cannot review their proceedings'. The same point arose in *Countess of Loudon* v. *Trustees on the High Roads in Ayrshire*. The trustees had been authorised by statute to suppress, or close up, any byroad which did not appear to them to be of importance to the public. There was an appeal from their judgment to the next meeting of the quarter sessions whose order and sentence was to be final and conclusive. The trustees had resolved to suppress a road which some members of the public wished to keep open. A bill of advocation was presented to the Court of Session as well as an appeal to the quarter sessions, and the question then arose as to the competency of the bill. The relevant part of the decision is recorded in these terms: 'The Court were of opinion, that the judgments of the quarter sessions were not liable to review on such points, as fixing the line of road, or the position of the toll bars, which were discretionary in their nature, and in the exercise of the powers exclusively committed to the Trustees. But it was on the other hand agreed, that a right to review, in the case of the smallest excess of power, was essential, and was not excluded by the words of the act. It could not be supposed (it was observed), that the trustees or Justices were meant to be themselves the sole and exclusive judges of the extent of their own powers, or that such jurisdiction, which might even be held to be in some measure unconstitutional, was intended to be given.'

Two points of significance are to be found in this passage. The first is the clear distinction which Lord Kilkerran observed between review on the merits and control of the process of decision making by the body to whom the merits of the decision have been entrusted. The second is the use of the words 'excess of power', and the insistence by the court that the trustees or justices were not the sole and exclusive judges of their own 'jurisdiction'. These expressions recur throughout the cases on this chapter of the law, and one can see here, even at the very earliest stage of its development, the emergence of a clearly defined principle that, where an excess or abuse of the power or jurisdiction conferred on a decision maker is alleged, the Court of Session, in the exercise of its function as the supreme court, has the power to correct it.

In *Heritors of Corstorphine* v. *Ramsay* it was held competent for the Court of Session to review a judgment of a presbytery in regard to schoolmasters, although their jurisdiction was declared to be final by the statute, if they refused to act, or if they exceeded their powers. Lord President Hope's opinion contains these passages at pp. 549 and 550: 'It is very true that the 43rd of the King [43 Geo. III c. 54] gave the exclusive jurisdiction as to schoolmasters to presbyteries alone. But that jurisdiction is exclusive only where they act in matters committed to them. But if they refuse to act at all, or go beyond their powers, they may be controuled by this Court … In other cases of privative jurisdiction, the Court of Session, as the Supreme Court of this country, has been in use to interfere, and to control. Thus, in the case of Commissioners of Supply refusing to split superiorities; — in the case of road trustees refusing to act; — and in the case of Courts of Lieutenancy exceeding their powers, the Court has interfered. In the case of road trustees from Aberdeenshire, this was most completely exemplified. The trustees refused to act, and to assess the damages due to a person through whose property the road went. The Court compelled them to do so. They then proceeded; and the heritor, not satisfied, brought the case before the Court by advocation, complaining of the proceedings, insofar as they proceeded on no proper evidence. The Court refused to sustain the advocation. The Court could compel the trustees to act; but having once done so, they had no power to interfere with what was done.'

Here again one can see a recognition of the distinction between the privative jurisdiction entrusted to the decision maker on the merits, with which the Court of Session cannot interfere, and control by the court where the decision maker refuses to act at all or goes beyond the powers which have been entrusted to him. The jurisdiction is seen here clearly to be a supervisory jurisdiction only. There is no conflict between the supervisory function and the exclusive or privative jurisdiction of the body whose decisions are open to supervision in this way.

These points were mentioned again in two further cases decided in the following decade. In *Ross* v. *Findlater* it was held that the Court of Session had jurisdiction to set aside the decree of a presbytery removing a schoolmaster, when they had failed to comply with the requisites of the statute. Lord Justice-Clerk Boyle at p. 520 explained the position of the court in these words: 'There has been manifest excess of power, and this, as the Supreme Civil Court, is bound to redress all the wrongs of the lieges, and to keep all inferior jurisdictions within the law. We are entitled to quash the proceedings of the presbytery, but without interfering on the merits of the question.'

In *Guthrie* v. *Miller* it was held that the court could not interfere with the exercise of the discretionary powers vested in commissioners of police under a local police Act, except in cases of excess of power or deviation from the statute. Lord Justice-Clerk Boyle said at p. 713: 'It did not appear to me that there was any clause in this act to exclude the review of this Court in a case of flagrant excess of power, or deviation from the statute... If the Court saw a case of wilful denial of rights under the statute, or a clear excess of power, we would interfere; but we cannot be called on to fix whether there is to be a lamp at this point, and a watchman at that.'

Lord Alloway at p. 713 is also instructive on this point: 'The doctrine laid down from the Chair as to jurisdiction cannot be disputed. The great distinction is that, when this Court has no previous jurisdiction, it requires express terms to exclude. But when there is no previous and radical jurisdiction, and the jurisdiction is created by the statute, the question comes to be determined on this ground, Have the parties intrusted with powers exceeded them? For while they keep within the bounds of the statute, which commits to them a discretionary power, unless excess of that power is pointed out, this Court cannot well interfere.'

This consistent line of authority in the Court of Session provided the background to a consideration of the matter in the House of Lords in *Campbell* v. *Brown*. This was a case about the dismissal of a schoolmaster. He was dissatisfied with the proceedings for his dismissal, and the question arose whether the Court of Session could review the judgment of the presbytery which, by the statute, was declared to be final without appeal to or review by any court civil or ecclesiastical. The argument for the schoolmaster was that the Court of Session had a jus supereminens which entitled the court to review the decision of the presbytery where there had been an informality in its proceedings. This argument was successful in the Court of Session, and on appeal to the House of Lords its judgment was affirmed on the ground that the Court of Session had a jurisdiction to review and set aside the proceedings of the presbytery where those proceedings had been irregular and informal. The following passage from the speech of Lord Lyndhurst L.C., at p. 448, is of particular interest and importance: 'But I apprehend that... a jurisdiction is given in this case to the Court of Session, not to review the judgment on the merits, but to take care that the Court of Presbytery shall keep within the line of its duty, and conform to the provisions of the Act of Parliament. There is in the Court of Session in Scotland that superintending authority over inferior jurisdictions, which is requisite in all countries, for the purpose of confining those inferior jurisdictions within the bounds of their duty; and the only question here is, whether this case is of such a nature and description as to justify the calling into action that authority of the Superior Court? Cases were cited at the Bar, and mentioned in the printed papers now on your Lordships' table, in which the Court of Session has exercised a superintending authority over inferior jurisdictions, when they have been guilty of an excess of their jurisdiction, or have acted inconsistently with the authority with which they were invested. Now, in this particular case, the power of final judgment is given to the Presbytery, under certain limitations and certain restrictions. The party is to be served with the libel, the necessary proof is to be taken, and unless the inferior tribunal pursue the course pointed out by the Act of Parliament, they have no authority to proceed to judgment; and if, without pursuing the course pointed out, they do proceed to a judgment, in that case all their proceedings will be so inconsistent with the authority with which they are invested, that the superintending authority of the Court of Session may be interposed, for the purpose of setting aside those proceedings.'

There is here an affirmation of the principle which defines the limits of the supervisory jurisdiction of the court. On the one hand there is no jurisdiction to review the judgment of the inferior tribunal or jurisdiction on the merits of the question which has been entrusted to them alone. On the other hand the court has authority to see that the decision taking body — the inferior tribunal or jurisdiction — keep within the limits of their duty and do not exceed the authority which has been given to them by the enabling power.

That was a case taken on the ground that the proceedings of the presbytery were irregular on the ground of an informality which was inconsistent with the enactment of the statute which gave them their authority. But the grounds upon which the decision of an inferior tribunal could be corrected were not limited to irregularities of any particular kind. As James Darling, *The Practice of the Court of Session* (1833) observed at p. 15: 'In cases even where the power of review is plainly excluded, the Session, as the supreme civil court of the kingdom, must necessarily still have jurisdiction to examine whether the inferior tribunals proceed according to the regulations of the statutes conferring on them the jurisdiction, and according to the ordinary principles of the common law.'

Examples are then given of various cases in which the court had exercised its authority to interfere on the ground of excess of power, assuming a jurisdiction beyond that conferred, omitting something enjoined by the statute or the irregular conduct of the proceedings. The author went on to say this: 'Wrongs of the above kinds must be redressed; and, besides, any thing done not in exact conformity with the provisions of a statute, is not a thing done in pursuance and execution of the statute, which is necessary to confine the matter to a particular jurisdiction... This jurisdiction of the Court of Session is evidently of a quite different nature from that of reviewing the merits of the cases which are intrusted to the inferior courts.'

These observations are important to an understanding of the distinction which must be made between the question of competency as to whether a decision is open to review by the Court of Session in the exercise of its supervisory jurisdiction, and the substantive grounds on which it may do so. The extent of the supervisory jurisdiction is capable of a relatively precise definition, in which the essential principles can be expressed. But the substantive grounds on which that jurisdiction may be exercised will of course vary from case to case. And they may be adapted to conform to the standards of decision taking as they are evolved from time to time by the common law.

Four cases in the latter half of the 19th century may now be mentioned to illustrate the extent of the supervisory jurisdiction as it had by now developed, and to show the range of decisions which may be subject to review. *Ashley* v. *Magistrates of Rothesay* was a case about the hours of opening and closing of inns and public houses in the Burgh of Rothesay. The magistrates made a resolution that all inns and public houses in the burgh were to close at 10 instead of 11 as required by the statutes, and they granted certificates to that effect at a meeting held for the granting and renewal of licensing certificates. The matter came before the Court of Session in an action of reduction and declarator. The defenders pleaded that the action was incompetent because review by the court had been excluded by the statute. It was held that when an inferior court exceeds its power the Court of Session may reduce its decree, although bearing to be under an Act which excludes reduction. Lord President Inglis explained the point at p. 716: 'Now, the plain answer to the objection founded upon in this section is, that the present is not a process of review, nor is it in a proper sense a stay of execution. It is a proceeding brought in the Court for the purpose of setting aside as incompetent and illegal the proceedings of an inferior Court, and the jurisdiction of this Court to entertain such an action cannot be doubted, notwithstanding the entire prohibition of review of any kind. This is not review, as I said before, but it is the interference of the Supreme Court for the purpose of keeping inferior courts within the bounds of their jurisdiction. The Magistrates having exceeded their powers under the statute their order, whatever it may be — or decision — is liable to be set aside.'

This decision was later affirmed in the House of Lords in *Macbeth* v. *Ashley*. In *Macfarlane* v. *Mochrum School Board*, a schoolmaster raised an action of reduction of a decision by a school board to remove him and that of the board of education by whom their judgment had been confirmed. He sought to do this on the grounds of deviation from the statutory procedure and of malice and oppression. The latter ground was held not to be relevant, but it was held that the court had jurisdiction in the action so far as based on relevant averments of deviations from the statutory procedure, although it had no power to review the judgment of a school board on its merits. Lord President Inglis said this at p. 98 of the argument presented to the court on competency: 'But the pleas which are stated both by the school board and by the Board of Education proceed upon a failure to distinguish between the review of a judgment of this kind of a Court of law and the reduction of such a resolution or sentence as we have before us on the ground of incompetency. The school board of a parish and the Board of Education are both of them the creatures of statute. They can do nothing except under statutory authority. They can exercise no power whatever, except that which is given to them by the statute; and if they do not conform to the conditions by which the statute authorises them to exercise that power then they are no longer acting under the statute, and their proceedings would be liable not to be reviewed but to be set aside as incompetent.'

In *Lord Advocate* v. *School Board of Stow*, the school board had resolved that it was necessary for additional school accommodation to be provided, and this resolution was confirmed by the board of education. But the school board then resolved that the carrying out of the former resolution should be delayed and they refused to comply with a requisition by the board of education to carry out their original resolution. The court, on the petition of the Lord Advocate, ordered the school board to comply with the requisition of the board of education. In his comment on the point of competency Lord Deas said this at p. 473: 'The first question is, what power have we to interfere? Looking to the terms of the Education Act, 1872, and particularly to those of the 28th and 36th sections, it appears to me that we have no power to interfere with the action of the Board of Education in a matter of the kind now in dispute, except in two cases — first, if it were plain that the board had refused or failed to apply their minds to the question of school accommodation in the particular parish, so as to come to an intelligent resolution on the subject, we might interfere to correct that abuse; or second, if the board had gone contrary to or outwith the statute, we might, in that case, also interfere to set them right.'

Finally in this group of cases there is *Forbes* v. *Underwood*, in which it was held in an appeal from the sheriff court that the Court of Session alone has jurisdiction to compel an arbiter to proceed. It was argued that the position of an arbiter was analogous to that of a public body such as road trustees refusing to act, in which case the Court of Session would interfere to make them proceed although it had no jurisdiction to direct them what to do. Lord President Inglis at p. 467 said this about the jurisdiction of the Court of Session: 'The position of an arbiter is very much like that of a Judge in many respects, and there is no doubt whatever that whenever an inferior Judge, no matter of what kind, fails to perform his duty, or transgresses his duty, either by going beyond his jurisdiction, or by failing to exercise his jurisdiction when called upon to do so by a party entitled to come before him, there is a remedy in this Court, and the inferior Judge, if it turns out that he is wrong, may be ordered by this Court to go on and perform his duty, and if he fails to do so he will be liable to imprisonment as upon a decree *ad factum praestandum*. The same rule applies to a variety of other public officers, such as statutory trustees and commissioners, who are under an obligation to exercise their functions for the benefit of the parties for whose benefit these functions are entrusted to them, and if they capriciously and without just cause refuse to perform their duty they will be ordained to do so by decree of this Court, and failing their performance will, in like manner, be committed to prison. Now, all this belongs to the Court of Session as the Supreme Civil Court of this country in the exercise of what is called, very properly, its supereminent jurisdiction.'

After considering the position of inferior judges and then of arbiters, he went on to say this at p. 469: 'Now, all these are considerations which require the most delicate handling by a Court that is called upon to enforce under the penalty of imprisonment the duty of the arbiter to go on and close the submission. I can hardly conceive anything more suitable for the interposition of the Supreme Court, or less suitable to the jurisdiction of an inferior Judge. It appears to me that the parallel between the position of an arbiter and the position of inferior Judges — Judges in the proper sense of the term — is complete, and that the two are quite undistinguishable in this question of jurisdiction.'

The importance of this case for present purposes is that it shows that the principle upon which the supervisory jurisdiction is exercised is not affected by distinctions which may exist for other purposes between public bodies and those who exercise a jurisdiction under a private contract. The public or private nature of the inferior body or tribunal is not decisive, nor is it necessary to inquire whether the decision of the inferior body or tribunal is administrative in character. The essential point is that a decision making function has been entrusted to that body or tribunal which it can be compelled by the court to perform. As counsel for the respondent pointed out, the tripartite relationship in these arrangements is significant. The essential feature of all these cases is the conferring, whether by statute or private contract, of a decision making power or duty on a third party to whom the taking of the decision is entrusted but whose manner of decision making may be controlled by the court.

This consistency of approach was maintained throughout the cases in this century which preceded the introduction of Rule of Court 260B. In *Moss Empires* v. *Walker*, an action for reduction of an entry in the valuation roll was held to be competent on grounds explained by Lord Kinnear at 1916 2 S.L.T., p. 218: 'Now, I apprehend that there can be no question at all of the jurisdiction of the Court of Session to entertain an action of that kind. Wherever any inferior tribunal or any administrative body has exceeded the powers conferred upon it by statute to the prejudice of the subject, the jurisdiction of the Court to set aside such excess of power as incompetent and illegal is not open to dispute.'

The scope of the expression 'any inferior tribunal or any administrative body' will be evident from the cases to which we have already referred. The common characteristic is not the nature of the tribunal or body as such but the entrusting to it of a decision making power or duty which must be exercised within the jurisdiction conferred upon it and is accordingly subject to supervision by the court.

In *McDonald* v. *Burns*, the Court of Session was willing to entertain an action as to whether the proceedings by which sisters were expelled from a convent in Edinburgh were regular and in conformity with the law and constitution of the Roman Catholic Church. It was recognised by Lord Justice-Clerk Aitchison that the judicatories of religious bodies in Scotland have their own exclusive jurisdictions and that their own decisions within their own sphere are final and binding upon their own members and not open to review unless in exceptional circumstances. Nevertheless, as he explained at 1940 S.L.T., p. 331, the court will entertain actions arising out of the judgments of ecclesiastical bodies where the religious association has acted beyond its own constitution in a manner calculated to affect the civil rights and patrimonial interests of any of its members and where, although acting within its own constitution, its procedure has been marked by gross irregularity such as would, in the case of an ordinary civil tribunal, be sufficient to vitiate the proceedings. The significance of this case is that it provides a further example of the supervisory jurisdiction being exercised by the court in a case where the jurisdiction was conferred on the inferior tribunal otherwise than by statute, and where the matter at issue could not be described as being in the area of public law.

The unimportance for this purpose of the distinction between public and private law can be seen also from the decision in *St Johnstone Football Club Ltd.* v. *Scottish Football Association Ltd.* The point at issue arose out of the articles of association of the S.F.A. to which the football club were subject as members of it, which empowered the council of the S.F.A. to fine or expel its members on grounds of which they were to be the sole judges. The case provides a clear example of the tripartite relationship to which we referred earlier, by which a decision making body — in this case the council — has been entrusted by an enabling body with a limited jurisdiction for decision taking in regard to others to which it must adhere. Lord Kilbrandon held, following *McDonald* v. *Burns*, that the Court of Session will entertain actions arising out of the judgments of the governing bodies of private associations, whether or not the civil rights and patrimonial interests of its members have been interfered with by the proceedings complained of, where a gross irregularity such as a departure from the rules of natural justice has been demonstrated. *Barrs* v. *British Wool Marketing Board, McDonald* v. *Lanarkshire Fire Brigade Joint Committee, Palmer* v. *Board of Management for Inverness Hospitals* and *Watt* v. *Lord Advocate* are all examples of quasi-judicial bodies and tribunals of various kinds being held to be subject to the supervisory jurisdiction of the court.

Mention should be made here of a case which lies outside the mainstream of this line of authority but to which counsel for the petitioner attached some importance in support of his argument that wherever a discretion is to be exercised the court may interfere to control the manner of its exercise. This proposition, which ignores the tripartite element inherent in the conferring of a jurisdiction or duty on a third party, is too broadly stated to be acceptable as an accurate definition of the supervisory jurisdiction. But counsel sought support for it in the observations of Lord President Clyde in *Governors of Donaldson's Hospital* v. *Educational Endowments Commissioners* at 1932 S.L.T., p. 421, where, after saying that all discretionary powers, without exception, must be used both reasonably and according to law, he said: 'Were it otherwise, there would be no difference between a discretionary power and an arbitrary one; and, if those upon whom a discretion is conferred exercise it, not reasonably or according to law, but arbitrarily, they are not using, but abusing, their discretion. Whenever this can be established as matter of fact, their acts become liable to be interfered with by a Court of law. The right and duty of the Court so to interfere — whenever, that is to say, discretionary powers are exercised either unreasonably or in a manner contrary to law — is illustrated by many cases, alike in the law of Scotland and in that of England, dealing with discretionary powers given to trustees under settlement and to magistrates under statute.'

That case, however, was one which had been presented to the court under the Educational Endowments (Scotland) Act 1928 for an opinion as to whether a proposed scheme was outwith the powers conferred on the commissioners. The argument was about the width of the discretionary powers of the commissioners, and the statutory background was a special one which makes it unwise to attach significance for present purposes to the passage which we have quoted. In any event these observations were directed to the substantive grounds on which the exercise of a discretion may be controlled rather than the question of crucial importance in the present case, which is to define the circumstances in which it is competent for the court in the exercise of its supervisory jurisdiction to exercise this control. These comments are best seen therefore in the same light as the observations of Lord President Emslie in *Wordie Property Co. Ltd.* v. *Secretary of State for Scotland*, 1984 S.L.T. at pp. 347–348, about the grounds upon which a decision taken by the Secretary of State in the exercise of statutory powers may be challenged as ultra vires. A discussion about the substantive grounds on which control is to be exercised should be kept separate from one about the competency of exercising that control.

Brown v. Hamilton District Council

We come now to *Brown* v. *Hamilton District Council* and to the observations of Lord Fraser of Tullybelton which were of such importance to the further development of the supervisory jurisdiction. But before examining what Lord Fraser said in that case it is worth pausing to notice the essential characteristics of this jurisdiction as revealed by the cases which we have described so far. The most striking feature is the consistency of approach over a period in excess of two centuries. This approach was both simple and understandable, untroubled by disputes about the scope of remedies or distinctions between public and private law which in England have given rise to much difficulty. Moreover the development of the law of Scotland in this field has not been on a case by case basis, as counsel for the petitioner invited us to find, but on the basis of principle. The principle is that where a particular matter has been entrusted to an inferior body or tribunal the Court of Session cannot substitute its own view for what that body or tribunal may decide; but it can nevertheless interfere in order to control any excess or abuse of power or failure to act within the limits of the jurisdiction which has been conferred. That supervisory jurisdiction may be appealed to in order to insist upon standards of rationality and fairness of procedure in addition to what may have been expressly required by the statute or by the contract by which the limits of the inferior jurisdiction have been defined. The only point of criticism was that to which Lord Fraser drew attention in *Brown*, 1983 S.L.T. at p. 418 and again in *Stevenson* v. *Midlothian District Council*, 1983 S.L.T. at p. 437, that the procedure for obtaining judicial review from the Court of Session was too slow and cumbersome and was in need of reform.

Before we examine these passages it is appropriate to observe the comments at the outset of Lord Fraser's speech at 1983 S.L.T., p. 414. Three points of importance are made on this page: first, that it has long been recognised in Scotland that the Court of Session has jurisdiction to exercise a supervisory control over inferior courts and tribunals in cases where there is no right of appeal from those courts or tribunals, and even in cases where appeal is expressly excluded by statute; secondly, that no difference of substance exists between the laws of England and Scotland in regard to the grounds on which judicial review may be open; and thirdly, that the supervisory jurisdiction over inferior courts and tribunals is vested exclusively in the Court of Session as the supreme court. There was nothing new in these remarks. All of them were amply vouched by previous authority, and there is no hint in anything said by Lord Fraser that the law of Scotland on these matters was in need of change. The respondents' argument in that case was that the supervisory jurisdiction of the Court of Session over bodies other than courts and tribunals was exclusive to this court only in respect of decisions which were judicial or quasi-judicial, and that administrative decisions were subject to a supervisory jurisdiction in the sheriff court. But Lord Fraser found few traces in the Scottish cases of a distinction being drawn between administrative and judicial decisions, and he held that the supervisory jurisdiction over decisions of administrative bodies, whether they were administrative, judicial or quasi-judicial, was privative to the Court of Session. Here again, what he said was entirely consistent with the authorities to which we have referred, and there is nothing here to disturb the pattern of consistency which is such a prominent feature of this long line of authority.

When he came to make his recommendation for procedural reform, however, Lord Fraser used expressions which have been relied upon in later cases as suggesting the limits for judicial review under the new rule. In *Brown*, 1983 S.L.T. at p. 418 he said: 'Secondly, it is for consideration whether there might not be advantages in developing special procedure in Scotland for dealing with questions in the public law area, comparable to the English prerogative orders.'

The phrase 'the public law area' and a reference later on the same page to 'the public law field' have attracted attention, as also have comments in *Stevenson* to the same effect, at 1983 S.L.T., p. 437, where Lord Fraser said: 'In the recent case of *Brown* v. *Hamilton District Council* I suggested that there might be advantages in developing or reviving special procedure in Scotland, comparable to the procedure under Order 53 of the Rules of the Supreme Court of England, for obtaining judicial review of decisions by public bodies. This appeal is a good example of a case where such procedure might have been useful.'

Now it is clear that it was not Lord Fraser's intention in these passages to define the extent of the supervisory jurisdiction of this court. He had said all that was necessary on this point in *Brown*, 1983 S.L.T. at p. 414. The context for these remarks was the entirely different one of concern about the time taken in the cases which were before him for the jurisdiction to be exercised. In *Brown's* case it had taken almost four years for a decision made in December 1978 to reach the House of Lords, yet the nature of the jurisdiction made it wholly unnecessary for the merits of the case to be gone into because all the court could do was to exercise its supervisory control. In *Stevenson's* case, where the notice was served in February 1978, it was five years before the case was resolved in the House of Lords.

His use of the phrases 'the public law area' and 'the public law field' should also be seen in the light of the fact that when the speeches in *Brown* were delivered on 25 November 1982 the judgments in two other cases about judicial review in England were also being delivered: see *O'Reilly* v. *Mackman* and *Cocks* v. *Thanet District Council*. Those two cases were also concerned with decisions by public bodies, the question being whether judicial review was the appropriate remedy. It was held in both of them that, since all the remedies under English law for the infringement of rights protected under public law could be obtained on an application for judicial review, subject to safeguards designed to protect public authorities from harassment, it would as a general rule be an abuse of process for a person to seek to establish by ordinary action that his public law rights had been infringed. No doubt the phrases used by Lord Fraser came readily to his mind as appropriate in that general context. One can accept that it was his particular concern that the remedies available to litigants in Scotland who took issue with decisions taken by public bodies in this country should not be at a disadvantage as compared with those in England because the procedure in Scotland denied ready access to the courts for the obtaining of the appropriate remedies. But it would be a mistake to assume from these few remarks that Lord Fraser intended to narrow the supervisory jurisdiction of the Court of Session from what it had previously been to a jurisdiction which was to be available only for exercise in the field which was recognised in England as being the field of public law.

Rule of Court 260B and subsequent cases

On 27 April 1983 a working party was set up under the chairmanship of Lord Dunpark with the following terms of reference: 'Having regard to the observations of Lord Fraser of Tullybelton in his speeches in *Brown* v. *Hamilton District Council* and *Stevenson* v. *Midlothian District Council*, to devise and recommend for consideration a simple form of procedure, capable of being operated with reasonable expedition, for bringing before the court, for such relief as is appropriate, complaints by aggrieved persons (1) against acts or decisions of inferior courts, tribunals, public bodies, authorities or officers, in respect of which no right of appeal is available, alleging that the acts or decisions are ultra vires, or that they have been done or taken without compliance with particular statutory procedural requirements; and (2) of failure of any body or person to perform a statutory duty, which it or he could be compelled to perform in terms of s. 91 of the Court of Session Act 1868.'

This working party assumed the title of the Working Party on Procedure for Judicial Review of Administrative Action. In para. 4 of its report it said: 'It is obvious from our terms of reference that the procedure which we recommend will be confined to disputes about the validity of acts done or decisions taken by tribunals and public bodies and their officers in the field of administrative law and to applications for the specific performance of a statutory duty by any body or person.'

Similar references elsewhere in the report indicate a concern only for decisions taken in this particular field of administrative law. And when it came to the terms of the new proposed rule, the working party proposed as the first of the new rules a provision whose effect would have been to limit the exercise of the supervisory jurisdiction under this procedure to 'acts or decisions of inferior courts, tribunals, public authorities, public bodies or officers acting in a public capacity'. The intention was that the new procedure should be used instead of any other form of process whenever an act or decision of one of the specified bodies or officers was to be challenged as unlawful for any reason. It is of particular interest, therefore, against this background that when the new rule 260B was made in due course by S.I. 1985 No. 500, in relation to proceedings commenced on or after 30 April 1985, no limit whatever was imposed by Rule of Court 260B (1) as to the bodies, officers or others to whose acts or decisions it was to apply.

The following characteristics of Rule of Court 260B may therefore be noted at this stage. First, since it was introduced by Act of Sederunt without any further enabling power having been conferred on the court by general legislation, it was a procedural amendment only which did not and could not alter in any respect the substantive law. Thus neither the nature or scope of the supervisory jurisdiction nor the grounds on which it may be exercised were affected by the introduction of this new rule. Secondly, it requires that all applications to the supervisory jurisdiction must be made only by means of the new procedure. The former procedure by way of summons or petition is no longer to be available in such cases. This makes it all the more important to observe that no change in the substantive law was being effected. To treat the procedure as available only in some cases appropriate for the supervisory jurisdiction and not others would risk leaving those other cases without a remedy, because no other procedure is available. Crucial to a proper understanding of the new procedure, therefore, is the generality of its application, since it applies to all cases where an application is being made to the supervisory jurisdiction of the court.

The simplicity of the rule and the success of the new procedure have nevertheless created difficulties. Perhaps because of a misconception about Lord Fraser's references to the public law field in *Brown*, and a tendency to think in terms of administrative law generally as illustrated by the report of the working party, there has been some confusion about the proper use in this field of English terminology and case law. It should be said at once in this chapter that, as Lord Fraser pointed out in *Brown*, 1983 S.L.T. at p. 414, there is no difference between the law of Scotland and the law of England as to the substantive grounds on which a decision may be challenged as ultra vires in proceedings of this kind. As Lord Fraser put it in *Brown* (1983 S.L.T. at p. 414): 'The decisions in the English cases of *Associated Provincial Picture Houses Ltd.* v. *Wednesbury Corporation* and *Anisminic* v. *Foreign Compensation Commission*, so far as they relate to matters of substance and not of procedure, are accepted as being applicable in Scotland: see *Watt* v. *Lord Advocate*.'

Lord President Emslie's remarks in *Wordie Property Co. Ltd.* v. *Secretary of State for Scotland*, 1984 S.L.T. at pp. 347–348, are to the same effect. The problem which has arisen in cases following the introduction of rule 260B is about the influence of English law on decisions about the competency of the procedure. Indications of a misunderstanding in this respect are to be found in *Connor* v. *Strathclyde Regional Council*. That case was concerned with a decision taken at a selection board of the education authority for the appointment of assistant head teachers in two schools. The application for judicial review was challenged on the ground of competency, and this argument was successful on a number of grounds. Counsel were agreed that it was appropriate to consider English law in regard to the question of competency, and the Lord Ordinary applied dicta in the English cases in order to arrive at this result. This led him to hold that the petition was incompetent because the actings of the board did not indicate a sufficient element of public law for them to be subject to judicial review. He went on to say, under reference to Lord Diplock's statement in *Council of Civil Service Unions* v. *Minister for the Civil Service* [1985] A.C. at p. 408 of the test which must be satisfied in England to qualify as a subject for judicial review, that the question of judicial review was still in the process of development, and that in the present state of the law the Court of Session had no power in the exercise of its supervisory jurisdiction to intervene 'in a situation where there is no element of public law arising which is sufficient to attract public law remedies'. But to describe the supervisory jurisdiction of the Court of Session as a public law remedy, and then to look for an element of public law as the test of whether it is available, is to introduce concepts which have had no part in the development of that jurisdiction in Scotland over the last two centuries. And there are indications of the confusion between the relevance of English law to the substantive grounds for review and its irrelevance to questions of competency, which was the only issue which the court in that case had to decide. The description of judicial review under Rule of Court 260B as a public law remedy led to the decision in *Safeway Food Stores Ltd.* v. *The Scottish Provident Institution* that, as the dispute in that case arose out of private arbitration, an action of reduction under the ordinary procedure was competent. But that decision was at variance with *Forbes* v. *Underwood*, to which no reference was made in that case. The confusion introduced by the argument that the procedure under Rule of Court 260B is concerned only with a public law remedy led to a decision which cannot now be supported as being correct.

Tehrani v. Argyll and Clyde Health Board

The most important of the cases since the introduction of the new rule, however, is *Tehrani* v. *Argyll and Clyde Health Board (No. 2)*. It was his concern about the implications of some of the things said in that case that was in the forefront of the Lord Ordinary's mind when he observed that he would welcome the opportunity which a reclaiming motion would give for a comprehensive consideration and statement of the scope of the court's supervisory jurisdiction.

The petitioner in that case was a consultant surgeon employed by the National Health Service for Scotland who had been suspended from duty following a complaint arising from his treatment of a patient. The health board investigated the allegations which were made against him, and in due course a committee of inquiry was set up by them to investigate these allegations and to report to the board. It was the board's decision to dismiss the petitioner summarily from his employment with them which the petitioner sought to challenge by way of judicial review. The board contended that the application was incompetent, but the Lord Ordinary repelled that plea and, having considered the arguments about the manner of the dismissal, held that it was unreasonable in the *Wednesbury* sense and granted decree of reduction. The board reclaimed and their plea to competency was sustained in the Inner House. But before examining the opinions which were delivered in the Inner House, we should say something about the reasons which the Lord Ordinary gave for holding that the petition was competent. This is because these reasons illustrate that some of the difficulties which the court has experienced in arriving at a clear understanding of the supervisory jurisdiction in the context of Rule of Court 260B are to be found also in his opinion and are not confined to things said in the course of argument in the Inner House.

It was submitted for the board in the Outer House that the dispute was essentially a matter of private law, being concerned with a breach of contract, and that it was not open to judicial review: p. 124L. It was recognised that the supervisory jurisdiction could extend to contracts of employment where an individual's employment was protected by statute, but since the petitioner's relationship with the board was one which was regulated by contract it was contended that the supervisory jurisdiction did not apply. Attention was drawn to the tendency to confine judicial review to what were called 'public law' matters. The Lord Ordinary was referred to the cases of *Connor* v. *Strathclyde Regional Council* and *Safeway Food Stores Ltd.* v. *The Scottish Provident Institution* which we have mentioned above. But he was not persuaded that the approach taken in these cases was correct, nor was he convinced that the distinction in English law between public law and private law in the context of judicial review applied in Scotland. He then turned to examine some of the previously reported cases in Scots law, especially *Forbes* v. *Underwood*, in order to determine the issue of competency. He observed that the dispute in *Forbes* concerned a matter which was purely one of private law and that this did not prevent the court from exercising its supervisory jurisdiction. He then said this at p. 126E: 'In my view, this case is authority for the proposition that where quasi-judicial machinery is stipulated in a private contract for use in certain circumstances, the court may exercise its supervisory jurisdiction.'

Counsel for the respondent in the present case said that they had no quarrel with that proposition so long as it was clearly understood that the quasi-judicial machinery was some body independent of the employer to whom the responsibility for decision taking had been delegated. But the expression used carried with it the risk of a misunderstanding, because the quasi-judicial machinery which the Lord Ordinary proceeded to identify was that of the board itself as the petitioner's employer. He rejected as illogical the board's argument that, while the committee which conducted the inquiry were open to judicial review, the board itself was not. It will be clear, however, from our analysis of the supervisory jurisdiction that there was a distinction which could logically be made. The committee was a body which had been set up by the board to which a jurisdiction had been committed. In its case the tripartite relationship between an inferior tribunal, the appointing body and the petitioner was established. But the board itself was not in that position. As the petitioner's employer it owed certain duties to him and in particular it owed him the duty to act fairly. But the performance of that duty was a matter to be regulated under the ordinary jurisdiction of the court according to the contract between employer and employee and was not amenable to judicial review. In *Sutcliffe* v. *Thackrah* [1974] A.C. at p. 737H, Lord Reid described the argument that, as all persons carrying out judicial functions must act fairly, therefore all persons who must act fairly are carrying out judicial functions as completely illogical: see also Lord Salmon at p. 759H. Yet that same fallacy is, with respect, apparent in the Lord Ordinary's reasoning at p. 126, where he said that the concepts of natural justice and unreasonableness are both aspects of judicial review and cannot be kept artificially apart. It was this association of ideas which led him to hold that the application was competent. He saw the functions of the board as being quasi-judicial, and thus subject to the requirements of natural justice, and thus amenable to judicial review. The fact was, however, that the board was not performing any function independent of its position as the employer of the respondent to whom it owed a duty to act fairly under its contract with him, and for that reason its duty to act fairly was not open to judicial review.

Two other points about the Lord Ordinary's approach should be noted here before we turn to the opinions in the Inner House. The first is that he made no mention of para. 197 of the petitioner's terms and conditions of service, which made provision enabling either party to terminate the contract without notice by reason of such conduct by the other party as enabled him so to treat it at law. This provision played an important part in the argument in the Inner House that the board were entitled to terminate the petitioner's employment without notice, provided his conduct had been such as to enable them to dismiss him summarily at common law. The second point relates to the Lord Ordinary's comment at p. 129F-G that cogent reasons had to exist for the step of summary dismissal to be taken and that the reasons for summary dismissal when compared with the alternative of dismissal with notice had to be particularly compelling. At p. 129L he said that the question for examination was whether any board acting reasonably in the circumstances would have concluded that the only course was to dismiss him forthwith. But this was in effect the *Wednesbury* test of unreasonableness, and in the Inner House it was held that it was the wrong test to apply to the contract. The proper question was whether a reasonable health board could reasonably have concluded that the petitioner was in material breach of contract so that they would be justified in dismissing him summarily. As Lord Murray pointed out at p. 141J-K, this was a pure matter of the law of contract without any public law element at all.

It will be apparent from what we have said so far that there were sound reasons for the decision reached by the Inner House that the petition was incompetent and that, in any event, even if it was competent it fell to be dismissed as irrelevant. According to the rubric at p. 119D, however, it was held that in deciding whether or not a petition for judicial review was competent the question was whether a matter of public law was raised in the application. If that was indeed the ratio of the decision it would be in conflict with the long line of authority in Scotland which preceded the introduction of rule 260B, and with the terms of the rule itself, which did not restrict the supervisory jurisdiction to what may loosely be described as the field of public law. It would also have the disadvantage of introducing into the law of Scotland a novel and uncertain test which even in England has given rise to such substantial difficulty. As Lord Wilberforce pointed out in *Davy* v. *Spelthorne Borough Council* [1984] A.C. at p. 276: 'The expressions "private law" and "public law" have recently been imported into the law of England from countries which, unlike our own, have separate systems concerning public law and private law. No doubt they are convenient expressions for descriptive purposes. In this country they must be used with caution, for, typically English law fastens, not upon principles but upon remedies.'

In our opinion, however, on a proper analysis of the opinions in the Inner House, this part of the rubric is inaccurate. The case is not to be read as having decided that the competency of an application to the supervisory jurisdiction of the Court of Session depends upon whether a matter of public law is raised in the application.

The argument for the board in the Inner House was that Rule of Court 260B fell to be read in a restricted sense, having regard to the mischief which it was intended to redress, and that, since Lord Fraser's remarks in *Brown* were clearly related to public law matters, the supervisory jurisdiction was exercisable only in the field of public administrative law. For the petitioner on the other hand it was accepted that the essential problem in the case was whether there were elements of public law in his contract of employment which would entitle him to a public law remedy: the Lord Justice-Clerk at p. 131L, Lord Wylie at p. 1361, Lord Murray at pp. 140C and 141B. The point was made that as a matter of principle the supervisory jurisdiction of the Court of Session could embrace not only public law matters but also private law to control voluntary associations or clubs, and that Rule of Court 260B did not expressly restrict its ambit to public law matters. But counsel were content to present their argument for the petitioner on the basis that for the purposes of that case the court did not have to choose between a restricted and a wider interpretation of the rule. They accepted that for the petitioner to succeed in his application he had to show that he was entitled to the public law remedy for which he contended. That being the nature of the argument it is not surprising that the Lord Justice-Clerk was satisfied that in that case it was not necessary to determine in any comprehensive way the scope of the Scottish procedure of judicial review under Rule of Court 260B, and that Lord Murray was able to reserve judgment on this point: see pp. 131L, 141B. For the reasons which we have explained earlier in this opinion these arguments were inconsistent with the Scottish authority on the scope and nature of the supervisory jurisdiction, and the terminology on which they were presented was liable to create difficulty. Any acceptance by the court of that terminology must, however, be regarded as strictly obiter in the circumstances, and the case is not to be taken as authority for the proposition that Rule of Court 260B is restricted in its scope to public law matters or is to be regarded only as a remedy of public administrative law. There is no indication in the Lord Justice-Clerk's opinion at p. 131K that he questioned the authority of cases such as *Forbes* v. *Underwood, McDonald* v. *Burns* and *St Johnstone Football Club Ltd.* v. *Scottish Football Association Ltd.*, where remedies were provided by the Court of Session in the exercise of its supervisory jurisdiction in the field of private law.

It is true that the Lord Justice-Clerk said at pp. 134L–135A that he was satisfied that in that case there were no public law elements in the petitioner's case which could give rise to any entitlement 'to a public law remedy such as judicial review'. We do not, with respect, agree that judicial review under Rule of Court 260B is properly to be described as a public law remedy. But that passage must be read in the context of the arguments which were presented to the court, and in any event for reasons which we shall come to it is plain that the description of judicial review as a public law remedy is not the ratio of the decision.

Lord Wylie's comments at pp. 137L–138A went further on this point. He said that the Lord Ordinary was wrong to decline to follow English authority in this field of law, having regard to what he had described as the distinctive origins and development of the remedies covered by judicial review in the two countries. He went on to say that the two procedures and the distinctive remedies provided were different but their purposes and the mischief for which they sought to provide remedies were the same in both jurisdictions. He agreed with counsel for the respondents that there was no good reason for differences between the two jurisdictions to develop in this field and added that it would be regrettable if they did. In our opinion, however, the origins and development of judicial review in the two countries are indeed different, as the Lord Ordinary was right to point out. One has only to look at what Lord Wilberforce said in *Davy* v. *Spelthorne Borough Council* which we have quoted above to see that these differences are fundamental. The English approach appears to be to fasten not upon principle but upon remedies, whereas the Scottish approach is based essentially upon principle. Moreover the choice of remedy has not in itself caused any difficulty in this country. The ordinary remedies of reduction, declarator and interdict are all available as a means of exercising the necessary control: see Lord Fraser in *Brown*, 1983 S.L.T. at p. 414, and Rule of Court 260B (4) in which the powers of the court are set out.

The argument in England has been whether cases which were in the public law field should be dealt with by ordinary action or by judicial review: see *O'Reilly* v. *Mackman*, in which at p. 285E Lord Diplock said that it would in his view as a general rule be contrary to public policy, and as such an abuse of the process of the court, to permit a person seeking to establish that a decision of a public authority infringed rights to which he was entitled to protection under public law to proceed by way of an ordinary action. What he saw as objectionable was the evasion by this means of the provisions of Order 53 of the Rules of the Supreme Court, which, for the protection of such authorities, prescribes a time limit for making the application for relief under that procedure. The nature of this debate is entirely different from that which has been taking place in Scotland since Rule of Court 260B was introduced. Furthermore, it is unnecessary for us to be troubled in Scotland by the distinction between public law and private law which has continued to create difficulty in England: see *R.* v. *Panel on Take-overs and Mergers, ex p. Datafin plc*, which illustrates the way in which what Lloyd L.J. described at [1987] Q.B., p. 845 as 'the new-found distinction between public and private law' continues to influence the developing law of judicial review in that country. There are obvious disadvantages in attempting to follow English authority in this field as it develops case by case, not the least of which is the uncertainty which this would create. We respectfully disagree therefore with Lord Wylie's comment in the passage to which we have referred. But, for the reasons already explained, we regard these remarks as obiter in the light of the argument presented in that case.

The petitioner's principal argument in the Inner House in *Tehrani* was that his case was similar to that of *Malloch* v. *Aberdeen Corporation*. And, as the Lord Justice-Clerk pointed out at p. 133L, he founded strongly upon the decision in that case. But there was an important distinction between the two cases, in that while in *Malloch* there was a special statutory provision which bore directly on the power to dismiss, namely s. 85 (1) of the Education (Scotland) Act 1962, the powers of dismissal in *Tehrani* were those set out in his terms and conditions of employment. There was an indirect link with the Secretary of State in that he had approved these terms and conditions. But, while he was no doubt exercising a jurisdiction in deciding whether or not to approve them, once they had been approved they were no longer amenable to judicial review, and decisions taken under them were challengeable only by means of the ordinary remedies available in respect of a contract of employment. This distinction was noted by the Lord Justice-Clerk at p. 134F-G, where he observed that merely to hold that a particular case was one where the principles of natural justice must be observed did not mean that the case was thereby elevated into the domain of public administrative law. We can find nothing in his discussion of this point with which we would disagree in principle, nor is there anything in the relevant passages in Lord Wylie's opinion at p. 137F-K or Lord Murray's opinion at p. 141G-H which is inconsistent with what we consider to be the correct approach. Lord Wylie drew attention at p. 137I to a passage in the opinion of Purchase L.J. in *R.* v. *East Berkshire Health Authority, ex p. Walsh* [1985] Q.B. at p. 176, where he drew attention to the danger of confusing the rights and remedies enjoyed by an employee arising out of a private contract of employment with the performance by a public body of the duties imposed upon it as part of the statutory terms under which it exercises its powers. Similar observations are to be found in the opinion of Sir John Donaldson M.R. in that case which were quoted by the Lord Justice-Clerk at p. 134H-L. We agree that these two issues are entirely distinct, and that if, in a case such as *Tehrani*, a public authority enters into a contract with its employees to give them rights under the terms of a contract of employment, a breach of that contract is a matter which must be dealt with under the ordinary jurisdiction by seeking contractual remedies and that it does not give rise to an entitlement to judicial review.

For these reasons we are in full agreement with the ratio of the decision in this case, which we consider to have been correctly decided. As already said, head (1) of the rubric goes further than is justified by the opinions, especially as the concession was made only in regard to the circumstances of that particular case and only the observations of Lord Wylie could properly be taken as having general application to all cases under Rule of Court 260B. The case should not be regarded as authority for the proposition that, in deciding whether or not a petition is competent under that rule, the question is whether a matter of public law has been raised in the application. The use of the expressions 'public law remedy', 'public law areas' and 'public administrative law' is inappropriate in the context of a discussion as to whether an application is competent under the rule.

Cases Subsequent to Tehrani

We must now deal briefly with two cases which were heard in the Inner House between the date when *Tehrani* was advised on 30 June 1989 and the hearing in the present case. These are *Watt* v. *Strathclyde Regional Council* and *Jackson* v. *Secretary of State for Scotland*.

The first of these cases was concerned with the pay and conditions of teaching staff employed by education authorities in Scotland. These had to be determined by a statutory body, whereupon each local authority was required to give effect to them insofar as they related to teachers in their employment. A statutory body had formulated a settlement relating to absence cover for teachers who were absent from their duties for more than three days which the respondent education authority was unwilling to implement. Yet the statute expressly required the education authority to give effect to the settlement. As Lord Clyde said in the course of his opinion, the decision of the education authority was one which cut across the statutory obligation, and it was in regard to this aspect of the case that an application was made for judicial review. The matter was complicated by the fact that on one view of the dispute between the teachers and their employers the issue was properly to be seen as one of contract, and it was for this reason that the Lord Ordinary held that the application for judicial review was not competent. But in the Inner House it was held that, while the ordinary contractual remedies were no doubt available in regard to such breaches of contract as might result, the decision itself not to give effect to the settlement was amenable to the remedy of judicial review. No one has suggested in the argument in the present case that *Watt* was wrongly decided in the Inner House. Indeed the respondents' counsel submitted that the application was clearly competent because the issue raised was one as to an excess of jurisdiction by the education authority. Our attention was, however, drawn to some of the dicta in the opinions of the Lord President and Lord Clyde which might cause difficulty if they were to be regarded as definitive of the supervisory jurisdiction under Rule of Court 260B. As the Lord President explained in the opening paragraph of his opinion, that case was dealt with as one of urgency, and the time available did not enable counsel to explore in argument the nature of the supervisory jurisdiction to any significant extent. Accordingly, where there is conflict between what was said in that case and the analysis of the supervisory jurisdiction in this opinion, the analysis in this opinion is to be preferred.

In these circumstances it is not necessary to deal in detail with the opinions in *Watt*, and we require to mention two matters only. The first is that the point made by the Lord President and Lord Clyde that the fact that the decision was of general application made it especially suitable for judicial review ought not in itself to be regarded as decisive of the question whether judicial review was appropriate. As junior counsel for the respondent pointed out, a decision which is of the appropriate character is amenable to judicial review whether it affects only one person or 100. The true significance of the point is that it revealed the nature or character of the decision as being one taken in the exercise of a statutory power or the implement of a statutory duty which, by its nature, was bound to affect all those in respect of whom the jurisdiction conferred by the statute was to be exercised. The second point is that Lord Clyde's comment that the petitioners' attack in that case was directed essentially at 'an alleged excess of power' was entirely consistent with the expressions used in the many Scottish cases prior to Rule of Court 260B, and it expresses very well the critical point in that case which showed that the decision was open to judicial review.

Jackson was an application for judicial review by an officer in the Scottish Prison Service of a decision by the Scottish Home and Health Department to defer his application to be permitted to retire on grounds of ill health from his post as governor in charge of a young offenders institution until disciplinary proceedings against him had been disposed of. The dispute was one about the proper constructions of provisions in the Civil Service Code which were treated as being, in effect, part of a contract of employment between the officer and the Secretary of State. No point of general importance is to be attached to this case on the point of competency, however, since no plea of competency was taken by the Secretary of State. The arguments were confined to the questions about the proper construction of the relevant provisions in the code. We were informed that it was not thought that any practical purpose would be served by taking the point on competency in that case, and it should be noted that the Lord Ordinary recorded at the end of his opinion that counsel had expressly refrained from presenting this argument, which was not raised in the Inner House.

Summary and Conclusion

We are now in a position, in the light of our examination of all these cases, to describe the principles by reference to which the competency of applications to the supervisory jurisdiction under Rule of Court 260B are to be determined. Counsel for the petitioner urged us not to attempt to do this, on the ground that it was better to allow the matter to develop on a case by case basis. Counsel for the respondent on the other hand said that there was no reason why we should not do so and that counsel for the petitioner's submission was based on a fundamental misconception about the nature of the supervisory jurisdiction. The question of competency was to be resolved by reference to principle. A case by case approach, he said, might be appropriate in England, but it was not the Scottish approach and it could only lead to continued uncertainty about the basis upon which the jurisdiction was to be exercised. In our opinion the principles are well settled, and no good reason has been advanced as to why we should not now describe them in order to remove the uncertainty and to correct misunderstandings which have affected discussions on this matter since the rule was introduced.

The following propositions are intended therefore to define the principles by reference to which the competency of all applications to the supervisory jurisdiction under Rule of Court 260B is to be determined:

(1) The Court of Session has power, in the exercise of its supervisory jurisdiction, to regulate the process by which decisions are taken by any person or body to whom a jurisdiction, power or authority has been delegated or entrusted by statute, agreement or any other instrument.

(2) The sole purpose for which the supervisory jurisdiction may be exercised is to ensure that the person or body does not exceed or abuse that jurisdiction, power or authority or fail to do what the jurisdiction, power or authority requires.

(3) The competency of the application does not depend upon any distinction between public law and private law, nor is it confined to those cases which English law has accepted as amenable to judicial review, nor is it correct in regard to issues about competency to describe judicial review under Rule of Court 260B as a public law remedy.

By way of explanation we would emphasise these important points:

(a) Judicial review is available, not to provide machinery for an appeal, but to ensure that the decision maker does not exceed or abuse his powers or fail to perform the duty which has been delegated or entrusted to him. It is not competent for the court to review the act or decision on its merits, nor may it substitute its own opinion for that of the person or body to whom the matter has been delegated or entrusted.

(b) The word 'jurisdiction' best describes the nature of the power, duty or authority committed to the person or body which is amenable to the supervisory jurisdiction of the court. It is used here as meaning simply 'power to decide', and it can be applied to the acts or decisions of any administrative bodies and persons with similar functions as well as to those of inferior tribunals. An excess or abuse of jurisdiction may involve stepping outside it, or failing to observe its limits, or departing from the rules of natural justice, or a failure to understand the law, or the taking into account of matters which ought not to have been taken into account. The categories of what may amount to an excess or abuse of jurisdiction are not closed, and they are capable of being adapted in accordance with the development of administrative law.

(c) There is no substantial difference between English law and Scots law as to the grounds on which the process of decision making may be open to review. So reference may be made to English cases in order to determine whether there has been an excess or abuse of the jurisdiction, power or authority or a failure to do what it requires.

(d) Contractual rights and obligations, such as those between employer and employee, are not as such amenable to judicial review. The cases in which the exercise of the supervisory jurisdiction is appropriate involve a tripartite relationship, between the person or body to whom the jurisdiction, power or authority has been delegated or entrusted, the person or body by whom it has been delegated or entrusted and the person or persons in respect of or for whose benefit that jurisdiction, power or authority is to be exercised.

We must now return to the facts of the present case, and to the question whether the petitioner's application to the supervisory jurisdiction can be regarded as competent. On this issue there is very little more to be said. There is no suggestion in the pleadings, nor was there at any stage in the argument, that the petitioner's concern is with the exercise of a jurisdiction, power or authority conferred on some third party who could be separately identified from his employer. No question has been raised as to any statutory or other restraint, whether by Parliament or any other body or person, on the exercise by the Scottish Prison Service of its discretion, through its personnel services division, on the matter at issue in this case. We can find nothing here, therefore, which could be said to raise a question about an excess or abuse of power or jurisdiction. There is an absence of any feature to place this case into any category other than that of a dispute between an employee and his employer about his conditions of employment. As the Lord Ordinary put it, the issue appears to be of the nature of a private dispute between the petitioner and the respondents arising from his terms of service. In the circumstances we consider that the Lord Ordinary was right to sustain the respondents' plea to the competency and to dismiss the petition.

On the whole matter, therefore, we shall refuse this reclaiming motion and adhere to the Lord Ordinary's interlocutor."

Notes

10–8 (1) This case must be taken as a starting point of any examination of the scope of judicial review. It has been subject to extensive comment and criticism: see *Stair Memorial Encyclopaedia*, Vol. 1, para. 205; W. Finnie, "Triangles as Touchstones of Review", 1993 S.L.T. (News) 51; C.M.G. Himsworth, "Further *West*? More Geometry of Judicial Review", 1995 S.L.T. (News) 127; Wolffe above; Finch and Ashton, pp. 229–249; G. Junor, "Judicial Review and the Intricacies of the Tripartite Relationship" (1995) 226 SCOLAG 126; and Himsworth in Hadfield (ed.) above.

(2) The concept of jurisdiction is the key to determining the scope of judicial review. Whether a decision is administrative, judicial or quasi-judicial does not appear to be relevant, nor does the nature of the decision-making body, nor are institutional factors such as the connection with the State nor the power of the body — for example, whether or not it monopolises an area of public life. Excess or abuse of jurisdiction which in turn is defined as the power to decide, delegated or entrusted by statute, agreement or other instrument, must be identified before judicial review is competent. Is this definition under or over inclusive?

Consider the position of trustees under a private trust deed. On the face of it, they would exercise a jurisdiction but would one normally consider judicial review procedure as being the method of control? In the Lord President's analysis there is concern to provide a coherent account of the supervisory jurisdiction and there is arguably an attractiveness in attempting to link the idea that only bodies exercising a jurisdiction are subject to judicial review on the usual grounds of review. Purely jurisdictional matters, such as simple *ultra vires* noted in Chapter 3, or error of law in Chapter 4, are integrally linked with the idea of a jurisdiction being exercised. The decision to withhold payment from West could hardly be seen as the exercise of a jurisdiction. However, so far as the other grounds of review are concerned, such as those relating to abuse and retention of discretion, detailed in Chapters 6 and 7 respectively, there does not appear to be any necessary link to the class of reviewable acts defined in *West*. If it was allowed, it would be competent to review decisions taken based on non-compliance with natural justice or which were inherently unreasonable or which were based on improper motives or irrelevant considerations, without there being any basis in the exercise of a jurisdiction. The decision carries with it the implication that the kind of decision complained of in *West*, which could in principle be reviewed on such grounds, are not susceptible to review. *West* can arguably be seen as an attempt both to clarify the basis of judicial review and to limit its scope.

(3) Notwithstanding uncertainty on the question of jurisdiction, the following bodies exercise **10–9**
a jurisdiction for the purpose of the test:

- Inferior courts and tribunals: see, for example, *McDonald v. Burns*, 1940 S.C. 376, extracted at para. 8–2 but there is no power to review the courts of the Church of Scotland on "all matters of doctrine, worship, government in discipline in the church": *Logan v. Presbytery of Dumbarton*, 1995 S.L.T. 1228; the Lyon Court: *Macrae's Trustees v. Lord Lyon King-of-Arms*, 1927 S.L.T. 285; the sheriff court in civil matters: *Adair v. Colville & Sons*, 1926 S.C. (H.L.) 51 and *Lothian Regional Council v. Lord Advocate*, 1993 S.C.L.R. 565 (fatal accident inquiry) although it would appear that where another remedy is competent — for example, reduction or suspension — judicial review of a decision of the sheriff is not competent; *Bell v. Fiddes*, 1996 S.L.T. 51 at 52 *per* Lord Marnoch and see now *Ingle v. Ingle's Trustee*, 1997 S.L.T. 160; the Justice of the Peace in civil matters: *Stakis plc v. Boyd*, 1989 S.C.L.R. 290. On *Bell* see V.M. Smith, "The Scope of Judicial Review Determined?" (1997) J.R. 122.

- Local authorities, whether in their legislative function, on which see *Robert Baird Ltd v. Glasgow Corporation*, 1935 S.C. (H.L.) 21, extracted at para. 2–47 or in their executive function: *Moss' Empires Ltd v. Assessor for Glasgow*, 1917 S.C. (H.L.) 1, extracted at para. 5–3.

- Government Ministers with delegated statutory power, whether legislative: *Air 2000 v. Secretary of State for Transport (No. 2)*, 1990 S.L.T. 335 or executive: *Lakin v. Secretary of State for Scotland*, 1988 S.L.T. 780 and *London and Clydeside Estates Ltd v. Secretary of State for Scotland*, 1987 S.L.T. 459, extracted at para. 9–7.

- Licensing boards: *Cinderella's Rockafella's Ltd v. Glasgow District Licensing Board*, 1994 S.C.L.R. 591, extracted at para.7–6; *Bass Taverns Ltd v. Clydebank District Licensing Board*, 1995 S.L.T. 1275, noted at para. 8–39; and *Brechin Golf and Squash Club v. Angus District Licensing Board*, 1993 S.L.T. 547.

- Other bodies with a jurisdiction delegated to them, including regulatory organisations: *Bank of Scotland v. Investment Management Regulatory Organisation Ltd*, 1989 S.C. 107; the Scottish Legal Aid Board: *McTear v. Scottish Legal Aid Board*, 1997 S.L.T. 108; monopolised public industries; *British Oxygen Co. Ltd v. South West Scotland Electricity Board*, 1956 S.C. (H.L.) 112, extracted at para. 8–14; rail authorities: *Highland Regional Council v. British Railways Board*, 1996 S.L.T. 274, noted at para. 6–6; political parties: *Brown v. Executive Committee of Edinburgh District Labour Party*, 1995 S.L.T. 985, noted at para. 11–7 and see now *Lally, Petitioner*, February 27, 1998, unreported; housing benefit review boards; *MacLeod v. Banff and Buchan District Housing Benefit Review Board*, 1988 S.L.T. 753; housing co-operatives: *Boyle v. Castlemilk East Housing Co-Operative Ltd*, 1998 S.L.T. 56. For further examples see *Stair Memorial Encyclopaedia*, Vol. 1, para. 234.

(4) Some powers of public authorities are derived from their capacity as a legal person **10–10**
rather than from an instrument. As noted by Daintith at para. 14–7 below, these powers can be
of great importance, but on the test in *West* they would apparently not be subject to review
unless such powers are delegated to such a person or body in terms of written instrument.
Arguably, the Criminal Injuries Compensation Authority falls into such a category and no doubt
has been expressed as to the competency of review of decisions of the board see, for example,
Rae v. Criminal Injuries Compensation Board, 1997 S.L.T. 291, extracted at para. 4–8 and
generally H.W.R. Wade, *Constitutional Fundamentals* (1980), pp. 47–48; R.D. Sutherland,
"Judicial Review and Criminal Injuries Compensation Authority" (1997) 241 SCOLAG 50 and
242 SCOLAG 72. The test in *West* does not appear to embrace the prerogative powers of the
Crown. It is accepted in Scots law that the courts can determine both the scope and manner of
exercise of prerogative power. *Burmah Oil Ltd v. Lord Advocate*, 1964 S.C. (H.L.) 117 and see
generally J.D.B. Mitchell, "The Royal Prerogative in Modern Scots Law" [1957] P.L. 304; W.
Wolffe, "Crown and Prerogative in Scots Law" in *Edinburgh Essays in Public Law* below;
Stair Memorial Encyclopaedia, Vol. 7, "The Crown", paras 720–721. In *C.C.S.U. v. Minister
for the Civil Service* [1985] A.C. 374 it was accepted by the House of Lords that in English law,
in principle, decisions taken by virtue of the prerogative were subject to judicial review albeit
questions of justiciability suggest that many decision will still remain unreviewable. Lord Roskill
observed (at 418):

"Prerogative powers such as those relating to the making of treaties, the defence of the realm, the prerogative of mercy, the grant of honours, the dissolution of Parliament and the appointment of ministers as well as others are not, I think, susceptible to judicial review because their nature and subject matter are such as not to be amenable to the judicial process. The courts are not the place wherein to determine whether a treaty should be concluded or the armed forces disposed in a particular manner or Parliament dissolved on one date rather than another."

The decision in this case would arguably have still been reviewable under the test in *West*, as it took the form of an Order in Council which could be treated as an instrument delegating authority. The question of reviewability of the prerogative was raised but not decided in *McDonald* v. *Secretary of State for Scotland (No. 2)*, 1996 S.L.T. 575 as the prerogative power in question (that of mercy) had been replaced by a statutory power which was reviewable. There have been a number of instances of review of prerogative power in English law. In *R.* v. *Secretary of state for the Home Department, ex p. Bentley* [1994] 2 W.L.R. 101 it was held that the prerogative power to grant a pardon for crime was subject to review and in *R.* v. *Secretary of State for the Home Department, ex p. Fire Brigades Union* [1995] 2 W.L.R. 464 the House of Lords held that it was an unlawful abuse of the common law prerogative power of the Home Secretary to set up a scheme for criminal injuries compensation outwith the statutory scheme provided by the Criminal Justice Act 1988. A decision to refuse the renewal of a passport was held amenable to judicial review in *R* v. *Secretary of State* v. *Foreign Commonwealth Affairs, ex p. Everett* [1989] 2 W.L.R. 224. Important prerogative powers do, however, still appear to be effectively exempt from judicial review. For example, in *R.* v. *Secretary of State for Foreign and Commonwealth Affairs, ex p. Rees-Mogg* [1994] 1 All E.R. 457 judicial review of the decision to ratify the Maastricht Treaty was sought but as the application related to a matter of foreign policy the court was not prepared to intervene. In *R.* v. *Ministry of Defence, ex p. Smith* [1996] 1 All E.R. 257 the Court of Appeal was not prepared to intervene in a decision by the Ministry of Defence to ban homosexuals from the Armed Forces. The case is extracted at para. 6–31.

For further examples see Finch and Ashton, pp. 245–249 and for an interesting general survey and comparison with the position in French law see D. Pollard, "Judicial Review of Prerogative Power in the United Kingdom and France" in *Administrative Law Facing the Future: Old Constraints and New Horizons* (P. Leyland and T. Woods eds, 1997), p. 297. For views suggesting that the scope of review in Scots law is potentially wider than that stated in Lord Roskill's speech see the contributed article "Prerogatives and Privileges in Scots Law", 1985 S.L.T. (News) 101.

10–11   (5) The provisions of the Scotland Act 1998 also have to be borne in mind. Consider the terms of section 53, extracted at para. 13–8. On one view, it might be possible to argue that prerogative powers under that section are exercised on the basis of a delegation from a statutory scheme so bringing those powers within the ambit of *West*. If that is the case, it is submitted that it is still unlikely to effect the *scope* of review and it is likely that questions of justiciability will still be important. The most significant prerogative powers, such as those relating to foreign policy or defence, are not within the devolved competence: Schedule 5, Part I, paragraphs 7 and 9, respectively. In relation to prerogative powers falling within devolved competence, it would be surprising if such powers which are accepted as reviewable in English law are treated as beyond review in Scots law. Arguably, until now, it was perhaps unnecessary for Scots law to have a coherent theory of the review of the prerogative power. Significant governmental decisions were made at Westminister and were generally reviewed in the English courts. With the coming of a Scottish Parliament and Executive, the Court of Session will have to develop a coherent theory of review of the prerogative power.

(6) Given its apparent rejection of the presence of an element of public law as being the cornerstone for a competent petition for judicial review, the decision in *West* would also seem to open the way to the review of decisions on which bodies which might be regarded as private. Although there is some academic comment to the effect that judicial review of a limited company is not appropriate, see A. Mennie, "Jurisdiction and Competency in Proceedings for Judicial Review", 1990 S.L.T. (News) 1 at 2. The decision in *St Johnstone Football Club* v. *The Scottish Football Association Ltd*, 1965 S.L.T. 171, referred to in *West*, involved such a company and no

doubt as to the competency of such an action was expressed. Moreover, unlike the decision in *Ferguson* v. *Scottish Football Association*, 1996 G.W.D. 11–601, noted at para. 3–3, which could be seen as a successful petition based on simple *ultra vires* alone, the decision in *St Johnstone Football Club* involved the court accepting arguments based on breach of principles of natural justice. Thus, it would seem competent to invoke grounds of challenge other than simple jurisdictional challenge even in the context of private organisations. It may be, however, that in the context of decisions made by private or domestic organisations or tribunals, that even if a tripartite relationship can be found, then the court will impose additional hurdles before it will intervene. Thus in *McDonald* v. *Burns*, discussed in *West*, it would appear that the court would only intervene in the circumstances envisaged by the Lord Justice-Clerk (Aitchison). The case is extracted at para. 8–2. More recently in *Gunstone* v. *Scottish Women's Amateur Athletic Association*, 1987 S.L.T. 611 Lord Prosser affirmed that in the context of a voluntary association, the court will only intervene where there had been a clear and demonstrable excess of power which had infringed the rights of its members or where there had been a gross procedural irregularity: see also *McDonald* v. *Council of St Andrews Ambulance Association*, Outer House, December 18, 1998, unreported. Similarly, it is not clear if the decision of a club which is owned by its members involves a jurisdiction for the purposes of the test in *West*: *Graham* v. *Ladeside of Kilbirnie Bowling Club*, 1990 S.C. 365. See also in the context of intervention in the affairs of a political party, *Brown* v. *Edinburgh District Labour* Party and *Lally, Petitioner* above. For a discussion of the rather different position in England see *R.* v. *Disciplinary Committee of the Jockey Club, ex parte The Aga Khan* [1993] 1 W.L.R. 909, C.A. and generally Finch and Ashton, pp. 237–238 and for the desirability or otherwise of judicial review being available in the context of domestic tribunals and private organisations see J. Alder, "Obsolescence and Renewal: Judicial Review in the Private Sector" in Leyland and Woods (eds) above; D. Pannick, "Who is Subject to Judicial Review and in Respect of What?" [1992] P.L. 1; and G. Borrie, "The Regulation of Public and Private Power" [1989] P.L. 552. For the possible impact of the Human Rights Act 1998, see para.6–18.

It was not long before the court had to consider the exact scope of the tripartite relationship.

Naik v. University of Stirling

1994 S.L.T. 449

"Samantha Devini Naik presented a petition for judicial review of a decision of the University of Stirling to exclude her from a course on which she was a student and requiring her to remove all her belongings from university buildings. **10–12**

The case came before the Lord Ordinary (MacLean) for a first hearing on the respondent's plea to the competency of the petition.

On 22 June 1993 the Lord Ordinary reserved the plea to the competency and allowed second hearing."

LORD MACLEAN: "The respondent is a body corporate established by royal charter on 14 December 1967, the terms of which are to be found on p 52 of the respondent's calendar for 1992–1993. Amongst the objects and powers declared by Her Majesty in the charter are the prescribing of rules for the discipline of the students of the university and the demanding and receiving of fees. On 31 July 1992 the secretary to the board of the respondent's school of management wrote to the petitioner informing her that the selectors, following her interview, offered her a place as a full time student on the course leading to the DTI Executive Diploma in Japanese on certain terms and conditions. One of the obligations she had to meet was the payment of the balance of the fees, namely the sum of £3,000, at registration on 7 October 1992. The secretary's letter is no 12/6 of process. On 13 August 1992 the petitioner accepted the offer of such a place on the terms and conditions stated. Her acceptance is no 12/7 of process. The petitioner duly registered as a student and so became a member of the respondent, but she failed to pay the balance of the fees. When she became a student the petitioner at the same time bound herself in terms of fees regulations, set out in the calendar at p 231, to pay the requisite fees on registration or in any case no later than three days after the beginning of the session.

By January 1993 the petitioner still had not paid the balance of her fees. In that month she avers that she had a meeting with Professor Gow who was director of the diploma course she was undertaking. He was also a director of the Scottish Centre for Japanese Studies and a vice principal of the university. She avers that she explained to him she was having difficulty in securing the necessary finance to meet the balance of her fees. After that meeting she sent to him a letter dated 29 January 1993 which is no 12/1 of process. The competing accounts of what took place between herself and Professor Gow, who throughout is said to have represented the respondent, are substantially set out in arts 6.2, 6.3, 6.4 and 6.5 together with the corresponding answers. I think it right to say that on any view some of what took place seems extraordinary. I have in mind particularly but not exclusively the respondent's averments about Professor Gow's view reached on the basis of what other students had said about a conversation overheard between the petitioner and her then boyfriend. The fact that there is a substantial dispute of fact between the parties was acknowledged by counsel who, if I did not uphold the respondent's first plea to the competency of this application for judicial review, were agreed that a second hearing would be required. The decision complained against is one which the petitioner avers was made on or about 18 February 1993 and that was to terminate her participation in the executive diploma course in Japanese studies. The respondent maintains that the decision was taken on 17 February 1993.

What is however reasonably clear is that Professor Gow wrote to the petitioner by letter dated 17 February 1993 (no 12/2 of process) in the following terms:

'Dear Ms Naik,

"I am writing to you formally in connection with the non-payment of your fees. You were awarded a bursary for part of your fees and, in January, I was informed by the Finance Office that you had not paid the outstanding amount. I discussed the matter with you and, given the circumstances you explained to me relating to your dispute with the bank, I agreed to discuss the matter further with the Finance Officer. It was a clearly stated condition of my discussion that you provide me with a letter stating that you would undertake, by monthly instalments, to pay the outstanding fees prior to departure for Japan. The first letter you provided clearly was not satisfactory and I instructed you to provide a revised letter of intent containing the conditions I outlined. This letter was not forthcoming and I have reluctantly to conclude that you do not intend to pay the outstanding amount. You have already had almost five months' tuition, received a bursary and I have given you every opportunity to resolve your financial problem. I therefore am not prepared to recommend the previous arrangement to the Finance Officer and I have decided to remove you from the course, effective immediate [sic]. I have passed my recommendation to the Finance Office and I am informing you in writing that you will not be allowed to take further classes unless there is an immediate payment of the full amount of outstanding fee. I am also instructing you to clear your things from the building and to leave as soon as possible."

He also wrote to her a second letter dated 18 February 1993 (no 12/3 of process) in the following terms:

'Dear Ms Naik,

"I have given the matter which we discussed yesterday regarding your continuation on the DTI course further and very careful consideration. I have sought advice and I have noted your behaviour during and after yesterday's meeting. I decided that my original decision that you leave the course due to non-payment of fees stands. You are therefore not permitted to attend any further classes and should remove your belongings from the DTI building as soon as possible."

There is a dispute as to when the petitioner received this letter. What is to be noted, however, from the second letter is that the petitioner's behaviour seems somehow to have become a component in the decision. I should add that the petitioner tendered a cheque for the outstanding balance at the finance office on 18 February 1993 but those in the office would not accept it from her. She avers in art 6.7 that the tendering of that cheque was sufficient compliance with the requirement in the letter of 17 February 1993.

The petitioner avers in art 6.8 that the respondent's decision to exclude her from the course and the university was based not merely upon non-payment of fees but upon matters relating to her conduct. Since her conduct was in issue the respondent was obliged to follow the provisions of its code of student discipline. It is admitted by the respondent that it did not follow its procedures relating to offences contained in the code of student offences set out in ordinance 2 which is to be found at p 93 and following of the university calendar. The petitioner, broadly, makes three submissions: (1) the decision of the respondent demonstrates procedural impropriety because it failed to follow its disciplinary procedures; (2) the decision of the respondent demonstrates a breach of natural justice in that it (a) failed to disclose the allegations made against her, (b) failed to allow her to answer them, especially where she had legitimate expectations in the light of the letter of 17 February 1993 that she would be allowed to pay the outstanding fees and take no further action in respect of her failure to do so earlier, and (c) left the decision to Professor Gow himself who might reasonably appear to have an interest in the decision; (3) the decision of the respondent was arrived at in a manner which no reasonable university authority would have employed.

There having been a caveat lodged, the petition came before Lord Cullen on 28 April 1993. The same counsel appeared then as appeared before me. I was informed that counsel for the respondent made a similar submission with regard to the competency of the petition before Lord Cullen as he made before me. Nevertheless, Lord Cullen granted an order for service and assigned 11 June 1993 as the date for the first hearing. Under the principles elaborated in *West v Secretary of State for Scotland* counsel for the respondent set out three propositions which he submitted were applicable in this case:

(1) The respondent was in the same position as the prison service in *West*. Its decision was not made in the exercise of a jurisdiction, power or authority which had been delegated or entrusted to it by any statute, agreement or other instrument.

(2) The decision was not made by a body or person which was identifiably separate from the respondent.

(3) In terminating membership of the university the respondent acted in the context of a bipartite relationship in which it exercised its own rules which governed one aspect of its legal relationship with one class of its members — that class being students.

Counsel for the respondent placed especial emphasis on what the court said in *West* (at p 651B-C), namely: 'Contractual rights and obligations, such as those between employer and employee, are not as such amenable to judicial review. The cases in which the exercise of the supervisory jurisdiction is appropriate involve a tripartite relationship, between the person or body to whom the jurisdiction, power or authority has been delegated or entrusted, the person or body by whom it has been delegated or entrusted and the person or persons in respect of or for whose benefit that jurisdiction, power or authority is to be exercised.' No such tripartite relationship existed, he maintained, in this case.

I confess that I have very considerable difficulty in understanding that in every case in which application is made to the supervisory jurisdiction of the Court of Session there must exist such a tripartite relationship. That seems to me to impose an inflexible and over formal restraint upon the court's jurisdiction. In this case, however, I consider that such a relationship, in relation to the matters in issue between the parties, can be discerned. The petitioner avers that this was not a mere case of non-payment of fees, as counsel for the respondent maintained, but was also a case involving her conduct and also to some extent the conduct of the respondent which she avers created a legitimate expectation in her. In my opinion this may not be a simple case of non-payment of fees by a student. It raises wider issues. It involves, in my view, the relationship of the Queen as the granter of the powers to the respondent and the fulfillment of these powers by the respondent to one of its members, namely a student. The respondent was empowered by Her Majesty to prescribe rules for the discipline of its students. It duly prescribed these rules but then, according to the petitioner, failed to observe them in relation to her when excluding her from her course in tertiary education. That failure in the circumstances set forth in the petition and answers falls comprehensively in my view within the principles of *West*. I would, however, wish to reserve my opinion on the question whether the decision to exclude a student from the university for non-payment of fees, without more, would be subject to the supervisory jurisdiction of this court. I will therefore reject counsel for the respondent's submission that this petition should be dismissed, but I will, consistently with what I have just said, reserve the respondent's preliminary plea directed to the competency of this application."

Notes

(1) For discussion of the case see C.M.G. Himsworth, 1995 S.L.T. (News) 127 at 129   **10–13** Himsworth suggests that in Lord MacLean's judgment there is

> "some scepticism about the comprehensive (and thereby inflexible) claims made for *West* tripartism as the determinant of the scope of review but a conviction that, in this instance, the use of the University's disciplinary powers fell within the *West* principles — although it is not made absolutely clear which 'principles' are being invoked."

Contrast with the approach taken by Lord MacLean in *Naik* with that of Lord Prosser in *Joobeen* v. *University of Stirling*, 1995 S.L.T. (Note) 120. On facts similar to *Naik* Lord Prosser stated (at 122F) that it would be "highly ironic, and paradoxical, if in Scotland we began to define competency in terms of pigeon holes." The petitioner urged upon his Lordship the view that the contractual origin of the dispute did not preclude judicial review. His Lordship seemed to accept that a contract did sometimes create a new legal relationship, different from that of mere contracting parties and such a case would exist where powers were granted by Parliament or perhaps in the case of the university, by royal charter. This suggests that a universal test is not appropriate. Much depends on the context of the case in question. In particular he said that.

"it seems to me that the real issues were not of a kind suitable for judicial review, but were matters of simple right and obligation, requiring the courts ordinary, and not supervisory jurisdiction".

In *McDonald* v. *Council of St Andrews Ambulance Association* below it was accepted that the constitution of the Association by Royal Charter was sufficient to found judicial review proceedings.

(2) In *McIntosh* v. *Aberdeenshire Council*, 1998 S.C.L.R. 435 Lord MacLean, in a petition for judicial review seeking reduction of a section 50 agreement under the Town and Country Planning (Scotland) Act 1972, observed that *Naik* was authority for the proposition that a tripartite relationship was not always necessary in every case of judicial review. However, once a planning agreement had been entered into, it was unlikely that a tripartite relationship would exist and that if the allegations of *ultra vires* were to be upheld, then that could only be done in the context of an ordinary action for reduction of the by then bilateral agreement: see too *Importa Ltd* v. *Tayside Regional Council*, 1994 G.W.D. 26–1542.

(3) The approach in *Naik* is consistent with the view that even if a body is in principle susceptible to judicial review, that does not entail that all functions of the authority are so. In *R.* v. *National Coal Board, exparte National Union of Mine workers* [1986] I.C.R. 791 decisions of the NCB were held amenable to judicial review in principle, in general terms, but management issues were not: see also *Smith* v. *Lord Advocate*, 1995 S.L.T. (Note) 379. (Not all aspects of fatal accident inquiry procedure are amenable to judicial review.)

(4) Do you agree with Lord McLean's interpretation of *West*? Is there anything in *West* which suggests that tripartite relationship is anything other than the exclusive basis for judicial review?

The most trenchant analysis of *West* to date has come in the troubled area of competency of the judicial review in the area of employment disputes involving those in the public sector. Contrast the next case with *Tehrani*.

Blair v. Lochaber District Council

1995 S.L.T. 407

10–14   "The petitioner was chief executive of the respondents. On 13th September 1994 a full meeting of the respondents passed a motion to suspend the petitioner from his duties. The petitioner brought a petition for judicial review of this decision in which he sought reduction, suspension and interdict. He averred that the decision had been ultra vires of the respondents as being in breach of certain provisions of the Local Government (Scotland) Act 1973 and of the respondents' own standing orders. The respondents pleaded inter alia that the petition was incompetent. Before the Lord Ordinary the respondents argued that judicial review was incompetent because there were contractual rights between the parties which could be enforced under employment legislation, and because the tripartite relationship which was necessary for judicial review to be invoked was lacking. The petitioner argued that a tripartite relationship was not essential for the exercise of judicial review and that it was appropriate here because what had occurred was an excess of power in the discharge of an administrative function. If a tripartite relationship was essential, then it existed here, with Parliament being the third party. In any event the existence of a contractual relationship between the parties did not preclude judicial review."

LORD CLYDE: "This is a petition for judicial review. It is raised by the Chief Executive of Lochaber District Council. He is an employee of that council. On 13th September 1994 the council passed a motion to suspend the petitioner from his duties on full pay and to ask the Director of Finance to assume responsibility as temporary Head of Administration. The suspension was to be during an investigation into allegations made in reports from certain internal auditors. The petitioner seeks orders of reduction, suspension and interdict on the ground that the decision was ultra vires of the council as being in breach of certain provisions of the Local Government (Scotland) Act 1973 and of the council's standing orders. The Dean of Faculty for the respondents made some observations about the remedies sought, questioning in particular the propriety of any order for suspension. Mr Reid, for the petitioner, said that he was not seeking interdict; eventually a reduction would be sought, but if the case could not be determined at the first hearing he wished an interim suspension.

The petition has come before me for a first hearing. Both the petitioner and the district council were represented by counsel, but no answers had been lodged by the respondents. It was pointed out that the first order did not call for answers to be lodged. Rule of Court 58.8, however, does allow the lodging of answers by a person intending to appear and, in my view, the present is a case where it would have been useful for formal notice to have been given in that way of the respondents' position. The Dean of Faculty at the start of the hearing explained that he proposed to challenge the competency of the application and, alternatively, if the application was competent, to argue that the council's actings had been intra vires. In the latter connection he proposed to make some reference to the factual background to the decision of 13th September. It seemed to me that at least the latter part of his proposal should be outlined in written answers so as to identify any factual issues which might exist between the parties, or to enable some agreement on the facts. The parties then proposed that the issue of competency should be debated first so that I could give a decision on that issue. I acceded to that course, recognising that it might only be a partial determination of the whole dispute. During the course of the hearing the respondents lodged answers together with a number of documentary productions so that some notice of the substance of the response is now available. The discussion which I have heard, however, was limited to the matter of competency. It was desired that in the interests of speed that matter should be isolated first and it is clearly desirable not to delay any decision upon it.

This is another case where an employee is seeking judicial review of a decision taken by his employer. In this case the employer is a local authority and the employee is their chief executive. This is an area of law which has given rise to some difficulty in the past. The cases of *Tehrani* v *Argyll & Clyde Health Board* and *Watt* v *Strathclyde Regional Council* are two particular examples. It was with the express purpose of removing uncertainty that the matter was explored in detail in the case of *West* v *Scottish Prison Service*. In the discussion before me attention was directed, in particular, to the propositions and points set out towards the close of the court's opinion in that case. The Dean of Faculty founded especially on point (*d*) at [p. 526E;] p. 651C:

'Contractual rights and obligations, such as those between employer and employee, are not as such amenable to judicial review. The cases in which the exercise of the supervisory jurisdiction is appropriate involve a tripartite relationship, between the person or body to whom the jurisdiction, power or authority has been delegated or entrusted, the person or body by whom it has been delegated or entrusted and the person or persons in respect of or for whose benefit that jurisdiction, power or authority is to be exercised.'

The first sentence of this passage was recognised by both parties as affirming that judicial review is not available where the issue is one of contractual rights and obligations as such. The matter in such cases can be met by the remedies ordinarily available. However, some divergence of view arose about the scope and meaning of the second and longer sentence in this paragraph. Mr Reid for the petitioner proposed two alternative approaches. He submitted that one or other of them had to be adopted in order to reconcile the decision in *West* with that in *Watt*.

The first of his two submissions was that the sentence was intended to be quite general in its application, with Parliament constituting the third party to the tripartite relationship. On this approach, Mr Reid submitted that there could be a statutory restraint imposed by Parliament on the exercise by a public authority employer of its discretion on the matter in issue in relation to an employee, especially one of high rank. The analysis thus fitted the present case, with Parliament, the council and the petitioner being the three parties and the council being subject to the statutory restraints set out in Schedule 7 to the Act of 1973. But this wide application of the tripartite approach was rejected by the Dean of Faculty. The wide analysis suggested by Mr Reid may well be thought to lack utility and could be taken as meaning little more than that all actings performed under statutory powers provided by Parliament may be open to judicial review. The Dean of Faculty described it as unnecessary and as going too far. It seems to me that this first construction is not without difficulty.

The second of Mr Reid's two constructions was that the concept was intended to deal at least primarily with the situation where there is a private employer who has conferred a jurisdiction on an independent quasi judicial body so as to extend the scope of the supervisory jurisdiction to the private sector as well as the public sector. The Dean of Faculty challenged that approach as illogical in that there was no reason for confining the concept to the private sector, given that the court has already discarded the utility of a distinction between actings in the public and in the private sectors. It seems to me unlikely that the sentence under discussion was intended only to refer to the private sector. It is not expressed to be so limited and indeed only a few lines later in the opinion the express reference to the absence of any third party in the context of the case before the court, which was a case reasonably to be regarded as in the public sector, seems to me to point against such a narrow construction.

The construction which commended itself to me is that for which the Dean of Faculty contended, the third of the alternatives put before me. As he pointed out, the sentence follows immediately on reference to contractual rights and obligations such as those between employer and employee. On the general layout of the articulated points presented in this passage of the opinion it is reasonable to conclude that the critical sentence is to be read in the context of contracts, including contracts of employment. There is no room for judicial review where there are contractual rights or obligations which can be enforced, at least as a matter of general principle. The tripartite relationship explains the availability of judicial review to an employee in cases where the decision-making process has been entrusted to a body other than the employer. As the Dean of Faculty submitted, there should be no difference in the applicability of judicial review in the context of contractual relationships whether they occur in the public or in the private sector. The point made in *West* is of application to both sectors but it relates to cases where there is a contractual relationship between the two principal parties. The Dean's submission was that the tripartite test is intended to cover conclusively all cases where the dispute is between employee and employer.

It appears, as Mr Reid pointed out, in tracing the use of the word tripartite through the court's opinion in *West*, that the word is used on [p. 514A;] p. 643 in a context which may be wider than that of contractual relationships but that does not, in my view, detract from the construction put forward by the Dean under reference to the context in which the word is used in the critical paragraph (*d*). It might seem curious that a defective decision taken by a body to whom the employer has entrusted the matter might be open to judicial review when the same defective decision taken by the employer would not be. The court in *West* explained that there is no illogicality, once the necessity for the tripartite relationship is recognised. It may be that a further reason could be that as between employer and employee there should be remedies available under the ordinary law but that in relation to the third body there may be no contractual basis for remedy and the supervisory jurisdiction should normally only be involved in the absence of any other available remedy.

However that may be, I must follow the guidance given in *West*. If, as the Dean submits, the tripartite test is conclusive in the context of employment contracts, then the petitioner fails here on competency. Mr Reid was not concerned to rest on one or other of his constructions of the critical passage but sought to present an altogether distinct basis for his case. There is no third party in the present case to whom the council entrusted the making of the decision; they made it themselves. On that approach, the petition is then incompetent.

However, Mr Reid for the petitioner submitted that the existence of the tripartite relationship was not an essential feature. In light of the approval of *Watt* in *West* he did not suggest that any tripartite relationship existed in the present case. As regards his alternative interpretations of the critical paragraph, he was able to say that on the first the test was satisfied in the present case and as regards the second, the test was irrelevant to the present case. However, his principal position was that in the present case there was an excess of power in the discharge of an administrative function. His main proposition was that where a public authority makes an administrative decision by means which are beyond their powers which prejudice an employee then that decision may be reviewed by the court in the exercise of the supervisory jurisdiction by way of judicial review. He accepted that if the case was one of a pure or straightforward relationship of employer and employee, judicial review would not be available. He also pointed out that the existence of a contractual relationship may not prevent recourse to judicial review and that is vouched by the case of *Watt*. He has admitted that the facts and circumstances of the present case took it beyond that of a pure or straightforward matter of contract and brought it within the scope of judicial review.

I pause at this stage to observe that it may be unsatisfactory to determine the applicability of the supervisory jurisdiction entirely on the circumstances of each case. In some cases such a course may be appropriate, especially where there is room to depart from a general rule. *Watt* could be seen as such a case. But while there may be exceptions to principles, it would seem more helpful that the matter should be determined by some guiding rule. However, I return to consider this alternative approach.

The approach can take the form of considering whether the decision in question is to be classified as an administrative decision or not. This is on the basis that judicial review is available for the challenge of administrative or judicial decisions. No one suggests that the present case is one of a judicial decision.

The Dean of Faculty invited me to define the characteristics of an administrative decision. He suggested that one had to examine the nature of the decision, its subject-matter and the capacity in which it was made. He submitted that a body was acting administratively if it was implementing a statutory obligation, or refusing it as in *Watt*, or performing a statutory function but the precise definition may remain somewhat elusive in the context of a body whose whole functions may be said at least to spring from statutory provisions. Mr Reid submitted that the capacity of the body cannot be the touchstone since in *Watt* the regional council was acting in the capacity of employer.

Mr Reid referred to other factors which he suggested pointed to the present decision being of an administrative character. One factor which was illustrated by the case of *Watt* was the imposition by statute of particular provisions in the contract of employment but that is not a factor looked to in the present case and I think Mr Reid simply referred to it as being one relevant possible consideration. Another factor which counsel put forward as relevant to the present case is the existence of a statutory restraint on the exercise of a local authority's powers, in the present case the procedural regulations contained in Schedule 7. The relevance of considerations of statutory restraint, at least in *West*, appears to be with regard to the exercise of a discretion. The present case, however, is not directed to attack the exercise of a discretion. What is challenged is the legality of the procedure which was followed. Indeed, the next of the factors detailed by Mr Reid was that the challenge was directed at an excess of power. As he pointed out under reference to *Guthrie* v *Miller*, excess of power has long been recognised as a ground for the intervention of the court under what is now known as the supervisory jurisdiction. But consideration of ultra vires actings, at least in the more narrow understanding of that expression, is not reserved to the supervisory jurisdiction. I do not see it as having any more particular significance in this context than any of the other identified grounds for judicial review.

One factor which Mr Reid highlighted was that the petitioner was a chief executive and could be seen as holding something like a public office. Under his contract of employment he is specifically made the 'proper officer' for a variety of statutory responsibilities, such as receiving legal proceedings (section 190 of the 1973 Act), executing deeds (section 194(1)), authenticating byelaws (section 202(3)) and signing the summons specifying the business to be transacted at meetings of the council (Schedule 7, paragraph 21(*b*)). He had himself certain disciplinary powers over junior employees. The case was thus different from any ordinary case of employer and employee. Mr Reid referred to *Malloch* v *Aberdeen Corporation* and found some support at pp. 104 and 119 for the proposition that at that stage in the development of this area of the law the status of senior officials may have been considered significant. But I am not persuaded that the status of the petitioner, so long as he is an employee, is of particular relevance to the issue before me. The petitioner is not the holder of a public office in the sense of having an appointment outwith the ordinary nature of an employment contract. As the Dean of Faculty pointed out, there is no statutory protection given to him and, as section 235(3) of the 1973 Act shows, it is for the local authority to decide who should be the proper officer for the various purposes detailed in that Act. It need not be the chief executive. The petitioner is subject to a personal contract between him and his employer and has the ordinary remedies under contract law. I am unable to distinguish the case on this ground.

Mr Reid also pointed to the fact that the decision was taken by the local authority meeting formally in full council, but the Dean of Faculty submitted that neither the place of the meeting nor the fact that it was taken by the full council, was relevant. A decision could be no less of an administrative character if it was taken by a committee of the council or by an official of the council under delegated powers. Conversely I find it hard to accept that all decisions of the full council are necessarily administrative decisions and I do not find this consideration persuasive in the present case.

I am reluctant to attempt any comprehensive definition of administrative decisions in the context of judicial review, but I consider that some distinction can be drawn in relation to the present case. The petitioner is aggrieved at the suspension of his employment. It is agreed that the council had power to suspend him. It is not expressed in writing but it was not disputed that it could be seen as a term implied in the petitioner's contract of employment. The power which the council were exercising in suspending him was a power which they had under the contract. It derived not from any statutory grant, but from the contract into which the parties had entered. On this approach the matter falls to be seen as one relating directly to the contractual relationship between the parties and the rights and the obligations which they had thereunder. What the petitioner is seeking to do is to enforce his right to work under his contract. The suspension which he alleges was illegally determined has breached that right. The true nature of the present dispute is in my view to be described as contractual rather than administrative. On this approach I am not persuaded in this case that recourse to judicial review is competent.

The Dean of Faculty contended that the petitioner had an alternative remedy under the ordinary law. He argued that the present question arose simply between an employee and his employer. In such a case the employee had a remedy under the employment legislation. The petitioner should wait to see if he would be exonerated and reinstated or dismissed. In the former case he would have suffered no loss. In the latter case he could seek redress before an employment tribunal. Mr Reid did not accept that an ordinary remedy was appropriate but I am not persuaded that the petitioner may not have a remedy in an alternative process. The Dean of Faculty referred to, and produced, a summons which had been prepared and signeted but not served in a possible action against the council by the petitioner arising out of his suspension, echoing something of the grounds of complaint made in the present petition and alleging inter alia breach of contract. This was described by Mr Reid simply as a fall-back position. I cannot comment on a process which has not even yet commenced, but it may at least suggest that a claim for an ordinary remedy might conceivably be formulated. It seems to me that, properly regarded, this case is essentially concerned with the regulation of the contract between the petitioner and the respondents and even on Mr Reid's suggested approach it is not a matter for the exercise of the supervisory jurisdiction. Even if the tripartite principle is not to be one of absolute application so that cases may be found... which only concern one employee and his employer which yet may be open to judicial review, although there is no third party involved, I do not consider that the considerations individually or cumulatively put forward by Mr Reid should cause the present case to qualify as such an exception. To take a different approach, the circumstances here do not seem to me sufficient to justify resort to the supervisory jurisdiction where a contractual remedy remains. The priority to be given to a contractual remedy should be recognised equally in relation to contracts by public bodies as well as private ones and the ordinary judicial processes may be expeditious enough to provide rapid remedies.

In the whole circumstances, accordingly, it seems to me that the present application for judicial review is not competent and I shall dismiss the petition."

Notes

10–15   (1) Lord Clyde clearly accepts that notwithstanding the different approaches put to him to determine the competency of the petition he "must follow the guidance given in *West*". However, like Lord Prosser in *Jobeen*, he seems to express doubt as to whether or not the tripartite test is to be taken as the exclusive basis of the availability of judicial review. His sympathy for the test of "administrative character", advanced by both parties, makes that clear. Yet an approach based on the nature of the dispute or the remedies sought as founding the basis of review does not appear in *West*. Himsworth, 1995 S.L.T. (News) 127, notes (at 131) that:

> "There remains the need for tests involving references inter alia to the statutory framework within which certain offices are created or otherwise regulated and to the availability of other 'ordinary' procedures and remedies. The justification, in both *Joobeen* and *Blair*, for the denial of judicial review on the grounds of the 'essential' nature of the dispute or of the remedy sought — without explanation of what constitutes that 'essence' in either case — shows the continuing gaps in the analysis."

He goes on to say:

> "A body's employment decisions (and presumably also any other contractual decisions) are reviewable if, in some undefined sense, they are 'administrative'. If that is not the re-admission of a 'public law' test, it is not at all clear what is."

The decision in *Malloch v. Aberdeen Corporation* is discussed at para. 8–6.

(2) In *Stannifer Developments Ltd v. Glasgow Development Agency*, 1998 S.C.L.R. 870 it was held that, on the basis of *Blair*, it was unsatisfactory to depart from the general rules on the applicability of the supervisory jurisdiction unless there was good reason to do so. Can *Blair* be interpreted in that manner? Is there any guidance given as to what might constitute a good reason? For the facts of this case see para. 8–12.

Lord Macfadyen made a distinction between the statutory power to dispose of property conferred by section 8 (1)(g) of the Enterprise and New Towns (Scotland) Act 1990 and decisions about how to invite and process offers and how offerors were to be treated when the offers were under consideration. While the former might amount to the exercise of a reviewable power, the latter decisions "were not… administrative decisions made in the exercise of any jurisdiction in the *West* sense" (at 890D). Note the use of the concept of "administrative decision".

(3) It may be, however, that some of the more difficult issues thrown up by tripartism will continue to be tempered by flexible interpretation of what is required to create a tripartite relationship. In *Rooney v. Chief Constable, Strathclyde Police*, 1997 S.L.T. 1261 judicial review was sought by a former police constable who had submitted his resignation to the Chief Constable. He sought declarator that the Chief Constable had failed properly to follow procedure in accepting his resignation and in refusing to accept his subsequent withdrawal of it. The Chief Constable argued that the petition was incompetent as the matter was one of contract only. Having considered the terms of section 26 of the Police (Scotland) Act 1967 relative to disciplinary powers and the regulations issued thereunder as well as non-statutory guidelines, Lady Cosgrove observed (at 1264):

"It is clear that while there is no room for judicial review where there are contractual rights or obligations which can be enforced, at least as a matter of general principle, the existence of a tripartite relationship explains the availability of judicial review to an employee in cases where the decision making process has been entrusted to a body other than the employer."

She found that a jurisdiction existed because matters of police discipline had been entrusted to the Chief Constable as distinct from the police authority and he was "an individual with separate identity from that authority". Moreover the procedures manual upon which the petitioner founded came

"from a higher authority and while they are not enshrined in statute or statutory instrument, it is clear from the terms… that the chief constable is being entrusted with the responsibility for ensuring that they are 'applied in each and every case' ".

(4) Does the apparent general exclusion of most employment and indeed contractual issues from judicial review proceedings suggest that the real basis for judicial review and underlying justification of the tripartite test is the availability of another remedy such as an application to an industrial tribunal in employment situations or ordinary action for reduction of a contract as in *Macintosh*? Consider the foregoing in light of the materials in this chapter on the availability of an alternative remedy.

(5) Consider again the principles enunciated by the Dunpark Working Party. Do you consider whether *West* has advanced or limited the application of those principles?

THE LIMITS OF THE SUPERVISORY JURISDICTION: APPEAL VERSUS REVIEW

Notwithstanding the uncertainty governing the scope of judicial review, it is no part of the court's jurisdiction to question the merits of the decision of an inferior body. The basis of review is the test of legality.   **10–16**

Pryde v. The Heritors and Kirk Session of Ceres

(1843) 5 D. 552

The Court of Session was asked to review the amount of poor relief awarded to a weaver's widow with seven children to support. A majority of the court required the heritors and Kirk Session to reconsider the sum awarded. The parish authorities had a statutory duty to provide for the "needful sustentation" of the family. They were in breach of that duty because they had made a provision which was so inadequate as to be reviewable in the same manner as an an ward which was "illusory". The majority of the court refrained from specifying the sum which should be awarded, but the Lord President referred to evidence about weavers' earnings collected by a parliamentary committee and suggested that an increase from 3s. 6d. per week to 6s. might be appropriate. Lord Cockburn, however, dissented.   **10–17**

LORD COCKBURN: "The first question is, 'Whether, generally, it is competent to bring under the review of the Court, by advocation or otherwise, the determinations of the heritors and kirk-session of a parish with regard to allowances for the poor?'

As this is put generally, and without reference to any particular case, it only admits of a general answer. And I am of opinion that there are cases in which it is competent to bring these determinations under the review of this Court. That is, it cannot be stated universally, that all review by this Court is absolutely excluded. I presume, for example, that the Court can always interfere to correct error in law. And, under this principle, I include the cases in which the heritors and session refuse to act; or in which, under pretence of performing their duty, they plainly show that they mean to evade it. Reported examples of this are given in the papers. If the heritors and session will not meet; or if after meeting they will not act; or if they only proceed in a manner so plainly elusory that it manifestly amounts to no proceeding at all; or if they go wrong in law, &c. &c., I have no doubt that they are liable to be controlled by the Supreme Court.

But this advances us very little towards a solution of the real point which it is wished to get settled, and which is only brought out in the two next questions. These are — 2d, Whether, after an allowance for a poor person has been fixed, 'on due enquiry,' by the heritors or session, 'it is competent to bring under the review of this Court the question as to the adequacy of such allowance?' and, 3d, 'Whether it is competent for this Court to ordain the payment of any particular rate of allowance for the poor.' These may, or rather must, be answered together; because in their practical results, as well as in their legal principles, they are inseparably connected.

I am of opinion, as to them both that all appeal to this Court against the sufficiency of the allowance is incompetent.

But under this I do not include the case of an allowance that is so elusory, as that in law it amounts to a plain refusal by the local authorities to do their duty. The advocator professes to think that this admits away the whole case of the respondent; because, says she, if the Court can interfere when the allowance is elusory, why not when it is grossly inadequate, which is all that she contends for. If the word elusory can only be used in the same sense with the words grossly inadequate, then I think that the Court cannot enlarge an allowance that is even elusory. But elusory is a term, and a thing, perfectly familiar to the law; and in its correct meaning it denotes something that is not done, but only pretended to be done. If a pauper, in seeking redress from this Court, can rest his appeal on the statement, that the parochial authorities have not exercised their discretion at all, but have evaded its exercise, this I think would justify the Court's interference; because it would be one form of the case in which these authorities had refused to act. My opinion merely goes this length, that wherever the heritors and session do conscientiously exercise their discretion, there any control by this Court is incompetent.

In considering this, it is absolutely necessary to look the matter fairly in the face, and to see distinctly what it is that the Court is asked to do. The advocator says, that 'as to this Court imposing any rate of taxation to provide for the payment of the allowances to the poor, that would seem to be unnecessary, and perhaps not strictly within the competency of the Court. The heritors and kirk-session are by statute bound to impose an assessment for this purpose; and perhaps all that the Court should do, would be to remit to them to perform their duty in this respect.' And she elsewhere argues, that even as to the amount of the allowance, all that it is necessary for the Court to do is, that, without itself fixing any particular sum, it will be enough that the heritors and session are made aware that the Court thinks that what they have allowed is too little. This hint she seems to suppose will always be taken, and every thing go on harmoniously.

I can indulge in no such hopes. If the kirk-session and heritors can be brought into this Court, and told judicially that what they have done is wrong, they are entitled to ask what will be right. If not, and if they are only to be instructed in general that they must give more, they may retire and add a mere mite to the former heap. This we may control again, by ordering still a little more; till at last, bit by bit, they come up to what we shall think proper. Or, it does not seem to be disputed, that they are entitled to adhere to their own opinion, and thus to compel the Court itself to fix the allowance, and consequently the assessment. So that, ultimately, it must resolve into a determination by the Court what each individual pauper shall get, and what the amount of the parochial tax shall be. And if an appeal be competent at the instance of the pauper for having these raised, I do not see how it can be doubted that an appeal must be equally competent at the instance of a minority of the heritors, or even of a single heritor, for having it lowered. These results seem to me to be all necessarily involved in the principle, that the Court has any control whatever over the discretion of the parochial body, in so far as the amount of the allowance is concerned…

It is said that the jurisdiction of this Court is not excluded. It is certainly not excluded in words. But it appears to me to be plainly excluded by the principle of the system. It is all a matter of artificial regulation. The poor have no right to maintenance at common law. The whole thing is entirely statutory. Now, there is no jurisdiction over the amount of the allowance given to this Court. If the poor could be considered as creditors on a fund with which the land was burdened for the payment of this their debt, the ordinary powers vested in the Court over all such matters of right might subsist where there was no positive exclusion. But this is not the correct view of the situation of the poor. They are supplicants for alms, of which the heritors and session are the almoners. It is argued that they have a legal right to 'needful sustentation.' But this is a mistake. They have only a right to such sustentation as certain persons, called heritors or members of kirk-sessions, shall, in their conscientious discretion, think needful.

And there is surely no want of analogous examples, in which the Court compels other Parliamentary boards to act, without having any power to prescribe the exact manner in which they are to act. Road trustees, police commissioners, managers of docks or harbours, &c. &c., can be compelled to do their duty, and can be corrected if they err in law; but are nevertheless entrusted by the legislature with a discretion within a given range, as to the amount and the application of assessments, with which discretion, independently of all direct exclusion, this Court cannot interfere. In the same way the Court has compelled arbiters, and persons appointed to distribute funds, to act, by deciding, or by making a distribution, without its being supposed that this implied any authority to prescribe what the decision or the distribution should be.

Indeed, a constructive exclusion of the jurisdiction of the Court of Session, seems to be implied in the considerations which have excluded the jurisdiction of the inferior courts. If the poor have a legal right, not merely to such sustentation as the session and heritors may approve of, but to such as they (the poor) can convince a separate power to be needful, how do the Sheriffs come to be excluded? It is idle to say (though this be the ground on which it is often put) that their interference would be inconvenient, and would lead to much provincial litigation; because mere expediency is not a legal argument. If a pauper be so far a creditor, as that he can resort to a court of law to enforce a particular amount of allowance as due to him in this character, upon what legal ground is it that the sheriff is not entitled to judge of this debt? And if they be not creditors, but mere applicants for charity, where is the difficulty of supposing that the legislature might reasonably subject them to some local discretion? It has been said, that, *quoad hoc*, the heritors and session are trustees, and that it is only the Supreme Court that can control trusts. But, in the first place, they are not trustees, and do not stand in any such position. And, in the second place, have sheriffs no jurisdiction over any debt which requires to be constituted against a trust? The sheriffs have been debarred, solely because the consequences of permitting the parochial distributors to be controlled in their disposal of claims, stood out more conspicuously in the case of a number of controlling courts, than it does in the case of one.

...The system has been working above two centuries yet while all our institutional writers state generally that the amount of the allowance must be fixed by the heritors and session, none of them say a word about there being any appeal to the Supreme Court against their decision. There is unquestionably no judgment, as yet, in support of such appeal. Several cases have been cited by the parties, on which there were incidental indications of opinion by individual Judges; but these come to nothing precise or positive; and in so far as relates to the amount of the relief, they are as much against such an appeal as in favour of it. It is impossible to say that a decision against the competency, will be repugnant to any express judgment already delivered. But it seems to me to be scarcely possible that this could have been the fact, if any such application to the Supreme Court had been competent. The advocator says, that the allowances to the poor by heritors have been 'shamefully inadequate;' and, on the other hand, nothing is more notorious than that thousands of heritors have immemorially been complaining that these allowances have been intolerably high. Yet, while both parties have thus been complaining, this is the first occasion in which any protection has been directly attempted to be obtained from this Court.

I am not moved by the supposed justice of either of these opposite complaints. Let the evil of the parochial boards being too liberal, or of their being too shabby, be as great as it may. The only just inference from this is, that it is a case for the interference of Parliament. It appears to me that no evil can be greater than what is implied in the proposed remedy, of controlling the discretion of these boards, by an appeal to the discretion of a Supreme Court. The needfulness of the sustentation to be given to every pauper in the country, can never be properly adjusted by such a tribunal. It is not Judges' work. 1. A Supreme Court can never have such knowledge as is necessary to enable it to do this business well; knowledge of the local circumstances of the parish, and of the personal circumstances, character included, of the applicant and his connexions. 2. The very understanding that such a review is competent, has every chance of overwhelming any Supreme Court with litigation unbecoming it. 3. And this litigation must be conducted by pursuers, all of whom are, or may be, on the poor's roll, and who therefore, paying little costs when they (or their agent) lose, try your Lordships with the tolerable certainty of throwing the expenses on the parochial funds, or officers, when they succeed. 4. The correction, in this way, of the errors of the parochial boards, must speedily be accompanied by the mischief of destroying the local respect and authority, without which they can be of little use.

I cannot believe that a power of review, necessarily carrying such defects along with it, can be legal. I am aware that it is said that they are all to be avoided by simply sustaining the jurisdiction of the Court, but resolving never, or almost never, to exercise it. It is supposed that declaring the competency will keep heritors and sessions in check; while frowning at all appeals will check the unreasonableness of the poor. This, I dare say, will do for a little. Just long enough to let each party feel its position. After this, it will not depend on the Court, but on them, whether the resolution can be kept or not. And I really cannot avoid saying, that to announce that a certain description of appeals is competent — but to add, that they will be so discouraged as to amount to a denial of that very competency in practice — is scarcely a legal mode of escaping from the evils admitted to attend the announcement.

On the whole, I do not think the redress now sought is due in law, and I have a confident anticipation that it will be found impracticable."

Notes

Lord Cockburn's speech is now generally accepted as representing the correct approach that should have been taken in that case: see also *Moss's Empires Ltd v. Assessor for Glasgow*, 1917 S.C. (H.L.) 1 at 1 *per* Lord Shaw of Dunfermline. Another way of expressing this general principle is that the court exercising its supervisory jurisdiction does not exercise an appellate role: see generally *Stewart v. Monklands District Council*, 1987 S.L.T. 630; J.D.B. Mitchell, *Constitutional Law* (2nd ed., 1968), p. 293; *Associated Provincial Picture Houses Ltd v. Wednesbury Corporation* [1948] 1 K.B. 223 at 228, extracted at para. 6–25 and Deans, pp. 136–137.

This distinction between appellate and supervisory jurisdiction is, however, not always clear cut and sometimes rights of appeal are based upon the accepted grounds of review: see, for example, the Licensing (Scotland) Act 1976, s. 39 (4) and the Civic Government (Scotland) Act 1982, s. 4, Sched. 1, para. 18 (7). Similarly, grounds of challenge such as procedural irregularity may be relevant both in an appeal and when judicial review of a decision is sought. To the extent that such matters are subject to appeal, review is not necessary, or indeed competent. On this generally see *Stair Memorial Encyclopaedia*, Vol. 1, paras 243–245.

LIMITS OF THE SUPERVISORY JURISDICTION: WHO CAN SEEK JUDICIAL REVIEW

10–18   Many people may feel that they have been affected by an administrative decision. Consider, for example, the decision in *Harvey v. Strathclyde Regional Council*, 1989 S.L.T. 612, noted at para. 6–15. A decision was made by the local education authority to close a school. The practical effects of this decision would have had an impact on a wide range of persons including pupils at the school, parents, those who worked at the school, as well as a broader range of interests such as those who were opposed to school closures in general or those who were concerned about the way in which public money was being used. Mrs Harvey, as a parent of a pupil at the school, was able to seek judicial review in the Court of Session. She had title and interest to sue. What of the other interests mentioned? How does the court decide whether or not to allow persons falling into these other categories access to the supervisory jurisdiction?

Nicol (D. & J.) v. Trustees of the Harbour of Dundee

1915 S.C. (H.L.) 7

10–19   The harbour trustees were authorised to operate ferry services on the River Tay. They proposed to use the ferries for pleasure cruises at times when they were not in operation as ferries. D. & J. Nicol, local ship owners, sought suspension and interdict with regard to the pleasure cruises. The House of Lords held that such uses were *ultra vires* since the use of the ships for pleasure cruises could not be interpreted as being reasonably incidental to the authorised purpose of running a ferry service. For comment on *ultra vires* and what is and is not "reasonably incidental" see para. 3–5. The passage extracted is, however, concerned with the capacity in which D. & J. Nicol pursued the action.

LORD DUNEDIN: "... I turn now to the question of title. The respondents maintained their title on a two-fold ground. They said (1) that they were rival traders, and that the competition of the appellants was injurious to them, as the appellants were enabled to undercut them in prices, and (2) that they were shipowners and 'harbour rate-payers' in the sense of the term as used in sections 8 and 10 of the appellants' Act.

On this matter there was in the Courts below some difference of judicial opinion. The Lord Ordinary held that there was a good title under heading (1) but not under heading (2). In the Inner House Lords Salvesen and Guthrie held that the title was good, Lord Dewar that it was bad, under both heads.

In the argument before your Lordships' House the respondent's counsel abandoned his contention under head (1). I think he was right in doing so. I agree with the judgment of Lord Low on this point in the *Clyde Steam Packet* case (*Clyde Steam Packet Co. Ltd.* v. *Glasgow and South-Western Railway Co.*, 1897, 4 S.L.T. 327), which is in accordance with the principle given effect to in the *Stockport* case in England (*Stockport District Waterworks Co.* v. *Mayor of Manchester*, 1862, 9 Jur. (N.S.) 266; 7 L.T. (N.S.) 545). In the phraseology of Scottish law, when a complainer can only say that he is a rival trader and nothing more, he qualifies an interest but not a title.

By the law of Scotland a litigant, and in particular a pursuer, must always qualify title and interest. Though the phrase 'title to sue' has been a heading under which cases have been collected from at least the time of Morison's Dictionary and Brown's Synopsis I am not aware that anyone of authority has risked a definition of what constitutes title to sue. I am not disposed to do so, but I think it may fairly be said that for a person to have such title he must be a party (using the word in its widest sense) to some legal relation which gives him some right which the person against whom he raises the action either infringes or denies.

The simplest case of all is where a person is the owner of something. That legal relation of ownership gives him the right to sue all actions which deal with the vindication or defence of his property. Next in simplicity comes contract, where the relation of contract gives the one party a right to insist on the fulfilment of the contract by the other. Generally speaking, persons who are not parties to the contract cannot sue upon it, but this rule suffers exception when there has been created what is known as a *jus quæsitum tertio*. A well-known instance of this will be found in the right of feuars to enforce building stipulations contained in the titles of other feuars, the law as to which was authoritatively explained by Lord Watson in the well-known case of *Hislop* v. *MacRitchie's Trs.* (1881, 8 R. (H.L.) 95).

This class of case also affords excellent examples of how there may be title without interest (*Gould* v. *M'Corquodule*, 1869, 8 M. 165), and of the way in which interest will be judged (*Earl of Zetland* v. *Hislop*, 1882, 9 R. (H.L.) 40, and *Mactaggart* v. *Roemmele*, 1907 S.C. 1318).

It would be useless, even if it were possible, to go on to enumerate in detail the various cases in which a title to sue may be found, so I pass at once to the class of cases which are analogous to the present. If any persons are in such a relation as to constitute them trustees, or if, without being technically trustees, they have a fiduciary duty to others, those persons to whom they owe a fiduciary duty will have a title to sue to prevent the infringement of that duty. Infringement of duty may consist in wrong dealing with property. These propositions are equally true whether the trustees or quasitrustees are individuals or voluntary associations or corporations.

Instances of such title to sue having been given effect to are to be found in numberless cases.

Thus, for instance, in *Row* v. *Patrons of Cowan's Hospital* (1825, 4 S. 276, N.E. 280), a guild brother was allowed to sue the trustees for reduction of an improper sale of property, his title being rested on the fact that under the trust a charity was to be maintained for decayed guild brethren, and although he had an appointment as one of a committee appointed by all the guild brethren, his title as an individual was affirmed by both Lord Alloway and Lord Justice-Clerk Boyle.

In *Rodgers* v. *Incorporation of Tailors of Edinburgh* (1842, 5 D. 295) a widow was allowed to raise the question of the appropriation of funds which would prevent her having the chance of her annuity being increased — a judgment which was practically repeated in *Morrison* v. *Incorporation of Fleshers of Edinburgh* (1853, 16 I). 86).

In *Baird* v. *Magistrates of Dundee* (1865, 4 M. 69) two burgesses were allowed to call to account the magistrates in their capacity as administrators of a mortification fund established for, *inter alia*, the educating the sons of poor burgesses.

In *Bruce* v. *Aiton* (1885, 13 R. 358) a fisherman who used a harbour was allowed to sue the proprietor of the harbour who levied dues thereon under an Act of Parliament for declarator that the proprietor was bound to keep the harbour lighted.

These cases I have quoted are not at all an exhaustive list, but are to be regarded merely as samples of the various relations in which title to sue has been maintained.

The only difficulty, and in truth the whole argument of the appellants depended upon this, arises out of the decision of this House in Lord Cottenham's time of the case of *Ewing* v. *Glasgow Police Commissioners* (1839, MacL. & Rob. 847), and consists not so much in a misunder-standing of the case as in the attempt to make it support a principle which it will not bear. Some preliminary explanation is necessary.

From the time of their creation the royal burghs in Scotland had possessed lands and other property which were designated by the name of the Common Good. The royal burghs are corporations by royal charter — it is not material save for accuracy's sake to note that in some cases there were subsequent Acts of Parliament — and the provost and magistrates of these burghs held the common good for the benefit of the inhabitants. The magistrates, however, were left as judges of what was for the good of the inhabitants, and sometimes from necessity and sometimes from less cogent motives, as time went on, much of the common good of the burghs of Scotland was alienated. Indeed, if the state of affairs to-day is taken it will be found that in the case of most of the Royal burghs in Scotland, by far the greater part of the common good has been dissipated.

Now it was to be expected that such transactions would be objected to by burgesses who had no part in them, and a good many cases are to be found in the books of attempts to call the magistrates to account. The decisions were conflicting, of which a somewhat naive account may be found in the note in Brown's Synopsis as to the decision in *Lang and Burgesses of Selkirk* v. *The Magistrates* in 1748 (M. 2515, Brown's Synopsis, p. 2560): 'A very elaborate argument tending to shew that private burgesses have neither title nor interest to pursue their magistrates for misapplication of the burgh revenues is to be found in this case. The Court pronounced opposite judgments; but before a final decision the suit was compromised.' At last, however, when the time came that the old hearings *in præsentia*, with the power of presenting unlimited reclaiming petitions, were brought to an end, and the Court divided into two Divisions, consisting of an Outer and an Inner House, and the decisions of the Divisions made final, save as appealable to the House of Lords, the controversy was finally settled by the case of *Burgesses of Inverury* v. *Magistrates* (14th Dec. 1820, F.C.), which settled that an individual burgess has no title to call on the magistrates for a general accounting as to the common good.

Then in 1837 came the case of *Ewing* v. *Glasgow Commissioners of Police (cit.)*. Glasgow had by this time obtained a Police Act, which imposed certain duties on the Commissioners established under it, and gave powers of assessment. These Commissioners opposed a certain water bill promoted by certain water companies in Parliament, and paid the expenses of the opposition out of the funds in their hands. Ewing, a resident in Glasgow, and as such liable to assessment, raised with others a suspension against the Commissioners seeking in general terms to have them interdicted from thus applying money raised by assessment. At the same time they raised an action of reduction of the resolutions by which the Commissioners had authorised the payment of the money with petitory conclusions attached, ordering them personally to pay back the moneys into the funds of the police establishment.

It is worthy of notice that in the discussions which followed, the bill of suspension seems to have got overshadowed by the action of reduction and payment, and got lost sight of. The Court of Session treated the matter somewhat strictly upon the conclusions in the reduction action; and the ground of judgment, which sustained a plea of no title to sue, is thus put by Lord Medwyn (15 S. 389, at p. 397): 'They (the pursuers) do not seek repetition to themselves but into the fund . . . This is not a question of levying but of misapplying funds levied for another purpose; and the levy for next year is not objected to.' With deference to Lord Medwyn, though this might be said of the conclusions of the reduction, it could not, I think, be properly said of the crave of the bill of suspension.

The case then came to this House, and was disposed of by Lord Cottenham. The cases cited were entirely the common good cases and none else. The judgment was affirmed, stress being laid on the decision of *Magistrates of Inverury* above mentioned.

Now the underlying view of the common good cases was undoubtedly this, that looking to the origin of the common good, and the wide range of discretion given to the magistrates in its management and application, the Crown, as represented by the Exchequer, could alone institute what one might now call an audit, and that no private burgess could be allowed to do so. Seeing that no such origin could be attributed to founds raised by assessment under a Police Act, and seeing that the Exchequer had never had, or proposed to have, any visitorial position as to said funds, (in the Act itself powers of objection were given to specific bodies and persons, and the Court of Exchequer was indicated as the Court before which certain of these objections should be brought), it is not altogether to be wondered at that doubts had been expressed as to the expediency of the judgment thus pronounced. (See Lord Kyllachy in *Conn* v. *Magistrates of Renfrew*, 1906, 8 F. 905, and Lord Johnston in *Sirling County Council* v. *Falkirk Magistrates*, 1912 S.C. 1281).

But the decision is a decision of this House of old standing, and cannot as a decision be interfered with. There is, however, no reason to take it as deciding any more than it necessarily decided, *i.e.*, in view of the particular conclusions contained in that action.

The appellants, however, wish to extract from that judgment the general proposition that if it is a corporation which commits an act of *ultra vires* no one can complain except the Crown, unless the act complained of has a direct injurious effect on some patrimonial interest of the complaining party.

Nor were these cases left to stand alone. In *Sanderson* v. *Lees* (1859, 22 D. 24) an individual burgess vindicated the right of the golfers of Musselburgh, he being after all only a potential golfer himself; and lastly in *Grahame* v. *Magistrates of Kirkcaldy* (1882, 9 R. (H.L.) 91), an individual burgess vindicated the right of recreation and bleaching, and Lord Watson in this House upheld his title, while pointing out that, in the matter of a general accounting for the common good, the *Magistrates of Inverury* case was still law. Finally, in the case of *Leith Dock Commissioners* v. *Magistrates of Leith* (1897, 25 R. 126), the Leith Dock Commissioners, in their capacity as rate-payers, presented a suspension against the proposed charging against the Public Health Assessments in Leith of the expenses of unsuccessful Parliamentary opposition to a Bill promoted by Edinburgh. Interdict was granted by the Court of Session, and on appeal to this House the appeal was dismissed (I. F. (H.L.) 65). It is worth noticing that the suspension in this case is practically indistinguishable from the neglected suspension in *Ewing's* case. The report does not shew it, but I have looked up the pleadings, and I find that no title and no interest were both pleaded by the defenders, and Lord Watson delivered the leading judgment. It is not likely that he had forgotten what he said in *Grahame's* case as to *Magistrates of Inverury (cit)*.

The reason for this attitude, I think, is not far to seek. At the time of *Ewing's* case, the doctrine of *ultra vires* had not been developed as it came afterwards to be, and the point was looked at from the point of view of a title to call to a general accounting. But a somewhat prophetic view may be found, in the opinion of Lord Glenlee, in the case of *Aitchison* v. *Magistrates of Dunbar* (1836, 14 S. 421), decided three years before *Ewing*. The action was brought by burgesses and town councillors against the magistrates to test the legality of an alienation of the burgh property. Lord Glenlee said: 'I do not rest on the circumstance that they are members of the Town Council, but that they complain as burgesses of the illegality of an alienation of the town's property. As the illegality of the act is asserted here I am not disposed to carry too far the distinction between burgesses and town councillors. I am inclined to think that at common law burgesses have an interest and title to look after matters of this sort.'

This case was disposed of by Lord Cottenham in *Ewing's* case by remarking that there was a title in a minority of the Town Council to challenge an act of the Magistrates and Council, and that the Lord Justice-Clerk put his opinion on that ground. But while that is true it does not notice the distinction between a calling to account and an objection to a specific act, and while I consider we cannot go back on the judgment in *Magistrates of Inverury* I think it is clear from the latter cases that even if it was a matter of the common good there might be room for distinction between objection to one specific *ultra vires* act and the general complaint of maladministration. A trace of such a distinction may be found in the old case of *Burgesses of Irvine* (1752, Elchies, Burgh Royal, No. 31), mentioned in the argument in *Inverury*, but for the reason I have given it was not at that time sufficiently appreciated.

The decision in *Magistrates of Leith* was followed in the recent cases of *Stirling County Council* v. *Falkirk Magistrates*, and *Farquhar & Gill* v. *Aberdeen Magistrates* (1912 S.C. 1281 and 1294), in which cases the case of *Ewing* was disinterred and sought to be overpled as here… .

I now turn to the circumstances of this case. As I said at the outset, I do not think any general pronouncement can be made as to when there is title and when there is not. But when I find that the respondents in the capacity of harbour ratepayers are members of the constituency erected by the Act of Parliament to elect the trustees, and as such are also persons for whose benefit the harbour is kept up, I cannot doubt that they have a title to prevent an *ultra vires* act of the appellants, which *ultra vires* act directly affects the property under their care. It is not only that loss of that property through improper acting may have the effect of imposing heavier rates on the respondents in the future, but, in the words of Lord Johnston, in the *Stirling County Council* case, as they have contributed to the funds which bought the property, 'they have an interest in the administration of a… fund to which they have contributed,' and a title flowing from that position and interest.

For these reasons I concur with the motion proposed by the Lord Chancellor."

Notes

Lord Dunedin's judgment has to be taken as a starting point of any discussion of the law of standing. It is an expression of the general rule of Scots law that in all civil proceedings a litigant must have title and interest. Title and interest are legally distinct concepts. If either is lacking, in effect the court is holding that there exists, as a matter of law, no dispute between the petitioner and the respondent. The implications and the adequacy of this approach are apparent in the next extract.

10–20

Scottish Old People's Welfare Council, Petitioners

1987 S.L.T. 179

10–21   LORD CLYDE: "The petitioners in this application for judicial review are a voluntary association called the Scottish Old People's Welfare Council, commonly known as Age Concern Scotland, and three of its office bearers. They seek to challenge the legality of a circular S48/85 which was issued by the chief adjudication officer appointed by the Secretary of State for Social Services under s. 97 (1B) of the Social Security Act 1975 as amended by s. 25 and Sched. 8 of the Health and Social Services and Social Security Adjudications Act 1983. They claim that certain instructions in the circular are erroneous in law and ultra vires. The petition was served on the chief adjudication officer and on the Secretary of State for Social Services. Answers have been lodged by the chief adjudication officer and it was on his behalf that a reply to the challenge has been presented.

The answers raised two matters which appeared to be of a preliminary nature, namely, a plea that the petitioners had no title or interest to sue and secondly, a plea that 'there being statutory rights of appeal available to claimants whose rights are adversely affected by the said interpretation of the said Regulations complained of, this petition should be dismissed'. At the start of the hearing the question was discussed whether at least the issue of locus standi should be isolated and dealt with first. Counsel for the petitioners contended that in the circumstances of this case the matter of locus standi was closely bound up with the merits of the case and required to be considered along with the whole matters in dispute. He accordingly opened on the merits of the case and I heard argument on the whole questions raised by each party.

[LORD CLYDE considered the merits of the case. Part of his opinion on the legality of the circular is extracted at para. 2–42. He concluded that the circular was lawful and continued (at 1832):]

I turn now to the question of title and interest to sue which as I have already noted was, in the submission of counsel for the petitioners, a matter which was mixed in with the merits of the case. His argument in that regard was based, very substantially, on the so called 'Fleet Street Casuals' case, *I.R.C.* v. *National Federation of Self Employed and Small Businesses Ltd.* where it was held that the question of locus standi should be taken together with the legal and factual context of the application. The case in my view requires to be taken with some caution in so far as it is dealing with the particular provisions of the English R.S.C. Order 53 and the meaning of the phrase 'sufficient interest' in rule 3 (5) of that Order for giving locus standi in matters of judicial review. Certainly there may be cases in Scotland where the issue of locus standi can only be resolved after a consideration of the merits of the case. An example is the case of *Baird & Co.* v. *Feuars of Kilsyth* but I am not persuaded that the approach which appears from some of the speeches in the 'Fleet Street Casuals' case, that as a general rule a favourable or adverse decision on the merits should determine the existence or absence of a locus standi, is applicable in Scotland. That approach seems to me to be closely linked to the particular rules of the English procedure. In my view, the matter of locus standi is logically prior to and conceptually distinct from the merits of the case. It is properly of a preliminary character even although there may be cases where it cannot be resolved without inquiry into the merits. I must add in relation to this matter and to what follows that I am not here dealing with an application for any interim order. Different considerations may well arise where only a prima facie title and case need to be established.

Counsel for the petitioners, founding upon the 'Fleet Street Casuals' case, urged me to adopt a liberal approach to the matter of locus standi. The procedural changes in England have evidently introduced a more liberal approach than was possible before in matters of judicial review in that jurisdiction, but the new Rule of Court 260B has not, and perhaps did not need, to make so major a change in Scotland While the new rule provides for a simplicity and flexibility of procedure, it does not in my view introduce any changes in the substantive law, nor, in particular, in the law of locus standi. I do not understand that any different rules on locus standi prevailed in Scotland in relation to the various procedures earlier used to invoke the supervisory jurisdiction of the court. Under rule 260B those procedures have been superseded by a single procedure, namely, the petition for judicial review. Where there is a single procedure it is to my mind reasonable to expect a single rule or principle for locus standi. Where there has in any event been a uniformity on that matter, there is no difficulty in concluding that a uniform principle should be applied in applications under rule 260B.

In the case of *D. & J. Nicol* v. *Trustees of the Harbour of Dundee* Lord Dunedin observed (1914 2 S.L.T., p. 420): 'By the law of Scotland a litigant, and in particular a pursuer, must always qualify title and interest.' In many cases it is possible to make a clear distinction between these two ingredients, but as Lord Dunedin himself observed in the earlier case of *Lindsay* v. *Summerlee Iron Co. Ltd.* (1907) S.L.T. at p. 308, title and interest often very much run into each other. In the case of *Adamson* v. *Edinburgh Street Tramways Co.* the considerations of right and title seem to be closely linked with each other. In *Adams* v. *Secretary of State for*

Scotland the issue of title to sue was not evidently disputed but the only averment was that the pursuers were women resident in Edinburgh, without, as it appears, further distinction between title and interest. In *T. Docherty Ltd.* v. *Burgh of Monifieth* the court had no difficulty in affirming the title of a building company who were owners of land in the burgh and ratepayers and who were being required by the council to build sewers which they alleged it was the statutory duty of the burgh to build, and no separate consideration was given to the respective issues of title and interest. More recently, in the case of *Wilson* v. *Independent Broadcasting Authority* the concepts of title and interest were clearly distinguished from each other. In the present case, the elements of title and interest seem to be distinguishable and I shall accordingly deal with them separately.

Before doing so, I should observe that in the course of the argument before me, both sides referred to several cases relating to matters of public right where the form of action had been that of an actio popularis. These were *Torrie* v. *Duke of Athol; Jenkins* v. *Robertson; Potter* v. *Hamilton; Grahame* v. *Magistrates of Kirkcaldy; Blackie* v. *Magistrates of Edinburgh*. These cases illustrate the proposition that no special interest is required of the member of the public who seeks to prosecute such an action. Thus a member of the public having the right to use a public road has the title and interest to sue in respect of it. But, as counsel for the respondent submitted, the present case is not one of an actio popularis in the proper sense and especially since that category of action is somewhat special and limited I am not prepared to apply without discrimination the approach taken in those cases to the problem in the present case. Decree in a true actio popularis is res judicata for all members of the public. I am not persuaded that that consequence follows in the present case, but that point was not explored in argument. The scope of the actio popularis in Scotland has hitherto been somewhat restricted but I do not find it necessary in the present case to consider or explore any possible extension or developments of it within the field of judicial review.

The essential element in the concept of title to sue as opposed to interest was described by Lord Dunedin in the case of *D. & J. Nicol* to which I have referred already, where he said that, for a person to have a title to sue, 'he must be a party (using the word in its widest sense) to some legal relation which gives him some right which the person against whom he raises the action either infringes or denies'. From the case of *Wilson* v. *Independent Broadcasting Authority* it appears that, where there is a duty owed by a public body to the public, an individual member of the public has title to sue and if he also has an interest he will have the right to do so.

In the present case counsel for the respondent did not argue that the action was incompetent, nor that there was no one who could properly apply for judicial review of the circular if it was erroneous in law. He conceded that that question was a justiciable issue and the matter on which the parties before me differed was on the definition of the class of persons who had a title let alone an interest to raise the point. Counsel for the respondent at one stage took up the extreme position of restricting the class to those persons who were claimants for the benefit in question, who qualified for the benefit and whose claims were determined in accordance with the advice given in the circular in question, although it may be that in so defining the class he was taking questions of title and interest together. At another stage I understood him to increase the class to include all persons who were claimants for the benefit in question. Counsel for the petitioners contended that this was a case of a public duty and any member of the public had title to sue. Both parties founded on various provisions of the legislative scheme. Reference was made in particular to s. 1 (1) of the Act of 1976 which I have quoted earlier, to s. 2 which provides that questions relating to supplementary benefit shall be determined by an adjudication officer or a tribunal or a commissioner and to s. 3 (1) of the Act which again I have-quoted earlier. Particular reference was also made to s. 27 of the Act which provides that it shall be the duty of the Secretary of State to make arrangements to ensure that adjudication officers exercise their functions in such manner as shall best promote the welfare of persons affected by the exercise of those functions. Reference was also made to s. 97 of the Social Security Act 1975 relating to adjudication officers and bodies and, in particular, to subs. (IC) imposing the duty on the chief adjudication officer to advise adjudication officers on the performance of their functions under that or any other Act.

Once it is accepted that the issue of the legality of the circular is justiciable, and that at least claimants for the benefit in question have a title to sue, I find it hard to see why the definition of the title, whatever the position may be about interest, should be so limited. The point does not have to be established in the present case but, in light of s. 1 (1) of the Act of 1976 and in relation to the administration of legislation which seeks to provide benefit to all members of the public whenever particular conditions are satisfied, I am prepared to proceed on the basis that, while every member may not have a right to sue because they have no interest to do so, they would at least have a title to do so. The purpose of the legislation is to make state benefit available to any member of the public who may qualify for it and it is not unreasonable to see the duty of the proper administration of the legislation as a duty owed to the public. On that basis it can be concluded that any member of the public has at least a title to sue and the only question remaining would be whether he had an interest to do so.

The present action has been raised not by a private individual as a member of the public, but by a voluntary association and this has given rise to further ground for challenge both upon the title and the interest of an unincorporated body to sue in matters of judicial review and in relation in particular to their title and interest to sue the present action. The constitution of the association known as Age Concern Scotland was produced to me and I find from it that the membership comprises local old people's welfare committees and clubs, certain voluntary organisations, professional organisations, individual members, honorary life members, office bearers, and representatives of certain particular bodies. In substance the membership is of a very considerable number of individual members of the public. The only reported precedent on this matter which was put before me was the case of *Macfie* v. *Scottish Rights of Way and Recreation Society (Ltd.)*. That was an actio popularis raised by a proprietor against certain members of the public to have it declared that his lands were free from certain alleged rights of way. Before defences were due the society, which was a limited company, sought to be sisted in the action. It was argued that each of the seven persons who had signed the memorandum of association was entitled to sist himself and there was no reason why the company should not do so. The court allowed the company to be sisted and the view was expressed that a judgment obtained against the society would be res judicata in a question with the public. I was informed that the society has subsequently litigated in matters of public right without challenge. It was suggested that the case was distinguishable in that the society was appearing as defender and was not a pursuer. It was, however, seeking to have itself introduced into the action as a minuter and I consider that counsel for the petitioners was right in submitting that the question was argued upon the principle of the society's title to sue.

No other Scottish authority was put before me to support or to contradict the proposition that, in the present case, the consideration that the petitioner was an association was per se fatal in the matter of title. It is evident that in England no difficulty appears to exist in that regard. An example is the 'Fleet Street Casuals' case to which I was referred. If the case is one where any member of the public has title to sue, I can see no reason in principle, and none was suggested to me in argument, why, simply because a group of members of the public combine to sue where each could do so as an individual, the mere fact of their combining together into an association should deprive them of a title. That much can, in my view, be taken from the case of *Macfie* notwithstanding that it was an actio popularis. Membership of a group was a consideration which weighed with the court in *Wilson* v. *Independent Broadcasting Authority* in the context of interest and in that context the consideration that a voluntary association has taken the initiative may well be a relevant consideration in assessing the importance or materiality of the issue. Accordingly, if the individual members of the public who directly or by membership of their local clubs have a title to sue as members of the public, I find it hard to see why the association to which they belong cannot sue. But this is not to hold that such an association necessarily acts in any representative capacity. *Macfie* was a case of an actio popularis and in that special context a representation of the public by one or more members of the public is recognised. Where an association sues in a case which is not an actio popularis in the proper sense of that term, then I am not at present prepared to hold that it acts in any representative capacity on behalf of the general public. In a case such as the present problems might well arise due to the possible difficulty of determining precisely the identity of all the individuals involved in the action and the practical application of the principle of res judicata could become difficult. Parties in the present case were, however, not concerned to go into the detail of the constitution and composition of the petitioners' association and I only express a general view on the point without any precise finding relating to the circumstances of the present case. In the event it is not necessary to do more. Counsel for the petitioners referred me to a recent unreported case in England, namely, *R.* v. *Secretary of State for Social Services and Chief Supplementary Benefit Officer, ex p. Child Poverty Action Group and Greater London Council* which was decided by Woolf J. on 30 July 1984 and by the Court of Appeal on 24 July 1985. In that case Woolf J. held that the Child Poverty Action Group had locus standi to sue as a body representing the interest of unidentified claimants who stood to be deprived of benefit because of a decision taken by the Secretary of State whose validity was challenged in the action. In the Court of Appeal, the question whether the group had a sufficient interest for the purpose of order 53 was expressly left open for decision. I am not required in the present case to consider further the development of any representative action in Scotland.

It is convenient at this stage to mention the respondent's second plea. In terms of reg. 71 of the Social Security (Adjudication) Regulations 1984 (S.I. 1984 No. 451) a right of appeal to an appeal tribunal against any determination of an adjudication officer is given to inter alios a person claiming, or in receipt of, supplementary benefit. There is provision for appeal from the tribunal to a commissioner and from there to the Court of Session. No right of appeal is given to the present petitioners as an association. There are, however, as the plea states, rights of appeal for claimants.

The respondent did not present any argument that the action was incompetent by virtue of the existence of the opportunity for appeal provided in the legislation. In particular, it was not suggested that any failure to exhaust the statutory remedy open to the individual claimant was in any way fatal to the attempt by the petitioners to seek judicial review. Counsel for the petitioners did contend in the course of his argument that the appeal process would be lengthy and slow to an extent which could cause difficulty or hardship, but no issue was joined on the question whether circumstances existed here which would justify resort to judicial review in the face of a statutory procedure for appeal. I accordingly express no view on the competency of the petition in respect of these matters. The second plea was only founded upon as providing support for the respondent's principal contention that it was only claimants who had title to sue. In that regard reference was made to the case of *Simpson* v. *Edinburgh Corporation*. The pursuer in that case had no right under the relevant legislation to object to a grant of planning permission and it was held that there was no title to challenge an allegedly ultra vires grant of planning permission. The relevant legislation in that case was found not to confer any right to insist in the action. It was argued here that since no right of appeal was given to the petitioners no duty was owed to them.

In the present case I am proceeding on the basis that the legislation does give rights to the public and it is common ground that at least some members of the public could have title and interest to seek judicial review. It was not argued that the appeal provisions ousted any such process or were an exclusive remedy. In these circumstances I see no reason why the existence of the appeal provisions should warrant the inference that only claimants have the title to challenge the alleged error. I note that in *Adamson* v. *Edinburgh Street Tramways* the title of the petitioners was sustained even although the corporation and others might also have been entitled to complain. Where the statute had not been complied with the company could not claim the benefit of it and there was no provision giving the corporation or anyone else an exclusive right and title to complain. The competency of the petition raised in *T. Docherty Ltd.* v. *Burgh of Monifieth* as well as the petitioners' title to sue were sustained despite the existence of alternative statutory means of redress.

I turn finally to the matter of interest which in the present case seems to me to be a distinct and essential ingredient for the petitioners' right to sue. I was referred to a passage in Lord Ardwall's opinion in *Swanson* v. *Manson* (1907) 14 S.L.T. at p. 738, for a statement of the reasons for the requirement of interest. His Lordship there said: 'The grounds of this rule are (1) that the law courts of the country are not instituted for the purpose of deciding academic questions of law, but for settling disputes where any of the lieges has a real interest to have a question determined which involves his pecuniary rights or his status; and (2) that no person is entitled to subject another to the trouble and expense of a litigation unless he has some real interest to enforce or protect.' The phrase 'his pecuniary right and his status' should perhaps in the light of *Wilson* be not regarded as an exhaustive or complete description of what may comprise an interest. At the one extreme there has to be excluded what Lord Fraser in the 'Fleet Street Casuals' case described as the desire of the busybody to interfere in other people's affairs (at p. 646) and on the other hand, to continue the quotation, 'the interest of the person affected or having a reasonable concern with the matter to which the application relates'. The interest must be such as to be seen as material or sufficient. The pursuit of an academic issue would not suffice, nor would an attempt to seek a general pronouncement of law on facts which were hypothetical. There must be a real issue. But the existence of a sufficient interest is essentially a matter depending upon the circumstances of the particular case. The variety of adjectives which are employed to describe the quality of interest required by the law reflects the difficulty of defining any single criterion.

The interest averred in the petition is in these terms: 'The objects of Age Concern Scotland are inter alia the promotion of the welfare of old people in Scotland and the establishment of policies to this end. They are particularly concerned with the availability of adequately heated accommodation for old people who are dependent upon state benefits and thus have an interest in any ultra vires actings of public officials which tend to make it more difficult for such persons to heat their homes.' In the course of the argument counsel for the petitioners submitted that a liberal view should be taken of the matter of interest. Following the 'Fleet Street Casuals' case he suggested in one branch of his argument that the existence or non-existence of the petitioners' interest would be determined by the question whether he was right or wrong in his attack on the merits of the case. As I have already indicated, I am not persuaded that that is a proper approach to the matter of interest in the present case. The question is whether in the circumstances of this case the petitioners have a sufficient interest to make their challenge on the validity of the circular.

It is not said that the association or any of its members have claimed the benefit in question or are intending to do so. Indeed while some of the members may be in a position to claim it is certainly not evident that all the members are potential claimants. The petitioners are not suing as a body of potential claimants but as a body working to protect and advance the interests of the aged. Their purpose in the present context is not to claim benefit for themselves or their members but to secure that benefit is available in all cases where they believe it is deserved. Further, while it may be that some of them would wish to claim, any claim is at present only prospective. There is no real issue at present on the construction of the regulation so far as the petitioners are concerned. I was indeed informed that no claims have been submitted so far by anyone at all following on the circular. The only case outstanding appears to be the case heard by the tribunal of commissioners and remitted by them to another tribunal for hearing. That hearing is to take place in a few weeks. At present the implementation of the circular is otherwise wholly in the future. How far, if at all, the advice it contains will be followed, or will require to be followed, remains to an extent uncertain. The situation is different from the recent case of *R.* v. *H.M. Treasury, ex p. Smedley* to which I was referred, where the interest of a taxpayer was held sufficient to entitle him to challenge a proposed payment of public money in a way which he believed was ultra vires. It is also different from the situation in the case of *Wilson* v. *Independent Broadcasting Authority*. In that case there was to be a referendum and the petitioners were voters who belonged to a group who believed that the vote should be cast in a certain way and who were campaigning to persuade others to vote in that way. It was held that they had a sufficient interest to challenge allegedly ultra vires actings which would hinder that campaign. In the present case the petitioners might be seen as campaigners but the allegedly ultra vires acting is not an interference with that campaign. In the present case it is not said that the petitioners nor their constituent individuals are all in need nor presently entitled to claim the benefit here in issue nor will benefit from any success in the present action. Where a member is a claimant or potential claimant, he or she will have the statutory right of appeal against an adverse decision. It was argued that success would not only lighten the burden of those of the association who might wish assistance with fuel bills but relieve the association itself of some burden in its own work of seeking to help their members. That seems to me to be too indirect a consideration to constitute an interest. There is of course no question about the sincerity of the concern and public spirited endeavour which the petitioners exercise in the interest of the deserving cause of the elderly but in my judgment their interest in the correctness of the circular in question is too remote to give them a right to challenge its validity.

In the whole circumstances I shall repel the petitioners' pleas and dismiss the petition. So far as the defender's pleas are concerned, I consider it sufficient to sustain his first and fourth pleas in law."

Notes

10–22   (1) On one level this case could be seen as a straight application of the approach taken by Lord Dunedin. Lord Clyde, however, in referring to *Baird & Co.* v. *Kilsyth Feuars* (1878) 6 R. 116, seems to accept that in certain circumstances the question of standing could only be resolved by looking at the merits of the case. Indeed in the view of A.W. Bradley, "Applications for Judicial Review — The Scottish Model" [1987] P.L. 313 at 319, in considering the question of the legality of the circular *first* to establish the class of persons entitled to sue and the nature of the interest in question, there may, notwithstanding Lord Clyde's assertion that standing was logically prior to and conceptually distinct from the merits, be "a blurring". The petitioners had title, but their interest was too remote. Given that "it is in the public interest that all official decisions should be made in accordance with the law" (*Stair Memorial Encyclopaedia*, Vol. 1, para. 308) and that Lord Clyde accepted that "the purpose of the legislation is to make state benefit available to any member of the public who may qualify for it... and it is not unreasonable to see the duty of the proper administration of the legislation as detailed to the public", he nevertheless interpreted the matter of interest as not being an interest in the legality of the application of the guidance, but on the authority of *Swanson* v. *Manson*, that "the interests must be seen to be as material or sufficient". Bradley indicated that the practical lesson to be learned here was that pressure groups should find a person with a direct financial interest in the issue.

(2) Typically, title will be held by an individual even if the duty is owed to a class of persons — for example, see *T. Docherty* v. *Burgh of Monifieth*, 1971 S.L.T. 13, extracted at para. 11–12. Similarly a trader has title to challenge conditions imposed on his licence by the local authority: *Rossi* v. *Edinburgh Magistrates* (1904) 7 F.(H.L.) 85, extracted at para. 11–4, but has no title to protect his business against unlawful competition by a public authority, as illustrated by *D. & J. Nicol*. Members of the electorate or candidates have title to seek judicial review of local and parliamentary elections: *Clark* v. *Sutherland* (1896) 24 R. 183 and this would include seeking a review of the procedure for revising parliamentary boundaries: *R.* v. *Boundary Commission for England, ex parte Foot* [1983] 1 All E.R. 1099, C.A.; to prevent the distribution by a local

authority of a leaflet in prima facie in breach of electoral law: *Meek v. Lothian Regional Council*, 1982 S.C. 84 and to prevent the televising of party political broadcasts in the week before a Scottish referendum on devolution: *Wilson v. Independent Broadcasting Authority*, 1979 S.C. 351; an applicant for a liquor licence has title to sue on the way in which the clerk to a licensing board handles the application: *Tait v. City of Glasgow District Licensing Board*, 1987 S.L.T. 340; and a bankrupt recipient of income support has title to challenge deductions made by the Secretary of State of repayment of a social fund loan paid before bankruptcy: *Mulvey v. Secretary of State for Social Security*, 1996 S.L.T. 229. For other examples see *Stair Memorial Encyclopaedia*, Vol. 1, paras 310–321. For the special test of "person aggrieved" in planning law see para. 12–19.

(3) The title of an individual and of an organisation representing such individuals cannot **10–23** always be readily separated. In *Cockenzie and Port Seton Community Council v. East Lothian District Council*, 1996 S.C.L.R. 209 the community council sought to challenge the decision by the council to demolish a swimming pool and sell the land. The district council contended that the community council had no title to sue. However, section 51(2) of the Local Government (Scotland) Act 1973 provided that:

> "In addition to any other purpose which a community council may pursue, the general purpose of a community council shall be to ascertain, co-ordinate and express to the local authorities for its area, and to public authorities, the views of the community which it represents, in relation to matters for which those authorities are responsible, and to take such action in the interests of that community as appears to it to be expedient and practicable".

This appears to be the kind of legal relationship referred to by Lord Dunedin in *D. & J. Nicol*. Similarly, a trade union has title and interest to sue as an organisation representing its members: *Educational Institute of Scotland v. Robert Gordon University*, *The Times*, July 1, 1996. Here the EIS challenged the university's decision to apply new conditions of service to teaching staff appointments. The EIS contended that the new conditions were *ultra vires*. Lord Milligan, in dealing with the plea taken by the university to the title of the EIS to sue, observed:

> "Where, as here, a trade union is able to allege that amongst its membership are persons who are likely to be adversely affected by an ultra vires decision of the respondents and that it is unrealistic for such members individually, both on timetabling and prospects of acceptance grounds, to challenge the decision individually, it seems to me that the trade union has not only an interest to challenge the decision but also title to do so. The governors of the respondents have a duty to comply with statutory requirements for conditions of service of persons employed by them and in my opinion the petitioners are amongst those having a title to see that the duty is performed".

For a discussion of these two cases see A.D. Murray, "Standing Up for the Scottish Public" (1997) J.R. 250. For an earlier case see *Association of Optical Practitioners Ltd v. Secretary of State for Scotland*, December 10, 1985, unreported, where the Association's title and interest in representing its members and challenging an executive decision fixing opticians' fees was not disputed and in older law *Glasgow and District Restaurateurs' and Hotel-keepers' Association v. Dollan*, 1941 S.C. 93 and *The Incorporated Society of Law-Agents in Scotland v. Clark* (1886) 14 R. 161. Notwithstanding the liberal approach to title in these cases, it has been held that an organisation representing the interests of taxi owners did not have title to challenge a proposed policy affecting its members: *PTOA Ltd v. Renfrew District Council*, 1997 S.L.T. 1112 and see also *Inverness Taxi Operators and Owners Association v. The Highland Council*, February 19, 1999, unreported.

(4) Even if the petitioner has title, interest must still be demonstrated, as shown by *Scottish Old People's Welfare Council*. In many cases, the interest will be pecuniary, patrimonial or proprietorial. Other interests have been accepted. In *Gunstone v. Scottish Women's Amateur Athletic Association* and *St Johnstone Football Club Ltd v. The Scottish Football Association Ltd* an interest in ensuring adherence to procedural fairness was held sufficient where there was no apparent financial loss. See para. 10–11 above.

Finch and Ashton at pp. 393–400 argue that the cases on interest fall into broad categories: the "narrow approach" where the person's individual rights have been infringed and the "broad approach" where the court determines that an individual is within a class entitled to enjoy a public right and is principally concerned with whether the decision challenged is lawful. In the former category it has been held that a community charge payer had no interest based on amenity to challenge a decision of a council to purchase a house to provide accommodation for disabled adults: *Wilson v. Grampian Regional Council*, 1993 S.L.T. 588; an individual has no interest to challenge the grant of a public house licence on amenity grounds, when his property was not sufficiently close to the public house: *Khan v. City of Glasgow District Licensing Board*, 1995 S.L.T. 332; an individual has no interest in enforcing planning control when there is no apparent adverse impact on his property: *Simpson v. Edinburgh Corporation*, 1960 S.C. 313; and a company has no interest to challenge grant of planning consent to a rival for a property on which it held planning consent already and where planning policy guidelines relied on by the company could not be said to be about the protection of specific commercial interests but about the proper approach to be taken to planning issues on the property in question: *Bondway Properties Ltd v. City of Edinburgh Council*, 1999 S.L.T. 127. *Scottish Old People's Welfare Council* can also be regarded as an application of this narrow approach.

Under the broad approach it has been held that three members of a group campaigning in a period leading up to a devolution referendum in Scotland had interest to sue for interdict to prevent a party political broadcast by the IBA: *Wilson v. Independent Broadcasting Authority*, 1979 S.C. 351; a local authority had interest to challenge the implementation of the Environmental Assessment Directive: *Kincardine and Deeside District Council v. Forestry Commissioners*, 1992 S.L.T. 1180; competitors of an applicant for the grant of a gaming licence had interest to ensure that the provisions of the Gaming Act 1968 were followed in the board's handling of the application: *Patmor Ltd v. City of Edinburgh District Licensing Board*, 1988 S.L.T. 850; the existence of a pending appeal against refusal of planning consent had been held to be an relevant interest: *Lakin v. Secretary of State for Scotland*, 1988 S.L.T. 780, extracted at para. 8–34; council employees criticised in a fatal accident inquiry by a sheriff had interest to challenge his decision: *Lothian Regional Council v. Lord Advocate*, 1993 S.L.T. 1132. If statutory appeal or objection procedures are in place which a petitioner for judicial review does not utilise, then the court is unlikely to hold that an interest in the broad sense exists: *Hollywood Bowl (Scotland) Ltd v. Horsburgh*, 1993 S.L.T. 241; *Matchett v. Dunfermline District Council*, 1993 S.L.T. 537.

Whether or not a narrow or broad approach is taken to the matter of interest, the petitioner must also show that the interest is sufficient in law. Accordingly any interest must be a live one so that where it was accepted that the validity of the approach taken in relation to the making of a benefit decision by the House of Lords in another case in circumstances in point with the petitioners, there was no interest in the petition which sought to have a social security appeal tribunal rehear the petitioners' challenge to their own decision: *Carrigan v. Secretary of State for Social Security*, 1997 G.W.D. 15-635; where a judicial review of a decision of the Parole Board was sought, sufficient interest existed notwithstanding that a rehearing of the decision in question was to take place as the first decision could have an effect on the pending decision: *Ritchie v. Secretary of State for Scotland*, 1998 G.W.D. 3-102. Where an interest is a future one, sufficient interest will not exist where it is hypothetical or academic. Thus in *Shaw v. Strathclyde Regional Council*, 1988 S.L.T. 313 a parent challenged the policy of the council to permit an automatic clothing grant per child in each school year. It was held that challenge based on the parent's apprehension about the fate of a further discretionary application in the same year raised a hypothetical point only. Contrast with *Air 2000 v. Secretary of State for Transport (No. 2)*, 1990 S.L.T. 335 where a company operating chartered air flights from Glasgow to Florida intended to apply for a licence to fly from Edinburgh to Florida but had not done so. The Secretary of State made rules compelling flights from Glasgow and Edinburgh to America to stop at Prestwick airport. It was held that the petitioners had title and interest to challenge the validity of the rules in relation to both Glasgow and Edinburgh routes as the matter was "of immediate and real concern" as their Edinburgh licence application was imminent.

10–24   (5) The decision in *Wilson v. Independent Broadcasting Authority*, referred to by Lord Clyde, is sometimes treated as being a citizen's action or *actio popularis*: see W. Wade and C. Forsyth, *Administrative Law* (7th ed., 1994, p. 712. However, C. Munro has noted. "Standing in Judicial

Review", 1995 S.L.T. (News) 279, that that decision has "nothing to do with the *actio popularis*, and depends on the general law of standing". The scope of the *actio popularis* appears to be restricted to certain ancient public rights, and essentially the existence of the public right in question — for example, a public right of way — is sufficient to qualify title and interest in itself. All that a person claiming infringement of the right requires to do is to demonstrate that he falls within the class entitled to enjoy the right: *Ogston v. Aberdeen District Tramways Company* (1896) 24 R. (H.L.) 8: see further, Finch and Ashton, pp. 400–403 and *Stair Memorial Encyclopaedia*, Vol. 1, para. 309. Sometimes statutory recognition is given to this — for example, the Local Government (Scotland) Act 1973, s. 133 (power of the local authority to institute legal proceedings in the interests of the inhabitants of its area). The scope of the *actio popularis* is therefore restricted and cannot be regarded as a citizen's action.

REFORM OF THE LAW OF STANDING

As will be seen from the foregoing extracts, the law of standing in Scotland is relatively restrictive. **10–25** In English administrative law, the test for standing is "sufficient interest": RSC Ord. 53, r. 3 (5), and a similar test was advocated by the Faculty of Advocates in its submission to the Dunpark Report. However, as issues of substantive law were outwith the report's remit, it could not be considered. Accordingly in England actions for judicial review have been held competent when raised by a wide range of special interest or pressure groups. In *R.v. Secretary of State for Employment, ex parte Equal Opportunities Commission* [1995] 1 A.C. 1 the EOC was entitled to challenge a decision on whether employment protection laws were indirectly discriminatory against women and therefore in breach of Community law on equal pay and equal treatment. In *R.v. Inspectorate of Pollution, ex parte Greenpeace Ltd (No. 2)* [1994] 4 All E.R. 321 it was held that Greenpeace had sufficient standing to challenge an attempt to vary the amount of discharge of radioactive waste from Sellafield and in *R.v. Secretary of State for Foreign Affairs, ex parte World Development Movement Ltd* [1995] 1 All E.R. 611 a pressure group sought to challenge the Government's payments to fund the Pergau dam where they alleged that the monies would be more properly spent in aiding a number of third world countries. That English law appears to be more favourable to such public interest challenges was also apparent in *R.v. Secretary of State for Scotland, ex parte Greenpeace Ltd*, May 24, 1995, Q.B.D. *per* Popplewell J. Greenpeace sought to challenge ministerial approval for Shell's proposals to dispose of the Brent Spar platform in deep water. On the basis of opinion from Scottish Queen's Counsel, it was accepted by the court that Greenpeace would have "very real difficulties in… establishing a right of interest, as such, before a Scottish court" and accepted that Greenpeace had sufficient interest in these proceedings to pursue the case in England even if a plea of *forum non conveniens* had been taken. For further discussion of the position in England see Munro above at 281–283. What are the arguments for reform of Scots law?

I. Cram, "Towards Good Administration — The Reform of Standing in Scots Public Law"

(1995) J.R. 332 at 334

"The Inadequacy of Restrictive Accounts of Standing
(1) Arguments for Restriction

> 'In administrative law, while it is in the public interest that all official decisions should be made in **10–26** accordance with law, it is not in the public interest that public authorities be required to show lawful authority for their actings at the instance of any litigious member of the public.'

Narrow accounts of standing tend to be found in what Feldman has called 'liberal individualist' political cultures, where the ultimate legal power is vested in a representative body (*e.g.* Parliament). In such a culture it is legitimate to use any lawful means to force that body to consider public interest matters prior to a decision being taken. However, once a decision has been reached after proper public debate, only those whose legal rights are infringed by the implementation of the decision are permitted to litigate. Those who cannot point to such an infringement are left to use the political arena, the media and, if appropriate, specialist grievance redress mechanisms like the parliamentary and local Commissioners for Administration to pursue their grievances. Under this account non-legal standards, such as the varieties of Citizen's Charter, might be seen as having a role to play when the administration acts improperly, but falls short of infringing any legal right possessed by the complainant. In this way the scarce resources of the courts can be preserved for the resolution of legal disputes, thus avoiding overtly political disputes and excluding the 'interfering busybody'. Ensuring that the litigant has a direct interest in the matter is said to guarantee that the court hears effective argument against any alleged impropriety. Narrow rules of standing are also said to bring about greater certainty for decision-makers and those who act in reliance upon the validity of such decisions. This point was evident in the recent landmark case south of the border, *R. v. Secretary of State for the Environment, ex p. Rose Theatre Trust Co. Ltd* [1990] 1 Q.B. 504 at 519] where Schiemann J. noted:

> 'Often the law provides a time limit or *other conditions* which have to be complied with before the court is empowered to quash an admittedly unlawful decision. The reason … is that in many fields, if it were otherwise, uncertainty and, at times, complete chaos would result' (emphasis added).

The view of judicial review commended here is one which prioritises the public interest in allowing the public administration to make and execute a regular flow of decisions without undue judicial interference. Instances of illegality are tolerated because of the heavy costs to the administration and others of first suspending and later amending an impugned decision.

(2) Restriction Undermined

Thus stated, narrow accounts of standing are difficult to sustain for two main reasons. First, inherent in the argument for restriction are certain assumptions about the availability of other mechanisms within the constitution to control executive illegality, which simply do not accord with the reality of executive accountability under the U.K. constitution, especially when viewed from a Scottish perspective. Secondly, the case for restriction on practical grounds relies upon unsubstantiated fear of large numbers of interfering busybodies and a dubious concern for the convenience of the administration and those who rely upon the validity of the administration's decisions and acts. These objections will now be set out.

The period 1979–90 in England and Wales witnessed a steady accretion of power in the hands of central government, as the functions of regional and local authorities were curtailed and central government's powers to control local spending were tightened. Ultimately, centres of political opposition at the Greater London Council and the other Metropolitan county councils were removed. One consequence of these policies was the resort in inner city areas to non-elected executive agencies such as Urban Development Corporations, or non-directly elected joint boards (as in the provision of fire, civil defence and transport services) to perform functions hitherto undertaken by local government. Little thought, however, appears to have been given to the question of how the new agencies might be made accountable, nor to the thorny issue of the desirability and extent of ministerial patronage.

In Scotland, a similar reorganisation was also underway. By 1982 Hogwood was able to describe a significant (if highly varied) pattern of executive bodies removed from direct political accountability. Further movement away from democratic control towards non-elected agencies and non-directly elected boards of appointees has now occurred in Scotland in the form of the Local Government etc. (Scotland) Act 1994. The Act is premised on the need for a single tier of local government and the supposed efficiency gains this will bring. The reforms have, however, encountered opposition on similar grounds to those met by earlier reforms, as a brief examination of the proposals relating to water and sewer-age and transport will make clear. In the case of water and sewerage provision, the responsibilities of elected regional councils have been transferred to three new water authorities whose membership is entirely within the gift of the Secretary of State. The Minister also appoints the members of another new body — the Scottish Water and Sewerage Customers Council — which will represent the interests of customers and potential customers of the new service. The Act further vests transport functions previously undertaken by Strathclyde Regional Council in a new agency — the Strathclyde Passenger Transport Authority — to be composed of appointees drawn from the members of constituent local authority areas. In what can be seen as a further (if only vaguely stated) threat to local democratic control, the Act empowers the Secretary of State to appoint the members of 'residuary bodies' and 'property commissions' to carry out, *inter alia*, such functions as are specified in the relevant ministerial order.

For some time now observers of the constitution have voiced concern at Parliament's seeming inability to control the executive. Today, large parliamentary majorities, control of the parliamentary timetable and a strong system of party discipline continue to limit the opportunities for opposition M.P.s to call the government to account. With respect to the system of scrutiny of the administration in Scotland, these problems find a more extreme expression. The Select Committee on Scottish Affairs, for example, has only been active in sporadic bursts. It sat between 1968 and 1972 and later from 1979–87, but was not re-constituted following the Conservatives' disastrous showing in the General Election of 1987, when just 10 Scottish M.P.s were returned to the Government benches in the House of Commons. After the modest recovery made by the Government in Scotland at the 1992 elections, the Select Committee was reconvened in June 1992, when it was eventually agreed that a Labour M.P. would be its chair. The committee's recent history suggests that its very existence is dependent upon the return to Westminster of a sizeable tranche of Scottish Conservative members willing to serve there. Few would claim that such an arrangement is defensible. The Government's latest thinking on the matter was outlined in a 1993 White Paper entitled 'Scotland in the Union — a Partnership for Good'. The scarcity of opportunity for detailed consideration of Scottish matters within the present system is recognised and a modest set of reforms, including changes to the way in which Scottish legislative proposals are examined, is proposed. An increase in the allocation of parliamentary time for oral questions to Scottish Office ministers (currently 15 minutes every four weeks) is also suggested. There is, however, nothing in the White Paper to remove the suspicion that the very existence of arguably the most powerful tool of scrutiny — the Select Committee on Scottish Affairs — is dependent upon sufficient numbers of compliant Conservative M.P.s.

Weaknesses in other mechanisms of control over the executive, such as the parliamentary and local Commissioners for Administration and, most recently, the Citizen's Charter, have been amply dealt with elsewhere. For present purposes, it is sufficient to note that, in addition to a lack of formal legal powers to enforce remedies, the parliamentary and local commissioners are further circumscribed by restrictions on the subject matter of complaint which may be investigated. Moreover, in the case of the English and Welsh local commissioners, the courts have not been slow to discover irregularities in investigations which have rendered the commissioners' reports *ultra vires*. As for the varieties of the newly promulgated Charter, it is the absence of new legal entitlements which prompts critics to downgrade their significance. In addition, there is no prospect of a challenge to administrative conduct by the Lord Advocate who, unlike the Attorney General in England and Wales, has no jurisdiction to act as representative of the public interest.

The case for limiting standing on the various practical grounds hinted at earlier may also be queried. First, as Cane has rightly pointed out, it is simply wrong to assume that because someone does not have a legal right which has been infringed he or she is not capable of presenting an effective argument against government misconduct. Secondly, there is no empirical evidence to suggest that hordes of frivolous litigants await the relaxation of standing rules to overwhelm the courts with their petty complaints. The conclusion reached by the most recent study by the Public Law Project of Judicial Review Trends in England and Wales was that there was a relatively low usage of the Order 53 R.S.C. procedure outside immigration and housing cases.

The case on administrative convenience grounds advanced by Schiemann J. in *ex p. Rose Theatre Trust Co.* can also be questioned. Even if it is assumed that the judges are capable of making assessments about administrative efficiency, the "costs" that concern them are surely short-term costs entailed in the disruption of a flow of decisions and, where review is successful, a quantifiable cost of correction borne by the taxpayer. Absent from this calculation are the benefits to accrue to the public at large from improved decision-making if standing was a less onerous hurdle to overcome."

Notes

(1) The foregoing analysis is clearly based on the inadequacy of existing political controls over the administration. On the face of it the existence of a Scottish Parliament should mean greater political accountability for decision makers and administrative bodies. Moreover, given the different ends of political and legal control, should the rules of standing depend on the effectiveness or otherwise of political remedies? This would arguably require the courts to become involved in gauging effectiveness, and it is not clear that the courts should do so, or indeed are equipped to do so. For comment on the parliamentary and local commissioners for administration and the Citizen's Charter see Chapter 16.

10–27

(2) In the *Rose Theatre Trust* case, a trust company was formed specifically for the purpose of preserving the remains of the Rose Theatre in London. Schiemann J. held that to challenge a ministerial decision not to list the site as an ancient monument in terms of the Ancient Monuments and Archaeological Areas Act 1979, the company lacked sufficient interest to do so. Since an ordinary citizen lacked interest, the formation of citizens into a trust company did not change

the position. In an article in [1990] P.L. 307, "Statutes, Standing and Representation", P. Cane criticised this case and argued (at 311) that:

> "True liberalisation of standing rules requires not only the applicants be accorded standing to represent interests which they share with many others, but also that standing be accorded to genuine representatives of interested persons, even if the only interest of the representative is to further the interests of the represented."

This case is the English equivalent of *Scottish Old People's Welfare Council*. That English law may have moved on can be seen perhaps from the subsequent cases referred to above. Moreover, what is lacking in the *Rose Theatre Trust* and indeed in *Scottish Old People's Welfare Council* and subsequent case law is arguably any analysis of the exact function of the rules of standing in administrative law. The acceptance of the test set out by Lord Dunedin in *D. & J. Nicol* is based on the merging of entitlement to a remedy and the right to apply for that remedy. This is to be contrasted with the position in public law where the public law litigant is required to show that the respondent public body has infringed one of the values embodied in the substantive heads of judicial review and also that some personal interest of his has thereby infringed thus giving a reason why "he should be allowed to complain in court of the abuse of power": Cane above at 313. These contrasting passages show that in administrative law the litigant is arguably in a disadvantaged position compared to the private law litigant. This restrictive approach is, as Cram notes (at 341) apparently in conflict with *West*, which on the face of it appears to "respond effectively to the dispersal of functions and powers hitherto seen as governmental", here quoting W. Wolffe [1992] P.L. 625 at 637.

It is also possible that actual practice may determine the extent to which problems over title and interest will continue to arise. Thus in the course of their research, T. Mullen, K. Pick and T. Prosser, "Judicial Review in Scotland Part I" (1996) S.L.P.Q. 366 at 380, believe that

> "a more generous approach to title and interest was taken in practice than the more restrictive reported cases would suggest ... Nor did (their) advisor survey suggest that there was concerns about standing... If in practice title and interest require this had become more relaxed than the older cases would suggest, this should be recognised more formally".

In this connection note the decision in *World Wildlife Fund for Nature Ltd v. Secretary of State for Scotland*, *The Times*, November 20, 1998 where no challenge to the title and interest of a pressure group was made in relation to their challenge to the approval of a funicular railway on a site of environmental significance. The Scottish Law Commission in its Twenty-Third Annual Report (1987–88), para 2.4, indicated that the question of the law of standing was being considered in light of *Scottish Old People's Welfare Council*. Its report is still awaited. Given judicial conservatism in this area it may well require intervention by the Scottish Parliament to bring about real reform. For further reading see *Stair Memorial Encyclopaedia*, Vol. 1, paras 308–323 and Finch and Ashton, pp. 387–406.

THE LIMITS OF THE SUPERVISORY JURISDICTION: THE AVAILABILITY OF AN ALTERNATIVE REMEDY

Bellway Ltd v. Strathclyde Regional Council

1980 S.L.T. 66

10–28   "On 10 March 1976 a regional planning authority in purported exercise of their powers under s. 179 (1) of the Local Government (Scotland) Act 1973 and s. 32 (1) of the Town and Country Planning (Scotland) Act 1972 directed the district planning authority to refer to them an application by a firm of builders to develop certain land owned by them. On 30 December 1976 the regional planning authority made a similar direction in respect of a further application by the said firm for approval of detailed plans. The district planning authority appealed to the Secretary of State for Scotland against the regional planning authority's direction of 10 March 1976, but the appeal was dismissed on 29 September 1976. The firm of builders raised an action for declarator that the said directions were null and void and for production and reduction of them on the ground that they were ultra vires. The regional planning authority pleaded inter alia that the pursuers had no title or interest to sue, and that the action was incompetent... .

The Town and Country Planning (Scotland) Act 1972 provides:... .

'33 ... (3) Where an appeal is brought under this section from a decision of a local planning authority, the Secretary of State, subject to the following provisions of this section, may allow or dismiss the appeal, or may reverse or vary any part of the decision of the local planning authority, whether the appeal relates to that part thereof or not, and may deal with the application as if it had been made to him in the first instance. (6) The decision of the Secretary of State on any appeal under this section shall be final.' "

LORD BRAND: "The pursuers in this action are a firm of builders who are carrying out the development of land owned by them at Redmoss Farm, Lennoxtown, and Frenchmill Farm, Milton of Campsie. The first and second defenders are respectively the regional and district planning authorities for the areas in which the pursuers' development is being carried on. The third defender is the reporter whom the first defenders appointed to hold a public local inquiry on 26 April 1977 into the pursuers' planning applications. The fourth defender is the Secretary of State for Scotland. Only the first defenders have lodged defences to the present action.

On 12 October 1973, the pursuers applied to Stirling County Council for planning permission to carry out residential and ancillary development at Redmoss Farm. On the reorganisation of local government the said application, which had not yet been determined, was transferred to the second defenders. On 5 October 1976, the pursuers applied to the second defenders for approval of details relating to their residential development at Frenchmill Farm and Redmoss Farm.

On 10 March 1976 the first defenders in purported exercise of their powers under s. 179 (1) of the Local Government (Scotland) Act 1973, and s. 32 (1) of the Town and County Planning (Scotland) Act 1972, directed the second defenders to refer to them for determination the pursuers' said application of 12 October 1973. The first defenders purported to exercise their said powers on the ground that: 'the proposed development raises a new planning issue of general significance to the Region of Strathclyde in that (a) no educational facilities may be available, and (b) it may be contrary to the Regional Development Strategy'. On 30 December 1976, the first defenders in purported exercise of their aforesaid powers directed the second defenders to refer to them for determination the said application of 5 October 1976. The first defenders purported to exercise their said powers on the ground that: 'the proposed development raises a new planning issue of general significance to the district of the Regional Planning Authority in that it may be contrary to the Regional Development Strategy'. The second defenders appealed to the fourth defender against the first defenders' said direction of 10 March 1976, but the appeal was dismissed on 29 September 1976.

In the present action the pursuers conclude inter alia for declarator that the said directions of 10 March 1976 and 30 December 1976, are null and void and for production and reduction of them. The grounds upon which it is alleged that the said directions are null and void are that they were ultra vires.

The case was debated in the procedure roll on the first, second, third and eighth pleas-in-law for the first defenders.

I shall deal first with the question of whether the pursuers have a title or interest to sue and with the question of competency which are raised by the first defenders' first and second pleas-in-law... .

The existence of an ultimate right of appeal had frequently been held to be a reason why proceedings should not be open to challenge by way of reduction (*Caledonian Railway Co.* v. *Glasgow Corporation*). Further, the pursuers had a second right of appeal by way of application to the Court of Session (Town and Country Planning (Scotland) Act 1972, s. 233). Reduction is not competent where other means of review are prescribed or have not been exhausted (*Adair* v. *Colville & Sons*, 1926 S.L.T., per Viscount Dunedin at p. 592). The pursuers must exhaust their statutory remedies before resorting to reduction... .

Counsel conceded that, if the legislature has prescribed the method by which a grievance is to be adjudicated upon, the jurisdiction of the court is excluded. But there is a presumption against the exclusion of the court's jurisdiction (*Brodie* v. *Ker*) and, if an ultra vires act is alleged, the provision for determination of the grievance does not protect a person's illegal acting from the restraint of the supreme court (*Caledonian Railway Co.* v. *Glasgow Corporation* (1905) 13 S.L.T., per the Lord President at p. 352). The pursuers' contention in the present case was that no valid directions were given. Therefore there could be no question of appealing against them. The statute provided a developer with the right to appeal against the refusal of planning permission and against the grant of planning permission subject to unacceptable conditions but it provided no method of determining a dispute of the present kind. Section 33 of the 1972 Act did not oust the jurisdiction of the court in relation to the reduction of an ultra vires act. The case of *Stringer* (supra) was of no relevance to the present situation. In *Stringer* the application to the court was to quash the decision of the Minister of Housing and Local Government which had affirmed on appeal the planning authority's refusal of planning permission. In the instant case the pursuers had no right of appeal at the present stage. Therefore they were entitled to obtain a remedy from the court.

In my opinion it is clear from the terms of the relevant statutory provisions that the pursuers have no title or interest to challenge the calling-in of their planning applications. In any event, they have no such title or interest at this stage. In terms of s. 179 (2) of the 1973 Act the district planning authority has a right of appeal to the Secretary of State against a calling-in and the Secretary of State, whose decision is final, is not required to consult or hear anyone other than the planning authorities (s. 177 (4)). On the other hand, when a planning decision has been made, the applicant, if dissatisfied, may appeal to the Secretary of State who 'may deal with the application as if it had been made to him in the first instance' (1972 Act, s. 33 (3)). The effect of these provisions, in my opinion, is that while the applicant has no intermediate right of appeal, he has an ultimate right of appeal at which he can be restored against any antecedent irregularity, invalidity or nullity. I respectfully agree with the opinion of Cooke J., in *Stringer* that, where a minister has power to deal with a matter de novo, he is entitled to deal with the application and to make a decision on it even though the decision appealed from is a nullity. It follows that the pursuers are not prejudiced by the decision to call in their applications. In any event, the remedy of reduction is not competent when other means of review are prescribed (see the speech of Viscount Dunedin in *Adair* v. *Colville & Sons*, 1926 S.L.T. at p. 592). Resort to this exceptional remedy can only be had when the prescribed procedures have been exhausted (see the opinion of Lord President Dunedin in *Caledonian Railway Co.* v. *Glasgow Corporation* at p. 1033). It follows that, even if the directions complained of were ultra vires, the present action is premature. It is not to be assumed that any prejudice suffered by the pursuers will not be remedied if the prescribed procedure is followed out.

For the foregoing reasons I shall sustain the first and second pleas-in-law for the first defenders and dismiss the action."

Notes

10–29   (1) Section 233 of the 1972 Act is now of course re-enacted in section 239 of the Town and Country Planning (Scotland) Act 1997, on which see para. 12–18. The principle articulated by the Lord Ordinary is one of long standing in Scots administrative law. The justifications for refusal of a petition on the grounds of the existence of an alternative remedy were examined in *Portobello Magistrates v. Edinburgh Magistrates* (1882) 10 R. 130. Here the Lord Justice-Clerk (Moncrieff) observed (at 137):

> "where a new and special jurisdiction is given to any Court the exercise of it must be regulated entirely by the conditions of the statute under which it is conferred, and that in the general case remedies which might have been competent in an ordinary civil process are not to be presumed or inferred to be given by the particular statute … on the other hand… where a well-known and recognised jurisdiction is invoked by the Legislature for the purpose of carrying out a series of provisions … without any specific form of process being prescribed, the presumption is that the ordinary forms of that Court are to be observed."

This is another way of expressing the distinction between appeal and review.

(2) Notwithstanding the apparently clear terms of the then rule 260B, there was at least some initial doubt as to the scope of the new judicial review procedure. For example, in *O'Neill v. Scottish Joint Negotiating Committee for Teaching Staff*, 1987 S.L.T. 648 the petitioner presented a petition for judicial review seeking reduction of two decisions of the *Scottish Joint Negotiating Committee for Teaching Staff*. The respondents took a plea to the competency of the petition arguing that the petitioner had failed to utilise the remedy given to her under section 3 (1), (3) of the Administration of Justice (Scotland) Act 1972 by referring the substance of the dispute to arbitration. In sustaining that plea the Lord Ordinary (Jauncey) noted (at 650):

> "It is perhaps sometimes forgotten by litigants that the Rule of Court 260 B, which instituted the expedited procedure for judicial review, provides no remedy or relief of which did not already exist. The supervisory jurisdiction of the Court of Session will continue to be exercised only in those cases in which it could have been exercised before the rule was introduced. That jurisdiction is not available as a general mode of appeal against decisions of tribunals or other bodies but is rather available in limited circumstances where no other means of review exist (*Brown v. Hamilton District Council*, Lord Fraser of Tullybelton at p. 414). It is certainly not available where other means of review are provided and those means have either not been made use of or have been used without success. (*Adair v. Caldwell and Sons* 1926 S.L.T., Viscount Dunedin at p. 592)."

As well as confirming the scope of the new procedure the foregoing emphasises the continuing relevance of case law prior to 1985: see also *Nahar v. Strathclyde Regional Council*, 1986 S.L.T. 570.

(3) Judicial review proceedings which were initially competent can become incompetent if the decision complained about under the judicial review proceedings in itself becomes subject to a statutory appeal. In *Strathclyde Buses Ltd v. Strathclyde Regional Council*, 1994 S.L.T. 724 an experimental traffic order under the Road Traffic Regulation Act 1984 was to be made. However, before the order was made, a bus company sought judicial review of the actings of the local authority and the Secretary of State for Scotland alleging that there was procedural impropriety leading to the decision to make the order. The bus company sought interdict against the local authority from proceeding further with the scheme and to suspend the Secretary of State's consent to it and it further intimated in its petition for judicial review of its intention to present a statutory appeal to the Court of Session in terms of para. 35 of Schedule 9 to the 1984 Act. The application for judicial review was sisted with an undertaking that the local authority would take no steps to implement the order without giving the bus company 14 days' notice. Some weeks later the local authority made the order but delayed its implementation for six weeks. The bus company appealed to the Inner House seeking interdict and thereafter quashing of the order and also recall of the sist in a petition for judicial review and seeking amendments expanding the grounds of challenge. The respondents took a plea to the competency and argued that the judicial review proceedings were now incompetent. The Lord Ordinary (Lord Cameron of Lochbroom) in sustaining that plea observed (at 727):

> "I am no doubt that the present proceedings as now framed are incompetent. I agree with counsel for the respondents that the matter begins with paras 35 and 37 of Sched 9 to the 1984 Act. The subject of the petitioners' present complaint is the making of the order on 13 January 1992. Paragraph 37 provides that an order such as that, shall not 'either before or after it has been made' be questioned in any legal proceedings except as provided by para 35. I observed that the petition as originally drafted was in part directed to complaint about procedure adopted by the first respondents in advertising an intention to make an order and the right to aggrieved persons to question its validity, which procedure purported to deprive the petitioners of their full statutory right within a period of six weeks from the making of the order to appeal to the Court of Session in terms of the 1984 Act. I do not decide whether proceedings under Rule of Court 260B (1) are competent for that purpose or not. However, at that stage, the order was not made. It has now been made. It is not, in my opinion, competent to convert these proceedings by amendment into a judicial review of the making of that order when the proper road is by way of an appeal under Rule of Court 290. The same result obtains whether regard is had to the terms of Rule of Court 290 (1) and to Rule of Court 260B (1) and (3) as a matter of court procedure, or whether the issue is looked at as a matter of substantive law, namely that the petitioners having availed themselves of their statutory right to appeal under the 1984 Act, are held to be limited to that avenue of challenge. Otherwise the anomalous result must obtain that the petitioners can at the same time pursue two actions on the same grounds in fact and in law in the same court and seek the same remedy in each. This would seem to offend against the principle of nemo debet bis vexari."

The petitioners had argued that the judicial review proceedings should be allowed to continue as they had uncovered materials which they would not have otherwise have been able to use and moreover it was somewhat speedier than a statutory appeal. However, it will be seen from the above that even if in substance there is unlikely to be any great difference in terms of the issues examined, as a matter of procedure, the requirement to exhaust an alternative remedy will be applied strictly. Note also the concern of the court to ensure that a respondent authority is not subject to the requirement of defending two sets of proceeding: see also *Kirkwood v. City of Glasgow District Council*, 1988 S.L.T. 430; *Chowdry v. Social Security Appeal Tribunal*, 1997 G.W.D. 40–2030; *Hussain v. Secretary of State for the Home Department*, 1997 G.W.D. 32–1635; and *Mensah v. Secretary of State for the Home Department*, 1992 S.L.T. 177.

For further reading see *Stair Memorial Encyclopaedia*, Vol. 1, paras 304–305; Finch and Ashton, pp. 224–229; N. Collar, "Judicial Review: The Significance of an Alternative Remedy" (1991) 36 J.L.S.S. 299; and C.T. Reid, "Failure to Exhaust Statutory Remedies" (1984) J.R. 185. The duty to exhaust an alternative remedy is however, not an absolute one as the following extract demonstrates.

Tarmac Econowaste Ltd v. Assessor for Lothian Region

1991 S.L.T. 77

10–30   "A former quarry came into occupation as a waste tip following the 1985 revaluation. The assessor altered the valuation roll by entering it in the roll as a tip with a net annual value of £9,000. Thereafter he issued two further notices intimating alteration of the roll, by making a new entry for a tip with a net value of £39,500 and by deleting the earlier entry. The occupiers, considering that the making of the further new entry and the deletion of the earlier entry were ultra vires of the assessor, petitioned by judicial review for reduction of the deletion and second entry. The assessor, as well as arguing that the steps taken had been competent under the provision about correction of errors [Local Government (Scotland) Act 1975, s.2] also sought dismissal of the petition on the ground that it was incompetent, the occupiers not having exhausted their statutory right of appeal to a local valuation appeal committee. The occupiers argued that it was not necessary to proceed by appeal to the committee since the allegation was of ultra vires actings by the assessor and also since the committee would have no power to reduce the notice of deletion."

The matter came before the Lord Ordinary, Lord Clyde, who after narrating the facts and statutory provisions continued:

LORD CLYDE: "... Reference was made during the argument to Rule of Court 260B (3) in relation to the proposition that the procedure for application for judicial review could not be made under Rule of Court 260B where a statutory means of appeal or review was open Rule 260B (3) of course only relates to the availability of the procedure introduced in that rule and does not affect the wider question of the competency of invoking a common law remedy Further, rule 260B (3) relates to applications to the court which is not immediately the question in the present case. In any event the argument presented by counsel for the assessor before me was based of the broader principle to the effect that the court will not grant redress in the exercise of it supervisory power where all statutory remedies have not been exhausted.

I was referred to a succession of cases where that principle has been considered or applied. The case clearly vouch the principle. In *Dante* v. *Magistrate of Ayr* and *Bellway Ltd.* v. *Strathclyde Regional Council* application to the court was incompetent In *Abercromby* v. *Badenoch* the statutory procedure had been exhausted and a common law remedy was competent. But it is also evident and indeed it was accepted by counsel for the assessor that the principle is not an absolute one but admits of exceptions. This was recognised in the case of *British Railways Board* v. *Glasgow Corporation* where, to use the language of Lord Justice-Clerk Wheatley, the exception to the operation of the principle was stated to arise in 'exceptional' or 'special' circumstances. It is not necessary to attempt any complete definition of what those circumstances might be. Lord McDonald in the Outer House in that case observed that recourse to the common law remedy would be incompetent 'unless the failure was due to ignorance owing to some irregularity of procedure on the part of the assessor or rating authority, to the fact that resort to the statutory remedy would, in the particular circumstances, be otiose or to some other special reason' (1975 S.L.T. at p. 48). Lord Wheatley observed (1976 S.C. at p. 239): 'Examples of such special circumstances would be averments of *ultra vires* or fraud'. One clear exception is where the complainer has been prevented from pursuing a statutory appeal through a procedural irregularity on the part of the authority. *Sharp* v. *Latheron Parochial Board* is an example of that and the correct basis of that decision, at least as stated in the Outer House and identified with approval in the House of Lords in *Moss' Empires* v. *Walker*, 1916 2 S.L.T. at p. 220, was that the ratepayer had not been given notice of the entry in the roll and so had no opportunity of appealing. As Lord Blackburn observed in the case of *Dante* v. *Magistrates of Ayr*, 1922 S.L.T. at p. 76: 'As the pursuer in this case has failed to exhaust his possible remedies and does not aver that his failure to do so was due to any irregularity on the part of the authorities in making up the Valuation Roll, or to any mistake of which he had no notice, I think it is incompetent for him to contradict the accuracy of the entry as he now endeavours to do.' Another situation is illustrated in *Hope* v. *Corporation of Edinburgh* where the court recognised that the statutory appeal involved an application to magistrates who would in the circumstances be judges in their own cause and accordingly allowed an application at common law. Another situation is where the statutory remedy is procedurally available but in the circumstances provides an inadequate method of resolving the issue. An example can be found in the case of *City Cabs (Edinburgh) Ltd.* v. *City of Edinburgh District Council*. There a statutory procedure was open by way of objection to individual applications for licences but the challenge which was being made against the licensing authority was against a general decision in relation to a large number of future licences. The argument on competency was not persisted in but the Lord Ordinary expressed the opinion that since competency was a matter for the court the appeal was competent and related to a matter which was not adequately covered by the statutory procedure.

Counsel for the petitioners founded particularly on the observation of Lord Wheatley which I have already quoted, to the effect that ultra vires actings were an example of an exceptional circumstance. He claimed that the present was a case of ultra vires actings. Counsel for the assessor submitted that the observation should not be construed as a general statement, covering all ultra vires actings. In its context it should be read as limited to the procedural irregularities of the kind which I have mentioned. Alternatively, counsel submitted that the proposition was too widely stated. Certainly it is clear that a valuation appeal committee can competently deal with some questions which could be considered in some sense as involving action ultra vires. Counsel suggested the example of the case of *Assessor for Strathclyde* v. *Dass Nicholas* where a question of the competency of an alteration to the roll purportedly made to correct a clerical error was determined by the valuation appeal committee and their decision was upheld by the appeal court.

As I have already observed it is not necessary in the present case to attempt any complete classification of the kinds of cases which should fall outwith the general principle. Given the recognition that an inadequacy in the statutory alternative may be a sufficient reason for recourse to be had to judicial review this is an area of law which may well be open to development in the interests of the provision of an effective procedure for redressing wrongs. But the court should be wary of trespassing on the jurisdiction of a tribunal which is competent to determine the matter in issue. In the present case the question at issue is the validity of the action taken by the assessor in March 1989.

It is not altogether easy to make a complete separation here between consideration of the competency of this application and of the validity of the assessor's actings because the resolution of the former question depends upon the nature and substance of the issues comprised in the latter. So far as the latter are concerned, counsel for the assessor sought to justify what had been done on two alternative bases. In the first place it was said that the assessor had acted wholly under s. 2 (1)(*f*) of the Local Government (Scotland) Act 1975. That section provides that "the assessor for any valuation area shall, as respects that area, at any time while the valuation roll is in force, alter the roll... (*f*) to correct any error of measurement, survey or classification or any clerical or arithmetical error in any entry therein". Alternatively it was submitted that he had made a new entry under s. 2 (1) (*f*) and then to avoid the existence on the roll of two entries had deleted one of them under s. 2 (1) (*h*). That paragraph obliges the assessor to alter the roll, '(*h*) by deleting therefrom (with effect from such date as the assessor thinks fit) any lands and heritages which cease to exist or which, for any other reason, are no longer appropriate for inclusion in the roll'. In support of the first argument he submitted that para. (*h*) related to the deletion only of lands and heritages as distinct from a deletion of an entry in the roll.

Counsel for the assessor explained that the reason why the assessor had proceeded by way of deletion of one entry and insertion of another was because it had been discovered that the subjects had been entered as being in the West Lothian District when they should have been entered in the City of Edinburgh District. The technical procedures used in the assessor's office were such that in order to make this correction the subjects had to be deleted from the section of the roll which related to West Lothian and inserted in the section of the roll which related to the City of Edinburgh. Counsel referred to s. 116 (6) of the Local Government (Scotland) Act 1973. That subsection provides that: [his Lordship quoted the terms of the subsection and continued:] But I do not find there a requirement that the roll be divided into such distinct sections that if an alteration of the identity of the appropriate district is required, a deletion and new entry must be made. Whatever procedures or techniques the assessor may adopt for the completing and maintaining of the valuation roll and whatever flexibility or lack of flexibility those procedures or techniques may have, the assessor is bound by the terms of the statute in the extent to which he may alter the roll when it is made up. Whatever the reason may have been for what was done, the question is whether those actings fall within the scope of the powers given to the assessor by s. 2 (1) of the Act. The immediate problem is whether that question can be or can adequately be resolved by a valuation committee by way of an appeal against the entry now in the roll.

In the present case the petitioners have lodged an appeal against the entry in the roll. It is not suggested that that appeal is incompetent. Counsel for the petitioners pointed out that while they had a right under s. 3 (2) of the Act of 1975 to appeal against a new entry they had no right to appeal against the deletion. While s. 3 (3) of that Act provides for notification of a deletion it does not allow for an appeal against such a step. But the petitioners are complaining not only about the new entry but also about the deletion of the former entry. The argument by counsel for the petitioners gained strength from the fact that the assessor sent out two notices in March 1989 several days apart, one notifying of the new entry and the other deleting the former entry. It seemed as if there were two distinct steps. On the other hand counsel for the assessor explained that the actual deletion and making of the entry in the revised form were all done as one step. In substance what the assessor was doing was substituting a corrected entry for an incorrect one.

I am not persuaded that the problems raised by counsel for the petitioners and in particular his inability to appeal against the deletion make it appropriate for this court to intervene at this stage. Each of the two approaches put forward by counsel for the assessor involve questions of competency of procedure which are within the jurisdiction of the committee. In my view the competency of the course taken by the assessor in March is matter which they can determine without the necessity for an appeal against the deletion. Counsel for the assessor as I understood him accepted that in an appeal against the new entry the petitioner was entitled to argue that the attempt to proceed under s. 2 (1) (f) or 2 (1) (f) and (h) was incompetent and that there had not been any error of the relevant kind to warrant the change and that the valuation was in any event incorrect. He also accepted that if the committee held the course taken by the assessor to have been incompetent then they would delete the entry. They could not resuscitate the former entry. On the other hand if they held the course to have been competent then they could proceed to consider how far if at all, the alteration in the roll was justified as having been made to correct some error of the kind specified in (f) and to consider the whole valuation. The details of the former entry would be available as a point of reference whereby the extent and nature of each alteration could be ascertained and its attributability to any of the errors specified in s. 2 (1) (f) ascertained. It is not averred and was not suggested in argument that there was any particular reason for the necessity of an appeal against the deletion in itself. So far as appears the petitioners' interest in the roll is solely in connection with rating and I do not understand that there would be any particular prejudice to them if the new entry was deleted and the former one not revived.

Since I am taking the view that it is a matter for the committee and not for me, it would be inappropriate to express any view on either of the approaches which have been suggested by counsel for the assessor. The matter is one which falls to be determined by a consideration of s. 2 (1) of the Act of 1975. In conclusion I take the view that at least as matters stand at present the application for judicial review is not competent and on that ground I shall refuse it."

Notes

10–31   (1) It will be seen from the foregoing that the basic test is that a petitioner will require to show that the statutory remedy is inadequate if a judicial review petition is to be competent. It is clear that exceptions to the general rule have not been exhaustively defined and the list given by Lord Clyde can only be regarded as illustrative. Other exceptions not noted include a statutory remedy not being privative in *Giles v. Baxter* (1849) J. Shaw 203, or where the parties' common law rights are in issue, thus in *Macdonald v. Singer Manufacturing Co. Ltd*, 1923 S.C. 551 where it was held that notwithstanding that wartime legislation set up a temporary tribunal to adjudicate on wage claims of workers in the munitions industry, it was nevertheless competent for such a worker to use the ordinary remedies of the court as the workers' right was characterised as a common law right to wages: see also *Pentland v. Henderson* (1855) 17 D. 542. Similarly in the field of planning law, in *Inverclyde District Council v. Inverkip Building Co. Ltd*, 1981 S.C. 401 a planning authority raised an action at common law for reduction of a planning permission granted by their predecessors. Lord McDonald took the view that section 42 of the Town and Country Planning (Scotland) 1972 (now see section 65 (1), (2) of the 1997 Act), did not provide an appropriate alternative to reduction: see also *Bovis Homes (Scotland) Ltd v. Inverclyde District Council*, 1982 S.L.T. 473 and compare *Bellway Ltd v. Strathclyde Regional Council* above. For comment see C. Reid (1982) S.P.L.P. 46 and for a similar decision under English planning legislation, see *Pyx Granite Co. Ltd v. Ministry of Housing and Local Government* [1960] A.C. 260. The courts may also disregard the existence of statutory remedy where there already exist clear grounds of challenge where the remedy in question would only exist at a later date when the issues may well have become academic: see *London and Clydeside Estates Ltd v. Secretary of State for Scotland*, 1987 S.L.T. 459.

(2) It will be noted from the excerpt that the court was concerned to ensure that the reference to *ultra vires* noted in *British Railways Board v. Glasgow Corporation* should not be taken to mean *ultra vires* in its broad sense as this would, of course, cover all forms of conduct which could give grounds for judicial review. If that were so then the rule requiring use of alternative

remedies would be robbed of its content. *Ultra vires* in this context means jurisdictional error where the subordinate body was clearly making a decision outwith its statutory powers: see also *Mensah v. Secretary of State for the Home Department*.

(3) Where a clear statutory duty exists requiring a person or authority to take action, then the Court of Session can grant a remedy under section 45 of the Court of Session Act 1988, whether or not there is another statutory method by which that duty could be ensured: see *T. Docherty Ltd v. Monifieth Burgh*, 1970 S.C. 200 extracted at para. 11–12.

(4) Exceptional circumstances justifying the use of judicial review where a series of circumstances not sufficient in themselves to justify an exception to the usual rule can exist if their cumulative effect is sufficient, as the next extract demonstrates.

Choi v. Secretary of State for the Home Department

1996 S.L.T. 590

"The petitioner was the holder of a British passport as a citizen of the British dependent territory, Hong Kong. He lived in Hong Kong with his mother until July 1992, when he came to the United Kingdom. Before travelling he had obtained an entry certificate until 31 October 1993 as a student for a single visit. He originally studied at a school in North Yorkshire, but was subsequently accepted for a college course in Aberdeen. He was living with C, who was said to be the petitioner's father, and who had remarried. In November 1992 the petitioner had applied for indefinite leave to remain. This application was refused in April 1993 and the petitioner appealed. In July 1993 he returned to Hong Kong to visit his mother. He came back to the United Kingdom in September 1993 to resume his studies. The petitioner had not obtained a new entry visa prior to his departure to Hong Kong or his return to the United Kingdom. His passport was removed and he was given a notice of temporary admission and asked to attend for interview, which took place at Aberdeen airport on 3 October 1993. C and his wife were interviewed first. The petitioner was interviewed later that afternoon. Notice of refusal of leave to enter was given on 5 October, along with directions for the removal of the petitioner to Hong Kong on 12 October. The reasons stated for refusal were that notwithstanding the extant conditions for leave to enter, the petitioner was to be treated as a new entrant and that the immigration officer was not satisfied that the petitioner intended to leave the United Kingdom on completion of his studies. The decision made no reference to the outstanding appeal. The petitioner sought judicial review of that decision on the grounds that the decision to treat the petitioner as a new entrant was ultra vires and illegal, that the decision was not reasonable, and that the circumstances of the interview were oppressive and in breach of natural justice. For the Home Secretary it was argued that the immigration officer was correct to treat the petitioner as a new entrant, and that as there was an appeal procedure available in terms of s. 13 of the Immigration Act 1971, the application for judicial review was incompetent. It was further argued that s 14(1) of the 1971 Act did not assist the petitioner as he had left the country voluntarily, and that in seeking to return as a student the petitioner was doing so in a different capacity from that in which he had originally been granted leave to enter."

LORD CAMERON OF LOCHBROOM narrated the facts and considered the argument that the petitioner had not used the appeal available under section 13 and continued:

"However it is said by counsel for the respondent that these matters could be addressed on appeal to an adjudicator and that following the line of authority beginning with *ex p Swati* the present application was incompetent, since there were no special circumstances which took the case out of the general rule that judicial review was not available when a statutory remedy was otherwise afforded to the petitioner and had not been exhausted. Accordingly she argued that the plea to competency should be sustained and the petition be dismissed. Counsel for the respondent cited as cases in which *Swati* had been followed in varied circumstances in England: *Doorga v Home Secretary; Suarez v Secretary of State for Home Department; Soon Ok Ryoo; Grazales v Secretary of State for Home Department, R v Secretary of State for the Home Department, ex p Pulgarin; R v Secretary of State for the Home Department, ex p Salamat*; and the case of *Kharrazi*. Counsel further submitted under reference to *British Railways Board v Glasgow Corporation* and *Tehrani v Argyll and Clyde Health Board* that the same principle applied in the law of Scotland.

Counsel for the petitioner accepted that the test stated in *Swati* was the appropriate test to determine the competency of the petition. He contended that there were here special circumstances. These arose not only from the issue whether all the material circumstances had been taken into account by the immigration officer, but also from the averments as to the manner in which the interview had been conducted, as a consequence of which the immigration officer had disabled himself from obtaining proper information as

10–32

to the relevant circumstances. Counsel pointed out the respondent did not argue at this stage that these averments were irrelevant or unfounded in fact. Counsel also made reference to *R v. Secretary of State for the Home Department, ex p Hindjou* and to my own decision in *Oghonoghor v Secretary of State for the Home Department*. A procedural impropriety could be such as to invalidate the decision of an immigration officer as was indicated in *Oloniluyi* by the Master of the Rolls. To require the petitioner to leave the United Kingdom before exercising his right to appeal against the decision of the immigration officer was also to deprive the petitioner of an opportunity properly to present his case in person before the immigration officer, which opportunity should have been available to him if the interview had been conducted fairly and properly. Counsel pointed to the averments relating to a request for the interview to be held in Glasgow and for the petitioner to be accompanied by a solicitor, to the limited notice of the interview in Aberdeen and to the criticisms made of the interviews themselves, all of which made the manner of procedure on the part of the immigration officer unusual to say the least. Furthermore, the effect of requiring the petitioner to leave the country before exercising any right of appeal against the immigration officer's decision, was to deprive him of the right personally to present his appeal against refusal of indefinite leave.

While I am not to be held as determining that all the submissions made by the petitioner are well founded on the merits, I am however satisfied that the accumulation of grounds averred both of procedural impropriety and of irrationality in this case are such as can constitute special circumstances of the kind which the courts have had in mind in setting out the general rule and the exception which may be made to it in permitting a judicial review where a statutory remedy is otherwise available and has not been exhausted. I find the decision of the immigration officer in relation to the refusal to grant leave to enter, standing the fact that the petitioner was a bona fide student with a course of education already available for which he had been accepted and for which payment had been made, against the background that there was an appeal against refusal of indefinite leave outstanding, surprising, to say the least, in that it bears to be based upon a determination that the petitioner would not leave at the conclusion of his course. Furthermore, I am also satisfied that in the light of the averments made as to procedural impropriety which are not at present attacked as irrelevant, it is arguable that the whole proceedings preparatory to the taking of the decision by the immigration officer may have been fatally flawed such as to make his decision irrational. As the decisions cited make clear, each case must turn upon its own individual facts and circumstances. None of the cases cited to me were in any sense analogous on their facts to the present case. Accordingly they can only act as guides as to the proper test to be applied in the particular circumstances arising in an application for judicial review. In the present case I am satisfied that notwithstanding the arguments presented upon the averments as they presently stand, the submissions for the respondent do not justify me in holding that this case is not one in which special circumstances arise such as to take the case out of the general rule."

Notes

10–33   The decision in *Choi* is of particular importance, given the context of human rights. Contrast *Choi* with the approach taken by the English courts in *R. v. Secretary of State for the Home Department, ex parte Swati* [1986] 1 W.L.R. 477, which was referred to in *Choi*. *Swati* has had a marked effect on the number of applications for judicial review in immigration cases. On this see M. Sunkin "What is Happening to Applications for Judicial Review?" (1987) 50 M.L.R. 432 at 444–447. Although accepting *Swati* as being relevant to determination of the issue, his Lordship clearly accepted that much depends on the particular circumstances of each case. Unlike the train of authority following *Swati* noted by Sunkin, there should be no general presumption that, in immigration cases, the existence of a statutory right of appeal being given undue weight should prevail. In *Sangha v. Secretary of State for the Home Department*, 1997 S.L.T. 545 the petitioner failed to establish an exceptional circumstance based on poor advice from an immigration adviser which led him to abandon his right of appeal. On the facts the courts failed to establish that this amounted to an exceptional circumstance. Moreover it emphasised what is inherent in *Choi*, that exceptional circumstances have to exist independently of the merits of the case: see also *Alagon v. Secretary of State for the Home Department* 1995 S.L.T. 381 and generally V.M. Smith, "The Scope of Judicial Review Determined?" (1997) J.R. 122 where it is argued in particular that the need for an effective remedy is consistent with Article 13 of the European Convention on Human Rights. Article 13 is not a Convention right for the purposes of the Human Rights Act 1998 or the Scotland Act 1998, on which see para. 11–40. For further general readings see *Stair Memorial Encyclopaedia*, Vol. 1, paras 304–305; Finch and Ashton, pp. 224–229.

DELAY IN SEEKING JUDICIAL REVIEW

Hanlon v. Traffic Commissioner

1988 S.L.T. 802

A group of holders of taxi operators' licences in Glasgow failed to challenge a decision **10–34** fixing a new scale of fees before the scale was implemented. There was a period of only three weeks for implementation but a large number of people had changed their circumstances on the basis of the changes. For example, new microchips had been fitted in all taxi meters and operators had made arrangements to implement the changes. Later a group of operators applied for judicial review on the ground that a breach of natural justice had occurred. The Act referred to by Lord Prosser is the Civic Government (Scotland) Act 1982. The respondent, the Traffic Commissioner, contended that the petitioners were barred from challenge by virtue of *mora*, taciturnity and acquiescence.

LORD PROSSER: "… On about 24 June 1986 the district council licensing committee approved a new scale of fares for taxis in Glasgow in terms of s. 17 of the 1982 Act. This determination was a review within the terms of that section, and was intimated to operators including the petitioners. By letter of 7 July 1986 agents on behalf of the petitioners appealed to the traffic commissioner in terms of s. 18 of the Act. The licensing authority lodged observations and a statement of reasons. The traffic commissioner did not hold a hearing or give the petitioners an opportunity to be heard or represented but in terms of s. 18 (3) (*b*) (i) declined to proceed, and issued a decision to that effect dated 8 August 1986. It is admitted that the traffic commissioner, in reaching that decision, relied on inter alia a letter from a body known as the Glasgow Taxi Trade Council ('G.T.T.C.'). It is also admitted that this letter was not shown to the petitioners and that they did not have the opportunity of making representations anent its contents. The traffic commissioner does not contest that he erred in relying on the letter from the G.T.T.C. without having given the petitioners the opportunity to comment on it. Moreover, it was accepted by counsel on behalf of the traffic commissioner that this error amounted to a breach of the requirements of natural justice.

The basis upon which it was contended that the decision should not be quashed, as would be the natural consequence of such a denial of natural justice, was twofold. First it was contended that the petitioners were barred from challenging the validity of the decision by mora, taciturnity and acquiescence. Secondly it was contended that even if there was no bar, the court should exercise a discretion to refuse the petitioners the remedy sought having regard to what were described as exceptional circumstances. Each of these contentions is perhaps more appropriate if advanced by persons who have been prejudiced or are liable to be prejudiced, as the traffic commissioner himself is not. On behalf of the petitioners, however, it was expressly stated that no objection was taken to these contentions being advanced by the traffic commissioner. Equally, it is to be observed that other taxi operators, who would have an interest in whether the order were to be quashed or not, have not been called in the present proceedings. Again however it was accepted that a sufficient picture of their interests could be provided by the respondent or by the district council, and no argument was advanced in relation to their absence.

As the denial of natural justice is admitted, there is perhaps no direct need to consider the terms of the letter from the G.T.T.C., or the part which it played in the decision which was reached by the traffic commissioner. Briefly however the position is this. [His Lordship then considered the duties of the traffic commissioner and continued:]

I turn to the contention that the petitioners are barred by mora, taciturnity and acquiescence. The decision was issued on 8 August 1986. After the procedures required by s. 18 (8) and (9) of the Act the new scale was brought into effect on 1 September 1986. Since then that scale has been operated by all operators in Glasgow, including the petitioners. Between the date of the decision and the actual introduction of a new scale of fares some three weeks elapsed, during which no indication was given by the petitioners to anyone that the validity of the decision was challenged. During that period, quite apart from the public advertisement of the impending change, a variety of steps were required by way of preparation for the change. In particular a change of the microchip in every meter had to be implemented and the meters tested in time for the coming into effect of the new scale. Moreover, after the scale had taken effect, the petitioners persisted in their failure to challenge the validity of the decision until the raising of the present petition. A letter had been written on 19 December 1986 seeking a sight of the G.T.T.C. letter. Some delay had occurred while the traffic commissioner consulted the writers of the letter to see if they objected to its being shown to the petitioners. They did object, and he refused such sight on 13 January 1987. It is however to be observed that the factual content of the letter was narrated in the decision letter itself, so that a reader of that decision would know what facts he proceeded upon and could see that this was derived from the letter which he expressly mentioned. The challenge to validity therefore did not depend on seeing the letter, and was open to the petitioners from the beginning. On 29 January, and presumably on the basis of the decision letter, it had been asserted on behalf of the petitioners that 'the information supplied by G.T.T.C. to the commissioner was quite wrong'. That contention (and the crucial complaint that an opportunity to respond and refute had been denied) could have been made at any time. The petition had only been lodged in June 1987, some 10 months after the decision and some eight and a half months after the new scale had been brought into effect. Throughout the whole of that time the petitioners would have been aware of what information the G.T.T.C. had supplied and would have been aware that the traffic commissioner had relied upon it. In these circumstances there was bar by taciturnity and acquiescence.

The nature of bar can of course be expressed in a variety of ways. I was referred to *Cairncross* v. *Lorimer; Stornoway Town Council* v. *Macdonald; Trades House of Glasgow* v. *Govan Heritors* and *Macfarlan* v. *Pringle*. These cases show that bar will very largely be a matter of circumstances, and I do not think that it would be helpful for me to try to produce a further formulation of the principle which is to be applied. On behalf of the petitioners it was emphasised that delay in itself will not suffice to produce bar. It was moreover contended that there would only be such bar where there was conduct on the part of the party indicating that he had truly abandoned an objection open to him in law; that this had occurred when he was in knowledge of the full circumstances giving rise to his right to object; and that his conduct had been relied upon and produced a material change of circumstances. Reference was made to *Assets Co.* v. *Bain's Trustees* and *Lees' Trustees* v. *Dun*. Moreover it might well be that the party would have taken certain steps "going along with" the situation which he claimed the right to challenge. Such conduct would not give rise to bar where those steps could be seen as the natural emergency measures which any businessman would take in order to avert disaster. Reference was made to *Bruce* v. *British Motors*.

While I do not think that these propositions can really be disputed, I have come to the view that in the present case the petitioners are indeed barred by acquiescence in respect of their failure to act before the scheme was given effect on 1 September 1986. It is clear that the requisite conduct for bar can consist in the negative conduct of standing by in silence, and that silence can indeed constitute an implied intimation that one is offering no opposition to the course of events. The fact that a large number of people will be affected by whether a given change is to occur or not will plainly be one consideration in determining whether silence implies acquiescence. Equally, if one is "going along with" a change for economic reasons while reserving one's right to challenge the new order, it appears to me that silence is unnecessary and indeed that silence will tend to negative any intention of challenge. The length of any delay before implications of acquiescence arise will be almost infinitely variable depending on circumstances. I am however in no real doubt that the natural inference from the petitioners' silence between 8 August and 1 September would be that they were accepting the decision of the traffic commissioner, which everyone was preparing to implement on the latter date.

It does not appear to me that the petitioners can claim that they lacked any requisite knowledge for the purposes of acquiescence, between the date of the decision and the date of the implementation of the new scheme. The decision letter carries on its face a clear indication of the breach of the rules of natural justice which gave rise to the petitioners' rights. Moreover I am satisfied that their silence can in a real sense be said to have induced the actions of others in bringing the new scheme into effect and as having been relied upon by them as indicating that the traffic commissioner's decision was final and not subject to challenge.

It was suggested that the silence could not really be seen as having induced the introduction of the new scheme, since in order to stop its coming into effect it would have been necessary for the petitioners to seek and obtain judicial review within the month of August. I do not however think that there is much substance in this line of argument, since the raising of proceedings and application for interim relief would have been possible and could have been effective to prevent the course which was being followed. There is perhaps more force in the argument that once the scheme had in fact been brought into effect, the continuing delay of the petitioners could not be seen as having induced any actions or as having been relied upon by others, since there would have been no alternative course open by that stage unless and until and decision were suspended or quashed. I am not however greatly concerned in relation to acquiescence with the delay in taking proceedings after 1 September. Although the delay before that date may not seem long it was in my view an unreasonable delay having regard to all the circumstances, and being coupled with full knowledge and implied reliance by others I see it as establishing acquiescence by mora and taciturnity. In these circumstances I consider that the petitioners are barred from seeking the present review and I accordingly uphold the respondents second plea and refuse the petition.

That being so, I do not find it necessary to rely upon the second ground advanced by the respondent for refusing the order sought. In support of the contention that I have a discretion in this respect reference was made to *Grahame* v. *Magistrates of Kirkcaldy*. Much emphasis was placed on the practical difficulties which could ensue if I were to reduce the decision and thus oblige the traffic commissioner to reconsider the question which arises under s. 18 (3) (*b*) (i). The effect of the reduction would be once more to suspend the operation of the new scale. The old scale would therefore revive and necessitate the reintroduction of some means of operating it. Depending on the result of the traffic commissioner's decision, and any appeal which he might allow to proceed, there might be the introduction of a new scale which would itself require practical introduction with new microchips and the like. Moreover the present scale would have to be reviews within 18 months from the date on which it came into effect, and there would thus only be a quite limited period before a new review if the new scale were allowed to run. The interests of other drivers would not be served by forcing them in the profitable summer period to revert to a long outdated and much lower scale. The remedy sought was an equitable one and I had a discretion to refuse to grant such a remedy....

In the present case the right which was denied was an important and substantive right. One reason for describing the remedy of reduction as 'equitable' is that such a denial of right demands a remedy on equitable grounds. The fact that the court must exercise a discretion does not in my view carry any implication that it can (far less that it should) deny a remedy to one whose rights have been infringed on the basis that others (whose rights have not been infringed) will suffer some prejudice because his right is upheld. If the present petitioners had not lost their rights by their own taciturnity and acquiescence, I see no reason why their abiding rights should be rendered worthless on such a basis. It does not appear to me that this is a case where they effectively lack an interest to enforce those rights. It is not a case which I see as analogous to cases where there is some minor encroachment on property and alternative remedies would be available insofar as there was a genuine interest. If the petitioners were not barred, I would have upheld their claim to the remedy of reduction without hesitation."

Notes

(1) This case and subsequent authorities are discussed by N. Collar, "Mora and Judicial Review", 1989 S.L.T. (News) 309 and 1992 S.L.T. (News) 335. Prior to *Hanlon* there appears to be no authority in Scots law for the plea of *mora*, taciturnity and acquiescence being used as a defence to judicial review. For a discussion of the position prior to *Hanlon* see C.T. Reid, "Mora and Administrative Law", 1981 S.L.T. (News) 253. Reid concluded, in the absence of the plea being recognised, that judicial review could have been sought a number of years after the decision complained of and would only be precluded by the expiry of the 20-year negative prescriptive period. Clearly this placed administrative authorities at something of a disadvantage. However, neither rule 58 nor its predecessor rule 260B, unlike the English RSC, Ord.53 (1), contains a time-limit as to when the petition for judicial review must be raised in the following terms:

10–35

> "An application for judicial review is to be made promptly, and in any event within three months from the date when grounds for the application first arose."

In *R. v. Stratford-on-Avon District Council, ex p. Jackson* [1985] 1 W.L.R. 1319 it was held that "promptly" meant no undue delay so that a period of even less than three months could in some circumstances still be relevant as a defence to judicial review proceedings or as a way of restricting the remedy available. Some relief is allowed in the case of applications for judicial review made outwith the three month period on grounds of "substantial hardship". It has been judicially recognised in *Pickering v. Kyle and Carrick District Council*, 1991 G.W.D. 7–361, that English authority on what constitutes delay may be referred to in terms of establishing whether a plea of *mora*, taciturnity and acquiescence is made out. In *Pickering* the reliance was placed on the English decision of *R. v. Dairy Produce Quota Tribunal for England and Wales ex p. Caswell* [1990] 2 A.C. 738.

(2) Collar is critical of the use of the doctrine of *mora*, taciturnity and acquiescence. He views it essentially as a private law doctrine and that it is in particular (at 310):

10–36

> "unsuitable for the needs of administrative law today. The involvement of large sections of the public in a single administrative decision must be contrasted with the participation of the two parties to a contract."

Collar also tentatively suggests that one can extract three propositions from *Hanlon* for a successful plea: (1) delay in raising legal action; (2) presumption of abandonment getting stronger as time passes; and (3) causing change of position in the respondent or a third party. There are difficulties with each of these elements. In relation to knowledge, it is not clear what knowledge is required, when it arises and what level of knowledge is required. The status of delay is also uncertain. In *Hanlon* it would appear that delay alone was not sufficient to set up a plea. Third-party prejudice has been a source of particular difficulty. Hanlon left open the question of whether third-party prejudice was needed for a successful a plea. In *Perfect Swivel Ltd v. City of Dundee District Licensing Board (No. 2)*, 1993 S.L.T. 112, reference was made to the question of prejudice *obiter* but no opinion was expressed as to whether prejudice was required. In *Conway v. Secretary of State for Scotland*, 1996 S.L.T. 689 again it was stated. *obiter*, that the key to the plea was prejudice to a third party. While prejudice will often be present as in *Hanlon* (and see also *Pickering* and *Atherton v. Strathclyde Regional Council*, 1995 S.L.T. 557), delay followed by a period of silence during which objection could have been made could be held to be contrary to the certainty required by good administration without the necessity of change of position or of specific prejudice being established, on which see now *Kwik Save Stores Ltd v. Secretary of State for Scotland*, 1999 S.L.T. 193 and for an earlier example see *Carlton v. Glasgow Caledonian University*, 1994 S.L.T. 549. No hard and fast rule can be set out to establish what is an inappropriate delay, Lord Johnston observed in *Kwik Save Stores Ltd* (at 196):

> "I am in no doubt that a challenge to a ministerial decision by way of judicial review is susceptible to the plea of mora being successfully sustained in appropriate circumstances where there is both material delay and ascertainable prejudice. Beyond that position, however, to define the matter as one of principle is extremely difficult since it seems to me that each case must turn on its own facts and it becomes to some extent a question of fact and degree. What may be a reasonable delay as a matter of time in one case may be wholly inappropriate in another but I do not consider that ministerial decision should be susceptible to challenge at any point in time after they have been made... I do consider that certainty in government is an important ingredient of good government, or at least the good administration of same. I also consider it relevant that no reason was advanced even at the bar why the period of time had elapsed... I approach the matter with regard to the position of the Secretary of State not by seeking to define what would have been a reasonable time to bring the challenge but rather upon the question of whether the lapse of time that has occurred in this case is unreasonable, and I consider that it is, particularly in the absence of an explanation that is satisfactory. I recognise on the issue of prejudice that the decision affects few people and a successful challenge would affect probably even less, namely only the petitioners. It does not seem to me that in itself detracts from the basic principle that delay in challenging a minister's decision, if unreasonable, is detrimental to good administration. The issue seems to me an intrinsic one, not to be judged by the consequences of a successful challenge, although they may be relevant upon the basis of the greater the consequences and the more people affected, the less reasonable it is to allow a delayed challenge to be made at all. I also in passing regard it as not immaterial that no intimation of a challenge was made to the minister who was not therefore even on guard that he might require to defend his decision."

In this case the owners of a store carried out building works before an application for building warrant had been determined. The local authority served a notice specifying that the works were contrary to building standards and an application for a building warrant was refused. The owners appealed to the sheriff, but that appeal was sisted until the Secretary of State considered whether or not the regulations on building standards should be relaxed. A year after the Secretary of State decided to refuse the application for relaxation, judicial review was sought of the Secretary of State's decision.

(3) In *Swan v. Secretary of State for Scotland*, 1998 S.C.L.R. 763 further observations on the question of delay in seeking judicial review of a decision were made. In implement of EEC Directive 85/337 of June 27, 1985, the Environmental Assessment (Afforestation) Regulations 1988 were made. These required that where an application was made for a grant or loan to forestry commissioners to plant forests in their area the commissioners were obliged to take into "consideration environmental information in respect of that project": regulation 3. Regulation 7 provided that the Minister of Agriculture, Forestry and Environment may of his own motion

give a direction that an environmental assessment be carried out in any case where the commissioners decided that such an assessment was unnecessary. This was such a case. On November 30, 1995 the Minister decided not to require an assessment. On December 5th the commissioners had entered into an agreement with the party to whom the grant was being paid. Planting began in January 1996 and was completed in April of that year after which the grant was paid. It was not until July 17, 1996 that the petitioners presented a petition for judicial review of the decision not to require an assessment, albeit they had complained to the European Commission on November 5, 1995 and had written letters intimating the possibility of legal challenge. At the first hearing, the respondent argued that the delay in seeking judicial review operated to the respondent's prejudice and to the prejudice of the recipient of the grant. This plea was upheld but the petitioners were successful when they reclaimed. The First Division did not consider that there had been prejudice to the respondents or the owner, nor acquiescence on the part of the petitioners. Five days had passed between the decision not to call in the application for environmental assessment and the award of the grant. During that time the petitioners had sought help from Brussels. There was uncertainty as to the legal position in light of *Kincardine and Deeside District Council v. Forestry Commissioners*, 1992 S.L.T. 1180, in relation to the way in which the directive had been implemented by the U.K. Government. Another important consideration was that where reliance on a national time-limit was alleged in relation to rights claimed under Community law, these rules should not make it impossible in practice or excessively difficult for a party to assert his Community law rights, on which see *Emmott v. Minister for Social Welfare* [1991] 1 E.C.R. 426. The Lord President (Rodger of Earslferry) commented (at 768):

"It is, of course, the case that judicial review proceedings ought normally to be raised promptly and it is also undeniable that the petitioners let some months pass without starting these proceedings. None the less, in considering whether the delay was such that the petitioners should not be allowed to proceed, we take into account the situation in which time was allowed to pass. In the first place, the petitioners had approached the authorities in Brussels and entertained the hope that the matter might be resolved in that quarter. Moreover, as we have just mentioned, the petitioners were in some doubt about the legal position in the light of Lord Coulsfield's decision. Their doubts, it was said, stemmed in part at least from the way in which the directive had been transposed by the government. We have explained that, in our view, the respondent was not prejudiced by any lapse of time before the proceedings began. In these circumstances we do not consider that any delay was such that the petitioners should be denied the right to pursue these proceedings.

In connection with the argument about delay we have also to take account of a far-reaching argument for the petitioners which is indeed based on their contention that the United Kingdom has failed to transpose the directive correctly and that the legal position remains in doubt as a result. The petitioners accepted, of course, that the European Court of Justice had recognised that, in cases involving Community law, national legal systems may enforce their own rules on time-limits for raising proceedings, provided that those rules do not make it either impossible in practice or excessively difficult for a party to assert his Community law rights. In *Emmott v. Minister for Social Welfare*. Case C-208/90 [1991] E.C.R. I–4269 at p. 4299, however, the Court of Justice appeared to decide that such national time-limits could not be invoked by a Member State where the Member State had failed to transpose a directive properly.

'21. So long as a directive has not been properly transposed into national law, individuals are unable to ascertain the full extent of their rights. That state of uncertainty for individuals subsists even after the Court has delivered a judgment finding that the Member State in question has not fulfilled its obligations under the directive and even if the Court has held that a particular provision or provisions of the directive are sufficiently precise and unconditional to be relied upon before a national court.

22. Only the proper transposition of the directive will bring that state of uncertainty to an end and it is only upon that transposition that the legal certainty which must exist if individuals are to be required to assert their rights is created.

23. It follows that, until such time as a directive has been properly transposed, a defaulting Member State may not rely on an individual's delay in initiating proceedings against it in order to protect rights conferred upon him by the provisions of the directive and that a period laid down by national law within which proceedings must be initiated cannot begin to run before that time.'

This passage suggests that, if the petitioners are correct in their contention that the United Kingdom has failed to transpose the directive correctly, the respondent, a Minister of the United Kingdom government, could not rely on any delay by the petitioners in initiating these proceedings. On that basis, whatever the facts relating to delay might be, it would be impossible to sustain any plea based on delay unless and until the court had reached a decision on the petitioners' case that the directive had not been properly transposed. The two issues would be inseparably intermingled. The court could therefore not decide at this stage whether the petitioners had failed to act promptly enough and delayed too long before raising the present proceedings."

RESTRICTION OF JUDICIAL REVIEW BY STATUTE

10–37 Parliament does not always welcome judicial control and there has been a long history of attempts to exclude challenge by the courts of administrative decisions by the insertion of "ouster clauses" in administrative schemes. One of the most recent is contained in section 28(5) of the Scotland Act 1998 to the effect that:

> The validity of an Act of the Scottish Parliament is not affected by any invalidity in the proceedings of the Parliament leading to its enactment".

One of the leading examples of the use of such an ouster clause occurred in the next extract. Anisminic Ltd challenged a decision of the Foreign Compensation Commission that it was not entitled to compensation for seizure of the property by the Egyptian Government. The Foreign Compensation Act 1950 provided that decisions of the Commission could not be "called into question in any Court of Law": section 4(4). For the full facts see para. 4–10 where the case is discussed in light of its relevance to jurisdictional control.

Anisminic Ltd v. Foreign Compensation Commission

[1969] 2 A.C. 147

10–38   Lord Reid: "… The next argument was that, by reason of the provisions of section 4(4) of the 1950 Act, the courts are precluded from considering whether the respondent's determination was a nullity, and therefore it must be treated as valid whether or not inquiry would disclose that it was a nullity…

The respondent maintains that these are plain words only capable of having one meaning. Here is a determination which is apparently valid: there is nothing on the face of the document to cast any doubt on its validity. If it is a nullity, that could only be established by raising some kind of proceedings in court. But that would be calling the determination in question, and that is expressly prohibited by statute. The appellants maintain that this is not the meaning of the words of this provision. They say that 'determination' means a real determination and does not include an apparent or purported determination which in the eyes of the law has no existence because it is a nullity. Or, putting it another way, if you seek to show that a determination is a nullity you are not questioning the purported determination — you are maintaining that it does not exist as a determination. It is one thing to question a determination which does not exist: it is quite another to say that there is nothing to be questioned.

Let me illustrate the matter by supposing a simple case. A statute provides that a certain order may be made by a person who holds a specified qualification or appointment, and it contains a provision similar to section 4(4), that such an order made by such a person shall not be questioned in any court of law. A person aggrieved by an order alleges that it is a forgery or that the person who made the order did not hold that qualification or appointment. Does such a provision require the court to treat that order as a valid order? It is a well-established principle that a provision ousting the ordinary jurisdiction of the court must be construed strictly — meaning, I think, that, if such provision is reasonably capable of having two meanings, that meaning shall be taken which preserves the ordinary jurisdiction of the court.

Statutory provisions which seek to limit the ordinary jurisdiction of the court have a long history. No case has been cited in which any other form of words limiting the jurisdiction of the court has been held to protect a nullity. If the draftsman or Parliament had intended to introduce a new kind of ouster clause so as to prevent any inquiry as to whether the document relied on was a forgery, I would have expected to find something much more specific than the bald statement that a determination shall not be called in question in any court of law. Undoubtedly such a provision protects every determination which is not a nullity. But

I do not think that it is necessary or even reasonable to construe the word 'determination' as including everything which purports to be a determination but which is in fact no determination at all…"

Notes

(1) Lord Reid's assessment of the intention of Parliament cannot go unquestioned. It was **10–39** perhaps very much the intention of Parliament that judicial challenge be excluded. Reaction to the decision came in the form of the Foreign Compensation Act 1969, s. 3, which provided for appeal on a point of law by way of stated case from the Commission to the Court of Session or the Court of Appeal. No appeal to the House of Lords was permitted and in terms of section 3(9) "determination" included "purported determination". Notwithstanding the failure of form of clause in the extract, the terms continued to be used. See, for example, section 44 of the British Nationality Act 1981 which provides that in relation to a decision to refuse British nationality "the decision of the Secretary of State … shall not be subject to appeal … or review in any court of law". This section came to be considered in *R.* v. *Secretary of State for the Home Department, ex parte Fayed*, [1997] 1 All E.R. 228, C.A. where, following the decision in *Anisminic* and *Attorney General* v. *Ryan* [1980] A.C. 718, Lord Woolf observed:

> "That to have effect such a decision has to 'come within the prohibition of appeal or review by an ouster clause of this type, the decision must be one which the decision making authority … had jurisdiction to make'."

For comment on this see S.C. Smith, "The Comprehensive Approach to Fairness", 1997 S.L.T. (News) 265.

The decision does not, however, mean that all attempts to prevent challenge must be sacrificed on the altar of judicial inventiveness. More limited clauses may be given effect.

Martin v. Bearsden and Milngavie District Council

1987 S.L.T. 300

"Paragraph 15 (1) of Sched. 1 to the Acquisition of Land (Authorisation Procedure) (Scotland) Act 1947 **10–40** entitles a person aggrieved by a compulsory purchase order who desires to question the validity thereof on certain specified grounds to make an application to the Court of Session within a certain period from the date on which notice of the confirmation or making of the order is first published. Paragraph 16 of the Schedule provides that subject to the provisions of para. 15, a compulsory purchase order shall not, either before or after it has been confirmed, made or given, be questioned in any legal proceedings whatsoever.

In a petition under the judicial review procedure in which the petitioners sought reduction of a compulsory purchase order and declaration in so far as the same affected heritage disponed to them, a question arose as to the efficacy of para. 16 in excluding the jurisdiction of the court to entertain the petitioners' application, which was not brought within the period required by para. 15."

LORD CLYDE: "… The respondent's argument on competency was based on the terms of paras. 15 and 16 of Sched. 1 to the Acquisition of Land (Authorisation Procedure) (Scotland) Act 1947. Paragraph 15 (1) provides as follows: 'If any person aggrieved by a compulsory purchase order desires to question the validity thereof, or of any provision contained therein, on the ground that the authorisation of a compulsory purchase thereby granted is not empowered to be granted under this Act or any such enactment as is mentioned in subsection (1) of section one of this Act, or if any person aggrieved by a compulsory purchase order… desires to question the validity thereof on the ground that any requirement of this Act or of any regulation made thereunder has not been complied with in relation to the order … he may, within six weeks from the date on which notice of the confirmation or making or the order… is first published in accordance with the provisions of this Schedule in that behalf, make an application to the Court of Session'. The paragraph then proceeds to provide for the steps which the court may take on any such application.

Paragraph 16 of the Schedule provides as follows: 'Subject to the provisions of the last foregoing paragraph a compulsory purchase order or a certificate under Part III of this Schedule shall not, either before or after it has been confirmed, made or given, be questioned in any legal proceedings whatsoever and shall become operative on the date on which notice is first published as mentioned in the last foregoing paragraph'.

Counsel for the respondent argued that the effect of para. 16 in the present case was to exclude any challenge other than one made under para. 15. The present application for judicial review was not an application under para. 15 and was accordingly incompetent. It may be noted in passing that applications under para. 15 may not proceed by way of the judicial review procedure by virtue of Rule of Court 260B (3) (*a*). Counsel founded upon the case of *Smith* v. *East Elloe Rural District Council*. That case concerned statutory provisions equivalent to those in the Act of 1947. The plaintiff in that case raised proceedings in 1954 for inter alia a declaration that a compulsory purchase order of 1948 was wrongfully made and in bad faith. It was held that the jurisdiction of the court was ousted by the plain wording of the prohibition in para. 16, the equivalent of para. 16 in Sched. 1 to the Act of 1947. Four of their Lordships took the view that para. 15 did not provide for a challenge on the grounds of fraud or bad faith. Lord Reid and Lord Somervell of Harrow went on to take the view that similarly para. 16 did not cover cases of fraud, and they dissented from the majority who held that the clear words of para. 16 ousted a challenge even on the ground of bad faith. All five of their Lordships appeared to recognise that para. 16 was effective to oust at least a challenge based on ultra vires actings in good faith. The case appears to give strong support to the respondent's contention that in the present case, where bad faith is not suggested, the application is ousted by para. 16.

Counsel for the petitioners argued that *Smith* came under some unfavourable comment in the case of *Anisminic Ltd.* v. *Foreign Compensation Commission*. He referred in particular to the observations of Lord Reid at p. 170G, Lord Pearce at p. 200H and Lord Wilberforce at p. 210F-G. In that case an ouster clause was held inapplicable to the challenge of a determination by the Foreign Compensation Commission on the ground that the determination was a nullity. But, as counsel for the respondent pointed out, *Smith* was not overturned in the *Anisminic* case and its authority was affirmed by Lord Kissen in *Hamilton* v. *Secretary of State for Scotland* and by the Court of Appeal in *R.* v. *Secretary of State for the Environment, ex p. Ostler. Hamilton* was concerned with paras. 15 and 16 of Sched. 1 to the 1947 Act. The pursuers sought to reduce a compulsory purchase order as being illegal and ultra vires in respect that the proceedings had been contrary to the requirements of natural justice. Lord Kissen held inter alia that the action was incompetent because the jurisdiction of the court was ousted by para. 16. He noted that *Smith* had not been reconsidered and that any doubt expressed about it in *Anisminic* related to the question of the effect of mala fides which was not in issue in *Hamilton*.

In *Ostler* the challenge to a road scheme order and a compulsory purchase order was made on grounds of want of natural justice and of bad faith verging on fraud. The court applied *Smith* and held that the application could not proceed. The case of *Anisminic* was distinguished by each of the three judges on a variety of grounds, but one common thread appears to me to have been the recognition that the circumstances in *Anisminic* opened up the question whether there was a decision at all, whether the tribunal had acted within its jurisdiction, while in *Smith* and in *Ostler* it was the validity of the procedure which was in issue: the decision was within jurisdiction and was one which could have been arrived at as a proper order.

Counsel for the petitioners, however, argued that neither *Hamilton* nor the English cases concerned the complaint of a failure to serve notice of a compulsory purchase order. His argument proceeded from the proposition that service of the order was a critical and crucial step in the statutory procedure and a condition precedent to the effectiveness of the order and the general vesting declaration. In that regard he founded on *McCowan* v. *Secretary of State for Scotland* and in particular on the observation of the Lord President in that case where in relation to the absence of service of the notice he said: 'Prima facie at least, this appears to amount to a failure to carry through the proper statutory procedure, which is a condition precedent to the compulsory acquisition of his lands' (1972 S.L.T. at p. 166). Counsel submitted that there was thus a fundamental defect which made the proceedings void. The defect was such as to prevent the owner from exercising his statutory rights and such as to annul the statutory procedure. He submitted that the present case fell within the reasoning followed by the court in *McDaid* v. *Clydebank District Council*, that the order was annulled, that the ouster did not operate and that the statutory code of appeal could not apply to persons who by the omission of the acquiring authority had not had notice of the order.

The case of *McCowan* does not in my view lay down that the omission of service of the order made it a nullity for the purposes of para. 16. The case was principally concerned with the question whether the failure could be solved by reference to s. 5 (3) of the Act of 1947. It was held that it could not be so solved. It was recognised that the provision for service was mandatory and the carrying through of the proper statutory procedure was referred to as a condition precedent to the compulsory acquisition of the land in question. That does not, however, seem to me necessarily to make the compulsory purchase order a nullity in the sense that para. 16 of Sched. 1 cannot apply to it. The question formulated by Lord Radcliffe in the case of *Smith* (at p. 770) still remains; has Parliament allowed the necessary proceedings to be taken to quash the order? While *Hamilton* did not concern a failure in service, it was nevertheless recognised that para. 15 related to some cases of nullity, and indeed Lord Kissen in the course of distinguishing the case from *Anisminic* said: 'In the statutory provisions which apply in this case there is a provision for quashing at least some kinds of null orders. I cannot see how it can be said, on the basis of *Anisminic*, that, as pursuers' counsel maintained, one kind of nullity can be remedied by the application of said para. 15 but all other kinds can be remedied by ordinary legal proceedings in the courts. If that was the intention of the statutory provisions which are under consideration in this case, it would have been easy to say so' (1972 S.L.T. at p. 239). In *Hamilton* it was held that para. 16 excluded the action.

The case of *McDaid* concerned certain enforcement notices which had not been served on the owners and lessees who were the petitioners as the statute, the Town and Country Planning (Scotland) Act 1972, required. The notices had been served on the occupier of the premises, which was also required by the statute, but the petitioners did not discover the existence of them until after the expiry of the statutory time for appeal to the Secretary of State. Section 85 (10) of the Act of 1972 states that: 'The validity of an enforcement notice shall not, except by way of an appeal under this section, be questioned in any proceedings whatsoever on any of the grounds specified in paragraphs (*b*) to (*e*) of subsection (1) of this section'. It was held by the First Division that the court's jurisdiction was not excluded by that provision where for reasons beyond the control of the petitioners the statutory procedure for appeal could not be used by them and that the notices were a nullity.

Counsel for the respondent submitted that the present case was distinguishable from that of *McDaid*. He drew attention to the differences in the statutory provisions for service and for appeal, and he argued that the absence of service in the present case did not have the effect so far as para. 16 was concerned which the absence of service of the enforcement notices was held to have in *McDaid* on the ouster clause with which that case was concerned. In my view he was correct in submitting that there is a valid and significant difference between the provisions in the two statutes.

Under para. 3 of Sched. 1 to the Act of 1947 the compulsory purchase order requires to be advertised in one or more local newspapers and notice of it requires to be served on every owner, lessee or occupier of the land in question. The advertisement and the notices must specify a period within which objections may be made. If there is objection, provision is made by para. 4 (2) of the Schedule for a public local inquiry or a hearing by a person appointed for that purpose. Thereafter the order may be confirmed, and further publication is required under para. 6 of the confirmation. Paragraph 15 makes express provision for application to the Court of Session by any person aggrieved who desires to challenge the validity of the order. For the making of such an application, an express time limit of six weeks is prescribed. Paragraph 15 also prescribes the remedies which the court may adopt. Paragraph 16 then contains the ouster of any legal proceedings questioning the order.

In the 1972 Act, s. 84 (1) provides for a planning authority to serve a notice under that section, referred to in the Act as an 'enforcement notice'. Section 84 (5) provides that the notice shall be served on the owner, lessee and occupier of the land to which it relates and any other person having an interest in that land. The notice specifies a period at the end of which it is to take effect (s. 84 (9)). Section 85 (1) entitles a person on whom an enforcement notice is served or any person having an interest in the land within the period specified in the notice to appeal to the Secretary of State against the notice on any of certain grounds set out beside letters (*a*) to (*g*) in the section. Provision is made by s. 85 (2) for a hearing by a person appointed by the Secretary of State for the purpose. Thereafter the Secretary of State determines the appeal and is empowered by s. 85 (5) to give any necessary directions. Section 85 (10) contains the ouster which I have already quoted.

It is to be noted that there is no provision in the 1972 Act corresponding with para. 15 of Sched. 1 to the 1947 Act. The respective provisions for recourse to the Secretary of State or the confirming authority seem to me broadly to correspond with each other, but after that stage of the procedure Parliament has expressly provided in the 1947 Act for an application to the court for challenge on the validity of the order within a stated time limit. In the context of such a time limit provision the provision for the exclusion of legal proceedings in para. 16 takes on a significance which s. 85 (10) of the 1972 Act does not have. While it may be possible to overcome the latter provision by application of the principle in *Anisminic* or the reasoning in *McDaid*, the same cannot, in my view, be done at least in the circumstances of the present case in relation to para. 16. It cannot be affirmed that para. 16 was not intended to cover an order which was open to attack on grounds of nullity. Nor in the framework of the scheme in Sched. 1 can it be affirmed that para. 16 does not exclude a person on whom the statutory notice has not been served.

Counsel for the respondent also submitted that the identification of the persons to be notified and given the right of appeal under the 1947 Act made the application of the reasoning in *McDaid* more difficult. Service of the enforcement notice is in terms of s. 84 (5) to be made on the owner, lessee and occupier of the land and on any other person having an interest in the land. A compulsory purchase order on the other hand requires to be advertised in one or more local newspapers and served on the owner, lessee and occupier. Appeal against an enforcement notice is open under s. 85 (1) to any person on whom the notice is served and any person having an interest in the land. Appeal against a compulsory purchase order is open under para. 15 to 'any person aggrieved', which, while it doubtless does not give an unlimited title for complaint, extends beyond those who had the right to have the order served upon them. The requirement for advertisement in addition to the serving of notice could attract interest in persons who had not had any notice served on them. In the context of the Act of 1972, where those who were to be served upon and those who had the right of appeal were so closely linked, the reasoning which was adopted in *McDaid* is more readily applicable than in the context of the Act of 1947. It seems to me that this adds further weight to the distinction which I have already noted.

A further ground of distinction put forward by counsel for the respondent lies in the effect of the defect complained of. In *McDaid* service can be seen as the essence of a notice. Section 84 (1) empowers the local authority in certain circumstances to 'serve a notice under this section'. Without service there is no notice. The purported enforcement notice which has not been served may thus be readily seen as an absolute nullity. A compulsory purchase order, on the other hand, is a means of authorising a compulsory purchase by a local authority. It requires first to be made, and then submitted and confirmed by the authority having power to authorise the purchase. Prior to submission, notice of it requires to be advertised and served on certain persons. The omission of service in that context does not seem to me to be of the same gravity as the omission to serve an enforcement notice. To put the matter in jurisdictional terms, it could be said that in failing to serve an enforcement notice an authority was not starting to exercise its jurisdiction at all. But the omission to serve a compulsory purchase order made within the powers of an authority could be seen as an error within the exercise of the authority's jurisdiction: it was an order which could have been made.

Counsel for the respondent argued that *McDaid* could not apply in the present case, because the petitioners were not persons who could have operated the provisions for appeal. It certainly appears that the petitioners had no interest in the land at the time of the compulsory purchase order and so could not have appealed, and in that respect the reasoning in *McDaid* does not apply to the petitioners themselves. But it seems to me that this point relates rather to their title to sue the present application than to the relevance of the case of *McDaid* to the circumstances of the present case. So far as title was concerned I did not understand it to be disputed that the petitioners were standing in the shoes of the trustees, and the trustees undoubtedly would have been able to challenge the order had they known of it.

In light of the authorities to which I have referred, it appears to me that the present application is rendered incompetent by virtue of para. 16 of Sched. 1. The provisions of that paragraph are clear and plain. The ground of challenge proposed here is that a requirement of the Act has not been complied with, namely the requirement for service in para. 3. That is specifically mentioned in para. 15 as a ground of challenge which may be made within the prescribed period of six weeks. In light of the provision for the appeal within the six weeks contained in para. 15, I take the view that the present application is excluded by para. 16. This seems to me to be a case which follows *Smith, Hamilton* and *Ostler* rather than *Anisminic* and *McDaid*. Both in *Smith* (Viscount Simonds at p. 748) and in *Ostler* (Lord Denning at p. 136) there was recognition of the policy of Parliament in relation to compulsory purchase orders that finality and security from challenge should be achieved in the public interest. The intention of para. 16 is in my view to exclude the kind of challenge which is made in the present case outwith the time limit expressly prescribed for the making of just such a challenge."

Notes

10–41   (1) The case is discussed in P.W. Ferguson, "The Limits of Judicial Review", 1987 S.L.T. (News) 306 and for a reply see T. Mullen, "Time Limit Clauses and Judicial Review — Some Further Thoughts" 1988 S.L.T. (News) 9. Ferguson suggests that *Martin* is not consistent with *Anisminic*, founding on the approach in *McDaid* v. *Clydebank District Council*, 1984 S.L.T. 162, arguing that "even an absolute prohibition against judicial review cannot prevent the courts from reversing a decision which is ultra vires" (at 306). His concern was that fundamental nullities should not be given any protection. Mullen, founding on the analysis of Lord Clyde, emphasised the need for certainty in administrative schemes. Similarly, E. Young and J. Rowan-Robinson, *Scottish Planning Law and Procedure* (1985) argue that *McDaid* would drive a coach and horses through such clauses (p. 336). Section 233 is now contained in section 239 of the Town and Country Planning (Scotland) Act 1997, on which see para. 12–18. Do you accept that there is a principled distinction between the clause found in *McDaid* and here? Some support for Ferguson's views might also be found in the JUSTICE-All Souls Report, para. 7.18, which argued that where a case of fraud or bad faith could be made out then the rule in *Smith* and *Ostler* should not apply, notwithstanding the lapse of a statutory time-limit. They argued that any remedy of damages against the individual responsible for the fraud may not sufficiently redress the wrong suffered. Note too, that it is not possible to invoke common law challenge by way of ordinary judicial review proceedings whether or not the six-week time-limit has expired: *Pollock* v. *Secretary of State for Scotland*, 1993 S.L.T. 1173. *McDaid* has not been followed in England: see *R.* v. *Collett* [1994] Crim. L.R. 607.

(2) Other forms of clause have been used. In *Institute of Patent-Agents* v. *Lockwood* (1894) 21 R. (H.L.) 61 a clause in a statutory instrument to the effect that it should be treated in law as "if enacted in this Act" put it beyond judicial control. However, that approach was disavowed in *McEwen's Trustees* v. *Church of Scotland*, 1940 S.L.T. 35 *General Trustees* at 359 *per* Lord President Normand and challenge along *Anisminic* lines would now be competent. The expression that a decision "shall be final" has also been used and, where directly effective European Community law rights are relevant to the decision, such a clause is unlikely to be upheld: *Johnston* v. *Chief Constable of the Royal Ulster Constabulary* [1987] Q.B. 129, on which see P. Oliver, "Enforcing Community Rights in the English Courts" (1987) 50 M.L.R. 881. If, however, such a clause is held to be effective then it would appear that even an appeal on a point of law would be precluded: *Re Racal Communications* [1981] A.C. 374, and would also overcome the possibility of an action of negligence against the decision maker: *Jones* v. *Department of Employment* [1989] Q.B. 1.

(3) There has been a degree of statutory intervention in relation to such clauses.

Tribunals and Inquiries Act 1992

"Supervisory functions of superior courts not excluded by Acts passed before 1st August 1958
12. . . . .

(2) As respects Scotland —

(a) any provision in an Act passed before 1st August 1958 that any order or determination shall not be called into question in any court, or

(b) any provision in such an Act which by similar words excludes any jurisdiction which the Court of Session would otherwise have to entertain an application for reduction or suspension of any order or determination, or otherwise to consider the validity of any order or determination, shall not have effect so as to prevent the exercise of any such jurisdiction.

(3) Nothing in this section shall apply —

(a) to any order or determination of a court of law, or

(b) where an Act makes special provision for application to the High Court or the Court of Session within a time limited by the Act."

Schedule 1 of the Act lists tribunals subject to this provision. It was originally contained in section 10 of the Tribunals and Inquiries Act 1958. Why do you consider that it has not been extended to legislation passed subsequent to August 1, 1958? For a recent example of a statutory scheme not subject to section 12 see section 7 (8) of the Interception of Communications Act 1985, which provides that decisions of the tribunal established for hearing complaints of breaches of the Act's provisions are as follows:

"decisions of the Tribunal (including any decisions as to their jurisdiction) shall not be subject to appeal or liable to be questioned in any court".

See also the Security Service Act 1989 and the Intelligence Services Act 1994 for similar provisions.

(4) On restriction of judicial control generally see *Stair Memorial Encyclopaedia*, Vol. 1,   **10–42**
paras 306–307; Finch and Ashton, pp. 407–416; Young and Rowan Robinson, pp. 332–339, 533–536; N.P. Gravells, "Time Limit Clauses and Judicial Review — Some Second Thoughts" (1980) 43 M.L.R. 173; J.E. Adler, "Time Limit Clauses and Conceptualism — A Reply" (1980) 43 M.L.R. 670; L.H. Leigh, "Time Limit Clauses and Jurisdictional Error" [1980] P.L. 34; and C.T. Reid, "Judicial Review and the Environment" in *Judicial Review: A Thematic Approach* (B. Hadfield, ed., 1995.)

JUDICIAL REVIEW IN PRACTICE

10–43   So far we have been concerned with the operation of judicial review from a strictly legal standpoint. Where issues of restriction of judicial review have been examined, we have been concerned with formal limitations such as title and interest to sue, delay or the restriction of control by statute. We now look at some of the practical ways in which access to judicial review can be controlled. We will go on to examine the impact of judicial review on local authorities. The following materials are drawn from detailed research carried out by the researchers at Glasgow University and published in T. Mullen. K. Pick and T. Prosser, '*Judicial Review in Scotland*' (1996). The extracts are taken from summaries of their work published in the *Scottish Law & Practice Quarterly*.

JUDICIAL REVIEW AND LEGAL AID

T. Mullen, K. Pick and T. Prosser, "Judicial Review in Scotland Part II"

(1997) 2 S.L.P.Q. 1 at 9

"Grant and refusal of legal aid applications
10–44   The most interesting and relevant questions arising from a study of the legal aid hurdle relate to the fairness of decision-making, in particular whether decisions to grant or refuse legal aid are appropriate, in the sense that the statutory criteria are correctly and reasonably applied. If decision-making were too strict and meritorious applications were refused, the legal aid system would be acting as an improper barrier to the redress of citizens' grievances against the administration. If decision-making were lax and allowed groundless applications, public authorities would be being subjected to an unnecessary burden of frequently defending perfectly lawful and reasonable actions in the courts.
       Statistics on the rates of granting and refusing legal aid cannot, of course, tell us whether legal aid decision-making is fair and reasonable, but they may shed some light on the question. Table 2 shows the number of applications submitted and the number and proportion granted, refused or abandoned. The table is derived from the results of initial applications and the 'Granted' column does not include applications granted after review.

Table 2: Rates of grant and refusal of applications for legal aid for judicial review						
	1992/93		1993/94		Total 1992–94	
	No	%	No	%	No	%
Received	176	100	222	100	398	100
Granted initially	41	23.3	68	30.6	109	27.4
Granted on review	17	9.7	16	7.2	33	8.3
Total grants	58	33	84	37.8	142	35.7
Refused	100	56.8	125	56.3	225	56.5
Abandoned	18	10.2	13	5.9	31	7.8

       In 1992/93, 23.3 per cent of applications were initially granted, 66.5 per cent were initially refused and 10.2 per cent were abandoned. If abandonments are excluded, the initial grant rate becomes 25.9 per cent and the refusal rate 74.1 per cent. In forty-seven cases, the solicitor applied for a review of a refusal, and seventeen of these were granted after review, pushing the overall success rate (excluding abandonments) to 36.7 per cent. In 1993/94, 30.6 per cent of applications were granted initially, 63.5 per cent were refused and 5.9 per cent were abandoned. If abandonments are excluded the grant rate becomes 32.5 per cent and the refusal rate 67.5 per cent. In sixty-four cases the solicitor applied for a review of a refusal, and sixteen of these were granted after review, pushing the overall success rate for 1993/94 to 40.2 per cent, excluding abandonments. Thus there is a sizeable difference in success rates on initial application as between the two years, which narrows once reviews are added in. Aggregating the figures for the two years it appears that, excluding abandonments, less than one-third of applications (29.7 per cent) are granted initially, and less than two-fifths (38.7 per cent) once successful reviews are added in.

It is instructive to compare these figures both with the rate of success in civil legal applications generally in Scotland and with those found in the study of legal aid applications for judicial review in England and Wales. Space does not permit detailed analysis of the figures, but the overall conclusion is that applications for legal aid for judicial review are granted far less frequently in Scotland than applications generally.

A comparison with decisions taken by the Legal Aid Board in England and Wales shows that, in that jurisdiction, in the period under study, nearly 67.7 per cent of judicial review legal aid applications were granted on a legal aid officer's initial decision. A further 6.7 per cent were granted on appeal, making an overall success rate of 74.4 per cent. This overall figure masks considerable regional variation — for example, the London office, which handles the largest number of applications, allowed 81 per cent of all applications including those granted on appeal, whereas the South East office granted only 27.3 per cent initially, rising to 39.4 per cent after appeals. Over all, it appears that the rate at which legal aid applications for judicial review are initially granted in Scotland is less than half the average rate in England and Wales (29.7 per cent compared to 67.7 per cent), and is comparable only to the lowest grant rates in the thirteen area offices there. The difference between rates is less after appeal/review but still surprisingly wide (38.7 per cent compared to 74.4 per cent).

What, therefore, explains these dramatic differences in success rates in two broadly similar jurisdictions operating broadly similar legal aid systems? We must emphasise that it is not possible to provide a clear answer to questions about the causes of the difference without direct scrutiny of legal aid case files, and the statutory confidentiality rule prevented this being done. However, there is some useful evidence available which is relevant to the inquiry. The full report contains a detailed analysis of which only an outline can be given here.

It seems unlikely that the dramatic differences between success rates in Scotland and England can be explained by particular differences in the substantive law, or the administrative environment, or other factors potentially affecting the level of need for judicial review as between the two jurisdictions. This appears to leave us with the conclusion that the major causes of the differences are more likely to be the result of one of, or some combination of, two possibilities. The first is that Scottish decision-makers are taking a more restrictive approach to granting legal aid than English decision-makers. The second is that the overall quality of applications submitted by solicitors in Scotland is substantially poorer. If the difference lies mainly in the decision-making, this in itself would be worthy of comment, but we would also wish to know to what extent the difference was explained by Scottish decision-makers being stricter than was appropriate or by English decision-makers being unduly lax as compared to an ideal standard of legal aid decision-making.

Most of the solicitors and advocates interviewed for the adviser survey had definite views on this issue. The majority of the solicitors were unhappy to some degree with legal aid decision-making, and some were very strongly critical. They complained that meritorious cases were refused legal aid, or that they had to expend a lot of effort convincing the Board to award legal aid in worthy cases. They suggested that there was a lack of relevant expertise among legal aid decision-makers in that they appeared not fully to understand the substantive principles of judicial review and the legislation and case-law relevant to particular statutory functions. Advocates' views were equally negative, but where the emphasis of their comments differed was in the belief that the poor quality of decision-making worked both ways, granting groundless applications as well as refusing worthy ones.

The view of the Board's staff is that, if the grant rate was substantially lower than it might be, this was primarily due to the standard of the applications. Certain faults recurred in a large proportion of applications, including documentation which was often badly reconciled, the omission of essential information, failure to focus the legal arguments to be relied upon, and failure to state why the decision was thought to be unlawful in terms of the accepted principles of judicial review.

None of this proves that the quality of legal aid decision-making is defective. But bearing in mind the considerable disquiet expressed by solicitors and advocates, and the fact that grant rates are much lower than in England and Wales, it appears that there is at least a case to answer and a need for further inquiry. Whether the explanation for the differences lies, as solicitors suggest, primarily in the decision-making process, or whether it lies in the quality of legal aid applications submitted by solicitors, it appears that Scottish residents seeking legal aid for the purposes of judicial review are not as well served as they should be, and that access to justice for the citizen is not on an equal footing in Scotland and England.

There is one feature of the English judicial review procedure — the requirement of leave to proceed — which might be having an impact on grant rates. Limited certificates are routinely granted in judicial review matters in England, whereas they would not be considered in an application for judicial review in Scotland. In all, 83 per cent of English grants were limited, the limitation usually being that the legal aid certificate is used initially only for the purpose of obtaining leave to seek judicial review. It may be that the decision to grant legal aid in borderline cases tends to be tipped in favour of the applicant because of the belief that the court will knock out groundless cases at the leave stage. This phenomenon may be making some contribution to the differential grant rates, but the research in England and Wales does not establish that it is a major cause of high grant rates, and it is unlikely that it can be the major cause of differences in grant rates as between the two jurisdictions. In fact our findings fit very well into the pattern of regional variation in England and Wales. If there were jurisdiction-wide features of the two legal aid systems which explained the differences in grant rates one would have expected regional grant rates in England and Wales to be consistently higher than in Scotland. The fact that there are such wide regional variations in England and Wales suggests that the explanation lies more in differences in administrative practice as between legal aid offices. It is also worth stating that if the combination of the leave requirement with the practice of granting limited certificates is reducing the ability of the English system to filter out unmeritorious legal aid applications, it provides a further argument against the introduction of a leave requirement in Scottish judicial review procedure.

The outcome of legally aided judicial reviews

In the first part of this article we noted that the court records appeared to indicate that there were not large numbers of groundless applications for judicial review being lodged *in general*. This conclusion also seems to apply to legally aided cases. We have not been able to follow up the actual cases on which the legal aid data discussed above are based, as many of them fall outside the period for which we examined court records. However, we are able to assess outcomes for the cases in our court database which appear to have been legally aided. The figures for the calendar years 1992 and 1993 would appear to be the most relevant.

If we use the measures of successful outcomes already described we find that in 1992, 53.5 per cent of legally aided petitions (23) were finally resolved with some degree of success for the petitioner. If cases otherwise taken out of court (which are impossible to classify in terms of outcome) are excluded from the analysis, the rate of success is 60.5 per cent. In 1993 rates of success appear to have dropped, with only 38.5 per cent of all legally aided petitioners (20) being to some degree successful, rising to 41.7 per cent if cases otherwise taken out of court are excluded. The 1993 figures are against the long-term trend, with the overall success rate for legally aided petitioners for 1988–1993 being 45.4 per cent (88), rising to 48.9 per cent if cases otherwise taken out of court are excluded.

In fact, the real rate of success is higher because the figures for final outcomes are affected by the peculiar features of immigration cases already discussed in the first part of this article. When allowance is made for this, success rates in legally aided cases appear much higher and the apparent drop in the success rate in 1993 can be explained away. Over all, the figures indicate quite respectable success rates for legally aided petitioners, and would tend to rebut any suggestion that legal aid decision-making is insufficiently do not do is reinforce the reverse hypothesis — that legal aid decision-making is too stric — although they are at least consistent with it."

There appear to be a number of significant issues involved in whether or not to grant legal aid. There appears to be some concern about whether there is adequate understanding of the tests in administrative law which an applicant might be invoking in their application. This is perhaps not surprising given that until 1985 judicial review was a little used procedure resulting in few applications for legal aid. The quality of decision making may improve simply due to experience.

KNOWLEDGE OF THE REMEDY

T. Mullen, K. Pick and T. Prosser, "Judicial Review in Scotland Part II"

(1997) 2 S.L.P.Q. 1 AT 13

"Survey of solicitors and lay advisers

10–45   The majority of solicitors in the sample reported at least some casework deriving from existing clients for whom they had acted on other matters, or from new clients making a direct approach to the solicitor on their own initiative. However, nearly half had never experienced this and derived their judicial review caseload solely from referrals from other agencies. Taking all the solicitors in the sample together, it is quite clear that the bulk of their caseload, which was primarily on the welfare law side of judicial review, was obtained by referral from lay advice agencies. The main sources of referral were Shelter and other specialist housing advice agencies, CABx, local authority social work departments (welfare rights officers and other social work staff), and the IAS.

Identifying cases as suitable for referral to solicitors

The role of lay advice agencies is crucial. They are clearly operating as gatekeepers in relation to judicial review. It appears that they are responsible for 'finding' the majority of cases for solicitors in the welfare law area. This places a heavy premium on the quality of advice given by lay advice agencies, in particular their ability to determine whether there might be a legal remedy for the client's grievance. The impression we have is that the ability of lay advisers to spot cases that are worth sending to solicitors as potential reviews is extremely variable. There may also be other factors at work which affea the propensity of advisers to refer cases to solicitors. Therefore, the level of activity on the welfare law side of judicial review is to a large extent determined by what the advice agencies do rather than by the extent of legal need.

The evidence for this general conclusion is, first, the comments made by those we interviewed. These were not unanimous, but many solicitors and some lay advisers suggested that many lay advisers are unaware of the possibilities that exist for judicial review. One solicitor who specialised in housing law described his experience in this way.

> 'No, I don't think we have had any CAB referrals. If I was asked to generalise on my experience, I would say we get a number of referrals from the CAB, but I cannot think of a single judicial review type referral, and I suspect that is because the CAB will try to pursue the matter through the normal housing channels first of all, and, secondly, I suspect they do not know that many of the administrative decisions of councils are open to judicial review ... it appears to be a well-kept secret among referral agencies.'

Another solicitor (who had been a welfare rights officer for a number of years) commented:

> 'I think one problem is on the social security side. People tend to concentrate on threatening judicial review because of delay and they are hooked on that one... focusing on that as if it was the only thing you could review, and not fully understanding the capacity to challenge the social fund inspector's decisions — only 14 challenges out of hundreds.'

> 'Social fund inspectors are a prime target and there you have a situation where people in the welfare rights industry take cases to the social fund inspector and stop at that point. They don't look at the decision critically. They don't seek professional legal advice and they don't consider whether or not it is worth challenging it ... There does not seem to be an awareness or proper training.'

There were many other comments in this vein.

The view that the ability of lay advisers to spot potential cases that are worth sending to solicitors as potential reviews is extremely variable is reinforced by the information derived from Court of Session and legal aid records which were discussed in some detail earlier in this article. These showed that the geographical distribution of relevant legal work is extremely patchy, and it does not appear possible plausibly to explain this distribution by reference to objective factors such as population size or local authority policies. Further reinforcement for the conclusion above comes from the impact study (discussed below) which shows that the number of judicial reviews mounted against local authority is a very uncertain indicator of the extent to which public authority decision-making complies with administrative law standards. It did not appear that the authorities most frequently reviewed were necessarily making more potentially reviewable decisions than other authorities who had largely escaped review.

It might be argued that the maldistribution of judicial review work merely indicate that there are problems with advising in general, without indicating whether they lid of the side of lay advisers or solicitors. Thus it is possible that many cases are being referred to solicitors who are then wrongly advising clients that they have no remedy. No doubt the low level of judicial review work in certain subject areas is caused by problems of both sides of the referral system. However, it seems more likely that non-referral is the greater problem, because we so often found that solicitors who were active in judicial review depended heavily on lay advice agencies for their caseload, and because of certain other characteristics of the lay advice network which will be discussed below.

The availability and quality of advice from lay agencies appears to vary according to subject-matter and geography. Our general conclusion is that the specialist housing advice agencies appear to perform much better on the whole than non-specialist agencies such as CABx.

However, as the example of social security shows, the proposition that specialist advice agencies are more successful at identifying potential judicial reviews than non specialist agencies is only true as a generalisation. Although this is a field well served by specialist agencies (both local authority and voluntary sector), the absolute number of petitions in social security matters and the number of legal aid applications are low. These figures tend to raise an inference that potential reviews in the social security field are being missed either by referral agencies or by solicitors not putting forward legal aid applications, and the information and opinions derived from our survey tended to support this inference.

The potential for judicial review in this field was illustrated by the experience of one solicitor and one welfare rights officer. The solicitor had a varied social security caseload which had included the following issues: delay in fixing social security appeal hearings various housing benefit matters, arguably illegal deductions of social fund loans from other benefits, and decisions made under the DSS *ex gratia* compensation scheme. This solicitor had more than one source of referral, but had received several dozen relevant referrals from a single welfare rights officer. The welfare rights officer concerned had neither special duties nor an extended catchment area. His cases were all derived from the area covered by his social work office, one of twenty-three in the Glasgow sub-region of Strathclyde Region. By contrast, most of the solicitors interviewed had received no referrals from welfare rights officers or other agencies in social security matters, and it was apparent that most other social work area offices did not even begin to approach this level of referral.

Solicitors' casework profile

With one or two exceptions, the solicitors interviewed had a relatively small caseload. Only a handful had had more than three or four cases proceed as far as a petition for judicial review in the Court of Session. For one or two, the actual litigation caseload was the DSS, all of which were settled by correspondence. However, for most solicitors there was not much more of the iceberg under water. The handful of actual judicial reviews they had conducted was a substantial fraction of their total relevant casework, ie, there were only a few more potential reviews which settled without going to court. The majority dealt with judicial review primarily in respect of a particular area such as homelessness or immigration control, with a few having a varied portfolio.

We interviewed several solicitors from law centres. Given that their avowed purpose is the satisfaction of unmet legal need, one might have thought that law centres would be very much to the fore in judicial review. In fact, law centres in general have not been particularly prominent in judicial review, although most have had some involvement. The law centre with the largest caseload is the Legal Services Agency, which had a larger caseload than nearly all the private sector firms interviewed. A number of special factors apply to the Legal Services Agency. Unlike the other law centres surveyed, it is a national organisation and has offices in Edinburgh and Glasgow. It had by far the largest staff complement (larger than many of the private firms interviewed) and the most varied portfolio of general casework. The most important of the special factors is that Shelter has sub-contracted to it the operation of the Shelter Scottish Housing Law Service (SHLS). This results in large numbers of referrals, particularly of homelessness cases. Between early 1994 and late 1995 solicitors at the Legal Services Agency had lodged more than a dozen petitions for judicial review derived from SHLS referrals, primarily homelessness cases. It would be going too far to say that this is a model which should be copied, but it indicates how the nature of arrangements for referral can apparently increase the level of judicial review in a particular area."

Notes

Clearly legal remedy is of little use if advisers are not aware of its potential application or its scope. Judicial review is peculiar in that, as will be seen from the table in the previous extract, many of those seeking the remedy fall within what is often regarded as being cases of "unmet legal need", such as housing, education, social security and similar "welfare" areas which are not regarded as being a traditional source of work for solicitors. This is perhaps reinforced by the fact that would-be petitioners will not perhaps regard their problem as a legal one and accordingly may not seek advice from a solicitor.

THE IMPACT OF JUDICIAL REVIEW

10–46   Decided cases only tell one side of the story when it comes to assessing the impact of judicial review on administrative bodies. In *Law and Administration* (1984), C. Harlow and R. Rawlings note that although "The number of cases is infinitesimal compared with the millions of decisions taken daily by public authorities" one court decision may affect "perhaps, thousands of similar cases" and that "The mere existence of judicial review and the creation of precedent may influence future administrative behaviour" (at pp. 258–261). This is in the context of the United Kingdom as a whole. What has been the Scottish experience? The following extract from the same article gives some indication of the impact of the remedy. Research was carried out in relation to two authorities on how they handled decisions and applications for housing by homeless persons during the period 1988–94.

T. Mullen, K. Pick and T. Prosser, "Judicial Review in Scotland Part II"

(1997) 2 S.L.P.Q. 1 at 20

"The two authorities dealt differently with petitions for judicial review. In authority A housing officials had chosen to bypass the legal department and dealt directly with Edinburgh agents. This was because they thought that they had greater expertise in the area of homelessness than the legal department, and were seriously dissatisfied with the nature of the service offered to them on housing law in general. The housing department has a relatively robust and combative approach to judicial review proceedings. Although they frequently revised decisions through the internal appeal procedure, when a decision had been confirmed through this procedure, their initial reaction was always to defend judicial review proceedings. It appeared that their confidence in their decisions was not in any way shaken by receipt of a petition for review. Indeed officials were prepared to argue to us that one of the decisions of the court which had gone against them was wrongly decided.

By contrast, the legal service in authority B had a substantial involvement in the conduct of judicial review proceedings. They tended not to become involved until a petition had been served on the council or proceedings were imminent. Once the legal service became involved, they managed the case, corresponding with Edinburgh agents, and obtaining any necessary information from the housing department. The legal department regularly found itself in the position of having less confidence in the soundness of the council's position than did the housing department. So, although most petitions were actually settled, this tended not to occur until proceedings had been live for some time and there had been a substantial exchange of correspondence with Edinburgh agents and some discussion of the issues in open court.

Of the ten petitions lodged in authority A, eight resulted in some measure of success for the petitioners in court, in the sense that either the petition was granted or the petition was dismissed on the basis that the council would reconsider its decision. Most petitioners ultimately obtained council accommodation as a result of taking legal action, including the two whose cases had 'failed' in court. There was only one case in which, having reconsidered its decision, the council reinstated an adverse decision finding that the petitioner became homeless intentionally. Therefore, although the council on occasion is willing to follow a 'successful' petition for review with a further decision to refuse to provide permanent accommodation, petitioners normally did obtain accommodation as a result of a petition being granted or a settlement achieved in court.

In seven of the ten petitions in authority B, the petitioner had some degree of success in court in that the petition was granted or settled on the basis that the council would offer accommodation or at least reconsider the application. Most petitioners ultimately obtained some form of accommodation from the council as a result of taking legal action. One of the three whose petitions were refused was allocated a council house shortly after the conclusion of proceedings on a discretionary basis. Six of the seven 'successful' petitioners were allocated housing by the council, the remaining case being one where reconsideration led to reinstatement of the original decision. However, there appears to have been more resistance to rehousing successful judicial review applicants than this brief summary suggests. In a number of cases the local offices to whom the responsibility had been allocated appear to have delayed allocating temporary accommodation because of reluctance to rehouse that particular petitioner, necessitating strongly-worded reminders from either housing headquarters or the legal service.

Most of the cases which were successful from the petitioner's point of view in both authorities raised doubts about the legality of the particular decision only and not the legality of council policy or procedures. However, a few cases clearly raised such issues. Authority A had one case which could be regarded as a test case. It established that they were applying the wrong test to determine whether a person had a local connection with their area by adopting a strict definition of family which was inconsistent with the definition of s 83 in the 1987 Act. As a result they had wrongly tried to refer the application to an authority in England. They had relied on an erroneous explanation of local connection appearing in the agreement on referrals adopted by COSLA and used by all Scottish local authorities. The council wrote to COSLA explaining the implications of the decision. No action had been taken by the time of local government reorganisation in April 1996, although the matter had received some consideration. The council itself intended to observe the court's ruling on the meaning of s 83 in future cases.

In another case the Lord Ordinary had made suggestions about the information which decision letters in a particular type of intentional homelessness case should contain. It was not clear whether this had any impact on the way decision letters were drafted.

It did appear that reaction to judicial review in authority B was not confined to reconsideration of specific decisions. The legal department on several occasions drew the conclusion that a particular judicial review revealed general deficiencies in the way in which decisions were taken. One notable example was the first of the crop of cases in 1992 in which the housing department received an application from a middle-aged man recently discharged from a mental hospital. He was advised (wrongly) that he could not be considered to be in priority need (on grounds of vulnerability) unless he produced medical certificates. A number of months passed without any final decision being made and an offer of accommodation was not made until after a petition for judicial review had been lodged.

The head of the legal service then wrote to the director of housing suggesting that the case highlighted deficiencies in the council's approach. This was the catalyst fur the introduction of a programme of training consisting of seminars on homelessness given by legal staff for housing staff which have been repeated at regular intervals. It appears also that the practice of effectively requesting applicants to obtain the evidence necessary to prove vulnerability in cases of poor mental and physical health was abandoned. Efforts had been made to reduce the delay in processing cases, but we did not attempt to measure change in the speed of processing applications over time.

Other attempts to achieve improvements across the board were less successful. The investigation of cases and the drafting of decision letters were areas of concern. These were often unhelpfully brief and did not always disclose the effective reason for a decision. At the conclusion of one set of proceedings in late 1993, Edinburgh agents suggested that there were lessons to be learned with regard to decision letters. The housing department agreed to take action to improve decision letters. Approximately ten months later (late summer 1994), the judge in a further petition, although refusing to reduce a decision that the petitioner did not have a priority need for accommodation, commented adversely on the decision letter which he thought was so uninformative that it would tend to provoke suspicion and lead to litigation. This judicial comment led the head of legal services to send a further memo to the director of housing suggesting that, since the decision letter was typical of the letters issued in all homeless cases, failure to have regard to the judge's comments would only leave the council open to challenge in future cases. Again, the director of housing responded positively, but from our scrutiny of ordinary case files, it appeared that in the spring of 1995 decision letters were no more detailed than they were before."

Notes

10–47   Within the decisions examined by the study, it will be seen that at least one of them, that of section 83 of the 1987 Act in relation to authority "A", might be regarded as one which "may influence administrative behaviour". Unsurprisingly, perhaps the bulk of the cases examined appear to be rather more mundane. With the exception of the specific example given in relation to authority "B" on priority need, it is perhaps difficult to escape the conclusion that judicial review may lead to a defensive culture in public administration, rather than a concerted effort to ensure that the decision making is improved by better training, greater knowledge of the law, and the availability of more sensitive internal review mechanisms.

M. Sunkin and A.P. Le Sueur, "Can Government Control Judicial Review?" (1991) 44 C.L.P. 161 made a study of administrative defensiveness. In particular the article discusses the establishment of an official group of high-ranking civil servants to assess the perceived growth in judicial activity. The steps to be taken to avoid judicial review included anticipating legal challenge rather than reacting to it, expressing decisions in legislation in the clearest possible terms, broadening legal awareness through a pamphlet "The Judge over Your Shoulder" and the development of closer links between administrators and government lawyers. Some attempt at a positive reaction to judicial review was also made, with legal awareness training "aimed at inculcating habits of good administrative conduct". The overall impression of the impact of judicial review and the guidance given was (at 175):

> "that if the new ethos is having an effect it is to encourage officials to become more cautious in their work and more aware of the need to explain and justify action."

Mullen, Pick and Prosser appear to reach a similar overall conclusion in stating that (at 23):

> "Our findings seem to support the familiar propositions that judicial review has a limited impact on public administration and that, if the goal of administrative lawyers is to ensure that there is respect for legality in all bureaucratic decision-making, attention needs to be paid to the internal processes and administrative culture of public authorities. The findings do not support the extreme view that judicial review is largely irrelevant".

JUDICIAL CONTROL UNDER THE SCOTLAND ACT 1998

We have noted that one of the Government's hopes was that sufficient scrutiny would be given to the *vires* of Acts of the Scottish Parliament before they became law and so there are mechanisms for the scrutiny of Bills by the members of the Scottish Executive and by the Presiding Officer, under section 31 (noted at para. 3–12), for reference of Bills at the pre-Assent stage to the Judicial Committee of the Privy Council under sections 32–36 and also the power of the Secretary of State to intervene in certain cases, where there is doubt as to the *vires* of Bill under section 35, on which see para. 6–38. Even with such scrutiny, doubts will still arise post-enactment as to the *vires* of Scottish legislation. Equally the *vires* of acts and decisions of the Scottish Executive, including subordinate legislation, will also be open to judicial scrutiny but, unlike primary legislation, will not be subject to any judicial scrutiny in advance. Note, however, that it is likely that the Parliament's delegated legislation committee will have power to raise concerns on the *vires* of delegated or subordinate legislation on which see para. 2–25.   **10–48**

Scotland Act 1998

ss. 33 (1)–(3), 34, 36 (4) (*a*)(*b*)

"Scrutiny of Bills by the Judicial Committee

33.— (1) The Advocate General, the Lord Advocate or the Attorney General may refer the question of whether a Bill or any provision of a Bill would be within the legislative competence of the Parliament to the Judicial Committee for decision.   **10–49**

(2) Subject to subsection (3), he may make a reference in relation to a Bill at any time during —
(a)   the period of four weeks beginning with the passing of the Bill, and
(b)   any period of four weeks beginning with any subsequent approval of the Bill in accordance with standing orders made by virtue of section 36(5).

(3) He shall not make a reference in relation to a Bill if he has notified the Presiding Officer that he does not intend to make a reference in relation to the Bill, unless the Bill has been approved as mentioned in subsection (2)(b) since the notification.

ECJ references

34. — (1) This section applies where —
(a)   a reference has been made in relation to a Bill under section 33,
(b)   a reference for a preliminary ruling has been made by the Judicial Committee in connection with that reference, and
(c)   neither of those references has been decided or otherwise disposed of.

(2) If the Parliament resolves that it wishes to reconsider the Bill —
(a)   the Presiding Officer shall notify the Advocate General, the Lord Advocate and the Attorney General of that fact, and
(b)   the person who made the reference in relation to the Bill under section 33 shall request the withdrawal of the reference.

(3) In this section 'a reference for a preliminary ruling' means a reference of a question to the European Court under Article 177 of the Treaty establishing the European Community, Article 41 of the Treaty establishing the European Coal and Steel Community or Article 150 of the Treaty establishing the European Atomic Energy Community.

Stages of Bills

36.…(4) Standing orders shall provide for an opportunity for the reconsideration of a Bill after its passing if (and only if) —
(a)   the Judicial Committee decide that a Bill or any provision of it would not be within the legislative competence of the Parliament,
(b)   a reference made in relation to the Bill under section 33 is withdrawn following a request for withdrawal of the reference under section 34(2)(b)…"

Notes

For discussion see C.M.G. Himsworth and C.R. Munro, "*Devolution and the Scotland Bill*" (1998), pp. 62–66, and by the same authors, *The Scotland Act 1998* (1999) pp. 46–51; and A.O'Neill, "The Scotland Act and the Government of Judges", 1999 S.L.T. (News) 61.   **10–50**

The scheme of the Scotland Act does not deal with issues of judicial competence, nor is there any attempt to legislate in advance for what parties and in which proceedings, issues of developed competence will arise. A multiplicity of examples could be imagined — citizens or groups of citizens making a challenge against a devolved institution, or a challenge by the U.K. Government to the *vires* of an Act of the Scottish Parliament, or a challenge by the Scottish Executive to an attempt by the U.K. Government to exercise the powers open to it under, for example, section 58 (extracted at para. 13–10). While it is conceivable that the typical forum will be judicial review in the Court of Session, that will not necessarily be the exclusive or only one. Issues of *vires* are just as likely to arise in the context of an appeal or indeed in ordinary civil litigation in the sheriff court where, for example, a defender in a reparation action argues that statutory liability imposed upon him by an Act of the Scottish Parliament is unlawful. A defence based on the *vires* of criminal legislation might also arise in the context of criminal proceedings. The scope for direct or collateral challenge (the defence of illegality on which see para. 11–20) is therefore considerable.

The only substantial intervention in this field is contained in section 98 and Schedule 6 to the Act by the creation of procedures relating to "devolution issues".

Scotland Act 1998

s. 98

"Devolution issues

10–51   98. Schedule 6 (which makes provision in relation to devolution issues) shall have effect."

Scotland Act 1998

Sched. 6, pts I, II, V

10–52   "SCHEDULE 6
DEVOLUTION ISSUES
PART 1
PRELIMINARY

1. In this Schedule 'devolution issue' means —
    (a) a question whether an Act of the Scottish Parliament or any provision of an Act of the Scottish Parliament is within the legislative competence of the Parliament.
    (b) a question whether any function (being a function which any person has purported, or is proposing, to exercise) is a function of the Scottish Ministers, the First Minister or the Lord Advocate.
    (c) a question whether the purported or proposed exercise of a function by a member of the Scottish Executive is, or would be, within devolved competence,
    (d) a question whether a purported or proposed exercise of a function by a member of the Scottish Executive is, or would be, incompatible with any of the Convention rights or with Community law,
    (e) a question whether a failure to act by a member of the Scottish Executive is incompatible with any of the Convention rights or with Community law.
    (f) any other question about whether a function is exercisable within developed competence or in or as regards Scotland and any other question arising by virtue of this Act about reserved matters.
2. A devolution issue shall not be taken to arise in any proceedings merely because of any contention of a party to the proceedings which appears to the court or tribunal before which the proceedings take place to be frivolous or vexatious.

PART II
PROCEEDINGS IN SCOTLAND

Application of Part II
3. This Part of this Schedule applies in relation to devolution issues in proceedings in Scotland.

Institution of proceedings

4 — (1) Proceedings for the determination of a devolution issue may be instituted by the Advocate General or the Lord Advocate.

(2) The Lord Advocate may defend any such proceedings instituted by the Advocate General.

(3) This paragraph is without prejudice to any power to institute or defend proceedings exercisable apart from this paragraph by any person.

Intimation of devolution issue

5. Intimation of any devolution issue which arises in any proceedings before a court or tribunal shall be given to the Advocate General and the Lord Advocate (unless the person to whom the intimation would be given is a party to the proceedings).

6. A person to whom intimation is given in pursuance of paragraph 5 may take part as a party in the proceedings, so far as they relate to a devolution issue.

Reference of devolution issue to higher court

7. A court, other than the House of Lords or any court consisting of three or more judges of the Court of Session, may refer any devolution issue which arises in proceedings (other than criminal proceedings) before it to the Inner House of the Court of Session.

8. A tribunal from which there is no appeal shall refer any devolution issue which arises in proceedings before it to the Inner House of the Court of Session; and any other tribunal may make such a reference.

9. A court, other than any court consisting of two or more judges of the High Court of Justiciary, may refer any devolution issue which arises in criminal proceedings before it to the High Court of Justiciary.

References from superior courts to Judicial Committee

10. Any court consisting of three or more judges of the Court of Session may refer any devolution issue which arises in proceedings before it (otherwise than on a reference under paragraph 7 or 8) to the Judicial Committee.

11. Any court consisting of two or more judges of the High Court of Justiciary may refer any devolution issue which arises in proceedings before it (otherwise than on a reference under paragraph 9) to the Judicial Committee.

Appeals from superior courts to Judicial Committee

12. An appeal against a determination of a devolution issue by the Inner House of the Court of Session on a reference under paragraph 7 or 8 shall lie to the Judicial Committee.

13. An appeal against a determination of a devolution issue by —

(a) a court of two or more judges of the High Court of Justiciary (whether in the ordinary course of proceedings or on a reference under paragraph 9), or

(b) a court of three or more judges of the Court of Session from which there is no appeal to the House of Lords.

shall lie to the Judicial Committee, but only with leave of the court concerned or, failing such leave, with special leave of the Judicial Committee.

PART V
GENERAL

Proceedings in the House of Lords

32. Any devolution issue which arises in judicial proceedings in the House of Lords shall be referred to the Judicial Committee unless the House considers it more appropriate, having regard to all the circumstances, that it should determine the issue.

Direct references to Judicial Committee

33. The Lord Advocate, the Advocate General, the Attorney General or the Attorney General for Northern Ireland may require any court or tribunal to refer to the Judicial Committee any devolution issue which has arisen in proceedings before it to which he is a party.

34. The Lord Advocate, the Attorney General, the Advocate General or the Attorney General for Northern Ireland may refer to the Judicial Committee any devolution issue which is not the subject of proceedings.

35. — (1) This paragraph applies where a reference is made under paragraph 34 in relation to a devolution issue which relates to the proposed exercise of a function by a member of the Scottish Executive.

(2) The person making the reference shall notify a member of the Scottish Executive of that fact.

(3) No member of the Scottish Executive shall exercise the function in the manner proposed during the period beginning with the receipt of the notification under sub-paragraph (2) and ending with the reference being decided or otherwise disposed of.

(4) Proceedings relating to any possible failure by a member of the Scottish Executive to comply with sub-paragraph (3) may be instituted by the Advocate General.

(5) Sub-paragraph (4) is without prejudice to any power to institute proceedings exercisable apart from that sub-paragraph by any person.

Expenses

36. — (1) A court or tribunal before which any proceedings take place may take account of any additional expense of the kind mentioned in sub-paragraph (3) in deciding any question as to costs or expenses.

(2) In deciding any such question, the court or tribunal may award the whole or part of the additional expense as costs or (as the case may be) expenses to the party who incurred it (whatever the decision on the devolution issue).

(3) The additional expense is any additional expense which the court or tribunal considers that any party to the proceedings has incurred as a result of the participation of any person in pursuance of paragraph 6, 17 or 27.

Procedure of courts and tribunals

37. Any power to make provision for regulating the procedure before any court or tribunal shall include power to make provision for the purposes of this Schedule including, in particular, provision —

(a) for prescribing the stage in the proceedings at which a devolution issue is to be raised or referred.

(b) for the sisting or staying of proceedings for the purpose of any proceedings under this Schedule, and

(c) for determining the manner in which and the time within which any intimation or notice is to be given.

Interpretation

38. Any duty or power conferred by this Schedule to refer a devolution issue to a court shall be construed as a duty or (as the case may be) power to refer the issue to the court for decision."

Notes

10–53 (1) Subparagraph (a) is the classic case of a devolution issue, where there is a question of competence as defined by sections 29,30 and Schedule 4 and 5 to the Act, on which see para. 3–10. Subparagraph (b) is concerned with the issue of whether or not a particular function has been conferred on the First Minister, on the Lord Advocate or on the Scottish Ministers and could conceivably include the situation where the function is being exercised by some "other" person such as a Minister of the Crown where the function has been wholly transferred to such a person by section 53 or 63, on which see paras 13–8 and 13–9 respectively. Subparagraph (c) is concerned with whether a function has been exercised properly. Powers transferred by section 53 are exercisable within "devolved competence" defined in turn by reference to the legislative competence of the Scottish Parliament by section 54, on which see para. 3–10. For further comments see Himsworth and Munro (1999), pp. 189–196.

(2) Part II deals with certain procedural matters. In addition to these procedures, of course, a devolution issue may be taken on appeal by use of normal appellate procedures. Detailed rules of court procedure in devolution issue cases are contained in (for the Court of Session), Act of Sederunt (Devolution Issues Rules) 1999, for the Sheriff court, Act of Sederunt (Proceedings for Determinations of Devolutions Issues Rules) 1999 and for the criminal courts in both solemn and summary matters Act of Adjournal (Devolution Issues Rules) 1999. Parts III and IV make parallel provision for England and

Wales and Northern Ireland in the context of devolution issues arising there. Part V must be read along with the next section.

Scotland Act 1998

s. 103

"The Judicial Committee
103. — (1) Any decision of the Judicial Committee in proceedings under this Act shall be stated in open court and shall be binding in all legal proceedings (other than proceedings before the Committee).

(2) No member of the Judicial Committee shall sit and act as a member of the Committee in proceedings under this Act unless he holds or has held —
(a)　the office of a Lord of Appeal in Ordinary, or
(b)　high judicial office as defined in section 25 of the Appellate Jurisdiction Act 1876 (ignoring for this purpose section 5 of the Appellate Jurisdiction Act 1887).

(3) Her Majesty may by Order in Council —
(a)　confer on the Judicial Committee in relation to proceedings under this Act such powers as Her Majesty considers necessary or expedient,
(b)　apply the Judicial Committee Act 1833 in relation to proceedings under this Act with exceptions or modifications.
(c)　make rules for regulating the procedure in relation to proceedings under this Act before the Judicial Committee.

(4) In this section 'proceedings under this Act' means proceedings on a question referred to the Judicial Committee under section 33 or proceedings under Schedule 6."

10–54

Notes

(1) As noted below, the Act gives important functions to the Judicial Committee of the Privy Council. We have already noted that section 33 of the Act gives the Privy Council jurisdiction to determine whether a Bill or a provision of a Bill was within the legislative competence of the Scottish Parliament and Schedule 6 provides that the resolution of devolution issues will ultimately be a matter for the committee.

(2) What do you consider the precise relationship of a ruling under section 33 and the ruling on a devolution issue under Schedule 6 to be? In particular, should a decision under section 33 on the meaning of a Bill or provision in a Bill be treated as a precedent binding on lower courts when a devolution issue is raised in that court?

(3) For further comment see Himsworth and Munro (1999), pp. 129–130 and for argument that the Lord Chancellor should not be entitled to sit in proceedings under this section see *Hansard*, H.L. Vol. 593, cols 1968–1972 and D. Oliver, "Devolution, The Privy Council and the Lord Chancellor" [1999] P.L. 1. For the detailed rules of procedure governing the determination by the Judicial Committee see the Judicial Committee (Devolution Issues) Rules Order 1999 and the Judicial Committee (Powers in Devolution Cases) Order 1999. These rules govern both references under section 33 above and section 103.

(4) For general reading on sections 98, 103 and Schedule 6 see T. Mullen and T. Prosser, "Devolution and Administrative Law" (1998) 4 E.P.L. 479; J. Hopkins, "Devolution from a Comparative Prospective" (1998) 4 E.P.L. 323;B. Hadfield, "The Nature of Devolution in Scotland and Northern Ireland: Key Issues of Responsibility and Control" (1999) 1 Edin. L.Rev. 3: C. Boyd, "Parliament and Courts" in *Devolution to Scotland: The Legal Aspects* (T. St J. N. Bates ed., 1997); J. McFadden, "The Scottish Parliament: Provisions for Dispute Resolution" (1998) J.R. 221; Himsworth and Munro (1998), pp. 62–68; and A. O'Neill, "The Scotland Act and the Government of Judges", 1999 S.L.T. (News) 61. Where a devolution issue arises which alleges an infringement of a Convention right, the next section is of significance.

10–55

Scotland Act 1998

s. 100 (1),(2),(4)

"Human rights

10–56   **100.** — (1) This Act does not enable a person —

   (a)   to bring any proceedings in a court or tribunal on the ground that an act is incompatible with the Convention rights, or

   (b)   to rely on any of the Convention rights in any such proceedings, unless he would be a victim for the purposes of Article 34 of the Convention (within the meaning of the Human Rights Act 1998) if proceedings in respect of the act were brought in the European Court of Human Rights.

   (2) Subsection (1) does not apply to the Lord Advocate the Advocate General, the Attorney General or the Attorney General for Northern Ireland…

   (4) In this section 'act' means —

   (a)   making any legislation,

   (b)   any other act or failure to act, if it is the act or failure of a member of the Scottish Executive."

Notes

10–57   As originally drafted, the test for standing to challenge an alleged breach of a right under the Scotland Act was a familiar one of title and interest. This was felt to be inconsistent with the victim test contained in section 7 (1) of the Human Rights Act 1998. As drafted, this carried with it the possibility of a two-tier system of standing felt to be undesirable. The section is currently drafted as a result of debate at the House of Lords committee stage: *Hansard*, H.L. Vol. 593, cols 417–428. For section 8 (3), (4) of the Human Rights Act 1998 see para. 11–43. On section 100 generally see Himsworth and Munro (1999), pp. 124–125. Subsection (3), which is concerned with the question of damages arising in relation to a breach of Convention right, is extracted and discussed at para. 11–34.

JUDICIAL CONTROL UNDER THE HUMAN RIGHTS ACT 1998

10–58   As with judicial control under the Scotland Act, this legislation does not make any radical innovation on the forms of judicial control available. Instead, it relies essentially on pre-existing mechanisms and superimposes upon them a number of specific provisions which will apply when it is alleged that a Convention right has been breached. Sections 7 and 9 are to be brought into force on a date to be appointed.

Human Rights Act 1998

s. 7

Proceedings

10–59   **7.** — (1) A person who claims that a public authority has acted (or proposes to act) in a way which is made unlawful by section 6(1) may —

   (a) bring proceedings against the authority under this Act in the appropriate court or tribunal, or

   (b) rely on the Convention right or rights concerned in any legal proceedings, but only if he is (or would be) a victim of the unlawful act.

   (2) In subsection (1)(a) "appropriate court or tribunal" means such court or tribunal as may be determined in accordance with rules: and proceedings against an authority include a counterclaim or similar proceeding.

   (3) If the proceedings are brought on an application for judicial review, the applicant is to be taken to have a sufficient interest in relation to the unlawful act only if he is, or would be, a victim of that act.

   (4) If the proceedings are made by way of a petition for judicial review in Scotland, the applicant shall be taken to have title and interest to sue in relation to the unlawful act only if he is, or would be, a victim of that act.

   (5) Proceedings under subsection (1)(a) must be brought before the end of —

   (a)   the period of one year beginning with the date on which the act complained of took place; or

(b)   such longer period as the court or tribunal considers equitable having regard to all the circumstances.

but that is subject to any rule imposing a stricter time limit in relation to the procedure in question.

(6) In subsection (1)(b) "legal proceedings" includes —

(a)   proceedings brought by or at the instigation of a public authority; and

(b)   an appeal against the decision of a court or tribunal.

(7) For the purposes of this section, a person is a victim of an unlawful act only if he would be a victim for the purposes of Article 34 of the Convention if proceedings were brought in the European Court of Human Rights in respect of that act.

(8) Nothing in this Act creates a criminal offence.

(9) In this section 'rules' means —

(a)   in relation to proceedings before a court or tribunal outside Scotland, rules made by the Lord Chancellor or the Secretary of State for the purposes of this section or rules of court.

(b)   in relation to proceedings before a court or tribunal in Scotland, rules made by the Secretary of State for those purposes…

(10) In making rules, regard must be had to section 9…"

Notes

(1) For definition of "public authorities" see section 6 (6), extracted at para. 6–17 Subsection   **10–60**
(1)(*b*) makes it clear that reliance on a Convention right can be made in the context of the existing judicial proceedings, including judicial review proceedings, and accordingly Convention rights may be relied upon, in both attack or defence or collateral proceedings. Subsection (1)(*a*) therefore deals with those situations in which an allegation of a breach of a Convention right is made and there is no other existing avenue for redress. As a safety net, the provision is unlikely to be frequently relied upon.

(2) Note the use of the expression "victim" in subsection (1),(3),(4) and (7). Article 34 of the ECHR (as modified by the eleventh protocol, formerly Article 25), and the case law thereunder, will provide the basis upon which the victim test can be interpreted. This has a number of consequences.

First, where a number of grounds of challenge are alleged in judicial review proceedings, some but not all of which involve violation of Convention right, there will be two tests for title and interest. The victim test will be used where a ground of action is based on breach of a Convention right, but where another ground of action is used, which does not involve such an allegation, then the domestic test of title and interest discussed below will fall to be used. Is it desirable that there be a duality of tests?

Secondly, to qualify as a victim, it will generally be necessary to show more than that a Convention right has been breached. The European Court of Human Rights has, however, applied a relatively flexible interpretation as to what might amount to a breach. Thus in *Open Door Counselling and Dublin Well Woman Clinic* v. *Ireland* (1993) 15 E.H.R.R. 244 at para. 44 the court accepted that women capable of having children were victims of a court order restricting abortion, since they "may be adversely affected by the restrictions imposed . . . [and] run a risk of being directly prejudiced by the measure complained of". In *Dudgeon* v. *United Kingdom* [1981] Series A, No. 45, (1982) 4 E.H.R.R. 149 at para. 41, the existence of legislation criminalising homosexual conduct in Northern Ireland "continuously and directly affects" the private life of a gay man and was therefore a breach of Article 8 of the Convention, even though he had not been prosecuted. Conversely, in some cases possible risk or effect will be insufficient. Thus in *Leigh* v *U.K.* [1984] 38 D.R. 74 the European Commission of Human Rights rejected the possibility that a journalist could be prosecuted for contempt of court as a victim of the rule preventing the disclosure of documents obtained on discovery (commission and diligence) to third parties. On the face of it something approaching a sufficiency of risk assessment or even possibly a blurring of merits with standing might have a role to play in establishing whether or not a person is a victim: see, for example, D. Feldman, "Public Interest Litigation and Constitutional Theory in Comparative Perspective" (1992) 55 M.L.R. 44 and R. Singh, *The Future of Human Rights in the United Kingdom* (1997), Chap. 7.

Potentially the most significant implication of the test is that the scope for challenge by public interest or representative groups where a breach of Convention right is alleged may well be foreclosed, and such litigants will effectively find themselves in the same position as under the ordinary rules of title and interest to sue. Thus in *Norris and National Gay Federation v. Ireland*, Application No. 10581/83 (1984) 44 D.R. 132 the Commission held that the Federation which worked for the rights and welfare of lesbians and gay men in Ireland was not as such directly affected by Irish legislation prohibiting male homosexual activity and could not claim to be a victim of it. See too *X (Union) v. France*, Application No. 99000/82 (1983) 32 D.R. 261 where it was held that a teaching union could not challenge a French measure requiring teachers and lecturers to reside in the town in which their school or university was situated. The restriction affected natural persons only, but not the union itself and in *Open Door Counselling Ltd* above, while the individual women were victims, Open Door itself was not a victim: see too *Purcell v. Ireland*, Application No. 154040/89 (1991) 70 D.R. 262.

For further discussion see J. Marriott and Danny Nicol, "The Human Rights Act, Representative Standing and the Victim Culture" [1998] E.H.R.L.R. 70; K. Campbell, "Human Rights Brought Home?", 1998 S.L.T. (News) 269 at 271; and D.J. Harris, M. O'Boyle and C. Warbrick, "*Law of the European Convention on Human Rights* (1995), pp. 633–634. Note, however, that in the view of the Lord Chancellor, third parties would not be precluded from "making submissions about the implications of Convention rights in written briefs" but this would be limited to situations where such a "written brief" is invited or accepted by the court: H.L. Deb., Vol. 583, col. 825 (November 24, 1997). This, however, has no statutory basis.

For further comment on such a brief, sometimes known as a Brandeis brief, see A. Henderson, "Brandeis briefs and the proof of legislative facts in proceedings under the Human Rights Act 1998" [1998] P.L. 563. The case law on the victim test will of course also be relevant to section 100 of the Scotland Act 1998 above.

(3) Note the time limits contained in subsection (5) and applicable only to proceedings brought under subsection (1)(*a*). In judicial review or other proceedings falling outwith subsection (1)(*a*), one will have to have regard to, in the case of judicial review, the case law on *mora*, taciturnity and acquiescence and in relation to other proceedings, procedural or substantive rules that may apply. Thus, where one claims damages as a result of a delict based on a personal injury which is characterised as a breach of the Convention right, the time-limit that will apply is two years less than the normal three-year period contained in section 17 of the Prescription and Limitation (Scotland) Act 1973. Conversely, it would appear that a victim of an alleged violation may rely on a Convention right when defending legal proceedings brought by or at the instigation of a public authority whenever those proceedings are brought.

For further discussion on time-limits for challenge see D. Nicol, "Limitation Periods under the Human Rights Act 1998 and Judicial Review" (1999) 115 L.Q.R. 216.

(4) Subsections (11) and (12) are concerned with questions of remedy and are noted at para. 11–44.

Human Rights Act 1998

s. 9 (1),(2)

Judicial acts

10–61   **9.** — (1) Proceedings under section 7(1)(a) in respect of a judicial act may be brought only —

(a)   by exercising a right of appeal;
(b)   on an application (in Scotland a petition) for a judicial review; or
(c)   in such other forum as may be prescribed by rules.

(2) That does not affect any rule of law which prevents a court from being the subject of judicial review."

Notes

10–62   (1) Section 9 (3)–(5) is noted in Chapter 11 at para. 11–44. Section 9 (1) means that no form of original action exists for breach of Convention right by a judicial act. A litigant will either have to require to go down the route of judicial review where that is competent or to appeal if that is available. Subsection (1)(*c*) leaves open the possibility of new procedures being developed. Subsection (1)(*a*) does not create any new right of appeal and subsection (1) (*b*) does not affect the procedural and substantive limitations on the scope of judicial review. Under *West* all inferior courts are of course subject to judicial review unless an alternative remedy exists, on which see *Bell v. Fiddes*, 1996 S.L.T. 51 above.

(2) It is not enough to consider the Scotland Act and the Human Rights Act in isolation. The interplay of these important pieces of legislation must be considered, particularly from the point of view of judicial control. A breach of the Convention right is both a violation of the Human Rights Act and in relation to an Act of the Scottish Parliament is outwith its legislative competence: Scotland Act, 1998, s. 29 (2) (*d*), as is the exercise of an Executive function, including the making of subordinate legislation in breach of a Convention right: section 54 (2) (*a*),(*b*), and see also section 57 (2). These provisions are extracted at paras 3–10, 3–11 and 13–9. The next extract explores the inter-relationship of the two Acts and suggests that some of the provisions are not wholly complementary.

A. O'Neill, "The Scotland Act and the Government of Judges"

1999 S.L.T. (News) 61 at 65

"Human rights Issues as Devolution Issues

Given that the question as to the compatibility of legislation emanating from the Scottish Parliament **10–63** and Executive with the rights incorporated by the Human Rights Act into UK law from the European Convention on Human Rights is also designated a 'devolution issue' under para 1 (a) and 1 (d) of Sched 6 to the Scotland Act, it is necessary to consider how the two statutes interact. Although the European Convention was incorporated into domestic Scots law in the same way as it was incorporated into the laws of England and Wales and of Northern Ireland, namely by the Human Rights Act 1998, with the creation of a Scottish Parliament the Convention is effectively given a different constitutional status in Scotland from the rest of the United Kingdom. Under the Scotland Act 1998, the rights guaranteed under the Convention will have the status of a higher law as against any legislation passed by the Scottish Parliament or by any member of the Scottish Executive. Given this different constitutional character, the European Convention is likely to have a more immediate and significant impact in Scotland than in the rest of the United Kingdom.

The Westminster Parliament has reserved to itself a list of a matters set out in Sched 5 to the Act. Any matter not specified in that Schedule is then in principle transferred to the competence of the Scottish Parliament. The new Parliament has thus has been accorded legislative competence in a broad range of domestic issues. These include health; education; local government; social work; housing; economic development; judicial appointments; civil and criminal law and procedure; the criminal justice and prosecution system; legal aid; prisons; police and fire services; the environment; agriculture, forestry and fishing. In England and Wales all of the above areas remain wholly within the competence of the Westminster Parliament. Primary legislation in these areas will therefore be subject only to the 'interpretative obligation' placed on the courts by s 3 (1) of the Human Rights Act 1998, to read and give effect to that legislation so far as possible in a way which is compatible with the Convention rights. Where the courts finds that a legislative provision cannot be interpreted in accordance with the requirements of the Human Rights Convention, the provision nonetheless remains valid, operative and enforceable. Under ss 10–12 of the Human Rights Act 1998, it is a matter for the Minister of the Crown, answerable to the Westminster Parliament, to decide whether and how to amend the offending provision, and whether or not to give it retrospective effect.

The contrast with the situation in relation to Scottish legislation is stark. Section 29 (2) (d) of the Scotland Act 1998 states that a provision of an Act of the Scottish Parliament will be deemed to be outside the competence of the Scottish Parliament and hence 'not law' insofar as it is incompatible with any of the European Convention rights or with Community law. Similarly, by virtue of s 57 (2) of the Act; 'A member of the Scottish Executive has no power to make any subordinate legislation, or to do any act, so far as the legislation or act is incompatible with any of the Convention rights or with Community law.' Thus, the courts will be required to strike down Scottish legislation that is found to contravene the incorporated Convention rights. Further, it will be for the courts and not the Holyrood Parliament to consider whether to limit the retrospective effect of any such ruling of invalidity under s 102 of the Scotland Act 1998.

However, since the courts are themselves defined as public authorities by s 6 (3) (a) of the Human Rights Act 1998, any decision limiting retrospectivity will itself have to be compatible with the rights guaranteed under the European Convention.

In relation to primary Westminster legislation, then, the manner of remedying any incompatibility between the law and Convention rights is under the Human Rights Act 1998 a decision for the Westminster Parliament and United Kingdom Executive. In relation to Scottish legislation, however, the manner of remedying any incompatibility between the law and the Convention rights rests with the courts before which the matter is raised. It is not, however, clear under which statute, the Human Rights Act or the Scotland Act, a court would be acting in considering a claim that a provision of Scottish legislation contravenes a Convention right. Section 7 (1) (b) of the Human Rights Act 1998 permits a person who claims that a public authority has acted or proposes to act in a way which is incompatible with a Convention right, to 'rely on the Convention right or rights concerned in any legal proceedings' before any court in the United Kingdom. Section 3 of that Act enjoins the court to treat any contravening provisions of 'subordinate legislation' (which includes both primary and secondary Scottish legislation) as 'invalid and unenforceable'. There is, however, no provision in the Human Rights Act for any variation by the court of the retrospective effect of the court's decision on incompatibility. There is no possibility for a fast track reference on the issue raised to higher courts. Final appeal against any decision on compatibility of Scottish legislation with the Human Rights Act 1998 would lie either with the House of Lords or, if the question were raised in Scotland in the course of criminal proceedings, with the High Court of Justiciary acting as a criminal appeals court.

If the incompatibility of the Scottish legislation with the Convention right as raised in the course of legal proceedings is characterised by the courts as a 'devolution issue' as defined in the Scotland Act, then the matter has to be intimated to the Lord Advocate and other relevant law officer for the jurisdiction of the United Kingdom in which the proceedings in question take place (paras 5, 16 and 26 of Sched 6 to the Scotland Act). The courts are then enjoined to consider whether and to what extent any decision on incompatibility should be made retrospective (s 102 (2) (a)). The court may also suspend its judgment to allow the identified defect to be corrected (s 102 (2) (b)). And the final decision on the question of the compatibility of Scottish legislation with the Convention rights, when this matter is raised as a 'devolution issue', would lie with the Judicial Committee of the Privy Council. Further, by virtue of ss 107 and 112 (1) of the Scotland Act a Minister of the Crown has the power to amend, even retrospectively (s 114 (3)), the offending Scottish provision by subordinate Westminster legislation to bring it within devolved legislative or executive competence, including into line with the requirements of the Convention.

It seems unlikely that the Westminster Parliament would have intended that the complex system of checks, references and balances that has been put in place by the Scotland Act in relation to the resolution by the courts of 'devolution issues' could simply be overridden in any case brought under the Human Rights Act where it is alleged in the course of any legal proceedings that a provision of Scottish legislation is incompatible with the Convention right. If the scheme of Sched 6 to the Scotland Act 1998 is to be preserved in the case of challenges based on incompatibility with Convention rights, either the Westminster Parliament or the courts will have to stipulate that for the purposes of s 7 (1) (b) of the Human Rights Act, the *only* reliance that can be made on Convention rights in relation to provisions of Scottish legislation is in the context of the matter raising a 'devolution issue' for the purposes of the Scotland Act. No direct human rights challenge could be made to any such ruling as not providing an effective remedy for the protection of Convention rights since this provision of the Convention, art 13, has not been incorporated into the Human Rights Act 1998. The paradoxical result of any such approach would be that secondary Scottish legislation passed by members of the Scottish Executive would receive more procedural protection from being set aside by the courts than would subordinate Westminster legislation made by Ministers of the Crown."

Notes

10–64   See also Lord Hope of Craighead, "Devolution and Human Rights" [1998] E.H.R.L.R. 367; T. Mullen and T. Prosser, "Devolution and Administrative Law" (1998) 4 E.P.L. 479; and A. Miller, "Human Rights and the Scottish Parliament" [1998] E.H.R.L.R. 260.

Chapter 11

JUDICIAL REMEDIES IN ADMINISTRATIVE LAW

It is, of course, of paramount importance in any legal system that the rights conferred on persons by that system can be enforced by way of the provision of a meaningful remedy. Scots law is peculiar in that the remedies available to the litigant in administrative law proceedings are essentially those available in the context of what might be termed ordinary litigation. This is in part a consequence of the rejection of Scots administrative law of any distinction between public law and private law and is to be contrasted with the position in England where the specialised public law remedies of certiorari, mandamus and prohibition have assumed particular importance. For an account of these see V. Finch and C. Ashton, *Administrative Law in Scotland* (1997), pp. 435–436. Where these remedies are invoked in the context of an application to the supervisory jurisdiction of the Court of Session, then they must be sought in the form of a petition for judicial review under rule 58 of the Rule of the Court of Session 1994. The emphasis in this chapter is on the use of these remedies in judicial review proceedings, albeit not exclusively. Where the supervisory jurisdiction is not being invoked then they are available in administrative law proceedings without recourse to judicial review procedure. Unless stated otherwise, or involving an application to the supervisory jurisdiction, the remedies are also available in sheriff court proceedings.

Discussion of specialised and non-judicial remedies such as statutory default procedures — for example, the Local Government (Scotland) Act 1973, s. 211(1) and audit provisions of the same Act in section 101 — are beyond the scope of this chapter but for comment thereon see *The Laws of Scotland: Stair Memorial Encyclopaedia*, Vol. 1, paras 336, 343; Vol. 14, paras 117, 882–900. In addition to these general remedies, we will also look at the application of the *nobile officium* in administrative law proceedings and will consider the specialised remedies introduced under the Human Rights Act 1998 and the Scotland Act 1998.

For a general discussion of remedies in Scots administrative law see Finch and Ashton, pp. 417–436 and *Stair Memorial Encyclopaedia*, Vol. 1, paras 324–335.

REMEDIES IN JUDICIAL REVIEW PROCEEDINGS

Rules of the Court of Session

1994 r. 58.4

"Powers of Court in Judicial Review

58.4 The court, in exercising its supervisory jurisdiction on a petition for judicial review may —

(a) grant or refuse any part of the petition, with or without conditions:

(b) make such order in relation to the decision in question as it thinks fit. whether or not such order was sought in the petition, being an order that could be made if sought in any action or petition, including an order for reduction, declarator, suspension, interdict, implement, restitution, payment (whether of damages or otherwise) and any interim order;

Notes

11–3   (1) It will be seen from the foregoing that there is a great deal of flexibility inherent in the remedies available. It is, however, ultimately for the court as to which remedy should be awarded. As the court can award a remedy, even if not sought by the petitioner, a petition will not fail simply because the wrong remedy has been chosen. Where a remedy sought by a petitioner may have undue consequences for public administration, then the court can tailor the remedy to balance the interests of the petitioner and the public authority in question. The balancing of those aims and an inherent need for flexibility were recognised by the Dunpark working party (para. 5):

> "The judge must have powers to grant any decree or make any order which he considers necessary in the interests of justice … every possible remedy should be made available in this process so that no ancillary litigation should be necessary."

(2) There is, however, one observation that the court's discretion as to the remedy should not be exercised lightly. In *Mecca Leisure* v. *City of Glasgow District Licensing Board*, 1987 S.L.T. 483 Lord Clyde stated (at 486) that: "the court should not compel a petitioner to accept a remedy not sought and not desired by him or her."

(3) The ability to obtain interim orders is highly important for practical reasons. Many decisions of public authorities have an immediate and adverse impact — for example, a spending decision alleged to be *ultra vires* a local authority, as in *Meek v. Lothian Regional Council*, 1980 S.L.T. (Notes) 61 or *Deane v. Lothian Regional Council*, 1986 S.L.T. 22 (a decision to close a school).

REMEDIES

DECLARATOR

Rossi v. Magistrates of Edinburgh

(1904) 7 F.(H.L.) 85

11–4   "By sec. 80 of the Edinburgh Corporation Act, 1900, as amended by sec. 57 of the Edinburgh Corporation Order Confirmation Act, 1901, it is enacted, that any person selling ice-cream (except in a duly licensed hotel) without a licence from the Magistrates, 'who are hereby empowered to grant the same,' for the house, building, or premises where such ice-cream is kept for sale or sold, shall be liable to a penalty, provided that such licence shall run from the date of issue until the 15th May ensuing, and upon renewal, from the date of expiry of the licence so renewed to the 15th May succeeding, 'unless the same shall be sooner forfeited, revoked, or suspended,' and that 'every person licensed … to sell ice-cream under the provisions of the Act who shall … sell ice-cream except during the hours between' 8 A.M. and 11 P.M. 'on any lawful day, or at such extended hour at night as the Magistrates may by special regulation, in particular cases and for reasons assigned, permit,' shall be liable in a penalty. The statute did not provide a form of licence.
       The Magistrates proposed that the licences to be issued by them to ice-cream vendors should contain the following conditions: — '1. That the said licencee shall not keep open said premises, or sell or permit the sale of ice-cream therein on Sunday, or on any other day set apart for public worship by lawful authority. 2. That the said licencee shall not keep open said premises, or sell or permit the sale of ice-cream therein before eight o'clock in the morning or after eleven o'clock at night. 3. That the said Magistrates, or any of them, may at any time suspend or revoke the licence.'
       In an action by an ice-cream vendor against the Magistrates for declarator that they were not entitled to issue, and that he was not bound to accept, a licence containing these conditions, in respect that the conditions were not authorised by the Act, *held (rev.* judgment of Second Division) that it was *ultra vires*, of the Magistrates to insert the conditions in the licences issued by them."

Lord Robertson: "… The first question is whether the proposed form of licence does or does not accurately state the restrictions imposed by the statute on dealers in ice-cream. It seems to me that it does not, and that it purports to impose on the dealers more restrictions than does the statute. I can find no warrant in the statute for forcing the dealer to close his premises at the hours during which he is forbidden to sell ice-cream, and I know of no principle upon which the Magistrates can be held entitled to eke out what they may consider a weak prohibition by imposing an additional one. The licence would compel a man who had a general baking or confectionery business to shut shop at the specified hours, merely because one (and it might be an unimportant) item of his business was ice-cream. If the Legislature should in the future come to estimate the importance of ice-cream higher than it seems to do at present, it may adopt the stringent measure proposed. But in the meantime the respondents must be content to keep pace with the Legislature.

I further think that the respondents, in the third condition, arrogate to the Magistrates a power not conferred on them.

As regards lawful days, I think Sundays are not, in the sense of the Act, lawful days, on the principle stated in this House in the case of *Phillips* v. *Innes* 2 Sh. and M.L. 465, 6 Sco. R.R. 647]. As regards the other days described in the proposed licence, I do not feel called on to discuss dubious questions about public fasts which have little or no practical importance, and shall only remark that it is quite out of place for a licensing body to put into the licence their gloss on the statute on such points, whether it be more or less probably correct. On the present point the respondents, I have no doubt with the best intentions, have gone out of their way to court discussion.

The next question is as to the form of action. Now, the substance of the matter is that the Magistrates have publicly threatened to impose and enforce on a lawful trade restrictions which are illegal. This being so, it would be unfortunate if it were necessary that a lawful trade should be interrupted and harassed by actual prosecution. It seems to me that the action of declarator, which is peculiar to the Scotch system, exactly meets the case. It is quite a mistake to assume that this trader requires to postulate what he has not got, namely, a licence, in order to find himself a title to sue. His title is his trade, which the respondents avow that they intend to interfere with by refusing to give a trader a licence except upon terms more onerous than the law allows. In my opinion the appellant has a perfectly good title to have those restrictions declared illegal."

Notes

(1) Stair described declarator as being a remedy which existed for "instructing and clearing **11–5** any kind of rights relating to liberty, dominion or obligation" (Stair, *The Institutions of the Law of Scotland*, iv, 3, 47). *Rossi* is a practical example of the application of the remedy. Clearly if Rossi had been required to await a formal decision on whether or not the conditions were lawful, his business could have been seriously damaged.

(2) The effect of a declarator may well be enough to resolve the issue. In *Ayr Magistrates v. Lord Advocate*, 1950 S.C. 102 a police authority obtained a declarator that a public inquiry into police reorganisation was irregular and to that extent prevented the proposed inquiry going ahead. Declarator will not, however, generally of itself be enough to deal with past wrongs that have been completed or future, apprehended wrongs. Declarator is, therefore, often sought in conjunction with other remedies, such as interdict in a case of apprehended future wrongs, or damages in the case of completed past wrongs. For a recent example of the flexible use of declarator along with other remedies see *Highland Regional Council v. British Railways Board*, 1996 S.L.T. 274.

(3) One of the most significant features of declarator in the context of its use as an administrative law remedy is that of the generality of its effect *Rossi* is an example of this. All persons in his position had the benefit of the decision even if they were not party to it. In *Rossi* the class of persons benefiting was relatively limited in scope but in *Edinburgh and Glasgow Railway Co. v. Meek* (1849) 12 D. 153 no fewer than 23 different public authorities were able to take action based on the way in which the court decided that a poor law assessment was to be made.

(4) The court will not, however, grant the remedy in the situation where the grievance in question is either hypothetical or too remote. In *Magistrates of Ayr v. Secretary of State for Scotland*, 1966 S.L.T. 16 Ayr magistrates sought an order declaring that both an order made under the Water (Scotland) Act 1946, ss. 15,16 was unlawful as was the decision to hold a public inquiry and for interim orders to that effect. The Secretary of State argued that the remedy was premature. Lord Fraser commented (at 18):

"The answer suggested by counsel for the pursuers was that the whole procedure followed by the first-named defender, including the publication of notice of his being about to make an order, was bad for the reasons averred ... that there is no evidence before the first-named defender entitling him to come to the conclusion that the conditions specified in section 15 or 16 of the Act are satisfied. But that is the very question which is raised by the first conclusion of the Summons and I am not in a position to decide it at this stage. Until I have decided whether the procedure taken by the Secretary of State is vitiated by the error averred ... I do not see how I can declare the rights of parties with regard to the holding of a local inquiry. It seems to me that what the pursuers are really asking me to do is to treat their averments, so far as relating to the first conclusion, *pro veritate*, and upon the assumption that those averments are correct, to make an order declaratory of their rights in relation to the second and third conclusions as to an inquiry. Such an order would be hypothetical ..."

His Lordship refused the motions for interim declarator and it is difficult to see situations in which such an interim order might be granted. It may have been more appropriate for the pursuers to have sought declarator together with interim interdict, as in *Highland Regional Council v. British Railways Board*, 1996 S.L.T. 274.

11–6　　(5) Note the terms of section 40(3)–(4) of the Scotland Act 1998, which provide that in any proceedings against the Parliament or any member thereof, the presiding officer or deputy, any member of staff of the Parliament or the Parliamentary corporation, the court "shall not make an order for suspension, interdict, reduction or specific performance (or other like order) but may instead make a declarator." Order includes an interim order: section 40(5). The purpose behind this is to provide some degree of privilege where the proceedings of the Scottish Parliament can be held without interruption from legal action. The effect of a declarator in this context is, however, uncertain. In the course of debate it was observed:

"It will, of course, be for the Parliament itself to decide how it should react to any such declaration. The Parliament would not be liable for contempt of court if it merely decided to take no action..." (*Hansard*, H.L. Vol 593. col. 2019).

SUSPENSION

Brown v. Executive Committee of the Edinburgh District Labour Party

1995 S.L.T. 985

11–7　　"Nine councillors of the City of Edinburgh District Council who were members of the council Labour Party group petitioned for suspension and interdict in respect of disciplinary proceedings brought against them which could have led to the withdrawal of the group whip and their subsequent ineligibility to stand for election as Labour candidates. Following a council meeting on 2 December 1993 a special meeting of the Edinburgh District Labour Party and its executive committee had been convened and on 6 December had passed a motion which was highly critical of the conduct of the nine councillors relating to the same matters which thereafter became subject to the disciplinary proceedings, which were to culminate in a hearing before the disciplinary authority on 11 January 1994. Under the rules of Edinburgh District Council Labour group the disciplinary authority was a specially convened joint meeting of the Labour group and the executive committee of the Edinburgh District Labour Party. The first ground on which suspension and interdict were sought was that the motion that had been passed on 6 December had been passed on a majority of 60 to one by individuals who included members of the disciplinary authority and that the motion disclosed a basis for a reasonable apprehension of something so prejudicial to a fair and impartial investigation of the questions to be decided by the disciplinary authority as to amount to a denial of natural justice. The second ground was that the nine councillors had not acted in a manner that had laid them open to competent disciplinary proceedings. The respondents argued that it was not competent for the courts to interfere in the internal affairs of a voluntary association, especially where, as here, there were appeal procedures provided, and also argued that, even if the disciplinary proceedings were without merit, that was no reason to prevent the members of the hearing from exercising their quasi-judicial authority fairly and so deciding."

Lord Osborne: "In this petition, the petitioners seek the remedies of suspension and interdict in relation to certain proceedings of a disciplinary nature which have been initiated against them. The circumstances in which the petition has been brought are set out fully in the petitioners' averments, which it is unnecessary for me to repeat here. On Friday 7 January 1991, there came before me a motion on behalf of the petitioners for an order for intimation and service and for interim interdict and interim suspension in terms of the prayer of the petition. At the hearing of that motion I had the benefit of a full argument from counsel for the petitioners and for certain of the respondents...

In a case such as this, where interim suspension and interdict are sought, these remedies can be granted only if two requirements are satisfied. These are, first, that there should exist a prima facie case for such remedies; secondly, that the balance of convenience must favour a grant. Accordingly, it is to these questions that I now turn.

Having regard to the fact that the petitioners are asking the court to interfere in the proceedings of a voluntary association, in this case the Labour group of Edinburgh District Council, it is, first of all, necessary to consider in what circumstances the court will take such a step. In my opinion, the words used by Lord Justice Clerk Aitchison in *McDonald v Burns*, although uttered in relation to a religious body, are equally apt here: 'The internal discipline of any such body is a matter of domestic concern, notwithstanding that status, or civil rights, may be involved, and it is only in extraordinary circumstances that the Courts will regard it as within their competence to intervene' (1940 SC at p 383; 1940 SLT at p 331).

Going on to consider what these extraordinary circumstances might be, he said that, speaking generally, there were two situations in which the courts would entertain actions: '(first) where the... association through its agencies has acted clearly and demonstrably beyond its own constitution, and in a manner calculated to affect the civil rights and patrimonial interests of any of its members, and (secondly) where, although acting within its constitution, the procedure of its judicial or *quasi*-judicial tribunals has been marked by gross irregularity, such fundamental irregularity as would, in the case of an ordinary civil tribunal, be sufficient to vitiate the proceedings. But a mere irregularity in procedure is not enough. It must be so fundamental an irregularity that it goes beyond a mere matter of procedure, and becomes something so prejudicial to a fair and impartial investigation of the question to be decided as to amount to a denial of natural justice' (pp 383–384 (pp 331–332)).

It will be seen that these observations are couched in the past tense. What I am dealing with here is, of course, what is said to be a threatened or apprehended wrong, rather than one which has already occurred. Be that as it may, it is perfectly proper, in my view, to test the character and quality of what is apprehended by reference to what the court has in the past characterised as a wrong after its occurrence.

In the present circumstances, in my opinion, nothing which has been said amounts to an allegation that the association has acted or is going to act clearly and demonstrably beyond its own constitution. In particular, I do not regard the second submission made on the petitioners' behalf to the effect that the petitioners had committed no offence which would entitle the respondents to initiate cl 10 proceedings, as falling into that category. In my view, that submission amounted to no more than the stating of a potential defence to such proceedings. For that reason, in my view, it deserves no further consideration in the present context.

However, the first submission made on the petitioners' behalf is of a different character. An apprehended denial of natural justice is exactly what is alleged in it. As I understood the submission, the essence of it is that at least some, if not all, of the members of the disciplinary body created by cl 10, namely 'a joint meeting of the Labour Group and Executive Committee of the District Labour Party', are persons who were present and supported the motion passed at the meeting of the Edinburgh District Labour Party held on 6 December 1993, which motion was highly critical of the conduct of the petitioners in the very matters which would be the subject of the contemplated disciplinary proceedings. These persons, it is submitted, must be seen as biased and as having prejudged the very issues which the disciplinary body is itself bound to consider in a fair and impartial manner.

The question for me is whether the circumstances founded upon amount to a basis for the reasonable apprehension of 'something so prejudicial to a fair and impartial investigation of the question[s] to be decided as to amount to a denial of natural justice'. In my opinion they do. Each member of the disciplinary body would be performing a judicial duty and would require to bring to the discharge of that duty an unbiased and impartial mind. If he or she has a bias which renders him or her otherwise than an impartial judge he or she is disqualified from performing that duty indeed, so jealous is the policy of the law of the purity of the administration of justice, that, if there are circumstances so affecting a person acting in a judicial capacity as to be calculated to create in the mind of a reasonable man a suspicion concerning that person's impartiality, those circumstances are themselves sufficient to disqualify, although in fact no bias exists. Further, when an allegation of bias is made out against one member of a collective body, that is sufficient to invalidate the decision of the whole body, in my opinion. Judged by these criteria, I have concluded that the petitioners have a prima facie case and that the court would be justified, in the circumstances of the present case, in granting the remedies sought, if the balance of convenience favours the petitioners. It appears to me that the terms of the motion passed by, among others, potential members of the disciplinary body, at the meeting of 6 December 1993, are, even making due allowance for the heat of political controversy, so seriously critical of the petitioners in relation to the relevant matters that those potential members must be seen as having prejudged the issues which are properly for that body. In any event, even if I were wrong about that, it appears to me that a reasonable man could not do other than entertain the gravest suspicion concerning the impartiality, in the relevant matters, of at least those members of the disciplinary body who were parties to the passing of the motion on 6 December 1993. That would be enough in the present context to satisfy the criteria mentioned. In this connection, it is appropriate for me to emphasise some of the language used: 'This District Labour Party condemns the nine Labour Councillors who defied the Labour Whip'; it is appalled that Labour Councillors would speak and vote in favour of a Conservative motion, in contravention of instructions from the General Secretary of the Labour Party in Scotland'; 'We therefore call on the District Labour Group and the Scottish Party to take all appropriate steps to ensure that there is no repetition of last week's disgraceful events....'

Turning now to the balance of convenience, I am satisfied that it favours the petitioners. If the court were not to intervene, the petitioners would immediately be subjected to disciplinary proceedings which might be thought likely to result in the withdrawal of the group whip from them, either indefinitely or for a specified period. If the former were the case, they would be disabled for at least six months, assuming nothing concerning any appeal, from seeking selection as Labour candidates in any election, and, in particular, in the contemplated elections for the new proposed single tier local authorities, which selections are shortly to occur. That, in my view, represents a serious disadvantage to them. On the other hand, the granting of the orders sought would simply delay the contemplated disciplinary proceedings until such time as the petition is finally determined. Thereafter, if appropriate, and depending on the decision reached, they might proceed. That appears to me to involve no discernible prejudice to the respondents.

In all these circumstances, I shall grant the petitioners' motion."

Notes

11–8   The remedy of suspension is not one that is commonly sought today, notwithstanding that rule 58.3 expressly preserves it as a competent remedy in judicial review proceedings. It was formerly a common remedy, particularly given its summary nature, and was particularly relevant in staying proceedings in lower courts and tribunals acting in excess of their powers: see *Stair Memorial Encyclopaedia*, Vol. 1, para. 330. It is often combined with an order for interim liberation in the context of immigration detention: Court of Session Act 1988, s. 47(1).

Interim suspension in *Brown* would only have prevented the enforcement of the disciplinary decision that had been arrived that and interim interdict was required to ensure that no further proceedings would be taken pending a full hearing of the case by the court. This basic weakness in the remedy perhaps explains its relative rarity.

IMPLEMENT

Forbes v. Underwood

(1886) 13 R. 465

11–9   LORD PRESIDENT: "The respondent, Donald Forbes, was outgoing tenant of the farm of Essick, in Inverness-shire, at Whitsunday 1884, and the appellant, Peter Underwood, was the incoming tenant. There were certain disputes between them in these capacities, which they referred to arbiters, and these arbiters had power to name an oversman in the event of their differing in opinion. The allegation of the pursuer in his petition in the inferior Court was, that the two arbiters had differed in opinion, but that one of them, Mr Winton, refused to sign a devolution to enable the oversman to dispose of the matter in dispute, and he brought his action for the purpose of having Mr Winton compeiled to go on and discharge the duty which he had undertaken as an arbiter, and to execute a minute of devolution in the event, which had occurred, of a difference of opinion between the arbiters. The prayer of the petition is to ordain Winton to concur with the other arbiter in executing a minute of devolution, that being the full remedy which the pursuer thought he required in the circumstances. But in addition to that he called Underwood as a defender. Of course he could not conclude against him to do anything as an arbiter, because he was not an arbiter but a party to the submission, and the only conclusion against him, therefore, in the prayer of the petition is to find him jointly and severally liable in expenses with the arbiter who refused to discharge his duty...

[U]nder the provision of the recent statute the other defender, Mr Winton, avails himself of this appeal to bring under review the interlocutors of the Sheriff in other respects; and he does so for the purpose of asking the Court to sustain his first plea in law, which is, that the Court — that is, the Sheriff — has no jurisdiction to try the question raised in this action. The question raised in this action is, whether Mr Winton has wrongfully failed to perform his duty as arbiter, and the remedy sought is a decree against him to compel him to do so. The question whether the Sheriff has jurisdiction in such a case is, I think, one of very great importance. The position of an arbiter is very much like that of a Judge in many respects, and there is no doubt whatever that whenever an inferior Judge, no matter of what kind, fails to perform his duty, or transgresses his duty, either by going beyond his jurisdiction, or by failing to exercise his jurisdiction when called upon to do so by a party entitled to come before him, there is a remedy in this Court, and the inferior Judge, if it turns out that he is wrong, may be ordered by this Court to go on and perform his duty, and if he fails to do so he will be liable to imprisonment as upon a decree *ad factum præstandum*. The same rule applies to a variety of other public officers, such as statutory trustees and commissioners, who are under an obligation to exercise their functions for the benefit of the parties for whose benefit these functions are entrusted to them, and if they capriciously and without just cause refuse to perform their duty they will be ordained to do so by decree of this Court, and failing their performance will, in like manner, be committed to prison. Now, all this belongs to the Court of Session as the Supreme Civil Court of this country in the exercise of what is called, very properly, its supereminent jurisdiction. It is not of very much consequence to determine whether it is in the exercise of its high equitable jurisdiction, or in the performance of what is sometimes called its *nobile officium*. But of one thing there can be no doubt, that in making such orders against inferior Judges, or statutory trustees, or commissioners, or the like this Court is exercising an exclusive jurisdiction — a jurisdiction which cannot possibly belong to any other Court in the country. It is enough to suggest the idea, that an inferior Judge should be called upon to ordain another inferior Judge to perform his duty — the very idea carries absurdity with it. It can be only the Supreme Court of the country that can possibly exercise such jurisdiction ...

I think if we consider the sort of question that may arise in an action to compel an arbiter to proceed to exercise the functions which he has undertaken by accepting a submission, we shall at once see that cases may arise, and generally will arise, of a very delicate kind, where the arbiter comes into Court to defend his conduct and to assign his reasons for refusing to exercise his functions. Various reasons may be stated by an arbiter for so doing; and various reasons have been stated in the cases which have been reported. An arbiter may come into Court excusing himself from proceeding further in a submission upon the ground that he accepted the submission believing that what he had to determine was a mere question of fact, and that unexpectedly it turned out that there were very delicate questions of law involved in the dispute between the parties which he considered himself totally unfit to solve. Another man comes into the Court and says he has a conscientious objection to proceeding further with the submission because he finds — what he was not at all aware of at the outset — that he really has an interest or bias in the matter referred to him, and that he cannot with satisfaction to his own conscience proceed to decide in the matter. In another case an interest may supervene, just as it did in the case of *Mackenzie*, and that would be a very sufficient reason for an arbiter declining to go further. Another case might be that the arbiter finds that since he accepted the submission his health, either mental or bodily, has rendered him not so capable of exercising those functions as he was when he undertook the duty. Now, all these are considerations which require the most delicate handling by a Court that is called upon to enforce under the penalty of imprisonment the duty of the arbiter to go on and close the submission. I can hardly conceive anything more suitable for the interposition of the Supreme Court, or less suitable to the jurisdiction of an inferior Judge. It appears to me that the parallel between the position of an arbiter and the position of inferior Judges — Judges in the proper sense of the term — is complete, and that the two are quite undistinguishable in this question of jurisdiction."

Notes

(1) This is an illustration of the power of common law of the Court of Session to compel an inferior authority to exercise its jurisdiction. On this see generally *Stair Memorial Encyclopaedia*, Vol. 1, para. 334 and J.A. McLaren, *Court of Session Practice* (1916), p. 119. *Forbes* was relied upon by the Lord President in West as an example of the scope of the court's supervisory jurisdiction. Insofar as the court's supervisory jurisdiction is not invoked when this remedy is sought, the sheriff court too can enforce an obligation or a duty. In *Brown v. Hamilton District Council*, 1983 S.L.T. 397, HL the remedy was sought in the sheriff court in the context of

11–10

enforcing a local authority to carry out its duties under the Housing (Homeless Persons) Act 1977. As no original right of appeal to the sheriff existed the litigant was effectively seeking to invoke the supervisory jurisdiction. No doubt was expressed as to the competency of the remedy of implement in the context of sheriff court proceedings not falling within the supervisory jurisdiction.

(2) Complementary to the remedy of implement is the procedure formerly set out in the Court of Session Act 1868, s. 91, and only available in the Court of Session, and which is now re-enacted in the Court of Session Act 1988 as follows.

Court of Session Act 1988

s. 45

"Restoration of Possession and Specific Performance

11–11   45. The Court may, on application by summary petition — ...

(b) order the specific performance of any statutory duty, under such conditions and penalties (including fine and imprisonment, where consistent with the enactment concerned) in the event of the order not being implemented, as to the Court seem proper."

T. Docherty Ltd v. Burgh of Monifieth

1971 S.L.T. 13

11–12   "The Burgh Police (Scotland) Act 1892, s. 219, as amended by the Burgh Police (Scotland) Act 1903, enacts that: 'The Commissioners shall from time to time...cause to be made under the streets and elsewhere, such main and other sewers as shall be necessary for the effectual drainage of the burgh...'. T. Docherty Limited, a development company, owned about five acres of land at Milton Park within the burgh of Monifieth. On this land they proposed to build 52 houses and streets leading to these houses. The necessary planning and other consents had been obtained. They presented a petition under the Court of Session Act 1868, s. 91 to ordain the burgh to cause to be made such main and other sewers as should be necessary for the effectual draining of the area of the petitioners' development. The petitioners averred that they were about to start building. The main sewer of the burgh of Monifieth ran near to, but outside, the petitioners' land. The respondents, the burgh of Monifieth, decided that the sewers which were necessary within the petitioners' land should be laid by the petitioners and at their own expense. They lodged answers to the petition in which they pled that the petitioners had no title to sue, and that the petition was incompetent and irrelevant."

Lord President (Clyde): "...Two preliminary points were argued to us. In the first place the respondents contended that the present action is incompetent. Under s. 91 of the Court of Session Act 1868, however, authority is given to the court upon an application by a summary petition to order specific performance of a statutory duty. The present proceedings are in the form of a summary petition, and, in my opinion, s. 91 of the 1868 Act can properly be invoked to enforce the provisions of s. 219 of the 1892 Act if the respondents are in breach of them. It was argued that this remedy was not available if some alternative method was provided in some other statute. But I see no warrant for this contention in the unequivocal terms of s. 91 of the 1868 Act. Reference was made in the course of the argument to the English doctrine of mandamus. But this never formed part of the law of Scotland. *Pasmore* v. *Oswaldtwistle Urban District Council* [1898] A.C. 387 was an action for mandamus, and cannot supersede the express terms of the Scottish Court of Session Act 1868. The point taken on competency is therefore an unsound one.

The second preliminary point was that the petitioners had no title to sue. But, in my opinion, when the petitioners are faced as they are with the decision of the town council that the sewers within the development area had to be laid by the petitioners from the individual house drains up to a point to be arranged with the burgh surveyor for connection to the main sewer of the burgh outside that area, the petitioners if they can show that this decision is in breach of the statutory duty of the burgh, do have a title to invoke the powers given by s. 91 of the Court of Session Act 1868.

In my opinion therefore there is no substance in either of these two preliminary points.

That brings me to the merits of the dispute between the parties. There is a general obligation imposed on the burgh under s. 219 of the Burgh Police (Scotland) Act 1892, as amended by the Burgh Police (Scotland) Act 1903, to construct from time to time such main and other sewers as shall be necessady for the effectual draining of the burgh, and the town council have power to carry these sewers through any lands in the burgh. This statutory obligation is stated in quite general terms, and there is no provision in the statutes imposing on an owner of houses nor upon a developer any duty to construct a branch or main sewer.

On the contrary in the normal case where a main or branch sewer runs within 100 yards of a house or an intended house about to be built, the duty of the owner of the house is to construct a covered branch drain or pipe to connect his house with the burgh sewer. (See ss. 238 and 239 of the 1892 Act, as amended by the 1903 Act). This provision points the distinction between the public sewer system which the burgh must create and administer, and the private pipe or drain which leads from the individual house into that system, and which remains the responsibility of the owner of the individual house.

It would be unfair, however, to require the local authority, and therefore the ratepayers, to construct and maintain a sewerage system which involved the construction of a branch sewer to serve a single isolated house situated a long way from any existing branch sewers as may often happen in fringe developments on the outskirts of the burgh. This is the reason for the 100 yards limitation. In a case where the distance between the burgh sewer and the house or proposed house is over 100 yards the sections of the statutes above referred to do not impose on the owner the duty of constructing a pipe or drain to the sewer, the town council are empowered to require him to lead his effluent into a cesspool and to maintain that cesspool until the burgh have constructed a branch sewer within 100 yards of his house. When the new sewer is made the town council are required under these sections to connect the cesspool to the sewer, the cost of this being recoverable from the owner of the house. The cesspool provision is obviously a temporary expedient to save the expense of the construction of a branch sewer until such time as a sufficient number of houses have been erected to justify a sewer if the area is to be effectually drained.

It was contended for the burgh that they had discharged their duty under the statutes by directing the petitioners to construct the sewers within the area to be developed for connection to the main sewer outside that area at a point to be arranged with the burgh surveyor. But, in the first place, the provision of sewers is exclusively entrusted to the burgh itself. They do not discharge their statutory function by directing someone else to perform it. The individual owner of a building or the developer of an area has no statutory obligation to construct sewers. His duty under the statute is to construct the individual pipes or drains from each house. In the second place there is no warrant in the statutes for the view that a developer, such as the petitioner, has any statutory duty to build sewers for the area of ground which he is developing and to lead his sewer to the edge of his land. The boundaries of the land owned are not in this connection in any way material. If they were, it would mean that a developer who himself develops an area with 50 houses in it would be under obligation to construct the sewerage system for that whole area; whereas if he sold each of the 50 plots and the houses were then built each proprietor would only have to lead his effluent out to the edge of his plot of ground. This was never the purpose or effect of the statutes. It is not the area of ground to be served but the individual house which is material in this connection.

Neither party to this application asked for a proof, but sought a decision from us on the pleadings. In a summary application such as this that would be the normal course. The question of the immediate necessity for a sewer in the area under consideration in this application may well be a question of circumstances. The petitioners have received planning permission, they aver that they are now about to commence work on the development, that the site is ready for work to begin, and that the men and equipment are ready to move in. It is obviously common sense that parties should know where they are, and that the new sewers in the area which have to be laid at an early stage should be constructed at the proper levels and in the light of the overriding obligation effectually to drain the whole burgh. On the other hand the petitioners' averments are not expressly admitted by the respondents, and no one can tell under modern conditions how long it will take to complete the whole development. It might be unfair on the burgh in these circumstances to impose on them an immediate obligation to build the sewerage system for draining the whole area. For it is conceivable that the development may never be completed, or that the whole system for the area may never be needed. In such circumstances some practical arrangement between the parties might well be reached which would be reasonable for both. Such an arrangement might be on the lines indicated in the note in Muirhead, *Municipal and Police Government in Scotland*, Vol. I, p. 406, whereby the petitioners would lay down the sewers in the development area at their own expense on lines and levels approved by the respondents, under an agreement with the latter that as soon as a specified proportion of the houses was erected the respondents would take over the sewer and pay the petitioners the price thereof. An arrangement of this sort would be a recognition of the burgh's statutory duty on this matter, while at the same time it would avoid their being compelled to carry out that duty before it becomes necessary.

In these circumstances, in my opinion, the first three pleas-in-law for the respondents should be repelled and in place of granting the prayer the court should make a finding that it is the duty of the respondents to provide such main and other sewers as shall be necessary for the effectual draining of the area of the petitioners' development at Milton Park within the burgh of Monifieth."

Notes

11–13   (1) This excerpt illustrates a number of points. The statutory duty must be clear and unequivocal. This is a question of statutory interpretation. An order will not be granted where, on a proper construction of the statute, the duty is in effect found to be discretionary or simply an exercise of the expression of a power. In *Tayside Regional Council*, Outer House, December 9, 1993, unreported the council sought judicial review of the decision of British Railways Board on the basis, *inter alia*, that the board was under a duty to maintain a crossing. Lord Prosser stated that:

> "Where a body is subject to the Court's supervision as a discretion, the Court will only take it upon itself to make a specific Order where that is seen as essential to the justice of the case. But where a body has a specific statutory duty, and the Court is being asked to ordain performance of that duty, the position seems to me to be very different."

T. Docherty Ltd also illustrates the proposition that unlike the position of the common law remedy of implement, the statutory remedy found in the Court of Session Act 1988 can be invoked, notwithstanding the existence of an alternative means of enforcing the duty. This view was reaffirmed in *Walker v. Strathclyde Regional Council* (No. 1), 1986 S.L.T. 523 when a group of parents sought to enforce the duty of the Education Authority under the Education (Scotland) Act 1980 to secure adequate and efficient provision of school education. The parents argued that the authority was failing its duty because of its failure to deal with the disruption caused to education by industrial action by teachers. Notwithstanding that under the 1980 Act the parents had a statutory remedy, the courts specifically accepted that the remedy under the Court of Session Act 1988 was competent. As in *Tayside Regional Council* the petitioner, however, failed on its merits. These two cases illustrate that notwithstanding the apparent utility of this remedy, its practical impact may be limited by the fact that most statutory duties are not expressed in unqualified terms. Notwithstanding that the remedy for enforcement of a statutory duty is referred to in rule 58. 4, it is doubtful whether or not a petitioner in judicial review proceedings will not still be required to exhaust an alternative remedy, on which see para. 10–29.

(2) Implement is not available against the Crown: Crown Proceedings Act 1947, s. 21. It has yet to be authoritatively decided whether action for enforcement of statutory duty can be brought against the Crown: *Carlton (Edinburgh) Hotel Co. Ltd v. Lord Advocate*, 1921 1 S.L.T. 126. If the statutory duty was one that binds the Crown, it may have to be decided whether the section was originally binding upon the Crown and its officers and if so whether it continues to bind the Crown: see generally *Stair Memorial Encyclopaedia*, Vol. 1, para. 335.

REDUCTION

British Oxygen Co. Ltd v. South West Scotland Electricity Board

1956 S.C. (H.L.) 112

LORD KEITH OF AVONHOLM: "In this case the respondents, the British Oxygen Company, Limited, complain that the appellants the South West Scotland Electricity Board (now the South of Scotland Electricity Board) have unduly discriminated against them in fixing certain tariffs for supplies of electricity for industrial purposes, known as industrial maximum demand tariffs. Three tariffs are in question, the first, operating as from 1st January 1952, superseded by the second, operating as from 1st October 1953, superseded in turn by the third, operating as from 1st April 1954. It will be convenient to call the respondents the pursuers and the appellant Board the defenders. The Central Electricity Authority were also called as defenders for any interest they might have and appear here as appellants, but they take no pleas distinct from those of the Board.

11–14

The action is based on subsection (8) of section 37 of the Electricity Act, 1947, which runs as follows: — '(8) An Area Board, in fixing tariffs and making agreements under this section, shall not show undue preference to any person or class of persons and shall not exercise any undue discrimination against any person or class of persons, and the Central Authority shall, in exercising their powers under this section in relation to the fixing of tariffs and making of agreements by Area Boards, secure compliance by Area Boards with this subsection.'

The conclusions of the summons are for declarator, in respect of each of the tariffs, that the defenders exercised undue discrimination against industrial users of supplies of electricity metered at or above a voltage of 6000, including the pursuers, contrary to the provisions of the Electricity Act, 1947, section 37 (8); and that the tariffs are illegal and *ultra vires* and of no force and effect: for production and reduction of the tariffs as applied to users metered at or above a voltage of 6000; and for payment by the defenders to the pursuers of the sum of £10,000 with interest at the rate of 5 per cent per annum from the date of citation until payment.

The Lord Ordinary held the averments of the pursuers to be irrelevant and dismissed the action. The Second Division has recalled the Lord Ordinary's interlocutor and allowed a proof before answer. It is against this judgment of the Second Division that the defenders have appealed to this House.

The question may be put thus: whether discrimination may not be exercised against one consumer and a preference given to another where both are charged the same rate in circumstances which justify a differential rate between them. If the answer is 'Yes' it would equally follow that, where the differential was too small, a like complaint could be made. For the reasons given I am not prepared to decide this matter in this case as a question of reluctancy the more so as I consider that only in vary exceptional circumstances would it be proper for this House to reverse an interlocutor of the Court of Session, allowing a proof before answer, which can only be appealed to this House with the leave of the Court of Session, on point which was never taken in the Courts below, and on which your Lordships have not had the benefit of the opinions of the Judges whose judgment is under appeal.

I should, before parting with this case, refer to certain other matters which were mentioned for the first time, but only slightly discussed. in the course of the appeal. The precise extent of the Court's jurisdiction to interfere with tariffs fixed by an Area Board is not easy to determine. But it may be questioned whether section 37 is an enactment that has the effect of nullifying tariffs containing an element of undue preference, or undue discrimination. Similar clauses have existed over the past hundred years in the Railway and Canal Traffic Acts and the Electricity (Supply) Acts and no case was cited to us where the effect of such a clause was held to render the tariff complained of null and void. It is the preference that is illegal, not the whole tariff. In most cases under earlier statutes the complaint was that somebody else's tariff was too low and no advantage would result to the complainer from wiping out the tariff altogether. The statute imposes a prohibition of undue preference or discrimination, and the normal method of enforcing such a prohibition would be interdict, or injunction, against the continuance of the undue preference, as illustrated, for instance, by cases under the Electricity (Supply) Acts. Further, the statutory procedure for fixing and revising tariffs raises a question whether the Courts can in any sense function as a tariff-fixing body and whether for this and other reasons a conclusion for repayment of overcharges can ever be an appropriate remedy. This is not a case under an equality clause, in which a claim for overcharges raises no serious difficulty. On these matters I express no concluded opinion. I mention them because the course which this whole case has taken has been of a very unusual character, and the fact that these points were raised for the first time during the hearing of this appeal suggests that they have had little, if any, proper consideration in the earlier stages of the case. There seems to me to be a serious question whether the whole form of action here is not misconceived.

I would dismiss the appeal."

Notes

11–15   (1) J. A. McLaren, pp. 82–84 makes a distinction between ordinary reduction and reduction of decrees. The former relates to the quashing of any contract or written instrument, the latter to the review of decrees of the Court of Session or inferior courts. This excerpt is, of course, an example of the former but both have relevance in administrative law, as A.W. Bradley states:

> "The grounds on which reduction may be sought in administrative law accordingly include all matters which render a decision of an inferior court, tribunal or public authority unlawful, ultravires, incompetent or in excess of jurisdiction" (*Stair Memorial Encyclopaedia*, Vol. 1, para. 325).

Thus, reduction has been allowed as a competent remedy where a breach of regulations is alleged, *Hayman v. Lord Advocate*, 1951 S.C. 621; material defects of procedure, *Goodall v. Bilsland*, 1909 S.C. 1152; allegations of bias and other breaches of natural justice, *McDonald v. Lanarkshire Fire Brigade Joint Committee* 1959 S.C. 141; and abuse of discretion, *Ashley v. Rothesay Magistrates* (1873) 11 M. 708. For other examples see *Stair Memorial Encyclopaedia*, Vol. 1, para. 325 and Finch and Ashton, pp. 423–426. Note that reduction is not a competent remedy in the sheriff court in any form of proceedings, although a matter can be raised *ope exceptionis* which could have given a ground for reduction and the sheriff has a discretion to order a separate action of reduction in the Court of Session: *Leggat Brothers v. Gray*, 1912 S.C. 230.

(2) The excerpt demonstrates in a negative manner the scope of the remedy. Reduction will not be awarded where a less radical remedy will resolve the grievance. Similarly, reduction may not be used as an appeal against the merits of a decision and may be withheld where a procedure for appeal existed but was not used or where it is premature in that the procedure for appeal may still be available at a later stage: see generally *Stair Memorial Encyclopaedia*, Vol. 1, para. 325. Reduction is, however, appropriate where the authority has prevented the litigant exercising a right of appeal: *London and Clydeside Estates Ltd v. Aberdeen District Council*, 1980 S.L.T. 81.

Underlying this approach is a concern that the consequences of allowing the remedy may go beyond remedying the wrong suffered and have a wider impact on the validity of administrative action. This is also apparent insofar as it is competent to award partial reduction where part of a decision is held to be unlawful. The scope of partial reduction does, however, depend on the context in which it arises. In planning law, for example, the scope of partial reduction is limited.

In *British Airports Authority v. Secretary of State for Scotland*, 1979 S.L.T. 197 the Court of Session had to consider whether or not a condition attached to a planning consent awarded by the Secretary of State was unlawful and if so whether all of the decision required to be reduced or only the offending condition. In determining the issue, the court had regard to section 233(4)(*b*) of the Town and Country Planning (Scotland) Act 1972, on which see now section 239 of the Town and Country Planning (Scotland) Act 1997. These provisions are discussed in greater detail in Chapter 12 but they provide a remedy which can be regarded as the statutory equivalent of reduction. As a matter of statutory construction the court held that it was not possible to sever this condition as part of the planning permission granted by the Secretary of State, but the court went on to consider the question of the effect of inept planning conditions generally. In particular the Lord President (Emslie) stated (at 204):

> "A number of English cases were cited to us — all actions for a declaration in respect of planning permission granted by a local planning authority subject to conditions — from which it may be taken that if a condition held to be ultra vires is important and not trivial there can be no question of quashing only that condition. The whole of the planning permission must be quashed on the view that it might not have been granted at all if it had been appreciated that the condition objected to could not properly be attached to it."

One of the English decisions referred to was that of the House of Lords in *Kingsway Investments (Kent) Ltd v. Kent County Council* [1971] A.C. 72 where Lord Reid stated (at 90) that:

> "[I]t is not surprising that there can only be severance of a contract in exceptional circumstances. But that is not so with regard to a unilateral licence or permission. Suppose that a planning authority purports to impose a condition which has nothing whatever to do with planning considerations but is only calculated to achieve some ulterior object thought to be in the public interest. Clearly, in my view, the condition should be severed and that permission should stand. But suppose, on the other hand, that a condition though invalid because ultra vires or unreasonable, limits the manner in which the land can be developed, then the condition would not be severable, for if it were simply struck out the result would be that the owner could do things on his land for which he never in fact obtained permission, and that would be contrary to the intention of the statute."

On severance in planning law generally see N. Collar, *Planning* (1994), pp. 191–192; see also *North East Fife District Council v. Secretary of State for Scotland*, 1992 S.L.T. 373.

(3) Severance has, however, been permitted in other contexts; see, for example, *John Darney* **11–16** *& Son v. Calder District Committee* (1904) 12 S.L.T. 546 in relation to a statutory consent and, in the context of an arbitration, *J. Miller and Son v. Oliver & Boyd* (1903) 11 S.L.T. 381. See also in the context of challenge to delegated legislation, *D.P.P. v. Hutchinson* [1990] 2 A.C. 783 and see paras 2–35 to 2–36.

(4) Partial reduction is competent notwithstanding that the decision in question may involve the proper approach as to the establishment of matters of fact. In *Smith v. H.M. Advocate*, 1994 S.L.T. 1161 judicial review was sought of part of a sheriffs determination relating to the conduct of two doctors involved in the care of a patient who died in a nursing home. The determination was reduced to the extent that it was held that the sheriff had erred in law in failing to distinguish the conduct of one of the doctors from the other and in effect treating the position of the two doctors in an identical manner: see also *Lothian District Council v. Lord Advocate*, 1993 S.L.T. 40. In deciding issues of fact the sheriff exercises a wide discretion. In the context of the supervisory jurisdiction the court does not seek to interfere with the merits of a decision, simply its legality. Is the power of severance actually or potentially contrary to the normal ambit of the supervisory jurisdiction? Is there a danger that the court will substitute its view of its merits in granting partial reduction?

(5) One of the most difficult issues raised by the question of reduction of a decision is the **11–17** issue of retrospective effect of nullification. Much discussion has centred around whether or not an *ultra vires* act can be regarded as "void" or "voidable". Thus an *ultra vires* act might be regarded as having no effect — for all purposes, a nullity. In contrast, an act which can only be set aside on appeal or in the context of an application to quash might only be regarded as voidable. On this generally see W. Wade and C. Forsyth, *Administrative Law* (7th ed., 1994), pp. 339–340. Voidness is a relative matter and so an *ultra vires* act may not be totally lacking in legal effect. In some situations, an *ultra vires* act might be ignored.

In *Dalgleish v. Livingston* (1895) 22 R. 646 at 657 *obiter, per* Lord Rutherfurd Clark, a landlord was entitled to ignore an order made by the Crofters Commission in proceedings to which he was not a party. Such cases are rare, however and it is generally advisable that reduction be obtained: *London and Clydeside Estates Ltd v. Aberdeen District Council* below. If a decision is not invalid in the sense that there is a patent defect, then the courts will act on the assumption that it is valid, unless or until it is set aside: *City of Edinburgh District Council v. Secretary of*

State for Scotland, 1985 S.L.T. 551, on which see para. 2–38, and see also *F. Hoffmann-La Roche v. Secretary of State for Trade and Industry* [1974] 2 All E.R. 1128. Finally, the doctrine of severance may allow a decision to be treated as partially valid.

Understood in this relative sense, the voidness of an act may have a number of consequences:

- It can be used as a defence to proceedings raised by a public authority: see defence of illegality above and also *Allingham v. Minister of Agriculture and Fisheries* [1948] 1 All E.R. 780.

- Statutory provisions purporting to prevent recourse to the courts will be interpreted as effective in preventing challenges to voidable Acts only: see paras 10–37 to 10–42.

- The availability of an appeal will not necessarily cure a void act: on this see *Calvin v. Carr* [1980] A.C. 574 below and *Brown v. Executive Committee of the Edinburgh District Labour Party*, 1995 S.L.T. 985 below.

The most authoritative recent discussion of the effect of retrospective nullification in Scots law occurred in *London and Clydeside Estates Ltd v. Aberdeen District Council*, extracted at para. 5–5. The most important speeches in this context were those of Lord Hailsham and Lord Keith. Lord Hailsham's speech is reproduced at above. Lord Keith stated:

"It is logical in the circumstances to consider first whether the Lord Ordinary and their Lordships of the Second Division were right in granting decree of reduction of the certificate dated 22nd October 1974. It was argued for the respondents initially that the notice as to rights of appeal required by article 3 (3) of the 1959 Order was something severable from the certificate itself. The certificate, so it was maintained, constituted a decision of the local planning authority which had a force and validity of its own unaffected by any failure to give the statutory required notice about rights of appeal. Reference was made to the decision of the Court of Appeal in *Brayhead (Ascot) Ltd. v. Berkshire County Council* [1964] 2 Q.B. 303, where it was held that the failure of a local planning authority, when granting planning permission subject to a condition, to give reasons in writing for the imposition of the condition as required by article 5 (9) of the Town and Country Planning (General Development) Order 1950 did not render the condition void. This was upon the ground, as stated by Winn J. at pp. 313–314, that while the requirement was mandatory in the sense that compliance with it could be enforced by mandamus, non-compliance did not render the condition void because that result was not required for the effective achievement of the purposes of the statute under which the requirement was imposed, and not intended by Parliament on a proper construction of that statute. In my opinion the argument is not assisted by the case referred to and is unsound. Article 3 (3) of the 1959 Order specifically states that any certificate issued under section 25 (4) (*b*) of the Act 'shall include' a statement in writing of rights of appeal. This is entirely contrary to any idea of severability, and the provision is clearly necessary for effectively achieving the obvious purpose that the applicant receiving the certificate should know what his rights are. The consequences of failure to inform him of these rights may be irretrievable, unlike the consequences of failure to state reasons in writing, which can always be put right at a later date without anything more serious than some inconvenience…

The final argument for the respondents on this branch of the case turned on the terms of section 26 (4) of the 1963 Act, which I have quoted above. That enactment gives a right of appeal where the local authority fails to issue a certificate within the prescribed time, upon the basis that a certificate in terms of section 25 (4) (*b*) is deemed to have been issued. In the event, so the argument ran, that the certificate actually issued in this ease is held to have been invalid, the situation is the same as if no certificate had been issued. Therefore section 26 (4) applies, under which no question of notification of rights of appeal arises. The appellants should have appealed to the Secretary of State within one month of the expiry of the period of two months from the receipt by the respondents of the appellants' application for a certificate. They did not do so, and therefore they have lost any right of appeal. In my opinion this argument also is unsound. In the first place it is to be observed that the argument is elided if decree is to be granted not only reducing the certificate actually issued but also ordaining the respondents to issue a new certificate in proper form. It is not an argument in favour of the validity of the certificate issued. Indeed, it requires that the certificate should have been totally void *ab initio* and that the respondents should be treated as having done nothing at all in response to the appellants' application. That would, in my opinion, be totally unrealistic. The respondents did issue a certificate, but it contained a defect enabling it to be successfully attacked as invalid. I do not consider that section 26 (4) applies to that situation. It applies where after the expiry of the time prescribed 'no certificate has been issued.' Here a certificate was issued which, though defective, was not a complete nullity. In this context use of the expressions 'void' and 'voidable,' which have a recognised significance and importance in certain fields of the law of contract, is to be avoided as inappropriate and counsel for the appellants founded on *James* v. *Minister of Housing and Local Government* [1966] 1 W.L.R. 135 and [1968] A.C. 409, and *London Ballast Co. Ltd.* v. *Buckinghamshire County Council* (1967) 18 P. & C. R. 446. In each of these cases a point arose regarding the validity of a conditional planning permission granted after the expiry of the period statutorily prescribed for doing so. It is unnecessary to examine the cases in detail. It is sufficient to say that in each of them opinions were expressed to the effect that a planning permission so granted was not necessarily voidable, but that it might be so in certain circumstances. That appears to me to be an unexceptionable statement of the law."

Does Lord Hailsham's speech give either the citizen or the public authority involved a clear indication as to the effects of breach of the statutory provision? The adequacy or otherwise of the test was considered at some length by P.P. Craig, *Administrative Law* (3rd ed., 1994), pp. 463/464. He accepts the need for some flexibility to mitigate the full effects of retrospective nullification but states, however:

"In so far as discretion is to be exercised, how we should express this in legal language? We have three options. The language of jurisdictional and non-jurisdictional either can be used to arrive at the desired conclusion; the terms void and voidable can be manipulated; or the discretion can appear at the remedial level. I would argue that the last of these is the most apt convenience on most occasions."

The need for clarity in judicial decision making requires that:

"It is for this reason, amongst others, that I am in favour of the exception operating in its discretion to refuse a remedy rather than in juggling of jurisdictional versus non-jurisdictional categories, or in a sleight of hand over the meanings of void and voidable. Both of these latter avenues suffer from three related defects. First, they conceal what is taking place. They provide a convenient mask for legal form to hide reality. Secondly, use of either of these avenues produces confusion by ascribing meanings to the same terms, meanings which when analysed make little sense. Thirdly, if the discretion is exercised via either of these routes there is a danger that what may have been intended as only an ad hoc exception to the norm of retrospective nullity, an exception is justified by the facts of the particular case, will become unintentionally generalised."

Are these approaches evident in Lord Hailsham's speech? Would prospective declarator avoid some of the problems caused by retrospective nullification? On this generally see C. Lewis, "Retrospective and Prospective Rulings in Administrative Law" [1988] P.L. 78.

It is not only academics who have had difficulty with Lord Hailsham's approach. In *R. v. London Borough of Tower Hamlets, ex parte Tower Hamlets Combined Traders Association* [1994] C.O.D. 325 Sedley J. held that the *ratio decidendi* of *London and Clydeside Estates Ltd* was found in the speech of Lord Keith. The proposition that the question of whether or not compliance with the procedural requirement rendered the decision invalid was a question of judgment and not discretion and depended on the significance of the requirement and not its effect on its imposition on the particular applicant.

(6) For a recent example of the application of Lord Hailsham's approach see *King v. East Ayrshire Council*, 1998 S.L.T. 1287. Here a mother of two children attending a denominational school petitioned for judicial review of the education authority's decision to close the school without referring the matter to the Secretary of State. She alleged that the education authority had applied the wrong test under the Education (Publication and Consultation Etc.) (Scotland) Regulations 1981. Although accepting that the education authority had erred in law, the First Division was not prepared to reduce the decision. **11–18**

"Even where a court is satisfied that an administrative body have erred in law in reaching their decision, the court is not bound to reduce that decision. As Lord Hailsham LC pointed out in *London & Clydeside Estates Ltd v Aberdeen District Council*, 1980 SC (HL) at p 31; 1980 SLT at p 86, the jurisdiction to grant decree of reduction of administrative decisions is 'inherently discretionary'. In particular it is relevant for the court to consider what practical effect the person seeking reduction will achieve if the decision is reduced. In *Malloch v Aberdeen Corporation* the appellant was a certificated teacher who was dismissed from his employment with the corporation. He sought reduction of the decision to dismiss him on the ground that he had not been given a hearing before being dismissed. The House of Lords held that he had been entitled to a hearing before being dismissed. Lord Reid accepted that, if it could have been clearly demonstrated that such a hearing could have made no difference and would therefore have been a useless formality, it might have been a good answer to the appellant's claim to have the decision to dismiss him reduced (at 1971 SC (HL), p 104; 1971 SLT, p 248) and Lord Simon left that point open (at p 123 (p 258)). Lord Wilberforce dealt with the same point in this way (at p 118 (p 255)):... .

It is recognised that the public interest in good administration requires that public authorities and third parties should not be kept in suspense as to the legal validity of a decision for any longer than is absolutely necessary in fairness to the person affected by it (*O'Reilly v Mackman* [1983] 2 AC at pp 280H-281A per Lord Diplock). Here the petitioner asks us to reduce the respondents' decision on a basis which would have been open to her from the outset, but which she did not advance then, preferring instead to use a different argument to attack their decision. This new attack is mounted 10 months after the judicial review proceeding began and over a year after the school was closed. Judicial review is a flexible procedure and the court can, of course, take account of new matters and grant different remedies from those which are originally sought. In an appropriate case that could be done even at a late stage, but in deciding whether to grant a remedy on a different basis the court must not lose sight of the wider interest in good administration which Lord Diplock describes. We have borne this wider interest in mind when considering the petitioner's new case for reduction. We have also had regard to the other circumstances which we have mentioned. In this unusual situation, even though it appears likely that the respondents failed to have regard to the historic attendance attendance figures when calculating the school's pupil capacity, we are satisfied that we should not reduce their decision."

For further examples of this flexible approach see *R. v. Chester City Council, ex parte Quitlynn Ltd, The Times*, October 19, 1983 and *Porritt v. Secretary of State for the Environment and Bramley London Borough* [1988] J.P.L. 414.

DEFENCE OF ILLEGALITY

Wandsworth London Borough Council v. Winder

[1985] A.C. 461

11–19   "Mr Winder, the respondent, was a tenant of a council flat in Wandsworth. In March 1981, the appellants, Wandsworth Borough Council, gave notice to the respondent, as they were required to do under s. 40 of the Housing Act 1980, that from April 1981 his rent would be increased from £12.06 to £16.56 a week. The respondent regarded the increase as unreasonable and paid only £12.06, plus an amount which he considered to be reasonable. When the appellants increased the rent in the following year he adopted the same stance. The appellants then took proceedings against the respondent in Wandsworth County Court claiming arrears of rent, and also claiming possession of the premises on the ground that the rent lawfully due had not been paid. The respondent defended the action on the ground that the appellants' decisions to make the increases, and the increases themselves, were so unreasonable that no local authority could have come to them and were therefore ultra vires. He also counterclaimed for a declaration that the notices of increase were ultra vires and void and of no effect, and for a declaration that the rent payable under the tenancy was £12.06 per week. The Court of Appeal allowed Mr Winder's appeal from the decision of the judge at first instance that the relevant paragraphs of his defence and the counter-claim should be struck out. The council appealed to the House of Lords."

LORD FRASER: "The respondent seeks to show in the course of his defence in these proceedings that the appellant's decisions to increase the rent were such as no reasonable man could consider justifiable. But your Lordships are not concerned in this appeal to decide whether that contention is right or wrong. The only issue at this stage is whether the respondent is entitled to put forward the contention as a defence in the present proceedings. The appellants say that he is not because the only procedure by which their decision could have been challenged was by judicial review under RSC Ord. 53. The respondent was refused leave to apply for judicial review out of time and (say the appellants) he has lost the opportunity to challenge the decisions. The appellants rely on the decisions of this House in *O'Reilly* v *Mackman*

[1983] 2 AC 237 and *Cocks v Thanet District Council* [1983] 2 AC 286. The respondent accepts that judicial review would have been an appropriate procedure for the purpose, but he maintains that it is not the only procedure open to him, and that he was entitled to wait until he was sued by the appellants and then to defend the proceedings, as he has done.

In order to deal with these contentions, it is necessary to consider what was decided by the House of Lords in those two cases. The question raised in *O'Reilly* was not the same as that in the present case, although of course, the circumstances were different.

...

There are two important differences between the facts in *O'Reilly* and those in the present case. First, the plaintiffs in *O'Reilly* had not suffered any infringement of their rights in private law; their complaint was that they had been ordered to forfeit part of their remission of sentence but they had no right in private law to such a remission, which was granted only as a matter of indulgence. Consequently, even if the board of visitors had acted contrary to the rules of natural justice when making the award, the members of the board would not have been liable in damages to the prisoners. In the present case what the respondent complains of is the infringement of a contractual right in private law. Secondly, in *O'Reilly* the prisoners had initiated the proceedings, and Lord Diplock, throughout in his speech, treated the question only as one affecting a claim for infringing a right of the plaintiff while in the present case the respondent is the defendant. The decision in *O'Reilly* is therefore not directly in point in the present case, but the appellants rely particularly on a passage in the speech of Lord Diplock, with whose speech the other members of the Appellate Committee agreed...

[His Lordship read from the judgment of Lord Diplock; the relevant paragraph, *ante*, beginning 'Now that...']

The last paragraph in that quotation shows that Lord Diplock was careful to emphasise that the general rule which he had stated in the previous paragraph might well be subject to exceptions. The question for your Lordships is whether the instant appeal is an exception to the general rule. It might be possible to treat this case as falling within one of the exceptions suggested by Lord Diplock, if the question of the invalidity of the appellants' decision had arisen as a collateral issue in a claim by the respondent (as defendant) for infringement of his right arising under private law to occupy the flat. But I do not consider that the question of invalidity is truly collateral to the issue between the parties. Although it is not mentioned in the appellant's statement of claim, it is the whole basis of the respondent's defence and it is the central issue which has to be decided. The case does not fall within any of the exceptions specifically suggested in *O'Reilly* v *Mackman* [1983] 2 AC 237. Immediately after the decision in *O'Reilly*, the House applied the general rule in the case of *Cocks* [1983] 2 AC 286. The proceedings in *O'Reilly* had begun before the Supreme Court Act 1981 (especially section 31) had been passed. The proceedings in *Cocks* were begun after that Act was passed, but for the present purpose nothing turns on that distinction. *Cocks* was an action by a homeless person claiming that the local housing authority had a duty to provide permanent accommodation for him. The council resolved that the plaintiff had become homeless 'intentionally' in the sense of the Housing (Homeless Persons) Act 1977. Consequently the plaintiff had no right in private law to be provided with permanent housing accommodation by the authority. The plaintiff raised an action in the county court claiming, inter alia, a declaration that the council were in breach of their duty to him in not having provided him with permanent accommodation. In order to proceed in his action he had to show as a condition precedent that the council's decision was invalid. This House held that the plaintiff was not entitled to impugn the council's decision in public law otherwise than by judicial review, notwithstanding that the effect of the decision was to prevent him from 'establishing a necessary condition precedent to the statutory private law right which he [was seeking] to enforce': see *per* my noble and learned friend Lord Bridge of Harwich at p. 294E. The essential difference between that case and the present is that the impugned decision of the local authority did not deprive the plaintiff of a pre-existing private law right; it prevented him from establishing a new private law right. There is also the same distinction as in *O'Reilly* [1983] 2 AC 237, namely, that the party complaining of the decision was the plaintiff.

Although neither *O'Reilly* nor *Cocks* [1983] 2 AC 286 is an authority which directly applies to the facts of the instant appeal, it is said on behalf of the appellants that the principle underlying those decisions applies here, and that, if the respondent is successful, he will be evading that principle. My Lords, I cannot agree. The principle underlying those decisions, as Lord Diplock explained in *O'Reilly* [1983] 2 AC 237, 284, is that there is a 'need, in the interests of good administration and of third parties who may be indirectly affected by the decision, for speedy certainty as to whether it has the effect of a decision that is valid in public law.' The main argument urged on behalf of the appellants was that this is a typical case where there is a need for speedy certainty in the public interest. I accept, of course, that the decision in the appeal will indirectly affect many of the appellants' tenants, and perhaps most if not all of their ratepayers because if the appellants' impugned decisions are held to be invalid, the basis of their financial administration since 1981 will be upset. That would be highly inconvenient from the point of view of the appellants, and of their rate-payers, and it would be a great advantage to them if persons who seek to challenge their decisions were limited to doing so by procedure under Order 53 . . . It may well be that such protection to public authorities tends to promote good administration. But there may be other ways of obtaining speedy decisions; for example in some cases it may be possible for a public authority itself to initiate proceedings for judicial review. In any event the arguments for protecting public authorities against unmeritorious or dilatory challenges to their decisions have to be set against the arguments for preserving the ordinary rights of citizens to defend themselves against unfounded claims.

It would in my opinion be a very strange use of language to describe the respondent's behaviour in relation to this litigation as an abuse or misuse by him of the process of the court. He did not select the procedure to be adopted. He is merely seeking to defend proceedings brought against him by the appellants. In so doing he is seeking only to exercise the ordinary right of any individual to defend an action against him on the ground that he is not liable for the whole sum claimed by the plaintiff. Moreover he puts forward his defence as a matter of right whereas in an application for judicial review, success would require an exercise of the court's discretion in his favour. Apart from the provisions of Order 53 and section 31 of the Supreme Court Act 1981, he would certainly be entitled to defend the action on the ground that the plaintiff's claim arises from a resolution which (on his view) is invalid: see for example *Cannock Chase District Council* v *Kelly* [1978] 1 WLR 1, which was decided in July 1977, a few months before Order 53 came into force (as it did in December 1977). I find it impossible to accept that the right to challenge the decision by a local authority in the course of defending an action for non-payment can have been swept away by Order 53, which was directed to introducing a procedural reform. As my noble and learned friend Lord Scarman said in *Reg* v *Inland Revenue Commissioners, ex parte Federation of Self-Employed and Small Businesses Ltd* [1982] AC 617, 647g 'The new RSC Ord 53 is a procedural reform of great importance in the field of public law but it does not — indeed, cannot — either extend or diminish the substantive law. Its function is limited to ensuring "ubi jus, ibi remedium".' Lord Wilberforce spoke to the same effect at p. 631A. Nor, in my opinion, did section 31 of the Supreme Court Act 1981 which refers only to 'an application for judicial review' have the effect of limiting the rights of a defendant sub silentio. I would adopt the words of Viscoun. Simonds in *Pyx Granite Co. Ltd* v *Ministry of Housing and Local Government* [1960] AC 260, 236 as follows:

It is a principle not by any means to be whittled down that the subject's recourse to Her Majesty's courts for the determination of his rights is not to be excluded except by clear words.

The argument of the appellants in the present case would be directly in conflict with that observation.

If the public interest requires that persons should not be entitled to defend actions brought against them by the public authority where the defence rests on a challenge to a decision by the public authority, then it is for Parliament to change the law.

I would dismiss the appeal."

Notes

11–20   (1) This case was concerned with the extent to which one could use the validity of an administrative act as a defence to enforcement proceedings, where the person to whom enforcement was directed had not yet taken action by seeking to have the act declared *ultra vires* by way of judicial review or, if a right of appeal had been available, by way of that procedure.

It was subsequently held that the rent increases were valid and an appeal to the Court of Appeal was dismissed: see *Wandsworth London Borough Council v. Winder (No. 2)* (1987) 19 H.L.R. 204. The difficulty that arose in *Winder* was that under English judicial review procedure, in light of *O'Reilly v. Mackman* [1982] 3 All E.R. 1124 (H.L.), it was generally accepted that only issues of public law could be invoked by judicial review procedure and that this was an exclusive procedure. This meant that one had to decide whether or not one's case raised a matter of public law and, if it did, to pursue judicial review as a means of resolving the issue. This difficulty was compounded by the fact that under English law, a petition for judicial review was to be brought within three months of the date of the decision being challenged. Those who opted for the wrong procedure could therefore find future challenge barred: see also *Roy v. Kensington and Chelsea and Westminster Family Practitioner Committee* [1992] 2 W.L.R. 239. The defence is recognised in Scots law, although there is not much in the way of recent authority: see *Stair Memorial Encyclopaedia*, Vol. 1, para. 331 and Finch and Ashton, pp. 364–365.

(2) Rule 58 seeks to provide an exclusive procedure for judicial review. Concern was raised by the Scottish Working Party of the Justice-All Souls Report to the effect that the difficulties found in *O'Reilly* might be relevant to Scots law: para. 6.47. This view did not, however, take on board the fact that existing Scots law, such as *North British Rail Co. v. Steel Co. of Scotland Ltd*, 1921 S.C. 252, was more consistent with the approach in *Winder* than in *O'Reilly*.

(3) It will be noted that as rule 58 is simply a procedural reform it cannot affect questions of **11–21** substantive right. However, does the lack of a time-limit for the seeking of judicial review in Scots law act as an argument for or against allowing the defence of illegality in civil proceedings? Moreover, notwithstanding the difficulties relating to the public/private law distinction, which are not an issue in Scots law, is the test set out in *West* sufficiently clear to justify a strict application of the exclusivity principle?

(4) There are in any event fairly serious limitations on the ability to use the defence and these will often arise in circumstances for which the defence might otherwise be considered. For example, statute may either restrict or exclude the availability of judicial review, on which see paras 10–34 to 10–42. Equally, failure to exhaust a statutory remedy may be relevant in limiting the scope of the defence, as in *Distillers Co. Ltd v. Fife County Council*, 1925 S.C. (H.L.) 15. An attempt was made by a ratepayer to challenge the validity of an entry in the valuation roll but only after the roll was finalised. This occurred in the context of enforcement proceedings for recovery of rates. It was held that it was not possible to use this as a defence as the matter should have been raised under the relevant rating appeal provisions of the legislation then in force: see too *R. v. Wicks* [1997] 2 All E.R. 801. *Distillers Co. Ltd* must now be read in light of *Tarmac Econowaste* and the other cases cited in Chapter 10. For further limitations on the defence see *Stair Memorial Encyclopaedia*, Vol. 1, para. 331.

(5) The use of the defence in the context of review of the actions of public authorities in enforcement of byelaws and regulations has a sound statutory basis in criminal law: see here the Criminal Procedure (Scotland) Act 1995, Sched. 3 and cases noted at paras 2–32 and 2–33. It has been held in England that if the successful defence of *ultra vires* of such a byelaw or regulations made out then this does not entitle the person acquitted to raise an action in tort against the arresting officer: *Percy v. Hall* [1996] 4 All E.R. 523. Until recently, in England, a defence based on procedural *ultra vires* to a criminal charge meant that the defendant had to seek a separate action for judicial review, but where the defence was based on substantive *ultra vires*, that could be used as a defence without separate judicial review proceedings: *Bugg v. D.P.P.* [1993] Q.B. 473. That approach has now been overruled: *Boddington v. British Transport Police* [1998] 1 W.L.R. 369.

(6) For discussion of this area generally see C. Emery, "The *Vires* Defence — '*Ultra Vires*' as a Defence to Criminal or Civil Proceedings" (1992) 51 C.L.J. 308 and "Collateral Attack — Attacking *Ultra Vires* Action Indirectly in Courts and Tribunals" (1993) 56 M.L.R. 643; A.W. Bradley, 2 "Collateral challenge to enforcement decisions — a duty to apply for judicial review?" [1997] P.L. 365; and C. Forsyth, "Collateral challenge and the foundations of judicial review: orthodoxy vindicated and procedural exclusivity rejected" [1998] P.L. 364.

INTERDICT

Meek v. Lothian Regional Council

1980 S.L.T. (Notes) 61

"Section 69 (1) of the Local Government (Scotland) Act 1973 provides: 'Without prejudice to any **11–22** powers exercisable apart from this section but subject to the provisions of this Act and any other enactment passed before or after this Act, a local authority shall have power to do anything (whether or not involving the expenditure, borrowing or lending of money or the acquisition or disposal of any property or rights) which is calculated to facilitate, or is conducive or incidental to, the discharge of any of their functions'. Section 83 (1) of the Act empowers a local authority to incur expenditure on contributions to charities, bodies providing public services and public appeals where such expenditure is thought to be in the interests of their area. Section 28 of the Employment Protection (Consolidation) Act 1978 provides inter alia: 'An employer shall permit an employee of his who is a member of an appropriate trade union to take time off … during the employee's working hours for the purpose of taking part in any trade union activity to which this section applies'.

On 26 November 1979 a regional council resolved to allow certain of its employees nominated by their trade unions time off work without loss of pay to take part in a 'National Lobby of Parliament' on 28 November. Members of the minority group on the council who had opposed the resolution applied to the court to declare the resolution null and void as being ultra vires and passed in mala fide and to interdict the council from implementing the resolution so far as allowing absence without loss of pay. On 27 November the pursuers moved the court to grant interim interdict. The motion was opposed by the regional council. Eodem die the Lord Ordinary (McDonald) granted the motion."

LORD McDONALD: "It was argued on behalf of the pursuers that the resolution was ultra vires because there was no power vested in the local authority to grant leave of absence for this purpose with pay. Where such an argument is presented one naturally turns in the first instance to the legislation which governs the powers and functions of local authorities. The appropriate statute in the present case is the Local Government (Scotland) Act 1973. I was referred in particular to s. 69 (1) of that Act which provides that a local authority shall have power to do anything which is calculated to facilitate or is conducive or incidental to the discharge of any of their functions. It was argued on behalf of the defenders that it was a matter which was calculated to facilitate or conducive or incidental to the discharge of their functions that they should support this lobby by making available such members of trade unions from their employees to be present and to demonstrate and that this entitled them to pay them for their activities. I would be slow at this juncture to form the opinion that this section of the Act which deals with subsidiary powers of local authorities was eve intended to be applied to a situation such as the present and I am of opinion that there is at least sufficient doubt about this matter at this stage to make it a relevant matter for further inquiry. I was also referred by counsel for the defenders to s. 83 of the same Act which is a miscellaneous section and does indeed provide a local authority with power to incur certain expenditure for certain purposes not otherwise authorised. The precise nature of these purposes is not spelled out but again I would have great hesitation in deciding at this juncture that this particular section authorised the defenders to make the payments which they seek to make in terms of their resolution. It was argued to me on behalf of the defenders that the doctrine of ultra vires was one which had to be applied reasonably and wherever anything may fairly be regarded as incidental to or consequential upon the things which the legislature has authorised then the doctrine ought not to be applied. I was referred in this connection to what Lord Selbourne said in the case of *Attorney General* v. *Great Eastern Railway Company* (1880) 5 A.C. 473. That case has obviously been considered on a great number of occasions. I have not had an opportunity of referring to all the cases in which it has been considered. My attention, however, was drawn to a recent expression of opinion to the effect that the words 'incidental to' should be applied with a narrow meaning and not as equivalent to 'in connection with'. I am content at this stage to accept that and I do not consider therefore that there is anything in what Lord Selbourne said in that case which necessarily prevents the pursuers being allowed to prove what they seek to prove in the present case....

The pursuers also have a case based upon mala fides and that proceeds upon averments that the resolution involved an unreasonable exercise of the defenders' powers; that they had acted upon irrelevant considerations in passing it; and that the majority of the councillors who voted for the resolution form part of a group opposed for political reasons to the government's proposed reductions in public expenditure. The averments go on to say that at a meeting on 26 November they had bound themselves to vote as a group for this purported resolution. There was, it is said, no material before the defenders at the meeting upon which they could honestly reach the conclusion that employees should be allowed time off work to lobby Parliament without loss of pay. Here again I am of the view that there is a matter which falls suitably to be investigated and in this connection I was referred to three cases: *Innes* v. *Royal Burgh of Kirkcaldy*, 1963 S.L.T. 325; *Roberts* v. *Hopwood* [1925] A.C. 578: and *Taylor* v. *Munrow* [1960] 1 W.L.R. 181. What is said in these cases is largely to the same effect, but I quote from that part of the judgment of Lord Cameron in the case of *Innes* v. *Royal Burgh of Kirkcaldy* where, having accepted that he requires to take the pursuer's averments pro veritate, he goes on to say: 'The only meaning I can give to that averment is that the majority group in the council entered on consideration of this case with their minds closed at least to one side of the matter, determined not to apply their unaffected judgment to the issue before them.' Accordingly I am of opinion that on both grounds the pursuers have properly raised an issue to be investigated. This now brings me to what is in the end of the day the only matter of importance at this stage, namely where does the balance of convenience lie? I am clearly of the view that it lies in favour of granting the interim order sought. If, for any reason, it turns out in the end of the day that the pursuers are erroneous in their averments or are unable to substantiate them then no doubt the appropriate payments can be made. It was argued on the other hand that some, if not all, of the proposed demonstrators would not go unless they were paid. At this late stage in the proceedings this seems somewhat undecided on their part and in any event I consider that less harm will be done if the interdict is granted in its present terms than if it is refused. I would like to emphasise that the terms of the interdict are extremely limited, they relate only to the question of time off work without loss of pay. There is of course nothing to prevent, as I understand it, those who wish to go taking time off work doing so. The only effect of this interdict is that at the moment they will not receive pay for the time whilst they are off work."

Notes

(1) *Meek* is an important example of the use of interdict in administrative law to restrain   **11–23**
ultra vires acts. Allegations of both simple *ultra vires* and abuse of discretion were made. The wrong in question was an apprehended one, but interdict is equally available where it is sought to prevent the continuation of the wrong: *Hay's Trustees v. Young* (1877) 4 R. 398 at 401 per Lord Ormidale. Interdict is a peculiar remedy in that it exists purely as a way of protecting existing rights or interests, it cannot be used to force an authority to exercise discretionary powers in a certain way: *Fleming v. Liddesdale District Committee* (1897) 24 R. 281 (discretion of committee to choose form of street lighting). Interdict can, however, be granted to stop the cessation of a service. In *Deane v. Lothian Regional Council*, 1986 S.L.T. 22 the Inner House granted interim interdict against a local authority to prevent it from carrying out the statutory procedure for opposing a denominational school: contrast with *Edinburgh Property Management Association v. City of Edinburgh District Council*, 1987 G.W.D. 38-1348. *Highland Regional Council v. British Railways Board*, 1996 S.L.T. 274 above is an example of the use of interdict to prevent the cessation of a railway service. It can be used to ensure that due care is taken in the exercise of a statutory duty: *Gavin v. Ayr County Council*, 1950 S.C. 197.

(2) Interdict is a discretionary remedy. As stated by Lord Deas in *Kelso School Board v. Hunter* (1874) 2 R. 228 at 232:

> "[It is] not to be given except for urgent reasons, and even then not as a matter or right, but only in the exercise of sound judicial discretion."

Where, however, the criteria for the grant of interdict are met, the court must grant the remedy: *Ferguson v. Tennant*, 1978 S.C. (H.L.) 19 at 47 *per* Lord Wheatley.

Although these dicta are of general application, in the context of administrative law they raise delicate questions of the balancing of public interest against private right. This found particular expression in relation to the reluctance of the courts to grant interim interdict where the substance of the issue involves interference with the parliamentary process or, at a lower level, public inquiry procedures: see, for example, *Ayr Magistrates v. Secretary of State for Scotland*, 1966 S.L.T. 16. Where questions of parliamentary privilege and the status of the Crown may be involved, equally the courts will often take the view that it is better that the substantive issues at stake should be aired freely without judicial restriction: see *Bilston Corporation v. Wolverhampton Corporation* [1942] 2 All E.R. 447. Interdict, including interim interdict, will not be available in relation to proceedings against the Scottish Parliament nor its officers or staff: see the Scotland Act 1998, ss. 40(3)–(5). Instead, declarator will be available.

(3) To obtain interim interdict, it is necessary to show that the balance of convenience   **11–24**
justifies it. Considerations which are relevant to the grant of refusal of interim interdict include the irreparable nature of the wrong alleged, *British Coal Corporation v. South of Scotland Electricity Board*, 1988 S.L.T. 446 (effect on market); considerations of natural justice or fairness, *Lockhart v. Irving* (see para. 9–5); and the cost of the implementation of the decision challenged, *Adams v. Glasgow Magistrates* (1868) 40 S.J. 524 (erection of public building). The presence of a clear conflict on the facts is not a conclusive factor in refusing interim interdict: *Falkirk Council v. Central Regional Council*, 1997 S.L.T. 1242. Special statutory considerations may, however, exclude or restrict scope for interim interdict, on which see *Central Regional Council v. Clackmannan District Council*, 1983 S.L.T. 666 (stop notice in planning law). The issue of balance of convenience is, however, secondary as to whether or not there is a prima facie case

in law for perpetual interdict. *Meek* is an example of this. However, the probability or otherwise of success on the law should not be taken too far, as noted by Lord Fleming in *Scottish Milk Marketing Board v. Paris*, 1935 S.C. 287 at 302,

> "In a petition for suspension and interdict at the instance of the Board against a registered producer, the petitioners craved for, *inter alia*, interim interdict against the respondent selling milk to certain customers without the petitioners' consent. The respondent held a producer-wholesaler's licence authorising him to sell milk to nondomestic consumers whose total daily supply did not exceed twenty gallons; but the petitioners maintained that this licence did not cover his dealings with the customers referred to; that the respondent had refused to accept the petitioners' conditions of contract for the supply of milk and was privately adjusting his own terms; that the respondent was in breach of the provisions of the Scheme; and that, pending the determination of the questions between the parties, the petitioners had no means of controlling the price paid for the respondent's milk. The respondent maintained that his licence covered the dealings referred to; that he was under no obligation to accept the petitioners' conditions of contract; and, in any event, that, even if he were in contravention of the Scheme, the Scheme itself provided the remedy for a contravention, and interdict was incompetent, or, at all events inappropriate. The Lord Ordinary... refused interim interdict ...
>
> LORD FLEMING: It is not in dispute that there are here questions which will require to be tried, and that the case must be continued for that purpose. I desire to express no opinion whatever on these questions which still remain for determination by the Court.
>
> The only point for consideration now is whether the petitioners are entitled to have interim interdict granted. In determining that matter it is the practice of the Court to consider where the balance of convenience lies. It was, however, argued on behalf of the respondents that the application for interdict was incompetent, and that interim interdict should therefore not be granted. It is clear that the Court has jurisdiction to regulate matters *ad interim* until that or any other question between the parties has been determined. If it was quite plain that the objection to the competency was well founded, that would doubtless be a good reason for refusing interim interdict. I assume that there is a serious question as to whether interdict is a competent remedy in this particular case, but the circumstances are quite special, and there is no authority precisely on the point. It cannot be said to be clear beyond all question that the objection to the competency is well founded, and I do not think the fact that it has been brought forward should prevent us from dealing with the application for interim interdict.
>
> In considering whether otherwise there is good ground for granting interim interdict I think it is legitimate to bear in mind that the petitioners are a statutory authority. In the interest of milk producers, and also, as I think, of the public generally, they are charged with the difficult duty of administering this Scheme. It is said that the actings of the Board which have given rise to the present proceedings are *ultra vires*. It is, of course, quite possible that a statutory body may act *ultra vires*, and if it does, and injury results to a private person, he will be entitled to redress. But it is not to be presumed that a public body acting in the public interest has exceeded its statutory powers. From the public point of view it would be unfortunate, if not disastrous, if anything were to prevent this Scheme functioning properly. I think it might lead to serious difficulty if milk-producers were permitted to disregard entirely the administrative directions of the Board until the validity of their objections had been finally determined. If the respondent had chosen, it seems to me he might have entered into a temporary arrangement with the Board which would have prejudiced neither his interests nor his rights. I agree that the petitioners are entitled to interim interdict."

Contrast with *Bell v. Secretary of State for Scotland*, 1933 S.L.T. 519. For the different position in English administrative law see *F. Hoffmann-La Roche & Co. A.G. v. Secretary of State for Trade and Industry* [1974] 2 All E.R. 1128.

(4) Where interim interdict is granted it is done *periculo petentis*: that is, the party who has obtained interim interdict will be liable in damages to the other party if, at final determination, the court holds him not entitled to interdict and the other party suffered loss: see, for example, *Bonnes v. West Lothian District Council*, 1994 G.W.D. 31-1888.

(5) Interdict, including interim interdict, is not available against the Crown or its officers: Crown Proceedings Act 1947, s. 21(1)(*a*), although declarator is available in section 43(*a*). Interdict was previously competent: *Bell v. Secretary of State for Scotland*, 1933 S.L.T. 519.

The issue of whether or not judicial review proceedings are "civil proceedings" within the terms of section 21(1)(*a*) was raised but not decided in *McDonald v. Secretary of State for Scotland*, 1994 S.C. 234. It is highly unlikely, however, that they would not be so treated if the matter arises for a future decision. Where, however, there is an allegation of breach of European Community law, interdict, including interim interdict is competent: *R. v. Secretary of State for Transport, ex parte Factortame* [1990] 2 A.C. 85 and see *Millar and Bryce Ltd v. Keeper of the Registers of Scotland*, 1997 S.L.T. 1000, on which see C. Bloch, "Interim Remedies Against the Crown Revisited", 1997 S.L.T. (News) 165 and generally see Finch and Ashton, pp. 464–469.

DAMAGES

Mallon v. Monklands District Council (sub nom. Kelly v. Monklands District Council)

1986 S.L.T. 347

"A young girl was put out of her home by her parents. She applied to the local housing authority for accommodation as a homeless person having a priority need. The authority wrongly decided that she did not have a priority need and accommodation was only provided six months later after an application for judicial review had been made. During the six month period the girl stayed first at a social work department short stay refuge for teenagers and then at a homeless unit. During this period the girl had become depressed. Her condition improved following the allocation of accommodation to her."

LORD JAUNCEY: "On 12 July 1985 Lord Ross reduced a decision of the respondents of 11 April 1985 that the petitioner, who was homeless, did not have a priority need for the purposes of the Housing (Homeless Persons) Act 1977 and ordered the respondents to secure that accommodation was made available for her in terms of s. 4(5) of that Act. The case now comes before me for proof on the petitioner's claim for damages of £1,000 resulting from the respondents' failure to perform their statutory duties under s. 4 (5).

11–25

The relevant history is as follows. For some time the petitioner's parents, who were both alcoholics, had abused the petitioner when she was at home, wrongly accused her of misdeeds and threatened to throw her out of the house. On one occasion the petitioner was so much affected by this behaviour that she slashed her wrists. From February 1985 the petitioner began to spend the evenings at a short stay refuge for teenagers run by the social work department of the Strathclyde Regional Council. On 4 April 1985 which was the eve of her 16th birthday, she returned home from the refuge in the company of a social worker to find her parents once again drunk. An argument ensued and she was told by her parents to leave the house. She then returned to stay at the refuge. On 9 April she made an application under the 1977 Act to the respondents for accommodation. On 11 April the respondents decided that the petitioner did not have a priority need for accommodation for the purposes of s. 2. The petitioner continued to stay at the refuge until 22 April when she removed to a homeless unit nearby which was run by the respondents. At this homeless unit the petitioner occupied a bed-sitting room on the second floor and shared washing and cooking facilities with other occupants. She remained there until 1 November although on occasion she returned to the refuge late at night and slept there when she was disturbed by young men shouting and otherwise creating outside the unit. However, in late September she was allocated a house by the respondents and on 7 October she signed the missives of lease therefor and received the key. The allocation of the house was made shortly after Lord Ross had on 24 September continued the second hearing for the purpose inter ali a of enabling the respondents to comply with the interlocutor of 12 July.

Evidence was given on behalf of the petitioner by Mrs Stevens, a qualified social worker employed by Strathclyde Regional Council in the short stay refuge, and by Mr Cran, another social worker who was the project leader at the refuge. The petitioner also gave evidence. The social workers who saw the petitioner on frequent occasions during the relevant period were perhaps better able to express an objective opinion as to her state of mind than was the petitioner. The picture which they painted was of a young girl who was very sad at times, was depressed and unsure of her future. The depression manifested itself in mild self mutilation of the arms and fits of anger and irrationality. For two or three weeks after the petitioner removed to the homeless unit she was quite happy but her depression returned after young men started to make nuisances of themselves outside the building. Her depression was described by Mrs Stevens as a reactive depression and not a medical problem. Certainly there was no evidence that the petitioner sought or required any medical advice or treatment while she was in the refuge or the homeless unit. Although the petitioner and the two social workers considered that the lack of any secure accommodation was a factor in her depression there is no doubt in my mind that other factors contributed as well. Indeed Mrs Stevens enumerated, in this order, five traumatic factors as contributing to her depression, namely, (1) the fact of being put of her home by her parents, (2) the possibility of her parents being taken to court and their younger children being put into care, (3) the fact that she did not have a house, (4) the fact that she had had to grow up in a matter of weeks and learn to cope with the department of health and social security and officialdom in general, and (5) that she very much minded not seeing her younger sister and worried about how she was being treated by her parents. However, not withstanding the existence of these other factors both social workers considered that the petitioner had changed remarkably since obtaining the keys for her house and that she was now happy, lively and purposeful in a way which she had not been before. From all this evidence I conclude that lack of secure accommodation was a substantial cause of the petitioner's insecurity and a factor contributing to her depression during the months prior to 7 October 1985.

Counsel for the petitioner submitted that most of the petitioner's anguish and depression was a consequence of the respondents' failure to perform their statutory duties consequent upon her application of 9 April and that an award of solatium of the order of the £1,000 claim would be appropriate....

In this case there is no doubt that the respondents' decision of 11 April did distress and depress the petitioner; the question is whether it did more and produced a recognisable psychiatric illness. The matter is finely balanced but having regard to the evidence of the two social workers I consider that the petitioner's self mutilation of her arms, her occasional anger and irrationality and withdrawal into herself were more than just normal reactions to the disappointment at not being allocated secure accommodation. I am satisfied that her general state of depression was a reactive depression which constituted a minor psychiatric illness and that it was in part due to the insecure situation in which she found herself.

I reject the respondents' contention which was stated but not developed to any extent in argument that the anguish and depression suffered by the petitioner were not reasonably foreseeable consequences of the respondents' failure to perform their statutory duties. I also reject the contention that the contribution of the respondents' failure to perform their statutory duty was so small as to be immeasurable. Equally I consider that the petitioner is ill founded in claiming that a sum of the order £1,000 would be appropriate compensation. I can only take a very broad axe to this problem but in my view a sum of £100 would adequately reflect the extent to which the respondents' failure contributed to the minor psychiatric illness suffered by the petitioner and for this sum I shall grant decree."

Notes

11–26   (1) Whether damages are available as a remedy in administrative law proceedings is to a great extent dependent on the underlying substantive law, whether of delict or contract, whether there has been a breach of statutory duty or misfeasance in office, on which see Chapter 14.

(2) In the context of judicial review proceedings, the award of damages in *Mallon* is relatively unusual. This stems from the fact that judicial review is generally concerned with jurisdictional control rather than compensation for wrong suffered. *Mallon* can be regarded as an example of a deliberate refusal to exercise jurisdiction. Generally, malice, bad faith or improper motive need to be averred before liability and damages will attach to a discretionary decision affecting an individual: see para. 6–11. Statute may also limit the scope for damages and sometimes this protection will extend to intentional misuse of powers: *Smith v. East Elloe Rural District Council* [1956] A.C. 736; *R. v. Secretary of State for the Environment, ex parte Ostler* [1977] Q.B. 122; and *Moore v. Secretary of State for Scotland*, 1985 S.L.T. 38.

(3) Where a claim for damages is sought in a petition for judicial review, it is desirable that the claim is properly averred and quantified on commencement of the proceedings, rather than included or expanded upon by amendment.

Shetland Line (1984) Ltd v. Secretary of State for Scotland

1996 S.L.T. 653

11–27   LORD JOHNSTON:... "(6) Even if there was a claim in negligence, in my opinion, it should not be pursued in an action relating to judicial review. At the end of his submission counsel for the petitioner was effectively arguing that he might have an action for reparation giving rise to a claim for damages. If so, it is clear to me that he should make that by way of separate action and not as an addendum to a petition for judicial review which started seeking a wholly different remedy, namely reduction of certain ministerial decisions. I appreciate that the Rules of Court permit damages to be awarded in proceedings for judicial review and that does appear to have happened on at least one occasion (*Kelly v. Monklands District Council*). In my opinion however, in this case, to allow the petition to be continued for such claim to be first averred and then quantified would create a procedural shambles There is presently no prejudice to the petitioners in this context as regards passage of time. If therefore the claim sought by counsel can be substantiated, the appropriate action will enable the very complex legal questions to be ventilated and also require quantification of damage. By the appropriate action I mean a separate action for reparation indicating the existence and breach of an alleged duty of care, between the parties. Despite counsel's submissions I do not consider that any decision as to the lawfulness of the decision itself turns on this question, which must relate to how the minister went about arming himself with the requisite knowledge."

Notes

For a discussion of damages generally see Finch and Ashton, pp. 433–434 and *Stair Memorial Encyclopaedia*, Vol. 1, para. 333.

THE EQUITABLE JURISDICTION OF THE SUPREME COURTS: NOBILE OFFICIUM

For the facts of the next extract see para. 54.   **11–28**

London and Clydeside Estates Ltd v. Aberdeen District Council

1980 S.C. (H.L.) 1

LORD FRASER OF TULLYBELTON:... "The next question is whether reduction of the certificate is the   **11–29**
appropriate remedy in the circumstances. Counsel for the respondents argued that whatever the appropriate remedy might be, it certainly was not reduction, because, he said, the *nobile officium* of the Court of Session was available to provide for what was a *casus improvisus*. The argument as I understood it was that a *casus improvisus* arose in this way. It is now too late for the appellants to make a fresh or amended application for a certificate because a reference has been made to the Lands Tribunal for Scotland, (which has replaced the Official Arbiter) to assess compensation — see section 25(2) of the 1963 Act. We were told that the Lands Tribunal had, at the request of both parties, made alternative assessments on different assumptions. I agree that it is too late for a fresh application. It is also too late, so it is said, for the respondents to issue a fresh or amended certificate because a certificate has to be issued within two months from the date of application (unless the period is extended by agreement) and after the expiry of the two months' period the local planning authority is *functus* and cannot issue a certificate. A complete impasse therefore arises comparable to that which existed in the case of *Maitland, Petitioner*, 1961 S.C. 291 when a licensing court could not be reconvened to pronounce an order that it had omitted to make per incuriam. The Court of Session resolved the impasse by an exercise of its *nobile officium*. For reasons that I shall explain, I do not agree that it is too late for the respondents to issue a proper certificate, but, even assuming that it is, I am of opinion that the argument is misconceived. The fact that Parliament has not provided for the legal consequences to follow from a failure to carry out the statutory procedure does not give rise to a *casus improvisus*. The consequences of such failure have to be ascertained according to the general rules of law. They may include a right to recover damages, or to have a document reduced, or to obtain a decree of declarator or some other redress but there is no impasse of the kind that has hitherto been regarded as suitable for solution by an exercise of the *nobile officium*. That is an exceptional power and the court 'does not view with favour its indefinite extension.' See MacLaren on Court of Session Practice p. 101. Its proper use as the Lord President pointed out in *Maitland, supra*, is 'to enable justice to be done where, *per incuriam*, some *formal step* [my italics] has been omitted' but it cannot be invoked 'even by agreement of all parties interested, to enable the court to supplement the statutory procedure by what would, in effect, be an amendment of a statute.' The proposal that the *nobile officium* should be invoked in the present case to extend the period either for issuing the certificate or for appealing against the certificate assumes that whichever period is to be extended is one which has been fixed by the statute or the order and which has expired. Otherwise no extension would be necessary. But an exercise of the power for such a purpose would be in order to get round the Act or the order and thus in effect to amend it. That would not be a proper exercise of the power."

LORD KEITH: "... It was suggested that recourse might be had to the *nobile officium* of the court. I regard that suggestion as entirely misplaced. The *nobile officium* does not exist to deal with matters of disputed right. Its chief object is to provide a means of rectifying obvious errors or omissions, principally of an administrative character, which cannot be dealt with in any other way. The present case is concerned with the appellants' right, disputed by the respondents, to require the latter to issue to them a certificate under section 25 (4) of the 1963 Act which is in proper form. That is a matter appropriate to be deals with by the ordinary process of law, and which does not in any respect concern the *nobile officium*. The argument for the respondents did not, in my opinion, come to grips at all with the appellants' contentions upon this matter of disputed right, let alone counter them successfully. These contentions must therefore prevail.

It remains to notice a submission for the respondents that the appellants should be put to proof of their averment that they were unaware of the time limit for appealing to the Secretary of State and this was the reason why their appeal was late. I reject that submission. The invalidity of the certificate derives from a defect of general application, and nothing turns on the state of the appellants' knowledge.

My Lords, for these reasons I would allow the appeal and dismiss the eross-appeal. Counsel for the appellants asked leave to further amend the second conclusion of the summons by substituting the word 'fresh' for the word 'amended' before the word 'certificate' in the fourth line, and such leave should be granted. Subject to that the appropriate order would be to recall the interlocutor of the Second Division dated 26th January 1979 in so far as it refused decree in terms of the second conclusion of the summons, and *quoad* that conclusion as amended to sustain the second and third pleas in law for the pursuer and to grant decree in terms thereof. The respondents will be liable to the appellants for costs in this House and also for all expenses in the Court of Session, apart from those for which the appellants were found liable to the second respondent by interlocutor of the Lord Ordinary dated 15th June 1978."

Notes

11–30   (1) The *nobile officium* has been described as the "ultimate equitable jurisdiction of the Court of Session as a Supreme Court", *Stair Memorial Encycolpaedia*, Vol. 1, para. 332. The tone of both speeches indicates a concern that the scope of this remedy should not be taken too far. This caution has a long pedigree. Stair was concerned that overreliance on the remedy "would render the subject insecure, and the power of the Lords too arbitrary" (*Institutions*, iv, 3, 1).

(2) The remedy would appear to be restricted to situations in which the ordinary procedure of the courts, including judicial review procedure, could not provide a remedy. The necessity of exhausting other remedies or establishing that no other remedy would be competent is apparent in the speech of Lord Fraser. In former times the distinction between the supervisory jurisdiction and the *nobile officium* was not clear and there are still isolated instances of the *nobile officium* being described as an aspect of the supervisory jurisdiction or even coterminous: see Lord McCluskey in *Royal Bank of Scotland plc v. Clydebank District Council*, 1992 S.L.T. 356 at 365 and see also *Forbes v. Underwood*, above. Given the inception of the new judicial review procedures in 1985 it is appropriate to regard the *nobile officium* as a distinct jurisdiction of the court.

(3) In *Ferguson, Petitioner*, 1965 S.L.T. 101 an electoral registration officer wrongly removed electors from the electoral roll. There was no procedure set out in the relevant statute to revise the electoral roll and the pressing need to do so was held to be a justification for exercising of the remedy: see also *R, Petitioner*, 1993 S.L.T. 910 and *Maitland* referred to in the foregoing extract. The *nobile officium* cannot extend statute nor can it derogate from it: *Smart v. Registrar General for Scotland*, 1954 S.C. 81. See also in the context of criminal law *Wan Ping Nam v. Federal German Republic Minister of Justice*, 1972 S.L.T. 220 and see generally *Stair Memorial Encyclopaedia*, Vol. 1, para. 332 and Finch and Ashton, p. 223.

REMEDIES UNDER THE SCOTLAND ACT 1998

11–31   The Scotland Act does not on the face of it affect the remedies we have looked at above. Instead, it presupposes that when the courts are asked to decide issues involving legislation of the Scottish Parliament or acts of the Scottish Executive, they will have regard to these standard remedies. However, constitutional policy considerations underlying the devolution settlement have demanded that a number of provisions must also be taken into account in assessing the range of remedies available to the courts. As we have noted in Chapter 10 in relation to procedures for judicial control of the Scottish Parliament and Executive, judicial review is likely to be one of the most significant forms of control. It is also likely that new provisions will have the most immediate impact in judicial review proceedings. However, unless otherwise stated, these provisions are general in effect and thus are equally applicable in other administrative law proceedings, statutory appeals or tribunal proceedings.

Scotland Act 1998

s. 40(3)–(5)

"Legal Issues
Proceedings by or Against the Parliament etc.
    (3) In any proceedings against the Parliament, the court shall not make an order for suspension, interdict, reduction or specific performance (or other like order) but may instead make a declarator.
    (4) In any proceedings against —
  (a)   any member of the Parliament,
  (b)   the Presiding Officer or a deputy,
  (c)   any member of the staff of the Parliament, or
  (d)   the Parliamentary corporation,
the court shall not make an order for suspension, interdict, reduction or specific performance (or other like order) if the effect of doing so would be to give any relief against the Parliament which could not have been given in proceedings against the Parliament.
    (5) References in this section to an order include an interim order."

11–32

Notes

    (1) The Scottish Parliament is, like the Westminster Parliament, an unincorporated association. Section 21 of the Act establishes a Parliamentary corporation which will be the body which will represent the Parliament in legal proceedings by or against it. The protection has been extended to others connected with the Parliament to avoid this protection being subverted: section 40(2), (4). On the possible scope of declarator see para. 11–6.

11–33

Scotland Act 1998

s. 100(3), (4)

"Human Rights
    (3) This Act does not enable a court or tribunal to award any damages in respect of an act which is incompatible with any of the Convention rights which it could not award if section 8(3) and (4) of the Human Rights Act 1998 applied.
    (4) In this section 'act' means —
  (a)   making any legislation.
  (b)   any other act or failure to act, if it is the act or failure of a member of the Scottish Executive."

11–34

Notes

    Tribunal means any tribunal in which legal proceedings may be brought: section 126(1). For discussion of the scope of Convention rights see Chapter 6 and for the scope of an award of damages under the Human Rights Act 1998 see above.

11–35

Scotland Act 1998, s. 102

"Powers of Courts or Tribunals to vary Retrospective Decisions

11–36   102. — (1) This section applies where any court or tribunal decides that —

(a)   an Act of the Scottish Parliament or any provision of such an Act is not within the legislative competence of the Parliament, or

(b)   a member of the Scottish Executive does not have the power to make, confirm or approve a provision of subordinate legislation that he has purported to make, confirm or approve.

(2) The court or tribunal may make an order —

(a)   removing or limiting any retrospective effect of the decision, or

(b)   suspending the effect of the decision for any period and on any conditions to allow the defect to be corrected.

(3) In deciding whether to make an order under this section, the court or tribunal shall (among other things) have regard to the extent to which persons who are not parties to the proceedings would otherwise be adversely affected.

(4) Where a court or tribunal is considering whether to make an order under this section, it shall order intimation of that fact to be given to —

(a)   the Lord Advocate, and

(b)   the appropriate law officer, where the decision mentioned in subsection (1) relates to a devolution issue (within the meaning of Schedule 6).

unless the person to whom the intimation would be given is a party to the proceedings.

(5) A person to whom information is given under subsection (4) may take part as a party in the proceedings so far as they relate to the making of the order.

(6) Paragraphs 36 and 37 of Schedule 6 apply with necessary modifications for the purposes of subsections (4) and (5) as they apply for the purposes of that Schedule.

(7) In this section —

'intimation' includes notice.

'the appropriate law officer' means —

(a)   in relation to proceedings in Scotland the Advocate General,

(b)   in relation to proceedings in England and Wales, the Attorney General.

(c)   in relation to proceedings in Northern Ireland the Attorney General for Northern Ireland."

Notes

11–37   (1) As the *ultra vires* doctrine is applicable to the Scottish Parliament and the Scottish Executive, the consequences of reliance on those acts by third parties in the event of successful challenge on grounds of *ultra vires* requires, as in the case of reduction at common law, a careful balancing of private and public interest. As with reduction at common law, the effect of challenge to a decision on parties outwith the immediate proceedings is a relevant consideration. Section 102(2)(a) suggests that the doctrine of severance is equally applicable in this context. Unlike reduction, it is competent for the court to correct a defect: section 102(2)(b). This would appear to be so whether this power is invoked in judicial review or other proceedings. This would suggest some inroad on the principle that judicial review is not a mechanism for appeal. Note the terms of subsection (3): could the court take into account benefits that might otherwise attach to parties or non-parties if no order is made? Note the particular provisions if the matter is raised in the context of a devolution issues. Devolution issues are discussed in Chapter 10 and Schedule 6 reproduced there. Paragraphs 36–37 of Schedule 6 relate to special provisions for expenses and for court procedure. The legislative competence of the Scottish Parliament is defined by section 29, which is noted in Chapter 3. "Subordinate legislation" has the same meaning as in the Interpretation Act 1978 and also includes an instrument made under an Act of the Scottish Parliament: section 126(1).

(2) Concern has been expressed as to the way in which this section gives courts and tribunals the power to "re-write law":

> "The controversial aspect of giving the courts a discretionary power to limit the retrospective effect of their judgments is that their decisions on the question of granting or refusing retrospective limitation or suspension will no longer be ones which can be presented as determined by purely

legal considerations, or seen as a purely objective application of the requirements of the rules. Rather, the question of whether or not to use their new prospective overruling power expressly requires the judges to take into account broad non-legal considerations, and to consider pragmatic arguments, put to them by the law officers, regarding the perceived consequences of those judgments. As guardians and interpreters of the law, the judges are natural authority. In non-legal matters, however, their views have no greater weight or privilege than others"
    (A. O'Neill, "The Scotland Act and the Government of Judges", 1999 S.L.T. (News) 61 at 62).

(3) Consider a situation where there is an allegation that an Act of the Scottish Parliament of the Scottish Executive is *ultra vires* because it is in breach of a Convention right. Compare and contrast the powers given to the courts in section 102 with those contained in section 4 of the Human Rights Act 1998. For further comment see O'Neill above.

Scotland Act 1998, s. 107

"Legislative Power to Remedy Ultra Vires Acts
    107. Subordinate legislation may make such provision as the person making the legislation considers necessary or expedient in consequence of — **11–38**
    (a)   an Act of the Scottish Parliament or any provision of an Act of the Scottish Parliament which is not or may not be within the legislative competence of the Parliament or
    (b)   any purported exercise by a member of the Scottish Executive of his functions which is not, or may not be, an exercise or a proper exercise of those functions."

Notes

(1) This is a broad power which gives a great deal of flexibility on the part of the U.K. **11–39** Government to remedy both defective legislation of the Scottish Parliament and defective acts and omissions of the Scottish Executive. The Government explained (*Hansard*, H.L. Vol. 593, cols 592–594) that the power might be used in a situation where after a judicial decision it was discovered that a provision of an Act of the Scottish Parliament was *ultra vires*. The amending power could be used to remedy the situation, including any consequential problems, such as any rights accrued or liabilities incurred by virtue of the offending act. Retrospective effect could be given, putting third parties in the position they would have been in before the flaw was discovered. Note, however, that it is not a prerequisite for the exercise of section 107 that a decision under section 102 from the court has been obtained. What do you consider the meaning of "a proper exercise" of functions to be? Is it confined to questions of devolved competence or simple ultra vires? Could the grounds of challenge noted in relation to abuse of discretion also be relevant? For comment on the procedure in relation to the making of subordinate legislation under this section see para. 2–12.

HUMAN RIGHTS ACT 1998

Article 13 of the European Convention on Human Rights provides that: **11–40**

"Everyone whose rights and freedoms as set forth in this Convention are violated shall have an effective remedy before a national authority notwithstanding that the violation has been committed by persons acting in an official capacity."

Article 13 means that there must exist an effective way of testing claims that a Convention right has been violated: *Silver v. United Kingdom* (1983) 5 E.H.R.R. 347. The National Authority must be able to correct or compensate for the violation: *Klass v. Federal Republic of Germany* (1979–80) 2 E.H.R.R. 214. Procedural rules securing the remedy must not stand in the way of its grant: *Vilvarajah v. United Kingdom* (1992) 14 E.H.R.R. 248. Article 13 has, however, not been created a Convention right under the 1998 Act. As explained by the Lord Chancellor, the remedies provided by the Act are intended to meet the obligations imposed by Article 13:

H.L. Official Report, Vol. 583, col. 475, November 18, 1997. The validity of the Lord Chancellor's assessment will of course require to be determined by the practical application of the remedial provisions of the Act.

Human Rights Act 1998.

s. 4

"Declaration of Incompatibility

11–41   4. — (1) Subsection (2) applies in any proceedings in which a court determines whether a provision of primary legislation is compatible with a Convention right.

(2) If the court is satisfied that the provision is incompatible with a Convention right, it may make a declaration of that incompatibility.

(3) Subsection (4) applies in any proceedings in which a court determines whether a provision of subordinate legislation, made in the exercise of a power conferred by primary legislation, is compatible with a Convention right.

(4) If the court is satisfied —

(a)   that the provision is incompatible with a convention right, and

(b)   that (disregarding any possibility of revocation) the primary legislation concerned prevents removal of the incompatibility,

it may make a declaration of that incompatibility.

(5) In this section 'court' means —

(a)   the House of Lords:

(b)   the Judicial Committee of the Privy Council:

(c)   the Courts-Martial Appeal Court:

(d)   in Scotland, the High Court of Justiciary sitting otherwise than as a trial court or the Court of Session:

(e)   in England and Wales or Northern Ireland, the High Court or the Court of Appeal.

(6) A declaration under this section ('a declaration of incompatibility') —

(a)   does not affect the validity, continuing operation or enforcement of the provision in respect of which it is given: and

(b)   is not binding on the parties to the proceedings in which it is made."

Notes

11–42   (1) For the scope of Convention rights see Chapter 6 Section 4 is not yet in force.

"Primary legislation" is defined as including any Public General Acts, any local and personal Act and any Private Act. Order in Council includes an order or instrument made under primary legislation to the extent to which it operates to bring one or more provisions of that legislation into force or amends any primary legislation, but which does not include any legislation of the Scottish Parliament, subordinate legislation under any such act or any subordinate legislation made by the Scottish Executive: section 21(1). In the context of an allegation of breach of a Convention right by the Scottish Parliament or Scottish Executive, this is treated as a devolution issue and would be subject to the procedure set out in Schedule 6 to the Scotland Act 1998, on which see Chapter 00. Note that court does not include a tribunal, albeit tribunals are obliged to take into account Convention rights in making a decision: section 2(1). Note that the sheriff court does not have jurisdiction to make such a declarator. Section 4 represents something of a constitutional novelty in Scots law. It is generally not competent to obtain a declarator as to the meaning of an Act of Parliament: *Orr v. Alston*, 1912 S.L.T. 95.

(2) The power to make a declaration of invalidity is permissive. This specialised declarator, like declarator at common law, is a discretionary remedy. Like common law declarator, it shares the characteristic that the wider public interest might be involved. That carries with it the implication that the public interest might require incompatible legislation to remain in force. However, given the relatively high threshold that requires to be met before declaration of incompatibility can be granted, it is submitted that only in exceptional cases would the remedy be refused.

(3) Note that declaration of incompatibility is not confined to judicial review proceedings, albeit that it is anticipated that this will be the typical forum. Such a declarator could be sought at first instance or an appeal to the courts detailed in subsection (5) and in any form of proceedings therein.

(4) In cases where there is no direct or indirect incompatibility with primary legislation, the remedy of an ordinary declarator would appear to be available from the court with competence to grant it.

(5) On section 4 generally see D. Feldman, "Remedies for Violations of Convention Rights Under the Human Rights Act" [1998] E.H.R.L.R. 691 at 698–701 and see also K. Campbell, "Human Rights Brought Home?", 1998 S.L.T. (News) 269 and A. Henderson, "Brandeis briefs and the proof of legislative facts in proceedings under the Human Rights Act 1998" [1998] P.L. 563.

Human Rights Act 1998

s. 8

"Judicial Remedies

8. — (1) In relation to any act (or proposed act) of a public authority which the court finds is (or would be) unlawful, it may grant such relief or remedy, or make such order, within its powers as it considers just and appropriate.   **11–43**

(2) But damages may be awarded only by a court which has power to award damages, or to order the payment of compensation, in civil proceedings.

(3) No award of damages is to be made unless, taking account of all the circumstances of the case, including —

(a)   any other relief or remedy granted, or order made, in relation to the act in question (by that or any other court), and

(b)   the consequences of any decision (of that or any other court) in respect of that act,

the court is satisfied that the award is necessary to afford just satisfaction to the person in whose favour it is made.

(4) In determining —

(a)   whether to award damages, or

(b)   the amount of an award,

the court must take into account the principles applied by the European Court of Human Rights in relation to the award of compensation under Article 41 of the Convention.

(5) A public authority against which damages are awarded is to be treated —

(a)   in Scotland, for the purposes of section 3 of the Law Reform (Miscellaneous Provisions) (Scotland) Act 1940 as if the award were made in an action of damages in which the authority has been found liable in respect of loss or damage to the person to whom the award is made;

(b)   for the purposes of the Civil Liability (Contribution) Act 1978 as liable in respect of damage suffered by the person to whom the award is made.

(6) In this section —

'court' includes a tribunal:

'damages' means damages for an unlawful act of a public authority; and 'unlawful' means unlawful under section 6(1)."

Notes

(1) Section 8 is not yet in force. Apart from the special remedy provided by section 4, the remedies available against a public authority are determined by the jurisdiction of the court dealing with the allegation of breach of the Convention rights. This means, of course, that in the case of the Court of Session, all of the common law remedies and specific statutory remedies, such as order for enforcement of a statutory duty, could competently be invoked under section 8. To determine the remedies available in the sheriff court or other courts or tribunals one will have to have regard to their pre-existing competence as to available remedies. Tribunals, of course, do not generally have available to them the remedies found in the ordinary courts. However, section 7(11) provides that the Minister who has power to make rules in relation to a   **11–44**

particular tribunal may, to the extent he considers it necessary to ensure that the tribunal can provide an appropriate remedy in relation to an act (or proposed act) of a public authority which is (or would be) unlawful, by order add to the relief or remedies which the tribunal may grant or the grounds on which it may grant any of them: section 7(11)(a),(b).

(2) Notwithstanding the terms of section 8 it would appear that it will still be incompetent to seek interdict or an order for specific implement against the Crown. However, the way would appear to be open to the litigant to argue that in an appropriate case involving the Crown in Scotland where a Convention right has allegedly been violated, there is in fact insufficient protection in national law for that right, perhaps thereafter raising the matter as a breach of Article 13 of the Convention at the European Court of Human Rights in Strasbourg. Alternatively this anomalous situation may pave the way for statutory reform of the question of remedies against the Crown by either the Scottish Parliament or the Westminster Parliament.

(3) The language of subsections (3) and (4) echoes that contained in Article 41 of the Convention (as amended by protocol 11; the previous provision was Article 50) which gives the European Court of Human Rights power to "afford just satisfaction to the injured party" only if it is "necessary" to do so. There would appear to be no material difference between Article 41 and subsections (3) and (4) and to that extent one must have regard to the case law on Articles 41 and 50. Whether it is necessary to make an award of compensation is a matter of discretion. Of particular weight will be the facts of the case in issue: *Guzzardi v. Italy* (1981) 3 E.H.R.R. 333, para. 114. The award of compensation has parallels with concerns underlying the award of damages in judicial review proceedings for finding of a violation does not of itself justify compensation. Where damages are to be awarded the European case law suggests that there must be a causal link between the damage suffered and the violation: *Philis v. Greece (No. 2)* (1998) 25 E.H.R.R. 417, para. 58, and that the wronged party should be put in the position they would have been in had the Convention not been disregarded: *Piersack v. Belgium* (compensation) (1985) 7 E.H.R.R. 251, para. 12. Although not limited to these, typically compensation covers legal costs and expenses, compensation for pecuniary loss, see, for example, *Weeks v. U.K.* 1998, ser. A, No. 145-A, para. 13, and compensation for non-pecuniary loss which is generally modest, see *Philis*. Subsection (5) allows a public authority to claim a right of contribution against any other person liable for the same damage. It is conceivable that situations might arise when more than one public authority has violated a Convention right; see, for example, *X & Y v. The Netherlands* (1986) 8 E.H.R.R. 235.

(4) Section 8 requires to be read along with section 6 as to the definition of a public authority. Section 6 is noted in Chapter 6. It follows from section 6 that as a court is also a public authority, the court would be acting unlawfully if it failed to develop *ordinary* principles of law in accordance with compatibility with Convention rights, even if litigation is taking place between private parties. This is significant. Accordingly, where, for example, an action is raised in delict against a public authority where no Convention right has been directly breached, the court, although applying the ordinary principles of delict in the assessment of liability and damages, will still require to have regard to Convention rights. This has already happened in pre-incorporation cases in relation to the assessment of damages, see, for example, *Derbyshire County Council v. Times Newspapers Ltd* [1993] A.C. 534, H.L. and *Attorney General v. Blake (Jonathan Cape Ltd, third party)* [1998] 1 All E.R. 833, C.A. (defamation).

(5) Note the additional limitation on the award of damages in respect of judicial acts contained in section 9(3), (4). Subsection (3) provides that in relation to proceedings in respect of a judicial act done in good faith, damages may not be awarded otherwise than to compensate a person to the extent required by Article 5(5) of the Convention. Article 5(5) is concerned with cases of "arrest or detention" in contravention of the Article. In such a case, the award is made against the Crown: subsection(5). If good faith is lacking, the test is as set out in section 8 and damages could be awarded on that basis. At common law, sheriffs and judges of the Supreme Court are immune from action even if they act in excess of jurisdiction or maliciously: *Russell v. Dickson*, 1998 S.L.T. 96, although magistrates have been held liable in certain circumstances: *McPhee v. McFarlane's Exr*, 1933 S.C. 163.

Human Rights Act 1998

s. 10

"Power to Take Remedial Action

10. — (1) This section applies if —   **11–45**
(a) a provision of legislation has been declared under section 4 to be incompatible with a Convention right and, if an appeal lies —
(i) all persons who may appeal have stated in writing that they do not intend to do so;
(ii) the time for bringing an appeal has expired and no appeal has been brought within that time; or
(iii) an appeal brought within that time has been determined or abandoned; or
(b) it appears to a Minister of the Crown or Her Majesty in Council that, having regard to a finding of the European Court of Human Rights made after the coming into force of this section in proceedings against the United Kingdom, a provision of legislation is incompatible with an obligation of the United Kingdom arising from the Convention.
(2) If a Minister of the Crown considers that there are compelling reasons for proceedings under this section, he may by order make such amendments to the legislation as he considers necessary to remove the incompatibility.
(3) If, in the case of subordinate legislation, a Minister of the Crown considers —
(a) that it is necessary to amend the primary legislation under which the subordinate legislation in question was made, in order to enable the incompatibility to be removed, and
(b) that there are compelling reasons for proceeding under this section, he may by order make such amendments to the primary legislation as he considers necessary.
(4) This section also applies where the provision in question is in subordinate legislation and has been quashed, or declared invalid, by reason of incompatibility with a Convention right and the Minister proposes to proceed under paragraph 2(b) of Schedule 2.
(5) If the legislation is an Order in Council, the power conferred by subsection (2) or (3) is exercisable by Her Majesty in Council.
(6) In this section 'legislation' does not include a Measure of the Church Assembly or of the General Synod of the Church of England.
(7) Schedule 2 makes further provision about remedial orders."

Notes

(1) Section 10 is not yet in force. Schedule 2 sets out the detailed procedure for the making   **11–46**
of a remedial order which except in cases of urgency, see Schedule 2, para. 2(b), requires to be approved by positive resolution of both Houses of Parliament by the end of 60 days from the laying of the draft order. A remedial order can amend primary legislation including primary legislation other than that which contains the incompatible provision and there are similar provisions in relation to the amendment or revocation of subordinate legislation: Schedule 2, paras 1, 2(a), (b). Note that subordinate legislation includes, along with the usual categories, Acts of the Scottish Parliament and orders, rules, regulations, schemes, warrants, byelaws or other instrument made by a member of the Scottish Executive but does not include Orders in Council made under the royal prerogative: section 21(1). Section 10 has been argued to be an "exceptionally drastic form of Henry VIII clause": Sir William Wade, "The United Kingdom's Bill of Rights" in *Constitutional Reform in the United Kingdom* (J. Beatson, C. Forsyth and I. Hare eds, 1998), p. 61 at pp. 66–67. As originally drafted, the then clause 10 of the Bill would have allowed amendment by order in all cases. This was criticised in the House of Lords and clause 10 was amended at the committee stage in the Commons in the form above: see H.L. Deb., Vol. 583, col. 1141, November 27, 1997 (Lord Simon of Glaisdale) and the Select Committee on Delegated Powers and Deregulation, Sixth Report (1997–98 H.L. 32), paras 23 and 27. For comment on Henry VIII clauses see paras 2–7 to 2–8.

To what extent do you think Sir William Wade's concern is justified? What meaning could be given to the phrase "compelling" in this context? Would a relevant consideration for the exercise of the Minister's discretion be practical considerations for example, the amount of parliamentary time available for full debate and primary legislative change? How readily do you think that the courts would intervene in challenging the Minister's assessment of whether the situation is "compelling"? This section also requires to be read along with section 107 of the Scotland Act 1998. Compare and contrast that section with the provisions of section 10.

Chapter 12

APPEALS

Parliament has often sought to improve upon existing methods of judicial control of administrative decisions. Judicial review in the Court of Session is not the sole method of control. Arguably of greater significance and impact are various rights of appeal against administrative decisions.

12–1

The procedures for appeal vary in their nature in effect and not all are judicial in character. We have noted already in Chapter 1, that in planning matters there exists an right of appeal to the Secretary of State, although usually a civil servant, known as a reporter, deals with the appeal. If a local authority resolves to make a byelaw, its decision is subject to appeal to the Secretary of State, on which see Chapter 2. In taking these decisions, the Secretary of State and his officials are subject to the principles of the supervisory jurisdiction of the Court of Session, whether at common law or by statute. In addition, many administrative decisions, particularly those of local authorities, are subject to appeal at a local level to the sheriff. Of great significance are, of course, the various forms of appeal in tribunal proceedings.

As a right of appeal depends on the existence of a statute creating such a right, the grounds of appeal are confined to those specified in or deduced from the statute and accordingly appeals must be distinguished from review by the Court of Session at common law. A central difference is that in an appeal the body hearing the appeal, including a court, may often substitute a different decision for that originally reached. For further discussion of the distinction between appeal and review see para. 10–17.

For general reading see *The Laws of Scotland: Stair Memorial Encyclopaedia*, Vol. 1, paras 337–342; V. Finch and C. Ashton, *Administrative Law in Scotland* (1997), pp 299–301, 198–211.

WHEN SHOULD A RIGHT OF APPEAL BE ALLOWED?

Report of the Franks Committee on Administrative Tribunals and Inquiries Part II: Tribunals in General

CMND. 218 (1957), paras 103–106, 107, 109, 110, 115, 116, 118, 119

"Appeal and Judicial Review

103. Most of the evidence which we have received has stressed the desirability of some form of appeal from tribunals of first instance, and many witnesses have advocated that at some stage there should be an appeal to the courts.

12–2

The Merits of a Right of Appeal

104. The existence of a right of appeal is salutary and makes for right adjudication. Provision for appeal is also important if decisions are to show reasonable consistency. Finally, the system of adjudication can hardly fail to appear fair to the applicant if he knows that he will normally be allowed two attempts to convince independent bodies of the soundness of his case.

An Appeal Structure for Tribunals

105. The first question is the extent to which appeals should lie to the courts or to further appellate tribunals. An appeal to the courts on matters of fact would not, we think, be desirable since it would constitute an appeal from a body expert in the particular subject to a relatively inexpert body. In the absence of special considerations we consider that the ideal appeal structure for tribunals should take the form of a general appeal from a tribunal of first instance to a second or appellate tribunal. By a general appeal we mean an appeal on fact, law or merits. We do not think that it is necessary for appeals to the second or appellate tribunal always to be heard orally. As a matter of general principle we consider that appeal should not lie from a tribunal to a Minister.

106. It is not essential to set up an appellate tribunal when the tribunal of first instance is so exceptionally strong and well qualified that an appellate tribunal would be no better qualified to review its decisions. Thus, for example, we see no need to provide for appeal to a further tribunal from decisions of Pensions Appeal Tribunals or the General Claims Tribunal. The evidence indicates no dissatisfaction with the absence of such appeal in these cases.

Appeals to the Courts on Points of Law

107. We are firmly of the opinion that all decisions of tribunals should be subject to review by the courts on points of law. This review could be obtained either by proceedings for certiorari or by appeal. If, as we recommend, tribunals are compelled to give full reasons for their decisions any error of law in such a decision would subject the decision to quashing by order of certiorari in England, and it is now clear that the fact that the decision of the tribunal may be expressed in the statute as 'final' does not oust this jurisdiction. The courts in Scotland do not, however, exercise this jurisdiction to quash a decision for error of law on the face of the record. Moreover, an application to quash a decision on this ground is quite different from an appeal on a point of law. In the former case the court can only quash the decision, while in the latter case the court may substitute, or in effect substitute, its own decision. Again, in the former case, the court must find the error, if it can, on the face of the record, for example in the notice of decision mentioned in the preceding Chapter; it cannot look at anything else. In the latter case the court can in addition look at the notes of the evidence given before the tribunal if the point of law is whether there was evidence on which the tribunal could in law have arrived at its decision. An appeal on a point of law is therefore wider in scope. For all these reasons we recommend that review by the courts of decisions of tribunals should in general be provided by making the decisions subject to appeal on points of law. We think, however, that special considerations arise in connection with the National Insurance Commissioner, the Industrial Injuries Commissioner and National Assistance Appeal Tribunals ...

109. The reasons which lead us to think that appeals on merits from National Assistance Appeal Tribunals are unnecessary (see paragraph 182) apply equally to appeals on points of law from these Tribunals. Accordingly we think that an exception to the general rule should also be made in the case of these Tribunals, leaving any review by the courts to be exercised by certiorari.

110. As we have already pointed out, there is in Scotland no remedy by way of certiorari to quash a decision for an error of law on its face. It may be, however, that no difficulties will arise in that certainly the Commissioners and probably National Assistance Appeal Tribunals, wherever they sit, are subject to the supervision of the English courts. If, however, this is not so an equivalent remedy should be provided in Scotland in these cases ...

115. There remains the question of the court to which appeals on points of law should lie. The possible alternatives are the Court of Appeal, the Divisional Court of the Queen's Bench Division, a nominated judge of the High Court, or the County Court. We think that there would be some advantage in concentrating appeals in the Divisional Court. This Court exercises general supervision and control over all inferior courts and tribunals in matters of jurisdiction. It is not only experienced in matters of jurisdiction but is constantly dealing with appeals on points of law, for example from Magistrates' Courts. The fact that it is almost invariably presided over by the Lord Chief Justice tends to ensure uniformity of approach and decision. By its constitution it commands great respect. Nevertheless we think that it would be wrong to lay down a hard and fast rule. In the case of the Lands Tribunal and the Transport Tribunal there seems no cogent reason for disturbing the present practice by which appeals lie to the Court of Appeal. In certain cases it may, as the Law Society suggests, be cheaper and simpler for appeals to lie to County Courts. Where a number of new tribunals is set up and there is likely to be a large volume of appeals on technical matters there is much to be said in favour of the appeals being decided by a nominated judge, as are appeals from Pensions Appeal Tribunals.

116. We do not necessarily intend that in every case there should be unrestricted recourse through the Supreme Court and up to the House of Lords. To permit this would in many cases be inconsistent, by reason of the expense and delay involved, with the purposes for which tribunals are established. We suggest that in each case there should be one further appeal on law, by leave, and no more ...

118. The reasons which have led us to recommend that an appeal should lie to a court of law from a tribunal sitting in England or Wales apply equally to a tribunal sitting in Scotland. The method of appeal in Scotland is either by way of stated case or on a full transcript of the evidence. We think, however, that the chairman's note of the evidence would suffice.

119. The Court of Session has no court similar to a Divisional Court of the High Court. Appeals from inferior civil courts and from the limited number of tribunals from whose decisions an appeal lies (for example Pensions Appeal Tribunals) are normally heard by the Inner House of the Court of Session. There is an exception to this practice. Appeals from Valuation Committees lie to the Lands Valuation Appeal Court. There are obvious advantages in such a specialised court where the volume of work is large, as in the case of valuation appeals. We have, however, no reason to suppose that the volume of appeals from any other group of tribunals would justify the setting up of a specialised court similar to the Lands Valuation Appeal Court and accordingly we suggest that appeals other than valuation appeals should be heard by the Inner House of the Court of Session. We suggest that an appeal should thereafter lie to the House of Lords only with leave of the Inner House of the Court of Session."

Tribunals and Inquiries Act 1992

s. 11

"Appeals from Certain Tribunals

11.–(1) Subject to subsection (2), if any party to proceedings before any tribunal specified in paragraph 8, 15(a) or (d), 16, 18, 24, 26, 31, 33(b), 37, 44 or 45 of Schedule 1 is dissatisfied in point of law with a decision of the tribunal he may, according as rules of court may provide, either appeal from the tribunal to the High Court or require the tribunal to state and sign a case for the opinion of the High Court.

(2) Subsection (1) shall not apply in relation to proceedings before industrial tribunals which arise under or by virtue of any of the enactments mentioned in section 136(1) of the Employment Protection (Consolidation) Act 1978.

(3) Rules of court made with respect to all or any of the tribunals referred to in subsection (1) may provide for authorising or requiring a tribunal, in the course of proceedings before it, to state, in the form of a special case for the decision of the High Court, any question of law arising in the proceedings; and a decision of the High Court on a case stated by virtue of this subsection shall be deemed to be a judgment of the Court within the meaning of section 16 of the Supreme Court Act 1981 (jurisdiction of Court of Appeal to hear and determine appeals from judgments of the High Court).

(4) In relation to proceedings in the High Court or the Court of Appeal brought by virtue of this section, the power to make rules of court shall include power to make rules prescribing the powers of the High Court or the Court of Appeal with respect to —
   (a)   the giving of any decision which might have been given by the tribunal;
   (b)   the remitting of the matter with the opinion or direction of the court for re-hearing and determination by the tribunal;
   (c)   the giving of directions to the tribunal;
   and different provisions may be made for different tribunals ...

(6) Subsection (1) shall apply to a decision of the Secretary of State on an appeal under section 41 of the Consumer Credit Act 1974 from a determination of the Director General of Fair Trading as it applies to a decision of any of the tribunals mentioned in that subsection, but with the substitution for the reference to a party to proceedings of a reference to any person who had a right to appeal to the Secretary of State (whether or not he has exercised that right); and accordingly references in subsections (1) and (4) to a tribunal shall be construed, in relation to such an appeal, as references to the Secretary of State.

(7) The following provisions shall have effect for the application of this section in Scotland —
   (a)   in relation to any proceedings in Scotland of any of the tribunals referred to in the preceding provisions of this section, or on an appeal under section 41 of the Consumer Credit Act 1974 by a company registered in Scotland or by any other person whose principal or prospective principal place of business in the United Kingdom is in Scotland, this section shall have effect with the following modifications —
      (i)   for references to the High Court or the Court of Appeal there shall be substituted references to the Court of Session,
      (ii)   in subsection (3) for 'in the form of a special case for the decision of the High Court' there shall be substituted 'a case for the opinion of the Court of Session on' and the words from 'and a decision' to the end of the subsection shall be omitted, and
      (iii) subsection (5) shall be omitted,

12–3

     (b)   this section shall apply, with the modifications specified in paragraph (a) —

          (i)   to proceedings before any such tribunal as is specified in paragraph 51, 56(b), 59 or 63 of Schedule 1, and

          (ii)   subject to paragraph (c) below, to proceedings before the Lands Tribunal for Scotland, as it applies to proceedings before the tribunals referred to in subsection (1);

     (c)   subsection (1) shall not apply in relation to proceedings before the Lands Tribunal for Scotland which arise under section 1(3A) of the Lands Tribunal Act 1949 (jurisdiction of the tribunal in valuation matters);

     (d)   an appeal shall lie, with the leave of the Court of Session or the House of Lords, from any decision of the Court of Session under this section, and such leave may be given on such terms as to costs or otherwise as the Court of Session or the House of Lords may determine …

    (10) In this section 'decision' includes any direction or order, and references to the giving of a decision shall be construed accordingly."

Notes

12–4   (1) The proposal that there should always be a right of appeal on the merits for a tribunal of first instance to an appeals tribunal has not been implemented. The Tribunals and Inquiries Act 1958 provided for appeal on a point of law in relation to the tribunals detailed in section 1 of what is now section 11 of the 1992 Act. Accordingly there is no automatic right of appeal from administrative decisions of an inferior tribunal and the only inherent method of control is judicial review. Note the proposal by the Franks Report that a general right of appeal on matters of fact or merits should exist and that the basic structure should be from a tribunal in the first instance to an appellate tribunal. However, the Franks proposals, in the main, remain unimplemented. One implication of this is that there is no coherent approach as to which court an appeal will lie or on the grounds in which people may be brought. For a general account see R. Wraith and P. Hutchesson, *Administrative Tribunals* (1973), pp. 3157–3161.

    (2) Among the tribunals subject to an appeal on a point of law are the social security appeal tribunals whose decisions are subject to appeal to the Social Security Commissioners and thereafter to the Court of Session, again on a point of law: Social Security Administration Act 1992, ss. 23,24. From a date to be appointed by the Social Security Act 1998, these provisions are to be repealed by s. 14 of the 1998 Act, which permits an appeal only on a point of law from a decision of the unified appeals tribunal to a Commissioner, thereafter to the Court of Session: ss. 14(1), 15(1); from an employment tribunal to the employment appeal tribunal: Employment Tribunals Act 1996, s. 21; and from an immigration adjudicator to the immigration appeal tribunal under the Immigration Act 1971, s. 20. As will be seen from section 11, sometimes appeal is by way of the procedure of stated case. This is common in income tax appeals but the procedure is not restricted to that area. The court can review questions of law, correct *ex facie* errors of law, correct decisions inconsistent with the evidence and correct decisions which are contrary to the only reasonable conclusion. Unless provided for in legislation, a party who requires a case to be stated must make the request before proceedings of the court or tribunal which he wishes to challenge are concluded: *McMahon v. Dunbarton County Council*, 1961 S.C. 126, unless another time-limit is provided or, where a stated case must be sought before proceedings are concluded, the period for appeal is 42 days after the intimation of the decision to the appellant: RCS 1994, r.41.20(1). A stated case should include the tribunal's findings of fact and the legal reasons for its decision. It is an error of law to state merely to state the evidence for a decision: *British Transport Commission v. Glasgow Assessor*, 1951 S.C. 404. An appellant is not entitled to have a case stated exactly in the terms he desires: *Forsyth-Grant v. Salmon*, 1961 S.C. 54. Questions of jurisdiction can be competently raised by stated case: *McCallum v. Arthur*, 1955 S.C. 188. On appeal by stated case generally see *Stair Memorial Encyclopaedia*, Vol. 1, para. 339; W.A. Wilson, "The Theory of the Case Stated" [1969] B.T.R. 231.

    (3) Not everyone, however, accepts the utility of rights of appeal in tribunal proceedings.

K.H. Hendry, "The Tasks of Tribunals: Some Thoughts"

(1982) 1 C.J.Q. 253 at 266

"Tribunals and the Courts

One more task of tribunals needs mention and in many ways it brings the gist of the above into focus: that task is to lighten the load of the ordinary courts. To put it negatively and perhaps more accurately, a purpose of the creation of Tribunals was expressly to avoid 'judicial justice.' The 1970/71 Holdsworth Club Presidential Address by Lord Hailsham expressed the view that the 'public' (*sic*) felt that many new questions were simply not for decision by the ordinary courts. The reason, says Lord Hailsham, was an inherent distrust of trial by judge alone as a method of deciding questions of fact or mixed question of fact and law. As a purely theoretical proposition in constitutional law, Hailsham condemned the proliferation of ad hoc tribunals as unhealthy; why could many of these cases, he asks, not be referred to the existing network of county courts? We return thus once again to the question of how we should view tribunals. Are they machinery of adjudication as Franks said they were? Are they machinery for administration? The answer is probably in shades of grey rather than black or white; they are machinery of adjudication within administration. The effect of Franks and the continuing work of the Council on Tribunals has been to hide the hybrid nature of tribunals; accordingly administrative lawyers have evaluated the performance and role of tribunals with normal judicial processes in mind.

Related to this and of the utmost importance are the powers of review and appeal that the ordinary courts have over the activities of tribunals. The real task of tribunals as presently constituted is to provide, cheap, informal, expert and speedy administrative justice. It must, therefore, be asked whether in the quest for judicialisation of administrative justice, the leap, by means of review or appeal, to judicial justice will, in certain cases, totally defeat the acknowledged virtues of adjudication by tribunals. This is a problem to be seen in terms of finality: the Tribunals and Inquiries Act provides that if a party before certain Schedule 1 Tribunals is dissatisfied with the outcome, he may appeal to the High Court, or require the tribunal to state a case for resolution by the High Court. Furthermore the Act seeks to preserve the venerable orders of certiorari and mandamus as methods of review. What is clearly implicit is the assumption that ordinary courts and legal profession are able to deal satisfactorily with the subject-matter involved. The most recent example of this perhaps misplaced trust is the Social Security Act 1980 which gives a right of appeal, with leave, on a question of law from a National Insurance Commissioner direct to the Court of Appeal which, with respect, is not unlike fitting a penny-farthing with an overhead camshaft and twin exhausts! What is glaringly ignored in all of this is that tribunals were set up to infuse certain decisions with policy factors which the courts by definition are ill-equipped to deal with.

It could, of course, be argued that review and appeal by the courts is a potentially important way of introducing order into administrative systems dominated by ad-hocery. Experience, unfortunately, has in many instances demonstrated the opposite. As Prosser has argued, the relationship between the courts and administration is a very complex one and that the intrusion of purely legal principles in administrative schemes could create chaos. Moreover, the 'test-case strategy' may be of little effect particularly where administrative practices, irrespective of the legal norms laid down by the courts, have basic governmental support. Prosser feels that whether or not a case has an effect will depend more upon traditional political forces at play in society and that the application of norms of judicial review are a relatively subordinate part of that process.

Furthermore, it is pre-eminently clear that the advantages of tribunals could be destroyed by the expense, complexity, lack of expertise and delay of the normal judicial process. Proposals for a more self-contained system of administrative justice such as Professor Robson's proposal for an Administrative Appeal Tribunal with a wide jurisdiction, not only to hear appeal from tribunals but also cases where a public authority prima facie appears to have acted in an unduly harsh, unjust or improper manner — or even Sir Carlton Allen's proposal for an Administrative Division of the High Court — have been given short shrift, primarily by the Franks Committee and ever since."

12–5

Notes

(1) Although Hendry refers to rights of appeal in the context of English practice his comments are equally applicable to Scottish conditions. (Social security appeals, from a date to be appointed, will be determined by the unified appeals to tribunal with an appeal thereafter to the Social Security Commissioner and ultimately to the Court of Session (in England the Court of Appeal): Social Security Act 1998, ss. 14, 15.) What alternatives could be constructed?

12–6

(2) From time to time some of the concerns picked up on in Hendry's article have, however, been given legislative form. Under Part III of the Social Security Act 1986, appeals were only established in respect of income support matters and payments from the cash-limited social fund which replaced the previous system of single payments and urgent needs payments made under the old supplementary benefits legislation in relation to social fund matters. Provision exists for a system of internal review by social fund inspectors. For discussion of the social fund and the new provisions of the Social Security Act 1998, see para. 1–14.

(3) Concern as to the use of judicial review in the absence of an appeal has been expressed by the Council on Tribunals.

Annual Report of The Council on Tribunals 1991–92 [Session 1992–1993, H.C. 316]

paras 2.2–2.5

12–7   "2.2 In accordance with the recommendations of the Franks Report, we have always held the view that there should be a right of appeal on a point of law from tribunals to the courts. In some recent proposals for legislation we have noted a tendency to regard the machinery of judicial review as an adequate substitute; we record one example of this at paragraph 2.16 below. In another such instance, the Government gave the availability of judicial review as their reason for making no provision for appeal from decisions of the Directors General in disputes under the Competition and Service (Utilities) Act 1992 (as to which, see paragraph 2.6 below). In our view, judicial review is not apt for the purpose of providing a route of appeal from tribunal decisions. Still less does the existence of the machinery of judicial review relieve the policy maker from the need to consider the establishment of a new tribunal system or other form of appeal machinery to consider appeals against administrative decisions. For that reason, as we note at paragraph 2.23 below, we rejected the option suggested in the Home Office consultation paper proposing the establishment of a Firearms Control Board that one possible means of dealing with appeals from the Board would be by way of applications for judicial review.

2.3 Given the tendency to which we have referred, we think it right to emphasise here the distinction between a right of appeal and judicial review. The judicial review jurisdiction is fundamentally different from an appellate jurisdiction, not least in its discretionary element. An appeals procedure is a means by which a public body may be brought within the control of the courts when an issue of substantive law is at stake, whereas judicial review is a supervisory jurisdiction by which the courts may find the decision-making process of a variety of public bodies to be unlawful. Although it is true that an error of law may found both a successful appeal and a successful application for judicial review, the latter is not concerned with the question whether a decision was 'right' or 'wrong', it is concerned rather with the question whether something has gone so badly wrong with the decision-making process as to make it unlawful or an abuse of power.

2.4 In this connection, we draw attention to the comments of the House of Lords in *Regina v Independent Television Commission, Ex parte TSW Broadcasting Ltd* (*The Times*, 30th March 1992). Lord Templeman said in that case:

'Parliament may by statute confer powers and discretions and impose duties on a decision-maker who may be an individual, a body of persons or a corporation. Parliament may or may not provide machinery for an appeal against a decision. The appeal machinery may be concerned with fact or law or both. The appeal machinery may or may not involve the courts of law. For example, Parliament has provided that an appeal on fact or law shall lie from an Immigration Officer to an Immigration Tribunal. Parliament has provided that an appeal on law only shall lie from the General or Special Commissioners of Income Tax to the High Court. Where Parliament has not provided for an appeal from a decision-maker the courts must not invent an appeal machinery. In the present case, Parliament has conferred powers and discretions and has imposed duties on the ITC. Parliament has not provided any appeal machinery. Even if the ITC makes mistakes of fact or of law, there is no appeal from their decision. The courts have invented the remedy of judicial review not to provide an appeal machinery but to ensure that the decision-maker does not exceed or abuse his powers.'

2.5 We trust that for the future departments will observe the distinction between a right of appeal and the discretionary remedy of judicial review, and not seek to rely on the existence of the latter in order to ignore the need for the former in appropriate cases.

Notes

As adverted to by Hendry, one way of resolving possible difficulties with the existence (or in view of the council's concerns lack) of the right of appeal to the courts on a point of law might be to create a general administrative appeals tribunal separate from the court structure. To some extent a degree of rationalisation has occurred in relation to some tribunals, such as the use of the presidential system. Similarly, the creation of the unified appeals tribunal might be viewed as an attempt to provide a more coherent system of appeal in social security matters, albeit subject to the scrutiny of the courts. However, there does not exist a general administrative appeals tribunal, such as that in Australia. Consider the following. **12–8**

The JUSTICE-All Souls Report on Administrative Law in the United Kingdom

paras 977–978

"9.77. We have considered whether there should be a single appeal tribunal similar to the AAT in place of the multitude of tribunals which exist at present. In our Discussion Paper the provisional conclusion which we reached on this proposal was as follows: **12–9**

Despite its apparent attractions, there are serious difficulties with the proposal for a general tribunal in this country. The sheer volume of statutory provisions conferring a discretion on Ministers, and a population of some 55 million, indicate that the potential jurisdiction of the general tribunal would be vast and the task of selection baffling. A more fundamental constitutional objection is that it would substitute for Ministerial answerability in Parliament an unaccountable policy-making tribunal.

On further reflection we do not think that the last sentence of the passage quoted is an adequate basis for rejecting an Administrative Appeals Tribunal or that it gives a fair picture of the achievements of that institution in Australia. No conflict of policy need arise. (It is really only with the immigration cases that there has been serious difficulty at times.) The most serious objection remains the problem of scale. For this reason we think it would not be sensible to dispense with the network of specialized tribunals and to replace them with a single administrative appeal tribunal. We do not consider that the adoption of such a system here would be either practicable, having regard to the much larger volume of business undertaken by tribunals in this country compared with that of the AAT, or productive when the gain is balanced against the disruption that such a change would cause initially. In our view effort should be directed towards the improvement of existing institutions in this field rather than towards their wholesale replacement. Improvement of the United Kingdom system is more likely to be achieved by the amalgamation, where appropriate, of existing tribunals as discussed in paragraph 9.72, and the extension of their jurisdiction.

9.78. But there remains the area of administrative decision-making from which there is no appeal on the merits. We think the first task is to ascertain the extent of this problem. We recommend that this inquiry should be one of the first tasks to be undertaken by the Administrative Review Commission, the establishment of which we recommended in chapter 4. We envisage that when the extent of this problem is ascertained, it can then be decided whether to provide an appeal on the merits in this area by further specialized tribunals or whether one general appeal tribunal would be better."

Notes

(1) The administrative review commission mentioned was to be independent of the Government and to have the task of commenting on proposed legislation and reforms and keeping an overview of the operation of the tribunal system. It would not, however, replace the Council on Tribunals, which would have a greater role in relation to day-to-day surveillance of tribunals in operation. Do you think it sensible that two bodies should exist? Should a single administrative appeal tribunal be established? **12–10**

(2) The JUSTICE-All Souls Committee also had cause to consider whether or not aspects of the tribunal system would comply with the U.K's obligations under the European Convention on Human Rights. Article 6(1) provides:

"In the determination of his civil rights and obligations or of any criminal charge against him, everyone is entitled to fair and public hearing within a reasonable time by an independent and impartial tribunal established by law."

The terminology is elastic and the words "determination of his civil rights and obligations" are clearly capable of covering a very wide range of subject matter. In *Le Compte v. Belgium* (1982) 4 E.H.R.R. 1 Article 6 was held to cover a decision to suspend a doctor from practice for three months. In reaching its decision, the European Court of Human Rights held that the right to a hearing which implicitly includes the right to a judicial determination of the dispute, includes a right to be heard on matters of fact as well as of law (at 19). This would seem to suggest that if the scope of review on matters of fact is limited, with the emphasis on appeals on points of law only, then judicial review procedure and many appeal procedures may be vulnerable to challenge. The report concluded (at 258) that the implication of *Le Compte* is that it is

> "not possible to conjure up a 'tribunal' on (as it were) a mosaic basis, by tacking the publicity of the High Court and its full examination of legal questions on to the factual investigation and exercise of discretion by some inferior body. All the requirements [of Article 6] must be satisfied in relation to one tribunal."

The full implications of this approach may now require to have worked out a domestic setting, given that Article 6 is now protected as a Convention right under the Human Rights Act 1998 and the Scotland Act 1998. Similarly Article 5(4) of the Convention has provided a basis for challenge. It provides that

> "Everyone who is deprived of his liberty by arrest or detention shall be entitled to take proceedings by which the lawfulness of his detention shall be decided speedily by a court and his release ordered if the detention is not lawful."

Tribunal procedure in the United Kingdom has been found lacking. Thus in *X v. United Kingdom* (1983) 5 E.H.R.R. 192, ECHR, it was found that procedures open to a patient to challenge continued detention did not meet the requirements of Article 5(4) and led to the creation of the mental health review tribunal system: the Mental Health Act 1983 and see also *R v. Secretary of State for Scotland*, 1999 S.L.T. 279, H.L. for a review of the legislation after *X*. For further challenge under Article 5(4) see also *Chahal v. United Kingdom The Times*, November 28, 1996, discussed at para. 8–44.

(3) Until 1993, no right of appeal from the immigration appeal tribunal to the courts existed. See the Annual Report of the Council on Tribunals 1990–91 (1991–92 H.C. 97), pp. 8–9, but see now section 9 of the Asylum and Immigration Appeals Act 1993.

Report of the Franks Committee on Administrative Tribunals and Inquiries Part IV: Administrative Procedures Involving an Inquiry of Hearing — General Questions

CMND. 218 (1957), paras 355, 356, 357–359

12–11   "355. Under present legislation the Minister's decision in the various procedures relating to land is final, subject in most cases to a right of appeal to the High Court, exercisable generally within six weeks of the decision, on the ground that the order in question (the compulsory purchase order, clearance order, etc.) is *ultra vires* or that the prescribed procedure has not been followed. It is provided that the decision shall not otherwise be questioned in any legal proceedings whatsoever. This right of appeal thus replaces any remedy by way of an order of certiorari. Where this right of appeal is not given, for example in the case of decisions on planning appeals, the action of the Minister could presumably be challenged in certiorari proceedings.

Appeal on Fact or Merits

356. Several proposals have been submitted to us, particularly by organisations representing members of the legal profession, for extending the scope of recourse to the courts against the Minister's decision. We do not propose to describe them in detail; it is fair to say that for the most part their broad effect would be to enable appeals to be brought additionally on the ground either that the inspector's report or the Minister's letter of decision contained errors of fact or that, in one respect or another, the Minister's decision was not 'reasonably' based upon the evidence at the inquiry and the facts found by the inspector.

357. Many of these proposals, particularly those which seek to apply a test of 'reasonableness' to the basis of the Minister's decision, would have the effect of introducing an appeal on merits against the

decision. We cannot regard such an appeal as appropriate. If, as we have already recommended, the parties are enabled to propose corrections to the inspector's findings of fact and the Minister is required to submit new factual evidence to the parties, there seems no need for an appeal beyond the Minister on fact.

358. Most of the witnesses who in their memoranda of evidence had proposed a wider scope of appeal to the courts agreed in oral evidence that, provided that the findings of fact were properly open to challenge before the decision and that the procedure was improved in other respects — notably by making inspectors independent of the deciding Minister and by requiring from the Minister, whenever possible, a statement of policy before the inquiry and full reasons for his eventual decision — then appeals to the courts against the Minister's decision could be restricted, as at present, to the two grounds of *ultra vires* and procedural defect.

Appeal on Law

359. There remains the question of an appeal on law. It is difficult to see how any question of law could arise other than a question of jurisdiction or procedure. The present form of appeal, covering these two matters, seems to us adequate, particularly since the scope for bringing appeals on grounds of alleged procedural irregularity will be wider if the various recommendations which we have made for strengthening and improving the procedure are adopted and, where appropriate, given statutory effect. This form of appeal should, however, be applied to decisions on planning appeals in the same way as it applies to decisions in other cases relating to land. We think that it would be reasonable to reduce, for example from six to four weeks, the limit of time for lodging appeals to the courts if a period of 14 days were allowed at an earlier stage for challenging the inspector's findings of fact. It is for consideration whether, following the lines of our suggestions concerning tribunals, all such appeals could not with advantage be made to the Divisional Court. There should then be one further appeal, by leave."

Notes

For further comment on the form of appeal prescribed in para. 355 see paras 12–16 to 12–23.   **12–12**

APPEALS TO THE SHERIFF

In Scotland, the sheriff has always exercised a wide variety of powers of an administrative   **12–13** nature, mainly in relation to local government. For a general survey see Report of the Committee on the Sheriff Court (the Grant Committee) Cmnd. 3248 (1967), Chap. 8 and Appendices 8 and 9. There is no uniformity as to the powers of the sheriff nor the procedures for making an appeal. According to A.W. Bradley, *Stair Memorial Encyclopaedia*, Vol. 1, para. 338, the powers fall into three main categories: (1) procedures for appeal to or confirmation by the sheriff of a decision where the sheriff has a broad discretion, including power to reconsider the merits of a decision; (2) appeals where the sheriff must find certain states of fact to exist before he can uphold the appeal; and (3) an appeal on specified grounds of *vires*, jurisdiction, fair procedure and error of law. The next extract is a general survey of the forms of appeal available, their rationale and also serves to highlight some of the concerns as to the propriety of an appeal existing at all.

C.M.G. Himsworth, "Scottish Local Authorities and the Sheriff"

1984 J.R. 63

"I. Introduction
In 1929 Lord Cooper (T. M. Cooper as he then was) wrote a paper entitled, 'The Limitations of the   **12–14** Judicial Functions of Public Authorities.' 'The practical question for us,' he said, 'and for every modern State, in the altered conditions of post-war life, is by what expedients the conflicting principles of *imperium* and *libertas* can best be reconciled, conformably with the genius of national and constitutional traditions.' He discussed the extent to which review by courts can operate as a partial restriction on administrative oppression and, in general, he advocated the use of a non-centralised administrative judge hearing appeals from the different types of public authority and, for reasons to which I shall be returning later, he strongly supported the use in Scotland of the ready-made judge of this type — the sheriff of the county. 'The

Sheriff,' he said, 'undoubtedly enjoys the confidence of the public, for his independence is beyond dispute and there is no room for the suspicion of bias in favour of the constituted authorities as against the public.'

This confidence in the use of the sheriff on appeal from local authority decisions is what this article seeks to discuss and, in some measure, to question. As we shall find, Lord Cooper has not been alone in holding the views that he did and what seems remarkable is not only that they appear to have gone substantially without challenge but also that there have been moves further to entrench the sheriff in the hearing of appeals from local authority decisions. Three developments are most prominent. The first is the call for a remedy on appeal for those denied accommodation by housing authorities under the Housing (Homeless Persons) Act 1977. The lack of an appeal of this sort was recognised (for England and Wales at least) as the Bill passed through Parliament. In the light of the operation of the Act, however, arguments for the creation of an appeal have continued, and for Scotland the principal suggestion appears to be that this should lie to the sheriff.

The second current development is in the field of education and school attendance. In Scotland school attendance orders made by education authorities may be taken on appeal to the sheriff by a 'person aggrieved.' The sheriff may then confirm, vary or annul the order and his decision is final. Over the years appeals have been taken to the sheriff under the predecessors of this provision and latterly the breadth of the sheriff's discretion in these cases and the actual decisions made (especially so far as they affect the implementation of educational policy) have caused concern. A review of this type of appeal has long been overdue and this was in effect acknowledged in an S.E.D. consultative paper published in 1980 where it was stated that 'there are no present proposals for changing the attendance order procedure which was, of course, intended to deal with failure to attend rather than parental choice of school.' A procedure originally aimed at recalcitrant parents who simply failed to ensure that their children attended at school had to be used as a means of implementing the policy of education authorities on catchment areas. An appeal to the sheriff may be appropriate to the first but not to the latter use. This point arose in the context of the paper's discussion of procedural proposals for the making of school allocation decisions which are now embodied in the Education (Scotland) Act 1981. The Act sets up the system for ensuring a degree of parental choice of school and involves a preliminary decision by the education authority, an appeal to a committee especially constituted by the authority and an appeal thereafter to the sheriff. The sheriff is obliged to confirm the education authority's original decision only if he is satisfied that one or more of the statutorily prescribed grounds of refusal of the parent's original request exists and 'that in all the circumstances it is appropriate to do so.' Otherwise the sheriff must refuse to confirm the authority's decision. The judgment of the sheriff is said to be final.

A third area is that covered by the Civic Government (Scotland) Act 1982. The purpose of the Act was to make general nationwide rules in place of those formerly contained in the Burgh Police (Scotland) Acts and in local legislation. A substantial part of the Act deals with local licensing powers (taxis, second-hand dealers, metal dealers, street traders) and appeals against refusals, conditions and suspensions lie to the sheriff. In the case of these appeals, however, the sheriff is entitled to uphold them only in the circumstances already prescribed for other licensing appeals under the Licensing (Scotland) Act 1976. Other provisions of the Act, however, also allow appeals to the sheriff and these are cast in more general terms. They include local authority powers in relation to buildings, stair lighting, and the use of open spaces and, in relation to these, the sheriff may simply order that the requirement appealed against shall be of no effect or that it shall have effect subject to modifications. The legislation imposes no limits upon the grounds for his order nor upon the considerations relevant to its making. Such a general form of appeal is by no means novel but it is interesting to see its retention in a new Act.

There are other areas in which the sheriff is already active in relation to local authorities and other public bodies and some of these will be mentioned later on. However, these new developments or potential developments in the fields of housing, education and 'civic government' highlight well enough the question of the appropriateness of the sheriff's function. What should be the proper role of the sheriff (if any at all) on appeal from local authority decisions? Local authorities are already subject to a wide variety of controls by way of appeal or review. In some cases the Secretary of State acts in an appellate capacity from local authority decisions and he has other powers to intervene in their activities. Audit procedures, in Scotland established under the Commission for Local Authority Accounts, are designed to restrain some types of illegal or otherwise unreasonable behaviour of local authorities. There is also the Commissioner for Local Administration with the power to investigate complaints of injustice in consequence of maladministration. And in the background there is the Court of Session with powers of judicial review and the courts in general to entertain ordinary civil proceedings against public authorities.

Where, if at all, should the sheriff fit into this overall pattern of control? The question is by no means completely new but, on the whole, it seems that such commentary as there has been (in Scotland and in relation to similar appeals to courts in England) has been confined to observing the wide variety of forms of appeal available, the anomalies which abound and that the lack of a consistent pattern is to be explained 'historically.' Otherwise one is left with the rather bland survey in the Grant Report and the more bombastic defence of the sheriff's position which has been expressed by the sheriffs themselves both judicially and extra-judicially.

My own attempt to define the proper role of the sheriff in relation to local authority functions (and, perhaps more importantly, the limitations upon that role) assumes that, although this will inevitably vary from one function to another, it is possible to adopt a general framework within which it can be understood. It assumes too that the concept of a 'proper role' has meaning and that it is understood to imply a measure of consistency of constitutional function. Sheriffs are appropriately allocated the function of reviewing local authority decisions only if this is consistent with the logic of the surrounding constitutional order. To some extent this may be determined by historical factors but it is likely that other criteria will dominate. Thus the starting-point of the discussion is to suggest that whatever form of supervision is proposed, the creation or retention of recourse to the sheriff in relation to either a new or continuing process of decision-making by a local authority entails the consideration of three interrelated questions: (1) Is there a need for any explicit form of supervision by a court at all? (2) If there is such a need, which level of court is to be selected? (3) Depending upon the answers to these questions, what should be the remit of the selected court? It is hoped that, as a result of looking at the suggested range of considerations to be taken into account and the range of answers to which they point, two conclusions may be drawn. The first, which is neither new nor surprising, is that the terms of the sheriff's remit should be drawn as precisely as possible to avoid confusion as to the extent of his powers. The second, which may be more controversial, is that, whatever the historical justification for such supervision, there cannot now be a case for the creation or continuation of forms of appeal or review which give to the sheriff the power to substitute his view of the merits of a policy decision for that of a local authority. These conclusions are discussed in the third and final part of the article. The second part deals with the questions of choice of court and remit. It is prefaced by a summary of the range of powers exercised by the sheriff in relation to local authorities in recent years.

II. The Sheriff's Supervisory Remit

A total account of the statutory provisions under which the sheriff acts in an appellate or other supervisory capacity in relation to local and other public authorities would be difficult to compile. In a Scottish Office memorandum on the 'Functions of the Sheriff in Scotland with particular reference to his administrative duties' submitted in evidence to the 1927 Royal Commission it is stated that: 'the administrative work of the Sheriff is so diversified in character, and borderline cases — where the administrative and judicial aspects tend to merge — so numerous, that an exact and exhaustive classification is scarcely possible.' Although the precise powers have changed in the last 50 years, the process of classification is not much easier today.

The Scottish Office memorandum went on to catalogue the administrative duties as follows: (1) *ex officio* appointments as, for instance, standing joint commissioner, tax commissioner and Commissioner of Northern Lighthouses; (2) the superintendence of the Sheriff courts themselves; (3) powers in relation to the preservation of law and order and particularly the police and the military; (4) duties in relation to Parliamentary elections including being returning officer; (5) the appointment of auditors, valuators and some local officials; and (6) a long list of miscellaneous duties including the holding of inquiries, duties in relation to wrecks and many functions under the Housing Acts, the Burgh Police (Scotland) Acts and so on. Evidence from the sheriffs themselves referred to the sheriff as a 'handyman' while the final Royal Commission report observed that the items of administrative business in the sheriff court amounted to roughly six times the amount of judicial business! Other substantial accounts of the administrative functions of the sheriff appear in *Green's Encyclopaedia of Scots Law*, W. J. Dobie's *Law and Practice of the Sheriff Courts in Scotland* and the report of the Grant Committee.

Since these older accounts were prepared, the sheriff's administrative duties have undergone some change. In terms of the Merchant Shipping Act 1894 sheriffs principal remain Commissioners of Northern Lighthouses. They have, however, ceased to be Parliamentary returning officers. Following the Local Government (Scotland) Act 1947 sheriffs lost their formerly important functions of confirming general local authority bye-laws. The sheriff's powers under the Police (Scotland) Act have lost their former significance and some other important functions have disappeared. The sheriff is not, for instance, any longer concerned with appeals against enforcement notices under the town planning code.

On the other hand some important powers remain. Under section 16 of the Social Work (Scotland) Act 1968 the sheriff reviews compulsory care resolutions and, as mentioned above, he hears appeals against attendance orders under the Education (Scotland) Act 1981. He is also available for appeals under the Housing (Scotland) Acts against demolition, closing, and improvement orders and repairs notices and under the Building (Scotland) Act 1959 persons aggrieved by *inter alia* the refusal of a warrant by a buildings authority may appeal to the sheriff. The sheriff may confirm, vary or quash the order 'as he thinks just and make such order in the matter as he thinks equitable.' Under the Water (Scotland) Act 1980 there is an appeal to the sheriff against a notice by a local council seeking to ensure the sufficient supply of wholesome water to a house. In the Slaughter of Animals (Scotland) Act 1980 there is an appeal under section 5(5) against the refusal or cancellation by a council of the registration of a private slaughterhouse. Recently under the Tenants' Rights, Etc. (Scotland) Act 1980 the sheriff has been designated to hear appeals against refusals of loans under the Act.

In addition, under the Local Government (Scotland) Act 1975 members of local valuation panels are appointed by the sheriff. The disposal of land forming part of the common good still has to be authorised by either the Court of Session or the sheriff and there is an interesting provision under which 'cases of difficulty,' arising out of the carrying into effect of any of the provisions in the Local Government (Scotland) Act 1973, may be referred to the sheriff for determination. The sheriff remains very important on appeal from local licensing decisions and many Local Acts continue to grant him wide powers.

With this outline of the current forms of shrieval supervision and intervention in mind, we return now to the questions which it was suggested at the end of Part I are necessarily involved when any decision to introduce or retain a specific form of statutory supervision is to be made.

The first is whether there should be provision for any form of supervision by a court at all, and, given the general pattern of controls which (unless they are specifically excluded) will apply in any event, it is assumed that those who wish to supplement those controls will have to make their case. They will have to show that there is a need to add to the degree of control imposed by the general political answerability of a local authority to its electorate; to the control imposed by the local government audit procedures; and to the control imposed by the Commissioner for Local Administration. Authorities are also subject to the general supervision of the Secretary of State who is empowered to investigate failure to discharge statutory duties and, normally following an inquiry, to issue default orders backed by the authority of the Court of Session. Important too are more direct forms of legal control over authorities and their officers and members. There is, for instance, the statutory code requiring declarations of interest by both members and officers upon pain of criminal prosecution and there are penalties for corrupt practices. More significantly, all forms of *ultra vires* action are subject to review by the Court of Session without specific provision to this effect and even, indeed, if a statute purports to remove the Court of Session's jurisdiction. Thus decisions which involve an excess or abuse of power; which are unreasonable (in its limited sense); or which are made in disregard of the principles of natural justice can be taken on review to the Court of Session. The question of whether or not these same jurisdictional issues could be taken instead to the sheriff court was at the heart of the case of *Brown v. Hamilton District Council*, in which it was decided that they lay exclusively with the Court of Session.

Thus, the general pattern of controls over local authority decision-making is fairly clear although their actual impact will vary from one type of decision to another. Audit, for instance, will be important only where expenditure is involved; ministerial default powers will be cumbersome or irrelevant in many situations involving individual decisions. On the other hand, the existence of these general controls coupled with the fact of a parliamentary grant of powers to local authorities in the first instance must throw the ball of additional controls into the court of those who propose them. Surely, otherwise, a decision made initially by a local authority should, at the same time, be finally made by it? Unless the addition of a further review or appeal may reasonably be expected to produce what in some sense would be a 'better' decision or to produce better decisions in a class of decisions taken as a whole, there can be little rational justification for it. It has to be established why the views of a court or tribunal acting in a supervisory role should be preferred to those of the original authority. And presumably the answer has to be seen in the supervising court's capacity, through its broader jurisdiction or greater expertise in a particular field, to provide better or more authoritative decisions.

Some types of expertise courts (and tribunals with a legally qualified membership) readily provide. Most obviously, they are skilled in the application of the law and it is not, therefore, surprising that there should be supervision by courts to curb illegality embracing, but not confined to, the jurisdictional issues of judicial review. It is understandable that provision is frequently made for the review of local authority decisions where legal errors are foreseeable and where they may have detrimental effects upon individuals. Respect for the rule of law requires this. But beyond the range of challenge on purely legal grounds it is far from clear what the justification is for the involvement of a court. Provision for review by the Secretary of State raises different questions. So too does review by a specialist tribunal — a device little used in the local government field. We return to the question of giving broader powers to a court when we discuss the specification of remit below.

Before doing so, a brief response to the second principal question raised earlier. It assumes a decision to provide supervision by a court but asks which level of court should perform the task and this quickly becomes a choice between the sheriff and the Court of Session. It is easy to see, however, that the use of the Court of Session to handle statutory appeals on grounds wider than questions of *vires* can have few attractions for, although at one time there was a form of general appeal from local authorities to the Court of Session, such a remedy today would appear too cumbersome and expensive for routine use.

The third principal question assumes a decision to use a court for the supervision of local authority decisions and that the court employed should be the sheriff court, but asks what the court's remit should be and how this should be statutorily expressed? The importance of this question is heightened by the uncertainty which has frequently arisen as to the nature of a sheriff's powers and also by the manner in which these powers have been used.

There are different ways in which the possible functions of a reviewing court may be categorised but they may for our purposes be very crudely divided into those which allow a court to review a decision on its merits and, where appropriate, to substitute one of its own devising and those which do not. If a court is confined to establishing the accuracy of material facts or the jurisdictional basis of an authority's actions or the wider legality of an action or decision, then the review of merits is not involved. (Or, to avoid undue naïvety, we should probably say that it is not overtly involved. The very process of review of facts, jurisdiction or law inevitably involves some scope for the introduction of some merits questions in the exercise of judicial discretion.) If a court is not so confined, its powers of review are much wider.

One would have thought that, since a legislative decision to confer narrower, more technical powers or, on the other hand, broad appellate powers crucially affects the constitutional function of the court, statutory power-conferring formulae would be quite unambiguous. But this has not generally been the case. A recent exception, however, is the appeal from licensing boards under the Licensing (Scotland) Act 1976. Section 39(4) of the Act provides that: 'The sheriff may uphold an appeal under this section only if he considers that the licensing board in arriving at its decision — (*a*) erred in law; (*b*) based its decision on any incorrect material fact; (*c*) acted contrary to natural justice; or (*d*) exercised its discretion in an unreasonable manner.' The formula may not be absolutely precise as to what will amount to an error of law, an incorrect material fact, or this statutory version of natural justice but what it certainly does is to exclude the power of the sheriff to reverse or modify a licensing board's decision simply because he considers it to be inappropriate. But section 39(4) is special in being so specific and in excluding so deliberately an appeal on the merits. Other appeal-conferring provisions (some now defunct, some surviving) have been nothing like so clear. Typically, at the suit of the 'person aggrieved,' the sheriff has the power to confirm, modify or reverse the earlier decision but with no further express guidance as to the grounds upon which the sheriff's decision should be made — although sometimes the statute is a little clearer in limiting the sheriff's powers. In the case of appeals against conditions on caravan site licences, for instance, the sheriff may vary or cancel a condition only if he is satisfied that it is 'unduly burdensome.' In appeals against advertisement enforcement notices, the sheriff can vary a notice if satisfied that it exceeds what is necessary for the restoration of the land involved or securing compliance with conditions. Appeals against resolutions assuming parental rights under the Social Work (Scotland) Act 1968 allow the sheriff rather more discretion. He may confirm the local authority's resolution (*i.e.* order that it shall not lapse) only if satisfied that one or other of the statutory grounds has been established (and still subsists) and that 'it is in the interests of the child to do so.' A rather similar formula was adopted in the Education (Scotland) Act 1981 which requires the sheriff to refuse to confirm the appeal committee's decision (and thus to allow the parent's appeal) unless satisfied that one or more of the specified grounds of refusal apply and that in all the circumstances it is appropriate to confirm their decision.

Whether or not the shrieval discretion permitted in these cases is appropriate is something to which we shall return, but its existence (even if not its extent) is clear enough from the words of the statutes involved. In other cases, it is left to the sheriff to deduce for himself (subject to supervision by the Court of Session) the extent of his powers. It becomes a matter of interpretation.

In some cases the main help in the process of interpretation has been derived from the statutory formulation of the remedy the sheriff is entitled to award. *General Billposting Co. Ltd. v. Glasgow Corporation* concerned an appeal against the refusal of an advertisement licence under a Glasgow Order of 1937 which authorised the sheriff to 'make such order in the premises and on such terms and conditions as to the sheriff may seem just.' Referring to this provision Sheriff Black said: 'I reject altogether the respondents' contention that I have no power to review their decision on the merits. That view, if sound, would render negative the obvious purpose for which an appeal is allowed and would deprive the provision that the sheriff may pronounce such order as seems just of any intelligible meaning.' In the same way the bye-law confirming powers of sheriffs were eventually acknowledged to include full powers to review on the merits despite earlier suggestions that sheriffs were confined to questions of law and jurisdiction or that the power to confirm or annul did not include a power to amend. Similarly a wealth of decisions has established that housing appeals against closing and demolition orders can appropriately raise questions of the merits of an order where the sheriff's power is 'to make such order in the matter as he thinks equitable… and… the [authority's] order may be confirmed, varied or quashed, as the sheriff thinks just.' Appeals against school attendance orders where the sheriff may 'confirm, vary or amend the order' have in some cases involved probing the expediency of an authority's order.

Sometimes reliance has been placed instead upon classifying the type of decision being made by the authority (and by the sheriff on appeal) in order to determine the scope of the sheriff's powers. The question of whether the sheriff is involved in an 'administrative' decision or a 'judicial' decision has been important in determining whether there is or should be a further implied right of appeal up from the sheriff to the sheriff principal or from sheriff principal to Court of Session and it has frequently been this issue which has forced discussion of the sheriff's role. If the sheriff is acting judicially his decision may be taken on appeal. If he acts administratively his decision (unless in some respect *ultra vires*) is final. The distinction between an administrative and judicial role for the sheriff has not always been easy to make. In the leading case of *Arcari v. Dumbartonshire County Council* which concerned planning enforcement orders, Lord President Cooper referred to the difficulties he had discussed earlier in *Glasgow Corporation v. Glasgow Churches' Council* about the 'multifarious functions which are more administrative or ministerial than judicial,' saying that it was difficult to judge whether functions were judicial and therefore subject to normal review thereafter or 'whether on the other hand the Sheriff is merely discharging a special and particular function confined to him alone. In every case the answer must be found in the provisions of the statute in question.'

Lord Cooper's opinion in the *Glasgow Churches' Council* case was also relied upon by Sheriff Macphail who in *Carvana v. Glasgow Corporation* decided that in an appeal against a refusal to renew a street trader's licence his role was administrative and he was, therefore, entitled to substitute his own opinion for that of the magistrates if he was satisfied that their decision was wrong. He could 'deal with the merits of the application as well as with purely legal issues.' In reaching that conclusion he derived support from the early Scottish case of *Allen & Sons Billposting Ltd. v. Edinburgh Corporation* and the English case of *Stepney Borough Council v. Joffe*. He also referred at some length to Professor Bradley's *Remedies in Administrative Law*:

'In many local government matters, either there is an appeal from the council's decision to the sheriff, or the council's decision requires to be confirmed by the sheriff before it comes into effect … Where an appeal lies to the sheriff against a local authority's decision, may this be considered a judicial remedy, or is it more akin to an appeal to a higher administrative authority? In conferring such power on the sheriff Parliament must be taken to be aware of the general nature of the sheriff's office… In the nature of things it is likely that a sheriff will be particularly alert to legal points relevant to jurisdiction and competence. But even in the case of the confirmation of bye-laws, it is now clear that the scope of the sheriff's decision is not confined to matters of judicial review and extends to the merits and expediency of the proposal. The scope and character of the sheriff's duties in matters such as these bears out the view cited with approval by Lord Cooper in the *Glasgow Churches* case.'

Sheriff Macphail set out the relevant section of Lord Cooper's opinion as follows:

'Scotland had (and still has) in the Sheriffs its own distinctive administrative and judicial officers of historic dignity and manifold responsibilities, amply equipped with local knowledge of the area to which they are severally attached. The great width and variety of the administrative and governmental functions discharged by the Sheriff under statute and at common law will be found by an examination of the illuminating article in the Encyclopaedia on "Sheriff" by the late Lord Wark, who was himself for many years a Sheriff … I respectfully adopt the opening sentences of that article: "The Sheriff in Scotland is both a judicial and administrative officer. In the former capacity he is the local judge of the bounds, and in the latter he is the King's representative and executive officer for civil affairs." All this has a twofold significance. On the one hand it explains why the Sheriff was, and still is, appropriately selected in many Scottish Acts as the confirming authority for bye-laws, and as the authority for the discharge of a multiplicity of other governmental functions which in England devolve on government departments or special officials. On the other hand it exposes the fallacy of the suggestion so earnestly pressed upon us that a remit to a Sheriff is a remit to a purely judicial officer, who is "only a lawyer," and on that account assumedly incapable of dealing with anything but purely legal issues.'

In addition to *Carvana*, some other modern cases have raised the administrative-judicial distinction. In a firearms certificate appeal the court took the opportunity to distinguish the position set out in an older case under an earlier Act, and to hold that the sheriff now performed a judicial role on appeal.

Thus the courts, over a long period of trying to interpret appeal-conferring formulae, have established that, given appropriate statutory language, sheriffs have the power and indeed the duty to take into account criteria wider than the merely legal and jurisdictional. This is not to say, however, that they have arrogated to themselves the freedom simply to do as they please with the decision before them. Far from it. Even in those cases where the courts have gone to some trouble to establish an administrative role for the sheriff they have not suggested a free hand and descriptions of his role are sometimes quite restrictive. In *Kaye v. Hunter* Lord President Clyde held that an appeal under the Firearms Act 1957, s. 2, was to the sheriff in his administrative and not in his judicial capacity and, therefore, that there was no appeal to the Court of Session. He distinguished the case, on the one hand, of the 'true *lis*' and, on the other hand, of the other type of appeal which was not really one on a point of law, not one for the 'weighing of considerations.' Where the sheriff is 'only entitled to interfere with what has been done provided he is satisfied that a discretion conferred by the statute has not been reasonably exercised, then the appeal to him is in his administrative capacity... For in this latter type of case the appeal is given by the statute not primarily to determine a legal issue which has arisen between two contestants, but to provide machinery to protect the ordinary citizen from a capricious or arbitrary exercise of a discretion.' Sheriff Macphail in *Carvana* viewed the appellate provision he was construing as one which: 'confers a right of appeal to the sheriff in his administrative rather than in his judicial capacity, in order that he may correct the determination of the magistrates and protect the rights of the traders and members of the other classes mentioned in Part V of the Act, if the magistrates should, perhaps from excess of zeal to maintain the high standards of honesty and good conduct among these classes, unreasonably deprive a person of the right to earn his living in the way in which he has been accustomed to do.'

Then, drawing upon the *Stepney* case (in which Lord Goddard referred to the need for an appellate court 'to pay great attention to the fact that the duly constituted and elected local authority have come to an opinion on the matter, and it ought not lightly, of course, to reverse their opinion') Sheriff Macphail concluded that: 'Although there is, in my opinion, an unrestricted right of appeal to the sheriff, the sheriff should not, I think, vary or reverse the decision of the magistrates' committee unless he is satisfied that their decision was wrong, and he should pay due regard to the competence of the magistrates in arriving at their decision.'

This declared unwillingness lightly to interfere with local authority decisions has been a recurring theme. Over a long period and in relation to many different types of local authority, sheriffs (or the Court of Session pronouncing upon sheriffs' functions) have, whilst asserting a wide power on appeal, nevertheless been keen to acknowledge the proper limits of these powers. Lord Low in *Allen & Sons Billposting Ltd.* has not been alone in using categories such as the unreasonable exercise of discretion, capriciousness or arbitrariness as the basis for overruling the original decision — categories which are not far removed from those firmly associated today with challenge for *vires* or breach of natural justice. In many cases the sheriff has appeared to concentrate upon and to prefer rejection or modification of a decision on the grounds of procedural defects or irregularity rather than on its substantive merits alone. When the sheriff does address the merits he frequently expresses a strong presumption that, in their assessment, the local authority came to the correct decision.

In many bye-law confirming cases sheriffs took a similarly deferential line. In *Rothesay Town Council — Petitioners* in 1898, the sheriff spoke of the 'responsible representatives of the community' and how he was bound to treat their bye-laws 'with the utmost respect, and to approach the consideration of them with the conviction that they represent the mind of the community expressed through their representatives.' And in *Biggar Town Council — Petitioners* in 1912, it was again to be the 'decision arrived at by the representatives of the community interested, acting under powers conferred on them by a recent statute' that should prevail over the sheriff's personal opinion. Similarly in cases arising under the interesting general appeal section in the Burgh Police (Scotland) Act 1892, there was an insistence that it should be construed very narrowly. In other areas too there has been reference to 'questions which pre-eminently fall within the province of the Town Council to decide'; to the sheriff not acting 'as dry nurse to all the communities in his sheriffdom in regard to their administrative work'; to the need to avoid subverting the principle of local government.

On the other hand, there have been other instances where sheriffs have insisted on the breadth of their powers. An example is the building line appeal in *Clark v. Lord Provost etc. of Edinburgh* where the sheriff said that: 'The only power given to me is to review the resolution, but the power is a wide and absolute one.... My function under subs. (2) is, I think, to judge whether the resolution, with its possible consequence that a strip of land will be taken, is fair and reasonable in the circumstances, and to hold a just balance between the public and general interest on the one hand and any possible invasion of or injury to private rights upon the other.' There are many, many reported cases in which sheriffs have made decisions clearly based on 'merits' following the hearing of evidence where there has been no reference at all to deference to local authority expertise. A 'benevolent' approach cannot be guaranteed and even where the primary statutory function of the local authority is acknowledged, the sheriff himself remains the judge of whether his views should prevail and it is to the appropriateness of this power that we turn in the final section.

III. The Merits of an Appeal on The Merits?

Even if it were to be universally accepted that a sheriff when exercising his powers in an administrative appeal should show respect for the type of authority from which the appeal comes and tend to defer to the exercise of that authority's discretion, the question still has to be asked whether there is any justification for an appeal which is formally unrestricted at all. For Lord Cooper, as indicated at the beginning of this article and as is clear from his decision in the *Glasgow Churches* case, this appellate jurisdiction of the sheriff was fully justified. As he said in his 1929 paper:

'The practice of constituting the "sheriff" as the appellate or confirmatory judicial authority in administrative questions is one of long-standing in Scotland, although serious inroads have latterly been made by the central departments. This change is deeply to be deplored. The sheriff undoubtedly enjoys the confidence of the public, for his independence is beyond dispute and there is no room for the suspicion of bias in favour of the constituted authorities as against the public. Being widely experienced in the performance of ordinary judicial work, the sheriff can be trusted not only to conduct the inquiry judicially and with cold impartiality, but also — and this is not less important — to create an impression that he is doing so. In addition he is in sufficiently intimate touch with local circumstances and requirements to be able to apply to the case a severely practical and intelligent scrutiny. The proceedings are conducted formally but expeditiously and in the wholesome light of complete publicity, while the decision is customarily embodied in a reasoned judgment. On the other side of the account it may be urged that the utilisation of the sheriffs as administrative judges cannot make for harmony and uniformity in the trend of decisions, and that the sheriff cannot bring to his task the specialised skill of the administrative expert. I am not satisfied that these criticisms are well-founded, or that, if they are, the objections are crucial. I have yet to see an administrative issue more complex and technical than those which are daily arising in the courts of law and are being satisfactorily determined. Equally, it is by no means clear that uniformity in a series of decisions relating to different circumstances and different local conditions may not be too dearly purchased.'...

In 1963, the committee chaired by Lord Grant was appointed to inquire into the sheriff court. In their memorandum of evidence to the committee submitted by the sheriffs, they discussed the 'administrative and other duties of the sheriff.' They set out some of the history of the sheriff's office and noted with approval that 'as regards administrative matters the powers of the sheriff have survived with little curtailment.' The sheriffs enumerated the administrative functions and concluded that: 'the above outline of duties performed by the sheriff although far from complete makes it clear that his office is very far from being a sinecure and that he performs a valuable and important part in the administration of justice and of local government in Scotland ... It is particularly necessary that the sheriff's status and precedence be maintained in his relations with the local authorities in his sheriffdom with whom he necessarily comes much in contact and whose decisions upon a wide variety of matters he has frequently to review. In our experience local authorities and their officials accept with respect the decisions of the sheriffs even when adverse to them and gladly concede to the sheriffs the status and precedence due to their ancient office.' To round off the memorandum as a whole the sheriffs concluded boldly that:

'It seems not out of place to express the impression which those of the present sheriffs with extensive experience of the office of sheriff powerfully have that any evisceration of the office of the sheriff would be deplored in the communities which they serve. It is a great constitutional office in the Scottish idiom. The sheriff is recognised and valued as the direct representative of the Sovereign within the bounds, charged as such with the protection of the interests of the individual citizen and as such clothed with the appropriate powers and responsibilities.'

The Report of the Grant Committee gave substantial support to these views: 'Most witnesses who commented on administrative work favoured the intervention of the sheriff in this field... we are satisfied that the sheriff should continue to discharge the very wide range of administrative and miscellaneous functions: he has done so for a long time, we have heard no complaints about the way in which the duties are performed, and there would be great difficulty in finding another authority, or combination of authorities, to carry out these duties in his place.'

Approving the tendency of legislation to confer upon sheriffs further quasi-administrative functions of the type they already discharged, the committee said they thought: 'the sheriff has three qualifications which determine his capacity to dispose of administrative or quasi-administrative work. First, he is a legally qualified professional judge, and therefore particularly competent to deal with matters having a legal content; secondly he operates in a particular locality and possesses local knowledge; thirdly, by virtue of his appointment he is independent of any public authority or private individual in his area. These characteristics are, *par excellence*, those of the arbiter in local disputes, and especially in disputes between public authorities on the one hand and private citizens on the other.'

The committee also acknowledged, however, that when decisions raised questions of law or policy of national interest they should be considered in a court or other tribunal having a national jurisdiction.

Equally appeals from administrative decisions which raised questions of fact but had no legal content might more efficiently be settled by an expert administrative tribunal than by a sheriff. The committee was able to take account of the Second Report of the Guest Committee on Scottish Licensing Law, which had recommended that appeals from licensing courts should not allow the sheriff to exercise a second discretionary decision on the merits of licensing applications. 'On matters of fact and policy the decision of the licensing court would in effect be final.' The Grant Committee agreed with the Guest Committee so far as that recommendation related to licensing appeals, but could not 'agree with those witnesses who propose that the same type of appeal should apply in all cases where a local authority administrative decision is appealed to the sheriff.' The committee went on to consider specific functions and, on the whole, recommended the maintenance of the existing position of sheriffs on appeal from decisions of local authorities.

The Grant Committee Report contains the most recent extensive discussion of the sheriff's administrative role and its conclusions remain the last comprehensive word on the subject. But how valid is their main proposal that appeals from local authorities, even if not confined to jurisdictional or other legal matters, should quite appropriately continue to go to the sheriff? It seems to me that this should no longer go unchallenged.

It may be that the sheer convenience of giving new appellate powers to the sheriff or, even more clearly, leaving existing appellate powers unaltered, will remain attractive. On the other hand, this factor of convenience must always be capable of being displaced by more weighty considerations and the process of trimming that has accompanied the recent development of the sheriff's administrative jurisdiction is evidence of this."

Notes

(1) See also C.M.G. Himsworth. *Local Government Law in Scotland* (1995), pp. 158–162 and I.D. Macphail, *Sheriff Court Practice* (2nd ed., 1998), Chap. 26. **12–15**

(2) To date, the suggestion that homeless persons should have a right of appeal to the sheriff has not been taken up, but in England there is an appeal on a point of law to the county court see the Housing Act 1996, s. 204.

(3) The decision *Kaye v. Hunter* referred to in the extract has now been overruled. In *Rodenhurst v. Chief Constable, Grampian Police*, 1992 S.L.T. 104 the holder of a shotgun licence appealed against the revocation of that licence by the Chief Constable. The sheriff upheld the decision but the appellant contended that a further appeal to the Sheriff Principal and the Court of Session was in fact competent. A court of five judges held that the decision in *Kaye v. Hunter* was incorrect. A true lis existed between the parties and the sheriff was not acting in an administrative, but a judicial, capacity. The reasoning in *Arcari v. Dumbartonshire County Council*, 1948 S.C. 62 was expressly approved: see also *Grieve v. Chief Constable, Lothian and Borders Police*, 1993 S.L.T. (Sh.Ct) 6 and *H.L. Friel & Son Ltd v. Inverclyde District Council*, 1995 S.L.T. 1310. *Kaye* was concerned with the situation where no express right of appeal was conferred by the relevant legislation. That is relatively unusual and more typically a right of appeal, usually to the Court of Session, will be expressly created see, for example, the Licensing (Scotland) Act 1976, s. 39(8) and the Civic Government (Scotland) Act 1982, s. 64(9), Sched. 1, para. 18(12). Where an appeal is by way of stated case on a question of law from the sheriff to the Court of Session, it is not competent to raise other matters on appeal, such as merits: *Dodds v. Ayrshire County Council*, 1954 S.C. 86.

(4) As noted in Chapter 4, in judicial review proceedings it is generally not open to the court to seek to review matters of fact, unless the factual matters are bound up with an error of law. In relation to statutory appeals the sheriff can sometimes uphold an appeal on the basis of a decision having made based on an incorrect material fact: see, for example, the Licensing (Scotland) Act 1976, s. 39(4) (liquor licensing) and the Civic Government (Scotland) Act 1982, s. 4, Sched. 1, para. 18(7) (licensing activities regulated by that Act, such as taxi licences); s. 64 (permission to hold a public procession); and s. 45, Sched. 2, para. 24(7) (licence to operate a sex shop). An incorrect material fact can include an erroneous inference from correct facts: *Art Wells (t/a Corals) v. Glasgow District Licensing Board*, 1988 S.C.L.R. 531 and see also *Sagnata Investments Ltd v. Norwich Corporation* [1971] 2 Q.B. 614, extracted at para. 7–12 for the

interplay of matters of fact and matters of policy in the context of an appeal. For further discussion see Sir C. Agnew, Q.C. and H.M. Baillie, *The Licensing (Scotland) Act 1976* (4th ed., 1996) and A. Hajducki, Q.C. and S. Stuart, "*Civic Government Licensing Law* (1994).

STATUTORY ULTRA VIRES

Town and Country Planning (Scotland) Act 1997

s. 238 (1)–(4)

12–16   "Proceedings for Questioning Validity of Development Plans and Certain Schemes and Orders
     238.–(1) If any person aggrieved by a structure plan or a local plan or by any alteration, repeal or replacement of any such plan desires to question the validity of the plan or, as the case may be, the alteration, repeal or replacement on the ground —
     (a)   that it is not within the powers conferred by Part II, or
     (b)   that any requirement of that Part or of any regulations made under it has not been complied with in relation to the approval or adoption of the plan or, as the case may be, its alteration, repeal or replacement,
he may make an application to the Court of Session under this section.
     (2) On any application under this section the Court of Session —
     (a)   may by interim order wholly or in part suspend the operation of the plan or, as the case may be, the alteration, repeal or replacement, either generally or in so far as it affects any property of the applicant, until the final determination of the proceedings;
     (b)   if satisfied that the plan or, as the case may be, the alteration, repeal or replacement is wholly or to any extent outside the powers conferred by Part II. or that the interests of the applicant have been substantially prejudiced by the failure to comply with any requirement of that Part or of any regulations made under it, may wholly or in part quash the plan or, as the case may be, the alteration, repeal or replacement either generally or in so far as it affects any property of the applicant.
     (3) Subsections (1) and (2) shall apply, subject to any necessary modifications, to a simplified planning zone scheme or an alteration of such a scheme or to an order under section 202, 203, 206, 207, 208 or 230 as they apply to any plan or an alteration, repeal or replacement there mentioned.
     (4) An application under this section must be made within 6 weeks from the relevant date."

Notes

12–17   (1) Sections 238–239 are in substance re-enactments of the provisions of the Town and Country Planning (Scotland) Act 1972, ss. 232, 233. Subsection (5) makes detailed provision for what is the relevant date in varying circumstances for the purposes of subsection (4). The limitations both as to the grounds of appeal and the period allowed for challenge were felt necessary in the view of the need for certainty in planning decisions. Similar provisions to those contained in sections 238 (and 239 below) are found in the Acquisition of Land (Authorisation Procedure) (Scotland) Act 1947, s. 1, Sched. 1, para. 15 (compulsory purchase orders) and the Roads (Scotland) Act 1984, Sched. 2, paras 2–4.
     (2) The statutory time-limit for lodging an application detailed in subsection (4) is a strict one and in *R. v. Secretary of State for the Environment, ex parte Kent* [1990] 1 P.L.R. 128 the Court of Appeal upheld a ruling by the Divisional Court that an appeal against planning permission granted for development near the appellant's home, where the appellant was not aware that the application had been made, could not proceed: see also *Okolo v. Secretary of State for the Environment* [1997] 4 All E.R. 242, C.A. The six-week rule has sometimes been subject to criticism by the courts, on which see *Smith v. East Elloe District Council* referred to in *McDaid v. Clydebank District Council*, 1984 S.L.T. 162. *McDaid* is extracted at para. 10–41 in relation to exclusion of judicial control and see also *Anisminic v. Foreign Compensation Commission* [1969] 2 A.C. 147, extracted at para. 10–38. Note that the right to challenge is exercisable only by an "aggrieved person", on which see notes to section 239 above.
     (3) An appeal under subsection (1) (*a*) and (*b*) might be viewed as substantive *ultra vires* and procedural *ultra vires* grounds respectively. This distinction can, however, be somewhat academic as a procedural irregularity may be regarded as falling outwith the powers conferred

by Part II as well as being a failure to comply with procedural requirements. Note that insofar as a simplified planning zone scheme where alteration thereof has been challenged, subsections (1) and (2) shall have effect as if they refer to Part III instead of Part II, subsection (6): see further, notes to section 239 above.

(4) The procedure that requires to be followed to make an application under section 238 bears comment. Under the Rules of the Court of Session 1994, RCS 41.19 an appeal must be made in the form set out in that rule and to the Inner House. Although section 238 simply provides for appeal to the Court of Session, in practice, all such appeals are dealt with by the Inner House. In England and Wales appeals are to the Queen's Bench Division of the High Court with an appeal thereafter to the Court of Appeal and the House of Lords on a point of law. Appeal to the House of Lords from the Inner House is competent. Which approach is preferable and why?

(5) Note the provisions of subsection (2) which permits an interim order suspending the operation of the plan or its alteration, repeal or replacement. If the court is satisfied that the statutory grounds of challenge have been established then it has discretion to order that the plan, its alteration, repeal or replacement be quashed in whole or in part: *Peak Park Joint Planning Board v. Secretary of State for the Environment and Imperial Chemical Industries* (1979) 39 P. & C.R. 361 and *Richmond-upon-Thames London Borough Council v. Secretary of State for the Environment* [1984] J.P.L. 24. Following on from this that where an error is not significant the court may exercise its discretion not to quash: *London and Clydeside Properties v. City of Aberdeen District Council*, 1984 S.L.T. 50 and see *Glasgow District Council v. Secretary of State for Scotland*, 1980 S.C. 150 noted above. In deciding whether to quash a plan, decision or order the court has "no power to vary or alter or remodel" an order or decision under review, on which see *British Airports Authority v. Secretary of State for Scotland*, 1979 S.C. 200 noted at p. 000 below. Standing the wording of subsection (2) (*b*) partial quashing is competent and for discussion of this power of severance see p. 000.

Town and Country Planning (Scotland) Act 1997

ss. 239 (1)–(3), (5)–(10)

"Proceedings for Questioning the Validity of Other Orders, Decisions and Directions
   239.–(1) If any person —
   (a)   is aggrieved by any order to which this section applies and wishes to question the validity of
          that order on the grounds —
          (i)   that the order is not within the powers of this Act, or
          (ii)   that any of the relevant requirements have not been complied
   with in relation to that order, or
   (b)   is aggrieved by any action on the part of the Secretary of State to which this section applies and
          wishes to question the validity of that action on the grounds —
          (i)   that the action is not within the powers of this Act, or
          (ii)   that any of the relevant requirements have not been complied
   with in relation to that action,
he may make an application to the Court of Session under this section.
   (2) Without prejudice to subsection (1), if the authority directly concerned with any order to which this section applies, or with any action on the part of the Secretary of State to which this section applies, wish to question the validity of that order or action on any of the grounds mentioned in subsection (1), the authority may make an application to the Court of Session under this section.
   (3) An application under this section must be made within 6 weeks from the date on which the order is confirmed (or, in the case of an order under section 65 which takes effect under section 67 without confirmation, the date on which it takes effect) or, as the case may be, the date on which the action is taken…
   (5) On any application under this section the Court of Session —
   (a)   may, subject to subsection (6), by interim order suspend the operation of the order or action in
          question until the final determination of the proceedings;
   (b)   if satisfied that the order or action in question is not within the powers of this Act, or that the
          interests of the applicant have been substantially prejudiced by failure to comply with any of
          the relevant requirements in relation to it, may quash that order or action.

12–18

(6) Paragraph (a) of subsection (5) shall not apply to applications questioning the validity of tree preservation orders.

(7) In relation to a tree preservation order, or to an order made in pursuance of section 183(4), the powers conferred on the Court of Session by subsection (5) shall be exercisable by way of quashing or (where applicable) suspending the operation of the order either in whole or in part, as the court may determine.

(8) References in this section to the confirmation of an order include the confirmation of an order subject to modifications as well as the confirmation of an order in the form in which it was made.

(9) In this section 'the relevant requirements', in relation to any order or action to which this section applies, means any requirements of this Act or of the Tribunals and Inquiries Act 1992, or of any order, regulations or rules made under this Act or under that Act which are applicable to that order or action.

(10) Any reference in this section to the authority directly concerned with any order or action to which this section applies —

(a)   in relation to any such decision as is mentioned in section 237(3)(e), where the Secretary of State confirms the notice in question, wholly or in part, with the substitution of another local authority or statutory undertakers for the planning authority, includes a reference to that local authority or those statutory undertakers;

(b)   in any other case, is a reference to the planning authority."

Notes

12–19   (1) There is no statutory definition of the expression "person aggrieved". According to Salmon J. in *Buxton v. Minister of Housing and Local Government* [1961] 1 Q.B. 278 only persons whose legal rights were infringed were entitled to bring proceedings where this expression was contained and see also *Simpson v. Edinburgh Corporation*, 1960 S.C. 313. This narrower approach was disapproved but not overruled by Lord Denning in *Attorney-General (Gambia) v. N'jie* [1961] A.C. 617 who stated (at 634) that the expression a "person aggrieved" is

> "of wide import and should not be subjected to a restrictive interpretation. They do not include, of course, a mere busybody who is interfering in things which do not concern him: but they do include a person who has a genuine grievance because an order has been made which prejudicially affects his interests."

Certainly, more recent case law has suggested that the liberal interpretation is to be preferred. In *Bizony v. Secretary of State for the Environment* [1976] J.P.L. 306 the term was held to include persons who had received notification of the inquiry and who had submitted observations and would have been entitled to appeal and in *North East Fife District Council v. Secretary of State for Scotland*, 1992 S.L.T. 373, the First Division held that several appellants who were present at the public inquiry and who made representations were within the scope of the expression "persons aggrieved". These decisions seem to establish that the courts are prepared to regard those persons whose legal rights are affected by decisions falling within the scope of section 238 or section 239 as "persons aggrieved" or those individuals who made written or oral representations at a public inquiry.

This flexible approach was confirmed by an extra division in *Cumming v. Secretary of State for Scotland*, 1993 S.L.T. 228. Here an appellant challenged a grant of outline planning permission for the development of a roadside service area together with a 40-bedroom lodge house, restaurant and parking for up to a 120 cars. The application had simply been advertised as a roadside petrol station and service area and the appellant argued that he did not make any objection to the original application as he had been misled by the advertisement. The court, in considering whether he was a "person aggrieved", considered that the central issue was whether the appellant was genuinely deprived by the procedure adopted in making representations which in the appellant's view would have affected the result. In adopting a broad brush approach where the description of the development in the planning application was sufficiently inadequate as to mislead a member of the public, the appellant was a "person aggrieved". However, the court made it clear that the case was decided upon its own facts and did not seek to lay down any guidelines or principles as to whether other individuals may or may not fall within the scope of the expression.

Similarly in *Lardner v. Renfrew District Council*, 1997 S.C. 104 the First Division. In this case the appellant did not object in writing or at an inquiry into proposed changes to a local plan which would have affected an area of land near his property. He argued that if the planning — proposals had been advertised in the local community centre, it was likely that he would have learned of the proposals during the consultation period. The proposals were, however, advertised widely in a number of other places close to his home and so it was difficult for him to argue that the consultation procedure had not been followed. There could therefore be no issue of breach of statutory duty on the part of the local authority. Accordingly in circumstances where no criticism was made in the procedures adopted and where the plan was advertised properly and gave adequate time for representations, including a public inquiry, the appellant was not a person aggrieved, for as the Lord President (Hope) stated (at 107):

> "there is a difference between *feeling aggrieved* and *being aggrieved:* for the latter expression to be appropriate, some external basis for feeling 'upset' is required — some denial or a front to his expectations or rights."

Is this consistent with *Cumming* and the more liberal case law? Does this approach add further complications to the concept of a "person aggrieved"?

(2) Note that as with section 238, only the person who is deemed to be "aggrieved" can challenge a decision. Can a planning authority be a person aggrieved? The position is not entirely clear. In *Strathclyde Regional Council v. Secretary of State for Scotland (No. 2)*, 1990 S.L.T. 149 the Court of Session ruled that a planning authority was a person aggrieved for the purposes of section 233 (now 239) and the earlier decision in *Strathclyde Regional Council v. Secretary of State for Scotland*, 1989 S.L.T. 821 was treated as unconvincing. In that case the council, dissatisfied with changes made to its structure plans by the Secretary of State, sought to challenge the validity of the changes. The Second Division had regard to earlier English authority in *Ealing Corporation v. Jones* [1959] 1 Q.B. 384 and since Parliament had the opportunity in the 1972 Act to make express provision for an authority to appeal against such alterations similar to the provisions contained in section 233 (now 239) but had not done so, the council could not be a "person aggrieved". In the later case the Lord Justice-Clerk (Ross) observed (at 153) that:

12–20

> "I remain of the opinion expressed in *Strathclyde Regional Council v. Secretary of State for Scotland* [in 1989] that the regional planning authority were not persons aggrieved within the meaning of s. 232(1) [(now section 238(1)]. Apart from anything else, as the structure plan contained a statement of the regional planning authority's policy and general proposals, I am satisfied that the regional planning authority could never qualify to be a person aggrieved by its own statement of policy and general proposals. That consideration, however, does not apply to s. 233."

This leaves open the question of whether or not a planning authority can be a person aggrieved under section 238 where it is not seeking to challenge its own policies but simply amendments or alterations or repeals to those policies made by the Secretary of State. The position in England might be different. In *Cook v. Southend Borough Council* [1990] 1 All E.R. 243 the Court of Appeal held that the expression "person aggrieved" was to be given its natural meaning and the authority would not have to show that the decision being challenged imposed any specific legal burden upon it in order to come within the scope of the expression. Lord Woolf drew an analogy between standing in judicial review proceedings and the concept of "person aggrieved" and suggested that the approach of the courts on appeal are the same (at 255A–B.) On that basis a planning authority would have title and interest to seek both judicial review and to invoke statutory review proceedings.

The scope of the grounds of challenge detailed in subsection (1) (*b*) and section 238(1)(*b*) were considered in the next extract. Although the next case is concerned with the statutory *ultra vires* clause in the context of a compulsory acquisition of property, the so-called "Ashbridge formula" has been held to be applicable in a planning context.

Ashbridge Investments Ltd v. Minister of Housing and Local Government

[1965] 3 All E.R. 371, C.A.

12–21   "Stalybridge Borough-Council declared an area to be a clearance area for the purposes of section 42(1) of the Housing Act 1957, on the ground that the houses therein were unfit for human habitation. This area included two adjoining terrace houses of similar appearance, numbers 17 and 19, Grosvenor Street, owned by the respondents. Subsequently the local authority made a compulsory purchase order in respect of the clearance area, which was coloured pink on the map of the order, and of certain adjoining land which was coloured grey on the map. The compensation payable in respect of the pink area (unfit houses) was less than that payable in the grey area. Following objections by the owners, a local inquiry was held. The Minister confirmed the order with modifications. One modification was the transfer of number 19 from the pink area to the grey area on the ground that it had lost its identity as a dwelling, and so was not a 'house'. The owners applied under Schedule 4, para. 2, to the Housing Act 1957, for an order quashing the compulsory purchase order in so far as it affected number 17, on the ground that it was not a 'house', or alternatively was not unfit for human habitation.

Mocatta J. (1965) 109 S.J. 474, held that the question whether number 17 was a 'house' was a question going to the jurisdiction of the Minister and that the court should receive evidence of the facts and reach its own conclusion thereon, and was not confined to the question whether the Minister, on the evidence before him could properly conclude that number 17 was a house. The Minister appealed."

LORD DENNING M.R.: [outlined the facts and continued:] "Now the owners make application to the High Court asking for the order to be quashed in regard to No. 17. They say that the Minister has gone outside his jurisdiction because No. 17 is not a house. It is no more a house than No. 19. The owners say that the court should receive evidence afresh on this point and should come to its own conclusion as to whether or no No. 17 is a house or not.

The Minister objects. He says: 'This is not a matter on which the court should receive fresh evidence at all, or go into the matter afresh. It is simply a case for the court to ask: Did the Minister have reasonable grounds or no for determining No. 17 to be a house?' The Minister concedes that, if he had no evidence before him such as to justify that finding, or if the materials before him were such that he could not reasonably come to the conclusion that it was a house then, of course, the court could interfere. The Minister also concedes that if he has erred in point of law the court can inquire into and quash his decision. But he says that this should be determined on the materials which he had before him, and not on fresh evidence. Mocatta J. has held that the court can look into the matter afresh and receive fresh evidence.

Section 42 of the Housing Act 1957, says: '(1) Where a local authority, upon consideration of an official representation or other information in their possession, are satisfied as respects any area in their district — (a) that the houses in that area are unfit for human habitation ... the authority shall cause that area to be defined on a map', and so on. It is apparent that the question 'fit or unfit?' is essentially one for the inspector and the Minister, and the courts would not ordinarily admit fresh evidence on it. But the owners say that, on the question of 'house or not a house', the court can and should look into the whole matter itself afresh.

In order to decide this question it is helpful to look at Schedule 3, para. 4(3). It says that 'If the Minister is of opinion that any land included by the local authority in a clearance area should not have been so included, he shall . . . modify it so as to exclude that land for all purposes from the clearance area.' It is clear, therefore, that the Minister can move the land from the pink into the grey if he thinks that it should not have been originally included in the pink area. It seems to me that, in order to determine this matter, the Minister must himself decide the question of 'house or not a house', just as he must decide 'fit or unfit'. The legislature has entrusted it to the Minister for decision. If it is not unfit, he can remove it from the pink to the grey. If it is not a house, he can likewise remove it from the pink to the grey.

Seeing that that decision is entrusted to the Minister, we have to consider the power of the court to interfere with his decision. It is given in Schedule 4, para. 2. The court can only interfere on the ground that the Minister has gone outside the powers of the Act or that any requirement of the Act has not been complied with. Under this section it seems to me that the court can interfere with the Minister's decision if he has acted on no evidence; or if he has come to a conclusion to which on the evidence he could not reasonably come; or if he has given a wrong interpretation to the words of the statute; or if he has taken into consideration matters which he ought not to have taken into account, or vice versa; or has otherwise gone wrong in law. It is identical with the position when the court has power to interfere with the decision of a lower tribunal which has erred in point of law.

We have to apply this to the modern procedure whereby the inspector makes his report and the Minister gives his letter of decision, and they are made available to the parties. It seems to me that the court should look at the material which the inspector and the Minister had before them just as it looks at the material before an inferior court, and see whether on that material the Minister has gone wrong in law. We were referred to two cases: *Re Butler, Camberwell (Wingfield Mews) No. 2 Clearance Order*, 1936 [1939] 1 K.B. 570 and *Re Ripon (Highfield) Housing Confirmation Order, 1938, White and Collins v. Minister of Health* [1939] 2 K.B. 838 [above, p. 193]. They were decided at a time when the report of the inspector was not open to the parties. There was no letter of decision. There was nothing but the formal order of the Minister. It was necessary, therefore, for affidavits to be received showing what was the material available before the Minister. They were received in those cases for that purpose. Nowadays, when the material is available, it seems to me that the court should limit itself to that material. Fresh evidence should not be admitted save in exceptional circumstances. It is not correct for the court to approach the case absolutely do novo as though the court was sitting to decide the matter in the first instance. The court can receive evidence to show what material was before the Minister; but it cannot receive evidence of the kind which was indicated in the present case so as to decide the whole matter afresh.

I think that the preliminary point taken on behalf of the Minister, namely, that this is not a matter for fresh evidence, ought to be upheld, and I would allow the appeal accordingly."

HARMAN L.J.: "... The judge before whom this matter came was, I think, misled by the two cases to which we have been referred. In *Re Ripon*, which on the face of it looks the nearest to this one, the decision eventually was that there was no evidence on which the Minister could have come to his conclusion. The terms of the Act were that if the land in question was part of a park it could not be included; that was not a matter for the opinion of the Minister or the satisfaction of the local authority, but was a statutory prohibition.

Therefore, it was necessary to see on what grounds the Minister had come to this conclusion, and as he had not been bound to give any reasons, nor to publish the report of his inspector, it was absolutely necessary to have some evidence to show what must have been the materials on which he so decided. Once they came out, it was seen that this was in fact part of a park and could not have been anything else. Therefore, there was no evidence on which the Minister could reach the conclusion which he did, and the order was quashed.

Now that does not seem to me to be an authority which involves anything here. It is true that the headnote states that the Court of Appeal held that a motion of this sort was a new and independent proceeding, and not a rehearing or a retrial. That, of course, we accept. But the fact that it is a new and independent proceeding does not mean that everything is necessarily open to the court. Some of the matters are left to the Minister, some are not. It is left to his opinion to decide whether a house is a house or another building, and it is left to his opinion also to decide whether it is or is not unfit for human habitation. In both those matters he relies on his inspector's view, and it is quite clear from the inspector's report in this case that he did take both those matters into his consideration... That being so, and it appearing from paragraph 4(3) of Schedule 3 that those matters are for the Minister's opinion, it would not be right for this court to substitute its opinion for that of the Minister; and I do not think there is any case which involves us in doing so....

We can interfere if the decision of the Minister was perverse and could not have been properly arrived at on the facts which his inspector gathered for him, but otherwise it seems to me that the legislature has entrusted that part of it to him, and not to us, and we should not interfere...."

WINN L.J. delivered a concurring judgment.

Notes

(1) For the equivalent Scottish provisions in relation to clearance area compulsory purchase orders see the Acquisition of Land (Authorisation Procedure) (Scotland) Act 1947, Sched. 1, para. 15(1).

12–22

(2) In *Smith v. East Elloe Rural District Council* [1956] A.C. 736, noted at para. 10–41, differing views have been expressed as to the scope of challenge under a statutory *ultra vires* clause. Lord Morton (at 754–755), Lord Reid (at 763) and Lord Somervell (at 772) held that it only covered claims that an order was *ultra vires* in the narrow sense of non-compliance with a statutory requirement, either substantive or procedural, but not allegations of bad faith or improper motive or *Wednesbury* grounds of challenge. However, Lord Radcliffe opined that they covered "any case in which the complainant sought to say that the order in question did not carry the

statutory authority which it purported to" (at 768) and Viscount Simonds inclined to the same view as Lord Radcliffe but preferred to leave the point open (at 752.) These observations were *obiter* as the issue in the case was whether any form of challenge could be made after the six-week period.

In *Webb v. Minister of Housing and Local Government* [1965] 1 W.L.R. 755 Lord Denning M.R., stated *obiter* that the "differing voices" in the House of Lords on the scope of the paragraph were "So differing that they give no clear guidance, or, at any rate, no guidance that binds us" (at 770).

The Ashbridge "formula" has been impliedly accepted by the Scottish courts. In *Wordie Property Co. v. Secretary of State for Scotland*, 1984 S.L.T. 345 the Lord President (Emslie) expressed the view that "little doubt" remains as to the scope of the statutory grounds of challenge. The test has been adopted in a number of subsequent cases: see, for example, *Howard v. Minister of Housing and Local Government* (1967) 65 L.G.R. 257; *British Dredging (Services) v. Secretary of State for Wales and Monmouthshire* [1975] 1 W.L.R. 687; *Seddon Properties v. Secretary of State for the Environment* [1978] J.P.L. 835; and *R v. Medicines Commission, ex parte Organon Laboratories Ltd* [1989] C.O.D. 479 (a case under the Medicines Act 1968, s. 107).

(3) In *Edwin H. Bradley & Sons Ltd v. Secretary of State for the Environment* (1982) 47 P. & C.R. 374 Glidewell J. observed that in *Ashbridge* Lord Denning was stating "exactly the same principles" as those formulated by Lord Greene M.R. in the *Wednesbury* case, (at 388). Is this analogy persuasive? In *R. v. Secretary of State for Transport, exp. de Rothschild* [1989] 1 All E.R. 933 Slade L.J. stated that the conventional grounds for challenging a compulsory purchase order were those set out in *Ashbridge* together with those derived from the *Wednesbury* test, thus indicating that they are distinct. Moreover, it is not clear whether the statutory grounds of challenge in *Ashbridge* embrace non-jurisdictional errors of law. In *Wordie Property Co. Ltd* above the Lord President appears to have thought so, observing that a decision will be challengeable under a statutory provision only "if it is based upon a material error of law going to the root of the question for determination". For further discussion on the distinction between jurisdictional and non-jurisdictional errors see the Chapter 4. Is Lord Denning's equation of errors which cause a Minister to act out with his powers the same as error of law? If his analysis is correct, is there any reason why a distinction requires to be drawn between appeals on points of law and applications to quash? In this connection compare sections 238 and 239 above with section 134 (appeal on points of law against enforcement notice) of the Town and Country (Planning) (Scotland) Act 1997.

(4) A number of points in relation to the second ground of challenge, failure to adhere to the procedural requirement, should be noted. First, "substantial prejudice" must be shown before a decision can be quashed. It is not necessary for the appellant to show that a decision would have been different if the statutory requirements had been adhered to, "the loss of a chance had been better off" is sufficient: *Hibernian Property Co. Ltd v. Secretary of State for the Environment* (1973) 27 P. & C.R. 197 *per* Browne J. at 200. Examples of substantial prejudice have included failure to serve notice of a making of a compulsory purchase order on the owners of part of land: *McCowan v. Secretary of State for Scotland*, 1972 S.C. 93; failure to give proper and adequate reasons for decision on a planning application: *Wordie Property Co. Ltd v. Secretary of State for Scotland*, 1984 S.L.T. 345 noted above; and *Paterson v. Secretary of State for Scotland*, 1971 S.C. 1 where a reporter's failure to provide proper findings in fact in his recommendation to the Secretary of State on a planning application which had gone to a public inquiry was held sufficient. Failure to make early objection to an alleged irregularity may suggest that no substantial prejudice has occurred: *Midlothian District Council v. Secretary of State for Scotland*, 1980 S.C. 210 and for comment see (1981) S.P.L.P. 17.

A literal interpretation of the formula would limit the need to show "substantial prejudice" to cases of non-compliance with procedural requirements under the second limb. However, in some such cases non-compliance would be so serious as to render the decision *ultra vires* under the first limb: see, for example, W. Wade and C. Forsyth, *Administrative Law* (7th ed., 1994) pp. 750–751. It has been suggested that on that analysis "substantial prejudice" under both limbs would be required: *Re Manchester (Ringway Airport) CPO* (1935) 153 L.T. 219 *per* Branson J, although this is not easy to reconcile with the views expressed in *Seddon Properties*. Note also the view that under the statutory formula the fact that the court "may" quash an order on one or other of the stated grounds gives the court a discretion of whether to intervene even when one of the grounds is clearly established. In *Peak Park Joint Planning Board* v. *Secretary of State for the Environment* below Sir Douglas Frank observed that the discretion not to quash will in general only be exercised if the point is technical and there is no possible detriment to the appellant. In *Richmond-upon-Thames London Borough Council* below Glidewell J. did not quash a grant of planning permission by the inspector (reporter) where the inspector was wrong to hold that a policy on the development of the land had been overridden but where there had been other considerable advantages in the development and where it would be a waste of time to send the matter back to the Secretary of State. Contrast with *Westminster City Council* v. *Secretary of State for the Environment and City Commercial Real Estates Investments* [1984] J.P.L. 27.

(5) Compare and contrast the test of substantial prejudice with the case law on "ordinary" procedural *ultra vires* discussed in Chapter 5.

12–23

(6) In *Seddon Properties* v. *Secretary of State for the Environment* (1981) 42 P. & C.R. 26 Forbes J. summarised the circumstances in which the court would be prepared to quash a decision under the statutory grounds as follows:

> "(1) The Secretary of State must not act perversely. That is, if the court considers that no reasonable person in the position of the Secretary of State, properly directing himself on the relevant material, could have reached the conclusion which he did reach, the decision may be overturned. See *e.g., Ashbridge Investments* v. *Minister of Housing and Local Government* [1965] 1 W.L.R. 1320, *per* Lord Denning M.R. at 1326F and Harman L.J. at 1328H. This is really no more than another example of the principle enshrined in a sentence from the judgment of Lord Greene M.R. in *Associated Provincial Picture Houses* v. *Wednesbury Corporation* [1948] 1 K.B. 223 at 230:
>
> 'It is true to say that, if a decision on a competent matter is so unreasonable that no reasonable authority could ever have come to it, then the courts can interfere.'
>
> (2) In reaching his conclusion the Secretary of State must not take into account irrelevant material or fail to take into account that which is relevant: see *e.g.*, again the *Ashbridge Investments* case *per* Lord Denning M.R. *loc. cit.*
>
> (3) The Secretary of State must abide by the statutory procedures, in particular by the Town and Country Planning (Inquiries Procedure) Rules 1974. These Rules require him to give reasons for his decision after a planning inquiry (r.13) and those reasons must be proper and adequate reasons which are clear and intelligible, and deal with the substantial points which have been raised: *Poyser and Mills Arbitration, Re* [1964] 2 Q.B. 467.
>
> (4) The Secretary of State, in exercising his powers, which include reaching a decision such as that in this case, must not depart from the principles of natural justice: *per* Lord Russell of Killowen in *Fairmount Investments* v. *Secretary of State for the Environment* [1976] 1 W.L.R. 1255 at 1263D.
>
> (5) If the Secretary of State differs from his inspector on a finding of fact or takes into account any new evidence or matter of fact not canvassed at the inquiry, he must, if this involves disagreeing with the inspector's recommendations, notify the parties and give them at least an opportunity of making further representations: (r.21 of the Scottish Inquiries Procedure Rules 1997)."

Other principles can be applied. If the Minister differs from an inspector on an inference of fact he must have sufficient material to enable him to do so, on which see *Coleen Properties* v. *Minister of Housing and Local Government* [1971] 1 All E.R. 1049 *per* Lord Denning M.R. at 1053C. If it is a matter of planning policy he is free to disagree with the inspector's conclusions or recommendations without having to notify parties and give them the opportunity of making further representation on the policy. He must, however, make it clear what the policy is and its relevance to the issues raised at any inquiry in accordance with the third principle above: *Pavenham (Lord Luke of)* v. *Minister of Housing and Local Government* [1961] Q.B. 172. For the Scottish Planning Inquiry Rules see para. 1–53.

Compare *Seddon Properties* with *London and Midland Developments* v. *Secretary of State for Scotland*, 1996 S.C. 155, noted at para. 6–16.

For further guidance on the exercise of the court's discretion to quash see the decision of the Court of Appeal in *Bolton Metropolitan Borough Council* v. *Secretary of State for the Environment* (1990) 61 P. & C.R. 343.

(7) For further discussion of statutory *ultra vires* see J. Alder, "Time Limit Clauses and Judicial Review–*Smith* v. *East Elloe* Revisited" (1975) 38 M.L.R. 274; E. Young and J. Rowan-Robinson, *Scottish Planning Law and Procedure* (1985), Chap. 21; *Stair Memorial Encyclopaedia*, Vol. 1, "Administrative Law" paras 340–342; Vol. 5, "Compulsory Acquisition and Compensation", paras 77–79; Vol. 23, "Town and Country Planning", paras, 270–276 and "Tribunals and Inquiries", paras, 942–948; and N. Collar, *Planning Law* (1999).

APPEALS ON QUESTIONS OF LAW

12–24   This is a typical ground of appeal. For example, there exists a right of appeal on a point of law to the sheriff under section 39 (4) of the Licensing (Scotland) Act 1976 from the decision of licensing boards and from licensing committees under the Civic Government (Scotland) Act 1982. There has also been an extension of rights of appeal from the decisions, on which see section 11 of the 1992 Act above.

It follows from this that it is necessary to draw a distinction between questions of law and questions of fact. This distinction may also be relevant where there is an allegation of jurisdictional error as the courts are less likely to find that there has been an error of fact than an error of law: see generally Chapter 4. The distinction has generated much case law but the courts have not adopted a consistent approach. Areas which have been major sources of case law in this field include workmen's compensation: *Nelson* v. *Allan Brothers & Co. (United Kingdom) Ltd*, 1913 S.C. 1003; town and country planning: *Bendles Motors Ltd* v. *Bristol Corporation* [1963] 1 All E.R. 578; and tax law: *Inland Revenue Commissioners* v. *Hood Barrs*, 1959 S.C. 273. Broadly stated, an issue is one of fact where its resolution is reliant on the reliability or credibility (but not admissibility) of evidence. Where resolution depends on probabilities, such as an inference from circumstantial evidence, that too is one of fact. However, an issue which depends on whether facts fall within a statutory description does not clearly fall into either category of fact or law and in different contexts has been characterised as a matter of law or of fact or of mixed law on fact or of fact and degree, on which see, for example, H. Whitmore [1967] 2 Federal Law Review 159. Which view is taken may well depend on how much control an appellate court wishes to exercise over an inferior court or tribunal. This clearly parallels the approach taken to error of law as a method of jurisdictional control in judicial review proceedings. Other factors which may be influential include whether the phrase can be regarded as an ordinary English expression: *Cozens* v. *Brutus* [1973] A.C. 854 and/or as a matter of degree, on which see *Bendles Motors Ltd* above.

For general reading see W.A. Wilson, "A Note on Fact and Law" (1963) 26 M.L.R. 609 and by the same author, "Questions of Degree" (1969) 32 M.L.R. 361; L.L., Jaffe, "Judicial Review — Question of Law" (1955–56) 69 Harv.L.R. ev. 239; E. Mureinik, "The Application of Rules: Law or Fact?" (1982) 98 L.Q.R. 587; J. Beatson, "The Scope of Judicial Review for Error of Law" [1984] 4 O.J.L.S. 22.

British Launderers' Association v. Borough of Hendon Rating Authority

[1949] 1 K.B. 462

12–25   "The Association was established to promote research and other scientific work in connection with the laundry and cleaning trades. It owned a site in Hendon with a laboratory block, an experimental laundry, a boiler house and other buildings. The rating authority demanded rates in respect of the site in 1946 for the first time in 20 years. The Association claimed they were exempt from rates by reason of section 1 of the Scientific Societies Act 1843. They appealed successfully on this point to quarter sessions. The Divisional Court reversed the decision of quarter sessions, on an appeal by case stated on a point of law, holding that the Association was not instituted 'for the purposes of science... exclusively', as required by section 1, but also for commercial purposes which were not merely incidental to the purposes of science. The Association argued that this was a question of fact from which there was no appeal to the Divisional Court."

DENNING L.J.: "... Mr Rowe says, however, that quarter sessions came to a conclusion of fact in his favour with which the Divisional Court should not have interfered. On this point it is important to distinguish between primary facts and the conclusions from them. Primary facts are facts which are observed by witnesses and proved by oral testimony or facts proved by the production of a thing itself, such as original documents. Their determination is essentially a question of fact for the tribunal of fact, and the only question of law that can arise on them is whether there was any evidence to support the finding. The conclusions from primary facts are, however, inferences deduced by a process of reasoning from them. If, and in so far as, those conclusions can as well be drawn by a layman (properly instructed on the law) as by a lawyer, they are conclusions of fact for the tribunal of fact: and the only questions of law which can arise on them are whether there was a proper direction in point of law; and whether the conclusion is one which could reasonably be drawn from the primary facts: see *Bracegirdle* v. *Oxley* [1947] K.B. 349 at 358. If, and in so far, however, as the correct conclusion to be drawn from primary facts requires, for its correctness, determination by a trained lawyer — as, for instance, because it involves the interpretation of documents or because the law and the facts cannot be separated, or because the law on the point cannot properly be understood or applied except by a trained lawyer — the conclusion is a conclusion of law on which an appellate tribunal is as competent to form an opinion as the tribunal of first instance.

... The question is whether the association was instituted for the purposes of science exclusively. That is, a conclusion of law to be drawn from the primary facts, particularly, but not exclusively, from the memorandum and articles of association, and involves questions of interpretation of those documents and of the Act. The Divisional Court were able, and indeed bound, to form their own opinion as to the proper conclusion to be drawn from those primary facts, and I find myself in entire agreement with them..."

BUCKNILL L.J. and JENKINS J. agreed.

Bendles Motors Ltd v. Bristol Corporation

[1963] 1 All E.R. 578

"Bendles Ltd permitted the installation by one J. Allcock, a veterinary surgeon and poultry farmer, of an egg-vending machine, free-standing on a base two feet seven inches square, on their garage and petrol filling station forecourt, which had a frontage of 120 feet and a depth of 15 feet. The local planning authority served an enforcement notice stating that it appeared that development had been carried out without permission and the site-owners appealed to the Minister of Housing and Local Government who ordered an inquiry. The Minister considered the evidence and arguments on the issues of law put forward at the inquiry, and concluded that the stationing on the site involved a change of use of the land on which the machine stood; that, while a petrol filling station was not a shop, the machine standing in part of the forecourt of the petrol filling station was of the nature of shop use; and, being satisfied on the facts that the introduction of the machine involved a material change of use, dismissed the appeal and upheld the enforcement notice.

12–26

Bendles Ltd appealed to the Divisional Court on a point of law.

Section 12(1) of the Town and Country Planning Act 1962 (now s. 55(1) of the 1990 Act) provided that development (for which planning permission was required) 'means the carrying out of building, engineering, mining or other operations in, on, over or under land, or the making of any material change in the use of any buildings or other land...' "

LORD PARKER C.J.: "... The Minister in his decision of August 31, 1962, recited the relevant parts of the inspector's report, and went on: '3. The Minister has considered the evidence and the arguments put forward at the inquiry on the issues of law. He notes that the machine is not attached to the freehold and is movable, though it is of substantial size and construction and is not normally intended to be moved about the site. It appears to the Minister that its stationing on the site involves a change of use of the land on which it stands. It is now necessary to consider whether the change of use is material.'

In the next paragraph he says: 'As to this it is to be observed that a petrol filling station is excepted from the definition of 'shop' in the Town and Country Planning (Use Classes) Order 1950, by article 2(2) of the Order. The machine stands in part of the forecourt of the petrol filling station and is of the nature of a 'shop' use. Moreover, although the space occupied by the machine is small in comparison with the total area of the forecourt, it attracts customers not necessarily concerned with the motoring service provided by the establishment and introduces a noticeably different element of use of the premises. The Minister is satisfied, on the facts, that the introduction of the machine on the site involves a material change of use of the land, for which the grant of planning permission is required.'

As this court has said on more than one occasion, the question of whether a change of use is a material change of use is largely a matter of degree and fact. In *East Barnet Urban District Council* v. *British Transport Commission* [1962] 2 Q.B. 484 after referring to this matter, I said (*ibid.* at 492): 'It is a question of fact and degree in every case and, when the matter comes before this court by way of case stated, the court is unable to interfere with a finding of the justices on such a matter unless it must be said that they could not properly have reached that conclusion.' That was dealing with a case stated from justices, but in my judgment the same is true of an appeal from the Minister himself. This court can only interfere if satisfied that it is a conclusion that he could not, properly directing himself as to the law, have reached.

That being so, one has to examine his decision with some care. Counsel for the site-owners has stated that there is a fatal error at the very outset in that the Minister is only considering the nine square feet, or whatever it may be, upon which the machine stands. Quite clearly, if one is looking at those nine square feet alone, there would be a change of use and undoubtedly a material change of use. Counsel says, and in my judgment rightly, that that is the wrong approach, and that in considering materiality one ought to consider the premises as a whole. It seems to me, however, that that is exactly what the Minister has done. It is true that he was referring to the fact that the stationing of this machine involves a change of use of the land upon which this machine stands, but he then goes on to deal with the matter of whether it is a material change, and for the purposes of deciding the material change it is clear that he is going beyond the nine square feet upon which the machine stands and is considering, if not the whole of the premises, at any rate the forecourt because he says in the next paragraph: 'Moreover, although the space occupied by the machine is small in comparison with the total area of the forecourt, it attracts customers not necessarily concerned with the motoring service' and so on.

The Minister having, therefore, properly directed himself on the law, this court could in my judgment only interfere if satisfied that the judgment was perverse in the sense that the evidence could not support it. That is going a very long way when one is dealing with planning considerations. I confess that at first sight, and indeed at last sight, I am somewhat surprised that it can be said that the placing of this small machine on this large forecourt can be said to change the use of these premises in a material sense from that of a garage and petrol filling station by the addition of a further use. It is surprising, and it may be, if it was a matter for my own personal judgment, that I should feel inclined to say that the egg-vending machine was *de minimis*; but it is not a question of what my opinion is on that matter, it is for the Minister to decide.

I cannot say that he was wrong in law in holding that the undoubted change of use of part of the premises did not amount to a material change of use of the whole. The Minister, in this case, has given a very careful decision, to which I find it unnecessary to refer in detail, but it is quite clear that with this type of machine coming on to the market it may well be that premises like garage premises may become used as shopping centres. The Minister in this case has not considered this as a case of *de minimis* and, that being so, I find it impossible to interfere. I would dismiss the appeal."

ASHWORTH and LYELL JJ. agreed.

Notes

12–27   (1) In *Birmingham Corporation* v. *Minister of Housing and Local Government* [1964] 1 Q.B. 178 it was held that the Minister had erred in law in holding that the intensification of the use of land could not constitute a material change of use: see also *Stringer* v. *Minister of Housing and Local Government* [1971] 1 All E.R. 65.

For further discussion of the meaning of "development" see Collar, pp. 71–83; Young and Rowan–Robinson, Chap. 6; and *Stair Memorial Encyclopaedia*, Vol. 23, Town and Country Planning, paras 64–99.

Edwards (Inspector of Taxes) v. Bairstow

[1956] A.C. 14, H.L.

12–28   "In 1946, Harold Bairstow and Fred Harrison, neither of whom had previously undertaken any transactions in machinery, purchased for £12,000 a complete spinning plant, agreeing not to hold it but to make a quick resale. Between then and February 1948, and after various negotiations, the plant was sold in separate lots at a profit of over £18,000. The General Commissioners of Income Tax found that this was not 'an adventure… in the nature of trade' so as to justify an assessment to income tax under Case I of Schedule D of the Income Tax Act 1918. The Inspector of Taxes appealed by case stated on a point of law to the High Court. The High Court and Court of Appeal (1954) 33 A.T.C. 131 rejected the appeal, treating the matter as a 'pure question of fact', but a further appeal was allowed by the House of Lords."

VISCOUNT SIMONDS: "… [I]n my opinion, whatever test is adopted, that is, whether the finding that the transaction was not an adventure in the nature of trade is to be regarded as a pure finding of fact or as the determination of a question of law or of mixed law and fact, the same result is reached in this case. The determination cannot stand: this appeal must be allowed and the assessments must be confirmed. For it is universally conceded that, though it is a pure finding of fact, it may be set aside on grounds which have been stated in various ways but are, I think, fairly summarized by saying that the court should take that course if it appears that the commissioners have acted without any evidence or upon a view of the facts which could not reasonably be entertained.

… [H]aving read and re-read [the facts found by the commissioners] with every desire to support the determination if it can reasonably be supported, I find myself quite unable to do so. The primary facts, as they are sometimes called, do not, in my opinion, justify the inference or conclusion which the commissioners have drawn: not only do they justify it but they lead irresistibly to the opposite inference or conclusion. It is therefore a case in which, whether it be said of the commissioners that their finding is perverse or that they have misdirected themselves in law by a misunderstanding of the statutory language or otherwise, their determination cannot stand. I venture to put the matter thus strongly because I do not find in the careful and, indeed, exhaustive statement of facts any item which points to the transaction not being an adventure in the nature of trade. Everything pointed the other way.…"

LORD RADCLIFFE: "… My Lords, I think that it is a question of law what meaning is to be given to the words of the Income Tax Act 'trade, manufacture, adventure or concern in the nature of trade' and for that matter what constitute 'profits or gains' arising from it. Here we have a statutory phrase involving a charge of tax, and it is for the courts to interpret its meaning, having regard to the context in which it occurs and to the principles which they bring to bear upon the meaning of income. But, that being said, the law does not supply a precise definition of the word 'trade': much less does it prescribe as detailed or exhaustive set of rules for application to any particular set of circumstances. In effect it lays down the limits within which it would be permissible to say that a 'trade' as interpreted by section 237 of the Act does or does not exist.

But the field so marked out is a wide one and there are many combinations of circumstances in which it could not be said to be wrong to arrive at a conclusion one way or the other. If the facts of any particular case are fairly capable of being so described, it seems to me that it necessarily follows that the determination of the Commissioners, Special or General, to the effect that a trade does or does not exist is not 'erroneous in point of law'; and, if a determination cannot be shown to be erroneous in point of law, the statute does not admit of its being upset by the court on appeal. I except the occasions when the commissioners, although dealing with a set of facts which would warrant a decision either way, show by some reason they give or statement they make in the body of the case that they have misunderstood the law in some relevant particular.

All these cases in which the facts warrant a determination either way can be described as questions of degree and therefore as questions of fact…

… If a party to a hearing before commissioners expresses dissatisfaction with their determination as being erroneous in point of law, it is for them to state a case and in the body of it to set out the facts that they have found as well as their determination. I do not think that inferences drawn from other facts are incapable of being themselves findings of fact, although there is value in the distinction between primary facts and inferences drawn from them. When the case comes before the court it is its duty to examine the determination having regard to its knowledge of the relevant law. If the case contains anything ex facie which is bad law and which bears upon the determination, it is, obviously, erroneus in point of law. But, without any such misconception appearing ex facie, it may be that the facts found are such that no person acting judicially and properly instructed as to the relevant law could have come to the determination under appeal. In those circumstances, too, the court must intervene. It has no option but to assume that there has been some misconception of the law and that this has been responsible for the determination. So there, too, there has been error in point of law. I do not think that it much matters whether this state of affairs is described as one in which there is no evidence to support the determination or as one in which the evidence is inconsistent with and contradictory of the determination, or as one in which the true and only reasonable conclusion contradicts the determination. Rightly understood, each phrase propounds the same test. For my part, I prefer the last of the three, since I think that it is rather misleading to speak of there being no evidence to support a conclusion when in cases such as these many of the facts are likely to be neutral in themselves, and only to take their colour from the combination of circumstances in which they are found to occur.

If I apply what I regard as the accepted test to the facts found in the present case, I am bound to say, with all respect to the judgments under appeal, that I can see only one true and reasonable conclusion. The profit from the set of operations that comprised the purchase and sales of the spinning plant was the profit of an adventure in the nature of trade ..."

VISCOUNT SIMONDS: "I must turn now to the question of the apparent divergence between the English and Scottish Courts and venture to approach it by a brief consideration of the nature of a problem which has many aspects, e.g. the finding of a jury, the award of an arbitrator, or the determination of a tribunal which is by statute made the judge of fact. And the present case affords an exact illustration of the considerations which I would place before your Lordships.

When the commissioners, having found the so-called primary facts which are stated in paragraph 3 of their case, proceed to their finding in the supplemental case that 'the transaction, the subject matter of this case, was not an adventure in the nature of trade', this is a finding which is in truth no more than an inference from the facts previously found. It could aptly be preceded by the word 'therefore'. Is it, then, an inference of fact? My Lords, it appears to me that the authority is overwhelming for saying that it is. Such cases as *Cooper* v. *Stubbs* (1925, 2 K.B. 753), *Jones* v. *Leeming* (1930 A.C. 415) and *Inland Revenue Commissioners* v. *Lysaght* (1928 A.C. 234; 44 T.L.R. 374) (a case of residence) amongst many others are decisive. Yet it must be clear that to say that such an inference is one of fact postulates that the character of that which is inferred is a matter of fact. To say that a transaction is or is not an adventure in the nature of trade is to say that it has or has not the characteristics which distinguish such an adventure. But it is a question of law, not of fact, what are those characteristics, or, in other words, what the statutory language means. It follows that the inference can only be regarded as an inference of fact if it is assumed that the tribunal which makes it is rightly directed in law what the characteristics are and that, I think, is the assumption that is made. It is a question of law what is murder: a jury finding as a fact that murder has been committed has been directed on the law and acts under that direction. The commissioners making an inference of fact that a transaction is or is not an adventure in the nature of trade are assumed to be similarly directed, and their finding thus becomes an inference of fact.

If that is, as I hope it is, a just analysis of the position, the somewhat different approach to the question in some, but by no means all, of the Scottish cases is easily explicable. For as the Lord President (Lord Normand) put it in *Inland Revenue Commissioners* v. *Fraser* (1942 SC 493, 501; 24 TC 498, 504): '... the commissioners here have either misunderstood the statutory language (which I think is the probable explanation of their error) or, having understood it, have made a perverse finding without evidence to support it.' He might equally well have said that the assumption that they were rightly directed in law was displaced by a finding which was upon that assumption inexplicable. The misdirection may appear upon the face of the determination. It did so here, I think, in the case as originally stated: for in effect that determination was that the transaction was not an adventure in the nature of trade because it was an isolated transaction, which was clearly wrong in law. But sometimes, as in the case as it now comes before the court, where all the admitted or found facts point one way and the inference is the other way, it can only be a matter of conjecture why that inference has been made. In such a case it is easy either to say that the commissioners have made a wrong inference of fact because they have misdirected themselves in law or to take a short cut and that they have made a wrong inference of law, and I venture to doubt whether there is more than this in the divergence between the two jurisdictions which has so much agitated the revenue authorities.

But, my Lords, having said so much, I think it right to add that in my opinion, if and so far as there is any divergence between the English and Scottish approach, it is the former which is supported by the previous authority of this House to which reference has been made. It is true that the decision of the commissioners is only impeachable if it is erroneous in law, and it may appear paradoxical to say that it may be erroneous in law where no question of law appears on the face of the case stated. But it cannot be, and has not been, questioned, that an inference, though regarded as a mere inference of fact, yet can be challenged as a matter of law on the grounds that I have already mentioned, and this is I think the safest way to leave it."

LORD TUCKER agreed with [the] speeches.

LORD SOMERVELL agreed with LORD RADCLIFFE.

Notes

(1) The approach in *Edwards (Inspector of Taxes)* v. *Bairstow* has been followed in a number **12–29** of other cases: see *R.v. Industrial Injuries Commissioner, ex parte Amalgamated Engineering Union (No.1)* [1966] 2 Q.B. 21 (whether an employee was injured "in the course of employment"); *Global Plant Ltd* v. *Secretary of State for Social Services* [1972] 1 Q.B. 139, *O'Kelly* v. *Trust House Forte plc* [1984] Q.B. 90 (whether contract was for "services" or of "service" held not to be a pure question of law); *Inland Revenue Commissioners* v. *Scottish & Newcastle Breweries Ltd*, 1982 S.L.T. 407, H.L. (application of the term "plant" for income tax purposes); *R. v. Social Fund Inspector, ex parte Connick* [1994] C.O.D. 75 (conclusion that incontinence pads were not "medical items" for the purposes of social security benefit, wrong in law). For arguments in favour of the approach see *Beatson* above and against, G.J. Pitt, "Law, Fact and Casual Workers" (1985) 101 L.Q.R. 217.

(2) Note also the decision in *Ferguson* v. *Secretary of State for Social Services*, 1989 S.L.T. 117, extracted at para. 4–5 that a box room was a "room" for the purposes of the supplementary benefit regulations. Note the reference in that case to the judgment of Lord Reid in *Cozens* v. *Brutus* [1973] A.C. 854 to the effect that the giving of a meaning to an ordinary English word is not a question of law at all, although the construction of a statute is a question of law. It is worth quoting Lord Reid's judgment more fully. He was concerned in this case with the meaning of "insulting" under section 5 of the Public Order Act 1936 and stated the following (at 861):

> "The meaning of an ordinary word of the English language is not a question of law. The proper construction of a statute is a question of law. If the context shows that a word is used in an unusual sense the court will determine in other words what that unusual sense is. But here there is in my opinion no question of the word 'insulting' being used in any unusual sense. It appears to me, for reasons which I shall give later, to be intended to have its ordinary meaning. It is for the tribunal which decides the case to consider, not as law but as fact, whether in the whole circumstances the words of the statute do or do not as a matter of ordinary usage of the English language cover or apply to the facts which have been proved. If it is alleged that the tribunal has reached a wrong decision then there can be a question of law but only of a limited character. The question would normally be whether their decision was unreasonable in the sense that no tribunal acquainted with the ordinary use of language could reasonably reach that decision.
>
> Were it otherwise we should reach an impossible position. When considering the meaning of a word one often goes to a dictionary. There one finds other words set out. And if one wants to pursue the matter and find the meaning of those other words the dictionary will give the meaning of those other words in still further words which often include the word for whose meaning one is searching.
>
> No doubt the court could act as a dictionary. It could direct the tribunal to take some word or phrase other than the word in the statute and consider whether that word or phrase applied to or covered the facts proved. But we have been warned time and again not to substitute other words for the words of a statute. And there is very good reason for that. Few words have exact synonyms. The overtones are almost always different.
>
> Or the court could frame a definition. But then again the tribunal would be left with words to consider. No doubt a statute may contain a definition — which incidentally often creates more problems than it solves — but the purpose of a definition is to limit or modify the ordinary meaning of a word and the court is not entitled to do that."

How does this compare with Lord Denning's comments in *British Launderers' Association*? The "ordinary English word" approach has not always been followed in criminal law as Lord Reid would have wished: see D.W. Elliott, "Brutus v. Cozens, Decline and Fall" [1989] Crim. L.R. 323. Note also the decision of the House of Lords in *Fitzpatrick* v. *Inland Revenue Commissioners* and *Smith (Inspector of Taxes)* v. *Abbott* both [1994] 1 W.L.R. 306. Here the question of whether spending by journalists in the purchase of newspapers and periodicals was incurred "in the performance of duty" employment was held to be a matter of law. This in turn allowed the House of Lords to make sense of different decisions made by income tax commissioners in separate cases in Scotland and England by overruling the English commissioners' decisions in favour of the taxpayers. Lord Browne-Wilkinson dissented, arguing that this was a matter of fact and subject to the principles in *Edwards (Inspector of Taxes)*. On this see A.A. Olowofoyeku, "In the performance of the Duties: Fact, Law, or Both?" [1996] B.T.R. 28. For another example of similar difficulties see *A.C.T. Construction Co.* v. *Customs and Excise Commissioners* [1981] 1 All E.R. 324.

12–30   (3) P.P. Craig, *Administrative Law* (2nd ed., 1989), commenting on *Edwards (Inspector of Taxes)* and the case law since that decision observed (at p. 126):

> "These examples demonstrate the pragmatic approach in operation… the initial denomination of the appeal as raising a question of law at all, and the standard to be applied in determining whether there has been an error. The influences guiding the judicial choice with respect to both topics are not difficult to discern. Where matters of real technical legality or broad principle are involved the courts will veer towards substitution of judgment. They will be influenced in addition by the comparative qualifications of the judiciary and that of the particular decision-maker for resolving the type of question posed, and also by the need to provide a uniform answer in an area where a number of lower courts or tribunals are interpreting the same term differently. By way of contrast there may be a large area in between technical legality and broad principle in which the court is content to allow the decision-maker the degree of latitude provided by Lord Radcliffe's test in the *Edwards* case. There is no reason why we should not continue to utilise both standards. Quite the opposite, the diversity of types of institutions to which a right of appeal on law is given would render any attempt to force them all under one standard rather than another inappropriate."

ERROR OF LAW

12–31   Once a point of law is established it is thereafter a question of whether or not there has been an error of law before an appeal can succeed. As we have noted in Chapter 4 the concept of error of law can include applying the wrong test in law as in *Watt* v. *Lord Advocate*, 1979 S.L.T. 137, extracted at para. 4–6; misconstruing a statute as in *Gordon* v. *Kirkcaldy District Council*, 1990 S.L.T. 644, noted at para. 4–13 or taking an irrelevant consideration into account as in *Padfield* v. *Minister of Agriculture, Fisheries and Food* [1968] 1 All E.R. 694, extracted at para. 6–13. Note also the equation by Lord Denning M.R. of error of law with grounds for statutory applications to quash in *Ashbridge Investments Ltd* above. A detailed analysis of the scope of error of law is beyond this work and the reader is referred to Chapter 4 for further reading. For present purposes three areas are worth noting: (*a*) whether a point as to *vires* could be raised on appeal as opposed to judicial review; (*b*) whether failure to give adequate reasons is an error of law; and (*c*) whether lack of evidence is an error of law. For discussion of the last point see paras 4–8 to 4–9.

QUESTIONS OF VIRES

Notes

12–32   There is no consistent train of authority on whether questions of *vires* can be raised on appeal. On one analysis, a decision which is *ultra vires* is no decision at all and accordingly the proper course is to seek judicial review, as there is no decision to appeal against: see, for example, *Henry Moss of London Ltd* v. *Customs and Excise Commissioners* [1981] 2 All E.R. 86 *per* Lord Denning M.R. (at 90); *Metropolitan Properties Co. (F.G.C.) Ltd* v. *Lannon* [1968] 1 W.L.R. 815; and see generally A.W. Bradley, "Applications for Judicial Review" [1981] P.L. 476. Underlying this approach is the principle of procedural exclusivity and, as we have noted at para. 11–20, in relation to the defence of illegality, Scots law appears to have been less troubled than English law in this area. Moreover, it is not necessarily the case that a decision, even if void, can be treated as having no effect, on which see *London and Clydeside Estates Ltd* v. *Aberdeen District Council*, 1980 S.C. (H.L.) 1 at 35 *per* Lord Fraser and at 44 and 93 *per* Lord Keith. The case is extracted and discussed at para. 11–16. For older law see *McIntosh* v. *Waite* (1891) 18 R. 582.

Equally there are other authorities which accept that questions of *vires* can be raised on appeal — for example, *Distillers Co. Ltd* v. *Fife County Council*, 1925 S.C. (H.L.) 15 and also *R.* v. *Inland Revenue Commissioners, ex parte Preston* [1985] A.C. 835, extracted above, where Lord Templeman observed (at 862) that in an appeal by a case stated on a point of law from the general commissioners or the special commissioners to the High Court the court:

> "can… correct all kinds of errors of law including errors which might otherwise be the subject of judicial review proceedings".

In *Chief Adjudication Officer* v. *Foster* [1993] A.C. 754 the House of Lords, overturning the Court of Appeal, held that the validity of income support regulations could be raised through a statutory appellate structure on the ground that the social security appeal tribunal's decision was "erroneous in point of law": see the Social Security Act 1975, s. 101 and now the Social Security Administration Act 1992, s. 23; and see generally D. Feldman, "Review, Appeal and Jurisdictional Confusion" (1992) 108 L.Q.R. 45 and A.W. Bradley, "Administrative Justice and Judicial Review: Taking Tribunals Seriously?" [1992] P.L. 185 on the decision of the Court of Appeal and D. Feldman and N.J. Wikeley, "Challenging the *vires* of Requlations" (1993) 109 L.Q.R. 544 and N. Harris, "Challenging the *Vires* of Social Security Regulations: *Chief Adjudication Officer v Foster*" (1993) 56 M.L.R. 710 on the House of Lords decision. See also *Nolan* v. *Leeds City Council* (1990) 23 H.L.R. 135 and for an earlier example *Scottish Milk Marketing Board* v. *Ferrier*, 1936 S.C. (H.L.) 39.

As we have noted in Chapter 10 issues of *vires* which amount to a devolution issue under the Scotland Act 1998 would appear to be able to be competently raised either in judicial review proceedings or on appeal.

FAILURE TO GIVE ADEQUATE REASONS

Crake v. Supplementary Benefits Commission

[1982] 1 All E.R. 498

"In two separate cases the Commission decided that the respective applicants were not entitled to a supplementary allowance on the ground that their resources and requirements were to be aggregated with those of a man with whom they were residing as they were 'living together as husband and wife' within Sched. 1, para. 3(1)(b) to the Supplementary Benefits Act 1976. In each case the decision was upheld by a Supplementary Benefits Appeal Tribunal. In the case of Mrs Crake the tribunal did not make any findings of fact, but merely summarised the history of the case and the parties' submissions, and gave as its reasons that most of the criteria specified in a supplementary benefit handbook for determining this question had been satisfied and that therefore C and the man were to be treated as living together as husband and wife. The tribunal did not state whether it accepted C's evidence that she was merely a housekeeper. C appealed, *inter alia*, on the ground that the tribunal had failed to give adequate reasons in accordance with its duties under r. 12(1) of the Supplementary Benefit (Appeal Tribunal) Rules 1971 or s.12 of the Tribunals and Inquiries Act 1971."

WOOLF J.: "… There was no formal request for reasons in this case and so perhaps the better approach is to look at it as if only the rule was applicable. However, whether one looks at the matter in the light of the rules or the Act, the situation is the same and there is an obligation on the tribunal to give reasons; and those must be reasons which are sufficient to indicate to the person who is in receipt of its decision why the tribunal came to the conclusion which it did.

It has got to be borne in mind, particularly with tribunals of this sort, that they cannot be expected to give long and precise accounts of their reasoning; but a short and concise statement in clear language should normally be possible which fairly indicates to the recipient why his appeal was allowed or dismissed; and it seems to me quite clear that when one looks at the findings of this tribunal together with the reasons for its decision, it falls far short of the standard which the Act requires.

First of all, when one analyses what are meant to be the findings of the tribunal on questions of fact, one finds that they are not any such thing. They are a citation of the history of the matter together with the

12–33

submissions of the parties, and the reasons for the decision are not as clear as they should be. Where a question whether a person is entitled to benefit or not arises which involves the issue whether persons are living together as husband and wife, it is important that a decision of that nature should grapple with the real issues which are before the tribunal. Frequently there will be a question of who the tribunal believes and it may be possible to give the very shortest reasons to make it clear that the decision has been reached because, notwithstanding what the appellant said before the tribunal, her evidence is not accepted and the tribunal prefers the other evidence which indicates the relationship as husband and wife went beyond, for example, that of mere housekeeper.

It is right to say that useful guidance is again given to tribunals on this precise matter in the Supplementary Benefits Appeal Tribunals Guide to Procedure, and having looked at that handbook it seems to me that if tribunals pay attention to what is said in that handbook they will not go very far wrong.

Having said that, the reasons here are, in my view, inadequate. It is next necessary to consider what the consequences of that are. I am afraid that here one enters into a position where the law is somewhat confused. The latest edition, which has just recently come out, of *de Smith's Judicial Review of Administrative Action* (4th ed., 1980), p. 151 deals with what are the consequences of the reasons not being in accordance with a statutory requirement in these terms:

> 'Unfortunately it is still far from clear what are the other legal effects of non-compliance with a statutory duty to give reasons for decisions. There is authority for the proposition that failure to give reasons, or to give adequate reasons, is not in itself an error of law entitling the court to set the decision aside.'

And then there is a reference to two cases in particular. One is *Re Allen and Matthews's Arbitration* [1971] 2 All E.R. 1259; [1971] 2 Q.B. 518 and the other is *Mountview Court Properties Ltd* v. *Devlin* (1970) 21 P. & C.R. 689 to which I will have to come back in a moment. The editor continues:

> '… if good and bad reasons for a decision are given, the decision should stand provided that the reasons are independent and severable. There is also authority (which it is submitted, is to be preferred) for treating material omissions as errors of law or as a failure to comply with the requirements of the legislation in question, and for regarding the adduction of legally irrelevant reasons as an excess of jurisdiction.'

In support of the alternative way of approaching the matter the editor relies in particular on *Re Poyser and Mills's Arbitration* [1963] 1 All E.R. 612; [1964] 2 Q.B. 467, *Givaudan & Co. Ltd* v. *Minister of Housing and Local Government* [1966] 3 All E.R. 696; [1967] 1 W.L.R. 250 and *United Kingdom Association of Professional Engineers* v. *Advisory, Conciliation and Arbitration Service* [1979] 2 All E.R. 478; [1979] 1 W.L.R. 570.

Those authorities have been cited to me together with a number of other authorities, and it seems to me that in approaching this question one must pay particular regard first of all to the *Mountview* decision. The facts of that case do not matter because it is a case involving a failure of the rent assessment committee to give reasons. In the course of his judgment Lord Parker C.J. said (21 P. & C.R. 689 at 695):

> 'For my part, I find it impossible to say that a failure to provide sufficient reasons of itself gives rise to the right of this court on an appeal to quash the decision of the committee. Secondly, it is to be observed that, quite apart from that, *Re Poyser and Mills' Arbitration* was really a case where, on the reasons stated, the proper inference was that there had been an error of law and that the arbitrator had misdirected himself. Of course, if they very insufficiency of the reason gives rise to a proper inference that there has been an error of law in arriving at the decision, then clearly it would be a case for quashing the decision.'

Cooke J. agreed with that judgment. Bridge J. said (at 695–696):

> 'It seems to me that there was here a lack of adequate reason for the decision, but I fully agree with my Lord and I add a word on this point because it seems to me to be a point of some importance: that a failure to give reasons pursuant to the duty imposed by section 12 of the Tribunals and Inquiries Act 1958 is not *per se* a ground on which the court could properly allow an appeal under section 9, the right of appeal being conferred upon a person who is dissatisfied in point of law with a decision. That language, and, indeed, any analogous language found in the statutes giving a right of appeal on a point of law, to my mind connotes that a successful appellant must demonstrate that the decision with which he is dissatisfied is itself vitiated by reason of the fact that it has been reached by an erroneous process of legal reasoning. Mr Slynn [as *amicus curiae*] concedes that there may in theory be cases where from a failure to give reasons one may legitimately infer, on a balance of probabilities, that the tribunal's process of legal reasoning must have been defective.'

And the judge goes on to say that at one stage in the argument he thought that was a case falling within that concession.

That decision of the Divisional Court has never been overruled and, in my view, it is binding on me. There are a number of cases where decisions have been set aside, among those being the decisions referred to by the editor of *de Smith* in the passage to which I have made reference, but when one looks at those cases they are in no way inconsistent with the *Mountview* case because they either turn on the particular statutory provision which gave the grounds for bringing the matter before the High Court in that case, or they turned on a statutory provision which was very different from the statutory provision which is under consideration here.

If there is a statutory right to have the decision quashed where statutory procedures have not been complied with and a person has been prejudiced, as in the *Givaudan* case, then of course once it is shown that those statutory requirements for the giving of reasons have not been complied with and an applicant has been prejudiced, it follows that the decision will be quashed.

Likewise, the *UKAPE* case was a case which contained a statutory provision which made it fundamental that there should be reasons for the decision of ACAS. Such an obligation cannot be implied here so as to make the tribunal's decision automatically a nullity if proper reasons are not given.

I would therefore still regard the *Mountview* case as being the main authority to be applied. However, it has to be applied in the light of the ten years which have elapsed since that case was decided. Over that period of ten years the approach of the courts with regard to the giving of reasons has been much more definite than they were at that time and courts are now much more ready to infer that because of inadequate reasons there has been an error of law, than perhaps they were prepared to at the time that the *Mountview* case was decided.

In other spheres there are numerous cases which have been before the courts where tribunals of all sorts have had to reconsider their decisions because the reasoning was inadequate. Therefore in practice I think that there will be few cases where it will not be possible, where the reasons are inadequate, to say one way or another whether the tribunal has gone wrong in law. In some cases the absence of any reasons would indicate that the tribunal had never properly considered the matter (and it must be part of the obligation in law to consider the matter properly) and that the proper thought processes have not been gone through.

In other cases it will be seen from the reasons given that there has been a failure to take into account something which should have been taken into account or that something which should not have been taken into account has in fact been taken into account. Again, in that situation, there will be an error of law which will justify this court interfering on an appeal on a point of law.

In the rare case where it is not possible to decide either way whether or not there is an error of law, then, in my view, this court has got a jurisdiction, as was indicated in the *Mountview* case, to remit the matter to the tribunal for reconsideration. That power arises because of the very wide terms of s. 13 of the Tribunals and Inquiries Act 1971, which is the Act which brings the matter before this court; and also because of the wording of R.S.C. Ord. 55, r. 7. There are great practical disadvantages in that course, as was stressed in argument before me, in relation to tribunals of this nature, because tribunals of this nature are informal bodies which cannot readily be reconvened and, indeed, if they are reconvened, may well have no recollection of the case which they herd; and so obviously the situations where it will be necessary to remit the matter will be limited. They can be limited if it is borne in mind that, as I have already stressed, this sort of tribunal cannot be expected to give the fullest and most detailed reasons, and a short and succinct statement is all that is required ...

[His Lordship then held that the reasons given suggested that the tribunal had misunderstood its role and was regarding itself as sitting as a review body rather than hearing an appeal on the merits. However, the Chairman's notes, admitted by virtue of R.S.C. Ord. 55, r. 7, made it clear that the tribunal was 'clearly concerned about the question of the merits'. Furthermore, it was open on the evidence for the tribunal to find that C was living with the man as husband and wife.]

Having approached the matter with the notes in mind I have come to the conclusion that notwithstanding the inadequacy of the reasoning of the tribunal, it would be wrong to allow this appeal on the grounds that the tribunal were approaching the matter in the wrong way."

Notes

(1) Section 12 of the Tribunals and Inquiries Act 1971 is now contained in section 10 of the   **12–34**
Tribunals and Inquiries Act 1992 and is in the following terms:

> "Judicial control of tribunals etc.
> Reasons to be given for decisions of tribunals and Ministers
>   10. — (1) Subject to the provisions of this section and of section 14, where —
>   (a) any tribunal specified in Schedule 1 gives any decision, or

(b) any Minister notifies any decision taken by him —

(i) after a statutory inquiry has been held by him or on his behalf, or

(ii) in a case in which a person concerned could (whether by objecting or otherwise) have required a statutory inquiry to be so held,

it shall be the duty of the tribunal or Minister to furnish a statement, either written or oral, of the reasons for the decision if requested, on or before the giving or notification of the decision, to state the reasons.

(2) The statement referred to in subsection (1) may be refused, or the specification of the reasons restricted, on grounds of national security.

(3) A tribunal or Minister may refuse to furnish a statement under subsection (1) to a person not primarily concerned with the decision if of the opinion that to furnish it would be contrary to the interests of any person primarily concerned.

(4) Subsection (1) does not apply to any decision taken by a Minister after the holding by him or on his behalf of an inquiry or hearing which is a statutory inquiry by virtue only of an order made under section 16(2) unless the order contains a direction that this section is to apply in relation to any inquiry or hearing to which the order applies.

(5) Subsection (1) does not apply —

(a) to decisions in respect of which any statutory provision has effect, apart from this section, as to the giving of reasons,

(b) to decisions of a Minister in connection with the preparation, making, approval, confirmation, or concurrence in regulations, rules or bye-laws, or orders or schemes of a legislative and not executive character, or ...

(6) Any statement of the reasons for a decision referred to in paragraph (a) or (b) of subsection (1), whether given in pursuance of that subsection or of any other statutory provision, shall be taken to form part of the decision and accordingly to be incorporated in the record.

(7) If, after consultation with the Council [Council on Tribunals], it appears to the Lord Chancellor and the Lord Advocate that it is expedient that —

(a) decisions of any particular tribunal or any description of such decisions, or

(b) any description of decisions of a Minister,

should be excluded from the operation of subsection (1) on the ground that the subject-matter of such decisions, or the circumstances in which they are made, make the giving of reasons unnecessary or impracticable, the Lord Chancellor and the Lord Advocate may by order direct that subsection (1) shall not apply to such decisions.

(8) Where an order relating to any decisions has been made under subsection (7), the Lord Chancellor and the Lord Advocate may, by a subsequent order made after consultation with the Council, revoke or vary the earlier order so that subsection (1) applies to any of those decisions."

Among the tribunals listed in Schedule 1 are the Criminal Injuries Compensation Board, the Lands Tribunal for Scotland, local valuation tribunals, mental health review tribunals and, in the field of social security, social security appeal tribunals. Unified appeal tribunals under the Social Security Act 1998 will also be included. In practice, many of the tribunals listed in Schedule 1 have their own rules of procedure which implement the duty to give reasons. Thus there exists a duty to give reasons under the Town and Country Planning (Inquiries Procedure) (Scotland) Rules 1997, r. 22, on which see para. 1–53 and see also the Social Security (Adjudication) Regulations 1995, regs 15(2), 23(2). In addition, licensing boards constituted under the Licensing (Scotland) Act 1976 are required to give reasons for certain of their decisions: section 18, as are committees constituted under the Civic Government (Scotland) Act 1982, s. 00. Note too the provisions of section 58 (5) of the Scotland Act 1998, reproduced at para. 13–10. The statutory duty to give reasons is discussed by M.B. Akehurst, "Statements of Reasons for Judicial and Administrative Decisions" (1970) 33 M.L.R. 154 and G. Richardson, "The Duty to Give Reasons: Potential and Practice" [1986] P.L. 437; *Stair Memorial Encyclopaedia*, Vol. 1, paras 291–192; and Finch and Ashton, pp. 351–358. For the development of the duty to give reasons at common law see paras 8–37 to 8–42.

12–35   (2) *Crake* is an example of the way in which an appellate court will give a decision maker a margin of error in giving reasons before a decision will be quashed for error of law. In *Glasgow District Council* v. *Secretary of State for Scotland*, 1980 S.C. 150 a decision of the Secretary of State to confirm that no planning permission was required to demolish a dangerous building, while based on an erroneous reasoning, was nevertheless upheld as other supportable reasons existed for the decision: see also *Andrew* v. *City of Glasgow District Council*, 1996 S.L.T. 814. A similar approach has been adopted in immigration appeals (*Dillon* v. *Secretary of State for the Home Department*, 1997 S.L.T. 842) and taxi licensing committees. (*R.* v. *Liverpool City Council, ex parte Liverpool Taxi Fleet Operators' Association* [1975] 1 All E.R. 379). It would also appear that where there is a statutory duty to give reasons, then the duty is confined to the reasons for the decision itself and not for any ancillary matter, such as procedure adopted leading to the decision in question (*J.A.E. (Glasgow)* v. *City of Glasgow District Licensing Board*, 1994 S.L.T. 1164). Note also the possibility of having the original body reconvened to give proper reasons. Sometimes as a matter of practice the court will seek such amplification: see, for example, *Calder* v. *Linlithgow Local Authority* (1890) 18 R. 48 and *Albyn Properties Ltd* v. *Knox*, 1977 S.C. 108 and compare *Iveagh* v. *Minister of Housing and Local Government* [1963] 3 All E.R. 817, C.A. and *Mountview*, referred to in the extract.

(3) Notwithstanding the restrictive approach exemplified by *Crake*, failure to give adequate reasons has been held to amount to an error of law in relation to decisions of a licensing board (*Brechin Golf and Squash Club* v. *Angus District Licensing Board*, 1993 S.L.T. 547); a local authority licensing committee (*McLuskie* v. *City of Glasgow District Council*, 1993 S.L.T. 1102); the discipline tribunal of the Law Society of Scotland (*McKinstry* v. *Law Society of Scotland*, 1996 S.C.L.R. 421); decisions of mental health review tribunals (*R.* v. *Mental Health Review Tribunal, ex parte Pickering* [1986] 1 All E.R. 99); an immigration adjudicator (*R.* v. *Immigration Appeal Tribunal, ex parte Iqbal (Iram)* [1993] Imm. A.R. 270); decisions of local authorities under homelessness legislation (*R.* v. *Westminster City Council, ex parte Ermakov* [1996] 2 All E.R. 302); and decisions of housing benefit review boards (*R.* v. *Lambeth London Borough Council Housing Benefit Review Board, ex parte Harrington*, *The Times*, December 10, 1996).

(4) The duty to give reasons under rule 22 of the Town and Country Planning (Inquiries Procedure) (Scotland) Rules 1997, reproduced at para. 1–53, has led to much case law in this area. A failure to give adequate and intelligible reasons may lead to a decision being quashed under sections 238 and 239 of the Town and Country Planning (Scotland) Act 1997 on the ground that the applicant's interests have been substantially prejudiced by failure to comply with a relevant requirement. Any reasons must be proper, adequate and intelligible and deal with the substantial points raised: *Wordie Property Co. Ltd* v. *Secretary of State for Scotland*, 1984 S.L.T. 345 and for an earlier example see *Albyn Properties Ltd* v. *Knox* above. Decision letters should not, however, be construed as statutes and should be read as a whole: *Wordie Property Co. Ltd per* Lord Cameron (at 356). In *Save Britain's Heritage* v. *Number 1 Poultry Ltd* [1991] 1 W.L.R. 153 Lord Bridge of Harwich observed that it was not possible for the courts to set out a general standard as to the adequacy of reasons required by the inquiry rules. In considering a passage from Woolf L.J's judgment in the Court of Appeal (reported at (1990) 60 P. & C.R. 539 at 545) he observed (at 166):

12–36

> "I certainly accept that the reasons should enable a person who is entitled to contest the decision to make a proper assessment as to whether the decision should be challenged. But I emphatically reject the proposition that in planning decisions the 'standard', 'threshold' or 'quality' of the reasons required to satisfy the statutory requirement varies according to who is making the decision, how much time he has to reflect upon it, and whether or not he had legal assistance, or depends upon the degree of importance which attaches to the matter falling to be decided. The obligation, being imposed on the Secretary of State and his inspectors in identical terms, must be construed in the same sense.
>
> The three criteria suggested in the dictum of Megaw J. in *Re Poyser and Mills' Arbitration* [1964] 2 Q.B. 467, 478 are that the reasons should be proper, intelligible and adequate. The application of the first two of these presents no problem. If the reasons given are improper they will reveal some flaw in the decision-making process which will be open to challenge on some ground other than the failure to give reasons. If the reasons given are unintelligible, this will be equivalent to giving no reasons at all. The difficulty arises in determining whether the reasons given are adequate, whether, in the words of Megaw J., they deal with the substantial points that

have been raised or, in the words of Phillips J. in *Hope* v. *Secretary of State for the Environment* 31 P. & C.R. 120, 123, enable the reader to know what conclusion the decision-maker has reached on the principal controversial issues. What degree of particularity is required? It is tempting to think that the Court of Appeal or your Lordships' House would be giving helpful guidance by offering a general answer to this question and thereby 'setting the standard' but I feel no doubt that the temptation should be resisted, precisely because the court has no authority to put a gloss on the words of the statute, only to construe them. I do not think one can safely say more in general terms than that the degree of particularity required will depend entirely on the nature of the issues falling for decision.

Whatever may be the position in any other legislative context, under the planning legislation, when it comes to deciding in any particular case whether the reasons given are deficient, the question is not to be answered *in vacuo*. The alleged deficiency will only afford a ground for quashing the decision if the court is satisfied that the interests of the applicant have been substantially prejudiced by it. This reinforces the view I have already expressed that the adequacy of reasons is not to be judged by reference to some abstract standard. There are in truth not two separate questions: (1) were the reasons adequate? (2) if not, were the interests of the applicant substantially prejudiced thereby? The single indivisible question, in my opinion, which the court must ask itself whenever a planning decision is challenged on the ground of a failure to give reasons is whether the interests of the applicant have been substantially prejudiced by the deficiency of the reasons given. Here again, I disclaim any intention to put a gloss on the statutory provisions by attempting to define or delimit the circumstances in which deficiency of reasons will be capable of causing substantial prejudice, but I should expect that normally such prejudice will arise from one of three causes. First, there will be substantial prejudice to a developer whose application for permission has been refused or to an opponent of development when permission has been granted where the reasons for the decision are so inadequately or obscurely expressed as to raise a substantial doubt whether the decision was taken within the powers of the Act. Secondly, a developer whose application for permission is refused may be substantially prejudiced where the planning considerations on which the decision is based are not explained sufficiently clearly to enable him reasonably to assess the prospects of succeeding in an application for some alternative form of development. Thirdly, an opponent of development, whether the local planning authority or some unofficial body like Save, may be substantially prejudiced by a decision to grant permission in which the planning considerations on which the decision is based, particularly if they relate to planning policy, are not explained sufficiently clearly to indicate what, if any, impact they may have in relation to the decision of future applications."

For discussion of this case see Sir Desmond Heap and M. Thomas, "The Need to give Reasons — But of What Kind?" [1991] J.P.L. 707 and see also *Bolton Metropolitan District Council* v. *Secretary of State for the Environment* (1996) 71 P. & C.R. 309. The need to consider the duty to give reasons in context was also apparent in *Safeway Stores plc* v. *National Appeal Panel*, 1996 S.L.T. 235. In an appeal against a grant of permission to sell pharmaceuticals in a supermarket, an appeal panel, which disagreed with the original decision, was required to indicate in specific detail the facts upon which they differed from the committee which had granted the permission. In the context of liquor licensing it would appear that where a licence is refused on the grounds of over provision, a reference to the board's knowledge of a particular locality in its statement of reasons was held to be adequate as the knowledge in question was general experience of the area in question, which an applicant for a licence might expect the board to take into account: *Mirza* v. *City of Glasgow Licensing Board*, 1996 S.L.T. 1029. In immigration law, where reasons are required, the reasons must be relevant to the issue, indicating the factual basis upon which the conclusion has been reached and the factors taken into account: *Zia* v. *Secretary of State for the Home Department*, 1994 S.L.T. 288 and also *Singh* v. *Secretary of State for the Home Department*, 1997 S.L.T. 164.

(5) The JUSTICE-All Souls Report criticised the typical statutory formulation of requirements to produce the statement of reasons. In its view the formulation allows the decision maker to produce a document which passes the test set by the court but still fails to reveal what findings were made or how issues of fact were resolved. It recommended that a statutory obligation to set out findings underlying the reasons should be required. A person provided with a statement of reasons could then ask for a supplementary statement if dissatisfied, backed up with the ability to go to court to obtain an appropriate order: see paras 3.58–3.59.

(6) The European dimension should not be forgotten. Article 190 of the Treaty of Rome   **12–37**
provides:

> "Regulations, directives and decisions of the Council and of the Commission shall be fully reasoned
> and shall refer to any proposals or opinions which were required to be obtained beforehand pursuant
> to this Treaty."

Thus vague, inadequate and inconsistent reasoning will lead to a decision being annulled:
Germany v. E.E.C. Commission [1963] E.C.R. 63. While this obligation applies principally to
Community institutions it is conceivable that the obligation could extend to national authorities
which are themselves applying Community law. Similarly, the provisions of the European
Convention of Human Rights and the Human Rights Act 1998 may also provide a further basis
for a "statutory" duty to give adequate reasons: *Thynn, Wilson and Gunnell v. United Kingdom*
(1991) 13 E.H.R.R. 666 requiring reasons to be given by the parole boards in connection with
decisions on parole of discretionary prisoners.

Chapter 13

THE CROWN

It is axiomatic that for rights of obligations to be conferred upon an entity, that the entity must have legal personality. In relation to central government, the way that this is achieved is by the legal fiction of the corporate entity of the Crown. The rights and obligations of the Crown are extensive and cover executive, legislative and judicial functions. The relationship between these areas is complex and political as well as legal considerations are relevant to a proper understanding of the issues. The unity and the common law power of the Crown from which they have evolved is known as "the Royal Prerogative" or "the Prerogative" and in so far as those powers have not been superseded by statute, it is those powers which are used by the Crown, its Ministers and servants in exercising these functions of Government. As always, one also has to consider the potentially very profound effects that the changes brought by the Scotland Act 1998 will have in this area, given the creation of a Scottish Executive to act on behalf of the Crown in those areas of devolved competence. In this chapter the concern is on a number of specific topics on which the Crown has specific impact in administrative law.

13–1

THE CROWN: DEFINITION

British Medical Association v. Greater Glasgow Health Board

1989 S.L.T. 493, H.L.

"A dispute arose between certain consultant surgeons and a health board about the appointment of a unit director. An agreement existed which set out procedures for resolving such disputes and which was binding on the consultants and the board. Notwithstanding that in accordance with the agreement, a panel had been convened to consider the dispute with a view to its resolution, the health board advertised for applicants for the position of director. The consultants presented a petition for suspension and interdict against the health board. The health board claimed that the petition was incompetent as they were entitled to Crown immunity under s. 21 of the Crown Proceedings Act 1947. The Lord Ordinary repelled the health board's contention and granted interdict and interim. A reclaiming motion was refused by the Second Division. The health board appealed."

13–2

LORD KEITH OF KINKEL: "I have had the opportunity of considering in draft the speech to be delivered by my noble and learned friend Lord Jauncey of Tullichettle. I agree with it, and would dismiss the appeal for the reasons he gives."

LORD BRANDON OF OAKBROOK: "For the reasons set out in the speech to be delivered by my noble and learned friend, Lord Jauncey of Tullichettle, I would dismiss the appeal."

LORD TEMPLEMAN: "For the reasons to be given by my noble and learned friend, Lord Jauncey of Tullichettle, I would dismiss the appeal."

LORD JAUNCEY OF TULLICHETTLE: "This appeal arises out of a dispute between consultants at the West of Scotland Regional Plastic Oral Surgery Unit at Canniesburn Hospital, Glasgow, and the Greater Glasgow Health Board. The sole issue raised by the appeal is whether a health board constituted under the National Health Service (Scotland) Act 1978 is entitled to immunity from interdict proceedings by virtue of s. 21 of the Crown Proceedings Act 1947. It is necessary to say no more about the dispute than that it concerned the appointment of a director of the unit. The Lord Ordinary (Prosser) granted interim interdict against the health board 'from interviewing candidates for the position of Director of the Plastic and Oral Surgery Unit, Canniesburn Hospital, Glasgow'. The interdict sought was at the instance of the British Medical Association who represent the consultants in dispute, and extended also to the appointment of a director, but in view of an undertaking by the health board to make no appointment until certain agreed disputes procedures had been exhausted, interdict against appointment became unnecessary. The health board reclaimed the Lord Ordinary's interlocutor but the Second Division refused the reclaiming motion.

The health board have now appealed. However in the interval which elapsed between the interlocutor of the Second Division of 10 March 1988 and the hearing of the appeal in this House the disputes procedures were exhausted and a director was appointed. It followed that the question of whether interim interdict should stand or be recalled had become academic. Nevertheless counsel for the appellants moved your Lordships to hear the appeal for two reasons, namely: (1) that a live issue still existed between the parties in relation to expenses in the courts below and costs in this House, and (2) that the question raised by the appeal was one of general importance which would be likely to arise again in disputes between the British Medical Association and its members on the one hand and health boards on the other.

Counsel for the respondents did not oppose this motion. Your Lordships took the view that as there was still a lis between the parties it would be proper to hear the appeal.

In addressing the question of whether a health board is entitled to immunity from interdict proceedings it is necessary in the first place to look at the relevant statutory provisions. Section 36(1) of the National Health Service (Scotland) Act 1978 provides: [his Lordship quoted the terms of s. 36(1) and continued:]

Section 2(1) of the Act of 1978 (as amended by para. 1 of Sched. 7 to the Health and Social Services and Social Security Adjudications Act 1983) provides, inter alia: [his Lordship quoted the terms of s. 2(1) set out supra and continued:]

Paragraph 1 of Sched. 1 to the Act of 1978 provides that a health board shall be a body corporate and shall have a common seal. Subsections (8) and (9) of s. 2 are in the following terms: [his Lordship quoted the terms of s. 2(8) and (9) and continued:]

Although health boards are creatures of the Act of 1978 the functions which they perform were previously carried out by regional hospital boards and boards of management under the National Health Service (Scotland) Act 1947. That Act imposed on the Secretary of State duties similar to those imposed upon him by s. 36(1) of the Act of 1978. Section 13 of the Act of 1947 was in the following terms: [his Lordship quoted the terms of s. 13 and continued:]

Section 13 of the comparable English Act, the National Health Service Act 1946, was in virtually identical terms. Section 21 of the Crown Proceedings Act 1947, which was later in time than the National Health Service (Scotland) Act 1947 is, so far as relevant, in the following terms: [his Lordship quoted the terms of s. 21 set out supra and continued:]

Against this statutory background counsel for the appellants propounded two alternative tests for determining whether a body fell to be treated as the Crown for the purposes of s. 21. In the first place the Crown extended to Her Majesty's government in the United Kingdom and those persons and bodies which are appointed or created to carry out exclusively the functions of the executive government. In the second place the Crown included a body, person or corporation whose essential activities were carried out exclusively in the performance of a duty or the exercise of a power which is imposed upon or vested in the executive government by statute or prerogative. Such a body might be a government agency. A health board, it was said, satisfied both these tests. In support of this argument counsel referred to a number of authorities as showing that the Crown embraces agencies which carry out the executive functions of government on its behalf. In *British Broadcasting Corporation* v. *Johns* Diplock L.J., in considering whether the B.B.C. were entitled to Crown immunity from payment of taxes, said, at p. 79: 'But to use the expression 'the Crown' as personifying the executive government of the country tends to conceal the fact that the executive functions of sovereignty are of necessity performed through the agency of persons other than the Queen herself. Such persons may be natural persons or, as has been increasingly the tendency over the last hundred years, fictitious persons — corporations. The question here is whether the B.B.C. carries on all or any of its activities as agent for the executive government. Are they carried out in the performance of a duty or in the exercise of a power which is imposed upon or vested in the executive government of the United Kingdom by statute or by the prerogative? (cf. *Pfizer Corporation* v. *Minister of Health*).'

In *Town Investment Ltd.* v. *Department of the Environment* Lord Diplock said, at p. 381A: 'Where, as in the instant case, we are concerned with the legal nature of the exercise of executive powers of government, I believe that some of the more Athanasian-like features of the debate in your Lordships' House could have been eliminated if instead of speaking of 'the Crown' we were to speak of 'the government' — a term appropriate to embrace both collectively and individually all of the ministers of the Crown and parliamentary secretaries under whose direction the administrative work of government is carried on by the civil servants employed in the various government departments. It is through them that the executive powers of Her Majesty's government in the United Kingdom are exercised, sometimes in the more important administrative matters in Her Majesty's name, but most often under their own official designation. Executive acts of government that are done by any of them are acts done by 'the Crown' in the fictional sense in which that expression is now used in English public law.'

Both these cases were concerned with Crown immunity and necessarily involved consideration of whether for general purposes a particular individual or body was the Crown.

Perhaps more germane to the present appeal is *Pfizer Corporation* v. *Minister of Health* which was concerned with whether the use of drugs by the National Health Service was 'for the services of the Crown' for the purposes of s. 46(1) of the Patents Act 1949. In the Court of Appeal Willmer L.J., after reference to certain sections of the National Health Service Act 1946, said, at p. 642: 'These provisions of the Act to which I have referred seem to me to lead inexorably to the conclusion that Regional Hospital Boards, Hospital Management Committees and Hospital Officers, in exercising their respective functions, are acting on behalf of the Minister for the purpose of discharging the duties laid by statute upon him, and are therefore carrying on services of the Crown.'

Diplock L.J. said, at pp. 652–653: 'The duty to provide hospital and specialist services is imposed upon the Minister. It is in its nature a duty which he can only perform vicariously through agents acting on his behalf. The Act requires him to do so through the immediate agency of the Regional Hospital Boards. The Regional Hospital Boards, being corporations, can themselves only do the physical acts involved in the provision of the services on behalf of the Minister, vicariously through their officers and servants. Any act done by an officer or servant of a Regional Hospital Board for the purpose of providing hospital or specialist services is accordingly done on behalf of the Minister in performance of the statutory duty which is imposed upon him. Their acts are acts of a Government department.

'Counsel for the plaintiffs placed considerable reliance upon section 13 of the Act, as showing that the Regional Hospital Boards exercise their functions as principals and not as agents of the Minister. But the section seems to me to be directed to quite a different matter. The National Health Service Act 1946 was passed before the Crown Proceedings Act, 1947. At that date the fact that a Regional Hospital Board was acting on behalf of a Minister of the Crown would have entitled it to shelter behind the immunity of the Crown from suit except by petition of right: see *Feather* v. *The Queen; Raleigh* v. *Goschen*. All that section 13 does is to re-assert that a Regional Hospital Board is acting on behalf of the Minister (i.e., on behalf of the Crown) but to provide that for the purpose of legal proceedings for the enforcement of rights and liabilities it shall be treated, notwithstanding that it is an agent of the Crown, as if it were acting as principal and shall sue and be sued in its own name. Such a provision would have been unnecessary unless a Regional Hospital Board, in exercising its functions under the Act, was acting on behalf of the Crown.

'It is not, in my view, necessary to determine whether the officers and servants of a Regional Hospital Board are strictly 'servants of the Crown'. It is sufficient for the decision of the present appeal that in administering or supplying drugs to in-patients or out-patients for the purpose of their treatment at National Health Service hospitals such officers and servants are acting on behalf of the Minister in fulfilment of his statutory duty to provide medical, nursing and other services required at or for the purposes of hospitals. The use of patented drugs for this purpose is thus, in my view, a use by a Government department.'

The Court of Appeal's decision that supply of patented drugs to hospital patients was for the service of the Crown was upheld by this House where the appellant conceded that doctors and nurses in National Health hospitals were to be treated as servants or agents of the Crown: see Lord Reid at p. 533. Counsel relied strongly on the dictum of Diplock L.J. at p. 653, that acts of an officer or servant of a regional hospital board 'are acts of a government department' in support of the proposition that health boards were the Crown or, in any event, agents of the Crown in a sense which identified them much more closely with the Crown than would a private agent be identified with his principal. He also referred to *Wood* v. *Leeds Area Health Authority* in which Sir John Donaldson, in the National Industrial Relations Court, having at p. 538 posed the question of whether National Health Service employees were servants of the Crown, referred to the National Health Service Act 1946 and to the passage from the judgment of Willmer L.J. in

Pfizer Corporation v. *Minister of Health* at p. 642, which I have quoted above, and concluded that the plaintiff, who was a National Health Service employee was in fact a Crown servant. If, it was argued, a National Health Service employee engaged and paid by a health authority was a Crown servant it must follow that the authority was itself the Crown or an agent thereof. Accordingly proceedings against the health authority were proceedings against the Crown. Reliance was also placed on (1) s. 138(5) of and Sched. 5 to the Employment Protection (Consolidation) Act 1978 which provided that for the purposes of certain parts of that Act health boards should not be regarded as performing functions on behalf of the Crown so that employment by them would not be Crown employment, and (2) s. 1(1)(*a*) of the National Health Service (Amendment) Act 1986 which is in the following terms: [his Lordship quoted s. 1(1) (a) and continued:]

These two statutory provisions, it was said, showed that for all purposes other than those therein referred to, health authorities were the Crown.

My Lords, these arguments were attractive, but I consider that they failed to address directly the critical question which is not whether health boards perform functions on behalf of the Crown — a matter which was not disputed by counsel for the respondents — nor whether health boards for the purposes of statutory immunity or other purposes fall to be treated as the Crown or as agents so clearly identified with the Crown that they are for all practical purposes indistinguishable therefrom, but whether the respondent's petition amounted to 'proceedings against the Crown' within the meaning of s. 21(1) of the Crown Proceedings Act 1947. The four authorities to which I have referred were not concerned with this point. That Act, as counsel pointed out, is not concerned with Crown immunity and who qualifies therefor, but in the words of the long title with 'the civil liabilities and rights of the Crown' and 'civil proceedings by and against the Crown'. Indeed, s. 40(2)(*f*) specifically provides that the presumption of Crown immunity from statutory liability is not to be affected. The two primary objects of the Act were (1) to enable a plaintiff in England to proceed against the Crown as of right instead of by petition of right, and (2) to subject the Crown in both England and Scotland to actions founded in tort and delict in the same way as other defendants and defenders.

Historically the position of the private litigant vis à vis the Crown differed in Scotland and England. While actions founded in tort and delict could be brought against the Crown in neither country, other actions could be brought as of right in Scotland, whereas in England it was necessary to proceed by petition of right. Indeed, interdict was available against the Crown in Scotland although such a remedy was, I understand, inconceivable in England. It could be said that Scots law took a more robust view of the individual's rights against the Crown than did the law of England. Had the present interdict proceedings been instituted against a regional hospital board after the passing of the National Health Service (Scotland) Act 1947 but before the coming into force of the Crown Proceedings Act 1947, no one could have suggested that they were incompetent. I refer briefly to this historical background because the Crown Proceedings Act 1947 is selective in its application to Scotland, and the historical background must be relevant to this selectivity.

My Lords, s. 21(1) of the Crown Proceedings Act 1947 provides that in any proceedings against the Crown the court shall not grant injunction or interdict but shall instead make a declaratory order. Section 21(2) is designed to ensure that subs. (1) is not circumvented by a litigant obtaining an injunction or interdict against an officer of the Crown which would have the effect of enjoining or interdicting the Crown. 'Officer' in relation to the Crown is defined by s. 38(2) as including 'any servant of His Majesty, and accordingly (but without prejudice to the generality of the foregoing provision) includes a Minister of the Crown'. It was not and in my view could not have been contended that a health board was an officer of the Crown for the purposes of s. 21(2). However the appellants' argument produces the curious result that whereas the Secretary of State is an officer of the Crown for the purposes of s. 21, a health board who carries out functions on his behalf is not an officer of the Crown but the Crown itself. In considering the scope of the proceedings to which s. 21 applies, regard must be had to s. 17(3) which provides: [his Lordship quoted the terms of s. 17(3) and continued:]

This section applies only to England, no doubt because provision already existed for suing the Lord Advocate as representing government departments by virtue of the Crown Suits (Scotland) Act 1857. However although this is a Scottish case, s. 17(3) is important as showing the sort of proceedings which Parliament had in mind in s. 21, namely proceedings against the appropriate government department or the Attorney General. It is, in my view, inconceivable that Parliament should have intended to fetter the right of the subject to obtain a prohibitory order more strictly in Scotland than in England, particularly when the historical background is remembered. Counsel for the respondents was, in my view, well founded in contending that the underlying approach in s. 17(3) and in the Act of 1857 was similar. Thus looking at the Crown Proceedings Act 1947 alone, it appears that Parliament intended that relief from prohibitory orders should only be available to the Crown in such proceedings as were instituted in accordance with s. 17(3) or with the Act of 1857.

However, this appeal does not turn solely on the provisions of the Crown Proceedings Act 1947 because s. 2(8) of the Act of 1978 provides that health boards should be liable in respect of any liabilities incurred in the exercise of their functions as if they were principals and should be sued in their own name. As I mentioned earlier, a similar provision appeared in the English and Scottish National Health Service Acts prior to the Crown Proceedings Act 1947, and if Parliament had intended that actions against regional hospital boards and hospital management committees should be treated as civil proceedings against the Crown, it would have been very simple to have so provided in s. 7(3) of the Crown Proceedings Act 1947. Section 2(8) of the Act of 1978 is prima facie inconsistent with the view that an action against the health board is a proceeding against the Crown for the purposes of s. 21 of the Crown Proceedings Act 1947. Counsel for the appellants sought to argue that subs. (9) of s. 2 of the Act of 1978 demonstrated that but for its provisions a health board would be entitled to claim Crown privilege in relation to recovery of documents. Even if that is the proper inference to be drawn, of which I am by no means certain, the mere fact that a health board, in exercising the functions imposed on the Secretary of State, could claim Crown privilege in relation to a document, cannot convert it into the Crown for the purposes of proceedings against it. When s. 2(8) of the Act of 1978 and ss. 17(3) and 21 of the Crown Proceedings Act are read together, the inference is inescapable that s. 21 was never intended to apply to proceedings against a regional hospital board or its successor, a health board. I am fortified in reaching this conclusion by the fact that the general purpose of the Crown Proceedings Act 1947 was to make it easier rather than more difficult for a subject to sue the Crown. To hold that the Act had clothed with immunity from prohibitory proceedings a body which prior to its passing would have enjoyed no such immunity would be to run wholly counter to its spirit. Furthermore, rather principle nor logic would appear to require that a body such as a health board should be granted such a privilege.

All three judges in the Second Division concluded that although a health board performed certain functions on behalf of the Secretary of State, it was not the Crown and therefore not entitled to protection under the Crown Proceedings Act 1947. I do not in any way criticise these conclusions, but I do not find it necessary to decide this case on so broad a basis, preferring to rely on a construction of the sections above referred to. I would therefore dismiss the appeal."

LORD LOWRY: "I have had the advantage of reading in draft the speech prepared by my noble and learned friend, Lord Jauncey of Tullichettle.

I agree with it and, for the reasons given by my noble and learned friend I, too, would dismiss this appeal."

Notes

(1) It is worthwhile contrasting the approach taken by Lord Jauncey with that adopted by the Second Division: **13–3**

> "A body which is acting on behalf of the Crown may be entitled to claim Crown immunity so long as it is acting on the instructions and at the direction of the Crown, but that does not mean that such a body falls to be treated as being the Crown" *per* the Lord Justice-Clerk (Ross), 1988 S.L.T. 538 at 540.

On that basis the definition of "the Crown" was straightforward:

> "Strictly speaking Her Majesty the Queen is the Crown, but she acts through her government, which is divided into a number of different departments with a Minister in charge of each... The Crown employs servants under the control of the Secretary of State to carry out the tasks necessary for the performance of the duties of the Secretary of State ... and their acts are the Minister's acts" *per* Lord Dunpark at 408.

The Secretary of State is therefore included as an officer of the Crown by the Act because he is at the same time "a servant of the Crown, paid by the Treasury and personally responsible for his own acts" *per* Lord Dunpark at 408.

Contrasted with Lord Jauncey's approach, which is preferable? Does Lord Jauncey's approach rely overly on interpretation of the specific statute being considered as compared with the broad constitutional principles noted by the Second Division?

(2) When the scope of government was relatively limited, the device of the Crown was certainly useful. However, with the greater scope of governmental power and function in this century, it is not always easy to establish if a governmental body can be regarded as a facet of

the Crown and this is the doubt that was raised and required to be decided in the above extract. Moreover, it may not even any longer be the case that the Crown is in fact coextensive with the state. In *Ross v. Lord Advocate*, 1986 S.C. (H.L.) 70 it was argued successfully by the Government that there was a distinction between the Crown and the state in order to justify not handing over any of the assets of the Trustee Savings Bank to the Exchequer. See Sixth Report for the Committee of Public Accounts 1987–88, Trustee Savings Bank — Rights of Ownership (December 1987) and see also *The Laws of Scotland: Stair Memorial Encyclopaedia*, Vol. 7, para. 753. Similarly, under European Community law a distinction between the "State" and the Crown must be drawn. Where an individual relies on a community measure as having direct effect it can be relied upon by individuals in national courts although the Member States failed in their obligation to implement it. As noted by Lord Donaldson in *Foster v. British Gas* [1988] 2 C.M.L.R. 697 at 700:

> "We have to look to European law to determine what kind of bodies constitute 'the State' for purposes of an EEC estoppel and to English law to determine whether any particular body can be said to be 'the State' as so defined".

It is clear that the State is obviously much bigger than the Crown and indeed a health board is for the purposes of direct effect "the State": see *Marshall v. Southampton and South-West Hampshire Area Health Authority (Teaching)* [1986] 2 All E.R. 584 and compare *Rainey v. Greater Glasgow Health Board*, 1987 S.L.T. 146.

13–4   (2) Generally bodies set up to carry out the functions of the Crown or of a Minister of the Crown and which were responsible thereto and subject to control by the Crown or a Minister are deemed to be an aspect of the Crown. Admittedly this is a somewhat vague test, but sometimes assistance is provided in the constituting enactment if it makes it clear whether the body is a Crown body so, for example, the Health and Safety Commission and the Health and Safety Executives are such: Health and Safety At Work etc. Act 1974, s. 10(7), but not the Oil and Pipelines Agency: Oil and Pipelines Act 1985, s. 1(3). One consequence of the functionalist approach is that where the objectives of a body are in substance commercial, then it is less likely to be treated as an aspect of the Crown. For example, the BBC (despite having a royal charter) is not an aspect of the Crown: *British Broadcasting Corporation v. Johns* [1965] Ch. 32, nor was the British Transport Commission: *Tamlin v. Hannaford* [1950] 1 K.B. 18, nor nationalised industries: *R. v. National Coal Board, ex parte National Union of Mineworkers* [1986] I.C.R. 791. Other relevant factors might include whether the body appears in the list of bodies mentioned in section 17(1) of the Crown Proceedings Act 1947, which although not applicable to Scotland, helps in determining the position of the body: *Lord Advocate v. Argyll County Council*, 1950 S.C. 304. Similarly, whether or not the body is subject to the jurisdiction of the Parliamentary Commissioner might also be relevant: Parliamentary Commissioner Act 1967, s. 4, Sched. 2 or whether its staff are declared to be civil servants, although not all servants of Crown bodies are necessarily civil servants, on which see *Stair Memorial Encyclopaedia*, Vol. 7, para. 757. Note too the provisions of Sched. 2, para. 7 of the Scotland Act 1998, which provide that an Order in Council may provide for the Scottish Parliamentary corporation to be treated to any extent as a Crown body for the purposes of any enactment. "Crown body" is defined as a body which is the servant or agent of the Crown, and includes a government department: para 7(3).

13–5   (3) Under the Next Steps initiative, the Civil Service (Management Functions) Act 1992 was passed enabling central departments to delegate their functions to executive agencies. Those to whom the powers are delegated, such as departmental heads or chief executives of agencies, are servants of the Crown. One of the consequences of the Act is that the Treasury Minister for the Civil Service can overturn the *Carltona* principle (on which see para. 5–13) as a condition of any delegation: section 1(3), and moreover the *Carltona* principle is extended by section 1(4) to cover authorisations to act in any other person other than a Minister. On this see, for example, *R. v. Secretary of State for the Home Department, ex parte Oladehinde*, para. 5–13. Where governmental functions are completely privatised, it is almost certainly the case that the function can no longer be regarded as one belonging to the Crown, albeit that for policy reasons a Crown servant is sometimes appointed to exercise a function over the undertaking in question, on which see, for example, the Criminal Justice Act 1991 (Contracted Out Prisons) Order 1993. See generally *Stair Memorial Encyclopaedia*, Vol. 7, para. 755 and V. Finch and C. Ashton, *Administrative Law in Scotland* (1997), Chap. 4.

THE CROWN: UNITY

As with any legal person, the inherent nature of the Crown means that it cannot in law find itself in conflict with another aspect of itself. Disputes where they arise are resolved internally and the courts presume that the interests of different aspects of the Crown are evaluated as part of the governmental function: *Crown Lands Commissioners v. Page* [1960] 2 Q.B. 274. This can lead to somewhat anomalous results. Thus in *R. v. W* [1998] S.T.C. 550, C.A. a prosecution for tax fraud was allowed to proceed even though the Crown as Inland Revenue had reached a compromise agreement with the alleged fraudster, on which see R. Rhodes, S. Stafford-Martin and M.J. Bridges, "The Indivisibility of the Crown" [1998] N.L.J. 747. However, the legal personality of the Crown has to be assessed in light of the legal system in which an issue is raised. Thus in *Sokha v. Secretary of State for the Home Office*, 1992 S.L.T. 1049 it was held that a litigant could not use the unity of the Crown to justify bringing proceedings in Scotland against the U.K. Minister when the Scottish court was *forum non conveniens*.

The concept of the unity of the Crown also requires to be reassessed in light of certain provisions of the Scotland Act 1998. Under section 44 of the Act, a Scottish Executive is created whose members shall be the First Minister: section 44(1)(*a*); Ministers appointed by the First Minister: section 47; and the Lord Advocate and the Solicitor General for Scotland: section 44(1)(*c*). Provision exists for the appointment for junior Scottish Ministers: section 49(1). The Scottish Executive is supported by its own civil service: section 51, although they will continue to be drawn from the Home Civil Service and continue to hold office under the Crown. These civil servants, together with the Scottish Ministers, are collectively known as the Scottish Administration: section 51(1). The general effect of the foregoing and the other provisions extracted and discussed below is to create a Scottish Administration for and on behalf of the Crown in Scotland. The political complexion of the Crown north and south of the border may of course differ, and the scope of disputes between these different aspects of the Crown is potentially, at least, considerably enhanced. It is beyond the scope of this work to provide a detailed commentary of the main provisions which establish the transfer of powers and functions to the Scottish Administration, those which are shared with the U.K. Government and those which are retained by the latter Government alone. For detailed commentary see C.M.G. Himsworth and C. Munro, *Devolution and the Scotland Bill* (1998) and by the same authors *The Scotland Act 1998* (1999) and R. Brazier, "The Scottish Executive" [1998] P.L. 212.

Scotland Act 1998

s. 52(1)

"Ministerial Functions
Exercise of Functions
    52. — (1) Statutory functions may be conferred on the Scottish Ministers by that name.   **13–6**
    (2) Statutory functions of the Scottish Ministers, the First Minister or the Lord Advocate shall be exercisable on behalf of Her Majesty.
    (3) Statutory functions of the Scottish Ministers shall be exercisable by any member of the Scottish Executive.
    (4) Any act or omission of, or in relation to, any member of the Scottish Executive shall be treated as an act or omission of, or in relation to, each of them; and any property acquired, or liability incurred, by any member of the Scottish Executive shall be treated accordingly.
    (5) Subsection (4) does not apply in relation to the exercise of —

(a)   functions conferred on the First Minister alone, or
(b)   retained functions of the Lord Advocate.
(6) In this Act, 'retained functions' in relation to the Lord Advocate means —
(a)   any functions exercisable by him immediately before he ceases to be a Minister of the Crown, and
(b)   other statutory functions conferred on him alone after he ceases to be a Minister of the Crown.
(7) In this section, 'statutory functions' means functions conferred by virtue of any enactment."

Notes

13–7   Acts of the Scottish Parliament will in due course confer most of the statutory functions referred to, although initially the powers vested in the Scottish Ministers will be those transferred by sections 53 and 54. Section 117 provides for a general modification of pre-commencement enactments to convert references to a Minister of the Crown to references to the Scottish Ministers. Subsections (3) and (5) make it clear that statutory functions are vested in the Scottish Ministers on a collective basis, but can be exercised by any member of the Scottish Executive. This does not, however, extend to functions conferred individually on the First Minister or on the "retained functions" of the Lord Advocate: subsection (7).

Scotland Act 1998

s. 53

"General Transfer of Functions
13–8   53. — (1) The functions mentioned in subsection (2) shall, so far as they are exercisable within devolved competence, be exercisable by the Scottish Ministers instead of by a Minister of the Crown.
(2) Those functions are —
(a)   those of Her Majesty's prerogative and other executive functions which are exercisable on behalf of Her Majesty by a Minister of the Crown,
(b)   other functions conferred on a Minister of the Crown by a prerogative instrument, and
(c)   functions conferred on a Minister of the Crown by any pre-commencement enactment,
but do not include any retained functions of the Lord Advocate.
(3) In this Act, 'pre-commencement enactment' means —
(a)   an Act passed before or in the same session as this Act and any other enactment made before the passing of this Act,
(b)   an enactment made, before the commencement of this section, under such an Act or such other enactment,
(c)   subordinate legislation under section 106, to the extent that the legislation states that it is to be treated as a pre-commencement enactment.
(4) This section and section 54 are modified by Part III of Schedule 4."

Notes

13–9   Note that only those powers which are within devolved competence as defined by section 54 are transferred by the foregoing. For section 54 see para. 3–11. Similarly the retained functions of the Lord Advocate are not transferred, nor are those functions exercisable with agreement: section 55; shared powers: section 56; community law and convention rights: section 57; property and liability: sections 59–62; and power to transfer functions: section 63. For transfer of functions from the Scottish Executive to a Minister of the Crown see section 108.
        Section 55 provides that any statutory provision or any other provision which provides for a Minister of the Crown to exercise a function with the agreement of, or after consultation with, any other Minister of the Crown, shall cease to have effect in relation to the exercise of the function by a member of the Scottish Executive by virtue of section 53. If that were not so, the Scottish Minister could be subject to the detailed control of a U.K. Minister of the Crown.

Section 56 provides for the joint exercise of powers by a U.K. Minister. The areas in which the U.K. Minister can do this are detailed in section 56(1)(*a*)–(*i*). Moreover, subsections (2) and (3) allow the U.K. Minister to extend the list of those functions by way of subordinate legislation, although subsection (3) provides that such an extension is only lawful if there has been no transfer of function to the Scottish Ministers. It is of course anticipated that U.K. Ministers and Scottish Ministers will work together in exercising joint powers in a co-ordinated manner. Any such agreement will have political rather than legal force, although there may possibly be scope for the application of the doctrine of legitimate expectation in judicial review proceedings.

Section 57(1) provides that although Scottish Ministers have power by virtue of section 53 to implement European Community obligations, a Minister of the Crown also retains the power to exercise any function in relation to Scotland for the purposes specified in section 2(2) of the European Communities Act 1972. This is another shared power. Although on the face of it, the Scottish Executive would be liable for any failure to implement a European Community obligation, given the ability of the U.K. Minister to intervene, it is possible that responsibility for any such failure would be shared. Interesting questions as to how any such liability might be apportioned could well arise. On relations with the European Union see *Scotland's Parliament*, CM. 3658 (1997) Chap. 8 and Himsworth and Munro (1998), Chap. 9

Section 63 provides that an Order in Council may provide for any function, presently exercised by a Minister of the Crown in regards to Scotland, to be exercised by the Scottish Ministers instead of by a Minister of the Crown: section 63(1)(*a*), or by the Scottish Ministers concurrently with a Minister of the Crown: section 63(1)(*b*), or by a Minister of the Crown only with the agreement of, or after consultation with, the Scottish Ministers: section 63(1)(*c*). This is a statutory expression of the views found in the White Paper, para. 2.7, that the Government would use powers under the legislation to confer on the Scottish Ministers an additional range of functions other than those conferred initially by sections 52 and 53. It is conceivable that the case law on consultation detailed in Chapter 5 could be relevant to subsection (1)(*c*). There may also be scope for the working of the doctrine of legitimate expectation in relation to subsection (1)(*b*). These could include some of the reserved matters in Schedule 5. It is beyond the scope of this section to examine section 63 in detail. Consider also the next section which brings into sharp focus the potential for conflicts, hitherto resolved at a political level, reaching the courts.

Scotland Act 1998

s. 58

"Power to Prevent or Require Action

58. — (1) If the Secretary of State has reasonable grounds to believe that any action proposed to be taken by a member of the Scottish Executive would be incompatible with any international obligations, he may by order direct that the proposed action shall not be taken.

(2) If the Secretary of State has reasonable grounds to believe that any action capable of being taken by a member of the Scottish Executive is required for the purpose of giving effect to any such obligations, he may by order direct that the action shall be taken.

(3) In subsections (1) and (2), 'action' includes making, confirming or approving subordinate legislation and, in subsection (2), includes introducing a Bill in the Parliament.

(4) If any subordinate legislation made or which could be revoked by a member of the Scottish Executive contains provisions —

(a)   which the Secretary of State has reasonable grounds to believe to be incompatible with any international obligations or the interests of defence or national security, or

(b)   which make modifications of the law as it applies to reserved matters and which the Secretary of State has reasonable grounds to believe to have an adverse effect on the operation of the law as it applies to reserved matters,

the Secretary of State may by order revoke the legislation.

(5) An order under this section must state the reasons for making the order."

13–10

Notes

13–11   For parallel provisions in relation to power to intervene to prevent a Bill in the Scottish Parliament from becoming law see section 35. International obligations include any international obligations of the United Kingdom other than obligations to observe and implement Community law or the Convention rights: section 126(10). Any Order made under subsections (1) and (2) attracts type I procedure under Schedule 7, *i.e.* subject to annulment by either House of Parliament and any such Order would be subject to judicial review. Orders under subsections (4) and (5) are also subject to type I procedure and similarly are subject to judicial review. For Schedule 7 see para. 2–19. Note in particular the test of "reasonable grounds", on which see para. 6–38 on a possible approach to the reasonable grounds test. Note too subsection (5), which creates a duty to give reasons for any such Order being made. See generally Himsworth and Munro, pp. 75–76.

It will be seen that the concept of the Crown is an important one in Scots law. Its importance has arisen not simply because of the need to identify and personify central government, whether in London or in Edinburgh, but also because whether or not a body is an aspect of the Crown has important consequences in law. Procedural peculiarities might apply in litigation, on which see Chapter 14; the question of remedies arising against the Crown raises difficulties, on which see para. 11–24; and of course the Crown is the source of prerogative power and only the Crown or a person authorised on its behalf can properly exercise such powers. Only the Crown can claim public interest immunity, on which see Chapter 15. For further examples of implications of a body being held to be a Crown body see *Stair Memorial Encyclopaedia*, Vol. 7, paras 720–740. However, one of the most significant consequences of a body being found to be an aspect of the Crown is the general immunity of the Crown from statute.

IMMUNITY OF THE CROWN FROM STATUTE

Lord Advocate v. Dumbarton District Council; Lord Advocate v. Strathclyde Regional Council

1990 S.L.T. 158, H.L.

"Petitions for Judicial Review
(Reported 1988 S.L.T. 546)

13–12   The Lord Advocate on behalf of the Secretary of State for Defence presented petitions for judicial review directed against Strathclyde Regional Council and Dumbarton District Council. The petition against Strathclyde Regional Council sought: (1) declarator that ss. 58, 59, 85, 87 and 141 of the Roads (Scotland) Act 1984 had no application to works carried out by or on behalf of the Crown, (2) declarator that a purported notice under s. 87 of the Act dated 17 March 1986 and addressed to Tarmac Construction Ltd. was null and of no effect, and (3) interdict against Strathclyde Regional Council or anyone on their behalf taking any steps to enforce that purported notice. The petition against Dumbarton District Council sought similar declarators in respect of ss. 19, 84 and 87 of the Town and Country Planning (Scotland) Act 1972 and purported enforcement and stop notices both dated 9 May 1986, and interdict against any steps being taken to enforce those notices. The various notices were concerned with a one mile stretch of the westernmost carriageway of the A814 road which was being used by contractors, Tarmac Construction Ltd., who had been instructed by the Ministry of Defence, acting through the Property Services Agency, to carry out fencing work at its submarine base at Faslane, Dunbartonshire, which was adjacent to the road.

On 25 March 1986 the Lord Ordinary (Cullen) *pronounced* interim interdict against Strathclyde Regional Council.

On 16 May 1986 the Lord Ordinary (Clyde) *refused* interim interdict against Dumbarton District Council but *granted* interim suspension of the enforcement and stop notices.

The petitions came before the Lord Ordinary (Cullen) on 12 and 13 June 1986 ...

On 4 September 1986 the Lord Ordinary (Cullen) *granted* the orders sought by the Crown.

The respondents reclaimed ...

On 5 February 1988 the First Division *allowed* the reclaiming motions and *refused* the prayer of each petition. (Reported 1988 S.L.T. 546.)

The Lord Advocate appealed to the House of Lords …

The appeal was heard before Lord Keith of Kinkel, Lord Griffiths, Lord Ackner, Lord Jauncey of Tullichettle and Lord Lowry on 9, 10, 11, 12 and 16 October 1989."

LORD KEITH OF KINKEL: "In 1985 the Ministry of Defence decided to erect an improved security fence at its submarine base at Faslane, Dunbartonshire. Part of the fence ran alongside the A814 road between Helensburgh and Gareloch head. The ministry's intention came to the notice of Strathclyde Regional Council as roads authority for the area, and the council (hereinafter referred to as 'Strathclyde') learnt that it was proposed to place temporary works on part of the A814 road in connection with the project. Strathclyde intimated to the ministry that this would require its permission as roads authority under certain provisions of the Roads (Scotland) Act 1984, but the ministry replied that these provisions did not bind the Crown. Early in 1986 the ministry, acting through the Property Services Agency, instructed contractors, Tarmac Construction Ltd., to carry out the fencing work. The contractors took possession of a one mile stretch of the westernmost carriageway of the A814 road by coning it off, and erected on it a temporary wire mesh fence 8 ft high and also a continuous metal safety barrier. They also placed within the area so enclosed portacabins and various building and other materials.

By letter dated 17 March 1986 Strathclyde gave notice to the contractors in terms of s. 87 of the Act of 1984 that by 25 March the various structures on the road must be removed and the road reinstated to its previous condition, failing which the council would itself do so in terms of s. 141 of the Act. A similar notice was at the same time sent to the Ministry of Defence.

Section 87 of the Act of 1984 provides: [his Lordship quoted s. 87(1) and (2) and continued:] Section 141 provides that where by notice under the Act a road authority has required works to be executed within a specified time, and the works are not timeously executed, then the authority may itself execute them. Section 59 of the Act, so far as material, provides: [his Lordship quoted s. 59(1) to (4) and continued:]

Following some negotiations between the ministry and Strathclyde, some adjustments were made to the works on the road which satisfied the latter that no traffic hazard existed, but they refused to withdraw the notice requiring that the works be removed.

In the meantime Dumbarton District Council, as local planning authority, had also joined in on the act. On 9 May 1986 this council ('Dunbartonshire') served on the Property Services Agency an enforcement notice under s. 84 of the Town and Country Planning (Scotland) Act 1972 requiring that all fencing and other materials should be removed from the A814 within 28 days after 9 June 1986, and the road restored to its former unrestricted use as a public highway. On the same date Dunbartonshire served on the Property Services Agency a stop notice under s. 87 of the Act of 1972 as amended requiring cessation of the unauthorised change of use.

Section 84 of the Act of 1972, as amended by s. 172(2) of, and Sched. 29 to, the Local Government (Scotland) Act 1973 provides, so far as material: [his Lordship quoted s. 84(1) and (2) and continued:] Section 87(1) of the same Act, as substituted by s. 4 of the Town and Country Planning (Scotland) Act 1977, provides: [his Lordship quoted s. 87(1) and continued:] By virtue of s. 20(1) of the Act, planning permission is required for the carrying out of any development of land, 'development' being defined by s. 19. It is not disputed that the works carried out by the Ministry of Defence contractors on the A814 constituted development of land within the meaning of that section.

In these circumstances the Lord Advocate, as representing the Secretary of State for Defence, presented in the Court of Session separate petitions for judicial review directed against Strathclyde and against Dunbartonshire. The Strathclyde petition sought (1) declarator that ss. 58, 59, 85, 87 and 141 of the Roads (Scotland) Act 1984 had no application to works carried out by or on behalf of the Crown, (2) declarator that the purported notice under s. 87 of the Act dated 17 March 1986 and addressed to Tarmac Construction Ltd. was null and of no effect, and (3) interdict against Strathclyde or anyone on their behalf taking any steps to enforce that purported notice. The Dunbartonshire petition sought similar declarators in respect of ss. 19, 84 and 87 of the Town and Country Planning (Scotland) Act 1972 and the purported enforcement notice and stop notice dated 9 May 1986, and interdict against any steps being taken to enforce these notices. In the Strathclyde petition interim interdict was granted by Lord Cullen on 25 March 1986, while in the Dunbartonshire petition Lord Clyde on 16 May 1986 refused interim interdict but granted interim suspension of the enforcement and stop notices. First hearings in the two petitions took place together before Lord Cullen on 12 and 13 June 1986, and on 4 September 1986 he found in favour of the Crown that it was not bound by the relevant enactments, and accordingly held that all the notices complained of were null and of no effect and granted permanent interdict as sought. The two councils reclaimed, and on 5 February 1988 the First Division (Lord Emslie, Lord President, Lord Grieve and Lord Brand) in each case recalled the interlocutor of the Lord Ordinary and refused the prayer of the petition, holding that the relevant enactments did bind the Crown. The Lord Advocate now appeals to your Lordships' House.

The improved security fence at the Faslane submarine base has now long since been completed, and the A814 road restored to its original condition. So in a sense the whole matter has become academic. But the question of expenses is still a live one, and the appeal raises a difficult issue of general importance with which it is appropriate that your Lordships should deal.

That issue relates to the principles which are properly to be applied by the court for the purpose of determining whether or not the Crown is bound by a particular statutory provision. It is to be observed at the outset that prior to the parliamentary union of England and Scotland in 1707 Scots law did not recognise any presumption that the Crown was not bound by general words in an Act of Parliament which were capable of applying to it. English law was to contrary effect, the earliest formulation of the rule being expressed in the maxim: 'Roy n'est lie per ascun statute, si il ne soit expressement nosmé' (Jenkins, Case LXXXIV). English influence began to infiltrate the law of Scotland through the Court of Exchequer, set up under the Act 6 Anne cap. 26, which provided by s. 6 that the court 'shall act, do and proceed, in any respect whatsoever, as the Court of Exchequer in England has used or practised to do in like cases in England'. Thus in *Advocate-General* v. *Garioch* the Scottish Court of Exchequer held that the Crown was not liable for national taxation. Other cases decided that the Crown was exempt from local taxation. In *Lord Advocate & Barbour* v. *Lang* it was held that the Crown was not liable under the Glasgow Police Act 1862 to maintain the foot pavement opposite the infantry barracks in Glasgow, the burden being treated as analogous to local taxation.

There are only two Scottish cases, outside the field of taxation and analogous burdens, which deal with the question whether the Crown is bound by statutory provision. The first is *Somerville* v. *Lord Advocate*, a decision of the First Division with consulted judges, making up the whole Court of Session. The commissioners of works and public buildings had purchased land within the burgh of Edinburgh and commenced to build upon it, without obtaining a warrant from the dean of guild court, an extension to the General Post Office. The procurator fiscal of the dean of guild court presented a petition in that court against the Lord Advocate as representing the commissioners for interdict against the works proceeding until a warrant had been obtained. The dean of guild repelled a plea of no jurisdiction and on appeal the whole Court of Session, with two dissentients, held that the dean of guild court had no jurisdiction over the Crown at common law and that there was nothing in the Edinburgh municipal statutes to indicate the Crown had consented to submit itself to that jurisdiction. Lord Kyllachy, however, examined in some detail the question whether, apart from the matter of jurisdiction, the Crown was bound by the relevant provisions of the Edinburgh Police Act 1879 and expressed the opinion that it was so bound in respect of lands other than those held jure coronae. This opinion was concurred in by three other of the judges and had the support of the dissenting judgment of Lord Kincairney. Lord Kyllachy said, at pp. 1064–1065: 'I am of opinion that this contention of the Board of Works is stated too broadly. The principle or rule of construction to which they appeal goes, as I read the authorities, no further than this — that by general words in an Act of Parliament the King may not be stripped of any part of his ancient prerogative or of those rights which are incommunicable and appropriated to him as essential to his regal capacity. These are the words of Dwarris, p. 524, and in Broom's Law Maxims, p. 68, they are adopted as a correct statement of the modern doctrine. The original maxim, no doubt, was — "Roy n'est lie per ascun statute si il ne soit expressement nosmé", but, at least in modern times, the interpretation of the maxim has been as stated. It is, of course, only since the Union that the doctrine applies to Scotland at all. There is no trace of any such doctrine as applied to the interpretation of the old Scotch statutes.

'The real question, therefore, is whether the statutory enactments referred to involve an invasion of the royal prerogative; and that depends upon this, whether it is part of the royal prerogative that the Crown shall be unrestricted in the use of its property; or, to put it perhaps more precisely, whether it is part of the royal prerogative that the Crown shall in respect of all lands and buildings acquired by it (although held not *jure coronae*, but on ordinary tenure) be exempt from all local regulations; and shall be so notwithstanding that these regulations may have affected the property before its acquisition, and may have been imposed by lawful authority for the public safety or the public health'; and later, at p. 1066: 'I conclude, therefore, that, as regards this property, the Crown is bound to obey all local regulations, whether statutory or arising at common law, which would have been binding on an ordinary owner, and in particular is bound to obey the regulation — imposed as above mentioned — which prohibits the erection within the city of new buildings without the previous warrant of the Dean of Guild Court. The result as regards the Crown rights is really the same as if under its titles the property was subject to a servitude *non aedificandi*, except with the sanction of the Dean of Guild. The property is in fact subject to a *legal* servitude to that effect.'

The second Scottish case is *Magistrates of Edinburgh* v. *Lord Advocate*. Under s. 67 of the Edinburgh Corporation Act 1906 the corporation had power, where certain conditions existed, to require that no building should be erected on vacant ground beside an existing street within 30 ft of the centre of the street. Section 78 of the Act, however, exempted from its provisions 'every building structure or work vested in or in the occupation of His Majesty'. The commissioners of works obtained from the dean of guild court warrant to erect buildings on the Royal Botanic Gardens, which were Crown property, within 30 feet of the centre of a public street. A first stage of the buildings was erected without objection by the corporation, but when it came to the second stage the corporation passed a resolution prohibiting the work and sought an interdict against its being proceeded with. This was refused by the First Division, the ground of the majority (Lord President Dunedin and Lord Kinnear) being that the Crown was exempted from the provisions of s. 67 of the Act by s. 78, while Lord Johnston took the view that the corporation, by permitting erection of the first stage of the buildings, were personally barred from objecting to the second. The primary issue in the appeal was whether s. 78 of the Act applied to future buildings or only to existing buildings, and the resolution of this issue in favour of the Crown constituted the ratio decidendi of the majority. However, in a passage of his opinion which was plainly obiter the Lord President considered the general question of whether the Crown was bound by a statutory provision. He said, at 1912 2 S.L.T., p. 134; 'But, then, the general question was argued for the Crown — the Commissioners of His Majesty's Works and Public Buildings hold for the Crown — that the Crown is not bound by any restriction of this sort contained in any local Act unless the restriction is *totidem verbis* imposed upon the Crown. While I do not think that that is quite true as a general proposition, I do not think it is necessary to go at length into this matter. I may say that I agree generally with the views expressed by Lord Kyllachy in *Somerville's* case, and I think the outcome of it is this: While I do not doubt that there are certain provisions by which the Crown never would be bound unless that were clearly expressed — such, for instance, as the provisions of a taxing statute, or certain enactments with penal clauses adjected, as, for example, certain provisions of the Motor Car Act, and so on — yet, when you come to a set of provisions in a statute having for its object the benefit of the public generally, there is not an antecedent improbability that the Crown will consent to be bound, and this, I think, would be so in the case of regulations which are meant to apply to all the land in a city, and where the Crown's property is not property held *jure coronae*, but has been acquired from a subject superior for the use of one of the public departments. While I think that is so, yet all legislation being primarily for the subject and not for the Crown, you must in some way or other gather that the Crown means to be bound. In the present case there is, I think, no antecedent improbability of the Crown being bound, and I say that the want of antecedent improbability is turned into a certainty the other way when you find, in a statute like this, saving clauses put in which deal with the Crown's rights. Therefore, looking at this statute, I come to the conclusion that, as regards property acquired from the subject, the Crown did intend to be bound by the restrictions in the Act, except in so far as it was exempted by the saving clauses, viz, sections 78 and 79.'

An Act of the United Kingdom Parliament may apply to the whole of the kingdom or only to particular parts of it. There would appear to be no rational grounds upon which a different approach to the construction of a statute might be adopted for the purpose of ascertaining whether or not the Crown is bound by it according to the jurisdiction where the matter is being considered. In the case of an Act in force over the whole of the United Kingdom the answer must be the same whether its application to the Crown in Scotland or in England or in Northern Ireland is in issue. It is not conceivable that Parliament could have a different intention as regards the application of the Act to the Crown in the various parts of the kingdom. Likewise, where Parliament is legislating for Scotland only it cannot, for that reason alone, be held to have a different intention from what it would have had if legislating for England only. So it is appropriate to turn for assistance to the more modern English cases where the present issue has been considered. In my opinion the law has developed to a point where it is not helpful to refer to writings of greater or less antiquity which discuss the prerogatives of the Crown.

A convenient starting point is *Gorton Local Board* v. *Prison Commissioners* (Note) which, though decided in 1887, was not reported till 1904. The Gorton local board sought to enforce against the prison commissioners, who proposed to erect houses for use as officers' quarters on land vested in them, certain provisions of a local byelaw made under the Public Health Acts. On a case stated by magistrates a court consisting of Day and Wills JJ. held that the board was not entitled to do so. Day J. said at p. 167: 'It is clear to my mind that this plot of ground is State property, and it is property therefore, in my judgment, over which the local authority can have no control whatever. It is property provided by the Crown, if I may use that expression, for the purposes of the Crown, and it is occupied by servants of the Crown, and, in my judgment, that property is to be entirely under the control of the Crown, and is not to be controlled by the local authority. There is certainly no express mention of the Crown so as to bind the Crown in the Public Health Act, 1875, and there is certainly no necessary implication that the Crown itself is to be bound. In the absence of express words the Crown is not to be bound, nor is the Crown to be affected except by necessary implication. There are many cases in which such implication does necessarily arise, because otherwise the legislation would be unmeaning. That is what I understand by "necessary implication." Here the Crown is not mentioned, and no necessary implication of any sort of kind arises, and it is clear that the Crown by its officials is quite competent to provide for the sanitary condition of these houses. It is quite competent to do all that it thinks fit to be done in the matter, and it is not to be controlled — that is, to my mind, a matter of the greatest public interest — the State is not to be controlled in the disposition of the property entrusted to the State for State management by any local authority whatever.' Wills J. said at p. 168: 'In my judgment, however anxious one may naturally be to confine the application of the prerogative within its legitimate limits, it seems to me that it is clear, from authority and from principles which are established beyond cavil and dispute, that the Crown is not bound unless it is expressly or by necessary implication named.'

These judgments were expressly approved by a court comprising Lord Alverstone C.J. and Wills J. in *Cooper* v. *Hawkins*, to which the report of the *Gorton* case is appended. The actual decision was that the Crown was not bound by s. 4 of the Locomotives Act 1865, by which local authorities were given power to make regulations as to the speed (not to exceed 2 m.p.h.) at which locomotives might pass through places subject to their jurisdiction.

Then in *Att. Gen.* v. *Hancock* it was held by Wrottesley J. that the Crown was not bound by s. 1(1) of the Courts (Emergency Powers) Act 1939, which prohibited the enforcement, except with the leave of the court, of any judgment for payment of a sum of money. Wrottesley J. said at p. 432: 'the true rule is probably, as has been put in argument, that the Crown often assents to legislation for itself and its subjects, but an Act does not apply to the Crown unless the Crown is specially named in it. It is only a short step from that proposition to the further one that the Crown is again to be regarded as being affected by an Act of Parliament when this is shown by necessary implication from the language of the statute. That being the rule, the question has come before the Courts for debate and decision from time to time in the last hundred years'. He then proceeded to examine a considerable number of reported cases and concluded, at p. 439: 'But, however that may be, the principle has been discussed and applied, or not applied, in a number of decisions during the last hundred years and the rule is now well laid down and clear that if an Act of Parliament would otherwise devest the Crown of its property, rights, interests or prerogative, it is not to be construed as applying to the Crown unless the Crown is mentioned either expressly or by necessary implication. In the statute under consideration here there are no special words naming the Crown and it is also clear that there is no necessary implication to be drawn from the words of the statute to involve the Crown.'

The next case is *Province of Bombay* v. *Municipal Corporation of the City of Bombay*. The Corporation of Bombay sought to lay a water main along a private road belonging to the provincial government under powers conferred upon it by the City of Bombay Municipal Act 1888. A judicial committee of the Privy Council which included Lord Macmillan, Lord Simonds and Lord Du Parcq, held that the Crown was not bound by the relevant provisions of the Act. The advice of the board was delivered by Lord Du Parcq, who said at p. 61: 'The High Court held, following previous decisions of its own, that the principle to be applied for the decision of the question whether or not the Crown is bound by a statute is no different in the case of Indian legislation from that which has long been applied in England. The parties concurred in accepting this view, and their Lordships regard it as correct. The general principle to be applied in considering whether or not the Crown is bound by general words in a statute is not in doubt. The maxim of the law in early times was that no statute bound the Crown unless the Crown was expressly named therein, 'Roy n'est lie par ascun statute si il ne soit expressement nosmé.' But the rule so laid down is subject to at least one exception. The Crown may be bound, as has often been said, 'by necessary implication.' If, that is to say, it is manifest from the very terms of the statute, that it was the intention of the legislature that the Crown should be bound, then the result is the same as if the Crown had been expressly named. It must then be inferred that the Crown, by assenting to the law, agreed to be bound by its provisions.'

Later he dealt with an argument that the Crown was bound by any statute passed for the public good, saying at pp. 62–63: 'It was contended on behalf of the respondents that whenever a statute is enacted 'for the public good' the Crown, though not expressly named, must be held to be bound by its provisions and that, as the Act in question was manifestly intended to secure the public welfare, it must bind the Crown. This contention, which did not meet with success in the High Court, was again raised before their Lordships. The proposition which the respondents thus sought to maintain is supported by early authority, and is to be found in Bacon's Abridgment and other text-books, but in their Lordships' opinion it cannot now be regarded as sound except in a strictly limited sense. Every statute must be supposed to be 'for the public good', at least in intention, and even when, as in the present case, it is apparent that one object of the legislature is to promote the welfare and convenience of a large body of the King's subjects by giving extensive powers to a local authority, it cannot be said, consistently with the decided cases, that the Crown is necessarily bound by the enactment. In the recent case of *Attorney-General* v. *Hancock* ... Wrottesley J. cited a series of decisions in which the Crown was held not to be bound although the statute in question was clearly for the public benefit. A plain and striking example is the case which their Lordships have already cited, *Gorton Local Board* v. *Prison Commissioners* ..., where it was held that a by-law, made under the Public Health Act, 1875, and clearly designed to safeguard the health of the public, did not bind the Crown, and gave the local board no control over one of His Majesty's prisons. In the present case the High Court disposed of the submission by a finding that, on the material before them, it was not shown to be for the public good that the Crown should be bound by the Municipal Act. This is, perhaps, not a wholly satisfactory way of dealing with the respondents' contention, which was, not that the court must consider whether it is for the public good that the Crown should be bound by a particular Act, but that wherever an Act is 'for the public good' it must be taken to bind the Crown. Their Lordships prefer to say that the apparent purpose of the statute is one element, and may be an important element, to be considered when an intention to bind the Crown is alleged. If it can be affirmed that, at the time when the statute was passed and received the royal sanction, it was apparent from its terms that its beneficent purpose must be wholly frustrated unless the Crown were bound, then it may be inferred that the Crown has agreed to be bound. Their Lordships will add that when the court is asked to draw this inference, it must always be remembered that, if it be the intention of the legislature that the Crown should be bound, nothing is easier than to say so in plain words.'

The attention of the board was drawn, possibly by Lord Macmillan, to the two Scottish cases of *Somerville* and *Magistrates of Edinburgh*, and in particular to the observations of Lord President Dunedin in the latter case about a possible distinction between land held by the Crown jure coronae and land acquired by it from a subject superior. In the light of further argument directed to the point Lord Du Parcq said, at pp. 64–65: 'In the present case it appears that the land of the Crown is not held jure coronae but, as has been said, was acquired from private owners, so that the dicta of the Lord President are directly in point. Their Lordships thought it right to require further argument on this aspect of the appeal, but, after careful consideration, remain of opinion that the law of England, and of India, is what they have stated it to be, and that no distinction can be drawn in such a case as the present between property held jure coronae and other property of the Crown. The view expressed in the Scottish cases had not been adopted in England, and does not seem to their Lordships to be in accordance with a body of English authority which, where an ancient doctrine of the common law of England is in question, ought in their Lordships' opinion to prevail. Their Lordships have accordingly considered the question before them in the light of the principle as they have stated it. In so stating it their Lordships believe that they have done no more than express in their own words a well-settled proposition of law, and they need only refer, in addition to the cases already cited, to *Hornsey Urban Council* v. *Hennell* ... and *Cooper* v. *Hawkins* ...

'After full consideration their Lordships can find no reason to say that, by necessary implication, the Crown is bound by the relevant sections of the Municipal Act.'

In *Madras Electric Supply Corporation Ltd.* v. *Boarland* the House of Lords was not directly concerned with the question whether the Crown was bound by an Act of Parliament. The point at issue was whether the Crown was included in the word 'person' in rule 11(2) of the Sched. D, Cases I and II rules in the Income Tax Act 1918 as amended. The rule provided that 'if at any time after the said April 5 any person succeeds to any trade, profession or vocation which until that time was carried on by another person' — then certain fiscal consequences followed. The Madras government had acquired the electricity undertaking of the appellants. If the word 'person' where first appearing in the rule included the Crown, then the appellants were subject to a balancing charge to income tax, but they escaped the charge if it did not. It was held that the word 'person' included the Crown by necessary implication. The essential reason was that Parliament could not reasonably have intended that a taxpayer disposing of his business should escape a balancing charge, or indeed be disentitled to a balancing allowance, merely because his successor did not happen to be liable for United Kingdom income tax. A successor which was not so liable might include not only the Crown but also a foreign corporation (see per Lord Reid at p. 691). In the light of the arguments presented, there was some discussion as to whether the Crown's immunity from taxation depended not on statutory construction but upon a right to override the terms of the statute deriving from the royal prerogative. Lord MacDermott regarded the matter as clearly one of statutory construction, saying at p. 685: 'My Lords, I consider the appellants to be right on this particular matter. Whatever ideas may once have prevailed on the subject, it is, in my opinion, today impossible to uphold the view that the Crown can find in the prerogative an immunity from tax if the statute in question, according to its true construction, includes the Crown amongst those made liable to the tax it imposes. The appropriate rule, as I understand it, is that in an Act of Parliament general words shall not bind the Crown to its prejudice unless by express provision or necessary implication. That, however, is and has long been regarded as a rule of construction, and such being its nature its application to the charging provisions of paragraph 1 of Schedule D seems to me to make an end of the respondent's submission on this aspect. In that paragraph the word 'person' is a general word capable of including the Crown, but there is no express provision and nothing by way of necessary implication to make it include the Crown, and so, as a matter of construction, it must be read in accordance with the rule as excluding the Crown.' Lord Reid took a similar view, saying at p. 690: 'it appears to me that a general taxing provision must be construed in the light of what Lord Blackburn called the 'implied exemption on the ground of prerogative.' A charging provision, which, on the face of it, would or could result in imposing a charge on the Crown, must be held inapplicable to the Crown unless the Crown is bound expressly or by necessary implication'. Lord Oaksey and Lord Tucker found it unnecessary to decide whether the Crown's immunity from taxation depended upon the construction of the statute or arose from the prerogative, while Lord Keith of Avonholm appears to have taken the view, at p. 694 that the Crown could rely on the prerogative to control the operation of the statute so far as it prejudiced the Crown.

In *Ministry of Agriculture, Fisheries and Food* v. *Jenkins* the ministry, owners of agricultural land in Wales, served notice to quit on the tenants with a view to using the land for forestry. The tenants served counter notices. By virtue of s. 24(1) of the Agricultural Holdings Act 1948 as amended, a notice to quit an agricultural holding, where a counter notice was served by the tenant, was of no effect unless the Agricultural Land Tribunal consented to its operation. However, under s. 24(2) such consent was not required inter alia where the notice was given on the ground that the land was required for a use, other than agriculture, for which planning permission had been granted under the Planning Acts 'or for which (otherwise than by virtue of any provision of those enactments) such permission is not required.' Under s. 87(2) of the Act it was declared that its provisions applied to land notwithstanding that the interest of the landlord or tenant thereof was held on behalf of His Majesty for the purposes of any government department. Section 12(2)(*e*) of the Town and Country Planning Act 1947 provided that the use of any land for purposes of agriculture or forestry (including afforestation) should not be deemed to involve development of the land. So afforestation was a use for which by virtue of a specific provision of the Planning Acts, planning permission was not required. The Court of Appeal held that the notice to quit was effective notwithstanding the absence of consent by the Agricultural Land Tribunal, on the ground that the Town and Country Planning Act 1947 did not apply to the Crown. The Crown did not require planning permission for that reason, and not by virtue of the provisions of section 12(2)(*e*) of the Act. Lord Denning M.R. said, at pp. 325–326: 'If the Crown desires to turn Crown lands over to afforestation, it does not have to get planning permission. That is quite plain. But why does the Crown not have to get planning permission? Is it by virtue of any provision in the Planning Acts? That is to say, is it by virtue of section 12(2)(*e*) of the Town and Country Planning Act, 1947, as it would be in the case of a private landlord? Or is it by virtue of section 87(2)(*b*) of the Planning Act of 1947? Or is it by virtue of the fact that it is the Crown and, as such, it is not bound by an Act of Parliament except in so far as it is included expressly or by reasonable implication?

'Looking at the whole of the Town and Country Planning Act, 1947, I am satisfied that the Crown does not need to get planning permission in respect of its own interest in Crown lands. The reason it is exempt is, not by virtue of any provision in the Act itself, but by reason of the general principle that the Crown is not bound by an Act unless it is expressly or impliedly included. Section 87(2)(*b*) does not exempt the Crown. It proceeds on the assumption that the Crown is already exempt. It says that, 'Notwithstanding any interest of the Crown in land being Crown land... any [planning] restrictions... shall apply and be exercisable in relation to the land, to the extent of any interest therein... held otherwise than by or on behalf of the Crown...' That provision assumes that the Crown is already exempt in respect of its own interest in Crown land. All it does is to make sure that other persons (e.g., its tenants) have to get planning permission in respect of their interests: and it preserves the Crown exemption in respect of its own interests.

'Coming back, then, to section 24(2)(*b*) of the Act of 1947, I hold that planning permission is not required by the Crown in order to use these lands for afforestation: and the reason why it is not required is because it is the Crown: and not by virtue of any provision in the Town Planning Acts. The Crown is entitled therefore to the benefit of section 24(2)(*b*) and it is unnecessary for it to get the consent of the Agricultural Land Tribunal. The notices to quit operate and are effective, even without the consent of the Agricultural Land Tribunal.' Danckwerts L.J. said at p. 326, in relation to the argument of counsel for the ministry: 'The basis of his argument is the indisputable one that the Crown is not bound by statute, unless it is expressly mentioned or involved by necessary implication. I think he is right in saying that there is nothing which does involve the Crown in that way in the Town and Country Planning Act, 1947. Accordingly, the claim of the Crown in the present case to be free from the question of consent is not based upon any provision in the Town and Country Planning Act.'

I come finally to *British Broadcasting Corporation* v. *Johns (Inspector of Taxes)*. That case was concerned with the liability of the B.B.C. to pay income tax. A number of issues were raised, of which the first was whether the corporation was exempt from taxation as an instrument of government, and the second was whether or not surplus funds remaining out of its grant from Parliament constituted profits of a trade. The Court of Appeal held that it was not exempt from taxation but that the surplus funds did not represent a 'profit' taxable under Sched. D. In connection with the first point, Diplock L.J. said, at pp. 78–79: '*The Crown immunity question*. The B.B.C. is liable to pay income tax under schedule D upon any annual profits or gains accruing to it from its activities if it is included in the expression 'any person' in section 122(1)(*a*) (i) and (ii) of the Income Tax Act, 1952. The question is thus one of construction of a statute. Since laws are made by rulers for subjects, a general expression in a statute such as 'any person', descriptive of those upon whom the statute imposes obligations or restraints is not to be read as including the ruler himself. Under our more sophisticated constitution the concept of sovereignty has in the course of history come to be treated as comprising three distinct functions of a ruler: executive, legislative and judicial, though the distinction between these functions in the case, for instance, of prerogative powers and administrative tribunals is sometimes blurred. The modern rule of construction of statutes is that the Crown, which today personifies the executive government of the country and is also a party to all legislation, is not bound by a statute which imposes obligations or restraints on persons or in respect of property unless the statute says so expressly or by necessary implication.'

In my opinion this statement by Lord Diplock accurately and correctly expresses the effect of the authorities. I consider it to be no longer a tenable view that the Crown is in terms bound by general words in a statute but that the prerogative enables it to override the statute. As to the considerations which may be applicable for the purpose of finding a necessary implication that the Crown is bound, it is clear that the mere fact that the statute in question has been passed for the public benefit is not in itself sufficient for that purpose. The observations of Lord Du Parcq in the *Province of Bombay* case at pp. 62–65, quoted above, are sufficient to lay to rest any contrary suggestion in the opinion of Lord Dunedin in *Magistrates of Edinburgh* at pp. 1090–1091. Similarly, the possibility of a distinction in the position of the Crown as regards lands held jure coronae and as regards lands held otherwise must be rejected.

The argument for the respondents in the present appeals accepts broadly the correctness of Lord Diplock's formulation, but contends for a qualification to the effect that it is unnecessary to consider whether a statutory provision binds the Crown expressly or by necessary implication where the provision would not in any event 'devest the Crown of its property, rights, interests or prerogative' — the words of Wrottesley J. in *Att. Gen.* v. *Hancock*, at p. 439. I do not myself consider that these words are to be taken as conveying any more than Lord Diplock's reference to 'a statute which imposes obligations or restraints on persons or in respect of property'. The very notion of a statutory provision being binding on a person connotes that that person's freedom of action is thereby in some measure constrained. The respondents' argument, however, would have it that it is only where the Crown's lawful freedom of action would be constrained that the presumption against application to the Crown comes into play.

The respondents' argument was accepted by the First Division. In the course of his opinion Lord President Emslie said, at p. 552: 'If I am not mistaken every case in Scotland and in England to which we were referred in which Crown immunity was considered was concerned with statutory provisions which, if they applied to the Crown, would prejudicially affect the Crown by, for want of a better word, divesting it of some of its existing rights, interests or privileges. In this case, however, it is not suggested that the Crown has any right whatever to occupy and erect structures and obstructions upon the land adjoining the submarine base — in this case the public road. It is not contended, accordingly, that the application to the Crown of the provisions of the statutes invoked by the respondents would encroach in any prejudicial way upon the Crown's rights, interests, or privileges. The question to be answered is whether upon a proper construction of the statute it can be affirmed that the Crown meant to be bound by the particular provisions. In order to answer that question it is essential to determine whether there is, as the Lord Ordinary held and as the petitioner contends, a special rule of construction which applies in the construction of all statutory provisions when the issue of Crown immunity has to be resolved, or whether, as the respondents contend, the special rule of construction only applies when the statutory provisions in question would bind the Crown to its prejudice.' The Lord President said later, at p. 553: 'In modern times, in my opinion, the application of the special rule is only required for the protection of the Crown where it is necessary to construe statutory provisions which would be likely, if applied to the Crown, to encroach upon its rights, interests and privileges. Unless, accordingly, I am compelled by binding authority or persuasive judicial opinion to follow the opinion of the Lord Ordinary I would say that the respondents are well founded in contending that the special rule of construction must be interpreted to fit modern circumstances, and that the modern formulation of the rule is that the Crown is not affected by statutory provisions which would bind it to its prejudice unless it is named expressly or by necessary implication.' Having considered the authorities the Lord President concluded that his formulation of the rule was correct.

If one accepts for the moment that the Lord President's formulation is correct in principle, it nevertheless remains to be considered whether it is to be applied narrowly, that is to say in relation to the particular act by the Crown which by the statutory provision in question it is sought to restrain, or whether it is to be applied broadly, namely by reference to a purview of all the acts on the part of the Crown which the terms of the provision are capable of covering. If some of these acts would otherwise be lawful then the provision may indeed bind the Crown to its prejudice.

There is no doubt that in the particular circumstances of this case the Ministry of Defence does not claim that it had any right to take possession of part of the A814 roadway and place upon it the various things that it did. Its pleaded claim to have done so under the prerogative for the defence of the realm has been abandoned. So if the statutory provisions founded upon by the respondents did apply to the Crown, the Crown's lawful freedom of action would not in these particular circumstances have been constrained. But it by no means follows that this consideration makes it unnecessary to consider whether the statutory provisions in question bind the Crown expressly or by necessary implication. There may be other circumstances where these statutory provisions would indeed constrain the Crown's lawful freedom of action. A statute must, in the absence of some particular provision to the contrary, bind the Crown either generally or not at all. There is no logical room for the view that it binds the Crown when the Crown is acting without any right to do so but not when the Crown does have such rights.

Turning first, then, to the appeal which involves the Roads (Scotland) Act 1984, it is to be asked whether, apart altogether from the Act, there are any circumstances under which the Crown might lawfully place obstructions on a public highway. At common law obstruction of a public highway is a public nuisance, and may in some circumstances be a private nuisance. However, the owner of premises adjoining a highway has at common law a right to place on that highway an obstruction, such as a scaffolding, which is necessary for the purpose of erecting or repairing a building, provided all reasonable steps are taken to minimise inconvenience to the public. The law of England is so stated in *Halsbury's Laws of England* (4th ed.), Vol. 21 (1973), para. 424, on the authority of *R.* v. *Jones.* I can find no similar statement in any Scottish textbook or decided case, but obvious considerations of practicality indicate that the same rule must apply in Scotland. In the event that a building abutting a highway had fallen into such a state of disrepair as to present potential danger to passers by, the law must surely permit the owner to take steps, necessarily involving the placing of shores on the highway, to alleviate the danger. The Crown as owner of a building abutting a highway must have the same right as any private owner.

I conclude, therefore, that there are circumstances under which the Crown might lawfully, apart from the Act of 1984, place obstructions on a public highway. Section 59(1), if applicable to the Crown, would take away its right to do so without the consent of the roads authority. Section 59(1) does not bind the Crown expressly, nor does it do so by necessary implication. There is nothing to indicate that if the Crown were not bound by it the purpose sought to be achieved by the enactment would in any material respect be frustrated. If s. 59(1) does not bind the Crown, then s. 87 does not do so either.

In addition there are, in my opinion, certain positive indications in the Act of 1984 that the provisions founded on were not intended to bind the Crown. By virtue of s. 2(1) the Secretary of State is the roads authority for trunk roads and certain other roads, and these roads are by subs. (4) vested in him for the purposes of his functions as such. In this context 'the Secretary of State' represents the Crown, and it cannot reasonably be held that in relation to the roads in question Parliament intended that the powers of ss. 59(3), 87 and 141 should be capable of being invoked by the Crown against itself. It is to be inferred that these sections are not intended to bind the Crown as regards roads vested in the Secretary of State. There do not appear to be any considerations suggesting that the parliamentary intention may have been different as regards roads vested in a local roads authority.

The conclusion that the provisions in question do not bind the Crown is not, in my view, contraverted by a consideration of s. 146(1) of the Act, which provides in effect that nothing therein shall apply in relation to land belonging to the Crown. The argument is that any such express saving would be unnecessary if the Crown were immune. But as Lord Du Parcq explained in the *Province of Bombay* case at p. 65, such saving provisions are commonly inserted ex abundanti cautela, and are not apt to support the inference that the Crown was in other respects intended to be bound.

The appeal which involves the Town and Country Planning (Scotland) Act 1972 is next to be considered. The judges of the First Division took the view that to hold that the Crown was bound by the relevant provisions of the Act in relation to development of land which was not Crown land would not involve any prejudice to the Crown, and that accordingly the Crown was to that extent bound by these provisions. The Lord President additionally expressed the opinion at p. 557 that support for that conclusion was to be found in s. 253(2) and (3) of the Act. The full terms of the section as amended by section 35 of the Town and Country Planning (Minerals) Act 1981, which is headed 'Crown land' are these: [his Lordship quoted s. 253 and continued:]

It is to be observed that there is no provision in the section which specifically exempts Crown land from planning control in relation to the interest therein of the Crown. Subsection (1)(*b*) enacts that all the provisions of the Act dealing with planning control shall apply to Crown land to the extent of any interest therein for the time being held otherwise than by or on behalf of the Crown. This positive enactment plainly proceeds on the basis that these provisions do not bind the Crown. Subsection (2) is dealing, and dealing only, with interests in Crown land which are held otherwise than by or on behalf of the Crown, because it is only these interests to which the provisions about planning control and compulsory acquisition apply. Even in relation to those interests the local planning authority does not have a free hand. It cannot act without the consent of the appropriate authority. Subsection (3) is concerned with land which was Crown land at a time when development was carried out on it by or on behalf of the Crown, but which has ceased to be such land. Ex hypothesi the development would have been carried out without planning permission, and but for this provision the Crown's successor in title would be subject to an enforcement notice requiring him to undo the development. Subsection (4) is a similar provision in relation to works carried out by the Crown on a listed building and having a similar purpose. Subsection (5) is a special provision restricting the serving of a purchase notice or listed building notice in respect of interests in Crown land held by persons other than the Crown.

These provisions, read as a whole, make it quite clear that the whole Act proceeds on the assumption that the Crown is not subject to any requirement of planning permission for development carried out by it. It is true that the ordinary contemplation is that any development carried out by the Crown would be carried out on Crown land. It may be doubted whether Parliament could ever have envisaged that the Crown might carry out development anywhere but on Crown land. There would be no need for the Crown to seek planning permission for development on land which it was proposing to acquire in the future, because once it had acquired the land it could carry out the development without planning permission. So I do not consider that there can be any question of a parliamentary intention that the Crown should be subject to the requirements of planning control in relation to land other than Crown land...

I return to the theme that a particular statutory provision must, in the absence of any specific indication to the contrary, bind the Crown either generally or not at all. Where the Crown is not expressly bound, there is no room at all for the view that it is not bound by necessary implication when acting within its rights but is so bound when acting without any right.

I am of opinion, however, that the Lord President's formulation of the applicable rule is in any event undesirable. It can rarely happen that the Crown is acting or proposing to act in a manner which, apart from the statutory provision sought to be invoked against it, is unlawful. If this should happen, it would, on the view which I have expressed above, be necessary to consider in some depth the question whether the provision in question would bind the Crown also in some situation where its act was lawful. This might involve the examination of the precise position as to the Crown's property, rights, interests and prerogative at the time when the relevant Act was passed, and perhaps also when some legislative predecessor of that Act was passed. This could be a difficult and inconvenient process. Accordingly it is preferable, in my view, to stick to the simple rule that the Crown is not bound by any statutory provision unless there can somehow be gathered from the terms of the relevant Act an intention to that effect. The Crown can be bound only by express words or necessary implication. The modern authorities do not, in my opinion, require that any gloss should be placed upon that formulation of the principle. However, as the very nature of these appeals demonstrates, it is most desirable that Acts of Parliament should always state explicitly whether or not the Crown is intended to be bound by any, and if so which, of their provisions.

My Lords, for these reasons I would allow both appeals and restore the interlocutors of the Lord Ordinary, under deletion of the orders for interdict. The respondents must pay the appellant's costs here and expenses in the Court of Session."

LORD GRIFFITHS, LORD ACKNER, LORD JAUNCEY OF TULLICHETTLE and LORD LOWRY issued concurring opinions.

Notes

(1) The approach taken by Lord Keith treats the issue of immunity from statute as an issue   **13–13**
of interpretation. This view is not consistent with that of Mitchell, *Constitutional Law*, pp. 180–184, who distils from his analysis of the case law including *Somerville* and *Magistrates of Edinburgh*, that in Scots law the Crown is bound by statute unless the statute states otherwise or its purpose would be frustrated. Mitchell's analysis considerably narrows the scope of Crown immunity. However, one has some sympathy for Lord Keith, for even the formulation of the Lord President is not entirely consistent with the supposedly traditional approach expressed by Mitchell. The Lord President's formulation would require the Crown to demonstrate

"prejudice" to its "rights interests and privilege". This goes beyond the test advocated by Lord President Dunedin in *Magistrates of Edinburgh*. Wolffe, below, has criticised this approach because of the difficulty in establishing any clear basis for the "interests" of the Crown, which leaves the question of prejudice as amounting to little more than a matter of circumstance and degree and which he argues, given the courts traditional deference to the claims of the Crown, would require very little to fulfil.

(2) Lord Keith's formulation, bringing as it does Scots law into line with English law, is not without its difficulties. In particular, how does one establish "necessary implication"? It would appear that anyone arguing that the Crown is bound by a statutory provision must demonstrate the purpose of the Act and show how any exemption would adversely affect the degree of frustration of its achievement. Unlike *Somerville* and *Magistrates of Edinburgh*, it is not enough to show that the statute was passed for the public benefit, with the onus of claiming exemption then falling to the Crown. Note, too, that express provisions exempting the Crown in some respects but not in others carry no implication that in those matter the Crown is bound: *Bombay Province v. Bombay Municipal Corporation* [1947] A.C. 58 at 65, P.C. Sometimes implication that the Crown is bound can be more readily established where, for example, an Act is directed at a specific class of person or where it imposes penalties or where a licence from a government department is required or where compulsory purchase powers are involved, on which see, for example, the Local Government (Scotland) Act 1973, s. 71. Servants and agents of the Crown share any immunity from statute which the Crown has so long as they are acting within the scope of their duties: *Bank voor Handel en Scheepvaart, N.V. v. Administrator of Hungarian Property* [1954] A.C. 584. Note the Crown Proceedings Act 1947, s. 31(1), which provides for the right of the Crown to take advantage of the provisions of an Act of Parliament although not named therein. In so far prerogative power is superseded by legislation, the Crown must comply with the statutory requirements assuming that the legislation does bind the Crown: *Attorney-General v. De Keyser's Royal Hotel Ltd* [1920] A.C. 508, H.L. There is the possibility of it re-emerging insofar as not replaced or qualified by statute: see *Burmah Oil Co (Burmah Trading) Ltd v. "Lord Advocate*, 1964 S.C. (H.L.) 117 *per* Lord Pearce and *De Keyser's Royal Hotel Ltd* at 539 *per* Lord Atkinson.

13–14   (3) Consider too *Burnet v. Barclay*, 1955 J.C. 34. This case was not cited in argument. The National Parks and Access to the Countryside Act 1949 gave local authorities power to make byelaws to designate nature reserves. A byelaw was passed forbidding discharge of a shotgun in a reserve. Here the accused was charged with such an offence, but most of the reserve in question constituted foreshore where the act had occurred. The accused contended first that the statute did not bind the Crown as there was no power to make byelaws adverse to the Crown's rights in the foreshore, although there were suggestion in the statute that the definition of Crown land was apt to cover the foreshore, but, more importantly: "the whole tenor of the statute, being, as it is, in the general public interest, points to an intention to encourage the creation of nature reserves". Since this purpose could not be carried out unless the foreshore was included, there was "no antecedent unlikelihood that the Crown would… consent to be bound." *per* Lord Justice-Clerk Thomson at 40.

This case appears to be consistent with *Somerville* and *Magistrates of Edinburgh* and is more recent than all but two of the authorities relied on by Lord Keith. It also carries with it the implication that even if the immunity were to be extended, it did not necessarily apply to the kind of statute in the extract, dealing with Crown activity not land owned by it.

(4) To what extent do you consider that the concept of the unity of the Crown was an underlying consideration in this case? Applying Lord Keith's own test of "necessary implication" did he give sufficient weight to the powers and duties of the local authorities in question in relation to their planning and roads function?

(5) Under European Community law, regulations or directives apply to the State as well as to the individual: E.C. Treaty, Art. 2. See in relation to public works contracts generally S. Arrowsmith, *A Guide to the Procurement Cases in the Court of Justice: Public Procurement in the European Community* (1992), Vol. II. Some legislation is, however, disapplied in relation to the State — for example, EC Treaty, Art. 48(4). So freedom of movement does not apply in

the public service although there are exceptions: *Lawrie-Blum v. Land Baden-Württemberg* [1987] 3 C.M.L.R. 389, E.C.J.; *E.C. Commission v. Luxembourg (Re Public Service Employment)* [1996] 3 C.M.L.R. 981, E.C.J.; and see generally *Stair Memorial Encyclopaedia*, Vol. 7, para. 743. The sex discrimination provisions in E.C. Council Directive 76/207 apply to the Crown as employer: *Marshall v. Southampton and South-West Hampshire Area Health Authority (Teaching) (No. 152/84)* [1986] 2 All E.R. 584, E.C.J.; [1986] 1 C.M.L.R. 688 and see also case No. 2 involving the same parties: [1993] 4 All E.R. 586, E.C.J.; [1993] 3 C.M.L.R. 293.

(6) The presumption of Crown immunity from statute has not been accepted in all Commonwealth jurisdictions; see in particular the approach in Australia on which see S. Kneebone, "The Crown's Presumptive Immunity from Statute: New Light in Australia" [1991] P.L. 361 which discusses the Dumbarton case and the leading Australian decision, *Bropho v. State of Western Australia* (1990) 93 A.L.R. 207; D. Kinley, "Crown Immunity: A Lesson from Australia?" [1990] 53 L.L.R. 819; and I.S. Dickinson, "Crown Immunity from Statute", 1990 S.L.T. (News) 61. On Crown immunity from statute generally see J.T. Cameron, "Crown Exemption from Statute and Tax in Scotland" (1962) 7 J.R. 191: J.D.B. Mitchell, "The Royal Prerogative in Modern Scots Law" [1957] P.L. 304; J. Wolffe, "Crown Immunity from Regulatory Statutes" [1988] P.L. 339 and by the same author "Crown Immunity from Legislative Obligations" [1990] P.L. 14; *Stair Memorial Encyclopaedia*, Vol. 7, paras 740–743; and Finch and Ashton, pp. 463–464.

LITIGATION INVOLVING THE CROWN

The development of rights of action against the Crown has differed between England and Scotland. In England the law was based on the view that the king could do no wrong and that the king could not be sued in his own courts. If these propositions were ever accepted in Scotland, they would have parted from it at an early stage as the Crown agreed to be subject to its own courts; see *A. v. B* (1534) Mor. 7321; *Somerville v. Lord Advocate* (1893) 20 R. 1050 and see generally J.R. Philip, "The Crown as Litigant in Scotland" (1928) 40 J.R. 238 and Lord Murray, "*Rex non potest peccare*", 1939 S.L. Rev. 1, 40 and Mitchell, above.   **13–15**

The main legislation governing the liability of the Crown today is the Crown Proceedings Act 1947, which was intended, in principle, to equate civil liability of the Crown to that of private individuals. The following are the main provisions in relation to the liability of the Crown in delict.

Crown Proceedings Act 1947

ss. 2, 38(2), 40(1)

"Part I. — Substantive Law.

2. LIABILITY OF THE CROWN IN TORT. — (1) Subject to the provisions of this Act, the Crown shall be subject to all those liabilities in tort to which, if it were a private person of full age and capacity, it would be subject —   **13–16**

    (*a*)   in respect of torts committed by its servants or agents;

    (*b*)   in respect of any breach of those duties which a person owes to his servants or agents at common law by reason of being their employer; and

    (*c*)   in respect of any breach of the duties attaching at common law to the ownership, occupation, possession or control of property:

Provided that no proceedings shall lie against the Crown by virtue of paragraph (*a*) of this subsection in respect of any act or omission of a servant or agent of the Crown unless the act or omission would apart from the provisions of this Act have given rise to a cause of action in tort against that servant or agent or his estate.

(2) Where the Crown is bound by a statutory duty which is binding also upon persons other than the Crown and its officers, then, subject to the provisions of this Act, the Crown shall, in respect of a failure to comply with that duty, be subject to all those liabilities in tort (if any) to which it would be so subject if it were a private person of full age and capacity.

(3) Where any functions are conferred or imposed upon an officer of the Crown as such either by any rule of the common law or by statute, and that officer commits a tort while performing or purporting to perform those functions, the liabilities of the Crown in respect of the tort shall be such as they would have been if those functions had been conferred or imposed solely by virtue of instructions lawfully given by the Crown.

(4) Any enactment which negatives or limits the amount of the liability of any Government department or officer of the Crown in respect of any tort committed by that department or officer shall, in the case of proceedings against the Crown under this section in respect of a tort committed by that department or officer, apply in relation to the Crown as it would have applied in relation to that department or officer if the proceedings against the Crown had been proceedings against that department or officer.

(5) No proceedings shall lie against the Crown by virtue of this section in respect of anything done or omitted to be done by any person while discharging or purporting to discharge any responsibilities of a judicial nature vested in him, or any responsibilities which he has in connection with the execution of judicial process.

(6) No proceedings shall lie against the Crown by virtue of this section in respect of any act, neglect or default of any officer of the Crown, unless that officer has been directly or indirectly appointed by the Crown and was at the material time paid in respect of his duties as an officer of the Crown wholly out of the Consolidated Fund of the United Kingdom, moneys provided by Parliament, the Road Fund, or any other Fund certified by the Treasury for the purposes of this subsection or was at the material time holding an office in respect of which the Treasury certify that the holder thereof would normally be so paid...

38. INTERPRETATION. — (1) Any reference in this Act to the provisions of this Act shall, unless the context otherwise requires, include a reference to rules of court or county court rules made for the purposes of this Act.

(2) In this Act, except in so far as the context otherwise requires or it is otherwise expressly provided, the following expressions have the meanings hereby respectively assigned to them, that is to say: —

'Agent,' when used in relation to the Crown, includes an independent contractor employed by the Crown;

'Civil proceedings' includes proceedings in the High Court or the county court for the recovery of fines or penalties, but does not include proceedings on the Crown side of the King's Bench Division;

'His Majesty's aircraft' does not include aircraft belonging to His Majesty otherwise than in right of His Government in the United Kingdom or the Scottish Administration;

'His Majesty's ships' means ships of which the beneficial interest is vested in His Majesty or which are registered as Government ships for the purposes of the Merchant Shipping Acts, 1894 to 1940, or which are for the time being demised or subdemised to or in the exclusive possession of the Crown, except that the said expression does not include any ship in which His Majesty is interested otherwise than in right of His Government in the United Kingdom or the Scottish Administration unless that ship is for the time being demised or subdemised to His Majesty in right of His said Government or Administration or in the exclusive possession of His Majesty in that right;

'Officer,' in relation to the Crown, includes any servant of His Majesty, and accordingly (but without prejudice to the generality of the foregoing provision) includes a Minister of the Crown and a Member of the Scottish Executive;

'Order' includes a judgment, decree, rule, award or declaration;

'Prescribed' means prescribed by rules of court or county court rules, as the case may be;

'Proceedings against the Crown' includes a claim by way of set-off or counterclaim raised in proceedings by the Crown and a member of the Scottish Executive;

'Ship' has the meaning assigned to it by section seven hundred and forty-two of the Merchant Shipping Act, 1894;

'Statutory duty' means any duty imposed by or under any Act of Parliament.

...

[*Proviso not applicable to Scotland, see section 51.* — ED.]

(5) Any reference in this Act to the armed forces of the Crown shall be construed as including a reference to the following forces: —

(*a*)   the Women's Royal Naval Service;

(*b*)   the Queen Alexandra's Royal Naval Nursing Service; and

(*c*)   any other organisation established under the control of the Admiralty, the Army Council or the Air Council.

(6) References in this Act to any enactment shall be construed as references to that enactment as amended by or under any other enactment, including this Act…

40. Savings. — (1) Nothing in this Act shall apply to proceedings by or against, or authorise proceedings in tort to be brought against, His Majesty in His private capacity.

(2) Except as therein otherwise expressly provided, nothing in this Act shall: —

(*a*)   affect the law relating to prize salvage, or apply to proceedings in causes or matters within the jurisdiction of the High Court as a prize court or to any criminal proceedings; or

(*b*)   authorise proceedings to be taken against the Crown under or in accordance with this Act in respect of any alleged liability of the Crown arising otherwise than in respect of His Majesty's Government in the United Kingdom or the Scottish Administration, or affect proceedings against the Crown in respect of any such alleged liability as aforesaid; or

(*c*)   affect any proceedings by the Crown otherwise than in right of His Majesty's Government in the United Kingdom or the Scottish Administration; or

(*d*)   subject the Crown to any greater liabilities in respect of the acts or omissions of any independent contractor employed by the Crown than those to which the Crown would be subject in respect of such acts or omissions if it were a private person; or

(*e*)   subject the Crown, in its capacity as a highway authority, to any greater liability than that to which a local authority is subject in that capacity; or

(*f*)   affect any rules of evidence or any presumption relating to the extent to which the Crown is bound by any Act of Parliament; or

(*g*)   affect any right of the Crown to demand a trial at bar or to control or otherwise intervene in proceedings affecting its rights, property or profits; or

(*h*)   affect any liability imposed on the public trustee or on the Consolidated Fund of the United Kingdom by the Public Trustee Act, 1906 (6 Edw. 7, c. 55),

and, without prejudice to the general effect of the foregoing provisions, Part III. of this Act shall not apply to the Crown except in right of His Majesty's Government in the United Kingdom or the Scottish Administration.

(3) A certificate of a Secretary of State: —

(*a*)   to the effect that any alleged liability of the Crown arises otherwise than in respect of His Majesty's Government in the United Kingdom;

(*b*)   to the effect that any proceedings by the Crown are proceedings otherwise than in right of His Majesty's Government in the United Kingdom;

shall, for the purposes of this Act, be conclusive as to the matter so certified.

(3A) A certificate of the Scottish Ministers to the effect that —

(a)   any alleged liability of the Crown arises otherwise than in respect of the Scottish Administration,

(b)   any proceedings by the Crown are proceedings otherwise than in right of the Scottish Administration,

shall, for the purposes of this Act, be conclusive as to that matter.

(4) Where any property vests in the Crown by virtue of any rule of law which operates independently of the acts or the intentions of the Crown, the Crown shall not by virtue of this Act be subject to any liabilities in tort by reason only of the property being so vested; but the provisions of this subsection shall be without prejudice to the liabilities of the Crown under this Act in respect of any period after the Crown or any person acting for the Crown has in fact taken possession or control of any such property, or entered into occupation thereof.

(5) This Act shall not operate to limit the discretion of the court to grant relief by way of mandamus in cases in which such relief might have been granted before the commencement of this Act, notwithstanding that by reason of the provisions of this Act some other and further remedy is available."

Notes

(1) The extract reflects the amendments made by Schedule 8, para. 7 of the Scotland   **13–17**
Act 1998.

(2) Until the decision in *Macgregor v. Lord Advocate*, 1921 S.C. 847, it appeared to be the case in Scots law that it was always competent to use the Crown in delict. This was not so in England. For commentary on the position prior to the decision in *Macgregor* and the decision itself see Philip above and Mitchell above.

(3) Particular difficulties arise in relation to who is a servant of the Crown. The approach of the Act is to define this in terms of payment from the consolidated fund. This would appear to have a restricted effect on the liability of the Crown. It would seem that for liability to apply it must be

shown that the wrongdoer was a servant in the ordinary sense, and that the additional condition of payment from the fund must be demonstrated. This would seem to exclude, for example, the liability of the Crown for a servant who is "borrowed" but not hired. 'For a modern example of this see *Cropper v. Chief Constable, Dumfries and Galloway*, 1998 S.L.T. 548 where it was held that a police officer seconded to the Scottish Crime Squad (subject to the direction of the Secretary of State for Scotland) but still paid by his original force and subject to the direction of his original superiors could not claim to be a servant of the Crown in relation to an injury sustained by a colleague from his original force as a result of alleged negligent driving on his part. For further difficulties in relation to the concept of a servant of the Crown, see P. Williams, *Crown Proceedings*, Chap. 2; H. Street, *Governmental Liability* (1953), pp. 25–46 and 48–50 and also G.H. Treitel, "Crown Proceedings: Same Recent Developments" [1957] P.L. 321 at 326–335 and *Stair Memorial Encyclopaedia*, Vol. 7, para. 757. If Crown service can be established, then the rules of vicarious liability apply in the normal way: *Hughes v. Lord Advocate*, 1963 S.C. (H.L.) 31.

(4) Note too the limitation on an action of reparation for breach of statutory duty under section 2(2). For the Crown to be liable, the duty must also be binding upon persons other than the Crown. Although this would not appear to affect the possibility of obtaining a declarator as to statutory duty, enforcement may be difficult. Such duties are normally generally phrased and it has been stated that the duty resting upon the Crown does not confer any enforceable right upon a particular individual who is within its ambit: *Griffin v. Lord Advocate*, 1950 S.C. 448 and for the older law *Craigie v. Hepburn*, Dec., 22 1809, F.C. It is only where a duty is specific that it could be enforced. For further discussion in relation to the difficulties of enforcing a statutory duty against the Crown see para. 11–13, and on this generally see Mitchell, pp. 309–310.

(5) Note section 40: nothing in the Act affects the personal liability of the sovereign in a private capacity. Moreover, the operation of the Act is confined to liabilities in respect of the Crown as being the Government in the United Kingdom and does not effect proceedings by the Crown in any other capacity. Provision is made for conclusive certification by a Secretary of State as to the capacity in which the Crown *did a* particular Act: section 38(3) and note section 38(3)(*a*), inserted by Schedule 8, para. 7 of the Scotland Act 1998 on the conclusiveness of acts of the Scottish Administration. The Crown and its servants may be able to plead the defence of Act of State in respect of action performed abroad. The scope of this defence is somewhat uncertain: *Nissan v. Attorney General* [1978] A.C. 179; see generally J.G. Collier, "Act of State as a Defence Against a British Subject" (1968) 26 C.L.J. 102 and Cane (1980) 29 I.C.L.Q. 681.

13–18   (6) The Crown Proceedings (Armed Forces) Act 1987 provides that section 10 of the 1947 Act, which deals with the special position of the Crown concerning delictual liability in relation to the armed forces, ceases to have effect except in relation to anything suffered by someone as a result of an act or omission occurring before May 15, 1987. Section 10 provides that no liability arises for death or injuries caused by a member of the armed forces of the Crown to other servicemen in the execution of his duties where the Minister certifies that the accident is attributable to service for the purposes of a pension award. It should be noted, however, that under the 1987 Act it is possible for the Secretary of State to revive the effect of section 10 of the 1947 Act when he considers it necessary or expedient to do so in the circumstances: section 2(2). For the position prior to the passing of the 1987 Act see *Pearce v. Secretary of State for Defence* [1988] 2 All E.R. 348 (no liability on the part of the Crown for illness developed as a result of nuclear weapons tests). See also *Adams v. War Office* [1955] 1 W.L.R. 1116 (when the Minister issues a certificate that the accident is caused to the serviceman for the purposes of a pension award, even if no award was made. Where certification is made, it is conclusive). For commentary on the 1987 Act see F.C. Boyd, "The Crown Proceedings (Armed Forces) Act 1987" [1989] P.L. 237.

(7) In relation to the liability of the Crown in contract, Scots law never experienced the difficulties found in English law where the special procedure of petition of right existed to allow an action to be brought against the Crown. See now section 1 of the 1947 Act, which brought English law into line with the position in Scotland. The substantive rules of contract law in relation to the Crown are, however, in some respects, significantly different from the ordinary rules as discussed above. Devolution to Scotland has also had its impact on this area.

Scotland Act 1998

s. 99

"Rights and Liabilities of the Crown in Different Capacities

99. — (1) Rights and liabilities may arise between the Crown in right of Her Majesty's Government in   **13–19**
the United Kingdom and the Crown in right of the Scottish Administration by virtue of a contract, by
operation of law or by virtue of an enactment as they may arise between subjects.

(2) Property and liabilities may be transferred between the Crown in one of those capacities and the
Crown in the other capacity as they may be transferred between subjects; and they may together create,
vary or extinguish any property or liability as subjects may.

(3) Proceedings in respect of _

(a)   any property or liabilities to which the Crown in one of those capacities is entitled or subject
      under subsection (1) or (2), or

(b)   the exercise of, or failure to exercise, any function exercisable by an office-holder of the Crown
      in one of those capacities,

may be instituted by the Crown in either capacity; and the Crown in the other capacity may be a
separate party in the proceedings.

(4) This section applies to a unilateral obligation as it applies to a contract.

(5) In this section —

'office-holder', in relation to the Crown in right of Her Majesty's Government in the United Kingdom,
means any Minister of the Crown or other office-holder under the Crown in that capacity and, in relation
to the Crown in right of the Scottish Administration, means any office-holder in the Scottish Administration,
'subject' means a person not acting on behalf of the Crown."

Notes

(1) The purpose of the section is to make clear that legal relations may be entered into   **13–20**
between the Crown in right of the U.K. Government and the Crown in right of the Scottish
Administration: *Hansard*, H.L. Vol. 594, col. 75. One of the main reasons for the provision is
that when a U.K. Minister of the Crown makes an order under section 58 above requiring
action to be taken by Scottish Ministers, the latter could competently seek judicial review of the
order and, on the other hand, for the U.K. Minister to enforce the order against the Scottish
Ministers, subject to the 1947 Act. "It was thought", the Lord Advocate continued, "that without
an express provision in the Bill, the view may be taken that the doctrine of Crown indivisibility
would prevent this" (col. 75).

(2) Under the Crown Suits (Scotland) Act 1857, section 1 authorises proceedings against
the Lord Advocate as representing the Crown or any public department. Unsurprisingly, the
Scotland Act 1998 has made amendments to the 1857 Act. Crown now includes the Scottish
Administration and the reference to the Lord Advocate contained in the Act is now changed to
"appropriate law officer", depending on whether the action is to be brought against the Lord
Advocate as the law officer of the Scottish Administration or the Advocate General for Scotland,
the new law officer created by section 87 of the Act to advise on matters of Scots law and
representing the U.K. Government in litigation. For further minor amendments see the Scotland
Act 1998, Sched. 8, para. 2. The definition contained in section 4 of "public department" is
incomplete but it would appear that it is limited by the *ejusdem generis* rule to those departments
and authorities which would be regarded as the Crown or Crown servants: *Lord Advocate v.
Argyll County Council*, 1950 S.C. 304, and to that extent some weight will be given to the
general test of control and to the English list of authorised departments authorised to sue and be
sued under the Crown Proceedings Act 1947, s. 17(1). The title of the Lord Advocate extends to
actions of the Crown outside the United Kingdom: *Burmah Oil Co. (Burmah Trading) Ltd v.
Lord Advocate*, 1964 S.C. (H.L.) 117. It is a consequence of section 5 that there is no need to
name the person holding the office of Lord Advocate: *Lord Advocate v. Black*, 1995 S.L.T. 540.
To the general rule that the Government is sued and sues in the name of the Lord Advocate,
there is an exception contained in section 1(8) of the Reorganisation of Offices (Scotland) Act
1939, which envisages legal proceedings against the Secretary of State in the name of the

"Secretary of State for Scotland". It is the practice where there is involvement of any department for which the Secretary of State is responsible to raise the action in those terms.

(3) Where an action is raised by the Lord Advocate or defended by him, he requires to have the authority of the public department in question but no private party can challenge that authority upon grounds that is has not been given. It would, however, seem to be competent to challenge on the ground that the public authority in question was not of the type covered by the 1857 Act: 108 H.C. Official Report, ser. 6, col. 260 (January 14, 1987).

Chapter 14

LIABILITY OF PUBLIC AUTHORITIES AND THE CROWN

Government in all its forms is exposed to the ordinary law. It enters contracts, it breaks them. It can cause injury intentionally or negligently in the carrying out of governmental functions. We have come to accept that under the rule of law in a democratic society, Government should not be afforded any special advantages or be subject to different rules of liability in reply to private individual's identities. This led the constitutional commentator, A. V. Dicey, to reject the concept of *droit administratif*, the special system of rules governing liability of Government under French law. In his view:

> "With us every official, from the Prime Minister down to a constable or a collector of taxes, is under the same responsibility for every act done without legal justification as any other citizen" (*Introduction to the Study of the Law of the Constitution* (H. W. R. Wade, ed., 10th ed., 1959, p. 193)

Such a view has echoes in early Scots law. For a general acount see J. D. B. Mitchell, *Constitutional Law* (2nd ed., 1968), Chap. 9 and by the same author, "The Royal Prerogative in Modern Scots Law" [1957] P.L. 304.

Like any legal person public authorities, whether the Crown, local authority, statutory body or nationalised industry can enter into contracts. Some are mundane and routine, such as the employment of staff or the purchase of property. Others can go to the very root of the purpose of the body in question or can be used as a tool of policy. Powers to contract may be conferred specifically by statute or more generally by statute, such as section 69 of the Local Government (Scotland) Act 1973 above, para. 3–19, and by common law, such as the general legal capacity of the Crown: Turpin, below, pp. 83–84.

On the contracts of public authorities and the Crown generally see J.D.B. Mitchell, *The Contracts of Public Authorities* (1954); C. Turpin, *Government Procurement and Contracts* (1989); S. Arrowsmith, *Civil Liability and Public Authorities* (1992) and *The Law of Public and Utilities Procurement* (1996); P.W. Hogg, *Liability of the Crown* (2nd ed., 1989), Chap. 8; C. Harlow and R. Rawlings, *Law and Administration* (1997), Chap. 9 and V. Finch and C. Ashton, *Administrative Law in Scotland* (1997), pp 83–91. As the general law of contract is of major significance to the contracts of public authorities, standard texts on Scots contract law are also of relevance, on which generally see W. McBryde, *The Law of Contract in Scotland* (1987) and S. Woolman, *Contract* (1994).

The following extracts explore a number of significant issues arising from the liability of the Crown and other public authorities in contract.

14–1

14–2

CROWN CONTRACTS

Rederiaktiebolaget Amphitrite v. The King

[1921] 3 K.B. 500

14–3   ROWLATT J.: "In this case the suppliants are a Swedish shipowning company who sue the Crown by petition of right for damages for breach of contract, the breach being that the ship *Amphitrite* was refused a clearance to enable her to leave this country, when she had entered a British port under an arrangement whereby she was promised that she should be given that clearance. Now undoubtedly the suppliants desired to get the clearest and most binding assurance that was possible. Their vessel was free; they might have employed her elsewhere; and they had experience of the difficulties encountered by foreign ships in getting away from this country when once they had come here. Accordingly they wrote on March 8, 1918, to the British Legation at Stockholm and asked whether, in the event of the vessel being put in trade between Sweden and England, the Legation could give them a guarantee that she would be allowed free passage without being detained in Great Britain. The Legation replied that they were 'instructed to say that the S.S. *Amphitrite* will earn her own release and be given a coal cargo if she proceed to the United Kingdom with a full cargo consisting of a least 60% approved goods'. That reply was given by the British Legation after consulting the proper authorities, and I must take it that it was given with the highest authority with which it could be given on behalf of His Majesty's Government. And the British Government thereby undertook that if the ship traded to this country she should not be subjected to the delays which were sometimes imposed. The letters in which that undertaking was contained were written with reference to an earlier voyage which was allowed to go through, the undertaking being on that occasion observed. But the undertaking was renewed with respect to the voyage in connection with which the present complaint arises by a letter from the British Legation, in which it was stated that 'the S.S. *Amphitrite* will be allowed to release herself in her next voyage to the United Kingdom' — that is to say, upon the same terms as before. Now under those circumstances what I have to consider is whether this was a contract at all. I have not to consider whether there was anything of which complaint might be made outside a Court, whether that is to say what the Government did was morally wrong or arbitrary; that would be altogether outside my province. All I have got to say is whether there was an enforceable contract, and I am of opinion that there was not. No doubt the Government can bind itself through its officers by a commercial contract, and if it does so it must perform it like anybody else or pay damages for the breach. But this was not a commercial contract; it was an arrangement whereby the Government purported to give an assurance as to what its executive action would be in the future in relation to a particular ship in the event of her coming to this country with a particular kind of cargo. And that is, to my mind, not a contract for the breach of which damages can be sued for in a Court of law. It was merely an expression of intention to act in a particular way in a certain event. My main reason for so thinking is that it is not competent for the Government to fetter its future executive action, which must necessarily be determined by the needs of the community when the question arises. It cannot by contract hamper its freedom of action in matters which concern the welfare of the State. Thus in the case of the employment of public servants, which is a less strong case than the present, it has been laid down that, except under an Act of Parliament, no one acting on behalf of the Crown has authority to employ any person except upon the terms that he is dismissible at the Crown's pleasure; the reason being that it is in the interests of the community that the ministers for the time being advising the Crown should be able to dispense with the services of its employees if they think it desirable. Again suppose that a man accepts an office which he is perfectly at liberty to refuse, and does so on the express terms that he is to have certain leave of absence, and that when the time arrives the leave is refused in circumstances of the greatest hardship to his family or business, as the case may be. Can it be conceived that a petition of right would lie for damages? I should think not. I am of opinion that this petition must fail and there must be judgment for the Crown."

Notes

14–4   (1) It is perhaps difficult to establish the ratio of this decision. The case is generally treated as being authority for the proposition that contracts which fetter the freedom of the executive function of the Crown are invalid. Given what we know about the limits on the remedies available against the Crown, such as interdict and implement, is this fear of fettering of discretion entirely justified? Is this immunity too widely drawn? It is also perhaps not clear why there should be a distinction between commercial and non-commercial contracts. See in particular Mitchell (1954) above at pp. 27–32, 52 and 57, particularly as the difference between the two may be difficult to discern. Arguably on the basis of this distinction the Crown is placed in a better position than other public authorities. This case must be taken to represent the starting-point for the examination of any Crown contract.

(2) Is the *Amphitrite* principle comparable with that applied in *Ayr Harbour Trustees* v. *Oswald* below? Should the test of incompatibility founded in the latter case be applied to the Crown? On this see Turpin above at p.24.

As with any contract, assuming the parties do have capacity to contract, the next issue that arises is the nature and extent of the obligations being undertaken. Here too the status of the Crown can be relevant.

Commissioners for Crown Lands v. Page

[1960] 2 Q.B. 274

"The Minister of Works, acting on behalf of the Crown, requisitioned in 1945 premises which had **14–5** been demised in 1937 by the Commissioner of Crown Lands for a term of 25 years. There was no express covenant of quiet enjoyment. The premises were derequisitioned in 1955. The Commissioners claimed the arrears of rent. It was conceded that the Crown was one and indivisible as lessor and requisitioning authority. The lessee claimed that she had been 'evicted', but the court held that there had been no 'eviction', merely the requisitioning of the lessee's right of occupation (for which compensation was payable to the lessee). One point was whether the re-entry was 'wrongful' as in breach of an *implied* covenant of quiet enjoyment. The Crown argued *inter alia* that the requisitioning was not done in the capacity of landlord, but as the Executive responsible for the government of the country."

DEVLIN L.J.: "…Has the Crown committed a fundamental breach of the covenant? To answer that question one must consider the true scope and object of the covenant in such a lease as this where the Crown is the grantor. On the face of it, and if the covenant is taken as read without any limitation, there has been a breach. The Crown has deprived the defendant of the enjoyment of the demised premises for a long and indefinite period, and has done so deliberately, and (if one ignores the compulsion of public duty) has done so of its own free will; its act was authorised, but was not required by the statute. But, it is said by the Crown, it is not an act done as landlord, and it lacks other necessary constituents of the act of eviction.

I think that it may well be that the covenant of quiet enjoyment is limited to acts that are done by the landlord in supposed assertion of his rights as landlord, and that other trespasses, however grave, are outside the covenant. But because the landlord in this case is also the Crown, I have found it on the whole simpler to answer the question in the case not by reference to any special limitation on the covenant of quiet enjoyment affecting all landlords, but by reference to the general limitation that affects all contracts or covenants entered into by the Crown, or for that matter by any other public authority.

When the Crown, or any other person, is entrusted, whether by virtue of the prerogative or by statute, with discretionary powers to be exercised for the public good, it does not, when making a private contract in general terms, undertake (and it may be that it could not even with the use of specific language validly undertake) to fetter itself in the use of those powers, and in the exercise of its discretion. This principle has been accepted in a number of authorities; it is sufficient to mention *Ayr Harbour Trustees* v. *Oswald* (1883) 8 App. Cas. 623; *Rederiaktiebolaget Amphitrite* v. *The King* [1921] 3 K.B. 500; *Board of Trade* v. *Temperley Steam Shipping Co. Ltd* (1926) 26 LI.L.R. 76; affirmed (1927) 27 LI.L.R. 230, C.A. and *William Cory & Sons Ltd* v. *City of London Corporation* [1951] 2 K.B. 476, C.A.

The covenant for quiet enjoyment in the present case is implied, and is not dissimilar to the contractual provision considered in the two cases last cited, which were both concerned with the implied obligation on one party to a contract not to interfere with the performance by the other party of his obligations under it. In *Board of Trade* v. *Temperley Steam Shipping Co. Ltd*, the Board were the charterers of the defendant's ship, and it was contended that they had prevented the defendants from making their ship efficient for her service under the charterparty because one of the Board's surveyors had refused a licence to do certain repairs…

I do not, however, rest my decision in the present case simply on the fact that the covenant for quiet enjoyment has to be implied. For reasons which I think will appear sufficient in the next paragraph, I should reach the same conclusion if the ordinary covenant was expressed.

In some of the cases in which public authorities have been defendants, the judgments have been put on the ground that it would be *ultra vires* for them to bind themselves not to exercise their powers; and it has also been said that a promise to do so would be contrary to public policy. It may perhaps be difficult to apply this reasoning to the Crown, but it seems to me to be unnecessary to delve into the constitutional position. When the Crown, in dealing with one of its subjects, is dealing as if it too were a private person, and is granting leases or buying and selling as ordinary persons do, it is absurd to suppose that it is making any promise about the way in which it will conduct the affairs of the nation. No one can imagine, for example, that when the Crown makes a contract which could not be fulfilled in time of war, it is pledging itself not to declare war for so long as the contract lasts. Even if, therefore, there was an express promise by the Crown that it would not do any act which might hinder the other party to the contract in the performance of his obligations, the covenant or promise must by necessary implication be read to exclude those measures affecting the nation as a whole which the Crown takes for the public good.

During the last war the Ministries of War Transport, Food and Supply were trading on a vast scale, and were also issuing orders under their statutory powers which quite frequently frustrated their own contracts, or those made by some other government department. The Minister of Supply, for example, might be found prohibiting all importation of a commodity of a sort which he had contracted to buy; or the Ministry of War Transport might fail to make cargo space available for another department's purchases. So far as I am aware, there is no case in which it has been contended that because of such action, the Crown was in breach of contract. That shows the general understanding under which such business was done. If at the time of making any such contract the 'officious bystander' had asked whether it was clear that the Crown was not undertaking to limit the use of its general executive powers, I think that there could have been only one answer. That is the proper basis for a necessary implication. I need not examine the question whether, if the Crown sought to fetter its future action in express and specific terms, it could effectively do so. It is most unlikely that in a contract with the subject, it would ever make the attempt. For the purpose of this case it is unnecessary to go further than to say that in making a lease or other contract with its subjects, the Crown does not (at least in the absence of specific words) promise to refrain from exercising its general powers under a statute or under the prerogative, or to exercise them in any particular way. That does not mean that the Crown can escape from any contract which it finds disadvantageous by saying that it never promised to act otherwise than for the public good. The distinction was clearly put by Roche J. in *Board of Trade* v. *Temperley Steam Shipping Co. Ltd*, 26 Ll.L.R. 76 at 78, where he said: 'I think and I hold that in this charterparty it is to be implied that the Crown should do nothing in connection with and in relation to and in the carrying out of the contract contained in the charterparty to prevent the shipowners from keeping the vessel seaworthy and to prevent them earning their hire. But I am utterly unable to imply in the charterparty a term or condition that the Crown should do nothing by virtue of some general legislation or by virtue of some executive action entirely remote from the charterparty and done by persons not connected with the performance of the contract directly or indirectly to bring about the results in question.' That is a different thing from saying that the Crown can never bind itself in its dealings with the subject in case it might turn out that the fulfilment of the contract was not advantageous. The observations of Denning J. in *Robertson* v. *Minister of Pensions* [1949] 1 K.B. 227, 231, on the doctrine of 'executive necessity' were, I think, directed to a case of that sort. Here we are dealing with an act done for a general executive purpose, and not an act done for the purpose of achieving a particular result under the contract in question.

I agree that the appeal should be dismissed."

"[Lord Evershed M.R. and Ormerod L.J. expressed no opinion on the effect of an express covenant, but agreed that an implied covenant of quiet enjoyment could not 'extend to prevent the future exercise by the Crown of powers and duties imposed upon it in its executive capacity by statute' (*per* Lord Evershed M.R., at 287) or 'be taken to go so far as to imply an undertaking by the Crown to refrain from exercising statutory powers in respect of the demised premises which the Crown may properly deem necessary' (*per* Ormerod L.J., at 289).]"

Notes

14–6   (1) What if the Crown had agreed expressly not to exercise the existing or future powers of entry under not just the legislation in issue, but any legislation? How would that compare with *Amphitrite*? Note that where the Crown seeks to terminate a contract before its expiry, then it is likely to be held liable in damages to the extent of any loss arising: *Kodeeswaran* v. *Attorney-General of Ceylon* [1970] A.C. 1111, P.C. disapproving *Mulvenna* v. *Admiralty*, 1926 S.C. 842.

(2) What is the position of those who act as contractors for the Crown? As a general proposition the rights of privileges of the Crown apply to a contractor carrying out work on behalf of the Crown provided they do what is reasonably necessary to do the specified purpose: *Darling* v. *Attorney General* [1950] 2 All E.R. 793, although no protection is conferred on such a contractor if liability arises outwith the scope of the contract: section 40(2) (*d*) of the Crown Proceedings Act 1947, and see *Hole* v. *Sittingbourne and Sheerness Railway Co.* (1861) 6 H. & N. 488. Where, however, the contract does not expressly state that work on behalf of the Crown has been carried out then no special protection is afforded: *Dixon* v. *London Small Arms Co. Ltd* (1876) 1 App. Cas. 632, H.L.

As noted in the introduction, the Crown can use its powers of contract not simply to carry out mundane activities such as employing staff or managing land, but also to secure policy goals. The following extract illustrates some of the issues raised by the use of the Crown's power of contract in such a manner.

T. Daintith, "Regulation by Contract: The New Prerogative"

1979 C.L.P. 41

"The anti-inflation policy pursued by the last Labour Government from 1975 to 1979 had **14–7** many striking features, but for lawyers, that which surely still demands discussion and analysis is the reinforcement of this 'voluntary' policy, until December 1978, by a programme of sanctions upon employers operated almost entirely without statutory support. During this period, an undertaking to comply with the policy was a prerequisite for the award of almost all government contracts and of some government industrial assistance; a known breach of the policy disqualified from consideration for such contracts and assistance; compliance with the policy was secured for the future as a legally enforceable term thereof. The purpose of this paper is not to discuss the details of the incomes policy, but to attempt to place the tools for its enforcement in an appropriate legal context, as an example — the most egregious to date — of the use by the Government of its contractual forms and procedures as an instrument of regulation of the behaviour of the subject.

Obviously, any government contract constrains, by law, the behaviour of both contracting parties, for the purpose of achieving their joint objective — the erection of an office building, say, or the provision of 10,000 pairs of wellington boots. In the traditional conception of contract, the legal obligations imposed are individualised by reference to this particular objective. With the widespread adoption, in ordinary commerce, of the standard form contract, the distinction between the consensual, individualised contract and the imposed, general regulation is already blurred. Government contracting shares fully in this movement but also, in the examples I wish to discuss, goes far beyond it; for it; for it incorporates, into standard terms and allocation procedures, clauses and requirements reflecting public interests which by their breadth and importance pass far beyond the mutual objectives of the contracting parties and which, therefore, might normally be promoted by statutory regulation. This is why the paper's title refers to prerogative: government has discovered means of using its increasing economic strength *vis-à-vis* private industry so as to promote certain policies in a style, and with results, which for a long time we have assumed must be the hallmark of parliamentary legislation: that is to say, officially promulgated rules backed by effective general compulsion. This means the power to rule without parliamentary consent, which is the hallmark of prerogative...

Such an inquiry falls naturally into two parts, corresponding to the two types of power related to government contracts: first, the power of Government to decide who will be its contractors, and on what terms; secondly, its power to control contractors' (and indeed subcontractors') behaviour in terms of the contract itself. These powers will be referred to respectively as *Precontractual* and *Contractual*.

Precontractual Powers

In discussing the precontractual phase, it is necessary to distinguish the position of the Crown — that is to say, the legal personification of central government — from that of most other public authorities. The reason is that the Crown enjoys a common law capacity to make contracts, while most other public authorities, being created by statute, only enjoy such contractual capacity as their constitutive statute allots them ...

To sum up, therefore, on the precontractual phase, in which the public authority is taking its unilateral decision as to who shall be its contractor and on what terms, the situation of the public authority, reflecting the common law respect for freedom of contract in general, is in domestic law one of almost complete discretion. This is so whether the power to contract is based in common law or in statute. The discretion is large enough to permit the pursuit of a wide range of regulatory policies through the contractual process — a very convenient discovery in a period of minority government. Such real legal constraints as exist are external, the product of the system of EEC law, operating on some central and local government contracts through the medium of co-ordination of contractual procedures, and on some of the contractual activity of public enterprises through the rules of competition policy.

Contractual Powers

Let us, then, look back over the different phases of the exercise of contractual powers by Government, to see what is the effect, in law, of using these powers, rather than statutory powers, as an instrument of public regulation. We have just noted that, with minor exceptions, the courts have applied, to the exercise of purely contractual powers, techniques of review of a type and intensity broadly similar to those which fill the pages of de Smith's *Judicial Review of Administrative Action*. At this stage, therefore, there is little to be gained, in terms of administrative freedom of manoeuvre, from the use of contractual techniques. But in the precontractual phase, in selecting contractual partners and deciding the terms it will offer them, the Government enjoys almost unfettered freedom and total immunity from judicial review by reason of the absence of general rules of domestic law to control this process. There are important constraints on this process stemming from the activity of the European Community in the fields of public procurement and of competition law, but their full potential, and the possibility of their operation in the domestic legal arena have not yet been adequately appreciated. In consequence Government enjoys far greater freedom and discretion in the elaboration of contractual schemes of regulation than it could reasonably hope to possess as the operator of a statutory scheme under powers conferred by Parliament. Moreover, even if Parliament might itself on occasion be prepared to grant Government such wide and ill-defined powers by statute, the availability to Government of the contractual option denies to Parliament the very possibility of discussing and deciding the issue. In a recent report, the parliamentary select committee on the ombudsman showed its sensitivity to the problem of contractual regulation in recommending that the ombudsman's powers be extended to enable him to look at the process of awarding government contracts. Consideration of this sensible proposal must not distract Parliament from the far more fundamental question of whether it is prepared to see a reduction of its formal supremacy by allowing Government to develop and ramify a technique of regulation in which legislative authorisation plays no effective part. It would be sad, but not surprising, if Parliament, at the time of its greatest real authority over Government in recent years, were to sit quietly by while Government fashioned for itself a new prerogative."

Notes

14–8   (1) As has been alluded to, the special power and position of the Crown has been used as a way of promoting government policy through contractual policy. On this see generally G. Ganz [1978] P.L. 333; R.B. Ferguson and A.C. Page, "Pay Restraint: The Legal Constraints" (1978) 128 N.L.J. 515; and C. Turpin, *Government Contracts* (1972), Chap. 9; on the fair wages clause see O. Kahn-Freund, "Legislation Through Adjudication: The Legal Aspect of Fair Wages Clauses and Recognised Conditions" (1948) 11 M.L.R. 269, 429 and *Stair Memorial Encyclopaedia*, Vol. 22, "Sources of Law", paras 223–246.

(2) Given the approach in *West*, it is doubtful whether the Crown's actions here are susceptible to judicial review. The tri-partite element central to *West* seems to be missing. Nevertheless in English public law, where such a test is not required, the position does not appear to be any different: see S. Arrowsmith, "Judicial Review and the Contractual Powers of Public Authorities" (1990) 106 L.Q.R. 277.

(3) The exercise of contractual powers is normally also excluded from review by the Parliamentary Commissioner for Administration, on which see Chapter 16. J.D.B. Mitchell, "The Royal Prerogative in modern Scots Law" [1957] P.L. 304 makes a distinction in the older Scots Law between Crown contracts which are exceptional and those which are ordinary. In the case of the latter, he argues that no special position should be afforded the Crown. In relation to the former, given the specialities, Crown privilege should apply, but it is for the Crown to establish the plea. Would this distinction be helpful in dealing with some of the difficulties faced by potential Crown contractors identified by Daintith? See, for example, *William Cory and Son Ltd* v. *London Corporation* below at para. 14–15 and *C zarnikow Ltd* v. *Centrala Handlu Zagranicznego Rolimpex* [1979] A.C. 351 at 370 *per* Lord Salmon (dissenting).

(4) One form of control over use of power by the Crown in relation to the awarding of contracts is the influence of European Community law. In "The Techniques of Government" in *The Changing Constitution* (J. Jowell and D. Oliver eds, 3rd ed., 1994), Chap. 8 at p. 232, Professor Daintith noted that:

> "While in its early years the Commission, as the Community's executive arm, naturally concentrated its attention on the removal of the most obvious regulatory and fiscal barriers, such as quotas and tariffs, it has more recently been able to focus on the less visible distortions of competition flowing from the use of State dominium, particularly through the granting of State aids, the favourable treatment of public enterprises (as by making capital available on advantageous terms) and discriminatory public procurement. All these feature strongly in the '1992' programme for the completion of the single market, embarked on in 1985. In consequence, decisions which once would have represented a highly discretionary exercise of dominium now need to be cleared with the Commission, and failure to do this may result in their reversal."

See also T. Daintith, "The Executive Power Today: Bargaining and Economic Control", in **14–9** *The Changing Constitution* (J. Jowell and D. Oliver eds 2nd ed. 1989), Chap. 8.

(5) Article 86 (now Article 82) of the E.C. Treaty, which prohibits abuse of a dominant position, has also provided a way of controlling the use of the Government's contractual power. In *Millar and Bryce Ltd* v. *Keeper of the Registers of Scotland*, 1997 G.W.D. 25-1265 Millar and Bryce sought interdict in suspension of a decision by the Keeper to terminate supply of hard copies of data from the Register of Inhibitions and Adjudications. For the purposes of interim interdict and suspension, the court was prepared to hold that Millar and Bryce had made out a prima facie case of breach of Article 86. See C. Bloch, "Interim Remedies Against The Crown Revisited", 1997 S.L.T. (News) 165.

(6) As noted at para. 13–18, the Crown Proceedings Act 1947 did not alter the liability of the Crown under contract in Scots law in any general sense, but it does have some relevance to specific areas. Section 50(2)(*d*), for example, provides that a government department cannot set off debts owed to another government department against a claim made against the department without the consent of the court: *Smith* v. *Lord Advocate (No. 2)*, 1980 S.C. 227. These provisions now apply to any such claim as set off as between a Scottish government department and a U.K. government department under the Scotland Act 1998, Sched. 8, para. 7(5).

PUBLIC AUTHORITY CONTRACTS

14–10　　Here we are concerned with the way in which the law deals with the contracts of public authorities other than the Crown. The Crown's powers derive generally from the common law, but the power of other public authorities is typically derived from statute. Where the Crown acts through statute, the following discussion is still relevant. This means that the *ultra vires* doctrine determines the capacity and powers of such bodies to contract. The cases which follow will show the inherent tension between on the one hand, the view that the public authorities must exercise their powers in the public interest and cannot fetter their freedom of action, with, on the other, the need for certainty on the part of those who enter into contracts with public authorities.

Ayr Harbour Trustees v. Oswald

(1883) 8 App. Cas. 623

14–11　　The Harbour trustees were given statutory powers compulsorily to purchase land for the management and improvement of a harbour. The trustees wished to acquire Oswald's land subject to an undertaking that they would not use the land acquired in such a manner as to interfere with the access from Oswald's remaining land to the harbour. The reason for this was to justify a lower sum being paid to Oswald as compensation. Oswald brought an action for a decree of declarator contending that the trustees' decision (recorded in a minute) was *ultra vires* and that the purchase should be made without the undertaking and for payment of the larger sum. On appeal by the trustees from the Court of Session, which had granted the relief sought:

LORD BLACKBURN: "… But in this case the trustees… endeavoured by a minute to fix once for all the way in which they and their successors in office would use their powers. And if they could at that time bind themselves by a bargain with Mr. Oswald, if he had agreed to it, and that agreement would prevent his land from being injuriously affected, I should be unwilling to hold that he could, by refusing his assent to that agreement, get compensation for the injury which he might have prevented. As Lord Shand says, 'he cannot insist on being injured that he may get money.' There are great technical difficulties in the way of working out this, but if I thought that his assent to the minute would have made the minute effectual to prevent the trustees and their successors from using their powers so as to injuriously affect the lands, I should have tried to overcome them. But I do not think that if Mr. Oswald had assented to the minute it would have bound the successors of the present trustees.

I think that where the legislature confer powers on any body to take lands compulsorily for a particular purpose, it is on the ground that the using of that land for that purpose will be for the public good. Whether that body be one which is seeking to make a profit for shareholders, or, as in the present case, a body of trustees acting solely for the public good, I think in either case the powers conferred on the body empowered to take the land compulsorily are intrusted to them, and their successors, to be used for the furtherance of that object which the legislature has thought sufficiently for the public good to justify it in intrusting them with such powers; and, consequently, that a contract purporting to bind them and their successors not to use those powers is void. This is, I think, the principle on which this House acted in *Staffordshire Canal* v. *Birmingham Canal*, and on which the late Master of the Rolls acted in *Mulliner* v. *Midland Ry. Co.* In both those cases there were shareholders, but, said the Master of the Rolls, at p. 619, 'Now for what purpose is the land to be used? It is to be used for the purposes of the Act, that is, for the general purposes of a railway. It is a public thoroughfare, subject to special rights on the part of the railway company working and using. But it is in fact a property devoted to public purposes as well as to private purposes; and the public have rights, no doubt, over the property of the railway company. It is property which is allowed to be acquired by the railway company solely for this purpose, and it is devoted to this purpose.'

This reasoning, which I think sound, is à fortiori applicable where there are no shareholders, and the purposes are all public…

There is only, I think, one further point on which I think it necessary to remark. The trustees are under no obligation to make erections on any part of the land. If they in the bonâ fide exercise of their discretion think it best for the interest of the harbour to leave the portion of the land between Mr. Oswald's land and the quay wall open as a road of access and wharf, they may do so. If they think it best to make erections there not inconsistent with the main purpose of leaving a road of access from York Street to near the gates of the wet dock, though injuriously affecting the frontage of Mr. Oswald's remaining land, they may do so. And it was strongly argued that the trustees at the present time in the exercise of their general administrative powers may fix what is to be done now; and that if they do so they practically fix what will be done for all time to come; if the present trustees now lay out an open road thirty feet wide, along the inner side of the land, erecting what erections they think advisable on other parts of the wharf, their successors can hardly be supposed likely to change this plan.

I think that it is quite true that as to all such things as from their nature must be done once for all at the beginning of the trust, the present trustees must bind their successors. And if the Act had required the trustees to make and maintain a road thirty feet wide upon the land taken along the north quay, I am by no means prepared to say that their successors could have closed the road they laid out and made a new one; something would depend on the very terms of the enactment. But such is not the enactment in this Act. And though I think that the mode in which the trustees now lay out the road of access and wharf will probably have great influence on the exercise of the discretion of their successors, and is therefore an element which ought to be, and I do not doubt was, considered by the oversman in fixing the fair compensation for the probable injury to the frontage, it goes, I think, no further.

I come therefore to the conclusion that the interlocutor appealed against should be affirmed and the appeal dismissed with costs."

LORD WATSON and LORD FITZGERALD also delivered speeches in favour of dismissing the appeal. Appeal dismissed

Notes

The ratio of this case has been the subject of debate. The test is a strict one, to the extent that where statutory power and contract touch upon the same subject matter, the contract will be void. There is no real further Scottish authority. The English courts have, however, in some cases decided to dilute the effect of *Oswald* or to distinguish it entirely as the next extract shows.

14–12

Birkdale District Electric Supply Co. Ltd v. Southport Corporation

[1926] A.C. 355

"In 1901 the appellants, an electricity company, took over, under an Electric Lighting Order (made under the Electric Lighting Acts), the local electricity supply undertaking from Birkdale UDC. Under a Supplemental Deed to the Main Deed of Transfer, it was agreed that the prices to be charged by the appellants to private consumers should not exceed those charged in the adjoining borough of Southport by Southport Corporation, which also operated an electricity supply undertaking. In 1911 Southport Corporation 'took over' Birkdale UDC. The appellants continued to supply the Birkdale area. In 1923, the Corporation applied for an injunction to restrain the appellants from charging prices in excess of the Southport prices (as had been done since 1921). The appellants argued that the 1901 agreement was an *ultra vires* fetter on their own power to fix the price (subject to statutory maxima) of electricity supplied by them. In the future they might be faced with a difficult situation, and need to raise their prices above those in Southport. The Corporation argued that the 1901 agreement was a business agreement which was not incompatible with the proper performance by the appellants of their statutory functions. The question of incompatibility had to be judged at the date of the agreement. The fact that the agreement might be improvident, and lead to lower profits, was a matter between the appellant company and their shareholders, but did not render the agreement *ultra vires*. Astbury J. dismissed the action ([1925]) 1 Ch. 63), but was reversed by the Court of Appeal ([1925] 1 Ch. 794). The company appealed to the House of Lords."

14–13

LORD SUMNER: "… Are… [the agreements] void at common law as being *ultra vires* the appellants, a trading company, incorporated to exercise statutory powers vested in them in the public interest under the authority of the Legislature? This is a doctrine, which it may be unwise to circumscribe within the limits of an inelastic definition. We have, however, a long series of decisions, extending over nearly a century, and at any rate illustrating the cases to which the rule has been understood to extend. With the exception of *York Corporation* v. *Henry Leetham & Sons* [1924] 1 Ch. 557 no case has been cited, in which a contract by a trading company to compound with a customer without limit of time for the price to be paid for services rendered to him, has been declared to be *ultra vires*, and we were told that the diligence of counsel had failed to find any other case. Certainly I have been able to go no further.

Hitherto the question has mainly arisen, where servitudes have been claimed over the property, which the alleged servient owner acquired under statutory authority and for the purposes of a public undertaking. In *R.* v. *Inhabitants of Leake* (1833) 5 B. & Ad. 469 a public right of way was alleged to exist over the bank of a drain constructed by statutory Commissioners and reparable as such by the inhabitants of Leake. In *Staffordshire and Worcestershire Canal Navigation* v. *Birmingham Canal Navigations* (1866) L.R. 1 H.L. 254 a right was claimed to have water discharged from the respondents' canal into the canal of the appellants at the bottom of a flight of locks connecting the two navigations… The right in these cases… was rested on prescription and not on express grant, but the argument, which prevailed, was that the theory of dedication to the public use rests on an implied grant but none could be implied, since even an express grant would have been void as being *ultra vires*.

Parallel with these decisions there is a line of cases, in which the servitude claimed has been upheld on the ground that a dedication would not under the circumstances have been incompatible with full observance of the terms and full attainment of the purposes for which the statutory powers had been granted. This principle is stated as early as *R.* v. *Inhabitants of Leake*, in which the dedication was upheld, and was acted on in *Grand Junction Canal Co.* v. *Petty* (1888) 21 Q.B.D. 273, a case of a public right of walking on a towpath, and in *Greenwich Board of Works* v. *Maudslay* (1870) L.R. 5 Q.B. 397, a case of a footpath along a sea wall… Parke J. says, in the *Leake* case, that, if the bank was vested in the Commissioners by statute, so that they were thereby bound to use it for some special purpose, incompatible with a public right of walking along it, they must be deemed to have been incapable in law of thus dedicating their property; otherwise they were in that regard in the same position as other landowners … In the *Grand Junction* case Lindley L.J. says, that such incompatibility is a matter of evidence, and, in practice, evidence has regularly been given and considered for the purpose of testing the question.

My Lords, I do not think that these cases assist the appellants in any way, but in most respects are against them, for they show that, in default of proof of incompatibility in the present case, some other consideration of a cogent kind must be found. The incompetence of the company is only an incompetence *sub modo*, beyond which the powers necessary to its operation may be freely exercised.

Ayr Harbour Trustees v. *Oswald* (1883) 8 App. Cas. 323 introduces a new matter and is nearer to the present case. Harbour trustees, whose statutory power and duty were to acquire land, to be used as need might arise for the construction of works on the coast line of the harbour, sought to save money in respect of severance on the compulsory acquisition of a particular owner's land by offering him a perpetual covenant not to construct their works on the land acquired, so as to cut him off from access to the waters of the harbour, or otherwise to affect, him injuriously in respect of land not taken but from which the acquired land was severed. It was held that such a covenant was *ultra vires*. Lord Blackburn's words should be quoted. 'I think', he says, 'that where the legislature confer powers on any body to take land compulsorily for a particular purpose, it is on the ground that the using of that land for that purpose will be for the public good. Whether that body be one which is seeking to make a profit for shareholders, or, as in the present case, a body of trustees acting solely for the public good… a contract, purporting to bind them and their successors not to use those powers, is void.'

Founding on this case, Russell J. held in *York Corporation* v. *Henry Leetham & Sons* [1924] 1 Ch. 557 that a contract, terminable only by the customer, to carry his traffic at a fixed annual sum was equally *ultra vires*. Just as the covenant in the *Ayr Harbour* case tied the hands of the successors to the then trustees, and prevented them from constructing works on the land acquired, however necessary they might have become for the proper management of the undertaking, so he held that the corresponding contracts with Leetham fettered the free management of the canal in perpetuity, no matter how urgent it might be to increase the revenues of the undertaking.

My Lords, I do not think that there is a true analogy between these cases. On examining the facts in the *Ayr Harbour* case it is plain that, in effect, the trustees did not merely propose to covenant in a manner that committed the business of the harbour to restricted lines in the future; they were to forbear, once and for all, to acquire all that the statute intended them to acquire, for, though technically they acquired the whole of the land, they were to sterilize part of their acquisition, so far as the statutory purpose of their undertaking was concerned. This is some distance from a mere contract entered into with regard to trading profits. The land itself was affected in favour of the former owner in the *Ayr* case just as a towpath is affected in favour of the owner of a dominant tenement, if he is given a personal right of walking along it. If the Ayr trustees had reduced the acquisition price by covenanting with the respondent for a perpetual right to moor his barges, free of tolls, at any wharf they might construct on the water front of the land acquired, the decision might, and I think would, have been different.

There is, however, another aspect of the *Ayr Harbour* case which ought to be loyally recognized. It is certainly some ground for saying that there may be cases where the question of competence to contract does not depend on a proved incompatibility between the statutory purposes and the user, which is granted or renounced, but is established by the very nature of the grants or the contract itself. It was not proved in the *Ayr* case that there was any actual incompatibility between the general purposes of the undertaking and the arrangement by which the particular proprietor was to be spared a particular interference with the amenities or the advantages of his back land. I think the case was supposed to speak for itself and that, in effect, the trustees were held to have renounced a part of their statutory birthright. The appellants, however, contend, and Russell J. appears to have thought, that your Lordships' House extended other principles, namely, those applicable to servitudes over land acquired, to mere contracts restricting the undertakers' future freedom of action in respect to the business management of their undertaking. This point of view ought therefore to be examined.

The appellants, as I understand them, say that the doctrine is not confined to the creation of servitudes or other derogations by grant from plenary ownership, but extends also to such covenants in perpetuity as may, in events not actually impossible, starve their undertaking and spell its ruin. Southport, they say, now standing in the shoes of the Birkdale Council as well as in its own (if I may somewhat distort their metaphor), has behind it the pockets of the ratepayers of both areas, and though these may be no more inexhaustible than their patience, at least they may prove deeper and more enduring than the paid-up or uncalled capital of the appellant company, or its shareholders' willingness to subscribe to new issues of debentures or of preference stock. The thing speaks for itself. The covenant is fraught with potential suicide for the covenantors, and so is *ultra vires*.

My Lords, this hypothesis is conceivable, though neither from the evidence nor the argument have I gathered why these machinations should be attributed to the respondents or be tolerated by their outraged ratepayers. Municipal finance is capable of much curious development, but I think that among ordinary ratepayers a passion to supply current below cost price to private consumers is purely academic. If it exists at Southport, I think it should be proved by testimony.

The argument must be either that it is one of the direct statutory objects of the Electric Lighting Order that the undertakers should make a profit or at least not suffer any loss, or else that this is an indirect statutory object, since, if the undertakers make no profit, they will either pursue the undertaking without zeal or will drop it, so soon as this imaginary rate-war exhausts their resources.

My Lords, I am afraid this is beyond me. It may be the policy of the Electric Lighting Acts to get trading companies to take up and work Electric Lighting Orders in hope of gain, but I cannot see that it is any part of the direct purposes of the Order, that money should be made or dividends distributed. The primary object of the Electric Lighting Order was to get a supply of electric energy for the area in question, a thing only feasible at the time by getting a trading company to undertake the business. It was not to secure that certain charges should be made or that certain results should be shown upon a profit and loss account. As for the indirect effect, which will follow if no money is made or enough money is lost, the Order itself imposes a maximum price for the current and conceivably, therefore, might itself lead to the exhaustion of the company's funds. How, then, can it be part of the legal objects of the grant of these powers, that they should never result in financial disaster? The Order is really as little concerned with the company's ultimate ability to continue the undertaking as with its earning of a profit. The latter is the company's own affair; the former will simply lead to the revocation of the Order and the grant of a more favourable one to someone else. If this is so, there is a wide and more than sufficient difference between the contract of the Ayr Harbour Trustees not to acquire all that they were intended to acquire, and that of the appellants to obtain the transfer of the Order by covenanting among other considerations for something, which obviously is not and may never be, incompatible with the fulfillment of all the purposes of the Order and most of the purposes of the company's trading as well.

In *York Corporation* v. *Henry Leetham & Sons* there were two navigations, both vested in the Corporation of York, which appear to have differed somewhat in their incidents, the Ouse Navigation and the Foss Navigation. The original Act of 1726, which authorized the former, empowered trustees to levy tolls on craft using the navigation when completed, and, for the purpose of constructing the navigation, authorized them to mortgage these prospective tolls and so to raise the necessary capital. The resources of the trustees were therefore of a character wholly different from those of a limited liability company. A later Act, that of 1732, fixed a schedule of rates and provided that all commodities carried 'shall' bear them, and that it should be lawful for the trustees to take the rates 'by this Act directed and no others', though, if the full revenue derived from these rates proved to be more than was required to maintain the undertaking, there was power to moderate them. The Act, which authorized the latter navigation, provided for the incorporation of a company having a capital of 25,400*l*. in 100*l*. shares and borrowing powers up to 10,000*l*. No distinction appears, from the judgment of Russell J., to have been drawn in argument between these two undertakings, but it is possible that the agreement in dispute, by which the undertakers compounded the rate with a particular customer, might be regarded as a direct breach of the mandatory charging clause of the Ouse Act of 1732, and consequently *ultra vires*. The same view could not arise on the Foss Act. The *ratio decidendi* of the judgment, however, proceeds entirely on the analogy of the *Ayr Harbour* case.

My Lords, with all respect to the learned judge, I am unable to adopt this reasoning. As I have said, it is no part of the intention of the Legislature that the appellants should make a profit or avoid a loss. If, again, the agreement is to be *ultra vires* at all, it must be *ultra vires* all through. In cases like the *Ayr Harbour* case the land acquired under statutory powers was fettered in the undertakers' hands from the time the agreement was made. In the present case the company's activities have not yet been and may never be impaired by the agreement at all. So far it may have been and probably has been safe and beneficial. How then, can it have been *ultra vires* hitherto? There is further, in my opinion, a wide distinction between the position of the appellants and of such undertakers as the Ayr Harbour Trustees. The scheme here is that a limited liability company, not deprived of its right, as such, to go into voluntary liquidation or otherwise to terminate its enterprise, obtained the Order with the Board of Trade's consent and with the like consent may part with it. In other words, the Board of Trade is here the constituted authority, by whose discretionary intervention the supply of electricity may be secured in the interest of the locality. This is a very different scheme from a constitution of undertakers, which under the same statute establishes their existence, confers their powers, and defines their purposes.

It appears to me that no line can be drawn between the agreement now in question and any ordinary trading contract, if the appellants are right in testing the validity of the contract by its ultimate and theoretic possibility of bringing upon them a crippling loss. I do not think that a speculation as to the possible effect of what they have done is a legitimate ground for relieving them from their bargain, and it seems to me that the appeal should be dismissed."

Notes

14–14   (1) In this case it would seem that incompatibility would only arise if property right was created by the contract. It is not clear whether the distinction between property rights and their contract and what might be termed ordinary rights is necessarily a valid one. On this generally see P. Rogerson, "On the Fettering of Public Powers" [1971] P.L. 288.

(2) In *British Transport Commission* v. *Westmorland County Council* [1958] A.C. 126 the issue of compatibility was raised in the context of whether a right of way by a statutory corporation had been competently granted. In response to argument by the Commission that compatibility could only arise if at no point it could be used at any future time or possibly interfere with the statutory purpose of which land was acquired, Lord Simonds stated (at 144):

> "to give to incompatibility such an extended meaning is in effect to reduce the principle to a nullity. For a jury, invited to say that in no conceivable circumstances and at no distance of time could an event possibly happen, could only fold their hands and reply that it was not for them to prophesy what an inscrutable Providence might in all the years to come disclose. I do not disguise from myself that it is difficult to formulate with precision what direction should be given to a jury. But, after all, we live in a world in which our actions are constantly guided by a consideration of reasonable probabilities of risks that can reasonably be foreseen and guarded against, and by a disregard of events of which, even if we think of them as possible, we can fairly say that they are not at all likely to happen. And it is, in my opinion, by such considerations as these, imprecise though they may be, that a tribunal of fact must be guided in determining whether a proposed user of land will interfere with the statutory purpose for which it was acquired."

It was further observed by Lord Radcliffe (at 155) that the approach of Lord Sumner in *Oswald* should not be taken too far:

> "it does not seem to me to offer much help in deciding which are the cases in which the principle of *Paterson's* case [(1881): 6 App. Cas. 833] and *Oswald's* case is to be applied, where, as he says,

'the very nature of the grants or the contract itself' provides the answer, and which are those many other cases in which the test to be applied is the humbler one of incompatibility proved by evidence. The birthright of a statutory corporation includes all those powers and rights with which it is thought proper to invest it at its creation: and I do not think it easy for a court of law to decide merely by the nature of the thing which of those powers are inalienably entailed and which can be disentailed and disposed of by ordinary grant.

In my opinion, we are bound to recognise that the principle of the these two cases cannot be applied in all circumstances and on all occasions to all statutory corporations and public bodies. That, indeed, has already been recognized by the decision of this House in the *Birkdale* case, in which the electric supply company had certainly made a contract which deprived themselves and their successors of power at any future time to raise the charges for their supply beyond the fixed limit, however much the needs of their undertaking might require it. It is of some importance to remember, when searching for a dividing line, that the two cases which 'spoke for themselves' were both concerned with defined areas of land of no great extent, and the possible consequence of renouncing powers over such areas could be stated as a matter of practical observation. But nothing like the same observation can be brought to bear when the factors of the problem are, on the one hand, all the general powers derived by a railway company from the Railway Clauses Consolidation Act, 1845, and, on the other hand, many miles of railway lines covering great varieties of setting. In such cases what I have called the pragmatic test is, I think, to be preferred…"

(3) In *William Cory & Son Ltd* v. *London Corporation* [1951] 2 K.B. 476 a distinction was drawn between a body trading for profit such as that in *Birkdale* and in *Oswald*, with a body performing a purely regulatory role. Here, the corporation as sanitary authority had contracted with Cory to have the latter remove refuse from the City of London by barge. As port health authority, byelaws were made by the corporation which were stringent in their effect and would have required expenditure of over £400 per barge. Cory argued that these byelaws were in breach of an implied term in the parallel contract not to do anything to prevent them performing an obligation under the contract. While accepting that such an implied obligation might exist, on the facts of this case no such term could be implied and so Cory was not entitled to treat the contract as rescinded, although it was accepted that the contract had been frustrated from the date the byelaws came into effect. Is the distinction between a body acting solely for public good and one acting for profit a meaningful one? Does it alleviate any of the difficulties associated with a strict application of the principle in *Oswald*? On this see Mitchell at p. 62.

14–15

(4) Another way of looking at the decision in *Cory* is that it asks the court to consider, in determining the extent of an authority's exercise of one of its powers, the extent to which it may legitimately inhibit its freedom as regards the exercise of another of its powers. A recent example of this occurred in *R.* v. *Hammersmith and Fulham London Borough Council, ex p. Beddowes* [1987] Q.B. 1050. Here a council resolution which purported to dispose of part of a rundown council estate to a private developer was made. In turn it was agreed that in the parts of the estate that the council retained, it would restrict the forms of letting that it would grant. It was observed by Fox L.J. (at 1064) that:

"If a statutory power is lawfully exercised so as to create legal rights and obligations between the council and third parties, the result will be that the council for the time being is bound, even though that hinders or prevents the exercise of other statutory powers."

This suggests that the exercise of one power may properly fetter the exercise of another and in itself will not provide a ground of challenge provided that the decision to exercise the power was taken properly, *i.e.* it does not constitute an abuse of power as detailed in Chapter 6. On this see also *Dowty Boulton Paul Ltd* v. *Wolverhampton Corporation* [1971] 2 All E.R. 277, noted in Chapter 4 in relation to error of law.

(5) The provisions of the Local Government (Contracts) Act 1997 have potential significance for the powers of local authorities to enter into contracts. The general policy of the Act is to encourage private finance initiative partnerships with local authorities and the private sector by removing concerns about the legal powers of local authorities to contract. For some of the case law giving rise to the concern see Chapter 3. The provisions of the Act apply, however, to *any*

contract entered into by a local authority with another person making available assets for services for the purposes of, or in connection with, the discharge of the function by the local authority: section 1(1). "Assets" are further defined by subsection (4) as meaning assets of any description, including land and buildings and plant and equipment. During debate, attempt was made to amend subsection (1) by attempting to widen it to cover all functions whether or not conferred by statute and for all reasonable purposes. This was rejected on the basis that it would involve a much wider and more contentious debate over whether there were non-statutory functions. Another proposed amendment sought to use wording drawn from section 69 of the Local Government (Scotland) Act 1973 (the equivalent English provision being section 111 of the Local Government Act 1972) and expand the meaning of "functions" in this section to include activities which are conducive or incidental to the functions as defined in section 69. This was rejected by the Minister on the basis that:

> "The amendment would enable authorities to enter into contracts with assets or services when relying on subsidiary powers under section 111, instead of primary powers … The amendment would therefore seem to widen the effect of the Bill, which is not our intention. The Bill does not add to local authority's powers" (*Hansard*, H.C. Vol. 297, col. 827).

Note too that subsection (1) actually narrows the scope of discretion which existed under section 69 and which is taken as general authority to enter all contracts. There is a degree of uncertainty as to the exact scope of the legislation, which is borne out by the fact that regulation 5 of the Local Authorities (Contracts) (Scotland) Regulations 1997 provides that where a certificate as to legal power under which it enters into the contract is issued, whether under section 69 or otherwise, the certificate requires to

> "specify in the certificate each statutory provision conferring a relevant function, or, where there are two or more relevant functions, the statutory provisions conferring the main relevant functions".

The regulations further specify that:

> "a function is a relevant function if the contract is calculated to facilitate, or is conducive or incidental to, the discharge of the function".

Contracts which are certified are presumed to be *intra vires*. To be a certified contract, the contract has to be issued under sections 3 and 4 and by section 4(3) the contract must be one operating for at least five years from the provision or making available of services, whether or not with assets, in connection with the discharge of the function of the authority. Note that *vires* includes the question of simple *ultra vires* as well as abuse of discretion: section 2(1). Section 3 sets out these certification requirements and specifies the matters that must be included in the certificate issued by the local authority: see also regulations 3,4 and 5 of the Local Authorities (Contracts) (Scotland) Regulations 1997 above. The presumption set up by the existence of certified contract can, however, be challenged through judicial review: sections 2, 5(1)(*a*). Provisions is made for challenge by way of audit review: section 5(1)(*b*). A certified contract is presumed to be valid for all purposes, unless and until a successful judicial review or audit review occurs. Moreover, even if judicial review or (audit review) is successful, the court can by having regard in particular to the likely consequences for the financial position of the local authority, and for the provision of services to the public, of a contract being found to be *ultra vires*, still order that the contract should be given effect: subsection (3). Note too the provisions of sections 6 and 7 in relation to relevant discharge terms. Discharge terms are terms in the certified contract or part of any other agreement entered into to the parties not later than the day of the contract and which provide for payment of compensatory damages or adjustment between the parties of any rights and liabilities relating to assets or goods provided under the contract or both of those things: section 2(2) (*a*)–(*c*), (3)(*a*),(*c*). Even if the certified contract is found to be *ultra vires*, subsection (4) provides that these discharge terms will have effect. Where no relevant discharge terms have been agreed then section 7(2) provides that the party suffering the loss is entitled to be paid by the local authority and the contract is valid until the time of the determination that it was invalid but had been ended by that time by exceptions of that party of a repudiatory breach by the local authority: subsection (2) (*a*),(*b*).

We have noted below the way in which central government through its legal personification in the Crown can use its contractual powers to pursue policy goals. However, the same freedom has not always been afforded to local government.

Local Government Act 1988

ss. 17, 18

"Public Supply or Works Contracts
Local and other public authority contracts: exclusion of non-commercial considerations

17.–(1) It is the duty of every public authority to which this section applies, in exercising, in relation to its public supply or works contracts, any proposed or any subsisting such contract, as the case may be, any function regulated by this section to exercise that function without reference to matters which are non-commercial matters for the purposes of this section.

(2) The public authorities to which this section applies are those specified in Schedule 2 to this Act.

(3) The contracts which are public supply or works contracts for the purposes of this section are contracts for the supply of goods or materials, for the supply of services or for the execution of works; but this section does not apply in relation to contracts entered into before the commencement of this section.

(4) The functions regulated by this section are —
(a)   the inclusion of persons in or the exclusion of persons from —
  (i)   any list of persons approved for the purposes of public supply or works contracts with the authority, or
  (ii)   any list of persons from whom tenders for such contracts may be invited;
(b)   in relation to a proposed public supply or works contract with the authority —
  (i)   the inclusion of persons in or the exclusion of persons from the group of persons from whom tenders are invited,
  (ii)   the accepting or not accepting the submission of tenders for the contract,
  (iii)   the selecting the person with whom to enter into the contract, or
  (iv)   the giving or withholding approval for, or the selecting or nominating, persons to be sub-contractors for the purposes of the contract; and
(c)   in relation to a subsisting public supply or works contract with the authority —
  (i)   the giving or withholding approval for, or the selecting or nominating, persons to be sub-contractors for the purposes of the contract, or
  (ii)   the termination of the contract.

(5) The following matters are non-commercial matters as regards the public supply or works contracts of a public authority, any proposed or any subsisting such contract, as the case may be, that is to say —
(a)   the terms and conditions of employment by contractors of their workers or the composition of, the arrangements for the promotion, transfer or training of or the other opportunities afforded to, their workforces;
(b)   whether the terms on which contractors contract with their sub-contractors constitute, in the case of contracts with individuals, contracts for the provision by them as self-employed persons of their services only;
(c)   any involvement of the business activities or interests of contractors with irrelevant fields of Government policy;
(d)   the conduct of contractors or workers in industrial disputes between them or any involvement of the business activities of contractors in industrial disputes between other persons;
(e)   the country or territory of origin of supplies to, or the location in any country or territory of the business activities or interests of, contractors;
(f)   any political, industrial or sectarian affiliations or interests of contractors or their directors, partners or employees;
(g)   financial support or lack of financial support by contractors for any institution to or from which the authority gives or withholds support;
(h)   use or non-use by contractors of technical or professional services provided by the authority under the Building Act 1984 or the Building (Scotland) Act 1959.

(6) The matters specified in subsection (5) above include matters which have occurred in the past as well as matters which subsist when the function in question falls to be exercised.

(7) Where any matter referable to a contractor would, as a matter specified in subsection (5) above, be a non-commercial matter in relation to him, the corresponding matter referable to —

14–16

(a)   a supplier or customer of the contractor;

(b)   a sub-contractor of the contractor or his supplier or customer;

(c)   an associated body of the contractor or his supplier or customer; or

(d)   a sub-contractor of an associated body of the contractor or his supplier or customer;

is also, in relation to the contractor, a non-commercial matter for the purposes of this section.

(8) In this section —

'approved list' means such a list as is mentioned in subsection (4)(a) above;

'associated body', in relation to a contractor, means any company which (within the meaning of the Companies Act 1985) is the contractor's holding company or subsidiary or is a subsidiary of the contractor's holding company;

'business' includes any trade or profession;

'business activities' and 'business interests', in relation to a contractor or other person, mean respectively any activities comprised in, or any investments employed in or attributable to, the carrying on of his business and 'activity' includes receiving the benefit of the performance of any contract;

'contractor', except in relation to a subsisting contract, means a 'potential contractor', that is to say —

(a)   in relation to functions as respects an approved list, any person who is or seeks to be included in the list; and

(b)   in relation to functions as respects a proposed public supply or works contract, any person who is or seeks to be included in the group of persons from whom tenders are invited or who seeks to submit a tender for or enter into the proposed contract, as the case may be;

'exclusion' includes removal;

'Government policy' falls within 'irrelevant fields' for the purposes of this section if it concerns matters or defence or foreign or Commonwealth policy and 'involve', as regards business activities and any such field or policy, includes the supply of goods or materials or services to, or the execution of works for, any authority or person having functions or carrying on business in that field and, as regards business interests and any such field of policy, includes investments in any authority or person whose business activities are so involved;

'industrial dispute' has, as regards a dispute in Great Britain, the same meaning as trade dispute in the Trade Union and Labour Relations Act 1974 and 'involve', as regards business activities and an industrial dispute, includes the supply of goods, materials or services to or by, or the execution of works for or by, any party to the dispute, any other person affected by the dispute, or any authority concerned with the enforcement of law and order in relation to the dispute;

'political, industrial or sectarian affiliations or interests' means actual or potential membership of, or actual or potential support for, respectively, any political party, any employers' association or trade union or any society, fraternity or other association;

'suppliers or customers' and 'sub-contractors' includes prospective suppliers or customers and sub-contractors; and 'supplier', in relation to a contractor, includes any person who, in the course of business, supplies him with services or facilities of any description for purposes of his business.

and 'employers' association' and 'trade union' have, as regards bodies constituted under the law of England and Wales or Scotland, the same meaning as in the Trade Union and Labour Relations Act 1974.

(9) This section is subject to section 18 below."

"Race relations matters

18. — (1) Except to the extent permitted by subsection (2) below, section 71 of the Race Relations Act 1976 (local authorities to have regard to need to eliminate unlawful racial discrimination and promote equality of opportunity, and good relations, between persons of different racial groups) shall not require or authorise a local authority to exercise any function regulated by section 17 above by reference to a non-commercial matter.

(2) Subject to subsection (3) below, nothing in section 17 above shall preclude a local authority from —

(a)   asking approved questions seeking information or undertakings relating to workforce matters and considering the responses to them, or

(b)   including in a draft contract or draft tender for a contract terms or provisions relating to workforce matters and considering the responses to them,

if, as the case may be, consideration of the information, the giving of the undertaking or the inclusion of the term is reasonably necessary to secure compliance with the said section 71.

(3) Subsection (2) above does not apply to the function of terminating a subsisting contract and, in relation to functions as respects approved lists or proposed contracts, does not authorise questions in other than written form.

(4) Where it is permissible under subsection (2) above to ask a question it is also permissible to make, it if is in writing, an approved request for evidence in support of an answer to the question.

(5) The Secretary of State may specify —

(a)   questions which are to be approved questions for the purposes of this section; and

(b)   descriptions of evidence which, in relation to approved questions, are to be approved descriptions of evidence for those purposes;

and the powers conferred by this subsection shall be exercised in writing.

(6) Any specification under subsection (5) above may include such consequential or transitional provisions as appear to the Secretary of State to be necessary or expedient.

(7) In this section —

'approved question' means a question for the time being specified by the Secretary of State under subsection (5) above;

'approved request for evidence' means a request for evidence of a description for the time being specified by the Secretary of State under that subsection in relation to an approved question;

'workforce matters' means matters falling within paragraph (a), but no other paragraph, of subsection (5) of section 17 above;

and any expression used in this section and section 17 above has the same meaning in this section as in that section."

Notes

(1) The scope of section 17 is broad. In terms of Schedule 2 to the Act, many public bodies **14–17** are subject to its restrictions, including local authorities and police authorities. Note also that in terms of section 19(7), specific authority is given to potential or former contractors for the purpose of bringing judicial review proceedings. Breach of the section in itself is not a criminal offence but is actionable by any person who in consequence suffers loss or damage.

Some guidance as to the terms of sections 17 and 18 has been afforded by government circulars. Thus DoE Circular 8/88 indicates that the section prohibits local authorities from banning contracts with contractors who have worked for nuclear missile bases, but does allow enquiry as to contractors' health and safety records. Similarly, local authorities are entitled to ask questions about behaviour under race relations legislation on the basis of a list of approved questions contained in Annex B to Scottish Development Department Circular 7/1988. In *C & E Campleman v. Clydesdale District Council*, 1992 G.W.D. 22–1280 poor financial status was held to be a commercial consideration whereas in *R. v. Islington London Borough Council, ex parte Building Employers Confederation* [1989] I.R.L.R. 382, Q.B. a clause requiring compliance with all of section 6 of the Sex Discrimination Act 1975 was unlawful.

(2) Another significant form of control over contracted powers of local authorities came in the form of compulsory competitive tendering. By Part III of the Local Government, Planning and Land Act 1980, direct labour organisations of local authorities were, before using the DLO for construction or maintenance work, required to put such work out to competitive tender. The principle of CCT was extended by the Local Government Act 1988, Pt, I, s. 1–16. Local authorities and certain other public authorities could only undertake certain activities if they could do so competitively. The activities referred to initially included refuse collection, cleaning and school catering: section 2(2). Other activities can be included: section 2(3). As with the provisions of the 1980 Act, requirements of CCT cover both works contracts and functional work as defined by section 3(2), (4). The local authority is subject to accounting and other financial objectives: sections 9(1), 10(1), 11(1). The Secretary of State has powers which parallel those contained in the 1980 Act in sections 13(1), (3), 14(1), (3) in relation to the issuing of a notice and directions as to how tendering is handled. Such a notice is subject to judicial review: *Ettrick and Lauderdale District Council v. Secretary of State for Scotland*, 1995 S.L.T. 996 (direction reduced on the ground that it was unreasonable as ill founded and unjustified). Note, however, that most of the CCT provisions of the 1980 and 1988 Acts have now been suspended: see the Local Government (Exemption from Competition) (Scotland) Order 1995, as amended by the Local Government (Exemption from Competition) (Scotland) Amendment Order 1998. In its place, the Government has put a system of Best Value. Provided that a local authority can

demonstrate that its services, whether works or functional, meet the criteria of Best Value, it is free to choose which method achieves those criteria, *i.e.* there is no compulsion to use tendering. Where a local authority does not adhere to Best Value, then the Secretary of State can reintroduce CCT. However, under Best Value not all of the provisions of CCT are suspended. Most importantly, the power of the Secretary of State to issue a notice and directions under the relevant provisions of the 1980 and 1988 Acts are retained as are the accounting provisions. For further details on CCT see *Stair Memorial Encyclopaedia*, Vol. 14, "Local Government", paras 901–1000 and C.M.G. Himsworth, *Local Government Law in Scotland* (1995), Chap. 6. It will be gathered that best value is to be put on a detailed statutory footing in Scotland. It will be a matter for the Scottish Parliament to consider. A detailed programme is contained in the White Paper *Modern Local Government in Touch with the People* and see now the Local Government Bill (1998–1999 H.C. 52) in relation to England and Wales. Scottish proposals are unlikely to differ radically from those contained in that Bill.

(3) Not only local government has been subject to tendering control. Central government agencies are also subject to competition by virtue of the "market testing" programme, on which see *Competing for Quality*, Cm. 730 (1991). Similarly, section 79 of Part II of the Deregulation and Contracting Out Act 1994 allows Ministers to make Orders enabling themselves or persons holding an office under a Public General Act to authorise any person, and this will generally be a commercial organisation, to undertake statutory or common law functions on behalf of the Minister or office holder in which to widen the range of central government activities subject to market testing. On this see M. Freedland, "Government by Contract and Public Law" [1994] P.L. 86 and "Privatising *Carltona*: Part II of the Deregulation and Contracting Out Act 1994" [1995] P.L. 21 and Finch and Ashton, pp. 83–91.

PUBLIC AUTHORITIES AND THE CROWN: DELICTUAL LIABILITY

14–18   Public authorities may both sue and be sued in delict. This liability is of interest to administrative lawyers because of the extent to which the ordinary principles of liability are, or should be, modified to take account of what is perceived to be the special position of public authorities. In many cases the position of the public authority should make no difference to its liability. There does not appear to be any difference between the liability applying to the driver of a lorry owned by a private employer or the driver of a lorry owned by a local authority. On the other hand, the position of public authorities is complicated because most of their powers and duties are usually derived from statute and therefore questions of *vires* arise. Also, statutory authority may be a defence to an action for delict. Similarly failure to perform a statutory power or duty or its negligent or malicious performance may create liability. For a general survey see Finch and Ashton, pp. 440–463; W.J. Stewart, *Delict* (3rd ed., 1998), p. 90; D. Brodie, "Public Authorities and the Duty of Care", 1996 J.R. 127; E. Galy, "Civil Liability of Public Authorities" [1986] 136 N.L.J. 435, 495; P.P. Craig, "Negligence in the Exercise of a Statutory Power" (1978) 94 L.Q.R. 428; J.J. Doyle, "The Liability of Public Authorities" [1994] 1 Tort L. Rev 189; S. Todd, "The Negligence Liability of Public Authorities: Divergence in the Common Law" (1986) 102 L.Q.R. 370; J. Sopinka, "The Liability of Public Authorities: Drawing the Line" [1993] 1 Tort L. Rev 123; and D. Brodie, "Liability of Public Authorities" [1997] Rep. L.B. 14–2 and "The Boundaries of Murphy: Part II" [1997] Rep L.B. 16–3.

THE DEFENCE OF STATUTORY AUTHORITY

14–19   Statutory authority as a defence may arise where the statute in question orders the conduct which is alleged to be harmful. It is more usual, however, for the statute simply to authorise or empower a course of action which would otherwise constitute an actionable delict. Unless the statute provides for some form of remedy or compensation then the injured party has no redress.

Bell v. McGlennan

1992 S.C. 41

"Action of Damages

James Bell raised an action against John McGlennan, the procurator fiscal for Kilmarnock, in respect of alleged damage caused to subjects at 27 Grange Terrace, Kilmarnock, Ayrshire, in the execution by Clifford James Jones, an officer of the radio investigation service of the Department of Trade and Industry, of a search warrant granted by the sheriff on 17 March 1989, in respect of physical damage to three items of radio apparatus seized under the warrant during their detention by the defender, and in respect of the detention of the radio apparatus from 19 March 1989 until 1 November 1989.

The case came for debate before the sheriff on 27 September 1990 ...

On 27 September 1990 the sheriff *dismissed* the action.

The pursuer appealed to the sheriff principal.

On 3 January 1991 the sheriff principal *refused* the appeal.

The pursuer appealed to the Court of Session...

The following opinion of the court was delivered by Lord McCluskey:"

14–20

LORD MC CLUSKEY: "... On 17 March 1989 the respondent by petition to the sheriff of North Strathclyde at Kilmarnock sought and obtained a search warrant. The petition (no. 9/1 of process, produced by the respondent) alleged that there was reasonable ground for suspecting that an offence under s. 1(1) of the Wireless Telegraphy Act 1949 was being or had been committed at premises at 27 Grange Terrace, Kilmarnock. That section inter alia makes it an offence for a person to establish or use any station for wireless telegraphy or to use any apparatus for wireless telegraphy except under and in accordance with a licence granted by the Secretary of State. The warrant was sought under s. 15(1) of the Wireless Telegraphy Act 1949 and authority was sought for Clifford James Jones, officer of the radio investigation service, Department of Trade and Industry (and others) to search those premises and to seize apparatus which appeared to have been used in connection with the alleged offence. Sheriff Croan granted the warrant as craved. On the same day, in the same court there was presented to the same sheriff a petition at the instance of the said Clifford James Jones, also seeking warrant for Clifford James Jones (and the same 'others' named in the earlier petition) to search the same premises for the same purpose under the same section. The said sheriff granted the warrant as craved in the second petition in terms of the Wireless Telegraphy Act 1949, as amended. The result was that two virtually identical warrants were granted on 17 March 1989. It was also common ground before us that the latter warrant (the one obtained on Clifford James Jones' petition) was executed by the said Clifford James Jones and that the warrant obtained on the respondent's petition was not used by anyone for any purpose: it disappears from the story and played no further part in anything that followed. On 19 March 1989, acting on the authority of the search warrant which he had petitioned for and obtained, Clifford Jones seized three CB tranceivers belonging to the appellant from the named premises, which were the appellant's premises. The appellant was left with a receipt in respect of the seizure. Thereafter the items seized were retained by those who had seized them until 1 November 1989 when they were returned to the appellant.

No criminal proceedings were taken against anyone following the seizure. Summary proceedings became incompetent on or before 17 September 1989 by virtue of s. 331 of the Criminal Procedure (Scotland) Act 1975. An abortive attempt was made by the respondent on 23 September to commence criminal proceedings, but the respondent soon realised that he had blundered and the purported complaint was not proceeded with. It is not in dispute that as no criminal proceedings were competently taken within the six month time limit allowed by s. 331 of the Criminal Procedure (Scotland) Act 1975 then, because of the terms of s. 83(1) of the Telecommunications Act 1984, the seized property should have been returned not later than six months after it was seized, i.e. not later than 19 September 1989. Against this background, adequately averred and — though this is not strictly speaking material — conceded and admitted by the respondent, the pursuer claims damages under four heads. He claims £56 in respect of damage to a garden gate caused, he avers, in the course of the execution of the search warrant. He claims £45 in respect of the cost of repairing two of the tranceivers which he avers had become damaged by dampness between the time they were seized and the time when they were returned to appellant's custody. He also claims a sum in respect of the loss of benefit for his CB licence for the year 1989 and a sum representing the loss of use of the apparatus for the 36 weeks during which the appellant was deprived of its possession.

Leaving aside for the moment the specification by the appellant in his pleadings of how any physical damage was done, we consider whether or not the appellant has averred enough to entitle him to a proof on the question of the responsibility of the respondent for the actings which are said to have caused the damage complained of. The appellant in his pleadings has, in our opinion, averred quite sufficient to justify his being allowed a proof before answer in respect of the responsibility of the respondent for the actings of those who obtained the search warrant which was executed, and, on its authority, seized the tranceivers and retained them until 1 November 1989. It is sufficient to point to the averments to the effect that the respondent himself applied for an identical search warrant on 17 March 1989 and obtained one, and that Clifford James Jones was the person whose oath was taken in support of the application and who was to be authorised to enter the appellant's premises to search for the apparatus to be seized. What appears to have happened is that that petition and warrant were effectively superseded by the petition brought by Clifford James Jones himself and the warrant granted by the sheriff to him. It may be that the respondent had doubts as to whether or not it was not competent for him to obtain such a warrant under s. 15(1) of the Wireless Telegraphy Act 1949, but we were not expressly told that and it is not of importance. Furthermore, the pursuer avers that shortly before the apparatus was returned he obtained a letter from the government department which had seized it indicating that they now had authority from the respondent to return the radio equipment; and, after the equipment was returned, the same government department advised the appellant in writing that the items seized had been held in safe custody 'until advised by the Procurator Fiscal Service'. As noted earlier, the respondent did not raise criminal proceedings against the appellant or anybody else within the six months allowed by s. 331, and some days thereafter a time barred complaint was served upon the appellant and then withdrawn. It was following these events that the respondent appears to have authorised the return of the seized equipment. There is thus ample in the pursuer's averments to enable the appellant to invite the court to hold the respondent and defender vicariously responsible for those who intromitted with the seized equipment between 19 March 1989 and 1 November 1989.

The main argument for the respondent in the court below was that s. 456 of the Criminal Procedure (Scotland) Act 1975 conferred immunity upon the respondent in respect of any acts done consequent upon the obtaining of the warrant, including damage to the garden gate, damage by storing in a damp place to the tranceivers, and the prolonged retention of the equipment. The submission was that any acts done by the respondent were done under Pt. II of the 1975 Act. Section 456 need not be quoted in full here but the material parts are as follows: [his Lordship quoted the terms of s. 456(1) continued:]

We should be reluctant to attempt to make an authoritative interpretation of this section because the debate before us as to its meaning was brief and unilluminating. There can be no doubt that, if s. 456 applied, both the sheriff and the sheriff principal were right in holding that the pursuer and appellant could not surmount the obstacle presented by s. 456 unless he averred that all three of the conditions imposed by paras. (*a*), (*b*) and (*c*) were met. The result should have been that, as the appellant had not made the necessary averments of imprisonment, quashing and malice, the plea to the relevancy (not the plea to the competency) should have been upheld. But what was not appreciated in the court below was that the acts of Clifford James Jones, for which the respondent may be held vicariously responsible and liable, may well not have been proceedings or acts under Pt. II of the 1975 Act at all, but, if anything, proceedings or acts done under the Wireless Telegraphy Act of 1949 as amended. On that view, s. 456 would have no bearing on the matter. This is an issue that must, in our opinion, be resolved after proof. Furthermore, though this is less important, it appears to us to be statable that para. (*b*) envisages that the proceeding or act must be of such a character that it is capable of being 'quashed'. That concept is one that can hardly be fitted to an act such as inflicting physical damage by the negligent handling or storage of a piece of radio equipment; it is not possible to conceive of the notion that the act of the procurator fiscal or his agent in, for example, dropping a transceiver and breaking it could be 'quashed'. It is thus at the very least arguable, in our opinion, that the words 'act done' in subs. (1) are not apt to cover every act which a procurator fiscal or his agent may do in the purported performance of the duties of prosecutor in the public interest. In particular, we have not so far been persuaded that these words are apt to confer an immunity in respect of the negligent handling of property belonging to a person against whom a search warrant is being executed. Thus the applicability of s. 456 to the circumstances of this case is in doubt. In the debates in the court below it was assumed by all concerned that all the actings in question were under Pt. II of the 1975 Act; but it is by no means clear that the actings in question were under Pt. II of the 1975 Act and not under s. 15(1) of the Wireless Telegraphy Act 1949. The petition in respect of which the relevant warrant was granted bears to be under the Wireless Telegraphy Act 1949 and makes no mention of the Criminal Procedure (Scotland) Act 1975. This is in contrast to the respondent's petition presented on the same day. The appellant averred and the respondent admitted in the closed record that the respondent had obtained a search warrant by petition in accordance with s. 310 of the Criminal Procedure (Scotland) Act 1975; it may be that that misled everyone in the court below to think that s. 456 applied. The discussion of the interpretation of s. 456 took place in that context. That discussion had been effectively superseded by the recognition and acknowledgment by the respondent's counsel that the relevant proceedings may not have been under Pt. II of the 1975 Act.

In relation to the retention (by persons for whom the respondent is relevantly averred to have vicarious responsibility) of the items seized and retained during the six months that followed their seizure we are of the opinion that the pursuer has made no relevant averments which would entitle him to damages for loss flowing simply from the retention from him during that period of the articles in question. The statutes in question (the 1949 and 1975 Acts as amended) make it abundantly plain that articles seized under a properly obtained search warrant could be retained for six months or for such longer period as was appropriate if proceedings were raised timeously. In the particular circumstances of this case it is plain from the appellant's pleadings that those who seized the goods were entitled to hold them from him for six months if the warrant itself was legally granted. In our view it is clear that there are no sufficient averments to the effect that the warrant under which the equipment was in fact seized was an illegal warrant or improperly obtained and we consider that no relevant basis has been made for a claim by the appellant in respect of loss during that period, being the loss flowing from the mere depriving the appellant of the equipment.

In relation to the retention from the appellant of the equipment during the period between 17 September 1989 and 1 November 1989 we consider that the appellant has made a claim which is relevant for inquiry; indeed no attempt was made by counsel for the respondent before us to justify the retention of the equipment during that period. It was accepted by counsel that the statutory authority for retaining the goods from their owner, the appellant, ceased at the expiry of the six months period. Furthermore, standing the terms of s. 331 of the 1975 Act, preventing any prosecution after the expiry of the same six month period, and s. 83(1) of the Telecommunications Act 1984, it could well be that those who retained the equipment during that time were acting beyond their statutory powers. In these circumstances it was accepted that s. 456 might confer no immunity in respect of being actings which were ultra vires. On that basis these actings in retaining the equipment without any statutory warrant could not be said to be 'under this Part of this Act' (words quoted from s. 456(1)). Counsel for the respondent also acknowledged that if the procurator fiscal stepped outwith his statutory powers and acted ultra vires he could not plead any special immunity based upon the common law. In particular, in a case where that had happened, it would not be necessary for a pursuer who was claiming damages in respect of the illegal detention of and damage to his property to aver malice and want of probable cause. It would be enough to aver illegal actings resulting in loss. In our view that is precisely what the pursuer has done in respect of the loss attributable to this period and we consider that his claim is relevant for inquiry."

Notes

(1) Where the act of a public authority would be a delict if committed by a private person **14–21** and it is *ultra vires* the authority, the defence has no application. Thus in *Smith v. East Elloe Regional District Council* [1952] C.P.L. 738 damages were awarded for trespass where a local authority had continued to requisition the plaintiff's property although the lawful purposes of the requisition (to house wartime evacuees) ceased. Conversely, a public authority may not argue in its defence that an act alleged to be delict was *ultra vires* and therefore one which it had no legal power to perform: *Campbell v. Paddington Corporation* [1911] 1 K.B. 869. It is always a matter of statutory interpretation as to whether Parliament has ordered the conduct in question and which therefore places a duty on the defender to act in the manner specified or has simply authorised the conduct by empowering the conferring authority to act: *R.H.M. Bakeries (Scotland) Ltd v. Strathclyde Regional Council*, 1985 S.C. (H.L.) 17 at 45 *per* Lord Fraser of Tullybelton.

(2) The issue of liability often depends on the precise expression of the statutory authorisation, and not necessarily on whether that authorisation is a power or a duty. Thus in *Metropolitan Asylum District v. Hill* (1881) 6 App. Cas. 193 general power to build a smallpox hospital did not confer a defence of statutory authority to permit nuisance. No specific site had been provided in terms of the empowering statute for the hospital to be built. If it had been, then the authority would have been under a duty to build such a hospital and that would have negatived the liability which would otherwise have existed. Most case law involves widely stated and general permissive powers as opposed to detailed statutory criteria.

(3) The defence does not, however apply where an act is carried out which need not have been performed at all or which does more damage than the necessity of the case requires. In *B. v. Forsey*, 1987 S.L.T. 681; 1988 S.L.T. 572, H.L. a patient complained that he had been unlawfully detained by a hospital. The hospital did have power to detain the patient under the terms of the

Mental Health (Scotland) Act 1984 but this was subject to a time restriction. The hospital detained the patient beyond that time and admitted that they were exceeding their statutory authority but argued that they were acting in good faith and in the patient's interest and that such a power existed at common law. In the face of express statutory provision, and the failure to establish a common law position, it was held that the hospital's actions, however well intentioned, were unlawful. See now, however, the Mental Health (Detention) (Scotland) Act 1991 and generally C.T. Reid, "Damages for Abuse of Power" [1989] P.L. 395 and Finch and Ashton, pp. 461–463.

NEGLIGENT EXERCISE OF POWERS AND DUTIES AND BREACH OF STATUTORY DUTY

14–22   Liability may arise for failure to perform statutory duties and for the negligent exercise of powers and duties. This is a difficult area as the case law over the years has seemed to go in a number of different directions. The difficulty for Scots law is compounded by the fact that much of the discussion has taken place in English courts, the most authoritative recent discussion being in the case of *X* below. It is therefore not clear to what extent Scots law is similar to or distinct from English law. When the issue has arisen at all in Scotland, it has typically been in the Outer House. The following extracts represent a general survey of the position.

Hallett v. Nicholson

1979 S.C. 1

14–23   LORD DUNPARK: "In this action the pursuers claim reparation from the defenders in respect of the death of their parents in a fire which occurred during the night 23rd/24th July, 1973, in the defenders' hotel in Oban when Mr and Mrs Hallett were occupying as guests a room on the top floor. The pursuers' claim is based on the defenders' failure to fulfil their duty to take reasonable care for the safety of their hotel guests by providing adequate fire precautions. In support of this claim the pursuers refer to a report made by an officer employed by the area fire authority following his inspection of the premises on the 2nd October, 1972, in which he stated that 'the means of escape provided fall well below the standards of modern day requirements.' The defenders deny liability and blame the third parties, in their capacity as statutory fire authority for the Oban area, for the death of Mr and Mrs Hallett on the ground that the third parties were in breach of a duty to take reasonable care for the safety of guests in the defenders' hotel. These averments have not been adopted by the pursuers, and counsel for the pursuers' case against the defenders should be disposed of by proof before answer. I heard debate on the procedure roll when counsel for the third parties moved me to sustain their plea that the defenders' averments against the third parties were irrelevant and for dismissal of the action in so far as directed against them.

I find it unnecessary to rehearse the averments which narrate the existence and non-existence of fire precautions in this hotel. The defenders' averments relating to the third parties' duty of care and breach thereof are derived from the duties imposed, and powers conferred, upon the third parties by the Fire Precautions Act 1971. Accordingly, before I consider the arguments presented to me, I refer to the relevant provisions of that Act. The preamble states it to be 'An Act to make further provision for the protection of persons from fire risks; and for purposes connected therewith.' The Act received the Royal Assent on 27th May 1971, and came into operation on 1st June 1972. Section I requires premises used for certain purposes, including the provision of sleeping accommodation, to have a fire certificate issued by the fire authority as defined in section 43(1). Section 5 of the Act relates to the application for, and issue of, fire certificates. When an application for a fire certificate with respect to any premises has been duly made to the relevant fire authority, section 5(3) imposes upon that authority the duties of causing to be carried out an inspection of the relevant building and, if satisfied as to the matters specified in the subsection, of issuing a fire certificate covering the relevant use of the building. Where the fire authority is not satisfied that the means specified in subsection (3) are such as may reasonably be required in the circumstances of the case in connection with the relevant use of the building, section 5(4) requires the fire authority to serve a notice on the applicant (a) informing him of that fact and of the steps which would have to be taken to satisfy the fire authority on the matters specified in subsection (3), and (b) notifying the applicant that the fire authority will not issue a fire certificate covering that use unless those steps were taken within a specified time. It also provides that a certificate shall be deemed to have been refused if it is not issued at the end of the time specified in the notice or extended by the fire authority. Section 6 governs the contents of fire certificates. Section 7 makes it an offence for the occupier of premises to use them for a purpose which requires a fire certificate without the necessary certificate. Section 8 prescribes procedure designed to ensure that an existing fire certificate is properly related to the conditions currently prevailing in the premises. Section 9 provides for appeals to the local sheriff court. Section 10 applies to premises being used for a purpose for which a fire certificate is required.

[His Lordship quoted sections 10(2, 18 and 19)]

The material admitted facts are as follows: —

(1) A fire certificate was required for the use of the defenders' premises as a hotel with effect from 1st June 1972.

(2) Prior to 1st June 1972 the defenders made a section 1 application for a fire certificate. The defenders aver that this was done in March 1972, but the third parties aver that the application was made on 24th May 1972.

(3) The defenders wrote to the fire master on 15th September 1972 (No. 21 of Process) in the following terms: — 'Further to my telephone call of to-day. As advised I have to change the boiler-room and oil tank from outside the building to inside and I also intend to make other alterations to comply with the Fire Precautions Act 1971. In the circumstances I would be grateful if I could have my premises inspected by you and also have your advice on location of the new boiler-room and in fact all other alterations. Intend having my architect present when you are here and I would be grateful if you would advise me of the date of your intended visit about a week beforehand so that I can make arrangements with him. I would like if at all possible to have the inspection by the 9th October 1972, as I close the Hotel for the winter months on that date and I would like to commence alterations right away as we re-open on the 7th April 1973.'

(4) On 25th September 1972 the firemaster replied as follows: — '*Fire Precautions Act* 1971. I refer to your letter of 15th September 1972, and your request for an inspection of the Esplanade Hotel, Oban, by one of my Fire Prevention Officers to give advice on complying with the above Act. One of my officers will be in Oban in Monday, 2nd October 1972, and will inspect your premises on that date. My Officer will contact you at the Hotel at 11 a.m.'

(5) On 23rd October 1972 the firemaster wrote to the first-named defender (No. 23 of Process) as follows: — 'As requested by you the above premises have been inspected by one of my Fire Prevention Officers with regard to general fire precautions and with a view to giving advice on meeting the standards of the Fire Precautions Act 1971. I enclose a copy of my Officer's report which will I trust be of value to you. If I can be of any further assistance please do not hesitate to contact me.'

(6) The copy Report is No. 24 of Process.

(7) *Quoad* Nos. 21 to 24 of Process the parties have renounced probation.

The defenders do not aver that they had any further communication with the third parties after October 1972. The defenders admit the pursuers' averments that there was a fire in the said hotel during the night of 23rd/24th July 1973 and that the pursuers' parents, who were occupying a room on the top floor of the hotel, died in the fire. These averments are not admitted by the third parties.

The defenders' case against the third parties is based on three alternative grounds. The main case is that, the defenders having applied for a section I certificate, the third parties were bound to carry out a section 5(3) inspection of the premises for the purpose of deciding whether or not to grant a certificate: that the extent of fire risk in the hotel was known to the third parties following their inspection on 2nd October 1972: and that this knowledge imposed upon the third parties the duty to take reasonable care for the safety of future hotel guests. The defenders then found upon three averments of fact as imposing upon the third parties the duty of advising the defenders not to open the hotel until all the measures recommended in their Report had been completed, and of making a section 10(2) application to the Sheriff Court at Oban before 7th April 1973 for an order prohibiting the use of the hotel for overnight guests until, in terms of section 10(2), such steps had been taken as, in the opinion of the court, were necessary to reduce the fire risk to a reasonable level. The three averments of fact upon which these duties are based are as follows: (1) that the third parties knew or ought to have known that the defenders intended to re-open the hotel on 7th April 1973: (2) that the third parties knew or ought to have known that all the measures recommended in their Report could not be completed by the said date or during the course of the 1973 season: and (3) that the risk to hotel guests was so serious that it could not be reduced to a reasonable level of safety until all the principal measures recommended in the Report had been completed...

Senior counsel for the defenders argued that, *esto* it was not a section 5(3) inspection, the third parties were in breach of this subsection of the Act. I do not agree. In the first place, the 1971 Act specifies no time limit within which the section 5(3) inspection must be made after receipt of the application for a fire certificate. I do not know whether the spate of applications for fire certificates in 1972 and the demand for structural work, such as the provision of fire doors, were so heavy that fire authorities decided that some period of grace was required before they began to operate subsections (3) and (4) of section 5 of the Act. *Esto* this was not a section 5(3) inspection, the reason is irrelevant because Parliament did not bind fire authorities to make such an inspection within any specific period after receipt of an application for a fire certificate. In the second place, a breach of the duty to inspect imposed by section 5(3) does not advance the defenders' case against the third parties as the defenders, rightly, did not contend that this breach was actionable at civil law. The peculiarity of the defenders' position is that, if the defenders had not specifically requested an inspection in their September letter and no inspection had been made by the third parties before the fire, they would presumably have had to found on the third parties' failure to perform a statutory duty of inspection within a reasonable time after receipt of the application, when the statute is silent as to time limit. They would, I believe, have had to use the same foundation if the fire had occurred before the inspection on 2nd October. These examples seem to me to illustrate the difficulty which the defenders have in deriving a duty of care from the duties and powers imposed upon the third parties by the 1971 Act.

The propositions upon which the defenders' case is founded may, I think, be put thus — although they were not so formulated —

(1) The 1971 Act was passed, as the preamble states. to make further provision for the protection of persons from fire risk.

(2) The Act and regulations required the defenders' hotel to have a fire certificate issued by the local Fire Authority.

(3) Fire Authorities have a statutory duty to inspect premises which have to have a fire certificate.

(4) The relevant fire authority inspected these premises and found them wanting.

(5) *Ergo* the third parties came under the common law duty of taking reasonable care to protect from injury future hotel guests, who they ought to have foreseen might be injured by fire unless the defenders implemented the inspector's recommendations.

(6) The Act laid upon the third parties the duty of enforcing its provisions *quoad* the defenders' hotel.

(7) As the third parties were empowered by statute to apply to the Sheriff for an order prohibiting the use of the building as a residential hotel until all the principal measures recommended in their Report had been completed, they were bound to discharge their common law duty by advising the defenders not to re-open the hotel in 1973 until all the said measures had been completed and, as they did not do that and ought to have known that the hotel was re-opened without the recommended measures being completed, by making the said application to the court.

Now, as Lord Wilberforce pointed out in *Anns* v. *London Borough of Merton* [1977] 2 All E.R. 492, H.L., the proximity test, which gives rise to a duty of care between parties *inter se* cannot be applied *mutatis mutandis* to a public authority with statutory duties and powers. I shall quote from the speech of Lord Wilberforce, but, before I do so, I table the propositions which I extract from the decisions of the House of Lords in *Anns* and in *Dorset Yacht Co.* v. *Home Office* [1970] A.C. 1004, as follows: —

(1) Acts or omissions committed by a statutory authority in the proper exercise of its statutory duties or powers do not found a cause of civil action (see *Sheppard* v. *Glossop Corporation* [1921] 3 K.B. 132).

(2) Acts or omissions which are committed by a statutory authority in the course of an improper exercise of its statutory duties or powers and which infringe the rights of third parties may be actionable at civil law.

(3) For such an exercise to be improper, it must be either (a) not authorised by statute or (b) not made *bona fide* in the interests of the public within the limits of any statutory discretion.

In *Anns* the House of Lords held that a local authority, who were responsible by statute for the supervision and control of the construction of buildings, could owe to the subsequent owners of such buildings the duty to take reasonable care that the buildings were soundly constructed. The headnote reads: 'The fact that an act had been performed in the exercise of a statutory power did not exclude the possibility that the act might be a breach of the common law duty of care. It was irrelevant to the existence of a duty of care whether what was created by the statute was a duty or a power; the duty of care might exist in either case. The difference was that, in the case of a power, liability could not exist unless the act complained of was outside the ambit of the power.' At page 500 of the report Lord Wilberforce, whose speech was approved by Lords Diplock, Simon and Russell, said this: — 'Although, as I have suggested, a situation of "proximity" existed between the council and owners and occupiers of the houses, I do not think that a description of the council's duty can be based on the "neighborhood" principle alone or on any such factual relationship as "control" as suggested by the Court of Appeal. So to base it would be to neglect an essential factor which is that the local authority is a public body, discharging functions under statute: its powers and duties are definable in terms of public not private law. The problem which this type of action creates is to define the circumstances in which the law should impose, over and above, or perhaps alongside, these public law powers and duties, a duty in private law towards individuals such that they may sue for damages in a civil court. It is in this context that the distinction sought to be drawn between duties and mere powers has to be examined. Most, indeed probably all, statutes relating to public authorities or public bodies contain in them a large area of policy. The courts call this "discretion", meaning that the decision is one for the authority or body to make, and not for the courts. Many statutes, also, prescribe or at least presuppose the practical execution of policy decisions: a convenient description of this is to say that in addition to the area of policy or discretion, there is an operational area. Although this distinction between the policy area and the operational area is convenient, and illuminating, it is probably a distinction of degree; many 'operational' powers or duties have in them some element of 'discretion.' It can safely be said that the more 'operational' a power or a duty may be, the easier it is to superimpose on it a common law duty of care.'

His Lordship went on to point out that local authorities are public bodies operating under statute with a clear responsibility (in the *Anns* case) for public health in their area, and that they must make their discretionary decisions responsibly and for reasons which accord with the statutory purpose. In pursuance of their public duties they must give proper consideration to the question whether they should inspect foundations of buildings before they are covered over. 'Their immunity from attack, in the event of failure to inspect... although great is not absolute. And because it is not absolute, the necessary premise for the proposition 'if no duty to inspect, then no duty to take care in inspection' vanishes. Passing then to the duty as regards inspection, if made. On principle there must surely be a duty to exercise reasonable care. The standard of care must be related to the duty to be performed — namely to ensure compliance with the byelaws. It must be related to the fact that the person responsible for construction in accordance with the byelaws is the builder, and that the inspector's function is supervisory. It must be related to the fact that once the inspector has passed the foundations they will be covered up, with no subsequent opportunity for inspection. But this duty, heavily operational though it may be, is still a duty arising under the statute. There may be a discretionary element in its exercise, discretionary as to the time and manner of inspection, and the techniques to be used. A plaintiff complaining of negligence must prove, the burden being on him, that action taken was not within the limits of a discretion *bona fide* exercised, before he can begin to rely on a common law duty of care. But if he can do this, he should, in principle, be able to sue.'

Lord Wilberforce summarised the position of a public authority by referring to the speech of Lord Diplock in *Dorset Yacht Co.* v. *Home Office* [1970] A.C. 1004, at pages 1064 *et seq*, and said, at page 503 of the report in *Anns*: 'My noble and learned friend points out that the accepted principles which are applicable to powers conferred by a private Act of Parliament, as laid down in *Geddis* v. *Bann Reservoir Proprietors* (1878) 3 App. Cas. 430, cannot automatically be applied to public statutes which confer a large measure of discretion on public authorities. As regards the latter, for a civil action based on negligence at common law to succeed, there must be acts or omissions taken outside the limits of the delegated discretion; in such a case 'its actionability falls to be determined by the civil law principles of negligence.' It is for this reason that the law, as stated in some of the speeches in the *East Suffolk* case [1941] A.C. 74. but not in those of Lord Atkin or Lord Thankerton, requires at the present time to be understood and applied with the recognition that, quite apart from such consequences as may flow from an examination of the duties laid down by the particular statute, there may be room, once one is outside the area of legitimate discretion or policy, for a duty of care at common law. It is irrelevant to the existence of this duty of care whether what is created by the statute is a duty or a power: the duty of care may exist in either case. The difference between the two lies in this, that, in the case of a power, liability cannot exist unless the act complained of lies outside the ambit of the power.'

The *Anns* case was sent to trial in order to determine whether or not any inspection of the relevant foundations had been made: if not, the circumstances in which no inspection was made: and, if an inspection was made, whether it was made by an inspector who, acting otherwise than in the *bona fide* exercise of any discretion under the Public Health Act, failed to exercise reasonable care to ensure that the byelaws applicable to the foundations were complied with.

Counsel for the defenders founded on the case of *Dutton* v. *Bognor Regis U.D.C.* [1972] 1 Q.B. 373 for the proposition that, as the third parties have a statutory duty of enforcing the provisions of the 1971 Act, they were in control of fire precautions in the defenders' hotel and that, in the exercise of that control, they owed the duty to take reasonable care to protect from injury by fire future guests in that hotel. I take this case to be an example of my proposition 3 (a), *supra*, namely, that it is an improper exercise of a statutory duty or power to perform an authorised act in an unauthorised manner, for example, negligently or so as to create a nuisance. So, in *Dutton's* case, the negligent inspection of the foundations of the house made by the council's surveyor involved the council in liability to the owner of the house for structural damage due to defective foundations.

In the present case there is no question of negligent inspection. The complaint is that, following upon the inspection made, the third parties omitted to take such action as was necessary to prevent the use of the premises in question as a residential hotel. The defenders do not found upon the third parties' failure to serve upon them the notice required by section 5 (4) of the 1971 Act. In any event the service of such a notice *per se* would not have prevented this cause of action from arising. The crux of the first ground of fault made by the defenders is the failure of the third parties either to advise the defenders not to re-open the hotel (upon which the defenders say they would have acted) or to exercise their statutory power to apply to the Sheriff for a closing order. This failure is, in my opinion, wholly within the area of the third parties' discretion, and there are certainly no averments made by the defenders from which it may reasonably be inferred that the *bona fide* exercise of this discretion required them to take the action above desiderated. It was submitted that 'may' means 'must', but I do not so read it in this section 10 (2). Although the Act does not specifically empower fire authorities to advise the occupiers of premises that the risk to persons in case of fire is so great that the premises ought to be closed to guests, it is obviously open to fire authorities to give such advice which, if acted upon, would render the section 10 (2) application unnecessary. But, if 'may' means 'must' in a situation where the fire authority knows that premises remained open, either because the advice to close was not given or because it was ignored, that does not assist the defenders.

It is important to note that under section 10 (2) of the 1971 Act fire authorities are not empowered to apply to the Court in terms thereof unless they are satisfied that the risk to persons in case of fire is so serious as to warrant prohibition or restriction of the use of premises. The defenders' bald averment that the risk to persons in case of fire in the defenders' hotel was so serious as to warrant such an application is, in my opinion, irrelevant for want of specification. All that follows from the prior averments of the defenders, namely, that the third parties had inspected the hotel and made certain recommendations, 'knew or ought to have known that all the recommended measures detailed in said Report could not be completed... during the course of the 1973 season,' and 'knew or ought to have known that the defenders intended to re-open the hotel on 7th April 1973,' is that the third parties knew the extent of the fire risk if nothing was done. The defenders aver that the third parties 'knew or ought to have known that said measures had not been taken by 7th April 1973.' It is not clear to me whether it is to be inferred from this averment that none of the said measures had then been taken and, if so, why the third parties knew or ought to have ascertained that this was the position. Assuming, however, that the degree of risk which existed at the time of the inspection in October had not been in any way reduced by 7th April 1973, the assessment of the gravity of that risk in relation to an application under section 10 (2) was solely a matter for the third parties. No amount of independent expert evidence, that the gravity of the risk was such as to warrant such an application, could advance the defenders' case against the third parties without averments sufficiently specific at least to open the question of whether the third parties' failure to make such an application was so improper an exercise of their discretion as to take this omission outwith the ambit of their powers. There are no such averments and, in their absence, I am of opinion that the first ground of fault alleged against the third parties is not relevantly averred...

The second ground of fault founded on is as follows: — '*Esto* it was reasonable for the third parties to be satisfied that the risk to hotel guests was not so serious that it could not be reduced to a reasonable level other than by the completion of all the said principal measures recommended in said Report... it was their duty to set out in said Report interim measures which could have been reasonably completed by the defenders by 7th April 1973 or which could have been observed during the 1973 season and which would have reduced the risk to hotel guests such as Mr. & Mrs. Hallett to a reasonable level of safety, namely that the smoke-screens and self-closing doors be installed; that the fire detection system be fitted; that the lift doors be protected; that the emergency lighting and (EXIT) signs be installed; that the fire extinguishers be installed, and that, until all the measures set out in said Report had been completed, a night watchman be employed.' I am of opinion that these averments are also irrelevant in respect that they ignore the stricture of Lord Wilberforce that a statutory authority is 'a public body, discharging functions under statute: its powers and duties are definable in terms of public not private law.' The 1971 Act does not empower, far less impose a duty upon, fire authorities to recommend interim measures. Accordingly, the duty alleged by the defenders does not even come within the area of the statutory discretion of the third parties. It seems to me to be based solely on the 'neighbourhood' principle without regard to the statutory functions of the third parties. If the third parties had recommended interim measures, they would have been acting outwith the ambit of their statutory powers, and the common law cannot, in my opinion, encroach upon the public law to the extent of requiring a statutory body to perform functions for which it has no statutory authority.

The third duty, which the defenders aver was incumbent upon the third parties, is based upon the assumption that the inspection made by the third parties was not made under the 1971 Act following upon the defenders' application for a fire certificate, but in pursuance of section I (1) (f) of the Fire Services Act 1947 in response to the defenders' written request for advice dated 15th September 1972. The section imposes upon every fire authority in Great Britain the duty of making provision for securing 'efficient arrangements for the giving, when requested, of advice in respect of buildings and other property in the area of the fire authority as to fire prevention, restricting the spread of fires, and means of escape in case of fire.' The relevant averments are as follows: 'It was in any event the duty of the third parties, having regard to the provisions of the Fire Services Act 1947 section I (1) (f) and the risk to hotel guests, to give the defenders advice not only on fire precautions and means of escape which they knew could not be implemented for 18 months, but also to give advice on those measures necessary to reduce the risk of fire to hotel guests to a reasonable level of safety during the period of 18 months prior to the completion of all measures in the Report. It was their duty to advise the defender on the introduction and observance of those interim measures herein before referred to'.

I need not deal with the situation which would have arisen if the defenders had asked the third parties for the advice which they allege it was the duty of the third parties to give them, because the defenders did not make this request. Their letter dated 15th September may reasonably be read as a request for advice only as to the alterations necessary to comply with the Fire Precautions Act 1971. In fact the advice given covered not only structural alterations to the premises but also general fire precautions with a view to meeting the standards of the Fire Precautions Act 1971 (see No. 23 of Process). Senior counsel for the defenders submitted that the fact that the defenders now alleged that the third parties were obliged to give to the defenders advice which they had not sought was not fatal to this ground of fault, which was based on the common law duty to take reasonable care to avoid an act or omission which might have as its reasonable and probable consequence injury to guests in the hotel. But this, in my opinion, is to extend the statutory function of the third parties to give advice, when requested, to the giving of advice which is not sought.

The duty of taking reasonable care to prevent injury to hotel guests lies upon the hoteliers. Parliament assisted them in the performance of this duty by affording them the expert advice of fire authorities if they applied for this. There is plainly no foundation in the 1947 Act for making a fire authority liable in reparation to third parties who are injured as a result of a hotelier's failure, for whatever reason, to act upon the advice given by a fire authority; nor is there any foundation for the proposition that a fire authority, in the exercise of its advisory functions, is bound to speculate upon which of the steps, which it has recommended, will be taken by the recipient and when they will be taken. In giving the advice which they did, the third parties, in my opinion, did all that they were required to do — indeed more than they were requested to do; thereafter it was the responsibility of the defenders to take such action as was reasonably necessary for the discharge of their duty to take reasonable care for the safety of guests in the hotel. According to the defenders' averments, they knew that all the measures recommended by the third parties could not be implemented during the 1973 season. If they wanted further advice from the third parties on interim measures, they could have taken up the offer of further assistance made by the firemaster in the letter dated 23rd October 1972 forwarding the said Report. In the absence of any request by the defenders for advice on interim measures, I am of opinion that the third parties were under no legal duty, either statutory or at common law, to give the additional advice which the defenders aver that they should have given.

I shall accordingly repel the fourth and fifth pleas-in-law for the defenders, sustain the first plea-in-law for the third parties and dismiss the action in so far as it is directed against them. *Quoad ultra* I shall order proof before answer."

Notes

(1) In *Bonthrone v. Secretary of State for Scotland*, 1987 S.L.T. 34 a fourth proposition to that of the three noted by Lord Dunpark, was added by Lord Grieve (at 41):   **14–24**

> "Where the exercise of a statutory power confers a discretion on the authority entitled to exercise it as to the manner in which, or the means by which, it is to be exercised, then if the discretion is exercised within the ambit of the power, and in bona fide, albeit the exercise of it can be shown to display an error of judgment, a person who suffers loss as a result of the exercise of the power will not have an action of damages against the authority which exercised it.
> [T]he taking of reasonable care in connection with the exercise of a statutory power… does not arise until the discretionary stage of its exercise has ceased and the executive stage has begun."

This is the articulation of the policy/operational distinction noted in *X* below and see *Stovin v. Wise* below. See too *Lamont v. North East Fife District Council*, 1987 GWD 37–1310; *Ross v. Secretary of State for Scotland*, 1990 S.L.T. 13 and *Wilson v. McCaffrey*, 1989 G.W.D. 1–37. Stewart (1998), p. 95 suggests that the "*Hallett/Bonthrone* formulation" is "different in style and perhaps in substance than the formulations … discussed in England" here referring to the next extract and *Stovin v. Wise*. Bear this comment in mind when reading the next extract and the rest of the materials in this chapter. Do you consider that a principled distinction can be made out? If so, is it a general difference in approach or simply a different way of handling specific aspects within arguments on liability such as the use of public interest to limit a duty of care?

X (Minors) v. Bedfordshire County Council

[1995] 3 All E.R. 353

14–25   The House of Lords heard appeals in five cases on the question of whether claims for negligence or for breach of statutory duty should be struck out. Two (*X (Minors)* v. Bedfordshire County Council and *M (A Minor) v. Newham London Borough Council*) concerned powers and duties in relation to the protection of children from abuse. The remaining three (*E (A Minor) v. Dorset County Council*; *Christmas v. Hampshire County Council* and *Keating v. Bromley London Borough Council* concerned powers and duties in relation to children with educational needs.

The five plaintiffs in *X* claimed damages for personal injury arising out of breach of statutory duty and negligence by the council in failing to protect them from parental abuse.

In *Newham* the plaintiff M and her mother claimed damages for personal injuries (psychiatric injury specified as anxiety neurosis) arising out of breach of statutory duty and negligence by the local authority, the area health authority and a consultant psychiatrist employed by the latter. They alleged that the psychiatrist and a social worker employed by the local authority had concluded that M had been sexually abused, but then mistakenly identified the abuser as the mother's cohabitee (who shared the same first name as the cousin whom M intended to identify). This led to the authority's obtaining court orders removing M from her mother, placing her in foster care and restricting the mother's access to her.

In *Dorset* the plaintiff, E, claimed damages for breach of statutory duty and negligence by the council, alleging that it had initially wrongly advised his parents and failed to diagnose that he suffered from a special learning disorder, and subsequently, after his difficulties were acknowledged, failed to take the appropriate steps.

In *Hampshire* the plaintiff (born in 1973) claimed damages against the council for negligence in the assessment of his educational needs. He alleged that his primary school headmaster had failed to refer him to the council for formal assessment or to an educational psychologist for diagnosis, notwithstanding his exhibiting learning difficulties consistent with dyslexia and behavioural problems. Furthermore, the council's teachers' advisory centre, to which he had been referred, had also failed to ascertain his difficulty. The failure to treat his condition had disadvantaged him in realising his potential and significantly restricted his vocational prospects.

In *Bromley* the plaintiff (born in 1971) claimed damages for breach of statutory duty and negligence against the council, alleging failure to place him at a reasonably appropriate school and to identify him as a child with special needs. He claimed damages for the alleged consequent impairment of his development and the disadvantage at which he was placed in seeking employment.

All the claims were struck out at first instance. The Court of Appeal allowed appeals against striking out as regards the claims in the education cases based on negligence. The House of Lords held that all the causes of anion should be struck out except those in respect of allegations of professional negligence against one authority directly in respect of its provision of a psychological advice service and against teachers and educational psychologists for whom defendant authorities were vicariously liable.

The leading speech was given by Lord Browne-Wilkinson, with whom Lord Jauncey of Tullichettle, Lord Lane, Lord Actcner and (subject to one point) Lord Nolan agreed.

Lord Browne-Wilkinson: "…

General Approach

Introductory — Public Law and Private Law

14–26   The question is whether, if Parliament has imposed a statutory duty on an authority to carry out a particular function, a plaintiff who has suffered damage in consequence of the authority's performance or non-performance of that function has a right of action in damages against the authority. It is important to distinguish such actions to recover damages, based on a private law cause of action, from actions in public law to enforce the due performance of statutory duties, now brought by way of judicial review. The breach of a public law right by itself gives rise to no claim for damages. A claim for damages must be based on a private law cause of action ...

Private law claims for damages can be classified into four different categories, *viz*: (A) actions for breach of statutory duty simpliciter (*i.e.* irrespective of carelessness); (B) actions based solely on the careless performance of a statutory duty in the absence of any other common law right of action; (C) actions based on a common law duty of care arising either from the imposition of the statutory duty or from the performance of it; (D) misfeasance in public office, *i.e.* the failure to exercise, or the exercise of, statutory powers either with the intention to injure the plaintiff or in the knowledge that the conduct is unlawful.

Category (D) is not in issue in this case. I will consider each of the other categories but I must make it clear that I am not attempting any general statement of the applicable law: rather I am seeking to set out a logical approach to the wide ranging arguments advanced in these appeals.

(A) Breach of Statutory Duty Simpliciter

This category comprises those cases where the statement of claim alleges simply (a) the statutory duty, (b) a breach of that duty, causing (c) damage to the plaintiff. The cause of action depends neither on proof of any breach of the plaintiffs' common law rights nor on any allegation of carelessness by the defendant.

The principles applicable in determining whether such statutory cause of action exists are now well established, although the application of those principles in any particular case remains difficult. The basic proposition is that in the ordinary case a breach of statutory duty does not, by itself, give rise to any private law cause of action. However a private law cause of action will arise if it can be shown, as a matter of construction of the statute, that the statutory duty was imposed for the protection of a limited class of the public and that Parliament intended to confer on members of that class a private right of action for breach of the duty. There is no general rule by reference to which it can be decided whether a statute does create such a right of action but there are a number of indicators. If the statute provides no other remedy for its breach and the Parliamentary intention to protect a limited class is shown, that indicates that there may be a private right of action since otherwise there is no method of securing the protection the statute was intended to confer. If the statute does provide some other means of enforcing the duty that will normally indicate that the statutory right was intended to be enforceable by those means and not by private right of action: *Cutler v. Wandsworth Stadium Ltd* [1949] A.C. 398; *Lonrho Ltd v. Shell Petroleum Co. Ltd (No. 2)* [1982] A.C. 173. However, the mere existence of some other statutory remedy is not necessarily decisive. It is still possible to show that on the true construction of the statute the protected class was intended by Parliament to have a private remedy. Thus the specific duties imposed on employers in relation to factory premises are enforceable by an action for damages, notwithstanding the imposition by the statutes of criminal penalties for any breach: see *Groves v. Wimborne (Lord)* [1898] 2 Q.B. 402.

Although the question is one of statutory construction and therefore each case turns on the provisions in the relevant statute, it is significant that your Lordships were not referred to any case where it had been held that statutory provisions establishing a regulatory system or a scheme of social welfare for the benefit of the public at large had been held to give rise to a private right of action for damages for breach of statutory duty. Although regulatory protection to those individuals particularly affected by that activity, the legislation is not to be treated as being passed for the benefit of those individuals but for the benefit of society in general. Thus legislation regulating the conduct of betting or prisons did not give rise to a statutory right of action vested in those adversely affected by the breach of the statutory provisions, *i.e.* bookmakers and prisoners: see *Cutler's* case [1949] A.C. 398; *R. v. Deputy Governor of Parkhurst Prison, ex p. Hague* [1992] 1 A.C. 58. The cases where a private right of action for breach of statutory duty have been held to arise are all cases in which the statutory duty has been very limited and specific as opposed to general administrative functions imposed on public bodies and involving the exercise of administrative discretions.

(B) The Careless Performance of a Statutory Duty — No Common Law Duty of Care

This category comprises those cases in which the plaintiff alleges (a) the statutory duty and (b) the 'negligent' breach of that duty but does not allege that the defendant was under a common law duty of care to the plaintiff. It is the use of the word 'negligent' in this context which gives rise to confusion: it is sometimes used to connote mere carelessness (there being no common law duty of care) and sometimes to import the concept of a common law duty of care. In my judgment it is important in considering the authorities to distinguish between the two concepts: as will appear, in my view the careless performance of a statutory duty does not in itself give rise to any cause of action in the absence of either a statutory right of action (Category (A) above) or a common law duty of care (Category (C) below).

Much of the difficulty can be traced back to the confusion between the ability to rely on a statutory provision as a defence and the ability to rely on it as founding a cause of action. The source of the confusion is to be found in the dictum of Lord Blackburn in *Geddis v. Proprietors of Bann Reservoir*, 3 App.Cals. 430, 455–456:

> 'For I take it, without citing cases, that it is now thoroughly well established that no action will lie for doing that which the legislature has authorised, if it be done without negligence, although it does occasion damage to anyone; but an action does lie for doing that which the legislature has authorised, if it be done negligently. And I think that if by a reasonable exercise of the powers, either given by statute to the promoters, or which they have at common law, the damage could be prevented it is, within this rule, "negligence" not to make such reasonable exercise of their powers.'

This dictum, divorced from its context, suggests that the careless performance of a statutory duty in itself gives rise to a cause of action for damages. But it has to be read in context.

In *Geddes* the defendants were authorised to construct and maintain a reservoir the water from which was discharged, via a new artificial watercourse, into an old watercourse which the defendants were authorised by the statute to widen and maintain. Water originating from the reservoir flooded from the old watercourse into the plaintiff's adjoining land, such flooding being due to the 'negligent' failure of the defendants to maintain the old watercourse adequately. The cause of action relied upon by the plaintiff is not clear from the report: it could have been either nuisance (including *Rylands v. Fletcher* (1868) L.R. 3 H.L. 330) or negligence. If the cause of action founded upon was in nuisance, the question was whether the statutory power to construct and maintain the works provided a defence to what would otherwise constitute an actionable wrong. It is well established that statutory authority only provides a defence to a claim based on a common law cause of action where the loss suffered by the plaintiff is the inevitable consequence of the proper exercise of the statutory power or duty: *Metropolitan Asylum District v. Hill*, 6 App.Cas. 193; *Allen v. Gulf Oil Refining Ltd* [1981] A.C. 1001. Therefore the careless exercise of a statutory power or duty cannot provide a defence to a claim based on a freestanding common law cause of action, whether in trespass, nuisance or breach of a common law duty of care. If Lord Blackburn's dictum in *Geddis*'s case, 3 App.Cas. 430, 455–456, merely refers to the circumstances in which statutory authority can be used as a defence it raises no problems.

In my judgment *Geddis*'s case is best treated as a decision that the careless exercise by the defendant of a statutory duty or power provides no defence to a claim by the plaintiff based on a freestanding common law cause of action. It was so treated by Lord Wilberforce in the *Gulf Oil* case who said [1981] A.C. 1001, 1011:

> 'It is now well settled that where Parliament by express direction or by necessary implication has authorised the construction and use of an undertaking or works, that carries with it an authority to do what is authorised with immunity from any action based on nuisance. The right of action is taken away: *Hammersmith and City Railway Co. v. Brand* (1869) L.R. 4 H.L. 171, 215 *per* Lord Cairns. To this there is made the qualification, or condition, that the statutory powers are exercised without "negligence" — that word here being used in a special sense so as to require the undertaker, as a condition of obtaining immunity from action, to carry out the work and conduct the operation with all reasonable regard and care for the interests of other persons: *Geddis* ...'

See also *Sutherland Shire Council v. Heyman* (1985) 157 C.L.R. 424, 458 and the article by Sir Gerard Brennan 'Liability in Negligence of Public Authorities: The Divergent Views' (1990) 48 *The Advocate* 842, 844–846.

[His Lordship then stated that the same position had been taken by the majority of the House of Lords in *Home Office v. Dorset Yacht Co. Ltd* [1970] A.C. 1004 (Lords Morris, Pearson and Reid) although Lord Diplock had adopted a different approach.]

In my judgment the correct view is that in order to found a cause of action flowing from the careless exercise of statutory powers or duties, the plaintiff has to show that the circumstances are such as to raise a duty of care at common law. The mere assertion of the careless exercise of a statutory power or duty is not sufficient.

(C) The Common Law Duty of Care

In this category, the claim alleges either that a statutory duty gives rise to a common law duty of care owed to the plaintiff by the defendant to do or refrain from doing a particular act or (more often) that in the course of carrying out a statutory duty the defendant has brought about such a relationship between himself and the plaintiff as to give rise to a duty of care at common law. A further variant is a claim by the plaintiff that, whether or not the authority is itself under a duty of care to the plaintiff, its servant in the course of performing the statutory function was under a common law duty of care for breach of which the authority is vicariously liable.

Mr Munby, in his reply in the *Newham* case, invited your Lordships to lay down the general principles applicable in determining the circumstances in which the law would impose a common law duty of care arising from the exercise of statutory powers or duties. I have no doubt that, if possible, this would be most desirable. But I have found it quite impossible either to detect such principle in the wide range of authorities and academic writings to which we were referred or to devise any such principle de novo. The truth of the matter is that statutory duties now exist over such a wide range of diverse activities and take so many different forms that no one principle is capable of being formulated applicable to all cases. However, in my view it is possible in considering the problems raised by these particular appeals to identify certain points which are of significance.

1. Co-existence of Statutory Duty and Common Law Duty of Care

It is clear that a common law duty of care may arise in the performance of statutory functions. But a broad distinction has to be drawn between: (a) cases in which it is alleged that the authority owes a duty of care in the manner in which it exercises a statutory discretion; (b) cases in which a duty of care is alleged to arise from the manner in which the statutory duty has been implemented in practice.

14–27

An example of (a) in the educational field would be a decision whether or not to exercise a statutory discretion to close a school, being a decision which necessarily involves the exercise of a discretion. An example of (b) would be the actual running of a school pursuant to the statutory duties. In such latter case a common law duty to take reasonable care for the physical safety of the pupils will arise. The fact that the school is being run pursuant to a statutory duty is not necessarily incompatible with a common law duty of care arising from the proximate relationship between a school and the pupils it has agreed to accept. The distinction is between (a) taking care in exercising a statutory discretion whether or not to do an act and (b) having decided to do that act, taking care in the manner in which you do it.

2. Discretion: Justiciability and the Policy Operational Test
(a) Discretion

Most statutes which impose a statutory duty on local authorities confer on the authority a discretion as to the extent to which, and the methods by which, such statutory duty is to be performed. It is clear both in principle and from the decided cases that the local authority cannot be liable in damages for doing that which Parliament has authorised. Therefore if the decisions complained of fall within the ambit of such statutory discretion they cannot be actionable in common law. However if the decision complained of is so unreasonable that it falls outside the ambit of the discretion conferred upon the local authority, there is no a priori reason for excluding all common law liability.

14–28

That this is the law is established by the decision in the *Dorset Yacht* case [1970] A.C. 1004 and by that part of the decision in *Anns v. Merton London Borough Council* [1978] A.C. 728 which, so far as I am aware, has largely escaped criticism in later decisions. In the *Dorset Yacht* case Lord Reid said [1970] A.C. 1004, 1031:

'Where Parliament confers a discretion the position is not the same. Then there may, and almost certainly will, be errors of judgment in exercising such a discretion and Parliament cannot have intended that members of the public should be entitled to sue in respect of such errors. But there must come a stage when the discretion is exercised so carelessly or unreasonably that there has been no real exercise of the discretion which Parliament has conferred. The person purporting to exercise his discretion has acted in abuse or excess of his power. Parliament cannot be supposed to have granted immunity to persons who do that.'

See also *per* Lord Morris, at 1037F.

LORD DIPLOCK,… took a rather different line, making it a condition precedent to any common law duty arising that the decision impugned should be shown to be ultra vires in the public law sense. For myself, I do not believe that it is either helpful or necessary to introduce public law concepts as to the validity of a decision into the question of liability at common law for negligence. In public law a decision can be *ultra vires* for reasons other than *Wednesbury* unreasonableness (*Associated Provincial Picture Houses Ltd v. Wednesbury Corporation* [1948] 1 K.B. 223) (*e.g.* breach of the rules of natural justice) which have no relevance to the question of negligence. Moreover it leads, in my judgment mistakenly, to the contention that claims for damages for negligence in the exercise of statutory powers should for procedural purposes be classified as public law claims and therefore, under *O'Reilly v. Mackman* [1983] 2 A.C. 237 should be brought in judicial review proceedings: see *Lonrho plc v. Tebbit* [1992] 4 All E.R. 280. However, although I consider that the public law doctrine of *ultra vires* has, as such, no role to play in the subject under discussion, the remarks of Lord Diplock were plainly directed to the fact that the exercise of a statutory discretion cannot be impugned unless it is so unreasonable that it falls altogether outside the ambit of the statutory discretion. He said [1970] A.C. 1004, 1068:

'These considerations lead me to the conclusion that neither the intentional release of a Borstal trainee under supervision, nor the unintended escape of a Borstal trainee still under detention which was the consequence of the application of a system of relaxed control intentionally adopted by the Home Office as conducive to the reformation of trainees, can have been intended by Parliament to give rise to any cause of action on the part of any private citizen unless the system adopted was so unrelated to any purpose of reformation that no reasonable person could have reached a bona fide conclusion that it was conducive to that purpose. Only then would the decision to adopt it be *ultra vires* in public law.'

Exactly the same approach was adopted by Lord Wilberforce in *Anns v. Merton London Borough Council* [1978] A.C. 728 who, speaking of the duty of a local authority which had in fact inspected a building under construction, said, at 755:

'But this duty, heavily operational though it may be, is still a duty arising under the statute. There may be a discretionary element in its exercise — discretionary as to the time and manner of inspection, and the techniques to be used. A plaintiff complaining of negligence must prove, the burden being on him, that action taken was not within the limits of a discretion bona fide exercised, before he can begin, to rely upon a common law duty of care.'

It follows that in seeking to establish that a local authority is liable at common law for negligence in the exercise of a discretion conferred by statute, the first requirement is to show that the decision was outside the ambit of the discretion altogether: if it was not, a local authority cannot itself be in breach of any duty of care owed to the plaintiff.

In deciding whether or not this requirement is satisfied, the court has to assess the relevant factors taken into account by the authority in exercising the discretion. Since what are under consideration are discretionary powers conferred on public bodies for public purposes the relevant factors will often include policy matters, for example social policy, the allocation of finite financial resources between the different calls made upon them or (as in *Dorset Yacht*) the balance between pursuing desirable social aims as against the risk to the public inherent in so doing. It is established that the courts cannot enter upon the assessment of such 'policy' matters. The difficulty is to identify in any particular case whether or not the decision in question is a 'policy' decision.

(b) Justiciability and the Policy Operational Dichotomy

14–29   In English law the first attempt to lay down the principles applicable in deciding whether or not a decision was one of policy was made by Lord Wilberforce in *Anns v. Merton London Borough Council* [1978] A.C. 728, 754:

'Most, indeed probably all, statutes relating to public authorities or public bodies, contain in them a large area of policy. The courts call this "discretion" meaning that the decision is one for the authority or body to make, and not for the courts. Many statutes also prescribe or at least presuppose the practical execution of policy decisions: a convenient description of this is to say that in addition to the area of policy or discretion, there is an operational area. Although this distinction between the policy area and the operational area is convenient, and illuminating, it is probably a distinction of degree; many "operational" powers or duties have in them some element of "discretion". It can safely be said that the more "operational" a power or duty may be, the easier it is to superimpose upon it a common law duty of care.'

As Lord Wilberforce appreciated, this approach did not provide a hard and fast test as to those matters which were open to the court's decision. In *Rowling v. Takaro Properties Ltd* [1988] A.C. 473 the Privy Council reverted to the problem. In that case the trial judge had found difficulty in applying the policy/operational test, but having classified the decision in question as being operational, took the view that as a result there was a common law duty of care. Commenting on the judge's view, Lord Keith of Kinkel said, at 501:

'Their Lordships feel considerable sympathy with Quilliam J.'s difficulty in solving the problem by reference to this distinction. They are well aware of the references in the literature to this distinction (which appears to have originated in the United States of America), and of the critical analysis to which it has been subjected. They incline to the opinion, expressed in the literature, that this distinction does not provide a touchstone of liability, but rather is expressive of the need to exclude altogether those cases in which the decision under attack is of such a kind that a question whether it has been made negligently is unsuitable for judicial resolution, of which notable examples are discretionary decisions on the allocation of scarce resources or the distribution of risks: see especially the discussion in *Craig on*

Administrative Law (1983), pp. 534–538. If this is right, classification of the relevant decision as a policy or planning decision in this sense may exclude liability; but a conclusion that it does not fall within that category does not, in their Lordships' opinion, mean that a duty of care will *necessarily* exist.' (Emphasis added.)

From these authorities I understand the applicable principles to be as follows. Where Parliament has conferred a statutory discretion on a public authority, it is for that authority, not for the courts, to exercise the discretion: nothing which the authority does within the ambit of the discretion can be actionable at common law. If the decision complained of falls outside the statutory discretion, it *can* (but not necessarily will) give rise to common law liability. However, if the factors relevant to the exercise of the discretion include matters of policy, the court cannot adjudicate on such policy matters and therefore cannot reach the conclusion that the decision was outside the ambit of the statutory discretion. Therefore a common law duty of care in relation to the taking of decisions involving policy matters cannot exist.

3. If Justiciable, the Ordinary Principles of Negligence Apply

If the plaintiff's complaint alleges carelessness, not in the taking of a discretionary decision to do some act, but in the practical manner in which that act has been performed (*e.g.* the running of a school) the question whether or not there is a common law duty of care falls to be decided by applying the usual principles, *i.e.* those laid down in *Caparo Industries plc v. Dickman* [1990] 2 A.C. 605, 617–618. Was the damage to the plaintiff reasonably foreseeable? Was the relationship between the plaintiff and the defendant sufficiently proximate? Is it just and reasonable to impose a duty of care? See *Rowling v. Takaro Properties Ltd* [1988] A.C. 473; *Hill v. Chief Constable of West Yorkshire* [1989] A.C. 53.

14–30

However the question whether there is such a common law duty and if so its ambit, must be profoundly influenced by the statutory framework within which the acts complained of were done. The position is directly analogous to that in which a tortious duty of care owed by A to C can arise out of the performance by A of a contract between A and B. In *Henderson v. Merrett Syndicates Ltd* [1994] 3 W.L.R. 761 your Lordships held that A (the managing agent) who had contracted with B (the members' agent) to render certain services for C (the Names) came under a duty of care to C in the performance of those services. It is clear that any tortious duty of care owed to C in those circumstances could not be inconsistent with the duty owed in contract by A to B. Similarly, in my judgment a common law duty of care cannot be imposed on a statutory duty if the observance of such common law duty of care would be inconsistent with, or have a tendency to discourage, the due performance by the local authority of its statutory duties.

4. Direct Liability and Vicarious Liability

In certain of the appeals before the House, the local authorities are alleged to be under a direct duty of care to the plaintiff not only in relation to the exercise of a statutory discretion but also in relation to the operational way in which they performed that duty.

14–31

This allegation of a direct duty of care owed by the authority to the plaintiff is to be contrasted with those claims which are based on the vicarious liability of the local authority for the negligence of its servants, *i.e.* for the breach of a duty of care owed by the servant to the plaintiff, the authority itself not being under any relevant duty of care to the plaintiff. Thus, in the *Newham* case the plaintiffs' claim is wholly based on allegations that two professionals, a social worker and a psychiatrist, individually owed professional duties of care to the plaintiff for the breach of which the authorities as their employers are vicariously liable. It is not alleged that the authorities were themselves under a duty of care to the plaintiff.

This distinction between direct and vicarious liability can be important since the authority may not be under a direct duty of care at all or the extent of the duty of care owed directly by the authority to the plaintiff may well differ from that owed by a professional to a patient. However, it is important not to lose sight of the fact that, even in the absence of a claim based on vicarious liability, an authority under a direct duty of care to the plaintiff will be liable for the negligent acts or omissions of its servant which constitute a breach of that direct duty. The authority can only act through its servants.

The position can be illustrated by reference to the hospital cases. It is established that those conducting a hospital are under a direct duty of care to those admitted as patients to the hospital (I express no view as to the extent of that duty). They are liable for the negligent acts of a member of the hospital staff which constitute a breach of that duty, whether or not the member of the staff is himself in breach of a separate duty of care owed by him to the plaintiff: *Gold v. Essex County Council* [1942] 2 K.B. 293, 301, *per* Lord Green; *Cassidy v. Ministry of Health* [1951] 2 K.B. 343, *per* Denning L.J.; *Roe v. Minister of Health* [1954] 2 Q.B. 66; see also *Wilsons & Clyde Coal Co. Ltd v. English* [1938] A.C. 57; *McDermid v. Nash Dredging & Reclamation Co. Ltd* [1987] A.C. 906. Therefore in the cases under appeal, even where there is no allegation of a separate duty of care owed by a servant of the authority to the plaintiff, the negligent acts of that servant are capable of constituting a breach of the duty of care (if any) owed directly by the authority to the plaintiff.

Striking Out

14–32   In all these cases the defendants are seeking to strike out the claims at an early stage, before discovery has taken place and before the facts are known. It is therefore necessary to proceed on the basis that the facts alleged in the various statements of claim are true. It must be stressed that these allegations are not admitted by the defendants.

It is must be stressed that these allegations are not admitted by the defendants.

Actions can only be struck out under R.S.C., Ord. 18, r. 19 where it is clear and obvious that in law the claim cannot succeed …

The Abuse Case

14–33   [His Lordship stated the facts of the *Bedfordshire* and *Newham* cases. He then summarised the powers and duties of local authorities to take children into care where, *inter alia*, they are at risk of being harmed (Children and Young Persons Act 1969, ss.1, 2; Child Care Act 1980, ss. 1, 2; Children Act 1989, ss.17,20(1), 47, Sched. 2). He noted that from April 1, 1991, there had been a statutory complaints procedure applicable to the Children Act provisions (Local Authority Social Services Act 1970, s.7B; Local Authority Social Services (Complaints Procedure) Order 1990 (S.I. 1990 No. 2244). His Lordship also referred to the Secretary of State's powers to give guidance and directions under the 1970 Act, ss.7, 7A, which were to be found in the publication *Working Together* (1991).]

The Claim for Breach of Statutory Duty: Category (A)

14–34   The Court of Appeal were unanimous in striking out these claims in both actions. I agree. My starting point is that the Acts in question are all concerned to establish an administrative system designed to promote the social welfare of the community. The welfare sector involved is one of peculiar sensitivity, involving very difficult decisions how to strike the balance between protecting the child from immediate feared harm and disrupting the relationship between the child and its parents. Decisions often have to be taken on the basis of inadequate and disputed facts. In my judgment in such a context it would require exceptionally clear statutory language to show a parliamentary intention that those responsible for carrying out these difficult functions should be liable in damages if, on subsequent investigation with the benefit of hindsight, it was shown that they had reached an erroneous conclusion and therefore failed to discharge their statutory duties.

It is true that the legislation was introduced primarily for the protection of a limited class, namely children at risk, and that until April 1991 the legislation itself contained only limited machinery for enforcing the statutory duties imposed. But in my view those are the only pointers in favour of imputing to Parliament an intention to create a private law cause of action. When one turns to the actual words used in the primary legislation to create the statutory duties relied upon in my judgment they are inconsistent with any intention to create a private law cause of action.

Thus, the duty imposed by section 2(2) of the Act of 1969 to bring care proceedings is made conditional upon the subjective judgment of the local authority that there are grounds for so doing. Similarly, the duty to receive a child into care under section 2(1) of the Act of 1980 only arises 'where it appears to a local authority' that the parents are prevented from providing properly for the child *and* that its intervention is necessary in the interest of the child. So far as the Act of 1989 is concerned, the duty relied on in section 17 is described as 'a general duty' which has two parts: (a) to safeguard the children and (b) 'so far as is consistent' with (a) to promote the upbringing of the children by their families. Thus not only is the duty not a specific one but the section itself points out the basic tension which lies at the root of so much child protection work: the decision whether to split the family in order to protect the child. I find it impossible to construe such a statutory provision as demonstrating an intention that even where there is no carelessness by the authority it should be liable in damages if a court subsequently decided with hindsight that the removal, or failure to remove, the child from the family either was or was not 'consistent with' the duty to safeguard the child.

All the duties imported by Schedule 2 to the Act of 1989 are to 'take reasonable steps' to do certain things. The duty to make inquiries under section 47 is limited to 'such inquiries as they consider necessary'. Thus all the statutory provisions relied upon in the *Bedfordshire* case are, as one would expect, made dependent upon the subjective judgment of the local authority. To treat such duties as being more than public law duties is impossible…

In the *Newham* case, the claim by the plaintiffs for damages for breach of statutory duty (Category (A)) was founded solely on sections 1 and 18 of the Act of 1980: the Act of 1989 was not in force at the relevant time. The claim was only faintly pursued by Mr Munby and, for the reasons given by Peter Gibson L.J. in the Court of Appeal [1994] 2 W.L.R. 554, 590, in my judgment it is ill founded.

For these reasons (which are in substance the same as those of the Court of Appeal), the claims in both abuse cases to the extent that they are based on a claim for damages for breach of statutory duty simpliciter were rightly struck out.

Direct Common Law Duty of Care Owed by the Local Authorities

In the *Newham* case it is not alleged that the borough council was under any direct duty of care to the plaintiffs: the case is based solely on the vicarious liability of the council and the health authority for the negligence of their servants.

14–35

In the *Bedfordshire* case, Mr Jackson formulated the common law duty of care owed by the county council as being 'a duty to children in respect of whom they receive reports of neglect or ill-treatment to take reasonable care to protect such children'. The first question is whether the determination by the court of the question whether there has been a breach of that duty will involve unjustifiable policy questions. The alleged breaches of that duty relate for the most part to the failure to take reasonable practical steps, *e.g.* to remove the children, to allocate a suitable social worker or to make proper investigations. The assessment by the court of such allegations would not require the court to consider policy matters which are not justiciable. They do not necessarily involve any question of the allocation of resources or the determination of general policy. There are other allegations the investigation of which by a court might require the weighing of policy factors, *e.g.* allegations that the county council failed to provide a level of service appropriate to the plaintiffs' needs. If the case were to go to trial, the trial judge might have to rule out these issues as not being justiciable. But since some of the allegations are justiciable, it would not be right to strike out the whole claim on this ground.

Next, do the allegations of breach of duty in the operational field all relate to decisions the power to make which Parliament has conferred on the local authority, *i.e.* are they all decisions within the ambit of the local authority's statutory discretion? I strongly suspect that, if the case were to go to trial, it would eventually fail on this ground since, in essence, the complaint is that the local authority failed to take steps to remove the children from the care of their mother, i.e. negligently failed properly to exercise a discretion which Parliament has conferred on the local authority. But again, it would not be right to strike out the claim on this ground because it is possible that the plaintiffs might be able to demonstrate at trial that the decisions of the local authority were so unreasonable that no reasonable local authority could have reached them and therefore, for the reasons given by Lord Reid in the *Dorset Yacht* case [1970] A.C. 1004, 1031 fall outside the ambit of the discretion conferred by Parliament.

I turn then to consider whether, in accordance with the ordinary principles laid down in the *Caparo* case [1990] 2 A.C. 605, the local authority in the *Bedfordshire* case owed a direct duty of care to the plaintiffs. The local authority accepts that they could foresee damage to the plaintiffs if they carried out their statutory duties negligently and that the relationship between the authority and the plaintiffs is sufficiently proximate. The third requirement laid down in *Caparo* is that it must be just and reasonable to impose a common law duty of care in all the circumstances. It was submitted that this third requirement is only applicable in cases where the plaintiffs' claim is for pure economic loss and that it does not apply where, as in the child abuse cases, the claim is for physical damage. I reject this submission: although *Caparo* and many other of the more recent cases were decisions where only pure economic loss was claimed, the same basic principles apply to claims for physical damage and were applied in, for example, *Hill v. Chief Constable of West Yorkshire* [1989] A.C. 53.

Is it, then, just and reasonable to superimpose a common law duty of care on the local authority in relation to the performance of its statutory duties to protect children? In my judgment it is not. Sir Thomas Bingham M.R. took the view, with which I agree, that the public policy consideration which has first claim on the loyalty of the law is that wrongs should be remedied and that very potent counter considerations are required to override that policy [1994] 2 W.L.R. 554, 572F. However, in my judgment there are such considerations in this case.

First, in my judgment a common law duty of care would cut across the whole statutory system set up for the protection of children at risk. As a result of the ministerial directions contained in 'Working Together' the protection of such children is not the exclusive territory of the local authority's social services. The system is inter-disciplinary, involving the participation of the police, educational bodies, doctors and others. At all stages the system involves joint discussions, joint recommendations and joint decisions. The key organisation is the Child Protection Conference, a multi-disciplinary body which decides whether to place the child on the Child Protection Register. This procedure by way of joint action takes place, not merely because it is good practice, but because it is required by guidance having statutory force binding on the local authority. The guidance is extremely detailed and extensive: the current edition of 'Working Together' runs to 126 pages. To introduce into such a system a common law duty of care enforceable against only one of the participant bodies would be manifestly unfair. To impose such liability on all the participant bodies would lead to almost impossible problems of disentangling as between the respective bodies the liability, both primary and by way of contribution, of each for reaching a decision found to be negligent.

Second, the task of the local authority and its servants in dealing with children at risk is extraordinarily delicate. Legislation requires the local authority to have regard not only to the physical wellbeing of the child but also to the advantages of not disrupting the child's family environment: see, for example, section 17 of the Act of 1989. In one of the child abuse cases, the local authority is blamed for removing the child precipitately: in the other, for failing to remove the children from their mother. As the Report of the Inquiry into Child Abuse in Cleveland 1987 (Cm. 412) said, at p. 244:

'It is a delicate and difficult line to tread between taking action too soon and not taking it soon enough. Social services whilst putting the needs of the child first must respect the rights of the parents; they also must work if possible with the parents for the benefit of the children. These parents themselves are often in need of help. Inevitably a degree of conflict develops between those objectives.'

Next, if a liability in damages were to be imposed, it might well be that local authorities would adopt a more cautious and defensive approach to their duties. For example, as the Cleveland Report makes clear, on occasions the speedy decision to remove the child is sometimes vital. If the authority is to be made liable in damages for a negligent decision to remove a child (such negligence lying in the failure properly first to investigate the allegations) there would be a substantial temptation to postpone making such a decision until further inquiries have been made in the hope of getting more concrete facts. Not only would the child in fact being abused be prejudiced by such delay: the increased workload inherent in making such investigations would reduce the time available to deal with other cases and other children.

The relationship between the social worker and the child's parents is frequently one of conflict, the parent wishing to retain care of the child, the social worker having to consider whether to remove it. This is fertile ground in which to breed ill feeling and litigation, often hopeless, the cost of which both in terms of money and human resources will be diverted from the performance of the social service for which they were provided. The spectre of vexatious and costly litigation is often urged as a reason for not imposing a legal duty. But the circumstances surrounding cases of child abuse make the risk a very high one which cannot be ignored.

If there were no other remedy for maladministration of the statutory system for the protection of children, it would provide substantial argument for imposing a duty of care. But the statutory complaints procedures contained in section 76 of the Act of 1980 and the much fuller procedures now available under the Act of 1989 provide a means to have grievances investigated, though not to recover compensation. Further, it was submitted (and not controverted) that the local authorities Ombudsman would have power to investigate cases such as these.

Finally, your Lordships' decision in the *Caparo* case [1990] 2 A.C. 605 lays down that, in deciding whether to develop novel categories of negligence the court should proceed incrementally and by analogy with decided categories. We were not referred to any category of case in which a duty of care has been held to exist which is in any way analogous to the present cases. Here, for the first time, the plaintiffs are seeking to erect a common law duty of care in relation to the administration of a statutory social welfare scheme. Such a scheme is designed to protect weaker members of society (children) from harm done to them by others. The scheme involves the administrators in exercising discretions and powers which could not exist in the private sector and which in many cases bring them into conflict with those who, under the general law, are responsible for the child's welfare. To my mind, the nearest analogies are the cases where a common law duty of care has been sought to be imposed upon the police (in seeking to protect vulnerable members of society from wrongs done to them by others) or statutory regulators of financial dealings who are seeking to protect investors from dishonesty. In neither of those cases has it been thought appropriate to superimpose on the statutory regime a common law duty of care giving rise to a claim in damages for failure to protect the weak against the wrongdoer: see *Hill v. Chief Constable of West Yorkshire* [1989] A.C. 53 and *Yuen Kun Yeu v. Attorney-General of Hong Kong* [1988] A.C. 175. In the latter case, the Privy Council whilst not deciding the point said, at 198, that there was much force in the argument that if the regulators had been held liable in that case the principles leading to such liability 'would surely be equally applicable to a wide range of regulatory agencies, not only in the financial field, but also, for example, to the factory inspectorate and social workers, to name only a few'. In my judgment, the courts should proceed with great care before holding liable in negligence those who have been charged by Parliament with the task of protecting society from the wrongdoings of others.

Vicarious Liability

14–36   [His Lordship then dealt with arguments that the defendant authorities were vicariously liable for the negligence of their staff.]

The claim based on vicarious liability is attractive and simple. The normal duty of a doctor to exercise reasonable skill and care is well established as a common law duty of care. In my judgement, the same duty applies to any other person possessed of special skills, such as a social worker. It is said, rightly, that in general such professional duty of care is owed irrespective of contract and can arise even where the professional assumes to act for the plaintiff pursuant to a contract with a third party: *Henderson v. Merrett*

Syndicates Ltd [1994] 3 W.L.R. 761; *White v. Jones* [1995] 2 W.L.R. 187. Therefore, it is said, it is nothing to the point that the social workers and psychiatrist only came into contact with the plaintiffs pursuant to contracts or arrangements made between the professionals and the local authority for the purpose of the discharge by the local authority of its statutory duties. Once brought into contact with the plaintiffs, the professionals owed a duty properly to exercise their professional skills in dealing with their 'patients', the plaintiffs. This duty involved the exercise of professional skills in investigating the circumstances of the plaintiffs and (in the *Newham* case) conducting the interview with the child. Moreover, since the professionals could foresee that negligent advice would damage the plaintiffs, they are liable to the plaintiffs for tendering such advice to the local authority.

Like the majority in the Court of Appeal, I cannot accept these arguments. The social workers and the psychiatrists were retained by the local authority to advise the local authority, not the plaintiffs. The subject matter of the advice and activities of the professionals is the child. Moreover the tendering of any advice will in many cases involve interviewing and, in the case of doctors, examining the child. But the fact that the carrying out of the retainer involves contact with and relationship with the child cannot alter the extent of the duty owed by the professionals under the retainer from the local authority. The Court of Appeal drew a correct analogy with the doctor instructed by an insurance company to examine an applicant for life insurance. The doctor does not, by examining the applicant, come under any general duty of medical care to the applicant. He is under a duty not to damage the applicant in the course of the examination: but beyond that his duties are owed to the insurance company and not to the applicant.

The position is not the same as in the case of the purchaser of property who is owed a duty of care by a surveyor instructed by the building society which is going to advance the money: see *Smith v. Eric S. Bush* [1990] 1 A.C. 831. In such a case the surveyor is only liable to the purchaser in negligence because he is aware that the purchaser will regulate his (the purchaser's) conduct by completing the purchase in reliance on the survey report. In the child abuse cases, even if the advice tendered by the professionals to the local authority comes to the knowledge of the child or his parents, they will not regulate their conduct in reliance on the report. The effect of the report will be reflected in the way in which the local authority acts.

Nor is the position the same as in *Henderson v. Merrett Syndicates Ltd* where, pursuant to a contract with the members' agents, the managing agents undertook the management of the insurance business of the indirect Names. The managing agents were held to be under a tortious duty of care to the indirect Names, notwithstanding that the managing agents were operating under the terms of a contract with a third party. But the duty of care to the Names in that case arose from, and fell within the ambit of, the terms of the retainer contained in the contract between the managing agents and the members' agents. The Names were not seeking to impose on the managing agents any obligation beyond that which the retainer itself required to be performed. So also in *White v. Jones* [1995] 2 W.L.R. 187.

In my judgment in the present cases, the social workers and the psychiatrist did not, by accepting the instructions of the local authority, assume any general professional duty of care to the plaintiff children. The professionals were employed or retained to advise the local authority in relation to the well being of the plaintiffs but not to advise or treat the plaintiffs …

Even if, contrary to my view, the social workers and psychiatrist would otherwise have come under a duty of care to the plaintiffs, the same considerations which have led me to the view that there is no direct duty of care owed by the local authorities apply with at least equal force to the question whether it would be just and reasonable to impose such a duty of care on the individual social workers and the psychiatrist.

For these reasons, in my judgment the professionals involved were under no separate duty of care to the plaintiffs for breach of which the local authorities could be vicariously liable.

Witness Immunity

14–37

[His Lordship then held that the psychiatrist in the *Newham* case was entitled to witness immunity from civil liability under *Watson v. M'Ewan; Watson v. Jones* [1905] A.C. 480 and *Evans v. London Hospital Medical College (University of London)* [1981] 1 W.L.R. 184.]

In the present case, the psychiatrist was instructed to carry out the examination of the child for the specific purpose of discovering whether the child had been sexually abused and (if possible) the identity of the abuser. The psychiatrist must have known that, if such abuse was discovered, proceedings by the local authority for the protection of the child would ensue and that her findings would be the evidence on which those proceedings would be based. It follows in my judgment that such investigations having such an immediate link with possible proceedings in pursuance of a statutory duty cannot be made the basis of subsequent claims.

Although anyone would have great sympathy for the plaintiffs in both these cases (if the allegations which they make are true), for these reasons I agree with the Court of Appeal that they have no private law claim in damages. I would dismiss both appeals.

The Education Cases
The Legislation

14–38   [His Lordship summarised the relevant statutory provisions. The Education Act 1944 as originally enacted imposed duties on local education authorities to provide sufficient schools having regard to the need to secure the provision of special educational treatment for pupils with any disability of mind or body, and to ascertain what children in their area require such treatment (ss.7, 8, 33, 34, 36). The Education Act 1981 introduced new arrangements whereby authorities were to have regard to the need for securing that special educational provision was made for pupils with special educational needs. Such pupils were to be identified and assessed and, if the authority was of the opinion that it should determine the special educational provision that should be made for them, it was to make a statement of educational needs. If the authority decided not to determine such provision, an appeal lay to the Secretary of State. Similarly, there was a right to appeal against the provision specified in a statement to an appeal committee and then to the Secretary of State (see the 1981 Act, ss.2, 4, 5, 7–9).]

The Dorset Case
[His Lordship summarised the facts.]

Common Law Duty of Care — Direct

14–39   … As to the claim based on the negligent failure to comply with the statutory requirements of the Act of 1981, it is in essence a claim that the authority was negligent in the exercise of the statutory discretions conferred on the defendant authority by the Act of 1981. The claim cannot be struck out as being not justiciable. Although it is very improbable, it may be that the exercise of the statutory discretions involved in operating the special needs machinery of the Act of 1981 involved policy decisions. The decision as to what should be included in the statement and what provision should be made is, by statute, a decision conferred on the defendant authority. Therefore, even if such decisions were made carelessly, the claim will fail unless the plaintiff can show that the decisions were so careless that no reasonable education authority could have reached them. Again, although it seems most improbable that this requirement can be satisfied, it is impossible to be certain until all the facts are known. Therefore the claim cannot be struck out at this stage on the grounds that it is not justiciable or the acts complained of fell within the statutory discretion.

The question, then, is whether it is right to superimpose on the statutory machinery for the investigation and treatment of the plaintiff's special educational needs a duty of care to exercise the statutory discretions carefully? I find this a difficult question on which my views have changed from time to time. In favour of imposing a duty of care is the fact that it was plainly foreseeable that if the powers were exercised carelessly a child with special educational needs might be harmed in the sense that he would not obtain the advantage that the statutory provisions were designed to provide for him. Further, for the reasons that I have given, a common law duty of care in the exercise of statutory discretions can only arise in relation to an authority which has decided an issue so carelessly that no reasonable authority could have reached that decision. Why, it may be asked, should such a grossly delinquent authority escape liability? However, I have reached the conclusion that, powerful though those considerations may be, they are outweighed by other factors.

First, in relation to the special statutory duties imposed by sections 2, 4, 5 and 7 of the Act of 1981, the exercise of the discretions involves the close participation of the parents who are themselves under a duty to cause the child to receive 'efficient full-time education suitable to his … ability and aptitude': section 36 of the Education Act 1944. The parents are themselves involved in the process of decision making and can appeal against decisions which they think to be erroneous. Although in the *Dorset* case the parents availed themselves of all the advantages of the statutory machinery, in the generality of cases to allow either the parents (on behalf of the child) or the child when he attains his majority to bring a claim alleging negligence by the authority in the making of the decision would be to duplicate remedies. Although in the present case this factor is not directly in point, if a duty of care is to be held to exist it must apply as much in relation to actions brought by a parent or child who has not used the statutory machinery as in the case of parents or a child who have.

Next, the number of cases which could successfully be brought for breach of such a duty of care would be very small since, as I have said, it would have to be shown that the decision impugned was taken so carelessly that no authority could have reached it. Yet, if a common law duty of care is held to exist, there is a very real risk that many hopeless (and possibly vexatious) cases will be brought, thereby exposing the authority to great expenditure of time and money in their defence. If there were no other remedy open, this is a price which might have to be paid in the interests of justice. But, in almost every case which could give rise to a claim for the negligent exercise of the statutory discretions, it is probable that, as in the present case, there will be an alternative remedy by way of a claim against the authority on the grounds of its vicarious liability for the negligent advice on the basis of which it exercises its discretion: as to which see below.

We were not referred to any category of case by analogy with which, in accordance with the *Caparo* principles [1990] 2 A.C. 605, it would be right to impose a direct duty of care on the authority in the exercise of its statutory discretions...

In my judgment, as in the child abuse cases, the courts should hesitate long before imposing a common law duty of care in the exercise of discretionary powers or duties conferred by Parliament for social welfare purposes. The aim of the Act of 1981 was to provide, for the benefit of society as a whole, an administrative machinery to help one disadvantaged section of society. The statute provides its own detailed machinery for securing that the statutory purpose is performed. If, despite the complex machinery for consultation and appeals contained in the Act, the scheme fails to provide the benefit intended that is a matter more appropriately remedied by way of the Ombudsman looking into the administrative failure than by way of litigation.

For these reasons I reach the conclusion that an education authority owes no common law duty of care in the exercise of the powers and discretions relating to children with special educational needs specifically conferred on them by the Act of 1981.

I turn then to the other duty of care which, it is alleged, the defendant authority owes directly to the plaintiff. There the position is wholly different. The claim is based on the fact that the authority is offering a service (psychological advice) to the public. True it is that, in the absence of a statutory power or duty, the authority could not offer such a service. But once the decision is taken to offer such a service, a statutory body is in general in the same position as any private individual or organisation holding itself out as offering such a service. By opening its doors to others to take advantage of the service offered, it comes under a duty of care to those using the service to exercise care in its conduct. the position is directly analogous with a hospital conducted, formerly by a local authority now by a health authority, in exercise of statutory powers. In such a case the authority running the hospital is under a duty to those whom it admits to exercise reasonable care in the way it runs it: see *Gold v. Essex County Council* [1942] 2 K.B. 293.

For these reasons, I can see no ground on which it can be said at this stage that the defendant authority, in providing a psychology service, could not have come under a duty of care to the plaintiff who, through his parents, took advantage of that service. It may well be that when the facts are fully investigated at trial it may emerge that, for example, the alleged psychology service was merely part and parcel of the system established by the defendant authority for the discharge of its statutory duties under the Act of 1981. If so, it may be that the existence and scope of the direct duty owed by the defendant authority will have to be excluded or limited so as not to impede the due performance by the authority of its statutory duties. But at this stage it is impossible to say that the claim under this head must fail.

Common Law Duty of Care — Vicarious

14–40

The claim is that the educational psychologists and other members of the staff of the defendant authority owed a duty to use reasonable professional skill and care in the assessment and determination of the plaintiff's educational needs. It is further alleged that the plaintiff's parents relied on the advice of such professionals. The defendant authority is vicariously liable for any breach of such duties by their employees.

Again, I can see no ground for striking out this claim at least in relation to the educational psychologists. Psychologists hold themselves out as having special skills and they are, in my judgment, like any other professional bound both to possess such skills and to exercise them carefully. Of course, the test in *Bolam v. Friern Hospital Management Committee* [1957] 1 W.L.R. 582 will apply to them, *i.e.* they are only bound to exercise the ordinary skill of a competent psychologist and if they can show that they acted in accordance with the accepted views of some reputable psychologist at the relevant time they will have discharged the duty of care, even if other psychologists would have adopted a different view. In the context of advice on the treatment of dyslexia, a subject on which views have changed over the years, this may be an important factor. But that said, I can see no ground on which, at this stage, the existence of a professional duty of care can be ruled out. The position of other members of the defendant's staff is not as clear, but I would not at this stage strike out the claims relating to them.

The position of the psychologists in the education cases is quite different from that of the doctor and social worker in the child abuse cases. There is no potential conflict of duty between the professional's duties to the plaintiff and his duty to the educational authority. Nor is there any obvious conflict between the professional being under a duty of care to the plaintiff and the discharge by the authority of its statutory duties. If, at trial, it emerges that there are such conflicts, then the trial judge may have to limit or exclude any duty of care owed by the professional to the plaintiff. But at this stage no obvious conflict has been demonstrated.

Finally, the defendant authority submitted that the damage claimed, being the cost of providing alternative fee paying education for the plaintiff, is not recoverable. In my view it is not appropriate to decide this point at the striking out stage: the matter will be better resolved at trial when the true facts are known.

My conclusion therefore in the *Dorset* case is that the defendant authority is under no liability at common law for the negligent exercise of the statutory discretions conferred on them by the Education Acts 1944 to 1981, but could be liable, both directly and vicariously, for negligence in the operation of the psychology service and negligent advice given by its officers."

The Hampshire Case
The Facts

14–41   [His Lordship stated the facts and held that the common law recognised a duty of care owed by a head teacher and an educational advisor to a pupil. There was no incompatibility between such a duty and the existence of the statutory special educational needs scheme. The authority would be vicariously liable for the negligence of such teachers in advising on and meeting the educational needs of pupils. The claim would be amended to allege that the failure to treat the plaintiff's dyslexia cause psychological damage sufficiently serious to constitute an identifiable mental illness. The claim should not be struck out.]

The Bromley Case

14–42   [His Lordship stated the facts and held (1) that breaches of section 8 of the Education Act 1944 (duty to provide sufficient schools) or the 1944 Act provisions concerning special educational treatment and the 1981 Act provisions (summarised above at p. 724) did not give rise to a civil action; (2) as in the *Dorset* case, there was no common law duty of care in relation to the exercise of statutory discretions under the 1944 and 1981 Acts; and (3) possible claims based on vicarious liability for the negligence of one or more professionals employed by the authority should not be struck out.]"

Appeals in the Bedfordshire and Newham cases dismissed; appeals in the Dorset and Bromley cases allowed in part; appeal in the Hampshire case and cross-appeal in the Bromley case dismissed.

Forbes v. City of Dundee District Council

1997 S.L.T. 1330

14–43   LORD NIMMO SMITH: "This is an action of reparation which came before me on procedure roll. The pursuer seeks damages from the defenders for loss, injury and damage allegedly sustained by her through the fault and negligence of the defenders. I note in passing that the defenders, whom I shall for convenience call 'the council', ceased to exist on 31 March 1996 and any liability on their part to make reparation to the pursuer passed to their statutory successors as local authority; but as no mention was made of this at procedure roll I shall continue to refer to the council as the defenders.

The circumstances in which the pursuer allegedly came to be injured may be summarised by quoting some of her averments in art 2 of condescendence, which are in these terms: 'On or about 12 July 1991, the pursuer, together with her four year old daughter, were [sic] shopping at the supermarket of William Low & Co plc at 274 Perth Road, Dundee. The supermarket has a car park at the rear. The car park is connected to Perth Road by inter alia Union Place. The front door of the supermarket faces northwards on to Perth Road. A concrete stairway leads westwards from the front door along the side of the supermarket down to Union Place. The pursuer together with her daughter left the front door of the supermarket. They began to descend the stairway. The stairway was steep. There were 10 steps down from the supermarket to Union Place. The going of the steps was not uniform. It varied from step to step and from left to right on each step. The variation in the going was unpredictable. The going on each step save the first was narrow, being less than 250mm. The rise between steps was not uniform. It varied between steps and from left to right... A person descending a stairway in a normal fashion establishes a "rhythm" in so doing. Such a "rhythm" anticipates consistency in underfoot conditions. The said stairway did not afford such consistency. The going and the rise in the steps varied. The pursuer lost her footing on the third step from the top (not counting the top landing). The third step from the top had a particularly narrow going. It varied from 220mm to 229mm. The pursuer lost her footing because of the said variations in the going and the rise, the steepness of the stairway, together with the narrow and variable going of the said third step. She lost her footing and fell. The pursuer fell on to her back. She bumped her back off the stairs as she fell. She fell to the bottom of the stairs."

The pursuer does not attribute any liability for this accident to the designers, builders, owners or occupiers of the stairway, none of whom were called as defenders. She attributes liability to the council by virtue of certain of their statutory functions. It is common ground between the parties that the supermarket and the stairway were built in or about 1977 or 1978, and that prior to construction the builders lodged with the council plans or drawings for the works together with an application for a building warrant. Such an application required to be made under the provisions of the Building (Scotland) Act 1959 ('the 1959 Act'), as amended to the date of the application. Section 3 (1) of the 1959 Act provides that for the purposes of the Act the Secretary of State may be regulations, referred to as 'building standards regulations', prescribe standards in relation to certain matters. By subs (2) (as amended by the Health and Safety at Work etc Act 1974) the standards prescribed under subs (1) are inter alia to be such as in the opinion of the Secretary of State can reasonably be expected to be attained in buildings of the classes to which they relate, having regard to the need for securing the health, safety, welfare and convenience of the persons who will inhabit or frequent such buildings and the safety of the public generally. Section 6 makes provision for the granting of building warrants. Subsection (3) thereof provides inter alia that a warrant for the construction of a building shall be subject to the condition that the building shall be constructed as described in the warrant (including any relative plans and specifications) and in accordance with the buildings standards regulations. Section 9 makes provision for the granting by the local authority of a certificate of completion after the completion of the construction of any building in respect of which a warrant has been granted. Subsection (2) thereof (as amended by the Health and Safety at Work etc Act 1974) provides that a buildings authority shall grant a certificate of completion in respect of any building if, so far as they are able to ascertain after taking all reasonable steps in that behalf, the building complies with the conditions on which the relative warrant was granted.

The regulations made under s 3, which are no longer in force but were in force at the material time, were the Building Standards (Scotland) (Consolidation) Regulations 1971 (SI 1971/2052) ('the 1971 Regulations'). While I shall refer later in more detail to other provisions of the 1971 Regulations, it is sufficient at this stage to quote from regs S3 and S4. Regulation S3 provided by para (2) inter alia that every stair should be constructed in straight flights having a uniform rise and going. (By reg S2 (1) 'rise' was defined as meaning 'the vertical distance between the tops of two consecutive treads or between the top of a tread and the top of a landing next above it'; and 'going' was defined as meaning 'the horizontal distance between the nosings of two consecutive treads or between the nosing of a tread and the nosing of a landing next above it'.) Regulation S4 provided that every stair forming part of an exit, access, private or other stairway should comply with the requirements set forth in the second, third, fourth or fifth columns respectively of the table following the regulation in relation to the corresponding head in the first column thereof. Columns (2) to (5) related respectively to exit stairways, access stairways, private stairways and other stairways. Head E in column (1) provided, in relation to the going on 'other stairways', that it should be 'at every part of the stair not less than 250 millimetres at the points 270 millimetres from each end of the tread'.

In arts 3 and 4 of condescendence the pursuer avers that prior to construction of the stairway and supermarket the builders lodged with the council plans or drawings for the works together with an application for building warrant. Prior to granting the application the drawings were checked by one of the council's building control officers. His purpose in checking the drawings was to determine whether the proposed works, as shown by them, would comply, when constructed, with the requirements of the 1971 Regulations. In respect of the stairway the only drawing lodged with the council was insufficiently detailed to allow the building control officer to determine whether or not the proposed works would so comply if constructed in accordance with the application for warrant. Notwithstanding this, the building control officer signed the application, and it was then stamped by the city engineer. The council thereby granted a building warrant for the supermarket building, including the stairway, on 10 October 1977. Following the granting of building warrant it was normal practice of building control officers to make numerous visits to the sites of work during construction. They did so with a view to ensuring by means of inspection that the works when completed complied with the 1971 Regulations. If any part of the works was not available for any reason during construction, normal practice was for such part to be made the subject of final inspection before the granting of a completion certificate. The building control officer carried out the relevant inspections prior to the granting of the completion certificate, which the council granted on 22 December 1978. No amendment was made to the original warrant, nor has any subsequent warrant been applied for. Accordingly, it is believed and averred by the pursuer that the stairs of the stairway have not been altered since their erection. At the time of their erection the stairway was part of a building. Accordingly it, including its individual stairs, required to comply with the 1971 Regulations. The stairway was not an exit stairway, an access stairway or a private stairway, and was accordingly an 'other stairway' for the purpose of reg S4 of the 1971 Regulations. It failed to comply with the standards set out in regs S3 (2) and S4...

After referring in art 5 to ss 6 (3) and 9 (2) of the 1959 Act, the pursuer avers that the accident was caused by breaches of duty on the part of the council and their building control officer. Since the main issue debated before me was whether the council in the circumstances owed any duty of care to the pursuer, and it was not suggested that any separate considerations were applicable to the role of the building control officer, I can summarise the averments in art 6 as follows. The pursuer alleges that it was the duty of the council to take reasonable care to see that the staircase was safe for persons using it and that the 1971 Regulations so far as relating to safety of persons using the stairs were complied with in respect of the building. The building control officer was under a duty to take reasonable care when checking the application for building warrant and relative documents 'to ensure that the stairway proposed was safe for persons using it insofar as affecting the safety of persons using the stairway [sic]'. He knew or ought to have known that the stairway would be used by members of the public such as the pursuer to descend, and that if it was erected without complying with the regulations referred to above, it could result in users such as the pursuer losing their footing and suffering injury. It was usual practice for a building control officer when checking an application for building warrant and supporting documents to ensure that the specification of any stairway therein would comply in all respects with the requirements of these regulations. It was his duty to raise with the applicant or his agent any failure of the application to demonstrate that the stairway would be in accordance with the regulations; not to issue the building warrant until the failure was remedied; to have carried out a proper inspection of the stairway to see that it was safe for persons using it before issuing a completion certificate; to see that, as constructed, the stairway complied with the regulations insofar as affecting the safety of persons using the stairway before issuing a completion certificate; and not to issue a completion certificate without having taken reasonable care to ascertain that the stairway was safe for persons using it. The pursuer concludes by averring that the accident was caused or materially contributed to by the breach of each and all of these duties...

The main issue between the parties was whether in the whole circumstances the council owed to the pursuer a duty of care. In submitting that no such duty was owed, counsel for the council referred to the provisions of the 1959 Act which I have quoted above. He accepted that the purpose of the statutory functions of the council under these provisions in respect of the granting of building warrants and completion certificates was to secure compliance with the provisions of the 1971 Regulations. The pursuer's case, however, was not one of breach of statutory duty, but at common law arising from the imposition of a statutory duty, or, more accurately, the exercise of that duty. In the case of *X (Minors) v Bedfordshire County Council*, Lord Browne-Wilkinson at [1995] 2 AC, pp 730H-731A said that the question in that case was whether, if Parliament had imposed a statutory duty on an authority to carry out a particular function, a plaintiff who had suffered damage in consequence of the authority's performance or non-performance of that function had a right of action in damages against the authority. It was important to distinguish such actions to recover damages based on a private law course of action, from actions in public law to enforce the due performance of statutory duties, now brought by way of judicial review. The breach of a public law right by itself gave rise to no claim for damages. A claim for damages must be based on a private law course of action. Lord Browne-Wilkinson went on to say that private law claims for damages could be classified into four different categories, viz: (a) actions for breach of statutory duty simpliciter (i e irrespective of carelessness); (b) actions based solely on the careless performance of a statutory duty in the absence of any other common law right of action; (c) actions based on a common law duty of care arising either from the imposition of the statutory duty or from the performance of it; (d) misfeasance in public office, ie the failure to exercise, or the exercise of, statutory powers either with intention to injure the plaintiff or in the knowledge that the conduct was unlawful. In further discussion of these categories, Lord Browne-Wilkinson said at p 735B-C, in respect of category (c) (the common law duty of care), that in this category the claim alleged either that a statutory duty gave rise to a common law duty of care owed to the plaintiff by the defendant to do or refrain from doing a particular act or (more often) that in the course of carrying out a statutory duty the defendant had brought about such a relationship between himself and the plaintiff as to give rise to a duty of care at common law. A further variant was a claim by the plaintiff that, whether or not the authority was itself under a duty of care to the plaintiff, its servant in the course of performing the statutory function was under a common law duty of care for breach of which the authority was vicariously liable. Statutory duties now existed over such a wide range of diverse activities and took so many different forms that no one principle was capable of being formulated, applicable to all cases, in determining the circumstances in which the law would impose a common law duty of care arising from the exercise of statutory powers or duties. In the present case, counsel submitted, the pursuer's averments brought the action within Lord Browne-Wilkinson's category (c).

Counsel pointed to the pursuer's averments that there was an inspection, but a failure to exercise reasonable care in carrying it out. The matter under consideration was therefore not one of policy, but was operational or executive, subject nevertheless to an element of discretion. The pursuer's case in relation to the inspection of drawings was irrelevant, as it was overtaken by the duty to check the stairway, as constructed, to see whether it complied with the regulations. The crucial element was what was done at the latest stage: inspection at the stage of construction superseded the earlier stage. The element of discretion in the operational sphere was conferred by s 9 (2). After discussion of the concept of reasonableness in this context, counsel indicated that he did not propose to advance submissions on the basis that the council's function under s 9 (2) was purely discretionary, although he did not concede the matter. So he based the rest of his argument on the proposition that the relevant actings were in the operational sphere, without reference to the question whether they were discretionary.

In respect of the existence of a duty of care, counsel referred to *Murphy v Brentwood District Council*, in which it was held inter alia that to hold that a local authority, in supervising compliance with the building regulations or byelaws, was under a common law duty to take reasonable care to avoid putting a purchaser of a house in a position in which he would be obliged to incur economic loss in the form of expense incurred in putting right a defect in its construction, was an extension of principle that should not, as a matter of policy, be affirmed. At [1991] 1 AC, pp 463–464, Lord Keith referred to the question whether a local authority owed any duty to persons who might suffer injury through a failure to take reasonable care to secure compliance with building byelaws, so far as extended to injury to person or health and (possibly) damage to property other than the defective building itself (which was not the question in that case). After saying that he preferred to reserve his opinion on the question whether any duty at all existed, he said: 'So far as I am aware, there has not yet been any case of claims against a local authority based on injury to person or health through a failure to secure compliance with building bye-laws.'

Counsel referred also to a passage, to the same effect, in the speech of the Lord Chancellor at p 457. Returning to the case of *X (Minors) v Bedfordshire County Council*, and Lord Browne-Wilkinson's category (c), counsel proposed to assume for present purposes that this case was concerned with the operational sphere. In discussing certain points which were of significance to his category (c), Lord Browne-Wilkinson said at p 739: 'If the plaintiff's complaint alleges carelessness, not in the taking of a discretionary decision to do some act, but in the practical way in which that act has to be performed... the question whether or not there is a common law duty of care requires to be decided by applying the usual principles i.e. those laid down in *Caparo Industries Plc. v. Dickman* [1990] 2 A.C. 605, 617–618. Was the damage to the plaintiff reasonably foreseeable? Was the relationship between the plaintiff and the defendant sufficiently proximate? Is it just and reasonable to impose a duty of care? See *Rowling v. Takaro Properties Ltd.* [1988] A.C. 473; *Hill v. Chief Constable of West Yorkshire* [1989] A.C. 53.

However the question whether there is such a common law duty and if so its ambit, must be profoundly influenced by the statutory framework within which the acts complained of were done.'

It was thus necessary to have regard to the principles which Lord Browne-Wilkinson derived from *Caparo Industries plc v Dickman* (the more usual phrase being 'fair, just and reasonable', rather than simply 'just and reasonable'), and also to the statutory framework. Counsel went on to refer to *Marc Rich & Co AG v Bishop Rock Marine Co Ltd*, in which it was held by a majority that whatever harm a plaintiff suffered, in order to determine the defendant's liability in tort for negligence the court had to consider the elements of foreseeability and proximity and whether it was fair, just and reasonable to impose a duty of care on the defendant. At [1996] AC, p 235 Lord Steyn, in rejecting a submission that in cases of physical damage to property in which the plaintiff had a proprietary or possessory interest, the only requirement was proof of reasonable foreseeability, said that certain observations of Lord Oliver in *Caparo Industries plc v Dickman*, seen in context, did not support this submission. They merely underlined the qualitative difference between cases of direct physical damage and direct economic loss. The materiality of that distinction was plain, but since the decision in *Dorset Yacht Co v Home Office*, it had been settled law that the elements of foreseeability and proximity as well as considerations of fairness, justice and reasonableness were relevant to all cases whatever the nature of the harm sustained by the plaintiff. In *Stovin v Wise*, which related to an alleged breach of a common law duty of care owed by a local authority by failing, before an accident had occurred, to take reasonable measures to reduce the dangers to road users at a road junction, Lord Hoffmann said: 'The trend of authorities has been to discourage the assumption that anyone who suffers loss is *prima facie* entitled to compensation from a person (preferably insured or a public authority) whose act or omission can be said to have caused it' ([1996] AC at p 949D).

Later he said that the distinction between policy and operations is an inadequate tool with which to discover whether it is appropriate to impose a duty of care or not. Even if the distinction is clear cut, leaving no element of discretion in the sense that it would be irrational (in the public law meaning of that word) for the public authority not to exercise its power, it does not follow that the law should superimpose a common law duty of care. He went on: This can be seen if one looks at cases in which a public authority has been under a statutory or common law *duty* [his emphasis] to provide a service or other benefit for the public or a section of the public. In such cases there is no discretion but the courts have nevertheless not been willing to hold that a member of the public who has suffered loss because the service was not provided to him should necessarily have a cause of action, either for breach of statutory duty or for negligence at common law."

Lord Hoffmann also said that whether a statutory duty gives rise to a private cause of action is a question of construction. It requires an examination of the policy of the statute to decide whether it was intended to confer a right to compensation for breach. Whether it can be relied upon to support the existence of a common law duty of care is not exactly a question of construction, because the cause of action does not arise out of the statute itself. But the policy of the statute is nevertheless a crucial factor in the decision. Lord Hoffmann then referred to the passage I have quoted above from the speech of Lord Browne-Wilkinson in *X (Minors) v Bedfordshire County Council*, and went on: 'The same is true of omission to perform a statutory duty. If such a duty does not give rise to a private right to sue for breach, it would be unusual if it nevertheless gave rise to a duty of care at common law which made the public authority liable to pay compensation for foreseeable loss caused by the duty not being performed. It will often be foreseeable that loss will result if, for example, a benefit or service is not provided. If the policy of the Act is not to create a statutory liability to pay compensation, the same policy should ordinarily exclude the existence of a common law duty of care.'

Lord Hoffmann also said that it appeared to be essential to the doctrine of general reliance (as discussed in *Sutherland Shire Council v Heyman* (1985) 157 CLR at pp 464 and 483) that the benefit or service provided under statutory powers should be of a uniform and routine nature, so that one could describe exactly what the public authority was supposed to do. Powers of inspection for defects clearly fell into this category. But it was also necessary to discern a policy which confers a right to financial compensation if the power had not been exercised.

In turning to the statutory framework, counsel said that there was no authority which held, contrary to his submission, that such legislation did give rise to a duty of care. In respect of the approach to the statutory provisions, counsel referred to three cases. In *Pullar v Window Clean Ltd* it was held that s 52 of the Edinburgh Corporation (Streets, Buildings and Sewers) Order Confirmation Act 1926, which made provision for the construction of buildings so as to admit of a window above the ground floor being cleaned from the inside of the room, could not properly be construed as a safety measure for the benefit of window cleaners, that it imposed no continuing duty upon occupiers and their successors, and accordingly that a failure to comply with its provisions did not give rise to a civil claim of damages by a window cleaner who sustained injury as a result of the failure. In *R v Deputy Governor of Parkhurst Prison, ex p Hague*, which related to certain statutory provisions providing for the segregation of prisoners, it was held that the question whether an enactment conferred private law rights of action on individuals in respect of its breaches depended on the intention of the legislature, and the fact that a particular provision was intended to protect certain individuals was not of itself sufficient to confer such rights. After reviewing the authorities Lord Jauncey said, at [1992] 1 AC, pp 170–171: 'My Lords, I take from these authorities that it must always be a matter for consideration whether the legislature intended that private law rights of action should be conferred upon individuals in respect of breaches of the relevant statutory provision. The fact that a particular provision was intended to protect certain individuals is not of itself sufficient to confer private law rights of action upon them, something more is required to show that the legislature intended such conferment.'

In *Lonrho Ltd v Shell Petroleum Co Ltd (No 2)* it was held that alleged breaches of the Southern Rhodesia (Petroleum) Order 1965 gave no cause of action in tort, since breach of a mere prohibition upon members of the public from doing what would otherwise be lawful was not enough to found such a right. The order in question created a statutory prohibition upon the doing of certain classes of acts and providing the means of enforcing the prohibition by prosecution for a criminal offence which was subject to heavy penalties including imprisonment. Lord Diplock said at [1982] AC, p 185:

'Where the only manner of enforcing performance for which the Act provides is prosecution for the criminal offence of failure to perform the statutory obligation or for contravening the statutory prohibition which the Act creates, there are two classes of exception to this general rule [ie the rule that where an Act creates an obligation, and enforces the performance in a specified manner, that performance cannot be enforced in any other manner].

'The first is where upon the true construction of the Act it is apparent that the obligation or prohibition was imposed for the benefit or protection of a particular class of individuals, as in the case of the Factories Act and similar legislation...

'The second exception is where the statute creates a public right (i.e. a right to be enjoyed by all those of Her Majesty's subjects who wish to avail themselves of it) and a particular member of the public suffers what Brett J. in *Benjamin v. Storr* (1874) L.R. 9 C.P. 400, 407, described as "particular, direct and substantial" damage "other and different from that which was common to all the rest of the public".'

On the basis of these cases counsel sought to formulate six propositions. The first of these was derived from the passage in the speech of Lord Jauncey in *R v Deputy Governor of Parkhurst Prison, ex p Hague*, which I have quoted and need not repeat. The next four propositions were derived from *Pullar v Window Clean Ltd*. The second was that if the legislature had provided no machinery by way of penalty or otherwise for enforcing compliance with the duty, there was a presumption that a civil right of action accrued to the person damnified by the breach. Thirdly, where there was such machinery, its existence did not necessarily deprive the injured person of a civil remedy. Fourthly, there was a presumption (or, as a preferable expression, a general rule — see the opinion of Lord Abernethy in *McArthur v Strathclyde Regional Council*, 1995 SLT at p 1136) that where a statute created an obligation and enforced performance of it in a specified manner, performance could not be enforced in another manner. This was subject to the two exceptions defined by Lord Diplock in *Lonrho Ltd v Shell Petroleum Co Ltd*. Fifthly, if the class of person for whose protection it was alleged that the duty was imposed was indefinite and difficult to define, that would tend to exclude a construction of the statutory provision which would give right to civil damages for breach. The sixth proposition was that one should look at the scheme of the Act as a whole, not just at the particular provision founded on. It was therefore necessary to look at the scheme of the 1959 Act and the 1971 Regulations.

In terms of its long title, the 1959 Act was inter alia 'an Act to make in respect of Scotland new provision for safety, health and other matters in respect of the construction of buildings'. The policy that lay behind the making of the building standards regulations could clearly be derived from s 3 (2) of the Act, which provided that in prescribing standards under s 3 (1) the Secretary of State was to have regard to the need for securing the health, safety and convenience of the persons who would inhabit or frequent the buildings to which the regulations would apply, and to the safety of the public generally. Reference was made to the opinion of Lord Cameron of Lochbroom in *Armstrong v Moore*, 1996 SLT at p 695E, where a similar approach was adopted. The 1959 Act contained no provisions in respect of civil liability. Section 19 imposed certain penalties (but not on a buildings authority). It should particularly be noticed that s 19A, which was added by the Health and Safety at Work etc Act 1974, had not yet been brought into force. This section, if enforced, would make certain breaches actionable: broadly speaking, breaches of warrants, orders or the Building Operations and Building Standards Regulations in the course of the construction, demolition or change of use of a building. This demonstrated that, apart from this provision, Parliament did not intend any civil liability to arise from the provisions of the 1959 Act. There was no provision which would make a buildings authority liable, and no basis for any suggestion that the authority should be liable. The purpose of the Act was to control those who carried out building works. It would be odd if no civil liability attached to such persons, unless and until s 19A was brought into force, but civil liability did attach to a local authority in respect of their functions under ss 6 and 9. These considerations, coupled with the imposition of criminal penalties under s 19, pointed away from the existence of any civil liability on the part of a local authority. Moreover it was not possible to define the class of persons to whom any duty of care might be owed. While there would obviously be persons who would use the stairway, they would not constitute a class in the necessary sense, because it would be large and difficult to define.

In addressing me on the tests derived from *Caparo Industries plc v Dickman*, counsel indicated that he did not intend to argue that in the circumstances of the case there was a lack of proximity between the pursuer and the council in the necessary sense. He proposed to assume for the purposes of the debate that there was such proximity, but he made no concession for subsequent procedural stages, and in particular reserved his position in the event of a proof before answer being allowed. This left two tests to consider. On the question of reasonable foreseeability, counsel referred to the well known passage in the speech of Lord Atkin in *Donoghue v Stevenson* at 1932 SC (HL), pp 44–45; 1932 SLT, pp 323–324, in particular the sentence: 'You must take reasonable care to avoid acts or omissions which you can reasonably foresee would be likely to injure your neighbour.' In *Taylor v City of Glasgow District Council* Lord Johnston said at 1996 SLT, p 704A, that the policy of the current law is effectively to protect local authorities when performing general public duties under general public statutes from a negligent performance of those duties in the sense of being liable for suit at common law. He then went on to observe that it was clear that questions of foreseeability do not arise. Counsel submitted that this, however, must depend on the circumstances of the particular case. He referred to the pursuer's averments about the dimensions of the steps, particularly the one from which she fell. Under reference to *McClafferty v British Telecommunications plc*, in which it was held that the projection of a manhole cover three quarters of an inch above the level of the surrounding pavement was not a foreseeable cause of injury, and *James v Preseli Pembrokeshire District Council* in which a similar conclusion was reached in respect of a 'trip' of about three quarters of an inch, counsel submitted that the departure from the measurements prescribed by the Building Standards Regulations was in the present case not great enough to make the risk of an accident reasonably foreseeable. Moreover, by the time she had reached the third step from the top, the pursuer had not been able to establish a rhythm (which was the subject of an averment by her) and it was not reasonably foreseeable that a departure from the specified dimensions would result in a fall. The danger arose, not from the step from which she fell, but from the danger of falling.

In addressing the question whether it was fair, just and reasonable that there should be liability on the part of the council, counsel repeated his references to the passages I have already mentioned in *Stovin v Wise, Murphy v Brentwood District Council* and *X (Minors) v Bedfordshire County Council*. He pointed out that the trend of the authorities was against the imposition of such liability, and there was no authority in favour of it, though he accepted that the absence of authority could not by itself be determinative. He advanced a number of further submissions. There would be no time limit for such liability. There could be circumstances in which the local authority could be liable, although any claim against the builders had become time barred. This could arise many years after the completion certificate had been granted. The duty, if it existed, was effectively owed to the world. The pursuer herself referred to 'members of the public'. Even if this was confined to such members of the public as used the stairway, this was still a very large class of people, which pointed against the existence of a duty of care. It would be unfair if the builders could not be sued, but the local authority could. The position arising from s 19A, which was not yet in force, was not definitive, because liability might arise separately, but it still constituted a contraindication. The likely effect of the imposition of a duty of care could be considered in broad terms. Local authorities had finite resources and if they came under a duty to inspect minutiae, in order to discharge such a duty, they would have difficulty in allocating their resources. Counsel accepted however that such a duty would not be absolute, because of the reasonableness qualification in s 9 (2). There would however be a tendency to discourage a local authority in the performance of their duties. If resources were finite, there was a risk that the attention of a building control officer would be focused on some matters to the detriment of others, so that the overall performance of the local authority's duties might suffer. At the least there would be delay and expense to applicants. In this connection counsel referred to the discussion of the 'danger of overkill' in *Rowling v Takaro Properties Ltd* [1988] AC at p 502. Finally, the pursuer's averments of fault sought to impose on the council and their building control officer duties which went beyond the duties of inspection which arose from the 1971 Regulations.

In reply to these submissions on the main issue, counsel for the pursuer addressed me, in the first place, on the question of reasonable foreseeability. He agreed that the authorities referred to by counsel for the council were applicable and that the tests derived from *Caparo Industries plc v Dickman* should be applied. I should only dismiss the action on the ground that there were no relevant averments of reasonable foreseeability if I was satisfied that the pursuer must fail. The pursuer offered to prove that the stairway was unsafe. *McClafferty v British Telecommunications plc* was a case which had been decided after proof. The submissions about the extent to which the dimensions of the stairway departed from those prescribed by the 1971 Regulations were based on the wrong approach. The question of reasonable foreseeability depended, not on the dimensions of one step, and the extent to which they departed from the prescribed dimensions, but whether the staircase as a whole constituted a reasonably foreseeable danger. It was only one aspect of this that the third step from the top was unsafe. It was unreasonable to look at this step in isolation. It was necessary to look at the whole stairway to see whether part of it gave rise to a risk of injury.

Turning to the question whether a duty of care existed, counsel submitted that it was incorrect to suggest that the only relevant stage was the carrying out of an inspection for the purposes of granting a completion certificate. The council had two opportunities to discover that the stairway did not conform to the regulations, and if they had taken either opportunity, there would have been no accident; so both failures contributed to the accident. If the drawing accompanying the application for building warrant was insufficiently detailed, that was insufficient to show that the building would comply with the Building Standards Regulations. For present purposes, it had been accepted by the council that their actings fell within the operational sphere, so questions of policy did not arise. Under reference to *X (Minors) v Bedfordshire County Council* he submitted that the case was concerned with the performance of statutory duties. *Stovin v Wise* referred to statutory powers, not duties. The pursuer's case was not based directly on the breach of a statutory duty. He was not saying that such a breach automatically gave rise to a right to claim damages. But a duty of care was brought into existence by reason of the statutory duties imposed on the defenders, so that they had a duty to take reasonable care to enforce those parts of the regulations which related to the safety of persons using the stairway. Under reference to the speech of Lord Browne-Wilkinson in *X (Minors) v Bedfordshire County Council* at p 739B, counsel disagreed with the suggestion that the statutory framework was a fourth test, additional to the three derived from *Caparo Industries plc v Dickman*.

Counsel then addressed me on the scheme of the 1959 Act. He did not accept that cases about direct civil liability for breach of statutory duty contained the appropriate tests. The basis of liability claimed here was different: see Lord Browne-Wilkinson's categorisation in *X (Minors) v Bedfordshire County Council* at p 730 and the passage in Lord Jauncey's speech in *R v Deputy Governor of Parkhurst Prison, ex p Hague* at pp 170–171, where Lord Jauncey was discussing breach of statutory duty (see also p 168). So counsel did not propose to make any direct comment on whether counsel for the council's propositions were correct in context. Instead he addressed particular points which had been made about the statutory provisions and allegedly negated the existence of any duty of care. He referred to the same provisions as I have mentioned above, and submitted that these provisions, especially s 9 (2), imposed a duty on the local authority to see that buildings were built in accordance with the 1972 Regulations. The qualification in s 9 (2), which required the local authority to do no more than take all reasonable steps, required to be tested objectively. Counsel advanced 12 factors for consideration:

(1) The scope of the duty incumbent on the defenders was specifically to make buildings comply with regulations promulgated inter alia for the safety of persons entering the building: see *Armstrong v Moore*.

(2) The pursuer fell within a clearly definable class of persons covered by the duty, that was the class of persons who would frequent the building: see s 3 (2) of the 1959 Act. This was the sort of class where a duty of care had already been recognised, for example consumers of a manufacturer's product, as in *Donoghue v Stevenson*, or persons entering on land, under the Occupiers' Liability (Scotland) Act 1960. The class was not exceptionally wide.

(3) The requirement on a local authority to take all reasonable steps to ensure that a building complied with the warrant was objective. Parliament must have envisaged that there must be scope for examination of the steps taken by a local authority after the event. It was difficult to see in what context that would be done, except in an action for damages. While an application for judicial review was a possibility, it was hard to see who would have the necessary interest to make such an application.

(4) It was not surprising that the statute itself made no provision for civil liability, where the local authority acted in a supervisory capacity and it would not therefore be expected that they would be directly liable for a breach of the building standards regulations. Section 19A of the 1959 Act envisaged that there would be a breach if a building did not comply with the regulations. This created strict liability if there was a breach of the regulations, with a result that such a breach would be actionable regardless of questions of reasonable care.

(5) The duty contended for was to take reasonable care to avoid personal injury. This was relevant to the question whether or not the duty existed. In *Murphy v Brentwood District Council* and *Caparo Industries plc v Dickman* different kinds of damage had been discussed, and it was important to recognise the type of damage which had arisen in the present case.

(6) There was no reason to make an exception in the present case for reasons of public policy, such as existed in *Hill v Chief Constable of West Yorkshire* per Lord Keith at [1989] AC, p 63. Here there was a limited duty, carried out in limited circumstances, and no more than the exercise of reasonable care was required.

(7) The absence of other cases of this kind in which liability had been recognised (see *Caparo Industries plc v Dickman* at p 618) might be because personal injuries were not often suffered by reason of the failure of local authorities to enforce regulations of this kind. In fact there had been recognition of the existence of such a duty by Lord Macfadyen in *Duff v Highland and Islands Fire Board*, where it was held that firefighters did owe a duty of care as there was a statutory duty imposed on fire authorities to make provision for firefighting purposes. The existence of a similar sort of duty had been recognised in *Adair v Magistrates of Paisley*. In that case the pursuer sought damages for injuries sustained by him through the collapse of a stand on a racecourse. He averred that the stand had been erected for the accommodation of the public by the Paisley Race Committee, but was defective in construction in various ways, in consequence of which it collapsed. The defenders were aware of the erection of the stand and it was their duty as commissioners under the Burgh Police (Scotland) Act 1892, in particular s 168, to have had the stand inspected; they had failed to do so, but had they done so the defects would have been discovered, the building condemned and the accident to the pursuer prevented. In allowing an issue the Second Division held that s 168 impliedly gave rise to a duty on those who were charged with the public interest in the matter to see that the stand was safe in the interests of the public. I was referred to various passages in the opinions which were delivered, but it is sufficient to quote from that of Lord Young at (1904) 12 SLT, p 107: 'Well, then, here is a duty placed by statute upon the public authority, who have the means of obtaining the best and most reliable assistance in discharging their duty, to take care of the public interest and safety in such a matter. The case of the pursuer upon that is that the defenders did not perform this duty. The pursuer undertakes to show that they did not cause the stand in question to be examined — and it is not alleged that they did — and also to show that such an examination would have led to forbidding the use of it until some alteration had been made.'

(8) There must be potent reasons to exclude a duty of care if the requirements of reasonable foreseeability and proximity were satisfied: see *X (Minors) v Bedfordshire County Council* at p 749. The passage in the speech of Lord Hoffmann in *Stovin v Wise* at p 949 was dealing with an omission to exercise statutory powers, not duties.

(9) There could be a duty incumbent on a public authority to prevent the commission of a wrong by another party: see *Home Office v Dorset Yacht Co Ltd*.

(10) The question of time bar was not a factor of any weight, as it could arise in any case.

(11) The same applied in connection with the failure to sue the builders.

(12) The existence of a common law duty of care would not interfere with the performance by a local authority of their statutory duty. So, a duty of care did exist to take reasonable care for the safety of persons such as the pursuer. Counsel indicated that he had not had prior notice of the criticisms of the specification of the duty of care in the pursuer's pleadings, and he would wish to consider proposing an amendment if I was minded, after consideration of this issue as a matter of principle, to allow a proof before answer.

In his second speech, counsel for the council concentrated on the 12 factors enumerated above. I need not refer to his submissions in any detail, except to note that under reference to *Adair v Magistrates of Paisley* counsel submitted that it was of no assistance. The nature of the statutory duty there was precise, and the allegation was of a failure to carry out any inspection, rather than to exercise reasonable care in carrying out an inspection. The case must be considered in light of the subsequent authorities from *Donoghue v Stevenson* onwards, particularly the recent cases in the House of Lords.

In my opinion the solution to the main issue, whether the council, in the circumstances, owed a duty of care to the pursuer, is to be arrived at by reference to the tests derived from *Caparo Industries plc v Dickman*, as further explained in *X (Minors) v Bedfordshire County Council*. As I have already indicated, it was not submitted, for the purposes of the procedure roll debate, that the necessary proximity between the council and the pursuer could not be discovered by reference to the pursuer's pleadings and, beyond noting that counsel for the council expressly reserved his position on this point should the action proceed further, I need say nothing more about it. My opinion on the test of reasonable foreseeability is that the pursuer has made sufficient averments to entitle her to a proof before answer on this point; I am certainly not satisfied that she would be bound to fail on this aspect of the case. It was not suggested by counsel for the council that the pursuer's averments in this regard were lacking in specification, so the question is whether, taking them pro veritate, an accident such as that sustained by the pursuer was not a reasonably foreseeable consequence of the alleged negligence of the defenders. I do not think it possible to answer this question without sufficiently detailed exploration of the facts in the course of evidence. I do not regard it as possible, without instruction from suitable witnesses, to reach a conclusion about what a reasonably careful local authority performing its functions under the 1959 Act ought reasonably to have foreseen as constituting a risk of danger to members of the public. Pavement cases are only of limited assistance, since such a case deals with projections above an otherwise relatively level walking surface. A stairway down which a person might fall appears to me to give rise to quite different considerations, and it does not seem to me to be possible to reach any conclusion either way as to the extent to which the dimensions of a particular step departed from those specified in the relevant provisions of the 1971 Regulations did or did not give rise to a reasonably foreseeable risk of danger. Moreover, I agree with counsel for the pursuer that it is not appropriate to look at one step in isolation. The step was only part of the stairway, and it would be necessary to look at it in relation to the whole stairway and any relevant surrounding circumstances to form any impression of the effect that its dimensions, related to other steps, and maybe other features of the stairway, would affect any person descending the stairway. I do not therefore think it appropriate to accede to counsel for the council's submissions on this point at this stage.

This leaves the question whether it would be fair, just and reasonable to impose a duty of care on the council. While I recognise of course that a breach of statutory duty which gives rise to injury may lead to a remedy in damages, I have derived little or no assistance for present purposes from consideration of cases where a potential liability in damages has been recognised. I was referred to no decision of the Inner House of the Court of Session which I would regard as binding on me for present purposes. *Adair v Magistrates of Paisley*, as I read it, did no more than recognise that a remedy in damages might arise directly from a breach of statutory duty which consisted of a failure to inspect. There was, however, no discussion in that case of the considerations which might arise if the claim for damages was based, not on breach of statutory duty, but on failure to exercise a duty to take reasonable care at common law in the performance of statutory functions. Moreover, that case was decided long before the House of Lords decisions which counsel were agreed that I should follow, and which I have indicated that I propose to follow. It appears to me to be of some significance that in no case has it been decided that civil liability on the part of a local authority may arise in a context similar to that in the present case. Given that the general trend is away from the imposition of civil liabilities on local authorities performing statutory regulatory functions, as can be seen from the passages quoted above, in my opinion it would be necessary to find clear indications in favour of such liability before it would be open to me to hold that the council could, in law, be regarded as owing any duty of care towards the pursuer. With all respect, I am not persuaded that such clear indications existed in *Duff v Highland and Islands Fire Board*.

The indications in this case all appear to me to point in the other direction. The council are not being sued as the designers, builders, owners or occupiers of the supermarket and stairway. The persons who fell into these categories, and who might be regarded, jointly or severally, as responsible for the physical condition of the stairway at the time of the pursuer's accident, are not parties to the action. The council's functions, as I see it, are properly to be regarded as placing the council in a secondary, though still important, category. This can be seen as being the intention of Parliament in the 1959 Act, s 19 of which does not subject a local authority to any criminal sanctions. Section 19A, if it were brought into force, would create a civil liability for certain breaches, but not breaches by a local authority in the performance of their functions relating to the approval of applications for building warrants and the granting of completion certificates. I deduce from these provisions that, apart from them, Parliament did not intend any civil liability to arise from the 1959 Act, particularly on the part of local authorities, and s 19A (whatever the reason for its not having been brought into force) is a clear contra-indication of any such intention in the case of local authorities. Although one of the policy considerations underlying the 1959 Act and the 1971 Regulations is the safety of the public, there is no authority for treating this as axiomatic. There may be civil liability to the public if a local authority are negligent in the performance of their statutory functions, but to establish that more is required. One requirement is that there should be a sufficiently determinate class of persons to whom a duty of care could be said to be owed. These must be fewer than the public at large. Counsel for the pursuer attempted to limit the class by reference to those who happened to use the stairway (or go into the supermarket, if they both formed parts of one building), but that limitation would only arise from random decisions of members of the public to use the stairway on any particular day in an indeterminate period after the granting of the completion certificate. This does not appear to me to create a class to whom a duty of care could arise in the granting of the completion certificate or at any earlier stage; it is not determinate in the way that, for example, the class of employees in a factory is determinate. Another consideration is that no absolute duty is imposed on a local authority under the 1959 Act. I agree with counsel for the pursuer that it is relevant to have regard both to the stage at which the application for building warrant is being considered and to the stage at which consideration is being given to the granting of a completion certificate. But s 9 (2) does no more than require the local authority to take reasonable steps in carrying out an inspection, and I do not regard the provisions relating to applications for building warrant as imposing any higher standard. Given that a local authority have finite resources, and must exercise their discretion, in the public interest, as to how best to use those resources, I would regard it as a form of interference which would tend adversely to affect the sound exercise of this discretion if the local authority felt it necessary to protect itself against claims for civil liability in this way. The safety of the public is important, and is expressly referred to in s 3 (2) of the 1959 Act; but it arises also in the context of the performance of many other statutory functions by a local authority, and I can see no reason why it should be regarded as giving rise to civil liability for negligent performance of statutory functions in the present case simply because it has been expressly mentioned. It would be necessary to establish a more unified doctrine, whether or not the safety of the public was expressly mentioned, before such liability could be said to exist. All the indications, as I have said, point in the opposite direction. I am not concerned in this case with liabilities in damages which might arise directly from breaches of statutory duty; as counsel for the pursuer made clear, and as the pursuer's averments show, the pursuer seeks to establish that a duty at common law was owed to her in the performance by the council of its statutory functions.

It was not suggested to me in this regard that the leading of evidence would assist in the resolution of what is essentially a question of law. In my opinion, as a matter of law, no duty of care was owed in the circumstances by the council to the pursuer, and for that reason the action is irrelevant. I shall accordingly sustain the first plea in law for the defenders and dismiss the action."

Notes

(1) *X* is clearly a very important decision. However, the guidance in *X* is of mixed value. Thus although there is discussion of breach of statutory duty, liability must be based on a common law duty of care and the question of policy arguments for and against the duty of care are helpful. More difficult is the failure to consider the fact that many of the matters of complaint were in fact about omissions and the general approach to be taken to discretionary decisions. The distinction between acts and omissions has not traditionally been a source of difficulty for Scots lawyers: see *Hallett* above and also *Maloco v. Littlewoods Organisation Ltd*, 1987 S.L.T. 425. These points were, however, addressed in the later judgment of the House of Lords in *Stovin v. Wise*.

14–44

(2) The case of *Duff v. Highland and Islands Fire Board*, noted in *Forbes*, was reported at 1995 S.L.T. 1362. A chimney fire was attended to by the fire brigade but restarted after they had left, causing the destruction of the house. Lord Macfadyen considered arguments to the effect that considerations of public policy prevented there being a duty of care owed by the fire brigade towards property owners. He considered the judgments in *East Suffolk Rivers Catchment Board v. Kent* [1941] A.C. 74 and *Hill v. Chief Constable of West Yorkshire* [1989] A.C. 53, the latter judgment being referred to in *X* and commented:

> "Counsel for the defenders is no doubt right in submitting that there is no statutory duty on a fire authority to fight an individual fire, or to exercise reasonable care in doing so. As I have already noted, however, there is in my view an underlying statutory duty to secure the services of a fire brigade and efficient arrangements for dealing with calls for assistance. In the *East Suffolk* case it was recognised that, even in the case of a mere power, an authority which chose to exercise the power came under a common law duty to take reasonable care not to inflict additional damage by doing so. I therefore do not regard the question of whether and to what extent a statutory duty exists as necessarily determinative of whether a common law duty of care exists.
>
> The public policy argument of counsel for the defenders depended on analogy with the law relating to the civil liability of police for negligence in the detection of crime. He cited *Hill v Chief Constable of West Yorkshire* [1989] AC 53, per Lord Keith at p 63, where it was held that as a matter of public policy the police were immune from action for negligence in respect of their activities in the investigation and suppression of crime; and a group of three more recent cases following *Hill*, namely *Alexandrou v Oxford* [1993] 4 All ER 328, *Osman v Ferguson* [1993] 4 All ER 344, and *Ansell v McDermott* [1993] 4 All ER 355. The proposition that the public policy considerations affecting the fire service are the same as those affecting the police appears to me to rest on nothing more than assertion. I recognise that there is a risk that the existence of potential liability in negligence may tend to encourage a defensive approach to their operations, but that seems to me to be an argument which could be deployed with at least as much force in the context of medical and other professional negligence, and there is no question of public policy excluding liability in those categories of case. It is no doubt right that in operational matters much must be left to the professional judgment of the firefighters, but that can be achieved by applying a test analogous to the professional negligence test in determining what amounts to negligence. It is going too far in my view to suggest, as counsel for the defenders did, that operational judgment should be immune from challenge."

Was Lord Nimmo Smith correct in his treatment of what was said in *Duff*? The presence of a basic duty on the part of the fire brigade was clearly important for Lord Macfadyen. Is it possible to construct such a basic duty on the facts of *Forbes*? While the builders or architects or occupiers have had more direct responsible the accident, did Lord Nimmo-Smith give sufficient weight to the fact that on local authority could issue a completion certificate and the consequences of certificate not being issued?

(3) Following *X*, the potential scope of civil liability for breach of statutory duty placed on a public authority has been narrowed considerably. Compare *X* with the dicta of Lord Lindhurst in *Ferguson v. Earl of Kinnoul* (1842) 9 Cl. and F. 251. In holding that a Presbytery was liable in damages for refusal to accept a presentee to a church, his Lordship noted that:

> "When a person has an important duty to perform, he is bound to perform that duty; and if he neglects or refuses to do so, as an individual in consequence sustains injury, that lays the foundation for an action to recover damages by way of compensation for the injury that he has so sustained."

Although Lord Lindhurst's statement is a general one, its ambit has been narrowed by *X*. Consider how *Mallon v. Monklands District Council*, 1986 S.L.T. 347 (see para. 11–25) might have been decided if the facts had arisen subsequent to *X*. In *R. v. Lambeth London Borough Council, ex p. Barnes* (1992) 25 H.L.R. 140 it was held that the continued failure of a local authority to house an applicant for accommodation under Part III of the Housing Act 1985 was a breach of statutory duty giving liability in damages: but see now *O'Rourke v. Camden London Borough Council* [1997] 3 W.L.R. 86. In *Clunis v. Camden and Islington Health Authority* [1998] Q.B. 978 it was held that section 117 of the Mental Health Act 1983 does not confer any right of action for damages for the alleged negligent release of a mental patient and in *Phelps v. Hillingdon*

Borough Council [1999] 1 All E.R. 421, again following *X*, no liability attached to an education authority for alleged negligent failure to diagnose dyslexia in a child in one of its schools. Performance of a statutory duty can of course be enforced under section 45(*b*) of the Court of Session Act 1988, on which see para. 11–11.

(4) On negligence and policy, do you agree with the policy arguments advanced by Lord Browne-Wilkinson and Lord Nimmo Smith? Are they sufficiently specific? Could they apply to a liability for negligence against doctors, for example? Contrast their Lordships' comments with those of Lord Macfadyen in *Duff* above and consider also the following comments of Lord Hamilton in *Gibson v. Chief Constable Strathclyde Police*, Outer House, February 26, 1999, unreported. Here the pursuer maintained that he had suffered injury as a result of the defender's failure to prevent the car in which he was travelling from crossing a bridge which had collapsed. The driver and other passenger had been killed. One of the arguments for the Chief Constable was that on the basis of *Hill*, public policy meant that the police owed no duty of care to someone in the pursuer's position. Lord Hamilton commented:

14–45

> "The third issue to be decided is whether no duty of care existed because it would not be fair, just and reasonable to 'impose' one in circumstances such as the present. In *Hill* v *Chief Constable of West Yorkshire*, Lord Keith at p. 63 expressed the opinion that another reason (that is, other than lack of proximity) why an action for damages in negligence should not lie against the police in the circumstances of that case was public policy. His Lordship identified a number of factors which bore on that matter. Some of those factors taken individually might apply in the present case. It is, however, important in my view to bear in mind the circumstances of the case in which those observations were made — in particular, the context of criminal investigation. His Lordship expressly approved the judgment of Glidewell L.J. in the Court of Appeal where at [1988] Q.B. pp. 75–6 reference was made to the implications for the criminal justice system of allowing civil actions of negligence to lie against the police arising out of the same subject matter. Reference was made by both Glidewell L.J. and Lord Keith to the basis for immunity held to exist in *Rondel* v *Worsley* [1969] 1 A.C. 191 (where the implications for the administration of criminal justice are obvious). The observations made by Lord Templeman in *Hill* v *Chief Constable of West Yorkshire* are also clearly concerned with the inappropriateness of an action of damages as a vehicle for inquiring into past failures by individual police officers in relation to criminal investigations. There is no justification, in my view, for lifting one or two of the factors referred to by Lord Keith and, if these happen to apply in another situation, to hold for that reason that it would not be fair, just and reasonable to impose (or maintain) a duty of care. As Mr McEachran pointed out, some of the factors relied on by his Lordship would equally apply to actions against medical men or other professionals. So far as I am aware, it has never been suggested that the diversion of precious time and energy from the care of the sick or the absence of any stimulus to perform better were individually or collectively grounds for conferring an immunity from suit on doctors or other health professionals, including those engaged in National Health Service practice. The listed criticisms made of certain earlier judgments by counsel for the plaintiffs in *Capital & Counties plc* v *Hampshire County Council* have, as Stuart-Smith L.J. said at p. 1044, considerable force. His Lordship also at p. 1044E–F observed (in relation to the position of the Fire Brigade) that the analogy with the police exercising their functions of investigating and suppressing crime was not close."
>
> Although in Scotland the police function in relation to the investigation and suppression of crime and that in relation to the protection of life and property stem from the same statutory provision, it does not follow, in my view, that the same considerations apply to both functions in relation to immunity from suit. In so far as English authority is concerned, I am unable, with respect, to accept the conclusion of Kennedy J in *Clough* v *Bussan* at p. 435 that, for the purposes of public policy, the one is really part and parcel of the other. Nor am I, with respect, convinced by the reasoning on the public policy issue in *Alexandrou* v *Oxford* or in *Ancell* v *McDermott*. These three last mentioned cases illustrate what might be regarded as a tide in the English courts towards a wide interpretation of Lord Keith's and Lord Templeman's observations in *Hill* v *Chief Constable of West Yorkshire*. That tide may now be running less strongly. *Swinney* v *Chief Constable of Northumbria Police* and *Capital & Counties plc* v *Hampshire County Council* may be indicative of such a change. Moreover, the decision of the Court of Human Rights in *Osman* v *United Kingdom*, together with the position adopted by the U.K. Government before that court that 'the exclusion was not a blanket exclusion of liability but a carefully and narrowly focused limitation which applied only in respect of the investigation and suppression of crime, and even then not in every case' (para. 144), may also lead to some reconsideration of the scope of the public policy immunity accorded to the police in some of the English decisions."

See also *Home Office v. Dorset Yacht Co. Ltd* [1970] A.C. 1004 at 1032–1033, *per* Lord Reid. Lord Hamilton went on to observe that in any event a distinction was held to be drawn between the criminal law and civil law responsibilities of the police and, moreover provided that due regard was paid to the judgment of the decision maker in question, the scope of public policy immunity, if it existed at all, should be narrowly drawn:

> "Likewise there is no close analogy, in my view, as regards the policy issue between the exercise by the police of their function of investigating and suppressing crime and the exercise by them of their function of performing civil operational tasks concerned with human safety on the public roads. It was not disputed that the police enjoy no immunity on public policy grounds in respect of the manner in which a constable drives his police vehicle or his motor cycle on the public roads. There would likewise be no immunity, in my view, in respect of the manner in which a constable in charge of directing traffic on such a road performed that function. Likewise, there is no immunity, in my view, in respect of the manner in which other civil road safety operational tasks are carried out by police officers where there is no inherent problem of conflict with instructions issued by superior officers or with duties owed to other persons. To adopt the language of Ward L.J. in *Swinney* v *Chief Constable of Northumbria Police* at p. 486 there is 'no overwhelming dictate of public policy' to exclude the prosecution of claims arising out of such circumstances. As Lord Macfadyen said in relation to the Fire Brigade in *Duff* v *Highland and Islands Fire Board* at p. 1363:
>
>> 'It is no doubt right that in operational matters much must be left to the professional judgement of the firefighters, but that can be achieved by applying a test analogous to the professional negligence test in determining what amounts to negligence. It is going too far in my view to suggest, as counsel for the defenders did, that operational judgement should be immune from challenge.'
>
> A similar approach was adopted by Lord Johnston (in relation to prison officers) in *McCafferty* v *Secretary of State for Scotland*.

Swinney v. Chief Constable of Northumbria Police [1996] 3 All E.R. 449 held that it was arguable that the police were owed a duty of care to an informant to keep confidential information supplied, including the informant's identity, secure. In *Ancell v. MacDermott* [1993] 4 All E.R. 355 a claim in respect of alleged police failure to deal adequately with a traffic hazard resulting from an oil spillage leading to a fatal accident was struck out. In *Alexandrou v. Oxford* [1993] 4 All E.R. 328 a claim in respect of an allegedly negligent response to a burglar alarm was dismissed and in *Capital and Counties plc v. Hampshire County Council* [1996] 4 All E.R. 336 the fire brigade was held liable where an officer negligently ordered a sprinkler system in a burning building to be turned off. Note too the reference to *McCafferty v. Secretary of State for Scotland*, 1998 S.C.L.R. 379 holding that no blanket immunity on policy grounds applied to prison officers dealing with the control of unrest in a prison.

14–46   (5) In *Osman v. Ferguson* [1993] 4 All E.R. 344 the House of Lords held principally on policy grounds that the police owed no duty of care to prevent injury to a person known to the police to have been threatened by a third party. The plaintiff alleged that his right under Article 6(1) of the European Convention on Human Rights, which secures to everyone the right to have any claim in relation to the civil rights and obligations brought before a court or tribunal, had been violated. The plaintiff went to the European Court of Human Rights. The European Court of Human Rights reasoned as follows:

> "149. The reasons which led the House of Lords in the *Hill* case to lay down an exclusionary rule to protect the police from negligence actions in the context at issue are based on the view that the interests of the community as a whole are best served by a police service whose efficiency and effectiveness in the battle against crime are not jeopardised by the constant risk of exposure to tortious liability for policy and operational decisions.
>
> 150. Although the aim of such a rule may be accepted as legitimate in terms of the Convention, as being directed to the maintenance of the effectiveness of the police service and hence to the prevention of disorder or crime, the Court must nevertheless, in turning to the issue of *proportionality*, have particular regard to its scope and especially its application in the case at issue. While the Government have contended that the exclusionary rule of liability is not of an absolute nature (see paragraph 144 above) and that its application may yield to other public policy considerations, it would appear to the Court that in the instant case the Court of Appeal proceeded on the basis that the rule provided a watertight defence to the police and that it was impossible to prise open an immunity which the police enjoy from civil suit in respect of their acts and omissions in the investigation and suppression of crime.

151. The Court would observe that the application of the rule in this manner without further enquiry into the existence of competing public interest considerations only serves to confer a blanket immunity on the police for their acts and omissions during the investigation and suppression of crime and amounts to an unjustifiable restriction on an applicant's right to have a determination on the merits of his or her claim against the police in deserving cases.

In its view, it must be open to a domestic court to have regard to the presence of other public interest considerations which pull in the opposite direction to the application of the rule. Failing this, there will be no distinction made between degrees of negligence or of harm suffered or any consideration of the justice of a particular case.... Furthermore, the applicants' case involved the alleged failure to protect the life of a child and their view that that failure was the result of a catalogue of acts and omissions which amounted to grave negligence as opposed to minor acts of incompetence. The applicants also claimed that the police had assumed responsibility for their safety. Finally, the harm sustained was of the most serious nature.

152. For the Court, these are considerations which must be examined on the merits and not automatically excluded by the application of a rule which amounts to the grant of an immunity to the police. In the instant case, the Court is not persuaded by the Government's argument that the rule as interpreted by the domestic court did not provided an automatic immunity to the police."

Note the use of proportionality. Arguably Scots law is closer to the test expounded by the European Court of Human Rights on the matter of policy as providing a basis for immunity, than the law which is found in *Hill* and *X*. *Forbes*, to that extent, may represent something of an anomalous position in Scots law. For comment on the domestic proceedings in *Osman* see J. Steele and D.S. Cowan, "The negligent pursuit of public duty — a police immunity?" [1994] P.L. 4, and on the impact of the ECHR generally, J. Wright, "Local Authorities, The Duty of Care and the ECHR" [1998] O.J.L.S. 1 and Lord Hoffmann, "Human Rights and the House of Lords" (1999) 62 M.L.R. 159.

(6) Negligence and Discretion: Underlying the court's concern about the imposition of a duty of care is its view that it may not be the appropriate accountability mechanism to deal with the way in which a statutory discretion has or has not been exercised. Often resource implications are involved and it might be more appropriate for decisions in relation to these to be reached by elected bodies and to be held accountable to the public through political means. This has led to a distinction between acts which might be regarded as operational and acts which are policy based. Operational acts implement policy decisions and it is at that level that liability if any should arise. This approach is exemplified by Lord Browne-Wilkinson in *X* and by Lord Dunpark in *Bonthrone* and in cases noted above. More recently there has been a shying away from the distinction as unworkable on which see *Stovin v. Wise* below.

(7) There are of course a great number of areas where liability on the part of public authorities **14-47** is readily recognised and a duty of care readily imposed. Thus public authorities as occupiers of land are subject to the Occupiers' Liability (Scotland) Act 1960; accidents involving vehicles owned by public authorities are dealt with by application of ordinary principles: *Watt v. Hertfordshire County Council* [1954] 1 W.L.R. 835. They may assume responsibility towards an individual as noted by Lord Hoffmann in *Stovin v. Wise*. However, identifying the line between areas where negligence is actionable and those where it is not is still problematic. Similarly the distinction between acts and omissions noted in *Stovin v. Wise* does not necessarily make it any easier to determine whether liability arises. Liability may be limited because of policy considerations even if harm is assumed to have happened, as in *X*, but equally at common law there are a number of positive obligations to act for the benefit of another. In *Gibson* above Lord Macfadyen adopted the dictum of Lord Browne-Wilkinson in *X* that:

"The question whether there is such a common law duty and if so its ambit, must be profoundly influenced by the statutory framework within which the acts complained of were done... Where no pre-existing relationship exists, failure to act may not whatever the moral obloquy, amount in law to a breach of any duty of care.... However, where (as here) a relationship does pre-exist, whether as an individual or with a limited group of persons, the distinction between acts and omissions becomes less important."

Of particular importance to Lord Macfadyen was the fact that he discerned under section 17 of the Police (Scotland) Act 1967 a general function of constables to protect in a civil context life and property which was in his view, an important consideration in establishing a duty of care. That duty extended "not only to the manner of the exercise of that control but, as *Wilson v. Chief Constable, Lothian and Borders Constabulary*, 1989 S.L.T. 97 illustrates in a different context, to the relinquishment of it".

14–48   (8) One of the most difficult areas in this field relates to liability for a negligent misstatement. Such liability was recognised in a leading case of *Hedley Byrne & Co. v. Heller & Partners* [1964] A.C. 465 where it was held that a duty of care could arise in respect of a misstatement which caused an economic loss. Liability will only exist where the person making the statement knows that it will be communicated to the pursuer, either individually or as a member of a specific class in connection with a particular matter and that it was likely that the pursuer would rely on it for the purpose of deciding whether or not to proceed with the matter in question: *Caparo Industries v. Dickman* [1990] 1 All E.R. 568 at 576 *per* Lord Bridge. In *Henderson v. Merrett Syndicates* [1994] 3 W.L.R. 761 it was noted that *Hedley Byrne* extended beyond provision of information to cover assumption of responsibility for a performance of a service for the pursuer. Public authorities have been held liable on the principle of *Hedley Byrne* for negligent statements and other acts in the following cases: *Ministry of Housing and Local Government v. Sharp* [1970] 2 Q.B. 223, negligent search of local land charges register; *Welton v. North Cornwall District Council* [1997] 1 W.L.R. 570, environmental health officer negligently required owners of food premises to undertake works which were unnecessary; *Lambert v. West Devon Borough Council, The Times*, March 27, 1997, negligent advice by building control officer that L could proceed with building works, although contrast this with *Tidman v. Reading Borough Council, The Times*, November 10, 1994 where it was held that a response by council officers to an informal planning enquiry by telephone did not give rise to a duty of care. In *Johnstone v. Traffic Commissioner*, 1990 S.L.T. 409 it was alleged that medical advice tendered by a senior doctor to the traffic commissioner, which led to the revocation of the pursuer's licence, was negligent. The defender argued, *inter alia*, that no duty of care was owed by the doctor as the advice in question had been tendered to the traffic commissioner, not the pursuer, and moreover that public policy was opposed to any duty of care arising. As a matter of relevancy, the Lord Ordinary (Cameron of Lochbroom) was not prepared to hold that no such duty could arise. In *W. v. Essex County Council* [1998] 3 All E.R. 111, C.A. a local authority made a statement to a foster family that a child sent to live with them did not present a physical threat to their own children. The child was a known sex abuser. It was alleged that abuse of the family's children occurred. It was held that while policy considerations may well have limited the common law duty of care in relation to the council's statutory duty to protect children, that did not apply to children not subject to its statutory duty of protection, such as the children in the foster family and liability could thereby arise.

Stovin v. Wise (Norfolk County Council, third party)

[1996] A.C. 923

14–49   In December 1988, the plaintiff, Thomas Stovin, was riding a motorcycle along Station Road, Wymondham, Norfolk, when he collided with a motor vehicle which was driven by the defendant, Rita Wise, out of a junction on his left. He was seriously injured. Although the junction was not a busy one, the county council as highway authority knew it to be dangerous because the view of road users turning out of the junction was restricted by a bank of earth on adjoining land. There had been accidents in 1976 and 1982 at the spot. In January 1988 the council wrote to the owner of the land, British Rail, suggesting that part of the bank should be removed and that the council would meet the cost of about £1,000. There was a third accident in March 1988. However, there was no response to the letter and the matter had not been followed up by the council by December.

The trial judge found that Mrs Wise was 70 per cent responsible and the council, brought in as a third party, 30 per cent responsible. The council's appeal to the Court of Appeal was dismissed ([1994] 1 W.L.R 1124). The council's appeal to the House of Lords was allowed by three to two (Lord Hoffmann, Lord Goff of Chievely and Lord Jauncey of Tullichettle; Lord Nicholls of Birkenhead and Lord Slynn of Hadley dissenting). The major speeches of the majority and minority were given, respectively, by Lord Hoffmann and Lord Nicholls of Birkenhead.

LORD HOFFMANN:

"4. Acts and Omissions

The judge made no express mention of the fact that the complaint against the council was not about anything which it had done to make the highway dangerous but about its omission to make it safer. Omissions, like economic loss, are notoriously a category of conduct in which Lord Atkin's generalisation in *Donoghue v. Stevenson* [1932] A.C. 562 offers limited help. In the High Court of Australia in *Hargrave v. Goldman* (1963) 110 C.L.R. 40, 66, Windeyer J. drew attention to the irony in Lord Atkin's allusion, in formulating his 'neighbour' test, to the parable of the Good Samaritan [1932] A.C. 562, 580:

> 'The priest and the Levite, when they saw the wounded man by the road, passed by on the other side. He obviously was a person whom they had in contemplation and who was closely and directly affected by their action. Yet the common law does not require a man to act as the Samaritan did.'

A similar point was made by Lord Diplock in *Dorset Yacht Co. Ltd v. Home Office* [1970] A.C. 1004, 1060. There are sound reasons why omissions require different treatment from positive conduct. It is one thing for the law to say that a person who undertakes some activity shall take reasonable care not to cause damage to others. It is another thing for the law to require that a person who is doing nothing in particular shall take steps to prevent another from suffering harm from the acts of third parties (like Mrs Wise) or natural causes. One can put the matter in political, moral or economic terms. In political terms it is less of an invasion of an individual's freedom for the law to require him to consider the safety of others in his actions than to impose upon him a duty to rescue or protect. A moral version of this point may be called the 'why pick on me?' argument. A duty to prevent harm to others or to render assistance to a person in danger or distress may apply to a large and indeterminate class of people who happen to be able to do something. Why should one be held liable rather than another? In economic terms, the efficient allocation of resources usually requires an activity should bear its own costs. If it benefits from being able to impose some of its costs on other people (what economists call 'externalities'), the market is distorted because the activity appears cheaper than it really is. So liability to pay compensation for loss caused by negligent conduct acts as a deterrent against increasing the cost of the activity to the community and reduces externalities. But there is no similar justification for requiring a person who is not doing anything to spend money on behalf of someone else. Except in special cases (such as marine salvage) English law does not reward someone who voluntarily confers a benefit on another. So there must be some special reason why he should have to put his hand in his pocket.

In *Hargrave v. Goldman*, 110 C.L.R. 40, 66, Windeyer J. said:

> 'The trend of judicial development in the law of negligence has been ... to found a duty to take care either in some task undertaken, or in the ownership, occupation, or use of land or chattels.'

There may be a duty to act if one has undertaken to do so or induced a person to rely upon one doing so. Or the ownership or occupation of land may give rise to a duty to take positive steps for the benefit of those who come upon the land and sometimes for the benefit of neighbours. In *Hargrave v. Goldman* the High Court of Australia held that the owner and occupier of a 600-acre grazing property in Western Australia had a duty to take reasonable steps to extinguish a fire, which had been started by lightning striking a tree on his land, so as to prevent it from spreading to his neighbour's land. This is a case in which the limited class of persons who owe the duty (neighbours) is easily identified and the political, moral and economic arguments which I have mentioned are countered by the fact that the duties are mutual. One cannot tell where the lightning may strike and it is therefore both fair and efficient to impose upon each landowner a duty to have regard to the interests of his neighbour. In giving the advice of the Privy Council affirming the decision (*Goldman v. Hargrave* [1967] 1 A.C. 645) Lord Wilberforce underlined the exceptional nature of the liability when he pointed out that the question of whether the landowner had acted reasonably should be judged by reference to the resources he actually had at his disposal and not by some general or objective standard. This is quite different from the duty owed by a person who undertakes a positive activity which carries the risk of causing damage to others. If he does not have the resources to take such steps as are objectively reasonable to prevent such damage, he should not undertake that activity at all.

5. Omissions in the Court of Appeal

[His Lordship rejected views adopted by members of the Court of Appeal (1) that this was an omission in the context of a positive decision to act analogous to the failure of a car driver to apply the

14–50

brakes (*per* Kennedy L.J. [1994] 1 W.L.R. 1124, 1138); and (2) that the highway authority's position was analogous to that of the occupier of premises in relation to visitors (Roch L.J. [1994] 1 W.L.R. 1124, 1139). As to (1), S's injuries 'were not caused by the negotiations between the council and British Rail or anything else which the council did': As to (2), the analogy was insufficient given that an occupier could normally take steps to keep out unwanted entrants; and where he could not, as where a public right of way lay across his land, it was established that there was no duty to take reasonable steps to make the way safe for users (*McGeown v. Northern Ireland Housing Executive* [1995] 1 A.C. 233, H.L.).]

6. Public Authorities

The argument that the council had a positive duty to take action giving rise to a claim for compensation in tort must therefore depend, as the judge and the Court of Appeal recognised, upon the public nature of its powers, duties and funding. The argument is that while it may be unreasonable to expect a private landowner to spend money for the benefit of strangers who have the right to cross his land, the very purpose of the existence of a public authority like the council is to spend its resources on making the roads convenient and safe. For that purpose it has a large battery of powers in the Highways Act 1980. These do not actually include a power which would have enabled the council to go upon the land of British Rail and remove the bank of earth. But there is power under section 79 to serve a notice requiring the bank to be removed. The power is conferred for the purpose of 'the prevention of danger arising from obstruction to the view of persons using the highway'. Although the allegation is not that the council failed to use this power (it probably would not have been necessary to do so), its existence shows that one of the purposes for which Parliament contemplated that the highway authority would spend its money was the removal of exactly the kind of obstructions which caused the accident in this case.

It is certainly true that some of the arguments against liability for omissions do not apply to public bodies like a highway authority. There is no 'why pick on me?' argument: as Kennedy L.J. said, at 1139, the highway authority alone had the financial and physical resources, as well as the legal powers, to eliminate the hazard. But this does not mean that the distinction between acts and omissions is irrelevant to the duties of a public body or that there are not other arguments, peculiar to public bodies, which may negative the existence of a duty of care.

(a) Negligent Conduct in the Exercise of Statutory Powers

14–51

Since *Mersey Docks and Harbour Board Trustees v. Gibbs* (1866) L.R. 1 H.L. 93 it has been clear law that in the absence of express statutory authority, a public body is in principle liable for torts in the same way as private person. But its statutory powers or duties may restrict its liability. For example, it may be authorised to do something which necessarily involves committing what would otherwise be a tort. In such a case it will not be liable: *Allen v. Gulf Oil Refining Ltd* [1981] A.C. 1001. Or it may have discretionary powers which enable it to do things to achieve a statutory purpose notwithstanding that they involve a foreseeable risk of damage to others. In such a case, a bona fide exercise of the discretion will not attract liability: *X (Minors) v. Bedfordshire County Council* [1995] 2 A.C. 633 and *Dorset Yacht Co. Ltd v. Home Office* [1970] A.C. 1004.

In the case of positive acts, therefore, the liability of a public authority in tort is in principle the same as that of a private person but may be *restricted* by its statutory powers and duties. The argument in the present case, however, is that whereas a private person would have owed no duty of care in respect of an omission to remove the hazard at the junction, the duty of the highway authority is *enlarged* by virtue of its statutory powers. The existence of the statutory powers is said to create a 'proximity' between the highway authority and the highway user which would not otherwise exist.

(b) Negligent Omission to Use Statutory Powers

Until the decision of this House in *Anns v. Merton London Borough Council* [1978] A.C. 728, there was no authority for treating a statutory power as giving rise to a common law duty of care. Two cases in particular were thought to be against it. In *Sheppard v. Glossop Corporation* [1921] 3 K.B. 132 the council had power to light the streets of Glossop. But their policy was to turn off the lamps at 9 p.m. The plaintiff was injured when he fell over a retaining wall in the dark after the lamps had been extinguished. He sued the council for negligence. The Court of Appeal said that the council owed him no duty of care. Atkin L.J. said, at 150:

> '[The local authority] is under no legal duty to act reasonably in deciding whether it shall exercise its statutory powers or not, or in deciding to what extent, over what particular area, or for what particular time, it shall exercise its powers ... The real complaint of the plaintiff is not that they caused the danger, but that, the danger being there, if they had lighted it he would have seen and avoided it.'

In *East Suffolk Rivers Catchment Board v. Kent* [1941] A.C. 74, 102 the facts of which are too well known to need repetition, Lord Romer cited *Sheppard v. Glossop Corporation* and stated the principle which he said it laid down, at 102:

> 'Where a statutory authority is entrusted with a mere power it cannot be made liable for any damage sustained by a member of the public by reason of a failure to exercise that power.'

There are two points to be made about the *East Suffolk* case by way of anticipation of what was said about it in the *Anns* case. First, Lord Wilberforce said [1978] A.C. 728, 757:

> 'only one of their Lordships [Lord Atkin] considered [the case] in relation to a duty of care at common law ... I believe that the conception of a general duty of care, not limited to particular accepted situations, but extending generally over all relations of sufficient proximity, and even pervading the sphere of statutory functions of public bodies, had not at that time become fully recognised.'

I must say with great respect that I do not think that this is a fair description of the reasoning of the majority. As a claim of breach of statutory duty had expressly been abandoned, it is hard to imagine what the majority could have thought was the alleged cause of action unless it was breach of a duty of care at common law. What the majority found impossible was to derive such a duty from the existence of a statutory power: to turn a statutory 'may' into a common law 'ought'.

The second point about the *East Suffolk* case is that Lord Atkin, who dissented, does not appear to have founded a duty of care solely upon the existence of the board's statutory powers. He appears to have held that by going upon the plaintiff's land to do work which the plaintiff himself could have done (see at 91–92) the board accepted a duty to execute the work with due dispatch. On this argument, the only relevance of the board's statutory powers was that it could have done the work. It had no statutory defence which would not have been available to a private contractor who had gone upon the land in similar circumstances. Whether Lord Atkin's reasoning is good or bad, it does not support the proposition that statutory powers can generate a duty of care which would not otherwise have existed.

The equally well known case of *Dorset Yacht Co. Ltd v. Home Office* [1970] A.C. 1004 also cast no doubt upon the general principle stated by Lord Romer in *East Suffolk*. The only reference to the case is by Viscount Dilhorne, at 1050G-H, in a dissenting speech. All members of the House plainly did not regard the case as one in which the alleged breach of duty was merely an omission to use a statutory power. The negligence was caused by something which the Borstal officers did, namely to use their statutory powers of custody to bring the trainees onto the island, where they constituted a foreseeable risk to boat owners, and then take no care to prevent them from escaping in the night. The case was therefore prima facie within *Mersey Docks and Harbour Board Trustees v. Gibbs*, L.R. 1 H.L. 93, and their Lordships were concerned only with whether the Crown had a defence on the grounds that the alleged breach of duty involved the exercise of a statutory discretion or whether the fact that the damage was caused by the criminal act of the Borstal trainees negatived the causal link with the Crown's breach of duty. Both these defences were rejected.

7. Anns v. Merton London Borough Council

This brings me to the *Anns* case [1978] A.C. 728. As this case is the mainstay of Mrs Wise's argument, I must examine it in some detail. The plaintiffs were lessees of flats in a new block which had been damaged by subsidence caused by inadequate foundations. They complained that the council had been negligent in the exercise of its statutory powers to inspect the foundations of new buildings. The council said that it owed no duty to inspect and therefore could not be liable for negligent inspection. The House rejected this argument. So far as it held that the council owed a duty of care in respect of purely economic loss, the case has been overruled by *Murphy v. Brentwood District Council* [1991] 1 A.C. 398. The House left open the question of whether the council might have owed a duty in respect of physical injury, although I think it is fair to say that the tone of their Lordships' remarks on this question was somewhat sceptical. Nevertheless, it is now necessary to ask whether the reasoning can support the existence of a duty of care owed by a public authority in respect of foreseeable physical injury which is founded upon the existence of statutory powers to safeguard people against that injury.

Lord Wilberforce, who gave the leading speech, first stated the well known two-stage test for the existence of a duty of care. This involves starting with a prima facie assumption that a duty of care exists if it is reasonably foreseeable that carelessness may cause damage and then asking whether there are any considerations which ought to 'negative, or to reduce or limit the scope of the duty or the class of person to whom it is owed or the damages to which a breach of it may arise'. Subsequent decisions in this House and the Privy Council have preferred to approach the question the other way round, starting with situations

14–52

in which a duty has been held to exist and then asking whether there are considerations of analogy, policy, fairness and justice for extending it to cover a new situation: see for example Lord Bridge of Harwich in *Caparo Industries plc v. Dickman* [1990] 2 A.C. 605, 617–618. It can be said that, provided that the considerations of policy etc. are properly analysed, it should not matter whether one starts from one end or the other.

On the other hand the assumption from which one starts makes a great deal of difference if the analysis is wrong. The trend of authorities has been to discourage the assumption that anyone who suffers loss is prima facie entitled to compensation from a person (preferably insured or a public authority) whose act or omission can be said to have caused it. The default position is that he is not.

This does not of course mean that the actual analysis in the *Anns* case was wrong. It has to be considered on its own merits. Lord Wilberforce had to deal with an argument by the council which was based upon two propositions. The first was that if the council owed no duty to inspect in the first place, it could be under no liability for having done so negligently. The second relied upon Lord Romer's principle in the *East Suffolk* case [1941] A.C. 74, 97: a public authority which has a mere statutory power cannot on that account owe a duty at common law to exercise the power. Lord Wilberforce did not deny the first proposition. This, if I may respectfully say so, seems to me to be right. If the public authority was under no duty to act, either by virtue of its statutory powers or on any other basis, it cannot be liable because it has acted but negligently failed to confer a benefit on the plaintiff or to protect him from loss. The position is of course different if the negligent action of the public authority has left the plaintiff in a worse position than he would have been in if the authority had not acted at all. Lord Wilberforce did however deny the council's second proposition. His reasoning was as follows, at 755:

> 'I think that this is too crude an argument. It overlooks the fact that local authorities are public bodies operating under statute with a clear responsibility for public health in their area. They must, and in fact do, make their discretionary decision responsibly and for reasons which accord with the statutory purpose; ... If they do not exercise their discretion in this way they can be challenged in the courts. Thus, to say that councils are under no duty to inspect, is not a sufficient statement of the position. They are under a duty to give proper consideration to the question whether they should inspect or not. Their immunity from attack, in the event of failure to inspect, in other words, though great is not absolute. And because it is not absolute, the necessary premise for the proposition "if no duty to inspect, then no duty to take care in inspection" vanishes.'

The duty of care at common law is therefore derived from the council's duty in public law to 'give proper consideration to the question whether they should inspect or not'. It is clear, however, that this public law duty cannot in itself give rise to a duty of care. A public body almost always has a duty in public law to consider whether it should exercise its powers, but that does not mean that it necessarily owes a duty of care which may require that the power should actually be exercised. As Mason J. said in *Sutherland Shire Council v. Heyman*, 157 C.L.R. 424, 465:

> 'although a public authority may be under a public duty, enforceable by mandamus, to give proper consideration to the question whether it should exercise a power, this duty cannot be equated with, or regarded as a foundation for imposing, a duty of care on the public authority in relation to the exercise of the power. Mandamus will compel proper consideration of the authority of its discretion, but that is all.'

A mandamus can require future consideration of the exercise of a power. But an action for negligence looks back to what the council ought to have done. Upon what principles can one say of a public authority that not only did it have a duty in public law to consider the exercise of the power but that it would thereupon have been under a duty in private law to act, giving rise to a claim in compensation against public funds for its failure to do so? Or as Lord Wilberforce puts it in the *Anns* case [1978] A.C. 728, 754:

> 'The problem which this kind of action creates, is to define the circumstances in which the law should impose, over and above, or perhaps alongside, these public law powers and duties, a duty in private law towards individuals such that they may sue for damages in a civil court.'

The only tool which the *Anns* case provides for defining these circumstances is the distinction between policy and operations. Lord Wilberforce said:

> 'Most, indeed probably all, statutes relating to public authorities or public bodies, contain in them a large area of policy. The courts call this "discretion" meaning that the decision is one for the authority or body to make, and not for the courts. Many statutes also prescribe or at least presuppose the practical execution of policy decisions: a convenient description of this is to say that in addition

to the area of policy or discretion, there is an operational area. Although this distinction between the policy area and the operational area is convenient, and illuminating, it is probably a distinction of degree; many "operational" powers or duties have in them some element of "discretion". It can safely be said that the more 'operational' a power or duty may be, the easier it is to superimpose upon it a common law duty of care.'

The *East Suffolk* case [1941] A.C. 74 and *Sheppard v. Glossop Corporation* [1921] 3 K.B. 132 were distinguished as involving questions of policy or discretion. The inspection of foundations, on the other hand, was 'heavily operational' and the power to inspect could therefore give rise to a duty of care. Lord Romer's statement of principle in *East Suffolk* was limited to cases in which the exercise of the power involved a policy decision.

8. Policy and Operations

Since *Anns v. Merton London Borough Council*, there have been differing views, both in England and the Commonwealth, over whether it was right to breach the protection which the *East Suffolk* principle gave to public authorities. In *Sutherland Shire Council v. Heyman*, 157 C.L.R. 424, 483, Brennan J. thought that it was wrong: one simply could not derive a common law 'ought' from a statutory 'may'. But I think that he was the only member of the court to adhere to such uncompromising orthodoxy. What has become clear, however, is that the distinction between policy and operations is an inadequate tool with which to discover whether it is appropriate to impose a duty of care or not. In *Rowling v. Takaro Properties Ltd* [1988] A.C. 473, 501 Lord Keith of Kinkel said:

14–53

'[Their Lordships] incline to the opinion, expressed in the literature, that this distinction does not provide a touchstone of liability, but rather is expressive of the need to exclude altogether those cases in which the decision under attack is of such a kind that a question whether it has been made negligently is unsuitable for judicial resolution, of which notable examples are discretionary decisions on the allocation of scarce resources or the distribution of risks ... If this is right, classification of the relevant decision as a policy or planning decision in this sense may exclude liability; but a conclusion that it does not fall within that category does not, in their Lordships' opinion, mean that a duty of care will necessarily exist.'

There are at least two reasons why the distinction is inadequate. The first is that, as Lord Wilberforce himself pointed out, the distinction is often elusive. This is particularly true of powers to provide public benefits which involve the expenditure of money. Practically every decision about the provision of such benefits, no matter how trivial it may seem, affects the budget of the public authority in either timing or amount. The *East Suffolk* case, about which Lord Wilberforce said in the *Anns* case [1978] A.C. 728, 757, that the activities of the board, though 'operational', were 'well within a discretionary area, so that the plaintiff's task in contending for a duty of care was a difficult one' is a very good example. But another reason is that even if the distinction is clear cut, leaving no element of discretion in the sense that it would be irrational (in the public law meaning of that word) for the public authority not to exercise its power, it does not follow that the law should superimpose a common law duty of care. This can be seen if one looks at cases in which a public authority has been under a statutory or common law *duty* to provide a service or other benefit for the public or a section of the public. In such cases there is no discretion but the courts have nevertheless not been willing to hold that a member of the public who has suffered loss because the service was not provided to him should necessarily have a cause of action, either for breach of statutory duty or for negligence at common law.

There are many instances of this principle being applied to statutory duties, but perhaps the most relevant example of the dissociation between public duty and a liability to pay compensation for breach of that duty was the ancient common law duty to repair the highway. The common law imposed this financial burden upon the inhabitants of the parish. But it saw no need to impose upon them the additional burden of paying compensation to users of the highway who suffered injury because the highway surveyor had failed to repair. The duty could be enforced only by indictment. This rule continued to apply when the duty to maintain was transferred by statute to highway authorities and was only abolished by section 1 of the Highways (Miscellaneous Provisions) Act 1961. Likewise in *Hill v. Chief Constable of West Yorkshire* [1989] A.C. 53 it was held that the public duty of the police to catch criminals did not give rise to a duty of care to a member of the public who was injured because the police had negligently failed to catch one. The decision was mainly based upon the large element of discretion which the police necessarily have in conducting their operations, but the judgment excludes liability even in cases in which the alleged breach of duty would constitute public law irrationality.

In terms of public finance, this is a perfectly reasonable attitude. It is one thing to provide a service at the public expense. It is another to require the public to pay compensation when a failure to provide the service has resulted in loss. Apart from cases of reliance, which I shall consider later, the same loss would have been suffered if the service had not been provided in the first place. To require payment of compensation increases the burden on public funds. Before imposing such an additional burden, the courts should be satisfied that this is what Parliament intended.

Whether a statutory duty gives rise to a private cause of action is a question of construction: see *R. v. Deputy Governor of Parkhurst Prison, ex p. Hague* [1992] 1 A.C. 58. It requires an examination of the policy of the statute to decide whether it was intended to confer a right to compensation for breach. Whether it can be relied upon to support the existence of a common law duty of care is not exactly a question of construction, because the cause of action does not arise out of the statute itself. But the policy of the statute is nevertheless a crucial factor in the decision. As Lord Browne-Wilkinson said in *X (Minors) v. Bedfordshire County Council* [1995] 2 A.C. 633, 739C in relation to the duty of care owed by a public authority performing statutory functions:

> 'the question whether there is such a common law duty and if so its ambit, must be profoundly influenced by the statutory framework within which the acts complained of were done'.

The same is true of omission to perform a statutory duty. If such a duty does not give rise to a private right to sue for breach, it would be unusual if it nevertheless gave rise to a duty of care at common law which made the public authority liable to pay compensation for foreseeable loss caused by the duty not being performed. It will often be foreseeable that loss will result if, for example, a benefit or service is not provided. If the policy of the act is not to create a statutory liability to pay compensation, the same policy should ordinarily exclude the existence of a common law duty of care.

In the case of a mere statutory power, there is the further point that the legislature has chosen to confer a discretion rather than create a duty. Of course there may be cases in which Parliament has chosen to confer a power because the subject matter did not permit a duty to be stated with sufficient precision. It may nevertheless have contemplated that in circumstances in which it would be irrational not to exercise the power, a person who suffered loss because it had not been exercised, or not properly exercised, would be entitled to compensation. I therefore do not say that a statutory 'may' can never give rise to a common law duty of care. I prefer to leave open the question of whether the *Anns* case was wrong to create any exception to Lord Romer's statement of principle in the *East Suffolk* case and I shall go on to consider the circumstances (such as 'general reliance') in which it has been suggested that such a duty might arise. But the fact that Parliament has conferred a discretion must be some indication that the policy of the act conferring the power was not to create a right to compensation. The need to have regard to the policy of the statute therefore means that exceptions will be rare.

In summary, therefore, I think that the minimum preconditions for basing a duty of care upon the existence of a statutory power, if it can be done at all, are, first, that it would in the circumstances have been irrational not to have exercised the power, so that there was in effect a public law duty to act, and secondly, that there are exceptional grounds for holding that the policy of the statute requires compensation to be paid to persons who suffer loss because the power was not exercised.

9. Particular and General Reliance

14–54   In *Sutherland Shire Council v. Heyman*, 157 C.L.R. 424, 483, Brennan J., as I have mentioned, thought that a statutory power could never generate a common law duty of care unless the public authority had created an expectation that the power would be used and the plaintiff had suffered damage from reliance on that expectation. A common example is the lighthouse authority which, by the exercise of its power to build and maintain a lighthouse, creates in mariners an expectation that the light will warn them of danger. In such circumstances, the authority (unlike the Glossop Corporation in *Sheppard v. Glossop Corporation* [1921] 3 K.B. 132) owes a duty of care which requires it not to extinguish the light without giving reasonable notice. This form of liability, based upon representation and reliance, does not depend upon the public nature of the authority's powers and causes no problems.

In the same case, however, Mason J. suggested a different basis upon which public powers might give rise to a duty of care. He said, at 464:

> 'there will be cases in which the plaintiff's reasonable reliance will arise out of a general dependence on an authority's performance of its function with due care, without the need for contributing conduct on the part of a defendant or action to his detriment on the part of a plaintiff. Reliance or dependence in this sense is in general the product of the grant (and exercise) of powers designed to prevent or minimise a risk of personal injury or disability, recognised by the legislature as being of such magnitude or complexity that individuals cannot, or may not, take adequate steps for their own protection. This situation generates on one side (the individual) a general expectation that the power will be exercised and on the other side (the authority) a realisation that there is a general reliance or dependence on its exercise of the power … The control of air traffic, the safety inspection of aircraft and the fighting of a fire in a building by a fire authority … may well be examples of this type of function.'

This ground for imposing a duty of care has been called 'general reliance'. It has little in common with the ordinary doctrine of reliance; the plaintiff does not need to have relied upon the expectation that the power would be used or even known that it existed. It appears rather to refer to general expectations in the community, which the individual plaintiff may or may not have shared. A widespread assumption that a statutory power will be exercised may affect the general pattern of economic and social behaviour. For example, insurance premiums may take into account the expectation that statutory powers of inspection or accident prevention will ordinarily prevent certain kinds of risk from materialising. Thus the doctrine of general reliance requires an inquiry into the role of a given statutory power in the behaviour of members of the general public, of which an outstanding example is the judgment of Richardson J. in *Invercargill City Council v. Hamlin* [1994] 3 N.Z.L.R. 513, 526.

It appears to be essential to the doctrine of general reliance that the benefit or service provided under statutory powers should be of a uniform and routine nature, so that one can describe exactly what the public authority was supposed to do. Powers of inspection for defects clearly fall into this category. Another way of looking at the matter is to say that if a particular service is provided as a matter of routine, it would be irrational for a public authority to provide it in one case and arbitrarily withhold it in another. This was obviously the main ground upon which this House in the *Anns* case considered that the power of the local authority to inspect foundations should give rise to a duty of care.

But the fact that it would be irrational not to exercise the power is, as I have said, only one of the conditions which has to be satisfied. It is also necessary to discern a policy which confers a right to financial compensation if the power has not been exercised. Mason J. thought in *Sutherland Shire Council v. Heyman*, 157 C.L.R. 424, 464, that such a policy might be inferred if the power was intended to protect members of the public from risks against which they could not guard themselves. In the *Invercargill* case, as I have said, the New Zealand Court of Appeal [1994] 3 N.Z.L.R. 513 and the Privy Council [1996] 2 W.L.R. 367 found it in general patterns of socio-economic behaviour. I do not propose to explore further the doctrine of general reliance because, for reasons which I shall explain, I think that there are no grounds upon which the present case can be brought within it. I will only note in passing that its application may require some very careful analysis of the role which the expected exercise of the statutory power plays in community behaviour. For example, in one sense it is true that the fire brigade is there to protect people in situations in which they could not be expected to be able to protect themselves. On the other hand they can and do protect themselves by insurance against the risk of fire. It is not obvious that there should be a right to compensation from a negligent fire authority which will ordinarily ensure by right of subrogation to an insurance company. The only reason would be to provide a general deterrent against inefficiency. But there must be better ways of doing this than by compensating insurance companies out of public funds. And while premiums no doubt take into account the existence of the fire brigade and the likelihood that it will arrive swiftly upon the scene, it is not clear that they would be very different merely because no compensation was paid in the rare cases in which the fire authority negligently failed to perform its public duty …

11. Duties of a Highway Authority

I return to consider whether the council owed a duty of care which required it to take steps to improve the junction. Since the only basis for such a duty is the authority's statutory powers, both specifically under section 79 of the Act of 1980 and generally to carry out works of improvement with the consent of British Rail, I will start by asking whether in the light of what the council knew or ought to have known about the junction, it would have had a duty in public law to undertake the work. This requires that it would have been irrational not to exercise its discretion to do so. The trial judge did not address himself to this question. He thought it was sufficient that, as he put it, 'a decision had already been taken to deal with the situation' in which 'budgetary considerations were not a restraint'.

The fact that Mr Longhurst and Mr Deller had agreed to do the work does not show that it would have been unreasonable or irrational for the council not to have done it. That is simply a non sequitur. The Court of Appeal seems to have reasoned that the 'decision' to do the work disposed of any question of policy or discretion and left only the operational question of when the work should have been done. But this too seems to me fallacious. The timing of the work and the budgetary year in which the money is spent is surely as much a matter of discretion as the decision in principle to do it. And why should the council be in a worse position than if Mr Longhurst had left Mr Deller's report at the bottom of his in-tray and forgotten about it? In that case, it is said, the council would have been in breach of its duty in public law to give due consideration to the exercise of its powers. Perhaps it would, but that does not advance the case far enough. It would still be necessary to say that if the council had considered the matter, it would have been bound to decide to do the work. One comes back, therefore, to the question of whether it would have been irrational to decide not to do it.

14–55

Furthermore, to say that a decision had been taken oversimplifies the situation. Mr Longhurst had not committed himself to any particular time within which the work would be done. There was, as Mr Deller said, a 'nil time scale involved'; he did not think it mattered whether the work took one, two or three years. At the time when the letter to British Rail was sent, the March 1988 accident with the police car had not yet happened. Nor was it notified to Mr Longhurst or Mr Deller when it did. The judge found that they would have displayed a greater sense of urgency if they had known about it. But the judge made no finding that the council should have had a system by which Mr Longhurst was notified of every accident on the roads of South Norfolk. Such a system would have been quite impractical. There were 3,500 personal injury accidents in Norfolk every year and their particulars were simply entered on a computer from which the Accident Studies Section in Norwich identified 'cluster sites' for special attention. No firm decision had been taken on expenditure either. Mr Deller thought that the work would cost less than £1,000, in which case it would have come within Mr Longhurst's discretionary budget for small works. But he said he could not be sure of the cost until he had consulted a design engineer: 'it could be lots and lots more'. This caution was justified by events. After Mr Stovin's accident, Mr Brian Meadows, who worked for the Accident Studies Section, inspected the junction and said that the bank could not be regraded within the budget for a low cost remedial scheme.

The judge, as I say, made no finding as to whether it would have been irrational for the council not to have done the work. The unchallenged evidence of Mr Reid, who was head of the Accident Studies Office, would have made it very difficult to do so. In evidence in chief, he was asked about the March 1988 accident:

> 'Q. So far as you are concerned, what difference, if any, would the significance of this accident have made in relation to priority given to carrying out work at this site, against the background of what had happened with British Rail? A. In practical terms, it would have made no difference at all to the priority within the accident remedial budget, because our attention and resources would have been directed to those many sites in the county which already had much higher accident records.'

There was no suggestion in cross-examination that this was an unreasonable, let alone irrational, attitude to take.

It seems to me therefore that the question of whether anything should be done about the junction was at all times firmly within the area of the council's discretion. As they were therefore not under a public law duty to do the work, the first condition for the imposition of a duty of care was not satisfied.

But even if it were, I do not think that the second condition would be satisfied. Assuming that the highway authority ought, as a matter of public law, to have done the work, I do not think that there are any grounds upon which it can be said that the public law duty should give rise to an obligation to compensate persons who have suffered loss because it was not performed. There is no question here of reliance on the council having improved the junction. Everyone could see that it was still the same. Mr Stovin was not arbitrarily denied a benefit which was routinely provided to others. In respect of the junction, he was treated in exactly the same way as any other road user. The foundation for the doctrine of general reliance is missing in this case, because we are not concerned with provision of a uniform identifiable benefit or service. Every hazardous junction, intersection or stretch of road is different and requires a separate decision as to whether anything should be done to improve it. It is not without significance that the Canadian cases in which a duty of care has been held to exist have all involved routine inspection and maintenance rather than improvements.

I have mentioned earlier that maintenance of the highway was, until 1961, a striking example of a public duty which involved no obligation to compensate a person who had suffered damage because of its breach. The power in section 79 of the Highways Act 1980, upon which the plaintiff principally relies to generate a duty of care, was first enacted as section 4 of the Roads Improvement Act 1925. It seems to me impossible to discern a legislative intent that there should be a duty of care in respect of the use of that power, giving rise to a liability to compensate persons injured by a failure to use it, when there was at the time no such liability even for breach of the statutory duty to maintain the highway.

In my view the creation of a duty of care upon a highway authority, even on grounds of irrationality in failing to exercise a power, would inevitably expose the authority's budgetary decisions to judicial inquiry. This would distort the priorities of local authorities, which would be bound to try to play safe by increasing their spending on road improvements rather than risk enormous liabilities for personal injury accidents. They will spend less on education or social services. I think that it is important, before extending the duty of care owed by public authorities, to consider the cost to the community of the defensive measures which they are likely to take in order to avoid liability. It would not be surprising if one of the consequences of the *Anns* case and the spate of cases which followed was that local council inspectors tended to insist upon stronger foundations than were necessary. In a case like this, I do not think that the duty of care can be used as a deterrent against low standards in improving the road layout. Given the fact that the British road network largely antedates the highway authorities themselves, the court is not in a position to say what an appropriate standard of improvement would be. This must be a matter for the discretion of the authority. On the other hand, denial of liability does not leave the road user unprotected. Drivers of vehicles must take the highway network as they find it. Everyone knows that there are hazardous bends, intersections and junctions. It is primarily the duty of drivers of vehicles to take due care. And if, as in the case of Mrs Wise, they do not, there is compulsory insurance to provide compensation to the victims. There is no reason of policy or justice which requires the highway authority to be an additional defendant. I would therefore allow the appeal."

Notes

(1) According to both Lord Hoffmann and Lord Nicholls, irrationality is a prerequisite of liability for a failure to exercise power. The bad faith test advocated in *Hallett* does not appear to be different in substance from the test of irrationality. In *Ross v. Secretary of State for Scotland*, 1990 S.L.T. 13 Lord Milligan, on facts similar to *Bonthrone*, expressly adopted the approach of Lord Grieve in *Bonthrone* in adopting bad faith as the only criteria upon which a policy decision could be stigmatised. He went on to consider the dicta of Lord Reid in *Home Office v. Dorset Yacht Co.* to the effect that for liability to arise "there must come a stage where the discretion is exercised so carelessly or unreasonably that there has been no real exercise of the discretion which Parliament has conferred". He also had regard to the decisions in *Rowling v. Takaro Properties Ltd* [1988] A.C. 473 and *Anns v. Merton London Borough Council* [1978] A.C. 728 below and concluded (at 19) that:

14–56

> "So far as terms other than bad faith are used in the cases cited with regard to the criterion for grounding an action in relation to exercise of ministerial discretion, I do not find the other terms used as being necessarily inconsistent with the requirement of bad faith. I find them rather as illustrating circumstances in which bad faith may be inferred. In any event, I consider that the authorities cited do not substantiate the contention for the pursuer that such action may relevantly be grounded on averments of irresponsibility alone."

Are the judges coming close to saying that only when no discretion existed — that is a duty to act was imposed — that failure to *do so* would be irrational and therefore culpable? The case law on enforcement of statutory duties is relevant in this context, on which see para. 11–13.

(2) On the matter of the policy/operational dichotomy, compare the views of Lord Browne-Wilkinson in *X*, Lord Dunpark in *Bonthrone* and Lord Hoffmann in *Stovin*. Do the approaches of the first two judges provide any guidance as to when the discretionary or policy stage of a decision has ended and the operational stage has commenced?

For further examples in English law of the distinction see *Haydon v. Kent County Council* [1978] Q.B. 343 and *Vicar of Writtle v. Essex County Council* (1979) 77 L.G.R. 656. For discussion of the distinction between policy and discretion and in particular whether it could cover any situation where the authority had an element of choice or whether it could only apply where issues involved were not suitable for consideration by a court see S.H. Bailey and M. J. Bowman, "The Policy Operational Dichotomy — A Cuckoo in the Nest" (1986) 45 C.L.J. 430; D. Oliver, "Anns v. London Borough of Merton Reconsidered" (1980) 33 C.L.P. 269 and C. Harley, "Public Bodies and Duty of Care in Negligence: *Stovin v. Wise*", 1997 J.R. 376.

(3) The court will not, however, readily infer the presence of difficult issues in the exercise of discretion or resource allocation in the absence of specific averments to that effect. In *Ireland v. Dunfermline District Council*, 1997 G.W.D. 10–405, the pursuer sued the council as a result of injuries sustained by falling into a footpath maintained by the council. It was not denied by the council that it was responsible for the footpath. It alleged that the case was not suitable for the jury trial the pursuers sought on the basis that difficult questions on the exercise of the council's discretion in relation to an argument based on a negligent omission to make the path safer were sufficiently complex to make the case inappropriate for jury trial. However, as the council had not specifically pled a case based on the resource allocation difficulties it alleged, the motion for jury trial was allowed.

14–57   (4) The status of the decision in *East Suffolk Rivers Catchment Board v. Kent* [1941] A.C. 74 in Scots law is unclear. An unusually high spring tide caused a river to overflow its banks causing damage to pastures. At first instance the judge held that the board's staff had inefficiently carried out repair works which could have prevented the flooding. The board had no duty to repair the beach but had power to do so and it was held that the board could not be made liable in damages. It was established as a matter of fact that repair works could have been carried out in 14 days and not the 178 days it actually took and given that the duty was limited to the avoidance of extra damage there was no causal link between the breach of that duty in the damage suffered, namely the continuation of the flooding for 164 days. The case was subject to criticism, particularly by Lord Wilberforce in *Anns* but standing Lord Hoffmann's speech in *Stovin*, it would appear now to represent good law subject to the qualification that an irrational failure to exercise a power may lead to liability and damages. In *Duff* above Lord Macfadyen described the *East Suffolk* case as unsatisfactory and expressly preferred the dissenting speech of Lord Atkin in that case. In *Johnstone* above Lord Wilberforce's treatment of *East Suffolk* was accepted by Lord Cameron of Lochbroom. For further comment on this case see M.J. Bowman and S.H. Bailey, "Negligence in the Realms of Public Law — A Positive Obligation to Rescue?" [1984] P.L. 277.

        (5) The decision in *Anns* was overruled in *Murphy v. Brentwood District Council* [1991] 1 A.C. 398, essentially on the ground that the loss suffered by the plaintiff was a pure economic loss and therefore not recoverable. This did at least open the possibility that an action might lie where there was a failure to inspect or there was a faulty inspection of a building which caused property damage or physical injury: see M. Giles and E. Szyszczak, "Negligence and defective buildings: demolishing the foundations of *Anns*?" [1991] L.S. 85; J.M. Arnott, "Defects in Building and Pure Economic Loss" (1989) 34 J.L.S.S. 183. Having regard to *X*, *Hallett*, *Forbes* and *Stovin* do you think it would be possible to argue that liability might arise? If so, what form of reliance on the part of the pursuer would have to be established, if any?

ABUSE OF PUBLIC OFFICE

Bourgoin S.A. v. Ministry of Agriculture, Fisheries and Food

[1985] 3 All E.R. 585

14–58   The plaintiffs, who were variously concerned in the production in France of frozen turkeys and turkey parts and in their sale and distribution within the United Kingdom, imported frozen turkeys and turkey parts into the United Kingdom under a general licence granted by the defendant. On September 1,1981, the defendant, purporting to act in the interests of preventing the spread of Newcastle disease into the United Kingdom, revoked the licence and replaced it with one which had the effect of prohibiting the importation of turkeys and turkey parts from France. The Court of Justice of the European Communities subsequently held that the withdrawal of the licence had constituted a contravention of Article 30 of the EEC Treaty and had therefore been *ultra vires*. In consequence of that decision the defendant issued a licence which permitted the resumption of such importation from November 1982. The plaintiffs claimed damages, alleging (under para. 23 of the amended statement of claim) that the withdrawal of the licence and the defendant's refusal subsequently to permit turkeys or turkey parts to be imported into the United Kingdom from France had caused the plaintiffs substantial loss and damage; that such loss and damage had been caused by the defendant's breach of his statutory duty under Article 30 and that such a breach sounded in damages (para. 24); that such loss and damage had been caused by the commission by the defendant of an innominate tort by so breaching Article 30, or acting contrary to its provisions, as to cause them injury (para. 25); and that the withdrawal of the licence had amounted to misfeasance in public office; in that the defendant had exercised its power to withdraw the licence for a purpose which, as it had known, was contrary to article 30 and/or was calculated to, and did, damage unlawfully the plaintiffs and/ or was not the purpose for which those powers had been conferred on the defendant (para. 26).

        On the trial of the preliminary issue whether paras 23–26 disclosed any causes of action, Mann J. found for the plaintiffs, holding that since Article 30 of the Treaty had direct effect, it conferred on persons injured by a contravention, even though arising from a breach of statutory duty, a cause of action in damages and that the defendant was liable to the plaintiffs for any damage which had flowed from the withdrawal of the licence as pleaded in paras 23 and 24, but, since the commission of an innominate tort as a formulation of a cause of action was obsolete, the claim in paras 23 and 25 did not disclose any cause of action; that in order to establish the tort of misfeasance in public office it was not necessary to prove that the defendant had been actuated by malice towards the plaintiff or had acted in bad faith but it was sufficient to show that the officer knew that he had no power to do that which he did and that his action would injure the plaintiff and subsequently did injure him and that paras 23 and 26 did disclose a cause of action.

The Court of Appeal allowed an appeal in part, holding (Oliver L.J. dissenting) that breach of Article 30 did not give rise to a cause of action in damages (although it would give rise to a right to judicial review). On the other points, the Court of Appeal agreed with Mann J.

OLIVER L.J.: "... The third way in which the case is formulated on the pleadings is as a claim for damages against the Minister for misfeasance in public office, a tort which was described by Lord Diplock in *Dunlop v. Woollahra Municipal Council* [1982] A.C. 158, 173E, as 'well-established'. That is not in dispute. The difference between the parties rests only in their respective appreciations of the essential ingredients of the tort. For the purposes only of the preliminary issue, it was accepted that the Minister's purpose in revoking the general licence was to protect English turkey producers, and that he knew at the time (i) that this involved a failure to perform the United Kingdom's obligations under Article 30; (ii) that the revocation would cause damage to the plaintiffs in their business; and (iii) that the protection of English producers from foreign competition was not one for the achievement of which powers were conferred on him by the enabling legislation or the Importation of Animal Products and Poultry Products Order 1980. The Solicitor-General's submission, however, was that it was an essential allegation, and one not made on the pleadings, that the Minister acted with the purpose of inflicting harm upon the plaintiffs. This has been referred to conveniently as an allegation of 'targeted malice'.

The court has been referred to a large number of cases both in this country and in Canada and Australia from which, it is said, the inference can be drawn that in order to constitute the tort it is necessary to show an improper motive specifically aimed at the plaintiff. The authorities were extensively reviewed by the judge and it would, I think, be a work of supererogation to repeat the exercise here. There are in certain of the older cases phrases in the judgments or pleadings which might be taken to suggest that 'targeted malice' was regarded as essential. I say 'might', because in my judgment they are entirely inconclusive. There are also strong indications in the other direction, particularly in the older election cases. For instance in *Cullen v. Morris* (1819) 2 Stark. 577, 587, Abbott C.J. observed:

'On the part of the defendant it has been contended, that an action is not maintainable for merely refusing the vote of a person who appears afterwards to have really had a right to vote, unless it also appears that the refusal resulted from a malicious and improper motive, and that if the party act honestly and uprightly according to the best of his judgment, he is not amenable in an action for damages. I am of opinion, that the law, as it has been stated by the counsel for the defendant, is correct.'

Again, he said, at 589:

'If a vote be refused with a view to prejudice either the party entitled to vote, or the candidate for whom he tenders his vote, the notice is an improper one, and an action is maintainable.'

Coming to more modern times there is the Privy Council case of *Dunlop v. Woollahra Municipal Council* [1982] A.C. 158, where the allegation was one of damage caused to the plaintiff by passing planning resolutions, which were in fact invalid, restricting the height of his proposed building. Paragraph 15A of the pleading was (so far as material) in these terms, at 169–170:

'the defendant was a public corporate body which occupied office and was incorporated by a public statute... and the defendant abused its said office and public duty under the said statute by purporting to pass each of the said resolutions with the consequence that damage was occasioned to the plaintiff.'

In delivering the judgment of the Board, Lord Diplock said, at 172:

'In pleading in paragraph 15A of the statement of claim that the council abused their public office and public duty the plaintiff was relying upon the well-established tort of misfeasance by a public officer in the discharge of his public duties ... [Their Lordships] agree with [the trial judge's] conclusion that, in the absence of malice, passing without knowledge of its invalidity a resolution which is devoid of any legal effect is not conduct that of itself is capable of amounting to such "misfeasance" as is a necessary element in this tort.'

Of this case Wade in his book on *Administrative Law* (5th ed., 1982), pp. 672–673, comments that the Privy Council held that the tort 'required as a necessary element either malice or knowledge… of the invalidity' a view which is in line with that expressed by Smith J. in *Farrington v. Thomson and Bridgland* [1959] V.R. 286, which was carefully considered by Mann J. in the course of his judgment in the instant case. Having concluded his review of the authorities, Mann J. concluded, *ante*, 740D–G:

> 'I do not read any of the decisions to which I have been referred as precluding the commission of the tort of misfeasance in public office where the officer actually knew that he had no power to do that which he did, and that his act would injure the plaintiff as subsequently it does. I read the judgment in *Dunlop v. Woollahra Municipal Council* [1982] A.C. 158 in the sense that malice and knowledge are alternatives. There is no sensible reason why the common law should not afford a remedy to the injured party in circumstances such as are before me. There is no sensible distinction between the case where an officer performs an act which he has no power to perform with the object of injuring A (which the defendant accepts is actionable at the instance of A) and the case where an officer performs an act which he knows he has no power to perform with the object of conferring a benefit on B but which has the foreseeable and actual consequence of injury to A (which the defendant denies is actionable at the instance of A). In my judgment each case is actionable at the instance of A and, accordingly, I determine that paragraphs 23 and 36 of the amended statement of claim do disclose a cause of action.'

For my part, I too can see no sensible distinction between the two cases which the judge mentions.

If it be shown that the Minister's motive was to further the interests of English turkey producers by keeping out the produce of French turkey producers — an act which must necessarily injure them — it seems to me entirely immaterial that the one purpose was dominant and the second merely a subsidiary purpose for giving effect to the dominant purpose. If an act is done deliberately and with knowledge of its consequences, I do not think that the actor can sensibly say that he did not 'intend' the consequences or that the act was not 'aimed' at the person who, it is known, will suffer them. In my judgment, the judge was right in his conclusion also on this point."

PARKER and NOURSE L.JJ. agreed with OLIVER L.J. on this point.

Notes

14–59   (1) On this area generally see A. Rubinstein, *Jurisdiction and Illegality* (1965), pp. 128–133; J. McBride, "Damages as a Remedy for Unlawful Administrative Action" (1979) 38 C.L.J. 323; C.T. Reid, "Damages for Abuse of Power" [1989] P.L. 395; and C.T. Reid, "Damages for Deliberate Abuse of Power", 1988 S.L.T. (News) 121.

(2) The concept of a specific delict for abuse of public office is relatively new in Scots law. In *Micosta v. Shetland Islands Council*, 1986 S.L.T. 193 Lord Ross had to consider whether or not a claim for damages against a harbour authority for improper use of the harbour master's powers could succeed. Micosta owned a bulk carrier based offshore at Sullom Voe. It was awaiting berthing instructions and had discharged ballast into the sea. This was a breach of the conditions of the charter and the harbour authority said it would issue a direction preventing the ship from loading cargo in light of that. The charterparty (the technical name given to contract for carriage at sea of goods) was cancelled on the basis that the contract was frustrated. The owners sought damages against the harbour authority on the grounds that their loss of profit arose from a deliberate misuse of the authority's statutory powers. Although failing on the merits Lord Ross, having reviewed the case law and in particular the decision in *Bourgoin*, noted:

> "The expression 'a tort which is called misfeasance in public office' sounds strange to Scottish ears. However, the question which arises is whether some equivalent would be recognised by the law of Scotland.
>
> Under reference to *Ashby v. White*, Professor Walker points out that there is no adequate Scottish authority on the question of recovering damages, at least nominal in amount, for the wrong of interfering with a public right or constitutional liberty (Walker, *Delict* (2nd ed.), p. 878).
>
> The validity of a claim such as that made by the present pursuers does not depend upon there being any precise Scottish authority. There is no such thing as an exhaustive list of named delicts

in the law of Scotland. If the conduct complained of appears to be wrongful, the law of Scotland will afford a remedy even if there has not been any previous instance of a remedy being given in similar circumstances. As Professor Walker puts it at p. 9: 'The decision to recognise a particular interest, and consequently to grant a remedy for its infringement, is a question of social policy, and the list recognised has grown over the years. In considering whether or not to recognise particular interests the courts have had regard to such factors as the moral obliquity of the defenders' conduct, the capacity of the parties to bear the loss, and the consistency of recognition with what is conceived to be public policy.'

In my opinion, deliberate misuse of statutory powers by a public body would be actionable under the law of Scotland at the instance of a third party who has suffered loss and damage in consequence of the misuse of statutory powers, provided that there was proof of malice or proof that the action had been taken by the public authority in the full knowledge that it did not possess the power which it purported to exercise. I have reached this conclusion on a consideration of the English authorities referred to above and having regard to the general principles applicable under the law of Scotland to abuse of legal process which are referred to by Professor Walker in chap. 24 of his work on *Delict*.

It follows that to succeed on the first ground of action, the pursuers would require to establish (1) that the alleged misuse of statutory power was deliberate; (2) malice or proof that the action had been taken by the defenders in the full knowledge that they did not possess the powers which they were purporting to exercise."

It is apparent from the formulation in *Bourgoin S.A.* and confirmation of the validity of that approach by Lord Ross that an authority will not be held liable where it has acted *ultra vires* but that it did so in a manner which could be regarded as amounting to a genuine and reasonable mistake. Accordingly in *Ballantyne v. City of Glasgow District Licensing Board*, 1987 S.L.T. 745 it was alleged that the board at one of its quarterly meetings had acted outwith its powers in refusing to accept as timeous an application for renewal of a licence. The refusal to consider the application resulted in there being a gap of around one month between the expiry of the previous licence and the eventual granting of a new one. The licence holder sought damages for the loss sustained during this period when their premises could not operate as normal. In the absence of malice (the first limb of the delict) or knowledge of *ultra vires* acting (the second limb of the delict), Lord Jauncey was not prepared to hold that an error of judgment, provided it had occurred in the context of a genuine and reasonable use of powers, would make a public office or a body liable. For an example based on the first limb see *B v. Forsey*, 1987 S.L.T. 681; 1988 S.L.T. 572, H.L. above where intent was established in connection with the detention of a mental patient beyond the period permitted by the relevant statute. Note too the approach of Clarke J. in *Three Rivers District Council v. Bank of England (No. 3)* [1996] 3 All E.R. 558 at 632 that intent to injure must exist and that mere recklessness is not enough to constitute intent.

(3) More difficult issues arise in the context of the second limb of this delict. The exact scope **14–60** of this was explored by Clarke J. in *Three Rivers District Council* above. Here, the plaintiffs were depositors with BCCI which was a commercial bank licensed by the Bank of England. It went into liquidation and the depositors sued the Bank of England alleging liability for misfeasance in public office in its performance of its duty to supervise banking operations in the United Kingdom and specifically by its failure to revoke BCCI's licence or alternatively that the licence had been granted wrongfully in the first place. A number of issues arose, including whether the bank was capable of being liable for this misfeasance and whether the depositors' losses were caused by the bank's acts or omissions. Clarke J. considered the decision in *Bourgoin* at length and in particular where Mann J. used the word "foreseeable" in the passage cited in Oliver L.J's judgment (at 568):

> "I think that he must have meant 'foreseen'. That is partly because there are three previous references either to 'foreseen' or to knowledge of the consequences and partly because it was an agreed fact (for the purposes of the issue to be determined) that the minister knew that his act would injure the plaintiffs in their business and the plaintiffs' case was that such knowledge was sufficient for liability. No one was suggesting that foreseeability of damage was enough. Thus, I do not think that Mann J was applying his mind separately to that question. He was principally concerned with whether malice (in the sense of targeted malice) was required or whether knowledge of absence of power would in certain circumstances be sufficient."

He also noted (at 569) that Oliver L. J's judgment was not to be interpreted as requiring for the second limb that the plaintiff prove that injuring the plaintiff was at least a subsidiary purpose of the defendant and that the defendant must know that his act will necessarily cause the loss suffered by the plaintiff. This approach would seem consistent with Lord Ross in *Micosta*. It would seem that it is sufficient to show that provided that the act could not be regarded as a genuine and reasonable one in terms of *Ballantyne*, then clear evidence of lack of knowledge of power, regardless of the existence or otherwise of an aim to injure, should be sufficient to impose liability. Invalidity will not, however, be taken to be coextensive with liability. Much will depend on the way in which Lord Jauncey's reliance on a genuine and reasonable mistake is interpreted. Support for that view can be found in the decision of the High Court of Australia in *Northern Territory v. Mengel* (1995) 69 A.L.J.R. 527 at 570–578 where it was noted that after a review of the case law, including *Bourgoin S.A.*, an official could not be held liable on the basis that he ought to have known that there was a lack of power. This narrower reading of *Bourgoin S.A.* was followed in the most recent case in the *Three Rivers District Council* litigation, that of *Three Rivers District Council v. Bank of England (No. 3), The Times*, December 10, 1998, C.A. where undue reliance on a rigid approach to the two-limb test was questioned. In the view of Hirst, L.J., the tort of misfeasance in public office was capable of judicial development at common law. The court should not set out an overly rigid test for establishing the constituent elements of the tort. Notwithstanding what was said in *Bourgoin S.A.*, in every case a deliberate and dishonest abuse of power by a public official who knew that a third party would suffer losses or inconsequence, or his reckless indifference to that occurring, had to be established. Undue reliance on the two-limb approach could obscure this fact. Accordingly, the appellants against the decision at first instance still had to establish the guilty state of mind on the part of the Bank of England and, on the facts, it was not reasonably arguable that in failing to regulate the BCCI, the bank had acted unlawfully and dishonestly, knowing that it would cause loss to the appellant.

(4) Liability exists regardless of whether the abuse of power by a public authority or officer is public or private in nature: *Jones v. Swansea City Council* [1990] 1 W.L.R. 1453. Given the rejection of the public/private divide in Scots law, this approach would seem to be valid here.

14–61   (5) It is of course the case that if an officer commits the delict, vicarious liability on the part of the employing authority still exists unless the officer is in fact acting independently and outwith the scope of his employment or duties: *Racz v. Home Office* [1994] 2 A.C. 45; *Taylor v. City of Glasgow District Council*, 1996 S.L.T. 701; and *Armstrong v. Moore*, 1996 S.L.T. 690.

(6) Do you agree that the widening of the scope of the second limb of the delict can be justified by the argument that "the absence of an honest attempt to perform the functions of the office... constitutes the abuse of the office": *per* Brennan J. in *Northern Territory v. Mengel* above and noted with approval by Clarke J. in *Three Rivers District Council*. As noted in *Bourgoin* and *Micosta*, negligence is not enough to establish misfeasance. In *Bourgoin*, *Three Rivers* and *Micosta* the injured parties were obliged to pursue misfeasance as no action would lie for breach of statutory duty and, on the authorities, no duty of care could arise: *Yuen Kun Yeu v. Attorney-General of Hong Kong* [1988] A.C. 175. There could of course be cases where loss caused by a public officer might arise in the context of a duty of care, on which see *X* above. Do you consider it necessary to continue with a separate limb based on intent to injure? Can any circumstance be imagined in which it will be necessary or advisable to seek to establish liability under this?

THE CROWN, DELICTUAL LIABILITY AND THE EUROPEAN DIMENSION

M. Upton, "Crown Liability in Damages Under Community Law — 1"

1996 S.L.T. (News) 175

14–62   "On 5 March this year, the European Court of Justice ('ECJ') issued a judgment in joined cases C-16/93 and C-48/93, *Brasserie du Pêcheur SA v Federal Republic of Germany* and *R v Secretary of State for Transport, ex p Factortame Ltd, The Times*, 7 March 1996....

The History of the Factortame Litigation

The judgment of 5 March is the seventh decision in the case of *R v Secretary of State for Transport, ex p Factortame Ltd* to have been reported since it was brought into court on 16 December 1988: see [1989] 2 CMLR 353 (QBD and CA); [1990] 2 AC 85 (HL); [1991] 1 AC 603 (ECJ and HL); and [1991] ECR I-3905 (ECJ). That does not include the related decisions in case C-3/87, *R v Ministry of Agriculture, Fisheries and Food, ex p Agegate Ltd* [1990] 2 QB 151; case C-216/87, *R v Ministry of Agriculture, Fisheries and Food, ex p Jaderow Ltd* [1990] 2 QB 193; and case 246/89, *Commission v United Kingdom* [1989] ECR 3125; [1991] ECR I-455.

Factortame is an application for judicial review brought by a number of companies who owned fishing vessels that were registered as British prior to the entry into force of Pt II of the Merchant Shipping Act 1988 and the Merchant Shipping (Registration of Fishing Vessels) Regulations 1988. The directors and shareholders of the companies are Spaniards. The 1988 Act and Regulations prevented the registration of the vessels under the new registration régime, because they provided that vessels managed or controlled from another country, or by foreign nationals, or by companies a given proportion of the shares of which were owned by foreign nationals, were ineligible for registration in the new register that was thereby established. Fishing vessels ineligible for registration were deprived of the right to fish in British waters.

Five of the earlier decisions concerned an application for an interim order that the regulations and Pt II of the Act be disapplied in respect of the applicants' vessels, pending a reference to the ECJ under art 177 of the EC Treaty. The questions referred were, in effect, whether the Act and Regulations were compatible with Community law. The Divisional Court made an interim order in the terms sought. The subsequent appeals to the Court of Appeal and the House of Lords concerned the competence of orders disapplying an Act of Parliament, and of interim injunctions against the Crown. In that regard, a second reference was made to the ECJ. The decision of the ECJ, as it was thereafter applied by the House of Lords, was that where the applicant founded upon a right granted to him by Community law, the rules of English law rendering those remedies incompetent were overridden, and, in the circumstances, the interim orders sought should be granted. (The decisions up to that point are sometimes referred to as '*Factortame I*'.)

The interim orders having been made, the cause itself required to be decided. To that end, the ECJ subsequently determined the *original* reference in July 1991, by holding that arts 52 and 221 of the EC Treaty did not allow a member state to impose conditions such as those of which the applicants complained. (That decision is known as '*Factortame II*'.) This in effect determined that the United Kingdom had acted in breach of Community law by enacting and enforcing the relevant provisions of the 1988 Act and Regulations. Consequent amendments to the 1988 Act were made by the Merchant Shipping Act 1988 (Amendment) Order 1989 (SI 1989/2006).

It hardly needs to be said *Factortame I* and *II* are now widely recognised as leading authorities on the relationship of national quotas under the Common Fisheries *Policy to the EC rules* prohibiting discrimination on the ground of nationality, on interim remedies in cases brought under Community law, and on the relationship of the European Communities Act 1972 to the principle of the sovereignty of Parliament.

The Third Reference to the ECJ

Not content with that mark on the law, and — more to the point — not having obtained reparation for the period during which they were allegedly prevented from fishing, the applicants have now gone on to obtain a decision on the circumstances under which a member state is obliged to pay damages to a person who has suffered loss as a result of that state's infringement of Community law.

From the outset the application for judicial review contained an application for damages. After the sundry procedure narrated above, the case went back to the Divisional Court, which on 18 November 1992 made a third reference to the ECJ. Two questions were referred. First, where national legislation infringed articles of the EC Treaty, were persons who had suffered losses as a result of those infringements of Community law entitled *as a matter of Community law* to compensation by that member state? Secondly, the Divisional Court sought guidance on the considerations (if any) that Community law required national courts to apply relative to claims in respect of, inter alia, loss of income, losses arising from forced sales of vessels, shares in vessels, and shares in companies owning vessels, and fines, bonds and legal expenses arising from criminal prosecutions, and to claims for exemplary damages.

Brasserie du Pêcheur

On reaching the ECJ *Factortame III* was conjoined with a case that had been referred by the German Federal High Court, the Bundesgerichtshof, viz *Brasserie du Pêcheur SA v Federal Republic of Germany*. This was an action of reparation brought by a French company that had allegedly been prevented from exporting to Germany beer that did not comply with the Biersteuergesetz ('Law on Beer Duty'). The German law had previously been found by the ECJ to be inconsistent with art 30 of the EC Treaty (case 178/84, *Commission v Federal Republic of Germany* [1987] ECR 1227). Thus in both cases the pursuers were seeking damages for loss caused by national legislation that infringed Community law.

Francovich

In the meantime, while *Factortame I* and *II* were proceeding, the question of a right to damages from a member state for failing to comply with Community law had come before the ECJ in joined cases C-6/90 and C-9/90, *Francovich v Italian Republic* [1991] ECR I–5357. Signor Francovich had suffered loss because Italy had failed to implement an EC directive. The absence of national legislation implementing a directive does not necessarily entail that an individual who would have benefited from such implementation cannot avail himself of the directive; for if the terms of the directive are sufficiently clear, precise and unconditional, then the ECJ has held that it gives an individual a right of action against the state and other public bodies. That is sometimes called 'direct effect'. The directive in question did not give Signor Francovich such a right. Consequently, his only recourse was to bring an action, not on the directive, but on art 189 of the EC Treaty, which obliges member states to implement directives.

When his case was referred to the ECJ, the Court said that 'the principle whereby a state must be liable for loss and damage caused to individuals as a result of breaches of Community law for which the state can be held responsible is inherent in the system of the Treaty … [but] the conditions under which that liability gives rise to a right to reparation depend on the nature of the breach of Community law giving rise to loss and damage' (pp 5414–5415, paras 35 and 38). In the particular case of a failure to implement a directive, the ECJ held that where (1) a directive entailed the grant of rights to individuals; (2) the contents of which rights could be identified from the directive; and (3) there was a causal link between the failure to implement the directive and the injured party's loss, then by virtue of Community law that party had a right to reparation. The Court said that the presence of those three conditions alone was sufficient to instruct liability. In the sense that liability does not depend on the seriousness of the failure to implement the directive, or on establishing fault, liability under *Francovich* may be described as 'strict'.

Francovich left some questions unanswered. The case was concerned only with failure to implement a directive. It was not concerned with the question of an infringement of any provision of the Community Treaties other than art 189, or of an EC regulation, or of any of the common law principles of Community law. It was subsequently interpreted in three different ways.

The narrowest interpretation was that the right to reparation was restricted to cases of failures to implement directives that did not have direct effect. A slightly broader interpretation was that it applied to a failure to implement any directive that sought to grant identifiable rights to individuals. The broadest interpretation was that it established a principle obliging a member state to pay damages for infringement of any rule of Community law, be its source a Treaty, a regulation, a directive, or be it a general principle of EC law. While a literal reading of the judgment clearly suggested that the third interpretation was the correct one, it left open the question of the conditions under which there would arise liability for infringements of Community law that did not consist in failing to implement a directive.

It can therefore be seen that *Francovich* on the one hand, and *Brasserie du Pêcheur* on the other, had this in common, that they both concerned failures to obtemper an article of the EC Treaty (arts 189, and 30 and 52, respectively); and this difference, that *Francovich* concerned a wrongful omission to legislate, whereas the UK and Germany in *Brasserie du Pêcheur* had committed positive acts of wrongful legislation.

The Decision of 5 March

In *Brasserie du Pêcheur*, the ECJ has now held, first, that it is a principle of Community law that member states are obliged to make reparation for loss caused to an individual by a breach of Community law that is attributable to that state. In doing so it explicitly rejected the narrowest, and approved the widest, of the three interpretations of the ratio of *Francovich*. Secondly, the Court held that that principle of liability applies even where the national legislature was responsible for the breach in question.

The decision goes into greater detail in setting out the precise conditions under which that obligation arises. Repeating what was said in *Francovich*, the Court observed that those conditions depended on the nature of the breach of Community law that was at issue. In particular, the Court said, they depended on the extent of the discretion that the member state had been entitled to exercise under Community law when it enacted the unlawful measure. In short, the wider the range of legitimate choices open to the member state, the less readily Community law would penalise it for selecting an unlawful option.

From that starting point, the Court said that, 'in the absence of Community harmonization', the German legislature had 'had a wide discretion… in laying down rules on the quality of beer put on the market'. Equally, in regulating the registration of fishing vessels, the UK Parliament had had a wide discretion, and, in relation to the regulation of fishing itself, at least 'a margin of discretion' (judgment, paras 48–49, pp 12–13).

In those circumstances, the ECJ decided that there are three criteria for there to be an obligation to make reparation: (1) the rule of Community law that has been infringed must have been intended to confer rights on individuals; (2) the breach of that rule must be 'sufficiently serious'; and (3) there must be a direct causal link between the breach of the obligation resting on the state and the pursuer's loss.

The presence of these conditions is both necessary and sufficient for liability under Community law, although national law may apply rules that are more favourable to the injured party.

The first criterion will seemingly be met wherever the Community law that has been broken has 'direct effect' (in the sense in which that expression was defined above); in the cases before it, the Court said that it was met by the relevant articles of the EC Treaty, arts 30 and 52.

On the second criterion, the Court said that a breach would be 'sufficiently serious' if the member state had 'manifestly and gravely disregarded the limits on its discretion' (para 55, p 13). This is probably the element of the test that will be fought over most fiercely in the future. The Court disavowed any intention of making negligence a necessary condition of liability. At the same time, the Court said that in deciding whether a breach was 'manifest and grave', the factors that could be considered included (i) the clarity and precision of the rule that had been breached; (ii) the measure of discretion which that rule left to the national authorities; (iii) whether the infringement and the loss that it caused had ben arrived at intentionally or involuntarily; (iv) whether any error of law was excusable or inexcusable; (v) any position taken by a Community institution that might have contributed towards the member state's so acting; and (vi) 'the adoption or retention of national measures or practices contrary to Community law' (para 56, p 13).

The Court added that where the infringement postdated a judicial ruling that made it clear that the member state was in breach of Community law, that would be sufficient to fulfil the second criterion. Beyond that, the application of these tests was a matter for the national courts in each case. With regard to the liability of the UK to Factortame Ltd and their co-applicants, the Court did however draw a distinction between the conditions relative to nationality that Britain had imposed — which it said were 'manifestly contrary to Community law' — and those relative to the residence and domicile of the owners and operators of fishing vessels — in relation to which the High Court would be entitled to take into account 'the assessments of the state of certainty of Community law made by the national courts' at the time, and 'the attitude of the Commission' (paras 61 and 63, pp 14–15). (The inclusion of the last factor is perhaps slightly odd, since outwith matters over which it has a quasi-judicial jurisdiction, the views of the Commission have as such no special legal authority.)

The third criterion, of causation, speaks for itself.

Quoad ultra, the Court pointed out, 'the conditions for reparation of loss and damage laid down by national law must not be less favourable than those relating to similar domestic claims and must not be such as in practice to make it impossible or excessively difficult to obtain reparation' (para 67, p 15). Those are of course the two established principles that regulate national remedies and procedures in actions brought to enforce Community rights.

The measure of recoverable loss remains in principle a matter for national law. All that the Court said on that topic that is of relevance to Scots law was that the extent of loss recoverable should be such as to ensure effective protection for the rights of the injured party, and determined by rules not less favourable than those applicable to similar claims under national law; that there was nothing to prevent the principle of mitigation of loss being applied; and that loss of profit should not be excluded from the allowable heads of damage.

British Telecommunications

The Court explained in *Brasserie du Pêcheur* that in cases of failure to implement directives, such as *Francovich*, strict liability applied because EC law imposes upon the member state 'obligations to achieve a particular result . . . which reduce its margin of discretion, sometimes to a considerable degree'. However, it seems that Community law will not always characterise as 'narrow' the degree of discretion that a member state exercises when implementing a directive. This is important, because it means that in an action of reparation in which the ground of action is a failure to implement a directive, the strict régime established by *Francovich* will not necessarily apply. For even since *Brasserie du Pêcheur* was decided, on 5 March, the law has moved on.

On 26 March, the ECJ issued its judgment in case C-392/93, *R v HM Treasury, ex p British Telecommunications plc*. This was a reference from the Queen's Bench Division in proceedings brought to reduce Sched 2 to the Utilities Supply and Works Contracts Regulations 1992 (SI 1992/ 3279). The regulations had been made by two Lords Commissioners of HM Treasury in order to implement the EEC Council Directive 90/531 anent public procurement procedures. The directive applies in terms to a number of named undertakings including, inter alios, British Telecommunications plc ('BT'), but not to contracts awarded by them in order to provide telecommunication services 'where other entities are free to offer the same services in the same geographical area and under substantially the same conditions'. The directive established a procedure for companies such as BT to notify the Commission when they were availing themselves of that exemption, and obliged them to keep records sufficient to enable them to justify the claim that the exemption applied. Schedule 2 to the UK regulations proceeded to define the services provided by BT to which the exemption did and did not apply. BT's complaint was that the directive had intended that it should be left to them to claim an exemption in the case of a given contract. The regulations identified a priori the cases to which the exemption applied. BT had thus been deprived of the discretion which the directive had intended should be conferred upon them.

The ECJ agreed with BT that, in that regard, the regulations did not correctly implement the directive. The question then arose of whether the UK was obliged to make reparation to BT for loss caused through the erroneous implementation of the directive. The Court's response was to refer to the decision in *Brasserie du Pêcheur*, and in particular to the rule that 'with regard to a breach of Community law for which a Member State, acting in a field in which it has a wide discretion in taking legislative decisions, can be held responsible', liability depends on the presence of the three conditions laid down in *Brasserie du Pêcheur*. 'Those same conditions' the Court continued, 'must be applicable to the situation… in which a Member State incorrectly transposes a Community directive into national law. A restrictive approach to state liability is justified in such a situation' (paras 39–40, p 10). In the instant case, the Court said that the national court could only conclude that the Lords Commissioners' error had not been a 'manifest and grave' breach of EC law, largely because the relevant article of the directive was 'imprecisely worded and was reasonably capable of bearing, as well as the construction applied to it by the Court in this judgment, the interpretation given to it by the United Kingdom in good faith and on the basis of arguments which are not entirely devoid of substance' (para 43, p 11).

Francovich Today

The decision in *British Telecommunications* appears to be of considerable significance for most of the cases in which, after *Francovich*, the UK may have been thought to face a possible obligation in reparation. Whether an error in implementing a directive is 'manifest and grave' will of course always depend on the facts of the case. What is important for future cases, however, is that *British Telecommunications* appears to state that, as a general rule in a question of whether reparation is owed, the implementation of a directive falls within an area of legislative activity in which a member state has a wide discretion. It would follow that in such a case the pursuer who seeks damages will always have to meet the test of a 'manifest and grave' breach of Community law. That is significantly different from the position under *Francovich*, where no such test applied.

Francovich concerned a total failure to take any steps to implement a directive. *British Telecommunications* applies in a case of 'incorrect transposition' of a directive. It seems unlikely that the Court intended the latter phrase to embrace a case like *Francovich*. If that is so, then strict liability applies to member states who take no steps to implement a directive, but on the other hand, a state which makes the attempt but gets it wrong is protected, inasmuch as unless its error is 'manifest and grave', it will not have to pay damages.

It might be thought that, taken together, *Brasserie du Pêcheur* and *British Telecommunications* create a situation in which a person injured by a total failure to implement a directive is in a significantly stronger position than someone whose loss flows either from a flawed attempt to do so, or from a breach of Community law unconnected with the implementation of any directive. However, it must be very doubtful whether the contrast between the two different tests will lead to results that differ from those that would obtain if the criterion of a 'manifest and grave breach' applied also to a total failure to implement a directive — for the simple reason that a total failure to implement must almost inevitably constitute a 'manifest and grave' breach of Community law.

It follows that it is academic that nothing in the latest decisions has expressly overruled *Francovich* by extending the 'manifest and grave' test to such a case. However, a more substantial issue that may need to be resolved is which test applies to a case like *Wagner Miret*.

Wagner Miret

In *Francovich*, the ECJ said that the three conditions that were sufficient to instruct liability applied in a case where a member state failed 'to fulfil its obligation under the third paragraph of Article 189 of the Treaty to take all the measures necessary to achieve the result prescribed by a directive' (para 39, p 5415). In principle, of course, a member state which does not enact a measure to implement a directive, and a member state which enacts a measure which purports to implement a directive but which in some respect fails to accord with the true meaning of the directive, have both failed to fulfil their obligations under art 189.

The same is of course true of a member state which, prior to a directive coming into force, has already enacted measures which it considers have the effect of implementing the directive, but which in fact fail in some respect to do so properly.

The latter situation arose in case C-334/92, *Wagner Miret v Fondo de Garantía Salarial* [1995] 2 CMLR 49 (decided on 16 December 1993), where the ECJ found that Directive 80/987, requiring member states to ensure that employees' rights were protected in the event of their employers' insolvency, did not exclude higher management staff from that protection. A pre-existing Spanish law ensured the necessary protection for most employees, but excluded higher management staff. The Tribunal Superior de Justicia of Catalonia asked the ECJ whether, in those circumstances, the Spanish state had to make good the loss sustained by a manager whose employer was insolvent. The Court responded that such staff were 'entitled to request the State concerned to make good the loss and damage sustained as a result of the failure to implement the directive in their respect' (para 24, p 64).

The decision in *Wagner Miret* was of course wholly consistent with the strict régime of liability established by *Francovich*. However, after *British Telecommunications* the question arises of whether a case in which a member state takes no steps to implement a directive because it believes that its pre-existing laws already reflect the requirements of the directive should be treated in the same way as a total failure to implement the directive, or as a case in which the action of the member state is equivalent to the 'incorrect transposition' of a directive, and therefore one in which the member state is, to quote *Brasserie du Pêcheur*, 'acting in a field in which it has a wide discretion in taking legislative decisions'; in which case liability depends on the presence of the three conditions laid down in that judgment. Technically, such a case appears to involve an omission equivalent to that in *Francovich*; as a matter of substance, it is obviously arguable that it is closer to *British Telecommunications*. The point may require judicial resolution.

Assessment of Brasserie du Pêcheur and British Telecommunications

The decision in *British Telecommunications* three weeks after *Brasserie du Pêcheur* confirms the impression that, compared with *Francovich*, the Court has now framed rules of liability for cases other than total failures to attempt to implement directives, in a manner that is considerably more favourable to the member state than to the pursuer. As was said above, the fact that the Court has not overruled *Francovich* seems in effect to be academic. What is significant is that the Court did not extend the strict régime of *Francovich* to the facts of *Brasserie du Pêcheur* and *British Telecommunications*. To that extent, the decision in *Brasserie du Pêcheur* is not in the terms for which counsel for Factortame Ltd and their fellow applicants contended, at least primarily, viz that the rule should be one of strict liability, as with *Francovich*. Indeed, the decision adopts criteria of liability that are comparable to those urged on the court by counsel for HM Government.

A difficulty with extending the rule of strict liability adumbrated by *Francovich*, was its apparent inconsistency with the case law on art 215 of the EC Treaty. Article 215 governs the delictual liability of Community institutions such as the Council and the Commission. Where those institutions make a law that is later found to be unlawful, the ECJ has held that art 215 means that, for there to be a duty to pay damages for consequent loss, the illegality must arise from a superior rule of law intended to protect the individual, and that the breach must be manifest and grave (case 5/71, *Zuckerfabrik Schöppenstedt v Council* [1971] ECR 975). In the decision of the Court of Appeal in *Bourgoin SA v Ministry of Agriculture, Fisheries and Food* [1986] 1 QB 716, Parker LJ had been only one of many commentators to remark upon the odd contrast that 'the *Schöppenstedt* formula' would make with a rule that member states, unlike Community institutions, were subject to strict liability. What the ECJ has now done is attempt to square the circle, by expressly equating the conditions of liability in *Brasserie du Pêcheur* with those in *Schöppenstedt*, on the basis that both are concerned with authorities exercising a wide discretion, and to leave *Francovich* as the exceptional case of strict liability.

The recent decisions may therefore be thought to suggest the development of an inchoate principle of 'judicial protection' of the taxpayer. For a member state such as the UK which has a very good record for implementing directives, but which faces a number of arguments that the terms of certain implementing measures do not comply with the true meaning of the relevant directives, the adoption of the same test in *British Telecommunications* is clearly good news. It is to be expected that the defence that any error was not 'manifest or grave' will be explored in, for example, the disputes over the former exclusion of employees of non-commercial undertakings from the scope of the Transfer of Undertakings (Protection of Employment) Regulations 1981 (SI 1981/1794), and over the test of 'reasonable practicability' in measures implementing the Health and Safety Directives.

It has, of course, to be said that the terms of the recent judgments do not bind the ECJ in respect of future decisions. Indeed, the mutability, or 'dynamism', of Community law is thought by some to be a virtue. The reason why *Francovich* has been so much discussed is because for the three previous decades the question it answered had in effect, if not also in principle, been a matter for national law. Some commentators thought that the decision in case 60/75, *Russo v AIMA* [1976] ECR 45 said as much, yet it was in truth ambiguous. Of course, ambiguity is itself as great a source of uncertainty as the possibility of retrospective restatement of the law. Community law may, unlike our own, be based entirely on written texts, but Luxembourg nonetheless has its equivalents of *Anns* and *Murphy*. As with *Murphy*, the latest decisions illustrate that changing trends in the law are not synonymous with the extension of liability. But if the past is any guide, the practitioner should not assume that they are the last word on the subject.

Francovich, Brasserie du Pêcheur and *British Telecommunications* are concerned only with the liabilities of *the state*. One obvious area in which to watch out for developments is that of the liability in private law of one individual to make reparation to another for loss caused as a result of a breach of a duty in Community law (cf *Garden Cottage Foods Ltd v Milk Marketing Board* [1984] AC 130; case C-128/92, *H J Banks & Co Ltd v British Coal Corporation* [1994] ECR I-1209; W van Gerven, 'Non-contractual Liability of Member States, Community Institutions and Individuals for Breaches of Community Law with a view to a Common Law of Europe', MJECL 1 (1994) 6).

The Context of Scots and English Law

How novel are the rules that *Francovich, Brasserie du Pêcheur* and *British Telecommunications* have introduced into Scots and English law?

In some respects, the approach that a national court must now adopt in assessing the liability of the Crown is not as new to Scots administrative law as one might at first think. Thus when *Brasserie du Pêcheur* directs attention to the 'excusability' of legislating in breach of a Community law, the Scottish courts have in fact already had some experience of determining whether reparation is owed by a public authority in the light of the question of whether a mistake of law was or was not a pardonable error: see e g *Edwards v Parochial Board of Kinross* (1891) 18 R 867 per Lord McLaren at p 869, and *Ballantyne v City of Glasgow District Licensing Board*, 1987 SLT 745, per Lord Jauncey at pp 747–748.

However, what *is* novel is the application of such criteria to legislation. 'Wrongful legislation' is an unfamiliar concept in the Scots law of delict because, unless it infringes the European Communities Act 1972, an Act of Parliament cannot be unlawful (unless, possibly, it infringes certain provisions of the Act of Union). In the case of persons other than Parliament who have the power to make measures that can be described as legislation (chief amongst whom are the General Assembly, Her Majesty in Council, Ministers of the Crown, the Court of Session, the High Court of Justiciary, local authorities, universities, and various statutory undertakers), the rules that they make *may* in principle be unlawful, either because they are ultra vires, or because of a procedural irregularity, or because they are unreasonable to the point of perversity. However, so far as the writer is aware, no one in Scotland has ever recovered damages for wrongful subordinate legislation. From first principles it can be said that in such a case there would be no entitlement to damages unless the legislator had acted in the knowledge that his conduct could injure the pursuer, and in bad faith; that is to say, either with malice or some other improper consideration as his motive, or in the knowledge that the legislation was unlawful. That is what is called in England 'misfeasance in public office' (cf *Micosta v Shetland Islands Council*, 1986 SLT 193, per Lord Ross at pp 198–199).

From the point of view of the applicants in *Factortame III*, the importance of the foregoing rules (as they apply in England) was that they meant that, unless there was a right to reparation that arose *as a matter of Community law*, they would be thrown back upon the tort of misfeasance in public office. In 1985 the Court of Appeal had decided in *Bourgoin SA* (in which the facts were analogous to the case against Germany in *Brasserie du PÊcheur*, except that an administrative rather than legislative measure was at issue) that as Community law then stood, a right to damages depended on establishing misfeasance in public office. The ECJ observed in *Brasserie du Pêcheur* that the criteria of that tort are 'such as in practice to make it impossible or extremely difficult to obtain effective reparation', bad faith 'being inconceivable in the case of the legislature'. Accordingly, applying the principle that national courts must provide effective means of enforcing rights in Community law, the Court held that it would be unlawful to require the applicants to establish the criteria of the tort of misfeasance in public office.

Brasserie du Pêcheur has been described above as favourable to defenders. However, if it is compared with Scots and English common law, the position at which Community law has now arrived is obviously vastly more favourable to pursuers, by obviating the former criteria for liability, while at the same time creating for the first time the possibility of reparation for loss caused by an Act of Parliament. That raises the bizarre question of whether in such an action Parliament must be called as a defender, which will be discussed in the subsequent article."

Notes

(1) In his subsequent article at 1996 S.L.T. (News) 211 Upton explored the appropriate **14–63** procedure to be used in bringing an action against the Crown and concluded that proceedings for damages would normally require to be brought by way of judicial review, with the litigant normally craving both reduction and damages, although that is not necessarily the exclusive way to proceed: see also C. Boch and R. Lane, "A New Remedy in Scots Law: Damages from the Crown for Breach of Community Law", 1992 S.L.T. (News) 145. For comment on damages and reduction see Chapter 11.

(2) The ambit of the doctrine discussed in the article has been expanded further in a number of subsequent cases. In *R. v. Ministry of Agriculture, Fisheries and Food, ex. p. Hedley Lomas (Ireland) Ltd* [1996] All E.R. (E.C.) 493, it was held that if, when the infringement occurred, the Member State in question was not called upon to make any legislative choice and had a limited or no discretion available to it, the fact of infringement of community law would be enough to create liability if the breach was sufficiently serious. Here, the Ministry refused to issue a licence for the export of live sheep to Spain in their belief that the treatment of sheep in Spanish slaughterhouses was contrary to Council Directive 74/577. The Ministry considered that the Spanish authorities had not fully implemented the directive. The U.K. Government was held to have little discretion at the time when it refused the licence and its failure to do so was sufficiently serious to create liability. Even if proof of non-compliance could be established, then that would not be enough to elide liability. The decision in *R v. HM Treasury, ex parte British Telecommunications plc* is now reported at [1996] 3 W.L.R. 203. Both that case and the decision in *Hedley Lomas (Ireland) Ltd* illustrate that any breach requires to be "sufficiently serious" before liability will attach. See also *Duff v. Minister for Agriculture and Food, Ireland, and the Attorney General* [1997] 3 C.M.L.R. 1034, where the Irish Supreme Court ruled that where a Minister had made a mistake of law in allocating milk quotas following a Community regulation, he had caused farmers damage and loss for which they were entitled to receive compensation. Similarly, in *R v. Secretary of State for Transport, ex parte Factortame (No. 5)* [1998] 1 All E.R. 736 the High Court and thereafter the Court of Appeal ruled that failure in transposition of the directive in question in that case was "sufficiently serious" as to merit compensation although this did not give rise to an entitlement to punitive damages. In the field of social security law, it has been held that even where a member state is liable for loss caused as a result of a breach of a community obligation, this does not entitle an individual affected to claim interest on arrears of social security benefit: *R v. Secretary of State for Social Security, ex parte Suttees* [1997] All E.R. (E.C.) 497, E.C.J. Moreover, a State cannot rely on domestic procedures and practices to avoid implementation of an obligation, if there is a time-limit for that to occur: see *Commission v. Belgium* [1988] E.C.R. 3271 and also *Dillenkofer v. Germany* [1996] T.L.R. 564 and on this area generally see Finch and Ashton, pp. 470–475.

(3) Under the Scotland Act 1998 the Scottish Executive is responsible for ensuring the **14–64** implementation in Scotland of European Union obligations. Typically this would be done by way of the passing of a subordinate instrument. Alternatively, the Scottish Executive could enter into arrangements for implementing E.U. proposals common to the whole of Great Britain or the United Kingdom by U.K. Ministers and Scottish Executive Ministers adopting the same formulae in separate instruments. As to liability for failure to implement an obligation, para. 5.8 of the White Paper noted:

> "Where EU obligations are to be implemented separately for Scotland, there will be arrangements with the UK Government to ensure that differences of approach are compatible with the need for consistency of effect; and to avoid the risk of financial penalties falling on the UK for any failure of implementation or enforcement. If any such financial penalties were imposed on the UK, or penalties arose from infraction proceedings, responsibility for meeting them would have to be borne by the Scottish Executive if it were responsible for the failure; and the same principle would apply to the other parts of the UK."

The terms of section 58 are the statutory expression of the above. Section 58 is extracted at para. 13–10. See also C.M.G. Himsworth and C. Munro, *Devolution and the Scotland Bill* (1998), Chap. 9.

Note the argument raised by Upton in the second of his articles that there may possibly be joint and several liability between the U.K. Government and the Westminster Parliament in relation to a breach of an E.U. obligation.

(4) Liability for failure to have regard to E.C. obligations rests not just on the kind of liability established in *Brasserie du Pêcheur S.A. v. Germany*. In *Booker Aquaculture Ltd v. Secretary of State for Scotland* [1998] T.L.R. 570 the pursuers' fish were ordered to be destroyed as a result of an order from the defender on the pursuers intimating to them the disease in the fish. They sought compensation but this was refused. The measures were taken under the Diseases of Fish (Control) Regulations, 1994 which in turn implemented Council Directives 91/67 and 93/53. Judicial review proceedings were raised, but reduction of the regulation was not sought. The matter was analysed as being one where E.U. law provided for compensation to persons who were permanently deprived of all appreciable value in their assets. As a result, in implementing of the regulation the United Kingdom should have noted that a regulation of such strictness was not required and having made it so strict, regard ought to have been taken account of the implicit principle of compensation, albeit that it was not mentioned in the directive. In these circumstances, where no discretion existed, there had to be compensatory mechanism. Declarator was granted to the effect that the defender's conduct was illegal. Damages, although not sought, were clearly competent.

(5) Consider also the effect of the Scotland Act 1998 and the Human Rights Act 1998, s. 6. Under the former, both the Parliament and the Executive cannot act in a way which is contrary to a Convention Right, whether by primary or subordinate legislation or by way of executive decision, on which see section 29 extracted at para. 3–10 and sections 54, 57(2), 58 noted at para. 3–11, 13–9 and 13–10 respectively. If *ultra vires* can be established, is there any reason in principle why an award of damages might not also be sought against the body in question? For discussion on the general approach to damages for breach of the ECHR see Chapter 11. Could such liability arise in a situation where there has been a *failure* to protect the Convention Right?

RESTITUTION

14–65   Restitution is of growing importance in relation in administrative law. In *Woolwich Equitable Building Society v. Inland Revenue Commissioners* [1993] A.C. 70 the citizens' right to recover money paid to a public authority under an unlawful demand was considered and expanded and in *Hazell v. Hammersmith and Fulham London Borough Council* [1992] 2 A.C. 1 interest rates swap and transactions entered into by local authorities and banks were held to be *ultra vires* leading to litigation by the local authorities to recover the money paid to the banks. These cases were of course decided in the context of English law.

It was not until the decision in *Morgan Guaranty Trust Co. of New York v. Lothian Regional Council*, 1995 S.L.T. 299 that the scope of restitution in Scots administrative law was examined. Here, the pursuers entered into a swap agreement with the defenders. The defenders were liable for interest at a fixed rate on a notional sum of £10 million and the pursuers were liable for variable rates of interest on that sum. Under the agreement the pursuers made payments to the defenders amounting to £368, 104.52. The pursuers sought repayment of this sum on the ground that the transaction had been *ultra vires* the defenders and was therefore void. The defenders relied on the terms of section 69 of the Local Government (Scotland) Act 1973 to plead that the transaction had been within their powers. In any event they also argued that if the transaction was void, the pursuers had no right to repayment as payment had been made under error of law as to the meaning of a public statute and there was binding authority from the Inner House to the effect that such payment was not recoverable: *Glasgow Corporation v. Lord Advocate*, 1959 S.C. 203. At first instance, the Lord Ordinary held that such a transaction was *ultra vires* on the basis of the authority in *Hazell* but standing the authority in *Glasgow Corporation*, could not hold that payments were recoverable. The matter therefore had to be considered by the Inner House. Until *Woolwich*, as a general rule while money paid under a mistake of law was not recoverable, money made under a mistake of fact was. However, after reviewing the case law, including *Glasgow Corporation*, the House of Lords held that:

> "the subject who makes a payment in response to an unlawful demand of tax acquires forthwith a prima facie right in restitution to the repayment of the money" (Lord Goff at 171).

Lord Goff explained the basis of this development known as the "*Woolwich* principle" in the following terms:

> "The justice underlying Woolwich's submission is, I consider, plain to see. Take the present case. The revenue has made an unlawful demand for tax. The taxpayer is convinced that the demand is unlawful, and has to decide what to do. It is faced with the revenue, armed with the coercive power of the state, including what is in practice a power to charge interest which is penal in its effect. In addition, being a reputable society which alone among building societies is challenging the lawfulness of the demand, it understandably fears damage to its reputation if it does not pay. So it decides to pay first, asserting that it will challenge the lawfulness of the demand in litigation. Now, Woolwich having won that litigation, the revenue asserts that it was never under any obligation to repay the money, and that it in fact repaid it only as a matter of grace. There being no applicable statute to regulate the position, the revenue has to maintain this position at common law.
>
> Stated in this stark form, the revenue's position appears to me, as a matter of common justice, to be unsustainable; and the injustice is rendered worse by the fact that it involves, as Nolan J. pointed out [1989] 1 W.L.R. 137, 140, the revenue having the benefit of a massive interest-free loan as the fruit of its unlawful action. I turn then from the particular to the general. Take any tax or duty paid by the citizen pursuant to an unlawful demand. Common justice seems to require that tax to be repaid, unless special circumstances or some principle of policy require otherwise; prima facie, the taxpayer should be entitled to repayment as of right.
>
> To the simple call of justice, there are a number of possible objections. The first is to be found in the structure of our law of restitution, as it developed during the 19th and early 20th centuries. That law might have developed so as to recognise a *condictio indebiti* — an action for the recovery of money on the ground that it was not due. But it did not do so. Instead, as we have seen, there developed common law actions for the recovery of money paid under a mistake of fact, and under certain forms of compulsion. What is now being sought is, in a sense, a reversal of that development, in a particular type of case; and it is said that it is too late to take that step. To that objection, however, there are two answers. The first is that the retention by the state of taxes unlawfully exacted is particularly obnoxious, because it is one of the most fundamental principles of our law — enshrined in a famous constitutional document, the Bill of Rights 1688 — that taxes should not be levied without the authority of Parliament; and full effect can only be given to that principle if the return of taxes exacted under an unlawful demand can be enforced as a matter of right. The second is that, when the revenue makes a demand for tax, that demand is implicitly backed by the coercive powers of the state and may well entail (as in the present case) unpleasant economic and social consequences if the taxpayer does not pay. In any event, it seems strange to penalise the good citizen, whose natural instinct is to trust the revenue and pay taxes when they are demanded of him."

(1) The exact scope of Lord Goff's approach is not clear. The Law Commission (Law Com. **14–66** No. 227) is of the view that it

> "may well be held to apply to all taxes, levies, assessments, tolls or charges, whether for the provision of services or not, collected by any person or body under a statutory provision which is the sole source of the authority to charge".

It is not:

> "limited to payments of tax or to Governmental or quasi-Governmental exactions, or to payments made in accordance with the demand. We believe the crucial element is that the payment is collected by any person or body which is operating outside its statutory authority, that is, it is acting ultra vires. The requirement of ultra vires is not in our view confined to the excess of statutory power but also extends to procedural abuses, abuse of power and error of law on the part of the charging authority" (paras 6.32–6.42).

(2) In *Morgan Guaranty* the Lord President (Hope), in giving the judgment of a court of five judges, was prepared to overrule the decision in *Glasgow Corporation* but did not feel it necessary to develop any new principle based on the approach in *Woolwich* or to adopt the *Woolwich* principle. His Lordship noted (at 315):

> "Concern may be felt that to reaffirm the decision that a payment not due may be recovered under the condictio indebiti irrespective of whether the mistake was one of fact or law may be too radical a departure from what has been thought to be the law of Scotland for so many years. I do not share that concern. The effect of the decision will require to be worked out in subsequent cases, but in one important field it has already been anticipated, although on other grounds, by developments in English law. In the *Glasgow Corporation* case the court was obviously much troubled by the effect on other transactions if a change in the interpretation of an Act of Parliament were to enable a party to open up a transaction which had been settled and completed on the law as it was then understood. The typical example might be thought to be where an unlawful demand for the payment of a tax or some other duty made by a public authority has now been found by judicial decision to have been unlawful. In the *Woolwich* case it has now been held, for English law, that there is a prima facie right in such a case to recovery. By overruling the decision in *Glasgow Corporation v Lord Advocate* we will be achieving the same result by reference to the principles of Scots law. I regard that as satisfactory, because it would be inequitable that a remedy which is now available in England in this important field of transactions between the citizen and a public authority should be denied here on the ground that it was not permitted by our law. By removing the error of law rule we will be providing a remedy which will prima facie be available in these cases, but whether it will or will not be given will depend in each case on considerations of equity."

(3) Just as the *Woolwich* principle might be regarded as having uncertain scope, so to the approach in *Morgan Guaranty* has been subject to scrutiny. The Scottish Law Commission (S.L.C.D.P. Nos 99 and 100) considered the implications of *Morgan Guaranty* in depth and contrasted it with *Woolwich*. In summary the Commission's views were that:

> "(1) The *Woolwich* case undermined that part of the decision in *Glasgow Corporation* which had held (following English cases) that a taxpayer does not have an automatic right, based on the Bill of Rights, to recover from the Crown undue tax paid in error.
> (2) The decision in *Morgan Guaranty* however neither introduced the *Woolwich* ground in Scots law nor recognised a new ground covering cases of the *Woolwich* type, ie payments to public authorities pursuant to *ultra vires* demands.
> (3) Nevertheless in *Morgan Guaranty* there are dicta recognising that such cases should indeed be actionable in Scots law and also dicta paving the way for the court to evolve a ground of repetition covering such cases.
> (4) The uncertainty and controversy surrounding the taxonomy of the grounds of repetition and associated *condictiones* makes it unclear what will be the scope and form of such a ground..."
> S.L.C. D.P. No. 100, (para. 2.44, pp. 50–51).

The impact of the decision in *Morgan Guaranty* has yet to be worked out. Of particular significance will be the extent to which the court handles the equitable considerations mentioned by the Lord President. First, under Scots law payment under error is recoverable only if the error is excusable: *Wilson and McLellan v. Sinclair* (1830) 4 W.S. 398 at 409. Secondly, wide judicial discretion to refuse payment on equitable grounds exists, particularly on the basis of the defence of change of position: S.L.C. D.P. No. 95, Vol. 2, para. 2.63. For other equitable defences see S.L.C. D.P. No. 100, paras 2.46–2.48.

14–67   (4) On the question of reform, the Scottish Law Commission rejected wholesale incorporation of the *Woolwich* principle into Scots law and questioned whether development by way of the extension of specific grounds of recovery was acceptable and whether a new type of approach based on a broader general ground of recovery should be examined as part of a general review of the law of unjustified enrichment: see S.L.C. D.P. No. 100, Part III, p. 256. The Scottish Law Commission has now published its *Report on Unjustified Enrichment, Error of Law and Public Authority Receipts and Disbursements* (S.L.C. No. 169) (1999), which makes recommendations on some of the topics raised in the discussion papers. First, while the Commission's provisional proposals to end the rule including recovery of benefits conferred under error of law were superseded by the decision in *Morgan Guaranty*, the court in that case was assisted by the work of the Commission in S.L.C. D.P. No. 95. Second, following its previous discussion paper, No. 99, and the decision of the House of Lords in *Kleinwort Benson v. Lincoln City Council* [1998] 3 W.L.R. 1095, the Commission recommended against the introduction of safeguard by statute to prevent persons who had paid an alleged debt in accordance with a settled in view of the law, which was later overturned by judicial decision, from recovering, lest a wide circle of closed transactions be opened up. Finally, the Commission reaffirmed its view that the ground of recovery in *Woolwich* did not require to be introduced in Scots law, because the Scottish courts would reach the same result at common law by relying on broader principles of recovery not restricted to *ultra vires* public authority receipts.

(5) There are some statutory provisions which expressly provide for repayment of overpaid taxes. For example, in *R. v. Tower Hamlets London Borough Council, ex parte Chetnik Developments Ltd* [1988] A.C. 858, section 9 of the General Rate Act 1967 was considered. The House of Lords held that judicial review of the council's refusal to exercise discretion under this section was available on the basis that the council had to have regard to irrelevant considerations — the financial circumstances of the council — both externally and internally. There is no exact counterpart of section 9 in Scotland although the Local Government (Financial Provisions) (Scotland) Act 1963, s. 20(1) imposes a duty of repayment of rates where an error of fact existed. Although the basis of judicial review in Scots law is based on the tripartite relationship detailed in *West*, *Chetnik* is at least persuasive authority that where a statutory power to refund exists then the exercise of discretion in relation thereto is amenable to judicial review and, standing the tripartite test, there seems no good reason why it would not be competent to seek judicial review of such a decision under Scots Law.

Other statutory provisions on recovery include sections 71 and 75 of the Social Security Administration Act 1992 and section 16 of the Jobseekers Act 1995, as amended by the Social Security Act 1998. Common law recovery of social security benefits is not precluded by the statutory scheme, on which see generally I. Nisbet, "Common law recovery of over payments social security benefits" (1998) 249 SCOLAG 45.

(6) On restitution and public authorities see P. Birks "Restitution from Public Authorities" **14–68** (1980) 33 C.L.P. 191 and "Restitution From The Executive" in *Essays on Restitution* (P. Finn ed., 1994), p. 164; A. Burrows, "Public Authorities, Ultra Vires and Restitution" in *Studies in the Law of Restitution* (A. Burrows ed., 1991); and W.J. Stewart, *The Law of Restitution in Scotland* (1992); on the *Woolwich Equitable* case see J. Beatson "Public Law, Restitution and the Role of the House of Lords" (1993) 109 L.Q.R. 1 and "Restitution of Taxes, Levies and Other Imposts: Defining the Extent of the *Woolwich* Principle" (1993) 109 L.Q.R. 401; on *Morgan Guaranty* see N.R. Whitty, "Ultra Vires Swap Contracts and Unjustified Enrichment", 1994 S.L.T. (News) 337; J.E. du Plessis and H. Wicke, "*Woolwich Equitable v. IRC* and the Condictio Indebiti in Scots Law", 1993 S.L.T. (News) 303; W.J. Stewart, "Restitution: First Thoughts on Swaps in Scotland", 1992 S.L.T. (News) 315; W.J. Stewart, *The Law of Restitution in Scotland* (1992) and supplement 1995; and W.J. Stewart, *Delict* (3rd ed., 1998), Chap. 13.

(7) Any payment made out of the Consolidated Fund without parliamentary authority is *ultra vires* and can be recovered by the Crown if it can be traced: *Auckland Harbour Board v. R.* [1924] A.C. 318 at 327 *per* Viscount Haldane. The English law commissioners observed that Lord Haldane's restriction of this rule to payments from the Consolidated Fund appears to be anomalous: see Law Com. No. 227, para. 17.2. If the limitation is to be based on public policy, namely the protection of public funds, it should apply to all *ultra vires* payments made by central government and so should apply to payments out of departmental budgets as well as payments out of the Consolidated Fund. Under the Scotland Act 1998, s. 64, a Scottish consolidated fund is established, and circumstances in which payments out of the fund might lawfully be made are detailed in section 65. For comment see Himsworth and Munro (1998), pp. 79–85 and (1999), pp. 81–91.

(8) A number of schemes exist in European Community law in relation to payments made unlawfully under Community provisions. Unlawful state aids are the prime example of such payments. For discussion of this complex area see S.L.C. D.P. No. 100, pp. 242–245.

Chapter 15

PUBLIC INTEREST IMMUNITY

It is a general principle in any legal action that all relevant evidence should be considered by the court. If the party holding that evidence is not willing to release it voluntarily the other party can seek an order to recover that evidence. The law recognises that, in some cases, there is a competing interest which should be set against the claim for recovery of evidence. One of these competing interests is that it is not in the public interest that the evidence be disclosed. Such a plea was formerly known as Crown privilege but, latterly, has been called either public interest privilege or public interest immunity. The development of the doctrine has been different in Scotland as compared to England and Wales. This is one of the areas of administrative law where Scots law appears to differ quite markedly in a number of material respects from English law.

    Although the development of the doctrine rests principally on the common law, statute has intervened to provide a structure within which a plea can be determined.

    Evidence, for the purpose of the plea, includes documents, notes of discussions video or audio tapes or physical items. The procedure for recovery is known as commission and diligence. For a general account see *The Laws of Scotland: Stair Memorial Encyclopaedia*, Vol. 17, paras 1148–1150; D. Sheldon, *Evidence: Cases and Materials* (1996), pp. 527–553; A. MacSporran and A. Young, *Commission and Diligence* (1996); A.B. Wilkinson, *The Scottish Law of Evidence* (1986), pp. 107–115; and D. Field and F. Raitt, *Evidence* (2nd ed., 1996).

15–1

GENERAL

Crown Proceedings Act 1947

s. 47

"**47.** Subject to and in accordance with Acts of Sederunt applying to the Court of Session and the sheriff court, commission and diligence for the recovery of documents in the possession of the Crown may be granted in any action whether or not the Crown is a party thereto, in like manner in all respects as if the documents were in the possession of a subject:

    Provided that —
    (i)   this subsection shall be without prejudice to any rule of law which authorises or requires the withholding of any document on the ground that its disclosure would be injurious to the public interest; and
    (ii)   the existence of a document shall not be disclosed if, in the opinion of a Minister of the Crown, it would be injurious to the public interest to disclose the existence thereof."

15–2

Notes

    F. M. McShane, "Crown Privilege in Scotland: The Demerits of Disharmony" (1992) 37 J.R. 256 states that section 47 had no substantive effect on the common law position, but simply abolished the difficulty in ordering the production of documents from the Crown as a party to an action. The equivalent English provision is found in section 28.

15–3

Administration of Justice (Scotland) Act 1972

s. 1(1), (4)

"Extended Powers of Courts to Order Inspection of Documents and Other Property, etc.

15–4   **1.** — (1) Without prejudice to the existing powers of the Court of Session and of the sheriff court, those courts shall have power, subject to the provisions of subsection (4) of this section, to order the inspection, photographing, preservation, custody and detention of documents and other property (including, where appropriate, land) which appear to the court to be property as to which any question may relevantly arise in any existing civil proceedings before that court or in civil proceedings which are likely to be brought, and to order the production and recovery of any such property, the taking of samples thereof and the carrying out of any experiment thereon or therewith . . .

(4) Nothing in this section shall affect any rule of law or practice relating to the privilege of witnesses and havers, confidentiality of communications and withholding or non-disclosure of information on the grounds of public interest; and section 47 of the Crown Proceedings Act 1947 (recovery of documents in possession of Crown) shall apply in relation to any application under this section in respect of a document or other property as it applied before the commencement of this section to an application for commission and diligence for the recovery of a document."

Notes

15–5   (1) This section covers the recovery of physical property, as in *P. Cannon (Garages) Ltd v. Lord Advocate*, 1983 S.L.T. (Sh. Ct) 50 where recovery of a blood sample was sought.

(2) Procedurally, when an issue of public interest immunity arises, if the Crown is party to the action it will make a direct objection: if not, a warrant to cite the Lord Advocate as representing the Crown will be granted. Where objection is made the most common mode is by way of a ministerial certificate.

(3) The Act refers to the sheriff court having the power of ordering recovery of evidence. However, the Act does not determine whether or not the sheriff court has power to determine a plea of public interest immunity. In *Central Land Board* below the tenor of Lord Keith's speech suggests that no such power exists, and Lord Normand expressed no opinion. I.D. Macphail, *Sheriff Court Practice* (2nd ed., 1998), para. 15.55 seems to accept that the power exists and there are sheriff court decisions where issues of public interest immunity arose, even if not requiring to be determined, without competency being doubted: see *P. Cannon (Garages) Ltd* above and *Davers v. Butler*, 1994 S.C.L.R. 717.

(4) Alongside the power contained in section 1, the courts have a power at common law to order recovery of evidence under commission and diligence procedure. For an example see *Admiralty v. Aberdeen Steam Trawling and Fishing Co. Ltd*, 1909 S.C. 335 noted in the next extract. The procedure for recovery at common law is, however, more restricted than that available under section 1 and for that reason is less frequently evoked. For general commentary see MacSporran and Young above.

GENERAL PRINCIPLES

The Corporation of the City of Glasgow v. The Central Land Board

1956 S.C. (H.L.) 1

15–6   "Glasgow Corporation brought an action against the Central Land Board for declarator that certain determinations of the Board in respect of development charges were *ultra vires*, and for their reduction. Proof having been allowed, the Corporation moved for a commission and diligence to recover various documents in the possession of the defenders which related to the determination of the charges. This motion was met by the lodging in process of a certificate by the Secretary of State for Scotland that some of these documents 'belonged to a class which it was necessary for the proper functioning of the public service to withhold from production'."

LORD NORMAND: "In this appeal the Corporation of the City of Glasgow are the pursuers and appellants. They raised the action to have it declared that certain determinations made by the Central Land board, the defenders and respondents, and purporting to determine certain development charges under the provisions of the Town and Country Planning (Scotland) Act, 1947, were *ultra vires*. The respondents contested the relevancy of the case, and after debate the Lord Ordinary allowed a proof before answer. Thereafter the appellants moved the Lord Ordinary to grant a diligence for the recovery of certain documents in the possession of the respondents and of the Board of Inland Revenue. About some of these there was no dispute, but there were others which the respondents declined to produce, and before the appellants' specification was debated the Secretary of State for Scotland granted a certificate that he had examined the disputed documents and had formed the view that on grounds of public interest they ought not to be produced because they belonged to a class which it was necessary for the proper functioning of the public service to withhold from production. The Lord Ordinary, after hearing parties, allowed the recovery of the undisputed documents only. The appellants reclaimed and the First Division of the Court of Session adhered to the Lord Ordinary's interlocutor. The scheduled interlocutors are those of the Lord Ordinary and of the First Division dealing with the recovery of documents: the Lord Ordinary's interlocutor allowing a proof before answer was not reclaimed against and there is no question upon it before the House.

The first question that the House must consider is whether the Central Land Board is a body which can claim the benefit of the Crown's right to certify that a document or class of document should not be produced because its production would adversely affect the public interest, or, to put it shortly, whether the Board is the Crown for this purpose. On this question I agree with my noble and learned friend on the Woolsack, and have nothing to add.

The next question is whether there is a rule of law by which the Scottish Courts are bound to give effect to the certificate of the Secretary of State, or whether these Courts have an inherent jurisdiction not to review the certificate but to override it. It is conceded that the Courts do not know the exigencies and conditions of the public service and cannot be in a position to say that the Minister, to whom the exigencies and conditions are known, was wrong in certifying that the public interest would be injured by the publication of documents called for by a party to a litigation. One of the considerations which may move a Minister to grant a certificate like the present is that publication would or might be injurious to that freedom and candour of communication in writing between the officers of a department, which are of great importance to public administration: and the responsible Minister or the head of the public department must be the judge whether the disclosure of documents would have an adverse effect by inducing among public servants a cautious timidity in expressing their views. The judgments of Lord President Dunedin, Lord M'Laren, Lord Kinnear and Lord Pearson in *The Admiralty v. Aberdeen Steam Trawling and Fishing Co.* are conclusive on this point, but these judgments do not deal explicitly with the question whether the Courts in Scotland have the power to override the ministerial certificate. If such a power does exist, it must be based on the ground that the fair administration of justice between subject and subject and between the subject and the Crown is a public interest of a high order, and that its protection is the care of the Courts.

In the hundred years before the case of *Duncan v. Cammell, Laird & Co.* was decided, there can be no doubt that the Scottish Courts were satisfied that they possessed the inherent power I am now discussing. In the present case the Lord Ordinary and Lord Russell were of opinion that the Scottish Courts retain that power. Lord Carmont was, I think, disposed to agree with that opinion but he felt constrained to bow to the decision in *Duncan v. Cammell, Laird & Co.* Lord Sorn also held that the rule of law laid down in *Duncan v. Cammell, Laird & Co.* was binding on the Court of Session in any situation contemplated in the judgment of the Lord Chancellor in *Duncan v. Cammell, Laird & Co.*, but not in other cases.

It was argued for the respondents that the case of *Earl v. Vass* decided in principle that the Courts in Scotland were bound to give effect to a ministerial certificate that production of a document would be contrary to the public interest. In that case the pursuer [Vass], who had been seeking employment under the Board of Customs, raised an action of damages against the Earl of Home on the ground that he had falsely and maliciously made insinuations to the Board against the pursuer's character and so caused the pursuer to lose the opportunity of employment under the Board. The Lord Ordinary granted diligence for the recovery of letters written by the defender to the Board and to the Treasury. The Inner House affirmed. In the House of Lords the Lord Chancellor, Lord Eldon, reversed the judgments. He did so after consulting the Lord Chief Justice, who stated that "he would not have permitted any such production as is here called for" for reasons of public interest. Lord Eldon heard no debate on the question which this House has now to decide and there was no appearance for the respondent. I can find in that case no authority for a general rule of law that the Scottish Courts have not the inherent power contended for. In Scotland the case has never been suffered to lay down any general rule. In *Henderson v. Robertson Vass* was referred to but it was treated as a decision of narrow scope and Lord Eldon's opinion that the Crown cannot waive the right to withhold documents was rejected.

So, in *Donald v. Hart*, Lord Justice-Clerk Hope, disallowing a call for a Crown precognition in an action for wrongous imprisonment directed against the Procurator-fiscal because malice did not appear in the issue, was free to say: "I am not prepared to say that there is no case for which the Court would not, when it was necessary for the ends of justice, and when malice is averred as to the precognition, order production of a precognition." From that time onwards for a hundred years there is a uniform tract of authority asserting the inherent power of the Court to disregard the Crown's objection to produce a document on grounds of public interest. It is necessary to refer to some only of the more important of these. In *Halcrow v. Shearer* the Court, consisting of Lord President Robertson, Lord Adam, Lord M'Laren and Lord Kinnear, granted diligence to recover a report on the character of a policeman made by the Procurator-fiscal to the Police Committee of the County Council although the Lord Advocate objected that its production would be prejudicial to the public service. It was ordered that the document should be transmitted to the Clerk of Court to lie *in retentis* and await the further order of the Court. This was done apparently in order to allow the Lord Advocate further time for consideration. The case, however, is not consistent with a rule of law that the Lord Advocate's objection, which had not been withdrawn, was conclusive. *Arthur v. Lindsay* was an action for defamation against a Procurator-fiscal in which the pursuer had relevantly averred that the defender had inserted in precognitions statements which had not been made by the pursuer and had shown the precognitions to persons who had no concern with the preparation or the trial of the case. The pursuer moved for diligence to recover the precognitions and the Lord Advocate objected on the ground that it would be prejudicial to the public service. The First Division refused the diligence. Lord President Robertson said: "They" (the precognitions) "are even of a high materiality, and it may be that the want of them will be prejudicial or even fatal to the pursuer's claim. But it is undoubted that private rights must sometimes yield to the requirements of general public policy, and it seems to me that the essential confidentiality of communications passing between a Procurator-fiscal and the head of the Criminal Department in Scotland is a paramount consideration." The Lord President referred to an admission said to have been made by the Crown in *Donald v. Hart* that the general rule might yield to some great and overwhelming necessity but he found that the case did not fall within that description. Lord Adam and Lord M' Laren agreed with the Lord President, and Lord M'Laren added this: "No doubt the Court has always maintained its power to make such an order in cases of emergency ... but this is qualified by the fact that no authority has been found where the jurisdiction was in fact exercised, and it is most unlikely that, while the criminal administration remains as at present, the Court ever will exercise this supplemental power." Lord Kinnear doubted whether the case was not one in which production of the precognition should have been ordered, but he was not prepared to override the Lord Advocate's objection. I think it is true that Lord President Robertson was disposed to hold that the recovery of a Crown precognition should never be ordered if it was opposed by the Lord Advocate, and it is also true that no case has been found where a Crown precognition was recovered when the Lord Advocate objected, but the Lord President did not deny the overriding power of the Court. In *Sheridan v. Peel* Lord President Dunedin, in granting an unopposed motion for diligence to produce, *inter alia*, a Crown precognition, said: "It is quite clear that where documents sought to be recovered are in the custody of the Lord Advocate or of the Crown officials, the only proper course is to intimate to the Lord Advocate. He may then consent to produce the documents, or refuse to produce them on grounds of public interest. If he refuses to produce them, the Court can be asked to ordain him to do so. There are probably very few instances in which the Court would order the Lord Advocate to produce documents which he thought it inexpedient to produce, but the power to do so has always been recognised as inherent in the Court." Lord M'Laren, Lord Kinnear and Lord Pearson concurred with the Lord President. In *Dowgray v. Gilmour* Lord President Dunedin referred to the steps which a party might have taken "for seeing if he could not make the Lord Advocate produce" a document in his possession, and he referred to his remarks in *Sheridan v. Peel.*

The next case is *Admiralty v. Aberdeen Steam Trawling and Fishing Co.* It arose out of a collision between a trawler and one of His Majesty's ships. The Admiralty objected to a motion for a diligence for the recovery of reports in its possession relating to the collision. The trawler owners argued that the Admiralty "could not plead that it would be contrary to the public interest to produce the documents called for." They did not argue that, if they were wrong on this point, the Admiralty's objection should nevertheless be overridden. The Court refused to order production, and the judgments of Lord President Dunedin and Lord Kinnear are important because they held that it is not for the Court to decide whether the production would be detrimental to the public interest and that that is a matter for the Board of Admiralty which alone had before it the necessary information. None of the learned Judges discussed the Court's inherent power to allow production in spite of the Lord Advocate's objection, but it cannot be inferred that they had changed the opinion they had all expressed so recently in *Sheridan v. Peel*. In *Henderson v. M'Gown* the First Division, reversing Lord Hunter, refused the defenders' crave for diligence to recover income tax returns. This was an action of damages in which the pursuer averred that his partners had falsely accused him of fraudulently understating the profits of the business managed by him. The defenders pleaded *veritas*. Many authorities, including *Earl v. Vass* and *Admiralty v. Aberdeen Steam Trawling and Fishing Co.*, were cited. The Court, before coming to a decision, consulted with the Judges of the Second Division. Lord President Strathclyde said: "Undeniably, certain expressions to be found in some of the opinions in the case of *Admiralty v. Aberdeen Steam Trawling and Fishing Co.* lend countenance to the Solicitor-General's contention, but, although the learned Judges in that case did not find it necessary to reassert the inherent power of this Court to order the recovery of a document, I cannot think that they intended to alter the law as it had previously been laid down and was generally understood, or to part with an inherent right in this Court which each of those Judges had on prior occasions expressly recognised. The true meaning and effect of the decision was that, when the objection is stated by the government department, this Court will not consider whether the objection is well founded or not; this Court will not consider the merits of that question, but will grant or refuse the diligence at their discretion." Having said that, he went on to consider whether the Court ought to exercise its inherent power in the case before it and decided that it should not. The same doctrine was reasserted by the Second Division in *Caffrey v. Lord Inverclyde* and by the First Division in *Rogers v. Orr.* It was, therefore, in 1939, a firmly established rule that in Scotland the Court has power to override the objection of a Minister or head of a government department that the production of a document would be contrary to public interest. The power has seldom been exercised and the Courts have emphatically said that it must be used with the greatest caution and only in very special circumstances. It was also a firmly established rule that the Court could not dispute the certificate and that the question whether production would be contrary to the public interest was for the Minister or the department concerned. The Courts have recognised that the refusal to exercise the jurisdiction to override the Crown's certificate may cause great injustice. It is, indeed, impossible to reconcile in all cases public interest and justice to individuals, yet the power is not a phantom power and in the last resort it is a real, though imperfect, safeguard of justice.

It was, however, contended by the Lord Advocate that *Duncan v. Cammell, Laird & Co.* has established that in England there is a rule of law by which the Courts are always bound to give effect to a valid certificate by the responsible Minister, or in some cases the head of a department, that production of a particular document either in itself or as forming an item of a class of documents would be contrary to the public interest, and that the same rule of law prevails in Scotland. He also contended that the judgment of Lord President Cooper in *M'Kie v. Western Scottish Motor Traction Co.* shows that after *Duncan's* case the Scottish Courts were at least weakening in their assertion of their inherent power.

I will assume the Lord Advocate's contention, so far as the law of England is concerned, is well founded, but so far as the law of Scotland is concerned it cannot, in my opinion, be sustained. *Duncan's* case was an appeal from the English Court of Appeal and in it no question of Scots law fell to be decided. It is not binding on the Scottish Courts nor, of course, on this House sitting as a Court of ultimate appeal in a Scottish case. What was said in *Duncan's* case about the law of Scotland was said *obiter*, and, though it is not binding on the House, must receive the most respectful consideration.

It appears from the speech of the Lord Chancellor that after the hearing the case of *Earl v. Vass* was brought to his notice. It was on that case and on *Admiralty v. Aberdeen Steam Trawling and Fishing Co.* that he formed the opinion that the Scots law was the same as that of England. The tract of authority which I have discussed was not brought to the notice of this House, and in particular the First Division judgment in *Henderson v. McGown*, delivered after consultation of the learned Judges of the Second Division, and its explanation of the *Aberdeen* case were never mentioned. In these circumstances I feel compelled to say that the Scots law did not receive sufficient consideration and that the observations upon it are of no weight. I cannot agree with Lord Carmont that the law of Scotland is to be altered by a side wind and that we are to have our long-established rules of law overturned by *dicta* pronounced without adequate citation Scottish authorities and without debate. I do not find in Lord Cooper's judgment in M'Kie any acceptance of *Duncan's* case as determinative of Scots law. His judgment leaves that case over for future consideration and he does not commit himself. The result seems to lead to the conclusion that there is a difference between the law of England and the law of Scotland on an important constitutional question. That is no new thing, for until 1947 it was the law of England that the Crown could not be required to give discovery of any documents in a suit against it — *Thomas v. The Queen* — and that was, in my opinion, never the rule in Scotland.

It now becomes necessary to consider whether the interlocutor appealed from should be reversed in whole or in part, and the diligence granted in whole or in part. The case is narrow, and I would not have been disposed to interfere if the Courts below had granted the diligence craved. But not one of the learned Judges was in favour of granting the diligence, on the footing that the inherent power of the Court was unaffected by *Duncan's* case, and I do not find that there are sufficient reasons for interfering.

I am for dismissing the appeal."

Notes

15–7   (1) *Duncan v. Cammell, Laird & Co.* [1942] A.C. 624 was an appeal to the House of Lords in England in an action by the widow of a man killed when a new submarine, the *Thetis*, sank during sea trials. She sued the shipbuilders but the Admiralty objected to the release of the plans of the submarine. It was decided that information could be withheld either on the grounds that its contents would damage the public interest or it belonged to a class of information which as a rule required to be withheld to safeguard the "proper functioning of the public service". The court also held, more significantly in light of *Central Land Board* that a certificate signed by a Minister making out such an objection was conclusive in all respects. As can be imagined, this led to the case being lost. There was considerable pressure in England to reconsider the inability to challenge a ministerial certificate: *Re Grosvenor Hotel, London Ltd (No. 2)* [1965] Ch. 1210. As can be seen from *Central Land Board*, it was argued that Scots law was the same as that found in *Duncan*, but without success.

(2) A matter which did not arise directly in *Central Land Board* was whether or not where an issue of public interest arose, the Crown was under a duty to make an objection or whether it simply had a discretion to do so. On the authority of *Admiralty v. Aberdeen Steam Trawling and Fishing Co. Ltd*, 1909 S.C. 335 it seems that the matter is one of discretion only.

The position in English law appears to be different. Indeed this was the source of much controversy in the light of the collapse of the *Matrix Churchill* prosecution. Here, a company and its directors were prosecuted for breaching government guidelines on exports to Iraq of materials which could be used for military purposes. In their defence it was contended that the Government was aware of the breach of guidelines and had done nothing. Four government Ministers signed ministerial certificates stating that documents needed by the defence belonged to a class which should not be released. One government Minister admitted that the Government was aware of the breach of guidelines and it was suspected that the Government was prepared to see innocent men go to prison. As a result of this the Scott inquiry was set up. The subsequent report was the Report of the Inquiry into Export of Defence Equipment and Dual use of Goods to Iraq and Related Prosecutions (1996). There was a conflict between the views of the Attorney-General based on Lord Scarman's view in *Air Canada v. Secretary of State for Trade (No. 2)* [1983] 2 A.C. 394 at 446 that:

> "The Crown, when it puts forward a public interest immunity objection, is not claiming a privilege but discharging a duty. The duty arises whether the document assists or damages the Crown's case or, if, as in a case to which the Crown is not a party, it neither helps nor injures the Crown. It is not for the Crown but for the court to determine whether the document should be produced."

However, Sir Richard Scott felt that the emphasis placed by the Attorney-General on the concept of duty was misplaced. Satisfaction as to the damage to the public interest must exist in the mind of the Minister before a claim is made. Support for the views expressed by Scott was subsequently found in *R. v. Chief Constable of the West Midlands Police, ex parte Wiley* [1994] 3 All E.R. 420. There it was observed by Lord Templeman (at 424) that:

> "It has been said that the holder of a confidential document for which public interest immunity may be claimed is under a duty to assert the claim, leaving the court to decide whether the claim is well founded. For my part I consider that when a document is known to be relevant and material, the holder of the document should voluntarily disclose it unless he is satisfied that the disclosure will cause substantial harm. If the holder is in doubt he may refer the matter to the court. If the holder decides that a document should not be disclosed then that decision can be upheld or set aside by the judge. A rubber stamp approach to public interest immunity by the holder of a document is neither necessary nor appropriate."

For a further discussion see G. Ganz, "*Matrix Churchill* and Public Interest Immunity" (1993) 56 M.L.R. 564; A. Tomkins, "Public Interest Immunity after Matrix Churchill" [1993] P.L. 650; M. Supperstone, "A new approach to public interest immunity?" [1997] P.L. 211; Rt Hon. Simon Brown L.J., "Public Interest Immunity" [1994] P.L. 579; and for the government response to the Scott Report and a discussion of the *Wiley* case see *Hansard*, H.C. Vol. 287, col. 949 (Dec. 18, 1996); H.C. Vol. 576, col. 1507 (Dec. 18, 1996). Note also the view expressed by the Lord Chancellor that as the difficulties found in *Matrix Churchill* do not appear to have arisen in Scotland, the new approach did not require to be applied here: *Hansard*, H.C. Vol. 287, col. 950.

(3) It is clear from *Central Land Board* that although the court can refuse a claim for public interest immunity, it cannot do so on the basis of an inspection of the information in question. This was something that was specifically confirmed in the earlier case of *Rogers v. Orr*, 1939 S.L.T. 403 at 405 where it was observed that:

15–8

> "In one somewhat peculiar case (*Carmichael* v. *Scottish Co-operative Wholesale Society*, 1934 S.L.T. 158) an objection was taken by the Lord Advocate on the ground of public interest, and the Lord Ordinary ruled that the document should be sealed up for his consideration and for his determination whether the public interest would be injured by its disclosure in Court. Now, I think that that is not a precedent to be followed, because it is really treating the question as one of confidentiality and not as a question of public interest. Even with the document before it the Court is not in a position to decide whether its production is contrary to the public interest, for that is a question which depends, or may depend, on circumstances not disclosed by the document itself."

Do you consider this reasoning convincing? Does the absence of the power to inspect strengthen or weaken the court's position in carrying out the balancing of public interest immunity with a competing public interest? Is the discretionary nature of a claim of public interest immunity in Scots law any more difficult to police as a result of this approach?

The position in England is again different. In *Air Canada v. Secretary of State for Trade (No. 2)* [1983] 2 A.C. 394 disclosure of government policy documents relative to the increase of landing charges at Heathrow airport was sought by Air Canada who were challenging the validity of increases in charges at the airport. They alleged that the Secretary of State for Trade had acted *ultra vires* and that the evidence of this would be found in the documents held by the Minister. Public interest immunity was claimed. Lord Fraser of Tullybelton (at 435) considered that:

> "The most that can usefully be said is that, in order to persuade the court even to inspect documents for which public interest immunity is claimed, the party seeking disclosure ought at least to satisfy the court that the documents are very likely to contain material which would give substantial support to his contention on an issue which arises in the case, and that without them he might 'be deprived of the means of ... proper presentation' of his case: see *Glasgow Corporation v. Central Land Board*, 1956 S.C. (H.L.) 1, 18, *per* Lord Radcliffe."

Lord Wilberforce (at 439) considered that:

> "The degree of likelihood (of providing support for the plaintiff's case) may be variously expressed: 'likely' was the word used by Lord Edmund-Davies in *Burmah Oil*: a 'reasonable probability' by Lord Keith of Kinkel. Both expressions must mean something beyond speculation, some concrete ground for belief which takes the case beyond a mere 'fishing' expedition."

Lord Edmund-Davies agreed with Lord Fraser's approach although he would have adopted a "likelihood" test for inspection. The minority, Lord Scarman and Lord Templeman, would not have limited inspection to cases where production would be likely to help the case with the party seeking production: they would have allowed it when it was necessary for the fair disposal of the case. However, on the facts of *Air Canada*, they too agreed that an inspection should not be carried out.

Is *Air Canada* of more assistance to the litigant than the approach in *Rogers*? In particular, how can one persuade a court to grant inspection of documents if some knowledge of the contents of the documents would appear to be required? It has been argued that *Air Canada* effectively strengthens the Government's position as it legitimises claims for public interest immunity by appearing to allow the litigant some scope for inspection. On this see T.R.S. Allan, "Abuse of Power and Public Interest Immunity; Justice, Rights and Truth" (1985) 101 L.Q.R. 200. Does the approach in *Air Canada* give sufficient weight to the "unknown circumstances" noted in *Rogers*?

15–9   (4) It is clear from *Central Land Board* that in Scots law only can the Crown assert public interest immunity. In England, following *D. v. National Society of the Prevention of Cruelty to Children* [1978] A.C. 171, the House of Lords granted immunity in respect of reports made to the Society on the ground that the disclosure would be contrary to the public interest without the intervention of the Crown. However, in *Higgins v. Burton*, 1968 S.L.T. (Notes) 52 the records of a child guidance clinic were not covered by public interest immunity on the basis that it was for the Crown to make out such a claim and failing intervention by the Crown, the court could not entertain it: see also *Kelly v. Kelly*, 1946 S.L.T. 208.

The most recent analysis of the position of claims by bodies other than the Crown came in *W.P. v. Tayside Regional Council*, 1989 S.C.L.R. 165. The regional council was sued by a foster mother for damages. She contracted hepatitis B from a child whose natural mother was a drug user and she sought to argue that the Social Work Department had knowledge of the natural mother's health. She needed documents to be disclosed to substantiate that argument. In granting the motion to recover Lord Sutherland made a number of observations about the nature of public interest privileges in Scots law (at 167):

> "Since 1968 there have been a number of decisions in England in which public interest privilege has been extended beyond national government to local authorities and to other bodies. In my

view decisions of courts in England in this field have to be treated with some caution. In the first place, it is only comparatively recently that the English courts have been prepared to hold themselves not bound by a ministerial certificate. Furthermore, in certain types of proceedings in England there appears always to have been a privilege attached to certain documents and I refer in particular to wardship proceedings. In the case of *D v. N.S.P.C.C.* public interest privilege was extended to the situation where a litigant sought to recover from the N.S.P.C.C. the name of an informer. It was held that because disclosure of the name of an informer would gravely damage the work of the N.S.P.C.C. public interest privilege should be extended to cover that situation . . . It is perhaps noteworthy that in the case of *Science Research Council* [[1980] A.C. 1028] Lord Scarman regretted the passing of the term 'Crown privilege' which in his view at least emphasised the very restricted area of public interest immunity. As he pointed out, the immunity exists to protect information the secrecy of which is essential to the proper working of the government of the state. Whatever may be the position in England I would respectfully adopt what was said by Lord Avonside in *Higgins*, and had it been necessary for the purposes of my decision in this case I would also have been inclined to hold that public interest privilege in the strict sense is confined to the privilege of the Crown and the Lord Advocate. I do not, however, consider that it is really necessary to divide confidentiality into separate compartments, namely public interest privilege and private confidentiality. The interest of an individual in his own privacy is in itself a public interest. Any breach of confidentiality which infringes the individual's right to his own privacy is accordingly to some extent at least a breach of public interest. What has to be balanced in every case is the breach of public interest against the interest that is seen in the need that impartial justice should be done in the courts of law and that a litigant who has a case to maintain should not be deprived of the means of its proper presentation by anything less than a weighty public reason. It is therefore apparent that each case will depend upon its own particular facts. If there is only going to be a minimal breach of the privacy of an individual the public interest in maintaining that privacy may be overcome without too much difficulty by the public interest in maintaining the impartiality of justice between litigants. If, on the other hand, a Minister of the Crown certifies that disclosure of a particular piece of information would be gravely prejudicial to the national security, the court would be very slow to hold that this public interest should be outweighed by the private requirement of a litigant. It has always been accepted in Scotland that there is no such thing as absolute privilege and in any case the court may overrule an attempt to prevent the disclosure of information even though there are strong grounds put forward in the public interest for preventing that information being disclosed. That being so, there appears to me to be no valid reason for a rigid compartmentalisation between public interest privilege on the one hand and confidentiality on the other. The ultimate position taken up by counsel for the respondents was that the law of Scotland recognises a claim for confidentiality if it is strong enough to outweigh any interest to favour recovery. I would agree with this proposition and it does not seem to me to be necessary for the resolution of the problem in any particular case to decide whether or not there should be a division between public interest privilege and ordinary confidentiality which depends upon public interest for its existence. Thus if a case arose in Scotland in which a party sought to recover from the R.S.S.P.C.C. the name of an informer, it would only be in very exceptional circumstances that such a motion would be granted. This would not be because public interest privilege is extended to the R.S.S.P.C.C. but because the nature of the work of that body is such that their claim to confidentiality would be awarded a high degree of protection."

Lord Sutherland's analysis would seem to suggest that where a claim by the Crown for public interest privilege is not made, then the issue will be treated purely as one of confidentiality. Does this suggest that any distinction between public interest privilege and confidentiality may well simply be a formalistic one? It would suggest that the burden of forcing disclosure may be significantly higher where the Crown invokes public interest immunity, although paradoxically, weightier issues of public interest could exist in a case where the Crown chooses not to make such a claim. It is possible to imagine a situation where a public interest claim conflicts with the views of the Crown. Could failure by the Crown to intervene be harmful to the public interest?

In *Davers v. Butler*, 1994 S.C.L.R. 717 the pursuer, a police officer, brought an action of damages for defamation against the defender alleging that a malicious report had been made about her to the Chief Constable. The Chief Constable lodged in process a sealed envelope containing documents relating to the complaint made. Warrant to cite the Lord Advocate was granted but he did not intervene. The Chief Constable contended that a motion to open the envelope should be opposed on the grounds of "public interest, confidentiality and privilege". It was contended by the pursuer that, standing no objection by the Lord Advocate, the Chief Constable had no locus to maintain any objection. The sheriff (Murphy) held, *inter alia*, since the privilege attaching to the documents was that of the defender, the Chief Constable was unsuccessful. However, he reserved his opinion as to whether or not the Chief Constable had locus to object to the disclosure of the documents although it was noted that the Scottish courts are very reluctant to grant to anyone other than the appropriate Minister of the Crown the right to assert a public interest. Standing further development to the approach in *W.P.*, the status of claims of public interest privilege by bodies other than the Crown in Scots law must, to some extent, remain uncertain.

The following cases are some of the more recent examples of the application of the claim.

Friel v. Chief Constable of Strathclyde

1981 S.C.1

15–10   "Police officers acting on information from an informer obtained a search warrant and searched the property of the petitioner in connection with the theft of a number of cases of whisky. The search was fruitless. The petitioner, who did not drink alcohol, was a respected local businessman. He believed that the information on which the police acted was given to them falsely and maliciously and without probable cause in order to damage his business standing and reputation. He wished to raise an action of damages against the informer, whose identity was unknown to him.

The petitioner therefore sought an order under sec. 1 of the Administration of Justice (Scotland) Act 1972 for the recovery of documents in the possession of the police force revealing the name of the informer. It was contended for the Chief Constable that there were insufficient averments to justify making an order. For the Lord Advocate it was contended that it would be injurious to the public interest to disclose the documents."

LORD MAXWELL: "This is a petition under section 1 of the Administration of Justice (Scotland) Act 1972 for an order, principally for recovery before the raising of an action of certain documents in the hands of the police. There is a reference in the petition to common law, as well as to the Act, but counsel for the petitioner accepted that he could not succeed unless he could bring himself within the Act. The petition is opposed by the Chief Constable of the force concerned and also by the Lord Advocate.

The petition narrates that on an evening in February 1979 officers of the Strathclyde Police called at the petitioner's home and stated that their visit was in connection with the theft of cases of whisky and that they had reason to believe that the cases were in the petitioner's house, garden or garage. They produced a search warrant and carried out a search, which proved fruitless. It is stated in the petition *inter alia* that the petitioner does not drink alcohol and has had no dealing in whisky and that the petitioner is a respected local businessman. The petitioner further avers: [His Lordship quoted from paragraphs 3 and 4 of the petition, and continued]. I was also referred to two letters addressed to the petitioner's solicitors by the Strathclyde Police. The first of these is a letter of 19th February 1979 and reads: — 'I refer to your letter of 14th instant regarding a search of your named client's premises by C.I.D. officers, I can only advise you that a consignment of whisky has been stolen and information came from a very reliable and respectable source that cases of what appeared to be whisky had been stored in your client's shed some time previously and were still therein. A search warrant was obtained and three cases of lemonade and some cans of lager were found in the shed. I am sure that your client as a law abiding citizen will recognise that the Police acted in good faith.' The second letter, which is dated 9th March reads as follows: — 'I refer to your letter of 21st February 1979 and previous correspondence with Chief Superintendent McCallum of Greenock. No insinuation was intended nor is such apparent to me in the letter of reply dated 19th February 1979 with regard to the property found in the shed at your client's premises. The search warrant in question was obtained on the basis of information which, although subsequently found to be incorrect as occurs on occasions, appeared to be given in good faith. It may well be that you can justify your allegation against the informant, but the negative search of your client's premises while clarifying the issue for the Police does not of itself suggest that the information was maliciously given. You will appreciate that information which comes into the hands of the Police must be treated with confidentiality, irrespective of its source and only weighty considerations of public interest would warrant the Chief Constable in exercising his discretion to divulge it. I regret that your client is aggrieved, but in the circumstances I am unable to accede to your request to divulge the information you seek.' Without going into the details of the 'calls' which are now sought to be enforced it was conceded that in substance what the petitioner seeks is an order to recover documents revealing the name of the person who gave the information on which the police proceeded. It is not suggested that the petitioner relies on any factual matter beyond that to which I have made reference.

Answers have been lodged on behalf of the police admitting that on information received they obtained a search warrant and made an unsuccessful search of the petitioner's premises for stolen whisky. They also state 'it is contrary to the public interest to divulge information given in confidence as to which matter the Police would follow the advice and instructions of the Lord Advocate.' The Lord Advocate also lodged Answers to which I shall refer in a moment.

Counsel for the Chief Constable, apart from certain criticisms of the details of the 'calls', confined his argument to the question of whether there is enough averred to justify an order under section 1 of the 1972 Act taking also into account the letters to which I was referred. Section 1 of the 1972 Act in subsection (1) is as follows: — 'Without prejudice to the existing powers of the Court of Session and of the sheriff court those Courts shall have power, subject to the provisions of subsection (4) of this section, to order the inspection, photographing, preservation, custody and detention of documents and other property (including, where appropriate, land) which appear to the court to be property as to which any question may relevantly arise in any existing civil proceedings before that Court or in civil proceedings which are likely to be brought, and to order the production and recovery of any such property, the taking of samples thereof and the carrying out of any experiment thereon or therewith.' The question at issue relates to the words 'likely to be brought.' At one point counsel suggested that a Court can only say that proceedings 'are likely to be brought' if he can aver facts which would make an action relevant if averred on a Record. I think that this is probably going too far. I disagree with counsel for the petitioner that such a contention would render the section, as regards proceedings not already in Court, meaningless. The section is to a large extent, at least, concerned with the preservation of evidence and other corporeal property as opposed to the ascertainment of facts, but I do not think that a discretion to give an order in respect that proceedings are likely to be brought can be read as requiring full averments of fact which would make a relevant action. There is a real question, however, as to whether it can be said that proceedings are likely to be brought where, as here, it is clear that they cannot be brought unless the order is granted. That is to say, where the ascertainment of matters essential to the bringing of proceedings, such as the identity of the prospective defender, is itself the object of the application. I do not consider it necessary or desirable to determine that question in this case. I was referred to an English case *Dunning v. United Liverpool Hospitals' Board of Governors* [1973] 1 W.L.R. 586, dealing with a similarly, but not identically, worded English Act. This is a case which incidentally I have been informed has been overruled on other grounds. My impression from that case is that the judges would have given an affirmative answer to the question in certain circumstances. James L.J. however, said: — 'In order to take advantage of the section the applicant for relief must disclose the nature of the claim he intends to make and show, not only the intention of making it, but also that there is a reasonable basis for making it. Ill-founded, irresponsible and speculative allegations or allegations based merely on hope would not provide a reasonable basis for an intended claim in subsequent proceedings.' I think that this would equally apply to an application for an order under section 1 of the 1972 Act on the ground that the proceedings 'are likely to be brought.' Assuming that the petitioner can use the section to 'are likely to be brought.' Assuming that the petitioner can use the section to discover his defender, as matter of degree I am of the opinion that he has not shown that proceedings are likely to be brought.

It is well settled that an informer is not liable for a false accusation, unless he is acting both from malice and without probable cause and that the presumption is that he has acted in good faith. (*Glegg on Reparation* (4th Ed.) 195). I was referred to a number of authorities on this matter, but need not cite them as the principle is not disputed. Senior counsel for the petitioner frankly admitted that he did not know and would not know unless I granted the order sought whether he could eventually make a case of malice and want of probable cause. He submitted, however, that having regard to what is said in the petition, particularly about the respectable character of the petitioner and the fact that he does not drink, and having regard to the police admission in the letters that they proceeded on information from a respectable source, a probability of malice and want of probable cause could be sufficiently inferred for present purposes. I do not agree. The fact that the police proceeded on information to make an investigation which turned out to be without justification does not, in my opinion, make it probable that the information was given maliciously. It may, for example, have been given under wholly innocent error or it may have been misunderstood or misinterpreted by the police or it may have been correct information from which the police drew a *prima facie* inference which was not in fact warranted. For these reasons, apart altogether from the Lord Advocate's objection, I would have refused this motion.

In his Answers to the petition the Lord Advocate states *inter alia* 'The Lord Advocate objects to the disclosure of said documents on the grounds that to do so would be injurious to the public interest. In so doing the Lord Advocate exercises the discretion of withholding documents afforded by the common law relating to Crown privilege expressly preserved by the provisos to section 47 of the Crown Proceedings Act 1947 and section 1(4) of the Administration of Justice (Scotland) Act 1972, which are referred to for their terms. Explained that said documents fall into a class of documents which must be afforded protection from disclosure on the grounds of public policy in order to enable the detection and prosecution of crime in Scotland to function efficiently and to allow citizens to offer assistance to the agencies of law enforcement secure in the knowledge that any such information will not be subject to public disclosure at a later date. For these reasons the Lord Advocate objects to the recovery of the documents.'

Counsel for the petitioner asked me to override the Lord Advocate's objection. On this matter I was given a most interesting and elaborate citation of authority going back to the early 19th century. I trust counsel will excuse me for not reviewing the authorities, but I consider it unnecessary to do so, since there is really no dispute on the law as it now stands except perhaps in emphasis.

It is accepted that the appropriate Minister can take objection to the production of documents in the hands of a public body on grounds of public interest. It is accepted in particular that the Lord Advocate can take objection to the production of documents in the hands of the police (*Rogers v. Orr* 1939 S.C. 492). It is accepted that the Court retains a discretionary power to order production of documents notwithstanding such an objection (*Glasgow Corporation v. Central Land Board* 1956 S.C. (H.L.) 1). It is accepted that this power has, in practice, rarely, if ever, been exercised. It is accepted that the Lord Advocate's objection can, as here, competently be based on the public interest in non-disclosure of a class of documents as opposed to a particular document.

Counsel for the petitioner contended that, where the objection is taken in respect of a class of documents, the Court, in considering whether to override the objection, can take into account not only the interests of the particular petitioner, but the interests of the public as a whole in so far as other members of the public might find themselves in the same position as the petitioner. I agree with that submission.

It was suggested for the petitioner that the Court's function was to balance competing interests. That is, I think, correct only in a limited sense. The Court does not, in my opinion, balance competing interests in the same way, for example, as it seeks to balance convenience in relation to interdict, and the reason for that is that the Lord Advocate has access to information which may not be available to the Court and the Court is bound to accept his assertion that there is an aspect of public interest to be protected. The matter was put thus by Lord Radcliffe in *Glasgow Corporation v. Central Land Board* 'I do not understand that the existence of the power involves that, in Scotland any more than in England, it is open to the Court to dispute with the Minister whether his view that production would be contrary to the public interest is well founded, or to arrive at a view contradictory of his, that production would not, in fact, be at all injurious to that interest. If weight is given to the argument that the Minister in forming his view may have before him a range of considerations that is not open to the Court and that he is not under any obligation to set out those considerations in public, I think that it must follow that the Minister's view must be accepted by the Court as incapable of being displaced by its own opinion. I understand the decision in *Admiralty v. Aberdeen Steam Trawling & Fishing Co.* 1909 S.C. 335 as a decision precisely to that effect and I do not think that there is anything in the later case of *Henderson v. McGown* 1916 S.C. 821 which conflicts with the earlier case as so understood. The power reserved to the Court is therefore a power to order production, even though the public interest is to some extent affected prejudicially. This amounts to a recognition that more than one aspect of public interest may have to be surveyed in reviewing the question whether a document which would be available to a party in a civil suit between parties is not to be available to the party engaged in a suit with the Crown. The interests of Government, for which the minister should speak with full authority do not exhaust the public interest. Another aspect of that interest is seen in the need that impartial justice should be done in the Courts of law, not least between citizen and Crown and that a litigant who has a case to maintain should not be deprived of the means of its proper presentation by anything less than a weighty public reason. It does not seem to me unreasonable to expect that the Court would be better qualified than the Minister to measure the importance of such principles in application to the particular case that is before it.'

The argument was put thus for the petitioner. If the Lord Advocate's objection is sustained as regards this class of document it means that those members of the public who find themselves, or may find themselves, in the petitioner's position are in effect being deprived of access to the Courts and there is an overriding public interest that all persons should have access to the Court. I think that is a somewhat emotive and inaccurate way of stating the matter. The petitioner has access to the Courts. What he is being deprived of is the exercise of the Court's power to order others to produce confidential documents. It may follow from this that he is unable to raise an action which might otherwise be available to him, but that happens frequently and from many causes and is not equivalent to a deprivation of access to the Courts.

In my opinion it is plain that the risk to law enforcement on which the Lord Advocate relies could be a very serious risk indeed. It is not for me to measure the risk because I do not have the information to do it, but I could not override the Lord Advocate's objection unless I was satisfied that there is another public interest at stake so substantial that the risk to law enforcement must take second place. I am completely satisfied that the risk that perhaps in this case and perhaps occasionally in future cases a person, who has been the subject of malicious slander by an informer, will find it impossible to pursue a civil remedy against the informer does not represent a matter of public interest which outweighs the risk on which the Lord Advocate founds. I shall accordingly, for this reason also, refuse the motion.

I should add two points. First, counsel for the petitioner relied heavily on certain *dicta* in *Henderson v. Robertson* (1853) 15 D. 292. I do not think that the case assists him since it was the informer in that case, not the Lord Advocate, who sought to invoke the public interest. Second, one of the calls in the petition, in addition to calling for certain documents, proceeds as follows: — 'and in any event an order ordaining the said Chief Constable to disclose the names and addresses of any informants referred to in the answers and the information relating to the petitioner upon which the said warrant was applied for and granted.' Even if I had been disposed to grant the other calls or any part of them I would not have granted this call. In my opinion it is clear that there is nothing in section 1 of the 1972 Act which authorises the Court to order anybody to disclose anything. The section is concerned with the preservation or production of things, including documents, and in my opinion it has nothing to do with ordering persons to disclose information which is available to them. I do not agree with the submission of counsel for the petitioner that this is a mere technical distinction. It is accordingly unnecessary for me to decide in what circumstances, even without objection by the Lord Advocate, it might or might not be competent to order disclosure of names nor is it necessary for me to refer to certain authorities cited to me on that matter."

A.B. v. Glasgow and West of Scotland Blood Transfusion Service

1993 S.L.T. 36

15–11   LORD MORISON: "This is an application by a person who avers that he became infected with human immune deficiency virus as a result of blood transfusions administered to him in 1986 by the respondents, the Glasgow and West of Scotland Blood Transfusion Service. The petitioner proceeds upon provisions contained in s 1 of the Administration of Justice (Scotland) Act 1972, and in effect he seeks an order of the court for disclosure to him and his legal advisers of the name and address of the person who donated the blood which was transfused. The petitioner's only purpose in seeking such an order is to enable him to raise an action of damages against the donor, on the ground that he negligently failed to disclose to the respondents his high risk of HIV infection, negligently failed to complete accurately a health questionnaire which donors are asked to complete, and negligently donated blood for transfusion knowing that there was a high risk of it being infected. If the donor were voluntarily to disclose his identity to the petitioner, there would be no need to obtain an order from the court, but he has not done so yet, and the petitioner is accordingly unable to raise an action against him, although he is suing the respondents on the ground that their screening procedures were inadequate.

The case came before the court on 13 December 1989 when there was appearance both for the respondents and for the Lord Advocate, on whom the petition had also been served. It was continued for a week to enable the Lord Advocate to consider his position in relation to the public interest which it was submitted might be affected by the disclosure sought. At the continued hearing on 20 December, the application was opposed both by the respondents and by the Secretary of State for Scotland as representing the public interest by virtue of his responsibility under the National Health Service (Scotland) Act 1978 to maintain and promote that service.

The Secretary of State opposes the disclosure sought, on the ground that it would be injurious to the public interest. That injury is particularised in answers to the petition lodged by him as follows: 'These documents [ie those which disclose the donor's identity]... fall within the class of documents which ought to be afforded protection on the ground of public policy in order to ensure that there is and continues to be a sufficient supply of donor blood to the health service nationally. Such supply is required for necessary and often emergency medical procedures in the treatment of illness (including injury). The Secretary of State has duly considered the matter and has concluded that any infringement of donor anonymity would put such supply at risk. Prospective donors, he has concluded, would be discouraged from providing donations by reasons of apprehension that they might be subjected to legal claims (whether justified or not) on the basis of some adverse effect resulting from the use of the blood for transfusion purposes.'

It is to be noted that this conclusion relates to any infringement whatever of donor anonymity. The disclosure which the petitioner seeks is confined to himself and his legal advisers. It is not to be assumed, and it was not contended, that if the petitioner raised an action against the donor, the donor's name would necessarily be disclosed to the public. The attitude of prospective donors upon which the Secretary of State is relying is exclusively the apprehension that they might be used, justifiably or not, in relation to their conduct, not that their names might be publicised.

Such apprehension is one which anybody whose conduct affects other persons might experience. In the case of blood donors there seems to me to be every reason to suppose that they are actuated by the very highest motives of altruism and commitment to the public welfare. It is not immediately apparent to me why such persons would be deterred from pursuing these motives by an apprehension that they might be unjustifiably sued. If on the other hand there are any persons who give blood without due regard to their responsibilities, the public interest would plainly be served if they were discouraged from doing so. But it was conceded on behalf of the petitioner that I was not entitled to investigate the validity of the conclusion expressed by the Secretary of State unless it appeared that the conclusion was patently unreasonable or had been expressed on an erroneous basis, and this obviously cannot be said in the present case. In view of the observations contained in the speeches of Lord Normand and Lord Keith in the case of *Glasgow Corporation v. Central Land Board*, I consider that this concession was rightly made. Whilst in Scotland the court has the inherent power to override the objection of a responsible minister based on the public interest, that power is not to be exercised upon the basis of an assessment of the merits of the objection. Thus in the present case there may well be matters upon which the Secretary of State has been informed of which I am not aware and which are not contained in the information before me. For present purposes I must accept that 'any infringement of donor anonymity' would put at risk the sufficiency of the national supply of donor blood.

On this assumption, the scope for any reasoned argument as to whether or not the Secretary of State's objection should be overridden is limited. On behalf of the petitioner it was submitted that his private right to sue the donor was of such 'magnitude' (to use the word employed by Lord Moncrieff in *Rogers v. Orr*, 1939 SLT at p 406) as to prevail over the public interest advanced by the Secretary of State. But the only right which the petitioner seeks to assert in the proceedings which he proposes is the right to claim damages, and although his claim is a very large one, it seems to me to be impossible to hold that such a pecuniary interest should prevail over a material risk to the sufficiency of the national supply of blood for purposes of transfusion. It was submitted also that there were other persons apart from the petitioner whose right to claim damages would similarly be affected if disclosure were not made. I can conceive of cases in which such a consideration might be material, but I was not informed that there is a large number of persons likely to be prejudiced by non-disclosure to them of the names of donors, and I do not think that this matter substantially affects the issue. It was further submitted that it was a matter of public interest that the administration of justice should not be selective. This is undoubtedly true, but such an argument could be advanced in any case where disclosure of relevant information is subject to ministerial objection and counsel were unable to inform me of any case in which such an objection had been overridden by the court. However I entirely agree that it is offensive to any notion of justice that persons should be deprived of the ability to claim damages from those by whose negligence they have been injured. If public policy requires this, it seems to me that it would be reasonable for public policy to provide also some alternative means of compensation.

Counsel for the petitioner also pointed out that the extent of the alleged risk to the public blood supply was not indicated by the objection. Contrary to submissions made on behalf of the Secretary of State, I consider that this is indeed a relevant consideration in determination of the issue which is before me. It seems to me that it would be much easier for the court to override an objection based on a slight risk to the public interest than one based on a substantial probability of damage to that interest. But it is obvious that the consequences of a national deficiency in the supply of blood for transfusion would be appalling. If there is any material risk of such an occurrence resulting from disclosure of the donor's name in the present case — and this is what I have to assume — it seems to me to be clear that the objection to that disclosure must prevail over the interests advanced on the petitioner's behalf.

For these reasons I shall refuse to pronounce the order which the petitioner seeks. It was agreed that if this were my determination, I should refuse the motion, dismiss the petition and order the return to the respondents of the documents recovered from them. I shall issue an interlocutor in these terms.

I should add that the respondents advanced arguments similar to those of the Secretary of State, to support their submission that the donor's identity should not be revealed to the petitioner. The respondents are providing a public service and they have an obvious duty (subject only to an order of the court) to promote that valuable service and to maintain the confidentiality of persons upon whom they rely to provide it. Nevertheless I consider that the court's approach to their objection would be different from that which applies to a ministerial objection based on the public interest. In particular, it would in my opinion be legitimate for the court to consider and assess the merits of the respondents' objection in light of the nature of the work which they perform, so as to determine whether or not the petitioner's interest should prevail over that objection. This would involve consideration of the quality of the evidence upon which the respondents rely, and it might also involve a determination whether their own procedures are adequate to support the immunity which they say ought to be accorded to donors. However on the view which I have formed in respect of the Secretary of State's objection, it is unnecessary for me to reach any conclusion as to the respondents' contentions, and I refrain from doing so."

Notes

15–12   The approach in *Friel* was applied in *Davers v. Butler* and *P. Cannon (Garages) Ltd v. Lord Advocate above*. In *Cannon* the pursuer sought access to a blood sample of an alleged drunk driver for use in a civil action for damage to a motor vehicle. The Lord Advocate intervened to claim public interest immunity based on the need to preserve the integrity of the supply of such evidence. Field and Raitt suggest that the nature of the remedy sought and the moral worth of the claim in question may well be relevant to the way in which the court assesses the competing interest and the weight it gives to the interest asserted against public interest immunity. Is this apparent in either *Friel* or *A.B.*? Is the suggestion in *A.B.* that the court could override a claim only if unreasonable or if expressed on an erroneous basis different from the approach in *Friel* and *Central Land Board*? Is there any scope for the court to investigate the way in which the Minister has determined what the public interest requires, even if it is careful not to challenge his conclusion on the substance of public interest?

CLASS CLAIMS AND CONTENTS CLAIMS

Conway v. Rimmer

[1968] A.C. 910

15–13   "The plaintiff, a former probationary police constable, began an action for malicious prosecution against his former superintendent. In the course of discovery, the defendant disclosed a list of documents in his possession or power, admittedly relevant to the plaintiff's action, which included four reports made by him about the plaintiff during his period of probation, and a report by him to his chief constable for transmission to the Director of Public Prosecutions in connection with the prosecution of the plaintiff on the criminal charge, on which he was acquitted, and on which his civil action was based.
    The Secretary of State for Home Affairs objected in proper form to production of all five documents on the ground that each fell within a class of documents the production of which would be injurious to the public interest."

LORD REID: "My Lords, these documents may be of crucial importance in this action. The appellant has to prove both malice and want of probable cause. If the probationary reports were favourable that may tell strongly in favour of the appellant on the question of malice, if they were unfavourable and were not prepared by the respondent they will tell strongly against the appellant on this issue. The respondent's report to the chief constable may well be decisive in the question of want of probable cause. If the respondent included in the report all relevant facts known to him and if no further relevant facts became known to him between the making of the report and the making of the charge, then advice by the Director of Public Prosecutions that prosecution would be justified would make it practically impossible to establish want of probable cause. But if relevant facts known to the respondent were not included the position would be very different.
    His Lordship set out the affidavit of the Home Secretary and continued: The question whether such a statement by a Minister of the Crown should be accepted as conclusively preventing any

court from ordering production of any of the documents to which it applies is one of very great importance in the administration of justice. If the commonly accepted interpretation of the decision of this House in *Duncan v. Cammell, Laird & Co. Ltd* [[1942] A.C. 624] is to remain authoritative the question admits of only one answer — the Minister's statement is final and conclusive. Normally I would be very slow to question the authority of a unanimous decision of this House only 25 years old which was carefully considered and obviously intended to lay down a general rule. But this decision has several abnormal features.

Lord Simon thought that on this matter the law in Scotland was the same as the law in England and he clearly intended to lay down a rule applicable to the whole of the United Kingdom. But in *Glasgow Corporation v. Central Land Board* [[1956] S.C. (H.L.) 1] this House held that that was not so, with the result that today on this question the law is different in the two countries. There are many chapters of the law where for historical and other reasons it is quite proper that the law should be different in the two countries. But here we are dealing purely with public policy — with the proper relation between the powers of the executive and the powers of the courts — and I can see no rational justification for the law on this matter being different in the two countries.

Secondly, events have proved that the rule supposed to have been laid down in *Duncan's* case is far from satisfactory. In the large number of cases in England and elsewhere which have been cited in argument much dissatisfaction has been expressed and I have not observed even one expression of whole-hearted approval. Moreover a statement made by the Lord Chancellor in 1956 on behalf of the Government, to which I shall return later, makes it clear that that Government did not regard it as consonant with public policy to maintain the rule to the full extent which existing authorities had held to be justifiable.

I have no doubt that the case of *Duncan v. Cammell, Laird & Co. Ltd* was rightly decided. The plaintiff sought discovery of documents relating to the submarine *Thetis* including a contract for the hull and machinery and plans and specifications. The First Lord of the Admiralty had stated that 'it would be injurious to the public interest that any of the said documents should be disclosed to any person.' Any of these documents might well have given valuable information, or at least clues, to the skilled eye of an agent of a foreign power. But Lord Simon L.C. took the opportunity to deal with the whole question of the right of the Crown to prevent production of documents in a litigation. Yet a study of his speech leaves me with the strong impression that throughout he had primarily in mind cases where discovery or disclosure would involve a danger of real prejudice to the national interest. I find it difficult to believe that his speech would have been the same if the case had related, as the present case does, to discovery of routine reports on a probationer constable.

Early in his speech Lord Simon quoted with approval the view of Rigby L.J., in *Attorney-General v. Newcastle-upon-Tyne Corporation* [[1897] 2 Q.B. 384] that documents are not to be withheld

'unless there be some plain overruling principle of public interest concerned which cannot be disregarded.'

And, summing up towards the end, he said:

'... the rule that the interest of the state must not be put in jeopardy by producing documents which would injure it is a principle to be observed in administering justice, quite unconnected with the interests or claims of the particular parties in litigation.'

Surely it would be grotesque to speak of the interest of the state being put in jeopardy by disclosure of a routine report on a probationer.

Lord Simon did not say very much about objections

'based upon the view that the public interest requires a particular class of communications with, or within, a public department to be protected from production on the ground that the candour and completeness of such communications might be prejudiced if they were ever liable to be disclosed in subsequent litigation rather than on the contents of the particular document itself.'

But at the end he said that a Minister

'ought not to take the responsibility of withholding production except in cases where the public interest would otherwise be damnified, for example, where disclosure would be injurious to national defence, or to good diplomatic relations, or where the practice of keeping a class of documents secret is necessary for the proper functioning of the public service.'

I find it difficult to believe that he would have put these three examples on the same level if he had intended the third to cover such minor matters as a routine report by a relatively junior officer. And my impression is strengthened by the passage at very end of the speech:

'...the public interest is also the interest of every subject of the realm, and while, in these exceptional cases, the private citizen may seem to be denied what is to his immediate advantage, he, like the rest of us, would suffer if the needs of protecting the interests of the country as a whole were not ranked as a prior obligation.'

Would he have spoken of 'these exceptional cases' or of 'the needs of protecting the interests of the country as a whole' if he had intended to include all manner of routine communications? And did he really mean that the protection of such communications is a 'prior obligation' in a case where a man's reputation or fortune is at stake and withholding the document makes it impossible for justice to be done?

It is universally recognised that here there are two kinds of public interest which may clash. There is the public interest that harm shall not be done to the nation or the public service by disclosure of certain documents, and there is the public interest that the administration of justice shall not be frustrated by the withholding of documents which must be produced if justice is to be done. There are many cases where the nature of the injury which would or might be done to the nation or the public service is of so grave a character that no other interest, public or private, can be allowed to prevail over it. With regard to such cases it would be proper to say, as Lord Simon did, that to order production of the document in question would put the interest of the state in jeopardy. But there are many other cases where the possible injury to the public service is much less and there one would think that it would be proper to balance the public interests involved. I do not believe that Lord Simon really meant that the smallest probability of injury to the public service must always outweigh the gravest frustration of the administration of justice.

It is to be observed that, in a passage which I have already quoted, Lord Simon referred to the practice of keeping a class of documents secret being 'necessary [my italics] for the proper functioning of the public interest.' But the certificate of the Home Secretary in the present case does not go nearly so far as that. It merely says that the production of a document of the classes to which it refers would be 'injurious to the public interest': it does not say what degree of injury is to be apprehended. it may be advantageous to the functioning of the public service that reports of this kind should be kept secret — that is the view of the Home Secretary — but I would be very surprised if anyone said that that is necessary.

There are now many large public bodies, such as British Railways and the National Coal Board, the proper and efficient functioning of which is very necessary for many reasons including the safety of the public. The Attorney-General made it clear that Crown privilege is not and cannot be invoked to prevent disclosure of similar documents made by them or their servants even if it were said that this is required for the proper and efficient functioning of that public service. I find it difficult to see why it should be *necessary* to withhold whole classes of routine 'communications with or within a public department' but quite unnecessary to withhold similar communications with or within a public corporation. There the safety of the public may well depend on the candour and completeness of reports made by subordinates whose duty it is to draw attention to defects. But, so far as I know, no one has ever suggested that public safety has been endangered by the candour or completeness of such reports having been inhibited by the fact that they may have to be produced if the interests of the due administration of justice should ever require production at any time.

I must turn now to a statement made by the Lord Chancellor, Lord Kilmuir, in this House on June 6, 1956. When counsel proposed to read this statement your Lordships had doubts, which

I shared, as to its admissibility. But we did permit it to be read, and, as the argument proceeded, its importance emerged. With a minor amendment made on March 8, 1962, it appears still to operate as a direction to, or at least a guide for, Ministers who swear affidavits. So we may assume that in the present case the Home Secretary acted in accordance with the views expressed in Lord Kilmuir's statement.

The statement sets out the grounds on which Crown privilege is to be claimed. Having set out the first ground that disclosure of the contents of the particular document would injure the public interest, it proceeds:

> 'The second ground is that the document falls within a class which the public interest requires to be withheld from production, and Lord Simon particularised this head of public interest as 'the proper functioning the of public service.' ''

There is no reference to Lord Simon's exhortation, which I have already quoted, that a Minister ought not to take the responsibility of withholding production of a class of documents except where the practice of keeping a class of documents secret is necessary for the proper functioning of the public service. Then the statement proceeds:

> 'The reason why the law sanctions the claiming of Crown privilege on the "class" ground is the need to secure freedom and candour of communication with and within the public service, so that Government decisions can be taken on the best advice and with the fullest information. In order to secure this it is necessary that the class of documents to which privilege applies should be clearly settled, so that the person giving advice or information should know that he is doing so in confidence. Any system whereby a document falling within the class might, as a result of a later decision, be required to be produced in evidence, would destroy that confidence and undermine the whole basis of class privilege, because there would be no certainty at the time of writing that the document would not be disclosed.'

But later in the statement the position taken is very different. A number of cases are set out in which Crown privilege should not be claimed. The most important for present purposes is:

> 'We also propose that if medical documents, or indeed other documents, are relevant to the defence in criminal proceedings, Crown privilege should not be claimed.'

The only exception specifically mentioned is statements by informers. That is a very wide ranging exception, for the Attorney-General stated that it applied at least to all manner of routine communications and even to prosecutions for minor offences. Thus it can no longer be said that the writer of such communications has any 'certainty at the time of writing that the document would not be disclosed.' So we have the curious result that 'freedom and candour of communication' is supposed not to be inhibited by knowledge of the writer that his report may be disclosed in a criminal case, but would still be supposed to be inhibited if he thought that his report might be disclosed in a civil case.

The Attorney-General did not deny that, even where the full contents of a report have already been made public in a criminal case, Crown privilege is still claimed for that report in a later civil case. And he was quite candid about the reason for that. Crown privilege is claimed in the civil case not to protect the document — its contents are already public property — but to protect the writer from civil liability should he be sued for libel or other tort. No doubt the Government have weighed the danger that knowledge of such protection might encourage malicious writers against the advantage that honest reporters shall not be subjected to vexatious actions, and have come to the conclusion that it is an advantage to the public service to afford this protection. But that seems very far removed from the original purpose of Crown privilege.

And the statement, as it has been explained to us, makes clear another point. The Minister who withholds production of a 'class' document has no duty to consider the degree of public interest involved in a particular case by frustrating in that way the due administration of justice. If it is in the public interest in his view to withhold documents of that class, then it matters not whether the result of withholding a document is merely to deprive a litigant of some evidence on a minor issue in a case of little importance or, on the other hand, is to make it impossible to do justice at all in a case of the greatest importance. I cannot think that it is satisfactory that there should be no means at all of weighing, in any civil case, the public interest involved in withholding the document against the public interest that it should be produced.

So it appears to me that the present position is so unsatisfactory that this House must re-examine the whole question in light of all the authorities.

Two questions will arise: first, whether the court is to have any right to question the finality of a Minister's certificate and, secondly, if it has such a right, how and in what circumstances that right is to be exercised and made effective.

A Minister's certificate may be given on one or other of two grounds: either because it would be against the public interest to disclose the contents of the particular document or documents in question or because the document belongs to a class of documents which ought to be withheld, whether or not there is anything in the particular document in question disclosure of which would be against the public interest. It does not appear that any serious difficulties have arisen or are likely to arise with regard to the first class. However wide the power of the court may be held to be, cases would be very rare in which it could be proper to question the view of the responsible Minister that it would be contrary to the public interest to make public the contents of a particular document. A question might arise whether it would be possible to separate those parts of a document of which disclosure would be innocuous from those parts which ought not to be made public, but I need not pursue that question now. In the present case your Lordships are directly concerned with the second class of documents...

It cannot be said that there would be any constitutional impropriety in enabling the court to overrule a Minister's objection. That is already the law in Scotland. In Commonwealth jurisdictions from which there is an appeal to the Privy Council the courts generally follow *Robinson's* case, [[1931] A.C. 704] and where they do not they follow *Duncan's* case with reluctance. And a limited citation of authority from the United States seems to indicate the same trend. I observe that in *United States v. Reynolds* [(1953) 345 US 1] Vinson C.J. in delivering the opinion of the Supreme Court said:

> 'Regardless of how it is articulated, some like formula of compromise must be applied here. Judicial control over the evidence in a case cannot be abdicated to the caprice of executive officers. Yet we will not go so far as to say that the court may automatically require a complete disclosure to the judge before the claim of privilege will be accepted in any case. It may be possible to satisfy the court, from all the circumstances of the case, that there is a reasonable danger that compulsion of the evidence will expose military matters which, in the interest of national security, should not be divulged. When this is the case, the occasion for the privilege is appropriate, and the court should not jeopardise the security which the privilege is meant to protect by insisting upon an examination of the evidence, even by the judge alone, in chambers.'

Lord Simon did not say that courts in England have no power to overrule the executive. He said (*Duncan's* case):

> ...'the decision ruling out such documents is the decision of the judge ... It is the judge who is in control of the trial, not the executive, but the proper ruling for the judge to give is as above expressed.'

that is, to accept the Minister's view in every case. In my judgment, in considering what it is 'proper' for a court to do we must have regard to the need, shown by 25 years' experience since *Duncan's* case, that the courts should balance the public interest in the proper administration of justice against the public interest in withholding any evidence which a Minister considers ought to be withheld.

I would therefore propose that the House ought now to decide that courts have and are entitled to exercise a power and duty to hold a balance between the public interest, as expressed by a Minister, to withhold certain documents or other evidence, and the public interest in ensuring the proper administration of justice. That does not mean that a court would reject a Minister's view: full weight must be given to it in every case, and if the Minister's reasons are of a character which judicial experience is not competent to weigh, then the Minister's view must prevail. But experience has shown that reasons given for withholding whole classes of documents are often not of that character. For example a court is perfectly well able to assess the likelihood that, if the writer of a certain class of document knew that there was a chance that his report might be produced in legal proceedings, he would make a less full and candid report than he would otherwise have done.

I do not doubt that there are certain classes of documents which ought not to be disclosed whatever their content may be. Virtually everyone agrees that Cabinet minutes and the like ought not to be disclosed until such time as they are only of historical interest. But I do not think that many people would give as the reason that premature disclosure would prevent candour in the Cabinet. To my mind the most important reason is that such disclosure would create or fan ill-informed or captious public or political criticism. The business of government is difficult enough as it is, and no government could contemplate with equanimity the inner workings of the government machine being exposed to the gaze of those ready to criticise without adequate knowledge of the background and perhaps with some axe to grind. And that must, in my view, also apply to all documents concerned with policy making within departments including, it may be, minutes and the like by quite junior officials and correspondence with outside bodies. Further it may be that deliberations about a particular case require protection as much as deliberations about policy. I do not think that it is possible to limit such documents by any definition. But there seems to me to be a wide difference between such documents and routine reports. There may be special reasons for withholding some kinds of routine documents, but I think that the proper test to be applied is to ask, in the language of Lord Simon in *Duncan's* case, whether the applied is to ask, in the language of Lord Simon in *Duncan's* case, whether the withholding of a document because it belongs to a particular class is really 'necessary for the proper functioning of the public service.'

It appears to me that, if the Minister's reasons are such that a judge can properly weigh them, he must, on the other hand, consider what is the probable importance in the case before him of the documents or other evidence sought to be withheld. If he decides that on balance the documents probably ought to be produced, I think that it would generally be best that he should see them before ordering production and if he thinks that the Minister's reasons are not clearly expressed he will have to see the documents before ordering production. I can see nothing wrong in the judge seeing documents without their being shown to the parties. Lord Simon said (in *Duncan's* case) that 'where the Crown is a party… this would amount to communicating with one party to the exclusion of the other.' I do not agree. The parties see the Minister's reasons. Where a document has not been prepared for the information of the judge, it seems to me a misuse of language to say that the judge 'communicates with' the holder of the document by reading it. If on reading the document he still thinks that it ought to be produced he will order its production.

But it is important that the Minister should have a right to appeal before the document is produced. This matter was not fully investigated in the argument before your Lordships. But it does appear that in one way or another there can be an appeal if the document is in the custody of a servant of the Crown or of a person who is willing to co-operate with the Minister. There may be difficulty if it is in the hands of a person who wishes to produce it. But that difficulty could occur today if a witness wishes to give some evidence which the Minister unsuccessfully urges the court to prevent from being given. It may be that this is a matter which deserves further investigation by the Crown authorities.

The documents in this case are in the possession of a police force. The position of the police is peculiar. They are not servants of the Crown and they do not take orders from the Government. But they are carrying out an essential function of Government, and various Crown rights, privileges and exemptions have been held to apply to them. Their position was explained in *Coomber v. Berkshire Justices* [(1883) 9 App. Cas. 61, H.L.] and cases there cited. It has never been denied that they are entitled to Crown privilege with regard to documents, and it is essential that they should have it.

The police are carrying on an unending war with criminals many of whom are today highly intelligent. So it is essential that there should be no disclosure of anything which might give any useful information to those who organise criminal activities. And it would generally be wrong to require disclosure in a civil case of anything which might be material in a pending prosecution: but after a verdict has been given or it has been decided to take no proceedings there is not the same need for secrecy. With regard to other documents there seems to be no greater need for protection than in the case of departments of Government.

It appears to me to be most improbable that any harm would be done by disclosure of the probationary reports on the appellant or of the report from the police training centre. With regard to the report which the respondent made to his chief constable with a view to the prosecution of the appellant there could be more doubt, although no suggestion was made in argument that disclosure of its contents would be harmful now that the appellant has been acquitted. And, as I have said, these documents may prove to be of vital importance in this litigation.

In my judgment, this appeal should be allowed and these documents ought now to be required to be produced for inspection. If it is then found that disclosure would not, in your Lordships' view be prejudicial to the public interest, or that any possibility of such prejudice is, in the case of each of the documents, insufficient to justify its being withheld, then disclosure should be ordered."

Notes

15–14   (1) Note the distinction between claims to privilege based on "class" and those based merely on "contents". This distinction has been recognised in Scots law: see *Friel* above and generally *Stair Memorial Encyclopaedia*, Vol. 10, paras 688–689. Thus, recovery has been denied documents falling within classes such as income tax returns, *Jenkins v. Glasgow Corporation*, 1934 S.L.T. 53; medical records of the Armed Forces, *Caffrey v. Lord Inverclyde*, 1930 S.C. 762; instructions to public officials, *Tierney v. Ballingall & Son* (1896) 23 R. 512; and reports on collisions at sea by a naval officer to the Admiralty, *Admiralty v. Aberdeen Steam Trawling and Fishing Co. Ltd*, 1909 S.C. 335.

Class privilege has been particularly significant in relation to the functioning of law enforcement agencies. Thus documents falling within information in the hands of those agencies protected by class immunity include reports to superior officers by constables, *Hinshelwood v. Auld*, 1926 J.C. 4; communications between the police and procurator fiscal including police reports and witness statements, *Campbell v. Gibson Maitland* (1893) 1 S.L.T. 127; and procurator fiscal's records and precognitions, *Sheridan v. Peel*, 1907 S.C. 577. On the last two see now *Hemming v. H.M. Advocate*, 1997 S.C.C.R. 257 below.

15–15   (2) Do you think that Lord Reid gave sufficient importance to the candour argument? Notwithstanding Lord Reid's reservations, candour was used as an argument to deny recovery in *Gaskin v. Liverpool Corporation* [1981] W.L.R. where a person claiming damages for negligence arising out of care received in a children's home sought recovery of documents relating to his time in care. It was held that candour was a relevant consideration in ensuring the proper function of the childcare service.

Similarly in *Campbell v. Tameside Metropolitan Borough Council* [1982] Q.B. 1065 where the teacher sued an education authority for injuries caused by a disruptive pupil. It was argued that the authority had not taken reasonable steps to protect her against such an attack. Here, however, the Court of Appeal was not prepared to accept that the value maintaining secrecy outweighed the considerable value the documents in question would have had for the teacher's case. Contrast the view expressed below by Lord Denning M.R. (at 1074) with those in *A.B.*:

> 'In these cases the court can and should consider the *significance* of the documents in relation to the decision of the case. If they are of such significance that they may well affect the very decision of the case, then justice may require them to be disclosed... But, if they are of little significance, so that they are very unlikely to affect the decision... then the greater public interest may be to keep them confidential.'

See also *Williams v. Home Office* No. 2 [1981] 1 All E.R. 1151.

(3) In *Burmah Oil Co. v. Governor and Co. The Bank of England* [1980] A.C. 1090 Burmah Oil sought to recover from the Bank of England documents which fell into a number of separate categories. They consisted of first, communications between Ministers relating to a formulation of government policy relative to the difficulties experienced by Burmah Oil and, secondly, communications between senior officials in various government departments and the Bank of England. It was contended that these fell within the "high" policy documents referred to in the speeches in *Conway*. The House of Lords considered that a case for inspection had been made out but, having inspected the documents, that they should not be disclosed. One of the arguments advanced by the Government was that candour prevented their disclosure. Lord Keith of Kinkel observed (at 1133):

> "The notion that any competent and conscientious public servant would be inhibited at all in the candour of his writings by consideration of the off-chance they might have to be produced in a litigation is in my opinion grotesque. To represent that the possibility of it might significantly impair the public service is even more so,... the candour argument is an utterly insubstantial ground for denying him access to relevant documents."

He also observed that it was important to maintain a distinction between candour and confidentiality and that:

> "I would add that the candour doctrine stands in a different category from that aspect of public interest which in appropriate circumstances may require that the sources and nature of information confidentially tendered should withheld from disclosure. *Reg. v. Lewes Justices, Ex parte Secretary of State for the Home Department* [1973] A.C. 388 and *D. v. National Society for the Prevention of Cruelty to Children* [1978] A.C. 171 are cases in point on that matter."

Lord Wilberforce (at 1112) was prepared to give some scope for the operation of candour:

> "It seems now rather fashionable to decry this [candour], but if as a ground it may at one time have been exaggerated, it has now, in my opinion, received an excessive dose of cold water. I am certainly not prepared — against the view of the minister — to discount the need, in the formation of such very controversial policy... for frank and uninhibited advice... from and between civil servants and between ministers."

On candour generally see J.M. Evans, "Civil Litigation Discovery — Public Interest Immunity and State Papers' (1980) 58 Can. Bar Rev. 360 at 368–372.

(4) The status of class claims and attempts to extend the recognised classes has been subject to criticism at two levels in England. First, the Scott Report made it clear that class objections could be relevant only to documents relating to policy formulation at a very high level in Government and were not relevant to the communications made in the *Matrix Churchill* case (para. G. 18.51). In response the Attorney-General made a statement to the House of Commons concerning the future use of class claims:

> 'Under the new approach, ministers will focus directly on the damage that disclosure would cause. The former division into class and contents claims will no longer be applied. Ministers will claim public interest immunity only when it is believed that disclosure of a document would cause real damage or harm to the public interest... the new emphasis on the test of serious harm means that ministers will not, for example, claim public interest immunity to protect either internal advice or national security material merely by pointing to the general nature of the document. The only basis for claiming public interest immunity will be a belief that disclosure will cause real harm' (*Hansard*, H.C. Vol. 287, col. 950).

Although a statement of practice and one which, standing the Attorney-General's comments noted earlier, does not apply to Scotland, there is now judicial authority to the view that class claims should be restricted. In *R. v. Chief Constable of the West Midlands Police, ex parte Wiley* [1995] 1 A.C. 274 an attempt was made to argue that class immunity applied to reports made under police complaints procedure, which reports were sought to be recovered by the complainants who were contemplating civil action against the Chief Constable for damages for assault. Lord Woolf, giving the leading judgment, reviewed the authorities from *Conway v. Rimmer* onwards and observed (at 305):

"Between the hearing in the Court of Appeal and the hearing before this House, as already indicated, the authority has accepted that in general the class immunity created by the *Neilson* decision can no longer be justified. However, in my opinion, this is the case, not because of any change in the balance of public interest or change in attitudes since the *Neilson* decision, but because establishing a class of public interest immunity of this nature was never justified. This lack of justification is part of the explanation for the problems which the courts have since had in finding a logical limit to the application of the class and creating a sensible balance between the interest of those involved in subsequent legal proceedings and the interest of those responsible for conducting the investigations into police complaints.

The recognition of a new class-based public interest immunity requires clear and compelling evidence that it is necessary. Yet as the present case has demonstrated, the existence of this class tends to defeat the very object it was designed to achieve. The applicants only launched their proceedings for judicial review to avoid the existence of a situation where their position would be prejudiced as a result of their not being given access to material to which the police had access. Their non co-operation was brought about because of the existence of the immunity. Mr. Reynold, on behalf of the applicants, made it clear that if there were to be disclosure of documents which came into existence as a result of the investigation, it would be inappropriate to grant injunctive relief. The restrictive nature of any assurance which could be given to a potential witness in relation to civil proceedings meant that it was unlikely to have significant effect on their decision as to whether to co-operate or not. The class was artificial in conception and this contributed to it having to be rigidly applied. The comments of Lord Taylor of Gosforth C.J. in *Ex parte Coventry Newspapers Ltd.* [1993] Q.B. 278. 292–293, which have already been cited, are likely to be equally appropriate in the great majority of cases. While I agree with Lord Hailsham of St. Marylebone's statement in *D. v. National Society for the Prevention of Cruelty to Children* [1978] A.C. 171, 230, that: 'The categories of public interest are not closed, and must alter from time to time whether by restriction or extension as social conditions and social legislation develop' in my opinion no sufficient case has ever been made out to justify the class of public interest immunity recognised in *Neilson*.

The *Neilson* case [1981] Q.B. 736 and the cases in which it was subsequently applied should therefore be regarded as being wrongly decided. This does not however, mean that public interest immunity can never apply to documents that come into existence in consequence of a police investigation into a complaint. There may be other reasons why because of the contents of a particular document it would be appropriate to extend immunity to that document. In addition, Mr. Pannick submitted that the report which comes into existence as a result of a police investigation into a complaint is a candidate for public interest immunity on a narrower class basis. Mr. Pannick did not, however, have available the evidence which would be needed to succeed on this submission. Although I have considerable reservations as to whether it would be possible to justify a class claim to immunity as opposed to a contents claim in respect of some reports, it would not be right to close the door to a future attempt to establish that the reports are subject to class immunity."

15–16   (5) Notwithstanding the scepticism for the development of new class claims expressed in *Wiley*, class claims have been upheld in *Taylor v. Anderton* [1995] 1 W.L.R. 447 (reports compiled by police officers dealing with complaints against other officers) and *Kelly v. Metropolitan Police Commissioner* [1997] T.L.R. 467 (police reports submitted to the prosecutor by investigating officers).

(6) It is perhaps possible to discern in Scottish case law a trend to limit the ambit of class claims and indeed the question of whether or not a class ever in fact existed. In *Anderson v. Palombo*, 1984 S.L.T. 332 the pursuer, a police officer, sought damages against the defender for defamation in relation to statements made in connection with a complaint by Palombo. Anderson made reference to previous unfounded complaints made by Palombo in his pleadings. Palombo argued that such police records were immune from disclosure. Lord McDonald held, however, that no such general immunity necessarily existed and much depended on the circumstances of each case.

Likewise, where action has been raised against a known person on the grounds of malicious information given to the prosecutor, it would not appear that any letters passing from the defender and the prosecutor or related paperwork are beyond recovery: *Sheridan v. Peel*, 1907 S.C. 577 above.

Similarly, where a question was put to a police officer by the defence as to the identity of a person who had allowed him to make observations from his house, an appeal was sustained on the basis that it had been wrongly disallowed: *Thomson v. Neilson* (1900) 3 F.(J.) 3. Contrast these cases with *Friel*. Is there a principle distinction? Perhaps the most striking example of the narrowing of a class claim came, however, in the next case.

Hemming v. H.M. Advocate

1997 S.C.C.R. 257

"Section 260 of the Criminal Procedure (Scotland) Act 1995 provides that a prior statement made by a witness shall be admissible as evidence of any matter stated in it if it is contained in a document and adopted by the witness as his evidence. 'Statement' is defined in s.262 of the Act so as to exclude precognitions other than precognitions on oath. **15–17**

Section 263(4) of the 1995 Act provides that a witness may be examined as to whether he has made a previous statement different from the evidence given by him at the trial, and that evidence may be led of that statement. A statement led under this section is not evidence of its contents and may be used only to discredit the witness's evidence.

The petitioner was charged on indictment with attempted murder. He presented a petition to the High Court seeking an order for the recovery of statements made by certain witnesses to police officers, on the ground that it was believed that they might have colluded in providing statements against the petitioner. The petition was opposed by the Crown on the ground that there was a general public interest in maintaining the confidentiality of such statements. It was also argued by the Crown that the purpose of recovering the statements was only to enable them to be used to attack the credibility of the witnesses."

Lord Osborne: "In the petition at the instance of William Charles Hemming, which came before me on Tuesday, 11th February 1997, it is averred that the petitioner maintains his innocence and intends to adhere to his plea of not guilty at the trial diet. It is further averred that, in order to prepare his defence against the charge, the petitioner requires to recover the records referred to in the annexed specification. Paragraph 4 of the petition was amended at the bar at the hearing of the petition. After this amendment it stood in the following terms.

> 'That the petitioner believes that the Crown witnesses Ruth Kerr, Ryan McCue, Daniel O'Donnell Senior, Daniel O'Donnell Junior and Paul O'Donnell may have colluded in providing their statements against the petitioner to the police. It is believed that the said belief will be supported by the terms of statements made by the said witnesses to police officers between 8th March 1996 and 12th March 1996.'

It is also averred in the petition that it is understood by the petitioner that the witness statements referred to are in the possession of the procurator fiscal at Edinburgh. In telephone conversations on 28th January 1997 he was called upon to produce these witness statements, but refused to do so. In these circumstances, an order of the court is sought for their recovery.

In presenting the petition counsel for the petitioner expanded upon the circumstances in which the order concerned was sought. He said that the witnesses named in the petition were present in the house mentioned in the libel at the time of the incident. In one way or another they were witnesses to it and its sequel. Following upon the incident, all these persons went into the house at 140 McDonald Road. According to a precognition, which had been taken in the course of the preparation of the petitioner's defence from Ryan McCue, there occurred a discussion involving or at least in the presence of all of these witnesses regarding what was to be said to the police. In the course of this discussion, it was alleged that Daniel O'Donnell Senior made certain suggestions to the other witnesses regarding what was to be said. In his precognition Ryan McCue indicated that he had given a statement to the police in terms which accorded with what had been discussed and suggested. Later he had given another statement to the police, which differed in its terms from the first.

It had emerged in the course of preparation of the petitioner's defence that Ruth Kerr had given more than one statement to the police. A police officer who had been precognosced had indicated that he had formed a certain view about the first statement which she had given to the police. She had subsequently given others. Her statements, although not in the possession of the petitioner, were said to differ the one from the other, as appeared from what had been gleaned in the course of preparation of the case.

It was submitted on behalf of the petitioner that it was of importance to the defence to attack the common account of the incident concerned which the witnesses mentioned had developed. In particular, it was important that the credibility of these witnesses should be attacked by means of the use of the provisions of section 263(4) of the Criminal Procedure (Scotland) Act 1995. That could not be done without the statements made by the witnesses concerned being available to counsel for the petitioner.

Furthermore, certain particular considerations arose in relation to the witness Ruth Kerr. It had already been indicated by the Crown to the petitioner's advisers that she had given three statements to the police. In the first she had imparted some information concerning the incident. In the second she had provided further information, including reference to a stab wound. In a third statement she had provided yet more material, in which she had indicated that the complainer Daniel O'Donnell Senior had been held over the bannister by the petitioner. She had admitted that she herself went into the house, obtained a knife and introduced it into the melée.

In the course of the precognition of certain police officers on behalf of the petitioner, indications had been given that the witnesses named in the petition had all given statements to the police, but the police had declined to impart information regarding the contents of those statements. It was in these circumstances that the petition was presented.

Against the foregoing background, it was submitted that it was in the interests of justice that the petition should be granted. There was no doubt at all that the application was competent at common law. In that connection reference was made to *H.M. Advocate* v *Hasson*. In that case Lord Cameron had held that an application such as this was competent; that the decision as to the relevancy of a call in a specification was a matter for the court; that the applicant ought to indicate in general terms the relation of the calls in the specification to the charge or charges in the indictment and the proposed defence; and that the calls in the specification should provide the commissioner with sufficiently clear guidance as to the documents of which recovery had been sought and authorised. All the requirements of that case were satisfied by the present application. It was of great importance that the statements of the witnesses specified should be made available for the purposes already outlined and for comparison purposes, having regard to the allegation that there had been collusion in providing statements against the petitioner to the police.

On behalf of the Crown the advocate-depute resisted the petitioner's motion. There was no dispute about the principles which were set forth in *H.M. Advocate v Hasson*, but it was plain that the material allowed to be recovered in that case was of a materially different character from that involved here. Thus no assistance could be got by the petitioner from the facts of that case.

Turning to the terms of the petition, it was submitted that the basis on which recovery was sought was vague. To say that certain persons 'may have colluded' was a weak allegation. Furthermore, on the basis of the account of the petitioner's position given to the court, the interest in the recovery of the documents concerned was limited to their use in the mounting of an attack on the credibility of the witnesses involved. The petitioner was asking the court to take a course which it had never previously taken, that is to say, to override an objection taken in the public interest by the Lord Advocate, although, of course, it was not disputed that the court had that power.

The advocate-depute next drew my attention to a number of cases which were of relevance to the issue for the court. In *McKie* v *Western S.M.T. Co. Ltd*, an action of damages for personal injuries, an attempt was made to recover a report made by a police sergeant to his superior officers in connection with a road traffic accident. Owing to illness, the sergeant had become permanently incapable of giving evidence. The Lord Advocate had objected to the production of the report on the ground that police reports regarding accidents had to be protected absolutely against publication at any time in the public interest. The court had held that, even if it had an inherent right to overrule objections to production stated by the Lord Advocate on behalf of departments of government, special weight had to be given to an objection taken by him in his capacity as head of the criminal administration in Scotland in relation to an entire class of documents, irrespective of their contents, and that his objection should be sustained on the view that police reports, like the report in question, must in the public interest be absolutely immune from the risk of disclosure. Reliance was also placed on *Hinshelwood* v *Auld*. It concerned notes taken at the time of an alleged offence by police officers for the purpose of preparing a police report. It had been held that their production could not be insisted upon by an accused person.

The only case known to the advocate-depute which dealt with a police statement was *H.M. Advocate* v *Ward*. In that case an attempt had been made to recover a very wide range of documentary material, including statements taken by the police from witnesses. The court had expressed the opinion that a general call for police statements was open to objection. However, in relation to certain particular specified statements, the court had continued the case to enable the Crown to consider its position. As a result of that opportunity, the position subsequently taken up by the Crown was that the statements referred to would be lodged as productions, in consequence of which the court made no further order.

The advocate-depute, in the context of discussion of this case, indicated that the Crown considered that it ought to reveal to defence advisers the occurrence of a change of position by a witness, but would not do so by means of providing copies of police statements, although it was accepted that, from time to time, the Crown itself lodged police statements as productions in criminal prosecutions where it was feared that a witness might depart in evidence from a position taken up in such a statement. Nevertheless, it was said that there was a public interest which the Lord Advocate considered should be protected in the privacy of a police statement.

Finally, reliance was placed on *Friel* v *Chief Constable of Strathclyde Region* ... The petitioner in that case had sought recovery of documents in the possession of the police which might have revealed the name of a police informer, since he believed that the information on which the police had acted in connection with a particular transaction had been given to them falsely and maliciously and without probable cause, in order to damage his business standing and reputation, in consequence of which he wished to raise an action of damages against the informer, whose identity was unknown to him. The court had refused to override the objection of the Lord Advocate in the circumstances of that case.

In conclusion the advocate-depute very fairly indicated that the Crown would do its utmost to assist the defence in relation to the contents of the statements involved here, stopping short of furnishing those statements to them.

Counsel for the petitioner, in reply, submitted that none of the authorities cited by the Crown suggested that police witness statements were a class of document protected by an overriding public interest. It was significant that in *H.M. Advocate* v *Ward* the court had not decided that there could never be recovery of such statements. Indeed, it had continued the case to enable the Crown to consider its position in relation to certain of the statements sought to be recovered. In the present case it was submitted that, while it was necessary for the court to recognise the public interest upon which the Lord Advocate founded in resisting the application, there was another aspect of the public interest which was of overriding importance, namely the public interest that the accused should have a fair trial and to avoid a miscarriage of justice. While the assistance which the Crown offered informally might enable some questioning to be undertaken of the witnesses concerned relating to prior statements, it would not enable counsel for the defence to cross-examine those witnesses to the necessary extent concerning the contents of prior statements. It was interesting that, in England, police statements were routinely made available to the defence.

Counsel for the petitioner next referred to sections 260 and 262 of the Criminal Procedure (Scotland) Act 1995. In these sections Parliament had provided, subject to the conditions there set forth, that any prior statement made by a witness should be admissible as evidence of any matter stated in it of which direct oral evidence by him would be admissible if given in the course of the proceedings. One of the conditions enacted was that the witness, in the course of giving evidence, had to indicate that the statement was made by him and that he adopted it as his evidence. It was provided by the Act of Adjournal of 1996, rule 21.4, that such a statement had to be authenticated by the method there specified. Section 262 provided for a wide definition of the word 'statement' for the purposes of section 260. It was quite plain that that definition would embrace a statement given by a witness to a police officer. That being so, it was necessary to conclude that Parliament had contemplated that police statements might be used in that way. That state of affairs tended to undermine the suggestion that there was an overriding public interest in the non-disclosure of such statements.

The advocate-depute in reply argued that the objection taken by the Crown in the present case was based upon the public interest in the detection and prosecution of crime. If the present application were granted, the floodgates would be opened and it would be possible in every case for a similar application to be made. The cases cited concerning the importance of the preservation of the confidentiality of police reports were relevant to the present issue, since, in substance, there was no difference between a police report and a police statement. Police statements were commonly appended to police reports sent to the procurator fiscal.

It was right to point out that in the Stair Encyclopaedia of the Laws of Scotland, vol. 10, paragraph 689, it was stated that, among the types of documents protected against public disclosure, were police reports and witness statements. The authority cited in support of this proposition was *Campbell* v *Gibson Maitland*. It had to be accepted that this authority did not appear to justify the proposition based upon it.

Turning to the argument of the petitioner, based upon section 260 of the Criminal Procedure (Scotland) Act 1995, it was submitted that the terms of the section did not assist the petitioner. While its provisions were designed to confer evidential status, in certain circumstances, upon prior statements made by a witness, it did not follow from the existence from those provisions that witness statements in the hands of the Crown would necessarily be recoverable by an accused person.

I did not understand there to be any significant difference of view between counsel for the petitioner and the advocate-depute regarding the legal principles which must be applied to an application such as the present one. In particular, it was accepted that the approach of Lord Cameron in *H.M. Advocate* v *Hasson* was correct. At p. 37 in the report of that case he affirmed the competency of such an application, saying:

'Such an application as this, cast in a form which is familiar in civil proceedings, is unusual in a criminal prosecution, but I do not think its competency in an appropriate case is now open to successful challenge.'

At p. 38 of the report his Lordship continued:

'The real difficulty in dealing with such an application as the present lies not in deciding as to its competency, but as to the relevance and width of the calls which are made and as to the accused's right to recover the particular documents covered by the calls in the specification. As the Lord Justice-General pointed out in *Downie* [v *H.M. Advocate*, 1952 J.C. 37; 1952 S.L.T. 159], there is the obvious initial difficulty in considering such a specification that it is not — as in civil procedure — related to adjusted pleadings. Beyond the indictment and (where rendered) the terms of a special defence, there are no written pleadings. Further, in the presentation of a defence very considerable latitude is necessarily allowed to an accused person and, in practice, it is often difficult, if not impossible, to discern *ab ante* the relevance of a particular document or piece of evidence. This means that the familiar tests of the legitimacy of a call for production of a document cannot be applied, nor, in particular, is it in consequence easy to recognise and reject a particular call as being of the character of a "fishing" diligence.'

At p. 39 of the same report Lord Cameron went on to explain the further consideration which would influence the court in reaching a decision on such an application. There he said:

'Although the situation has been materially changed by the introduction of criminal legal aid, the problem remains for solution of deciding which documents are or are not recoverable and the limits of such recovery.'

Referring to a passage in the then extant edition of Renton and Brown, his Lordship continued:

'On this point the late learned editor of the edition expresses the opinion '... that, in general, statement by the accused's responsible adviser that the document in question is required for the conduct of the defence should be regarded by the Court as sufficient'. As at present advised, I would regard this as too broad and bald a statement of the law, and I am not prepared to accept it as an adequate or sufficient test of the relevancy of a call for production of documents in the hands of third parties, especially when themselves not on the list of witnesses for the Crown or defence... I think something more than the mere *ipse dixit* of a responsible adviser is required, even if it be only an indication in general terms of the relation of the call to the charge or charges and the proposed defence to them.'

Turning from these general considerations in relation to the recovery of documents in criminal proceedings, the approach to be adopted where the Crown stated a public interest objection to recovery was fully and carefully examined by Lord Maxwell in *Friel* v *Chief Constable of Strathclyde Region*. At pp. 7–8 of the report his Lordship said this.

'It is accepted that the Court retains a discretionary power to order production of documents notwithstanding such an objection (*Glasgow Corporation* v *Central Land Board*, 1956 S.C. (H.L.) 1). It is accepted that this power has, in practice, rarely, if ever, been exercised. It is accepted that the Lord Advocate's objection can, as here, competently be based on the public interest in non-disclosure of a class of documents as opposed to a particular document.

'Counsel for the petitioner contended that, where the objection is taken in respect of a class of documents, the Court, in considering whether to override the objection, can take into account not only the interests of the particular petitioner, but the interests of the public as a whole in so far as other members of the public might find themselves in the same position as the petitioner. I agree with that submission.

'It was suggested for the petitioner that the Court's function was to balance competing interests. That is, I think, correct only in a limited sense. The Court does not, in my opinion, balance competing interests in the same way, for example, as it seeks to balance convenience in relation to interdict, and the reason for that is that the Lord Advocate has access to information which may not be available to the Court and the Court is bound to accept his assertion that there is an aspect of public interest to be protected. The matter was put thus by Lord Radcliffe in *Glasgow Corporation* v *Central Land Board*: "I do not understand that the existence of the power involves that, in Scotland any more than in England, it is open to the Court to dispute with the Minister whether his view that production would be contrary to the public interest is well founded, or to arrive at a view contradictory of his, that production would not, in fact, be at all injurious to that interest. If weight is given to the argument that the Minister in forming his view may have before him a range of considerations that is not open to the Court and that he is not under any obligation to set out those considerations in public, I think that it must follow that the Minister's view must be accepted by the Court as incapable of being displaced by its own opinion. I understand the decision in *Admiralty* v *Aberdeen Steam Trawling and Fishing Co.*, 1909 S.C. 335 as a decision precisely to that effect, and I do not think that there is anything in the later case of *Henderson* v *McGown*, 1916 S.C. 821 which conflicts with the earlier case as so understood. The power reserved to the Court is therefore a power to order production, even though the public interest is to some extent affected prejudicially. This amounts to a recognition that more than one aspect of public interest may have to be surveyed in reviewing the question whether a document which would be available to a party in a civil suit between parties is not to be available to the party engaged in a suit with the Crown. The interests of Government, for which the minister should speak with full authority do not exhaust the public interest. Another aspect of that interest is seen in the need that impartial justice should be done in the Courts of law, not least between citizen and Crown and that a litigant who has a case to maintain should not be deprived of the means of its proper presentation by anything less than a weighty public reason. It does not seem to me unreasonable to expect that the Court would be better qualified than the Minister to measure the importance of such principles in application to the particular case that is before it." '

Further important guidance in relation to these matters is contained in *McKie* v *Western S.M.T. Co. Ltd.* At p. 215 of the report Lord President Cooper said this in relation to the position of the Lord Advocate.

'While it may still be legitimate, notwithstanding the decision in *Duncan* v *Cammell Laird* [[1942] A.C. 624] and the provisions of section 47 of the Crown Proceedings Act, 1947, to continue to affirm the power of the Court to override the views of the Executive (or at least to take the full responsibility for the decision to refuse production) in cases in which the public interest is pleaded by ordinary departments of government, I cannot but feel that special considerations apply to the weight attaching to such a plea when stated by the Lord Advocate in his capacity as head of our native system of criminal administration, in relation to the entire class of documents, irrespective of their contents, which embody reports by the police to their superior officers and ultimately to the Crown authorities. It seems to me to be indispensable to the efficient working of the system of detection and prosecution of crime in Scotland that the officers making such reports or communications should know *when they are making them* that they are protected by absolute immunity from the risk of subsequent disclosure.'

It is in the light of these accepted principles that I have approached the problem which arises in this case. Accordingly, standing what was said, particularly in *Friel* v *Chief Constable of Strathclyde Region*, the public interest objection having been taken by the Lord Advocate in the present case, it is necessary for me to accept that to grant the order sought would cause damage to the public interest. It is not possible for me in this court to seek to review the judgment formed by the Lord Advocate in that respect. In these circumstances, I consider that the question for me is whether there exists some other aspect of the public interest, of an overriding nature, which should be recognised by the court.

In my opinion, there is no doubt whatever that there exists a fundamental aspect of the public interest which requires the court to ensure that, in crimunal proceedings before it, so far as possible, justice must be done and miscarriages of justice avoided. That responsibility of the court involves the duty to see that, in such proceedings, there should be a fair hearing, in which a full opportunity is afforded to an accused person to undertake a critical examination of the Crown's case against him and, in particular, to challenge, in cross-examination, the quality of the evidence adduced to support it. Plainly, the ability to use the provisions of section 263(4) of the Criminal Procedure (Scotland) Act 1995 is crucial to the provision of such an opportunity.

In assessing whether the aspect of the public interest which I have just described is, or is not, of an overriding nature, the main difficulty which arises is that it is necessary to try to compare the easily comprehended damage which the petitioner and others who might find themselves in a similar position would suffer if the order sought and others like it were refused, with the much less easily discernible damage to another aspect of public interest, which I must accept would occur if the order sought were to be granted. I have given this problem the most anxious consideration. The conclusion which I have reached is that the particular aspect of the public interest which I have identified and described is of a high and overriding nature. It is for these reasons that I consider I ought to grant the order sought."

Notes

(1) Precognitions, other than those on oath would appear not to be recoverable. Is there a logical distinction between precognitions and statements of the kind in issue here? See P.W. Ferguson, "Disclosure in Criminal Proceedings", 1997 S.L.T. (News) 181.

15–18

(2) *Hemming* came to be considered by a Full Bench in *McLeod, Petitioner*, 1998 S.L.T. 233. Here, the accused was charged with offences under the Misuse of Drugs Act 1971. His night-club had been raided and a number of people including the accused were detained and questioned by the police. The detainees' responses were recorded on a *pro forma* questionnaire. The accused sought to recover the questionnaires but the Crown refused, maintaining that they fell within a class of privileged documents because of their confidentiality. At first instance a petition to recover the questionnaires was rejected but in the subsequent hearing written submissions were received by the court from the Crown which stated (at 239D):

> "The Crown accept that it would no longer be right to claim confidentiality in respect of police statements merely because they belong to a class of documents which has traditionally enjoyed protection from disclosure."

The onus would still be on the accused to justify that the documents were "likely to be of material assistance to the proper preparation or presentation of the accused's defence" (at 244K–L). In *Hemming* the witness statements would have been recoverable under this test as Lord Osborne's formulation is not materially different from this test. Although the onus remains with the accused, the Crown is, however, subject to a duty of disclosure of "any information which supports the defence case... and it extends to information which supports any known or statable defence or which undermines the Crown case" (at 243L–244A). McLeod had contended that there was a right to general disclosure of any information helpful to the defence. The court under reference to Article 6(1) of the ECHR said that all that the Convention requires is that only material evidence for and against the accused need be revealed: *Edward v. UK* (1993) 15 E.H.R.R. 417, para. 36 and *Foucher v. France* (1998) 25 E.H.R.R. 234, para. 36 and see Lord Hamilton at 246A–B. Scots law also appears to be consistent with the test set out in Part I of the Criminal Procedure and Investigations Act 1996, the leading English statute in this area: see also V. Finch and C. Ashton, *Administrative Law in Scotland* (1997), pp. 492–498.

Notwithstanding the apparently more rigorous approach to claims of public interest immunity in criminal cases, do you consider it should have any scope at all in this area? For the arguments for and against see Sir Richard Scott, "The Use of Public Interest Immunity Claims in Criminal Cases" (1996) 3 Web Journal of Current Legal Issues, Part I. On *McLeod*, see P.W. Ferguson, "Disclosure: The Prosecutors Duties", 1998 S.L.T. (News) 233.

15–19   (3) Public interest immunity is now regarded as an aspect of the debate over freedom of information. Partly in response to the results of the Scott inquiry, the Conservative Government issued a Code of Practice on Access to Government Information. The current code came into effect on February 1, 1997 and applies to all bodies which are subject to the jurisdiction of the Parliamentary Ombudsman. Under the code such bodies have an obligation to:

• Publish facts and the analysis of facts which form the backdrop to government policy.
• Publish explanatory material and departments dealings with the public.
• Give reasons for administrative decisions.
• Give full information as to how services are run, who is responsible for them and complaints and redress procedures.
• Release in response to specific requests information relating to government policies, actions and decisions.

Set against this general principle of disclosure, Part II of the code lists 15 exemptions to the basic principle in favour of disclosure, which include, unsurprisingly, defence, security and international relations, internal discussions and advice (the candour argument), the privacy of an individual, law enforcement in legal proceedings and information given in confidence. The code does not, however, "alter present practice covering disclosure of information before courts" (para. 10), which would include public interest privilege. However welcome, the impact of the code is, perhaps, limited. In its first year only 41 complaints were made to the Ombudsman in relation to the code: see the Second Report of the Select Committee on the Parliamentary

Commissioner for Administration, Open Government (1996, H.C. 84), para. 56. For the most recent figures and the Parliamentary Commissioners' views on the proposals for reform of Freedom of Information, see para.16–12. For the current Government's proposals in relation to freedom of information see *Your Right to Know: The Government's Proposals for A Freedom of Information Act*, Cm. 3818, and for comment thereon see P. Birkinshaw, "An 'all singin' and all dancin' ' affair: the new Labour Government's proposals for freedom of information" [1998] P.L. 176.

For discussion of the government proposals see the Third Report of the Select Committee on Public Administration (1997–98 session), H.C. 398I and Minutes of Evidence H.C. 398 iii-v and for the government response see the Fourth Special Report of the Committee (1997–98) 1020 H.C. Note the view expressed in the Third Report, para. 46 that it will be for the Scottish Parliament and Executive to confirm as to what extent the Government's proposals should be implemented in relation to areas within devolved competence. At the time of submission a Freedom of Information Bill which broadly reflects the government's proposals was introduced in the House of Lords: see 1998–99 H.L. Bill 10. This is a Private Bill. Without government support it is unlikely to become law in the current parliamentary session.

'The United Kingdom Government has published a draft Freedom of Information Bill and a consultation paper: see Cm. 4355 (1999). The Scottish Executive has no immediate plans for Freedom of Information legislation in the current session of the Scottish Parliament although it has announced that it will publish a Code of Practice on Freedom of Information pending formal legislation. For discussion of the proposals both at U.K. and Scottish level, and the possible relevance of the Human Rights Act 1998, see the article by the Advocate General, Dr Lynda Clark Q.C., M.P., "Freedom of information: new rights, new remedies & new parliament" (1999) 200 SCOLAG 59.

Chapter 16

OMBUDSMEN AND OTHER COMPLAINTS MECHANISMS

The concept of an Ombudsman as someone who enquires into claims of poor administration has its origins in Sweden. Through the activities of JUSTICE, a U.K. Ombudsman, known as the Parliamentary Commissioner for Administration, was established by legislation in 1967 (the Parliamentary Commissioner Act). This in turn was followed by the Health Service Commissioner for Scotland (The National Health Service (Scotland) Act 1972), and for England and Wales (The National Health Service Re-organisation Act 1973), and in local government, the Commissioners for Local Administration (The Local Government Act 1974) for England and Wales and for Scotland (Part II of the Local Government (Scotland) Act 1975). Section 91 of the Scotland Act 1998 provides that the Parliament shall make provision for the investigation of complaints in relation to the actions of the Scottish Executive and Scottish Administration and certain other bodies, falling within areas of devolved competence. Transitional and temporary provisions have created a Scottish Parliamentary Ombudsman: the Scotland Act 1998 (Transitory and Transitional Provisions) (Complaints of Maladministration) Order 1999, which is discussed below. The provisions of the 1967 Act are, however, of continuing importance in Scotland, because the Parliamentary Commissioner for Administration (the PCA) will continue to have a role to play in relation to complaints made against bodies not within devolved competence. Moreover, it is likely that the practice and procedure, if not the institutional features of the PCA, are likely to be reflected in any permanent Scottish arrangements.

16–1

The Parliamentary Commissioner for Administration was initially concerned with investigating complaints referred to him by Members of Parliament of "maladministration" by central government departments. His jurisdiction has, however, been extended to encompass over 70 Non-Departmental Public Bodies as well as "Next Steps" agencies. His jurisdiction was extended further by the Parliamentary Commissioner Order 1999.

Although beyond the scope of this chapter, the role of other ombudsmen should not be overlooked. For example, there is now a Scottish Legal Services Ombudsman created by the Law Reform (Miscellaneous Provisions) (Scotland) Act 1990 to investigate the way in which complaints against members of the Faculty of Advocates, the Law Society of Scotland and the Scottish Conveyancing and Executries Board have been handled by those bodies. The powers of this Ombudsman have recently been enhanced by the Scottish Legal Services Ombudsman and Commissioner for Local Administration in Scotland Act 1997, giving him power to compel any of these professional bodies to publicise the fact that they have failed to comply with any recommendation on how a complaint could have been better handled and the reasons for their failure to do so: sections 2, 23 (8)–(10). For further reading on his role see V. Finch and C. Ashton, *Administrative Law in Scotland* (1997), pp. 181–183. The financial services industry has been a rich source of ombudsmen. Some of these ombudsmen rest entirely on voluntary agreement among the organisations concerned, such as the Insurance Ombudsman established in 1980. The Banking Ombudsman is similar, but the jurisdiction of the Building Societies Ombudsman is in part based upon requirements laid down by the Building Societies Act 1986. While these ombudsmen may be viewed as private institutions and not of immediate concern to administrative lawyers, it is arguable that some of their original methods of investigation may be of relevance to Public Sector Ombudsmen, particularly the Parliamentary Ombudsmen, in developing a range of efficient techniques: on this see, for example, A.R. Mowbray, "Ombudsmen: the Private Sector Dimension" in *Edinburgh Essays in Public Law* (W. Finnie, C.M.G. Himsworth and N. Walker eds, 1991), p. 315 and R.W. Hodges, "Ombudsman and Other Complaints Procedures in the Financial Services Sector in the U.K." (1992) 21 Anglo-Am. L.R. 1. For a recent major study of the phenomenon and the parallels that can be drawn in the field of public law see R. James, *Private Ombudsmen and Public Law* (1997).

Finally, regard should also be had to the existence of a European Ombudsman created by the Treaty on European Union (the Maastricht Treaty) who can receive complaints from citizens of the Union alleging that they have suffered maladministration at the hands of a Community institution (but not the Court of Justice or the Court of First Instance acting in their judicial role): see E.C. Treaty, Article 138e, as amended. Details of the work of this Ombudsman and the Annual Report can be obtained on the Internet from http:www.europa.eu.int and see also E.A. Marais (ed.), *The European Ombudsman* (1994) and the Fourth Report of the Select Committee on the European Community (1997–98 H.L. 18).

For further general reading on the ombudsmen technique see JUSTICE-All Souls Report, Chap. 5; P. Birkinshaw, *Grievances, Remedies and the State* (2nd 1994); Finch and Ashton, Chap. 7; P.P. Craig, *Administrative Law* (3rd ed., 1994) pp. 127–138 C. Harlow and R. Rawlings, *Law and Administration* (1997), Chaps 12, 13; G. Drewry, "The Ombudsman: Parochial Stopgap or Global Panacea?" in *Administrative Law Facing the Future: Old Constraints and New Horizons* (P. Leyland and T. Woods eds, 1997), p. 83.

THE PARLIAMENTARY COMMISSIONER FOR ADMINISTRATION

Parliamentary Commissioner Act 1967

ss. 1–12, Scheds 2, 3

"Appointment and Tenure of Office

1. — (1) For the purpose of conducting investigations in accordance with the following provisions of this Act there shall be appointed a Commissioner, to be known as the Parliamentary Commissioner for Administration.

(2) Her Majesty may be Letters Patent from time to time appoint a person to be the Commissioner, and any person so appointed shall (subject to [subsections (3) and (3A)] of this section) hold office during good behaviour.

(3) A person appointed to be the Commissioner may be relieved of office by Her Majesty at his own request, or may be removed from office by Her Majesty in consequence of Addresses from both Houses of Parliament, and shall in any case vacate office on completing the year of service in which he attains the age of sixty-five years.

[(3A) Her Majesty may declare the office of Commissioner to have been vacated if satisfied that the person appointed to be the Commissioner is incapable for medical reasons —
(a)   of performing duties of his office; and
(b)   of requesting to be relieved of it.]...

Salary and Pension
2. — (1) There shall be paid to the holder of the office of Commissioner a salary at the rate (subject to subsection (2) of this section) of £8,600 a year.

(2) The House of Commons may from time to time by resolution increase the rate of the salary payable under this section, and any such resolution may take effect from the date on which it is passed or such other date as may be specified therein ...

(5) Any salary, pension or other benefit payable by virtue of this section shall be charged on and issued out of the Consolidated Fund.

Administrative Provisions
3. — (1) The Commissioner may appoint such officers as he may determine with the approval of the Treasury as to numbers and conditions of service.

(2) Any function of the Commissioner under this Act may be performed by any officer of the Commissioner authorised for that purpose by the Commissioner [or may be performed by any officer so authorised —

16–2

(a)   of the Health Service Commissioner for England;

(b)   of the Health Service Commissioner for Scotland; or

(c)   of the Health Service Commissioner for Wales].

(3) The expenses of the Commissioner under this Act, to such amount as may be sanctioned by the Treasury, shall be defrayed out of moneys provided by Parliament.

Appointment of Acting Commissioners

[**3A**. — (1) Where the Office of Commissioner becomes vacant, Her Majesty may, pending the appointment of a new Commissioner, appoint a person under this section to act as the Commissioner at any time during the period of twelve months beginning with the date on which the vacancy arose.

(2) A person appointed under this section shall hold office during Her Majesty's pleasure and, subject to that, shall hold office —

(a)   until the appointment of a new Commissioner or the expiry of the period of twelve months beginning with the date on which the vacancy arose, whichever occurs first; and

(b)   in other respects, in accordance with the terms and conditions of his appointment which shall be such as the Treasury may determine.

(3) A person appointed under this section shall, while he holds office, be treated for all purposes, except those of section 2 of this Act, as the Commissioner.

(4) Any salary, pension or other benefit payable by virtue of this section shall be charged on and issued out of the Consolidated Fund.]

Departments, etc., Subject to Investigation

[**4**. — (1) Subject to the provisions of this section and to the notes contained in Schedule 2 to this Act, this Act applies to the government departments, corporations and unincorporated bodies listed in that Schedule; and references in this Act to an authority to which this Act applies are references to any such corporation or body.

(2) Her Majesty may by Order in Council amend Schedule 2 to this Act by the alteration of any entry or note, the removal of any entry or note or the insertion of any additional entry or note.

(3) An Order in Council may only insert an entry if —

(a)   it relates —

   (i)   to a government department; or

   (ii)   to a corporation or body whose functions are exercised on behalf of the Crown; or

(b)   it relates to a corporation or body —

   (i)   which is established by virtue of Her Majesty's prerogative or by an Act of Parliament or on Order in Council or order made under an Act of Parliament or which is established in any other way by a Minister of the Crown in his capacity as a Minister or by a government department;

   (ii)   at least half of whose revenues derive directly from money provided by Parliament, a levy authorised by an enactment, a fee or charge of any other description so authorised or more than one of those sources; and

   (iii) which is wholly or partly constituted by appointment made by Her Majesty or a Minister of the Crown or government department.

(4) No entry shall be made in respect of a corporation or body whose sole activity is, or whose main activities are, included among the activities specified in subsection (5) below.

(5) The activities mentioned in subsection (4) above are —

(a)   the provision of education, or the provision of training otherwise than under the Industrial Training Act 1982;

(b)   the development of curricula, the conduct of examinations or the validation of educational courses;

(c)   the control of entry to any profession or the regulation of the conduct of members of any profession;

(d)   the investigation of complaints by members of the public regarding the actions of any person or body, or the supervision or review of such investigations or of steps taken following them.

(6) No entry shall be made in respect of a corporation or body operating in an exclusively or predominantly commercial manner or a corporation carrying on under national ownership an industry or undertaking or part of an industry or undertaking.

(7) Any statutory instrument made by virtue of this section shall be subject to annulment in pursuance of a resolution of either House of Parliament.

(8) In this Act —

(a)   any reference to a government department to which this Act applies includes a reference to any of the Ministers or officers of such a department; and

(b)   any reference to an authority to which this Act applies includes a reference to any members or officers of such an authority.]

Matters Subject to Investigation

5. — (1) Subject to the provisions of this section, the Commissioner may investigate an action taken by or on behalf of a government department or other authority to which this Act applies, being action taken in the exercise of administrative functions of that department or authority, in any case where —

(a)   a written complaint is duly made to a member of the House of Commons by a member of the public who claims to have sustained injustice in consequence of maladministration in connection with the action so taken; and

(b)   the complaint is referred to the Commissioner, with the consent of the person who made it, by a member of that House with a request to conduct an investigation thereon.

(2) Except as hereinafter provided, the Commissioner shall not conduct an investigation under this Act in respect of any of the following matters, that is to say —

(a)   any action in respect of which the person aggrieved has or had a right of appeal, reference or review to or before a tribunal constituted by or under any enactment or by virtue of Her Majesty's prerogative;

(b)   any action in respect of which the person aggrieved has or had a remedy by way of proceedings in any court of law;

Provided that the Commissioner may conduct an investigation notwithstanding that the person aggrieved has or had such a right or remedy if satisfied that in the particular circumstances it is not reasonable to expect him to resort or have resorted to it.

(3) Without prejudice to subsection (2) of this section, the Commissioner shall not conduct an investigation under this Act in respect of any such action or matter as is described in Schedule 3 to this Act.

(4) Her Majesty may be Order in Council amend the said Schedule 3 so as to exclude from the provisions of that Schedule such actions or matters as may be described in the Order; and any statutory instrument made by virtue of this subsection shall be subject to annulment in pursuance of a resolution of either House of Parliament.

(5) In determining whether to initiate, continue or discontinue an investigation under this Act, the Commissioner shall, subject to the foregoing provisions of this section, act in accordance with his own discretion; and any question whether a complaint is duly made under this Act shall be determined by the Commissioner.

[(6) For the purposes of this section, administrative functions exercisable by any person appointed by the Lord Chancellor as a member of the administrative staff of any court or tribunal shall be taken to be administrative functions of the Lord Chancellor's Department or, in Northern Ireland, of the Northern Ireland Court Service.];

[(7) For the purposes of this section, administrative functions exercisable by any person appointed as a member of the administrative staff of a relevant tribunal —

(a)   by a government department or authority to which this Act applies; or

(b)   with the consent (whether as to remuneration and other terms and conditions of service or otherwise) of such a department or authority,

shall be taken to be administrative functions of that department or authority.

(8) In subsection (7) of this section, "relevant tribunal" means a tribunal listed in Schedule 4 to this Act.

(9) Her Majesty may be Order in Council amend the said Schedule 4 by the alteration or removal of any entry or the insertion of any additional entry; and any statutory instrument made by virtue of this subsection shall be subject to annulment in pursuance of a resolution of either House of Parliament.]

Provisions Relating to Complaints

6. — (1) A complaint under this Act may be made by any individual, or by any body of persons whether incorporated or not, not being —

(a)   a local authority or other authority or body constituted for purposes of the public service or of local government or for the purposes of carrying on under national ownership any industry or undertaking or part of an industry or undertaking;

(b)   any other authority or body whose members are appointed by Her Majesty or any Minister of the Crown or government department, or whose revenues consist wholly or mainly of moneys provided by Parliament.

(2) Where the person by whom a complaint might have been made under the foregoing provisions of this Act has died or is for any reason unable to act for himself, the complaint may be made by his personal representative or by a member of his family or other individual suitable to represent him; but except as aforesaid a complaint shall not be entertained under this Act unless made by the person aggrieved himself.

(3) A complaint shall not be entertained under this Act unless it is made to a member of the House of Commons not later than twelve months from the day on which the person aggrieved first had notice of the matters alleged in the complaint; but the Commissioner may conduct an investigation pursuant to a complaint not made within that period if he considers that there are special circumstances which make it proper to do so.

(4) [Except as provided in subsection (5) below] a complaint shall not be entertained under this Act unless the person aggrieved is resident in the United Kingdom (or, if he is dead, was so resident at the time of his death) or the complaint relates to action taken in relation to him while he was present in the United Kingdom or on an installation in a designated area within the meaning of the Continental Shelf Act 1964 or on a ship registered in the United Kingdom or an aircraft so registered, or in relation to rights or obligations which accrued or arose in the United Kingdom or on such an installation, a ship or aircraft.

[(5) A complaint may be entertained under this Act in circumstances not falling within subsection (4) above where —
(a)   the complaint relates to action taken in any country or territory outside the United Kingdom by an officer (not being an honorary consular officer) in the exercise of a consular function on behalf of the Government of the United Kingdom; and
(b)   the person aggrieved is a citizen of the United Kingdom and Colonies who, under section 2 of the Immigration Act 1971, has the right of abode in the United Kingdom.]

Procedures in Respect of Investigations
7. — (1) Where the Commissioner proposes to conduct an investigation pursuant to a complaint under this Act, he shall afford to the principal officer of the department of authority concerned, and to any person who is alleged in the complaint to have taken or authorised the action complained of, an opportunity to comment on any allegations contained in the complaint.

(2) Every such investigation shall be conducted in private, but except as aforesaid the procedure for conducting an investigation shall be such as the Commissioner considers appropriate in the circumstances of the case; and without prejudice to the generality of the foregoing provision the Commissioner may obtain information from such persons and in such manner, and make such inquiries, as he thinks fit, and may determine whether any person may be represented, by counsel or solicitor or otherwise, in the investigation.

(3) The Commissioner may, if he thinks fit, pay to the person by whom the complaint was made and to any other person who attends or furnishes information for the purposes of an investigation under this Act —
(a)   sums in respect of expenses properly incurred by them;
(b)   allowances by way of compensation for the loss of their time,
in accordance with such scales and subject to such conditions as may be determined by the Treasury.

(4) The conduct of an investigation under this Act shall not affect any action taken by the department or authority concerned, or any power or duty of that department or authority to take further action with respect to any matters subject to the investigation; but where the person aggrieved has been removed from the United Kingdom under any Order in force under the Aliens Restriction Acts 1914 and 1919 or under the Commonwealth Immigrants Act 1962, he shall, if the Commissioner so directs, be permitted to re-enter and remain in the United Kingdom, subject to such conditions as the Secretary of State may direct, for the purposes of the investigation.

Evidence
8. — (1) For the purposes of an investigation under this Act the Commissioner may require any Minister, officer or member of the department or authority concerned or any other person who in his opinion is able to furnish information or produce documents relevant to the investigation to furnish any such information or produce any such document.

(2) For the purposes of any such investigation the Commissioner shall have the same powers as the Court in respect of the attendance and examination of witnesses (including the administration of oaths or affirmations and the examination of witnesses abroad) and in respect of the production of documents.

(3) No obligation to maintain secrecy or other restriction upon the disclosure of information obtained by or furnished to persons in Her Majesty's service, whether imposed by any enactment or by any rule of law, shall apply to the disclosure of information for the purposes of an investigation under this Act; and the Crown shall not be entitled in relation to any such investigation to any such privilege in respect of the production of documents or the giving of evidence as is allowed by law in legal proceedings.

(4) No person shall be required or authorised by virtue of this Act to furnish any information or answer any question relating to proceedings of the Cabinet or of any committee of the Cabinet or to produce so much of any document as relates to such proceedings; and for the purposes of this subsection a certificate issued by the Secretary of the Cabinet with the approval of the Prime Minister and certifying that any information, question, document or part of a document so relates shall be conclusive.

(5) Subject to subsection (3) of this section, no person shall be compelled for the purposes of an investigation under this Act to give any evidence or produce any document which he could not be compelled to give or produce in [civil] proceedings before the Court.

Obstruction and Contempt

9. — (1) If any person without lawful excuse obstructs the Commissioner or any officer of the Commissioner in the performance of his functions under this Act, or is guilty of any act or omission in relation to any investigation under this Act which, if that investigation were a proceeding in the Court, would constitute contempt of court, the Commissioner may certify the offence to the Court.

(2) Where an offence is certified under this section, the Court may inquire into the matter and, after hearing any witnesses who may be produced against or on behalf of the person charged with the offence, and after hearing any statement that may be offered in defence, deal with him in any manner in which the Court could deal with him if he had committed the like offence in relation to the Court.

(3) Nothing in this section shall be construed as applying to the taking of any such action as is mentioned in subsection (4) of section 7 of this Act.

Reports by Commissioner

10. — (1) In any case where the Commissioner conducts an investigation under this Act or decides not to conduct such an investigation, he shall send to the member of the House of Commons by whom the request for investigation was made (or if he is no longer a member of that House, to such member of that House as the Commissioner thinks appropriate) a report of the results of the investigation or, as the case may be, a statement of his reasons for not conducting an investigation.

(2) In any case where the Commissioner conducts an investigation under this Act, he shall also send a report of the results of the investigation to the principal officer of the department or authority concerned and to any other person who is alleged in the relevant complaint to have taken or authorised the action complained of.

(3) If, after conducting an investigation under this Act, it appears to the Commissioner that injustice has been caused to the person aggrieved in consequence of maladministration and that the injustice has not been, or will not be, remedied, he may, if he thinks fit, lay before each House of Parliament a special report upon the case.

(4) The Commissioner shall annually lay before each House of Parliament a general report on the performance of his functions under this Act and may from time to time lay before each House of Parliament such other reports with respect to those functions as he thinks fit.

(5) For the purposes of the law of defamation, any such publication as is hereinafter mentioned shall be absolutely privileged, that is to say —

(a)   the publication of any matter by the Commissioner in making a report to either House of Parliament for the purposes of this Act;

(b)   the publication of any matter by a member of the House of Commons in communicating with the Commissioner or his officers for those purposes or by the Commissioner or his officers in communicating with such a member for those purposes;

(c)   the publication by such a member to the person by whom a complaint was made under this Act of a report or statement sent to the member in respect of the complaint in pursuance of section (1) of this section;

(d)   the publication by the Commissioner to such a person as is mentioned in subsection (2) of this section of a report to that person in pursuance of that subsection.

Consultations between Parliamentary Commissioner and Health Service Commissioners

[**11A.** — (1) Where, at any stage in the course of conducting an investigation under this Act, the Commissioner forms the opinions that the complaint relates partly to a matter within the jurisdiction of the Health Service Commissioner for England, Wales or Scotland, he shall —

(a)   unless he also holds office as that Commissioner, consult about the complaint with him; and

(b)   if he considers it necessary, inform the person initiating the complaint under this Act of the steps necessary to initiate a complaint under [the Health Service Commissioners Act 1993].

(2) Where by virtue of subsection (1) above the Commissioner consults with the Health Service Commissioner in relation to a complaint under this Act, he may consult him about any matter relating to the complaint, including —

(a)   the conduct of any investigation into the complaint; and

(b)   the form, content and publication of any report of the results of such an investigation.

(3) Nothing in section 11(2) of this Act shall apply in relation to the disclosure of information by the Commissioner or any of his officers in the course of consultations held in accordance with this section.]

Investigation by the Commissioner

[**11B** — (1) For the purposes of this Act, administrative functions exercisable by an administrator of the Criminal Injuries Compensation Scheme ("Scheme functions") shall be taken to be administrative functions of a government department to which this Act applies.

(2) For the purposes of this section, the following are administrators of the Scheme —

(a)   a claims officer appointed under section 3(4)(b) of the Criminal Injuries Compensation Act 1995;

(b)   a person appointed under section 5(3)(c) of that Act;

(c)   the Scheme manager, as defined by section 1(4) of that Act, and any person assigned by him to exercise functions in relation to the Scheme.

(3) The principal officer in relation to any complaint made in respect of any action taken in respect of Scheme functions is —

Provision for Secrecy of Information

11. — (1)...

(2) Information obtained by the Commissioner or his officers in the course of or for the purposes of an investigation under this Act shall not be disclosed except —

(a)   for the purposes of the investigation and of any report to be made thereon under this Act;

(b)   for the purposes of any proceedings for an offence under [the Official Secrets Act 1911 to 1989] alleged to have been committed in respect of information obtained by the Commissioner or any of his officers by virtue of this Act or for an offence of perjury alleged to have been committed in the course of an investigation under this Act or for the purposes of an inquiry with a view to the taking of such proceedings; or

(c)   for the purposes of any proceedings under section 9 of this Act;

and the Commissioner and his officers shall not be called upon to give evidence in any proceedings (other than such proceedings as aforesaid) of matters coming to his or their knowledge in the course of an investigation under this Act.

[(2A) Where the Commissioner also holds office as a Health Service Commissioner and a person initiates a complaint to him in his capacity as such a Commissioner which relates partly to a matter with respect to which that person has previously initiated a complaint under this Act, or subsequently initiates such a complaint, information obtained by the Commissioner or his officers in the course of or for the purposes of investigating the complaint under this Act may be disclosed for the purposes of his carrying out his functions in relation to the other complaint.]

(3) A Minister of the Crown may give notice in writing to the Commissioner, with respect to any document or information specified in the notice, or any class of documents or information so specified, that in the opinion of the Minister the disclosure of that document or information, or of documents or information of that class, would be prejudicial to the safety of the State or otherwise contrary to the public interest; and where such a notice is given nothing in this Act shall be construed as authorising or requiring the Commissioner or any officer of the Commissioner to communicate to any person or for any purpose any document or information specified in the notice, or any document or information of a class so specified.

(4) The references in this section to a Minister of the Crown include references to the Commissioners of Customs and Excise and the Commissioners of Inland Revenue.

(a)   in the case of action taken by a claims officer, such person as may from time to time be designated by the Secretary of State for the purposes of this paragraph;

(b)   in the case of action taken by a person appointed under section 5(3)(c) of the Act of 1995, the chairman appointed by the Secretary of State under section 5(3)(b) of that Act; or

(c)   in the case of action taken by the Scheme manager or by any other person mentioned in subsection (2)(c) of this section, the Scheme manager.

(4) The conduct of an investigation under this Act in respect of any action taken in respect of Scheme functions shall not affect —

(a)   any action so taken; or

(b)   any power or duty of any person to take further action with respect to any matters subject to investigation.]

Interpretation

12. — (1) In this Act the following expressions have the meanings hereby respectively assigned to them, that is to say —

'action' includes failure to act, and other expressions connoting action shall be construed accordingly;

'the Commissioner' means the Parliamentary Commissioner for Administration;

'the Court' means, in relation to England and Wales the High Court, in relation to Scotland the Court of Session, and in relation to Northern Ireland the High Court of Northern Ireland;

'enactment' includes an enactment of the Parliament of Northern Ireland and any instrument made by virtue of an enactment;

'officer' includes employee;

'person aggrieved' means the person who claims or is alleged to have sustained such injustice as is mentioned in section 5(1)(a) of this Act;

'tribunal' includes the person constituting a tribunal consisting of one person.

(2) References to this Act to any enactment are references to that enactment as amended or extended by or under any other enactment.

(3) It is hereby declared that nothing in this Act authorises or requires the Commissioner to question the merits of a decision taken without maladministration by a government department or other authority in the exercise of a discretion vested in that department or authority...

Schedule 2

DEPARTMENTS, ETC., SUBJECT TO INVESTIGATION

Note

As amended by the Parliamentary Commissioner Order 1999 (S.I. 1999 No. 277), with effect from
    March 15, 1999.

Accounts Commission for Scotland
Advisory Board on Family Law
Advisory Committee on Novel Foods and Processes
Advisory, Conciliation and Arbitration Service
Advisory Council on Public Records
Agricultural Dwelling House Advisory Committees
Agricultural Wages Committees
Ministry of Agriculture, Fisheries and Food
Apple and Pear Research Council
Arts Council of England
Arts Council of Great Britain
Arts Council of Wales (Cyngor Celfyddydau Cymru)
Scottish Arts Council
Authorised Conveyancing Practitioners Board
Boundary Commission for Northern Ireland
British Council
British Educational Communications and Technology Agency
British Hallmarking Council
British Library Board
British Museum
British Potato Council
British Tourist Authority
Broadcasting Standards Commission
Building Societies Commission
Bwrdd yr Iaith Gymraeg (Welsh Language Board)
Certification Officer
Charity Commission
Central Rail Users' Consultative Committee
Civil Aviation Authority
Civil Justice Council
Civil Service Commission
Clinical Standards Advisory Group
Coal Authority
Commissioner for Protection Against Unlawful Industrial Action

Commissioner for the Rights of Trade Union Members
Committee for Monitoring Agreements on Tobacco Advertising and Sponsorship
Committee of Investigation for Great Britain
Committee on Standards in Public Life
Commonwealth Institute
Commonwealth Scholarship Commission in the United Kingdom
Community Development Foundation
Consumer Panel
Consumers' Committee for Great Britain under the Agricultural Marketing Act 1958
Co-operative Development Agency
Countryside Commission
Countryside Council for Wales
Crafts Council
Crofters Commission
Crown Estate Office
Customs and Excise
Data Protection Registrar
Ministry of Defence
Design Council
Development Commission
Docklands Light Railway
East Midlands Region Electricity Consumers' Committee
Eastern Region Electricity Consumers' Committee
Education Assets Board
Central Bureau for Educational Visits and Exchanges
Office of the Director General of Electricity Supply
The Department for Education and Employment
English National Board for Nursing, Midwifery and Health Visiting
Environment Agency
Equal Opportunities Commission
Export Credits Guarantee Department
Office of the Director General of Fair Trading
British Film Institute
Fleet Air Arm Museum
Food Advisory Committee
Food from Britain
Football Licensing Authority
Foreign and Commonwealth Office
Forestry Commission
Friendly Societies Commission
Registry of Friendly Societies
Further Education Funding Council for England
Gas Consumers' Council
Office of the Director General of Gas Supply
Geffrye Museum
Gene Therapy Advisory Committee
General Teaching Council for Scotland
The Great Britain-China Centre
Health and Safety Commission
Health and Safety Executive
Department of Health
Higher Education Funding Council for England
Historic Buildings and Monuments Commission for England
Historic Royal Palaces
Home Office
Home-Grown Cereals Authority
Horniman Museum and Gardens
Horserace Betting Levy Board
Horticultural Development Council

Housing Corporation
Housing for Wales
Human Fertilisation and Embryology Authority
Imperial War Museum
Central Office of Information
Inland Revenue
The International Rail Regulator
Intervention Board for Agricultural Produce
Investors in People UK
Land Registry
Legal Aid Board
The following general lighthouse authorities —
(a) the Corporation of the Trinity House of Deptford Strond;
(b) the Commissioners of Northern Lighthouses
Local Government Boundary Commission for Scotland
Local Government Commission for England
London Region Electricity Consumers' Committee
London Regional Passengers' Committee
Lord Chancellor's Advisory Committee on Legal Education and Conduct
Lord Chancellor's Department
Lord President of the Council's Office
Marshall Aid Commemoration Commission
Meat and Livestock Commission
Medical Practices Committee
Scottish Medical Practices Committee
Medical Workforce Standing Advisory Committee
Merseyside and North Wales Region Electricity Consumers' Committee
Midlands Region Electricity Consumers' Committee
Milk Development Council
Millennium Commission
Monopolies and Mergers Commission
Museum of London
Museum of Science and Industry in Manchester
Museums and Galleries Commission
National Army Museum
National Biological Standards Board (UK)
National Consumer Council
National Debt Office
National Employers' Liaison Committee
National Endowment for Science, Technology and the Arts
National Film and Television School
National Forest Company
National Gallery
National Galleries of Scotland
Department of National Heritage
Trustees of the National Heritage Memorial Fund
Office of the Director General of the National Lottery
National Library of Scotland
National Lottery Charities Board
National Maritime Museum
National Museum of Science and Industry
National Museums of Scotland
National Museums and Galleries on Merseyside
National Portrait Gallery
National Radiological Protection Board
National Rivers Authority
Department for National Savings
Office for National Statistics
Natural History Museum

Nature Conservancy Council for England
Joint Nature Conservation Committee
New Millennium Experience Company Ltd
New Opportunities Fund
Commission for the New Towns
Development corporations for new towns
North Eastern Region Electricity Consumers' Committee
North Western Region Electricity Consumers' Committee
Northern Ireland Court Service
Northern Ireland Human Rights Commission
Northern Ireland Office
Occupational Pensions Board
Occupational Pensions Regulatory Authority
Oil and Pipelines Agency
Ordnance Survey
Parliamentary Boundary Commission for England
Parliamentary Boundary Commission for Wales
Parole Board
Parole Board for Scotland
Director of Passenger Rail Franchising
Pensions Compensation Board.
Office of Population Censuses and Surveys
Post Office Users' Council for Northern Ireland
Post Office Users' Council for Scotland
Post Office Users' Council for Wales
Post Office Users' National Council
Probation Board for Northern Ireland
Office of the Commissioner for Protection Against Unlawful Industrial Action
Registrar of Public Lending Right
Public Record Office
Office of Public Service ...
Qualifications Curriculum Authority
Commission for Racial Equality
Rail Regulator
Central Rail Users' Consultative Committee
Rail Users' Consultative Committee for Eastern England
Rail Users' Consultative Committee for North Eastern England
Rail Users' Consultative Committee for North Western England
Rail Users' Consultative Committee for Scotland
Rail Users' Consultative Committee for Southern England
Rail Users' Consultative Committee for the Midlands
Rail Users' Consultative Committee for Wales
Rail Users' Consultative Committee for Western England
Red Deer Commission
Department of the Registers of Scotland
General Register Office, Scotland
Remploy Ltd
Biotechnology and Biological Sciences Research Council
Economic and Social Research Council
Engineering and Physical Sciences Research Council
Medical Research Council
Natural Environment Research Council
Particle Physics and Astronomy Research Council
Council for the Central Laboratory of the Research Councils
Residuary Bodies
Reviewing Committee on the Export of Works of Art
Office of the Commissioners for the Rights of Trade Union Members
Royal Air Force Museum
Royal Armouries Museum

Royal Botanic Garden, Edinburgh
Royal Botanic Gardens, Kew
Royal Commission on Historical Manuscripts
Royal Commission on the Ancient and Historical Monuments of Scotland
Royal Commission on the Historical Monuments of England
Royal Marines Museum
Royal Mint
Royal Naval Museum
Royal Navy Submarine Museum
Office of Her Majesty's Chief Inspector of Schools in England
Office of Her Majesty's Chief Inspector of Schools in Wales
Scientific Committee on Tobacco and Health
Scottish Agricultural Wages Board
Scottish Children's Reporter Administration
Scottish Community Education Council
Scottish Consultative Council on the Curriculum
Scottish Council for Educational Technology
Scottish Courts Administration
Scottish Environment Protection Agency
Scottish Homes
Scottish Further Education Funding Council
Scottish Further Education Unit
Scottish Higher Education Funding Council
Scottish Legal Aid Board
Scottish Natural Heritage
Scottish Office
Scottish Qualifications Authority
Scottish Record Office
Scottish Screen Ltd
Scottish Studentship Selection Committee
Scottish Water and Sewerage Customers' Council
Sea Fish Industry Authority
Sir John Soane's Museum
Council for Small Industries in Rural Areas
Department of Social Security
Central Council for Education and Training in Social Work
South Eastern Region Electricity Consumers' Committee
South of Scotland Region Electricity Consumers' Committee
South Wales Region Electricity Consumers' Committee
South Western Region Electricity Consumers' Committee
Southern Region Electricity Consumers' Committee
Sports Council
Scottish Sports Council
Sports Council for Wales
Staff Commission for Wales (Comisiwn Staff Cymru)
Standing Dental Advisory Committee
Standing Medical Advisory Committee
Standing Nursing and Midwifery Advisory Committee
Standing Pharmaceutical Advisory Committee
Stationery Office
Tate Gallery
Teacher Training Agency
Office of the Director General of Telecommunication
English Tourist Board
Scottish Tourist Board
Wales Tourist Board
Board of Trade
Department of Trade and Industry
The Simpler Trade Procedures Board

Traffic Director for London
Agricultural Training Board
Clothing and Allied Products Industry Training Board
Construction Industry Training Board
Engineering Industry Training Board
Hotel and Catering Industry Training Board
Plastics Processing Industry Training Board
Road Transport Industry Training Board
Department of Transport
Treasure Valuation Committee
Treasury
Treasury Solicitor
United Kingdom Atomic Energy Authority
United Kingdom Ecolabelling Board
United Kingdom Register of Organic Food Standards
United Kingdom Xenotransplantation Interim Regulatory Authority
Unrelated Live Transplant Regulatory Authority
Urban development corporations
Urban Regeneration Agency
Victoria and Albert Museum
Wallace Collection
Development Board for Rural Wales
War Pensions Committees
Office of the Director General of Water Services
Welsh Office
Westminster Foundation for Democracy
Wine Standards Board of the Vintners' Company
Women's National Commission
Yorkshire Region Electricity Consumers' Committee
Youth Justice Board"

Schedule 3

MATTERS NOT SUBJECT TO INVESTIGATION

1. Action taken in matters certified by a Secretary of State or other Minister of the Crown to affect relations or dealings between the Government of the United Kingdom and any other Government or any international organisation of States or Governments.

2. Action taken, in any country or territory outside the United Kingdom, by or on behalf of any officer representing or acting under the authority of Her Majesty in respect of the United Kingdom, or any other officer of the Government of the United Kingdom other than action which is taken by an officer (not being an honorary consular officer) in the exercise of a consular function on behalf of the Government of the United Kingdom ...

3. Action taken in connection with the administration of the government of any country or territory outside the United Kingdom which forms part of Her Majesty's dominions or in which Her Majesty has jurisdiction.

4. Action taken by the Secretary of State under the Extradition Act 1870 or the Fugitive Offenders Act 1881, the Fugitive Offenders Act 1967 or the Extradition Act 1989.

5. Action taken by or with the authority of the Secretary of State for the purposes of investigating crime or of protecting the security of the State, including action so taken with respect to passports.

6. The commencement or conduct of civil or criminal proceedings before any court of law in the United Kingdom, of proceedings at any place under the Naval Discipline Act 1957, the Army Act 1955 or the Air Force Act 1955, or of proceedings before any international court or tribunal.

6A. Action taken by any person appointed by the Lord Chancellor as a member of the administrative staff of any court or tribunal, so far as that action is taken at the direction, or on the authority (whether express or implied), of any person acting in a judicial capacity or in his capacity as a member of the tribunal.

6B. — (1) Action taken by any member of the administrative staff of a relevant tribunal, so far as that action is taken at the direction, or on the authority (whether express or implied), of any person acting in his capacity as a member of the tribunal.

(2) In this paragraph, 'relevant tribunal' has the meaning given by section 5(8) of this Act.

6C. Action taken by any person appointed under section 5(3)(c) of the Criminal Injuries Compensation Act 1995, so far as that action is taken at the direction, or on the authority (whether express or implied), of any person acting in his capacity as an adjudicator appointed under section 5 of that Act to determine appeals.

7. Any exercise of the prerogative of mercy or of the power of a Secretary of State to make a reference in respect of any person to the Court of Appeal, the High Court of Justiciary or the Courts-Martial Appeal Court.

8. Action taken on behalf of the Minister of Health or the Secretary of State by a Regional Health Authority, an Area Health Authority, a District Health Authority, a special health authority, except the Rampton Hospital Review Board… the Rampton Hospital Board, the Broadmoor Hospital Board or the Moss Side and Park Lane Hospitals Board, a Family Practitioner Committee, a Health Board or the Common Services Agency for the Scottish Health Service, by the Dental Practice Board or the Scottish Dental Practice Board, or by the Public Health Laboratory Service Board.

9. Action taken in matters relating to contractual or other commercial transactions, whether within the United Kingdom or elsewhere, being transactions of a government department or authority to which this Act applies or of any such authority or body as is mentioned in paragraph (a) or (b) of subsection (1) of section 6 of this Act and not being transactions for or relating to —

(a)   the acquisition of land compulsorily or in circumstances in which it could be acquired compulsorily;

(b)   the disposal as surplus of land acquired compulsorily or in such circumstances as aforesaid.

10. — (1) Action taken in respect of appointments or removals, pay, discipline, superannuation or other personnel matters, in relation to —

(a)   service in any of the armed forces of the Crown, including reserve and auxiliary and cadet forces,

(b)   service in any office or employment under the Crown or under any authority to which this Act applies; or

(c)   service in any office or employment, or under any contract for services, in respect of which power to take action, or to determine or approve the action to be taken, in such matters is vested in Her Majesty, any Minister of the Crown or any such authority as aforesaid.

(2) Sub-paragraph (1)(c) above shall not apply to any action (not otherwise excluded from investigation by this Schedule) which is taken by the Secretary of State in connection with:

(a)   the provision of information relating to the terms and conditions of any employment covered by an agreement entered into by him under section 12(1) of the Overseas Development and Cooperation Act 1980 or

(b)   the provision of any allowance, grant or supplement or any benefit (other than those relating to superannuation) arising from the designation of any person in accordance with such an agreement.

11. The grant of honours, awards or privileges within the gift of the Crown, including the grant of Royal Charters."

Notes

16–3   (1) The bodies in Schedule 2 include those now subject to the PCA's jurisdiction by virtue of the Parliamentary Commissioner Order 1999. "Maladministration" was the key concept in determining the jurisdiction of the Ombudsman as he came to be known, during the passage of the 1967 Act. The Leader of the House of Commons, Richard Crossman M.P., accepted that there was no definition of maladministration contained in the Act but suggested that maladministration could include "bias, neglect, inattention, delay, incompetence, inaptitude, perversity, turpitude, arbitrariness, and so on": H.C. Deb., Vol. 754, col. 51 (1966). This description is sometimes known as the "Crossman catalogue". The concept itself had its origins in the important JUSTICE report, The Citizen and Administration (1961). The underlying emphasis was that the concept did not allow the Commissioner to encroach readily upon the exercise of discretionary power by examining the merits of the decisions. From time to time criticism of the concept has been raised. G. Marshall, "Maladminstration" [1973] P.L. 32 concluded (at 34) that "the view (that certainly follows from the Crossman catalogue approach) that maladministration may be inferred from, and can consist in, a complete lack of merits implies that the distinction between merits and maladministration drawn in the 1967 Act is incoherent...".

In 1977 JUSTICE issued a report, Our Fettered Ombudsman, suggesting, as did Marshall, that maladministration should be abandoned and that the PCA should investigate "unreasonable, unjust, or oppressive action" by government departments. This view was rejected by the Select Committee on the PCA as it did not believe that the creation of a new jurisdiction would enable the Parliamentary Commissioner to deal with any matter that had not already come under his authority: Review of Access and Jurisdiction (1977–78 H.C. 615). In 1994 the PCA, while expressing the view that the definition of maladministration is inherently limited, suggested that the Crossman catalogue could be supplemented with other examples, including unwillingness to treat the complainants with respect; refusal to answer reasonable questions; knowingly giving advice which was misleading or inadequate; and showing bias, whether on terms of colour, race, sex or other grounds: see Annual Report for 1993–94, para 7: (1993–94 H.C. 290). The courts have also recognised the open-ended nature of the term: see, for example, Lord Denning M.R's discussion in *R. v. Local Commissioner for Administration for the North and East area of England, ex parte Bradford Metropolitan City Council* [1979] Q.B. 287.

(2) It was clearly the intention of Parliament that the work of the PCA was to be confined to matters of procedure, and this is clearly borne out by section 12 (3). A classic example of procedural error occurred in the *Sachsenhausen* case reported in the Special Report of the PCA (1967 H.C. 54). Twelve victims of Nazi persecution had been denied compensation by the Foreign Office under its rules of distribution and the PCA found that there had been many procedural defects which had led to the reputations of the claimants being damaged. The Foreign Secretary argued that the principle of a ministerial responsibility was being eroded by the investigation but the Select Committee stressed the importance of the role of the PCA in examining complaints of this kind: (1967–68 H.C. 258), paras 13–16. From time to time the PCA does, however, accept that his remit includes the so-called "bad decision or bad rule". A bad decision is one "which, judged by its effect on the aggrieved person appears to be thoroughly bad in quality, he might infer from the quality of the decision itself that there had been an element of maladministration in the taking of it and asked for its review": para. 14.

The bad rule arises where injustice and hardship are caused despite the fact that the rules had been properly applied: para. 17. For further comment see A.W. Bradley, "The Role of the Ombudsman in Relation to the Protection of Citizens' Rights" (1980) 39 C.L.J. 304.

For a further consideration of the way in which the concept of maladministration has been used see the discussion below on the casework of the Ombudsman.

(3) In 1993 the Select Committee on the PCA published a report on The Powers, Work and Jurisdiction of the Ombudsman (1993–94 H.C. 33). Among its recommendations were that complainants should continue to be referred by M.Ps. This was because this filter was supported by M.Ps themselves and also because of the constitutional argument that the M.P. had a special role in pursuing complaints on behalf of the public against the Executive "notwithstanding the development within public bodies of an array of direct access complaint and redress mechanisms for the citizen": para. 75. The committee also felt that the Ombudsman should be able to act where a matter was raised with him by the committee even though no individual complaint had been made to any M.P., and moreover that as the "current system of jurisdiction is both bureaucratic and confusing" (para. 50), the 1967 Act should be amended to provide that the PCA would have jurisdiction over all central government bodies unless specifically excluded. The Government was unwilling to accept the proposal for complaints being activated by the committee as it would "represent a fundamental change in the concept that his basic role is to investigate and suggest redress for people's grievances" (1993–94 H.C. 619), para. 18 and that with regard to the proposed jurisdictional change the Government would "look carefully" at that proposal but priority should be given to publicising the existing jurisdiction of the Ombudsman. The Select Committee returned to some of the issues raised in its 1993 Report in its First Report for the session 1998–99; H.C. 136. It was concerned about the apparent fall in

16–4

the number of cases received by the PCA in the period covered by his 1997–98 Report. In particular, in every year up to 1996 his workload rose, but in 1997 it fell. For example, in 1996 he was considering 2,816 cases, 1,933 of which were new but in the period covered by the report, of the 2,551 cases being investigated only 1,459 were new. The Ombudsman could only speculate about the reasons in his discussion with the committee (at para. 5):

> "Is it the new Parliament, a lot of new M.Ps who may have a different method of working? Is it that they do not understand what my office can do? Is it that they are dissatisfied with the service we provide, in which case we had better do something about it?"

The committee was sufficiently concerned that it wrote to all members reminding them of the service provided by the Ombudsman but it also queried whether the "MP filter" was the best way of ensuring that the complaints were properly dealt with. This is a topic which it hopes to address in a forthcoming inquiry.

(4) Another trend in recent years has been the creation of internal complaints to officers or ombudsmen. These individuals have different powers and titles. The Inland Revenue and the Customs and Excise have an "adjudicator" and Companies House has a "complaints adjudicator". The Select Committee on the PCA has criticised such persons being termed Ombudsman when the department or agency in question is subject to the jurisdiction of the PCA (1993–94 H.C. 33), para. 28. Notwithstanding the creation of these officials, the jurisdiction of the PCA in these departments is still active. For further discussion see D. Oliver, "The Revenue Adjudicator: A new breed of Ombudsperson?" [1993] P.L. 407 and P.E. Morris, "The Revenue Adjudicator — The First Two Years" [1996] P.L. 309. Morris concluded (at 321) that the scheme is to be praised for its openness, fairness and effectiveness but had concerns over perceived independence and accountability.

THE WORK OF THE PARLIAMENTARY
COMMISSIONER — WORKLOAD

PCA Annual Report for 1997–98

(1998–99 H.C. 846)

[See diagram on opposite page.]

Cases received, screened and investigated 16–15

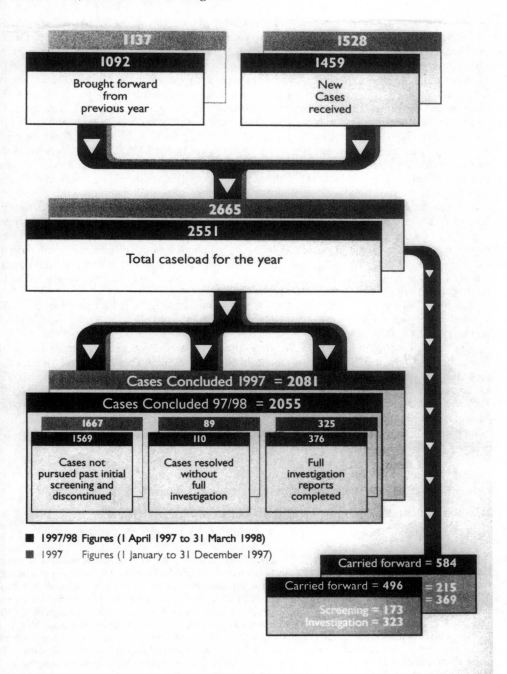

1137
1092
Brought forward
from
previous year

1528
1459
New
Cases
received

2665
2551
Total caseload for the year

Cases Concluded 1997 = 2081
Cases Concluded 97/98 = 2055

1667
1569
Cases not
pursued past initial
screening and
discontinued

89
110
Cases resolved
without
full
investigation

325
376
Full
investigation
reports
completed

■ 1997/98 Figures (1 April 1997 to 31 March 1998)
■ 1997   Figures (1 January to 31 December 1997)

Carried forward = 584
= 215
= 369

Carried forward = 496
Screening = 173
Investigation = 323

Notes

16–6   (1) 2,551 complaints were received by the PCA of which 1,679 were rejected or discontinued. 716 complaints did not relate to administrative matters; 204 complaints related to issues where the complainant had a right of appeal to a tribunal; 107 complaints were outside the PCA's jurisdiction; and 27 complaints involved public service personnel matters. The workload of the PCA peaked in 1996 with 2,816 cases being investigated, on which see 1995–96 H.C. 296. We have already noted the concerns of the Select Committee on possible reasons why there was a drop in the PCA's workload. Apart from the problems associated with the M.P. filter, the committee is also concerned that the public may be dissatisfied with the service and are simply not using it. It cites delay in completing investigations as a possible reason. In 1992, for example, the average time taken to investigate was 53 weeks, but in 1997–98 it was 100 weeks. While there are often reasons explaining delay in individual cases, the committee went on to recommend that the Ombudsman should set, as his ultimate aim, that all cases should be resolved within six months of their arrival in his office and that the Government and he should work together to eliminate obstacles in achieving this aim. Among key issues raised in achieving this include the resources available to him, particularly staff, and that the departments should respond fully and urgently to requests for information, one of the "good reasons" for delay: para. 9. It also went on to recommend that in his next Annual Report, the Ombudsman should provide a table showing the age profile of cases currently under investigation. This is because to date, Annual Reports simply indicate how many cases are received in any one year and are carried forward to the next year, but not the age of the cases: para. 10.

(2) In 212 of the cases upheld by the PCA as demonstrating maladministration, a remedy beyond simply an apology was obtained. Financial redress varied from £6.02 to £50,044.30 and totalled £437,000.

(3) The Department of Social Security and its related agencies accounted for 1,243 complaints, of which 578 related to the Child Support Agency. Two complaints were made against the Scottish Legal Aid Board and 23 complaints were outstanding against the Scottish Office, of which 16 were rejected or discontinued. On average, complaints made against the DSS and the Inland Revenue amounted to almost 50 per cent of all complaints. The administration of social security and the Inland Revenue are, with minor exceptions, not within the devolved competence of the Scottish Parliament and the Scottish Executive.

THE WORK OF THE PARLIAMENTARY
COMMISSIONER — CASE WORK

R. v. Parliamentary Commissioner for Administration, ex parte Dyer

[1994] 1 All E.R. 375

16–7   "Miss Dyer had complained to her M.P. (Rt Hon. Roy Hattersley) about a number of matters concerning her claims for various benefits administered by the Department of Social Security. Mr Hattersley had referred her complaints to the P.C.A. who had decided to investigate some of them. In his report the P.C.A. found that Miss Dyer had suffered maladministration and he criticised the local office of the Department for various mistakes in its handling of her claims. The Department apologised and made an *ex gratia* payment of £500. The P.C.A. considered these remedies to be a satisfactory outcome to his investigation. However, Miss Dyer was not satisfied and sought judicial review of the P.C.A.'s decision not to reopen his investigation into her complaints. She alleged that the P.C.A. had acted unlawfully by: (1) deciding to investigate some of her original complaints (rather than investigating all of them), (2) giving the Department an opportunity to comment on the factual accuracy of his draft report (whilst denying her such an opportunity) and (3) regarding himself as being precluded from reopening an investigation once he had issued a report."

SIMON BROWN L.J.: "…This is the first substantive application for judicial review of the P.C.A. to come before the courts (an application for leave in an earlier case having been refused). The first question raised for decision upon it concerns the proper ambit of this court's supervisory jurisdiction over the

P.C.A. Mr Stephen Richards on his behalf submits to us that, certainly so far as the P.C.A.'s discretionary powers are concerned, this court has no review jurisdiction whatever over their exercise. In the alternative he submits that the court should intervene only in the most exceptional cases of abuse of discretion, essentially on the same limited basis held by the House of Lords in *Nottinghamshire C.C. v. Secretary of State for the Environment* [1986] 1 All E.R. 199; [1986] A.C. 240 and *Hammersmith and Fulham London B.C. v. Secretary of State for the Environment* [1990] 3 All E.R. 589; [1991] 1 A.C. 521 to be appropriate in the particular area of decision-making there in question.

The resolution of this initial jurisdictional issue clearly depends essentially on the legislation which created the P.C.A.'s office and governs the discharge of his functions...

As to his wider proposition — that this court has literally no right to review the P.C.A.'s exercise of his discretion under the 1967 Act (not even, to give the classic illustration, if he refused to investigate complaints by red-headed complainants) — Mr Richards submits that the legislation is enacted in such terms as to indicate an intention that the P.C.A. should be answerable to Parliament alone for the way he performs his functions. The P.C.A. is, he suggests, an officer of the House of Commons, and, the argument runs, the parliamentary control provided for by the statute displaces any supervisory control by the courts. Mr Richards relies in particular on these considerations: first, the stipulation under s.5 that a complaint must be referred to the P.C.A. by a member of Parliament before even his powers of investigation are engaged; second, the requirement under s. 10(1) to report back to the member of Parliament (and, in certain circumstances, to each House of Parliament — see s.10(3)); third, the requirement under s.10(4) annually to lay a general report before Parliament; fourth, the provision under s.1(3) of the Act for the P.C.A.'s removal from office only in the event of addresses from both Houses of Parliament. Mr Richards points also to the P.C.A. being always answerable to the select committee.

Despite these considerations I, for my part, would unhesitatingly reject this argument. Many in government are answerable to Parliament and yet answerable also to the supervisory jurisdiction of this court. I see nothing about the P.C.A.'s role or the statutory framework within which he operates so singular as to take him wholly outside the purview of judicial review.

I turn next, therefore, to Mr Richard's alternative and narrower submission that, by analogy with the two House of Lords cases already mentioned, the courts should regard their powers as restricted with regard to reviewing the P.C.A.'s exercise of the discretions conferred upon him by this legislation.

I need cite one passage only from the speeches in those two cases, this from Lord Bridge's speech in *Hammersmith and Fulham London B.C.v. Secretary of State for the Environment* [1990] 3 All E.R. 589 at 637; [1991] 1 A.C. 521 at 597:

> 'The restriction which the *Nottinghamshire* case [1986] 1 All E.R. 199; [1986] A.C. 240 imposes on the scope of judicial review operates only when the court has first determined that the ministerial action in question does not contravene the requirements of the statute, whether express or implied, and only then declares that, since the statute has conferred a power on the Secretary of State which involves the formulation and the implementation of national economic policy and which can only take effect with the approval of the House of Commons, it is not open to challenge on the grounds of irrationality short of the extremes of bad faith, improper motive or manifest absurdity. Both the constitutional propriety and the good sense of this restriction seem to me to be clear enough. The formulation and the implementation of national economic policy are matters depending essentially on political judgment. The decisions which shape them are for politicians to take and it is in the political forum of the House of Commons that they are properly to be debated and approved or disapproved on their merits. If the decisions have been taken in good faith within the four corners of the Act, the merits of the policy underlying the decisions are not susceptible to review by the courts and the courts would be exceeding their proper function if they presumed to condemn the policy as unreasonable.'

Mr Richards concedes that the analogy between the position considered there and that arising here is not a very close one. He submits, however, that the underlying rationale for restricting the scope of judicial review in those cases applies also here. Although, as counsel recognises, the P.C.A.'s functions are manifestly not political, nevertheless, he submits, the provisions here for parliamentary control afford this case a comparable dimension.

This submission too I would reject. There seems to me no parallel whatever between, on the one hand, decisions regarding the formulation and implementation of national economic policy — decisions 'depending essentially on political judgment... for politicians to take... in the political forum of the House of Commons' — and, on the other hand, decisions of the P.C.A. regarding the matters appropriate for investigation and the proper manner of their investigation.

All that said, however, and despite my rejection of both Mr Richard's submissions on the question of jurisdiction, it does not follow that this court will readily be persuaded to interfere with the exercise of the P.C.A.'s discretion. Quite the contrary. The intended width of these discretions is made strikingly clear by the legislature: under s.5(5), when determining whether to initiate, continue or discontinue an investigation, the commissioner shall 'act in accordance with his own discretion'; under s. 7(2), 'the procedure for conducting an investigation shall be such as the commissioner considers appropriate in the circumstances of the case'. Bearing in mind too that the exercise of these particular discretions inevitably involves a high degree of subjective judgment, it follows that it will always be difficult to mount an effective challenge on what may be called the conventional ground of *Wednesbury* unreasonableness (see *Associated Provincial Picture Houses Ltd v. Wednesbury Corp.* [1947] 2 All E.R. 680; [1948] 1 K.B. 223).

Recognising this, indeed, one may pause to wonder whether in reality the end result is much different from that arrived at by the House of Lords in the two cases referred to, where the decisions in question were held 'not open to challenge on the grounds of irrationality short of the extremes of bad faith, improper motive or manifest absurdity'. True, in the present case 'manifest absurdity' does not have to be shown; but inevitably it will be almost as difficult to demonstrate that the P.C.A. has exercised one or other of his discretions unreasonably in the public law sense…

Recognising the full width of our jurisdiction but with those considerations in mind I turn to Miss Dyer's grounds of challenge.

As to her contention that the P.C.A. investigated some only of her original grounds of complaint, that is undoubtedly the case. But is she entitled to criticise the P.C.A. for taking that course? More particularly, was the P.C.A. acting outside the proper ambit of his discretion under s.5(5) of the 1967 Act in doing so?…

In my judgment, the P.C.A. was entitled in the exercise of his discretion to limit the scope of his investigation, to be selective as to just which of Miss Dyer's many detailed complaints he addressed, to identify certain broad categories of complaint (the six main aspects as he called them) and investigate only those. Inevitably such an approach carried the risk that some of the problems which Miss Dyer complained of having experienced with the local office would continue, and that indeed is what Miss Dyer says has occurred. But no investigation should be expected to solve all problems for all time and it cannot in my judgment be said that the approach adopted here by the P.C.A. was not one properly open to him.

Turning to Miss Dyer's complaint that the draft report was sent to the department for comment on the facts but not to her, the respondent's evidence indicates that this is a practice which has existed for 25 years, and is known to and acquiesced in by the select committee. The reasons for it are explained as follows. First, that it is the department rather than the complainant who may subsequently be called upon to justify its actions before the select committee and, if it is shown the draft report and does not point out any inaccuracy, it will then be unable to dispute the facts stated in it. Second, the practice affords the department an opportunity to give notice in writing to the P.C.A., as expressly provided for by s.11(3) of the 1967 Act, of any document or information the disclosure of which, in the opinion of the relevant minister, would be prejudicial to the safety of the state or otherwise contrary to the public interest. Third, sight of the draft report gives the department the opportunity to propose the remedy it is prepared to offer in the light of any findings of maladministration and injustice contained in it. The commissioner can then include in his final report what that proposed remedy is and indicate whether he finds that it satisfactorily meets the need.

Miss Dyer recognises, I think, that the same reasons do not exist for sending the draft report to her. Indeed, having regard to s.11(3), it could not be sent to her unless and until it had already been cleared by the department. Therefore, to graft on to the existing practice a need to show the draft report to complainants too would introduce a further stage into the process. Does natural justice require this? I do not think so. As Lord Bridge said in *Lloyd v. McMahon* [1987] 1 All E.R. 1118 at 1161; [1987] A.C. 625 at 702:

> 'My Lords, the so-called rules of natural justice are not engraved on tablets of stone. To use the phrase which better expresses the underlying concept, what the requirements of fairness demand when any body, domestic, administrative or judicial, has to make a decision which will affect the rights of individuals depends on the character of the decision-making body, the kind of decision it has to make and the statutory or other framework in which it operates.'

Assuming, as I do, and indeed as Mr Richards concedes, that the P.C.A. makes 'a decision which will affect the rights of' Miss Dyer, it should nevertheless be borne in mind that it is the department and not her who is being investigated and who is liable to face public criticism for its acts. I cannot conclude that fairness here demanded that she too be shown the draft report. Rather it seems to me that the P.C.A., in determining the procedure for conducting his investigation as provided for by s.7(2), was amply entitled to consider it appropriate to follow his long-established practice.

I come finally to Miss Dyer's complaint about the P.C.A.'s refusal to reopen this investigation. This I can deal with altogether more shortly. It seems to me that the P.C.A. is clearly correct in his view that, once his report had been sent to Mr Hattersley and the DSS (as required by s.10(1) and (2)), he was *functus officio* and unable to reopen the investigation without a further referral under s.5(1). Section 5(5), as already indicated, confers a wide discretion indeed; it does not, however, purport to empower the P.C.A. to reopen an investigation once his report is submitted. It would seem to me unfair to the department and outside the scheme of this legislation to suppose that the P.C.A. could do as Miss Dyer wished…

It follows that, in my judgment, none of Miss Dyer's grounds of challenge can be made good and this application accordingly fails…"

Notes

(1) In an article, "The extent and depth of judicial review of the decisions of the Parliamentary Commissioner for Administration" [1994] P.L. 347, by Norman Marsh, chairman of the committee which had proposed the creation of the PCA, Simon Brown L.J's reasoning concerning Miss Dyer's allegation that it was unlawful for the PCA to allow the department to comment on the actual accuracy of his draft reports was criticised (at 349):

16–8

> "The impression given by this part of Simon Brown L.J.'s judgment is almost that the underlying purpose of the Parliamentary Commissioner Act is to give government departments a better opportunity to refute accusations of maladministration made against them."

(2) Although the basis for judicial review is of course different in England, it is quite clear that the jurisdiction exercised by the PCA falls within the Lord President's description of a jurisdiction amenable to judicial review discussed in *West v. Secretary of State for Scotland*, 1992 S.L.T. 636, extracted at para.10–7. The first judicial review of a report issued by the PCA occurred in *R. v. Parliamentary Commissioner for Administration, ex parte Balchin* [1996] E.G.C.S. 166, Q.B.D. *per* Sedley J. Here the complainant's home had been affected by planning blight caused by a proposed road scheme. The complaint was about the actions of the Department of Transport which had confirmed the scheme. The PCA rejected the applicant's complaints but the court held that he had acted unlawfully in failing to have regard to the relevant consideration of whether, if the department had brought a new statutory power to pay compensation to property owners to the attention of the highway authority, then the applicant might have received compensation.

(3) As we have noted, an investigation by the PCA takes an average of 100 weeks to complete and this is one of the reasons why many M.Ps do not refer more cases to him: R. Mays, "25 years of the Ombudsman" (1992) 195 SCOLAG 185. Note also the results of a questionnaire survey by the Select Committee where 54.3 per cent of M.Ps stated that they "never" or "hardly ever" read PCA reports (1993–94 H.C. 33-I), para. 25 and see also R. Rawlings, "The MP's Complaints Service" (1990) 53 M.L.R. 22 and 149. The PCA responded to the issue of delay in completing investigations by reporting in 1993 that where a department offers immediate redress to a complainant after the approach by the PCA he will pass information on immediately to the M.P. and so a complainant may receive redress well in advance of completion of the formal investigation: Select Committee Report on Powers, Functions and Jurisdiction of the PCA, Vol. I (1993–1994 H.C. 33-I), p. VIII. The PCA has set himself a target of nine months for completion of investigation: Annual Report 1994, App. B.

(4) The most detailed report produced by the PCA to date concerned the Barlow Clowes affair of 1989. The Barlow Clowes companies collapsed in 1989 leaving many elderly people without savings. Many of these people thought that they were investing in safe government stocks. A quarter of all M.Ps received complaints from around 18,000 savers affected by the collapse and 12 M.Ps referred the matter to the PCA. Barlow Clowes had been set up in the 1970s and at that time the Department of Trade and Industry was required by the Prevention of Fraud (Investments) Act 1958 to perform the regulatory function of inspection and the issuing

of licences for those providing investment opportunities. The DTI had allowed the company to operate for 10 years without a licence. In 1984 the company applied for a licence and the DTI tried to bring it within the framework. The licence was granted in 1985 and was renewed until 1987. The existence of a partnership operating in Jersey came to light and the licence was withdrawn on that basis. The Jersey firm was significantly involved in the fraud. The PCA found substantial maladministration in five crucial areas. The Government rejected most of the criticisms of the DTI but agreed to make *ex gratia* payments of almost £150 million. For discussion and analysis see W. Wade and C. Forsyth, *Administrative Law* (7th ed., 1994), p. 99 and R. Gregory and G. Drewry, "Barlow Clowes and the Ombudsman" [1991] P.L. 192 and 408 and for the report itself see the Annual Report for 1989 (1989–90 H.C. 353).

For another other major investigation, this time into complaints about alleged planning blight arising from the Channel tunnel rail link, see the Special Report of the PCA, The Channel Tunnel Rail Link and Blight (1994–95 H.C. 193). He found maladministration in the way in which the Department of Transport dealt with several claims for compensation for alleged blight. The department refused to accept the PCA's finding of maladministration, and he felt compelled to issue (for only a second time in his history) a special report under section 10 (3) of the 1967 Act. The Select Committee recommended that the department accept the findings: (1994–95 H.C. 270). To date the Government has still not been prepared to accept the finding of maladministration although it has been prepared to reconsider its position on compensation, on which see the Second Report of the Select Committee, The Channel Tunnel Rail Link and Exceptional Hardship — The Government's Proposals for Redress (1996–97 H.C. 453): R. James and D. Longley, "The Channel tunnel rail link, the Ombudsman and the Select Committee" [1996] P.L. 38.

(5) As well as reporting on the outcomes of complaints made, the PCA also reports on examples of good administration and practice he has found in the course of his investigations and of course matters of concern to which he wishes attention to be drawn. One of the most significant areas in which the PCA is involved relates to the giving of advice by government departments. The number of cases involving such advice now accounts for around 20 per cent of his case load. It is with this area that the next extract is concerned.

A.R. Mowbray, "A Right to Official Advice: The Parliamentary Commissioner's Perspective"

[1990] P.L. 68

16–9   "In the context of our contemporary society, it is inevitable that a great deal of sought after information is located within government departments, particularly where they are responsible for generating the detailed provisions that govern today's numerous administrative programmes. Therefore, a vital element in the relationship between citizens and the state concerns the nature of the obligation on the latter to provide advice to citizens regarding matters falling within the competence and expertise of those departments.

Of all the administrative grievance-handling agencies, it is the Parliamentary Commissioner for Administration (hereafter the P.C.A. or the Commissioner) who has contributed the most towards the development of a citizen's right to advice from the government in our modern public law ...

Today, the importance of the right to advice is reflected in the fact that during recent years advice cases have represented approximately 20 per cent of all the investigations published by the P.C.A. in his selected case reports (see table below).

Year	Number of Reported Cases	Number of Advice Cases
1985	59	12
1986	63	13
1987	51	9
Totals	173	34

The Scope of the Right to Advice

A study of the Commissioner's published cases during 1985–1987 enables us to delimit the boundaries of the right as currently enforced by the P.C.A. A clear example of the principle that individuals have a right to advice is given by a complaint against the DHSS. The complainant asked an officer at the local office whether he would be entitled to an increase in his supplementary benefit payments if he was to take out a mortgage on a new house. Because of a confusion over case papers the office failed to provide the complainant with a reply to his request and subsequently the building society refused to grant the complainant a mortgage. The P.C.A. concluded that the department's failure to provide the requested information meant that the complainant's criticisms were fully justified. Moreover, the P.C.A. has adopted a wide usage of the concept of 'advice'. He treats both the provision of essentially factual information to individuals (*e.g.* the extent of a complainant's pension contributions) and the expression of officers' opinions as amounting to statements of advice. Officers' opinions can be about matters of current departmental policy (*e.g.* whether a company's short-time working schedule complied with existing departmental rules governing the payment of unemployment benefit) or future situations involving the department (*e.g.* the level of benefits an individual would receive if she began reclaiming social security allowances in several months' time).

(a) The Subject-Matter of Official Advice

Of the 34 advice cases published during 1985–1987, the overwhelming majority concerned what may be termed personal queries, where individuals sought advice from departments about their eligibility for public benefit (21 cases) or liability to make a payment to the state (four cases)...

(b) The Form of Official Advice

... In half the cases studied (17), the relevant advice took the form of a personal letter sent to the complainant. A typical example of advice being presented in such a form arose in a case involving the overseas branch of the DHSS. The complainant was a United Kingdom citizen who had taken up employment in France and he sought advice from the department about his future entitlement to retirement pensions in Britain and France. The department wrote expressing their views on the levels of pensions he could expect from both countries under European Community regulations. Later the complainant received a much lower French pension than the DHSS had predicted and he complained to the P.C.A. The Commissioner found that the department had inadvertently misinterpreted the E.C. regulations.

The second most common form of advice was that of oral statements (14 cases). This type of advice was normally given in two distinct circumstances. First, in response to a personal visit by a citizen to departmental premises. An example occurred where a managing director went to his local VAT office to discover if a proposed purchase of manufacturing assets would be liable to tax. He was informed by the officer at the counter that VAT would be payable; but the District Surveyor later determined that tax was not due. The other context in which oral advice was obviously present was where an individual telephoned the department for advice. For example, a complainant telephoned his local DHSS office to seek advice on social security benefits he could claim whilst undergoing a M.S.C. training course. In reply the officer expressed a view as to what types of benefits would be payable. When it subsequently transpired that not all these benefits were available the P.C.A. was asked to investigate.

Lastly, in three of the cases studied, advice took the form of leaflets and booklets published by the department. In a case against the Department of Employment, a woman complained that she satisfied the conditions required for employment under the Job Release Scheme, administered by the department, as explained in an official leaflet. But the department refused to allow her to take up such a post, because they asserted that she did not meet all the requirements laid down for the scheme. The P.C.A. upheld her complaint, noting that,

> 'there was nothing in the leaflet then current to suggest that eligibility was also governed by other rules... the leaflet was clearly misleading in this respect and the Principal Officer of D.E. has acknowledged that it should have provided a clearer definition of the term "unemployed".'

In such a case the offending advice was directed towards sections of the community at large...

The Quality of Official Advice

As members of the public have a prima facie right to advice concerning their personal queries about programmes being administered by departments, what is the quality of the advice they can expect from officials? The P.C.A. has invoked the adaptable concept of maladministration to condemn advice which he considers to be defective. Incorrect and misleading statements were the most common forms of defects found in the cases studied, 10 cases involving incorrect advice and eight misleading advice. Although the

16–10

Commissioner has not provided specific definitions of these terms, we can gain an understanding of his usage by examining the substance of his criticisms in individual cases.

The P.C.A. equates the notion of 'wholly wrong' with the term 'incorrect' as a characteristic of defective advice. For example, after a complainant received a reduction in his social security benefits he queried the level of his new payments with the department. The local office replied that the change was caused by the fact that the department would now be paying his rent and rates directly to the local authority. Subsequently, it emerged that this was not the true position and his benefits had been reduced because his wife had become entitled to a pension in her own right. The P.C.A. noted, 'it is clear from my investigation that ... the local office did inform the complainant quite specifically and *quite wrongly*, that from November 22 he would no longer have to pay rent and rates.'

In contrast, the Commissioner uses the term 'misleading' advice in relation to statements which are partially wrong, with the consequence that the citizen is unable to comprehend his true position. An example involved a case where a woman was receiving benefits from the DHSS including a higher long-term scale rate of supplementary benefit. The claimant asked the local office what her entitlements would be if she were to register for a training course and then later reclaim social security benefits. The office replied that her attendance on the course would have no effect on her future eligibility for supplementary benefit. Some months later, after completing the course, the woman reapplied for supplementary benefit, but was awarded only a lower rate payment, because the rules provided that where a person receiving a higher rate benefit stopped claiming the benefit for more than eight weeks they were subsequently entitled only to the lower rate. The P.C.A. considered that the office had given the complainant misleading advice and criticised them 'for their failure to provide the complainant with a *full and correct* explanation of the consequences of her planned attendance on the TOPS course'.

'Inadequate' advice also results in citizens being incompletely informed of their true position. The P.C.A. found that the DHSS had provided a widow with inadequate advice about her eligibility for invalidity benefit by failing to warn her of the need to submit medical evidence regularly to the local office. The difference between misleading and inadequate advice, therefore, appears to be that the former category contains statements which are partially erroneous whereas in the latter case the advice is correct but incomplete...

The Injustice Suffered Through Reliance on Defective Official Advice

According to section 5(1)(a) of the Parliamentary Commissioner Act 1967, the P.C.A. can investigate complaints only where, *inter alia*, the complainant claims to have 'sustained injustice in consequence of maladministration'. So if the P.C.A. is to uphold a citizen's complaint in regard to defective advice he must also find that he or she has sustained an injustice through relying or acting upon the advice. In contrast to the Local Ombudsman, the P.C.A. tends not to make an express finding of both maladministration and injustice, but instead concludes that he upholds the citizen's complaint. However, according to the substance of his reports in this context, the P.C.A. has generally equated injustice with a tangible and direct financial disadvantage experienced by the citizen relying upon the defective advice.

The most common form of financial disadvantage experienced by complainants was a loss of state benefits, which occurred in eight of the 34 cases. One example involved a woman who suffered from agoraphobia with the result that she could not use public transport. The complainant asked the DHSS mobility allowance unit if she was entitled to any form of benefit to help pay the cost of taxi fares to work. The unit informed her that she was not entitled to mobility allowance and failed to provide her with a leaflet listing other available benefits as their internal procedures required. Eight months later the complainant was awarded one of these other benefits, the existence of which she had discovered from a magazine. The P.C.A. criticised the unit's failure and approved the payment of an *ex gratia* sum equivalent to the lost eight months' benefit...

Conclusions

16–11   What then are the contours of the right to advice from departments of state as currently enforced by the P.C.A.? Provided citizens have complied with a series of preliminary obligations, including the full disclosure of relevant information and the seeking of advice at the earliest opportunity, they can legitimately expect answers to the overwhelming majority of queries concerning the application of departmental programmes to their personal circumstances. If the answers are incorrect, misleading or inadequate, the P.C.A. will characterise the department's conduct as amounting to maladministration. He will then determine whether the citizen has suffered a direct financial loss through acting or relying upon the defective advice. Where such a loss is established the P.C.A. will then treat the citizen as having sustained an injustice in consequence of maladministration. A suitable remedy will then be recommended by the P.C.A., in most cases involving the department in making a quantified *ex gratia* payment to the citizen to compensate for his or her loss.

The only significant weakness discovered in the P.C.A.'s response to advice complaints was the lack of clarity in his reports regarding the calculation of the level of financial loss suffered by citizens and the corresponding compensation required to alleviate the injustice. The inclusion of a more precise assessment of the extent of the pecuniary loss flowing from the defective advice would end any lingering suspicion that the P.C.A.'s calculations are based more on subjective inclination than objective evaluation ...

Despite persistent criticisms of the notion of 'maladministration', the reports disclose that the indefinite nature of the concept has enabled the P.C.A. to develop and refine its application to cover virtually all forms of departmental advice concerning personal queries about collective consumption programmes. Furthermore, the success of the P.C.A. in securing redress for justified complaints (financial compensation was paid in 20 cases), means that despite his lack of formal coercive powers the P.C.A.'s findings in advice cases satisfy the minimum jurisprudential requirements of a right. As Stoljar explains, 'you cannot have a right unless it can be claimed or demanded or insisted upon, indeed claimed effectively or enforceably'. [S. Stoljar, *An Analysis of Rights* (1984), pp. 3–4.] The achievements of the Commissioner in relation to advice complaints certainly enable individuals effectively to insist upon the provision of accurate advice within the limits elucidated in this article.

Finally, we can assess the value of this right in the context of the continuing debate over freedom of information in the United Kingdom. Marsh observes that one justification put forward by proponents of a statutory right of access to government information is that the current position reflects:

> 'disequilibrium between the state with its command over a wide field of information and the private organisation or individual, from whom information of all kinds is demanded by the state, from which, however, information can only be obtained with difficulty, or not at all.'

Against this backdrop, the right to official advice has the potential to help redress that imbalance on the level of dealings between individuals and departments, because it can assist a citizen in discovering his or her position in relation to the administrative norms governing specific programmes. However, the right only extends to those activities which fall within the P.C.A.'s jurisdiction and it fails to provide a general right of access to governmental information for interested citizens (qua campaigners, journalists or academics) where they are not directly affected by a particular administrative scheme. Therefore, whilst the right is clearly not a substitute for a balanced Freedom of Information Act, it offers a modest ray of sunshine in an otherwise gloomy landscape of increasing official secrecy."

Notes

(1) The right to advice is one of a number of norms developed by the PCA in his casework. **16–12** Professor Bradley, "The Role of the Ombudsman in Relation to the Protection of Citizens' Rights" (1980) 39 C.L.J. 304 at 310, has concluded that:

> "the British Ombudsman has developed principles, standards and rules of what he believes to constitute good administration, since otherwise no notion or maladministration could have emerged. As the process of investigation and report continues in every fresh case, so the individual complainant receives the benefit of the Ombudsman's enforcement of the rules and principles which have emerged from the previous case-work. And it may not be pressing this analysis too far to conclude that the individual citizen thus acquires what may properly be called new rights to the maintenance of a certain quality of administration."

For examination of the Ombudsman's views on the use of administrative guidance see A.R. Mowbray, "The Parliamentary Commissioner and Administrative Guidance" [1987] P.L. 570. Here Mowbray considered the role of the PCA in relation to certain forms of administrative "rule". In particular, the role of the P C A in relation to policy guidance, procedural guidance and interpretative guidance was examined and he concluded (at 585):

> "the P.C.A. has helped to protect the vital rights, interests and duties of citizens from some of the adverse effects of the creation and application of administrative guidance by departments. His role has been particularly valuable in cases where the relevant guidance had not been published and consequently it would have been virtually impossible for the citizen to seek a judicial remedy."

For further examination of some of the problems surrounding informal administrative rule making see Chapter 2.

(2) The PCA also has a role to play in the field of freedom of information. As noted in Chapter 15, there now exists a Code of Practice on Access to Government Information. It applies to all bodies subject to the jurisdiction of the P C A. Commenting on his role in his report for 1997–98 he observed that the number of complaints of maladministration about refusal of access to government information "has continued to be small". 27 complaints were received in 1997–98 (28 in 1997); and 25 reports on completed investigations (including one discontinuation) were issued (and 22 in 1997): para 1.13. While welcoming the possibility of a Freedom of Information Act, with those alleging a breach of the Act being able to take their complaints to a Freedom of Information Commissioner, he was (at para. 1.15):

> "concerned that the creation of yet another public sector complaints authority will make an already complex and fragmented system still harder for complainants to use and understand… What is essential, in my view, is that I — and other Public Sector Ombudsmen — should continue to be able to investigate complaints of maladministration which have a freedom of information element without putting complainants to additional time and trouble."

The role of the P C A also now requires to be re-assessed in light of the creation of a Scottish Parliament and Executive.

Scotland Act 1998

s. 91

"Maladministration

16–13   **91.** — (1) The Parliament shall make provision for the investigation of relevant complaints made to its members in respect of any action taken by or on behalf of —

  (a)   a member of the Scottish Executive in the exercise of functions conferred on the Scottish Ministers, or

  (b)   any other office-holder in the Scottish Administration.

(2) For the purposes of subsection (1), a complaint is a relevant complaint if it is a complaint of a kind which could be investigated under the Parliamentary Commissioner Act 1967 if it were made to a member of the House of Commons in respect of a government department or other authority to which that Act applies.

(3) The Parliament may make provision for the investigation of complaints in respect of —

  (a)   any action taken by or on behalf of an office-holder in the Scottish Administration.

  (b)   any action taken by or on behalf of the Parliamentary corporation.

  (c)   any action taken by or on behalf of a Scottish public authority with mixed functions or no reserved functions, or

  (d)   any action concerning Scotland and not relating to reserved matters which is taken by or on behalf of a cross-border public authority.

(4) In making provision of the kind required by subsection (1), the Parliament shall have regard (among other things) to the Act of 1967.

(5) Sections 53 and 117 to 121 shall not apply in relation to functions conferred by or under the Act of 1967.

(6) In this section —

'action' includes failure to act (and related expressions shall be read accordingly).

'provision' means provision by an Act of the Scottish Parliament; and the references to the Act of 1967 are to that Act as it has effect on the commencement of this section."

Scotland Act 1998 (Transitory and Transitional Provisions) (Complaints of Maladministration) Order 1999 (as amended by the Scotland Act 1998 (Transitory and Transitional Provisions) (Complaints of Maladministration) Amendment Order 1999)

16–14   The Secretary of State, in exercise of the powers conferred on him by section 112(1), 113, 114(1) and 129(1) of the Scotland Act 1998 and of all other powers enabling him in that behalf, hereby makes the following Order:

Citation and Commencement

1. This Order may be cited as the Scotland Act 1998 (Transitory and Transitional Provisions) (Complaints of Maladministration) Order 1999 and shall come into force on the principal appointed day

Interpretation

2. — (1) In this Order —

'the 1967 Act' means the Parliamentary Commissioner Act 1967

'the Act' means the Scotland Act 1998;

'action' includes failure to act and related expressions shall be construed accordingly;

'authority subject to investigation' shall be construed in accordance with article 8;

'listed tribunal' means a tribunal which is either a Scottish public authority which is listed in Schedule 1 or a cross-border public authority which is listed in Schedule 2;

'officer' includes employee;

'Parliamentary Commissioner' means the Parliamentary Commissioner for Administration;

'person aggrieved' shall be construed in accordance with article 9(1) (b);

'the Scottish Commissioner' means the Scottish Parliamentary Commissioner for Administration appointed in accordance with article 4,

and action taken in the exercise of functions of an authority subject to investigation includes a reference to action taken by any of its members or officers or any members of its staff.

(2) Unless otherwise provided, any reference in this Order to a numbered article or Schedule is a reference to an article or Schedule bearing that number in or to this Order and any reference in an article to a numbered paragraph is to a paragraph bearing that number in that article.

Duration of this Order

3. This Order, unless previously revoked by the Secretary of State, shall cease to have effect on the day appointed by or under an Act of the Scottish Parliament, and different days may be appointed for different purposes.

Scottish Commissioner

4. — (1) For the purpose of conducting investigations in accordance with the following provisions of this Order, there shall be appointed a Scottish Commissioner.

(2) Her Majesty may from time to time appoint a person to be the Scottish Commissioner.

(3) Subject to the following paragraphs, the Scottish Commissioner shall hold office during good behaviour.

(4) A person appointed to be the Scottish Commissioner may be relieved of office by Her Majesty at his own request, or may be removed from office by Her Majesty in consequence of a resolution of the Parliament that he should be removed from office on the ground of misbehaviour, and shall in any case vacate office on completing the year of service in which he attains the age of 65 years.

(5) Her Majesty may declare the office of Scottish Commissioner to have been vacated if Her Majesty is satisfied that the person appointed to be the Scottish Commissioner is incapable for medical reasons of performing the duties of the office and of requesting to be relieved of it.

Status

5. — (1) The Scottish Commissioner shall be regarded as holding office under Her Majesty and as exercising his functions on behalf of the Crown.

(2) Service as the Scottish Commissioner or as a member of staff of the Scottish Commissioner shall not be service in the Home Civil Service.

Remuneration, Allowances and Pension

6. — (1) Subject to paragraphs (2) and (3), there shall be payable to the Scottish Commissioner —

(a)   such salary; and

(b)   such allowances in respect of his expenses under this Order (including his expenses under articles 7 and 11(3)),

as the Parliament may, by resolution, from time to time determine and a resolution under this paragraph may take effect from the date on which it is passed or from such other date as may be specified in the resolution.

(2) Where a person is both Parliamentary Commissioner and Scottish Commissioner, he shall not be entitled to any salary as Scottish Commissioner.

(3) The salary payable to a holder of the office of Scottish Commissioner shall be abated by the amount of any pension payable to him in respect of any public office in the United Kingdom or elsewhere to which he had previously been appointed or elected.

(4) The Parliament may make provision for the payment of pensions, gratuities or allowances to, or in respect of, any person who has ceased to hold the office of Scottish Commissioner and such provision may, in particular, include provision for —

(a)   contributions or payments towards provision for such pensions, gratuities or allowances; and

(b)   the establishment and administration (whether by the Parliamentary corporation or otherwise) of a pension scheme.

(5) The Parliamentary corporation shall determine the other terms and conditions of appointment of the Scottish Commissioner.

(6) The amounts payable to the Scottish Commissioner under paragraph (1) and any amounts payable by virtue of paragraph (4) shall be paid by the Parliamentary corporation.

Staff

7. — (1) The Scottish Commissioner may appoint such staff as he considers necessary to assist him in the exercise of his functions.

(2) It is for the Scottish Commissioner to determine the terms and conditions of appointment of his staff, including arrangements for the payment of pensions, gratuities or allowances to, or in respect of, any person who has ceased to be a member of his staff.

(3) In particular, the Scottish Commissioner may make provision for —

(a)   contributions or payments towards the provision for such pensions, gratuities or allowances; and

(b)   the establishment and administration (whether by the Parliamentary corporation or otherwise) of a pension scheme.

(4) Any function of the Scottish Commissioner may be exercised by —

(a)   a member of his staff;

(b)   an officer of the Parliamentary Commissioner; or

(c)   an officer of the Health Service Commissioner for Scotland, of the Health Service Commissioner for England or of the Health Service Commissioner for Wales,

if authorised by the Scottish Commissioner for that purpose; and references in any enactment (including this Order) to a member of the staff of the Scottish Commissioner include any person exercising any function of his by virtue of sub-paragraph (b) or (c).

Authorities Subject to Investigation

8. The persons, bodies and authorities subject to investigation by the Scottish Commissioner are —

(a)   any member of the Scottish Executive;

(b)   any other office-holder in the Scottish Administration;

(c)   the Parliamentary corporation;

(d)   any Scottish public authority with mixed functions or no reserved functions which is listed in Schedule 1;

(e)   any cross-border public authority which is listed in Schedule 2,

and references in this Order to an authority subject to investigation are references to any such person, body or authority.

Matters Which May be Investigated

9. — (1) Subject to the provisions of this article, the Scottish Commissioner may investigate any action taken by or on behalf of an authority subject to investigation if —

(a)   the action was taken in the exercise of administrative functions of that authority;

(b)   a written complaint is duly made to a member of the Parliament by a member of the public who claims to have sustained injustice in consequence of maladministration in connection with the action so taken ('the person aggrieved'); and

(c)   the complaint is referred to the Scottish Commissioner, with the consent of the person who made it, by a member of the Parliament with a request to conduct an investigation thereon.

(2) The Scottish Commissioner may not question the merits of a decision taken without maladministration by an authority subject to investigation in the exercise of a discretion vested in that authority.

(3) A member of the Scottish Executive is subject to investigation by the Scottish Commissioner only in respect of any action taken by or on behalf of that member in the exercise of functions conferred on the Scottish Ministers or of functions conferred upon the First Minister alone.

(4) A cross-border public authority which is listed in Schedule 2 is subject to investigation by the Scottish Commissioner only in connection with any action concerning Scotland and not relating to reserved matters taken by or on behalf of that authority.

(5) The Scottish Commissioner shall not conduct an investigation in respect of any action in respect of which the person aggrieved has or had —

(a)   a right of appeal, reference or review to or before a tribunal constituted by or under any enactment or by virtue of Her Majesty's prerogative; or

(b)   a remedy by way of proceedings in any court of law, unless the Scottish Commissioner is satisfied that, in the particular circumstances, it is not reasonable to expect the person aggrieved to resort or have resorted to it.

(6) The Scottish Commissioner shall not conduct an investigation in respect of any matter mentioned in Schedule 3 to the 1967 Act and, for this purpose —

(a)   the references in paragraphs 5, 7 and 8 of that Schedule to the Secretary of State shall be read as if they included a reference to a member of the Scottish Executive;

(b)   the definition in paragraph 6B(2) of that Schedule of 'relevant tribunal' shall be read as including a listed tribunal; and

(c)   the references in paragraphs 9 and 10 of that Schedule to a government department or authority to which the 1967 Act applies shall be read as if they included references to an authority subject to investigation.

(7) The Scottish Commissioner shall not conduct an investigation in respect of any action taken by or on behalf of Scottish Homes in respect of any of its actions as a landlord.

(8) For the purposes of this article, administrative functions exercisable by any person appointed as a member of the administrative staff of a listed tribunal —

(a)   by an authority subject to investigation; or

(b)   with the consent (whether as to remuneration and other terms and conditions of service or otherwise) of such an authority,

shall be taken to be administrative functions of that authority.

(9) In determining whether to initiate, continue or discontinue an investigation, the Scottish Commissioner shall, subject to the preceding provisions of this article, act in accordance with his discretion.

Complaints

10. — (1) A complaint may be made under article 9(1)(b) by any individual or body of persons (whether or not incorporated) except —

(a)   the Parliamentary corporation;

(b)   a local authority or other authority or body constituted for purposes of the public service or of local government;

(c)   a body constituted for the purposes of carrying on under national ownership an industry or undertaking or part of an industry or undertaking;

(d)   any other authority or body whose members are appointed by Her Majesty or by any Minister of the Crown or government department or by a member of the Scottish Executive, or whose revenues consist wholly or mainly of money provided by Parliament or sums payable out of the Scottish Consolidated Fund (whether directly or indirectly).

(2) A complaint shall not be entertained by the Scottish Commissioner unless made by the person aggrieved himself, except that —

(a)   where an individual by whom a complaint might have been made has died, or is for any reason unable to act for himself, the complaint may be made by his personal representatives or a member of his family or any other individual or any body suitable to represent him; and

(b)   where a body by whom a complaint might have been made is for any reason unable to act for itself, the complaint may be made by an individual, or another body, suitable to represent it.

(3) A complaint shall not be entertained by the Scottish Commissioner unless —

(a)   it is made to a member of the Parliament not later than 12 months after the day on which the person aggrieved first had notice of the matters alleged in the complaint, but the Scottish Commissioner may conduct an investigation pursuant to a complaint not made within that period if he considers that there are special circumstances which make it proper to do so; and

(b)   the person aggrieved is resident in the United Kingdom (or, if he is dead, was so resident at the time of his death) or the complaint relates to action taken in relation to him while he was present in the United Kingdom or on an installation in a designated area within the meaning of the Continental Shelf Act 1964 or on a ship registered in the United Kingdom or an aircraft so registered, or in relation to rights or obligations which accrued or arose in the United Kingdom or on such an installation, ship or aircraft.

(4) Any question whether a complaint is duly made or referred to the Scottish Commissioner shall be determined by him.

Investigation Procedure

11. — (1) Where the Scottish Commissioner proposes to conduct an investigation pursuant to a complaint referred to him, he shall afford to —

(a)   the particular authority subject to investigation; and

(b)   any person who is alleged in the complaint to have taken or authorised the action complained of,

an opportunity to comment on any allegations contained in the complaint.

(2) The investigation shall be conducted in private but in other respects the procedure for conducting the investigation shall be such as the Scottish Commissioner considers appropriate in the circumstances of the case, and, in particular, the Scottish Commissioner —

(a)   may obtain information from such persons and in such manner, and make such inquiries, as he thinks fit; and

(b)   may determine whether any person may be represented, by counsel or solicitor or otherwise, in the investigation.

(3) The Scottish Commissioner may, if he thinks fit, pay to the person by whom the complaint was made and to any other person who attends or supplies information for the purposes of an investigation such sums in respect of expenses properly incurred by them, and such allowances by way of compensation for the loss of their time, in accordance with such scales and subject to such conditions as may be determined by the Parliamentary corporation.

(4) The conduct of an investigation shall not affect —

(a)   any action taken by the authority concerned; or

(b)   any power or duty of that authority to take further action with respect to any matter subject to the investigation.

Evidence

12. — (1) For the purposes of an investigation, the Scottish Commissioner may require any of the following persons to supply information or produce documents relevant to the investigation —

(a)   any member, or officer or member of the staff, of the authority subject to investigation, including, in particular, where that authority is an authority mentioned in article 8(a) or (b), any office-holder in the Scottish Administration or member of the staff of the part of the Scottish Administration concerned; or

(b)   any other person,

who in his opinion is able to supply such information or produce such documents.

(2) For the purposes of any investigation the Scottish Commissioner shall have the same powers as the Court of Session in respect of —

(a)   the attendance and examination of witnesses (including the administration of oaths and affirmations and the examination of witnesses abroad); and

(b)   the production of documents.

(3) No obligation to maintain secrecy or other restriction on the disclosure of information obtained by or supplied to persons in Her Majesty's service, whether imposed by any enactment or by any rule of law, shall apply to the disclosure of information for the purposes of an investigation by the Scottish Commissioner —

(4) The Crown (whether in right of Her Majesty's Government in the United Kingdom or in right of the Scottish Administration) shall not be entitled in relation to any investigation by the Scottish Commissioner to any such privilege in respect of the production of documents or the giving of evidence as is allowed by law in legal proceedings.

(5) No person shall be required or authorised by virtue of this Order to supply any information or answer any question relating to proceedings of the Cabinet or of any committee of the Cabinet, or to produce so much of any document as relates to such proceedings; and for the purposes of this paragraph a certificate issued by the Secretary of the Cabinet with the approval of the Prime Minister and certifying that any information, question, document or part of a document so relates shall be conclusive.

(6) Subject to paragraphs (3) to (5), no person shall be compelled for the purposes of an investigation by the Scottish Commissioner to give any evidence or produce any document which he could not be compelled to give or to produce in civil proceedings before the Court of Session.

Obstruction and Contempt

13. — (1) Where —

(a)   a person, without lawful excuse, obstructs the Scottish Commissioner or any member of his staff in the performance of his functions; or

(b)   a person does any act or fails to take any action in relation to an investigation which, if that investigation were a proceeding in the Court of Session, would constitute contempt of court, the Scottish Commissioner may apply by petition to the Court of Session for that person to be dealt with for contempt.

(2) Where such a petition is presented, the Court of Session may inquire into the matter and after hearing —

(a)   any witnesses who may be produced against or on behalf of the person alleged to have committed the contempt; and

(b)   any statement that may be offered in defence,

may, if satisfied that a contempt has been committed, deal with that person in any manner in which it would deal with him if he had committed the same contempt in relation to the Court of Session.

(3) Nothing in this article shall be construed as applying to the taking of any such action as is mentioned in article 11(4).

Reports

14. — (1) Where the Scottish Commissioner conducts an investigation or decides not to conduct an investigation, he shall send to the member of the Parliament by whom the request for investigation was made (or, if he is no longer a member of the Parliament, to such member as the Scottish Commissioner thinks appropriate) a report of the investigation or, as the case may be, a statement of his reasons for not conducting an investigation.

(2) Where the Scottish Commissioner conducts an investigation, he shall also send a report of the investigation to the authority subject to investigation and to any other person who is alleged in the complaint to have taken or authorised the action complained of.

(3) If, after conducting an investigation, it appears to the Scottish Commissioner that injustice has been caused to the person aggrieved in consequence of maladministration and that the injustice has not been, or will not be, remedied, he may, if he thinks fit, lay before the Parliament a special report on the case.

(4) The Scottish Commissioner shall annually lay before the Parliament a general report on the performance of his functions and may from time to time lay before the Parliament such other reports with respect to those functions as he thinks fit.

(5) For the purposes of the law of defamation, the following are absolutely privileged —

(a)   the publication of any matter by the Scottish Commissioner in making a report to the Parliament for the purposes of this Order,

(b)   the publication of any matter by a member of the Parliament in communicating with the Scottish Commissioner or any member of his staff for those purposes or by the Scottish Commissioner or any member of his staff in communicating with such a member for those purposes;

(c)   the publication by the Scottish Commissioner to a member of the Parliament or by that member to the person by whom a complaint was made of a report or statement under paragraph (1); and

(d)   the publication by the Scottish Commissioner to the authority or other person mentioned in paragraph (2) of a report sent to that authority or that person under that paragraph.

Confidentiality of Information

15. — (1) Information obtained by the Scottish Commissioner or a member of his staff in the course of or for the purposes of an investigation shall not be disclosed except —

(a)   for the purposes of the investigation and of any report of it under this Order;

(b)   for the purposes of any proceedings for —

(i)   an offence under the Official Secrets Acts 1911 to 1989 alleged to have been committed in respect of information obtained by the Scottish Commissioner or a member of his staff;

or

(ii)   an offence of perjury alleged to have been committed in the course of an investigation by him;

(c)   for the purposes of an inquiry with a view to the taking of any of the proceedings mentioned in sub-paragraph (b);

(d)   for the purposes of any proceedings under article 13.

(2) Neither the Scottish Commissioner nor any member of his staff shall be called upon to give evidence in any proceedings (other than proceedings referred to in paragraph (1)) of matters coming to his or their knowledge in the course of an investigation.

(3) A member of the Scottish Executive or, as the case may be, a Minister of the Crown may give notice in writing to the Scottish Commissioner with respect to —

(a)   any document or information specified in the notice; or

(b)   any class of document or information so specified,

that, in the opinion of that member of the Scottish Executive or of that Minister, the disclosure of that document or information, or of documents or information of that class, would be prejudicial to the safety of the State or otherwise contrary to the public interest. In this paragraph references to a Minister of the Crown include references to the Treasury, the Commissioners of Customs and Excise and the Commissioners of Inland Revenue.

(4) Where such a notice is given neither the Scottish Commissioner nor any member of his staff shall be authorised or required to communicate to any person or for any purpose any document or information specified in the notice, or any document or information of a class so specified.

(5) Where —

(a)   the Scottish Commissioner also holds office as the Parliamentary Commissioner or as a Health Service Commissioner ('a Commissioner'); and

(b)   a person initiates a complaint to him in his capacity as a Commissioner which relates partly to a matter with respect to which that person has previously initiated, or subsequently initiates, a complaint to him in his capacity as the Scottish Commissioner,

information obtained by the Scottish Commissioner or a member of his staff in the course of, or for the purposes of, investigating a complaint to him in his capacity as Scottish Commissioner may be disclosed for the purposes of his carrying out his functions in relation to the other complaint.

Consultation and Co-operation with Other Commissioners

16. — (1) Where the Scottish Commissioner, at any stage in the course of conducting an investigation, forms the opinion that the complaint relates partly to a matter which could be the subject of an investigation —

(a)   by the Commissioner for Local Administration in Scotland under the Local Government (Scotland) Act 1975 or

(b)   by any of the Health Service Commissioners under the Health Service Commissioners Act 1993 or

(c)   by the Parliamentary Commissioner under the 1967 Act,

he shall consult the appropriate Commissioner about the complaint and, if he considers it necessary, he shall inform the person initiating the complaint of the steps necessary to initiate a complaint to that Commissioner.

(2) Where a Commissioner consults with another Commissioner in accordance with this article, the consultations may extend to any matter relating to the complaint, including —

(a)   the conduct of any investigation into the complaint; and

(b)   the form, content and publication of any report of the result of such an investigation.

(3) Where an authority which is subject to investigation by the Scottish Commissioner is also an authority to which the 1967 Act applies, the Scottish Commissioner and the Parliamentary Commissioner shall co-operate with each other to any such extent as appears appropriate when exercising any function in relation to the authority.

(4) Nothing in article 15 applies in relation to the disclosure of information in the course of consultation or co-operation under this article.

Modifications of Enactments

17. — (1) In the 1967 Act —

(a)   in subsection (2) of section 3 (administrative provisions) the reference to any officer of the Health Service Commissioner for Scotland authorised as mentioned in that subsection shall be read as if it included a reference to any member of staff so authorised of the Scottish Commissioner;

(b)   in section 11(2A) (provision for secrecy of information), the reference to a Health Service Commissioner shall be read as if it included a reference to the Scottish Commissioner;

'(c)   in section 11A (consultations between Parliamentary Commissioner and the Health Service Commissioners) the reference —

(i)   in subsection (1) to the Health Service Commissioner for Scotland shall be read as if it included a reference to the Scottish Commissioner;

(ii)   in subsection (1)(b) to the Health Service Commissioners Act 1993 shall be read as if it included a reference to this Order; and

(iii)   in subsection (2) to the Health Service Commissioner shall be read as if it included a reference to the Scottish Commissioner; and'.

(d)   in section 11B (the criminal injuries compensation scheme), the reference to the Secretary of State in subsection (3)(a) shall be read as if it included a reference to the Scottish Ministers.

(2) The following enactments shall be read as if references to the Parliamentary Commissioner included references to the Scottish Commissioner:-

(a)   Part III of Schedule 1 to the House of Commons Disqualification Act 1975;

(b)   section 134(3)(c) of the Mental Health Act 1983;
(c)   section 115(3)(c) of the Mental Health (Scotland) Act 1984;
(d)   section 123(8)(c) of the Social Security Administration Act 1992;
(e)   section 117(8)(e) of the Social Security Administration (Northern Ireland) Act 1992;
(f)   section 79(1) of the Deregulation and Contracting Out Act 1994;
(g)   rule 62B of the Prisons and Young Offenders Institutions (Scotland) Rules 1994;
(h)   Part I of the Schedule to the Scottish Parliament (Disqualification) Order 1999.

(3) In the Local Government (Scotland) Act 1975 —
(a)   in section 31(1) to (4), the references to the Parliamentary Commissioner and to any provision of the 1967 Act shall be read as if they included references to the Scottish Commissioner and to this Order; and
(b)   in section 31(5), the reference to section 11(2) of the 1967 Act shall be read as if it included a reference to article 15(1) of this Order.

(4) In section 2(3) of the Tribunals and Inquiries Act 1992, the reference to the Parliamentary Commissioner being, by virtue of his office, a member of the Council on Tribunals and of Scottish Committee of that Council shall be read as if it included a reference to the Scottish Commissioner.

(5) In the Health Service Commissioners Act 1993 —
(a)   in sections 17 and 18 and paragraph 6 of Schedule 1, the references to the Parliamentary Commissioner shall be read as if they included references to the Scottish Commissioner; and
(b)   in section 18(1)(b) the reference to the 1967 Act shall be read as if it included a reference to this Order.

(6) In Schedule 1 to the Public Supply Contracts Regulations 1995 the reference to the office of the Parliamentary Commissioner for Administration and the Health Service Commissioners shall be read as if it included a reference to the office of the Scottish Commissioner.

(7) In each of the following enactments the reference to the 1967 Act shall be read as if it were a reference to this Order:-
(a)   paragraph 8 of Schedule 4 to the Town and Country Planning (Scotland) Act 1997;
(b)   paragraph 7 of Schedule 3 to the Planning (Listed Buildings and Conservation Areas) (Scotland) Act 1997; and
(c)   paragraph 7 of Schedule 1 to the Planning (Hazardous Substances) (Scotland) Act 1997.

(8) In Schedule 2 to the Official Secrets Act 1989 (Prescription) Order 1990, the reference to the Parliamentary Commissioner shall be read as if it included a reference to the Scottish Commissioner, and the reference to the officers of the Commissioner shall be read as if it included a reference to the staff of the Scottish Commissioner.

Transitional and Savings Provisions
18. — (1) On the principal appointed day, there shall be transferred to the Scottish Commissioner —
(a)   any complaint made in relation to any of the authorities mentioned in article 8(d) which has been referred to the Parliamentary Commissioner under section 5(1) of the 1967 Act and which has not been determined by him before that day; and
(b)   any investigation pursuant to any such complaint.

(2) On the principal appointed day, there shall be transferred to the Scottish Commissioner —
(a)   any complaint made in relation to any of the authorities mentioned in article 8(e) which concerns such action as is mentioned in article 9(4) and which has been referred to the Parliamentary Commissioner under section 5(1) of the 1967 Act but which has not been determined by him before that day; and
(b)   any investigation pursuant to any such complaint.

(3) For the purposes of this article —
(a)   a complaint is determined by the Parliamentary Commissioner if he has decided —
        (i)   to conduct an investigation pursuant to the complaint and the investigation is concluded; or
        (ii)   not to conduct an investigation into the complaint; and
(b)   an investigation is concluded if he has reported the results of that investigation as mentioned in section 10(1) of the 1967 Act.

(4) Where a complaint or an investigation is transferred by virtue of paragraph (1) or (2), the Scottish Commissioner shall send to the member of Parliament by whom the complaint was referred and the request for an investigation was made (or if he is no longer a member of Parliament, to such member as the Scottish Commissioner thinks appropriate) a report of the investigation or; as the case may be, a statement of his reasons for not conducting an investigation and article 14(5)(b) and (c) shall apply to a member of Parliament as it applies to a member of the Parliament.

(5) A transfer by virtue of paragraph (1) or (2) shall not affect the validity of anything done (or having effect as if done) by or in relation to a complaint or an investigation by the Parliamentary Commissioner before the principal appointed day.

(6) Anything (including legal proceedings) which, on the principal appointed day, is in the process of being done by or in relation to the Parliamentary Commissioner may, so far as it relates to anything transferred by virtue of paragraph (1) and (2), be continued by or in relation to the Scottish Commissioner.

(7) Anything done (or having effect as if done) by or in relation to the Parliamentary Commissioner for the purposes of or in connection with anything transferred by virtue of paragraph (1) or (2) shall, if in force on the principal appointed day, have effect as if done by or in relation to the Scottish Commissioner in so far as that is required for continuing its effect on or after the principal appointed day.

Schedule 1
Articles 2(1) and 8(d)
SCOTTISH PUBLIC AUTHORITIES SUBJECT TO INVESTIGATION
BY THE SCOTTISH COMMISSIONER

Accounts Commission for Scotland
Community Learning Scotland
Court of the Lord Lyon
Crofters Commission
Dairy Produce Quota Tribunal for Scotland
Deer Commission for Scotland
General Teaching Council for Scotland
Independent Schools Tribunals for Scotland
Lands Tribunal for Scotland
Local Government Boundary Commission for Scotland
Meat Hygiene Appeals Tribunal any of whose members was appointed by the Secretary of State for
    Scotland or by the Scottish Ministers
National Galleries of Scotland
National Library of Scotland
National Museums of Scotland
Parole Board for Scotland
Rent Assessment Committees for Scotland
Royal Botanic Garden, Edinburgh
Royal Commission on the Ancient and Historical Monuments of Scotland
Scottish Agricultural Wages Board
Scottish Arts Council
Scottish Children's Reporter Administration
Scottish Consultative Council on the Curriculum
Scottish Council for Educational Technology
Scottish Environment Protection Agency
Scottish Further Education Funding Council
Scottish Further Education Unit
Scottish Higher Education Funding Council
Scottish Homes
Scottish Land Court
Scottish Legal Aid Board
Scottish Medical Practices Committee
Scottish Natural Heritage
Scottish Qualifications Authority
Scottish Screen
Scottish Sports Council
Scottish Studentship Selection Committee
Scottish Tourist Board
Scottish Water and Sewerage Customers Council

Schedule 2
Articles 2(1), 8(e) and 9(4)
CROSS-BORDER PUBLIC AUTHORITIES SUBJECT TO INVESTIGATION
BY THE SCOTTISH COMMISSIONER

British Library Board
British Potato Council
British Tourist Authority
Central Bureau for Educational Visits and Exchanges
Clinical Standards Advisory Group

Committee of Investigation for Great Britain
Community Development Foundation
Construction Industry Training Board
Consumers' Committee for Great Britain
The Criminal Injuries Compensation Appeals Panel
Criminal Injuries Compensation Authority
Design Council
Engineering Construction Industry Training Board
Food from Britain
Forestry Commissioners
Home-Grown Cereals Authority
Horticultural Development Council
Intervention Board for Agricultural Produce
Joint Nature Conservation Committee
Meat and Livestock Commission
Milk Development Council
Museums and Galleries Commission
National Consumer Council
National Radiological Protection Board
Plant Varieties and Seeds Tribunal
Police Information Technology Organisation
Rail Users' Consultative Committee for Scotland
Sea Fish Industry Authority
United Kingdom Sports Council
Unrelated Live Transplant Regulatory Authority"

Notes

(1) Insofar as the Parliamentary Ombudsman has jurisdiction to do so, he will continue to **16–15** operate on a U.K. basis. In Scotland the scope of his jurisdiction will be restricted to the reserved areas of Government which will include significant and important areas of complaint, such as the administration of the tax and social security system, as well as continuing to have a role in relation to more specialised bodies such as the Registrar of Public Lending Rights, research councils and the Data Protection Registrar. Most functions exercised by the Scottish Office and subject to the scrutiny of the P C A will be transferred to the Scottish Ministers and will cease to be subject to his supervision. The same consideration apply to devolved quangos and other bodies and it is anticipated that these will be deleted from Schedule 2 to the 1967 Act. However, cross-border public authorities will remain subject to the Parliamentary Ombudsman insofar as their functions do not concern Scotland or relate to reserved matters: subsection (3)(*d*). The purpose of section 91(5) is to ensure that the functions of Ministers of the Crown under the 1967 Act are not transferred by virtue of section 53, on which see p. 000, to the Scottish Ministers. C.M.G. Himsworth and C.R. Munro, *The Scotland Act 1998* (1999) suggest that the need for subsection (5) suggests that the subject matter of the 1967 Act is not, or not entirely, reserved. The Act is not directly protected by Schedule 4, and para. 10 of Part I of the Schedule does not prevent an Act of the Scottish Parliament from modifying or conferring power by subordinate legislation to modify any enactment for or in connection with section 91. The authors suggest that the Scottish Parliament might be able to amend aspects of the 1967 Act, such as the rules of access to the PCA: see p. 116.

(2) It is anticipated that the Order will in due course be replaced by an Act of the Parliament. However, it is quite clear that whatever approach is ultimately taken, it is likely to be heavily modelled on provisions of the 1967 Act. Indeed, section 91(4) makes it clear that the provisions of the 1967 Act have to be taken into account in any scheme that is created. The principal appointed day is 1st July 1999: The Scotland Act 1998 (Commencement) Order 1998. It is worth comparing Schedules 1 and 2 to the Order with Schedule 2 to the 1967 Act: see the extent of removals from the PCA's jurisdiction as well as those bodies and departments still subject to

this jurisdiction. Article 9 of the Order clearly reflects the provisions of the 1967 Act both as to what can be investigated and the procedure by which this is done. Note in particular the retention of the concept of "maladministration" and the use of an M.P. filter. Note also the exclusions from jurisdiction, including matters detailed in Schedule 3 to the 1967 Act. Note also the time-limit for the making of a complaint of 12 months detailed in article 10, the detailed provisions on procedure and evidence contained in articles 11 and 12, and the provisions in relation to the making of reports contained in article 14. It is not yet clear whether the Scottish Ombudsman will have a role in relation to freedom of information. The Scottish Executive has announced that a Scottish Freedom of Information Act will form part of its legislative programme, but in the interim a Code of Practice on Freedom of Information will be issued and it will be expected that the bodies subject to it will adhere to the code. The Advocate General, Dr Lynda Clark Q.C., M.P. has suggested that given that Scotland is a small jurisdiction, there is an argument for combining the office of Scottish Parliamentary Ombudsman with the oversight of any Freedom of Information Act, rather than by creating a Scottish Freedom of Information Commissioner: "Freedom of Information: new rights, new remedies and the new parliament" (1999) 260 SCOLAG 59. Compare with the views of the PCA above at para. 16–12.

THE LOCAL GOVERNMENT OMBUDSMAN

16–16   The Local Government Ombudsman, or more correctly the Commissioner for Local Administration in Scotland, was created in Part II of the Local Government (Scotland) Act 1975. The Commissioner is appointed by the Crown on the recommendation of the Secretary of State after consultation with the bodies representing the local authorities, typically the Convention of Scottish Local Authorities (COSLA): section 21(2). As originally conceived, the Commissioner was subject to a "councillor filter" for complaints but since the Local Government Act 1988, Sched. 3, para. 13, direct access has been permitted. The abolition of the filter system has resulted in an increase in the number of complaints received. The jurisdiction of the Ombudsman includes not only local authorities but also some other bodies which are subject to investigation. For example, committees or joint boards, the members of which are appointed by one or more local authorities; any person or body which discharges any of the functions of a local authority under arrangements made with the authority; licensing boards and children's panel advisory committees are included. For an exhaustive list of the authorities subject to investigation see section 23. Her Majesty may by Order in Council extend the application of the jurisdiction of the Commissioner to any authority which is established by or under statute and which has power to levy a rate or to issue a requisition. To date no such Order has been made: subsection (3). Broadly speaking the jurisdiction of the Commissioner is based on the terminology in the Parliamentary Commissioner Act 1967. Accordingly, complaints that members of the public have "sustained injustice in consequence of maladministration in connection with action (including failure to act) taken by or on behalf of an authority . . . being action taken in the exercise of administrative functions of that authority": section 24 (1), fall to be investigated. A number of areas are, however, excluded from his jurisdiction.

Local Government (Scotland) Act 1975

s. 24 (4)–(9)

"Matters Subject to Investigation

16–17   (4) A complaint shall not be entertained unless it was made to a member of any authority concerned within twelve months from the day on which the person aggrieved first had notice of the matters alleged in the complaint, but the Commissioner may conduct an investigation pursuant to a complaint not made within that period if he considers that there are special circumstances which make it proper to do so.

(5) Before proceeding to investigate a complaint, the Commissioner shall satisfy himself that the complaint has been brought, by or on behalf of the person aggrieved, to the notice of the authority to

which the complaint relates and that that authority has been afforded a reasonable opportunity to investigate, and reply to, the complaint.

(6) The Commissioner shall not conduct an investigation under this Part of this Act in respect of any of the following matters, that is to say, —

(a) any action in respect of which the person aggrieved has or had a right of appeal, reference or review to or before a tribunal constituted by or under any enactment;

(b) any action in respect of which the person aggrieved has or had a right of appeal to a Minister of the Crown; or

(c) any action in respect of which the person aggrieved has or had a remedy by way of proceedings in any court of law:

Providing that the Commissioner may conduct an investigation notwithstanding the existence of such a right or remedy if satisfied that in the particular circumstances it is not reasonable to expect the person aggrieved to resort or have resorted to it.

(7) The Commissioner shall not conduct an investigation in respect of any action which in his opinion affects all or most of the inhabitants of the area of the authority concerned.

(8) Without prejudice to the preceding provisions of this section, the Commissioner shall not conduct an investigation under this Part of this Act in respect of any such action or matter as is described in Schedule 5 to this Act.

(9) Her Majesty may be Order in Council amend the said Schedule 5 so as to exclude from the provisions of that Schedule such actions or matters as may be described in the Order; and any Order made by virtue of this subsection shall be subject to annulment in pursuance of a resolution of either House of Parliament."

Notes

The areas contained in Schedule 5 include commencement or conduct of civil or criminal proceedings in any court; action taken by a police authority or joint police committee in connection with investigation or prevention of crime; contractual or commercial transactions of any authority; action taken in respect of appointments or removals, pay, discipline or other personnel matters; and the giving of instruction in any educational establishment managed by an education authority, including all schools and further education authorities and the conduct, curriculum and internal organisation, management and discipline in any of these establishments; and anything done or not done before May 16, 1975. The jurisdiction was extended by section 7 (1) of the Scottish Legal Services Ombudsman and Commissioner for Local Administration in Scotland Act 1997 to enable him to consider complaints against a member or officer of an authority.

16–18

The Commissioner, along with his English and Welsh counterparts, has, on a number of occasions, sought to extend his jurisdiction. When the Widdicombe Committee met to examine *The Conduct of Local Government Business*, Cmnd. 9797 (1986), the Commissioners argued that there be:

(1) An extension of jurisdiction to cover contractual, commercial and personnel matters;

(2) Power be given to the local Ombudsman to investigate without having received a complaint from a member of the public;

(3) Direct access by complainants.

16–19

In his Annual Report for the year ending March 31, 1986, which was cited to the committee, the Scottish Ombudsman argued (at para. 2) that:

> "Complaints about action taken in contractual or other commercial transactions of a local authority should be capable of investigation ... Ombudsmen would, as at present be required to respect the fact that a Local Authority must not be criticised if it is simply exercising its discretion properly, but if, for example, a trader or firm is deprived of the chance to compete in providing goods and services to a Local Authority by prejudice or incompetence, this should be open to investigation. The matter becomes all the more important as Local Authorities are encouraged to require to privatise their functions."

In relation to personnel matters, in his Annual Report for 1983–84, the Scottish Ombudsman drew attention to the fact that the exclusion meant that he was not entitled to investigate matters, "even those relating to appointment procedures, where the complainant is unable to benefit from the procedures applying to officers in post", and in his review of Part II of the 1975 Act he stated that there was no redress available for persons aggrieved by the way in which local authorities operate their selection procedures or the administration of pensions and urged an extension of his jurisdiction on the ground of fairness to deal with these matters in view of the importance of local authorities as employers and for the many who depend upon local government's superannuation schemes: see Appendix III to Minutes of Meeting of Convention of Scottish Local Authorities Policy Committee, January 4, 1985, para. 14. COSLA has, however, to date been opposed to an extension on the basis that there are adequate legislative safeguards. The Widdicombe Committee accepted the argument for investigation of commercial transactions but was only willing to recommend that complaints about appointment procedures be within the Ombudsman's jurisdiction, but not general personnel matters. As indicated above, direct access was granted in 1988 but as regards the other possible changes, the Government felt (in relation to commercial transactions) that (the Government's Response to the Report of the Widdicombe Committee of Inquiry, Cm. 433 (1988), para. 6.27):

> "Ombudsmen — Central and Local — are concerned with inter-action between the executive arm of government and the general public. Actions taken by public bodies in buying and selling goods and services are fundamentally different. The Law already provides various safeguards and remedies for the parties involved in such commercial transactions, and there is no case for providing further protection through the local Ombudsmen ..."

By the same reasoning, the Government rejected the propriety of investigating personnel complaints. The ability of the Ombudsman to initiate an investigation without a complaint received was also rejected. The Government was concerned that the Ombudsman would be seen as a watchdog with a roving commission. The Government did, however, give new power to published general guidance to local authorities on good administrative practice and this has been enacted in section 23 of the Local Government and Housing Act 1989.

For a major empirical account of the work of the Scottish Ombudsman down to 1990 see J.G. Logie and P.Q. Watchman, *The Local Ombudsman* (1990) and for a more concise account see C.M.G. Himsworth, *Local Government Law in Scotland* (1995), Chap. 8; Finch and Ashton, pp. 179–181; *The Laws of Scotland: Stair Memorial Encyclopaedia*, Vol. 14, "Local Government", paras 133–200.

THE LOCAL GOVERNMENT OMBUDSMAN — JUDICIAL CHALLENGE

R. v. Local Commissioner for Administration for the South, ex parte Eastleigh Borough Council

[1988] 3 All E.R. 151, C.A.

16–20   A property owner complained to the English Local Government Ombudsman that Eastleigh Borough Council had failed properly to inspect the building of a defective sewer connected to his house as required by the Building Regulations 1976. The Ombudsman produced a report (extracts of which appear in the judgment below) in which he stated that the council had not inspected the sewer at the relevant stages of its construction and, therefore, the sewer had not been thoroughly inspected. He went on to find that the property owner had sustained injustice as a consequence of maladministration. He did, however, accept that even if a final inspection of the sewer had been carried out properly, he could not be certain that the defect would have been discovered. On that basis, he recommended that the council pay only a part of the costs of the work needed to remedy the problem. The council sought judicial review of the report on the grounds that it was contrary to section 34(3) of the Local Government Act 1974, in that the Ombudsman had questioned the discretionary decision taken without maladministration by the council and also that it was contrary to section 26 (1) of the same Act, in that he had made a report when it was not certain that the complainant had in fact suffered injustice as a consequence of an act of maladministration. In the High Court, Nolan J. upheld the council's argument but refused to grant a declaration to that effect. The council appealed against refusal of this remedy and the Ombudsman cross-appealed against the findings of *ultra vires*.

LORD DONALDSON OF LYMINGTON M.R.: "... The ombudsman's conclusions are stated in paragraphs 30 and 31 of his report:

> '30. In my view good administration dictates that the council should carry out an inspection under the Building Regulations in respect of all stage inspections for which they have received notice from the owner or builder as the case may be. Where inspections have not been made at a particular stage I consider that special attention should be given on the final inspection to remedy the omission. In the case of drains it is a relatively easy matter to carry out a full test, such as a ball test or its equivalent, at the final inspection stage and I consider that a council have a duty to ensure that this is done because a final inspection should mean that, so far as the council are concerned, they have with reasonable diligence and expenditure of officer time found no defect under the Building Regulations. I am satisfied that in this case the private foul sewer in question was not fully or thoroughly inspected. The defects in piping discovered as a result of the soil and vent pipe test should have alerted officers to the possibility of other defects in the pipe work.
>
> 31. I find, therefore, that the complainant has sustained injustice as a result of the council's maladministration. However, I cannot say, categorically, whether had the council carried out the final inspection in accordance with the dictates of good administration, the trouble at the centre of this complaint would not have arisen. Equally, I have taken account of the argument that with synthetic piping of the sort employed in this case soil compaction can cause undulation at a later date. I have also considered the fact that the original fault was the builder's and that that (and the council's fault) occurred some years ago. On the other hand the final inspection was, in my view, incomplete and the council could have become aware of the problem at an early stage because of the difficulties experienced by the owner of house 3. Having considered these factors I feel on balance it would be inequitable to ask the council to defray the whole cost of the necessary remedial work. Accordingly, upon the residents' agreement to pay a proportion of the reasonable cost, I consider that the council themselves should take the action which the Assistant Director of Technical Services commended to the residents (see paragraph 29, above).'

The action referred to in paragraph 29 consisted of exposing that part of the sewer which lay between two manholes and adjusting the pipe work to eliminate the undulation.

The Ombudsman's Cross-appeal

Section 34(3)
This subsection is in the following terms:

> 'It is hereby declared that nothing in this Part of this Act authorises or requires a Local Commissioner to question the merits of a decision taken without maladministration by an authority in the exercise of a discretion vested in that authority.'

'Maladministration' is not defined in the Act, but its meaning was considered in *R. v. Local Commissioner for Administration for the North and East Area of England, ex p. Bradford Metropolitan City Council* [1979] Q.B. 287. All three judges (Lord Denning M.R., at 311, Eveleigh L.J., at 314, and Sir David Cairns, at 319) expressed themselves differently, but in substance each was saying the same thing, namely, that administration and maladministration in the context of the work of a local authority is concerned with the *manner* in which decisions by the authority are reached and the *manner* in which they are or are not implemented. Administration and maladministration have nothing to do with the nature, quality or reasonableness of the decision itself.

The key to this part of the cross-appeal lies in identifying the policy decision of the council in relation to the inspection of drains. This was, as I have stated, to inspect at four of the more important of nine stages in construction. It did not condescend to the nature of the inspections ...

Nolan J. read paragraph 30 of the ombudsman's report, which I have set out in full, as questioning the merits of that policy. I do not so read it. I can best illustrate my understanding of that paragraph by adding words which render explicit what, in my judgment, is implicit:

> 'In my view good administration dictates that the council should carry out an inspection under the Building Regulations in respect of all stage inspections for which they have received notice from the owner or builder as the case may be. [However I recognise that, on the authority of *Anns'* case [1978] A.C. 728 to which I have referred at length earlier in this report, it was open to the council in the exercise of their discretion and taking account of the competing claims of efficiency and thrift to decide to inspect on fewer occasions. This the council has done and I accept its decisions. That said] Where inspections have not been made at a particular stage I consider that special

attention should be given on the final inspection to remedying the omission. [In saying this I am not calling for an expenditure of time and effort which would nullify the council's discretionary decision on the resources to be devoted to building regulation inspections.] In the case of drains it is a relatively easy matter to carry out a full test, such as a ball test or its equivalent, at the final inspection stage… [The choice of test must be a matter for the council's officers and I would not criticise them for not using the ball test, if they had used some equivalent test. However an air pressure test, such as the council's officers used, is not such an equivalent, because it only reveals whether or not the sewer is watertight. It tells the inspector nothing about its gradient or its ability to self-clear and efficiently carry away matter discharged into it as required by regulation N10.] I consider that [this is of considerable importance and that] a council have a duty to ensure that this is done because a final inspection [if the council decide to make one, as this council did] should mean that, so far as the council are concerned, they have with reasonable diligence and expenditure of officer time found no defect under the Building Regulations. I am satisfied that in this case the private foul sewer in question was not fully or thoroughly inspected [in terms of the council's own 1977 policy. Even if in other circumstances a lesser inspection might have been justified in terms of that policy] the defects in piping discovered as a result of the soil and vent pipe tests should have alerted officers to the possibility of other defects in the pipe work.'

So read, and I do so read it, paragraph 30 loyally accepts the council's discretionary decision on the inspection of drains. It simply criticises the way in which that decision was implemented. I do not, therefore, think that this complaint by the council is made out.

Section 26(1)

This subsection is in the following terms:

'Subject to the provisions of this Part of this Act where a written complaint is made by or on behalf of a member of the public who claims to have sustained injustice in consequence of maladministration in connection with action taken by or on behalf of an authority to which this Part of this Act applies, being action taken in the exercise of administrative functions of that authority, a Local Commissioner may investigate that complaint.'

… [I]t does mean that he cannot report adversely upon an authority unless his investigation reveals not only maladministration, but injustice to the complainant sustained as a consequence of that maladministration.

The mischief at which this subsection is directed is not difficult to detect. Every local authority has living within its boundaries a small cadre of citizens who would like nothing better than to spend their spare time complaining of maladministration. The subsection limits the extent to which they can involve the ombudsman by requiring, as a condition precedent to his involvement, that the complainant shall personally have been adversely affected by the alleged maladministration. If he was not so affected, he did not himself suffer injustice. If he was, he did …

Like Nolan J., I am loath to criticise a busy Local Commissioner on merely semantic grounds, but I think that he laid himself open to criticism by finding maladministration in paragraph 30 and then proceeding, without any explanation, to his conclusion of consequential injustice.…

…[I]n the end I have come to the conclusion that the ombudsman was intending to say that, whilst there could be no absolute certainty that a proper inspection would have revealed the defects and it was a possibility that the undulation occurred after the date of the inspection, on the balance of probabilities he was satisfied that the defects were present at the time of the inspection, that a proper inspection would have revealed them and that he was therefore satisfied that the complainant had suffered injustice in consequence of the maladministration.

An ombudsman's report is neither a statute nor a judgment. It is a report to the council and to the ratepayers of the area. It has to be written in everyday language and convey a message. This report has been subjected to a microscopic and somewhat legalistic analysis which it was not intended to undergo. Valid criticisms have been made, particularly of paragraph 31, but in my judgment they go to form rather than substance and, notwithstanding occasional dicta to the contrary, judicial review is concerned with substance. I would therefore allow the ombudsman's cross-appeal.

The Council's Appeal

As Parker and Taylor L.JJ. are minded to dismiss the ombudsman's appeal, it is necessary to consider the council's appeal. I would allow it.

Nolan J. considered that there was no need for any declaration that the ombudsman had exceeded his remit by contravening the limits upon his jurisdiction set by section 34(3). He said that this was a free country and that there was nothing to prevent the council responding to the report with equal publicity. He concluded by saying that, since Parliament had not thought it necessary to create a right of appeal against the findings in the Local Commissioner's report, and in the absence of impropriety, it seemed to him that the courts ought not to provide the equivalent of such a right by judicial review.

I have to say that I profoundly disagree with this approach. Let me start with the fact that Parliament has not created a right of appeal against the findings in a Local Commissioner's report. It is this very fact, coupled with the public law character of the ombudsman's office and powers, which is the foundation of the right to relief by way of judicial review.

Next there is the suggestion that the council should issue a statement disputing the right of the ombudsman to make his findings and that this would provide the council with an adequate remedy. Such an action would wholly undermine the system of ombudsman's reports and would, in effect, provide for an appeal to the media against his findings. The Parliamentary intention was that reports by ombudsmen should be loyally accepted by the local authorities concerned. This is clear from section 30(4) and (5), which require the local authority to make the report available for inspection by the public and to advertise this fact, from section 31(1), which requires the local authority to notify the ombudsman of the action which it has taken and proposes to take in the light of his report and from section 31(2), which entitles the ombudsman to make a further report if the local authority's response is not satisfactory.

Whilst I am very far from encouraging councils to seek judicial review of an ombudsman's report, which, bearing in mind the nature of his office and duties and the qualifications of those who hold that office, is inherently unlikely to succeed, in the absence of a successful application for judicial review and the giving of relief by the court, local authorities should not dispute an ombudsman's report and should carry out their statutory duties in relation to it.

If Nolan J. thought that the publication of his judgment in favour of the council was itself an adequate remedy, he did not say so, and, in any event, I think that he would have been mistaken, because this by itself does not relieve the council of its obligations to respond to the report in accordance with section 31(1) and, assuming that the report should never have been made, it is wrong that the council should be expected to respond.

I would grant a declaration in terms which reflect the decision of this court on the ombudsman's appeal against the decision of Nolan J."

PARKER L.J.: "… On a fair reading of the whole of paragraph 30 it appears to me that the ombudsman is not concluding that there was maladministration because there was no inspection at all nine stages, but merely that the inspections of the sewer which were called for by the policy of inspecting at the four most important stages were not fully or thoroughly carried out. This conclusion was not dependent upon the view expressed in the opening sentence and indeed it could not have been because the policy did call for drain inspections, indeed two drain inspections…

I conclude therefore that the ombudsman's conclusion in paragraph 30 was valid, but if the council felt it necessary to seek some declaratory relief with regard to the opening words of the paragraph I would be prepared to consider granting it.

I turn to the second question raised on the cross-appeal, namely, whether the conclusion that the complainant had suffered injustice as a result of the maladministration can be sustained. This depends upon paragraph 31 of the report. Had the ombudsman stopped at the first sentence, I should have had no doubt that the decision was sustainable. It seems to me abundantly clear that the complainant had suffered injustice if the failure to inspect properly led to the subsequent expenditure and the ombudsman could in my view easily have determined that it had. It is submitted however that, having stated his conclusion in the opening sentence, he proceeds to negate it and that the paragraph read as a whole really amounts to this: 'I cannot say whether the failure to inspect led to the expenditure, but as the council were at fault it would be fair that they should contribute to the cost of remedial measures.' For the ombudsman it is submitted that this is not so and that on a fair reading the paragraph says no more than: 'I cannot be absolutely sure, but on the balance of probabilities I conclude…'

I regret to say that, unlike Lord Donaldson M.R. I cannot accept this construction. It appears to me that to do so involves applying legal concepts of differing standards of proof in order to uphold a paragraph which, like its predecessor, must be broadly considered. I have, despite its opening words, been able, by a broad reading and the correctness of the ombudsman's directions to himself on the law, to uphold the conclusion in paragraph 30. In the case of paragraph 31 I am unable to do so.

I would therefore dismiss the cross-appeal and allow the appeal."

TAYLOR L.J.: "… The crucial issue therefore is whether the ombudsman's findings in both paragraphs 30 and 31 of his report can be upheld and his cross-appeal thus allowed. I agree with Nolan J. that both paragraphs contain findings which cannot be justified.

[Regarding paragraph 30.] In my judgment its tenor shows the ombudsman to be trespassing into the field of discretion by laying down what policy as to inspections the dictates of good administration require, and what tests the council ought to ensure are carried out. That is quite different from finding that a test specifically required by the council's policy has not been carried out or has been carried out inefficiently. I therefore agree with Nolan J. that the ombudsman was in breach of section 34(3) of the Local Government Act 1974 in his conclusion that maladministration was established.

As to paragraph 31, I agree with Parker L.J. Only by straining the language used by the ombudsman and attributing to him speculatively considerations as to the burden of proof, could one render his finding on causation sound. I do not think such straining and speculation is justified.

Accordingly I conclude that in respect of both paragraphs 30 and 31 of the report, Nolan J. reached the correct conclusions. I would therefore dismiss the cross-appeal and allow the council's appeal."

Notes

16–21   (1) The equivalent Scottish provisions to sections 34 (3) and 26 (1) are sections 32 (2) and 24 (1) of the Local Government (Scotland) Act 1975. The restrictive approach adopted by Parker L.J. and Taylor L.J. has been the subject of criticism. M. Jones observed, "The Local Ombudsmen and Judicial Review" [1988] P.L. 608 at 615:

"In *Eastleigh*, the court's interpretation of section 34 (3) affirms the orthodox view, and the legislature's intent, that the Commissioners ought not to usurp the policy-making discretions of democratically elected authorities; [nevertheless] the local ombudsmen ... may continue to find maladministration in the processes by which discretionary decisions are made upon grounds which closely resemble the *Wednesbury* principles of review employed by the courts — relevancy, proper purposes and so on. And there may still be room for a finding of maladministration where a Commissioner considers that the terms of an authority's policy transcend the bounds of reasonableness, and step into perversity, capriciousness, or what the courts now term 'irrationality'."

On the issue of whether the complainant suffered injustice caused by maladministration, A.R. Mowbray noted, "Maladministration and the local ombudsmen" (1988) 132 S.J. 1442 at 1444:

"The division of opinion on this question by the Court of Appeal again clearly reflected differing judicial attitudes towards the margin of appreciation to be accorded to the local ombudsman in performing his functions. Lord Donaldson was willing to allow the ombudsman a wide latitude of freedom because, in his opinion, the ombudsman was not required to produce the kind of reasoned decision expected of a superior court of law. But the majority were unwilling to make similar allowances when scrutinising the ombudsman's logic. Therefore, if the local ombudsman is to avoid such criticisms in the future his reports will have to adopt a more precise and definitive form of reasoning."

Is the distinction between merits and maladministration readily explicable? In his Annual Report for 1985–86 (at para. 10) the Scottish Ombudsman shed some light on some of the difficulties faced by complainants in grappling with the distinction:

"where maladministration cannot be found, but the complainant feels aggrieved by the merits of the decision; convincing complainants that this is the position in their particular case is by no means an easy task, as they tend to think my office is a court of appeal against their Local Authority ... The main source of misunderstanding is that my office does not exist to adjudicate on the merits of local authority policies and individual decisions — but only to say whether the process of reaching the decision was fair, took account of all the relevant facts and ignored irrelevant facts, and was taken without bias, and in accordance with current policy, and in the proper exercise of the local authority's discretion."

(2) Judicial review of the decision of the Ombudsman was also successful in *R. v. Commissioner for Local Administration, ex parte Croydon London Borough Council* [1989] 1 All E.R. 1033. The Local Ombudsman investigated a complaint by parents about the way in which an education appeal committee, established by the council, rejected their appeal regarding the school which their daughter should attend. The Ombudsman concluded that the committee

had been guilty of maladministration by giving undue weight to council policy regarding school admissions. The council sought judicial review of the report arguing, *inter alia*, that the Ombudsman should not have investigated this complaint as the parents had a remedy before a court of law under section 26(6) of the Local Government Act 1974. For the Scottish equivalent see section 24(6) (*c*) of the 1975 Act above.

In the judgment of Woolf L.J., the Ombudsman must consider whether the complainant comes within the terms of section 26(6) both before and during the course of investigation. Moreover, (at 1045):

> "The Commissioner should also have well in mind... that his expertise is not the same as that of a court of law. Issues whether an administrative tribunal has properly understood the relevant law and the legal obligations which it is under when conducting an inquiry are more appropriate for resolution by the High Court than by a commissioner, however eminent".

It follows from the terms of section 24 (6) (*c*) and by implication, subsection (6)(*a*), (*b*), that where a right of appeal or other remedy has been exercised it is impossible for the local Ombudsman to exercise power to investigate a complaint for he can hardly form the view that it was unreasonable for the complainant to resort to the remedy when he has already done so. Where developers had already exercised their right of appeal to the Secretary of State for Scotland against a decision by a planning authority under provisions of the Town and Country Planning (Scotland) Act 1972, the local Ombudsman rejected these complaints as outwith his remit: see the Annual Report 1980, para 44. However, where a complainant has exercised his right of appeal to a tribunal, Minister or court, the Ombudsman may nevertheless decide to investigate the complaint if it raises matters other than the substantive matter of the appeal. For example, in *Central Regional Council* (Inv nos 185/80 and 237/80), a regional council contended that the Ombudsman had no power to investigate a complaint about the replacement of a Roman Catholic school on the grounds that the Parent Teachers' Association had made representations in respect of a road, which would affect the school, at a public inquiry into the council's structure plan. However, the Ombudsman formed the view that as matters raised by the association at the inquiry related to planning matters and not the wider issue of provision of education, the council's objection fell to be repelled.

(3) The strict logic of the approach in *Croydon London Borough Council* was also apparent in *R. v. Commissioner for Local Administration, ex parte H (A Minor)*, *The Times*, January 8, 1999, Q.B.D. *per* Turner, J. In judicial review proceedings H's local education authority was ordered to assess the special educational needs promptly and to give speedy consideration to all suitable alternatives for his future education. However, the Commissioner for Local Administration refused to investigate H's complaint that the authority had failed to provide him with appropriate education. In particular, H wished the Commissioner to intervene in order to enable him to be compensated for maladministration which had necessitated the original judicial review proceedings. He sought an order of mandamus (the English equivalent of Scots remedy of enforcement of a statutory duty, on which see para. 11–13) requiring the Commissioner to investigate the complaint and also a declaration that section 26 (6) (*c*) of the 1974 Act did not prevent an investigation by the Commissioner where no remedy was available in judicial review proceedings for a complaint of maladministration, and that he had a discretion to investigate, even where the subject matter of the complaint had been raised in earlier judicial review proceedings, where those proceedings did not include a remedy for past maladministration. In dismissing the application, the court held that the correct interpretation of section 26 (6) (*c*) was that the Commissioner was not concerned with the remedies but with the action taken by local authorities in the exercise of the administrative functions. The Commissioner could not interfere where the court had jurisdiction other than in cases where it was not reasonable to expect the complainant to resort to a right or remedy which was otherwise available.

(4) The question of whether or not it is reasonable to expect the complainant to resort to an alternative remedy would appear to depend very much on which person any appeal or review is directed to. Thus, the Local Ombudsman has never exercised his discretion to investigate matters which could be brought before either a statutory tribunal or a Minister of the Crown, a

16–22

consequence, no doubt, of the belief that these remedies were set up to provide a citizen with an accessible and inexpensive means of challenging local government decision making. Consider here the materials on tribunals and inquiries and rights of appeal discussed in Chapters 1 and 12. Is that view justified? He has, however, exercised his discretion in a number of cases to investigate complaints where a remedy by proceedings in court would be permitted where he has formed the opinion that for reasons of expense or personal hardship the legal remedy open to the complainant is more apparent than real. In assessing reasonableness, Logie and Watchman concluded that the Ombudsman takes into account a number of factors; the nature of the complaint (particularly if no issue of legal liability arises), the nature and cost of the remedy (thus in at least one case the challenge to legality of the council policy which would have required judicial review was considered by the Ombudsman: *Midlothian District Council* (Inv no. 218/81); hardship to the complainant and the action of the authority (where a district council repudiated liability for damage caused by a pipe burst in empty adjoining premises without giving any reasons for doing so, the local Ombudsman accepted that irrespective of any action for compensation which might be available, there was evidence of maladministration: *City of Glasgow District Council* (Inv. no 249/82). Compare Lord Woolf, writing extrajudicially in *Protection of the Public Image — A New Challenge* (1990), pp. 90–91, who argued that the Ombudsman should have an express power to refer an issue to court, whether before, during or after investigation,

> "either because there is a point of law of significance involved or because the court is in a better situation to provide the remedy than he is."

To date there have been no Scottish cases on judicial review of decisions of the Local Ombudsman and it is tempting to conclude that this is because local authorities in Scotland at least, readily accept a finding of maladministration. However, the next note suggests that such complacency may be misplaced.

16–23   (5) There have been a number of cases where the Ombudsman has found a local authority guilty of maladministration but the authority fails to provide an acceptable remedy. Consequently, the Local Ombudsman argued before the Widdicombe Committee that, as in Northern Ireland, where a local authority failed to provide a suitable remedy, then the complainant should have the right to go to the sheriff court or county court for a binding judicial order of compensation or other remedial action. This proposal was accepted by the committee: para. 9.69. At about the same time, the Select Committee on the PCA proposed a system for dealing with local authorities who failed to provide a remedy. It suggested that where a council failed to provide suitable remedy then the leaders of the council could be called to give evidence before the committee: Local Government Cases: Enforcement of Remedies (1985–86 H.C. 488) However, the Government rejected judicial enforcement because "local authorities might be less willing to co-operate, and an investigation would become increasingly formalised, lengthy, legalistic and costly". The Select Committee's idea was also dismissed as it "is unlikely to be readily acceptable to local government who do not see themselves as accountable to Parliament — though recognising that they operate within a statutory framework laid down by Parliament": the Government's Response to the Report of the Widdicombe Committee of Inquiry, paras 6.21– 6.23. Are these reasons convincing? Local government matters are of course within the devolved competence of the Scottish Parliament. It will be interesting to see whether the Parliament takes any steps to strengthen the local Ombudsman's powers.

(6) Some reform did, however, occur under Part II of the Local Government and Housing Act 1989. New sections were inserted in the 1975 Act, namely sections 29 (2A), (2B). Where a report finds injustice in consequence of maladministration existing then the relevant local authority must consider the report and notify the Ombudsman of the action it proposes to take within three months. If the authority does not notify the Ombudsman, or he is not satisfied with the action taken, he may issue a second report. Again the authority must consider and notify the Ombudsman on its action regarding the second report. If the Ombudsman is still not satisfied with the authority's conduct he may publish an account of his recommendation in two editions of a local newspaper. By 1990 18 second reports had been issued amounting to 6 per cent of total findings of maladministration. However, from the 1993– 94 report to the 1997–98 report, no further reports have had to be issued.

(7) How then should the overall effectiveness of the Ombudsman be assessed? Writing in his report for 1995–96, the Ombudsman concluded (at pp. 31–32):

"In evaluating effectiveness it is necessary to bear in mind the very limited resources available. While it remains for others to judge, it appears that the Ombudsman has become increasingly effective in resolving disputes and can legitimately claim to have been instrumental in bringing about changes in administrative practice."

Others are less sanguine. Himsworth observed (at pp. 150–151):

"It has become one of the orthodoxies of the study of ombudsmen and their impact that it is first necessary to decide what their purpose is. Only then can there be established the criteria, the yardsticks against which the success of the institution may be measured. Broadly, there are two such purposes proposed. On the one hand, the ombudsman may be seen primarily as a mechanism for the resolution of individual complaints, in which case the principal criteria of success are the number of complaints handled and the number of investigations completed. On the other hand, the ombudsman's main purpose may be seen as seeking to improve systematically the quality of administrative practice. On this view, the numbers of individual complaints made and injustices righted are much less important. Rather, success would be measured in terms of the improvements in practice made across the whole range of administrative bodies under scrutiny as a result of the ombudsman's intervention.

However, even with this distinction in mind, analysis of the impact of the local ombudsman in Scotland is quite difficult. It is, for instance, not easy to assess the significance of the numbers of complaints handled. In 1993–94, only one report of an investigation involving a regional council was issued and there was a finding of both maladministration and injustice. In ten cases involving district councils (out of thirteen investigated) the complaint was wholly or partially upheld. These numbers (fourteen investigations completed in a year) are not large. At the other end of the scale, a total of 1008 complaints were received during the same year but 785 complaints were rejected (about one-half without inquiry of the authority concerned and the other half after inquiry) without formal investigation — mainly because no maladministration or injustice was specified in them. However, the category of complaints in which the ombudsman found most satisfaction were those resolved by offers of settlement by the authority concerned and without the need, therefore, for formal investigation. In 1993–94, there were 183 in this category. This was lower than the 224 in the year before and the ombudsman's comment was that the fall was attributable to a decline in the volume of complaints about housing (which were relatively susceptible to informal settlement) but a rise in those about planning (which were more intractable). Also in relation to planning, however, the ombudsman made separate reference to the issue by the Scottish Office of a planning advice note containing guidance on how authorities should handle planning applications involving development contrary to a development plan. The processing of such applications had been the cause of many complaints to the ombudsman and, although the most tangible response to his concerns came from the Scottish Office rather than from authorities themselves, there is no doubt that it should be measured as a success on the yardstick of administrative procedural reform."

He went on to identify other factors which were significant in assessing the role of the Ombudsman, including the existence of other complaints mechanisms and the introduction of published standards under the Citizen's Charter. Similarly the "privatisation" of many hitherto local authority functions, such as housing, have decreased the scope for the Ombudsman's role.

THE WORK OF THE LOCAL OMBUDSMAN

The Local Ombudsman: Annual Report 1997–98

"2. An Overview
    Number of Complaints   **16–24**
2.1 In the year to 31 March 1998, 902 complaints were received compared to 873 in the previous year.
2.2 Complaints were received against every local authority bar one as detailed in Appendix I.
2.3 While the number of formal complaints made remained fairly static, informal contact with the office increased substantially. Staff handled 932 telephone enquiries compared to 654 in 1997.

Subjects of Complaint

2.4 Housing and Planning continued to give rise to the largest and second largest percentage of complaints although both reduced slightly in number.

2.5 Of the 902 complaints received
- 289 related to housing (296 in 1996/97)
- 151 involved planning matters (161 in 1996/97)
- social work complaints increased from 41 to 49
- finance related complaints fell from 68 to 61

2.6 A breakdown of complaints received by subject matter is shown in Chart I. The manner of their disposal is contained in Appendix 2.

Chart 1:

COMPLAINTS BY SUBJECT 1997/98

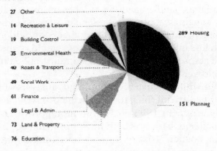

Outcome of Complaints

2.7 Of the 923 complaints determined
- 16 involved bodies outside jurisdiction
- 18 related to matters which cannot be investigated (for example personnel matters or contractual issues)
- enquiries were made of the local authority concerned in 485 cases
- a total of 216 complaints were satisfactorily resolved without the use of formal powers
- in 17 cases formal investigations were commenced

Formal Investigations

2.8   The number of formal investigations reported on was 18
- in 10 reports maladministration with injustice was found
- 2 reports resulted in findings of no maladministration
- 6 investigations involving 7 complaints were discontinued when the authority involved took action to remedy the matter.

2.9 A breakdown of formal investigations by subject matter is contained in Chart 2. An analysis of their outcome can be found at Appendix 3 with individual case reports listed in Appendix 4.

2.10   No further reports required to be issued.

Chart 2:

COMPLAINTS INVESTIGATED BY SUBJECT 1997/98

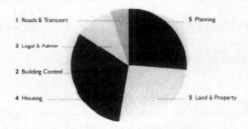

Notes

(1) Some reports are lengthy and complex and others are short. A copy of the report must be   **16–25**
sent to the complainant, to the authority concerned and, where relevant, to the councillor who
originally referred the complaint. Generally speaking the persons involved in the complaint are
not named in the report although the Ombudsman has general power to mention a person's
name where it is necessary to do so but only after taking account of the public interest as well
as the interest of the complainant and any others concerned: section 28 (3). There is also a
specific obligation (provided it is not unjust to do so) to mention the name of the councillor
involved in maladministration where his or her conduct constitutes a breach of the National
Code of Local Government Conduct: section 28 (3) (A).

(2) A survey undertaken for the local ombudsmen for England and Wales in 1995–96 revealed
that 59 per cent of social groups A, B and C were aware of the complaints service but only 32
per cent of ethnic minority groups had such an awareness. To date, no detailed survey has been
carried out by the Scottish Ombudsman, but it would be surprising if the findings were
substantially different.

(3) In his 1997–98 Report, the Ombudsman for the first time had cause to name a member
of a local authority for breach of the National Code of Conduct. The circumstances related to
the handling of a planning application. The complainant alleged that the council had not followed
its policy and acted inconsistently in its handling of the application. It emerged that an individual
councillor, who was also involved in an official capacity for the trust who owned the property
subject to the application, took part in its determination and in his capacity as housing convenor
agreed to provide a substantial sum of money to the housing association seeking the planning
permission. There was no declaration of interest. In the view of the Ombudsman, this constituted
a breach of the National Code of Conduct. In noting the local authority's reaction the Ombudsman
stated it was

> "disappointing. Whilst satisfying the terms of the Act by providing a remedy for the person who
> had suffered injustice it would have been more appropriate for them to have also reaffirmed the
> need for members to adhere to the terms of the Code rather than expressing concern about the
> action which I had taken."

In response to the Government's proposals contained in its consultation paper, "A New
Ethical Framework for Local Government in Scotland", on which see para. 9–18, the
Ombudsman stated that he was not in favour of the proposed Standards Commission dealing
with complaints arising from breach of the code. Rather than removing such matters from his
jurisdiction he felt that:

> "there would be considerable merit in building on existing arrangements and resources rather than
> establishing another organisation with investigatory powers similar to my own. There could be
> role for a Standards Commission to deal with penalities and enforcement but I do not consider
> that fragmenting the arrangements for processing and investigating complaints against local
> authorities and their members is either in the best interests of complainants or indeed those
> complained against. In my view the current proposals may lead to confusion and unnecessary
> duplication."

(4) The time taken for a report to be made averaged four months, 13 days in the 1996–97
period and four months, four days in the period under report. There were 195 files still open at
the end of the year. Formal remedies obtained by the Ombudsman included £5,000 compensation
for distress and worry and the costs of a delayed building warrant. Local negotiated settlements
for the period under report included agreement to pay a grant of £5,411 and a housing transfer
being granted owing to noisy neighbours.

(5) Besides investigation of complaints, the Ombudsman, like the PCA, sees his role as also
including the promotion of good administrative practice. Since his 1996 Report, the Ombudsman
has reported on specific examples of good practice and seeks to raise the awareness of principles
of good administration. In his 1997–98 Report the Ombudsman commented that the development

of good administrative practice had arisen by combination of the publication of formal reports and by his raising issues with bodies best placed to give advice. Moreover, there had been many instances of authorities reviewing and amending their practices and policies in light of individual complaints. He observed that (at p. 12):

> "while the resolution of individual complaints is satisfying these procedural changes are particularly gratifying in that they underline the wider impact of the office and confirm its role as more than a complaints handling mechanism".

COMPLAINTS MECHANISMS

16–26   The Parliamentary and Local Government Ombudsmen are two aspects of the wider field of administrative complaints mechanisms. They are also formal mechanisms and it would be wrong to ignore the many less formal ways of resolving grievances. Various studies have been done of nature and impact on some of these mechanisms. In the field of local government see, for example, N. Lewis and P. Birkinshaw, "Taking Complaints Seriously: A study in Local Government Practice" in *Welfare Law and Policy* (M. Partington and J. Jowell eds, 1979), p. 130; M. Seneviratne and S. Cracknell, "Consumer Complaints in Public Sector Services" (1988) 66 Public Administration 181; and Birkinshaw. Chap. 2. On the way in which M.Ps deal with complaints see generally R. Rawlings, "Parliamentary Redress of Grievance" in *Public Law and Politics* (C. Harlow ed., 1986), p. 118 and by the same author "The MP's Complaints Service" (1990) 53 M.L.R. 22 and 149.

Although informal ways of resolving complaints are widely accepted as part of current administrative practice, they are not always regarded as welcome. The Council on Tribunals has objected a number of times to the introduction of internal review mechanisms instead of a formal right of appeal to an independent body or tribunal: see, for example, Annual Reports for 1989–90 (1990–91 H.C. 64), paras 1.6–1.10 and 1990–91 (1991–92 H.C. 97), paras 3.25–3.28. P. Birkinshaw, "Decision-making and its Control in the Administrative Process — An Overview" in *Law, Legitimacy and the Constitution* (P. McAuslan and J.F. McEldowney eds, 1985), p. 151 suggests (at pp. 164–165) that government departments often adopt informal mechanisms for dealing with complaints to avoid "a more rigorous and formal statutory process of hearing grievances or complaints".

To date, perhaps the most important new innovation in the field of complaints mechanisms is the philosophy underlying the Citizen's Charter, Cm. 1599 (1991).

The Citizen's Charter: Raising The Standard

Cm. 1599 (1991)

"The Principles of Public Service
16–27   Every citizen is entitled to expect:
•   **Standards**
Explicit standards, published and prominently displayed at the point of delivery. These standards should invariably include courtesy and helpfulness from staff, accuracy in accordance with statutory entitlements, and a commitment to prompt action, which might be expressed in terms of a target response or waiting time. If targets are to be stretched, it may not be possible to guarantee them in every case; minimum, as well as average, standards may be necessary. There should be a clear presumption that standards will be progressively improved as services become more efficient.

•   **Openness**
There should be no secrecy about how public services are run, how much they cost, who is in charge, and whether or not they are meeting their standards. Public servants should not be anonymous. Save only where there is a real threat to their safety, all those who deal directly with the public should wear name badges and give their name on the telephone and in letters.

•   **Information**
Full, accurate information should be readily available, in plain language, about what services are being provided. Targets should be published, together with full and audited information about the results achieved.

Wherever possible, information should be in comparable form, so that there is a pressure to emulate the best.

• **Choice**
The public sector should provide choice wherever practicable. The people affected by services should be consulted. Their views about the services they use should be sought regularly and systematically to inform decisions about what services should be provided.

• **Non-discrimination**
Services should be available regardless of race or sex. Leaflets are being printed in minority languages where there is a need. In Wales public bodies are aware of the needs of Welsh speakers.

• **Accessibility**
Services should be run to suit the convenience of customers, not staff. This means flexible opening hours, and telephone inquiry points that direct callers quickly to someone who can help them.

• **And if things go wrong?**
At the very least, the citizen is entitled to a good explanation, or an apology. He or she should be told why the train is late, or why the doctor could not keep the appointment. There should be a well-publicised and readily available complaints procedure. If there is a serious problem, it should be put right. And lessons must be learnt so that mistakes are not repeated. Nobody wants to see money diverted from service improvement into large-scale compensation for indifferent services. But the Government intends to introduce new forms of redress where these can be made to stimulate rather than distract from efficiency."

The Scottish Office Development Department Inquiry Reporters Unit

CHARTER STANDARD STATEMENT
"IF YOU ARE INVOLVED IN AN APPEAL, YOU ARE ENTITLED TO EXPECT THE REPORTERS UNIT: —
1. To Provide an Efficient Service
• By ensuring that at each stage within the Unit's control, the processing of a case receives prompt and   **16–28**
careful attention from the relevant case officer.
• The Unit's targets are to process appeals delegated for decision by the Reporter within the following periods:

Planning Appeals
Cases determined by the written submissions procedure — 80% of decisions to be issued within 28 weeks of receipt of appeal.
Cases determined following public local inquiry — 80% of decisions to be issued within 48 weeks of receipt of appeal.

Enforcement Notice Appeals
Cases determined by the written submission procedure — 80% of decisions to be issued within 32 weeks of receipt of appeal.
Cases determined following public local inquiry — 80% of decisions to be issued within 48 weeks of receipt of appeal.

Advertisement Consent Appeals
Cases determined by the written submissions procedure — 80% of decisions to be issued within 21 weeks of receipt of appeal.
For other, less common, types of delegated appeal, we would seek to achieve the same targets as those set out above for planning and enforcement notice appeals, according to whether the case involves enforcement and/or a public local inquiry.
Where it appears that a particular case is unlikely to be completed within the appropriate target, the Unit will write to the appellant and the planning authority towards the end of the period to inform them of the situation, unless this is already known, to give the reasons for the delay, and to indicate wherever possible when the case is likely to be completed.
The target periods for completing cases will be reviewed regularly, with a view to reductions wherever possible.

2. To be Fair
•   By dealing with all casework in an open, fair, and impartial manner. The determination of appeal cases will be based on the planning merits of the proposed developments, having regard to the approved development plan, relevant published government guidance, the written submissions of the parties and/or evidence led at a public inquiry.

3. To Help You
•   The Unit will provide clear forms, leaflets, and our explanatory booklet '*Planning Permission Appeals in Scotland*'
•   The Unit will clearly identify the staff with whom you are dealing in letters, phone calls, or in a meeting
•   The Unit will give you such further information and explanations as you may require, by telephone, office visit, or in writing, by contacting the address, phone, or fax number given below
•   The Unit has private interview rooms available if you wish a member of the staff to explain the procedures to you
•   Our staff will be courteous at all times
•   Our location is in central Edinburgh, close to the bus and train stations.

COMPLAINTS PROCEDURES
    If you are aggrieved by the *outcome* of a planning decision made on behalf of the Secretary of State, and you consider that the decision is outwith the Secretary of State's planning powers, or that you have been substantially prejudiced by a failure to comply with any requirement of the relevant statutory procedures, you may apply to the Court of Session within 6 weeks of the decision to ask the Court to quash the decision. If that happens, the defect must be remedied, and a further decision issued.
    If you are dissatisfied with any aspect of the *service* provided by the Inquiry Reporters Unit, you should proceed as follows:-
    First get in touch with the person in the Unit dealing with your case to let them know of the problem, and to see what immediate action can be taken...
    If for any reason you remain dissatisfied, please write to the Chief Reporter at the same address
    It will help us to investigate your complaint if you set out the facts as fully as possible in writing. We will acknowledge your complaint immediately on receipt, will investigate it properly, and will aim to reply within two weeks.
    You may also contact your Member of Parliament (or if you prefer it any other MP) and ask for your complaint to be passed to the Parliamentary Commissioner for Administration (the Parliamentary Ombudsman) who is entirely independent of the Government. However he can only act when asked to do so by a Member of Parliament.
    On the other hand, if you are satisfied with the service we have provided, wish to highlight some exceptional performance, or you have any other suggestion to make about the service, or how it could be improved, the Chief Reporter would be happy to hear from you."

Notes

16–29   (1) The Charter applies to all public services, including government departments and agencies, local authorities, the health service, the court, emergency services and important private sector utilities. The Charter has had specific impact in a number of these areas. Thus, there is an accepted link between Next Steps Agencies and performance standards under the Charter. To quote G. Drewry, "Mr Major's Charter: Empowering the Consumer" [1993] P.L. 248 at 250:

> "The Charter has become a prominent feature of the agendas of the Next Steps agencies and of the framework agreements that define their performance targets".

    In the field of local government, the Accounts Commission for Scotland has been given additional powers to ensure that local authorities collect and publish information on performance standards which are then published in league tables of performance. The Commission is also entitled to give directions to local authorities as to how this information is to be published so as to allow appropriate comparisons between different authorities: the Local Government Act 1992, ss. 1, 2. The first statutory direction was issued in December 1992 and stipulated performance indicators across the fields of education, social work, roads, police, housing and other services. In addition, the Commission now has powers to ensure when auditing a local authority accounts, that arrangements are in place for collecting and publishing the information prescribed by the Commission and, in addition, the Commission is obliged to carry out "value for money" studies to enable it to determine what directions should be given to local authorities and what comparative information it should publish: section 3. See generally Himsworth, pp. 133–136 and *Stair Memorial Encyclopaedia*, Vol. 14, para. 884.

(2) In 1995, the then Conservative Government published a special report in review of the first four years of the programme. By then there were around 40 Charters covering key public services, such as the Taxpayers' Charter from the Inland Revenue. The report also recognised the Charter Mark Award Scheme for excellence and innovation in public service. By then some 227 awards had been made to a number of public sector organisations and private utilities: see the Citizen's Charter: The Facts and Figures, Cm. 2970 (1995). The link between the Charter programme and the Conservative Government's underlying approach to public services was encapsulated in the statement (at 9.42) that:

> "privatisation of public sector industries and organisations has also achieved a major improvement in the efficiency and value of services to businesses and households. Privatisation has meant real pressure on costs; and it has meant major improvements in service standards; and it has secured a major increase in infrastructure investment."

(3) The Charter Standards statement from the inquiry reporter's unit is a typical example of the practical application of Charter principles. In its 1996–97 Report, The Citizen's Charter (1996–97 H.C. 78), the Public Service Committee expressed concern that it was not always clear whether the citizen understood what the Charter could achieve and recommended (at para. 41) that the

> "citizens charter unit (which is attached to the Cabinet Office and which has responsibility for promoting Charter principles) ensure that Charters make clear what is a right, which is capable of being enforced, and what is merely a target that services aspire to meet".

They were critical of Charters which mixed promises mainly of concern to users (such as the quality of the process of using the service) and promises which are of a broader interest, to citizens as a whole. For example, in the BMA's Patient's Charter, different approaches to delivery of a public service are expressed. Matters of best practice, such as standards of accommodation are dealt with; so are statutory entitlements, such as access to medical records; targets relating to waiting times for treatment; and finally broader policy objectives, such as community support. The first can be regarded as a commitment about how the service is to be run, the second about matters of legal entitlement, but the third and fourth are essentially political promises. The committee recommended (at para. 40) that:

> "charters should in future make clear the distinction between standards concerning the level of service, and standards which are based on a political allocation of resources".

How would you categorise the statements contained in the inquiry reporter's statement? The report was also critical (at para. 8) of the tendency to associate Charter programmes with the emphasis on value for money as

> "value for money will always need to be set aside for the improvements and services that users want. We recommend that the Government clarify the role of the Citizen's Charter programme by stating unequivocally that it is about using all available resources to ensure the best quality of service to the citizen, and does not encompass other aspects of public service reform such as the means by which that service is delivered."

Is it meaningful to draw a distinction between the "means" and the "ends"? Among further specific recommendations, the committee proposed that the Local Government Act 1992 be amended to enable authorities to choose between publication of the data themselves or in a local newspaper and also that the Act should enable the Accounts Commission and in England the Audit Commission to require publication of details of past performance and future targets as well: para. 66. On performance indicators generally, the committee was concerned that little research had been done into the impact of performance indicators and in particular that they should not be used in isolation without a true understanding of their meaning. It recommended that the Citizen's Charter Unit commission research into the impact that such indicators have had on individual services: para. 68.

16–30   (4) It is difficult to assess the real value of the Charter Programme, because any assessment must be based on the acceptance or otherwise of the political philosophy underlying the Charter. For example, Professor Drewry above has commented (at 256):

> "One's view of the merits of the Citizen's Charter depends on one's views about the political philosophy to which it relates. Disciples of Public Choice will presumably welcome it as a desirable move to redress an imbalance of power between the providers and the consumers of public services; those who do not subscribe to such a philosophy may nevertheless be willing to recognise the Charter as a logical extension of recent policy tendencies — though those who are hostile to those tendencies may see it as a cynical way of squeezing extra productivity out of a rapidly shrinking and over-stretched public sector."

Others have expressed more particular concerns over the efficacy of the programme — for example, its standards are not legally binding and the legal rights of customers or users of the service are not increased. It is not always clear whether the quality of information supplied is of a high standard — is information on the time taken to answering the telephone significant? Third, there is perhaps a danger that administrators will concentrate overlay in trying to meet performance indicators in certain areas of their service, but neglecting others. Finally, the cost involved in implementing the Citizen's Charter could arguably be used to improve service.

See generally M. Connelly, P. McKeown and G. Milligan-Byrne, "Making the Public Sector More User Friendly? A Critical Examination of the Citizen's Charter" (1994) 47 Parliamentary Affairs 23. For a further critical assessment see Birkinshaw, p. 18. For views in support of the Charter see W. Waldegrave, *The Reality of Reform and Accountability in Today's Public Service* (1993); A. Barron and C. Scott, "The Citizen's Charter Programme" (1992) 55 M.L.R. 526; and R. Bellamy and J. Greenway, "The New Right Conception of Citizenship and the Citizen's Charter" (1995) 30 Government and Opposition 469. For a general account of the Charter see Finch and Ashton, pp. 96–98 and Harlow and Rawlings, Chap. 5.

Index